The First

American Frontier

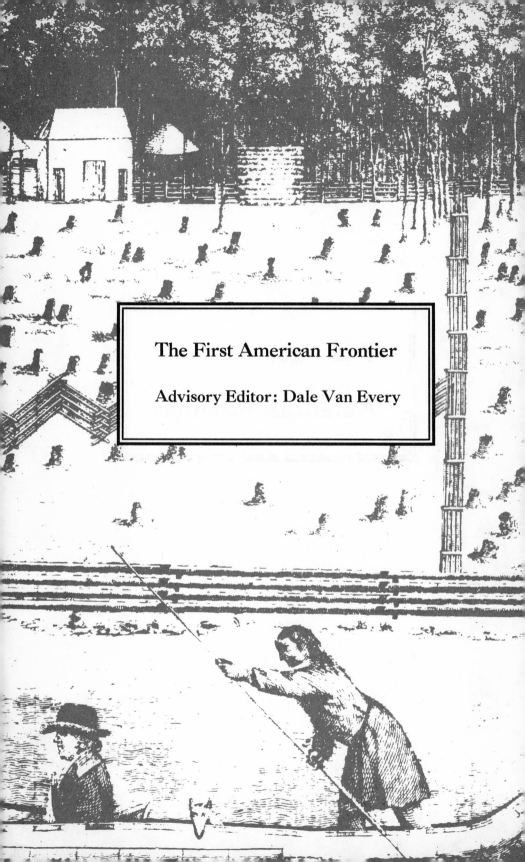

The First American Frontier

Advisory Editor: Dale Van Every

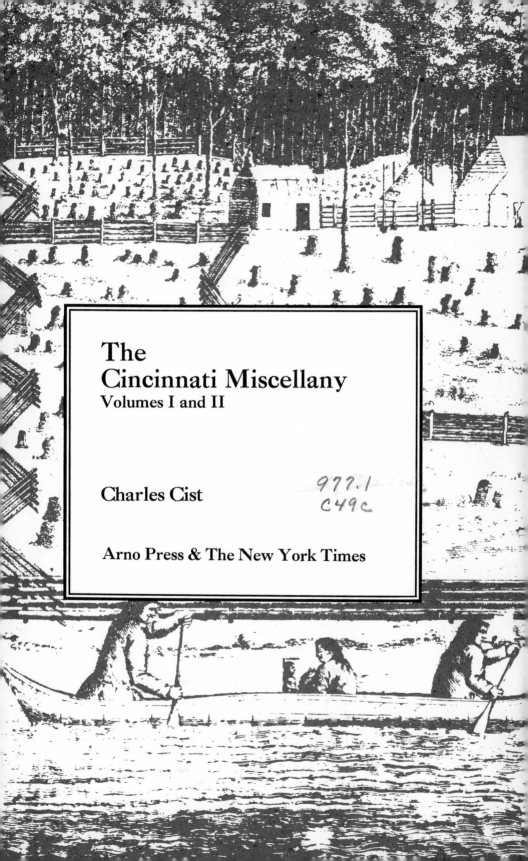

The
Cincinnati Miscellany
Volumes I and II

Charles Cist

Arno Press & The New York Times

Reprint Edition 1971 by Arno Press Inc.

Reprinted from a copy in
The State Historical Society of Wisconsin Library

LC # 72-146381
ISBN 0-405-02832-6

The First American Frontier
ISBN for complete set: 0-405-02820-2

See last pages of this volume for titles.

Manufactured in the United States of America

THE

CINCINNATI MISCELLANY,

OR

ANTIQUITIES OF THE WEST:

AND

PIONEER HISTORY AND GENERAL AND LOCAL STATISTICS

- COMPILED FROM THE

WESTERN GENERAL ADVERTISER,

FROM OCTOBER 1st. 1844 TO APRIL 1st. 1845.

VOLUME 1.

BY CHARLES CIST.

CINCINNATI:
CALEB CLARK, PRINTER.

1845.

CINCINNATI MISCELLANY.

CINCINNATI, OCTOBER, 1845.

Estill's Defeat.

One of the most remarkable pioneer fights, in the history of the West, was that waged by Captain James Estill, and seventeen of his associates on the 22d March, 1782, with a party of Wyandot Indians, twenty-five in number. Sixty three years almost, have elapsed since; yet one of the actors in that sanguinary struggle, Rev. Joseph Proctor, of Estill county Ky., survived to the 2d Dec. last, dying in the full enjoyment of his faculties in the 90th year of his age. His wife, the partner of his early privations and toils, and nearly as old as himself, deceased six months previously.

On the 19th March, 1782, Indian rafts without any one on them, were seen floating down the Kentucky river, past Boonsborough. Intelligence of this fact was immediately despatched by Col. Logan to Capt. Estill, at his station fifteen miles from Boonsborough, and near the present site of Richmond, Kentucky, together with a force of fifteen men, who were directed to march from Lincoln county to Estill's assistance, instructing Capt. Estill, if the Indians had not appeared there, to scour the country with a reconnoitring party, as it could not be known at what point the attack would be made.

Estill lost not a moment in collecting a force to go in search of the savages, not doubting, from his knowledge of the Indian character, that they designed an immediate blow at his or some of the neighboring stations. From his own and the nearest stations, he raised twenty-five men. Joseph Proctor was of the number. Whilst Capt. Estill and his men were on this expedition, the Indians suddenly appeared around his station at the dawn of day, on the 20th of March, killed and scalped Miss Innes, daughter of Captain Innes, and took Munk, a slave of Capt. Estill, captive. The Indians immediately and hastily retreated, in consequence of a highly exaggerated account which Munk gave them of the strength of the station, and number of fighting men in it. No sooner had the Indians commenced their retreat, than the women in the fort (the men being all absent except one of the sick list) despatched two boys, the late Gen. Samuel South and Peter Hacket, to take the trail of Capt. Estill and his men, and, overtaking them, give information of what had occurred at the fort. The boys succeeded in coming up with Capt. Estill early on the morning of the 21st, between the mouths of Drowning creek and Red river. After a short search, Capt. Estill's party struck the trail of the retreating Indians. It was resolved at once to make pursuit,

and no time was lost in doing so. Five men of the party, however, who had families in the fort, feeling uneasy for their safety, and unwilling to trust their defence to the few who remained there, returned to the fort, leaving Capt. Estill's party, thirty-five in number. These pressed the pursuit of the retreating Indians, as rapidly as possible, but night coming on they encamped near the *Little Mountain*, at present the site of *Mount Sterling*. Early next morning, they put forward, being obliged to leave ten of the men behind, whose horses were too jaded to travel farther. They had not proceeded far until they discovered by fresh tracks of the Indians, that they were not far distant. They then marched in four lines until about an hour before sun set, when they discovered six of the savages helping themselves to rations from the body of a buffalo, which they had killed. The company was ordered to dismount. With the usual impetuosity of Kentuckians, some of the party fired without regarding orders, and the Indians fled. One of the party, a Mr. David Cook, who acted as ensign, exceedingly ardent and active, had proceeded in advance of the company, and seeing an Indian halt, raised his gun and fired. At the same moment another Indian crossed on the opposite side, and they were both levelled with the same shot. This occurring in view of the whole company, inspired them all with a high degree of ardor and confidence. In the meantime, the main body of the Indians had heard the alarm and returned, and the two hostile parties exactly matched in point of numbers, having twenty-five on each side, were now face to face. The ground was highly favorable to the Indian mode of warfare; but Capt. Estill and his men, without a moment's hesitation, boldly and fearlessly commenced an attack upon them, and the latter as boldly and fearlessly (for they were picked warriors) engaged in the bloody combat. It is, however, disgraceful to relate that, at the very onset of the action, Lieut. Miller, of Capt. Estill's party, with six men under his command, "ingloriously" fled" from the field, thereby placing in jeopardy the whole of their comrades, and causing the death of many brave soldiers. Hence, Estill's party numbered eighteen, and the Wyandots twenty-five.

The flank becoming thus unprotected, Capt. Estill directed Cook with three men to occupy Miller's station, and repel the attack in that quarter to which this base act of cowardice exposed the whole party. The Ensign with his party were taking the position assigned, when one of them discovered an Indian and shot him, and the three retreated to a little eminence whence they thought greater execution could be effected with less danger to themselves, but Cook continued to advance without noticing the absence of his party until he had discharged his gun with effect, when he immediately retreated, but after running some distance to a large tree, for the purpose of shelter in firing, he unfortunately got entangled in the tops of fallen timber, and halting for a moment, received a ball which struck him just below the shoulder blade, and came out below his collar bone. In the mean time, on the main field of battle, at the distance of fifty yards, the fight raged with great fury, lasting one hour and three quarters. On either side wounds and death were inflicted, neither party advancing or retreating. "Every man to his man, and every man to his tree."—Capt. Estill at this period was covered with blood from a wound received early in the action; nine of his brave companions lay dead upon the field; and four other were so disabled by their wounds, as to be unable to continue the fight. Capt. Estill's fighting men were now reduced to four. Among this number was Joseph Proctor.

Capt. Estill, the brave leader of this Spartan band, was now brought into personal conflict with a powerful and active Wyandot warrior.—The conflict was for a time fierce and desperate, and keenly and anxiously watched by Proctor, with his finger on the trigger of his unerring rifle. Such, however, was the struggle between these fierce and powerful warriors, that Proctor could not shoot without greatly endangering the safety of his captain. Estill had had his righ arm broken the preceding summer in an engagement with the Indians; and, in the conflict with the warrior on this occasion, that arm gave way, and in an instant his savage foe buried his knife in Capt. Estill's breast; but in the very same moment, the brave Proctor sent a ball from his rifle to the Wyandot's heart. The survivors then drew off as by mutual consent.—Thus ended this memorable battle. It wanted nothing but the circumstance of numbers to make it the most memorable in ancient or modern times. The loss of the Indians, in killed and wounded, notwithstanding the disparity of numbers after the shameful retreat of Miller, was even greater than that of Capt. Estill.

It was afterwards ascertained by prisoners who were recaptured from the Wyandot, that seventeen of the Indians had been killed, and two severely wounded. This battle was fought on the same day, with the disastrous battle of the Blue licks, March 22d, 1782.

There is a tradition derived from the Wyandot towns, after the peace, that but one of the warriors engaged in this battle ever returned to his nation. It is certain that the chief who led on the Wyandots with so much desperation, fell in the action. Throughout this bloody engagement the coolness and bravery of Proctor were unsurpassed. But his conduct after the battle has always, with those acquainted with it, elicited the warmest commendation. He brought off the field of battle, and most of the way to the station, a distance of forty miles, on his back, his badly wounded friend, the late brave Col. Wm. Irvine, so long and so favorably known in Kentucky.

In an engagement with the Indians at the Pickaway towns, on the Great Miami, Proctor killed an Indian Chief. He was a brave soldier, a stranger to fear, and an ardent friend to the institutions of his country. He made three campaigns into Ohio, in defence of his country and in suppressing Indian wars. He had fought side by side with Col. Daniel Boone, Col. Calloway, and Col. Logan.

He joined the Methodist Episcopal Church in a fort in Madison county, Ky., under the preaching of Rev. James Hawkes. He was ordained by Bishop Asbury in Clarke County, Ky., 1809. He had been a local preacher more than half a century, and an exemplary member of the Church for sixty-five years.

He was buried with military honors. The several military companies of Madison and Estill counties, with their respective officers, and more than a thousand citizens, marched in solemn procession to the grave.

City Changes.

The changes which the surfaces of cities undergo in the lapse of time, from the appearances they presented in a state of nature, are inconceivable to those who contemplate merely the present scene. No one would suppose by the existing surface of the intersection of Market and Fourth street, Philadelphia, that a water course ever ran there. Equally remarkable are some of the changes which fifty years, and even less have wrought on the surface of Cincinanti. in the early part of the present century, Broadway, opposite John's cabinet warehouse, was the centre of a pond, three or four acres in extent to which the early settlers resorted to shoot ployers.

The original level of Main street, on the hill may be judged by observing the range of the windows in the second story of the saddler shop and store of J. S. Fountain, next door to the South-East corner of Main and Fourth streets. If the window nearest Fourth street be narrowly examined, it will be discerned to have been once a door, of which the lower part is now built up, and it needed, as may be noticed from the general level beyond Fourth street, but a step or two to bring the occupant to the level of the street, as it originally stood. In the final grading of Main street, it will be seen that Major Ferguson who built, and still owns the premises, has been constrained to accommodate himself to that grade, by converting the space below into a regular story. The general level of upper Main Street, extended as far south as nearly the line of Third street, part of the original surface of the ground being preserved in some of the yards north of Third street to this date.— It will readily be imagined what an impediment the bluff bank overhanging the lower ground to the south, and repeatedly caving in on it, must have created to the intercourse between the two great divisions of the city,—hill and bottom.— But this statement, if it were to end here, would not give an adequate idea how far the brow of the hill overhung the bottom region, for it must be observed, that while the hill projected nearly forty feet above the present level where its edge stood: the ground on Main street opposite Pearl and Lower Market streets, corresponded with the general level of those streets, which must have been between thirteen and fourteen feet below the present grade. The whole ground from the foot of the hill was a swamp, fed partly from a cove which put in from the Ohio near what is now Harkness' foundry, and in high water filled the whole region from the hill to within about one hundred and fifty yards of the Ohio in that part of the city, from Walnut to Broadway,—in early days the dwelling ground, principally, of the settlers, as it still is the most densely built on and valuable part of Cincinnati.

One of the first brick houses put up in this city, is the well known *Hopple* tobacco establishment on Lower Market street, still standing, and occupied in that line. This building, though of brick, and three stories high also, one of those stories being covered over in the repeated fillings up of Lower Marker street, *is built upon boat gunnels.* The building was put up under the superintendence of Caspar Hopple, still living, and a fine specimen of the early pioneers; and a little incident in its history may be worth recording in illustration of the point I started with, the changes of grades and surfaces which city improvements have wrought. Fourteen feet above what then constituted the sill of his door, he placed the joists of the next story, and while that tier was laying, our old fellow citizen *Jonathan Pancoast* passed by, and after gazing at the improvement, without comprehending its design, asked of Mr. Hopple what he meant by what he was doing. Mr. H. observed that as accurately as he could judge, that would be the proper range of the floor, when Lower Market street would be filled to its proper level, to correspond with what he supposed would prove the final grade of Main street, opposite.— When the first filling of Lower Market street took place, Mr. H. was compelled to convert some five feet deep of the lower story into a cellar, to which he had access by a trap door still in existence, and after the establishment at the present grade, of that street, the level at which he had built his joists, corresponded exactly to its purpose, giving him a sill at his door and a cellar of the ordinary depth with one, as already described, below it.

Nearly opposite on the West side of Main st., on the scite of J. S. Bates & Co's. hat warehouse, Capt. Hugh Moore, another of our surviving pioneers, had a building occupied by him as a store for the sale of such goods as were required by the wants of the early settlers. This was an erection of boat planks for the inside walls, lined with poplar boards, with boat gunnels also for foundation. The building was perhaps thirty-six feet deep, and twenty in front. A clapboard roof sheltered its inmates from the weather. This was the only building Mr. Moore was able to secure for his purpose, houses and stores being as difficult to obtain in those days as at present. When he had bargained for the house, which he rented at 100 dollars per annum, and which with the lot 100 feet on Main, by 200 on Pearl street, he was offered in fee simple at 350 dollars, he brought the flat boat which was loaded with his storegoods from the Ohio, via. Hobson's choice, not far from Mill street, up Second or Columbia streets, and fastened the boat to a stake near the door, as nearly as can be judged, the exact spot where *the museum lamp post now stands, at the corner of Main and Pearl streets.* It would be as difficult for the new comer to Cincinnati, to comprehend and realize this, as for the settlers of those days to have anticipated the changes which have been made in that region, as vast if not as rapid as those effected by the *genii* of *Alladdin and his lamp.*

The First Currency of the West.

In the early days of Cincinnati, as throughout the whole West, considerable difficulty existed in making change. The first currency was raccoon and other skins. This lasted but a short time, the establishment of the garrison and the campaigns against the Indians bringing a fair supply of specie into the country. This being however, either gold or Spanish dollars, did not relieve the natural difficulty of making change in the same currency. In this perplexity, the early settlers *coined* cut money, that is to say the dollar was cut into four equal parts, worth 25 cents each, or again divided for 12½ ct. pieces. This was soon superceded by a new, and more profitable emission from the same mint, which formed an additional quarter, or two additional eighths *to pay the expense of coinage.* This last description of change, which was nicknamed *sharp shins,* from its wedge shape, became speedily as redundant as were the dimes in 1841, when they ceased to pass eight and nine for a dollar, and of course equally unpopular. I remember as late as 1806, that the business house in Philadelphia in which I was apprentice, received over one hundred pounds of cut silver, brought on by a Kentucky merchant, which went up on a dray under my care to the United States mint for recoinage, greatly to the loss and vexation of the Western merchant. Smaller sums than 12½ cts. were given out by the retailers of goods, in pins, needles, writing paper &c. Bartle who kept store on the scite of the Cincinnati Hotel, had a barrel of copper coins brought out in 1794, which so exasperated his brother storekeepers that they had almost mobbed him, and the same feeling of contempt for copper money existed here in those days, which even yet exposes a storekeeper to insult in offering them to a certain description of customers.

Early Military Posts.

The following notes are dated Fort McIntosh. This was one of a chain of Posts first established in early days, for the defence of the Western Frontiers, extending defence for the settlements of which Fort Ligonier Penna. was the easternmost point, and Fort Finney at Jeffersonville, was the termination at the west. The immediate succession west of Ligonier were Forts Pitt —now Pittsburgh, McIntosh—on the Ohio between Pittsburgh and Beaver; and Harmar at the mouth of the Muskingum river, opposite Marietta.

Major J. P. Wyllys to Lieut John Armstrong.
FORT McINTOSH, April 29, 1785.
SIR:
I can send you but five men to relieve your party, which must answer until the arrival of more troops, which can not be long. I wish you to send on the men belonging to the three companies at this port, by Mr. O'Hara's large boat, which will be down to-morrow. Maj. Doughty will be at Fort Pitt in order to inspect the military stores there. You will doubtless afford him every assistance in your power,
I am sir, with esteem,
your most ob't and humble serv't.
J. P. WYLLYS, Maj. Comd.

Major N. Fish to Capt. Armstrong.
FORT McINTOSH, May 31, 1785.
DEAR SIR:
Your letter of the 29th inst. I have received, and thank you for your attention to the business therein mentioned. Your little council with the Indians, and gratuity made to them meet my approbation; and I am well pleased to find that you have got rid of them upon so easy terms.

I have been engaged here in a similar way.— Scotash, a Wyandot Chief, son of the half king of that nation, together with two Delawares and a Mingo, have been in council with me these two days, and are very friendly. I have promised them six pounds of tobacco, and some Wampum, which cannot be obtained at this Garrison. I have therefore directed them to apply at Fort Pitt, and beg you to procure those articles of the contractor or elsewhere, and deliver them to the bearer.

Don't suffer any disappointment to take place, but at all events let the tobacco and a string of Wampum be furnished them.
I am sir, your most ob't.
and humble servant,
N. FISH.
P. S. You will please to furnish them with provisions during their stay at Fort Pitt, and about eight days allowance when they depart to subsist them on their journey.

Major G. Doughty to Captain Armstrong.
McINTOSH, 4th May, 1786.
MY DEAR SIR:
I am this moment embarking for Muskingum, I have to request you will hand the enclosed to Col. Harmar and Capt. Ferguson on their arrival.
Maj. Wyllys tells me you have some paper, which was drawn for the Garrison of Muskingum; he says it was sent to you to be exchanged; be so good as to send it to Muskingum the first opportunity, there is not a sheet at that Post. Maj. Craig has promised to send me some as soon as it arrives. I wish you to jog his memory, lest he should forget.
God bless you
my dear sir, adieu,
G. DOUGHTY.

Maj. J. F. Hamtramck to Capt. Armstrong, Commander at Fort Pitt.
McINTOSH, May 22nd., '86.
SIR:
I will be obliged to you if you will send me by the first opportunity (if you have them in public store) two sithes and hangings, two pickaxes, one dozen of fascine hatchets, four spades or shovels, and six planting hoes. We are going to work at a garden.
I have the honor to be sir,
your most obedient,
J. F. HAMTRAMCK.

A Proclamation.

By William Henry Harrison, Major General in the army of the United States, and commanding the eighth Military District.

An armistice having been concluded between the United States and the tribes of Indians, called Miamies, Potawatomies, Weas, Eel River Miamies, Ottoways, Chippeways and Wyandots, to continue until the pleasure of the former shall be known, I do hereby make known, the same to all whom it may concern. This armistice is preparatory to a general council, to be held with the different tribes; and until its termination, they have been permitted to retire to their hunting grounds, and there remain unmolested, if they behave themselves peaceably. They have surrendered into our hands, hostages from each tribe, and have agreed immediately to restore all our prisoners in their possession, and to unite with us in the chastisement of any Indians, who may commit any aggressions upon our frontiers. Under these circumstances, I exhort our citizens, living upon the frontiers to respect the terms of the said armistice, and neither to engage in, nor countenance any expedition against their persons nor property, leaving to the Government, with whom the Constitution has left it, to pursue such course with respect to the Indians, as they may think most compatible with sound policy, and the best interest of the country.

Done at Detroit, this 16th day of Oct. 1813.

WILLIAM HENRY HARRISON.

[SEAL.]

A true copy.

C. S. Todd.—Extra A D Camp.

Col. John Armstrong.

In one of his memorandum books—1782 he says:

"Oct. 31st, at 3 o'clock P· M., marched from Harrison to *Cabin* point, in Surry county, 12 miles, and pitched tents at 8 o'clock P. M. 1st Sept. at 10 o'clock A. M., marched 12 miles to Surry Court House. The recrossing the James River, and marching this route, was in consequence of an account that a French fleet was in the bay; at 10 o'clock the account was confirmed by a letter to Gen. Wayne—2nd, marched 6 miles to Cabin point; at 10 o'clock A. M. two frigates and thirty boats made their appearance, and at 10 o'clock P. M. the French landed 3000 men on James Island—3rd, at 9 o'clock A. M., went on board the French boats and crossed the James River—at this place the river is 3 miles wide, and took a position between Green Spring and James Town, leaving our baggage and tents standing on the other side of the river with one Virginia regiment to assist in transporting over. At 5 o'clock P. M. there came on a heavy rain, the troops marched one mile to Green Spring, where we lay without shelter after getting very wet. 4th, marched at 5 o'clock A. M., 8 miles to Williamsburgh, James City county, where we were reviewed by the French General—at night retired into the College. 5th, marched one mile back in order to give the men an opportunity of washing their linen—where we lay without shelter. 6th, marched through Williamsburg to Burrill's mills, 5 miles into York county—the morning of the 7th, the enemy's horse came up to our pickets but were obliged to retire, leaving one sword, cloak, and pistol. 8th, at 10 o'clock A. M. was relieved by a detachment commanded by Gen. Muhlenburgh—marched 6 miles in rear of Williamsburgh, and formed a junction with the light infantry, and French troops—at 9 o'clock P. M. was alarmed by two of the French centinels firing—false alarm. 9th, at 10 o'clock A. M. received our tents and baggage, and encamped. At 5 o'clock P. M. was reviewed after which the American officers marched in a body to the French camp, and were introduced by the Marquis La Fayette to Major Gen. St. Simon, and others of the French gentlemen.

"Virginia, Sept. 19, 1782. Pierce Butler Dr. one Beaver Hat on a bet respecting the surrender of Lord Cornwallis."

1781.

In his orderly book is found dated Hd. Qrs. 8th July, 1781.

The General in acknowledging the spirit of the detachment commanded by Gen. Wayne, in their engagement with the total of the British Army, of which he happened to be an eye witness. He requests Gen. Wayne and the officers and men under his command, to receive his best thanks. For the bravery & destructive fire of the Riflemen engaged, rendered essential service. The brilliant conduct of Major Galvan, and the continental detachment under his command entitle them to applause.

The conduct and exertions of the field and other officers of the Pennsylvania line, are rare instances of their gallantry and talents, &c.

Camp Cooper's Mills, 9th July, 1781.

Gen. Wayne's orders. It is with the highest pleasure that Gen. Wayne acknowledges the intrepidity and fortitude with which the advance corps composed of between 7 and 800 men under his command attacked the whole British army on their own ground, and in their own encampment, and from that emulation and firmness so conspicuous in every officer, and soldier belonging to the cavalry, artillery, infantry and riflemen, the General is confident, that had the whole army been within supporting distance, victory would have inclined to our arms &c.

Head Qrs. Williamsburgh, 8th Sept. Here fol·

lows the Gen. order of Lafayette.

"Oct. 20. 1781. The General congratulates the army upon the glorious result of yesterday, the generous proof which his christian majesty has given of his attachment to the cause of America must force conviction in the minds of the most decided among the enemy, relatively to the decisive good consequences of these alliances, and inspire every citizen of these States with sentiments of the most unalterable gratitude."

He was at West Point 5th Aug., 1779.

Carlisle, 24th June, 1782. In Virginia 19th April, 1782.

Wyoming, 24th March, 1784, and up to 20th April, 1784.

Commands at Pitt, Dec., 1785 to March 1786.

On 15th Dec. ,1785, he is ordered to the command of Fort Pitt, and remains till some time in 1786, when he is ordered to the command of Fort Finney Rapids of Ohio.

Commands at Fort Finney, Aug. 1786.

Fort Hamilton, 1791, 2d and 3d.

A Genuine Scene with Abernethy.

About a year and a half before the death of Mr. Abernethy, a big fellow, a clerk in a brewer's establishment, went to consult that eminent man, when the following conversation took place between them:—The patient, who had a very crazy frame, but a sound understanding, said, upon entering the parlor, and seeing a little odd looking man with the knees of his breeches loose, I want to speak to Dr. Abernethy. Doctor—I am no doctor; what brings you here? I came for advice to be sure. You don't think I came to ask you how you do? Hah! muttered Abernethy, evidently pleased with meeting a congenial customer; no, I hope not; but there's no use of your coming to me for advice—you won't take it. Yes I will. I'll be hang'd if you do. I'll be hang'd if I dont. What trade are you?—A butcher, or a publican or a coster-monger? Not a bit of it; you're all wrong; I am a brewer's clerk.—What they call a broad cooper? I am a collecting clerk. Worse and worse. Nothing can satisfy fellows of your kind, you'll drink beer till you burst.

Show me your tongue. The patient immediately obeyed, by lolling a large yellow, furry tongue over his chin. Bad, said Mr. Abernethy, very bad. You were drunk last night? No, I wasn't. So much the worse, for the state of your tongue must then proceed from habitual drinking.

You are always drunk, and you don't know it. You drink what you fellows call "heavy wet!" No, I don't. I drink ale, because I wish to serve my employers. To serve your employers! Then you pay for what you drink? No, I don't. I happen to be in one of the first houses in London. Then if you stay much longer with them, they will be one of the last. Here (pulling some of his *specific* pills out of a drawer,) take one of these every other night, and diminish your ale from gallons to half-pints. But you won't remember what I say to you?— Yes, I will. No, you won't. You have no

memory. I have as good a memory as you.— I'll get off a hundred lines in Milton's Paradise Lost, with you any day. Aye. Pandemonium? You are always dreaming of the devil and all his angels; isn't that it? No, it isn't; but I often feel a palpitation of the heart, or the headache, without being a bit lumpy. Nonsense! How can a fellow who lives upon ale, have either head or heart? You have stomach and guts enough. Really, sir, I get very much depressed, particularly when I can't get in the debts of the house. It is always cold morning with me then. Well, I advise you to take the pills, and take exercise, and have mercy upon your employers and yourself. Good morning. As the patient was walking out of the room, Mr. Abernethy said—Stay, where are you doing business? Over the water. Well, take a cab. Why so? You just said exercise is good for me. Yes, but between this and your place of business, there are twenty public houses, I am greatly afraid of the shortness of your memory. When shall I call again? Do as I tell you, and I never need see your face more. I'll come, if I don't improve, but I trust we shall never meet again this side of the grave. If ever we do, I hope you'll repeat the hundred lines from Milton, I'll be satisfied with that instead of a fee. There, (ringing the bell and whistling,) that'll do, but give me another call.

French Police.

The French Police is very indifferent, except for political purposes, then it is unrivalled, and go in what circle of society one may, he never can be certain that any expressions he may drop against the powers that are, will not be duly communicated, and registered against him at the *Quai de Jerusalem.* One of the most popular saloons of the fauxbourg St. Germain, is that of Madame Delamarque; it is a sort of neutral ground where men of all parties meet & converse freely on the prominent topics of the day.— Colonel Rattin, one of those worthies who gained their epaulets in the Spanish Legion, recently obtained the *entrée*, but on his first appearance the busy tongue of scandal whispered that he was a *Mouchard*; or, to speak more plainly, a public spy. The hostess perceived the sensation created by her new guest, and was indignant when she learned the cause. "He shall leave the house," said she, "unless he gives a perfect explanation;" and forthwith gave him an invitation to follow her to her boudoir, where she at once broached the matter. "Colonel, I do not wish to offend you, nor know how to express myself, but these people say you are sent here —by—the" "Go on, Madame, you excite my curiosity." "Oh, I really cannot believe it, but they say you are sent here by the Police."— "Indeed, Madame, nothing can be truer."— "And you have the effrontery to avow it?"— "Yes, Madame, I am sent here to ascertain—" "To ascertain! it is infamous." "Hear me, Madame, to ascertain *if you earn the fifteen thousand francs which the Police pay you for spying your guests.*" "Ah! you know it?" "Pshaw, Madame, is it not my business? Madame Delamarque re-entered her drawing-room some few minutes afterwards, leading by the hand the Colonel, upon whose countenance was painted wronged innocence. "Ladies and gentlemen," said she, "I have had a perfect explanation with the Colonel, and am happy to say that the report concerning him is groundless. I answer for him—*as for myself!*"

Cincinnati--Its Name and Plat.

CINCINNATI, Oct. 5th. 1844.

DEAR SIR:—

At the close of a conversation which passed between us a few weeks since respecting the original plan and name of the place, which is now familiarly called the Queen City of the West; you requested me to furnish you with such reminiscences in relation to that subject as my early residence in the West might enable me to give.

You are aware that I was not among the first adventurers to the Miami Valley. When the settlement of it began I had not finished my education; but I commenced my journey to join the little band of adventurers as soon as my professional studies were closed, which was in the Spring, after the treaty of Greenville, in 1795, had terminated the Indian war: of course the town had been laid out and the settlement of it commenced, before my arrival, It had. however, made but little progress, either in population or improvement; though it contained a larger number of inhabitants than any other American Village in the territory, excepting Marietta; and if you take into the account, the officers and soldiers of the garrison, and others attached to the army, it very much exceeded the population of that place.

Most of the persons who saw the town laid out, and put up the first cabins erected in it, were here when I came, and were my earliest companions and associates. Without professing an unusual share of curiosity, it is natural to suppose, that I learnt from them, correctly, the few and simple historical facts of the place which for good or ill, I had selected for life as my residence. By way of comparison it may be said, that the facts connected with the recent location of the Cincinnati Observatory—the donation made by our distinguished fellow-citizen N. Longworth Esq—the ceremony of laying the corner stone of the edifice, by the venerable sage and patriot of Quincy, and the name of Mount Adams then publicly given to it, are not more distinctly known, as matters of history, than were the facts of the laying out, establishing and naming of the town of Cincinnati. at the time to which I refer. They were a subject of enquiry by every stranger who came to the place, and every person in the village could recite them. There was but one version of the story, which was this, that M. Denman of New Jersey entered into a contract with Col. Robert Patterson of Lexington, and John Filson, a Surveyor in the employ of Judge Symmes, to lay out the land opposite the mouth of Licking river, then the exclusive property of M. Denman. A plat of the contemplated town was made out and Losantiville agreed upon as its name; but before any step was taken to carry that contract into effect, and before a chain had been stretched on the ground, Mr. Filson was killed by the Indians, not having done any thing to fulfil his part of the contract; in consequence of which it was forfeited, and the projected town fell through. This is all that was ever done towards the establishment of a town by the name of Losantiville, yet as was natural the settlement then just beginning, was for some time, called by the intended name of the projected town.

Early in the next season, Mr. Denman entered into a new contract with Col. Patterson and Israel Ludlow, to lay out a town on the same ground, but on a different plan from the one formerly agreed upon. To that town they gave the name of Cincinnati, and by that name it was surveyed and known in the fall of 1789.

I was informed by Judge Turner, one of the earliest adventurers to the West, that he had seen both plats, and that the general outline and plan of division were nearly the same in both, but that the first or Filson plat, to which the name of Losantiville was to have been given, set apart two entire blocks for the use of the town, and that it gave as a public common, all the ground between Front street and the river, extending from Eastern Row to Western Row, then the extreme boundaries of the town plat: and it is impressed upon my mind, though I cannot say what caused that impression, that on the first or Filson plat, Front street was laid down nearer to the river, or made more southing in its course Westward, than we find it on the plat of Cincinnati. I was also informed that some of the names which had been selected for streets of the Losantiville plan, were given to streets on the plan of Cincinnati, and that others were rejected. This circumstance may account for a fact, which is no doubt remembered by many now living in the city, that after Joel Williams had become proprietor, by purchasing the right of Mr. Denman, and had determined to claim the public common, as private property, an unsuccessful effort was made to change the names of some of the streets on the genuine plat of Cincinnati by substituting others, taken from the plat of Filson. That attempt created some temporary difficulty in the minds of persons not correctly informed, as to the true history of the town, and many took the precaution of inserting both the names in their deeds and contracts.

But independent of these facts, it must be evident that the name of the town could not have been changed after the town had been established, named and surveyed. The territorial statute of December, 1800, which I advocated and voted for in the Legislative Council, made it the duty of the proprietors of every town which had been laid out in the territory, before that time, to cause a true and correct map, or plat thereof to be recorded in the Recorder's office of the county in which it lay, within one year after the passage of the act, under a heavy penalty.

The name of the town constitutes as important a part of the plat of it, as the names of the streets or the numbers of lots, and the title to property acquired in it, is affected as much by error, mistake or uncertainty, in the one, as in the other; it was therefore considered important for the security of property holders that a true record should be made of these matters, and of every thing else appertaining to the plat, precisely as they were when the town was established and the sale of the lots commenced. Hence, the law required a true and correct plat—in other words, the original plat, without change or variation, to be recorded.

When the plan of Cincinnati was recorded by Israel Ludlow in 1801—the original proprietors were all living, he being one of them. It is therefore impossible to suppose, that he did not know what the original plat contained—or that he acted without authority—or that he would falsify the plat by placing on it any name other than the one originally given to it. I was intimately acquainted with Col. Ludlow who recorded the town plat, and was professionally consulted by him as to the requirements of the statute. He was very much annoyed by the interference of Joel Williams, a sub-proprietor, who insisted on making innovations, or changes in the original plat, calculated to favor a claim he was setting up to the public common for landing. I gave it as my opinion that Mr. Williams not being an original proprietor, or even a resident of the country when the town plat was formed and established, and having had no agency in the formation of the original plan of the town, could not be presumed to know what it was: and moreover, that the statute did not recognize him as having any other or greater authority to interfere in the matter, than any other individual who had become the purchaser of a single lot.

The result was, that each of those individuals prepared and lodged in the recorder's office, a plat of the town, affirming it to be a true copy from the original, unfortunately perhaps—certainly without legal authority, the recorder placed both plats on the record, but the community soon became satisfied, that the plat prepared and certified by Col. Ludlow, was alone to be relied on.

This, however, has no other bearing on the subject matter of our conversation, than arises from the fact, that each of them affirmed Cincinnati to be the true, original name of the town.

The controversy between them continued for several months, and was marked with great warmth. On one occasion it terminated in a violent personal conflict, in which the original plat of the town, made and agreed to by the proprietors at Limestone, in the winter of 1788-9, bearing on its face the name of Cincinnati, was torn in pieces; each party retaining a part of it. In this alteration Col. Ludlow took the ground, that Williams was an unauthorized intruder, and that the statute made it his duty as an original proprietor, to record the plat, correctly and faithfully as it came from the proprietors; neither adding to, subtracting from or altering any thing, which was on it when it was agreed to and signed by the proprietors.

To show how firmly he adhered to that principle, I will mention one case. The ground bounded by Broadway, Front street, Main street and the River, had been publicly given, and set apart by the proprietors with his knowledge and concurrence as a common for the use of the town forever. This fact he knew and affirmed, but because the word common had not been written on the map within the lines enclosing that donation or elsewhere, he refused to insert it on the copy made for the recorder, and yet it is affirmed by implication that he deliberately made out, and placed on record a plat of the town, affirming it to be a true copy of the original, knowing that it contained a name altogether different from the one which had been in the first instance adopted, and entered on the plat.

I will state farther, that at an early period, professional duty made it necessary for me to investigate the facts connected with the origin and establishment of Cincinnati, which did not extend to any other individual then or now living, and it so happened that the performance of that duty, was required at a time when the town was almost in its incipient state, and when all the original proprietors, and most of the first adventurers and settlers were living within the village or in places easily accessible.

Without presuming to claim more of tact or industry than belongs to the profession generally, it may be presumed, considering the sources of correct information then within my reach, that I must at least, have ascertained the name of the place, the establishment and history of which I was investigating.

It has been already intimated, that Joel Williams, soon after he purchased the proprietary right of Mr. Denman set up a claim to the common before described, alleging it to be private property, reserved by the proprietors for future disposition. On the strength of that pretence, he erected a brick house on the north-west corner of the tract in question. In consequence of this movement a number of the most public spirited of our citizens, Martin Baum, Jesse Hunt and General Findley taking the lead, raised a fund by subscription, to defend and sustain the right of the town. I was employed to collect and perpetuate the testimony applicable to the case; and you will not hesitate to believe, that in executing that commission, my enquiries were directed to the original proprietors and to such other persons as were likely to have any knowledge of the facts, touching the laying out of the town, and the matters contained on the original plat. I mention this to show that there was something more than curiosity prompting me to this investigation of the early history of the town, which ought to entitle it to credence.

Now let any person ask himself what description of facts were likely to be disclosed in the course of such an examination, and the answer will be precisely such as were stated in the preceding part of this letter, if they existed, although they could not have any bearing on the matter then in controversy. On the supposition that they did not exist, was there a sufficient motive to induce anybody to fabricate them? It would be difficult to assign a reason in favor of an affirmative answer.

You will perceive, that to sustain the right of the town to the common, it was necessary to prove the correctness of the plat recorded by Ludlow, which affirmed Cincinnati to be the true, original, and only name of the town. In pursuing that enquiry, the facts came out that there had been a previous project for laying out a town, the name which was to have been Losantiville, but that that project had fallen through.— As that matter had no relation to the subject, I was specially investigating, it was not noticed in the depositions, but omitted as irrelevant.

Having said thus much on the subject of our conversation, I will state as information which may be interesting, if not useful, that in Nov. 1794, Samuel Freeman purchased the unsold interest of Robert Patterson in the town section and fraction—that in March 1795, Joel Williams purchased the unsold interest of Mr. Denman, and in Nov. 1803 he also purchased of Samuel Freeman the proprietary interest acquiring by his purchase from Col. Patterson, by which he owned and represented two shares, or equal third parts of the unsold lots and ground in the section and fraction.

You are no doubt, acquainted with the fact, that by an arrangement between Judge Symmes and the first proprietors of the town, he was to retain the title in trust for them, and to execute deeds to the purchasers of lots, on their producing certificates of the respective purchases, signed by any two of the proprietors. You have also, it is presumed, heard that all those certifi-

cates, of which no record has been preserved, were consumed in the conflagration of Judge Symmes' house. These facts connected with the sale of Freeman's entire proprietary right to Joel Williams, may possibly account for the link which is said to be wanting, in the chain of title to part of the ground, lying west of the town plat, now held under Joel Williams. That fatal fire may have consumed the documents required to make out a complete paper title.

This conjecture is in some measure corroborated by a reference to the peculiarities of Mr. Williams, who had an active mind—was somewhat eccentric—possessed a vein of humor and could at times be very sarcastic. He was however quite illiterate and unusually careless, and having great confidence in Judge Symmes, he generally relied on him as a friend and adviser, though on one or two occasions, there was some serious misunderstanding between them. I was frequently engaged for him, in his legal controversies, and it so happened, that a paper required in his cause was found in the keeping of Judge Symmes. I have several times, when calling on him for papers, seen him open and examine the contents of his desk which gave me an opportunity of knowing, that even the most valuable of his papers were kept in a very careless and slovenly manner, and I have often thought, that it would have been better for him, if all his papers had been in the safe keeping of a guardian or friend; and particularly so, as every person who had been a purchaser of a town property, was exposed more or less to the consequence of his carelessness; resulting from the peculiar manner in which titles to property, within the town section or fraction, though beyond the limits of the town plat, were to be obtained. To illustrate my meaning—there have been cases in which non-residents have purchased lots, obtained their certificates, and left them in the hands of Judge Symmes, without calling for deeds after the burning of the Judge's house, and the consequent destruction of their evidence of title, and other persons, by a fresh purchase, or otherwise, have become the legal owners of the same lots.

Very respectfully,

J. BURNET,

Charles Cist.

Early Brickmaking.

July 4, 1791. Received of the hands of Wm. McMillen, Esquire, one of the Justices of the Peace, in and for the county of Hamilton, the sum of sixteen dollars, in full of a fine, upon information at my own proper inst., levied against Reuben Read, of Cincinnati, *Brickmaker*, for selling spirituous liquor, contrary to an act of the Territory of the U. S. N. W. R. O.

By me, JOS. SAFFIN.

It would seem by the above, that brick were made here in less than two years, *ab urbe condita*.

Gas an "Obsolete Idea,"

In the *Advertiser* of the 4th Sept. under the head "IMPORTANT DISCOVERY," I announced the fact that a new species of light far surpassing the Drummond in intensity, was about to make its appearance in our city, and would be submitted to the public inspection, so soon as the necessary letters patent were obtained for the discovery. It was stated that an hall light, of ordinary size for table use, had enabled print to be read at the distance of three hundred feet, *the glass* in this instance, *being rendered semiopaque by grinding*. This had become necessary to *reduce* the intensity of light, for practical purposes, the full brilliancy being equal to that of the sun at noon day. It was stated, also, that a tower 200 feet high or even less, would suffice to light the whole city, and that the tower when built could be lighted at an expense of three undred dollars. Fin ally, it was alleged that this discovery had been tested for the past five months. When I stated all this, I was perfectly aware that the account would stir up a vast amount of incredulity. As my friend Wesley Smead, the banker says, and the remark evinces profound knowledge of temporal matters, "In the affairs of *this* world, men are saved not by *faith* but by the *want* of it." Hence I was prepared to expect and even to justify the sceptical air with which many received the announcement, and the knowlng look with which others quizzed me, for being *sucked in*, as they phrased it, to usher it forth to the community,

I have now the pleasure to say that all this is true, and that, as in the case of the Queen of Sheba, *the half has not been told*. At that time I was not at liberty to say more, but now state—

1. That this light is *Magneto electrical*.

2. That it is produced by permanent Magnets, which may be increased to any indefinite extent. The apparatus now finishing by the inventors or discoverers in this case will possess twenty magnets.

3. That it supplies a light whose brilliancy is insupportable to the naked eye.

4. That a tower of adequate height will enable a light to be diffused all over Cincinnati, equal for all practical purposes to that of day.

5. That this light when once set in operation will continue to illuminate without *one cent of aditional expense*.

6. And lastly, that the inventors in this process have nearly solved the long sought problem, PERPETUAL MOTION. They suppose they have accomplished this, which I doubt, although there is as much evidence for it as I conceive can be furnished to the existence of *Mesmerism or Animal Magnetism*, sufficient to convince others if not myself.

I suppose this light will prove *the great discovery* of modern times. It is needless to add how much it gratifies me that *Cincinnati* is the place and two of its native sons, *J. Milton Sanders*, and *John Starr*, the authors of the discovery. Mr. D. A. Sanders has gone on to Washington for letters patent, and on his return, public exhibitions will be made of its astonishing capabilities.

The *Whale*, that great sea lubber, has been elbowed out of the community by the *hog*, the great land lubber. Gas for public use has superceded both—alas for them all when doomed to be reckoned among the things that were!

I have not time to specify the many uses to which light, independent on combustion may be applied, and will merely suggest as one, its perfect adaptedness to mining, in which respect it is far superior in efficiency as well as security to Sir Humphrey Davy's safety lamp. Its aid to the Daguerreotype art alone is invaluable.

Equivoques of our Language.

The English language is wonderfully equivocal. A servant girl, once fatigued with the labors of a hard day's employment, exclaimed, "She wished she was a *mistress*, for she was tired of being a *maid*."

I remember in Philadelphia, in my boyish days an old skinflint named Conrad Weckerly, much such a man as Hathaway of our city.—Although rolling in wealth, he denied himself many of the ordinary comforts of life. One day having treated himself, in an urwonted fit of generosity to a *sheep's pluck*, the cheapest article in market, he was carrying it home on a skewer, when he was met by a tenant of his, who to curry favor with him, observed that nothing was better than *sheep's pluck*. "Nutting petter as sheep's pluck. Dat ish great mishtake," replied Cooney indignantly and with much emphasis, "*Sheep's pluck* is petter as *nutting*."

Quartering on the Enemy.

In 1839, it may be recollected, vigorous efforts were made, in the City Council, for the suppression of coffee houses, by raising the price of license to some applicants, and utterly refusing them to the rest. To counteract this, the coffee house interest came in applying for tavern licences; in many cases, where they had neither stalls for horses, nor beds for travelers. By this course, two advantages were gained. Twenty-five dollars was the usual price for tavern licences, while the coffee house keepers paid from seventy-five to three hundred dollars; and the assumption of the innkeeping character secured them one more day in the week to sell liquors, the coffee houses being restricted from selling on the Sabbath.

Among others who came in for licences to keep tavern, were Evans and Levering, of the Cincinnati Hotel, and their application was resisted by myself, with others, on the ground that this description of houses might entertain travelers, so far as to secure the tavern character, but that they were not the less coffee houses on that account, selling liquors being their principal business, and that it would be fraudulent on our part to give them a license at twenty-five dollars, while we charged avowed coffee houses, but a few doors off, who did not sell one-tenth as much at their bars, as high as 300 dollars. Sufficient interest was made at the board, however, to pass this application through in the mode desired by the applicants. *Jonah Martin*, of the 3rd ward, and myself, were, probably, the most active and obstinate in this case; of course, on different sides. I incurred, naturally enough, the displeasure of the proprietors of that house, and was informed, even after the application proved successful, in no ambiguous terms, that I should *catch goss*, on the first suitable opportunity.

I had been eastward, and, on my return, made acquaintance on board the steamboat with an interesting party of travelers, who concluded to put up at the Cincinnati Hotel, where one of them had previously lodged. I accompanied them up from the boat to the house, proposing to see them again, and to shew them the various objects of interest in the place. While I was addressing a few parting words, I noticed that the firm was at my elbow, and and appeared as if waiting an opportunity to accost me. I was under no apprehension of violence, but expected and dreaded abusive language, particularly as strangers were present. As I was about to depart, one of these gentlemen addressed me with a polite request to stop and take dinner with them, which I considered ironical, but quietly declined, on the plea that I had not yet seen my family, and was now on my way home. They persisted in the application with such sincerity and earnestness that I knew not what to make of the scene, and as the party added its solicitations, I said I would return for that purpose, as soon as I had found the family well. I must own my curiosity was strongly piqued to see what was meant.

At the regular hour, dinner being ready, we were all led to the eating room, one of the proprietors doing the honors at the head of the table, and the other attending to supply the guests. Among these, I was distinguished by choice selections of the desirable parts of a fine turkey, and still finer roast pig, "Shall I help you to *this?*" "Shall I help you to *that?*" were the questions put to me continually. In short, had I been Governor of the State, I could not have received greater attentions, and was wondering what all this could mean, when the question,— 'Will you have a glass of ale, *Mr. Martin*, let the cat out of the bag. I was enjoying a feast of fat things on the credit of my opponent, *Jonah Martin*, for whom I was mistaken then, as I have often been since. The mystery was solved, and vowing internally to hold myself a dinner elsewhere in debt to Mr. M; as soon as I could retire with decency, I made myself sufficiently scarce.

N. B. This was the first public dinner given to me in my life, as it probably will be the last.

MORAL. As long as you live, quarter on the enemy.

Unwritten History.

JOHN ROSS, long and well known to the American people as the distinguished Cherokee Chief, arrived here on Monday last. He was accompanied by his bride, an accomplished and charming woman, whom he has lately made his own, thus adding by his marriage relation, a new link to the chain of friendship which has so long bound him to the *pale faces.*

His visit to this city is calculated to revive recollections of the past, which have slept for fifteen years. Cincinnati having been at that date the *theatre*, and many of its most distinguished citizens the *victims* of a singular and most daring imposture. An individual calling himself General Ross, and personating the son of the great Cherokee, by dint of forged letters, a consummate share of impudence, and that gullibility which characterises the American people, where titled foreigners are concerned, obtained access to the first circles of Cincinnati, and made himself for nine days—a nine days wonder and bubble—the observed of all observers. Judges of our Courts waited on him. Distinguished members of the bar rode out with him to show him every thing remarkable. A candidate for Congress accompanied him on the Sabbath to the Wesleyan Chapel. One of our distinguished *literati* escorted him to the theatre, after having taken an entire box, so as to shut out the profane and vulgar from the company of the General. Military officers of high distinction shared his bed-room, *perhaps his bed*, the chambermaid testifying that of the two beds in the room, but one appeared to have been slept in. In short, there was as great a *sensation*, as the French call it, produced by this visit, as when John Quincy Adams or Old Hickory himself, were at Cincinnati. The feeling was as intense, if not so diffused throughout all classes. The nose of the stranger at Strasburg, recorded by Sterne, was a mere circumstance in creating excitement, compared to the anxiety to obtain a sight of, and exchange greetings with, General Ross. He was a tall, good-looking fellow, of about three and twenty, with black straight hair, and coppery face, but in many respects, speech especially, indicating African rather than Indian extraction, and African he proved to be. But let me not anticipate. Parties were made for him evening after evening, always of the most select character, and happy the gentleman or lady who were admitted to the favored circle. One evening, at General ——'s, another at the Shakspeare Coffee House, a third at the house of a great millionaire, and lastly at Major ——'s.

"How happily the days of Thalaba passed by." One incident is all I have space to individualize. In the midst of all this *empressement*, a well known and respectable gentleman approached to bask in the sunshine of the General's countenance "I hope, General, you will do me the honor of calling on me, in the course of your stay." "I will do myself the pleasure, if possible," replied the General, with all suavity, where shall I find you Sir? I am at No. 45, Main Street—you will find the sign over the door, ***** *****, Merchant Tailor. Ah! said the General, on reflection, I am afraid I shall not have time. This was the *cut* direct.

There is no telling how long the General might have enjoyed the consideration so liberally awarded him, had not temptations which proved too strong decoyed him into improper society for one of such distinguished rank as himself.— There is a story in the *Arabian Nights Entertainments* of a cat transformed into a beautiful Princess, who was slipping into bed on her wedding night, and heard a mouse nibbling in the room. Nature proved too strong for habit. The Princess leaped out of bed and became again a cat. So with the General, as my readers will perceive.

A party, the last which his traveling engagements permitted him, as he said, to attend, was made for him by a distinguished civil officer, pesident in Cincinnati. The guests, ladies and gentlemen, had all regularly assembled and been nearly an hour kept in suspense by the non-appearance of General Ross. Still they waited, and still he came not. The host in an agony of anxiety, called his waiter, Jo Fowler. Jo, said he, jump on a horse and ride down to the Cincinnati Hotel and see what detains the Gen-

eral. Give my compliments, and tell him that we are all impatient to see him. Dont lose an instant. If massa pleases, said Fowler, who was as shrewd a fellow as lives, white or black, I think I can find the General and not go so far to hunt. Where? said the host. If I dont mistake, said Jo, he is down at a Nigger dance in the bottom. Surely, said the master, the General would not associate in such places. Sociate or not, replied Fowler, sturdily, de General got a good deal affinitude wid dem Darkies. He's half nig any how, said Jo, chuckling. Fowler being despatched, found the truant as he expected at a dance house on Columbia st, with his slippers off, dancing and playing the *jaw bones* or Castanets.

Jo made his report to the horror of all the party, who slipped off, one by one, as quietly as possible. The General of course immediately became, as Webster called Nick Biddle, an exploded idea, and " fell from his high estate weltering" in disgrace. To speak less poetically, next morning General Ross was in the hands of the constables, one of whom finding out that he had a master at Alexandria on Red River, took him to that place as a runaway slave. On application to the owner for the reward which it was supposed had been duly earned, his master flew into a violent passion and threatened to prosecute the constable for bringing the fellow back. Here, said he, I have been in hopes never to see the rascal's face again, and there seems to be no getting rid of him. Clear out and take him along within six hours, or the neighbors here will lynch you. That fellow, says he, is too smart to live in these diggings.

This is the last authentic tidings ever heard here of the distinguished General Ross.

Cincinnati Artists.

I doubt if there be more skill or ingenuity in existence at any place than in Cincinnati. A few facts will place this in a strong light.

Sheppard and Davies, who make the gold pens, are also cutters of names on punches. There is no work superior to their's anywhere. I have seen a seal bearing this impression—SEVENTH ANNUAL FAIR OF THE OHIO MECHANIC'S INSTITUTE, cut by them in a circle so small that four of them would no more than cover a half a dime, and *yet every letter had its appropriate bold and hair strokes*. These men are self-taught, and never had an hour's instruction in their business.

We have all heard of Daguerre's chemical pictures. They have been taken for exhibition throughout the world, and it was said when they were shown here, that it was impossible for such paintings to be made by any one else. They were indeed of singular beauty and magnificence. Well, one of our young Cincinnatians, T. Winter, set to work, and after the preparatory labors of 3 months to perfect his materials brought out chemical pictures, equal to Daguerre's, one of them indeed, in the judgement of New York connoisseurs,—Belshazzar's feast—surpassing its rival of Daguerre's.

Some of my readers who attended the exhibition of the last Mechanics Institute must have noticed the air pumps, on the speaker's desk. One of these was made by the celebrated Tronghton, of London, whose scientific skill is known wherever the English language is spoken, or English commerce penetrates. It belongs to the Institute, having been purchased in days when we were as afraid to give Cincinnati artists orders for air pumps, as we are now to trust them with furnishing us with a telescope for our Observatory. Well,—one of our philosophical instrument makers here, Mr. James Foster, jr., of such modest merit, that he is hardly known out of the sphere of his own circle of acquaintance, sent in for exhibition, an air pump of his own manufacture, *superior in every respect*, to the London article, and pronounced so by every votary of science present, who saw the performance of the two. A brief statement shall show conclusively in what that superiority consists.

A gallon receiver was exhausted of its air by the London pump in fifteen minutes, and the operator was as thoroughly *exhausted himself*, under the exercise, so severe was it. The same operation was then performed by the Cincinnati instrument in less than one minute, and with remarkable ease. In fact five strokes of this pump so far exhausted the air in a pair of hemispheres laid together, that the strength of five men was insufficient to pull them apart. The London instrument cost, I believe, about $140, the Cincinnati one, $35, just one-fourth the price of its rival, and in every respect its inferior. Never was a competition more fairly made, and a trial more conclusive and satisfactory to those present.

I place my prediction on record here, while I am on the subject, that a short time only can elapse before we shall find our great Munich telescope surpassed by some of our optical instrument makers here. I shall state only one more case.

The *Daguerre* art, as every one knows, originated in France, and from the reputation of that country, in science, and the fine arts, it might have been inferred that its Daguerrotypes are the best in the world. But this is so far from the fact that all Americans who have been to Paris, express their disappointment in this respect. Miner K. Kellogg, declined sending from Italy, a daguerrotype of himself to his friends, under the acknowledgement that in none of its cities could one be executed that would do to show along side of Cincinnati work, of the same nature, and when he had it taken at last on a visit to Paris, and sent it to his friends in this city, they all agree that the only comparison to be made of that portrait and those made here as a work of art, is the difference in favor of ours. Mr. E. C. Hawkins, who has succeeded admirably in this art, and that *without an hour's instruction from any artist*, and but for some useful hints received from Mr. Morse, of the *Electro Magnetic Telegraph*, owes nothing of his art to a soul living, turns out work which has no equal elsewhere, as far as I know or can learn. If any man doubts this, let him visit Mr. H. and examine his specimens. Instead of those portraits we have heretofore seen, visible in one light, and in one light only, and absolutely invisible in all others, and when seen imaging a corpse rather than a living human being, we can see their faces as faithfully portrayed in expression as mezzotint in fullness of light and shade, and when required with the exact tints and hue of the most roseate cheeks. Mr. H.'s portraits have another advantage over all others, that have fallen under my notice—they may be invisible in one light, but they are visible *in all others*, reversing the usual order of things in this respect.— The result of all this is that he frequently takes likenesses of those who, until they see his, are prejudiced against daguerrotypes entirely. While I was at his rooms a few days since, I saw two gentlemen sitting for their portraits, who stated to him that they had refused to sit for them in Philadelphia, when on there, and probably should never have had them taken anywhere, if they had not visited his rooms. I could say more on these subjects, but content myself with ending as I began:—It may be well doubted if more skill and ingenuity exists anywhere among mechanics or artists than in Cincinnati.

The Power of Kindness

No man hath measured it—for it is boundless; no man hath seen its death—for it is eternal. In all ages of the world, in every clime, among every kind, it hath shone out, a bright and beautiful star, a beaming glory!

Look at the case of Saul and David. Bitter and blasting jealousy filled the heart of Saul—and he "sought to take the young man's life." With hellish hate, he hunted him, even to the dens and caves of the earth. But David conquered his enemy—even the proud spirit of haughty Saul, he humbled.

And how? Not with sword and spear—not with harsh words and coarse contumely, for these did never touch the heart with gentle influence. No, but with a weapon, simple as the shepherd's sling, yet sure as the arrow of death. 'Twas kindness! This killed rankling hatred, and left Saul to live. And when it had done its work, Saul said to David, "Thou art more righteous than I, for thou hast rewarded me good, whereas I have rewarded thee evil." Was not here a victory, more glorious, more godlike, than a Wellington ever knew?

See Joseph, in the hands of his wicked brethren. For a few pieces of paltry silver, they sold him into Egypt. Providence, in kindness, broke the bands which held him in slavery, and made him a ruler there. Famine spread over the land her dark mantle, and the cruel brethren of Joseph hungered They went to Egypt for corn. And how acted Joseph? More than once he filled their sacks, and returned them their money, and then he made himself known. "I am Joseph, your brother, whom ye sold in Egypt!" Here was kindness, forgiveness. And it crushed to death the spirit of jealousy, that had once made him a slave. He had conquered.

Come farther down in the world's history, and tell me, what word of all those spoken by the "meek and lowly Jesus"—the 'Prince of Peace," the "Savior of the world"—was best calculated to soften and subdue the hard hearts of his persecutors? Are we not pointed to the cross on Calvary? Are we not asked to listen to the soft, sweet tones of that voice, "Father, forgive them?" O, here was kindness.

Look over our extended country at the present day. What has changed those miserable hovels of other days, where misery and wretchedness had dwelt, into the neat and beautiful abodes of plenty and peace? What has kindled anew the flame of love and affection, in hearts long estranged and freezing with coldness? What has made happy the homes of thousands of wives, and tens of thousands of children? What, in short, has been the great propellant of the late temperance reformation, which has carried joy and gladness all over the land? What, but kindness?

Reader, have you an enemy whom you would make a friend, a neighbor who needs repentance, a fallen brother, whom you would restore to sobriety and virtue? Forget not the power of KINDNESS.

I AM GOING TO BE A MAN!--The Editor was visiting some time since in a family where he saw a little lad, about four years old. Calling the little fellow to him, 'Well, my little boy,' said he, 'what do you intend to be when you grow up?' He had asked the question a great many times before, and some boys told him they meant to be farmers, some merchants, and some ministers. But, what do you think was the answer of this little boy? Better than all of them, 'I mean to be a man!' said he. It will matter very little whether he is a farmer, or a merchant, or a minister, if he is a man,—he will be successful, and be loved and respected.— The editor has known some persons who never became men, but were great boys after they had grown up. Ask your teacher, children, what makes a man, and then, like this little boy, aim to be one.

Hear what Robert Burns says:

"What though on homely fare we pine,
   Wear hoddin-gary. and a' that,
Gie fools their silks, and knaves their wine,—
   A man's a man, for a' that,
For a' that, and a' that,
   Their tinsel shows and a' that,
The honest man, though e'er sae poor.
   Is King of men for a' that."

First Promissory Note.

The following is probably the first obligation given in Cincinnati; at any rate, it is doubtless the oldest one now extant.

"On or before the 15th April next ensuing, I, Thomas Pecke, promise for myself, my heirs, &c., to deliver and pay to Hugh McClellan, or as'ns, one cow and calf, otherwise, one cow with calf to the valuation of five pounds, Penn. currency.

Witness my hand, at Cincinnati, where s'd cow is to be delivered to s'd McCllend, &c. this 28th June, 1790.

THOMAS PECK.

Test.
   THOMAS RICHARDS,
   ASA PECK,
               Endorsed."

Command you may, your mind from play, any moment in the day.

Covington.

Adjacent to every large city, will be found smaller ones, and suburbs, to accommodate those who desire to reside beyond the tumult and dust of a metropolis. Such is Covington to Cincinnati.

Wonderful as has been our own advance in prosperity. it is hardly more remarkable than that of our neighbor. Major Bush, a man of respectability, who resides in Kentucky, opposite North Bend, and who was one of the pioneer settlers, assured me that he could have taken up - any quantity of farming land in and adjacent to Covington, at five pounds—$13,33—the hundred acres.

In fact, he was offered two hundred acres, including the point at the intersection of Licking and the Ohio rivers, as an inducement to settle there. These two hundred acres must now be worth considerably more than a million of dollars, if even sold at Sheriff's sale.

Rattle Snakes.

I remember the day when the danger of rattle snake bites was seriously felt and urged as an objection to a removal to the West. From what I know of the notions current eastward on this subject, I have no doubt that many emigrants felt a terror of rattlesnakes hardly inferior to that they entertained respecting the savages themselves. To this day, it is currently reported by most of our friends in the Atlantic cities, and in Europe, as devoutly held an article of faith as any fact of record in the Bible, that the bite of the rattle snake inflicts certain death. One of the last cautions I received on leaving the parental home, was to take care always to wear boots when out in the woods, and avoid all places where these reptiles were supposed to lurk.

Now, the whole popular notion on this subject, is a vulgar superstition, which must fade away in the increasing light of the age, and will some future day, rank among the belief in love philtres, the mad dog stone, the Phœnix rising from its ashes, the corpse bleeding afresh at the touch of the murderer, and various other common notions, most of which have been long since exploded, and the residue shortly will be. The simple fact is, that the bite of the rattle snake is rarely fatal, and no more dangerous than the sting of the honey bee, which, in some constitutions, will produce as severe and painful swelling as the rattlesnake's bite, although unaccampanied with the sickening sensations, which attend the last.

My residence for many years, has been in Western Pennsylvania, a country infested by the reptile, and during that whole period, I never heard of a death resulting from its bite, except one—that of a Mrs. Klingensmith, in Westmoreland County—in a settlement and population of three hundred thousand souls. In her case, its effects were greatly aggravated, if not rendered fatal by an enfeebled constitution. The usual remedy is, to drink sweet milk which vomits the patient, and relieves the deadly nausea following the bite. This or some other emetic is all I ever knew applied, in the hundreds of cases that occurred during my ten or twelve years dwelling in those regions. I well remember the merriment created there by my reading some recipes which I had found in the newspaper, such as go the rounds of the press in later days. My auditors felt as we should do in reading a recipe for the cure of a musquito bite.

The popular prejudice on the subject has no doubt grown out of the imperfect knowledge of the habits and character of animals, possessed by the natural historians of the last century.— Buffon, Goldsmith, and others of that day, wrote down not the result of their own observa-tions, but what they believed, and they were credulous enough to believe all they had been told on this and kindred subjects. It is only necessary to peruse the pages of Alexander Wilson, or Godman, or Say, or Audubon, to perceive that the past generation knew hardly anything accurately of the habits and nature of the animal world. How I became enlightened on such points, may be infered from the following narrative:

I was keeping a store in one of the towns in Western Pennsylvania, and having made acquaintance with a young fellow about my own age, a farmer, some five miles off, accompanied him home. One Saturday noon, on his own pressing invitation to spend the residue of the day in the country. It was a delightful day in July, and I enjoyed the walk and the scenery. With the hospitality which belongs to the American farmer, and that personal kindness which would not take on such matters, No, for an answer, it was insisted I should stay through the night.

The dwelling was a log cabin of a single room and loft, with an outhouse used for cooking in. The room which, as Goldsmith says, "sufficed a double debt to pay," served by day for a dining room and parlor, and as a bed chamber by night. On one side two bedsteads headed against each other, while a broad coverlet depending from the unplastered joists, answered for a screen and partition all the demands of decency and convenience. In one of the beds slept the young man and myself, in the other, his mother and sister, a young woman grown.

I was roused out of sleep towards morning, by the girl calling, Mother! mother! and listening further, heard her say in a low tone of voice, as if unwilling to disturb the stranger,

"There's a snake in the bed."

The old woman observed, "You have been dreaming, Fanny, go to sleep again."

Presently I heard the girl speaking in the same tone as before, "Mother, I am snake bit."

"Well," said the mother quietly, "get up, then, and light a candle." The girl did so, seized a stick, used to poke the fire, the mother having risen in the mean time, and killed the reptile in the act of crawling out to the floor to make his escape. The snake was thrown out of the door, and the parties went back to bed.

As for myself, I thought and felt faster than I ever did before in all my life. First, I wondered how people could go back to a bed after having just killed a snake in it. It would not astonish my readers now, more than at that time it did me. Then I tasked my memory how long persons lived after they were bit, and conjectured whether the girl would live till morning. At any rate, I hoped she would not die before I could get away from the house. All at once I reflected that there might be a snake in my bed also. From the crown of my head to the soles of my feet, my whole flesh quivered at the thought. As the poet says, "I was distilled to jelly with my fears." I sprang out of bed with a single leap, as quick and as softly at the same time as possible, made to the door, and finding it a clear and moonlight night, decided to step off, and make tracks home. In the act of dressing in the dark, however, I made a noise, which woke my companion, who missed me, and springing up asked what I was doing. I replied,

"I am going home."

"Wait till breakfast, and I will go with you," said he. Finding me still dressing, he asked, "What is the matter? are you sick?"

"No, but I am uneasy and want to go home."

"Have you dreamt anything wrong."

"No, but still I am very uneasy." At last I said "there was a snake in the other bed, and I was afraid."

"Afraid of what?" said he, laughing, "it could not bite you there, and there is none in our'n you may depend."

He then pressed me to stay till breakfast, saying he would sit up by the fire with me till morning, since I was afraid to go to bed again, assuring me, however, there was no danger, that it wasn't *often* that snakes got into bed with people, though it was natural for such a cold creature to try and warm itself; that if Fanny had only laid still and made no fuss, the snake would not have bit her, and more of such views of the case, with which it may be supposed, I had little sympathy. I staid, however. We had an excellent breakfast on venison steak, and Fanny, who, if she was to live, I supposed in the language of that country, would have been *bedfast*, for at least six weeks to come, waited on table as though nothing had occurred. Not a word was said on the event of the night, although it was hardly a moment out of my thoughts, all the time I was there.

Two days afterwards, she brought to the store a crock of butter, and a basket of eggs, to trade.

"Fanny," said I, "is this you? Why, I was afraid I should hear of your death before this time." She laughed and said,

"Rattlesnakes never kills any body."

And so I found out, after I remained long enough in the country to overcome my prejudices. She added that Jem, her brother, had lifted the puncheons of which the floor were made, after I went, and killed two rattlesnakes, there, They were both full grown. Next time I saw *Jem*, he amused himself, and the neighbors present, greatly, with the story. They obviously pitied my *cowardice*, but contented themselves with saying, when I got used to the country I would not mind a *snake bite* any more than a *flea bite.*

By what I have since seen South, in the Mississippi country, I have no doubt that the poison of the rattlesnake, and still more of the copperhead snake, is more virulent. The effluvia of these reptiles is absolutely sickening. The introduction into new settlements of hogs, which feed on them, serves to keep down their increase, and but for their dens in crevices where they cannot be followed, they would soon be extirpated from this source.

The hog is not more a glutton than an epicure, as any one knows, who is familiar with his habits, and there is nothing more delicious than the rattlesnake, at least when broiled on coals, as I know from experience. I have made many a meal on bull frogs, as well as eaten occasionally rattlesnakes, and hold that man's taste cheap, who regales himself with an opossum or rabbit, when he can enjoy such delicacies as these.

It is also a popular error, that the rattlesnake always warns with his rattle before he wounds. This led Dr. Franklin to consider him a generous enemy, and desire his adoption as our national emblem, rather than the Bald Eagle, which he considered a sneaking thief, plundering other birds of the prey they had taken. All this is a fallacy.

I doubt, greatly, from what I have seen, and learned of those who know his habits, whether the rattle snake ever bites as long as he has a chance to escape. It is his alarm doubtless which prompts him to rattle. At any rate, he is obliged to coil himself up before he can spring, which, with the sound of the rattle, usually serves to put the passer by on his guard.

Relics of the Past.
Ft. Washington, May 24th, 1792.

Dear Sir,—I have received your several favors by Capt. Peters and Mr. Hartshorn, and note the contents. Ward carries on some of the deficient articles out from the Quarter Master's department, and the balance, as far as they can be provided, will be sent out by the next convoy. The cooper cannot be spared from this Post.

I applaud the plan and progress of your buildings, and wish you to extend and to complete them, because I shall spend much of my idle time with you after our chief arrives. You should contrive some plan for cooling of wine, and preserving fresh meat, and butter, milk, &c. Mrs. W. and my sons set off for Philadelphia between the 5th and 10th of next month. The almighty Brigadier General has, I believe, conceived some jealousy of me; he may make the attempt, but shall not violate my rights with impunity.

The contractors must find men to drive his cattle, in my opinion, and that point is now before the Executive for their decision.

The difficulties respecting thé abstracts are easily removed. Open columns for the Quarter Master's department, and for extra allowances to fatigue, &c., artificers, wagoners, packhorsemen, (other than the contractors) come under the former. That you have not received the proceedings of the General Court Martial, is an omission which distresses me; the fault is Mr. Wade's, and is accidental.

In addition to our mounted Infantry, I am authorized to organize and levy a corps of 100 mounted riflemen, for the purpose of escorts. I recommended this plan last February.

I am sorry Capt. Kersey's drummer should march without my orders. I will send you the rifle powder and blank cartridges, and approve your idea of the appropriation, but we have no rifles. You have an undoubted right to cut up any party of the enemy who may be found lurking in the vicinity of your post.

Hardin and Truman left us day before yesterday, the former for Sandusky, the latter for the Maumee. I think it is equivocal, what may be the event, but do expect they will return.

I am, dear Sir,
Sincerely yours,
JAS. WILKINSON, B. Gen.

Jno. Armstrong, Esq.,
Capt. Comni ·   Hamilton.

Population of Cincinnati.

I am frequently asked my estimate of the population of Cincinnati. The late city election affords a pretty fair criterion of the number of our inhabitants, and its results agree with what the increase in buildings would indicate. In October 1840, election, this city polled 6,340 votes, being as full a vote to the population as has ever been given here. On Tuesday last, that vote was augmented to 9738, an increase of 54 per cent. in four years. A proportionate increase of inhabitants would give us 70,636 souls, as the result.

This it must be recollected is strictly within our corporate limits. If we add our adjacencies, as is done in Philadelphia, Pittsburg, St. Louis, &c., we cannot number less than 94,000, and in doing this I do not embrace a foot of ground west of our city boundary. I choose, however, as I have always done, to include in our city estimate only the Southern precinct of Mill Creek, and Fulton Township, which are absolutely suburbs of ours, and separated from us only by imaginary lines. In these bounds

there is unquestionably a population of 84,000 souls.

Let us now contemplate our progress for the last fourteen years:

Year	Population
1830	24,831
1831	26,071
1832	28,014
1833	27,645
1834	29,005
1839	42,529
1840	46,382
1841	50,650
1842	56,680
1843	62,817
1844	70,636

being, since 1840, an increase of 11 per cent. per annum, a duplication of our population in 7½ years. What this will lead to by the census of 1850, may be understood by the following comparative table, carrying on, in the first column, an annual increase from 1830 to 1840, of 6¼ per cent., and following out in the second the increase from 1840 to 1850 at the rate for the last four years, say 11 per cent.

1830	24,831	1840	46,382
	1,552		5,101
1831	26,383	1841	51,483
	1,649		5,663
1832	28,032	1842	57,146
	1,752		6,286
1833	29,784	1843	63,432
	1,862		6,977
1834	31,646	1844	70,409
	1,978		7,744
1835	33,624	1845	78,153
	2,101		8,596
1836	35,725	1846	86,749
	2,233		9,542
1837	37,958	1847	96,291
	2,372		10,595
1838	40,330	1848	106,883
	2,521		11,757
1839	42,831	1849	118,640
	2,677		13,050
	45,508	1850	131,690

This seems extravagant, but both the data and the calculations invite scrutiny, and defy dispute. I have been greatly ridiculed in 1840, after completing the census, for saying that I expected 100,000 would be found in 1850 within our city limits. I based this on a much lower rate of increase than has taken place within the last four years, and which must, *at least*, continue for the six years to come. What was considered absurd in 1840, it is now apparent upon the lowest probabilities, must be exceeded for 1850.

Provision Market of Cincinnati.

There has hardly been a period since the settlement of Cincinnati, in which the means of living,—the marketing articles of the place for example—were not abundant; and except during the great *soap-bubble* year 1837, correspondently cheap. Mr. John Shays the father of the pork-packing business here, put up pork in 1827, and I well recollect cart loads upon cart loads of spare-ribs, such as could not be produced any where at the east, or beyond the Atlantic, drawn to the water's edge and emptied in the Ohio to get rid of them. The influx of Germans and the rapid increase of inhabitants from 1830 onwards, gradually opened a market for these delicacies, as they would be esteemed if they were scarcer and costlier, & obviated such scandalous waste; but even yet a man may get a market basket filled with tender-loins and spare-ribs for a *dime*. Read this, ye eastern epicures! I cannot expect *you* to believe it, although every body in Cincinnati knows its truth.

Apropos of spare-ribs. There is a pleasant story extant on the subject. One of our citizens from Philadelphia and long a resident here, on his arrival in Cincinnati became an inmate with Mrs. G——, who keeps boarders. After boarding some months there, being in company with a friend, and the conversation falling on such subjects. "What a splendid table my landlady Mrs. G—— keeps," said the new comer. "Ah!" observed his acquaintance, "She must have lately got to keeping it. I boarded there formerly and never had poorer fare at any place. What does she give you?" "Why, to say nothing of other luxuries, we get spare-ribs for breakfast as much as four or five times a week, and the finest I ever tasted in my life." "Well," replied his friend drily, "If your landlady knew you were so fond of them, I suppose she could give you them *every* morning of your life. You don't appear to know that they cost her nothing. The fact is she can get a basket filled at any pork house in the city, by sending for it and not pay one cent." This was enough for the Philadelphian. Fond as he was of spare-ribs, the idea of eating what cost nothing, was too much for his imagination. As long as he boarded there, he never again touched the article.

I have got off my subject, which was the cheapness of provisions here. 1823 I think was a period of plentiful crops and uncommonly low prices. A farmer in the habit of dealing with Mr. Shays had brought in a waggon load of potatoes, for which he could find no purchaser in market. He then drove down to the store on Front street, and observing that the people did not seem to want potatoes, offered them successively at 12½, 10 and finally at 6¼ cents per bush-el. Mr. Shays had told him at first that he did not want potatoes, and at last remarked, when he found the man pressing them on him, that he had five thousand bushels then in the cellar, and thought it likely they would all spoil on his hands. The farmer was in a peck of troubles. His last chance was gone. "Well," said he, "I don't like the idea of taking a load of potatoes home, and *being its you*, I shant charge you any thing, and must try to make it out of you in some other trade." "Why," replied Shays, *being its you, if you will help down with them into the cellar, you may leave them.*"

This was accordingly done.

Bull Frogs.

"FORTY THOUSAND TAME FROGS!—The ascent to the peak of Teneriffe, made by Mr. Wise, our Minister to Brazil, and others from the U. S. frigate Constitution, on the 4th of July last, is described at great length and with much beauty and vivacity of style, in a letter in the Boston Atlas, of Monday, by Lieut. J. B. Dale, one of the party. Among other notable things celebrated, the writer notices a huge cistern in the richly embellished garden of the American Consul, from whence at twilight, issued the music of 40,000 tame frogs, cultivated with care for their musical talents."—*Times.*

I extract the above as an introduction to my experience on the subject of *Frogs*. Any person who has passed by ponds or marshes in the appropriate season, that would listen to the variety and extent of the music made by these *amphibia*. must suppose that it was produced by one hundred times the number of the actual performers in the concert; and let any one employ boys in such regions to catch them for table use, as is common in certain parts, he will find their numbers come far short of his estimate. The 40,000 in the extract from the *Atlas*, if reduced to an actual count would probably not reach fifty. The following narrative will shed some light on the subject.

Mr. George Sutton, formerly of Pittsburg, and well known there in that city, some thirty years since, as a practical joker, was extensively in business in 1814, and during that year and the next I was in his employ as clerk, in which capacity I witnessed many amusing scenes, in which he usually bore a conspicuous part. He had his periodical subjects of *boring*, and at the time to which I allude, his great hobby for that purpose was *bull frogs*.

Among our customers of that date, was a long, slabsided, gangling fellow from the Western Reserve, named Oviatt, who brought us in, three or four times a year, an assortment of beeswax, ginseng, popularly called *sang*, feathers, and other notions in the line of trade. He had made his purchases, and was proposing a contract for potash, as a means of enlarging his dealings, and finished by regretting that he had nothing else to supply us with. On this hint, Sutton spake, for it was like bringing fire from the flint, a single stroke sufficed.

"Have you any bull frogs in your neighborhood? I would not mind taking a few thousand put up in barrels, if you could supply them."

"Bull frogs! Mr. Sutton, what do you want with bull frogs."

"Why sir, I have a correspondent down at Baton Rouge, who has left a standing order with me for ten barrels, and I can't find any place where I can get it filled. I would make it worth any man's while to contract with me for the article."

"Well, now, Mr. Sutton, I vow to gracious there's *millions* in our neighborhood—but you are quizzing me, I snore."

"Upon my honor," replied Sutton, "I am perfectly serious. I will take ten or five barrels, or even two, and give fifty dollars a barrel to any gentleman who would contract with me."

Oviatt's eyes sparkled at the prospect.

"Well, Mr. Sutton, if you say so, I will put you up ten barrels—perhaps your friend may want more—and I hope you will give me the preference, if so. But you are not boring me, Mr. Sutton, I hope."

"My dear sir," said Sutton, "rest assured that I have long been at a loss to get the order filled, and am perfectly serious." Mr. Wahrendorf—his book-keeper—was directed on the spot to draw the memorandum in contract form, and Oviatt folding it away carefully in his pocket book, and doubtless calculating deeply on making a brilliant speculation out of us, as he seized the reins and sprang to the seat of his Yankee wagon, said:

"Don't forget, if your friend should want *twenty* barrels, to let me know in time."

We heard nothing from Oviatt for months, and by the time he made his re-appearance in Pittsburg, Sutton had some new subject on the carpet, and had lost sight of the bull frogs. Not so with me. I anticipated something amusing, being well aware, as was Sutton, in making the contract, that by the time the frogs would be caught, the millions would shrink into hundreds. I was silent, however, until Oviatt's purchases had been made, his produce credited, the account adjusted, and himself ready to start. I then remarked:

"One thing is forgot. Do you recollect our contract, Mr. Sutton, for the Baton Rouge house, for bull frogs?"

"I do declare," said Sutton, "I had almost forgot. What about it, Mr. Oviatt. Are they ready?"

The contractor looked as if he could have crept through an auger hole. He began to whimper like a school boy expecting a whipping—I hope Mr. Sutton you will let me off on that contract. I declare to gracious, I had forty boys out for six weeks, sir, day and night, and I never got more frogs than filled a barrel six inches high, and had to give it up at last. My dear sir, said Sutton, you have no idea of the disappointment. We never get a letter from these Frenchmen that they do not remind us of the bull frogs. They say the price is no object only get the frogs. Besides, I told them you could send them twenty barrels. My dear sir, if you can't make out on fifty dollars, I will give you a hundred dollars a barrel; so don't think of giving up. Put on more boys and give them better wages. Mr. Cist—calculate for our friend Oviatt what he can afford to give a dozen, supposing he pays twenty dollars a barrel. Its of no use, Mr. Sutton, replied Oviatt with a most rueful expression of face, and a deep sigh, I know it aint. It takes a power of hind legs to fill a barrel. In short the frogs must have disappeared, for they can't be found and unless you have a mind to ruin my family, bursting into tears, you will let me off. If you do said he, a thought suddenly striking him; Mr. Sutton, I'll bring you as fine a cheese as ever came out of the reserve. My dear sir, said Sutton, overcome by the scene, I wish to take advantage of no man. I see you have done your best, and my friends Menager & Co., must do without the frogs. I will explain the circumstances to them, and I hope they will be satisfied. If not, I will bear the consequences myself. As to the Cheese, never mind it.—We'll have a glass of beer, to reconcile all things. Here, Dick," said he, calling his man of all work, "go out to Mr. Neal's and get a gallon of beer, of Shiras' best."

Oviatt, smiling through his tears, at his lucky escape, drove off—doubtless vowing, internally, to be more careful with his next contract.

A Revolutionary Anecdote.

The following history of William Bancroft, in revolutionary days, may be read by some, with satisfaction, and is worthy to be kept in remembrance among the noble deeds of those times. It was related some years since by Mr. Bancroft, a slight notice of which is in Gordan's History of the American Revolution.

"When on a tour to the West, I met with the subject of this notice at New York. The grateful remembrance of the soldiers of the revolution by our country, became the subject of conversation. After there had been an interchange of opinion among us, Mr. Bancroft observed that he had applied to Congress for a pension, but owing to the circumstance that his name was stricken off the roll, before he had served nine months, to serve Gen. Washington in a more hazardous relation, he could not obtain it; tho' he thought his circumstances and his claims for consideration were as great as any soldier's. He then related the following history of his life:

"I was born in Woburn, north of Boston. At the age of 14, I was sent to Boston and put behind the counter. I was warmly attached to the whig cause, and at the age of 16 was obliged to leave town. I then enlisted in the army as a soldier for three years. I studiously endeavored to understand my duty in my relation, and I thought I was a proficient, at least, as much so as the other soldiers. One day, immediately after Washington's arrival at Brookline, I was detached by the officer of the day, among the guard. It so happened that I was placed as a sentinel before the General's quarters at 9 o'clock. About 10 o'clock, the General's carriage drove up, which I knew as a soldier, but not as a sentinel. I hailed the driver—

'Who comes there?'

He answered, 'Gen. Washington.'

'Who is Gen. Washington?'

He replied, 'the Commander of the American Army.'

'I don't know him; advance and give the countersign.'

The driver put his head within the carriage, and then came and gave me the countersign.

"The countersign is right,' I replied, 'Gen. Washington can now pass.'

The next morning the officer of the guard came to me and said, 'Gen. Washington has commanded me to notify you to appear at his quarters precisely at 9 o'clock.'

'What does he want of me?'

'I don't know,' replied the officer.

In obedience to his order, I went to his quarters at the time appointed; but my mind was greatly harrassed to know whether I had discharged my duty aright the night previous. I gave the alarm at the door and a servant appeared.

'Inform Gen. Washington,' said I, 'that the person whom he ordered to his quarters at 9 o'clock, is now at the door.'

The servant made the report, and immediately came and bade me come in, and conducted me to the General's room. When I entered he addressed me—

'Are you the sentinel who stood at my door at 10 o'clock, last night?'

'Yes, sir, and I endeavored to do my duty.'

'I wish all the army understood it as well as you do,' said the General. This relieved the burden on my mind.

The General then continued, 'Can you keep a secret?'

'I can try.'

'Are you willing to have your name struck from the roll of the army, and engage in a secret service at the hazard of your life, for which I promise you forty dollars a month?'

'I am willing to serve my country in any way you may think best.'

'Call here precisely at 7 o'clock this evening and I will give you further instructions.'

I then retired, and precisely at 7 o'clock I returned. The General presented me with a sealed letter without any superscription. He asked me if I had ever been on Roxbury Heights. I told him I had, and at his request I described the level ground on the top. He gave the countersign lest I should not be able to return before the sentinels received it; and on the way converse with no one, and if I should observe any person who appeared to notice me particularly,

not to go on the height, until out of his sight. And when I had ascended to the height, I must look round carefully, and if I discovered any person I must keep at a distance from him and suffer no one to take me. If every thing appeared quiet, I must go to the west side of the plain, there I should see a flat rock which I could raise by one hand, and a round stone about four feet from it; I must take the round stone and place it under the edge of the flat rock, which would raise it high enough to put my hand under it. 'You must then feel under the rock," said the General, 'till you find a second hollow, if there is a letter in it, bring it to me, and put this in the same place.'

Having received my instructions, I made my way for the height, and nothing occurred worthy of note, except that I found the rock and the stone described, and in the hollow a letter, sealed without any superscription. I then adjusted the rock and placed the stone as I found it. I returned to the General's quarters, and delivered the letter I found under the rock. He then said—

'You may retire and appear at seven o'clock to-morrow evening.'

This I did for some time, carrying and bringing letters, without being annoyed in any respect.

At length I observed a person at some distance traveling the same way I was going, and he eyed me with more attention than was pleasing to me. I took rather a circuitous route, and when I came on the height, I was confident I saw two persons, if not more, descend the hill on the opposite side among the savins. I went even to make the discovery, but could see no one. This I told the General on my return. He upbraided me for my presumption. He said, 'they might have sprung on you and taken you. Never do the like again.'

When I returned the next evening, he gave me a stricter charge than before. There was nothing occurred till I ascended the height; I then plainly saw three persons dodge behind the savins; I hesitated what to do. I placed my head to the ground to obtain a clearer view of the opposite side. In an instant three men rushed from behind the savins on the other side in full run to take me. I rose and ran with all my speed. No Grecian in their celebrated games exerted themselves more than I did. I found one of the three was a near match for me. When I came to the sentinel, he was not more than six rods from me. I gave the countersign without much ceremony. The sentinel then hailed my pursuer, who turned on his heel and fled. I went to the General's quarters, and on presenting this letter, I said—

'Here is the letter you gave me,' and then related the above story to him.

He told me I might retire and need not call on him again till he should give me notice. He strictly charged me when in company or in camp to make myself a stranger to the movements of friends or foes, never to enter into any dispute about the war or the army, but always be an inquirer.

In about a week the General sent for me, and I repaired to his quarters at the usual hour. He inquired if I was ever down on what was then called Cambridge Neck. I told him I had been there twice. He then handed me a letter as usual, and said—

'Go to the lower house and enter the front door, and when you enter the room if there be more than one person present, sit down and make yourself a stranger; when all have gone out of the room but one, then get up and walk across the room repeatedly; after you have passed and re-passed, he will take a letter out of his pocket and present it to you, and as he is doing this you must take this letter out of your pocket and present it to him. I charge you not to speak a word to him on the peril of your life. It is important you observe this.'

I went to the house, and on entering the room, I found but one man in it, and he was at the corner of the room. He rose at my entering. I immediately commenced my travel across the room, and eyeing him attentively.— The third time I passed he put his hand into his pocket, took out a letter and extended it toward him. With his other he took hold of my letter, and I did the same with his. I then retired with a bow, and returned to the General. We could well recognize each other,though we were not allowed to speak. This mode of communication continued for some time.

One evening, as this man was presenting his letter he whispered so me,

'Tell Gen. Washington the British are coming out on the Neck to-morrow morning at two o'clock.'

When I delivered the letter to General Washington, I addressed him thus:

'General, the person who delivered this letter to me whispered and said—

'Tell General Washington the British are coming out on the Neck to-morrow morning at two o'clock.'

The General started and inquired,

'Was it the same person you received letters from before?'

'Yes sir.'

He then broke the letter and read it, after which he asked,

'Did you speak to him?'

'No sir.'

Then saying,Stop here until I return," he took his hat and cane and locked the door after him. He was gone nearly an hour and a half.

When he returned, he said, 'I do not know that I shall need your services any more; you will continue about the encampment and I will allow you the same pay you now have.'

Having nothing to do, I had the curiosity to ramble about the army and vicinity to find the man who whispered to me,but I never saw him. Whether that whisper was fatal to him I know not. The injunction on me was tantamount to it in case of disobedience. I continued with the army till they left Cambridge, when I was discharged.

Fire Engines.

In the last "Advertiser," I expressed a conviction that the fire engine Cincinnati, lately built by Mr. C. H. Paddack,in this city, would prove, on trial, of equal or superior power and excellence to the "Fame," just received from Philadelphia, whose performance was recorded in the same paper. That trial was made last Saturday afternoon, and in all respects has justified my anticipations,and demonstrated publicly the gross impolicy and impropriety of sending abroad for fire apparatus.

The distance to which the Cincinnati threw water at her first effort, was, according to one measurement, 201, and by another, 214. At the lowest figures, allowing for the difference of measurement in length of pipe, &c., the distance was precisely that of the Fame, at her farthest performance, while the wind, which blew smartly in puffs on that occasion, gave that engine great advantage in the measurement. The Cincinnati cast water several feet over the spire of the Second Presbyterian church, on Fourth street, at the first trial, but it being apparent that no accurate judgment could be formed of heights in open air, no effort was made to exceed the first attempt. Her first performance in throwing upwards, exceeded the first performance of the same nature by the Fame, at least twenty feet, and equaled the fourth trial of that engine, as far as the eye could be made a judge.

Of course, trials of engines not made under circumstances precisely alike, afford no satisfactory test of superiority, nor do I believe either of the exhibitions referred to afford the best tests, since some engines may be made to throw as far as others, which are yet decidedly inferior in other respects. If doubts remain in the particular case of these two engines, let them be tried together before judges, composed of members of the fire department, and not belonging to either company. I have no doubt that not only the Cincinnati, but the Deluge, the Constitution, and a new Engine, building by Mr. Cummings, of our city, will prove able to put the question of superiority at rest.

As this is a somewhat exciting subject just at this time, I desire to state distinctly that the views expressed by me upon it, are not directed to promote the interests of Messrs. Paddack, or Cummings,but refer to the great duty of giving our home manufacture the preference, where equal excellence exists, since not only our pecuniary interests, but high moral considerations rest on the establishment of this principle. It is superfluous,after what we have seen at the Mechanics' Institute exhibitions, to insist that Cincinnati possesses in her mechanics and artists as much ingenuity and skill as can be imported from other places. But it will be in vain to offer engines or anything else, here, if we bring the same article from Philadelphia; for how can we expect to sell to our neighbors in the West, an article we ourselves repudiate.

This brings me one step farther in the argument. The Jefferson Co., at least some of the members, allege that it is nobody's business where they buy apparatus. As other companies are about to purchase new engines, it may be proper to discuss this point. How then, are the expenses of our Fire Companies borne, and who are the actual and virtual owners of the apparatus? Take the case of this Company for example. They allege that they obtained from the whole community but five dollars and ten cents, which were contributed by two individuals.

Their inference, therefore is, that the public have no claim upon them, such as would spring from pecuniary support. How is this? The city builds them an engine house, from which they derive revenue in the shape of rent, and an appropriation is made by the City Council, of one thousand dollars for the purchase of fire apparatus. I say nothing of the firemen's fairs, concerts, and soirees, to which the public so liberally contribute, because I cannot tell whether the Jefferson Co. have derived any revenue from this source. Have the public, then no right to say that the Fire Companies are bound to give a preference to our own engine builders, if they can make an article equal to those at the East?

We have three manufactories of Fire apparatus here, who deserve the patronage, and so far as public sentiment can be made to operate, will receive it.

Flax Seed Oil Cake.

Late developments of chemical science, prove that articles of food, are flesh, or fat forming in proportion to their deficiency or abundance of oleaginous matter. Thus peas and beans, which constitute the food of swine in England, are 30 per cent. flesh, and 52 per cent. fat forming articles, while in Indian corn 12 1-2 per cent. forms flesh, and 77 per cent. fat—the wastage on the first description of food being 18 per cent., and but 11 per cent. in the last. In point of fact, we find, as might be expected, therefore a greater degree of solidity in the English pork than in ours, and a far inferior coating of fat.

These facts serve to explain why *mast* as it is called, so readily fattens hogs.

One important result follows this subject. The increasing product of flax seed, and its market here must furnish one of the most important and efficient agents in fattening, the cake which is left in grinding out oil. As soon as it shall become known by experience, as it must, that oil cake possesses aliment for fattening more abundant, and at a lower price than other articles with which it competes, the amount made here will find a market on the spot. What that amount is, may be inferred from the fact that C. R. Miller & Co., of our city, alone manufacture near 1,000,000 lbs. annually.

To Readers.

I commence with this day's Advertiser, the publication of a very interesting article, "Recollections of a Voyage to Italy." It bears every mark of truth on its face, and the attention of my readers is solicited to the series.

I have to acknowledge various acts of kindness from my brother editors in Cincinnati in their comments on my enterprise, and in giving currency to my articles through the medium of their columns. These have *generally* been credited to me, and when they have not been, I am willing to attribute it to accident. As regards my co-laborers in this department of public teaching, being on good terms with them all, I am in the position of the butler in the Vicar of Wakefield" "I read," said he, "all the politics that come out. The Daily, the Public, the Ledger, the Chronicle, the Evening, and the Post, the seventeen Magazines, and the two Reviews, and though *they hate each other, I love them all.*"

As regards the Advertiser itself, my only regret is, that it is too popular for my interest, being extensively picked up and carried off by interlopers before my subscribers can get to peruse it. This, flattering as it appears, is doing me a serious injury. The paper costs but $2 per annum, and there is hardly one who cannot afford to pay for it. There is another and bolder class of depredators, for whom I am on the look out—out-door thieves, who take it off the knockers, and from front doors. As soon as I can get proper testimony, such persons shall be prosecuted for the offence.

Recollections of a Voyage to Italy in 1800

In the early part of my life, I was accustomed to pass my winters in Philadelphia, and the rest of the year in the country. I spent the greater part of 1799 in rambling through the wilderness which now forms the States of Ohio, Indiana, Illinois and Missouri. I hunted with the Indians, slept in their wig-wams, and was half tempted to remain with them. I am not conscious of being unstable in my pursuits; but when a lad, I was suffered to run wild, and even to those who have been more rigidly trained than myself, there is something very pleasing in changes and transitions, which, whether they are from "grave to gay" or from "lively to severe," are interesting from their contrasts, and strike our feelings as the lights and shades of a picture do our eyes. Among the Indians, who had seen me bring down a turkey on the wing with a single rifle ball, I had the reputation of being a good hunter, and capable of enduring much fatigue; but my companions in the city considered me as a mere Sybarite, and seldom found me out of bed before noon.

One reason of my indolence was, that I had nothing to do, and no one to direct me how to employ the passing hour. We may be "stretched on the rack of a too easy chain." I found that I yawned much more than those of my acquaintance who had something to occupy or interest them. I sometimes thought myself capable of better things. "I really do not know what to do with myself this summer," said I to my acquaintance, as we were sauntering along the street. "I really do not know where to go. I am tired of the city and yet I linger here, as if I had something to attach me to it. I have rambled in the country till there is little of novelty to attract me there. I cannot mount my horse without some greater inducement than riding for an appetite; and as to my horse, I have not seen him since I came here, although that is so long, that if he is alive I fancy the charge for his keeping must amount to at least the sum which I paid for him; and, indeed, unless the grooms ride him, he may have forgot the use of his limbs."

"If you are tired of both city and country," said my companion, "go to Europe." "You are fond of poetry, painting, and music—go to Italy." "Upon my word," replied I, "it might be very pleasant, and I think, I should like it." "Then I will make some enquiry about a ship to some port there, and will let you know if I can hear of one." "Be it so," said I, "I will obey your bidding, should you direct me even to "call spirits from the vasty deep." A few days afterwards he told me that a ship was ready to sail, bound to Leghorn. All I had to do was to send my trunk on board.

A ship was new to me. I had seen our great lakes, which resemble the ocean; but I had never seen the ocean. I was not, however, as ignorant of either, as an officer of the western army, who accompanied me to Philadelphia the preceding autumn. He was born on the frontier of Pennsylvania, and when about ten years of age, his father's family was surprised by the Indians, his father and some others killed, and he taken to one of the Indian towns, where he was adopted in an Indian family. The boy grew up among them; but his relations discovered him, and with difficulty prevailed upon him to return to his former home and associates. A lieutenant's com mission was procured for him, and he joined the western troop in a campaign against the Indians, in which he was much distinguished for his gallantry.

He had obtained a furlough, and accompanied me to the city. We arrived at night; the next morning he was out at daylight, and it was with difficulty that he found his way back to his lodging. He said that he would with more readiness have found his way through fifty miles of woods, than through five squares in the city. The following day he told me that he had seen a very large ship *marching* down the river; but he wished me to go to the Delaware with him, for it was the most singular river he had ever seen—one part of the day it ran one way, and at another time it ran another way,—he was sure of it; for he had been several times at the wharves, and had seen it running different ways with his own eyes. I found that he had not heard of the tide, and it was difficult to make him comprehend it. But to return to myself.

On the 23d of June the ship was ready to sail, and I shipped on board of her at the wharf, and she dropped down to New Castle, where she came to, to take the Captain on board, who, having something to execute, had been detained at Philadelphia after her sailing. Early the next morning the Captain came on board, and I found that he had already met with some adventures on his way. One of the sailors taking leave of his companions, had got into a frolic, and when the ship left the city, he was missing. As he was an excellent seaman, the Captain was unwilling to leave him behind, and after much search had found him, and, to use his own phrase, had chartered a chaise to take them to New Castle. It was dark when they crossed the ferry at Wilmington. The ground, in wet weather, is knee deep in mud. I was well acquainted with it; for, when a boy, I had spent many a day in shooting snipes in the marshes in that neighborhood; and thought it a good feat with a double barreled gun to kill two rising at the same moment, and flying in different directions.

After crossing the ferry the Captain found the

darkness increased by a thick fog which covered the flats, so that in a little time he could not see the horse before him; the consequence of which was, that driving too much on one side of the road, a wheel of the chaise got on the descending ground, and the Captain and his *compagnon de voyage,* were both thrown into a ditch full of deep water; but as water was their element, they probably came out like Commodore Tiunnion, invigorated by their immersion.— With much difficulty they got the chaise into its proper position, and as the Captain was unwilling to make any more summersets, he placed the sailor in the chaise, with, as he said, a brace in each hand, to follow, while he waded through the mud to *con*—explore—the way. Whenever the Captain found himself getting into the ditch on his starboard hand, he would call to Jack "port"—to which Jack would reply, with true nautical precision " port it is, sir," and pull the poor horse short up with the rein in his left hand. They got into New Castle, covered with mud, about one o'clock in the morning, and the Captain, as he did not like to come on board " unanointed and unannealed," changed his dress, and appeared among us in a very gentlemanly garb.

The ship was the Louisa, a letter of marque, mounting twelve guns, but appearing to have eighteen, six of them being what the sailors called Quakers; that is, very pacific ones, made of wood. She was commanded by Thomas Hoggard, and had a crew of thirty men. It was during our war with the French, and the owners of the ship had armed her, as a protection from the French privateers, which it was supposed she might fall in with.

The first sight of the ocean must strike the rudest breast with an impression of awe. Its immensity, and even its monotony, is sublime. But the appearance was not entirely new to me. I had seen the great lakes with their "blue, trembling billows, top'd with foam," apparently as shoreless as the ocean itself. The ship, however, and my companions were all novel, and when the pilot took his leave, I felt strongly the sensation which every one must feel who leaves a home which contains many who are extremely dear to him. We were outside of the Capes, and the breeze blew fresh and chill. There were many things to be arranged about the ship, at which the sailors busied themselves, and to the whistling of the wind among the rigging, was added the frequent piping of the boatswain, as orders were given to perform different evolutions. I put on my great coat, and remained on deck. The ship went rapidly through the waves. The spray dashed over our bows, while a train of phosphoric light sparkled in her wake. Velocity gives an impression of power, and produces delightful sensations.

Some French writer mentions a countryman of his, whom he met in Arabia, who had grown as wild as the Arabs themselves, who told him that nothing was so delightful to him, as to be mounted on an Heirie, and in full speed in the Desert. Strange as this may appear, I can readily believe it. But this feeling partly arose from the solitude in which he was placed, enabling him to fancy himself a more important part of creation, than he would have thought himself to be in the midst of a crowd.

I recollect the effect of the solitude of the western prairies, and can recall the thrill of mingled pain and pleasure which it produced by the consciousness of being alone in them. The horizon, without a tree, as unbroken as the ocean —the clear and cold moon within an hour of setting—a silence that could be felt, interrupted by the howl, at long intervals, of a solitary wolf, which seemed two or three miles distant. I never thought of the line of Campbell, "The wolf's long howl on Oonalaska's shore," without recollecting him of the Prairies. On shipboard there was no solitude, everything was bustle and noise. I went forward and cast my eyes over the bow, and enjoyed the dashing of the spray, as the ship's head was buried in the waves, out of which she rose like a feather, giving a powerful idea of the resistance of a fluid, which could so lightly repel a body of upwards of three hundred tons burthen.

Looking ahead, something, at first dimly descried became more and more distinct, and I soon found it to be a ship, approaching in an opposite direction to our course. Apprehensive that I might alarm my companions improperly, I remained long enough to be fully convinced of the nature and situation of the object in view, when going to a sailor who was engaged at something near me, "I said, "there is a vessel!" Jack turned to me, but made no answer. I repeated, "There is a vessel before us." Still no reply, but I heard one of the crew a little distance, ask another, "What does he say?" The wind was fresh, and the ship having a good deal of sail, heaved considerably, which together with her high bulwarks, and the bellying of the sails, prevented the sailors from seeing the approach of the stranger. I was apprehensive that the two ships would strike against each other; and suddenly conceiving that the inattention paid to what I said might be occasioned by my expressing myself in a dialect not understood on board ship, I called out "a sail ahead!" The man nearest to me promptly sprang forward, and seeing he danger, repeated my call in a voice like a trumpet, the helm was instantly clapped hard up, and the two ships, almost touching, and on different tacks, dashed by each other like the wind. The tars themselves felt it a narrow escape, and the one whose attention I had roused, exclaimed, after holding his breath, until we were fairly clear, "d—n my eyes, but that was touch and go!" We suppose that we had been unnoticed by the other ship. Not a word was said on either side. Many vessels, in all probability, are annually lost by coming in collision with each other on the ocean.

I have never been sea-sick, but the wind was chilly, and the sea rough, and I felt a slight qualmishness that intimated to me the propriety of retiring to my couch, where I slept as well as I could expect to be permitted to do, by the pitching of the vessel, and in a situation so novel. When I went on deck, in the morning, I found everything in excellent regulation. The sun had risen in an unclouded sky; the gale of the preceding evening had moderated to a fine breeze, and blew from a favorable point, and the Captain, with a very good natured countenance, was pacing the deck, apparently pleased
" To see
The gallant ship so lustly
Furrow the green sea foam."
We were out of sight of land. The sky and the sea were all that the eye found to rest upon; and the variety consisted of the foam-crested billows of the one, and the differently shaped and tinged clouds, which passed across the face of the other.

On shipboard, the character of the persons composing the family is of much importance to our comfort. I think it is Johnson who observed, that to be at sea is to be imprisoned with the chance of being drowned, excepting that, in prison you are very likely to meet with the most agreeable company. I, therefore, looked around to see how I was situated. The inmates of the cabin were, besides myself, the Captain, two mates, and an Italian gentleman, as a passenger. Of the latter, I recollect nothing, but that he sang agreeably, and appeared to have a tolerably favorable opinion of himself. The Captain's appearance told you that he was a sailor. He was about forty years of age; his idiom peculiarly that of his profession, so that at a table he would desire a person to *scull* that plate to him, &c. Of the mates, I at that time took little notice; I supposed them your everyday kind of sailors, with but little knowledge beyond that of their profession, but I was not a physiognomist, if I had been, I would easily have discovered in one of them, "the hand to do, the heart to dare."

I soon found that it would be useful to endeavor to occupy myself with something, in order to prevent my time from hanging heavily on my hands, and I told the captain that I would like to learn how to navigate a ship, and tasked his good nature to tell me the names and give me an explanation of the uses of the different parts of the rigging, and, in return, I would take upon me all the astronomical calculations necessary to ascertain his longitude. He expressed himself very willing to communicate the knowledge which he possessed of the subject which I was desirous of being acquainted with; but said it would be well not to ask questions of the sailors, who would form a very unfavorable opinion of one so ignorant as not to know the difference between the main brace and main top bowline. It was therefore agreed, that all my questions should be asked of him, and I was so apt a scholar, that in less than a fortnight, I ventured, under his particular instruction to give an order about some part of the working of the ship, and got through it with a pretty good tone. I was so much emboldened by this, that after having repeatedly gone aloft, begining with the main top, to which I took care at first to ascend by the weather shrouds, I had the hardihood, on the command to reef top sail being given, to make an essay to get on the main topsail-yard, during a squall, but in this essay, I found that I had over-rated my abilities; for when on the yard, as the ship pitched with great violence, it required the aid of a sailor on each side to enable me to maintain my position; and when I found myself safely on deck, I made a vow to abandon all yard arms during the remainder of my voyage.

I had a great inclination to see a storm at sea. It is related of some celebrated marine painter —I might say Vernet, but am not sure it was he; and it was most probably some one of the Dutch school—that when the ship in which he sailed, was in danger, and he lashed to the mast, while the sailors beheld their situation with the greatest apprehensions, he viewed it merely as a picture, and was delighted with the effect of the scene, and engaged, in imagination, in transfering to the canvass, the magnificent swell of the foaming billows. My curiosity did not lead me so far as to wish to be in any danger; I was therefore willing to put up with a very moderate storm, and not disposed to insist on the mast being carried away, or the ship left a wreck. One night, one of the officers awoke me with the information that there was a fine gale of wind, and some lightning to be seen, which it was worth going on deck for. I accordingly got up. The sea did not, as we are told by voyagers it frequently does, run mountains high; but it certainly ran very lofty. The ship lay to under a stay-sail, which was the only sail set. The wind did not merely whistle, but whizzed through the rigging with such force, that, together with the roaring of the waves, it was difficult to distinguish the words of a person exerting his voice, to me; and the lightning flashed in such streams that, considering the artillery on deck, and the iron in all parts of the ship, it appeared to me that we should scarcely escape it. There was no bustle on board. The ship had been made *snug*.— The rain fell in sheets; but the sailors, who were accustomed to "bide the peltings of the pitiless storm," seemed very much unconcerned in the midst of a scene which might have been sufficient to terrify a landsman. As for the mate, whose watch it was, he looked as if he could have said with the boatswain in the Tempest, "Blow till thou burst thy wind, if room enough;" while, for myself, I might be excused if I

"Ey'd the shrouds and swelling sail,
With many a benedicite."

I, however, felt sufficient composure, for when I went on board, aware that scenes of this kind in which there was no danger might appear to an eye unaccustomed to them in a very fearful light, I determined to take my tone, as much as possible, from the aspect of the sailors around me, and therefore looked to their countenances, rather than to the billows, in order to form my opinion of the risk, and seeing them very tranquil, I readily became so myself. I cannot say much about the storm, although I believe it might be considered as a pretty specimen of foul weather, "fair is foul, and foul is fair;" other voyagers have seen much sublimer ones.

But I don't like storms, and detest tempests, which, I suppose, are in the scale of comparison, as the superlative to the comparative. I would not give one Zephyr for a thousand Austers, Euruses, or Boreases.

The rising and setting of the sun, when his full orb is seen just over the horizon, is very fine; and moonlight nights are delightful. The moon has been the theme of poets in all ages, and nothing can equal the soothing and tranquilizing effects of its clear light at sea. In the dewy freshness of the night, I have gazed for hours upon its fine aspect on the waves, as they danced and sparkled in its brilliancy, which marked a broad path for the vessel to the verge of the horizon. Nothing can be more delightful than this effect when the weather is fine, and the wind fair; for then there is no noise of orders given or bustle to execute them, to mar your meditations; and the consciousness of speeding on your course, the tranquility on board, and the gentle dashing of the wave as it breaks against the ship's bows, and passes along her sides in glittering foam, harmonizes deliciously with the "night's regent," when "riding at her brightest noon." At a late hour of the night, when the *mid-watch* had been some time on their duty, the helmsman at his post, attentively eyeing the needle by which his course is directed, and which has been exquisitely compared to the sensitive heart, that

"Turns at the touch of joy or woe,
And turning, trembles too,"

the officer in command, pacing the quarter deck with a regular and monotonous step; the crew silent, or the indistinctly heard voice of some one narrating his adventures, or a tale which he has heard or read, to his listening companions; all together form a picture which I have felt very powerfully on my heart and imagination. In these fine evenings, a sailor who can tell a good story is a valuable acquisition to his shipmates, who are not, in general very fastidious about style, provided he will give them sufficient incident. I was on deck late one night, all sail was set, and the wind fair on the quarter, when hearing some thing on the forecastle, which from the tone of the speaker appeared to be some tale of his adventures, I went forward, that I might be a partaker of it and stood unseen in the shadow of the foresail. I found the speaker whose comrades were seated around him, narrating to them a tale which he had read in the Arabian Nights; but having forgot the words he was obliged to give it in his own phraseology. He told them of the king of Persia's son, who having fallen in love with the Emperor of China's daughter, had been seperated by some malignant *Ginny.* Here he was interrupted by the question of what was a *Ginny;* this he could not tell, but supposed it to be a conjurer. That the young woman fell sick, and her lover discovering her, sought to introduce himself as a "foreign doctor," who could cure all maladies, but on the nurse informing her that a foreign doctor wished to see her, the princess swore, "d—n her eyes, if he should come within a boat-hook's length of her." The story which lasted nearly an hour, was all in this style, and extremely well relished by the auditors; and by none more than myself. I wished I could repeat it to you throughout, in the manner in which I heard it.

MARRIAGES.

On the 10th inst., by A. Drury, Mr. WM. BURROWS, of Cincinnati, Ohio & Miss MATILDA CULBERTSON, of Kenton Co., Ky.

On the 15th inst., by the same, Mr. EPHRAIM D. MERRELL and Miss ELLEN E. ROBINSON.

On the same day, by Rev. Mr. Orr, Mr. JOHN WILLIAMS of this city, and HARRIET LEATHERS, daughter of Capt. P. Bliss. of Covington, Ky.

On the 16th inst., by Rev. James E. Wilson. Mr. THOS. J. FINCH and Miss ELIZABETH H. CARR, of Alleghany city. Pa.

On the 17th inst., by Rev. Mr. Lowry, Mr. SAMUEL WINALL and Miss LYDIA WOOLSEY, both of this city

DEATHS.

On the 13th inst., Mrs SARAH A., wife of John W. Sullivan and second daughter of WM. P. Willams, aged 24 years.

At St. Charles, Mo.. Rev. J. H. FIELDING, President of the St. Charles College, on the 15th inst.

In this city, on the 16th inst., Mr. ERASMUS BENSON.

On the 18th inst., of the Bronchitis, in the 5th year of her age, Helen, daughter of George W. and Susan L. Phillips.

Cisterns, and Well and Cistern Pumps.

I recollect the period in Cincinnati when the old fashioned cistern of cooper work was all that the great mass of our citizens had to depend on as a receptacle for water. The great depth and consequent expense of wells forbade a resort, in early days, to such a medium of supply. As the water works became extended over the city, the public has felt less interest in constructing cisterns, and except along the north and west lines of our city, they are now rarely built. I hold this to be great impolicy. There is a comfort and luxury in cistern water, now that cisterns are cemented with hydraulic lime, for which nothing else is a substitute. The water is here preserved at an uniform temperature throughout the year, rendering it more acceptable, either in summer or winter, than that which flows from the hydrant. It is, besides, a purer and of course wholesomer article. I say nothing on the subject of the protection cisterns afford families in the earlier stages of a fire, when a bucket full obtained on the spot, and at an instant, is of more value than hogsheads full at a later period of its ravages. It is well known, too, that the supply of river water is inadequate to the consumption of the city, even where hydrants exist. On occasions, too, that supply is entirely shut off. Under these considerations, it will be seen, that no family, if possible, should be without a cistern. They are now built inconceivably cheap; as low, I learn, as ten dollars for a small one.

If cisterns are built, we necessarily want pumps. Of these, there is a variety made in Cincinnati, all more or less convenient and efficient. But examining, of late, the public pump, on Lower Market street, I incline to think it among the best.

This is Van Allen's patent, and extensively manufactured by Messrs. Wardell & Atkinson, on Hopple's Alley, in our city. They are of wood, the tubes coated with a composition to preserve them, which appears as impenetrable as metal. The joints are of iron screws, which hold with a firmness that defies the strain always created in pumping, and secures an air tightness not attainable in wooden joints. Two excellencies I notice in these pumps. The valve being perfectly loose, clears itself at every stroke of the piston, and the valve seat being concave, it becomes impossible for any substance to get fastened between the valve and the seat, as is so frequently the case on the ordinary principle. The importance of this will be readily understood by those who have been annoyed by gravel, &c. being carried up in pumps, and lodging in the bucket.

Mr. Wardell, in the establishment to which he belonged, in Philadelphia, I learn, has made and sold fifteen thousand of these pumps.

The Well, on Lower Market street, is 52 feet deep, and the pump there has been in constant service for the last 18 months, in perfect order all that time.

Wardell & Atkinson also build cisterns, furnish and set grates, furnaces and chimney pots.

Marriage Licences.

In the list of marriages of this week, there is "Married, by the Rev. James F. Wilson, THOMAS J. FINCH to Miss ELIZABETH HOLMES CARR, of Alleghany City, Pa."

There is an incident connected with this event worthy of remark. I was assured by the groomsman, as he handed me in the notice of the marriage, that such was the influence of the scene on his feelings, that but for the want of a marriage license, he should have stepped forward and become a principal also, instead of playing second fiddle on the occasion.

This confession speaks volumes, and determines me to go for the repeal of marriage licences, as soon as I can get time to agitate the subject. Here is a youthful pair, fitted to ornament society in the family relation, ready to plight their vows, and the State steps in, like the Dutch Squire, in Pennsylvania, with "vare ish mine tollar?" banishing all the romance of fond affection, compelling the impatient lover to wait "the law's delay,"and interposing a veto from the exercise of which even Old Hickory, in the plenitude of his iron will, would have shrunk. Here are two congenial spirits separated, perhaps never more to meet, who, but for the pre-requisite of these hateful licences, might have 'like kindred drops been melted into one.'

On these and other considerations, I go for the repeal of the marriage license system. What right, I would seriously ask, has society to interpose even the slightest obstacle in the shape of expense or delay to the establishment of that relation on which its whole well-being depends?

Millerism.

This delusion has been producing here as elsewhere, its appropriate effects. Friend Eshelby knocked off on Saturday, declining to take any more measures. Those of the brethren who are carpenters have locked up their chests of tools, and other mechanics have laid down work also. As the day approaches, to which they look forward as the consummation of all earthly things, the faithful adventists continue nearly the whole time, day and night at the Tabernacle, corner of John and Seventh sts. What the consequences will prove when the 23rd shall have passed away and the 24th dawn upon us, it is fearful to contemplate. These believers have been gathered out of every Christian church in the land, and yet I have no doubt, a majority of them will be brought when they behold the fallacy of their calculations, to the awful conclusion that the Bible is a lie. Well was it prophesied of such, *"They be blind leaders of the blind,"* and both must fall into the ditch.

One of the brethren whose wife did not hold the same views, came into the breakfast room and said he believed he should not work any more, and should employ the few days that remained in preparation for the great event. After sitting some time and seeing no signs of breakfast, he inquired how soon it would be ready, when his wife replied, that she thought as he did, and concluded to cook nothing more, particularly as the apostolic injunction to the church was, "If a man will not work neither shall he eat." He hesitated a little while and then added, If you will get me some breakfast I will go to work again.

Relics of the Past.

The following letter from Capt. Armstrong, to General Wilkinson, derives much interest from the incidents relative to Lieutenant, now General Gaines, refered to therein. The last letter of Wilkinson's published, desires Armstrong to advise Gaines, then Ensign, of his promotion to a Lieutenancy. By this it will be seen that General Gaines has been more than fifty-two years in continued service, a length of time which perhaps has no parallel in military history. He is probably the only commissioned officer who survives of Wayne's army of the west, and undoubtedly the only one still on the military roll.

FORT HAMILTON, June 1, 1792.

Dear Sir:—Your letter of the 24th May, came duly to hand, I am pleased with the idea of having much of your company this summer. I have happily anticipated your wishes. I have a cellar adjoining the well, and in part of it a cistern that contains about four hundred gallons, which I fill with water once every day, which serves to keep the cellar cool, and answers the purpose of a fish pond. The pleasing idea of being received into the arms of friendship in Philadelphia must, in some measure, lessen the fatigues of the long journey your lady is about to undertake. I sincerely wish her a pleasant and safe passage.

Will you come and eat strawberries with us? If we had a cow you should have cream also Green peas we have in abundance; if you could spare some radish seeds, their produce would hereafter serve to ornament your table. Four of the cattle left for the supply of this post, broke from the drove some days since, took the road for Fort Washington, and could not be overtaken by the party on foot who pursued them as far as Pleasant Run. One other this morning swam across the river, and is so wild that Mr. Ewing has crossed to shoot him; there is, therefore, only one bullock remaining, he will give the garrison about four days' provision.

You will, no doubt, receive by this express a letter from Lt. Gaines, inclosing two orders relative to the —— of this garrison. Should he inclose you the orders of the 25th and 31st of May, any thing that may appear ambiguous therein, will be explained by the following relation. I had filled the cistern already spoken of in the evening, in order to give the water the night to settle, for the use of the troops next day. Mr. Gaines drew the plug and emptied it. As the drawing three or four hundred gallons of water is attended with much fatigue, by way of reprimand I observed to Lt. Gaines, that if directing him to attend the filling and emptying it would have any other effect than to hurt his feelings, I would direct his attention thereto for a month. His reply was, that he would disobey such an order, the issuing of which will be the cause of a complaint. *He is young in service, and will learn better.* I have read him this part of my letter, and referred him to the 18th chapter of the Baron's instructions.

From the list of appointments accompanying your list, I see there are but three brigadiers appointed. I think the law says four, and I hope means yourself.

Respectfully,
Your ob't Serv't,
JOHN ARMSTRONG.

Brig. Gen. JAMES WILKINSON.

Benjamin Franklin.

I have, in my possession, a file of the Pennsylvania Gazette, for a series of years, beginning at 1744, just a century since. The earliest years bear the imprint, "Philadelphia, printed by B. Franklin, Post-Master, at the new Printing Office near the Market." The first number bears date August 16, 1744, and displays the effigy of the British Lion with the motto, "Mercy, Justice." Every thing about the paper is remarkable. Negro women and men are as freely advertised for sale, as they would be in a Louisiana paper of the present day. Dutch and Irish servants are advertised in some places for sale, and in others, as runaways from their masters. Other advertisements equally characteristic of the times, abound. But the great leading topic for thought is, "Here is a newspaper, published in the then principal city of the United States, extending its circulation over half the inhabited continent, and the composition, press-work, editing, and even the mailing—for these papers bear his well known writing on the address—all performed by one man; by a man, who, by the force of his unaided energies, became identified with the history of his age and country, in politics, science and literature." And the paper, a weekly sheet, only one fourth the size of the "Advertiser," but adequate, probably, to the wants and desires of the age. What a wonderful revolution has the press wrought in later days!

Fuel.--Coal.

As the season of laying in Coal for the winter consumption is at hand, I wish to call public attention, once more, to the fact, that we have, in the Pomeroy Coal mined, in our own vicinity, an article which ought to supercede the highly bituminous coal of Pittsburg and Wheeling—first, because it affects the lungs much less, and secondly, because it does not disfigure our house fronts as much as the rival articles. I press this matter with great earnestness, from the strong desire I have that the great and increasing consumption of Coal, as fuel, here, should not become the means of staining and discoloring our fair city. This is a matter, I hold,in which the whole community has a deep stake, and one by which our prosperity, as well as our pride, are affected—much of the rapid growth of Cincinnati resulting from its beautiful appearance, which is constantly attracting strangers to settle in the place.

MARRIAGES.

On the 20rd inst., by the Rev, E. W. Sehon, C. A. GARRETT, of the firm of C. A. Garrett & Co., and Miss ELIZA A. JORDAN, all of this city.

On the 23d' inst., by the Rev, N. L. Rice, Mr.P. M. FARNSWORTH, of the Atlas Office, and Miss MARTHA FULTON, eldest daughter of Robert Fulton, Esq., all of this city.

On the 23d inst., by the Rev. Hart Judah, Mr. ISAAC LIEBENSTEIN and Miss ADELINE WOLF, both of this city.

In Covington, Ky., on the 23d inst., by the Rev. Mr. Bayless, Mr. JOHN G. WEBB and Miss PAMELA PAYNE, all of this city.

On the 24th inst., by Rev. Mr. Deering, Mr. ALEXANDER C.CHRISTOPHER and Miss SUSAN JONES, daughter of Wm. H. Steele, all of this city.

On Fifth Day, the 24th inst., in Friends' Meeting, JAMES TAYLOR and ELIZABETH C. daughter of the late Wm. Shipley.

DEATHS.

On Friday morning, Oct. 18th, 1844, at the house of her uncle,Nathan Stewart,on Sycamore St., south of 8th, Miss Jane F. Tuley, of Scarlet Fever, aged 21 years.

Monday evening, at 10 o'clock, in the 35th year of his age, Mr. Wm. Ryall, formerly a native of Halifax, Novia Scotia.

On Wednesday afternoon, 23d inst., at half-past 3 o' clock, Amelia A. Cnamplin, daughter of Matthew F Champlin.

On the 21st inst., after a severe illness of a few days VANNELIA JAMES, infant daughter of James R. and Angelina Smith.

Changes in Transportation.

It is but a few years since, that the mackerel and herring put up at the east in the fall, only reached us in Cincinnati at the opening of the spring business, there being felt too great a risk in the circuitous and tardy route of the shipment of its being intercepted by the closing of navigation either of the Ohio or the canals One among many evidences of a change in this respect, I noticed on Wednesday last, the 23rd inst., in a row of barrels of herring and mackerel, inspected and branded October, 1844, and lying opposite Elliott's. Lower Market. Those who relish the luxury of a fat mackerel, but a few days in salt, can appreciate the benefits which our modern approximations eastward are conferring on us.

Mike Fink.

BY HIRAM KAINE.

In the interval between the first commencement of trade and travel on the Ohio and Mississippi rivers, and the introduction of steamboats, a race of men, with peculiar and distinct habits and manners, sprang into existence upon the silent waters. They were composed of old Indian fighters, who, on the return of peace, could not abandon their predatory habits, and of refugees from more civilized classes of society, who saw an attraction in the wild life of adventure led by the Boatmen. No trace is now left of them,—as the steamboat-man of the present day is no more like his keel-boat progenitor, than the "hand" on a fishing-boat is like a salt water sailor. We will not undertake to say in whose favor this difference would operate. It is very possible that while much of the blunt sincerity and courage of former times has degenerated into ruffianism, society. at least along the rivers, has gained by the safety of its property from lawless pillage.

As Mike was the last, so was he the most celebrated of all the "River men." To this day there is scarce a town or city between Pittsburgh and New Orleans, that has not some tradition in which he bears a conspicuous part. He appears to have been a man of great personal strength and courage, and of singular energy of character.

From what we have been able to learn, Mike was born about the year 1780, in Allegheny co., Pa.; and his early adventures in the city of Pittsburgh, were of themselves sufficient to form a volume of wild romantic interest, illustrative of the bloody character of the Indian wars.

While a mere stripling, Mike enlisted in a corps of scouts, a body of men who "fought the Indians in their own way," and exulted in the capture of a scalp, as much as did their savage enemies, Many were the bloody and desperate conflicts in which they were engaged; and here Fink displayed those admirable qualities of courage and fortitude, for which he was afterwards so famous. One of his adventures, while a scout, is worthy of a recital; and it was one which he himself used to tell with great pride.

"As he was creeping along one morning with the stealthy tread of a cat, his eye fell upon a beautiful buck, browsing on the edge of a barren spot three hundred yards distant. The temptation was too strong for the woodsman,and he resolved to have a shot. at every hazard. Re-priming his gun and picking his flint, he made his approaches tn the usual noiseless manner. At the moment he reached the spot from which he, meant to take his aim, he observed a large savage, intent upon the same object, advancing from a direction a little different from his own, Mike shrunk behind a tree with the quickness of thought, and, keeping his eye fixed on the hunter, waited the result with patience. ' In a few moments the Indian halted within fifty paces, and leveled his piece at the deer. In the meanwhile, Mike presented his rifle at the body of the savage, and at the moment the smoke issued from the gun of the latter, the bullet of Fink passed through the Red man's breast: he uttered a yell and fell dead at the same instant, with the deer. Mike re-loaded his rifle, and remained in his covert for some minutes, to ascertain whether there were more enemies at hand, he then stepped up to the prostrate savage, and having satisfied himself that life was extinguished, turned his attention to the buck, and took from the carcass those pieces suited to the process of jerking."

In the progress of years, however, the great West began to fill up with a white population; and the tribes either retiring or making peace the occupation of the scouts was gone. Some of them settled down as farmers,—others still ranged the woods as hunters—but by far the greater number commenced trading on the river. Among this latter number was *Mike Fink*, who by his superior courage and dexterity, soon became the most famous of all his companions. By the phrase, trading on the river, our readers are not to understand the system of commercial intercourse which now covers the Western waters with floating palaces. A broad low flatboat, with a "cabin" erected in the centre, in which the crew slept upon straw, propelled by long poles, constituted the only vehicles for transportation. Upon these "dug outs," the richest cargoes were often taken from Pittsburgh to New Orleans; and though anything but secure guardians to the property along the river, we believe there is no example on record, of dishonesty towards their employers by the boatmen. *Mike's* standing, in this particular, is thus summed up in the fragment of a work, a few leaves of which have been sent to us by a friend, entitled, "The Last of the Boatmen,"—"Every farmer on the shore, kept on good terms with Mike; otherwise there was no safety for his property. Wherever he was an enemy, like his great prototype Rob Roy, he levied the contribution of Black mail for the use of his boat. Often at night, when his tired companions slept, he would take an excursion of five or six miles, and return before morning, rich in spoil. On the Ohio he was known among his companions by the appellation of the "Snapping Turtle," and on the Mississippi he was called the "Snag."

This was the palmy period of Mike's career. He was in all but name, a king. Law,—he recognised none, save his own wishes, while he possessed unbounded influence over his comrades. His personal appearance at this period is thus described in the sketch before us:—"He was leaning carelessly against a large beech, and as his left arm negligently pressed a rifle to his side, presented a figure that Salvator would have chosen from a million, as a model for his wild and gloomy pencil. His stature was upwards of six feet, his proportion perfectly symmetrical, and exhibiting the evidence of Herculean powers. To a stranger he would have seemed a complete mulatto. Long exposure to the sun and weather, on the lower Ohio and Mississippi, had changed his skin; and but for the fine European cast of his countenance, he might have passed for the principal warrior of some powerful tribe. Although at least fifty years of age, his hair was as black as the wing of the raven. Next to his skin he wore a red flannel shirt, covered by a blue capote ornamented with white fringe. On his feet were moccasins, and a broad leathern belt, from which hung suspended in a sheath a large knife, encircled his waist.

His wonderful skill with the rifle, was not among the least imposing of Mike's claims to the admiration and obedience of the wild people among whom he lived. Various stories of the singular precision of his aim, are still extant. While passing Wheeling once, a negro was walking up from the beach with a small pitcher upon his head. Although at a considerable distance, the unerring rifle knocked the vessel from its resting-place, to the no small amusement of his companions. Another feat is thus narrated of him:—

"Mike, followed by several of his crew, led the way to the beech-grove some distance from the landing. I invited my fellow-passengers to witness the scene. On arriving at the spot, a stout, bull-headed boatman, dressed in a hunting-shirt, but bare-footed, in whom I recognised a younger brother of Mike, drew line with his toe, and stepping off thirty yards, turned round fronting his brother, took a tin-cup which hung from his belt, and placed it on his head. Although I had seen this feat performed before, I acknowledge 1 felt uneasy whilst this silent preparation was going on. But I had not much time for reflection ; for this second Albert exclaimed—

'Blaze away, Mike, and let's have the quart.'

My 'compagnons de voyage,' as soon as they recovered from the first effect of their astonishment, exhibited a disposition to interfere. But Mike, throwing back his left leg, levelled the rifle at the head of his brother. In this horizontal position the weapon remained for some seconds as immoveable as if the arm which held it was affected by no pulsation.

'Elevate your piece a little lower, Mike, or you will pay the corn,' cried the imperturbable brother.

1 know not if the advice was obeyed or not. But the sharp crack of the rifle immediately followed, and the cup flew off thirty or forty yards, rendered unfit for future service. There was a cry of admiration from the strangers, who pressed forward to see if the fool-hardy boatman was really safe. He remained as immoveable as if he had been a figure hewn out of stone. He had not even winked, when the ball struck within two inches of his skull.

'Mike has won!' I exclaimed. And my decision was the signal which, according to their rules, permitted him of the target to move from his position. No more sensation was exhibited among the boatmen, than if a common wager had been won. The bet being decided, they hurried back to their boat, giving me and my friends an invitation to partake of 'the treat.'

Another feat he used himself to narrate with much relish. Once, while floating down the middle of the stream, he discovered a negro, with his foot upon the fence, watching the boat as it passed.

'That nigger's heel is entirely too long for use. Who'll bet I can't trim it from here?' said Mike.

A quart was instantly staked,—and Mike, slowly raising his rifle to his shoulder—the "nigger" was saved several inches of leather in after times.

But it would fill a volume to detail half of the strange legends of which Mike was the hero; and we must close our researches into his history, for the present.

Animal Magnetism.
No. II.

I have said that many of the occult workings of nature, as observed in Pennsylvania, are not less wonderful than the mesmeric phenomena, and that as they establish the great fact of the universal sympathetic principle which pervades all nature, they corroborate the general truths of Animal Magnetism and Neurology.

A dislike to lengthen an article already too long, forbade my resorting to specifications in my last article on this subject. I have, therefore, exposed myself to cavils and doubts as to the matters of fact which are involved in the various modifications of the mesmeric, or great sympathetic science, as they exist in Pennsylvania, and probably elsewhere. Be it my employment now, to furnish a narrative of individual cases, which rest on the testimony of men resident here and whose veracity and intelligence cannot be impeached by any man in the community. Their names can be had on application to me.

Many years since, said my informant on one of these points, I kept store in Baltimore. Myself and a clerk in my employ, were one evening sitting at supper, when an inmate of the family burst into the room with, Oh! Mr. D., Mrs. Morrison's child is just scalded dreadfully, and cannot live. Mrs. Morrison was one of our neighbors. Let us go over to her house, said Mr. G., the clerk, I can cure the scald. I stared at him, but on his rising to go over, went along. There was the child scalded as badly as I ever saw a human being, and in perfect agony. The mother had bathed it in oil, and bandaged it over, but the screams continued and were dreadfully distressing. Madam, said G., please take off these bandages. What for, said the mother.— I can extract the fire if you do. She declined. I added my request to that of my clerk. The bandage was removed and the appearance of the body was awful. I had no idea that the child could live twenty-four hours. As soon as it was entirely stripped, G. leaned over it, breathed on it, and said a few words in a low tone. The child hushed up instantly, and not even a moan or a sob followed. Come said Mr. G., the pain is gone, let us go back to supper.

The scald healed in a few days. I never could get him to tell me how he operated the cure; when I spoke to him on the subject, he always contrived to change it. He could also stop bleeding at a moment's notice, and without a failure.

Another very remarkable faculty he possessed, which was, that if the names of two persons were handed on a piece of paper to him, he could invariably tell which would first die.

Hear the testimony of a second witness, as respectable a man as any in Cincinnati, or anywhere else. I had a fine horse which had the *hokes*, said my informant, and I took him to a celebrated farrier in our neighborhood, to be cured. Besides being cut in the eye for this complaint, he was bled to reduce the fever which accompanied it. The operation being delicately and skilfully performed, took up nearly the whole morning, and by the time it was completed, the dinner was ready, of which I was invited to partake. I was, however, unwilling to lose sight of the horse, who was bleeding freely, and hesitated to comply. It was a summer day, and the door to the dinner room which led to the yard, was wide open, and I was enabled by a slight movement of the head, to keep my eye almost at the same moment on both the farrier and my horse. The horse appeared considerably exhausted with the loss of blood, and being a valuable one, I became alarmed, and told the operator that he would bleed to death. No danger replied he, that is the life of the cause. I persisted, however, and told him he must come out and we would bandage him up, so as to stop the bleeding. Oh! said he, if that is what you want, I can do it here just the same. So saying, he turned himself on his chair at the table, and without rising from his seat, repeated something, and perhaps made some motions, and the blood which had been running a steady stream, stopped flowing, instantaneously. I am certain not another drop fell after my attention was directed to the horse. I have seen other persons who could also stop bleeding, in a manner equally remarkable.

In 1814, I resided on Diamond Alley, Pittsburg, said another person to me, a very intelligent man, where I kept the most extensive livery stable in the place. The water which was used for the horses, had become unfit for further service, and we had dug a new well, in sinking which, we went a great depth, and after all the water was not fit to use. As it had cost much trouble to dig it so deep, the disappointment was great, and I was the more annoyed at the circumstance, by the fact, that absolutely I did not know what to do next. In this perplexity, an individual who proved to be a well digger by profession. came along, and after examining the premises, remarked to me that I should have dug *there*, pointing to a spot about five feet along side. I was so provoked with him, in my then excited and worried state of feeling, that I told him petulantly, that he only said so because he wanted a job of well digging. Well, said he, Mr. B., I will dig this well where I set my stick, and if I do not find first rate water at half the depth, I will charge you nothing for the job. Very well, said I, catching at the suggestion as a relief to my anxiety, although I had not a particle of expectation of success, set to work then. He did so, and at precisely the depth previously indicated, he came to water so pure, that for years afterwards, the citizens for three squares off carried water to their tables from it. The two wells were so near each other that the earth of the second one dug was thrown into the first. I paid him his bill and added a five dollar note as a present. I never paid money with greater pleasure.

I will conclude the subject for the present with my own experience in the Divining rod. My friend and quondam partner, Joseph Jonas, Esq., called on me to ascertain if I could find water in the Synagogue lot on Broadway, where it was needed for the ritual of their religious services. Having prepared myself, I went, and examining the premises carefully, I found water within two or three feet of the east wall of the house of worship. Here, said I, is abundance of water, and judging from indications, I should expect that if a well be dug here, the water will flow over the curb. That, said he, is the very thing we want. It is desirable for the purpose of making it a water of purification, that it should be a running water. I concluded to trace its course beyond the limits of the lot, which was rendered difficult by the built-up condition of the lots to the east. After spending three or more hours in the enterprize, I succeeded in getting outside of the dwelling, and following the course towards Schnetz's Garden, on descending the hill just at its foot, I found it issue in quite a large spring, of whose existence I was ignorant. I have no doubt that if the well had been dug in the Synagogue lot, it would have spoiled the outlet of the spring.

But we need not go to Pennsylvania for facts on this subject. Dr. T., an intelligent physician of North Bend, has had many cases lately of chills and fevers in that vicinity, springing from drawing the water off the canal, during the autumnal seasons. His remedy—and it proves a very successful one—is to tie a string around the right arm and left leg or around the left arm and right leg, just as the chill is about to come on, by which means he succeeds invariably in averting the paroxysm.

I repeat it, what is there in Animal Magnetism more wonderful than these things? and, I may add, better attested or more susceptible of being accounted for on natural principles.

Another number will be devoted to Chiromancy and its kindred operations, which I propose to compare with the Neurological and Clairvoyant phenomena.

Review.

Mason's Juvenile Harp. In nothing, scarcely, is the spirit of improvement and change so characteristic of the age we live in, more strongly manifested, or more strikingly illustrated than in the world of letters. Formerly, years of scrutiny and critical examination could alone entitle a work to the honor of being received as a "Standard," on the subject of which it might treat; and when so received, it could with difficulty be displaced by any newer candidate for favor, even in cases where the superiority of the new-comer over its predecessor, was evident to the most superficial observer.

In schools, the very antiquity of "Dilworth," and "Pike," and "Morse," in Spelling, Arithmetic, and Geography, were assigned as a reason for the preference entertained in their favor, and the opposition to the earlier class of improved modern works in those studies. But that day has gone by, and as extremes generally meet, the fault *now* is, that so numerous and so varied are the books that rapidly succeed each other, in every branch of science and education, that teachers and others are puzzled to decide in making a choice from the number, and are scarcely allowed time to give those selected for use, the trial that is needful to test their merits and pronounce upon their claims to be regarded as standard authorities.

This improvement in works designed to convey elementary instruction to the mass is probably in nothing more apparent than in those which embrace the science of sacred music. A few years ago, and the "Old Colony," "Bridgewater," "Dyers," and "Cole's Collections," were standards of musical skill and taste in the eastern portion of our land; while, beyond the "*patent notes*" of the "Missouri Harmony," and the "Western Lyre," we, of the West, knew little or nothing of this delightful branch of science. But a vast revolution has since then taken place, and works alike creditable to the talents and taste of their compilers have multiplied in our midst, till the musical wants of the west, no less than of the east, are now as fully supplied are those of any other department of study. Conspicuous among the *Pioneers* in this reform, have long been the Messrs. MASON, and by their various publications devoted to the advancement of sacred music, they have, it is believed contributed more than any others to the improved state of that art in our country.

The JUVENILE HARP, which has just been issued in a superior style, by WM. T. TRUMAN, of this city, is designed to take the place, as a musical collection for *youth*, which has been by general consent assigned to Mason's *Sacred* Harp, among our collections of church music—a popular compendium of such compositions as will please the greatest number. It is a neat volume of 208 pages, pocket size, and contains 140 songs, suitable for juvenile singers, comprising in one volume most of the best compositions of that class, which previously were scattered through several separate publications.— From a cursory examination of the book, the music appears to be well arraigned & judiciously selected, the only fault which is noticed being the insertion of a few pieces of little merit, apparently written for the occasion, and inserted to fill out the desired number of pages. But there is quite enough of that which is really good, to make the work fully worth its cost to the purchaser.   *

Street Perplexities.

I have already stated that I have frequently been mistaken for Jonah Martin, having once got a dinner on his account for coffee-house services in a case where he advocated the license and I opposed it. The story is in the Advertiser of the 2nd inst. One of the richest circumstances in the case I was not made aware of, until a few days since. The proprietors of the Hotel did not find out the mistake, although six years had passed, until they read that narrative.

Some few weeks ago, I had business over the canal, and fell into a conversation with one of my German acquaintances there, which was commenced in that language by myself, knowing that the individual spoke English with difficulty. After keeping it up for some ten minutes, we were about to part, when my friend remarked, slapping me on the shoulder,—"Well Mr. Martin, so long I knows you, I neffer know you talk Detch pefore." "I cant speak German very well," said I, "and, may be, next time we meet, you cant get me to speak it at all. It is just as I feel in the humor." I said this, in hopes that on his next meeting with Jonah, that he would insist on *his* speaking German *again.*

But it is not my only difficulty that I am mistaken for Martin, as I am not unfrequently accosted as Mr. Funk, which leads into more serious perplexities, of which the following may serve as a specimen:

"Good morning,' said a good- looking countryman to me. 'What is wheat worth now?' 'About 65 cents, I believe,' was my reply, wondering at the same time why I should be appealed to for the statistics of the grain market.— 'Well, said my querist, 'if we should elect Mr Clay this fall, I am in hopes I shall get a better price for it. I was silent, not wishing to enter into politics with a stranger, and in the street. But he would not let me off. 'What do *you* think?' said he. I observed that I thought the Presidential election had nothing to do with the price of produce. 'How!' exclaimed he, 'why I always thought you was a Whig, Mr. Funk.' 'I am neither Mr. Funk nor a Whig,' said I testily; 'and if you were to look sharp, you would see the difference; Funk wears gold spectacles, and the Democracy carry the gold. *when they have any,* in their pockets. Good bye.'

Wood County, Ohio.

I have to acknowledge the receipt of two notes, giving the desired information to my query in last Advertiser as to the etymology of Wood, one of the counties in Ohio, one of which, the fullest, follows:

DEAR SIR:

In your paper of this morning, you inquire the origin of the name of Wood County. It was probably named after Col. Wood, of the engineers, in the U. S. Army, who was killed at Fort Erie. He was a very distinguished man—was the principal engineer in Gen. Harrison's army, in the campaign of 1813, and planned the celebrated sortie, which was so successful, so far as the plan was pursued, and the orders of the Commander-in-Chief obeyed, and so disastrous in the end, in consequence of a departure from those orders. In 1814, he was with the army of Gen. Brown, in the brilliant campaign on the Niagara, and was conspicuous In all the leading events. He was killed in the sortie from Fort Erie, towards the close of that campaign. His reputation was very high. Few men of his age and rank stood so well with the army and the country; and his premature fall was greatly lamented. He was well known to all the leading men of Ohio, of that day, and he served with many of them in the N. W. Army, and they would have been very apt to perpetuate his name by attaching it to the soil.

ONE OF YOUR READERS.

C. CIST.

French Literature.

I regret to see advertised, by book-sellers as respectable as Desilver and Burr, of our city, a French periodical "*L'Echo des Feuilletons,*" of which I ask and will accept nothing further as evidence of its character than that the infamous Madame George Sand is announced as one of the contributors. This woman, in whom an immoral life well illustrates immoral principles, has done more to corrupt the youth of Paris, at the present day, than any one of her cotemporaries. If the 40,000 subscribers in that city attest the general corruption of morals there, and 9000 more in our own country, expose their families to the same influence, it is sufficiently to be deplored. For myself, as the conductor of a periodical, I lift the warning voice to caution my readers how they suffer the writings of Madame Sand, and her kindred spirits of evil, to enter their families under the seductive plea "that being led on unconsciously by the charms of the subject, they will, unawares, make rapid progress in the language." Rather, I apprehend, to make rapid progress in losing that delicacy and purity which is the pride and glory of American women.

Animal Magnetism.

She was a fine strapping young woman enough, dressed half and half between a fine lady and a servant maid; but as sly looking a baggage as you could select from an assortment of gipsies, and, unless her face belied her, quite capable of scratching a Cocklane ghost. Indeed something came across me that I had seen her before; and if my memory don't deceive me, it was at some private theatricals contrary to law. For certain she could keep her countenance; for if the outlandish figure of a doctor, with his queer face, had postured, and pawed, and poked towards me, with his fingers, for all the world like the old game of "My grandmother sends you a staff, and you are neither to smile nor to laugh," as he did to her, I should have burst to a dead certainty, instead of going off, as she did into an easy sleep. As soon as she was sound the Count turned round to me, with his broken English—

'Ladies and gentlemen,' says he, 'look here at dis young maidens, Mizz Charlot Ann Ellzabet Martin'—for that is his way of talking—'wid my magnetismuses I tro her into von state of sombamboozleism"—or something to that effect, Mizz Charlot Ann, dou art a slip.'

'As fast as a church, Mister Count,' says she, talking and hearing as easy as broad awake.

'Ferry good,' says he. 'Now, I take dis boke —Missis Glasse Cokery—and I sall make the maidens read some little of him wid her back. Dere he is bytween her shoulder. Mizz Charlot Ann, what you see now mit your eyes turned de wrong way for to look?'

'Why then,' says she, 'Mr. Count, I see quite plain a T. and an O. Then comes R. and O and S, and T; and the next word is H, and A and I, and R.'

'Ferry goot,' cries the Count over again.— Dad is to rost de hare. Ladies and gentlemen, you all hear? As Gott is my shudge, so is here in de boke. Now, den, Mizz Charlot Ann, vons more. Vot you taste in your mouse?'

"Why, then, master,' says Charlotte Ann, 'as sure as fate, I taste sweet herbs chopped up small!'

'Very goot, indeed! but vot more by sides de sweet herrubs?' 'Why,' says she, 'its a relish,a salt and pepper, and mace—and let me see— there's flavor of currant jelly.'

'Besser and besser,' cries the Count. 'Ladies and gentlemen, are not dese vonderfools? You shall see every wort of it in the print. Mizz Charlott Ann, vot you feel now?

'Lawk-a.mercy, Mister Count,' says she, there's a sort of stuffy feel, so there is, in my inside!'

'Yaw! like von fool pelly! Ferry goot! Now vou feel vot?' 'Feel! Mr. Count,' said she 'Why I don't feel nothing at all the stuffines is clean gone away!'

'Yaw, my child!' says he, dat is by cause I take away the cokery boke from your two shoulders. Ladies and gentlemens, dese are grand powers of magnetismus! Ach himmel!

As Hamlet says, dere more in our philosiofies dan dare is in de heaven or de earth! Our mutter Nature is so fond to hider face! But von adept, so as me, can lifet up her whale!'-*Hood.*

The Right Hon. T. B. Macaulay, Member of Parliament.

Thomas Babington Macaulay is the son of Zacharia Macaulay, well known as the friend of Wilberforce, and though himself an African Merchant, one of the most ardent abolitionists of slavery. In 1818, T. B. Macaulay became a member of Trinity College, Cambridge, where he took his Bachelor's degree in 1822. He distinguished himself as a student, having obtained a scholarship, twice gained the chancellor's medal for English verse, and also gained the second Craven Scholarship, the highest honors to classics which the University confers. Owing to his dislike of mathematics, he did not compete for honors at graduation, but nevertheless he obtained a fellowship at the October competition open to graduates of Trinity, which he appears to have resigned before his subsequent departure for India. He devoted much of his time to the "Union" Debating Society, where he was reckoned an eloquent speaker.

Mr. Macaulay studied at Lincoln's Inn, and was called to the bar in 1826. In the same year, his "Essays on Milton" appeared in the Edinburgh Review; and out of (then Mr.) Jeffrey's administration of that paper, arose, an intimate friendship. Macaulay visiting Scotland soon afterwards, went to circuit with Mr. Jeffrey. His connection with the Edinburgh Review has continued at intervals ever since.

By the Whig Administranion, Mr. Macaulay was appointed Commissioner of Bankrupts.— He commenced his parliamentary career about the same period, as member of Colne in the reform parliament of 1832, and again for Leeds in 1834, at which time he was Secretary to the India Board. His seat, however, was soon relinquished, for, in the same year, he was appointed member of the Supreme Council in Calcutta, under the East India Company's new charter.

Arriving in Calcutta, in September, in 1834, Mr. Macaulay shortly assumed an important trust, in addition to his seat at the Council. At the request of the Governor General, Lord Wm. Bentick, he became President of the commission of five, appointed to frame a penal code for India ; and the principal provisions of this code have been attributed to him. One of the enactments, in particular, was so unpopular among the English inhabitants, as to receive the appellation of the "Black Act." It abolished the right of appeal from the local courts to the supreme court at the presidency, hitherto exclusively enjoyed by Europeans, and put them on the same footing with natives, giving to both an equal right of appeal to the highest provincial courts. Inconvenience and delay of justice had been caused by the original practice, even when India was closed against Europeans in general, but such practice was obviously incompatible with the rights and property of the natives under the new system of opening the courts to general resort. This measure of equal justice, however, exposed Mr. Macaulay, to whom it was universally attributed, to outrageous personal attacks, in letters, pamphlets, and at public meetings.

The various reforms and changes instituted by Lord W. Bentick and Lord Aukland, were advocated in general by Mr. Macaulay. He returned to England in 1838.

Mr. Macaulay was elected member for Edinburgh on the liberal inierest in 1335; and being appointed Secretary at war, he was re-elected the following year, and again at the general election of 1841. No review of his political career is here intended, although, in relation to literature, it should be mentioned that he opposed Mr. Sergeant Talfourd's copy-right bill, and was the principal agent in defeating it. As a public speaker, he usually displays extensive information, close reasoning and eloquence; and has recently bid fair to rival the greatest names among our English orators.— His conversation in private is equally brilliant and instructive.

Mr. Macaulay may fairly be regarded as the first critical and historical essayest of the time. It is not meant to be inferred there are not other writers who display as much understanding and research, as great, perhaps greater, capacity for appreciating excellence, as much acuteness and humor, and more subtle powers of exciting, or of measuring the efforts of the intellect and the imagination, besides possessing an equal mastery of language in their own peculiar style; but there is no other writer who combines so large an amount of those qualities, with the addition of a masterly style, at once highly classical and most extensively popular. His style is classical because it is correct, and is popular, because it must be intelligible without effort, to every educated understanding.— *Horne's New Spirit of the Age.*

The University at Glasgow and its Discipline.

It is remarkable, (says Kohl in his travels in Scotland) that while the number of students in the other universities of Great Britain has always been on the increase, those of the " Universitas Glasguensis " has steadily decreased. Between the years 1820 and 1826 there were here nearly 1600 students, and now there are only 1000, among whom, as also in Edinburgh, there are many from the British colonies. In the English universities of Oxford and Cambridge all students must belong to, or declare allegiance to the established church, on which account, those seminaries of learning contain fewer from the frequently dissenting colonies of Great Britain, than do the Scottish universities. The faculty of Medicine draws the greatest number of students, and therefore, the regulations and restrictions for the students in this faculty, are especially mild. It has been often remarked, that the youth of the freedom-loving English nation are subjected to a discipline so severe, that the youth of our country would, on no account, submit to it. Such a censor, for example, as sits here, in Glasgow, by the side of each professor, could not be introduced into one of our universities. It is the duty of the censor to watch the behaviour of the students during the lectures, and to note any ill behaviour or insubordination. A very common offence against which he has to animadvert, is that wide spread passion in all English schools, the considering the writing-tables as good material for exercises in engraving, and the execution of all sorts of design upon it. I found, in the lecture-room at Glasgow large placards threatening all such artists with heavy punishments. It is a curious subject of investigation for the psychologist, how is it that our wild, disorderly students, who would not allow such restrictions to be laid on them, should often in after life be metamorphosed into such obedient citizens, whilst from the British youth, treated and overlooked as schoolboys, such obstinate and powerful opponents to government should arise. Under the head Humanity, here, as with us, is understood philology; or rather, as philology here is confined at Latin and Greek, the study of these two languages, and especially the former, the latter, Greek, being much less zealously pursued in England then in Germany.— "A professor of humanity" is a teacher in Latin. In the middle ages, when Latin was, indeed, the herald of all the muses, this appellation was sufficiently applicable and appropriate. But now all such old appellations, which have lost their significance, should be allowed gradually to drop away, like the old feudal titles among the nobility. The new light of humanity, which has risen among the nations of Europe, through the zealous and industrious study of nature, has made its way here, but slowly, through the old Latin humanity. It is but lately that they have established a professorship of Natural History. Only since 1818 have they a separate professor of Chemistry. Up to that time, only a lecturer was tolerated on this branch of science, so all important in Glasgow. There are other new professional chairs, but the old chairs have still many privileges, as, for example, free lodgings in the college, and the like. The new professional chairs, about nine of which have been founded since 1816, are carrying on a war at this present time with the old ones, with whom they wished to be placed on an equal footing. They demand free lodgings, and a voice in the internal regulations of the college, which, up to the present time, they have not obtained.— But it is more than probable they will soon be placed on equal terms. Natural distinctions and limitations are also being gradually laid aside. Formerly none but Scotchman were allowed to be professors. Hudgisson (Hutchinson?) was the first Irishman whom they admitted, and now there are one or two professors from Ireland in that high school. This is a remarkable fact: and I do not believe that we, in Germany, have any conception, that the different subjects of the kingdom of Great Britain have been accustomed to make such distinctions among themselves.

Biography of Col. John Armstrong.

Col. John Armstrong, was born in New Jersey, 20th April, 1775. At the commencement of the Revolutionary war, having gone to Philadelphia to dispose of a load of wheat, for his father, he found that recruits were enlisting for the service of the U.S., and when he returned home said to his father he felt inclined to join the army, if it met his approbation. The inquiry was made, "in what capacity," to which he replied, "*as a private soldier.*" After a moment's reflection, the old gentleman said, "I would prefer you should have some command, but if you think your country needs your service, you have my permission.

John arranged his little affairs, and started next morning to Philadelphia, where he joined the army. In a short time he was made Sergeant, and from 11th Sept., 1777, to the close of the revolution, served as a commissioned officer in various ranks.

On the disbanding of the army, he was continued in the service. Was commandant at Wyoming in 1784, at Ft. Pitt in 1785, and 1786,and from 1786 to 1790, in the same capacity, at the Garrison, at the Falls of Ohio. In the spring of 1791, he returned to Philadelphia to recruit his force, with a view to the approaching campaign in the North West, under the command of Col. Josiah Harmar, reached Ft. Washington in August of that year, and marched thence with the main body of troops. He afterwards participated in the campaign, under General St. Clair, and was in command at Ft. Hamilton, until the spring of 1793, when he resigned.

During the Revolution and Indian wars, he served a period of 17 years, was in 37 skirmishes, 4 general actions, and one siege. Among which were the battles of Stony Point, Trenton, Princeton, and Monmouth, and the siege of Yorktown, in Virginia.

His service in the Revolutionary war was extremely severe. While on the Pennsylvania lines, his men were often relieved in consequence of the excessive fatigue, while he himself remained in active service, to the constant annoyance of the enemy. At one time he stationed his men behind a stone wall, enclosing a grave yard. Having a fine horse,he had rode up to the vicinity of Tarlton's encampment, when a number of horsemen gave him chase. Reining his horse so as to allow his pursuers to come very near him until he was approaching the point where his men were secreted, he gave spur, and leaving his pursuers behind, they were fired upon by his party, while he rode round the lot and entered at a gate on the opposite side.

At another time, directing his men to be governed as to the position they were to assume by the waving of his hat, he approached very near the enemy's encampment, his intended retreat being round a mill pond, but finding himself intercepted in that direction, his only chance of escape was to cross the forebay of the mill, where if the stretch would have proven too great for his horse to leap, he must lose him and cross on the timbers. On approaching it, unwilling to lose an animal which had so often proved useful to him, he gave him the spur and cleared the forebay, which none of his British pursuers were willing to attempt. Before they could reach him round the pond, he was snugly in ambush with his men in a thicket ready to receive them.

He often remarked that he never knew himself alarmed but once during his command, and that was while grazing his horse in a meadow,

and resting his men, an hundred British horse had unobserved passed up a drain and were within fifty yards when first observed. His command being only 25 men, the odds were as four to one against him, and in an open field, but affecting a smile, he said, "My brave fellows stand fast and we will laugh at them,"-- "reserving fire till within 20 steps, then fire front platoon." His order was obeyed, the fire given, the enemy's lines broken and thrown back,and forming in his rear. Ordering his second platoon "face to the right about," a second fire was poured in, and the horse were again broken, and so successively by platoons,until the enemy finding themselves regularly cut off by every fire, and *the little band standing firm without the loss of a man*, withdrew at a gallop.

At another time, a regiment of the enemy having been stationed on either side of a lane protected by a stone fence, where he must pass to avoid a swamp which was impassable, he drilled his men so that but two were together at a time, each passing forward ten steps, then waiting till the next came up,& so on until all reached a point near the enemy, the night being very dark. In an audible tone, he then ordered "the right and left wing, to flank out and surround the enemy!" by which the enemy were surprized and confused, when he hastily pressed his *"right and left wing"* of 25 men through the lane undisturbed. Although other incidents equally interesting might be given, let these suffice.

After the close of the Revolution, he passed over the mountains to the western wilds. While stationed at the Falls of Ohio, he and his little force in the garrison rendered essential service in protecting the inhabitants of Kentucky from the depredation of the savages, frequently following them into the interior, and reclaiming horses stolen from the Kentucky side. And at one time saving the garrison at Vincennes from starvation, by his fortitude and exertions.

Several attempts to supply them having been foiled by the savages. When he came near the rapids of the Wabash, anticipating an attack from the Indians at that point, he despatched three of his men with the intelligence to Colonel Hamtramck, commanding at the post, and requesting the Colonel to meet him at that point, with such force as could be spared from the garrison. He had not proceeded far up the river until they found two of the men in a canoe tomahawked and scalped, one of them having the communication to Col. Hamtramck. Another party was then sent forward by land to the Fort, and a portion of the men sent to collect wood and bark, to be placed in piles on a sand bar near the rapids. At night the fires were kindled, making a show of a large encampment, but neither the men nor provisions were there; the boats were quietly fastened among the willows at another point, and the men lodged on shore *without fires*. The second despatch fortunately reached the Fort. Colonel Hamtramck mustered his whole force, leaving the women and children with a very few (it is believed not more than three) men in possession of the Fort, and pressed forward to meet the provisions, intending in case they had been taken by the Indians, to make an attack upon them and retake the supplies. Descending the river, in periogues, and descrying the fires on the bar, they supposed them to be the fires of the enemy. While he was giving directions to his men, having approached near enough he was hailed by Armstrong, and brought to. A careful watch was kept during the night, and at an early hour Hamtramck giving the entire control to Armstrong, new hands were put to the poles, and the rest set on shore. The boats were pressed forward with uncommon energy, and by 11 o'clock reached the Fort in safety, to the no small joy of all concerned, and especially those who belonged to the Post, who having had supplies intended for their relief twice cut off by the savages at the Rapids, were now, for a time, placed beyond want, for which service they were indebted to the exertions and management of Col. Armstrong.

The Indians were making frequent excursions into Kentucky, during the time of Armstrong's command at Fort Finney, (situate on the Indiana bank, at the lower end of what is now known as the old town of Jeffersonville.) With a view to prevent the savages from passing the river and bringing off horses from Kentucky. Armstrong built a block house at the mouth of Bull creek, on the Indiana shore, which commanded a view of their crossing places, at what is now known by the names of the Grassy Flats, and 18 mile Island bar, at both of which, particularly the flats, the river was fordable at a low stage.

While his men were engaged in building the block-house, he with his tomahawk girdled the timber on about three acres of land, on top of the hill, opposite the Grassy Flats, and planted peach seeds in the woods. When the first settlers came to the Illinois Grant, and landed at the *big rock*, designated as their landing place, now well known by boatmen, in the fall after Wayne's treaty, they found the timber dead and fallen down, and the peach trees growing among the brush and bearing fruit. The settlers cleared away the brush, and this *woody orchard* supplied them with fruit for some years. There are at this time, persons living who were of these settlers, and saw this wilderness orchard. This settlement was long known as "Armstrong's Station."

In Harmar's campaign he suffered severely In the action fought under the command of Col. Hardin, near where Ft. Wayne now stands, he lost 31 men out of 39 of his command. The militia having been thrown into disorder, suddenly retreated, leaving Captain Armstrong to contend at the head of a decidedly unequal force. The Captain and most of his men stood their ground, anticipating a rally of the militia, in which they were disappointed, when the Captain after shooting an Indian in the act of scalping the last man he had on the field, threw himself in the grass between an immense oak stump and log which had been blown down where he remained about three hours in daylight. At night the Indians went to their war dance, with him in gunshot of where he laid. Desiring to sell his life as dear as possible, he at one time tho't of attempting to shoot a chief, who he could distinguish by his dress and trinkets in the light of the fires. Taking his watch and compass from their fobs, he buried them by the side of the log where he lay, saying to himself some honest fellow tilling this ground many years hence may find them, and these rascals shan't have them. Finding, however, great uncertainty in drawing a *bead* by cloudy moonlight, and that of the fires at the dance, and thinking it possible he might escape, in which case they would be useful to him, he dug them up and replaced them in his fobs. Soon after, being satisfied that there were Indians very near him, and conscious that they would prefer taking him prisoner to shooting him, should he cock his gun, and on attempting to escape, be discovered, he could wheel and shoot before the Indian would attempt to shoot, upon which he cocked his rifle; the Indian near him began to rattle in the leaves and mimick ground squirrels and perwink. The Captain cautiously moved, and on the third step was so distinctly discovered by the Indians that the savage yell was given, when everything was instantly silent at the dance. The Captain then took to his heels, springing the grass as far as practicable to prevent tracking. After running a short distance, he discovered a pond of water in, to which he immediately jumped, thinking there would be no tracking there. Seating himself on a bog of grass, with his gun on his shoulder, and the water round his waist, he had not been in the pond five minutes when the whole troop of Indians, foot and horse, were around the pond hunting for him. Using his own expression, "such yells I never heard. I suppose the Indians thought I was a wounded man, that their yells would scare me, and I would run and they would catch me, but I tho't to myself I would see them d—d first; the Indians continued their hunt for seven hours, until the moon went down, when they retired to their fires."

"The ice was frozen to my clothes, and very much benumbed, I extricated myself from the pond, broke some sticks and rubbed my thighs and legs to circulate the blood, and with some difficulty at first, slowly made my way thro' the brush. Believing the Indians would be traveling between their own and the American camp, I went at right angles from the trace about two miles to a piece of rising ground, thinking to myself it is a cold night, if there are any Indians here, *they* will have fire, if I can't see their's they can't see mine, and fire is necessary for me. I went into a ravine where a large tree was blown up by the roots, kindled a fire, dried myself, and laid down and took a nap of sleep. In the morning, threw my fire in a puddle of water, and started for camp."

Capt. A. being a first rate woodsman, and conversant with the Indian habits, when he came to open wood, passed round it, in wet ground walked logs, and stepped backwards to prevent being tracked. About half way from the battle ground to the American Camp, he discovered three Indians coming along the path meeting him, he squatted in the hazle bushes, about 20 steps from the trace, and the Indians passed him undiscovered. Said he, "I never so much wished for two guns in my life. I was perfectly cool—could have taken the eye out of either of them, and with two guns should have killed two of them and the other rascal would have run away, but with one gun thought it best not to make the attack, as the odds was against me, as three to one."

Reaching the vicinity of the ground where he had left the main army the day before, the day being now far spent, he expected soon to meet with those he had left there, but was suddenly arrested in his lonely march by the commencement of a heavy battle, as he supposed, at the encampment. Hesitating for a moment, and then cautiously moving to a position from which he could overlook the camp, instead of seeing there his associates in arms from whom he had then been separated two days, a different scene was presented. The savages had full possession of the American camp ground. Is it possible, said he, that the main army has been cut off. Having been these two days without eating a mouthful, except the breakfast taken early in the morning of his leaving camp, he began to reflect upon what should be his future course. Much exhausted from fatigue, without food, alone in the wilderness, far removed from any settlements and surrounded by savages, the probability of his escape was indeed slight, but duty to himself and country soon determined him upon the attempt. At this moment the sound of a cannon attracted his attention. He knew it was a token for the lost men to come in, and taking a circle, passed in the direction from whence the sound came, and arrived safely at the camp; the army had changed position, from the time he had left, to a point two miles lower down the creek, which presented ground more favorable for encampment. The dusk of the evening had arrived when he got to camp, greatly to the surprize of his acquaintance, who had numbered him with the men who had fought their last fight. Col. Armstrong in speaking of this engagement and the heavy loss in his command, always evinced much feeling, saying "the men of my command *were as brave as ever lived; I could have marched them to the mouth of a cannon, without their flinching.*" Much difference of opinion has been expressed by writers and authors as to the place where this battle was fought; but the memorandum kept by Col. Armstrong, and now found in his own hand writing, of the march of Harmar's Army from Ft. Washington, fixes beyond doubt the place to be near the St. Mary and St. Joseph, a few miles from Ft. Wayne in Indiana.

Col. Armstrong was well known as a Soldier and woodsman. The importance to the country, of a tour of exploration and examination of the Western wilds, of the number of the Indians, the location of their towns, &c., becoming manifest; the charge of this hazardous enterprise was given to and accepted by him. On the 20th Feb. 1790, Gen. Harmar notifies him that he is to make the tour, provided the Governor of the Western Territory judges it advisable. If not, he is to return from Vincennes, and explore the Wabash—make particular examination of the communication of that river with Lake Erie—depth of water—distances, &c., and if it can be done with safety, proceed to the Miami village. He immediately started on this tour, and proceeded up the Missouri some distance above St. Louis, *not with an army to deter the savages, nor yet an escort, but entirely alone!* It was his intention to examine the country of the upper Missouri, and cross the Rocky Mountains—but, meeting with some French traders, was persuaded to return in consequence of the hostility of some of the Missouri bands to each other, as they were then at war, that he could not safely pass from one nation to another. Returning then as he was directed, to Post Vincennes, he called on Hamtramck for an escort—whose force being small, desired to know the extent of the escort, Armstrong replied, "an escort of two friendly Indians." The Indians being called out, he selected from among them, judging for himself their characters—the choice proved to be that of a father and his son. With these he traversed the then wilderness of Illinois and Indiana—his savage companions proved to be faithful, and in every way a good selection for the object he had in view.

After completing this exploration, he returned to Fort Washington and discharged *his escort.*—

This was a tour of great hazard and exposure of constitution; the notes taken by him of the country, the quality of the soil, and water courses, are evidence that he anticipated that the country would ere long, be populated by white men. And here may be introduced an anecdote to show his opinions on that subject.

While stationed at the Falls of Ohio, having just returned from an excursion after a party of Indians, he was making some notes of the country over which he had travelled, when his brother came to see him, who enquired what he was doing, and on being informed, remarked, "you are giving yourself much trouble for no benefit —you will never live to see this country settled. The reply was, "*I expect not only to live to see this country settled, but to see vessels built at this place, and freighted for Europe!* He did see the country settled, and four vessels lying at anchor below the Falls at one time—none of them were however, built at that point, but before his death a large steam boat, the "United States," was built at the Jeffersonville ship yard. From one of his memorandums, it seems he was at the Falls preparing for this exploring expedition on 27th Feb., 1790, was at Vincennes 18th March, 1790; at Fort Washington 28th July, 1791, preparing for the campaign under Gen. St. Clair.

Of his participation in Harmar's campaign mention has already been made. He again went out in the campaign of Gen. St. Clair, at the time of the battle, was some distance from the scene of action, having been sent back with Hamtramck's regiment to protect the provision. On the opening of the fire, they made press march for the battle ground, but met the army retreating—when they covered the rear, and assisted the men who were wounded or given out. Col. A. dismounted from his horse and placed on him two men, who could travel no farther.— After some time, they came up to Capt. John S. Gano—who had given out and seated himself on a log, the two men on the horse having rested, they gave place to Gano—and alternating, in this way many men were saved who must otherwise have perished by the savages' tomahawk, or in the flames—returning from this expedition he was put in command at Fort Hamilton.— Most of the fortifications at that post were erected under his superintendance there, he took charge of the wounded, provided for them until they were able to go forward to Fort Washington. Of the service here, the letters of St. Clair are highly complimentary; he continued in command here until the spring of 1793, when he resigned, and soon after married a daughter of Judge Goforth of Columbia. When Gen. Wayne came west, he urged Col. Armstrong to take

command of a regiment, expressing great confidence in his bravery, and regretting the loss of so well tried an officer and soldier. Having then a family and his constitution failing from hardships and exposures in the service of his country for a period of 17 years, he declined service in this campaign. Soon after his retirement he was appointed Treasurer of the North Western Territory. His first commission as Treasurer, is dated 13th Sep., 1796. Another commission to the same office is dated 14th Dec., 1799.— He served also, as one of the judges of the Court of Hamilton county, and many years as magistrate in Columbia, where he resided from 1793 to the spring of 1814, when he removed to his farm opposite the Grassy Flats, in Clark county, Indiana, and died there on the 4th February, 1816, after a confinement of five years and 24 days; during which time he was unable to walk unless supported by persons on either side of him —his remains were interred on that farm where a monument is placed to mark his resting place

---

Millerism--The Finale here.

I feel it my duty to record the late exhibitions of Millerism, as far as they have been made in Cincinnati, as part of the history of the times.

For the last eighteen months the delusion has been spreading west, and was propagated here with great industry and zeal by Himes, Jacobs and others. As a part of its influences, the Midnight Cry was established and circulated gratuitously. Religious services, originally commenced and carried on for a length of time at the Cincinnati College edifice, have been maintained with a degree of feeling and devotedness, worthy of a purer and better grounded faith, and as the numbers of the believers increased, and their resources augmented by the addition of men who were possessed of means, the Tabernacle, a broad building of 80 feet square, uncouth in outward appearance, but well adapted for their purpose otherwise, was erected. This building is capable of seating two thousand persons on benches.

It will be recollected, that Miller, the author of this movement, predicted originally, that the *second advent,* or consummation of all things, would take place with the close of 1843. When that period passed, it became necessary to assign a new one, or abandon the faith. It was then discovered that the termination of the Jewish year, on the last day of Nisan, or the 23d March, 1844, was the proper date. After the fallacy of this calculation was demonstrated by the result, it was finally concluded that the long expected advent would be the day of Jubilee—according to Jewish chronology, the 10th day of the seventh month—which brought us at the last day and hour to midnight of the 22d of October,

All these periods were referred to in succession, in the Midnight Cry, and so firmly was the faith of the Millerites fixed on the last calculation, that the number published Oct. 22d, was solemnly announced to be the last communication through that channel to the believers. In this progress of things, both in the press and the tabernacle, as might have been expected, deeper exercises of mind, among the Millerites, was the result, and within a few days of the 22d, all the brethren had divested themselves of their earthly cares, eating, drinking and sleeping only excepted. Chests of tools which cost forty dollars were sold for three. A gold watch worth one hundred dollars was sacrificed for one fifth the value. Two brothers of the name of Hanselmann, who owned a steamboat in company with Capt. Collins, abandoned to him their entire interest in it, alleging they had nothing farther to do with earthly treasures. John Smith, an estimable man, once a distinguished member of the Baptist Church, and a man of considerable property here, left it all to take care of itself. A distinguished leader in this movement, shut up his shop and placed a card on his door, " *Gone to meet the Lord*"—which, in a few hours, was irreverently replaced by some of the neighbors with " *Gone up.*"

One of the believers, the clerk of one of our Courts, made up his business papers to the 22d, and left later business to those who were willing to attend to it. Another, a clerk in one of the city banks resigned his position in order to devote his entire attention to second advent preparations. And others settled up their worldly business, paying their debts, as far as was in their power, and asking forgiveness of their unpaid creditors, where they were unable to discharge the account. Others, again, spent weeks in visiting relations and friends for the last time, as they supposed. In short, after all these things, all ranks and classes of the believers assembled at the Tabernacle on the night of the 22nd and 23rd successively, to be ready for the great event.

In the meantime, considerable ill feeling had been engendered among the relatives of those who had become infatuated with these doctrines, as they saw their wives, or sisters or daughters led off by such delusions, to the neglect of family duties, even to the preparing the ordinary meals, or attending to the common and every day business of life. The spirit of Lynching was about to make its appearance. Crowds upon crowds, increasing every evening, as the alloted day approached, aided to fill the house or surround the doors of their building. A large share were ready to commence mischief so soon as a fair opportunity should present itself.

On last Sabbath, the first indications of popular displeasure broke out. Every species of annoyance were offered to the Millerites at the doors of the Tabernacle, and even within its walls, on that and Monday evening—much of it highly discreditable to the actors. At the close of an exhortation or address, or even a prayer by the members, the same tokens of approbation, by clapping of hands and stamping of feet, as are exhibited at a theatre or a public lecture, were given here, interspersed with groans of *Oh Polk! Oh Clay!*—shouts of, Hurrah for Clay, Hurrah for Polk, Hurrah for Birney; and loud calls of " move him," " you can't come it," varied occasionally with distinct rounds of applause. A pigeon was let into the Tabernacle also, on Monday evening to the general annoyance. On Tuesday the crowds in and outside the building, still increasing, and not less than twenty-five hundred persons being within the walls, and nearly two thousand in the street adjacent, a general disturbance was expected. But the Mayor and police had been called on, and were upon the ground, and distributed through the crowd.— The clear moonlight rendered it difficult to commit any excess irresponsibly; and above all, *Father Reese*, venerable for his age, erudition and skill in theology, and his magnificent beard, occupied the great mass outside the doors, as a safety-valve to let off the superfluous excitement. At nine o'clock the Millerites adjourned, as it proved *sine die*, going home to watch at their respective dwellings, for the expected advent.— They held no Tabernacle meeting on Wednesday evening, to the disappointment of the crowd which assembled as usual, to which, by way of solace, *Reese* again held forth. At 9 o'clock, the out-door assembly dispersed, also without day.

Wednesday evening having dissipated the last hopes, and confounded all the calculations of the " Adventists," they have since, to a great extent, resumed that position in the community which they previously held. The carpenter has again seized his jack plane, the mason his trowel, and the painter his brush. Eshelby has tied on anew the leather apron, and brother Jones again laid hold of the currying knife. The *clerk* in the bank, whose post was kept in abeyance until he should recover from his delusion, is again at his desk, and *John the Baptist*, by which well known soubriquet, one of the principal leaders is designated, has gone back to his houses and his farms, content to wait, as other Christians are willing, for the day and hour to come, as the CHART has pointed it out.

In most popular delusions, the leaders are crafty, designing and dishonest men, and the mass honest dupes. I have watched this movement in every stage of its progress, and believe that all concerned, " Priest and people alike," were sincere in their convictions. As respects the extent to which the delusion spread, and the consequences to its followers and to those who were connected with them as families, there is nothing new in the result. History records fifty or more similar extravagances, which, on account of the greater ignorance of our fathers, were on a more extensive scale. I conclude with a synopsis of one of these, by which, it will be seen that man is the same in all countries and in every age.

William Whiston, a divine, astronomer and writer of considerable eminence, in the early part of the last century, prophesied, on a given day, the destruction of the world by its coming in collision with a comet then visible. A general consternation was the result. In London, not less than fifty thousand packs of cards were burned, and seven thousand kept mistresses married in one day. The archbishop, at Lambeth, was applied to for a form of prayer suitable to the event. The Governor of the Bank of England gave it in charge to the officers of the Fire Engine companies to keep a good look out for the Bank. The theatres were closed, and the Churches could hardly contain the multitudes that rushed to them. The mob compelled the Captain of a lighter in the Thames, loaded with gun powder, to commit his freight to the river. Every vessel in port was filled with the crowd, who sought refuge on water as the safest place in the impending danger. The sailors, of which there are always vast numbers in London, as is the custom on board ships that are not expected to survive, dressed themselves in their best clothes, and drinking, to drown all consciousness, filled the streets with riot and alarm by day and night. In short, a general consternation pervaded all ranks and classes of society. Such is human nature in every age.

Popular Education.

Mr. Cist—*Dear Sir:*—Knowing the deep interest you feel in the Common School enterprize of our city, I take pleasure in presenting you with the fifteenth "Annual Report" of the Trustees and Visiters, embracing, among other things, the laws and ordinances under which the Schools are conducted.

The friends of education have much to hope for from these Schools. Since their commencement they have been gradually growing up into system* and emphatically pointing, at no distant day, to a "Central High School," which shall complete the series.

While on this subject, I will mention, that an individual in the city has liberally offered to be one of *ten*, who will give $1000 each, for the establishment of a "Central High School" for the educating of boys, to be taken, under certain

regulations, from the Common Schools of the city. The new establishment to embrace the 4 collegiate classes, and to give as thorough an education as any institution in the land; thereby carrying out the system as it exists in our public Schools, of entire equality in the education of the youth of this community.

The Trustees of the Hughes Fund, it is hoped, will yet unite on some plan with the Trustees of the City Schools, to establish a Central High School for girls, taken from the Common Schools, by which all those who may desire, may receive a finished education without going from home to obtain it.

These contemplated institutions, with the Woodward and Cincinnati Colleges, will entitle our city to rank high in the estimation of those who may make the facilities for education the reason for selecting this city as a place or permanent residence. Let the appeal, then, be made to the lover of western enterprise, the lover of his country, the lover of his race, to come forward at once, and meet this noble proposition of a citizen, to establish a "Central High School." Cannot nine men be found in this city who will delight to enroll their names as brethren in this noble enterprise? I send you the name of the first, to be used on any proper occasion.

One of the Trustees of Com. Schools.

Ancient Marriage Licence.

[SEAL.] By his EXCELLENCY the Right Honorable JOHN Earl of DUNMORE, Captain General and Governor in Chief in and over the province of New York and the Territories depending thereon in America, Chancellor and Vice-Admiral of the same.

To any Protestant Minister of the Gospel,

Whereas, There is a mutual purpose of Marriage between *Charles Morse* of the City of New York, *Gentleman* of the one party, and *Margaret Collins* of the same city, *Widow* of the other party, for which they have desired my License and have given Bond upon condition that neither of them have any lawful let or impediment of Pre-contract, affinity or consanguinity, to hinder them from being joined in the holy bonds of Matrimony, these are therefore, to impower you to join the said Charles Morse and Margaret Collins in the holy bonds of Matrimony, and them to pronounce them Man and Wife.

Given under my hand and the prerogative seal of the province of New York, at Fort George, in the City of New York, the twelfth day of April, in the eleventh year of the reign of our Sovereign Lord, George the Third, by the grace of GOD; of Great Britain, France and Ireland, King, Defender of the Faith, &c., Annoq. Domini 1771.   DUNMORE.
By his Excellency's command,
P. W. Banyar, Surr.

Executed the 13th April, by John Siegfried Geroch, Minister of Christ Church.

On this document I comment,

1. That this John, Earl of Dunmore, is the same notorious individual who figured as Governor of Virginia, at the breaking out of the American Revolution.

2. That at that date none but *Protestant* ministers of the Gospel were authorized to marry in this country. This was the statute law of Great Britain, and its provisions extended to the colonies.

3. Can any of my New York readers point out the scite of *Fort George?*

4. What an absurdity is the whole system of marriage licences, availing nothing but to put fees into the hands of public officers.—*Ib.*

Foreign Correspondence.

LONDON, August 1, 1844.

MY DEAR SIR:—I have just returned from an extensive tour through the Mid-land and Northern counties of England; and as I have seen and learned much of this beautiful but ill-governed island, I cannot refrain from troubling you with some of my lucubrations.

The diversified and picturesque scenery—the beautiful and secluded villages—the magnificent and gorgeous habitations of the nobility, fill the mind of the traveller with emotions of wonder and delight. The whole country seems to be one beautiful garden. Every thing is in order, from the palace of the peer, to the hovel of the peasant. It is one of the distinguishing characteristics of the English peasantry, that their houses, however humble, are the abodes of neatness. Even in the wretched and miserable huts which are every where scattered over this lovely land, there is a straining at appearances which indicate how strongly home is implanted in the bosom of an Englishman. In the abodes of the rich, order, utility, refinement and luxury prevail, to a degree wholly inconceivable by the unsophisticated backwoodsman. If it were possible for man to shut his eyes to the misery and wretchedness which constantly obtrude themselves upon his notice, he might well deem this an earthly paradise. But, amid all the beauty, profusion, splendor and gorgeousness which surround him, the appaling fact is ever staring him in the face, that misery and disease, and crime, are here triumphant.

During my sojourn in the North, I was an eye witness to a scene of great interest, in the opening of the Newcastle and Darlington Junction Railway. It was an event of great importance to the surrounding country, and had drawn together a vast assemblage of people from various parts of England. Besides, there were some important historical facts connected with locomotion developed, which I think worth knowing and worth recording.

The celebration of the opening of the road, took place on Thursday June 17 at Newcastle upon Tyne. By means of this road, a direct and uninterrupted communication has been opened between London and Newcastle, the distance between the two places being 305 miles. At 5 o'clock in the morning of that day, a special train left Euston 'square London, and at half-past 2 P. M. arrived at Gateshead on the banks of the Tyne, and opposite to Newcastle. The average rate of running was about forty miles an hour. This was an extraordinary and unprecedented achievement in the history of railroads. One train which arrived was upwards of 350 yards long, and contained between 8 and 900 passengers. It was drawn by three engines. Never before, have I witnessed such an exhibition of the mighty power of steam, or of the wonderful skill and enterprise of man. It was a scene, once beheld, never to be forgotten.—Upon the arrival of this train the excitement and enthusiasm was intense; and as car after car was delivered of its living freight, the spectators gazed in astonishment, and wondered from whence the living mass of human beings came.

What a proud spectacle this must have been to one man who witnessed it, and who might have exclaimed to the assembled thousands:—'Behold! I have done this!'

About forty years ago, a poor, but honest and industrious man worked at a steam engine in a colliery belonging to Lord Ravensworth near to Newcastle upon Tyne. He had an inventive genius, and untiring application. He devoted himself with great assiduity to the fulfilment of his daily task. His intervals were devoted to the improvement of the mechanical business under his control. Those intervals were short for he frequently rose at one o'clock in the morning for the purpose of commencing his accustomed task. But he persevered, and success attended his efforts. Many and important improvements were made to his engine; but as yet, they brought him no mitigation of his constant toil. At length an idea gleamed in upon the uninstructed mind of this laborious man—"What if this mighty stationary wizard could be made to move." The thought startled him at first with its wild image, but it soon took the shape of reality. Still no step could be taken without money—and he was poor. Time rolled on. The mighty workings of genius were at last triumphant. Lord Ravensworth, the owner of Killingworth colliery furnished funds to construct an engine—it was the first Locomotive Engine that was ever built, and in honor of the noble individual who had as nobly used his wealth, it was called "My Lord." This was thirty-two years ago. The great achievement of the age was accomplished; and now burst forth the stupendous intellect which had been for years groping in the gloom of a coal pit. After laying down various railroads, and completely establishing the practicability of his invention, he was sent for to plan the line of the Liverpool and Manchester Railroad. He then pledged himself to obtain a speed of ten miles an hour; and although he felt conscious that there was no limit to the velocity of his engine, yet he was afraid to avow it. It was a hard matter for him to keep it down to that, but he said it had to be done. It now became necessary to apply to Parliament for a charter, and he was deputed to appear before a Committee.—One of them thought he was mad; others that he was a foreigner; but he was determined to succeed, and genius and perseverance triumphed over incredulous and purse-proud stupidity. Each succeeding year witnessed new triumphs—until his fame had become a part of the fame of his country—his, as imperishable as hers. Step by step he had risen from the obscurity of his station, and by the vigor of his intellect, conferred immortal honor upon the name of George Stephenson.

What a lesson this man's history might impart to those who are conscious of superior powers, yet chilled by adverse circumstances. If he had not persevered, the rail road might yet have been an iron path for horses to jog upon, instead of being made what it is, the conqueror of time and space.

Upon the arrival of the various trains at the station at Gateshead, and after the conclusion of some civic ceremonies, about 500 gentlemen sat down to a sumptuous dinner. Among the distinguished individuals present, Mr. Stephenson was the "observed of all observers." He was there upon the spot which had witnessed his early toils, and his mighty triumph—he was amidst the poor who had toiled by his side, and the noble, who were honored by his friendship. How various were the emotions of his heart, when beholding what he had accomplished.

I might extend this letter to a much greater length, but I am fearful of wearying your patience. If what I have written should be acceptable, I shall, at a future time, trouble you again. This is a vast field for the study of man. Since I have been here, I have observed some astonishing anomalies in the peer and peasant. They shall form the subject of another letter. Adieu.   Yours,   D.

Anecdote.

When Mr. Sanders, one of the patentees in the recent discovery of *magneto electric light*, laid his specification before H. L. Ellsworth, the head of the department, that gentleman remarked, I am in the habit every day of seeing something ingenious or remarkable offered for patents, but this is of greater importance than anything I have seen for years, and if it came from any other place than *Cincinnati*, I should be disposed to consider it a great humbug. But there seems to be no limits to your enterprise and energy. It was only last week one of your citizens applied for a patent for a new mode of rendering lard, in which the whole hog of three to four hundred weight is put into an iron tank, and comes out hoofs, hide, and bones, an entire mass of lard! And as the sailor who was blown up at the theatre, and supposed it was a part of the performance, remarked, I wonder what you are going to shew *next!—Ib.*

Etymologies of County names in Ohio.

Of the 79 Counties of Ohio, Washington, Adams, Jefferson, Madison, Monroe, and Jackson, 6;—commemorate the Presidents of those names. Carroll, Fayette, Franklin, Greene, Henry, Hancock, Hamilton, Knox, Morgan, Montgomery, Marion, Mercer, Putnam, Stark, Trumbull, and Warren, 16;—are named after the heroes and statesmen of revolutionary date. Butler, Clark, Crawford, Darke, Hardin, Logan, and Wayne, 7;—record the names of those to whom Ohio has been indebted, on the battlefield, for her emancipation from Indian violence and massacre. Preble is called after a gallant sailor, as is Ross, after an able statesman, both of a later date, say 1806. Allen, Brown, Clinton, Harrison, Holmes, Lawrence, Perry, Pike, and Shelby, 9;—bear the names of the heroes of the last war. Williams, Paulding, and Van Wert, honor the memory of the patriotic and incorruptible captors of Maj. Andre. Two derive their appellations from Governors of Ohio. Meigs and Lucas.

Of Indian originals, we have but 16;—Ashtabula, Cuyahoga, Coshocton, Delaware, Erie, Geauga, Hocking, Huron, Miami, Muskingum, Ottawa, Pickaway, Scioto, Sandusky, Seneca, and Tuscarawas, many of them having the same name with streams, lakes, and bays, in their limits or neighborhood. The names of 11 indicate some peculiarity in location, quality of soil, or character of surface, as Belmont, Champaign, Clermont, Fairfield, Highland, Lake, Licking, Portage, Richland, Summit, and Union. The names—Guernsey, and Gallia, serve to point out the fatherland of the first settlers in these Counties. Athens, and Medina, are Asiatic names, absurdly and inappropriately applied in our State, unless the location of an University, at the first may redeem its share of that reproach. Columbiana, and Lorain, are, I presume, corruptions of Columbia, and Lorraine, both unsuitable names, although for different reasons. One name, that of Wood, defies my scrutiny. Will Mr. Scott, of the Toledo Blade, shed light on its origin?

Can it be named after Judge Reuben Wood?

Of all those who have furnished names for these Counties, three individuals only survive, Andrew Jackson, of Tennessee, James Ross, of Pittsburg, and Robert Lucas, of Piketon, Ohio.

The Progress of "Light."

Unexpected difficulties have been and yet are delaying the exhibition of the *magneto electric* light, lately discovered in our city. It is necessary that 6,000 feet of copper wire should be wrapped with cotton in the manner of bonnet wire, to insulate the conducting wires which are cylindrical and spiral. There is no machine here for such purposes and the inventors are driven to the alternative of constructing one for themselves, which will probably delay them two weeks more, or commence operations at Philadelphia, New York, or Boston, where the wire can be covered in 24 hours. Nothing but absolute necessity will drive them to this last course. They think with me, that the city of their nativity has the stronger claim to be the first in witnessing the glories of this discovery

From Cist's Advertiser.

Capture of O. M. Spencer, by Indians.

The following letter from Gen. Wilkinson to Col. Armstrong, refers to the capture, by Indians, of Oliver M. Spencer, one of the early settlers of the Miami Valley, and father to Henry E. Spencer, Mayor of our city.

Spencer, then a boy of eleven, had been on a visit to Cincinnati, from Columbia, where he then lived, to spend the 4th of July here, and having staid until the 7th, set out in a canoe with four other persons who were going to Columbia.— About a mile above Deer Creek, one of the men much intoxicated, made so many lurches in the canoe as to endanger its safety, and Spencer, who could not swim, becoming alarmed, was at his earnest request, set ashore, as was also the drunken man, who was unable to proceed on foot, and was accordingly left where landed. The three in the canoe, and Spencer on shore, proceeded on, but had hardly progressed a few rods, when they were fired on by two Indians. A Mr. Jacob Light was wounded in the arm, and another man, name unknown, killed on the spot, both falling overboard, the man left on shore tomahawked and scalped, and Spencer, after a vain attempt to escape, was carried off by the savages, and taken out to an Indian village, at the mouth of Auglaize, where he remained several months in captivity. The tidings of these events were taken by Light, who swam ashore a short distance below, by the aid of his remaining arm, and Mrs. Coleman, the other passenger, who, though an old woman of sixty, and, of course, encumbered with the apparel of her sex,

was unable to make any efforts to save herself, but whose clothes floating to the top of the river probably buoyed her up in safety. It is certain, at any rate, incredible as it may be thought by some, that she floated down to Cincinnati, where she was assisted to shore by some of the residents here.

Spencer, after remaining nearly a year among the Indians, was taken to Detroit, where he was ransomed, and finally sent home, after an absence, in various places, of three years, two of which he passed among his relatives in New Jersey. He resided, subsequently, in the city, where he held various offices of trust and honor, and died on May 31st, 1838.

FORT WASHINGTON, July 7th 1792.
JOHN ARMSTRONG ESQ:

Dear Sir,—I send out to apprize you that, this day about noon, a party of savages fired on a party consisting of two men, a women and Col. Spencer's son—about one and a half miles above this, and on this side of the river—one man killed, the other wounded but not mortally, and poor little Spencer carried off a prisoner. I sent out a party who fell in with their trail in Gen. Harmar's trace about six miles from this, and followed it on the path about two miles farther, when the men failing with fatigue, the Sergeant was obliged to return—master Spencer's trail was upon the path—this is a farther answer to the pacific overtures, and makes me tremble for your hay. I pray you if possible to redouble your vigilance, and on Monday morning early Captain Peters will march with his company and six wagons to your assistance— send me twenty horses the moment Peters reaches you, and I will be with you next day— in the meantime, your cavalry should scout on both sides of the river, and your rifle men be kept constantly in motion—adieu,

Yours

JAS. WILKINSON, Brig. Gen.

Drawing School.

Amidst the various facilities afforded in this city for a good education, we have hitherto been deficient in a school for drawing, calculated to commence with the elements and carry the learner out, as his genius and taste may justify, into the higher branches of the art.

That deficiency is now supplied, by a competent instructor in this department Mr. M. ROSIENKIEWICZ, who has opened at his room on 4th street west of the Council Chamber, a school for drawing and design. Mr. R. comes recommended to some of our most respectable citizens as a gentleman and artist. As respects the last, in my judgment, he needs no other testimony than his own exquisite productions which ornament the walls of his room, two of which, a boat, leaving a vessel at anchor, for the adjacent shore, and a perspective of Greenock surpass in beauty any thing I remember to have seen in water colors.

Mr. R. is a stranger, on every score deserving encouragement. He is a native of Poland, of a land at the bare mention of whose name the pulse of every lover of liberty beats quicker, of a land which sent us a Kosciusko and a Pulaski, with hundreds of subalterns, in the hour of our country's danger to fight her battles. When we have it in our power to repay the obligation in the only manner in which we can repay it, by affording encouragement to the fine genius and taste of one of her worthiest sons, let us not neglect the opportunity. I doubt not, that Mr. R. will be extensively sustained as soon and as far as he becomes known. As his best introduction to the community I recommend the public to visit his rooms and make his acquaintance.

Chronology for the week.

Nov.1 1756, Earthquake at Lisbon which cost more than seventy thousand persons their lives. The second shock laid the city in ruins. The bed of the river Tagus was in many places raised to the surface, a large new quay with several people on it sank to an unfathonable depth. At the time of this earthquake, Loch Lomond and Loch Ness, two beautiful lakes in Scotland, were uncommonly agitated, and the latter after flowing and ebbing for an hour, spread over the northern bank, a space of thirty feet. At the Hot Wells at Bristol in England the water became red as blood and so turbid that it could not be drank. The water of a common well which had previously been perfectly clear became perfectly black at the same time, and remained so for sixteen days. The natural course of the river Avon was reversed on this occasion and many other remarkable effects were observed which appeared to be connected with the same cause. The entire duration of this earthquake was six minutes.

2nd. 1519, Reformation in Germany by Martin Luther.

3rd 1534, Henry VIII constituted by his Parliament head of the Church of England. Synod of Dort assembled 1618.

4th 1794, Organization of the British Missionary Society. Defeat of Gen. St. Clair by the Indians 1791.

5th 1605, Gunpowder plot, discovery of the

7th 1665, The first English newspaper made its appearance at Oxford England.

R. R. M.

Profane Swearing.--A Lay Sermon.

On my way to my office, a few mornings since I passed the driver of a dray, who had considerable difficulty in getting his horse to obey his orders. He seized him, at length, by the head, violently enraged, and belabored him with his whip handle, interlarding his abuse with, God damn your soul! God damn you! and much other profane language of the sort.

I felt grieved, both for the horse and the driver, which last was still a mere youth; but knowing by experience what little it avails to address a *maniac*, whether he be so under the influence of passion ardent spirits, or permanent mental derangement. I passed on, resolving to speak to the drayman on the subject, at a suitable opportunity, and meditating deeply on the scene.

Here thought I, is a young man who believes his horse has a soul, and yet, probably, is ignorant he has one himself. A man who, perhaps, never prays at home, and yet prays publicly in the streets. A man who never asks a blessing at his meals, or on his repose at night, and doubtless never prays unless to supplicate a curse upon his horse, or some fellow being.— What a *bundle* of *inconsistencies* is human nature!

Other reflections suggested themselves to me in further meditating on the subject. Would this youth as willingly have asked, publicly, for blessings on his horse, or on himself, or his fellow being? Did he ask in faith? Did he expect a favorable answer to his prayers? Was he aware that the damnation of the horse's soul involved the destruction of his body? Was he willing to lose his horse's service entirely and forever, on the present provocation? What a *tissue* of *absurdities* is human nature!

Following out the theme, I asked myself, whether this was not a topic of rebuke to christians as well as profligates. How many religious people shrink from praying in public, even for blessings, while this poor fellow was so deeply engaged invoking curses in a similar exercise. How far short in fervency is the most ardent prayer, I recollect to have heard lately, when compared with the earnestness of this drayman. Truly the *children of this world* are not only wiser, but frequently more in earnest than the *children of light.*

After all, there is an essential difference in prayer. The ploughing and the dray driving of the wicked is sin, and their prayer, however fervent,not being in a right spirit,and directed to right objects, avails nothing. It is the effectual fervent prayer of a righteous man,only,which availeth much.

And so I dismiss the subject for the present.

The Guano Islands.

It is stated in late foreign journals, that the famous product of *Guano* is keenly exciting the spirit of adventure amongst speculators, and that between forty and fifty English vessels have sailed from England to bring guano from the rocky islands on the West coast of Africa. The

West India planters, it seems, have begun to use it freely for their sugar canes, and so successfully (it being supposed they would require large quantities) that numerous vessels have been sent to procure loads of it for the West India market.

Immense beds of guano are known to exist on two of the islands lying on that desert and uninhabited coast, which stretches from the southern point of the Portuguese possessions of Congo, almost to the grand Orange river, the northern boundary of the British possessions at the Cape; and as rain rarely if ever falls along this coast, it is probable that the guano will be found to have been collecting in the same manner on the whole of the islands along it, for centuries.

A Liverpool paper in reference to the same subject says:

A writer in one of the London papers wishes to know whether there is not some danger of this article being subjected to an export duty in Africa as well as in South America, but we may certainly dismiss his fears, for there are no inhabitants along the coast, except lions and other beasts of prey, amongst which Custom-house officers are not to be found; and as for the islands, their only inhabitants are the sea birds which produce the guano, and which, if they take toll at all, take it in the form of flesh and blood, for it is a fact that the first guano searchers who landed on these islands had to fight as fiercely with the birds for their cargoes as Eneas and his companions had to fight with the Harpies of old in defence of their dinners.

With regard to the effect of Guano as an admirable fertilizer, we have seen it stated in the Durham (Eng.) Chronicle, that during the last season, an *old land* grass-field, upon which the substance had been tried, produced two excellent crops of hay. The manure was applied at the rate of one cwt. per acre. The first dressing took place in March last, and a second immediately after the first crop had been led. The cost of each dressing was about 12s per acre. The produce of the first crop averaged about 2½ tons per acre; and the second two tons.

Thunder.

Thunder claps are the effect of lightning, which causes a vacuum in that portion of the atmosphere through which it passes; the air rushing on to restore the equilibrium may cause much of the noise that is heard in the clap. An easy experiment on the air pump illustrates this: Take a glass receiver open at both ends, over one end tie a piece of a sheep's bladder, wet and let it stand till thoroughly dry. Then place the open end on the plate of the air pump, and exhaust the air slowly from under it. The bladder soon becomes concave, owing to the pressure of the atmospheric air on it, the supporting air in the receiver being partly thrown out.—Carry on the exhaustion, and the air presses at the rate of fifteen pounds on every square inch. The fibres of the bladder being no longer capable of bearing the pressure of the atmospheric column upon the receiver, are torn to pieces, with a noise equal to the report of a musket, which is occasioned by the air rushing in to restore the equilibrium.—Imagine a rapid succession of such experiments, on a large scale, and you have a peal of thunder, the rapture of the first bladder being the clap. But the explosion of the gasses, exygon and hydrogen, of which water is composed, will also account for he noise.

Power of the Memory.

In distinguished men the thorough awakening and vigorous exertion of the mind has more to do with their eminence than is generally thought. In most men the intellectual energies slumber, or are but half put forth. A correspondent of the New York Tribune, writing from Rome, relates some anecdotes of the eminent linguist Cardinal Mezzafonti, which illustrates this truth.

Mezzafonti is able to speak 52 languages. The Pope attributes his extraordinary powers in this respect to miraculous aid. A friend of the Cardinal's informed the writer that he took the same view of the case; which, with the circumstances mentioned below, shows that his powers as a linguist did probably receive, when extraordinary exertion was demanded, a remarkable impulse and developement.

He states that when an obscure priest, in the North of Italy he was called one day to confess two foreigners condemned for piracy, who were to be executed the next day. On entering their cell he found them unable to understand a word he uttered. Overwhelmed with the thought that the criminals should leave this world without the benefits of religion, he returned to his room resolved to acquire their language before morning. He accomplished his task, and the next day confessed them in their own tongue. From that time on, he says, he had no difficulty in mastering the most difficult language. The purity of his motive in the first place, he thinks, influenced the Deity to assist him miraculously. A short time since a Swede, who could speak a patois peculiar to a certain province of Sweden, called on him in that dialect. Mezzafonti had never heard it before, and seemed very much interested. He invited him to call on him often, which he did, while the conversation invariably turned on this dialect. At length the Swede calling one day, heard himself, to his amazement, addressed in this difficult patois. He inquired of the Cardinal who had been his master, for he thought, he said, there was no man in Rome who could speak that language but himself. "I have had no one," he replied, "but yourself—I NEVER *forget a word I hear once.*

Narrow Escape.

When we read in the history of battles, to what dangers the commanding officers are at times exposed in leading their troops into an engagement, it becomes matter of surprise, how they escape with life, and in particular instances without even a wound. Marlborough, Wellington, Napoleon, Washington and Jackson, have been remarkable for having exposed themselves greatly in this respect, yet according to my recollection of all these, Napoleon is the only one who was ever wounded in battle and his wounds were few and not severe.

But there are dangers incidental to such cases, unseen and unrecorded in many instances, which increase the hazard of life to such a degree as to satisfy even a careless observer of the fact that their lives are under the care of an overruling providence which reserves them for future usefulness. We are all familiar with the fact, as declared by an Indian chief on the treaty ground, that he had three times taken deliberate aim, during the battle which ended in "Braddock's defeat," at Washington, then commanding the provincials, and missed every time.

The following anecdote relating to the same individual is not so generally known. It may be found in a well attested note to page 122 of Bisset's continuation of history, vol. II.

Col. Ferguson of the British army, who lay with part of his riflemen on the skirts of a wood in front of Gen. Knyphausen's division, writing to his brother Dr. A. Ferguson, the day after the battle at Brandywine creek, states, "We had not lain long when a rebel officer, remarkable by a hussar dress, passed towards our army, within a hundred yards of my right flank, not perceiving us. He was followed by another dressed in dark green and blue, mounted on a good bay horse, with a remarkably large high cocked hat. I ordered three good shots to steal near to them and fire at them, but the idea disgusted me; and I recalled the order. The hussar in returning made a circuit, but the other passed within a hundred yards of us; upon which I advanced from the wood towards him. Upon my calling, he stopped, but after looking at me, proceeded. I again drew his attention, and made a sign to him to stop, leveling my piece at him; but he slowly continued his way. As I was within that distance at which, in the quickest firing, I could have lodged half a dozen balls in or about him, before he was out of my reach; I had only to determine, but it was not pleasant to fire at the back of an unoffending individual, who was acquitting himself very coolly of his duty; so I let him alone. The day after, I had been telling this to some wounded officers who lay in the same room with me, when one of our surgeons, who had been dressing the wounded rebel officers, came in and told us, that they had been informing him, that Gen. Washington was all morning with the light troops, and only attended by a French officer in a hussar dress, he himself dressed and mounted in every point as above described. I am not sorry that I did not know at the time who it was.

The Pardoning Power.

It must be obvious, that the power originally given to the highest authority, to protect the innocent merely, has under a variety of influences, become perverted to the injury of the public interest and is tending rapidly to jeopardize the public safety. It becomes then time for the community to interpose and insist that the power should be exercised only in its legitimate department, and no longer be made the means of returning to the bosom of society, in many cases, directly after their conviction of the basest or most flagitious crimes—the scoundrels, who in the face of legal ingenuity, difficulty of proving what every body knows to be true, and the false sympathies of juries have been sent at length to the Penitentiary where they should long since have been immured.

Acting Governor Bartley introduced a rule no doubt with the best of motives which I think increases the evil he proposed to remedy,—the facility with which persons convicted of crimes obtain through their friends signatures to petitions for pardons. He required public notice to be given in every case, that such application would be made, calculating probably that when the case did not deserve a favorable hearing that the community would exert themselves to defeat it. But this was not placing the subject in its proper attitude. There is an active interest enlisted on behalf of the convict, while the public welfare remains in the neglected province of every body's business.

I agitate this subject now that we have a new Governor under whose administration I trust that a convict who has had a fair trial and *all the evidence in his favor present which exists,* will be made to serve out the period for which he was sentenced, and as we have no right to expose our Governor to influences which we ourselves can hardly withstand, let the legislature pass a law by which the signers to a petition for the pardon of a convict shall be held answerable for his future good behaviour in the penalty of one thousand dollars, to be collected from any of the signers. I guarantee that responsible men will become more careful under such circumstances what they sign.

Another abuse connected with this subject, is a practice prevalent at Columbus, perhaps elsewhere, of the Governor pardoning a convict, a few days prior to the expiration of his sentence, so as to restore him to the rights of citizenship. I hold this, if possible, deserving still greater censure than the abuse of which I have been already complaining. If the law disfranchises a man for crime, by what moral right does the Governor evade its requirements. Is he not sworn to execute and support the laws? And are we who have borne unblemished characters, willing to go to the polls, it may be, along side of individuals of this description and find our right of suffrage neutralized and nullified by such scoundrels. I feel at the moment of writing this, almost the same degree of indignation which made my blood boil on seeing an infamous counterfeiter deposite his vote along side of mine at the Sixth Ward on Friday last, and I now say what every friend to good order in society should say with me, that no candidate for Governor shall receive my support hereafter who does not pledge himself to set his face against these abuses.

The following narrative which I derived from Governor Corwin himself, in reply to my asking him how he could justify it to his conscience, to let loose on society such fellows as he had lately pardoned, from Cincinnati, sheds light on the whole subject. You do not know, said the Governor, how far the community are to blame rather than the executive. I will give you an instance. Not long since, a man was convicted of arson in B...... county, and sent to the penitentiary. In a few days a petition for pardon came on, setting forth that there was great reason to doubt the man's guilt, that it was believed that an alibi, could be substantiated in the case, and various other reasons urged to induce the exercise of official clemency. The petition was signed by the Judges, members of the bar, county commissioners, and respectable citizens at large. The very jury which convicted him, and the prosecuting attorney who officiated at the trial, signed it. It appeared a clear case. But I had been so often imposed upon, or attempted to be, that I paused to reflect. What is your name? said I to the bearer. He gave it, and I knew it to be that of one of the most respectable citizens of the county. I glanced over the signatures; why is not your name to the petition? He replied that he did not know the facts in the case to be as stated; and on further conversation, admitted that he did not believe the statement. Very well, I shall have inquiries made upon this subject, before I interfere. I did so, and to my utter astonishment ascertained that the whole affair, was thus managed to get the county clear of the expense of supporting the convict.

I wrote such a letter as the case deserved to such of the parties as I knew, and recommended to the prosecuting attorney, to resign his office. What a mockery of justice do such scenes present. Is it any wonder that the community so often of late years, takes the law into its own hands.

Winter's Chemical Diorama.

Our townsman, R. WINTER has returned from the East, with his *chemical pictures*, which he has been exhibiting for the last thirteen months, in Boston, New York, and Baltimore. with distinguished success. He is now among his early friends, who feel proud that the defiance to produce such pictures as Daguerre's, which was publicly made by *Maffei and Lonati*, who exhibited them here, was taken up, and successfully accomplished by a Cincinnati artist.

Nothing can be more perfect than the agency of light and shade, to give life and *vraisemblance* to these pictures. They are four in number. The Milan Cathedral, at Midnight Mass. The Church of the Holy Sepulchre, at Jerusalem. Belshazzar's Feast, and the Destruction of Babylon. These are all fine, each having its appropriate excellencies, but the rich, yet harmonious coloring in the two last, has an incomparable effect, which must strike every observer. But the pen cannot adequately describe the triumphs of the pencil, the eye alone must be the judge.

Exhibition on Fourth, below Main Street, Miller's buildings.

Early Jails, &c.

The great range of power lodged in the hands of Territorial Governors, and which St. Clair, from his millitary habits and personal character, was disposed to stretch to its full extent, the kindred influence which a garrison stationed here, with a force originally outnumbering greatly the settlers, naturally had upon the whole community, and the difficulty if not impossibility of obtaining redress elsewhere, for abuses or authority committed here, all, naturally led to many irregular and summary proceedings, in the early days of Cincinnati.

As a Gallows stood in 1795, on Walnut below Fifth street, the presumption is, that it had not unfrequently been made use of, although there is little pioneer lore on this subject, and its victims must have been distinct from the military corps, in which deserters are shot, not hung.— But in those days, the gallows, the pillory, and the whipping post, were appendages of civilized society, two of them in the further advance of civilization driven out of existence, and the third in a rapid process of extinction. Several of our citizens survive, who have witnessed not only these structures, but also the administration of justice under their operation. Jonah Martin, while a youth, was present when Sheriff Goforth inflicted the *"forty stripes save one,"* upon a woman convicted of setting fire to haystacks, and

Mr. Samuel Stitt, witnessed the same punishment applied to another woman guilty of theft, by the hands of Levi M'Clean, the deputy Sheriff and jailor at that time. It must not be inferred, however, that the infliction was as severe as it appeared to be. Goforth was a man of great humanity, and even M'Clean, although jailor, pound keeper, butcher, and constable, four hard hearted avocations, played on the fiddle and taught singing school.

Men are not steel, but *steel* is bent,
Men are not flints, even *flint* is rent,

And Levi, unless his prisoners rebeled on his hands, or he had himself taken a glass too much, in which case he would turn in and take a flogging frolic among his *pets*, without making much distinction between debtors and criminals, was rather a good natured fellow, than otherwise.

The first jail here was built early in 1793, and as every thing else in the early days of Cincinnati, was located to accommodate the convenience of the bottom interest. It was, therefore, built upon Water street, west of Main street. Although a mere log cabin, of a story and a half in height, and probably sixteen feet square, the ground in its neighborhood being cleared out, it was distinctly visible from the river. Small as it was, it was amply large enough to accommodate the prisoners, most of whom were in for debt. Neither were its inmates kept strictly within its limits, or even those of the yard adjacent, the prisoners visiting around the neighborhood throughout the day, taking care to return in time to be locked up at night, and on the approach of the Sheriff, scampering home in a great fright, like so many rats to their holes.

This was the Jail referred to in the following letter of Judge Symmes to Wm. McMillan, Esq., now published for the first time:

NORTH BEND, Dec. 28th, 1792.
Dear Sir;
I hope, that by this time the jail is begun and going on briskly. I hear that the people of Cincinnati are voting on this question—whether the jail shall be built on the first bottom or the second bank? If you will allow us at North Bend to vote also, our voice is for the second bank most decidedly. Our reasons are—the ground will be had much cheaper—fuel will be had easier and at less expense—the situation will be more elevated and healthy, in addition to its more magnificent appearance—the soil is much more dry—the prisoners will at no time be drowned in a fresh like pigs in a sty—a great expense will be saved in carting the timber—it is or soon will be more in the centre of the town. It will be more convenient than Cincinnati for the people of the other villages in the county. Water may be had by digging a well which ought to be within the liberties

of the prison, and if it stood on the banks of the Ohio, a well will be necessary that privileged prisoners for debt allowed the liberty, might draw for themselves. But, if interested motives are to direct our votes, the inhabitants of North Bend vote that the prison be built on Congress green,* a most elegant situation.

Sir, your most obd't servant.
JOHN CLEVES SYMMES.
WM. McMILLEN, Esq.

As greater space became requisite for immuring within the walls of a jail that increase of prisoners which kept pace with the increase of the town, a new jail of hewed logs and lapt-shingle roof, two stories high, and larger than its predecessor, was erected within less than two years, at the S. E. corner of Walnut and Sixth street, on the lot now occupied by an apothecary store. Its size was 15 by 20 feet. Late in 1795, the building was moved with 8 yoke of oxen, by the public teams in charge of Captain John Thorp, quarter-master in the public service, assisted by Mr. John Richardson, to the lot at the corner of Church Alley and Walnut street, now in the tenancy of H. & J. Koch, tailors. It was from this "*dungeon keep*" that the following pathetic notice issued, being published in the "Cincinnati Spy," of November 4, 1799:

'Those indebted to Dr. Himes, are desired to remit the sums due—he being confined to jail *deprives him of the pleasure of calling personally* on his friends—they will therefore oblige their unfortunate friend, by complying with this request without loss of time. Hamilton county prison, Oct. 29th, 1799."

* The public ground in front of the village of North Bend,

I am indebted to a correspondent, who is obviously a professional man for the following rebuke. I sit corrected.

MR. EDITOR:

Your paper has recently contained an editorial remark, under the head of Marriage Licences, in which you tell a story of a groomsman who would have got married himself, under the influence of the moment, if he had had a license. And from your closing remark about it, that here were congenial spirits prevented from a union of bliss, because the law interposed a delay and an expense for a marriage license, many persons may suppose you were serious in reprehending the law as an evil and a burden. Society is already too prone to hold the marriage tie too lightly, and inconsiderate engagements are, doubtless, encouraged by the facility with which divorces are dispensed from our courts, and even by our Legislature, in face of the Constitution, which says that no law shall be passed impairing the obligation of contracts.

If it is in seriousness you ask, what right has society to interpose even the slightest obstacle in the shape of expense or delay, to the establishment of that relation on which its whole well-being depends? I would as seriously answer, that the well-being of society, gives an undoubted right to prescribe all salutary regulations, on every matter connected with that well-being. It is of moment to society that marriages shall not be made without consideration; and it is of moment to the parties, that a ready and cheap mode of proving their marriage, should exist. For the sum of seventy-five cents, the Clerk issues the marriage license, and makes a record of the marriage, a certificate of which, the person solemnizing it, is bound to return to him within three months. Proof of actual marriage is often needed in connection with the rights of property, and that proof is thus furnished with certainty and cheapness. If your groomsman, in a fit of excitement, would have committed matrimony, with a kindred lunatic, and on the morrow's morn, the delusion was so far spent, as to leave no desire of renewing the perpetration, they might well thank the "law's delay," as a benign rescue from a life of wretchedness.

So, Mr. Editor, I think you ought not to speak lightly in your columns, on such sober matters, for many persons may misunderstand you, and be misled by your respectable authority.   VINCTUS.
October 31st, 1844.

Early Conveyances.

The following, together with that great paramount title, undisturbed possession for twenty-one years, is the right by which is held property of great value here, 100 feet by 200, comprehending Luck's tavern scite, and that of the two frames on the north upon Sycamore, between Third and Fourth Streets, and running west to Mayor's Alley, in the centre of the block. Of so little value was it considered fifty years ago, that the assignment from Cook does not even specify the assignee.

Know all men, by these presents, that I, Jonathan Fitts, do hereby bind myself, my heirs, &c., to hold and defend to *Peyton Cook*, my right, title, and claim to a town lot, in Cincinnati, viz: No. 61. The right of said lot to said Fitts have, by these presents vested in said Cook. for value received, this 28th August.
                               JONATHAN FITTS.
Test.
    John Vance,
                    (Endorsed,)
I do hereby assign my right and title to the within said lot, for value received, as witness my hand and seal, this 25th Jan., 1791.
Testas.   PEYTON COOK.
    B. Brown.

Relic of the Past.

Capt. Jno. Armstrong to Gen. James Wilkinson.

Ft. Hamilton, 13th July, 1792. 10 o'cl'k.

Dear General—Capt. Barbee, is this moment arrived. The packet accompanying this will no doubt, inform you of every particular from the advanced posts, the loss of all the cattle from Ft. Jefferson, &c.

One man taken prisoner on the 19th October, 1791, belonging to the detachment of Federal troops, then under my command, and one taken the 4th November, 1792, in Gen. St. Clair's defeat, are also here. They made their escape from an Indian village, 50 miles above the Miami, on the St. Joseph's, passed that village the second day, and on the morning of the third, reached Fort Jefferson. They came through the field or place where our army was defeated, and say that their different Flags from us have been received at the Auglaize river, and the messengers were then tomahawked—that the last was a Captain—poor Truman.

I expect all my hay will be in stack to-morrow. All is well here.

Sketch of the Life of John Bush.

John Bush was born in Winchester, Virginia, on the 21st of March, 1767. His father, Philip Bush, was a Captain under the then Col. George Washington, at the time he capitulated to the French and Indians, at the Little Meadows, in which campaign he imbibed a great dislike to tee French, which accounts somewhat for an anecdote which occurred at his tavern, in Winchester, in 1797. The present King of France, Louis Phillippe was, during the winter of that year, with his brother, &c., *incognito,* He called ed at Bush's house and ordered a room and dinner. He was shown into the dining room.— When dinner was announced, it was found he had secured the doors to prevent intrusion, and had of course shut out the boarders. Upon an explanation being demanded, he declared himself and company to be *gentlemen,* who wished to dine by themselves. He was told by Mr. Bush that none but gentlemen dined at his house, and that for his insolence he must seek other quarters. His horse was ordered, his baggage produced, and he was obliged to leave the house.

This anecdote was published in the papers of the day. In 1788, John Bush (as did many of the enterprising and chivalrous sons of Virginia) came to the bloody ground to make it his permanent home, and lived in the family of Col. Thomas Marshall, of Fayette, now Woodford county. He was engaged in many of the dangerous scouting parties that went in pursuit of the marauding Indians, and once in a company of only four, two of which were sons of Col. Marshall.

He volunteered in the expedition of Gen. Harmar, in 1789,, crossed the river at Cincinnati, and marched to Fort Wayne—volunteered in the army, and went with the troops engaged in both days' battles with the Indians. On the first day. he commanded an advanced guard of 20 men, with orders by Major Fountaine, to charge any body of Indians the spies might discover and fire upon. He asked the Major what he was to do if he came upon a *large body* of Indians. Fountaine demanded to know if he was afraid? No, Sir, I am not afraid, but wish to know my duty, was the reply. Well, Sir, if you fall upon 10,-000 Indians, it is your duty to charge through them and form at their backs. The detachment, as is known, were drawn into ambuscade and defeated, and about one-third, including many of the best spies and soldiers, were killed. After the Indian town had been burned, Harmar's army commenced its usual march for the settlement and encamped about 6 miles off. Col. Hardin solicited permission to return to the town with another detachment and surprise the Indians, which being granted, volunteers were again called for, excusing those who had been in the first day's engagement. Maj. Fountaine went to Bush and requested him to go. He agreed, provided they would get him a very fine horse, belonging to one Nelson, which being procured, he marched with Harmar and reached the town just before day. The detachment divided into two parties, Bush with that of Cols. Hall, McMullen, and Fountaine. When it became light enough to see, a number of Indians were discovered some fifty or an hundred yards in advance. Fountaine, as Bush thinks, without giving the word *charge*, in his eagerness, charged alone, and was shot, and fell from his horse. The Lieutenant of the troops advanced and ordered the charge, but was followed by only four men, Bush, Titus Mershon, and two named Moore. When reaching the place where Fountaine lay, they were fired on by the Indians, and all wounded but the Lieutenant. Bush had his sword knocked out of his hand. and a ball grazed his cheek and cut off part of his queue. They then returned; but a reinforcement coming up, the Indians gave way, and many of them were killed in crossing the St. Joseph. They were followed by the horsemen. On reaching the opposite bank, Bush saw an Indian leave the rest, which he followed and took prisoner; some of the troop coming up they cut him down beside Bush's horse. He cursed the fellow for a coward, and turned his horse and rode towards the firing that had commenced under Cols. Hardin and Willis. Upon coming in sight, he found himself in the rear of the Indians, and Hardin's troops firing directly towards him. He then tried to turn them on the right flank; but, in ascending a small rise, he met 50 or 60 Indians, who halted & fired at him just as he turned his horse, the ball passing through his coat. He then attempted to pass on the left, but found the Indian flank reached to the river. His next effort was to retreat to the rear, where he soon met several horsemen, who told him there was a body of Indian horsemen approaching in that direction—they having, as he since supposed, become alarmed at seeing some of their own men.—He now determined to charge through the Indian lines and join Hardin, which he accomplished in safety, followed by his few associates. On passing the Indian town he saw a very large Indian behind a tree. and prepared to strike him with his sword, but, the Indian, turning the tree just at the moment, saved himself. Hardin's men were begining to give way, but seeing the men charge through the Indians, they rallied and fired again, but were soon compelled to retreat. During the retreat the horsemen were directed to ride as far as they could with safety to the rear and bring up the men that were going out.

At one time during this dangerous employment, Bush got mired in a swamp, with a man behind him. He made the man get off, but not being able to extricate the horse, he got off himself, and remained trying to get him out till two Indians came up and took the man prisoner.— He then sprang out of the swamp and was fired at by the Indians, which alarmed the horse so that he cleared the swamp and was regained and mounted.

On his return to Fort Washington, he crossed the river to the Kentucky side, now Covington, and passed the night there. In the course of the night, his horse was stolen. Next morning he re-crossed the river, reported his horse as lost, returned and walked to Georgetown the same day. A few years after, he married the daughter of John Craig, the Commandant of Bryant's Station.

In 1794, he settled in the bottom opposite Gen. Harrison's future log cabin residence at North Bend, with whom he was on terms of intimacy, as early as '97, and for whom he had always interchanged an unchangeable friendship.

He had four children, (three sons of whom survive,) by his first wife. In 1813, he married a sister of Ex-Governor Noble, by whom he has had 21 children, 8 of whom survive. Between his first and last there is about 40 years difference.

He still resides in Boone county, Kentucky, and although in reduced circumstances, he has never received a cent by way of pension—Congress having passed no law granting any to Harrison's soldiers.

The Methodist Preacher.

LOOKING TOWARD MY NEW APPOINTMENT.—Up to the close of Conference, I have kept faithfully the forty dollars reserved for the purchase of a horse so soon as I should reach my new circuit. But over and above that I have not five dollars, and wife and children all want new shoes, and my boots have given way at the side. They have been twice half-soled, and the uppers wont stand it any longer. My only coat is all threadbare, and white at the seams. That, however, is no matter, it will look well enough back in the woods, although it has rather a shabby appearance here among so many shining new black coats. But, besides the absolute want of shoes and boots, it will cost us all of thirty dollars to get to our new home. Where, then, is the horse to come from? Be still, desponding heart! The Lord will provide. You go forth in his cause, and he will take care to supply the armour, if you will always keep it bright and whole! Yes—yes—weak, timid, trembling soldier of the cross! The Captain of your salvation will go before you, and lead you on to certain victory. Only be faithful: look not back for a moment; but press forward.

I have just had a talk with brother T———. He called in very kindly to give me all the advice, encouragement, and instruction that he could, in regard to my new appointment; and also to furnish me with a list of the names of some of the prominent brethren. There is no parsonage provided for the preacher's family. Nor do the people pay the rent for one. But a log cottage, he says, with a little patch of ground for a garden and pasturage, can be had for about twenty dollars a year. A cow will cost as much more, But where is the money to buy her to come from? Ah, me! If I had just about as much as it costs three or four of the sisters here for ribbons and laces, how rich I should be. The elegant dinner-set, upon which our food is served here every day, the good sister told my wife, cost eighty dollars. There was a plainer set for sixty; but the first set had a gold band, and she liked it best and gave twenty dollars more, for the sake of the gold band. Now, just the price of that gold band on the dinner-set would buy me a cow. Ah, me! These thoughts trouble me. But hush! hush! poor, doubting, murmuring heart! *Thou shalt not covet thy neighbour's wife, nor his man-servant, nor his maid-servant, nor his ox, nor his ass, nor any thing that is thy neighbour's.* If the good Master has prospered our brother and sister in their basket and store, I ought to be thankful to him on their account, that he has given them the good things of life with a liberal hand.

I met old father H———y this morning, with his cowhide shoes and leather strings, wool hat, coarse coat, and shirt collar unbound with a neckcloth. It is two years since I last saw him. We talked for half an hour about matters and things. He is no happier than when I last met him. Not so happy I think. The luxurious living of our rich professors troubles his soul. He has lifted his voice against it faithfully, and enforced his precepts of temperance and moderation by a rigid, self denying example, but it is all of no avail. There is no diminution of the evil he complains of. His own perverse heart, too, causes him great affliction. The bitter things which he is daily compelled to write against himself, humble his soul to the dust. He finds, he says, every day, lower and lower depths of evil in his own heart, the discovery of which fills his soul with the deepest anguish. Dear, good old man! His troubles and his trials *here*, will, I trust, make him richer *there*. I cannot, however, coincide with him in all his positions. I cannot follow him in all his examples. The bounties provided by nature—her delicious fruits—sweet flowers—honey from the rock—were not 'all made in vain; or, only for those who look not for good things beyond this world. They are all for us, if in our power to obtain them, and to me, it seems a greater sin to put aside the blessings thus provided by our Father's hand, than to receive them, and use them with thankfulness.

But he is sincere, and the Lord looks at the heart. I wish more of us had a portion of his self-denying spirit. I am sure I need some of it to enable me to bear up more patiently than I do. I do wish I could never feel troubled about anything—that I could really say from the heart: 'Thy will, not mine, be done.' I often say as much with the lips—but, alas! it is, I fear, only from the teeth outward.

I had written thus far in my journal, when my wife came in, and holding a stout bundle in her hand said, with a cheerful smile,

' What do you think this contains, dear?'

'I don't know, I'm sure,' I said. 'What does it contain?'

'You shall see,' was her reply, as she unrolled it. There were three pairs of shoes a piece for the children, and three pairs for wife, enough to last them all the next year. Then there were four frocks a piece for the little ones, and four new gowns for wife, besides various other matters, such as muslin for underclothes, and nice warm Canton flannel, and stockings!

'Not all for us?' I exclaimed, in astonishment, as Mary displayed these before my eyes.

'Yes, all for us. May the Lord reward sister A——— for her goodness—we cannot.' Tears of thankfulness were in her eyes.

'Amen!' I responded, fervently. In the next moment my heart smote me for what I had thought and written about the gold bands on the dinner set. Several times since I have turned to the page of my journal where it lies recorded, and taken up my pen to erase it. But I have as often determined to let it remain. It presents a true history of my feelings, and I cannot blot it out.

After supper that evening—the last we were to spend in the kind family of brother and sister A———, brother A——— began to ask about my new circuit, and how I expect to get along on it. I felt a little delicacy about replying to his questions—for I could not speak very encouragingly, and I never like to make a poor mouth. But he was in earnest, and cornered me so closely that I had to tell all the truth about the means the circuit afforded, and my own poor condition.

'And so you still have your 'horse money' safe?' he said, smiling after he had got all out of me.

'Yes, that still remains untouched. But a part will have to go for stage hire. That can't be helped. Though I doubt not, something will turn up, and that I shall get a horse after I get there easily enough. Horses don't cost much in that section of the country, and then to add to what is left after paying our fare, I hope to receive about ten dollars for the sale of some things at the old place, left in the care of a good brother. It will all come right, I know, brother A———. It always has come right.'

'No doubt,' he said. 'The Lord will provide.'

Brother A—— seemed thoughtful after he had said this. After sitting for a little while, he said. rising,

'Come, brother B——.'

I followed him up stairs, into his chamber. He closed the door, and then opened a large mahogany wardrobe, well stocked with clothes. 'You and I are near about the same size,' he said, taking down a black frock coat, that was very little worn. 'Try on this and see how near it will come to fitting you. I have not worn it for some months, and it is a pity to let the moths get into it. There!' he continued, as I drew on the coat, 'it fits you just as well as if it had been made for you, and scarcely shows the wear it has had. Let me see,' he added, turning again to the wardrobe, 'what else we have here. Ah! this is just the thing for you!' bringing out an overcoat, made of stout beaver cloth. 'You will want just such a thing as this next winter. It will keep you as warm as toast while riding among those snowy hills. I found it almost too heavy for me last winter. But to ride in it will be the dandy.'

He did not stop here. Two pair of good pantaloons, as many vests, and a pair of excellent boots, were added to these. I tried to thank him, but my voice was so husky that I could not articulate distinctly. The remembrance, too, of what I had thought and written down about the gold bands on the dinner-set, with other reflections not clothed in words, choked me. He did not stop here. Next morning as I shook hands with him, and bade him farewell, he left two pieces of coin in my hands, saying as he did so, with a smile;

'Don't touch the 'horse money,' brother B——. A minister can't walk around his circuit.'

Excellent man! May the Lord reward him? As for me, I feel humbled before my Master, for my want of faith. So many—many times has he brought me safely out of the wilderness into a clear place, and yet I am unwilling to trust him.

Mutton and no Mutton.

It is odd enough that a sheep, when dead, should turn into mutton, all but its head; for, while we ask for a leg or a shoulder of mutton, we never ask for a mutton's head. But there is a fruit which changes its name still oftener; grapes are so called while fresh; raisins when dried, and plums when in a pudding.

Recollections of a Voyage to Italy in 1800

The language of a thorough sailor, is *sui generis*, and much of it is unintelligible to the uninitiated. It was sometime before I could comprehend readily all the phrases which I heard. In performing many parts of the duty on shipboard, it is customary for the sailor to answer the order by repeating the words in which it is given; as in directing the steersman, hard-a-port, he replies, hard-a-port it is, sir. The steward having misbehaved himself, the Captain turned him before the mast, and took a smart active fellow in his place. Just after he had got into his new berth, I desired him to brush my coat, then on me, which he began to perform so gently that I could scarcely feel him, and I exclaimed. with a little impatience, Brush away, Tom. Changing his hand instantly, to a manner which resembled curry-combing a horse, he repeated, Brush away it is, sir; and was pursuing his operation with so much energy, that I was obliged to moderate him, by saying, I am afraid you mistake me for the main mast, Tom. I was pleased with the sailors, and found them to be the frank, honest, and jovial, good-natured fellows, which they are generally reported to be.

The monotony of sea life renders every accidental variety interesting. A sail discovered in the horizon, or any distant and cloud-like land calls the attention of all on board. The latter is sometimes useful as well as pleasant, and serves to mark the sailor his position on the chart. On the 29th of July, we passed the Azores, or Western Islands. *Pico*, except its top, which rose above them, was shrouded by the clouds. From its height condensing the vapors that float around it, I suppose this is frequently the case. Moore mentions the same thing when he passed it·

"The only envious cloud that lowers,
Hath hung its shade on Pico's height."

There was a fine effect produced on Terceira, by the sun shining brilliantly on one part of it while the rest appeared deluged by a heavy shower of rain. The climate of these Islands must be delightful,

On the 7th of August a sail was visible from the mast head, astern of us, and steering our course. She was seen the whole of the next day and appeared in chase of us, close by the wind. The following morning finding her within a few miles of us, the captain ordered the ship to be tacked and stood for her; when alongside she proved to be brig Huntress from New York bound to Leghorn. On the ensuing day we made the land, which proved to be Cape Spartel, on the Barbary coast. The wind was light and fair, and I went aloft to have a better view of the scenery which we were approaching. I observed something which appeared to be a large white rock on the shore, directly ahead of us and had seen it for at least half an hour, when some one made it out to be the sails of a large ship, approaching us, close hauled; but we still could not ascertain what she was, till having approached within two or three miles, she changed her course, and we perceived her to be a vessel of war; in a short time, having tacked again, she came alongside, and proved to be the British frigate Topaz.

Cape Spartel is one of the head lands which form the straits of Gibraltar: Trafalgar is the other. The outline of both coasts is very varied, and distant mountains are seen over the lower lands near the shore; but to an American, accustomed to behold the hills and mountains of his own country clothed with towering forests, the bare and rugged hills of both shores present the appearance of great sterility. A this time the wind was fair, and there was every prospect of passing the straits without any difficulty; but the wind suddenly came round to the east, and blew with great violence for several days, so that we tacked from one cape to the other, without making any headway. I became very tired of it, and could have exclaimed *fortiter occupa portum*, with all my heart. I felt all the tedium which Horace mentions. In this situation we spoke the brig Greyhound from Boston, and the Huntress, which had parted company rejoined us. Till our arrival off Cape Spartel, the voyage might be considered as a very pleasant, although a slow one, the winds in general, being moderate and the weather fine. But we now paid pretty dearly for our former ease, being beat about from cape to cape without being able to get within them.

On the morning of the 19th, we observed several vessels at anchor under the lee of Cape Spartel, and as we had very strong gales, accompanied by a rough sea, the captain determined to bear away, and come into the smooth water under the lee of the land. As we approached it, he said to me, that he thought I would be able to catch some fish, and directed one of the men to bring me some fishing lines, which I got ready, and waited for the opportunity of trying my luck, when the ship should be hove to. We had not reflected on the possibility of any of these vessels being enemies, and were approaching them with great confidence, when a large brig that lay rather in shore of the others, got under weigh, and at the same time hoisted the French flag. I saw it the instant it began to ascend, and turning to the Captain, who was near me, said, "I believe we should have other fish to fry than those we expected to catch." "By Jove!" exclaimed he, "A French man-of-war brig." All hands were piped, the ship tacked, and in five minutes had as much

sail on her as she could carry. As soon as this was done, the decks were cleared, the men called to quarters, the guns double-shotted, and every thing prepared for action, the brig being in chase of us. The other vessels, although two or three of them were armed, kept their positions. Conjectures were now hazarded, about what the brig could be. She showed eighteen guns. "I'll swear," said one of the mates, "that some of the vessels under the land are not French built ships." "In that case," says another, they "must be her prizes." "If she has taken and manned so many prizes," said the Captain, "she cannot have many men left on board, and if she hasn't, she might not be an overmatch for us." "If we could take her," said the first Mate, "we should be able to capture all her prizes; that would be a glorious haul of prize money!" In ten minutes it was all arranged. The conjectures were communicated to the crew, and the determination to take the French brig and all her prizes, was received by them with three cheers, so animating that I myself felt a little of their spirit. The ship was then hove to, and she stood for the brig, under reefed topsail; on which, the brig hauled her wind, took in sail, and then tacked again for us. We were directly close along side of each other, when, behold, down came the French colors, and in their place an English ensign was displayed. I heard one near me exclaim, in a tone of great mortification, "d—n it, she's not a Frenchman after all!" It was easily to perceive the honest fellow thought he had lost a large sum of prize money by the transformation of the national ensign.

Our ship had been well armed before leaving port; and although the number of her men was small in proportion to her guns, yet they were sufficient to work the guns on one side. I have said she had thirty men, but this included her officers. Her twelve guns were six-pounders. One part, which is usually neglected in merchant ships, had been well attended to; that is, the security of her quarters. The space between the outer and inner planks above deck, was stuffed full of seasoned hoop poles which, from their elasticity, formed an admirable defence against shot; and above the wood work, iron staunchions to the height of a man's head, filled with old cables.

On the passage, the crew had been frequently exercised at their guns, in which exercise I had participated; and my shipmates acknowledged that I could beat them at a target with a musket or pistol and single ball. Indeed, it would have been singular had I not had some superiority over them at these weapons; for I have been very fond of shooting from my childhood, and can recollect having my gun when so small as not to be able to hold it without a rest. The Captain said he saw no reason why a person who was so expert with a musket, should not be a good marksman with a cannon, and offered me, in case of an action, the command of a gun. "Very well," said I, "If we should be compelled to fight, it would be less awkward to be busy than to be idle. What is considered the most honorable position?" "The quarter deck, for it is usually the most dangerous," said he. Of course, I could do nothing else than take a quarter deck gun.

During our conjectures about the supposed French brig and her prizes, I had taken particular notice of the spirited manner of the first mate; and the animation which he displayed at the expected rencontre. It was he, who expressed his mortification at seeing the English in the place of the French ensign. He was about twenty-two years of age, born in Nantucket, out of which he sailed when but eight years old, on board of a whaler, in a voyage round Cape Horn. There is no better school for a seaman than these voyages. He who is accustomed to pursue his enormous prey amidst the icebergs of Hudson's Bay, or the rocks of Terra del Fuego, can bid defiance to any thing. He had been at sea, with but few intermissions ever since. I had taken little or no notice of him during the voyage. Nothing had occurred to bring him out. It could easily be seen that he was a good sailor, and perfectly at home at all parts of his duty: but this had very little interest for a landsman, and I had seldom spoken to him. The trite adage of *nimium ne crede colori*, applies to many men who seem better than they are, but Charles Ramsdell was better than he seemed to be. He was not only an expert sailor; but a brave, frank, and honorable fellow.

During the following night, the wind moderated, and the next morning (the 20th) became fair, and we stood into the straits of Gibraltar. At 4 A. M. Tarifa bore N. W. Ceuta point, S. E. by E. and the rock of Gibraltar N. E.

I was very soundly asleep when Ramsdell came to awaken me, and said, "I think that we shall have a battle; there are several French privateers near us." "Well," said I, "I shall hear you when you begin, and that will be time enough to get up." "No," replied he, "you had better see that the men are ready at your gun; I am very certain that you will be wanted there shortly." I laid a few minutes longer, till thinking that it would not be to my credit, if my companions should imagine me more disposed to remain snugly in my birth, than to join them, I got up. On repairing to the deck, I saw several vessels under the Spanish shore, which were pointed out to me as French and Spanish priva-

teers and gun-boats. There were at that time four American brigs in sight—one was near the Spanish shore; the other three astern of us.—Two of the latter were the Huntress of New York, and the Greyhound of Boston. The brig near the shore appeared to be unarmed. One of the privateers boarded her. and sent her under the guns of a fort. Several sails were visible far astern of us, which we supposed to be a fleet we had seen under Cape Spartel. Some of the privateers stood for these. while two of the largest bore down on the brigs astern of us. It was the duty of our captain, as it is the duty of all commanders of merchant vessels, to avoid an action. The breeze was fair, but light, and we had all sail set. I find by the log-book, a copy of which is before me, that the remarks were made only to three o'clock in the morning, at which time we were going at the rate of only two knots (or miles) an hour; but the current, which always sets from the Atlantic into the Mediterranean, favored us. The privateers sailed remarkably well. The hindmost one began to fire on the brig nearest to her, which being unarmed, and seeing no prospect of escape, hauled down her colors and hove to for the privateer to board her. I felt very much like a person who sees a venomous snake in the act of swallowing a beautiful bird. The quarter guns had been run out of the stern-port. I asked the captain to give me permission to fire a shot at the privateer, to which he assented, but said it was too far off for me to hit. I aimed the piece and fired; the shot struck in the true direction, but short of her, on which she immediately hove to for her consort to come up to her, which she did in a few minutes, (the brig not having been boarded, but lying to with her topsail to the coast,) and after some consultation they both neglecting the brigs which they could easily have taken, as they were unarmed, bore directly down on us. Each of them, as we afterwards ascertained, carried two long brass twenty-four pounders, which worked on slides, and were served by regular artillerists, in her bows: and as they came down on us, these were fired with very excellent aim; and that at a distance, which from the inferior size of our guns, we did not think it expedient to answer. The effect of this distant fire is, I think, more unpleasant than that of a closer action. You see the gush of smoke from the gun; you know you are in the spot aimed at; a twenty-four pound ball is on its way to you; you can count eight or ten deliberately before it reaches the spot, and before it is decided whether it strikes you or not. For my part, I endeavored to persuade myself, that this would not strike me; but apprehensive that if one of those shot came through the stern it would bring a volley of splinters with it, I jumped on the taffrail, and sat there endeavoring to judge of the distance by counting the seconds which elapsed from the firing of the gun till the shot passed, which it did with a whiz, which I did not find quite such pleasant music as Charles XII, declared the first volley of musket balls which he heard, to be. It was thought best to retain our fire till the enemy should be quite near us. I had remarked a good many holes made in onr sails, and ropes cut away by the round shot, when my attention was attracted by a sputtering noise, and I was just going to ask the captain what it was, when catching me by the arm, he said, "they are firing grape, get from the taffrail." It was my duty to obey, which I did without the slightest demur. I think I can recollect my feelings at the time, very well.— I had in the course of the voyage more than half an inclination to see an action: but then I should have prefered having the control of both its duration and intensity. As it was, I could not help seeing that we were greatly outnumbered, the consequence was, a very hesitating mood whether I should like it or not. I had never seen a battle. It was worth something to see one. It is not every day we have an opportunity; but this was misty and chilly—that kind of weather we call raw, and I had not eaten my breakfast; and let me tell you, that a breakfast before a battle is not to be despised. I fancy no one likes to fight before breakfast; and I knew not how to get mine. The wheel had been unshipped, and the tiller ropes rove through blocks in the cabin; and the cook was stationed there to assist in working the ship: the steward was at one of the guns. If I was again in such a situation, I would advise a different disposition of affairs. While I was in this blank humor, Ramsdell said to me, with as much glee in his countenance as if he had just been partaking of an excellent sea-pie and a can of grog, (by the way there was no grog given to the men before the action; that was another error.) "I'll warrant, we'll knock the dust out of these fellow's jackets, if they come along side of us." From the size of the enemy's vessels, I was not quite so certain of the correctness of this declaration as he appeared to be. They were up with us in as short a time as he desired, and before I could make up my mind whether I wished them in our vicinity or not. Their fire was returned with spirit. The wind was light, but fair for Gibraltar, the batteries and shipping of which, were within sight, having by this time emerged from the straits and passed Europa point. The captain thought it best to keep the sail on the ship, and continue the course, although we fought under great disadvantage by doing so, as we were able to reply to their fire with the two stern guns only. The captain apprehended, that the priva-

teers might suspect that a running fight would place us within the protection of the British batteries, before its conclusion, and therefore would attempt to carry the ship by boarding, and he directed the boarding nettings to be triced up, which placed us all as it were in a cage; but the enemy threw such showers of grape and cannister upon us, that in a quarter of an hour's time, the boarding nettings were cut away in all directions, and the rigging was so torn to pieces, that the ship became perfectly unmanageable, and she drifted without our having any power of directing her course. About this time the ensign was shot away from the mizen peak, and fell on deck. The Frenchmen supposed we had struck, and both vessels began to cheer; but a continuation of our fire soon convinced them that they had been mistaken, and a very smart sailor, of whose name I recollect only the first part, which was Tom, without waiting for orders, snatched up the ensign, ran up the mizen shrouds, and tied it fast. It was not, however, long before the mizen shrouds were shot away, and it fell a second time, when the part of it which was left being torn to ribbands, was run up to the fore top gallant mast head, and displayed such a tattered escutcheon that it would have been impossible to tell what nation it belonged to.

The vessels of the enemy were long and low, and built for sailing, and full of men. In the disabled situation of our ship, one of them took a position directly under our stern, and within fifty yards of us; the other lay on our larboard quarter, about double that distance.— We could not give the least direction to our ship; but as the current set us to the eastward, and the wind though light was fair, and assisted our drifting, it was evident that it was necessary only to fight long enough for the ship to be carried into such a situation, that if the privateers should at last succeed in capturing her, they could not get her against wind and current to Algiers; but would have to take her to the British vessels of war, which we could see, very composedly viewing all our troubles from Gibraltar. I do not hesitate to acknowledge that after the engagement had lasted an hour or more, I was sufficiently satisfied with its duration and effects, and I should not have objected to some of the British vessels coming to partake of the honors to be obtained; on the contrary, I cast my eyes several times in the direction of Gibraltar, when the smoke would permit me to see it, and felt no small degree of surprise at the tranquility with which the combat appeared to be viewed. But the sailors and soldiers on that station, are accustomed to see and hear cannonading, and custom does wonders, or they might not have considered it any part of their business.

"What do you stop for?" said Charles the XIIth, to his Secretary, who, looking much aghast, had suspended his writing at a time when the king was dictating to him. "The bomb, sire!" exclaimed the Secretary, alluding to one which the moment before had fallen through the roof, and whose fuse was hissing its preparation to explode. "What has the bomb to do with your business? Go on with the letter," said his majesty. So I suppose the British sailors minded their business and left us to get on with ours.

The Frenchmen in consequence of their vicinity and their vessels being lower than ours, were very much exposed to our shot. We could bring but one cannon to bear on them; but they were completely within the effect of our muskets, and during the action I looked at them repeatedly with much astonishment, and could not help saying to myself, 'it is really surprising that they are not all killed yet!" They certainly bore the fire with much fortitude and perseverance, and took a great deal of beating. The Captain of one of them had but one arm; but with that he flourished his sword in fine style, and was constantly encouraging his men. Twice I levelled a musket at him, and as often thought it was a pity for the poor fellow, who behaved so well, and turned it on others; but notwithstanding my humanity, before the action was over, he got a ball in his remaining arm, from some other person. One of the stern guns being overloaded, (for there is a strong temptation to fill them to their muzzles with canister shot,) in its recoil canted over, and as I took a handspike to assist in bringing it to its proper position, the Captain applied his shoulder to it to assist me. At that moment a grape shot which came through the port hole, struck him in the upper part of his breast, and passed through his body, as he leaned in a stooping position. He fell, and the first Mate, who was close by me, assisted to take him below into the cabin. I have mentioned an Italian passenger: when the engagement was likely to take place, the Captain thinking he appeared to have no inclination to take part in it, veiled his desire that he should remain below, by telling him that he would be much obliged by his assisting the cook who was stationed in the cabin, at the tiller ropes; to this he assented, and I had neither seen nor thought of him after, till I went into the cabin where he and the cook were placed, with the tiller ropes in their hands, although the ship had long ceased to obey any direction from them. They were both crying lustily, but from different motives. The one from simple apprehension of danger, the other at what he conceived to be the degradation of being placed in a post of less danger than he was entitled to from his experience. He was an old man, with a rough and weather-beaten face, had served his country in the revolutionary war, and lost one leg on board a privateer. It was owing to the latter circumstance, that the Captain supposing his activity impeded, and his ability not equal to his inclination, had sent him below. His companion said nothing; but, perhaps, he thought the more.

While I was endeavoring to place the Captain in as easy a position as possible, Ramsdell observing the hatchway leading from the cabin to the magazine, which was directly under it, open, & the gunner beneath, by its light, very composedly filling his cartridges from open casks of powder, drew an old sail over it. At this time one of the privateers ran aboard of us, and endeavored to enter her men, over the stern, and through the cabin windows, two of which had been left open. Those who made the attempt over the stern, first entered our boat which hung there, and which being very much cut to pieces with shot, when a number of the Frenchmen entered, gave way, and dropped them into the sea. Those who attempted the cabin windows were very unceremoniously pushed back, without any regard, on their side to the grace of attitude, for which their countrymen are so celebrated, and without much concern on our part whether they gained their ship, or joined their companions who had just tumbled into the waves. The old cook bore a hand in this, and used a pike with infinite good will. The dead lights were then got into their places. All this kept us a considerable time below, and when it was accomplished, we ran on deck. I was up first, and was much astonished at the appearance of affairs there. There were but three of our men to be seen. I stood like a goose; I think so, because I felt like one. I could not imagine what had become of the men. To me it was all incomprehensible. Ramsdell was on deck the instant after me. He comprehended the whole thing at a glance, and with a presence of mind which I then thought and still think wonderful, he ran forward to the forecastle, and stooping at the hatchway, called like a trumpet, and in the pure nautical style, "D—n your limbs, why are you skulking below, when the Frenchmen are making all sail they can away from us." If he had told them, as was the case, that at that moment the Frenchmen were lashing their bowsprit to our starboard mizen rigging, they might not have been extremely obedient to a command to come on deck; but Ramsdell supposed that any information of that nature was unnecessary, and that they might be left to trust their eyes in that particular, when they came on deck. Perhaps he uttered the only words which would have brought these fellows in an instant to their duty. As it was, they rushed on deck as fast as they could push each other through the hatchway. Let me do them the justice to say, that they had not discovered the slightest disposition to flinch from their guns till Ramsdell and I left the deck. He left to assist in carrying his commanding officer below, and did not expect to be absent a minute. When in the cabin he could not leave it till the magazine was secured; for a wad coming in at the cabin windows might have blown up the ship; and when that was done, the window had to be closed. By the time the crew got aft, the enemy were climbing over our quarters, and were properly met and repulsed with boarding pikes. An officer, distinguished by an epaulet, (I do not know what right any one on board a privateer had to wear it, unless he belonged to the artillerists on board) was shot on our side and fel overboard.

Early Politics.

Cincinnati, Dec. 24th, 1804.

MUCH RESPECTED SIR:

When I left New York on the 25th June, I proceeded on to Philadelphia in the Stage, from Philadelphia to Newcastle in Delaware State, from thence to Frenchcreek, and then in packet to Baltimore, where I arrived on the 29th at 12 o'clock, P. M. On the 30th I attended the horse-market, and bought a Maryland poney, got him rigged and trimmed, and on the 1st day of July I parted with my friend Mr. Williamson, and set my face towards the westward, no other company than my Maryland poney. I overtook and passed many on the road who were travelling to the Westward, but some I did not like their company, some travelled too fast and others too slow—I chose to go on one steady gait, and therefore travelled by myself, and arrived at Columbia on the 18th of July, at 10 o'clock P. M.—was very sick four days on the road, so that I could not travel. I was eighteen days travelling from New York to Columbia, which Sir, was a much shorter time than you calculated I would take. My sickness on the road was owing to my getting wet frequently—I rode through a great deal of rain. The next morning after my arrival I went to see Edward, I found himself, wife and child, all well—we were glad to see each other—I delivered him the bundles, letters and messages delivered to my charge, and was glad to find the bolting cloth did not get wet, rubbed, or in anywise injured. I have been sick since my return nearly two months, am now well—my father and mother have both been dangerously ill, with an intermitting fever, but have greatly recovered—my father is very much broke in consequence of it, and finds old age crowding on him very fast— he has been honored lately by the citizens of the State with an appointment of Elector of President and Vice President of the U. States, and met the other Electors at Chillicothe [the seat of Government of the State] on the 5th instant, and was highly pleased in having it in his power to give a vote to Jefferson as President, and to his old fellow citizen, Governor Clinton, as Vice President. The State of Ohio has two Senators and one Representative in Congress; consequently had a right by the Constitution to choose three Electors, which they did; who met at Chillicothe and gave three republican votes. It is pleasing to see the republican interest throughout the Union increasing so rapidly; I hope it may never cease until the whole world is republican, and not even then, The Fed's. triumph greatly about the little State of Delaware, having elected three Aristocrats in Congress—*poor souls.* The Legislature of this State now in session are all Republican, the Federalists here are silent, scarcely attend elections.— I was glad to find by the New York papers that your city has not been visited by the fever as heretofore.

I have weekly been expecting to hear something of Bonaparte's expedition, but have not heard anything decisive. I am somewhat at a loss what to say about that man; he for a long time appeared to be extending the victorious arms of France, in favor of Liberty, but has at length bartered the people out of their rights. If he had exerted himself in establishing a Government upon the firm basis of Republicanism, giving the people all the elective privileges possible—then his name would have been handed down to posterity and enrolled among the worthies, but now he must be despised by the friends of Liberty. The people of France are a restless people—I have no doubt but their government will change and Buonaparte yet tremble at the sight of the Guillotine.

I have sent you by this day's mail some of the newspapers printed at this place, and at Chillicothe—one containing the Governor's message. The first private conveyance I will send you a copy of the constitution and a map of the country. Edward was here yesterday, himself and family are well.

I would, sir, have wrote you before, but have not been able to use the pen until lately. Please sir, to give my most respectful compliments to Mrs. Meeks, and Messrs. Joseph and John Meeks.

With much respect and regard,

I have the honor to be, sir, your

friend and ob't. servant,

AARON GOFORTH.

COL. EDWARD MEEKS:

A statement of votes given for Electors of

President aud Vice President at the late election in this State.

Republican.

Nathaniel Massie	2593
William Goforth, Sen'r.	2502
James Pritchard	2475

Federal.

Bazaleel Wells	364
John Reily	320
B. I. Gilman	190
John Carlisle	80
Doubtful, John Bigger	176

Bank Note Engraving in Cincinnati.

Although every one who handles bank notes, must have remarked the high degree of improvement to which, as works of Art, these engravings have been brought, few persons seem aware, that it is not only by the advance in skill among artists, but by the aid of machinery, that this branch of the Fine Arts, has reached its present order of excellence.

It is generally supposed, also, by the community, that the various notes issued by the Banks in the Western States, are engraved altogether in the Atlantic cities. This is a great but a very natural mistake. Rawdon, Wright, & Hatch, the great engraving establishment at New York, extensively supply banks, through the Atlantic States, but the whole of the engraving for those of the west, which bears their name, is executed at the branch in Cincinnati, in charge of their representative here, Mr. Wm. F. Harrison. That this is done in a stile of excellence, equal to any at the East, an inspection of the various specimens of engraving, which may be seen at the establishment, will satisfy any person competent to judge.

How it is that engravers here, with a much less force in numbers, and only four years in operation, can execute work in a style equal to any of the great eastern engraving houses, is one of those problems only to be solved by that great engine of modern days, LABOR SAVING MACHINERY, which with the adjuncts of the combination and permutation principle, leaves the mind of the Artist free for the creation of forms of beauty and taste, which, under the old system required the use of his hands and head also to elaborate and execute. Let me go into details.

The dies are first engraved on pieces of soft steel, of sizes varying with the subject, which are called *bed pieces*, the figures being, of course, sunk into the plate. These bed pieces being then carbonized or hardened, a roll of soft steel is passed over the plate, and indented with the engraving by means of a transfer press, capable of supplying a seven tons' power, one lever of which rolls the cylinder, while another presses it. The roll also is then hardened by the same process, as was the bed piece, and serves in turn

to transfer the subject in its original form, to a steel or copper plate, which is then passed to receive its finish into the hands of the letter engraver, and it is then ready for the printing press. Duplicates of the engraved cylinders are made by the Cincinnati establishment for the New York house, or by the New York establishment for the branch here, as the case may be, these cylinders or dies being common to both concerns. Of these, there are in the office in Cincinnati, more than one thousand, each of which presents in the face of the circle four or five figures of vignettes, denominations, or letter press as the case may be. These dies bear the same relation to the old style of bank note engraving, as moveable types to the Chinese system of block printing or the first efforts of Faust or Guttemberg, and it is by the combinations and changes which may be multiplied by this means to any indefinite extent, that an infinite variety in elegance of pattern as well as ample security from counterfeiting results, and a plate of the most elaborate character and finish can be supplied to order in three days, which it formerly would have taken as many months to execute.

It is difficult to convey to one who has not examined the specimens in this establishment, a just idea by description of the various checks in the way of counterfeiting afforded here. Some of these, however. are obvious, when suggested to my readers. The various denominations bear upon their several vignettes, in the number of prominent figures, the number in value also. Thus for example, a Five dollar bill has the ornament at the head or in the body of the note, composed of five distinct female figures, gracefully grouped, and the figure 5 at the border is ingeniously constituted of five seperate and distinct fancy figures. So with the Two and the Three. Again, the word "*Five*" is, in some patterns incorporated into every figure in the note, or letter of the title. Under these and other guards and checks, it becomes impossible to alter a small note to a larger one. In some cases the denomination is chemically printed or stained into the very fibre of the note in red letters, by a process of their own, which it is impossible either to imitate or to alter without destroying the note. Their United States Treasury notes afford a splendid specimen of this sort.

Having stated that the titles, devices, denominations, and letter press which are of boundless variety, are four or five thousand in number, it may be easily judged what exhaustless combinations of embellishment and security may be wrought out here by the taste and the skill of an accomplished artist. If twenty-six letters of the alphabet may be combined to fill thousands of pages no two of which are alike, what combinations may not be expected from more than four thousand figures and devices?

Skill in bank note engraving is of vital importance, both for the protection of the banks and of the public, as every one must have felt, who recollects engravings of the Mount Pleasant and Lancaster banks, of our own State, and many of the plates of the Bank of the United States, in all which cases it was always difficult and sometimes impossible to detect the counterfeits from the inferior execution of the genuine notes. What Rawdon, Wright, & Hatch can do, and have done, may be inferred from one or two facts:

When the Bank of Upper Canada went into operation, a large share of its capital being owned in England, that interest secured the engraving of the notes to London artists. The notes when offered in Buffalo, where Canada paper usually circulates freely, could not be put out without difficulty from the general apprehension that they were counterfeits, so inferior was the work to that of our best engravers, and a new set of plates were ordered of Rawdon, Wright, & Hatch, specimens of which I saw at the office, to supply their circulation in the United States at least.

It was news to me, as it probably will be to my readers, that this firm engraves the checks of Rothschild; Baring, Brothers, & Co., Brown, Brothers & Co., Roche & Co., and others, eminent bankers in London, Paris, Dublin, and other commercial cities in Europe. Why they enjoy this preference, may be judged from the following circumstance:

We all recollect M. Alexandre de Vattemare, and his system of cosmopolite exchanges. On his visit to this country, he obtained among other exhibitions of the American Arts, a copy of the various specimens from this firm of their bank note and check engravings. These naturally attracted much attention in a city like Paris, and *Galignani's Messenger*, a journal of the highest reputation, wound up its criticism on the subject, by saying that these engravings entirely surpassed any thing that could be produced on the continent.

It must be apparent, from what I have said, that this Cincinnati establishment is prepared and qualified to execute bank note plates of equal excellence, at as reasonable prices, and on as short notice as any other in the United States.

Western Literary Journal.

I have to acknowledge the receipt of "The Western Literary Journal and Monthly Review" for November, being the first number of that periodical. The columns of the Advertiser do not afford space for a suitable notice of its con-

tents, consistently with the claims of other things.

I like the tone of morality, and the American and Western feeling it exhibits. Its lot is cast on one of the noblest theatres in the world for its purpose, and if faithful to its present promise, a long course of usefulness is before the "Journal." Beyond this I do not feel disposed to speak of it at present. Six months will give that method and arrangement to its design and consistency, and distinctness to its character, which no first number of a periodical can present.

Our Country—One Hundred Years Ago.

I commence this week a series of brief extracts from the Pennsylvania Gazette, published in Philadelphia by Benjamin Franklin, a file of which commencing August 30, 1744, more than one hundred years since, is in my possession. I add such comments and explanations as are likely to illustrate the various subjects. The whole will serve to shed light on the darkness of the past.

Aug. 30, 1744, a message from Governor Clinton, Governor of the *province* of New York, on the opening of the General Assembly of the Colony "*Die Lunae*," 20 Aug., 1744. It would make perhaps half a column of the "Advertiser.' In those days Governors confined their Messages strictly to the affairs of their own respective provinces, an example worthy of their successors in the States at the present day. Gov. C. was doubtless of the same family with Geo. Clinton, one of our early Vice Presidents, and Dewitt Clinton, Governor of New York during the early part of this century.

Great Britain being at war with France, the colonies were extensively engaged in Privateering, and advertisements of prize vessels with their cargoes make their appearance regularly in the "Gazette." Here is a notice on the same subject.

"To all gentlemen and others that are inclined to go on a privateering voyage against the enemies of the Crown of Great Britain. This is to give notice that the Brigantine Raleigh, now fitting out at Norfolk in Virginia, commanded by Capt. Walter Coode, mounting 12 guns with 120 small arms, 120 pair pistols, 120 pair cutlashes, and 120 pair cartouche boxes, with all other warlike stores, and six months provision; to be manned with 120 men, will be in order to receive men on board by the 5th September, and with all expedition will proceed on such a cruise as may be judged likely to prove most advantageous to all parties concerned. Durham Hall for the company."

"Four likely negro men and one woman, all young, fit for plantation business, to be sold by Wm. Bell, below the Drawbridge, near Powell's wharf." Negro slavery existed at that date, it seems, in Pennsylvania.

Runaways of convicts sold in the colonies, are advertised also. "An English servant man, Thomas Goodson; a Welsh servant lad, Morgan Jones; a native Irishman, Patrick O'Cadden," &c. &c.

Fashions of the day. "Thomas Cattinger, staymaker from London, has removed to Chesnut near Front street, and keeps the sign of the Green Stays, where all sorts of stays may be had on reasonable terms."

"To be made or sold by Matthews and Charlton, Peruke makers in Chesnut Street Philadelphia. Perukes of English hair of any sort, color, or make, viz; *Tyes, Bobs, Majors, Spencers, Foxtails or Twists.* They also make *Curls* or *Tates,* for ladies or others, made of their own or English hair at the shortest notice as cheap as in London."

Pope the poet. "London, May 8, we hear that Alexander Pope. Esq., who died a few days ago, has appointed the Lord Visc. Bolingbroke, and the Earl of Marchmont to be his executors."

The names of vessels on the shipping list are very characteristic of the times, "The Charming Sally, Two Pollies, Rosanna, New Susannah, Increase, Relief, Tryal, Mulberry, Alice and Mary, Delight, Unity, Little Gipsey, Good Intent, Lovely Lass, &c."

"Just published and to be sold by B. Franklin, at the New Printing Office near the Market. The Grand Treaty held at the town of Lancaster with the Indians of the six nations, in June, 1744. Price, eighteen pence. Also, "The Chronicles of the Kings of England, written in the manner of the Ancient Jewish historians, by Nathan Ben Saddi, a priest of the Jews," written, doubtless, by Franklin himself.

"To be sold, Curriers Oil, Chockolate, Indigo, &c, by John Leech, near *the church,* Philadelphia."

It might be hence infered, that they had but one church in Philadelphia at that date. This was far, however, from the fact.

Ancient names and styles of dry goods, "Mantua and padusoys, calimancoes, plain & striped tammies, hairbines, alapeens, duroys, ribbed druggets, turkets, florettas, nonesopretties, worsted shaggs, shalloons, madrepoors, sawns, chittabully baftas, gurrahs, mamoodies, seersuckers, &c., for sale by John Morgan." We need a dictionary of fashions badly. What will the next generation understand by *Roorback* cassimeres.

"London July 8. Yesterday the treasure taken by Admiral Anson consisting of 208 chests of silver, 18 chests of gold, and 20 barrels of gold dust, was carried through our city in 32 waggons, preceded by a kettle drum, trumpets, and French horns, guarded by the seamen, commanded by the officers, and was lodged in the tower. On the first waggon was the English colours with the Spanish ensign under it, and every third or fourth waggon carried some trophy of honor taken from the Spaniards in the South Sea as well as the Acapulco ship."

It appears from the face of the "Gazette" and his own autobiography, that Franklin set the types, did the press work, mailed and addressed the papers, and as postmaster forwarded them to his subscribers.

Besides all these, an advertisement "Very good *lamblack* made and sold by the printer hereof," serves to show that he doubtless made his own printing ink, which is more than can be said of his successors in *"the art conservative of arts."*

Review.

The Pictorial History of the United States u America—By John Frost, L. L. D., 2 vols. royal octavo. This is a work *got up* (to use the technical phrase) in a very superior style. The Publishers have evidently felt that every thing about about these volumes should be such as patriotism and good taste would equally approve. The paper, typography, binding, and pictorial illustrations are all such as should belong to a publication which must form a part of the library of every family, which can afford its purchase.— The current of narrative flows full and gracefully, while the ornamental character of the work will doubtless invite the attention of youth to the subject, and obtain for it a more gracious reception than would probably be yielded it under a less showy appearance.

Although the question I asked, respecting the etymology of Wood County, has been already answered in the columns of the Western General Advertiser, the following communication derives interest from the historical record contained in the closing part:

URBANA, O., 30th Oct., 1844.

MR. C. CIST:

Dear Sir—Your paper of 23rd Oct., contains an article on the names of Counties in which you say the name of Wood, defies your scrutiny.— Your question whether it can be named after Judge Reuben Wood, is meant, I suppose, to express doubt and possibility.

The County was named after Col. Eleazer D. Wood, a gallant officer of the last war, who was distinguished in the sortie of Fort Meigs, and who fell at the head of his regiment in the sortie from Fort Erie, on the 17th Sept., 1814. He was also distinguished as the officer who discovered and reported to Gen. Harrison, the fact of the enemy being formed in open order, at the battle of the Thames, which led to the order for Col. Johnson's celebrated charge with his mounted men.

The name of the County was doubtless conferred by Gen. Harrison, who was a member of the Ohio Senate, in 1820, when the County was created. The "New Purchase," as then called, embracing all the country north of the old Indian Boundary,was, at the same time divided into Counties,as follows:—Van Wert, Mercer,Putnam, Allen,Hancock, Hardin,Crawford. Marion, Seneca, Sandusky, Wood, Henry, Paulding, and Williams. It is probable that he suggested most of the names; and I have heard him state that the names of Paulding, Williams, and Van Wert, suggested by him, were objected to for want of euphony, and, I think, for want of distinction in the persons,

Yours respectfully,

J. H. J.

Growth of the City.

In a late number of the Advertiser a calculation was made, predicated on the votes given at the General election on the 8th ult., which pointed out 70,636 as the population at this time within our corporate limits. This estimate seems corroborated by the late presidential election also.

As a means of judging the growth of particular districts of our city, the population may be distributed among the wards as follows:

	1844.	Census of 1840.
First Ward,	4963	8869
Second do	8929	5370
Third do	8048	7325
Fourth do	7264	6087
Fifth do	10863	9341
Sixth do	7094	4577
Seventh do	8950	4743
Eighth do	7416	new ward
Ninth do	8109	new ward

70,636

In comparing these tables it must be recollected that since 1840, two new wards, the 8th and 9th have been added. That the first ward now comprehends but a small although compact part of what originally bore that name, that the second is the only ward which has gained any territory: that the third, fourth and sixth wards have each lost a part of their territory since, and that the fifth is reduced one half nearly in its breadth, and the seventh has lost four-fifths of its original limits. With these allowances it will be seen that the principal growth of our city is in the 5th, 6th, 7th, 8th and 9th wards, in other words, that its increase has been mainly in the northern and western regions of Cincinnati.

City Buildings.

A new style of building fronts—of which there are two specimens on Fourth street, east of Plum, in the dwelling houses just putting up by S. S. Smith, and S. C. Parkhurst,—is just becoming introduced here. It is a variety of white lime stone or marble from the Dayton quarries, and will, I have no doubt, be generally employed for this purpose in future.

Our city is not only rapidly increasing its buildings, but is imbibing a purer taste in the display of its buildings, public and private. We are all under obligation to Bishop Purcell, for the introduction of the Dayton limestone,which in the new Cathedral, I believe, he was the first in the city, to make use of for ornamental purposes.

Anecdote of Lough, the Sculptorr.

When Mr. Lough, the sculptor, "whom not to know argues yourself unknown," first arrived in London, his purse was an exact antithesis to his mind, for the first was certainly trash, but the latter pregnant with the beauties of his art, which he has since stamped on his creations. He took lodgings in a humble habitation (a shoemaker's we believe,) and there commenced forming the clay which eventually became his "Milo rending the oak." The magnificent work is, as every one doubtless knows, of large dimensions—not quite colossal, but certainly too large to be comfortable in an attic. The sculptor worked on, and completed it all but the upper portion, which required greater height, How was this to be managed? He would not leave his work incomplete, but what could be done? The thought at last struck him to break through the roof of the apartment, which, after sundry qualms, he ventured to do. His invariable custom had been to keep the door locked; and now came the awful moment to make known to his landlord the dilapidation which had occured to his property. With fear and trembling the poor sculptor led him to the room, expecting the most summary legal punishment for the injury he had committed. When the shoemaker, however, beheld his work, he was enraptured with its beauty that he said not a word about the injured ceiling, and gave him a pair of razors—all the poor fellow had at that moment to offer—as a memento that the kindly feelings of a man in so humble a rank of life were thus called forth at the sight of Mr. Lough's first great production. We need hardly add at what value the gift is to this day estimated.

MARRIAGES.

On the 12th inst., by the Rev. E. W. Sehon, Mr. Wm. C. Whicher and Miss Sarah N. Patterson, of this city.

On the 14th inst., by Elder James Challen, Mr. John Dennhard and Miss Minerva Blair, all of this city.

On the 14th inst., by Rev. Asa Drury, Henry Snow, Esq.. and Miss Catharine L. Lynd, daughter of Rev. Dr. Lynd.

On the 14th inst., by Elder Wm. P. Stratton, Major George Hawpe, of Henry co., Tenn.. to Miss Rebecca Wilson, of Mill Creek township, Ohio.

On the 13th inst., by Rev. E. T. Collins, Pius Chambers, of this city, and Hannah Chamberlain, of Springdale.

On the 14th inst. by the Rev. E. S. Southgate, Mr. Thomas Buist, of this city, and Miss Missouri Eliza, daughter of David Downard, Esq., Campbell co., Ky.

DEATHS.

On the 17th, of inflammation of the lungs, Anna T. Cist, eldest daughter of the Editor of the Advertiser.

In this city, on the 19th inst., Michael Pugh, formerly of Lancaster, Ohio.

On Tuesday night, at his residence on Longworth st.. Mr. B. Ezekiel, aged 58.

CORRESPONEENCE.

CINCINNATI, Nov. 22, 1844.

DEAR SIR:

In the laudable effort you are making to collect and perpetuate historical facts, will you suffer me to suggest, that you cannot be too careful in discriminating between statements that are well authenticated, and such as are of doubtful veracity. It has been frequently said, and with some truth, that in the second and third generations of new settlements or colonies, an endless variety of legends are fabricated, with more or less plausibility, which are recited and repeated till they acquire a sufficient amount of confidence to be adopted and recorded as matter of history, although they are unsupported by evidence, and are frequently at variance with known and well authenticated facts.

I have often thought that caterers for future historians, have a heavier responsibility on their consciences, than historians themselves, because it is their duty to investigate the truth of all the statements they receive, before they adopt them as true, and give them their sanction; and because the historian, who is neither more nor less than the compiler of facts thus collected, and sanctioned by the chroniclers of the day, is justified in assuming them to be true, taking it for granted that they have been fully examined, and sufficiently tested by those who have committed them to record. In consequence of the carelessness of those who undertake to collect and preserve detached portions of recent history, many of the historical works now extant, are so blended with fiction, as, in a great measure, to destroy their value. Statements furnished by those who do not profess, personally, to know their truth, should not be received, or sanctioned, unless they are accompanied with evidence sufficient to attest their authenticity. There is such a propensity in human nature to believe and give currency to fable and fiction, as ought to put the editors of periodical publications on their guard. There is also a great disposition to exaggerate; in proof of which, I refer you to the fact, that stories originally simple, and devoid of interest, after they have been often repeated, assume a character of much importance.

Memory is also, more or less treacherous and deceptive; always liable to lose the distinctness of original impressions, and in its recollections, to mingle mere legendary tales with authentic facts. There is also on the minds of most men, a desire, springing from a laudable disposition, to give the best coloring to incidents that affect themselves, or their friends. This often prompts them, innocently, to exaggerate, and sometimes purposely to misstate the truth. In short, there are so many avenues to misrepresentation, and so many temptations to falsify, that with all the care and circumspection that can be made use of, much matter, either wholly fabricated, or so materially discolored, and distorted, as to have but little resemblance to the truth, will find its way into the most carefully managed, and impartial of our periodical journals.

I have often reflected on this subject, and deprecated the consequences, that are to follow the loose and careless manner in which communications, purporting to be narratives of past events, are received and recorded as authentic, and as such, transmitted to the future historian. He, as a matter of course, receives them as true, having no reason to suspect their verity, or means of testing it, if suspected.

The most effectual way of guarding against this evil, is for every one who is in any manner connected with the press, to make it a rule not to admit anything to the pages of his publication, which has not a reliable voucher for its authenticity. The truth is, that our editors are too fearful of wounding the feelings of their contributors, and under that influence, sometimes receive and publish communications without a responsible name. The task of distinguishing between fact and fiction, between candid and inflated narrative, is often difficult, and sometimes impossible. There are, however, some general principles, which, if observed, will serve to lessen the evil.

When a statement is made of any past occurrence, in which the narrator had no agency, and of which he was not an eye witness, the source from which he derives his information should be carefully investigated. In like manner, if the facts must have taken place anterior to the time when he could have had cognizance of them; if they occurred before his birth, or during his infancy, the same precaution should be taken, and in either case, the evidence corroborating the statement, should be preserved with it. The importance of excluding fiction and falsehood from historical works, being so universally admitted, it is surprising that there should be so much apathy, and such a want of vigilance on the part of those who are professedly collectors of historical materials. History is read not only to ascertain what has been but to know the results of what has been. It is read to learn the wisdom acquired by other men —to be taught what may be expected to follow any given state of things, by knowing what the same state of things has heretofore produced. We read it to learn and profit by the experience of past ages; we proceed on the principle, that like causes produce like effects—that what has been may be—and we often shape our course by the teachings of history, because we believe experience to be a safe guide in all matters to which it applies. The study of history is not intended for amusement merely, but to enable us, by knowing what has been the course of those who have lived before us, and what were its results, to avail ourselves of their experience without the risque of their experiments.

History has been denominated philosophy, teaching by example, and the study of it, the acquisition of wisdom derived from the experience of preceding ages; but if it be mingled with fiction and falsehood, it ceases to be a reliable guide, for this plain reason, that we do not see the true causes of effects, in consequence of error in the establishment of facts alledged to have produced them.

These thoughts have occurred to my mind, and I am induced to present them to your consideration, by the circumstance of having lately read two historical sketches, one of which was published in Kentucky more than twenty years ago, and the other, very recently, in your paper. The first is entitled a narrative of the remarkable adventures of Jackson Johonnet, and is full of astonishing feats, performed by the hero of the tale. It sets forth, that he was born at Casco Bay, that his parents were poor; that he left them on the first day of May, 1791, being then seventeen years of age; that he proceeded to Boston, where he met with a recruiting officer, and that having listened to his conversations on the pleasures of a military life, the chances for promotion in the army, and the grand prospect of making great fortunes in the Western country, he was induced to enlist. It further informs us that in the beginning of July he left Boston to join the western army; that on his arrival at Fort Washington, he was ordered to Capt. Phelon's company, and that in a few days thereafter he set out on the expedition under Gen. Harmar. It tells us also, that on the fourth of August, he was taken prisoner on the Wabash river, and carried to the Upper Miami villages; that the Indians informed him of the destruction of Gen. Harmar's army, and exhibited scalps taken on that occasion; that having endured distress and suffering indescribable, he made his escape on the thirteenth of August, that on the eighteenth he fell in with a scouting party from Fort Jefferson, and that having performed feats sufficient to immortalize his name, he joined the expedition under Gen. Harmar.

Without pursuing the narrative further, let me advert to the surprising fact, that at the early period to which he refers, when the country was almost entirely destitute of improvements to facilitate travelling, troops could march on foot from Boston to Cincinnati, and having refreshed at that place, proceed to the Wabash river through an Indian wilderness, between the beginning of July, when he marched from Boston, and the fourth of August, when he was ta-

ken prisoner. It is also matter of surprise, that on the fifth of August he saw scalps taken by the Indians at the destruction of he army of General Harmar, and that in the succeeding month he marched under him, on his expedition against the Miami villages, situated at, and near the junction of the St. Mary's and the St. Joseph's Rivers, where Fort Wayne was afterwards erected. You recollect that Col. Harmar received his commission in 1789 — that he marched from Fort Washington against the Miami villages in September, 1790—that after sustaining what, I think, is improperly called a *defeat*, he returned to Fort Washington in October, by slow and easy marches; and that, early in the spring of 1791, he retired from the army and General St. Clair was appointed Commander in Chief. This was about three months before Mr. Johonnet enlisted for the avowed purpose of going on the expedition, under General Harmar, and six months after that expedition terminated.

I will now make a remark or two on the article which appeared in your paper of the 16th inst, entitled "Biography of Colonel John Armstrong," with whom I had a long personal acquaintance, and of whom I can say that he sustained the character of a brave officer; but it is matter of regret that the writer of the article has not given a more full and connected account of his military services, by which a better estimate might have been made of their merit, and of their service to the country. Had he pursued that course, much additional interest would have been given to the narrative. We should, in that case, have known when, where, and on what occasions those feats of bravery he relates were performed, and might have seen their influence on the military operations of the army, and what other portion of the troops were engaged in them.

No person will be disposed to question the substantial truth of the narrative, yet every one would have been better able to estimate the importance of the facts stated, if they had been given more specifically, and in a more connected form.

The article contains some errors which the writer will readily see, and promptly correct, as they are no doubt inadvertent. In the first place, it is impossible that the Colonel could have been born in 1775, and enlisted as a soldier in 1777—nor could he have been recruiting troops, in Philadelphia, in the spring of 1791, with a view to the approaching campaign, under Col. Harmar, for the manifest reason, that that campaign took place in the fall of 1790. I know that he was in Harmar's expedition. He was then a Lieutenant in the army, and had the command appertaining to an officer of that grade.

The narrator tells us that "he enlisted as a private soldier and that from the eleventh of September, 1777," (which seems to have been the period of his enlistment,) "to the end of the war, he served as a commissioned officer in various ranks."

This, to say the least, is a statement too vague. The writer should have told us, what commissions he held and when they were granted. This might have been done with a little trouble, as all such appointments are matters of record. I am aware that at the close of the revolutionary war, he was permitted to remain in service, but I have no document on hand, from which I can now ascertain the rank he then held. In September, 1789, about six years after the close of the war of the revolution, having continued uninterruptedly in service he received the appointment of a Lieutenant, on the nomination of President Washington, which appointment was confirmed by the Senate in June 1790; three months before Gen. Harmar marched on his expedition.

He continued to hold the rank of a Lieutenant till March, 1791, when he was promoted to a Captaincy. In that capacity he served till 1793, when he resigned and left the army.

Soon after his resignation he received the commission of a Colonel in the militia of the territory, which he held in 1796, when my acquaintance with him began. For some years thereafter, I belonged to his regiment, having the honor of being a private in Captain Cutter's company, in which I mustered regularly, without promotion, for about twenty years.

If an apology be due for having introduced my own name on this occasion, it may be found in the fact that the incidents spoken of relate to primitive times, when a *private militia-man* was considered of some importance to the settlement.

Very respectfully, yours,
J. BURNET.

Mr. Charles Cist.

Relics of the Past.

Capt. John Armstrong to Gen. James Wilkinson.

Fort Hamilton, Nov. 15th, 1792.

Dear General:

Your letter of the 12th inst come duly to hand. From the unfinished state of the building you have ordered to be erected, we could not possibly spare a second tenm from the Port, and the one sent in was of little worth—every exertion is used to complete the building as soon as possible; but unfortunately for us, we have lost two days this week in consequence of the wet weather. Our mason is sick, and one other of the sawyers, so that both saws are idle; the celler unfinished, as also the plastering your rooms; the doors are hung, just finished, floor laid, and partition up, so that you can lodge therein. The building for the reception of forage is also up, ; and on Monday we shall raise the rafters, but plank will still be wanting. The Magazine is finished excepting the hanging of the doors, and under-pining. Nothing further has been done to the Stables. The meadow is cut and the hay in stack. Major Smith has no doubt mentioned the circumstance of a boy being fired on and chased at his post; also an attempt to carry off the cattle by removing the pickets. Capt. Barbee will no doubt inform you of the rencounter between one of his men and a savage—the villains are doubtless watching the road, it will therefore be very unsafe for Major Story's express to keep it any part of the way; if they do it should be in the night time.

I have thought proper sir, to detain at this Port, four of the Columbia militia, whose terms have not expired, to serve as spies to apprize us of the approach of our enemy—who being disappointed in their favorite object, [stealing horses] would embrace a secondary one, that of taking scalps, The number of small parties employed daily in the woods will, I hope justify the measure.

First Ward--Cincinnati.

I have just completed the enumeration of buildings in this ward, and find that there are within its bounds 15 public buildings and 720 dwellings, shops, store houses, mills and offices—total 735. Of these 551 are built of brick, and 184 are frames.

Of these public buildings, there are one Fire Engine house, an Observatory—one Bank,—the Commercial—a Theatre—the Seminary of *"Soeurs de notre dame"*—the Post Office, and nine Churches, to wit: Christ Church on Fourth st.,—Wesleyan Chapel on Fifth—Welsh church on Harrison—-Disciples' church on Sycamore—Fourth Presbyterian church on High st.—Welsh church on Lawrence st.—Jews Synagogue on Broadway—Bethel and True Wesleyan, African churches.

Of these buildings there were at the close of the year 1842,

	Stone	Bricks	Frames	Total
	1	463	163	627
Built in 1843, "	0	22	4	26
do 1844, "	1	71	10	82
Total	2	556	177	735

It will be seen that the number of buildings in the First ward for 1844 surpasses that of 1843 more than 3 to 1. I suppose that to be a proportion of this year over the last which few other wards can maintain.

The first ward embraces a territory heretofore densely built in such of its parts as were at all built on, which accounts for the last year's building extending to no more than 26 houses; and it is principally by building east of the Canal, and a few scattered open spots in the ward that the additions this year have been made.

The buildings of each year improve on their immediate predecessors, as a general rule, in value, beauty, and convenience. Among those of 1844, a fine block put up by A. Irwin, the mansion house of E. S. Haines, a block at the corner of Pike and Symmes, and various single buildings are observable for their fine appearance.

Baum street, on a range with Lock street, and in its rear, a new street, has been opened during the present year, and is filling rapidly with buildings; and High street, which for years seemed to have no connection between its eastern and western point, is grading down at a rate which before many months will throw into occupancy a section of the city valuable, because contiguous to its canal and ship-yard business operations.

The Observatory is progressing rapidly to its completion, and promises to become an object of distinguished notice and interest to strangers, especially travelers on the Ohio.

Twenty years ago I stood on part of the present Observatory premises, surveying the City, then a place of two thousand houses, and fifteen thousand inhabitants, hardly one-fifth of its present population and buildings. As I had never been on it since till yesterday, it may easily be conceived, what a change and a progress the scene which lay before my view presented.— Twenty years hence the city will doubtless exhibit from that point, the view of a dense mass and wide extent of buildings. through which the eye will seek in vain for objects so distinct as to locate any particular spot—our Court House and church steeples only excepted.

Relief for the Destitute.

A society has been lately formed and is getting into operation under the most favorable auspices, whose object it is to provide employment for the poor during the winter season. It proposes,

1. To procure a wood yard,

2. To provide wood, which shall be sawed and split at the yard, by those who cannot obtain other employment.

3. The labor to be paid for at a less rate per cord than the regular prices in the street.

4. The wood to be sold at an uniform price through the year.

5. Purchasers may be supplied with any amount, not less than the value of ten cents.

6. The refuse wood or that which cannot be split, to be given to the poor.

The following advantages are expected to result:

1. Daily employment to the poor would be furnished at a rate which would subsist them until more lucrative business offers.

2. The wood being cut up and thereby seasoned for immediate and convenient use, would save trouble and time to the purchaser.

3. Its sale in small quantities, will enable persons of limited means to supply themselves from week to week, and adapt the quantity to the convenience of storing it.

4. The uniformity of price would protect the purchaser from speculators on the article.

Whatever tends, as this must, to throw the poor on their own industrial resources and enable them to help themselves, must command sympathy and support to the enterprise. I doubt not that much good will result from this movement. Relief in one shape to the necessities, in another to the affluent.

Wanderings of Intellect.

The following incoherent jumble was actually taken down from an address by an individual in one of our lunatic asylums. It may be more immethodical, but it is fully as reasonable as the speculations of *Gen. Price,* and the expression in the second paragraph, "Let all the people say Amen, and let the military present arms," is just half way between the sublime and the ridiculous.

"O! my good Mr. Vanderbilt,—thou paragon of philosophy,—bottle-washer to the Khan of Cochin China,—emperor of Illinois,—and Stargazer general:—it gives me true delight to hear that the seven stars are made of brass nails, and that his Excellency, Don Pedro, in his late expedition to South America, overturned the soap tub of Inca Capac, the deliverer, in conformity to an ancient decree of the Senate of the United States, which declares that cob-webs shall not obscure the moral law.

But, to return from this digression—let all the people say Amen;—and let the military present arms. Away with Aldebaran—away with obstructions in the milky-way:—the era of rice-cakes and verdigris puddings has arrived—the very nurslings cry out *donner carriere a son esprit!* —cities are swallowed up in gingerbread— physic is nonsense to doctors,—all is vanity and vexation. The magistrate and the fiddler dabble where Leviathan sings epic poems to Job and the Seven Muses. Give me a tamarind stone,—give Sampson Agonistes the right ear of Jenny Tompson—Tompson Jenny O!—for O! my dear countrymen, my purpose is fixed; here I stand in the tribune of the Chamber of Deputies, crying from the dome of St. Sophia, rise O! ashes of Timour the Tartar—sprinkle with ketchup gravy the hoary beard of Chislar Aga. May the President of these United kingdoms of Massachusetts and Baltimore live in perpetual extacy:—live O King forever—and may his constant drink be new cider.

Sweet are the rose-buds of affection;—poor dear Mary—she is dead, dead—as a door-nail; she has gone, and I am all alone and alone, saith the poet. This is the true cause of the whirling round of the head. Sir,—gentlemen of the Jury, and ladies all, hear ye—the cat's in the meadow, the cow's in the corn—Ladies are the cream of the pan, made for making water gruel—the companions of sophomores,—to be sold at a bargain:—bank stock by the ounce,—who deals in magic?—where is the land of Gomorrah? Who sups upon whalebone soups? Show me the lusus naturæ, the dog with two tails—the mad astronomer, the monkey dressed in a lion skin jacket—show in derision Madame Malibran, the ne plus ultra of China gongs, gongs, gongs.

Speak out the words of sober Soprana. fathers and countrymen. Sing songs to Woden, the god of stone pipes, ring the bells for joy—the etat major has swallowed the central market, and two dozen and four crossed boys have burned their hats in a gally-pot—America, happy, happy land.

The weather is fainter and more elastic; the rain distils through the bung hole of a flour barrel—all the sorrel top gentlemen must hereafter haul in their horns when the orator rides on a wooden horse.

Early Duels in the United States.

It is a little remarkable that the first duel fought in the United States, was in staid, sober New England, and still more, that the actors in this folly were servants. Two individuals of this description fought with swords—a lady, as usual, being in the case. Neither, however, being mortally wounded; the General Court, by way of example, directed them to be tied, neck and heels, and exposed for twenty-four hours, to the ridicule and scoffs of the bystanders.

The following submission of a law case to the arbitrament of wager by battle, which took place in New England also, is not so generally known.

The conflicting claims of two towns in Connecticut,—Lyme, and New London,—to certain lands, once gave rise to a mode of adjusting the title, of which I apprehend no trace can be found in the common law, or the codes of the civilians. The land, says Dr. Dwight, though now of considerable value, was then regarded a trifling object. The expense of appointing agents to manage the cause before the legislature, was considerable, and the hazard of the journey was no trifle.

In this situation, the inhabitants of both town-ships agreed to settle their respective titles to the lands in controversy, by a combat between two champions, to be chosen by each for that purpose. New London selected two men, of the names of Picket & Latimer; Lyme committed its cause to two others, named Griswold, and Ely. On a day, mutually appointed, the champions appeared in the field, and fought with their fists, till victory was declared in favor of each of the Lyme combatants. Lyme then quietly took possession of the controverted tract, and has held it undisputed to the present day.

Early Bread Baking.

The early bakers of Cincinnati, supplied families with loaf bread, which was paid for in flour, pound for pound. Of these business transactions, we have the following examples:

Wm. & M. Jones, advertise in the Western Spy, of August 27, 1800, "that they still carry on the baking business, and as *flower* is getting cheap, they have enlarged their loaf to four pounds, which is sold at one-eighth of a dollar per loaf, or flour pound for pound, payable every three months."

The following accounts were brought in by the parties, in settlement before a magistrate.

"David J. Poor,

To David Vanderpool, Dr.

1803		
Sept. 8.	To baking 69 loaves of bread, weighing each 2 3-4 lbs.,190 lbs., for which you agreed to give me as many pounds of flour,	6,00
" 9.	To 31 lbs. bread; for this I was also to have as many pounds of flour,	93
" 11.	To 57 lbs. bread, to be paid as above	1,71
	Dr.	$8,64."

"David Vanderpool in accompt with David J. Poor.

To 1 barrel of flour, 196, 2½c	$4,90
Cash, $1,00, damages (bread short of weight) $1,00	2,00
	$6,90

Cr.		
By 69 loaves bread, 2½ lbs. each, 172 lbs. at 2½ cts. per lb.,	4,30	
30 lbs. bread, 2½	75	
57 " " "	1,42½	6,47½

Balance due David J. Poor,	42½
½ pint bitters,	12½
	55."

Flour, as most housekeepers are aware, increases greatly in weight in the process of baking So much so as to produce 265 lbs. bread from a barrel—196 lbs.—of flour. Inferior flour will not make as great a turn out as superfine. This is not owing to the weight of water employed in making it up, as some unreflecting persons suppose, for the moisture is of course evaporated in baking, but by the great absorption of oxygen which takes place in that process. Chr. Ludwig, of Philadelphia, during the revolutionary war, supplied the continental troops with bread, delivering as many pounds of bread as he received pounds of flour, much to the astonishment of Gen. Washington, who supposed he was working for nothing.

After all, the true economy is *home made and baked bread*, and the perfection of bread in point of flavor, is that which is *baked in brick ovens*.

Revolutionary Incident.

It is instructive as well as interesting to turn aside occasionally from current incidents to glance at the history and the men of the past. The following anecdote is of this description, and refers to two of the most distinguished men of their times, and is very characteristic of the parties.

An unhappy difference had occurred in the transaction of business between the general and his much respected Aid, which produced the latter's withdrawal from his family. A few days preceding this period, Hamilton had been engaged all the morning in copying some despatches, which the General, when about to take his usual rounds, directed him to forward a soon as finished.

Washington finding, on his return, the despatches on the table, renewed his directions in expressions indicating his surprise at the delay, and again leaving his apartment, found, when he returned, the despatches where he had left them. At this time, Hamilton had gone out in search of the courier, who had been long waitings when he accidentally met the Marquis de Lafayette, who, seizing him by the button, (as was the habit of this zealous nobleman,) engaged him in conversation; which, being continued with the Marquis' usual earnestness, dismissed from Hamilton's mind for some minutes, the object in view. At length, breaking off from the Marquis, he reached the courier, and directed him to come forward to receive his charge and orders.

Returning, he found the General seated by the table, on which lay the despatches. The moment he appeared, Washington, with warmth and sternness, chided him for the delay; to which Hamilton mildly replied, stating the cause; when the General rather irritated than mollified, sternly rebuked him. To this Hamilton answered, "If your excellency thinks proper thus to address me, it is time for me to leave you." He proceeded to the table, took up the despatches, sent off the express, packed up his baggage, and quitted head quarters.

Although Washington took no measures to restore him to his family, yet he treated him with the highest respect, giving to him the command of a regiment of light infantry, which now formed a part of La Fayette's corps.

Cincinnati Horticultural Society.

A splendid show of Chrysanthemums, was on parade last Wednesday, at the Society rooms, of great variety and extent. This is the last and perhaps most beautiful flower of the season, and we depart from beholding its glories as if we had taken leave of Flora, for six months. A fine mottled Chrysanthemum from the collection of Joseph Cook, called "*the Queen,*" and a Philadelphia variety, appropriately named "*the William Penn,*" from the garden of Jacob Hoffner at Cummingsville, particularly attracted my notice.

Comparative Growth of the East and the West.

It seems impossible to possess our Atlantic brethren of the causes of the rapid growth of the West, and many of them, like the traveller in the fable, who waited for the river to run out, that he might have an opportunity to cross it, appear to expect that we shall in some reasonable time, for which they are waiting with commendable patience, have passed the rapid growth which has characterised our progress hitherto, and increase thenceforth in the same proportion with themselves.

A comparative table of the progress of New York and Cincinnati is subjoined, that the fallacy of such views may be made apparent. I select New York, as affording for the last forty years the most rapid advance in population of any city in the Eastern States.

New York.	Cincinnati.
1697 —— 4,302	
1731 —— 8,628	
1756 —— 10,380	
1771 —— 21,863	
1790 —— 33,131	
1800 —— 60,489	1800 —— ,750
1810 —— 96,372	1810 —— 2,540
1820 —— 123,706	1820 —— 9,602
1830 —— 203,007	1830 —— 24,831
1840 —— 312,710	1840 —— 46,382
1844 —— 375,980†	1844 —— 70,634†
1850 —— 469,075§	1850 —— 131,690§
1860 —— 656,678*	1860 —— 290,000*
1870 —— 875,570*	1870 —— 565.000*
1880 —— 1,069,462*	1880 —— 1,000,000*
1890 —— 1,283,354*	1890 —— 1,500,000*

† Population in the ratio of late Presidential election.

§ Do. in proportion for six years to come.

* Probable population of both cities at those dates.

I am aware of the ridicule which it is easy to cast upon such speculations on the future as these, but I intrench myself on the fact that a less ratio of increase than is now actually taking place, will suffice for these results, and that there never has been any calculation made, hitherto, of progress to Cincinnati, or to the West at large which has not fallen short of facts, when the period future for which they had been made, was reached. And I am not alone in these views.

Second Ward---Cincinnati.

The Second Ward is one of the oldest and most densely built Wards in the city, and is probably four fifths occupied with permanent buildings. My enumeration of dwellings, etc., is as follows:

Public buildings, 22. Dwellings, workshops, store-houses, offices; brick, 825; frame, 214; total, 1061.

Of the public buildings, there are two banking houses—the Lafayette and Franklin Bank; an Orphan Asylum for girls: St Peter's. The Cincinnati and Medical Colleges; the Mercantile Library. One of the Public Schools and the Classical Academy of the New Jerusalem Church, all of brick, and thirteen Churches. The First, Second, and Sixth, and Central Presbyterian Churches. The Unitarian, Universalist, and Restorationist Churches. St. Pauls, Episcopal, Methodist Protestant, Associate Reformed, and Burke's Churches. The New Jerusalem Temple, and two African Baptist Churches, one on Baker street, the other on Third street: all these are of brick, except the last and Burke's church.

Of these buildings, there were, at the close of the year 1842,

Brick,	721.	Frames, 205.	Total, 926.
Built, '43	27.	6.	33.
do '44	97.	5.	102.
	845.	216.	1,061.

The buildings of 1844, in this, as in the First Ward, exceed those of 1843 in the proportion of three to one, and lead me to expect a larger amount of house building to have been made in the city, than the highest estimate I have hitherto made.

Among the best improvements in this Ward, a block, on the lower side Fifth, west of Race, Judge Wright, and Messrs. Febiger Parkhurst, Smith, Probasco, Stevens; two houses belonging to Messrs. Cameron, all on Fourth street, are more or less remarkable for excellence or beauty.

This Ward is central to the city, and Fourth street has been for years becoming the most desirable street in the city for private residences. The streets in the Second Ward are generally spacious; the plateau elevated and airy, and its residents are within reach of markets, schools, churches, public meetings, and general business to a degree of convenience, which no other Ward possesses.

A Chinese English Epistle.

I am indebted for the following, to the person addressed, now in Cincinnati, who has the original in his custody. As a curiosity, especially to the thousands here who have never seen any thing of the sort, I publish it. Dr. Parker refered to in the letter, is the Missionary of the American Board of Foreign missions at Canton.

QUANGTONG, 23rd YEAR, 5th MOON, 10th DAY.

MY GOOD FRIEND:

How fashion insi hab got this morning? Hab catchee little more better? What thing Dr. Parker talkee 'long you? He hab show you true what thing insi?

My thinkee spose any man show you catchee that Gin go 'long that water spose you wantee catchee No 1 fine that he talkee small chilo play pigeon. No got reason all same one foolo.

Spose my all the same for you sick, my must wantee too muchee chin chin, that large Josh. My thinkee he can savvee that pigeon more better for Dr. Parker little. No 'casion you talkee insi. So eh. Cause any man can savvee hab got reason talkee. Have hear any news come from that America si? Too muchee piecee man shew my hab got two piecee ships talkee Don Juan go 'long that Paulina hab begin long teem before walkee this side. Just now he no hab got Macao si.

Don Juan have begin that No 15 day, that No 1 moon, Europe counter and Paulina have all the same fashion No 19 day, any man thinkee he must come Macao direcly. Can see, can savvee. That no my pigeon, that hab Josh pigeon.

Just now must finishee, no got teem talkee any more long you. My Chin chin, you catchee more better chop chop. So fashion talkee

Your good friend,

C. F. HOWQUA.

F. A. R * * * * * * * * *, Esq.

at Messrs. Russell & Co. Canton.

TRANSLATION OF THE ABOVE.

CANTON, May 10th. 1843.

My Good Friend:

How are you (what is the state of your insides) this morning. Have you got a little better. What does Dr. Parker say to you. He has (no doubt) shown you correctly, (what is wrong inside.) My opinion is, that if any man recommends you to take gin and water, to get perfectly well, (No. 1 fine) that he talks childish, (as unfit as a child to attend to the business.) He is as unreasonable as a fool.

Suppose I was as sick as you are, I would want very much to burn incense (chin chin) to that great Josh (the Idol.) I think he (Josh) knows that business (what is the matter with you) a little better than Dr. Parker. There is no occasion for you to doubt this (talk inside) because any one will see I talk reasonably.

Have you heard any news from America (shores.) Several men have told me that there are two ships, named Don Juan and (go long.) Paulina started to come here long since. They have not reached Macao [shore.] The Don Juan started the 15th January, European reckoning, and the Paulina the 19th, same reckoning. It is to be supposed they will arrive soon. As soon as we see we shall know. It is Josh's business not mine.

I must now close as I have no time to write any more to you. In hope you will get better very soon. So writes your good friend,

C. F. HOWQUA.

F. A. Ř * * * * * * * * *, Esq.

at Messrs. Russell & Co. Canton.

Glossary.—Pigeon, means business; catchee, to get or bring, go long, with or and; chin chin, good wishes or prayer. Josh, the Idol, or heathen God; chop chop, very quick.

Winter's Chemical Dioramas.

I alluded briefly to these delightful pictures last week. As works of art as well as ingenuity they are of a very high order of excellence. The coloring, the perspective, the light and shade and their successive changes under the various lights in which they are presented, are extremely striking and impressive. It is rare that a scenic illusion is so perfect. You see the Cathedral at Milan in the moonlight of midnight. Mass is celebrating within the walls. A bell faintly tinkles in the great distance apparently before you, in tones of perfect keeping with the scene. It is difficult to realize that you are beholding a picture—so perfectly are the eye and ear led captive.

I am not in the habit of noticing spectacles and exhibitions, most of them being of questionable influence on the morals and habits of society, if not worse. These are of a different character and effect as is felt in the decorous attention and quiet, with which they inspire the spectators. No one can contemplate the visiters in their seats, without seeing at a glance that they are of a more intellectual if not moral class than usually attend theatrical exhibitions.

Mr. Winter has exhibited these pictures in our Atlantic cities, with marked success, and will shortly take them to Europe.

Fancy Soaps.

This is a new article of manufacture in Cincinnati, at least of later date than those embraced in the last census, at which period there was nothing of the kind cluded in the statistics. There are now four establishments here in which it is made, Winans & Co., M. David, V. Tarde and M. Friedlander, which last makes about half the entire quantity manufactured here. The four factories employ twelve hands, and produce an aggregate of 500 lbs. daily, in value annually 30,000 dollars. This is a small amount as a branch of manufactures, but it is of such descriptions of business that many departments of our productive industry are composed, which contribute in the aggregate, heavy additions to the more important and extensively manufactured articles.

The Advantage of getting "a Sub."

It is stated in the Natchez Free Trader, that Tim Greene, now one the oldest printers in Virginia, was drafted for service in the Revolutionary war; but believing with Jack Falstaff that "discretion was the better part of valor," at the expense of a watch and a pretty round sum of money, he procured a substitute, who answered at the first enrollment to the name, as well as the place, of Tim Greene. In the first battle after the enrollment Greene's substitute was killed, and thus the name of the principal went upon the books of the war department as slain. Under the pension law the children of that old slain soldier, Tim Greene, who is even now alive, have for years received the substantial gratitude of their country.

MARRIAGES.

At Exeter, N. H., 12th inst, by the Rev. Mr. Hurd, Rev. John P Cleveland, D D., of Cincinnati, to Juliana, daughter of the late Capt. Chamberlain.

On the 14th inst., by John Jones, Esq., Mr. Thomas Hunly to Miss Jane Hunly. all of Columbia Township.

On Thursday evening, Nov. 14th, by Rev. W. H. Walker, Mr. John Potts to Miss Eliza Martha Duncan—all of this city.

By the same. on Sunday the 17th inst, at the house of Mr. Chamberlin, in Madison, Ia., Jacob Wentling to Miss Matilda Gassling, all of Cincinnati.

On the 17th, by the Rev. Abel C. Thomas, Mr. B. R. Alley to Miss Augusta Hilton, all of this city.

On the 17th inst. by the Rev. J. Aldrich, Mr. William Oliver Helm to Miss Catherine Virginia Reister, of Reistertown Ma.

On the 17th inst., by the Rev. John F. Wright, Mr. Cornelius Molster to Miss Sarah Ann Finch, all of this city.

On Thursday evening, the 21st inst, by the Rev. E. W. Sehon, John W. Punshon to Miss Ruth Langdon.

At Friends' Meeting Fifth day; 21 inst., Wm. H. Malone to Jane G. Kinsey, both of this city.

On Friday morning, by the Rev. Edward Purcell, Mr. Auguste Labrot, of France, to Miss Elizabeth, daughter of Capt. J. H. Cromwell, of this city.

DEATHS.

On Tuesday afternoon, the 19th inst. at the residence of Mr. N. P. Iglehart, after a severe illness of one week, Joseph Gray, of Pleasant Run, Butler County, Ohio, in the 38th year of his age.

At Mount Auburn, 21st Nov., at 5 o'clock. Mr. Janez Elliot, aged 39 years.

Thursday, Nov. 21st, of Consumption, Elizabeth, consort of Nathaniel Holley, Sen.

In this city, on Friday morning, an infant son of Crafts J. Wright, Esq.

Tuesday. Nov. 26th. Charles Allison, youngest son of Allison Owen, aged 2 years.

CINCINNATI MISCELLANY.

CINCINNATI, DECEMBER, 1844.

Our Cincinnati Artists.

MR. CIST:—In a late letter from a citizen of Kentucky, recently at Florence, a slur is cast on our Queen city, as extending no patronage to the numerous artists who have done honor to the West, and naming Powers and Kellogg, as instances. Mr. Kellogg, when he left Cincinnati for Italy, did not rank as high as some of our younger artists for genius, though really calculated in time, to eclipse them all. Powell and Reed were mere boys, and supposed to possess more genius than Kellogg. But Kellogg, in addition to genius, has that, without which, genius can seldom excel—untiring industry, perseverance, and ambition. If he fails it will not be because he will not toil day and night, and live, if necessary, on a crust of bread. He belongs to a class of artists who require no patronage, and I am led to believe that more promising artists are ruined by patronage than are benefited by it. If I wanted to destroy a young artist of great promise, I would engage him to paint my portrait; pay him a high price for it, and recommend him to require the same compensation from all others. It would be a greater favor to give him 100 dollars for painting four pictures, than the same price for one. But we must pardon the Kentucky letter writer, as a little envy is excusable, in a citizen of his state. We have reduced their great emporium, Louisville, into a country village, and they have done so little to encourage the arts themselves, that poor human nature will scarcely let them laud others. Mr. Wickliffe's letter, nevertheless, is creditable to the artists, and his own talents, and I am not disposed to censure selfish feelings from which I do not find myself exempt. But has Cincinnati given no evidence of a due appreciation of the talents of Powers? Months since, some of her citizens made him an offer of 3000 dollars for his Eve, understanding that was the price. They would have given him more. The offer was not then accepted, for the sale of his Greek Captive had relieved his necessities, and placed him in funds to meet future expenses.—He declined the offer, as he was relieved from embarrassment, and resolved on sending his Eve, Fisher Boy, and a copy of his Greek Slave to the United States for exhibition, and they may be expected daily. Mrs. Clevenger, the widow of the Sculptor, was recently in our city, and stated that the Greek Captive was more admired by her husband and others, than any other work of Powers. If, therefore, Mr. Preston has bought the statue of Eve, it is subject to its being first exhibited in the United States for the benefit of Powers, and no person is more worthy of possessing it—for Mr. Preston was among the first to appreciate the unrivalled genius of Powers. Nor was he content with a proper estimate of his talents. He aided him in his exertions, with great liberality. R. H. Wilde, Esq., now of New Orleans, was among the first to put a proper estimate on the genius of Powers, and herald his fame; and was an efficient actor in the late meeting of the citizens of New Orleans, to engage Powers to make a statue of Franklin. But Powers is not a mere sculptor. He meets the proper definition of a genius—one calculated to excel in any art, but whose mind circumstances direct into a particular channel. Powers' first essay was as a Yankee clock maker's assistant. His employer thought him equal to any branch of art, and recommended him to Dorfeuille who placed in his hands the Poem of Dante, and requested him to make a representation of the Infernal regions. It was done. Had the genius of Powers been directed to Literature, as writer he would have excelled. If the Kentuckian had censured Congress for fostering Italians, without genius, the censure would have been well merited. Clevenger died, with his death hastened, if not occasioned, by his embarrassments, and some of the citizens of Boston deserve great praise, for their liberality in paying his debts, and aiding his widow, since his death.

A motion was made in Congress at the last session, to employ Powers to execute busts of our Presidents, at $500 each. Time was, when such an engagement would have been a great favor, and it would have added to his reputation, to be engaged by our Government, though their taste was not in high repute, from their employment of foreign artists, of talents far inferior to several of our countrymen. But in a pecuniary point of view, the engagement would not now aid him.

If he had leisure to devote to busts, a higher price is paid him by European travellers. For in this department, the world has never produced his superior. As Clevenger nobly said of him: "The bust of Judge Burnet, by Powers, surpasses mine, for it is speaking," and it is in the expression that Powers stands without a rival. It is to be hoped, that our government will now engage Powers on some work, that may add to his reputation as well as profit. I would advise those who admire fine portraits, to call at Mr. Soule's room, on the south side of Fourth street, between Main and Walnut streets. It is true, there are great objections against him. He is not from *foreign* parts. Has never travelled beyond the smoke of his own chimney, and moreover, charges only forty dollars, for better portraits than our citizens have paid one hundred for. But as the country is now supposed to be bankrupt from the success of the progressive Democratic party, this objection may be overlooked.　　　　　　　　　　A CITIZEN.

Fulton Bagging Factory.

My readers will doubtless recollect that the WASHINGTON BREWERY owned by Mr. Schultz, with other buildings on the west was destroyed by fire on the morning of the 6th ult. The Fulton Bagging Factory adjacent on the eastern side was at one time threatened with a similar fate; but the wind contrary to its usual wont, being from the east, that edifice escaped with the loss of its west wall, third story front, its roof and upper floor, with considerable machinery in the third and fourth stories. Having been three times exposed to fire from its first erection and repeatedly to floods, its foundations have been thoroughly tested, and if the establishment needed a device, it might now be entitled to assume the noble one of a ducal house in Scotland, *a lighted taper* blown by the wind, with the motto, FRUSTRA—*In vain.*

To repair these damages involved the rebuilding of the west wall, the brick work in front from the second story, with the reflooring of the third and fourth floors and the reroofing of the whole building. This was promptly effected under the superintendence of Mr. Seneca Palmer one of our longest and best known architects and contractors in whose hands the work progressed with such rapidity that in twelve days from the calamity the looms and spinning machines were again in motion.

I observe in the *Times* that Mr. Gliddon the lecturer on Egypt, stated in reference to the pyramids, that one peculiarity in their construction was that they were all built from the top downwards. Whether this be merely a play upon words, I shall not undertake to say, but it is a fact and literally so, that in rebuilding the FULTON BAGGING FACTORY, Mr. Palmer put on the roof in the first place, as a means of protection to the edifice and its remaining contents, building up one pillar or fresh support at a time and taking down the defective wall pieces in sections as the new replacements went up. This delicate operation, which placed the parties at the mercy of high winds, not unusual in November, has been safely and successfully accomplished, and the building is to say the least, as substantial and strong as when originally built.

I know not why this establishment should be termed the *Fulton* rather than the *Cincinnati* Bagging Factory, as it is within our city limits.

Tax on Attornies and Physicians.

In 1826 the legislature of Ohio made Attorneys and Counsellors at law, together with Physicians and Surgeons subject to a tax, placing them in the same category in that identical act of assembly with *horses, mules and jackasses.* I copy the docket entry of our Court of Common Pleas in the premises.

CINCINNATI, February 20, 1827.

In pursuance of the statute in such case made and provided, the Court list the attornies and counsellors at law, and physicians and surgeons practising their several professions, within the county, and resident therein, who have practised their profession within the State for the period of two years, and affix to each the sum of five dollars, as a tax to be paid agreeably to the statute,—supplementary to the several acts regulating the admission and practice of physicians and surgeons within this State, and file the same, and direct a duplicate of the same to be filed, with the Treasurer of the county.

Attornies and Counsellors of Law.

1 David K. Este.	17 John S. Lytle.
2 *Bellamy Storer.*	18 *J. W. Piatt.*
3 Joseph S. Benham.	19 N. G. Pendleton.
4 *Nathaniel Wright.*	20 *E. S. Haines.*
5 David Wade.	21 *J. G Worthington.*
6 *William Greene.*	22 W. H. Harrison, Jr.
7 William Corry.	23 *Samuel Findlay.*
8 Charles Hammond.	24 Moses Brooks.
9 Samuel R. Miller	25 J. Madeira.
10 Nich. Longworth.	26 *Dan'l Van Matre.*
11 Thomas Hammond.	27 Isaiah Wing.
12 Samuel Lewis.	28 Nathan Guilford.
13 Dan Stone.	29 Benj. F. Powers.
14 *Charles Fox.*	30 *James W. Gazlay.*
15 Elijah Hayward.	31 D. J. Caswell.
16 Jesse Kimball.	32 Hugh M'Dougal.

Physicians and Surgeons.

1 Samuel Ramsay.	14 John Cranmer.
2 E. H. Pierson.	15 Jno. Morehead.
3 Jesse Smith.	16 John Sellman.
4 V. C. Marshall.	17 James W. Mason.
5 Guy W. Wright.	18 Abel Slayback.
6 John Woolley.	19 F. C. Oberdorf.
7 Lorenzo Lawrence.	20 J. M. Ludlum.
8 J. W. Hagerman.	21 E. Y. Kemper.
9 Jedediah Cobb.	22 C. Munroe.
10 Josiah Whitman.	23 Edward H. Stall.
11 Beverly Smith.	24 J. E. Smith.
12 Isaac Hough.	25 Dan'l. Drake.
13 C. W. Barbour.	26 Wm. Barnes.

The physicians and surgeons of the county of Hamilton are seperated from this catalogue.

What changes have seventeen years brought in this list. Of the attorneys, Este, Longworth, Lewis and Pendleton have retired from professional business, Stone, Hayward, and Powers, have removed from Cincinnati; Brooks, Wing and Guilford have changed their profession, and with the exception of the ten in italic, who still survive, the residue are no longer living.

With the physicians, death has been busier still. Dr. Cobb has removed from the city, and

Drs. Moorhead, Drake, Oberdorf and Ludlum it is believed are all who survive out of twenty-six who were in active practice seventeen years since. What is to account for the greater mortality among the medical than in the legal class?

CORRESPONDENCE.

Washington and Hamilton.

Mr. Cist—Sir:

The Revolutionary Incident contained in your paper of the 20th Nov., agrees very nearly with what I have heard detailed as the story of the difference between General Washington and his aid. The tradition, however, is incorrect in some some particulars, especially in exaggerating the neglect of Hamilton,—and the General's want of temper:—and in setting forth that the General made no effort to restore Hamilton to his family.

The true version of the story is given in a letter of Col. Hamilton's written to his father-in-law, Gen. Schuyler, within two days after the occurrence, which I send you for insertion in your paper.   J. H. J.

Urbana, 25th Nov.

Head-Quarters, }
New Windsor, February 18, 1781. }

My Dear Sir: Since I had the pleasure of writing you last, an unexpected change has taken place in my situation. I am no longer a member of the General's family. This information will surprise you, and the manner of the change will surprise you more. Two days ago, the General and I passed each other on the stairs:—he told me he wanted to speak to me. I answered that I would wait upon him immediately. I went below and delivered Mr. Tilghman a letter to be sent to the commissary, containing an order of a pressing and interesting nature.

Returning to the General, I was stopped on the way by the Marquis de La Fayette, and we conversed together about a minute on a matter of business. He can testify how impatient I was to get back, and that I left him in a manner which, but for our intimacy, would have been more than abrupt. Instead of finding the General, as is usual, in the room, I met him at the head of the stairs, where accosting me in an angry tone:—" Colonel Hamilton, (said he,) you have kept me waiting at the head of the stairs, these ten minutes:—I must tell you, sir, you treat me with disrespect." I replied without petulancy, but with decision, " I am not conscious of it, sir, but since you have though it necessary to tell me so, we part." " Very well, sir, (said he,) if it be your choice," or something to that effect, and we seperated. I sincerely believe my absence, which gave so much umbrage, did not last two minutes.

In less than an hour, Tilghman came to me in the General's name, assuring me of his great confidence in my abilities, integrity, &c., and of his desire, in a candid conversation, to heal a difference which could not have happened but in a moment of passion. I requested Mr. Tilghman to tell him,—1st, That I had taken my resolution in a manner not to be revoked. 2d, That as a conversation could serve no other purpose than to produce explanations mutually disagreeable, though I would certainly not refuse an interview, if he desired it, yet I would be happy if he would permit me to decline it. 3d, That though determined to leave the family, the same principles which had kept me so long in it, would continue to direct my conduct when out of it. 4th, That, however, I did not wish to distress him, or the public business, by quitting him before he could derive other assistance by the return of some of the gentlemen who were absent. 5th; And that in the meantime, I depended upon him to let our behavior to each other be the same as if nothing had happened. He consented to decline the conversation, and thanked me for my offer of continuing my aid in the manner I had mentioned.

I have given you so particular a detail of our difference from the desire I have to justify myself in your opinion. Perhaps you may think I was precipitate in rejecting the overture made to an accommodation. I assure you, my dear sir, it was not the effect of resentment; it was the deliberate result of maxims I had long formed for the government of my own conduct.

I always disliked the office of aid-de-camp, as having in it a kind of personal dependence. I refused to serve in this capacity with the Major General, at an early period of the war.— Infected, however. with the general enthusiasm of the times, an idea of the General's character overcame my scruples, and induced me to *accept his invitation* to enter into his family. * * It has been often with great difficulty that I have prevailed upon myself not to renounce it; but while, from pure motives of public utility, I was doing violence to my feelings, I was always determined if there should ever happen a breach between us, never to consent to an accommodation. I was persuaded that when once that nice barrier, which marked the boundaries of what we owed to each other, should be thrown down, it might be propped again, but could never be restored.

The General is a very honest man. His competitors have slender abilities and less integrity His popularity has often been essential to the safety of America, and is still of importance to it. These considerations have influenced my past conduct respecting him, and will influence my future. I think it is necessary he should be supported.

His estimation in your mind, whatever may be its amount, I am persuaded has been formed on principles, which a circumstance like this cannot materially affect; but if I thought it could diminish your friendship for him, I should almost forego the motives that urge me to justify myself to you. I wish what I have said, to make no other impression than to satisfy you I have not been in the wrong. It is also said in confidence, as a public knowledge of the breach would, in many ways, have an ill effect. It will probably be the policy of both sides to conceal it, and cover the seperation with some plausible pretext. I am importuned by such of my friends as are privy to the affair to listen to a reconciliation; but my resolution is unalterable.

Very sincerely and affectionately,
I am, dear sir,
Your most obedient servant,
A. HAMILTON.

Our Country One Hundred Years ago.

I resume my extracts from Franklin's Pennsylvania Gazette of 1744-5:

"Just imported from Bristol in the ship Catharine. A parcel of likely men servants, to be sold by Edward and James Shippen."

"For sale; a billiard table. Enquire on Samuel Hastings, on Front street; In Quaker Philadelphia!"

"Whereas I, the subscriber, living on Strawberry Alley, intend (God willing) to begin the German evening school, at the beginning of October, next ensuing,all persons inclining to learn the above language are hereby invited,and they shall be duly attended and instructed after the shortest and easiest method. J. Shippey. N. B. Book-binding of all sorts is done in the best manner and at a most reasonable rate, at the above place."

Literature of the age. "Lately published at Boston, and to be sold by B. Franklin, in Philadelphia, price one shilling, the American Magazine, containing,

Motion inseparable from matter, with the moral improvement.

Man's life a continued round of hurry and amusement.

A remarkable instance of true friendship.

The blessings of plenty.

The art of not thinking; a satire.

An essay on the wisdom of Providence, &c." Very different subjects from those that fill Godey, or Graham, or the Democratic Review of the present day.

"Notice is hereby given that plumbing, glazing and painting is to be performed in the cheapest and best manner by Eden Haydock, late from old England, at Paul Chanders' on Second street."

"New York lottery tickets sold by B. Franklin; price 30 shillings each."

"To be sold at auction. At the widow Jones' coffee house, on Water street, on Monday, the 26th inst., two thirty-thirds of the privateer ship, MARLBOROUGH, now on her cruise, and of four negroes on board, belonging to her owners, with the benefit of her cruise from this term. One thirty-third to be set up at a time.

"Twenty pistoles reward. Dropt yesterday afternoon, between Philadelphia and Frankford, a small oznabrig bag, containing two hundred and ninety-five pistoles and one moidore."

The pistole, at that period, was as regularly the coin of value, in advertisements, as the dollar appears now.

"To be sold by Nathaniel Allen, cooper in Philadelphia, choice beef and pork, in barrels.

White slavery. "Sundry young men and lads, servants —lately imported from England—to be disposed of by Wm. Attwood, on reasonable terms."

"Just published and to be sold By the printer hereof, a journal of the proceedings of the detection of the conspiracy formed by some white people, in connection with negro and other slaves for burning the city of New York, in America, and murdering the inhabitants: which conspiracy was partly put in execution by burning his Majesty's house in Fort George, within the said city, on Wednesday, the 18th of March, 1741, and setting fire to several dwellings, and other houses therein, within a few days succeeding.— And by another attempt made, in prosecution of the same infernal scheme,by putting fire between two other dwelling houses in the same city, on the 15th day of February, 1741, which was accidentally discovered and extinguished. Containing a narrative of the trials, condemnation, execution, and behaviour of the several criminals, at the gallows and stake, with their several speeches and confessions.

By the Recorder of the city of New York. The stake! Were any of them burned?

"To be sold by John Ord, at his shop, at the corner of Gray's Alley, on Front street in the house where John Armit lived, a neat assortment of Irish linens. Stint ware by the crate, &c." Quere? Crockery ware.

"To be sold; a likely mulatto boy who has had the measles and small pox. Enquire at the Post Office."

"Very good English window sash, 8 by 10, to be sold cheap, by James Claypoole, on Walnut street, Philadelphia." It seems by this advertisement, that in Philadelphia, sixty-four years after its being built, and within twenty-five years of the breaking out of the revolutionary war, even window-sashes were imported from England. How much more dependent were the colonies for articles which required machinery for their manufacture.

"Stationery of all sorts to be sold at the Post Office."

I notice that from the 1st January to the 22d March, Franklin dates the year 1745-6—aftei which 1746. Twelve advertisements fill up that department in the Gazette. Three new ones on an average per week; and this for the only paper south of Boston, on the whole continent,and in a city 64 years old and now numbering 300,- 000 inhabitants!!

Ohio, Pennsylvania, and New York.

The late Presidential vote in these three States after having served political purposes becomes deeply interesting as statistical data. That vote serves to shew that Pennsylvania is maintaining the movement by which, at the last census, she had been threatening New York with regaining her original political ascendancy in the National scale.

The following table points out the relative progress from census to census of two of these States.

	N. York.	Increase.	Penn.	Increase.
1790	340,000		434,000	
1800	586,000	72 pr. ct.	602,000	38 pr. ct.
1810	959,000	62 "	810,000	34 "
1820	1,372,000	43 "	1,049,000	29 "
1830	1,918,000	40 "	1,340,000	28 "
1840	2,428,000	26 "	1,274,000	28 "

Let me place the subject in another light. The growth of Pennsylvania from 1820 to 1830, was 290,000; whereas from 1830 to 1840 it was 376,000, showing the difference in the increase of two decades of 77,000. Whereas New York *fell off*, during the same period, from 546,000, to 540,000.

It may appear strange that New York, after gaining on Pennsylvania, for forty years, in the great race for power and political consequence, should now, without any apparent reason for the change, be found falling behind her. I suppose the following explanatory statement may suffice.

The agricultural interest is that which is first developed in every settlement,and it is only when *that* is fully brought out, that the manufacturing and mining interests become properly attended to; new markets are then opened for the products of the soil in the feeding of these later interests, and increased production is stimulated by higher rates for produce. The greater extent of tillable land gave New York early an advantage which has resulted in the prodigious strides she has been making from 1790 to 1830, about which period, the mining and manufacturing resources of Pennsylvania began to manifest themselves, and create a re-action in growth and progress, which promises to restore that State to its

original position in advance of New York. The same state of things occurred in England in the course of the last twenty years, and aided efficiently in the overthrow of the rotten borough system. In the readjustment of the representation in Parliament, it was discovered, that the agricultural interest in the South had lost its former relative importance, and the manufacturing and still more the mining interests in the North, were assuming a consequence from the increase of population there, which no one was prepared to expect.

I deem this view of the tendency of things of vast importance in its application to our own State. The mineral wealth of Ohio. in iron, coal, and salt especially, is of vast, and as yet comparatively unknown and undeveloped extent. I shall take up this subject shortly in a seperate article.

The late returns confirm all my calculations, for censuses future as regards these three States, which I made in 1840. I shall close this article by republishing my views, at that date.

	Ohio.	Pennsylvania.	N. York.
1840	1,519,000.	1,724,033.	2,428,921.
1844	1,734,458.	1,985,033.	2,611,342.
1850	2,250,000.	2,150,000.	2,950,000.
1860	3,100,000.	2,600,000.	3,450,000.
1870	3,900,000.	3,100,000.	3,900,000.

The statements for 1844 are founded on the late Presidential vote. The estimates for 1850, are those proportions carried out to that date, and the later calculations have resulted from following out the probable progress of each State at those respective dates.

An American Church at the Giant's Causeway.

Many of my readers will remember the Rev. Jonathan Simpson, who visited Cincinnati not many months ago, in the prosecution of his effort to gather, throughout the United States, among emigrants from the north of Ireland, especially, the means of erecting a Presbyterian house of worship, at Port Rush, in the immediate vicinity of the Giant's Causeway. That building has been finished and was opened for religious exercises on the 29th September last.

There are some facts connected with this case which render it remarkable. The church has been built by the contributions of Irishmen dwelling in New York, Baltimore, Philadelphia, Albany, Pittsburgh, Cincinnati, Louisville, Nashville, Charleston, S. C., and Easton, Pennsylvania, sixty pounds only being raised in the neighborhood of Port Rush.

It is intended to record those benefactions on a marble tablet, opposite the outer door on the inner gable, as a monument of gratitude for what Trans-atlantic Christians have done for their weak congregation; "beloved for their fathers' sakes."

The pulpit or desk, it is stated, has been constructed in the American fashion, and though much of a novelty, is well liked by all who see it.

The entire contributions in the United States were 5465 dollars. Of this New York gave 1038, Albany 250, Philadelphia 900, Easton 40, Baltimore 980, Pittsburgh 615, *Cincinnati* 350, Louisville 292, Nashville 189, Charleston 245.

Third Ward--Cincinnati.

In the enumeration of buildings in this ward, I find there are 1162 dwelling houses, workshops,public stables, store houses, mills and offices. Of these 720 are of brick, 2 are of stone, and 434 are frames. Besides these there are six public buildings. The Botanico Medical College, and Bethel Chapel, the city water works, an engine house, and two public school houses. Of these buildings there were at the close of 1842:

	Stone 2	Bricks 585	Frames 345	Total 932
Built in 1843	0	" 69	" 44	" 113
Built in 1844	0	" 71	" 46	" 117
Total	2	725	436	1162

There seems to be little increase in building this year over the last so far as numbers are concerned. But some of the buildings in this ward erected in 1844 are immense piles of masonry in extent. Such are the new buildings of Messrs. Harkness, Griffey &c., which not only cover a great space of ground, but are 5, 6, and 7 stories high. And the quality and size of the dwellings are improving year after year, in this as well as in other parts of Cincinnati. Four-fifths of this ward is built up to its utmost capacity.

The third ward is the great hive of Cincinnati industry, especially in the manufacturing line. Planeing machines, iron foundries, breweries, saw mills, rolling mills, finishing shops, bell and brass foundries, boiler yards, boat building, machine shops, &c. constitute an extensive share of its business.

Fourth Ward--Cincinnati.

This is one of the oldest sections of the city, and embraces a large share of the heavy business of the city, within its limits. My enumeration of its buildings is as follows: Public buildings, 4; dwelling houses, offices, work-shops, and store-houses, 1,207. Of these 4 are built of stone, 652 of brick and 551 are frames. Of these buildings there were at the close of the year 1842,

	Stone 4	Brick 536	Frames 495	Total 1045.
Built in '43,	" 0	" 45	" 14	" 59.
do '44,	" 0	" 75	" 42	" 117.
Total	4	656	551	1211.

·The public buildings in the Fourth Ward are the Ohio Life Insurance and Trust Company;— Third Presbyterian Church, one of the Public School houses; and an Engine House.

The Fourth Ward has been for years in a state of suspended animation, and with little signs of improvement. Second, or Columbia street, was left, for a long period, at a grade which shut out the improvement its contiguity to the business region of Cincinnati, should have located within its limits. In addition to this, the great flood of 1832, laid it under water to such a depth, that steamboats actually passed down some of its streets, and its western borders were overflowed from eight to twelve feet. This calamity drove the dwelling-house building, especially the elegant and spacious portion of it to the hill. and left the river region in a languishing state, until within the past year, or within eighteen months, by which time the absolute want of room elsewhere, for business purposes, and the increasing trade of Cincinnati, gave an impulse to warehouse building in the eastern and southern parts of the Ward, which is filling them up with many and extensive improvements, in blocks as well as single houses. Such store houses as the block of Geo. H. Bates & Co., at the corner of Walnut and Front streets; Stephen J. Wade's block, at the south west corner of Front and Walnut, and John H. Groesbeck's, at north west corner of the same ; two fine buildings at the corner of Walnut and Second; Wm. C. Stewart & Co's block on Second street, between Main and Walnut street, and a few other single buildings, are of a character for strength, spaciousness and convenience, for which we have hitherto had few or no parallels. These are all built with substantial door posts, and lintels, faced in every direction with cast iron, handsomely ornamented, which give a beautiful finish to the wide doorways they protect. A new and capacious foundry,of Messrs. Goodhue & Co, on Elm street, adds to the valuable erections in the Fourth Ward. Such, in fact is the character and extent of the last eighteen months improvements, as to constitute a value of buildings here much greater than the previous erections for fifteen years, and, if we except the Pearl street buildings, for twenty. The necessary consequence of any given improvement is, that it begets neighboring ones, and I have no doubt that Front and Second streets, west of Walnut, now present opportunities for a profitable investment of funds, beyond almost any other region in the city. And I so judge because the heavy business of Cincinnati must extend beyond its present limits, and it has no other direction to spread out in than the region I refer to. Connected with the improvements already made and preparing the way for more, Second street west has been filled up ten to twelve feet, admirably graded, and now forms a direct connection with the White Water Canal basin, much of the produce landed at which, must, for a few year, be drayed up by this avenue, to the business regions of the Third and Fourth Wards.

A Panther Hunt in Pennsylvania.

Conrad Sock was one of the old settlers of the north branch of Susquehannah, in one of its wildest sections,and in his time has killed more panthers and bears than usually falls to the lot even of pioneers. The following is an account of one of his panther hunts taken down from his own lips:

The settlement on the mountain here is very scattered, and there are no inhabitants for a considerable distance back from the road. I heard that a person had been hunting, and said that he had seen three panthers; upon which I called on him, and he told me, that at a certain place, on Spring Brook, about ten miles from this, he had came across three panthers, and had tried to fire at them, but could not get his gun to go off. I thought the fellow was a coward, that only part of his story was true, and that he had been afraid to fire at them; but as I knew exactly the place which he described (for I had been frequently there on hunting excursions) I tho't I would go and see whether there had been any panthers there. So, I started off next morning with my dog. You know what a terrible thicket of laurel,and spruce, and hemlock there is about here; well, it is as bad all the way to the place where the fellow said he saw the panthers. At last, however, I got to it, and sure enough the panthers had been there. There was a little snow upon the ground, and I found where they had killed a deer, and eaten part of it; but I knew that after I had been at the place they would not go back to it again; for a panther will never touch his game a second time, if anything else has been at it. So, I marked which way they went, as it was two days since they had been there, and I did not know how long I might be in the woods in chase of them, I thought it would be best to go home, and get a supply of provisions for a good long hunt, and then take a fresh start. But it was almost night; I struck a fire, and laid down till morning. As soon as it was light, I started off, taking my back track, to go home, and got about half way, when, behold! I came right to the panthers' tracks! They had crossed the path I had made in the snow, the day before. I knew they had crossed in the day time, for it had been warm and the snow had melted a little, and I could easily tell that they had crossed my path before night. So, I started on the track and followed till almost evening, when I saw a light place in the woods, and going into it, I found I was on a road about three miles from home. I then concluded it would be the best way for me to go home that night, and get my knapsack of provisions as I had intended; for I did not know but what the devils might keep me running after them a whole week; and I was determined, if I once started them, to give them no time to rest or kill game, as long as I could see to follow them, let them go where they would; and sometimes they lead one an infernal long chase.

So, home I went, filled my knapsack with provisions, and started out with that dog, that is lying by the stove there—not the white one—the spotted one. He is a good fellow for a panther, and likes hunting as well as I do! Well, as I said, as soon as it was daylight next morning, out I went, and got on the track again where I had left it the evening before, and followed it all day long, up one valley and down another, over hills and through laurel swamps, till just before sunset,when I came on a fine buck which the panthers had killed and partly eaten, and which was still warm. They had killed him where he lay. He had never got up. He had been lying behind a large hemlock tree, which was blown down; and it appeared by the marks in the snow; as if they had smelt him, crawled up close to him, jumped over the tree, and seized him in his bed. They always take their game by surprise. They never make more than two or three jumps after it; if it then escapes, they turn off another way. They had eaten as much as they wished of the buck, and after getting their bellies full, they appeared to have been in a very good humor: for their marks shewed where they had played about, and had jumped up and down all the small trees around. They did not know who was after them. I had not expected to come on them so soon, and had pushed ahead without any caution, so that they had heard my approach, and I soon found, by the appearance of things, that they must have started away just as I came up; for instead of keeping together as they had done all day before, they had set off in different directions. I thought it was sunset, and that I had better encamp where I was; for they would hardly come back in the night to claim their buck; but first, I thought I would look a little more around, to see which track it would be best to follow in the morning; and so just went a little way into the swamp, which was close by me, when, only think! one of the curses had been watching all the time, and I heard him start within ten rods of me! but the laurel was so thick that I could not see him, As soon as he started,away went the dog after him, full yelp. Well, I stood still, and there was a glorious threshing among the laurels; when all at once I heard the panther take up a tree. I heard his nails strike the bark the first dash he made. It was a beautiful still evening; and I said to myself: I have one of you anyway; and I ran as hard as I could through the thicket, tumbling over logs, and scrambling through the laurels,until I came to where Toby was, barking and jumping, and shaking his tail, and looking mightily tickled, at having got one of them up the tree. Well, I soon saw the panther lying at his full length on a limb—it was on a very large hemlock. I did not know well what to do: for it was now so late that I could scarcely see the foresight of my rifle, and I could not see the notch of the hindsight at all; but as I knew my gun, I thought I had better venture a shot, rather than keep watch at the tree all night; and so I drew up,and took the best aim I could and fired away. Well the devilish rascals never stirred. I said to myself, I am sure I can't have missed you. In a short time I saw a motion in his tail, which hung over the limb on which he lay, and directly after I could hear his nails gritting on the bark, and I saw his body begin to slide round the limb till at last he slung fairly under it, suspended by his claws, and in a minute after he let go his hold and down he came, souse! so nearly dead that when I ran to keep Toby from taking hold of him (for they are devilish thing to fight and can tear a dog to pieces in no time)I found him unable to stretch out a claw. I knew that I could find the place again, and so I just let him lay where he fell, and I went back to the buck, and made a good fire and layed down there till morning. But first I cut some good slices off the buck and roasted them for supper. He was a fine fat fellow and killed as nicely as a butcher could have killed him. I don't like to eat part of a deer which has been killed by the wolves —but a panther is a different thing.

Well, the next morning I started bright and early and I soon came on the tracks of the other two panthers. It appeared as if they had been tracing about separately, and had kept around the swamp nearly all night; but at last they got together and started off. As soon as I got on the track I followed it briskly, till about noon, when I started them afresh, and letting out Toby they and he, and I, all ran as fast as we could; but they got about a quarter of a mile ahead of me, when dash! one of them took up a tree;—which I soon knew by the manner of the dog's barking. Oh! said I, I've got another one!—When I came up to the dog, there, sure enough, was a panther up a tree, shaking his tail and looking just like a cat when she is about to jump on a mouse; but, says I, my fine fellow, I'll soon put a stop to your jumping. So I ups with my rifle, and down he came, as dead as if he had never been alive. Well! I skinned him and fastened his skin to my knapsack, and away I started after the other one

The last fellow did not like to travel without his companions. I suppose he wondered what had become of them. He kept dodging about, first one way, then another, as if he expected them to come up with him; but he had another kind of companion hunting for him. Well, as I said, after I skinned the second one, I started after the third, and in about two hours I roused him from behind a log, and Toby and he had a fine run for about ten minutes. I stood still; for I thought maybe the panther would take a circuit to hunt for the other ones, and—so he did; but the dog was so close to him, he thought it best to tree; in torder, I suppose, to see who, and how many were after him. As soon as I knew, by the barking, he had treed, away I ran, and soon got on the track. I took notice of it on a leaning tree, which I ran past, to the dog, who was about ten rods farther, looking up at a large hemlock, and making a great racket. I looked up: but I could see no panther. I went off a little where I could see every limb; but the devil a panther was there. Why, said I, this can be no ghost, to vanish in this way; he must be on some of these trees; but let us go where I last saw the track. So I went back to the leaning tree, where I had last seen the track. It was a pretty large hemlock, which had fallen against another; and looking up, there I saw the fellow sure enough, crouching right in the crotch, where the leaning tree lay across the other, close down, so hidden by the limbs and green leaves of the hemlock, that I could see only a small part of his body. In running to the dog, I had gone right under him. Although I could see but little of him from the place where I stood, yet as I was sure that what I saw was his shoulders, I did not wait to see any more of him, but I took a fair sight and drew my trigger. Well: he did not budge! I looked at him for some time, but he did not stir. I was sure I had shot him thro'

—I thought it a pity to waste any more lead on him. His tail hung over the crotch of the large tree, and there was a smaller tree which grew up close to the crotch, and I thought I could climb up the little tree, so as to catch his tail and see whether he was dead or no; but just as I was about half up, I saw his tail begin to move, and before I could get to the ground, his head, and foreparts slid over the crotch, and down he came as dead as a door-nail. So I skinned him, and went back to the one I killed first, and skinned him, and got home that night. And I sent word to the fellow who saw them by the Spring Brook, that if he would come to me I would shew him the skins of his three panthers." P.

A Hint.

At some places I visit, the dogs, who are among the most insignificant of their species, fly at me on my approach, making such a barking, that I can neither hear those I call upon, nor they me. While thus annoyed, I feel disposed to kick, when the owner, mistaking the feeling of vexation for that of fear, interposes. " Oh, don't be afraid—he won't bite you, sir "—It is unpleasant to be worried with the barking of such apologies for dogs, but it is distressing to be supposed apprehensive of their bite.

What an illustration is this of some human beings with whom we come, at times, in contact!

MARRIED,

At Greendale, on the 26th inst, by the Rev. T.O. Prestcott, J. FORD DESILVER to LAVINIA M. GEIGER, daughter of the Rev. M. M. Carll, of Philadelphia.

On Thursday evening, Nov. 28th, by Elder Wm. P. Stratton, Mr. JOHN DUNSETH to Miss MARY HAT, all of his city.

On Thursday morning, 28th Nov., by Rev. Mr. Prestley, Mr. THOMAS H. MINOR, to Miss REBECCA, daughter of James R. Baldridge, Esq., all of this city.

On Thursday evening, Nov. 28th, by the Rev. Mr. Cleaveland, EDWARD R. TILLOTSON to AUGUSTA, daughter of Stephen Schooley, Esq.

On Thursday, the 28th, by Elder James Challen, JAMES L. BRINDLE to Miss MARION BROWN.

On Thursday morning, Nov. 28th, by the Rev. N. L. Rice, Mr. JOHN S. STANSBURY to Miss CAROLINE E. BURCH.

On Thursday, the 28th inst, by the Rev. E. T. Collins, Dr. JOHN C. MAGGINI, of Fayetteville, Brown county, Ohio, to MARY ANN, daughter of Capt. P. McCloskey of this city.

On Sunday afternoon, Dec. 1st, by Elder Wm. P. Stratton, Mr. JOHN SWEAT to Miss MATILDA MOORE, all of this city

---

DIED,

On Monday, Nov. 25th, MARIANA MARGARET, eldest child of Alexander and Jane Anne Johnston—aged 3 years and 3 months.

On Saturday, Nov. 30th, 1844, Mrs. JULIA ANN ROLL, aged 25 years, wife of Edward C. Roll.

On Saturday morning, HARRIET, youngest daughter of Samuel N. and Ellen Ruffin, aged 3 years and 9 months.

On Sabbath morning, of Chronic disease of the heart, ANNE, wife of John W. Hartwell.

On Monday evening, the 2d inst.. in the 77th year of his age, MOSES DAWSON, Esq., many years a resident of this city, and editor of the Cincinnati Advertiser. Mr. D. was a native of Ireland and an associate of Dr. Drennan and others, in their gallant but unsuccessful efforts to give Ireland her place among the nations of the earth.

FUNERAL NOTICE.

The Funeral of Moses Dawson, Esq.. will take place this day, Wednesday, December 4th, at 2 o'clock, P. M. from the residence of his son, Mr Thomas Dawson, on Third street. between Walnut and Vine.
The friends of the family are requested to attend with out further notice.

Churches, and Religious Societies in Cincinnati.

Roman Catholic. *St. Peter's Cathedral*, Sycamore between 5th and 6th,; officiating clergy, Very Rev. E. T. Collins, Rev. E. Purcell and J. B. Wood. *Holy Trinity* church, 5th, between Smith and Park streets; Rev. Francis L. Huber and William Unterthiner. *St. Mary's* church, corner of Clay and 13th streets; Rev. Joseph Ferneding, Clement Hammer and Andrew Tusch. Cincinnati is an episcopate of this church. Rt. Rev. J. B. Purcell, Bishop of the Diocese.

Protestant Episcopal. *Christ* church, 4th between Sycamore and Broadway; Rev. J. T. Brooke, Rector. *St. Paul's* church, 4th between Main and Walnut; Rectorship vacant. *Grace* church, 7th, between Plum and Western Row; Rev. Richard S. Killin Rector. *Trinity* church, officiating minister, Rev. Ethan Allen.

Presbyterian—Old School. *First*; Main between 4th and 5th; J. L. Wilson, D. D., Rev. S. R. Wilson. *Fourth*; High street, near Corporation line, vacant. *Fifth*; corner 7th and Elm, Rev. D. K. McDonald. *Central*; corner 4th and Plum; Rev. N. L. Rice, pastors.

Presbyterian—New School. *Second*; Fourth, between Vine and Race; John P. Cleaveland, D. D. *Third*; Second street, between Walnut and Vine; Rev. Thornton A. Mills. *Sixth*; Sixth, between Main and Walnut, anti-slavery; Rev. Jonathan Blanchard. *Tabernacle*; Betts between John and Cutter streets; Rev. John C. White,. pastors. *George Street*; At Engine House, Geo. street; Lyman Beecher, D. D., temporary supply.

Reformed Presbyterian. George between Race and Elm streets; Rev. William Wilson, pastor,

Associate Reformed Presbyterian; Sixth between Race and Elm; Rev. James Prestley. pastor.

Baptist. *Ninth St.* church; Elder S. W. Lynd, pastor. First Baptist; corner 9th and Elm; Elder T. R. Cressey, pastor. *College street* church; College street, between 6th and 7th; Elder W. H. Brisbane, pastor. *Pearson Street* church; Pearson, between 5th and 6th; Elder Lewis French, pastor.

African Union—Baptist; Baker, between Walnut and Vine; Elder Charles Satchell, pastor.

Zion—Baptist; Third, between Race and Elm; Elder Wm. Shelton, pastor.

These are regular Baptists. The second in order, is on an abolition basis. The two last are congregations of colored people.

Baptist Christian Disciples. Sycamore between 5th and 6th streets; Elder David S. Burnet, preacher. Sixth, between Smith and Mound, Elders B. S. Lawson, M. D., Wm. P. Stratton and George Tait, preachers. Engine House, Vine, between Front and Second streets; Elder James Challen, Preacher, Jefferson Hall church, Vine between Court and Canal; Elder Jasper J, Moss, preacher.

Episcopal Methodist, *Wesley Chapel*, Fifth street, between Sycamore and Broadway; Rev. John F. Wright. *Morris Chapel*, Western Row, between Fourth and Fifth; Rev. Geo. W. Walker. *Ninth Street Chapel*, Ninth street, between Race and Elm streets, Rev. Wm. P. Strickland. *Asbury chapel*, Webster, between Main and Sycamore; Rev. Asbury Lowry.— *German Mission chapel*, Race, between Thirteenth and Fourteenth streets, Rev. Wm. Ahrens. *City Mission*, Rev. George W. Maley.— *African New Street*—colored—New east of Broadway; Rev. J. Reynolds, preacher in charge.

Methodist Protestant Churches, south side of Sixth, between Vine and Race streets, and Elm near Northern Row; Rev. James E. Wilson, and Oliver H. Stevens, ministers.

New Wesleyan; Ninth, between Main and Walnut; Rev. Hiram S. Gilmore, J. W. Walker, and Silas H. Chase, preachers. African. corner of Harrison and Pike, Rev. Smith Clements. Bethel African Methodist, Sixth, east of Broadway; Rev, M. M. Clarke, preacher.

Friends' Meeting Houses. Fifth between Western Row and John.

New Jerusalem Temple, Longworth, between Race and Elm streets; Rev. T. O. Prescott, minister.

First Congregational—*Unitarian*—south-west corner of Race and Fourth streets. Rev. James H. Perkins, minister.

Universalist church. Walnut, between Third and Fourth streets, Rev. Abel C. Thomas, Minister. First Restorationist church; Race, between Fifth and Sixth streets; Rev. Daniel Parker, minister.

German Lutheran churches, *Zion*, Bremen, between Fifteenth and Northern Row. Rev. J E. W. Braasch. *St. John*, Sixth between Walnut and Vine streets; Rev. Augustus Kroell.— *Northern*, Walnut, between Eighth and Ninth streets; Rev. A. W. Suhr, English Lutheran, Fourth, between Main and Sycamore streets; Rev. Abraham Reck. German Reformed churches, north west corner Walnut and Thirteenth sts., Rev. J. Becher; Elm street, opposite Orphan Asylum; Rev. F. M. Raschig; Vine, between Fourth and Fifth streets, Rev. Philip Hauser, ministers.

These are all German Protestant churches, Mr. Reck's congregation, with services in the English language.

Second Advent Tabernacle, corner John and Seventh streets, Elders J. Jacobs, and Henry A. Crittenden, ministers.

United Brethren in Christ; corner of Fulton

and Catharine streets; Rev. Francis J. Whitcomb, minister. Welsh Calvinistic Methodist church, north side of Harrison street: Rev. Edward Jones, pastor.

Welsh Congregational, corner of Lawrence and Symmes: Rev. John Jones, pastor.

The services of these churches are in Welsh

Jewish Synagogues. *Kal a Kodesh Beni Isroel.* Broadway , between Harrison and Sixth, Joseph Jonas, parnas; corner Walnut and Sixth , A. Fechheimer, parnas.

Bethel Chapel, Front, between Main and Sycamore.

Mormon church, Andrew L. Lamoureaux priest.

Christian church, Fourth,between Stone and Wood; vacant.

There are then, it seems, sixty-one churches, with their appropriate edifices, or places of worship, in Cincinnati. I have no means of comparing our religious privileges with any other city in the United States than N. York,which had at the latest computation,190 churches, and Washington city, 25. The number of churches is however, no fair criterion of the state of morals and religion to any given community ; for New York has but one church for 2.000 of her population, while Washington ha one for every 1000 of hers; yet there can be no doubt that Washington is much lower in the scale of morals and religious observances than New York.— Indeed, I conceive it, during the session of Congress, one of the most immoral communities in our whole country.

The First step to Office.

In new settlements a start is usually given to public men, by electing them to some office in the militia, or to that of a justice of the peace. The following document serves to show how the people of Ohio, before they possessed any political existence, obtained their local magistrates. It will be seen by this memorial that Gov. Morrow has been in office more than forty five years. He has been a member of the Territorial Legislature, of the Assembly and Senate under the State organization, a representative to Congress, and member from Ohio of the Senate of the United States, and Governor of the State. He has repeatedly been chosen elector of President heading the ticket for that purpose.

To the Governor of the N. W. Territory of the U. States.

The Petition of a number of inhabitants of the third entire range of the Miami purchase, near the Little Miami, humbly sheweth that there has not yet been any person commissioned as a Justice of the Peace in this neighborhood. Your petitioners consider themselves as laboring under some inconveniencies on that account, and

being met on this 30th day of August (for appointing and recommending military officers)— judged it proper to recommend a suitable person to the Governor for Justice of the Peace,— They were encouraged therein by the Governor in many instances, indulging the people with the privilege of appointing by sufferage for of fice. They therefore unanimously elected Jeremiah Morrow to recommend to the Governor, as a person suitable, and well qualified for the office of Justice of the Peace; and we, your petitioners pray that the Governor would grant him a commission as soon as convenient, if in your wisdom it may be proper—and your petitioners as in duty bound will ever pray.

August 31st, 1799.

CERTIFIED BY THE JUDGES OF ELECTION,
Alexander Kirkpatrick,
Jas. McClellan.

SUBSCRIBER'S NAMES.

Jas. Martin,	Jno. Lewart,
Sam'l. Erwin,	Jno. Linky,
Uzal Bates,	Thos. Espy,
Jno. Meeker,	Isaac Shields,
Jno. Patterson,	David Espy,
Jas. Keen,	Wm. Keefe,
Ares Keen,	James Shield,
Seth Bates,	Jas. Kenedy,
Jno. McClellan,	Jno. Parkhill,
Wm. Harper,	Allen Cullum,
Jno. Demass,	Thos. Crawford,
Wm. McClellan,	Daniel Sickle,
John Bigham,	Jas. Rolf,
Martin Fernor,	Dan'l. Briney,
Jno. Gaugh,	David Lemon ,
Samuel Leward,	Peter Tetrick.

Review.

TOWNDROW'S GUIDE to CALIGRAPHY.

Every branch of science, art, and literature is now systemized as well as simplified for the benefit of learners. It is to be regretted that the simplification does not extend to the nomenclature of subjects. A treatise on corns is now called podography. Mesmerism is neurology, and the caligraphy at the head of this article is in plain English, penmanship.

Mr. Towndrow has, with great propriety divided his guide into a series of seven books, calculated by example, to take the beginer from the elements of the art. No. 1 is designed for the formation of single letters and their components; and for the purpose of securing their proper proportion and space, the copies are ruled with transverse lines for the letter breadths.— This is obviously an important aid and guide to young beginers, with whom proper spacing is one of the last things mastered.

In No. 2, the principle of proper spacing is carried forward to words. In both these books the writer is confined to letters of one range in which there are none used above or below these letter lines. This appears to preserve to pupils the natural position of the hand in writing.

No. 3, takes us by monosylables into fine or joining hand. The spacing guides are employed here also. No. 4, is devoted to words of several syllables, capital letters, and figures. In No. 5, we have an entire line as copies. No. 6 is the same reduced to a finer size. No. 7. The final exhibition of the system is afforded in employing the learner to carry out by two line copies, any necessary continuous writing, an entire letter for example.

The principle of teaching habitually, correct notions of spacing each way, is never lost sight of in these books.

This series seems to be in general use in many important places in New England, and I do not see why it may not be found equally useful here.

INTRODUCTION to AMERICAN LAW, designed as a first book for students. By Timothy Walker, late Professor of Law, in the Cincinnati College. The objects of this publication appear to be two-fold. It is at once a guide-book for students, commencing the legal profession, and a compendious, general view of a subject of which it becomes necessary for the great mass of society to possess correct notions. It is not designed to supercede other elementary works, but to prepare the way for their study, and its claim, therefore is rather to usefulness than to novelty.

The great merit of such a work as far as the author succeeds in it, is obviously the condensation of the great variety of details that are embraced in the Science of Jurisprudence, within the compass of a single octavo in such shape that its elements and principles, shall bear in the compression the same proportion, as well as relation to each other, as they did to the subject at large. To present these in full and harmonious proportion, and at the same time with proper perspicuity, it must be apparent is no light undertaking. My own experience in statistics teaches that no man can condense accurately and proportionately on any given subject, without an ample understanding, not merely of that subject at large, but of all its details, and on a theme of such extensive range, as that which this book epitomises. The knowledge of the writer must be full, various and accurate, or he will not fail to manifest the fact, that however competent he may be to do justice to most of its parts, he is not equal to the whole.

It is hardly necessary here, where Judge Walker is so well and favorably known, to say how far he has succeeded in the effort. The popularity it possesses with better judges than I can assume to be, must be its recommendation to the public at large.

MR. CIST:

In your paper of the 4th inst., a writer over the signature of "A Citizen," attempts to defend the honor of the Queen City, from a reputed "slur," cast upon it by Mr. Wickliffe, in a letter that he wrote from Tuscany to the National institute at Washington, in which he charges upon Cincinnati the fact, that she is willing to claim her artists and their fame, but not to support them. The defence is a curious one, for the writer goes on to give the best of evidence, of the truth of Mr. Wickliffe's charge.

It is well known, that Kellogg was obliged to resort to his talents for music, in order that he might obtain the means necessary to defray travelling expenses. After years of absence he returned, expecting at least, to be able to make a living from the labors of his brush, but was sadly disappointed, and his desire to visit Florence, was fostered and aided, by his friends the other side of the Alleghenies.

"A citizen" asks "has Cincinnati given no evidence of a due appreciation of the talents of Powers?" I say, no—if a mere offer to purchase his Eve, by two or three individuals, is evidence, then the honor and credit of the self-styled Queen City, is easily satisfied. However, the offer is all that in this instance she can pride herself upon; and a proud claim she makes, indeed, to the credit of patronizing one of her own sons, along side of Charleston, S. C., who has sent him an order for a statue of Mr. Calhoun, and New Orleans, for one of Franklin. Mr. Preston has purchased of Mr. Powers, his statue of Eve, and "A Citizen," gets out of this part of his defence by saying, "Mr. Preston was among the first to appreciate the unrivaled genius of Powers." It appears he was first in his patronage too,—leaving the slow and reluctant charity of the Queen City to come after, when Mr. Powers had mastered his pecuniary difficulties, in a foreign land, and taken his station as one of the first sculptors of the world.

"A Citizen" would have done some credit to the city, if he had have mentioned the order sent to Kellogg by some of our public spirited citizens, for an Altar piece, for the new Cathedral. It is the first order of a public nature, that our citizens have sent, out of the city, and she should have the credit of it. It vexes me to see a city or State, after an individual has rendered himself famous by his unaided exertions and genius, meanly sneak in, and claim to divide with him his renown. "A Citizen," shall not aid in doing this, if my pen can prevent it—at least until they prove their claim to a just share, by their future conduct. We are too much in the habit of felicitating ourselves upon the fame of the Queen City, and her artists, without once thinking that we are enjoying ourselves at not one penny's expense.

If the truth were known, and the amount of capital we possess was made apparent to the world, upon which we are doing so large a business, we should be rendered bankrupt, without the aid of the "progressive Democracy."

VERITAS.

Cin. Dec. 6.

Improved Style of Building.

I have already referred to the houses built side by side on Fourth street, by Messrs. S. S. Smith and S. C. Parkhurst. The latter is now finished, and its appearance far exceeds my highest anticipations. The house has yet to be built which is to deprive this beautiful mansion of its character as the handsomest in exterior of any in the city, unless his neighbor, Mr. Smith whose dwelling has a larger front, and is getting ready in the same style, shall be found, when finished, to surpass it. I would call public notice to the elegant simplicity of the cornice, in the last named dwelling.

Fourth street is the only street in the city, running east and west, which is blocked at each termination, and it seems probable it will always remain thus. This circumstance protects it from being a thoroughfare for drays, wagons, and other loaded vehicles, which mar the cleanliness and smoothness, and block up the passages of many of our streets. It is destined, on this account, to become, for years, the most delightful promenade ground in the city.

Bills of Exchange.

In my article last week of Bank Note engraving, I had not room to speak of the specimens of Messrs. Rawdon, Wright and Hatch's check and promisory note work, of which there are various beautiful specimens in Cincinnati. I recollect, however, and would refer to one fine check pattern, which combines simplicity and elegance in design, with felicitous execution in a high degree. It may be seen and the blanks had at W. T. TRUMAN'S, Museum buildings, on Main street.

MARRIAGES.

In this city on Sunday evening, Dec. 8, Mr. THOMAS HILTON to Mrs. ANN MORTON, of this city.

DEATHS.

At his residence at Bethel, Clermont county, Ohio. last Saturday, the Hon. THOMAS MORRIS, formerly U. S. Senator from this State, and lately the candidate of the Liberty Party, for the Vice Presidency.

On Monday morning, Dec. 9, at about 3 o'clock, Miss ADELIA ANN GOSHORN, of Congestive Fever.

On Monday, 9th inst., Mrs. SARAH A. NELSON HARRIS, daughter of David Nelson, of Lancaster, Penn., and wife of Nathaniel Harris, of this city, in the 28th year of her age.

Recollections of a Voyage to Italy in 1800.

In the midst of all this confusion I saw a mischievous little dog, of about twelve or fourteen, who had displayed throughout the action as much glee as if it was all a frolic, make a dart at one of the port holes. "What is the matter, Ned?" said I. "Why, sir, one fellow was firing through the port, but he has my boarding-pike with him." After repeated attempts to board and finding his post very uncomfortable, our antagonist endeavored to cut loose his lashings; but in this he failed; all who attempted it were shot, till at last his men fairly took to their heels and ran below. Now would have been our turn to board, but we could not spare the men, as the other privateer had ranged itself along-side during the close contest with her companion, and threatened us with an attempt to board from that side. This was the first time during the action we were able to get all our guns to bear on her, and the firing had become very animated, when a slight squall (the breeze which was very light in the beginning of the action, had now freshened considerably) striking the head-sails, which hung flapping in all directions, brought our ship round, and the bowsprit of the privateer, which was lashed to her, unable to bear the strain, or probably being injured by our shot, swept short off, and we saw, in an instant, she was loose from us. Her crew perceived it also, and hastened on deck, made some sail on her, and stood away from us, attended by her comrade, and was saluted with three cheers by our men.

I have often been surprised at the length of time which we hear of battles lasting, and the little destruction of life on one or the other side. This action was fought nearly all the time close aboard, and it lasted upwards of eight glasses, that is four hours. Our ship was literally cut to pieces in her spars, sails, and rigging, and yet, to our astonishment, not a man but the Captain touched. I counted the marks of the grape shot in the lower masts, and the foremast, which had the least, had upwards of forty. The situation of the ship would be best known by the report of two naval officers, who made a survey of her when she arrived into Gibraltar, on account of the under-writers. I quote their words, for I preserved a copy of the document. After condemning almost all her spars, as unfit to be used again, they say: "We have likewise examined the standing and running rigging, and find the whole of it shot and cut, except of the former, the forestay, mainstay, and bob-stay; and of the latter, the starboard mainbrace, the reef-tackle and mizen stay-sail halyards." Those who know the rigging of a ship, will from such a statement conceive the situation of this one; and yet, I repeat it, not an individual of the crew was touched but the Captain. The loss of our antagonist was far different. We saw a number lying dead and wounded upon their decks, and many were pushed overboard from our stern and quarters, three of whom, with marks of boarding-pikes about them, floated into Gibraltar, where they were buried two of three days after. When the privateers left us, they stood over to Algesiras. While in Gibralter I saw a resident of Algesiras, who said he was there when they arrived, and that he saw twenty dead bodies landed from one of them.— Two men whom he had had in his employment, and who left him a few days previous,were with them; one was killed and the other sent to the hospital desperately wounded.

The privateers were full of men, so that a shot could scarcely go amiss. One of them mounted two twenty-four pounders, brass guns, on slides, and ten nine pounders, besides swivels; the other had ten guns, two of them like the others, working on slides. These guns, we were informed, were worked in both vessels by regular artillerists,nearly all of whom were killed. It might have been one of their officers that wore the epaulet. To soften the disgrace of the defeat our antagonists reported in Algesiras that our ship was a British transport of eighteen guns, with three hundred troops on board and that she had fought part of the action under American colors. The colors they could not deny, for they were plainly seen from Algesiras,although it was impossible to tell in their ragged state what they were. Our ship was unquestionably saved by the attention which had been paid to the strengthening of those parts which screened the men. A person could not spread his hand from the main chains aft, and on the stern without touching holes made by grape-shot; but the shot had penetrated only through the outer plank, and had lodged among the hoop poles. No man could have remained on deck, had not that protection been there. "The better part of valor," in more ways than one, "is discretion." The action saved the three brigs. They made the best of their way, and their sails were seen hull down to leeward.

After the action was over, I looked on my companions, and could scarcely tell one from the other; the smoke and powder having made them as dingy as so many colliers. The first thing to be attended to was to get something to eat and drink, and Ramsdell who took command of the ship, directed the cook and steward to produce their supplies, "make a bucket of grog steward" said he, "and my lads drink what you will, but take care not to drink too much; we may have something more to do yet; for I see some gun boats coming out of Algesiras. "Oh." replied one of the men, "I'll engage we can beat as many of those fellows as can lie between us and the rock." After a hearty breakfast, the men went to splicing the ropes, so as to set some sail that would assist them in getting the ship into the harbour of Gibraltar, from which we now saw a number of boats and barges putting off to us. They were soon alongside, and hailed to say that they would assist in towing us in. I then first saw that Ramsdell as well as myself, had made some remarks about their dilatoriness; for, he declined their offer in rather a gruff tone, and said their assistance might have been of some use an hour or two ago.

As soon as the anchor was dropped, the ship was filled with British officers; among whom was the Governor, General O'Hara, who having enquired for the person in command of the ship, said to him, "I am an old man as you see," taking off his hat, and showing his fine white hair, "and have seen many actions both by sea and by land, but I have never before seen a little ship so gallantly defended as this has been." And in the evening, the admiral on the station, whose name I forget, sent to request Mr. Ramsdell to go on board of his ship where he received him with great politeness, and said, "a letter from me may not be amiss, to show your owners and under-writers what I think of your conduct to day."—He then sat down and wrote a note, the purport of which was, that after a most gallant defence of several hours against a very superior force, within sight of the garrison of Gibraltar, and some of his majesty's ships laying there. Mr. Ramsdell had conducted his ship into port, in her dismantled state, in a very seaman-like manner. This, we supposed, was an unusual tribute of praise, elicited from an English Admiral in favor of the commander of a merchant vessel of a different nation.

Captain Hoggard languished for some time of his wound, and died. He was buried with great respect; a long train of British officers attending his funeral. The American flag was laid upon his coffin as a pall. It was intended to use the ship's ensign, but as there was only about two-thirds of it remaining, Ramsdell said it would look like ostentation to display the tattered banner, and another was borrowed for the occasion.

The cargo on board the ship was very valuable; much of it was insured in England, and I since heard that the underwriters at Lloyd's presented the widow of Captain Hoggard with one thousand dollars, and that some of our own Insurance Companies had made her presents also. These gifts are creditable to those who presented them, and have every useful effect upon the sailors who are expected to defend the vessel and cargo; besides which in the present case, the action saved the three American brigs that were astern of us when it commenced.

Conversing one day with Ramsdell about the action; "for my part," said he, "I had determined not to be taken alive. Last year I was taken in the straits. Our ship carried six guns; we had but twelve men; and we were attacked by two French privateers. I was first mate. I thought we could beat anything. I was foolish enough to be very anxious that they should come up with us, as the Captain carried all the sail he could, on the ship, to escape; but they outsailed us, and got alongside. They commenced firing at a distance, while we reserved our fire till they came close; we then took in sail, and prepared to engage, and I have often laughed frequently since at our preparation. Not knowing where we should be attacked, and wishing to be ready at all points, we run two guns out of the stern ports so that we had two astern, and but two on each side. When we rounded to, and the Captain asked, are you ready fore and aft! it was replied instantly, all ready, sir; and on his giving the word, well, *now, then*; we fired a whole broadside, two guns at them; bang! bang! and to it we went. The engagement lasted nearly three glasses, by which time we had three men killed, and our rigging very much cut up, and there appeared no hope of escape when the Captain said to me; 'Mr. Ramsdell, I am afraid we'll have to strike at last; for, if they kill many more of our men, we shall have none left to a work a gun." "I am afraid so" said I, "for we can make no sail on the ship," "Well, then, haul down the colors," said he; upon which I looked round, and behold! we had forgotten to hoist them, and had been fighting all the time without any; so, I had to go into the cabin, get the ensign and hoist it, and we fought another glass, during which we had another man killed, in order to let the Frenchmen see it, before we pulled it down. They boarded us directly from all sides and were so enraged at our resistance, and at having some of their men killed, that instead of giving us some credit, which, if they had been brave men, or anything but privateersmen, they would have done, the scoundrels beat those of us who were left, in such a manner I thought they would have killed every one of us. I swore then that I never would be taken alive, by those kind of land pirates."

I took up my quarters at a very pleasant hotel, and as the ship was obliged to remain there from the 20th of August to the 12th of October, to refit, I found sufficient amusement at so very interesting a place. Gibraltar has been sufficiently described, and my narration shall be confined to the incidents of the voyage. The Governor, as a mark of particular favor, permitted the ship to be hauled into the King's dock to be repaired, and directed that she should be supplied with anything she should want, and

which could not be obtained elsewhere, out of his majesty's stores. This was understood, however, not to be without paying for them; and I think it cost eight or ten thousand dollars to repair the damages done to the ship in part of one morning. The day after the action, I went on board to see how the ship looked, and to speak to the crew, several of whom I found with black eyes and the mark of bloody noses, and on inquiring the cause, was told, having too great an allowance of grog, the evening before, they had had a battle royal, but they said it was all for love, and there appeared to be no resentment harbored among them for the consequences. While the ship remained at Gibraltar, greater privileges of passing the gates of the garrison were given to her crew, than any other sailors; and it was found that men who belonged to other vessels, and who wished to pass the guard at unusual times, on being asked what ship they belonged to, were in the habit or answering: "The Louisa."

On the 12th of October, the ship being sufficiently repaired, we sailed from Gibraltar, bound up the Mediterranean, having two ships of eighteen guns each, from Liverpool, in company. In the evening of the next day, we discovered three sail of large ships standing across our course; one of them, a frigate, made a signal, which was obeyed by the two Liverpool ships, who hove to for her; but seeing that the direction in which the largest sailed would bring us along side of her, Captain Ramsdell thought he would prevent any delay by continuing his course, and speaking her instead of the frigate, for which the ships in our company had laid to; he accordingly stood on, and when within hailing distance, took his speaking trumpet, to be in readiness to answer a hail which he expected; but no hail was made and the strange ship which proved to be the Minotaur, of 84 guns, was manœuvred as if with the intention of running our ship down, which was very nearly effected.

It appeared afterwards, that the Louisa was mistaken for an English ship, and that the frigate had communicated that the three were all English, and according to etiquette to be preserved by merchant ships, to those of his majesty's navy, we should in such case have hauled up for the frigate to examine us. It was with difficulty that our ship avoided the immense bulk which brushed by us, our yardarms being about on a level with her quarter deck.

At the same time we were hailed with a long string of most virulent execrations, and asked why we had not hove to for the frigate. Ramsdell was a good-natured, good-hearted fellow; off duty, he would scarce have been known for a sailor; on duty, he felt "all as one piece of his ship."

His temper was roused by the apparent attempt to run us down, and when this was succeeded by the hail I have mentioned, he threw his trumpet on the deck, with the greatest indignation, and cried, "I'll be d——— if I answer such a hail as that! no, I'll not answer, if the ship is sunk under me for not doing it." At this moment we saw a boat lowered from the Minotaur. I said to him, "They will fire into us, if you don't heave to." We were then under top-sails. "I don't care," he answered, "I'll neither answer nor heave to; they may fire if they please." By this time, the boat, manned with fifteen or twenty men, was pulling after us; the evening was growing dark fast. The officer in the boat was continually calling out: "Why don't you heave to? Why don't you heave your main-top sail aback?" When we approached the large ship, Ramsdell had taken in sail, and intended to heave to for her. He now could easily, by hoisting sail, have left the boat which was in chase; but he would neither hoist nor take in sails: he merely said, let him come alongside if he can. At last, by great exertions, he got alongside. Ramsdell then ordered the main topsail aback, and lanthorn on deck; "but," he said, "throw no rope to them; let the fellow who commands come on board the best way he can; and suffer no one else to come on board." The officer, with great difficulty, scrambled up the side, and exclaimed as he reached the deck, "I never saw English sailors behave in this manner before." "You are not on board of an English ship," said Ramsdell. "how dared you to hail me in the manner you did?" "Not on board of an English ship?" said the officer with great astonishment, "what ship am I on board of?" "Of an American ship, and if I should treat you as you deserve, I would take you and your boat's crew along to the port I am bound to, and there let you find your way back to the ship as well as you could. "Sir," said the officer, "this has been a mistake; we were told by a signal from the frigate that this was an English ship." "And if it were an English ship, had you any right to hail her like a pirate! Go, sir, to your boat, and tell the Captain of your ship that I expected to find an English officer always a gentleman: and if he asks you who formed so wrong an opinion of him, tell him Charles Ramsdell, of the American ship, Louisa." By this time guns were fired and blue-lights burned for the boat; and the officer took his departure in a tone somewhat different from the one he had on his arrival.

Here we parted from the Liverpool ships. "If," said Ramsdell, "we are to be treated thus by every British ship of war we meet, merely because we are in their company, we had better cut the connexion, and have nothing to do with them."

On the following morning we fell in with a brig from Boston, bound up the Mediterranean; with the commander, who wished to keep in our company, Ramsdell was acquainted. The next morning we saw a vessel standing across our course, which when she approached to within about two miles, appeared to be reconnoitering us, upon which the ship laid to for her to come down. When she came within long gun shot, she showed Spanish colors; and fired a gun which we answered by showing our colors and firing a gun to leeward. We now found her to an armed ship, of eighteen guns, apparently full of men. She again stood towards us, and came to at about half gun-shot.

I was leaning on the quarters looking at her, when Ramsdell took me by the arm, and said, walk forward a little, the fellow will try and throw a shot between the main, and mizen, just over the place where you stand. Directly a gun was fired, the shot of which struck the water close by our stern, and the ship then came alongside of us, and sent her boat aboard. Our men were all at their quarters, I had taken my old station, and while their officers went into the cabin to look at the ship's papers. some of the Spaniards from the boat were suffered to come on deck. One of them asked a sailor, in very broken English, for some tobacco. "Here's my tobacco box," said the sailor, with a very sour phiz, taking a musket which stood by him, and striking the butt of it against the deck. "Is not this," asked the other, "the ship that had an action with two French privateers in the straits, about two months ago!" "Why do yon ask?" said the sailor. Because, I know her; I was on board of one of the privateers." "Ah ha! shipmate," said the tar, "if you know her so well you had better advise Jack Spaniard to keep a greater offing."

The officer had not been long in the cabin, before we heard some high words. It appeared, that on examining the ship's papers, he thought, or affected to think, that there was some deficiency in them, and talked of taking the ship in to Alicant. "The less you say on that subject the better," said our Captain, bundling up his papers; "Come, sir I must go on deck; I can't be detained here any longer by you;" on which he came from the cabin, very angry, and very unceremoniously leaving the other to follow. The officer, who was in high wrath at such cavalier treatment, went to his boat uttering something in Spanish, which I took to be a string of oaths, & saying something in broken English to Ramsdell, which he understood as a threat of firing into us. In the meantime, they in the Spanish ship had obliged the captain of the brig to go on board with his papers, which they detained, but suffered him to go back in his boat to the brig.

In this situation the Captain of the brig hailed, and said that the Spaniard had detained his papers, and was going to take the brig into Alicant. Ramsdell ordered four men to jump into the boat. "What, sir," said the first mate, shall I do, if they detain you?" "You can fight your ship, Mr. Bennet! "Oh, then I know what to do," said Bennet; and as soon as the Captain was on board the Spaniards, he ordered the main-topsail to be filled, and ranged along side, within twenty yards of the Spanish vessel, all hands at the guns, and a fellow who could play on the fife, piping Yankee Doodle. We learnt afterwards, that the Captain, on going into the cabin, saw the brig's papers on the table, and seized them without any ceremony. There were several officers, who attempted to stop him; but he drew his cutlass, and forced his way on deck. Here we saw a great bustle, and a number of muskets presented at him, and at the same time heard him hail, "Mr. Bennet, fire a broad side right where I stand." Bennet in a minute would have obeyed the order, but we supposed that some of the men who were hemming him in, understood what he said; for they gave way instantly, and he jumped on board the boat, and was rowed to the ship. As soon as he reached the deck, he hailed the brig—"Capt. Davis, I have got your papers; make sail, and if this scoundrel offers to prevent you, I will sink him." Davis was very alert in obeying the directions of his friend: no impediment was offered, and both vessels stood on their former course.

The conduct of the Spaniards, appeared to be very unjustifiable. The papers of both the ship and brig were all very full and fair. A number of Frenchmen were observed on board the Spaniard; and some of our men suspected it to be a French vessel; but in this I think they were mistaken. She was well armed, and some of our men, who were stationed in the tops, counted upwards of an hundred men on deck,— The conduct of Ramsdell, may be considered rash, but it was successful, and success is sometimes the only difference between the hero and madman.

There were many cruisers in our way up the Mediterranean, and I had several opportunities of observing the spirit of our crew. One day we discovered a sail standing for us. In a little time, she was ascertained to be a brig-of-war, of 18 guns. From her rigging the sailors said she was French. Ramsdell hailed the brig in company, and told her to get a considerable offing, in case the vessel coming down on us should prove an enemy. He then took in sail and hove to for her, all the men at their quarters. In this situation, the strange vessel manoeuvred as if to run astern of us. No colours were displayed on either side. Ramsdell suppo-

sing she would cross the stern of our ship, stationed some men so as to wear round at the moment she should do so, by which she would find herself along side instead of astern of us: but at the moment this was expected, she ran along side close aboard, and hoisted an English flag; but before the flag was displayed, and while she was ranging alongside, our sailors said, she is an English brig. She hailed, "Where are you from? Where bound to? What brig is that in company? Have you seen any Frenchmen?" And on receiving answers to these questions, she went off without making any further examination. I afterwards asked one of our sailors, "How did you know that to be an English brig?" "Oh, no Frenchman would run alongside of us as she did."—Well how did he know our ship to be an American? We might have been a French ship, and had a person who spoke English, on board to answer his questions." "Yes, that is very true; but he knew we were an American, for no French ship of our force, would have laid to for him to come alongside of us." I might mention in justification of our men's opinion of the rigging, that on our hailing to know what brig it was, we were answered the Mondovi, which from the name was probably a French built one.

At another time, we were chased, very perseveringly, the wind right ahead, from daylight till noon, by a corvette built ship. She tacked whenever we did, and outsailed us. The captain and supercargo of the brig in company, dined that day on board of the ship. By the time we sat down to dinner, the superiority of the vessel in chase could be fairly ascertained from the deck." The fellow will be up with us by dark," said Ramsdell, "whether Frenchman or not." However that need not spoil our dinner; we should fight none the better with empty stomachs." After dinner we went on deck; the chase was about a league from us. The captain said to our guests, "Gentlemen, you had better go on board your brig—keep a good distance to windward; and if you do so, and this should prove to be a Frenchman, though he may take us, I think we will put it out of his power to take you. At the rate we have gone, he would be alongside of us in the night; we cant avoid that; but as I like to see what I am about, I will save him the trouble of any further chase, and stand down to speak to him while we have daylight." Our guests went away in their boat; but the boat directly came back with the four men who had rowed it, and desiring to speak to the Captain, they told him, that with the permission of Captain Davis, they had come to offer their services on board, in case the ship in chase should prove to be an enemy. "You are honest fellows, stout sailors, and true yankees." said he; come on board, and take your stations, at the guns, we may have need of all the aid we can get before the day is over." All things were ready for action, and the ship under topsail stood down towards the chase. When we ranged alongside she proved like the former one, an English vessel; but we were told she had been taken from the French, and retained her original spars and rigging. An officer came on board from her, and seeing our men at their guns, turning round to the captain, and said, "surely sir, you did not intend to engage our ship with your force."— "Certainly, I did," said the captain, "but you know I did not think it one of his majesty's ships that we were running down upon."

One morning at day light, we found ourselves close by two armed cutters. They were smart looking black little things, exactly alike, of ten guns each, and full of men. They hoisted English colours. The one nearest hailed with a trumpet large enough, at least with a tone loud enough, to have belonged to a line of battle ship. "Ho! heave your main-top—sail aback, till I send my boat aboard of you!" Ramsdell, who was standing beside me looking at them, somewhat nettled by being hailed in that manner by a vessel of the size, imitating the provincial twang, generally supposed to belong to some of the eastern people, and drawling his words, replied,—"Ho! what's that you say neighbor?" Our neighbor who appeared to understand the derision intended, again hailed with a still deeper roar than the former one, "heave your main top-sail aback, or I'll fire a broad side into you!" "Why, now, I guess, cried Ramsdell, still drawling in his former tone, "that would be very unkind of you; for you might cut away some of my rigging, and then you would see who would pay the piper." By this time the other cutter hailed in a more respectful manner, and Ramsdell said, "Well, my little fellow, as you appear to know how to behave yourself, you may come on board."

On the 3rd of November, we arrived off Leghorn, where we we were brought to by the British frigate Mermaid, and informed that the French troops were in Leghorn, which rendered it impossible for the ship to enter, in consequence of which it was judged prudent to put into Elba till information could be obtained of the situation of Leghorn; the ship therefore bore away for that island, since celebrated as the short residence of the modern Charlemagne. On the evening of the 5th we came to in the outer harbour of Porto Ferrajo, with the small bower anchor; but that not holding, in consequence of heavy squalls, we let go the best bower also; notwithstanding which the ship began to drive, and before daylight, being almost on the rocks, under the light house, we were obliged to hoist both anchors, and get the ship under weigh in order to take a station higher up in the harbour, where the bottom might be better holding ground. It blew in violent squalls, and we were obliged to tack from point to point, making little or no headway. Just at day light, the fort fired a gun, without shot; we supposed it to be a morning gun, and paid no attention to it: but in a few minutes afterwards, as we were tacking ship, two or three more, shotted, were fired in quick succession at us. We could not heave to; the ship was in the greatest danger of going on the rocks at the time, and the stupid fellows in the fort appeared to think that we were escaping out of instead of trying to get into the harbour. In this dilemma, I told the captain that if he would order some men into the boat, I would endeavor to stop the firing on us. The men were sent into the boat, and I jumped in after, and told them to row right up to the battery, on arriving at which, I was directed to go round a point higher up the harbour, to the officer of the port. This I did, and told him who we were, and what was our difficulty. I was treated with great politeness, and asked if I wished any refreshment; I requested some coffee and breakfast for my men, and was admiring the promptitude and alacrity with which my request was granted, when a guard of soldiers entered the room and told me rather roughly, that I and my men, must go with them, which I did without hesitation, thinking that they wished to conduct me to the governor or some superior officer of the place, instead of which, they led us to a very uncomfortable looking mansion, whose interior did not belie its outside, consisting of one large room floored with brick, and desiring us to walk in, fairly turned the key on us. The grating of the lock made me whistle a long *whew,* and called forth other exclamations from my companions. My anxiety was shortly after very much increased by hearing several cannon fired in the direction I supposed the ship to be. I was utterly unable to conjecture what was the cause of this, and remained in great uncertainty and anxiety for an hour or two, when one of the men peeping through a crack in the door saw an English naval officer at a little distance, which he informed me of, and knocking at the door, I desired the sentinel to call him to me. He was the Captain of a frigate, then lying in the harbour. I told him who I was, and the awkward situation in which I was placed. Make yourself easy, sir, said he, you shall be here but a very few minutes. He left me, and directly after the British consul came, who told me that I and my men were at liberty, and desired me to accompany him to a hotel near his home, where I would find all the accommodations I might want. From him I learnt that our ship had been in great danger of being driven on the rocks, which was the occasion of her firing several guns, as signals of distress. She had let go her anchors, but drifted with them all ahead, in consequence of the extreme violence of the squalls, and was obliged to cut her cables. A number of boats had gone to her assistance, among which were four from the British frigate, Sancta Theresa, the master of which had got on board of her, but being unable to gain his boat, had been taken out to sea. "But," said he, "she will soon be back, and in the mean time command whatever is in my power to procure you." I felt very grateful for such kindness from a perfect stranger, and proffered in a situation where it was so much needed.

The next day came, and the next, and the next, but no ship came with them. I ascended the highest ground several times a day, and looked out for her with great solicitude. On the evening of the third day, while I was pacing backwards and forwards on the pavement before the hotel, hearing the rapid approach of horses, I looked up, and behold, the Captain leaped from a horse and seized me by the hand. "Why, Ramsdell! where did you come from? where's the ship?" At Port Lougone, two leagues from this, where having lost all our anchors, and twenty times escaped the rocks, we at last brought the ship up with a couple of guns instead of anchors. You'll see the master of the frigate, whom we took along with us, and he'll tell you that he never had such a jaunt in all his life.— But here is a bundle of your clothes; I thought you would want them, and be rather uncomfortable till you knew what had become of us, therefore, as soon as the ship was secured, I got these rags, and that fellow who can't understand a word I say to him, and we have come here like a couple of flying proas."

From this place a few days afterwards, I crossed in a sparonaro to Piombino in Tuscany.

Poor Ramsdell! he was an excellent seaman, possessed of the greatest presence of mind, of the most determined courage, and the most affectionate heart, I frequently delight in recollecting him. It is that feeling which induced me to write this narrative of the events which occurred while I was in his company, and in which I have been obliged to mention myself oftener than I would have done, could I have avoided it.

I say poor Ramsdell! The next voyage was his last. He had command of a ship, and is supposed to have been lost in a severe gale of wind in the Atlantic. Neither vessel nor crew were ever heard of.

I know nothing of his parentage or connexion, except, that they lived in Nantucket.

R.

Dying Operations.

This is one of many descriptions of business carried on in Cincinnati, the importance of which is underrated because the public at large is not familiar with its actual character and extent, it being usually considered merely the redying of stained or faded articles of dress of small value, enabling many persons thereby, to preserve appearances at a trifling expence.

The dying business of this city employs eighteen hands in some twelve establishments. I propose by way of illustration of the whole business to sketch the dye-house operations of WM. TEASDALE, the most extensively engaged in this line of business.

His establishment is at the corner of Gano and Walnut streets, and employs five to six hands constantly. It is one of the oldest dye-houses in Cincinnati, and Mr. T. has resided on Walnut street some ten years.

There are here eight copper dye kettles, of sizes varying from 75 to 350 gallons with furnaces to each, besides a boiler of 250 gallons capacity to supply steam for the cylinders on which the work undergoes its finishing processes. The aggregate capacity of the kettles is 1250 gallons. These cylinders, which are copper, with tinned surfaces, are on a scale equally large. They are four in number, and range from 5 to 7½ feet in length, with a circumference, of from 5 to 10 feet each.

The articles brought in for dying, after undergoing scouring where necessary, are plunged in the dye-kettles, and after undergoing that operation, are then rinsed out and taken to the dying house. This is a room warmed by flues carried under the floors, which of course serves to warm every part of it. The dyed goods are then taken up stairs where they are carefully examined and if found perfect are wetted and spread upon the cylinders, where under the contractile influence of heat the work is finished. Lastly the goods are taken to the presses where they are disposed between press papers as book work sheets from the printing office.

I have said that it is a mistake to suppose that it is the dying of second hand articles, which constitutes the principal, or indeed any important part of this business, although such an impression is generally prevalent. Large quantities of silk, woolen and cotton goods which have been discolored by keeping or accident, or have become unfashionable in color or pattern are redyed, being sent by storekeepers, not only in Cincinnati, but from cities and country towns abroad, extending as far off as Cleaveland to the Lakes; Pittsburg to the east, and Nashville, St. Louis and New Orleans to the west and south-west, with all the intermediate places

The redying of merchandize injured by casualties to steamboats alone is a heavy item in the business. It is a great mistake which prejudices the public mind on this subject, in supposing that these fabrics are usually dyed in the raw material. Silks are so undoubtedly, but it is rare that either cotton or woolen goods are dyed otherwise than in the web or cloth, although various artifices are resorted to on this point to deceive purchasers.

Mr. Teasdale's dye stuffs, soap, &c. cost him annually more than one thousand dollars. His consumption of stone coal during the same period is more than 2500 bushels.

Every lot of goods—not each piece, but all that is left at one time, which is occasionally ten or fifteen pieces, is numbered and delivered by that number on the production of a ticket given the owner on receipts of the articles. These numbers extended in 1842 to 4064, in 1843 to 4641, and will this year exceed 4850.

Besides these dying operations an extensive business is carried on here in renovating or scouring by machinery, carpets for families, hotels and steam boats. During each summer season, more than 3000 yards pass through his hands for this purpose.

As to the quality of the work it is at least equal to any turned out in the Atlantic cities. Articles of his dying exhibited at the fair of the Mechanics Institute have taken the premium for three successive years. Those who noticed his sewing silks at the last exhibition will recollect the richness of tint and glossy appearance of that article.

The preparations for executing job work in Mr. Teasdale's dye-house have been pronounced by persons from New York and Boston, familiar with the subject, to be on a scale as extensive as any in the United States, and the kettles and cylinders of greater capacity than have fallen under their notice, in any similar establishment.

Relics of the Past.
Jas. Henry to Arthur St. Clair, Jr. Esq.
DETROIT, September 12th, 1799.

DEAR SIR:

I received yours of the 17th August, which gave me pleasure. I shall make it a point to give the information you request to Lafferty, &c. I have just returned from a visit to my friends in Pennsylvania; was in Philadelphia two weeks, great apprehensions of the fever—no public amusements; as I passed through the country observed many in military habits;—recruiting parties in every village. I have a younger brother appointed a Captain in the 10th regiment, who has nearly recruited a company at Lancaster—seen all our old friends at Pitts-burgh, did not spend much time with them; division among them since last election for Congress; was much surprised on my return to this part to hear you had no circuit this Summer; often thought of you during my absence, re gretting it so happened; as I supposed then I should not have the pleasure of seeing you when at Detroit. I now anticipate that satisfaction in the Spring, when, with the assistance of a bottle or two of wine, and a *quantum sufficit* of segars, we will settle the interests of the contending parties in Europe, not forgetting to secure those of our own country. The parties in Pennsylvania are indeed making every exertion each to secure the election of its favorite candidate. I hope for the honor of the State, that Mr. Ross may be elected. I was almost ashamed to acknowledge myself a Pennsylvanian, after the second insurrection in Northampton county.

We jog on here at an easier gait than we of late have been accustomed to—not so much cavilling and disputing: you will have the pleasure of seeing Col. Strong and Mr. Sibley, who will give you our domestic news.

Do, when you have a leisure moment, write to me; it will give pleasure to a man, who highly esteems you. Make my respectful compliments unto your father, and believe me, dear Arthur,   Always yours, &c.
                    JAS. HENRY.

Levels in the West.

The following levels may be useful to refer to, as exhibiting the general surface of the West, and I have, therefore, put them on record in this shape:

Lake Ontario is	282	feet above tide water.
" Erie	283	do
" Huron	296	do
" Superior	314	do
Beaver, Penn.	127	feet above lake Erie.
Akron, Ohio,	395	do
St. Mary's, O.,	398	do
Fort Wayne, Ind.,	181	do
Lockport, Ill.,	30	do
Ft. Winebago, W.T.	144	do

The general fall of the Ohio River, is thus pointed out:

Low water in the Ohio, at Pittsburg, 140 feet above Lake Erie.

Portsmouth, 94 feet. Cincinnati, 133 feet. Evansville, 245 feet—all *below* Lake Erie.— This is of course a fall in the River Ohio, from Pittsburg to Evansville, of 335 feet, in 792 miles, equal to but six inches in the mile. This is a descent much less than is really supposed to be the fact, but these are the results of actual surveys and measurements, in the Surveyor General's office for this District.

Relics of the Past.

Gen. Anthony Wayne, to Col, John Armstrong.
The following letter speaks for itself. I attach a *fac simile* of Wayne's signature as a specimen, not merely of the penmanship, but as a sign manual, that corresponds exactly with the bold and dashing character of the writer.

CAMP HOBSON'S CHOICE.
May 12, 1793.

DEAR SIR:

I have been favored with a copy of a correspondence between you and Gen. Wilkinson, also with your letters subsequent thereto of the 28th March, 2nd ultimo and 7th instant.

I sincerely lament the loss of an officer of known bravery and experience, especially at this *crisis* when we really are in want of many such.

But your own act of resignation, together with your letter and certificate paving the way to it. copies of which are enclosed, have effectually foreclosed any further military investigation on this subject.

Your resignation was also announced to me by the Secretary of war, in a letter of the 20th ultimo, in which is the following paragraph, viz:

"I have received letters from Gen. Wilkinson of the 4th March, by which it appears that Armstrong has resigned. I conceive in case of vacancies, the officers clearly entitled to those vacancies are to fill them as soon as they occur."

Thus you see this business is done with, but as you express a wish to make another campaign Que: could you—or would you, undertake to raise a corps of mounted volunteers, for a given period—whose pay and emoluments will be as follows, viz:

The non-commissioned officers, one dollar per diem, and the privates 75 cents, each person finding his own horse, arms and accoutrements, and at his own risque—and 75 cents per diem in lieu of rations, and forage provided he furnish himself therewith. The President, was by law authorized to appoint the officers—that power he has vested in me, their pay and other emoluments, exclusively of fifty cents per diem for the use and risk of their horses,—will be the same as that of officers of corresponding rank in the Legion.

Let me hear from you upon this subject, and believe me to be with much esteem and regard

Your most ob't.
and humble servant,

CAPT. JOHN ARMSTRONG.

The Fulton Bagging Factory.

This is the title of a large manufacturing establishment, which ought rather to have been called the *Cincinnati* Bagging Factory, as its whole operations are within the city limits. Its site has been for many years the theatre of manufacturing business, originally as a woollen factory, then a machine shop, and in later days occupied as a factory of rail-road cars. It was originally a moderate sized building, and for various reason suffered to become dilapidated; but was some three years ago rebuilt and enlarged, by Messrs. WM. M. WALKER & Co., and converted into a Bagging Factory, on the most extensive scale. Another chapter in the vicissitudes to which it has been exposed is, that on the morning of Sabbath, the 6th October, it was again subjected to the ravages of fire; in the destruction by that element of SCHULTZ's *Brewery*, and a factory or two to the west. This damage which pretty much destroyed the upper stories of the building, with their contents, was, however, promptly and thoroughly repaired, and on a late visit of mine to the premises, there appeared hardly any vestige of the injury left. A single publication in the *Cincinnati* ATLAS of a year ago, comprises, however, all that the Cincinnati press has ever published of the character and operations of this extensive and important manufactory; I feel, therefore, disposed to gather what has been thus published, enlarging and correcting the article, by bringing it down to the close of 1844, and leaving my intelligent readers to draw their own inferences on the subject.

The FULTON BAGGING FACTORY is 137 by 40 feet on its floors, and three stories in height;—the third being occupied as a machine shop, in which the Company has built her entire machinery. These consist of thirteen looms and one hundred and four spindles, with the necessary frames for preparing the hemp for spinning.

The process of manufacturing commences on the lower floor, where the hemp, in the condition in which it comes from the farm, passes through a Cylinder Heckle, which reduces and straitens the fibre, and returns it in a lap some eighteen feet long. It is then successively subjected to a large and small drawing frame, from which last it passes out in a continuous stream,folding over and over, like liquid iron at furnaces, into light cans or boxes, in which it is carried to the spinning frames. It is then spun, warped, dressed, and woven on power looms, and lastly calendered, and formed into rolls, by a process which serves at the same time to measure it. The whole of these operations. *including the measurement*, being performed by steam. The spinning frames have machinery connected with them, which indicate, with perfect accuracy, each individual's amount of work.

This establishment consumes 800 tons, equal to 6300 bales of Hemp per annum, and the raw material is supplied from Kentucky and Missouri, in perhaps, equal quantities. It produces annually, 800,000 yards Bagging and 100 tons of Bale Rope. These statistics proclaim the magnitude of the business—what the character of the manufacture is, may be inferred from the fact that there is not a single piece of Bagging unsold at this time. It is at once more even in texture and uniform in weight, than that which is spun and woven by hand, being forty-five inches wide, and weighing twenty-six ounces to the yard, and, without any doubt, they turn off here more than in any factory in the world where Bagging is of equal substance.

The Factory gives employment to fifty-five girls, and forty-five men and boys. The prices I understand to be at Lowell, 1.75 cents per week as the nett rate of wages,exclusive of boarding, for the girls. and 70 cents per day as that of the men,

ROBERT C. WINTHROP, of Boston, gives the following as the average of wages in the Merrimack mills, in the month of June, in five successive years, viz:

1840. Females $1,92 per week.
" Males 80 cts. perday. $20 80 month.
1841. Females 2,27 "
" Males 78 " 20 02 "
1842 Females 2.30 "
" Males 84 " 21 81 "
1843 Females 2.16 "
" Males 79 " 20 54 "
1844 Females 2.24 "
" Males 87 " 22 66 "

The Northampton Gazette states that the females in the Ware factories have $4 per week —board $1,25 out; males $1 per day, board at $1,75 per week out.

As a friend to the cause of domestic manufacturers, while I rejoice to learn that the proprietors are doing well, I feel a deeper sympathy in the welfare of the larger class—the operatives—and find that while the expenses of living to a family are much less here than in Massachusetts, the wages are fully as high. On this point I will add one fact. A little girl at this establishment, quit work on Saturday, at 2 o'clock, having woven thirty cuts, equal to 1530 yards from Monday morning for which she was paid twenty cents per cut, being six dollars for less than as many days' employment.

Under the foreign competition in Bagging,following the peace of 1815,the article was brought down to fifty cents per yard, at which price our Manufacturers to a great extent gave up the contest. But the tariff of 1816 invigorated them for another struggle; and, under the protection offered by the tariffs of 1824,1828, and even the Compromise Act of 1832 and more lately by the tariff of 1841, with improvements made in machinery, the home competition has reduced the price of Bagging from fifty cents to eleven cents —a rate which cuts off entirely the Dundee and India manufacture.

As the article of Bagging and Bale Rope forms an important element of national industry and a covering to two and a half millions of bales of cotton, the great staple of the United States, it may be of interest to present its statistics:

	YARDS.
350 Hand Looms in Kentucky, make	6,880,000.
Fulton Bagging Factory, Cincinnati,	800,000.
Power Looms at Maysville	700,000.
Do at Louisville	1,400,000.
Do at New Albany	200,000.
Do in Missouri	220,000.
Yearly manufactured,	10,200,000.

This is within three million yards of what is annually required for the cotton crop; and the deficit is supplied with foreign Bagging, which still finds its way to the South Atlantic ports, where they have so long been accustomed to a lighter and closer fabric, that American Bagging has hitherto stood no chance, although, unquestionably, a better, as well as a cheaper article.

The factory is warmed by steam, which secures an uniform temperature, throughout the rooms,much to the health and comfort of the operatives. It is also lighted by Gas of its own manufacture, in which respect it stands alone among the various Bagging Factories of the United States. The value of these means of light and heat, as regards economy, safety from fire, and efficiency, is very great. The Gas works, which are on a novel principle, and constructed by Mr John Crutchett, lately settled in Cincinnati, are remarkable for simplicity and ingenuity, occupying in the Engine room, a space not greater than four by eight feet. They are of 500 burner capacity, although 80 burners are actually in use, and the raw material employed is lard, of which an inferior quality answers every purpose —of this article, twenty-five pounds are consumed every night. The Gas works were put in operation in less than three weeks from their commencement.

A great saving is effected by the use of Gas. Twelve hours make a days work, but from the first of October to the first of April, after allowing for meals, the average of sufficient day-light to work by, is not over eight hours and a half, so that the Gas affords an actual saving during that period, of more than one fourth the entire expense of carrying on the Factory.

Within the last year by the enlargement of the Gasometer the establishment has been enabled to use Gas cold, which has effected a saving of 50 per cent, in the expense of the article. In other words 80 burners cost them one fourth less than 55 did, a year since.

One respect in which I contemplate our manufacturing industry gives it a strong claim to my good wishes. The extent to which we have been able in the United States, to prosecute successfully so many branches of mechanical ingenuity, in the face of the lower wages, redundant capital, and governmental patronage of Europe, especially Great Britain, so as in fact to exclude the foreign manufacture, has satisfied me, as it ought to satisfy others, that it is not necessary, even in order to make money out of them, to grind and degrade the working classes of society. In Cincinnati, at any rate, operatives can be found, who occupy their proper position in the community, respected for their industry, energy, and steadiness.

In connection with this article, I may state that in less than sixty days, a new Bagging Factory of equal capacity and extent with the present will be put in operation, at the west end of Covington, opposite our city, by M. J. Blair, one of our own citizens.

Early Bank Dealings in the West.

The readers of American history will recollect the stamp act, the earliest in the long list of grievances which finally drove our fathers to arms and to the establishment of our American independence. Such is the force of names and the influence of associations in the mind of man, that a violent prejudice against the raising duties by stamps upon promissory and negotiable notes, has always existed in the bosoms of the American people, and although twice in our national history, the *quasi* war with France, under the administration of the elder Adams, and again during the last war with Great Britain, resort was had to this means of raising a revenue; it contributed greatly to break down the Administration in the first case, and required all the popularity and strength of the then dominant party to sustain themselves under the odium of the measure. As this species of taxation lasted but a short period in each case; there are thousands in the community ignorant of the fact that such stamp duties ever existed here. The following are evidences not only of that fact, but are curiosities in early dealings and early banking in many of their features.

PHILADELPHIA, JULY 21 1801.

Six months after date I promise to pay Messrs Boggs and Davidson or order without defalcation, One hundred and twenty-nine dollars and sixty-nine cents value received.

JOHN M'CULAGH.

Stamp with 13 stars in centre. "COM. REV. U. S. "XXV CENTS" National eagle with 25 cts. in a scroll.

CINCINNATI, February 19th 1802.

I proms for to Pay or Cause for to Be payd unto John M'Cullagh the Just and full Sum of thurtey six Dollars the tanth of october Naxte in Suing the Date heer of and I will Dalevr good flowar according to the Layes of our tartary at Market prize at the mouth of grate Mama the is to be recd in Decharge of the above Sum.

ateste,   TOM SMITH.

SAM'L M'CULLAGH.

Eagle and Shield. "TEN CENTS." Stamp as above. "X CENTS."

CINCINNATI, March 19th 1816.

Thirty Days after date we or Either of us promise to pay Ethan Stone for the use of the Bank of Cincinnati twelve Dollars without Defalcation Negotiable and Payable at Said Bank, for value rec'd.

CHARLES TUSTIN.

EDW'D HORROCKS.

Eagle and Shield. "FIVE CENTS

There is one matter worthy of notice in this document. It is endorsed Charles Tustin 19 | 23 April, being four days of grace. Was his the bank custom in those days?

Steamboat Yorktown.

It is not often I notice in print the steamboats, of which it suffices to say generally that they always attest the skill and ingenuity of our Cincinnati mechanics. But the YORKTOWN, a newly finished boat, which leaves our wharf this day for N. Orleans, is such a paragon among the travelling palaces of the Ohio and Mississippi, that I cannot forbear sketching some of her distinctive points.

The YORKTOWN has been just built and finished here, for plying regularly between Cincinnati and New Orleans. Her hull was built by Litherbury & Lockwood; joiners, Kessler and Funk. Engine builders, Niles & Co. Her bell of 450 lbs. weight and fine tone, from the foundery of G. W. Coffin. Her measurements and equipments are as follows. Length 182 feet, breadth of beam 31 feet, water wheels 28 feet in diameter, length of buckets 10 feet 3 inches, and 28 inches wide. Hold 8 feet. She has 4 boilers, 30 feet long, and 42 inches in diameter, double engines, and two 24 inch cylinders, with 9 feet stroke; she draws 4 feet light, and hardly more than 8 feet with 550 tons freigh', her full cargo. She has 40 state rooms and of course 80 berths, all appropriated to cabin-passengers; the boat officers being provided with state rooms in the pilot house. This arrangement affords the officers opportunity of attending to their appropriate duties without the annoyance and interference of others and dispensing with that *regular nuisance* the SOCIAL HALL protects the gentlemen and especially the ladies on board, from the effluvia of Cigars, which, in ordinary cases taints the whole range of the cabins.

The state rooms are spacious, capable of being well ventilated, with commodious stools which afford seats independent of those for the tables. Each berth has its upper and lower mattress.— To the ladies cabin there are permanent skylights, and a lower range of moveable lights by which the supply of warm or fresh air in the ladies rooms is regulated at pleasure. The cabin seats are armed chairs, which being two feet in breadth afford ample space at the table, and protect the feeble and infirm from being crowded or elbowed at meals. The chains and other iron fastening work usually projecting in every direction to the annoyance of passengers at all times—at night especially—are here disposed of out of the way and generally out of sight. Such are the arrangements for convenience and comfort on board the YORKTOWN, that there are few persons who command at home the *agremens* which are provided here, and the only thing I object to in the boat, is the danger of its rendering her passengers unsatisfied with the measure of their enjoyments at home. by the force of contrast. Sound judgment and taste have dictated all the details. Every thing about her is of the best quality and highest finish, and strength, convenience and elegance are every where apparent. The floors are carpeted in exquisite taste. Even the folding doors which admit to the ladies cabin, with their rich pannel work can hardly find a rival in the mansions of the aristocracy in our Atlantic cities.

The YORKTOWN is supplied with two of Evans' Safety Guards, one to each outside boiler, and her tiller and bell ropes are all of wire.— An hundred feet of hose is ready at a moment's notice to convey a torrent of water to the most extreme part of the boat. The hurricane roof is covered with sheet iron, and a half a dozen water casks, constantly filled, are at hand there, for immediate use in case of fire. The seventy-two table chairs are connected with life preservers beneath the seats, of such buoyancy that each chair has been tested to float two persons. All the doors and window shutters—nearly five hundred in number—are on litting hinges and can be detached at a moment's notice. Each of these can buoy up a passenger in case of necessity until assistance could arrive.

Her Engine is equal in all respects to the general superiority of this boat over her rivals in this trade. I cannot go into details on this and other points without extending this article beyond reasonable bounds, but must not, however, omit to notice as of great importance that her shafts and cranks are of *wrought iron*. This is the first introduction of wrought iron for such purposes on steamboats. Steam boat shafts should never have been made of any thing else.

I hazard nothing in the assertion that there has never yet floated a boat equal in all respects to the Yorktown upon the Ohio or Mississippi, and that the whole building, finishing and furnishing interest at Pittsburg, Wheeling, Louisville or St. Louis may be defied to exhibit her match. It will be time enough for her to be surpassed here when she can be rivaled elsewhere. If this statement appears extravagant to any man of intelligence, let him visit the boat, and if he does not find my details correct, and fifty things besides found equally remarkable and interesting which I have not space to describe, I will again defer the conclusion to which I have come as to her superiority in every thing, almost, to any boat afloat or in port.

The YORKTOWN has not cost her owners, Kellogg & Kennett and T. J. Halderman, less than 33,000 dollars. She will be commanded by the last named gentleman, with Mr. George Gassaway, clerk.

Captain Halderman has enjoyed the reputation for years of being one of those favored individuals, who are always in luck. Whenever he is ready to start he always takes a rise of water along; has generally his share of passengers and if these happen to be few in port, he is sure to overtake vessels aground, or lying by with broken shafts, or in some difficulty which gets him their passengers. Let who may, miss, he always hits the right time, and the right port. I never understood how he enjoyed that reputation, till I visited and examined the *Yorktown*.— All his arrangements are such as to command preference and success, as far as man can control events. This is the secret, probably, of his *luck*, as far as the luck exists.

French Literature.

I regret to see advertised, by book-sellers as respectable as Desilver and Burr, of our city, a French periodical "*L'Echo des Feuilletons,*" of which I ask and will accept nothing further as evidence of its character than that the infamous Madame George Sand is announced as one of the contributors. This woman, in whom an immoral life well illustrates immoral principles, has done more to corrupt the youth of Paris, at the present day, than any one of her cotemporaries. If the 40,000 subscribers in that city attest the general corruption of morals there, and 9000 more in our own country, expose their families to the same influence, it is sufficiently to be deplored. For myself, as the conductor of a periodical, I lift the warning voice to caution my readers how they suffer the writings of Madame Sand, and her kindred spirits of evil, to enter their families under the seductive plea "that being led on unconsciously by the charms of the subject, they will, unawares, make rapid progress in the language." Rather, I apprehend, to make rapid progress in losing that delicacy and purity which is the pride and glory of American women.

Review.

URANOGRAPHY, or a *Description of the Heavens!* 12mo. pp. 366, and *Atlas of the Heavens* by E. Otis Kendall, Professor of Mathematics and Astronomy, in the Central High School of Philadelphia.

A popular treatise of astronomy, including, the modern discoveries, and embracing the observations of the elder and younger Herschell,in England and Struve and Maedler,in Germany,has long been a desideratum for the advanced classes in astronomy, in our Schools and Colleges. These with the "Atlas of the Starry Heaven," by the celebrated Littrow, serve to give a distinctive character to this treatise on astronomy, which, with the "Atlas," will be found, I doubt not, better adapted for a text book in schoolst than those to which we usually have access.

The publishers deserve credit for the character of the paper and typography of the publication, and the plates or drawings, as the author terms them, which illustrate it, in my judgment, surpass in clearness and beauty, anything of the kind in use.

The Widow's Mite.

"I want to give the widow's mite," said an old lady worth her thousands, as she handed *ten cents* to give the bread of life to millions perishing in ignorance and sin.

Said a gentleman of a large income, "I suppose I must give my mite," as he very reluctantly handed a *dollar* to one collecting funds to send the gospel to the destitute.

It is not uncommon for those who receive the offerings of the people for the Lord's treasury, to hear such allusions to the poor widow whose benevolence is recorded in Mark xii. 41–44.— The example is evidently quoted with self-complacency, and as an apology for giving a very small sum, far below the ability God has given. Is it intended as a cloak for their covetousness, or do they really think that the *smaller* the sum the more acceptable it is to God? It was not the *smallness* of what she gave that drew forth the commendation of the Savior, but the greatness of her benevolence. The rich gave of their abundance, a part only of their surplus; she gave all she had, yea, all her living.

The measure of benevolence is not the amount *given*, but the amount *left* from which the offering is taken. No person can exceed the poor widow in benevolence. How few come up to her! How many would call it an act of imprudence to imitate her! None can properly claim to imitate her till they give all they have, *yea, all their living.*   A. S.

Steam made Putty.

I find Steam becoming applied to a great variety of purposes as a working agent, of which the last generation never dreamed. One of these is to work up Putty, in which there is so much labor saving, that Mr. J. Glascoe, as appears by his advertisement in the Cincinnati Gazette, is able to sell the article at 4 cts. wholesale, and 4½ and 5 cts in smaller quantities,less than one half what the article sold at a year or two since. At these prices Cincinnati must supply putty for the entire region north, west and south of us.

Some idea of the reduction in prices building materials, are constantly undergoing here, may be formed from the fact that the putty used in the glazing of the Cincinnati College cost at *wholesale* twenty-five cents per lb., six times the price at which Mr. G. is selling an article of equal quality.

Chinese Gratitude.

An English merchant of the name of C——, resided in Canton and Macao, where a sudden reverse of fortune reduced him from a state of affluence to the greatest necessity. A Chinese merchant, named Chinqua, to whom he had formerly rendered service, gratefully offered him an immediate loan of ten thousand dollars, which the gentleman accepted, and gave his bond for the amount: this the Chinese immediately threw into the fire, saying, "When you, my friend, first came to China, I was a poor man, you took me by the hand, and assisting my honest endeavors, made me rich. Our destiny is now reversed; I see you poor, while I am blessed with affluence." The bystanders had snatched the bond from the flames; the gentleman sensibly affected by such generosity, pressed his friend to take the security, which he did, and then effectually destroyed it. The disciple of Confucius, beholding the increased distress it occasioned, said he would accept of his watch, or any little valuable, as a memorial of their friendship. The gentleman immediately presented his watch, and Chinqua, in return, gave him an old iron seal, saying, "Take this seal, it is one I have long used, and possesses no intrinsic value, but, as you are going to India to look after your outstanding concerns, should fortune further persecute you, draw upon me for any sum of money you may need, sign it with your own hand, and seal it with this signet, and I will pay the money."—*Forbes' Oriental Manners.*

CINCINNATI MISCELLANY.

CINCINNATI, JANUARY, 1845.

The Fifth Ward.

My enumeration of this Ward is as follows Public buildings 13; Pork and ware houses, dwellings, offices, work shops, mills, &c., 1552, of which there are bricks 825, frames 727.

Of these buildings there were at the close of

1842	Bricks	649	Frames	663	Total	1312.
Built in '43	"	85	"	35	"	120.
" '44	"	125	"	51	"	176.
		859		749		1608.

The public buildings in the Fifth Ward are, one of the Public Schools on Ninth street; a school for German Catholic children, Talbott's school room, and the Methodist Female Seminary, tho last three of which are new buildings.— The German Methodist, on Race street, the Ninth street Baptist, St. Mary's church—Roman Catholic, St. John, Zion and Northern German Lutheran churches, one on Bremen st. one on Sixth street, and the last on Walnut street, the German Reformed, corner Walnut and Thirteenth, and the True Wesleyan on Ninth street. The Methodist Book Rooms, and an Engine House.

Of these Zion and the True Wesleyan are erections of 1844. Three fourths of the buildings put up this year in this ward are in the section south of the canal. The reverse was the case last year. Much of the building from 1840 to 1842 inclusive was put up by persons, of limited resources, or built as a means of employment, under the great depression of business during those years. But the buildings of later date not only in this ward, but throughout the city have been built for capitalists as investments, or for men of resources, for their own occupancy, and the buildings of this year are, therefore, of a higher order, in size and expensive finish.

An additional foundry put up by Miles Greenwood, and a new one by Davis & Bail: a new brewery by Fortman & Co; three valuable blocks at the corner of Walnut and Eighth sts. various fine store houses on Main street, and a number of handsome private dwellings, interspersed throughout the ward, enter into this year's improvements. Three fourths of this ward is built up entirely.

English Refinement.

It is the fashion for English travelers to speak of the barbarisms of the United States, especially of the West. National character every where has its shades, and there are blemishes, doubtless, on the escutcheon of American manners. If there be however, a feature in the national character of my country peculiar to itself, it is respect to woman kind. A woman among stran-gers any where in this country, is secure of kindness, attention and respect from all classes of society, however poor or friendless she may be: and I hazard nothing in asserting, that in no part of the United States, would the CHALLENGE below, which is copied from an English newspaper, have been *offered*, *accepted*, or permitted to take place.

CHALLENGE.

I, Elizabeth Wilkinson, of Clerkenwell, having had some words with Hannah Hyfield, and requiring satisfaction, do invite her to meet me on the stage, and box me for 3 guineas; each woman holding half a crown in each hand, and the first woman that drops the money to lose the battle. She shall have *Rare sport*.

ACCEPTANCE.

I, Hannah Hyfield, of Newgate-Market, hearing of the resoluteness of Elizabeth Wilkinson, will not fail, *God willing*. to give her more blows, and show her no favor; she may expect a good thumping.

CHRISTMAS ANTHEM.

BY LEWIS J. CIST.

I.

When Christ the Prince of Peace was born,
    Glad hymns of praise the blest employ;
And Bethlehem's plains, that hallowed morn,
    Were vocal with the notes of joy:
Through highest Heaven, a lofty strain
    Of blest hosannas, loudly rang;
While down to earth, an Angel-train
    The tidings bore, as thus they sang:—
"Glory to God on high be given !
On earth is born the Lord of Heaven;
Good will to men, and heavenly peace
To day begin, and never cease ! "

II.

The Shepherd bands, their flocks who watch
    On blest Judea's plains by night,
The sacred anthem hear, and catch
    The heavenly numbers with delight;
With holy awe, as floats above
    The tide of song o'er Bethlehem's plain,
They list to catch the notes of love,
    And echo back the sacred strain:—
"Glory to God on high be given !
On earth is born the Lord of Heaven ;
Good will to men, and heavenly peace
To-day begin, and never cease ! "

III.

On Bethlehem's hallowed plain, no more
    Judea's Shepherds keep their watch,
Or wake from slumber, as of yore,
    Angelic harmonies to catch;
Yet still, with joy and holy mirth,
    On this glad day the faithful bring
Their offerings at a Saviour's birth,
    And still the sacred Anthem sing:—
"Glory to God on high be given !
On earth is born the Lord of Heaven;
Good will to men, and heavenly peace
To-day begin, and never cease ! "

CHRISTMAS DAY, 1844

Coleman and his Eolian Attachment.

It is interesting and instructive to trace the buffetings with fortune, which in their earlier career so many ingenious men have maintained for years, sometimes for half their lives, and few coming off victorious so early in the battle as the subject of this notice.

Coleman's first appearance in public was at Albany and Troy, in which places he played on the accordion, then but lately introduced into notice. He had been from childhood remarkable for musical talent, and as far as it favored his musical taste, for mechanical ingenuity also. While thus engaged, he devoted his leisure hours to the construction of an Automaton accordion player, in which he met with signal success, and his exhibitions were well attended in both those cities. He then proceeded to New York with the Automaton, but on hoisting the package in which it was boxed up, out of the hold of the vessel, by some act of carelessness in the boat hands, it fell, and the mechanism was so much injured as to discourage Mr. Coleman from any attempt to repair it. It is probable that having tested what could be done in this line, he needed some new stimulus to his mechanical ingenuity. At this period he is described by my informant, as a young man of good sense, and rather modest, if not diffident in his deportment, and at no one stage of this part of his life earning more than a mere subsistence.

He resumed his Accordion on which he played with uncommon taste, as a means of support, and appears to have been experimenting during the time he could spare from his regular business, upon what in a more perfect shape, and at a later date became his EOLIAN ATTACHMENT. For this, when it was finished he secured letters patent, and *Gilbert* a piano manufacturer of Boston, who had been long and in vain endeavoring to drive Chickering's Pianos out of the market, gave him 25,000 dollars for the right of making and vending in Massachusetts alone. From Boston Coleman proceeded to New York, where Nunns and Clark offered him for the same right to the residue of the United States 25,000 dollars in cash, and 50,000 dollars payable in instalments out of every piano which they should make on this principle, or for every instance in which the Eolian Attachment should be added to any Piano in use. This offer was accepted. As the invention came from the hands of Coleman, it bore about the same relation to what the professional taste and skill of Nunns and Clark moulded it into, as Fulton's first steamboat probably did to the last effort of Cincinnati boat building—the YORKTOWN. The principle and the music were there to their hands, the full adaptation to the piano for convenience and ornament they had to adjust and create.

As soon as Messrs. Nunns & Clark had completed a piano on this principle, Coleman put off to London with the instrument, and opened rooms for its exhibition. He became instantly all the rage. Nobility and gentry, the wealthy, the fashionable, the world of musical taste, artists and dilletanti all rushed to hear and to admire, for these were here synonimous. Even Royalty and its inseperable shadow in the persons of Queen Victoria and Prince Albert gave largely of their gracious presence at his levee.

The last tidings of Mr. Coleman are, that in conversation with my informant, he said he had no earthly doubt of making a million of dollars in London out of his "Attachment." If he should be disappointed in this, which is not probable, with the 100,000 dollars he has received and is yet to get in the United States, he will nevertheless *not be left in absolute poverty*. He intends visiting the continent as soon as he has gathered in his *London* harvest.

Here is a man ten years ago, who probably could not have commanded credit for twenty dollars, and if he lives a few years, can draw his checks by the hundred thousand dollars at a time. His *Eolian Attachment* will be in his hands what Dr. Johnson described Thrale's brewery to be, the potentiality of growing rich beyond the dreams of avarice.

It will be news to some of my readers, that at Mr. T. B. Mason's ware rooms, Fourth street, east of Main, they can hear this delightful instrument,—and when they hear they will no longer wonder that the lucky hit made by Coleman, when he invented his Eolian attachment, is leading him to fame and fortune.

He that is born to be hung will never be shot.

There are few of the citizens of Philadelphia whose recollections extend as far back as 1807 or 8, but will remember *George Helmbold,* of that city, who edited at that period, the TICKLER, and after the close of the war of 1812-15, the INDEPENDENT BALANCE. In these publications, especially the first, with much wit, was mingled great scurrility and personal abuse, which kept the editor, as might be expected, in perpetual difficulties and brawls. *Helmbold* was a large man, of great strength and firm nerve, and unless worsted by numbers, generally came out of these scrapes with flying colors. But going often to the well breaks the pitcher at last, and the editor, as might be expected in such a case, finally broke down. He enlisted in 1812, as a private soldier, went on to the Canada lines, and applying himself to his duty strictly, was soon promoted to the post of sergeant, in which capacity, he signalized himself on every occasion which called him out.

At the battle of Brownstown in 1813, the company commanded by Captain Baker, was placed in the front of that severe engagement and after all the commissioned officers and nearly half the men were either killed or wounded the command devolved on *Helmbold*, then orderly sergeant to the corps. The shot from the English in their entrenchments, and from the Indians in ambush, was so galling as to compel the American commander to charge bayonets on the enemy, and *Helmbold* at this critical juncture filled with more than his usual ardor, invigorated every part of the line, within reach of his Stentorian voice, by exclaiming, " *Rush on! Rush on! the gallows will claim its rights!*"

The effect was electrical! this unprecedented battle cry was passed along the line—the march became a quick step—the quick step a run, and the enemy broke in all directions, without attempting to cross bayonets with the assailants.

For less signal, cool, and determined bravery, than this, *Junot* was raised from being a drummer to a General's command, and finally became Duke of Abrantes, and one of the Marshals of Napoleon's empire.

Store Dealings in Early Days.

The following bills of goods sold by Francis Willson, the earliest storekeeper at Columbia in this county. serve to show what it cost the pioneer settlers for whiskey and tobacco. These are the first wants in the early stage of frontier life, and they make accordingly the first items in Mr. Laird's purchase. Whiskey at 25 cents per quart, and tobacco at 40 cts per lb, were heavy taxes on the industry as well as health and correct habits of the pioneers. They may both be bought now at one fourth those prices, or even less.

Laird's bill is a striking proof how large a share of our wants are artificial. It may be classified thus. Playing cards, 73 cts; whiskey, 25 cts.; tobacco, 20 cts.—*useless and pernicious.* Hair ribbon, 60 cts.—*useless* simply. White flannel, 120 cts.—*useful.* Irish linen and cambric, 5 dollars 75 cts.—*luxuries* merely.

In part payment of this bill, Laird who seems to have been a tailor, makes an *entire suit of clothes*, for which he is allowed *three dollars.*— Truly, to buy *cheap* and sell *dear* seems to be some people's only idea of making money.

Serns, who appears by the credits to have been a farmer, gets nearer the worth of his money. Sugar even at 33 cts, and chocolate at the same price, although high in price, were probably seldom used, or only when company visited the cabin. Shawls and handkerchiefs must be worn; and fustian, a durable though homely article was not too costly at 60 cts. per yard. The tins, that is tin cups, were indispensable to house keeping and at a fair price, 12½ cts.

COLUMBIA, December 11th, 1792.

ROBERT LEARD:

To Francis Willson, Dr.

1 quart of whiskey,	*L* 0, 1*s*, 10*d.*
14th. 1-2 a pound of Tobacco,	0, 1, 6.
22d. 6½ y'ds Irish linen, at 6s pr y'd 1, 19, 0.
1-2 yard of Cambric,at 1¾ pr y'd 0, 4, 2.
2 y'ds white flannel,at 4s6d pr y'd 0, 9, 0.
1 pack of playing cards at 0, 3, 0.
June. 1793.
25th. 3 y'ds of hair ribband,at 1s6d y'd 0, 4, 6.
29th. 1 pack of playing cards, at 0, 2, 6.

Total,	3, 5, 6½.
By making a suit of clothes, at	1, 2, 6.
Remainder,	2, 3, 0½.

COLUMBIA, Jan. 1st, 1793.

Joshua Serns, Dr.

To Francis Willson,

1 pound of Sugar at	£2 6
1 do Chocolate at	2 6
3 Tins at 11d.	2 9
24th 1 Cotton Shawl at	10 0
1 do Handkerchief at	4 0
10th 4 yds. Fustian at 4s. 6d.	18 0
7 buttons at 2d,	1 2
1 skain of sewing silk, at	1 0
	2 ⌊1 11

By Butter,	£4 3	
By Cash,	4 8	
By Corn,	1 6	
	10 5	10 5
Remains due,		£1 11 6

Ladies' Fair at the College Hall.

The ladies of the *Central Presbyterian Church*, commenced last evening a FAIR, for the sale of useful and ornamental articles of their own manufacture, with a view to aid the various benevolent operations of that Society. They are provided, I observe, with the usual attractions of *hot coffee* and *bright eyes, glee in the cheeks* and *glees on the lips*, which make up the assortment in such cases.

My present object is—as a dealer in statistics—to refer to the establishment for the occasion, of a new periodical "THE CHRISTMAS GUEST," *Mrs. R. S. Nichols*, Editor; of which No. 1 made its appearance on last evening, as No. 2 will upon this. It. is a neat sheet and well filled by the editor and her numerous contributors, with appropriate articles. many of them of marked ability. Indeed, I have never read any publication, got up on so short a notice, of higher merit. Two or three of these articles are copied to-day into my columns as specimens.

Among the various articles exhibited at this Fair, are certain Essence bags, &c., ornamented with engraved fancy designs printed on silk and satin, from the Engraving rooms of W. F. Harrison, at the corner of Main and Fourth streets. The delicacy and beauty of these various devices attract general admiration and notice.

I trust that this *Ladies' Fair* will be adequately sustained. Its objects are such as appeal to our best sympathies, and a tithe of one or two days profits in the ordinary business of life, could not be spent by the visitors at this season of hilarity and enjoyment, more judiciously than at these tables.

From the *Christmas Guest*,

Pioneer Hardships.

Those who are now in the enjoyment of the plenty which pours in by wagons, railroads, and canals, cannot realize the destitution of the first settlers before they had got the farms cleared, and the cleared land under fence and cultivation.

The first improvements made in *Columbia* were the means of supplying *Cincinnati* and the garrison at *Fort Washington* with sustenance for some time, perhaps for two seasons, 1789 and 1790, before crops were raised within the city limits.

TURKEY BOTTOM, one and a half mile above the mouth of the Little Miami, was a clearing of 640 acres made ready to the hands of the whites when they commenced the settlement of the country. The Indians had cultivated it for a length of years up to the period of Major Stites' settlement, although part of this extensive field had been suffered to grow up by neglect in honey and black locust, which became literally, as well as figuratively, "thorns in the sides," to the early settlers. This ground was leased by Stites to six of the settlers for five years and with a clearing of Elijah Stites and other settlers of six acres more, furnished the entire supply of corn for that settlement and Cincinnati for that season. Nothing could surpass the fertility of the soil, which was as mellow as an ash heap. Benjamin Randolph planted an acre, which he had no time to hoe, being obliged to leave the settlement for New Jersey. When he returned he found an hundred bushels of corn ready for husking.

Seed corn, and even corn for hommony, and in the form of meal was brought out of the Kentucky settlements, down the Licking, and occasionally from a distance as great as Lexington.

While those who were best off were thus straitened, it may readily be supposed that others must have suffered still greater privations.-- The women and their children came from *Columbia* to Turkey Bottom to scratch up the bulbous roots of the bear-grass. These they boiled, washed, dried on smooth boards, and finally pounded into a species of flour, which served as a tolerable substitute for making various baking

preparations. Few families had milk, and still fewer bacon, for a season or two.

In 1789, Gen. Harmar sent Captains Strong and Kearsay to Columbia, to procure corn for their soldiers. They applied to James Flinn, understanding he had 500 bushels for sale. Flinn refused to sell to the army, having the previous year, when he resided at Balleville, below Marietta, not been able to get his pay for a supply he had furnished the troops at Fort Harmar, in consequence of the removal to some other station of the officer who made the purchase. Strong remarked, if we can't get corn we shall have to retreat on starvation. While they were talking and with great earnestness, Luke Foster, since Judge of the Hamilton Court of Common Pleas, came up and inquired the difficulty. Captain Strong replied the difficulty is, that the troops have been for nine days on half rations, and the half rations are nearly out, and we are starving for corn. Foster agreed then to lend the garrison one hundred bushels, to be returned the next season. How badly off they were the next season. may be judged by the fact, that Mr. Foster had to ride down to Cincinnati *six* times to get nineteen bushels of it!

Judge Foster gave me the following history of the crop, which enabled him to supply the wants at Fort Washington. He had run out of seed corn, and the only one of the neighbors, who could supply him with the quantity he wanted---less than a peck---happened also to be out of corn meal. As Foster had a small quantity of this last, an exchange was promptly made of thirteen pint cups full, pint for pint. The corn was planted, three grains in a hill, this supply serving to seed two and a half acres. The crop had not been put in early, and it was a dry season, but such was the character of the soil, and the condition it was in, that barely turning up the earth to the hills served to keep it in moisture. What a lively idea does it give of the progress of Cincinnati, with its 70,000 inhabitants that the individual is yet living and in the enjoyment of vigor and health, who planted the first crop of corn, which served to supply the wants of a whole community, here.   C. C.

The Christmas Guest.

Room, courteous Readers, room in your hearts, and among your Christmas festivities, for a stranger Guest. Plain and unpretending, unheralded and uninvited, the Unknown appears before you. If the calls of courtesy and hospitality are unheeded, we *know* that you will listen eagerly to the spurring dictates of curiosity, and extend a welcome to our little Guest. You know, oh kindest reader, that this uncalled visiter has a Fairy Budget, that has never been exposed to the public eye. Whether the pack consists of real gems, or only the false glitter of the tinsel, shall be left for your decision.— Should the Guest, however, repay its generous entertainers, by contributing to their entertainment at this happy season, one object of its errand will have been fulfilled. Should its silent voice lead one erring or desponding soul to the God of light, and life, and hope, it will have accomplished a glorious mission. We ask, then, a welcoming hand, and a corner of your heart, kind friends, for the stranger Guest.

[*Christmas Guest.*

From the Christmas Guest.
SONG FOR THE SABBATH.

WRITTEN DURING ILLNESS.

Worship, worship, heart of mine,
   All thy lowly incense offer,
Though before no sacred shrine,
   Still the grateful incense proffer:
Flowing from a contrite heart,
   Stealing from the world apart,
Praising though oppressed by pain,
   ONE who heals the fevered vein.

Worship! worship, spirit mine,
   Though thy trembling accents falter,
God shall strengthen thee with wine,
   From the sacrificial altar;
Praise him for his mercies all—
   On the faithful Saviour call,
Knowing, though oppressed by pain,
   He can cool the fevered vein.

Worship! worship, body mine,
   If thy earthly strength's decaying,
Thou shalt not in darkness pine,
   Faith a fair foundation's laying
For thy mansion in the skies—
   Upward then direct thine eyes,
Showing the oppressed by pain,
   God can heal the fevered vein.

R. S. N.

From the Christmas Guest.
GOOD NIGHT.

Good night, it is a simple phrase,
But sweeter than the minstrel's lays,
Or pleasant sounding words of praise,
   To me it seems,
When breathed by one whose cheerful voice,
Is like old music rare and choice,
He whispers low, "good night, rejoice
   In pleasant dreams."

Good night, ah then I feel alone,
And seek to wake again the tone,
As if my heart had jealous grown,
   Of slumbers light.
Lest they exclude me from the breast
On which I now confiding rest,
And murmur back the words so blest—
   Good night, good night!
R. S N.

Paper Huckstering.

There are certain paper establishments which profess to supply the public with their own manufacture, and are at the same time busily engaged in buying up paper from establishments

abroad, and raising the price on purchasers.— I only want to get the facts authenticated, and the names of parties, that I may exhibit these paper hucksters and forestallers in their true colors. I am promised these facts in a few days.

Customs of Society Fifty Years Since.

The following tavern bill incurred by Gen. St. Clair and two other persons, sheds light on the past. The bill it seems was *a club*, that is, to be divided between three, and it appears to have been settled by St. Clair, the residue after Lincoln's receipt, being the General's notes. Jacob —— appears to have been one of the three, St. Clair of course another, and the third, alas! is lost forever to the record. It seems the other two paid up their share. The account is made in Pennsylvania currency 7s 6d to the dollar. The items in the bill will remind a reader who has read Shakspeare, of Falstaff. 'Oh monstrous, four' shillings, "worth of bread to all this" eating and drinking. But St. Clair compared with Harmar and others was a perfectly temperate man, and probably the "illustrious missing" drank the brandy, &c.

Mr. ST. CLAIR, Co.   Dr.
To Joseph Lincoln,

	£	s	d
21 Meals at 1s 6d,	1	11	6
3 Dinners and club 7s 6d,	1	2	6
3 Dinners and club 3s 6d.		10	6
3 Pints wine.		12	0
2 Half pints brandy,		5	0
4 do. P. brandy,		6	0
Washing,		7	6
Paper,		1	6
For keeping horses,	3	12	0
1 Venison ham,		2	0
Bread,		4	0
Logings,		3	6
½ bushel oats,		6	0
19 p brandy,		3	6
2¼ lbs. cheese,		2	3
Victuals &c.		3	0
	£9	12	1

D. C.
Brandy &c,   32 12
                 62½
                 32 74½

Received payment, 21st Oct, 1798, at Marietta.   JOSEPH LINCOLN.

Paid Lincoln	$32	74½
" Thomson	4	50
" Salt Works	1	50
" For corn		19
" Grimes	3	50
" Ferriage		50
" Heddlestones	1	60
" Jeremiah Hunt	7	37
	3) 52	20½
	17	40

Rec'd. of Jacob   18 Dolls.
Rec'd. of St. Clair   1 50 cents.
Rec'd. of St. Clair   16 00 at Cincinnati.

Cincinnati Wood Company.

I have been deeply interested in an enterprise lately started up, for the two-fold purpose of supplying the poor and persons in straitened circumstances, with wood and temporary employment. This is the CINCINNATI WOOD COMPANY, whose contemplated operations, I referred to, two or three weeks since, and which has since procured a lot on the White Water Canal, below Smith street. enclosed it, with a substantial fence, and nearly filled it with wood.— This lot—170 feet by 100—has been leased for three years, from *Nicholas Longworth*, at $200 per annum. Four hundred cords of wood are already laid in, and laboring hands destitute of employment elsewhere, find it here in assorting sawing, splitting and piling the wood into ranks for customers.

I have not time this week to give a view of all the features of this establishment, which I see plainly is destined to accomplish, not only all that its benevolent projectors contemplated to do for the destitute, but may effect good, in other respects which I supposed never entered into their calculations. The feature I shall present to-day is the relief of the poor by the supply of wood, and employment to those who are suffering for the want of both. And the manner in which the society operates is as judicious as the object is important. A man destitute of employment applies for work. His name is entered on a register kept for the purpose, with his occupation or profession, where he has one. He is set to work at wages so low, as not to tempt any person, who can get work in the community at large; and as soon as any more profitable employment out of the yard is found by himself, or by his employers for him, he leaves the premises to make room for fresh hands. If he has a wife, who would like to do washing, or a boy or a girl whom he is disposed to hire out, they are entered on the books, accordingly, and, as soon as possible, provided with places.

There are many persons in straitened circumstances willing to buy wood in small quantities, who are not able to buy a load at a time, and are put to all manner of inconveniences, and loss of time, which to poor, as well as rich, is loss of money, to make shifts for supplies of this article. To such individuals, this wood-yard offers any quantity, from ten cents to a dollar's worth, which they can carry in their arms, or on a wheelbarrow, without losing time in getting it sawed or split or incur the risk of buying wood, some part of which they cannot use in small stoves, or if they buy half a cord it is delivered to them of the best quality, sawed and split, taken into their yards, and piled up, all at less expense, as well as to greater convenience than they could get it at any other place. Nor is this all. They are protected by the company arrangements, from being exposed to a rise in the price of wood, to which they are usually subject in the ordinary mode of supply. It is hardly necessary to say that those who get but a dime's worth, get as much wood for their money proportionally, as those who lay out a dollar, or five dollars for the article.

This system, it will be perceived, helps the poor by enabling them to help themselves.— Present employment is afforded, until more profitable business can be obtained, and numbers are thus enabled to find business, who could not have obtained it through any other medium.— By way of illustration of this subject, three hands, after sawing wood, at fifty cents a day, were directed to situations of attending masons at a dollar per day, and they have now men sawing wood, fitted for other employment, who know not where to get it, and who will be taken to more profitable business, as soon as their qualifications become known to those who need their services elsewhere.

Next week I shall exhibit another important feature of this company's operations.

Temperance Statistics.

In examining some old newspapers for other purposes, my eye rested on the annexed article with all the deep feeling of personal interest.

From the Genius of Temperance.

The following is as instructive as it is remarkable. We have it from a source we consider authentic.

In the year 1813, the first company of Washington Guards of Philadelphia, commanded, by Capt. Condy Raguet, marched to defend the shores of the Delaware from the English. The company numbered 130 men divided in messes of 6 and 7 men each. It so happened that one mess of seven men drank none of their rations of spirits or other articles. They were in camp seven months and when the peace took place, the company was disbanded. Seventeen years afterwards a call was made for assembling the survivors of the company, and it was found that 33 were living, and 7 of that number were the mess that drank no liquor, when in camp; 5 of them were present at the meeting, and letters were read from two others stating their reasons for not being at the meeting; one resided in Cincinnati, and the other in some other part of Ohio. No other mess could number more than two living members.

The gentleman who gave me this information is one or the mess of seven spoken of, and every word may be relied upon as fact. I am acquainted with some of the members and I believe the whole number is now living. After the meeting held three years ago, a pamphlet was published giving a history of the company, services, &c., &c., which I believe may be obtained from C. Raguet,　　　　　　　T. H. S.

Philadelphia, July 3, 1833.

Of the individuals besides myself, composing this mess I can only recollect three, namely

Thomas I. Wharton, now an eminent member of the Philadelphia bar, James Correy, Cashier successively of the United States Branch, and the Merchant's and Manufacturer's Banks of Pittsburgh, of the Bank of North America, in Philadelphia; and now of the Planter's Bank of Tennessee, at Nashville; and Thomas A. Marshall, formerly, perhaps still of Marcus Hook, Pa., all of whom are yet living, as I believe the whole mess to be. If Mr. Wharton, to whom I shall send a copy of this article, can afford me the desired information, whether they be all living, I do not doubt he will do so. With the exception of Mr. Correy and myself, if living, they reside probably in and near Philadelphia. It is not often seven men shall start together in the race of human life, and push on for fifty-two years, as these seven have done, without one or more giving out, before they have reached that distance in the course.

Robert Burns and Lord Byron.

I have seen Robert Burns laid in his grave, and I have seen George Gordon Byron borne to his; of both I wish to speak, and my words shall be spoken with honesty and freedom. They were great, though unequal heirs of fame; the fortunes of their birth were widely dissimilar; yet in their passions and in their genius, they approached to a closer resemblance; their careers were short and glorious, and they both perished in the summer of life, and in all the splendour of a reputation more likely to increase than diminish. One was a peasant, and the other was a peer; but nature is a great leveller, and makes amends for the injuries of fortune by the richness of her benefactions; the genius of Burns raised him to a level with the nobles of the land; by nature, if not by birth, he was the peer of Byron. I knew one, and I have seen both; I have hearkened to words from their lips, and admired the labours of their pens, and J am now, and likely to remain, under the influence of their magic songs. They rose by the force of their genius, and they fell by the strength of their passions; one wrote from a love and the other from a scorn of mankind; and they both sang of the emotions of their own hearts with a vehemence and an originality which few have equalled, and none surely have surpassed. But it is less my wish to draw the characters of those extraordinary men than to write what I remember of them; and I will say nothing that I know not to be true, and little but what I saw myself.

The first time I ever saw Burns was in Nithsdale. I was then a child, but his looks and his voice cannot well be forgotten; and while I write this I behold him as distinctly as I did when I stood at my father's knee, and heard the bard repeat his Tam O'Shanter. He was tall and of a manly make, his brow broad and high, and his voice varied with the character of his inimitable tale; yet through all its variations it was melody itself. He was of great personal strength, and proud too of displaying it; and I have seen him lift a load with ease, which few ordinary men would have willingly undertaken. The first time I ever saw Byron was in the House of Lords, soon after the publication of Childe Harold. He stood up in his place on the opposition side, and made a speech on the subject of Catholic freedom. His voice was low, and I heard him but by fits, and when I say he was witty and sarcastic, I judge as much from the involuntary mirth of the benches as from what I heard with my own ears. His voice had not the full and manly melody of the voice of Burns; nor had he equal vigour of form, nor the same open expanse of forehead. But his face was finely formed, and was impressed with a more delicate vigour than that of the peasant poet. He had a singular conformation of ear, the lower lobe, instead of being pendulous, grew down and united itself to the cheek and resembled no other ear I ever saw, save that of the Duke of Wellington. His bust by Thorvaldson is feeble and mean; the painting of Phillips is more noble and much more like. Of Burns 1 have never seen aught but a very uninspired resemblance—and I regret it the more, because he had a look worthy of the happiest effort of art; a look beaming with poetry and eloquence.

The last time I saw Burns in life was on his return from the Brow-well of Solway; he had been ailing all spring, and summer had come without bringing health with it; he had gone away very ill; and he returned worse. He was brought back, I think, in a covered spring-cart, and when he alighted at the foot of the street in which he lived he could scarce stand upright. He reached his own door with difficulty. He stooped much, and there was a visible change in his looks. Some may think it not unimportant to know, that he was at the time dressed in a blue coat with the dress nankeen pantaloons of the volunteers, and that his neck, which was inclining to be short, caused his hat to turn up behind, in the manner of the shovel hats of the Episcopal clergy. Truth obliges me to add, that he was not fastidious about his dress; and that an officer, curious in personal appearance and equipments of his company, might have questioned the military nicety of the poet's clothes and arms. But his colonel was a maker of rhyme, and the poet had to display more charity for his commander's verse than the other had to exercise when he inspected the clothing and arms of the careless bard.

From the day of his return home, till the hour of his untimely death, Dumfries was like a besieged place. It was known he was dying, and the anxiety, not of the rich and the learned only, but of the mechanics and peasants, exceeded all belief. Wherever two or three people stood together, their talk was of Burns and of him alone; they spoke of his history, of his person, of his works, of his family, of his fame, and of his untimely and approaching fate, with a warmth and an enthusiasm which will ever endear Dumfries to my remembrance. All that he said or was saying—the opinions of the physicians, (and Maxwell was a kind and a skilful one,) were eagerly caught up and reported from street to street, and from house to house.

His good humor was unruffled, and his wit never forsook him. He looked to one of his fellow volunteers with a smile, as he stood by the bed-side with his eyes wet, and said, "John don't let the awkward squad fire over me." He was aware that death was dealing with him; he asked a lady who visited him, more in sincerity than mirth, what commands she had for the other world—he repressed with a smile the hopes of his friends, and told them he had lived long enough. As his life drew near a close, the eager yet decorous solicitnde of his fellow townsmen increased. He was an exciseman it is true—a name odious, from many associations, to his countrymen—but he did his duty meekly and kindly, and repressed rather than encouraged the desire of some of his companions to push the law with severity; he was therefore much beloved, and the passion of the Scotch for poetry made them regard him as little lower than a spirit inspired. It is the practice of the young men of Dumfries to meet in the streets during the hours of remission from labour, and by these means I had an opportunity of witnessing the general solicitude of all ranks and of all ages. His differences with them in some important points of human speculations and religious hope were forgotton and forgiven: they thought only of his genius—of the delight his compositions had diffused—and they talked of him with the same awe as of some departing spirit, whose voice was to gladden them no more. His last moments have never been described; he had laid his head quietly on the pillow awaiting dissolution, when his attendant reminded him of his medicine and held the cup to his lips. He started suddenly up, drained the cup at a gulp, threw his hands before him like a man about to swim, and sprung from head to foot of the bed—fell with his face down, and expired without a groan.

Of the dying moments of Byron we have no very minute nor very distinct account. He perished in a foreign land among barbarians or aliens, and he seems to have been without the aid of a determined physician, whose firmness or persuasion might have vanquished his obstinacy. His aversion to bleeding was an infirmity which he shared with many better regulated minds; for it is no uncommon belief that the first touch of the lancet will charm away the approach of death, and those who believe this are willing to reserve so decisive a spell for a more momentous occasion. He had parted with his native land in no ordinary bitterness of spirit; and his domestic infelicity had rendered his future peace of mind hopeless--this was aggravated from time to time by the tales or the intrusion of travellers, by reports injurious to his character, and by the eager and vulgar avidity with which idle stories were circulated, which exhibited him in weakness or in folly. But there is every reason to believe, that long before his untimely death his native land was as bright as ever in his fancy, and that his anger conceived against the many for the sins of the few had subsided or was subsiding. Of Scotland, and of his Scottish origin, he has boasted in more than one place of his poetry; he is proud to remember the land of his mother, and to sing that he is half a Scot by birth, and a whole one in his heart. Of his great rival in popularity, Sir Walter Scott, he speaks with kindness; and the compliment he has paid him has been earned by the unchangeable admiration of the other.-- Scott has ever spoken of Byron as he has always written, and all those who know him will feel this consistency is characteristic. I must, however, confess, his forgiveness of Mr. Jeffrey was an unlooked-for and unexpected piece of humility and loving kindness, and, as a Scotchman, I am rather willing to regard it as a presage of early death, and to conclude that the poet was "fey," and forgave his arch enemy in the spirit of the dying Highlander—"Weel, weel, I forgive him, but God confound you, my twa sons, Duncan and Gilbert, if you forgive him." The criticism with which the Edinburgh Review welcomed the first flight which Byron's muse took, would have crushed and broken any spirit less dauntless than his own; and for a long while he entertained the horror of a reviewer which a bird of song feels for the presence of the raven. But they smoothed his spirit down, first by submission, and then by idolatry, and his pride must have been equal to that which made the angels fall if it had refused to be soothed by the obeisance of a reviewer One never forgets, if he should happen to forgive, an insult or an injury offered in youth—it grows with the growth and strengthens with the strength, and I may reasonably doubt the truth of the poet's song when he sings of his dear Jeffrey. The news of his death came upon London like an earthquake; and though the common multitude are ignorant of literature or feeling for the higher flights of poetry, yet they consented to feel by faith, and believed, because the newspapers believed, that one of the brightest lights in the firmament of poesy was extinguished forever.— With literary men a sense of the public misfortune, was mingled, perhaps, with a sense that a giant was removed from their way; and that they had room now to break a lance with an equal, without the fear of being overthrown by his impetuosity and colossal strength. The world of literature is now resigned to lower, but, perhaps, not less presumptuous poetic spirits. But among those who feared him, or envied him, or loved him, there are none who sorrow not for the national loss, and grieve not that Byron fell so soon, and on a foreign shore.

When Burns died I was then young, but I was not insensible that a mind of no common strength had passed from among us. He had caught my fancy, and touched my heart with his songs and poems. I went to see him laid out for the grave; several elderly people were with me. He lay in a plain unadorned coffin, with a linen sheet drawn over his face, and on the bed, and around the body, herbs and flowers were thickly strewn according to the usage of the country. He was wasted by long illness,— but death had not increased the swarthy hue of his face, which was uncommonly dark and deeply marked—the dying pang was visible in the lower part, but his broad and open brow was pale and serene, and around it his sable hair lay in masses, slightly touched with gray, and inclining more to a wave than a curl. The room where he lay was plain and neat, and the simplicity of the poet's humble dwelling pressed the presence of death more closely on the heart than if his bier had been embellished by vanity and covered with the blazonry of high ancestry and rank. We stood and gazed on him in silence for the space of ten minutes—we went, and others succeeded us; there was no rushing and justling though the crowd was great; man followed man as patiently and orderly as if all had been a matter of mutual understanding —not a question was asked—not a whisper was heard. This was several days after his death. It is the custom of Scotland to "wake" the body—not with wild howlings and wilder songs, and much waste of strong drink, like our mercurial neighbors; but in silence or in prayer; superstition says it is unsonsie to leave the corpse alone; so it is never left. I know not who watched by the body of Burns—much it was my wish to share in the honor—but my extreme youth would have made such a request seem foolish, and its rejection would have been certain.

I am to speak of the feelings of another people, and of the customs of a higher rank, when I speak of laying out the body of Byron for the grave. It was announced from time to time that he was to be exhibited in state, and the progress of the embellishments of the poets' bier was recorded in the pages of an hundred publications. They were at length completed, and to seperate the curiosity of the poor from the admiration of the rich, the latter were indulged with tickets of admission, and a day was set apart for them to go and wonder over the decked room and the emblazoned bier. Peers and peeresses, priests, poets, and politicians, came in gilded chariots and hired hacks to gaze upon the splendor of the funeral preparations, and to see in how rich and how vain a shroud the body of the immortal had been hid. Those idle trappings in which rank seeks to mark its altitude above the vulgar belonged to the state of the peer rather than to the state of the poet: genius required no such attractions; and all this magnificence served only to divide our regard with the man whose inspired tongue was now silenced forever. Who cared for Lord Byron, the peer, and the privy counsellor, with his coronet, and his long descent from princes, on one side, and from heroes on both; and who did not care for George Gordon Byron, the poet, who has charmed us, and will charm our descendants with his deep and impassioned verse. The homage was rendered to genius, not surely to rank, for lord can be stamped on any clay, but inspiration can only be impressed on the finest metal.

Of the day on which the multitude were admitted, I know not in what terms to speak— I never surely saw so strange a mixture of silent sorrow and of fierce and intractable curiosity. If one looked on the poet's splendid coffin with deep awe, and thought of the gifted spirit which had lately animated the cold remains, others regarded the whole as a pageant or a show, got up for the amusement of the idle and the careless, and criticised the arrangements as those who wished to be rewarded for their time. and who consider that all they condescend to visit, should be according to their own taste. There was a crushing, a trampling, and an impatience as rude and as fierce as I. ever witnessed at a theatre, and words of incivility were bandied about, and questions asked with such determina- tion to be answered, that the very mutes, whose business was silence and repose, were obliged to interfere with tongue and hand between the visitors and the dust of the poet. In contemplation of such a scene many of the trappings which were there on the first day were removed on the second, and this suspicion of the good sense and decorum of the multitude called forth many exclamations of displeasure, as remarkable for their warmth as their propriety of language. By five o'clock the people were ejected, man and woman, and the rich coffin bore tokens of the touch of hundreds of eager fingers—many of which had not been overclean.

The multitude who accompanied Burns to the grave, went step by step with the chief mourners: they might amount to ten or twelve thousand. Not a word was heard, and though all could not be near, and many could not see, when the earth closed on their darling poet forever, there was no rude impatience shown, no fierce disappointment expressed. It was an impressive and mournful sight to see men of all ranks and persuasions and opinions mingling as brothers, and stepping side by side down the streets of Dumfries, with the remains of him who had sang of their loves and joys and domestic endearments, with a truth and a tenderness which none perhaps have since equaled. I could, indeed, have wished the military part of the procession away—for he was buried with militaryhonors--because I am one of those who love simplicity in all that regards genius. The scarlet and gold: the banners displayed; the measured step, and the military array, with the sound of martial instruments of music, had no share in increasing the solemnity of the burial scene: and had no connexion with the poet.—I looked on it then, and consider it now as an idle ostentation, a piece of superfluous state, which might have been spared, more especially as his neglected and traduced and insulted spirit had experienced no kindness in the body from those lofty people, who are now proud of being numbered as his coevals and countrymen. His fate has been a reproach to Scotland; but the reproach comes with an ill grace from England. When we can forget Butler's fate—Otway's loaf—Dryden's old age, and Chatterton's poison cup, we may think that we stand alone in the iniquity of neglecting pre-eminent genius. I found myself at the brink of the poet's grave, into which he was about to descend forever—there was a pause among the mourners, as if loth to part with his remains; and when he was at last lowered, and the first shovelful of earth fell on his coffin lid, I looked up and saw tears on many cheeks where tears were not usual.—The volunteers justified the fears of their comrades by three ragged and straggling volleys. The earth was heaped up, the green sod laid over him, and the multitude stood gazing on the grave for some minutes' space, then melted silently away. The day was a fine one; the sun was almost without a cloud, and not a drop of rain fell from dawn to twilight. I notice this, not from my concurrence with the common superstition, that "happy is the corse that the rain falls on," but to confute a pious fraud of a religious Magazine, which made heaven express its wrath at the interment of a profane poet, in thunder and in lightning and in rain. I know not who wrote the story, nor do I wish to know, but its utter falsehood thousands can attest.

A few select friends and admirers followed Byron to the grave; his coronet was borne before him and there were many indications of his rank; but, save the assembled multitude, no indications of his genius. In conformity to a singular practice of the great, a long train of their empty carriages followed the mourning coaches: mocking the dead with idle state, and impeding the honester sympathies of the crowd with barren pageantry. Where were the owners of those machines of sloth and luxury; where were the men of rank among whose dark pedigrees Lord Byron threw the light of his genius, and lent the brows of nobility a halo to which they were strangers? Where were the great Whigs? Where were the illustrious Tories? Could a mere difference in matters of human belief keep those fastidious persons away? But, above all, where were the friends with whom wedlock had united him? On his desolate corpse no wife looked, and no child shed a tear. I have no wish to set myself up as a judge in domestic infelicities, and I am willing to believe they were separated in such a way as rendered conciliation hopeless; but who could stand and look on his pale, manly face, and his dark locks which early sorrows were making thin and gray, without feeling that, gifted as he was, with a soul above the mark of other men, his domestic misfortunes called for our pity as surely as his genius called for our admiration.---When the career of Burns was closed, I saw another sight; a weeping widow and four helpless sons; they came into the streets in their mournings, and public sympathy was awakened afresh; I shall never forget the looks of his boys, and the compassion which they excited. The poet's life had not been without errors, and such errors, too, as a wife is slow in forgiving,—but he was honored then, and is honored now, by the unalienable affection of his wife, and the world repays her prudence and her love by its regard and esteem.

Burns, with all his errors in faith and practice was laid in hallowed earth, in the church-yard of the town in which he resided; no one thought of closing the church gates against his body, because of the freedom of his poetry, and the carelessness of his life. And why was not Byron laid among the illustrious men of England, in Westminster Abbey? Is there a poet in all the Poet's Corner who has better right to this distinction? Why was the door closed against him, and opened to the carcasses of thousands without merit and without name? Look round the walls, and on the floor over which you tread, and behold them encumbered amd inscribed with memorials of the mean and the sordid, and the impure, as well as of the virtuous and the great. Why did the Dean of Westminster refuse admission to such an heir of fame as Byron? if he had no claim to lie within the consecrated procincts of the Abbey, he had no right to lie in consecrated ground at all. There is no doubt that the pious fee for sepulture would have been paid; and it is not a small one. Hail to the Church of England, if her piety is stronger than her avarice.   M.

Cincinnati Periodical Press.

A list and description of our periodical literature, may serve as one indication, among others, of the progress of Cincinnati, and the extent to which, as compared with other cities, her population is brought within the influence of the press, at once the exponent and moulder of public sentiment.

At the commencement of the last year, there were thirty-five periodicals of all descriptions, in existence here. Of these the Sun, Commercial and Volksbuhne have become extinct or merged in other papers. The Cincinnati Washingtonian and the Ohio Temperance Organ have become consolidated in one paper, bearing both titles.

There are now published here 12 Daily papers devoted to various objects as follows.

1. The Cincinnati Gazette, J. C. Wright and J. C. Vaughan, editors. L'Hommedieu & Co. proprietors.

2. The Cincinnati Chronicle, E. D. Mansfield editor. Pugh, Harlan and Davis, publishers.

3. Cincinnati Atlas, Guilford and Russell, editors and proprietors.

4. Enquirer and Message, Brough & Robinson, editors and publishers.

5. Cincinnati Morning Herald, G. Bailey Jr. editor and publisher.

6. The Daily Times, J. D. Taylor, editor; Calvin Starbuck, proprietor.
All political or commercial.

7. Cincinnati Daily Bulletin, J. V. Loomis, editor, Loomis, Browne and Young proprietors.

8. Cincinnati American Republican, E. D. Campbell editor; C. A. Morgan & J. L. Brown proprietors.

9. The People's Paper, Swim and Pickering publishers.

10. The Volks Blatt, George Ritz editor; Stephen Molitor publisher.

11. The Freisinnige, J. Scho editor and proprietor.

12. The Deutsche Republikaner, Charles F. Schmidt, editor and proprietor.

Of these Dailies nine are in the English, and three in the German language. The Gazette, Atlas, Chronicle, and Republikaner are Whig, and the Enquirer and Message, Volks Blatt, and Freisinnige, are Democratic in politics.

The Bulletin and the American Republican are what are popularly termed Native American papers.

The Herald is the organ of the Liberty party. The other two are generally silent on politics, on which subject they profess neutrality.

The Gazette, Chronicle, Atlas, Times, Enquirer and Message, American Republican, and Herald among the English, and the Volks Blatt, and Republikaner, of the German prints, also publish weeklies, and the Gazette, Atlas and Chronicle issue a tri-weekly edition.

13. Cincinnati Prices Current, W. D. Gallaher editor.

14. Cincinnati Prices Current, J. B. Russell editor,

15. Cincinnati Prices Current, A. Peabody editor.

16. The Western General Advertiser, Charles Cist editor and publisher, C. Clark printer.

17. The Watchman of the Valley, Rev. Epaphras Goodman editor and proprietor.

18. The Star in the West, Rev. J. A. Gurley editor and proprietor.

19. The Catholic Telegraph, Rev. Edward Purcell editor; Daniel Conahan agent.

20. The Western Christian Advocate, Rev. Charles Elliott editor; Revs. J. F. Wright and Leroy Swormstedt publisher.

21. The Wahrheits Freund, J. J. Max. Oertel editor; Hermann Lehmann, publishers.

22. The Apologete, Rev. Wm. Nast editor; Rev's. J. F. Wright and Leroy Swormstedt publishers.

23. The Ohio Temperance Organ and Washingtonian, Walter Smith & Co. editors and proprietors.

24. The Western Midnight Cry, E. Jacobs editor; J. V. Himes publisher.

25. The Christian Politician, Dr. Wm. H. Brisbane, editor and proprietor.

26. The Disfranchised American, A. M. Sumner, editor.

Fourteen Weeklies unconnected with daily issues.

The first four, as their titles indicate, are devoted to mercantile business purposes. The Watchman is New School Presbyterian. The Star in the West is Universalist. The Telegraph and Wahrheit's Freund are Roman Catholic. The Christian Advocate and Apologete are Episcopal Methodist. The Ohio Temperance Organ and Washingtonian advocate the Temperance cause. The Midnight Cry is Millerite; the Christian Politician is the advocate of reform in morals, politics and religion; and the Disfranchised American advocates the cause of the colored people of Cincinnati.

27. The Botanico—Medical Recorder, A. Curtis, M. D. Botanic Practice;—semi-monthly.

28. The Ladies Repository and Gatherings of the West, same editors and publishers as the Christian Advocate. Literary and Religious.

20. The Missionary Herald, American Board of Commissioners for Foreign Missions; George L. Weed publisher. Missionary.

30. Western Farmer and Gardener, Charles Foster editor and proprietor. Agricultural.

31. Facts for the People, G. Bailey, jr. editor. Liberty party advocate.

32. Counterfeit Detector, H. H. Goodman and Co. editors; Charles Goodman publisher.

33. Youths' Visiter, Mrs. M. L. Bailey editor. Literary.

34. The Western Journal of Health. Medical.

35. The Western Lancet, L. M. Lawson, M. D., editor. also Medical.

36. The Semicolon, Robinson and Jones publishers. Literary.

37. The Reformer and High School Messenger. Devoted to the elevation of the colored people, H. S. Gilmore and J. W. Walker, editors; A. G. Sparhawk publisher.

38. The Western Literary Journal, A. Z. C. Judson and L. A. Hine, editors and proprietors. Literary.

39. The Retina, published in Cincinnati and Hamilton. New Jerusalem Church principles.

40. The Law Journal, Timothy Walker editor; Desilver and Burr publishers.

There last thirteen are monthlies.

I doubt if any city on the American continent can exhibit such an array and aggregate of intelligence, social, professional, religious and political, as may be found in this list. And in saying this, I do not include in the comparison, as might justly be done, the disparity in age, population, wealth and professional business, between Cincinnati, and Boston, New York, Philadelphia, Baltimore or New Orleans.

Of the Dailies of 1843, three no longer exist, and are replaced with two new ones. Of the Weeklies, two are united, lessening the number one, and three new ones are added. The Monthlies have increased from eight in 1844 to thirteen by the establishment of five new ones.

Cincinnati Fire Engines.

On the 25th ult, the CINCINNATI Engine was taken out for trial by its members, at the corner of 8th and Elm sts.; she threw the distance of 212 feet through a pipe 6 feet long, being 42 feet further than at the trial by judges between her and the Fame. This movement brought out the FAME, which after the Cincinnati left the ground, made her appearance there, and succeeded in throwing 202 feet. The Fame is the Philadelphia engine lately brought out to this city; the Cincinnati is from the Engine Factory of C. H. Paddack one of our own Engine builders. It will be recollected that the chambers of the Cincinnati, are 8¼ and those of the Fame 8½, on the Boston scale of power affording an advantage of five feet at least to the latter engine; they are both 9 inches stroke.— The Fame cost the company who own her, two thousand dollars; the Cincinnati cost but sixteen hundred. At the trial by judges about a month since the Fame threw 16 feet farther than the Cincinnati, the latter engine reaching only the distance of 170 feet. Neither engine performed on that occasion to do justice to their respective builders.

The simple statement of these facts furnishes its own comment.

Quaker Ingenuity.

Innumerable are the stories told of Quakers. more properly Friends, and furnishing a comment on the half line of Pope—"a Quaker sly."

A Sailor, half drunk inquired the price of a hat, which a Quaker offered for sale. The price was named, and objected to as too high. *As I live!* said Broadbrim, I cannot afford it thee for less. Well then, retorted the sailor, live more savingly and be d——d to you. Friend, rejoined the hatter, I have sold hats for five and thirty years, and thou art the first to find my secret out. Take the hat at thy own price.

Jacob Longstreth who I knew in Philadelphia many years ago as a dashing hickory Quaker, joined the Shakers at Union village, in Lebanon county Ohio. The Society dealt with Mr. James Johnston, on Main street, who did their business for years, and perhaps still does it.— Longstreth had once brought in a lot of garden seeds, which he could not dispose of, the market being overstocked, and left them therefore with Mr. J. who failed that season to sell them, on the same account. The seeds were forgotten by all parties for four or five years. Longstreth being one day at Mr. Johnston's store he was reminded of the seeds and requested to take them away as useless. *Jacob* said nothing, but putting a box or two under his arm posted along Lower Market street, and in the course of repeated trips, disposed of the entire lot, realizing some three dollars a box on perhaps thirty boxes.— "Well James think what I got for these seeds," "a hundred dollars I believe!" Why, said Mr. J. you surely would not attempt to sell seeds that were too old to grow. Why, said Jacob,

I exchanged them for dry goods—*real old* shopkeepers, and I should think *old seeds* are worth as much as *old goods.* "And did no one ask you if they were fresh." "Only in one place."— "And what did you say?" "Say—why friend does thee think we *salt our seeds?.*" That answer sufficed.

One of the Yarnalls of the Quaker family of that name in Philadelphia, sailed on a merchant voyage to one of the Mediterranean Ports. It was during our difficulties of 1805, with the Barbary powers, and the vessel was armed. This however was nothing to Yarnall, who was merely super-cargo. I knew him well, although I have forgotten his surname—I think it was Nathan. He was a brawny, broad chested fellow of six feet in height & strength. that for any thing else than lifting was flung away upon a man of his pacific principles. Off the Barbary coast they were chased by Tripolitan cruizers repeatedly, but the good sailing of their vessel generally saved them a conflict. In one instance, however, they were overtaken and fired into by a Tripolitan well armed and manned. The American vessel returned the fire with spirit.— In the midst of the engagement Yarnall was facing the deck with the spirit of a man deeply interested, but who did not think it right to interfere, glancing his eye occasionally at the firing of the men on board his own ship, and watching its execution on the enemy. Satisfied at length that one of the guns was elevated too much, he became uneasy, checked himself once or twice, and at length unable to stand it any longer, James, said he, thee is wasting thee owner's powder and ball. Dont thee see thee shoots too high? James profited by the suggestion to the sorrow of the Turks, who perceiving they could make no decided impression by their guns, after several abortive attempts, succeeded in boarding their opponent. A desperate scuffle ensued, and Nathan finding the battle likely to go against his friends,in considerable agitation accosted one of the Turks. "Friend, thee has no business here," and finding that the barbarian as might be expected, paid no attention to the expostulation,seized him from behind, grappling him under the armpits, with as much apparent ease as a terrier dog would lay hold of a rat, and taking him to the vessel's side dropped him overboard, adding "*I hope thee can swim!*" After disposing of two or three more in this same way, the American sailors inspirited by this unexpected diversion in their favor, succeeded in driving the boarders back to their own vessel, and in compelling them to sheer off, foiled of their object, Nathan could never tell whether these men got to shore or to their own vessel, and as it was in the middle of the Mediterranean, it was at any rate a charitable *hope.*

Christmas Living.

On Christmas day last, a show of beef was made at S. Berresford's stall, such as has rarely been exhibited any where. Think of a stand ing rib, 5½ *inches* thick *of fat* in its thinnest part; and the *kidney fat* 12½ *inches through.* This extraordinary bullock was fattened by Douglass Lewis of Bourbon county, Kentucky, a region which produces as fine beef as any in the wide world.

I was shown last Friday at the same stall, a superb saddle of mutton also, which Mr. B. has since sent off to Columbus to fill up its measure of usefulness, and wipe off the reproach inflicted by Judge Wright in one of his senior editor letters, that no good thing can come into Columbus. The editor who is not only a Judge in *law* but in gastronomy, will be obliged to retract, I suspect.

Statistics.

A correspondent of the Cincinnati Chronicle of the 24th ult., having alleged that after counting three times the buildings put up in 1844 for the *Second Ward,* they fell far short of the statement on that subject, in CIST'S ADVERTISER copied in the *Chronicle,* I addressed a note to that office asking the writer's name. This was refused, on the ground that their correspondent wished his name to be unknown. On Saturday last, the same article, substantially, appeared in the Gazette, and will doubtless go the rounds of the city press; the purpose of the writer, or of those who put him forward to gratify their *private griefs,* being obviously to provoke a controversy with me.

With an individual who thus *skulks,* I can have no controversy, nor will the assurance of the publishers of the Chronicle, that he is a man of *responsible* character, suffice me. *Responsibility* and *no answer* are contradictory terms. as Webster's dictionary as well as common sense, and usage of words will satisfy every one. A man may be wealthy, of general intelligence, and of great influence in society, who cannot be responsible on this subject. Unless he is familiar with it, and too honest to misstate, he is not responsible, *even if known*: much more so, while unknown.

It may be said, it does not require special qualifications to count houses. I admit it: But there are other things in issue. The Second ward has been repeatedly changed in its boundaries, and the last change has added territory to it. How do I know, or any one else, that this writer knows its boundaries. It is necessary also to agree upon some common principle of computation, so as to determine what belongs to thi year, to the last, or to the next. It is then necessary to apply these principles or rules to a laborious and patient ascertainment, what build ings enter into the erections of 1844. These and other preliminaries must be settled before an issue of correctness can be made up by me with any one. How are they to be adjusted between two persons, one of whom is unwilling to be known to the other, or to the public?

What the testimony of the writer is worth may be told when he gives his name; what his reasoning is worth may be judged by one of his arguments, which 1 give as a specimen of the case. A block of houses may have *several tenements*, it is however, but *one building*. That is to say, that the rows on Fifth street, between Race and Elm street, at the corners of Walnut and Fourth, and Plum and Longworth streets, and others of the some character, are each one building, and must count accordingly. I shall not waste argument or time with such reasoning. When our eastern cities, who put up their 1200 to 1600 houses per annum, a large share in blocks of thirty to fifty, reckon by this rule, I will agree to adopt it.

I do not feel myself called upon, at this time to vindicate my statements on this or any other subject, and am willing that the public shall judge whether myself or an anonymous accuser be worthy of credit.

Fancy Squirrels.

It is well known that cats and rats are extensively used in some countries as articles of food. The *olla podridas* of Spain and Italy, are composed in part of cats, fattened for the purpose; while rats and other vermin are regular articles of consumption in the Canton and other Chinese markets. But it is not so well known that these articles are in use in many parts of our own country, principally by foreigners. Dr. T. a physician of Butler county, Penn., and a native of Holland, was extravagantly fond of cats which he fricasseed or smothered in onions.— Although as honest as steel in every thing else, it was notorious that he had slight scruples in making free with his neighbors cats, which disappeared rapidly, most of them being traced by the pelts and loose fur to the Dr's. residence.— The ladies of Woodville, near which he resided made a general outcry on the Dr's. taste as well as lamentation for the fate of their feline inmates, and wanted their husbands to interfere. These however did not think it worth while to quarrel with so useful and necessary a man as the Doctor for the sake of a few cats; he being a very pleasant and popular neighbor otherwise.

I am reminded of the circumstance by a rumpus kicked up in the 5th street market a few days since. It seems that a farmer from Colerain township brought in a lot of rats which he sold for squirrels a few market days since,—

They brought him five cents each. The affair leaked out in the neighborhood, and a man of the same name being accused with it, it almost occasioned a fight. I should like to know who bought these squirrels; that the problem might be solved whether public prejudice deprives us of an addition to the existing luxuries of our Cincinnati markets.

An Aid-de-camp Extempore.

On the 18th of June, the battle of Waterloo was raging fiercely. Napoleon and Wellington were in the midst of their "great game," and each intently regarded the "moves" upon the complicated and chequered field. Squadron after squadron bore down upon our gallant infantry as the big waves rise and break upon our level shore, and then retire in unavailing fury and dispersing foam. Then followed the devastating fire of artillery, rending our brave and living masses in gory fissures, which were closed as soon as made, or avoided by a change of attitude, and then again came the fierce rush of the horse and enthusiastic foe, with cuirass and uplifted sabre, to be as often repulsed by a steady fire of musketry, or checked or routed by our own resolute and strong armed cavalry.

Confident in the strength of his numbers and the success of other days, Napoleon departed not from his favorite and furious system; as firm in purpose as conscious of the unfailing means which he possessed for supporting it.— Wellington saw the devastating havoc made upon his advanced battalions, while he coolly dispatched aid-de-camp after aid-de-camp from point to point—from position to position preparing for various consequences—to remedy unfavorable aspects—availing himself of casual results or fresh intelligence—until his whole staff had left him. The directing spirit of the British line sat, apparently as upon a review day, directing his eagle glance over the field, as though penetrating the dense smoke which arose from hard fought encounters, and distinguishing individuals among the countless figures mingling in the bloody conflict. The handglass was constantly at his eye, and his favorite charger "Copenhagen," seemed conscious of the importance of good behavior upon that momentous day.

A few paces in the rear of his Grace, and mounted upon a Flemish nag, sat an unpretending young man, with a ruddy countenance and in "mufti," deliberately contemplating the scene of human strife in which he took no part, nor in which, from his demeanor, one might imagine he was very deeply interested. He wore a dark surtout. with drab trousers and buff gaiters; a hat of less dimensions than was the fashion of the day, inclined a little over the left ear, from under which, for it was firmly fixed upon his head, some wiry, sandy colored hair, just shewed its edges. In his hand he held a stout cotton umbrella with which he ever and anon evinced his dislike to the slightest curvetting on the part of his horse by a thump on the flank.

Here was an odd figure of peace and quietude, in strange contrast to the surrounding din of war and conflict. Occasionally he would rise in his stirrups, as fresh shouts of onslaught reached his ear, or sudden peals of cannon from a fresh quarter attracted his attention. Then settling down in the saddle, he would wait complacently the result, or watch, with an undisturbed countenance and amazing "sang froid," the course of a stray shot, furrowing the earth a few yards left or right of his person.

Suddenly his Grace turned quickly round as though seeking somebody to whom he would deliver an order, when his eye rested on the unmilitary personage whom we have described; it then glanced in other directions, and again returned to the daring but passive spectator.

"Who and what are you, sir?" inquired the commander in quick, authoritative accent.

"Me, sir?" replied his companion out of arms, bestowing a blow upon the flank of his animal. "My name is Jones. I am travelling agent to Smith and Jenkins, of Holburn, in the hardware line.

Here was a pause, during which the Duke seemed for a second, "but" a second, to withdraw his mind from the immense responsibility of his situation, when the last speaker continued:

"I was at Brussels for orders and understood there was to be a fight, so I came to see it. I am rather thinking if I don't mind, I shall have to pay for this horse which I have only borrowed for the occasion. There," pointing to some scattered earth, "that shot would have spoiled my day's pleasure; but I shall see it out."

"Mr. Jones," said his Grace, "I want an order conveyed to a certain position; would you serve your country and oblige me by delivering it?"

"Oh dear, yes!" instantly replied the bagman, with another whack upon the beast. I don't mind giving it a bit, what is it?"

Hereupon the Duke pointed out the quarter, bidding him inquire for General ———, and communicate to him a certain command.

"But it is a question whether he'll believe me," observe the bagman, half doubtingly.

"Take this ring," added the Duke, giving him a signet, and a minute after the traveller was on his way amidst the battle, with an order in which the firm of Smith and Jenkins had no participation.

The General's eye followed him as he escaped the bullets, and took his course over more than one field, and many hundred dead and dying. In due time, the effects of the order was manifest, and the "service" was done. Nothing more was seen of the adventurous bagman. The Duke made many inquiries for 'Mr. Jones,' but in vain, and he at length came to the conclusion of his having fallen with other "good men and true."

Many years had elapsed when a servant at Apsley house announced the name of a visiter, one Mr. Jones. The Duke happened to be disengaged, and gave permission for him to enter his presence, when who should present himself but the "civil" hero of Waterloo, who with scarcely any change of costume from that which was worn on the memorable day, advanced, saying—"I am Mr. Jones, if your grace remembers a trifling service." "I remember a great and personal one, my dear sir," said his Grace, interrupting him and shaking his hand, "how can I serve you?"

"Why, I am of the firm of Smith and Jenkins, in the hardware line, and the honor of your patronage, and government patronage"—

"I shall not fail to exert myself in your behalf," said his Grace; "but what became of you immediately after you delivered your order to General ———?"

"Why I can scarcely tell." Mr. Jones looking up to the ceiling. "At first I got into the corner field among one regiment—then over the hedge among another—then into the wrong reserve among the French—then my horse was killed—then back again among a square, whilst the fight lasted between your horse soldiers and Bonaparte's horse soldiers, (and yours beat 'em fairly,) and then I got out of a charge, and "hid up" a bit! and after that I was sometimes in one place and sometimes in another; but had nothing to do with the "fight," and so I did'nt much join one side nor the other.

The Duke kept his word. If some of the government clerks of the present day, when they stir for the hundredth time their winter office fire, can find leisure to examine their pokers they will find stamped thereon "Smith, Jenkins and Jones, makers."

Paul Jones.

So much has been published respecting this extraordinary man, that there is little which is interesting respecting him left, at the present day for gleaners of history, or anecdote.

The following, although not absolutely new, is not generally known, and merits preservation:

"In the year 1801, two of the largest frigates in the world lay near each other in the Bay of Gibralter. It was a question which was the largest. Some gave it that the *American* President (commodore Dale) had it in length, and the *Portuguese* Carlotto (commodore Duncan) in breadth. Each commander had a wish to survey the vessel of the other and yet these gentlemen could never be brought together. There was a shyness as to who should pay the first visit. There is no more punctilious observer of etiquette than a naval commander, jealous of the honor of his flag, on a foreign station. A master of ceremonies, or a king at arms, is nothing to him at a match of precedency. The wings of a ship are the college in which he obtains this polite acquirement, and when he comes to run up his pennant, we may be sure that a very professor in the courtesies flaunts upon the quarter deck. Dale was a good-humored fellow, a square strong set man, rather inclined to corpulence, jolly and hospitable. His pride in the command and discipline of his squadron, and the dignity of his diplomatic function, as the paramount of his station in the Mediterranean, formed a gentle bridle on his easy intercourse and openheartedness. Now he thought that the Portuguese commodore should "cale vurst," (parson Trulliber has it so,) as having been earliest at the station. This was mentioned to Duncan, (a fine hard bitten old seaman by the way,) and he forthwith laid down his punctilio in a manner that put an end to all hopes of an intimacy, or of a friendly measurement of the two ships. "Sir," said he, "as Commodore Duncan of the Portuguese navy, I would readily call first upon Commodore Dale of the American navy; but as Lieutenant Duncan of the British navy, I cannot call upon a gentleman who served under the pirate Paul Jones."

This awoke my curiosity, and the next time I was in company with commodore Dale, he, perceiving that my conversation led that way, readily met me in it. He had been with Jones in the Ranger, as well as in the Bon Homme Richard. What follows is from his recital.

Paul Jones *wanted* (as the Bow-street runners

say) Lord Selkirk, to try upon him the experiment practising on President Laurens in the Tower; and if Laurens had suffered, Lord Selkirk, or any other great man they could get hold of, would have been put to death. Lord Selkirk was only preferred as being considered by his supposed residence to be the readiest for capture. Jones was surprised and displeased at the family plate being brought on board, but the returning it would have been too serious a displeasure to his crew. It was sold by public auction at Cadiz, bought in by Jones, and sent back, as we have known.

Commodore Dale thus related the action of the Serapis. The "Bon Homme Richard" was an old East Indiamen, bought and fitted out at a French port, and so christened out of compliment to Franklin, then in Paris, one of whose instructive tales is conveyed under such a title. Having originally no ports in her lower decks, six were broken out, (three on a side,) and fitted with six French eleven-pounder guns. On the upper deck she had twenty-four or twenty-six of small calibre. She had a numerous crew to which[were added some recruits of the Irish brigade, commanded by a lieutenant—now a general officer in the British service. Fontenoy was one instance, and this action was another, of the gallantry of these unfortunate gentlemen whom an invincible hereditary feeling had driven into the service of the French monarch.—When the last of their protectors was dethroned, honor brought them gladly over to the standard of their country.

In this vessel with the Alliance, American frigate of 36 guns (a fine regular ship of war) and the Pallas, French frigate of 32, Paul Jones started on a marauding expedition,only differing from that of Whitehaven, as being on a larger scale. It was his intention to amerce the northeastern ports of England, in heavy pecuniary ransoms, or to destroy the shipping and building as far as could be effected. He had intelligence, or believed so, of the exact number of troops stationed in those different places. Leith was the first great object. Entering the Firth, they seized upon a Scotch fishing boat. The owner was refractory, but they terrified him into the office of pilot. The wind became adverse; they reached Inchkeith, but could not weather it, and had to stand out again. Making the land next to visit Whitby and Hull, they fell in with a large convoy,which dispersed while the ships of war (Serapis 44, captain Pearson, and Percy 20 guns, captain Piercy) which protected it, stood out to engage them. The determination was mutual; there was a deal of hailing from the Serapis,to the really *strange* ship which approached her. They closed, and the Bon Homme, by Jones' order, was made fast to the Serapis,—While these were thus closely engaged the Alliance worked round the two ships, pouring in raking broadsides, which Paul Jones finding equally injurious to his own ship, if intended for the Serapis, put an end to by ordering the Alliance off, and she lay by during the action while the Pallas was engaged with the British sloop of war. The cannonade was to the advantage of the Serapis, and gradually silenced the fire of the Bon Homme. The latter wished, and expected once to be boarded; the British boarders were about to enter but returned, deterred at the superior number lying waiting for them, and purposely concealed, as far as might be, under the gangway. Lieutenant Dale, on going below, found two of the three guns on the fighting side silenced and the crew of the other vying with the crew of a British gun opposite, which should fire first. The British were quickest and that gun was knocked over also.— He returned slightly wounded and much fatigued to the upper deck, and was seated on the windlass,when the explosion which blew up the deck of the Serapis, all aft from the main hatchway, gave the victory to the Bon Homme. For this success they were indebted to the officer and party of their marines. Seated out on the yards grenades were handed along, dropped by the officer into the hatchway of the Serapis, and at last caught to some ammunition.

Paul Jones, crippled and afflicted with the gout, was seated, during the affair, in a chair, on the quarter deck. Dale boarded the Serapis with a few men. As he made his way aft, he saw a solitary person leaning on the taffrail in a melancholy posture, his face resting upon his hands. It was Captain Pearson. He said to Dale, "The ship has struck." While hurrying him on, an officer came from below, and observed to Captain Pearson, that the ship alongside was going down. "We have got three guns clear, Sir, and they'll soon send her to the devil." It's too late, Sir, call the men off, the ship has struck." *I'll go below, Sir, and call them off;"* and he was about to descend, when Dale interfering, said, *'No. Sir, if you please you'll come on board with me."* Dale told me if he had let that officer go below, he feared he would have sunk them, as the Bon Homme was old, settling in the water, and in fact, went to the bottom that night.

Paul Jones was, in Commodore Dale's opinion, a very skilful, enterprising officer, but harsh and overbearing in disposition.

He was afterwards taken into the service of the Empress of Russia, and was to have had an important command against the Turks. Greig, however, and the other British officers in her service memorialed against it. They would neither associate nor serve with him, and, if she had not got rid of him, would have left her fleets.

Wherever Paul Jones was born. I have understood, from what I thought good authority, that he was apprentice in a coal vessel, in the employ of Mr. Wilson, at Whitehaven. It is told of him, that quarreling with a fellow apprentice, he took an opportunity to anoint the lad's head with a tar-brush, and then set it on fire.

MARRIAGES.

On the 24th inst., by the Rev. A. C. Thomas, Mr Christian Seidert to Miss Sarah T. McKim, both of this city.

On Tuesday the 24th, by Rev. Mr. Sehon. Mr. John Walker, to Mrs. Adeline A. French, all of this city.

On Tuesday the 24th, by Elder W. P. Stratton, Mr. Thomas C. Rensford to Miss Margaret R. Williams, all of this city.

On Wednesday the 25th inst., by the Rev. Abel C. Thomas, John C. Gaskill to Miss Catharine Singer, all of this city.

On Thursday the 26th Inst., by the Rev. Mr. Walker, Thomas B. Hubbell to Miss Elizabeth Ann Benson, all of this city.

DEATHS;

On Thursday morning, the 19th inst., at his residence in Batavia, Clermont County, Hon. Thomas J. Buchanan, after an illness of a few days.

In this city, at the resdence of Rev. L. French, on Monday the 23d inst, Mr. H. H. Smoot, of Consumption.

At his residence in Covington, on Thursday, the 26th inst., Hon. William Wright Southgate.

Sixth Ward--Cincinnati.

This is the south-west section of Cincinnati. It is somewhat in the shape of a wedge, of which the point is at Mill Creek, Sixth street, and the river forming the sides, and its eastern line, the butt. Its enumeration of buildings, follows:— Public buildings,ten. St, Aloysius orphan asylum, on 4th street,Gas works,public school house,two Friends' meeting houses, Morris Chapel, Trinity church, on Fifth street, Christian church, on Fourth, Baptist church, on Pearson street, and an Engine house, on Fifth. The entire number of buildings of the ward is 1063; 495 of which are of brick, and 568 are frames.

Of these there were at the close of 1842.

Bricks. 249.	Frames, 501.	Total,	750.
Built in 1843, 157.	" 39.	"	196.
" 1844, 89.	" 23.	"	117.
495.	568.		1063.

This is the only ward in the city through which I have gone, in which the buildings of this year, fall short of those put up in 1843. As an offset to this, it should be recollected that more buildings were put up last year, in the Sixth Ward, than in any other in Cincinnati.

Several fine improvements have been made during the current year here. Among these are the steam saw-mill of Baily and Langstaff, Thayer's Phoenix distillery,a Brewery on Smith street, south of the canal, a Rolling Mill, on 3d west of Smith, an Iron Wire, and Leaden Pipe factory, near the Gas works, Walter's bedstead factory, on Smith, near Front, and above all, the Cottonmill of Messrs Strader & Co,of which there is nothing in capacity, convenience,and substantial character, its equal this side of Lowell ,Mass. All these are of brick; a large number of fine brick dwellings, interpersed through the ward have also been erected this year, among which I have room only to specify two on Fourth st., opposite the Public school house, put up by Dr. Almy.

I observe that the work of grading Sixth st,, west of Park to its termination at Mill Creek which cannot be greatly short of a mile, is rapidly progressing. It will prepare the way, for a great amount of house-building on the western end of that street, heretofore neglected on account of former difficulty of approach from the west,and I have no doubt will at least add fifty buildings next year to Sixth street west of Mound.

A splendid improvement is in progress, also at the west end of Longworth street, which bids fair for completion in the spring. This is the erection of a row of ten dwelling houses in modern style,faced with marble and ornamented with verandahs, and balconies. This and the elevation of the scite, must make these buildings one of the most conspicuous, as well as striking

objects to arrest the eye of the traveler, and will be visible even from the steamboats.

I estimate one half of this ward built upon. It is probably the only ward in Cincinnati, where the frame buildings are more numerous than those of brick.

Seventh Ward--Cincinnati.

This is another of the larger and more populous of the Wards. It lies between the Fifth and Eighth Wards, and extends from Sixth street, north to the corporation line. Three-fifths of it is built up, according to my estimate.

The public buildings are: The Commercial Hospital; Cincinnati Orphan Asylum; Engine House on George street. Churches, The Methodist Protestant on Elm; Fifth Presbyterian corner Elm and Seventh; Elm street Baptist corner Elm and Ninth; German Reformed on Elm; Second Advent Tabernacle corner John and Seventh; Reformed Presbyterian, George between Race and Elm; Grace Church—Episcopal--Seventh between Plum and Western Row; Ninth street Methodist Chapel, and the Roman Catholic Cathedral, now nearly finished. —12.

The entire number of buildings in the Seventh Ward, is 1311, of which, 610 are bricks, and 701 are frames.

Of these, there were at the close of 1842:

	Bricks, 352	Frames, 588	Total, 940
Built in 1843,	112	40	152
" 1844,	146	73	219
	610	701	1311

This ward has received its full share in the beauty and importance of the buildings added the current year to Cincinnati. Among these are a large block of four or five spacious three story business buildings, at the corner of Elm and Sixth, with five fine dwellings in the rear, fronting on George street. Some fine private dwellings at, and near the corner of Court and Elm streets, and various other buildings interspersed through the ward. The larger share of its improvements are north of the canal, the contrary being the fact, as already stated, in its adjacent ward east—the Fifth. Pleasant street to the south, and parts of 14th, Hopkins, and John streets, are undergoing great improvements in their grade, in the latter cases imparting that elevation to the lots, which contributes so distinctly to the beauty of Fourth street on its upper side, from Plum to Park street, west. The great building of the Seventh Ward, however, is the CATHEDRAL, which has been progressing now for four years, steadily but slowly, as became the massive and permanent character of the improvement. The Plum street front has been closed up with walls of Dayton marble, breast high, and surmounted with neat and well.

finished railings, with necessary openings and gates facing the Cathedral entrances. The railing is continued on the north side the whole depth of the Cathedral, where it is succeeded by brick walls on the north-west and south sides of the entire enclosure, comprehending the dwellings erected for the clergy, attached to the diocese. I suppose there is nothing belonging to that denomination, in the United States, which will compare with this Cathedral when finished, so far as the exterior is concerned. It has cost far less, I should judge, than the metropolitan one at Baltimore, which is an unsightly pile, while this is a truly magnificent structure.

In this Ward as in the *Sixth*, I have found as I probably shall also find in the *Eighth*, an excess of frame over brick buildings. This is occasioned by the circumstance, that nearly all the early buildings in that part of the city which now constitutes these wards, were put up of frame. The tearing down of Frames to make way for Bricks, and the great excess of new bricks over new frame buildings, will increase the disparity between the two, each succeeding year of our building operations.

Eighth Ward--Cincinnati.

This is the north-west territory, and the only region of our city in which the built up part is less than that which remains yet to built. If any individual who has lived here five to ten years, to say nothing of longer residents, and as far back as the shortest period named can remember it as an irregular surface of commons, brick-yards, pasture grounds, and market vegetable gardens, were to visit it now, he would be at a loss to find his way through the cuttings down and fillings up of the streets, the putting up of buildings in all directions, and various other changes which would leave him in doubt whether this was the region he once knew.

The public buildings in the Eighth Ward, are in number, 7. The Engine House on Cutter street. The Pest House. The Tabernacle on Betts street. The United Brethren's Church, Fulton street. The Disciples' Church on Sixth street. The Public School House on London and Clinton streets. Of these, the Clinton street School house, and the Engine house have been built during the year which has just passed.

The entire number of buildings in the Eighth Ward, is 1164—bricks, 403; frames, 761.

Of these there were at the close of 1842,

	Bricks,		Frames,		Total,	
	145		604		749	
Built in 1843,	138	"	51	"	189	
" 1844,	120	"	106	"	226	
	403		761		1164	

Very extensive improvements in grading some

of the streets preparatory to paving, and in the actual paving of others have been made. Of these, the filling up of London from Cutter street, perhaps twelve hundred feet west, the cutting down of Freeman, Betts and Hopkins streets, all on the most extensive scale of thorough and efficient calculation for the future, may serve as specimens. A great number of fine dwellings of brick, with not a few charming frame cottages more delightful with their spring and summer shrubbery accompaniments, than the most splendid mansions on Broadway, have been put up during the year 1844.

Lever Lock Factory.

The making of Locks—now an extensive and important fabric here, was commenced in Cincinnati some ten or twelve years since, by ABEL SHAWK,, one of our most enterprising and ingenious mechanics, who judging rightly that the foreign article could be superceded only by locks of a decidedly superior quality, set to work and produced a series of fastenings for buildings, entirely different in material, construction, finish and strength from the English locks, and surpassing them in the same measure as they were different.

To understand this, it is necessary only for those who have seen them, to recall to mind the locks that were in use thirty years ago, defective in exactness of fit to the respective parts; with imperfect springs; with handles which could not hold the knobs permanently; latches that were liable to overshoot themselves; and keys filed into a multiplicity of wards which as they wore by use, either forced the corresponding wards of the lock out of their places, or became themselves unable to pass them; and continually getting out of order, to the constant loss and inconvenience of housekeepers. Even the *Scotch spring* locks, as they were called. which were doubtless a great improvement on the common lock, retained nevertheless many of the disadvantages referred to. It was reserved for American ingenuity, by abandoning the use of iron as far as possible; improving the form of the spindle and knob, and the mode of securing them together, furnishing efficient springs, and applying the tumbler principle to the bolt throughout these locks and latches, substituting for the old system of wards, solid bitts to the keys, in which the edges were filed to fit corresponding and substantial guards in the locks, that the foreign article has been driven from use in the city, and to a great extent in the whole west.

Since the commencement of *Mr. Shawk's* operations, five or six factories of the same kind have been established, most of which are in successful operation. His own—always the most important and extensive of them all—passed a year or two since into the hands of Messrs. *Glenn & McGregor*, who have well sustained the high reputation *Shawk* acquired for his locks, and added some important improvements to the manufacture. Among these is an ingenious and effective change in the shape of the key, whose wards are now taken off the nose in lieu of the sides. I shall refer to this change again, in the progress of this article.

The best idea of manufacturing operations here can probably be afforded by commencing with the successive stages of the fabrication of locks, latches, &c.

The first process as it commences in the basement, is the rough casting in brass of levers, tumblers, bolts, striking plates and knobs being the several parts of the locks and latches made here, and of the keys belonging to the locks. Of all these Messrs. Glenn and McGregor have an almost infinite assortment according to size and pattern. In the second story of the factory, the frames and covers of the lock, the only parts made of iron are cut by steel dies out of iron plates of suitable thickness, punching out the bolt, latch, and follower holes, the plate being then bent up to form the edges of the lock.

This operation is accomplished by the energies of a lever press, made by Miller and Carlton of our city. Of such force, as under the mere pressure of the hand to cut with great smoothness iron even 5-16 inch in thickness.

In another part of the same floor, the work of finishing the keys is also performed. These are usually varied at the side of the bit, but by one of those improvements in the mechanic arts going on continually here, they are now formed at its edge or nose, which allows of the same or a greater range in fitting, and tends less to injure the strength and durability of the key, by weakening it where it is already weakest, as was formerly the case. The manner in which the changes and combinations are formed of more than 180 different shapes and sizes of keys, may be varied to such an extent as to defy the possibility of fitting any other key to them than its appropriate one, or one made purposely to supply its loss. This is accomplished by cylindrical floats, which form the various modifications and varieties at the nose of the key. It must be obvious that a check is thus interposed to the use of skeleton keys, in picking locks which did not exist in the old mode.

The inside work is of Prince's metal a compound of copper and block tin, which renders it tougher than brass of which it is generally supposed to be made. A variety of ingenious bank door, tool chest, and pad locks fabricated by Messrs. Glenn and McGregor, were shown me, deserving of notice here, but which can be better appreciated by examination than description. It might suffice to say that a simplicity as well as an exactness of mechanism, are manifest in all these, which is the best guarantee of their being highly efficient now, and of their capacity of being kept so for years. One feature of their detector bank lock is remarkable. It not only defies tampering with, twelve tumblers being required to be raised, which no skeleton key can accomplish. But such is the exactness required to imitate the genuine key, that the thickness of a slip of bank paper, as was made apparent in my presence, sufficed when added to the size of *its own key* to prevent that key from opening the lock to which it belonged. It is worthy of notice that no locks of their make have been picked during the late burglaries in Cincinnati, where the neglect, or rather ignorance of house-keepers, did not invite the operations of the picklock, by leaving the key *improperly* in the door. When I say improperly, I mean leaving the key in the position it occupies in locking the door with the bit to the jamb side of the keyhole, which permits a wire bent for the purpose to pass through, catch the handle of the key, and to open the door from outside. This cannot be done if the key after locking is turned so far round in the lock as to leave its bit on the opposite side, the wire in that case, interfering with the repassing of the key in unlocking. After all the safer way is to take the key out entirely.

At this factory are made also all sorts of bell rope fixtures, & also club-foot apparatus for correcting that deformity. There are fourteen hands employed in this establishment, who turn out annually 10,000 dollars worth of locks latches &c. Now there are five more factories in Cincinnati of this nature, and the entire aggregate of their force may be estimated at thirty-five hands, and the value of their products, of 25,000 dollars. It must be observed, this does not include the heavy operations of *Miles Greenwood* in the lock line; his being principally made of cast iron could not well be included in these statistics.

Cincinnati Wood Company.--No. 2.

I have presented a brief view of the operations of this Company, so far as they are calculated to assist and relieve the poor, the primary object of their labors. There remains another feature of this establishment, which I had not room to touch in my last number, and will now notice.

Families who buy wood as most of us do, a load or a cord at a time, are subject to imposition in every stage of the dealing, from the bargaining for a load, to its final piling up, when sawed and split in the yard or the cellar. Those who have the means to pay for a years supply at once, and space to stow it away, can protect themselves. It is one job and no more to contract with the large dealer, for 15 or 20 cords, to stipulate the price for sawing, splitting, and piling, and in these various processes detect or guard against extortion or imposition in any of these departments. But they who buy a load or a cord merely, and generally at the moment of need, must sometimes take it of a quality, and at a price which they would not if they had a choice; will have crooked and knotted sticks imposed on them, some of which cannot readily be split, and must go to waste; and must pay at times 50 per cent. higher for sawing and splitting on the spur of the moment, than their wealthy neighbor who chooses his time and mode of purchase, and bespeaks his wood of a man in whom he can confide.

All this and more, this Company I see clearly, will obviate by their operations. They deliver into your yard or cellar, wood of just the quality you want, with the unprofitable pieces taken out, and the residue sawed and split to the length and size you desire, and at a price never higher and generally much cheaper than you can get in any other mode. For example: you order a cord of best hickory or sugar tree for immediate use; it is delivered into your cellar and piled up, at 4 dollars per cord. Now if you are fortunate enough to obtain at your first search, hickory wood at the canal or river, at 2 50 cents, perfectly straight, sound, and free from forks, if you find a perfectly honest wagoner, who will deliver you full loads, and at 50 cents per cord; if you get none of it lost on the way by carelessness of his driver; if you get a man to saw it twice at 50 cents per cord, who will not take advantage of your absence to saw some of it but once, and a man to split it at the same price; all which are the lowest possible rates at which these things are done; then wood may be bought as cheap, but no cheaper, than of the Company. But if you fail in a single one of these points, your wood costs you higher;—greatly so, if you fail in many or all these.—Wood costs frequently much higher than 2 50, if first rate, and the charge to many parts of the city is 62½, 75, and even 87½ cents per cord for hauling; most of the sawing is paid for at 37½ cents each time, and splitting unless of the easiest kind always costs more than sawing. It is easy to see then, that in a regular course of dealing, wood can be here supplied, 20 to 25 per cent. cheaper than at the public stands, and at a greater difference when the article is scarce, the Company selling always at regular and permanent prices. The effect of this will be, as its operations are becoming felt in the community, that persons will leave their orders at a yard, where there is no motive to deal otherwise than

justly and liberally, rather than with individuals in the market space of whom they know nothing, and we shall see the system of forestalling and huckstering wood now prevalent, so long a curse not to the poor merely, but to persons in moderate circumstances, broken up as all huckstering ought to be, and the persons engaged in it driven to regular and more honest employment.

I commenced this article with the view of calling public attention and support to an institution which, enabling the poor to help themselves, deserves sympathy and patronage. But the views presented in this number, rendering it palpable that every dollar laid out in stock is a saving of so much or more by persons able to contribute, in the purchase of their own supplies, that I am satisfied self interest alone will bring out all the funds necessary for the enlargement of its operations so as to meet the wants of the whole city.

CORRESPONDENCE.

Cincinnati, Jan. 7th, 1845.

Mr. Cist, Sir :—

I have read, with great interest, the "Recollections of a Voyage to Italy, in 1800," lately published in your Advertiser, partly from the spirit stirring character of the incidents, but still more from my long and thorough intimacy with Charles Ramsdell, the hero of the narrative, who was all the writer described him to be. We were school-boys together, on the island of Nantucket, and at that early period, Charles was the same master spirit among his youthful associates, as he appears in that narrative, and would doubtless have approved himself more fully if he had survived a few years to take part in the naval warfare of the last war with Great Britain. There were but two families of the name, to my knowledge, there, the heads of which were James and William Ramsdell. I do not believe their relationship was very close, if any existed at all. Charles was the son of William, having a brother of that name also, and resembled his father rather in character and conduct than in features. He went to sea as a cabin boy first, in a ship commanded by Zenas Coffin, in 1791, sailed as mate in 1798 and 99, and it must have been in the voyage narrated by your correspondent, that he had his portrait taken in Europe, and sent home to his mother on the Island.

The old woman who lived to the age of one hundred, and died only a year since, was of Quaker origin and prejudices. She was much gratified with the picture, Charles being a favorite, of course, with her, as he was more or less with every body else. He was represented standing on the quarter deck with a spy-glass in his hand: and so far Mrs Ramsdell was pleased with what she saw; but her pacific feelings revolted from the guns which made their appearance on the deck, as represented in the picture. "I wish," said she, "those things had not been there."— I was present when she received it, and remember its whole appearance. Ramsdell was lost at sea, as the writer states, and could not have been more than 23 or 24 years of age, when he perished in the vigor of his usefulness.

Yours,   N.

Derivations.

I have been asked by a correspondent the derivation of *Buck*-wheat. As a Pennsylvanian, of which State that grain is an important item in the *cereals*, I felt bound to devote a few moments of leisure to the subject. But alas! the minutes became hours before I accomplished my undertaking, to which Webster and Johnson were called on,—to no purpose—for assistance.

The names of the family of grains, wheat, buckwheat, rye, oats, spelts, with the generic name corn, are all of Saxon origin. Buckwheat is a corruption rather than a translation of *Buchwaizen*, the first syllable signifying beech,the tree of that name, whose nuts the kernel of the grain so much resemble in shape. The grain therefore, might be properly called *beech* wheat. While on the subject of derivations, I remember an ingenious suggestion made by a friend more than thirty years ago, which I have never seen published. An individual using the vulgarism *Hand*irons, was corrected by another in being told to say *And*irons. My friend who was present observed that the last was doubtless the accredited orthography as well as pronunciation, but considered one as incorrect as the other, believing both to be corruptions of *End*-irons, that is, irons to receive the ends of the firewood.

Election Returns of 1814.

The annexed papers exhibit the whole vote of the City—then town—of Cincinnati thirty years since. It seems one hundred and forty-one votes, constituted the electoral force of the place at that date. The City vote last election, nearly reached ten thousand. What an increase! more than seventy fold, in that space of time.— Wingate's tavern, at which the poll was held, was on Main below Fifth, where Denniston's tavern at a later date was kept. The whole City voted at one poll—the Mayor's Office on Third street—as late as the Presidential election of 1824, after which the City was divided into four Wards, which dissected Cincinnati north and south by Third, and east and west by Main street.

After the lapse of twenty years, we are just as much crowded at each poll of the nine Wards, as the City then was at one. What a prodigious increase in that space of time.

The names of survivors are in italics:

—

CINCINNATI, April 4th, 1814.

At an election held at John Wingate's tavern, for Corporation Officers, the following persons were ticketed for, viz:

PRESIDENT.

Samuel W. Davies,	122	Daniel Symmes,	19

RECORDER.

Griffin Yeatman,	124	John Andrews,	14
A. Pharis,	1	Solomon Sysco,	1
Dan'l. Drake,	1		

SELECT COUNCIL.

Jacob Burnet,	133	William Corry,	132
Samuel Stitt,	122	*Davis Embree*,	103
John S. Wallace,	80	William Irwin,	79
Jacob Wheeler,	77	*N. Longworth*,	68
Joseph Ruffner,	62	John Andrews,	60
Andrew Burt,	14	N. Reeder,	14
Jonathan Pancoast,	1	*Griffin Yeatman*,	1
Benjn. Mason,	2		

ASSESSOR.

John Mahard,	135

COLLECTOR AND MARSHALL.

James Chambers,	132
Josiah Conklin,	1

ICHD. SPINING, ⎱ Judges of
GEO. SULLIVAN,⎰ Election.

Attest:

W. S. HATCH, ⎱
THOS. HECKEWELDER, ⎰ Clerks,

Enclosed is the return of an election for Corporation Officers, held at Wingates tavern, on 4th April, inst. When the following persons were declared duly elected to the respective offices.

President of Select Council—SAM'L. W. DAVIES.
Recorder—GRIFFIN YEATMAN.
Select Council—Jacob Burnet,
                        Wm. Corry,
                        Sam'l. Stitt,
                        Davis Embree,
                        John S. Wallace,
                        William Irwin,
                        Jacob Wheeler.
Assessor—John Mahard.
Collector and Marshall—James Chambers.

Attest   THOS. HECKEWELDER,⎱ Clerks of
              W. S. HATCH: ⎰ Election.

4th April, 1814.

The Early Scouts of Cincinnati.

We, the subscribers, having engaged as Spies, Scouts, and Messengers, in the service of the United States, to be stationed at Forts Hamilton, St. Clair, and Jefferson, do covenant, bind, and oblige ourselves, to receive, obey, and as far as may be in our power, carry into effect, all the lawful commands which may from time to time be given to us by the Commandant of the post, where we may respectively be stationed, for and in consideration of which, we are by a-greement with L't. Col. Comm't. Wilkinson, to be subsisted with a Continental Ration per day to each of us—and are to receive one dollar for every day of our service, from the time of muster until discharged.

As witness our hands at Fort Washington, the 12th of May, 1792.

> DAN'L. GRIFFIN,
> JNO FLETCHER,
> DAN. CAMPBELL,
> JOSIAH CLAWSON,
> RESIN BAILY,
> JOSEPH SHEPHARD.

Fish from the Lakes.

For years, at repeated intervals, efforts have been made to introduce the *white fish*, of our great lakes into market, here and at other places, as a substitute for the shad of the Susquehanna and the Connecticut. These efforts have proved a failure. Nothing can exceed the beauty and tempting appearance of these fish, on their first receipt and retail sale. But they have a flavor which cannot be weil and distinctly described, although every one who has tasted them recognises it afresh on every trial. This is contended by many, finally, to be in the nature of the fish, and I believe the experiment of sale, for this year, is as decided a failure as heretofore.

For myself I entertain no doubts, that the flavor referred to, and which must ever form an objection to the use of this article is not incident to the white fish themselves, but results from the character of the salt in which they are pickled. This is the *Onondago*, the only description of salt I have seen in the Lake country, and which having been used in the packing of pork has occasioned the loss of large quantities of that article, some few years since, and effected its own banishment from our markets, except for salting butter, for which use its beautiful appearance recommends it, although I have no doubt, it is the great cause why butter put up in the west does not keep as well as in the east.

The injurious properties of the *New York Salt*, —and that *from Liverpool* is nearly as worthless— arise from the use of quick or fresh-slacked lime which is employed in the vats and even in the kettles, while boiling, to precipitate the iron, of which there is enough to discolor western salt although it neither affects its taste, or injures its preservative properties. In this use, the lime combines with the carbonic acid, which is one of the constituent parts of the brine, forming the carbonate of lime, which imparts an injurious taste, and neutralises the antiseptic properties of salt: in both ways, rendering the fish unfit for market, and still more so for keeping.

It is to be desired that some of the putters up of fish on the Lake shores, would supply themselves with salt from New York city or the Kanawha Salines. I have no doubt that the extra cost of either of these, would be more than repaid by the higher price and permanent demand they would find for fish put up with such salt.

I address this subject to my brethren of the quill in the Lake cities and towns, and recommend to their perusal, an elaborate report of Col. Benton's, drawn up for the use of the Senate, in 1838, on the *nature, use, and properties of salt.*—This document, if not within their reach otherwise, can doubtless be readily procured on application to their representatives in congress.

Relics of the Past.

Capt. John Armstrong to Gen. Jas. Wilkinsson.

> FORT HAMILTON, 1st May, 1792.

Dear General:—

I was honored with your letter of yesterday, by the Express, which gave me great relief, as my apprehension with respect to his safety, had given me painful sensations. M'-Donald, whom I sent to head quarters, on the 23d of April, carrying the despatches of Jefferson and St. Clair is either killed or taken. I am anxious for the safety of this, but conceive it my duty until you order otherwise, to send forward those letters from the out-posts, be the danger ever so great. I have as yet lost no men although the enemy have been frequently seen around us.

The building I have already began, when finished, will contain all the flour now here. Shall I proceed to erect one of the other bastions? those buildings add much to the strength of the garrison, but getting up the timber will be attended with some danger. Capt. Cushing's men arrived yesterday, and with those sent forward on the 20th, will return this evening:— when they left St. Clair, those from Jefferson had not arrived, although expected the day before,—

If this communication is kept up by soldiers who being unacquainted with the woods must keep the road, I am fearful we shall lose many of our men. I wish it might occur to you as proper to have two woodsmen at each Post for that purpose. The proceedings of the court martial, wherof Capt. Ford was President, were forwarded by M'Donald, and from a presumption that the President did not take a copy, I have directed the Judge Advocate, to forward one to Captain Ford, by this express. Please to inform me if Major Zeigler's resignation has been accepted.

Major Wyllys, the writer of the following, was in the United States service, employed in the West. He was out in Harmar's campaign, acting with Major Fountaine as seconds in command to Col. Hardin, in which capacity they shared the dangers to which his regiment was exposed in the surprize by the Indians, of the first day, and in the conflict of the next, fell victims to the rifles of the savages, Fountaine being pierced with eighteen balls.

FORT McINTOSH, 3rd May, 1786.

Sir:—I send you ten dollars by the bearer—also, some letters to the Minister at War—and one to Col. Harmar—which I wish you to take care of. It is probable Col. Harmar is on his way—I have directed the letter to Philadelphia, and I had rather it should remain than miss him on the road; use your judgment as to the probability of its reaching him before he arrives.

I cannot take my leave of you, without assuring you of the high sense I entertain of your strict attention to your duty since you have commanded at Fort Pitt.

I am, sir, with esteem,

Your most ob't. and humble serv't,

JNO. P. WYLLYS, Maj. 1st A. Reg.

Lieut. JOHN ARMSTRONG.

"Cincinnati in 1841."

Many of my readers will remember that in 1841 and 1842, I forwarded a considerable number of my publication, "Cincinnati in 1841," on account of purchasers here, to their friends in the British Isles. Hardly an opportunity occurred, but that from twelve to thirty copies were sent off at a time. Other persons here forwarded the book themselves to a great extent, and in examining my lists, I find that not less than five hundred copies have been sent to various parts of England, Scotland and Ireland.

From time to time since, I have been in the receipt of gratifying evidence, that the transmission of a publication like this, giving full and various information respecting the advantages presented at Cincinnati to emigrants, has answered many valuable purposes. As a specimen of western typography and engraving, it has elevated our character in these respects abroad, and I hazard nothing in saying, what I have abundant evidence before me to conclude as a fact, that Cincinnati is more fully and accurately known in many parts of the British isles and the ports of embarkation for German emigrants, through the medium of this and other statistical information—such as the columns of the Chronicle and other city papers, for instance impart, than any other place in the United States.

A week or two since, I was informed by Mr. Procter, of the firm of Procter and Gamble, that the copy of the publication I refer to, which he

forwarded his father, in Herefordshire, England, fell into the hands of two young men, whom it decided to visit this country, with the intention of making Cincinnati their residence. They arrived here accordingly, and have told Mr. P., that great as were their expectations, they have been amply fulfilled. They give Cincinnati the preference of any City they have seen in America.

Clevenger's bust of Harrison.

This is the bust of a western President, by a western artist, and both by residence and otherwise, identified forever with Cincinnati. Clevenger died prematurely, just as his talents were winning him fame, employment and support, and has left a destitute family, almost whose only possessions from which they can expect to realise money, is this work of his. Where should that bust be permanently placed with as much appropriateness as in Cincinnati? The price is five hundred dollars, which it is proposed to raise in one dollar subscriptions, from our citizens; the bust is to be disposed of as the subscribers may direct. For this purpose a subscription paper has been opened at the office of Burt and Greene, on Third street, which I trust the public spirit of the community will fill up at once. As we have never done anything directly for our artists let us not neglect this opportunity.

Chronology of the Week.

Jan. 1st. Union between Great Britain and Ireland, 1800. Tennessee admitted into the United States, 1796.

2nd. Edmund Burke born, 1730. Lavater died, 1801.

3rd. Gen'l. Monk died, 1670. Wm. Pitt died 1806. Battle of Trenton, 1777.

4th. Roger Ascham died, 1568.

5th. Duke of York died, 1827.

6th. Festival of the EPIPHANY from the Greek *Epiphaneia*, an appearance or Apparition, is kept in commemoration of the manifestation of our Savior to the Gentiles, first observed, A. D., 813, —old Christmas day.

7th. Fenelon died, 1715.

8th. Battle of New Orleans 1815. St. Lucian's day, the first named Saint in the Romish Calendar, was a presbyter at Antioch and suffered martyrdom under Maximinian, 211.

Organ Building.

My friend Koehnke, I find, is extending his business and customers, as his operations are becoming known. He is now at work on four organs, one of which, is for a Parlor, the others for Churches. His Organs compare advantageously wherever taken, with those in use, being not only superior in richness and sweetness of tone, but vastly cheaper in price. A reference to my advertising columns, will exhibit a certificate of the Organist and Vestry of the Episcopal Church, at Marietta, which lately supplied itself with one of his Organs.

The Constitution.

The following lyric, by O. W. Holmes, M. D. was published in the Boston Daily Advertiser, when it was proposed to break up the frigate Constitution, as unfit for service:

Ay, tear her tattered ensign down!
Long has it waved on high,
And many an eye has danced to see
That banner in the sky;
Beneath it rang the battle shout,
And burst the cannon's roar:
The meteor of the ocean air
Shall sweep the clouds no more!

Her deck, once red with heroes' blood,
Where knelt the vanquished foe,
Where winds were hurrying o'er the flood
And waves were white below,
No more shall feel the victor's tread,
Or know the conquered knee;
The harpies of the shore shall pluck
The eagle of the sea!

O, better that her shattered hulk
Should sink beneath the wave;
Her thunders shook the mighty deep,
And there should be her grave;
Nail to the mast her holy flag,
Set every thread-bare sail,
And give her to the god of storms,
The lightning and the gale!

Indian Sense of Propriety.

Some years ago, I think in 1800, I had the pleasure of meeting in Italy with Mr. Ellis, formerly governor of Georgia, when under the British crown. He delighted in recollections of the colony; I recollect, in speaking of the acute conceptions of the native Indians. his relation of the following circumstance.

After some difficulties that had occurred between the white settlers and the aborigines, in which several skirmishes had taken place, he succeeded in restoring peace; and, as was customary in such cases, the Indian chiefs were invited to the government house, to receive presents of arms, &c. The principal chief, however, did not appear on the day appointed. The delivery of the presents was postponed until all expectation of his arrival was abandoned.—They were then divided among those who did attend. A few days afterwards the chief arrived. The governor expressed to him his regret that he had not come in time to receive a part of the presents; and, as he was very desirous of propitiating his good will, he told him he would send by a packet, just ready to sail, for certain arms, &c., of superior workmanship, which he named, and that as soon as the packet should return from England, he should be sent for to re-

ceive them. The Indian expressed his obligation and returned to the forest.

On the arrival of the packet a messenger was sent to the chief, who was received by the governor in a room in which the various articles that had been named to him were all arranged. They were splendid arms, and savage finery;—but although articles best calculated to captivate his heart, his eyes glanced around the room with apparent unconcern, and he made no observations respecting them. The governor, apprehensive from his manner that he was not satisfied with the presents, desired the interpreter to ask him if the articles did not equal his expectation, He replied, yes. Why then, proceeded the interpreter, do you not thank him for them? The chief appeared to reflect for a moment, when fixing his eyes on the querist, he said: Six months ago, I was here. The governor then promised me these things—when he promised them, then he gave them. I then thanked him for them; were I to thank him now, would it not appear as if I had doubted the fulfilment of his promise.   R.

The Western Literary Journal.

The second number of the *Western Literary Journal* lies before me. The brief examination which editorial *leisure*, or rather the want of it, has permitted, induces me to think favorably of it. There is in it no want of a due proportion of able writers and interesting subjects. Mrs. Dumont's essay on "Female Training," is a forcible, just, eloquent and indignant plea for the rights of her sex to every educational privilege possessed now by males, and must find an echo in the breast of every lover of justice. There is also a valuable article by W. D. Gallagher, upon our Common Schools, rich in statistics and inductions.. There is a sufficient proportion of light and fancy reading, besides, to suit the cheap literature relish of the age. On the whole, every reader will find something to his taste when he sits down to this mental dinner table.

MARRIAGES.

ON Dec. 24th, by the Rt. Rev. Charles P. McIlvaine, D. D., James J. Butler of Cincinnati, to Cornelia Rutgers, daughter of the late Rev. Lewis P. Bayard of New York.

On the 31st ult., by the Rev. T. A. Mills, John N. Cosgrove of South Bend, Indiana, to Miss Susan Gardner of this city.

On the 31st ult., by Rev. Mr. Strickland. Mr. Cornelius Vancamp of Reading, O., to Miss Mary Hand, of this city.

On Jan. the 1st, inst, by the Rev. Abel C. Thomas. Mr. Calvin R. Starbuck, Proprietor and Publisher of the Cincinnati Daily Times, to Miss Nancy Webster.

On the 2nd inst, by the Rev. Mr. Kroel, Mr. Edward Fisher to Miss Charlotte Burghart, all of this city.

DEATHS.

ON the 31st Dec., Henry, son of J. A. James, aged 11 months.

In this city, 1st inst., Mr Andrew Coffman.

On 2nd of Jan., of disease of the heart, Rebecca, only daughter of Christian Donaldson, of Cincinnati, in the 20th year of her age.

In this city on the 6th inst., of Inflammatory Rheumatism, Christopher Marshall, son of Mr. C. M. Baxter, aged 18 months.

Indian Warfare--The Whetzels.

Among the early settlers, who have figured in the pioneer history of the west, one entire fa mily, that of the Whetzels, figures conspicuously. I have devoted some time to the comparison of various notices of the four brothers, who con stituted that family, and re-writing many inci dents in their history, to correspond with the corrections of Major Jacob Fowler, still surviving, and a resident of Covington, Kentucky, who was in early days an associate of Lewis and Jacob, two of these brothers. Some of the existing accounts represent old Whetzel, with his wife and small children, to have been killed, tomahawked, and scalped by the Indians. This was true only as respects the old man, but the wife survived and married again, and the children escaped by being providentially absent.

Major Fowler states that the family lived on a farm on the road from Catfishtown—now Washington, Pennsylvania, and Wheeling, Virginia, so close to the line that it was a matter of doubt in those days, which Whetzel belonged to, Pennsylvania or Virginia. Old Whetzel was a Maryland or Pennsylvania German, but had been one of the earliest settlers on the frontiers, and disdaining the usual precaution of placing his family on one of the stations or forts, which were to be found at convenient distances thro'- out that region of the country, had erected a cabin on his plantation, and occupied it while cultivating the farm. The family consisted of himself and wife, with his sons, Martin, Lewis, Jacob, and John, respectively 15, 13, 11, and 9 years of age. There were three or four small children besides, who had been left with some friends, that day, in the adjacent fort, to which John had also been despatched on an errand, when a party of savages surrounded the house forced open the temporary defences, killing and scalping the old man, and carrying off as prisoners, according to their custom with children o that age, the boys, Lewis and Jacob. The mo- ther made her escape in the confusion of the scene. Martin, the oldest son, had been out hunting, at the time. All three of these boys were stout and active for their age, the training on the frontiers, at that date, being such as to call out boys to do much of men's work, as soon as they were able to handle an axe, or steady a rifle.

In the attack on their house, Lewis received a slight wound from a bullet, which carried a- way a small piece of the breast bone. The second night after their capture, the Indians en- camped at the Biglick, twenty miles from the river, in what is now Ohio, and upon the waters of McMahon's Creek. The extreme youth of the boys induced the savages to neglect their usual precautions, of tying their prisoners at night. After the Indians had fallen asleep, Lewis whispered to his brother to get up, and they would make their way home. They started, and and after going a few hundred yards, sat down on a log. "Well," said Lewis, "we can't go home barefooted. You stay here, and I will go back and get a pair of moccasins for each of us." He did so, and returned. After sitting a little lon- ger; "Now," said he, "I will go back and get one of their guns and we will then start." This was accordingly done. Young as they were, the boys were sufficiently expert with tracking paths in the woods, to trace their course home, the moon enabling them, by her occasiona glimpses, to find the trail which they had fol- lowed from the river. The Indians soon disco- vered their escape, and were heard by them hard on their heels. When the party in pursuit had almost overtaken them, they stepped aside in the bushes and let them pass, then fell into the rear and travelled on. On the return of their pursuers, they did the same. They were then followed by two Indians on horseback, whom they eluded in the same manner. The next day they reached Wheeling in safety, crossing the river on a raft of their own making; Lewis, by this time, being nearly exhausted by his wound. When they got to the Virginia side, and ascer- tained thei father's death, they vowed to shoot every Indian that fell in their way, as long as they lived; and fearfully was this vow kept, as might be expected from the energy and activity displayed at so early an age.

The following narrative goes to show how much has been effected by the skill, bravery, and activity of single individuals, in the parti- zan warfare, carried on against the Indians, on the western frontier. Lewis Whetzel's educa- tion, like that of his cotemporaries, was that of a hunter and a warrior. When a boy he adopted the mode of loading and firing his rifle as he ran. This was a means of making him very destructive to tne Indians afterwards.

In the year 1782, after Crawford's defeat, Lewis Whetzel, then only eighteen years of age, went with Thomas Mills, who had been in the campaign, to get a horse, which he had left near the place where St. Clairsville now stands. At the Indian Spring, two miles above St. Clairs- ville, on the Wheeling road, they were met by about forty Indians, who were in pursuit of the stragglers from the campaign. The Indians and the white men discovered each other about the same time. Lewis fired first and killed an In- dian; the fire from the Indians wounded Mr. Mills, and he was soon overtaken and killed.— Four of the Indians selected out Whetzel, drop- ped their guns and pursued him. Whetzel load- ed his rifle as he ran. After running about half a mile, one of the Indians having got within ight or ten steps of him Whetzel wheeled round and shot him down; ran on, and loaded as before. After going about three quarters of a mile further, a second Indian came so close to him, that whon he turned to fire, the savage caught the muzzle of his gun, and, as he expressed it, he and the Indian had a pretty severe wring for it; he succeeded, however, in bringing the muzzle to the Indian's breast, and killed him on the spot. By this time he as well as the Indians were pretty well tired: but the pursuit was continued by the two remaining Indians; Whetzel, as before, loading his gun, and stopping several times during the latter chase. When he did so, the Indians treed themselves. After going something more than a mile, Whetzel took advantage of a little open piece of ground, over which the Indians were passing. a short distance behind him, to make a sudden stop for the purpose of shooting the foremost, who got behind a little sapling which was too small to protect his body. Whitzel shot, and broke his thigh, the wound, in the issue, proving fatal. The last of the Indians then gave a little yell and said: 'No catch dat man—gun always loaded,' and gave up the chase, glad, no doubt, to get off with his life. This was a frightful and well managed fight.

These Indians, in succession, were near enough to have despatched Whetzel with tomahawks, but their determination to take him alive, for burning at the stake, blinded their judgment, and enabled him to effect his escape. It is said that Lewis Whitzel, in the course of the Indian wars in the neighborhood of Wheeling alone, killed twenty-seven Indians, besides a number more, along the frontier settlements of Kentucky.

The United States Navy.

I observe in an Eastern print, the following project, which it is therein alleged to be the purpose of the Navy Department, to recommend to Congress as an improvement in our naval service. If adopted it would carry us in that department, fifty years forward in one single movement:

"Of all the rumors the most gratifying is, that the contemplated lines of steamers from Boston, Philadelphia, and New York to London, Liverpool and Havre, and from New Orleans to the West Indies and Spanish America, are to be set in motion as soon as possible.

The United States is to man completely and constantly, with officers, seamen and apprentices, some say ten years, others indefinitely; and allow them to carry the mails for their own benefit, and on these cheap terms, a company or companies of ship builders and merchants are ready to construct suitable steamers and keep up monthly returns.

The national character of these vessels, and their perpetual presence in the principal foreign ports will give valuable and efficient protection to our seamen.

It is said that whenever capitalists are willing to provide suitable vessels to run at stated and regular intervails, the United States will, under the new naval system, furnish as ample a complement of men, and as many guns as the owners are willing to provision and support. We have 6000 men now under government pay in the naval service. These would man a couple of frigates, the revenue vessels, and nearly, or quite one hundred steamers.

One hundred steamers passing at stated intervals to foreign ports carrying every where, in honor and usefulness, the United States flag, would do infinitely more credit to the national character, and would cost the Union less than the Mediteranean squadron managed as now; only occupied in cruising from one point to the other, their officers making parties, dancing, gambling, and carousing in harbor, and expending their ennui at sea, in acts of cruelty to their sailors.

The navy as now constituted, does not earn its salt; it has nothing to do, and naught is always in mischief. Yet its annual expenditure is equal to the whole expenses of our government, when administered with honesty and economy."

Commerce with the East.

They are beginning Eastward gradually to appreciate the value of the Western business.— By the time light on this subject spreads from Buffalo to Boston, we shall have the railroads finished which is now making to connect Cincinnati with the Lake Erie.

Railroad from Sandusky to Cincinnati.

An effort is now making to raise the necessary funds, $500,000, to complete this important work. The evidence that the stock will be very productive, is so abundant and so conclusive that we do not doubt it will be speedily taken by capitalists in New York, Boston and other cities.

The distance by this route is but 200 miles from Lake Erie to Cincinnati. Two companies are engaged in the enterprise. One, the Mad River and Lake Erie, is building the road from Sandusky City to Springfield, on the National Road, 40 miles west of Columbus—a distance of 132 miles. The other is called the little Miami Co., and is constructing a railway from Springfield to Cincinnati—a distance of 88 miles.— The latter company will have 64 miles of their road completed by the first of July, 1845, 40 of which, from Cincinnati Northward, are now in operation.

On the Mad River and Lake Erie road, 40 miles are also completec and doing a profitable business, and 40 more are so far advanced that $70,000 will finish the road. Within the limit of ten miles on either side of the line of the road, there are 350,000 inhabitants, mostly cultivating as fine a soil as the sun shines upon. Cincinnati already contains 70,000 inhabitants, and for the first 100 miles north of that city, there is an average of one factory or mill every mile on the line of the road.

This great improvement once completed, and we can go from this city to the Queen City of the Ohio valley in 36 hours, and to Louisville in a little over two days. The travel between the Southwest and the north and east by this route is quite incalculable. The country is admira bly adapted to the construction of a railway from Sandusky to Cincinnati, and the distance can easily be made in 10 or 12 hours- Below Cincinnati, the Ohio river is always navigable for steamers, except a few weeks in the winter.

The travel from the lower and upper Mississippi, Missouri, Southern Illinois, Indiana, and from the valleys of the Cumberland and Tennessee rivers, the latter of which runs into northern Alabama and Georgia, will all come north to the Atlantic cities by this route.

The intercourse between the northern and southern portions of the Union, will be much increased by the the opening of this easy and cheap thoroughfare between the great lakes and the 20,000 miles of navigable rivers at the southwest.

If the owners of the railway from this to Boston have any spare capital, they can hardly invest it better than to take stock in the road from Sandusky to Cincinnati. We speak advisedly on this subject when we say that a large portion of the immense valley of the Ohio, up that river to Wheeling, and thence to Baltimore, and still farther up to Pittsburgh and thence to Philadelphia, will turn north at Cincinnati, when a railway will take them to Lake Erie in twelve hours. That this travel would add largely to the present income of the railroad between this and Boston no one can doubt.—*Buffalo Com.Advertiser*

Relics of the Past.

To His Excellency, Arthur St. Clair, Esq., Governor of the north western Territory of the U States.

The humble petition of Francis Desruisseaux Bellecour, most humbly sheweth, that your petitioner hath for many years past acted at Detroit by appointment of the former government, as Public Notary for a number of years to the universal satisfaction of the individuals,, and the then government. After or immediately on the government of the United States taking place here, I was appointed to the same office of public Notary by Col. Sargent. But still, notwithstanding, I am deprived of the benefit of that office by individuals, having their notarial acts performed before the present proto notary and clerk of the court, which deprives me of the means of supporting a helpless family.

I therefore pray your excellency, to grant me the said office for the county of Wayne, exclusively of any other persons.

And your petitioner, as in duty bound, will pray. Being of your Excellency,

The most obedient, and humble servant,

F. D. BELLECOUR,
Notary Public
DETROIT, 7th January, 1799.

To the Hon. Arthur St. Clair, Esq., Governor of the north western Territory.

January 10, 1799.

DEAR SIE:—We., a number of inhabitants situated in the aforesaid Territory and county of Hamilton, between the waters of Eagle and Strait Creeks, and thereabouts, being at a great distance from a Magistrate, or Justice of the Peace—a greivance which we consider ourselves to labor under, we therefore have thought proper to petition your Honour for Alexander Martin, to be commissioned in such an office, as we look upon him to be an honest, well meaning man, and a citizen here amongst us, whom we have selected far that purpose. This, dear sir, being our grievance, a removal of which we, your petitioners, humbly pray.

Matthew Davidson.	Wm Woodrufl.
Thos. M'Connell.	Geo J Jennings.
Joseph Lacock.	Ichabod Tweed.
Isaac Ellis.	Amos Ellis.
Wm M'Kinney.	Jas Henry.
Wm Forbes.	Wm Moore.
Geo M'Kinney.	Isaac Prickett.
Jacob Miller.	Tom Rogers.
John Mefford.	Wm Long.
John Caryon.	Joseph Moore.
Wm Lewis.	Benjamin Evans.
Fergus M'Clain.	Jacob Nagle.
Richard Robison.	Lewis Sheek.
Henry Rogers.	John Philips.
Thomas Ark.	James Prickitt.
Valentine M'Daniel.	James Young.
Uriah Springer.	

Bell and Brass Foundry.

This is an important item of manufacturing industry in Cincinnati, and of increasing value. Its importance consists not more in the amount of industry which it stimulates, than in the incidental aid it supplies to other business, by concentrating to this point, the entire demand for bells north, south, and west of us. In 1840 there were eight of these establishments, with sixty-two hands, which have been increased at this date to twelve foundries, with one hundred and six hands, all engaged in the various operations of casting and finishing of articles in brass, of which the article of bells is of the greatest magnitude, affording an aggregate value of $135,000 for the past year. As an example of its character and operations, I select the business, for the last two years, of G. W. COFFIN, at the *Buckeye Foundry*, on Columbia street, whose bell business is of greater magnitude than all the other establishments combined, but whose brass business, generally, would not constitute more than an average of the general aggregate. In 1843, Mr. Coffin made, all to order,

36 steamboat bells, from		$150 to 706	each.	
8 plantation	do	50 to 360	do.	
3 foundry	do	150 to 350	do.	
11 college academy, and				
school house bells,		50 to 350	do.	
1 court house,		350	do.	
1 engine house,		326	do.	
38 church	do	80	3,363	do.

Besides 206 of lighter sizes of which no register has been kept. The whole weighing 40647 pounds, including the iron works connected therewith—worth more than twenty thousand dollars. The entire operations in brass, in this foundry reached the value of $31,000.

During the year 1844, there have been made bells here for steamboats

S. B. Maria,	500.	Charlotte,	326.
L. Flinn,	150.	Paul Pry,	82.
Mendota,	325.	Isaac Shelby,	200.
Lynx,	150.	Princess,	450.
Gov. Jones,	500.	Lowndes,	326.
B. Franklin,	7,327.	New World,	450.
Dan'l Boone,	150.	Superb,	450.
Harkaway,	326.	Hamer,	326.
Fashion,	200.	Belle Zane,	150.
Reindeer,	326.	Lama,	182.
Red Rover,	500.	Pike, No. 7,	550.
Gazelle,	150.	Juniata,	110.
Little Rock,	200.	Wave(Kanawha)	110.
Meteor,	326.	Arkansas No 4,	525.
Fort Wayne,	426.	Lady Madison,	326.
Lodi,	326.	Yorktown,	500.
Alex. Scott,	500.	St. Mary,	325.
Hard Times,	500.	Cincinnati,	326.
J. E. Roberts,	100.		

37 steamboat bells, weighing 11,598.

2 for barges. 62.

31 PLANTATION AND FARM BELLS.

150 82 326 80 50 336 25.
200 50 150 50 50 220 25.
110 82 110 82 50 326 82.
150 60 100 60 82 200
100 60 100 150 3,406.

6 Foundry, Factory, Turner and Engine Shop Bells.

82 110 120 31 50. 82 375.

9 School House and College.

50 80 50 200 25.
80 326 100 80 1001.

8 Court House and Fire Engine House.

326 326 500 750.
326 750 326 326 3630.

57 Churches.

150 60 150 200 150 110 450.
450 50 450 356 110 220 150,
150 50 200 450 110 200 326.
200 82 150 326 750 450
326 700 450 150 350 450
450 82 326 100 450 200
110 1800 110 200 750 326
500 200 200 700 110 82
326 500 200 110 2000 1000 19,758.

21 Hotels.

31 31 31 25 50 31 31.
25 31 31 31 31 31 50.
50 31 60 31 50 694.

The value of bells made in the BUCKEYE *Brass and Bell Foundry* for the past year was 31,000

dollars; of all manufactured articles of brass and bell metal, 39,000 dollars, being an increase of 25 per cent in the business of 1843. I presume there is a proportionate increase in the other establishments, Mr. Coffin being in bells, and theirs in brass foundry generally. He is about to put up a new Foundry, where bells only will be made.

I note two or three remarkable facts in connection with these statistics.

One of the bells cast this season was for the Roman Catholic Church at Mobile, a large share of its raw material, being the old bell, perhaps the oldest in the United States, which was cast at Toledo, in Spain. One eighth part of this bell was made of pure silver, fourteen hundred and seventy Spanish dollars being employed for that purpose. The whole of this precious article went into the new bell also. Mr. Coffin considers it one of the finest toned ones he ever heard rang.

Another singular fact connected with this statement is, that the bell which had been made for the Fulton Bagging Factory in 1842, was consumed, or at least so far destroyed, in the fire of October last, that not a vestige of it was to be found. The only reasonable conjecture respecting its fate, is that as the cupola, with the roof below, were burnt before the rest of the building, that the bell in melting spread out upon the sheeting and remaining roof, among the ashes into particles so minute as to be absolutely lost.

Early Annals.

To the Honorable Arthur St. Clair, Governor of the north western Territory.

January 10, 1799.

DEAR SIR:—We, a number of inhabitants, situated between the waters of Eagle and Strait Creeks, and thereabouts, in the aforesaid Territory and county of Hamilton, being destitute of malitia officers, such as Captain, Lieutenant, and Ensign, we therefore have thought proper to petition your Honour for such, and have selected Thomas M'Connell for Captain, John Mefford, Lieutenant, and Amos Ellis, Ensign, if your Honour shall think proper to commission them in that office; This, dear sir, being the desires for which we, your petitioners, do humbly pray

Abel Martin.	Tom Ash.
George M'Kinney.	Wm Moore.
William M'Kinney.	Ben
F orgy MClure.	Isaac Ellis.
Henry Rogers.	Jacob Nagle.
N McDaniel.	Geo J Jennings.
Jno Henry.	Uriah Springer.
Thomas Dougherty.	Joseph Jacobs.
John Redmon.	Samuel Tweed.
William Forbes.	William Lewcas.
Jas Pricket.	Jacob Miller.
John Caryon.	Walter Wall.

Thomas Rogers.

The Last of the Girtys.

BY CHARLES CIST.

THE early commerce of the Ohio river for some years was confined to the transportation of Western produce on flat-boats, which were built at various points from Cincinnati to Elizabethtown, on the Monongahela. The high rates of wagonage across the mountains, led many persons early to contemplate and some of them to engage in the taking up in keel-boats and subsequently by barges, various articles, groceries especially, which could be bought to good advantage at New Orleans, at that period the only outlet for the whisky, flour and tobacco of the West.

From 1800 to 1817, and occasionally even at a later date, the barges or bargees, as they were termed by the French of the Mississippi country, performed so far as they could the services rendered afterwards by steamboats. They were built like the keel-boats which our low water season brings down still from Pittsburgh and Wheeling, but much broader as well as longer, being 75 to 120 feet in length, with a breadth of beam from 15 to 20 feet, sufficing to carry from 60 to 100 tons. A cargo box served to protect the merchandize from the weather, and a space in the stern of about 8 feet in length, partitioned off from the rest of the boat, and called by courtesy a cabin, afforded some degree of privilege in sleeping hours to the captain and his *patroon*, by which name the steersman of the boat was known. The roof of the cabin sloped slightly to the stern, and was the station by day of that officer in steering the barge. These vessels carried generally two masts, occasionally but one, their principal dependence being in a large square sail forward, to enable them, when the wind was in the right direction, and of sufficient force to make more rapid progress as well as to ease the hands, in the laborious process of rowing in such a current as that of the Mississippi. A barge usually carried from thirty to fifty men, with as many oars, suitable spaces being left in stowing the cargo, principally towards the bow, for their employment. Where the shore or beach permitted, the cordelle was also resorted to. This was a stout rope, which being fastened to the mast, was carried along the beach, on the shoulders of the whole boat's crew, stationed at regular distances. Where the shore was lined with trees, as was often the case, and a beach did not present the opportunity of cordelling, and the current bore hard on the rowers, the yawl, with which these boats were always provided, was sent out ahead with a coil of rope, one end of which was made fast to a tree, or even a snag in the river, and while the boat was pulling up to the fast, a fresh coil was started ahead, to be secured to some new object for the same purpose. This was called warping. Lastly, these barges, like the keel-boats, had setting poles, which being brought to the shoulders of the men, and resting on the bed of the river, afforded ample purchase in propelling boats. Poles, however, were generally employed on the Ohio, the bolder shores and yielding bed of the Mississippi rarely rendering their use in that river expedient. It must be observed that these various changes in the mod of working the barges up greatly relieved th

crew, on the physical principle of resting one set of muscles by the employment of another set. All these various contrivances, however, were an immense expenditure of labor as compared with results, the usual rate of progress up the Mississippi, unless aided by a breeze, being hardly three miles an hour running time. It might naturally be supposed that the severe and protracted toil of propelling boats under such circumstances particularly against the current and along the shores of a river like the Mississippi, would disgust those whose curiosity or ignorance led them to engage in it, and render it difficult even under high wages to secure a constant supply of hands. On the contrary, however, allurements of a roving life, freedom from the restraints of civilized society and settled employment,—in short, what in the West is expressively termed "*range*," are temptations which are irresistible to a certain class of minds to be found every where. Nor was the picture without its lights as well as shades. If they had hard work and protracted confinement, they had regular resting places on the route when they relaxed in the dance or in drinking frolics from their habitual toils, debasing themselves in excesses which served voyage by voyage to sink them nearer and nearer to the level of brutes. Of course there were exceptions, but the general tendency as well as effect was to the ruin of the morals still more even than the health of those who led this kind of life.

The first race of boatmen were the spies and scouts, whose employment ceased when Wayne, at the battle of the Fallen Timbers and the treaty of Greenville, gave repose and safety to the settlers of the West. Most of them had become unfitted for the pursuits of agriculture—a few followed the chase for subsistence when they could pursue the savage no longer as an occupation, but of the mass, part had imbibed in their intercourse with the Indians, a sympathetic contempt, as well as disrelish, for regular and steady labor; and the others were like the refugees to King David, at the cave of Adullam, being either in distress, or in debt, or discontented with the state of things forming around them. A boatman's life was the very thing for such individuals. From the nature of their movements, they felt themselves scarcely responsible to the laws, as indeed they actually were not, except at New Orleans, where the motley crew, whether residents or strangers, have always been kept with the curb bit in the mouth and the rein drawn tightly up.

With these men were gradually incorporated fresh accessions of recruits, most of whom were bankrupt in character as in purse—whose conduct had made them liable to the whipping-post and the jail, in some cases even to the gallows, in their former residences. These were a race of younger individuals, who served to keep the ranks full as the veterans dropped off in the service. The graphic pen of Morgan Neville has given celebrity to Mike Fink, one of these river characters, to whose exploits as a marksman, Mr. Neville has done justice; but to whose character otherwise, he has done more than justice, in classing him with the boatmen to whose care merchandize in great value was committed with a confidence which the owners never had cause to repent.—

This was true of those who had charge of the boat; but did not apply to Fink, who was nothing more than a hand on board, and whose private character was worthless and vile. Mike was in fact an illustration of a class of which I have spoken, who did not dare to show their faces in their early neighborhoods or homes.— Just such a fellow as Bill Lloyd in the narrative which follows, in every respect but his courage. Mike's whole history in Missouri, proves this, and especially is it made manifest in the closing scene of his existence. He takes the life of an unarmed youth, whom he had raised from a child, in a drunken fit of jealousy, probably without cause, and when reproved indignantly for his conduct, by one of his comrades, draws his rifle to his shoulder to kill him also, provoking the quicker movement, which, in self defence, deprived himself of life.

The following narrative, for which I am indebted to one of our steamboat captains, a man of strict veracity, gives an incident in the story of one of these early boatmen, JAMES GIRTY by name. My informant, as will be seen, had it from the narrator's lips.

Girty was a native of Western Pennsylvania, nephew to the Girtys, *Simon* and *George*, famous and infamous, as renegades from the whites to the Indians, and instigators of many of the atrocities committed on the frontier settlements, as well as on the defenceless prisoners who fell into the hands of the savages. The name of Guthrie, a very general one in Scotland and Ireland, pronounced Guttrey in the western part of Pennsylvania, and corrupted still farther in the case of this family, into Girty, was the name of his forefathers. The neighborhood of Pittsburgh, across the Allegheny river, was the stamping ground, as the early settlers called it, of the Girtys, and the scenery of that neighborhood still attests their former residence. Girty's Hill is some four or five miles north of the city, and Girty's Run flows along its base. A wilder country, in its natural features, within even twenty years, would hardly be found in any part of the State.

JAMES GIRTY was a man, said my informant, of about the usual height, of uncommon strength, activity and courage. What in ordinary men, is made up of ribs, in his case was a broad as well as thick sheet of bone. I had heard of this as a fact, and verified it myself, during a trip I made with him, in which he took a fit, and it became necessary for me to rub his chest and sides with whiskey, salt, and pepper, the only remedies the boatman's medicine chest supplied. During the whole period referred to, as the era of barging, I do not recollect him out of employment, either as captain or patroon of a barge. He was never known to have a hand unless he first ascertained whether he could and would fight. As to himself, although he sought no quarrel, he felt himself able to fight any man that could be found any where, and was never known to have been *whipt*.

The last boating he did, was steering a boat for me from the mouth of Cumberland to Nashville. During this voyage he was attacked with sickness, under which he finally sunk, dying at Nashville in 1820, under my care. He appeared conscious, as I was, from the first, that he would not recover.

On one of my visits, I told him that I had heard some imperfect accounts of an adventure he had in Natchez, and would like to have the facts accurately, upon which he gave me the following narrative:

"In the year 1814 I was captain of the barge Black Snake, belonging to the Poyntz's at Maysville. I started with the barge, about two thirds loaded, for New Orleans, in the latter part of November. When I reached the mouth of Cumberland, I found a considerable quantity of arms belonging to the United States, which had been despatched from Pittsburgh for the troops engaged under General Jackson, in the defence of New Orleans. They had been taken down thus far, depending on an engagement made with Ben Smith of Cincinnati, under which he contracted to deliver them within a given time at New Orleans. The government agent had been waiting some days for Smith, who had not yet made his appearance; and finding an opportunity offering, and fearing they would be needed, immediately decided to send them by me. I made all possible despatch, and happily succeeded in reaching New Orleans with my precious freight on the 3d January, 1815. Eager to have a hand in the approaching battle, I reported myself immediately to Gen. Jackson, who gave me the appointment of Captain, with authority to impress into service the whole body of barge and keel-boat men in port. I entered on the work without delay, and with great activity and success. You know as much as I can tell you of the glorious 8th. After every thing in the shape of a red coat had disappeared, I discharged the remaining part of the cargo and crew, for which last I had no further use until I could get a freight up the river, which I did not get until the latter part of May, when I hired a crew and started for Pittsburgh. I reached Natchez in June. It was the custom of those days to give the hands a holiday at Natchez, one at the mouth of the Ohio, and one also at Louisville or Shippingsport. It was four o'clock in the afternoon that we threw up our poles and fastened our bowlines at Natchez. The men were eager for a dance, and some would not wait even for their supper, scampering off for the dance-houses under the hill. I got my supper and went up also. I looked on until 11 or 12 at night, when finding all my entreaties to get them back to the boat unavailing, I left them, some engaged in dancing, others betting with the gamblers on the *Roulettes*, and went on board the Black Snake.— As the day dawned, all hands were also at their posts, but in a wretched plight, many of them having their heads badly cut and bruised.

It seems the gamblers had won all their money, and a fight ensued, in which those gentry came off victorious. After breakfast, I judged by the threats of the hands, and other circumstances, that it would be advisable to get the Black Snake under way; but on giving orders to that effect, not a man would raise a pole, until he had had his accustomed frolic out, and I was compelled to give way, determining in my own mind, to leave at 4 o'clock, when the day of privilege would be out. When that hour came, it was of no use to propose starting, none of the men would budge, until they had obtained revenge; and they had privately agreed that they would not assist me up any further, if I would not go with them and help them whip the gamblers.

I saw there was no alternative, and after supper, I repaired with my whole crew to the dance house, armed with knives, chopping axes and setting poles. The gamblers had expected us and were prepared with pistols, knives, and rifles, for the fight. The *scrimmage* commenced without exchanging a word. At first they gave us hard usage, but their ammunition was soon spent, and they gave way, bearing three of their number off who were killed in the scuffle. One of our men was mortally wounded, who made out to walk to the boat, where he died in half an hour. We cut cable and crossed the Mississippi, worked the Black Snake three miles up the river, and came to for the night. About day-light next morning, while burying the dead man, the Sheriff of Adams county and a posse of almost an hundred men, came up and made us all prisoners.

They left a man of the party in charge of the barge, and took us all down to the ferry-boat and across to Natchez, where we were brought before a judge and tried. No evidence being found against any but myself and Bill Lloyd, one of my hands, the rest of the crew were set free, while Bill and I were sent to Washington jail; my barge was sent on, and I was detained to stay in jail until Court, which was to sit the first Monday in October. After I had been in jail about two weeks, one of the Associate Judges of the Court by which I was to be tried, came out to Washington to see me. I found in him an old Pennsylvania acquaintance, on whom I had some claims. He gave me poor encouragement, telling me he feared the Court would not let me out on bail. I told him I had $2,700, which I could leave with my security. Still he discouraged me. He said the evidence was point-blank against me and Lloyd, but promised he would call again, ordering the jailor to see that I did not want for anything that lay in his power to give, and bade me good-bye. In about a week, he came again, and told me he had succeeded in making it a bailable case of $3,000, and had also obtained a man to go my security. The door was opened. I gave the Judge $2,700 and the necessary security. The Judge advised me to leave immediately, and never show myself in Natchez, saying he would willingly pay the $3,00, if I would keep away. I told him I would be in Washington at the sitting of the Court, if I lived—on this I was determined. That afternoon I wrote a letter to a friend of mine in Natchez, who was a woman that kept a dance-house—now living and wealthy, and, of course, respectable—requesting her to get clear of the evidence against me. I received an answer to this next morning, assuring me I need fear nothing; that I might make my appearance at the proper time with perfect safety, for there would be no one present to witness against me. I left Natchez the same day, on foot, for Pittsburgh, which I reached the latter part of July. I lost no time collecting money, and gathered up $1,500, and started in a large covered skiff on my return to Natchez. This was the last of August. My skiff had two pair of oars, and I took three yankees on board to work their passage as far as Cincinnati, and the

oars were plied night and day till we got there. At Cincinnati I hired a man to help me the rest of the way down; by the time we reached Louisville, however, he got tired and ran off. I went over the Falls by myself, and landed at Shippingsport in search of another hand, and the first man that met my eye was Bill Lloyd. You may guess my astonishment. My first words were, "Why, Bill, how did you get here?" "Why, I walked the most of the way." "Well, how did you get out of jail?" "Oh," said he, "it got so d—d sickly among the thieving scoundrels in there, that the jailer was glad to open my door to get me to take charge of the sick. I opened the door for the rest, and all went out that could walk out, and then I walked off to the mouth of Tennessee, and there I got a chance to push up on that keel-boat there," said he, pointing to it. "Well, Bill, you need not fear anything while you are with me," I remarked; "I am going back to stand my trial, and I want to hire a hand to help me down. The river is low, and if I don't get some good hand to help me row, I fear I shan't get there in time." In short, I agreed to give Bill a dollar a day, and to let him off at Walnut Hills; so he came on with his horn and blanket, and we were off in a jiffy. Bill was a worthless fellow, and I knew it, but he was a stout and good oarsman. He had not been long with me, till he found out that my chest was heavy, and I watched him close. When we were near the mouth of the Ohio, he became dissatisfied, and objected to going any further towards Natchez, proposed to go trapping up the Mississippi, insisting there could be a great deal made on the Missouri, with other suggestions of the sort. I paid little attention to his statements or arguments, keeping on down the Mississippi, and told him, if he wanted to stop, to do so; as for me, I should go on to Natchez. He said no more until we were in the bend above Beef Island, when he broke out afresh, accusing me of suspicioning him of a wish to rob me. I told him I was not afraid of him in any shape. A fight ensued, which I knew must end in the death of one or the other, with the skiff and my money for the victor's spoils. After much struggling, I put him over board. I set the blade of an oar against him, shoving him off from the skiff, then thrusting the oar to him, told him to save his life. He made no other reply, than to clench the oar and throw it back to me, telling me to 'go to hell,' and swimming about fifty yards, safely reached the head of Beef Island. I landed at Natchez at one o'clock, and on the morning of the first Monday in October, I left the skiff, and with my chest on my shoulder, walked up to the dance-house. My friend was still up, as were several more. I deposited my chest with her, and looking around the room, I espied the most important witness against me. I turned to her, reminding her of the promise she had made me. She told me she had been trying to get rid of him all summer; that he was the only evidence against me left in the country, and that she would yet get him out of the way. I observed the time was short, and calling him forward, told him I would give him five hundred dollars to leave the place that morning, and not appear against me. He swore there was no use to talk to him, for he had braved the worst of the yellow-fever for the purpose of remaining there and appearing against me, and I might depend upon it, he would be on the spot when called to testify. My friend said, never fear, all would be right; and as I was about bidding her and witness good-bye, proposed that we should take a gin-sling together. She mixed one for witness, one for me, and one for herself. Having all drank, I started for Washington, and reached there by 9 o'clock. Being quite tired, I lay down on the door-step and directly fell fast asleep and did not awake until the sheriff, calling the Court awoke me. Every body seemed astonished at my presence. My case was the first one called. I answered to my name, and when the judge enquired of me if I was ready for trial, my counsel did not happen to be present, and I answered that I was as ready then as I ever should be; that I had no evidence when I was sent to jail, and had none now. The attorney for the State directed the sheriff to call his witnesses, to see if he was ready for trial, who called 11 names in succession, not one of whom was present, but some one answered, name by name, as they were called, what had become of them. Some had left the country, and some had died of the yellow fever, until the name of the one I had left in Natchez was called, and the answer was that he died that morning at half past eight. There being no evidence against me, I was, of course, discharged, and returned the same evening to Natchez. I asked my friend what had caused the fellow's death who was to have been the witness. She said she supposed it was in the course of nature, nor could I, then or afterwards, get any satisfaction from her on this point. Next day, I called on my security, settled my business with him, then went to my friend's house, opened my chest, and counted out $500 for her. She perceived what I was doing, and told me, if I wanted to make her my enemy for life, I could have a chance, and if I dared to offer her money, she would blow my brains out. I made several excuses to induce her to take the money, saying that I owed it to her honestly for her kind treatment of me, and that I did not mean anything dishonorable by it. She remained resolute, and said if I wanted to continue friends with her, I must not offer her money. I then bade her good-bye, and before dark, my chest and skiff and myself were all on the way to New Orleans."

Such was Girty's narrative. And though such a man at this day, would not be entrusted with any important charge, in his time thousands of dollars' worth of property and money were confided to his care, and accounted for, to the perfect satisfaction of his employers; nor was he ever known to break an engagement, or abuse a trust in his pecuniary dealings. The narrative itself is put upon record as a correct picture of the river men, and the times in which they flourished.

West. Lit. Journal.

A Pork Story.

As this is "killing time," we may be excused for telling a hog story.

Some years since, B. B. who is a fine judge of hogs, and has dealt in the article, and is rather a cute chap withal, made a contract with a packer to furnish him a lot of fat hogs by a given day. The day came round, and found B. on the road within 8 or 10 miles of Cincinnati with a fine drove of fat hogs; but the price had risen since the contract was made, and that contract was in writing. To get over it and sell the hogs at the highest price, was a job that tax ed B's wits to the utmost; but he succeeded. Galloping ahead of the hogs, he went to the packer, and called him out, when the following chat ensued:

"Mr. O," says B. "you must lend me three or four hands to help in with those hogs."

O. "Why so?"

B. "Because I can't get them into town without; they have got so wild there is no driving them. I left the boys minding them in a field about 8 miles back, and must have some help or they will all run off.

O. "Run off! Why I agreed with you for *fat* hogs, to weigh so much."

B. Well they *are* big hogs, and will weigh that, but they are as wild as Injins. They run like all the world.

O. Well but fat hogs dont run that way.— When did you start from Hamilton?

B. Why this morning to be sure! Did you think I was going to be a week driving them in? Come send out the h ands, and let's get them in to town.

O. I tell you I did'nt agree to take such hogs.

B. Did'nt you agree for hogs that would weigh so much? These will do it; and if you want the hogs, just send the men out with me, and they shall be here in two hours.

O. Well but I can't take hogs that will travel that way. You had better take them somewhere else.

B. Yes, but we have a written agreement; and I must hold you to it.

O. I did'nt want such hogs I tell you, and we must break the article.

B. Well, if you won't have them I must sell them somewhere else; but they are mighty big hogs—only a little wild. But tear up the paper if you don't like it.

The paper was torn up, and the next morning B. drove in a rare lot of fat hogs, and sold them for a dollar a hundred more than agreed for with O.— *Hamilton Intelligencer.*

CINCINNATI, FEBRUARY, 1845.

The Sleeping Wife.

Delicious task to sit and watch
The breathing of a sleeping wife,
And mark the features of that state
Dividing Death from Life.
How sweet her slumber! on her lids
The angel—Peace—hath set its seal;
And to her couch the guard forbids
An envious care to steal.

How beautiful! She would compel
The tribute of a stoic's kiss;
Angelic purity might dwell
In such a shrine as this.
And here it dwells—unstained and bright,
Though half concealed by modest fear;
Yes, were this soul disrobed this night,
There were an angel here.

How sweet her slumber! None but those
Whom Heav'n hath numbered for its bliss,
Have promise of such calm repose—
Such perfect rest as this.
Unconscious of the woes and cares
That weigh us down in waking hours,
Her gentle spirit only wears
A burden now of flowers!

She dreams! Her radiant features speak
Of themes that waken deep delight,
And smiles adorn her lip and cheek—
Smiles beautiful and bright.
Oh! could I lift the jealous veil
That doth those joyous thoughts conceal,
The spotless page a sinless tale
Would presently reveal.

And hark! Her parting lips disclose
Some cherished secret long repressed:
Mark how her cheek with blushes glows—
How heaves her swelling breast!
She breathes a *name* amid her dream—
The soul of love is in the tone!
Her cheeks with deeper blushes teem:
That name—*it is my own!*

Joy! joy! my bliss is perfect now—
The boon I craved is mine—is mine;
Upon my bended knee I bow,
And thank thee, God Divine!
By night or day—awake—asleep,
The signals of her love I see:
I know that love is pure and deep,
And centered all in me.

A TENDER HEART.—A certain man in Vermont once said that his children were the most tender-hearted beings that he ever knew, and on being asked what made him think so, said— 'Because they always cry when I *ask them to get a bucket of water.*'

Ninth Ward—Cincinnati.

This is the north east section of our city, extending from Sixth street north, to the corporation line, and Main street east, to the First Ward, a few years since, and the largest portion of its surface was then built on. Two thirds of it is now occupied with improvements.

The public buildings of this ward, are in number fourteen, as follows: St. Xavier and Woodward Colleges, Court House. and public offices adjacent, public school house. on Franklin st.: Jail; Baptist church, on Webster st, Episcopal, on Pendleton st, Methodist, on Webster, and Catholic on Sycamore streets, colored Methodist church, on New st., Engine houses, on Sycamore and Webster streets. Of these the Engine house on Webster street, and the Episcopal church are recent erections.

The entire number of buildings in the Ninth ward are 1212; bricks 478, frames, 732, stone 2.

Of these there were, at the close of 1842:

	Bricks	Frames	Stone	
	352.	663.	0	1015.
In '43,	81.	34.	0.	115.
In '44,	45.	35.	2.	82,
	478.	732.	2.	1212-

On the opposite side of the "Advertiser" will be found a general summary of the building operations of Cincinnati.

Investments for Capitalists.

It seems difficult to impress Capitalists abroad, with correct views of the subject of investments here. Nor is it any wonder, while there are hundreds here, with abundant resources, who prefer investing surplus funds in bank stock or in mortgages, producing them 8 to 10 per cent. per annum. A few facts which I can authenticate by a reference to the individuals alluded to, will set this short-sighted policy in its true light.

A year ago the vacant corner of Walnut and Fourth streets, belonging to the First Presbyterian Society, was offered on perpetual lease, at public sale. The property was 99 feet on Fourth Street, by 36 on Walnut, with the privilege of air and light from a space of ten feet in the rear, to be kept open forever for the common benefit of the Fourth street property, and the Cincinnati College, its neighbor to the north. It brought 10 dollars per front foot on Fourth St. Messrs. Sanford & Park, who leased 33 feet including the corner, put up two buildings, which cost when finished, 3950 dollars. They occupy the corner with their store, counting room, manufacturing and ware rooms in the basement, for which space they paid on Fourth Street, east of Main, 650 dollars, and if the question were put in that shape, would give a higher rent for their present tenement. They rent in double rooms, the residue for six hundred and ninety-nine dollars, with the certainty when any of the tenants leave the premises to re-rent at higher rates. As a proof of which for the storeroom adjoining their own, which is included in the above statement at 200 dollars, they have been offered 250 dollars per annum for ten years, if they would lease it so long a term of years.

Let us bring this operation to a focus as follows:

Value of rents,	699	
Corner building,	650	
	——	1349
Deduct taxes and insurance	104	
Ground rent,	330	434
		——
		915

Affording more than 23 per cent profit on the investment, with the certainty of a future advance.

Let me cite another case.

Every one knows the property on Broadway, South of the Holmes House, at the intersection of that street with Columbia and Second streets, and divided from the Hotel by a 10 foot alley.— It was destroyed not long since by fire, with the exception of the Columbus house, a brick at the corner, the residue being frames. Mr. Clement Dietrich, the proprietor of the south half of the property destroyed having engaged Mr. Seneca Palmer, one of our architects by contract to rebuild the property, Mr. P. with the public spirit which belongs to that profession, prevailed on the other property-holders to unite with Mr. Dietrich in putting up substantial and uniform buildings to correspond with the appearance of the corner when repaired and finished. The result to the public is, that spacious business accommodations, and ornamental buildings are put up in place of the insignificant improvements which would have been made. The result to the owners is a permanently profitable investment of money which they could not have made as well in any other shape.

Let me make a synopsis of the case.

C. Dietrich.

Cost of four lots and houses	13,000	
Less insurance money	2,187	1,0813
	——	
Three new buildings, with repairs and adding one story to corner		5650
		——
		16,473
Of these two rent at	$1100	
Two will fetch	950	2,050
	——	

If we deduct the insurance money from the expense of the late improvement, as it ought to

be, the raising one story and repairs costing the greater part of it, then the nett cost would be 3473 dollars, a sum which would be made up by the rents after deducting taxes and insurance in a less space of time than two years.

O. W. Stevens owns the house next door

north which cost with the lot		4600
The storeroom rents for	300	
The house as much more	300	
P. P. & R. C. Turpin own	——	600
the building next the alley which with the lot cost them		5250

It rents at 700 dollars per annum.

The entire cost of the block is then	$26.323

And the aggregate of the rents is $3350, being at the rate of 12¾ per cent. per annum in the investment. It must be remembered also that those rents will be augmenting constantly, in the nature of the case.

I propose next week to exhibit other modes of safe and profitable investments for which I have not room in an article already larger than I contemplated to make it.

The Whaling business.

Just as I was making up last week's "Advertiser," and too late to use the information, I received the annual exhibit of the whaling business in the United States, with the following note attached to it:

"The whale fishery is alive yet, in spite of lard oil- Yours, A WHALER."

I owe this favor, undoubtedly, to the articles on lard oil, whose statistical character gave them extensively the range of the periodical press in the United States, and I can truly assure the unknown writer that he has laid me under obligations, by the valuable, full, and interesting table sent, and which want of space in this print, alone withholds from my columns.

A synopsis of it follows.

The imports into the United States, for 1844 were:

Sperm oil.	Whale oil.	Whalebone.
Bbls. 139,544.	Bbls. 252,047.	lbs. 2,532,445.
1843 166,985.	206,721.	

The supplies of 1844 were brought in 238 ships, barques, brigs, schooners, and sloops principally of the first class. The whaling voyages lasting for a length of time averaging three years, two thirds of the vessels employed are not included in this table. The whole number of whalers is 695, the increase during the last year being fifty vessels of 18508 tonsburthen.

I rejoice in the prosperous condition of this important trade. The whale fishery is the great nursery of American sailors, and it has served to prepare many of our naval heroes for usefulness and honor in the national service. It was in this school that *Charles Ramsdell*, whose spirit stirring biography I gave so lately to the public, in these columns, was trained, as are thousands of other gallant and energetic spirits.

But it is in vain that our eastern brethren shut their eyes to the tendency of the lard oil manufacture. As a means of light, it is atonce cheaper, pleasanter, and of rapidly enlarging power of production. The increase of vessels for the whale voyages is in the growth of the leather business, a heavy and important manu-facture speading over the whole United States, and which grows, and must continue to do so, with the general advance of the country. This is evident from the fact that it is the increase in whale or tanner's oil, which has furnished freights for these vessels. That article has averaged 34½ cents at New Bedford, for six years past, a price at which it may defy the competition of lard oil, while sperm oil, which was in 1839, at an average of 1,03 cts., had gradually sunk by the close of 1843 to 63 cents. The average of 1844, it is true, had improved to 88 cts. This is owing to the general revival of business, and confidence among dealers, which has produced the same state of things, with respect to lard oil, and raised its price 10 per cent already. now that the season for the accumulation of raw materials has only commenced. At any rate, there is room and use in the world for both sperm and lard oil.

Dyers and Painters Colors.

Modern chemistry is the touch of Midas turning everything to gold, and some of the changes in color, taste, and properties, which natural substances undergo in the crucible, the re tort and the furnace, are such as puzzle plain men of sound understandings, not familiar with the magic of the science. Who that surveys *Piperine*, a crystallized substance, looking like roll brimstone split up, would imagine that it was the extract and principle of the black pepper, with whose smell and taste his daily dinner makes him familiar, or that the paper which wraps up the package of goods he has just purchased was made of straw, which grew on his own or his neighbor's farm, or that the ivory-black which serves him for paint, was made purely out of old bones.

Among the recent additions to our manufacturing industry, Mr. Charles Dummer has commenced the manufacture on an extensive scale, of colors, for dyers and painters, such as *Prussiate of potash; Chrome Yellow and Green*; *Paris, Antwerp and Mineral Blue.* The chromes are not new articles of manufacture here, Mr. R. Conkling, on Court street. being already engaged largely in the business, but the other arti-

cles have heretofore been brought from abroad under the disadvantage to the community, that what is ordered from the east *may* be good, and ordinarily is of fair quality, while the corresponding manufacture here *must* be either better or cheaper, or both, if designed to supercede it.

Prussiate of potash, which ought rather perhaps to be called *blue oxyde of potash*, is a cheaper and more efficient coloring substance than the indigo which it replaces in dying. It is employed, in large quantities, in woollen factories, and calico print establishments at the east, and serves also for rendering iron as hard as steel.

The other articles named, are used by painters, paper stainers, and oil cloth, fancy printing ink, and paper manufacturers, for whom they furnish blue and yellow of the deepest and most brilliant tints, with all the intermediate shades.

All these articles are made chiefly of animal substances, such as blood, hoofs, horns, old leather, &c., and when we reflect on the immense amount of such offal, which annually runs to waste, in the Mill creek, and Deer creek valleys it will readily be understood that this establishment is prepared to operate on the most extensive scale.

As things now are, the principal markets for these products must be sought east, although I doubt not the lapse of a few years will supply an abundant demand in Cincinnati and the west. What the future operations of this and other establishments must become in point of magnitude, may be judged from the fact that already, in the infancy of the business, *Mr. Dummig* consumes, in his manufacture, two thousand pounds of animal substances, and nearly one thousand pounds of potash daily. Seven hands are here employed, and the operations go on, day and night.

Specimens of these articles are left at my office, which I shall be pleased to show to those who take an interest in the subject. Their appearance itself will recommend them beyond anything I can say, but on the subject of their quality, I must relate one little incident. Mr. D. manufactured a supply of one of these articles for one of our heavy druggists, a man thoroughly acquainted with dye stuffs, expecting to be paid the price of the eastern article, whatever that might be. That price proved to be 45 cents per lb. at that time. The Druggist examined it very carefully and then remarked: "The price as you see by this price current," shewing it to him, "is 45 cents, but for such an article as this I cannot think of giving you less than 60 cts;" and paid him accordingly.

Such establishments, in which labor forms almost every thing, and raw materials almost nothing, of the value of manufacturing deserve the support of every well wisher to the prosperity of Cincinnati. Had the immense banking patronage to our pork business, which in the course of twenty years had swallowed up almost every man engaged on it, leaving the pork house, as the only assets, been diverted to manufactures of similar descriptions. Cincinnati wo uld now have been one of the most important manufacturing point in the United States. Every one can readily see that a department of industry, which gives 85 per cent to the farmer for raw material and divides 15 per cent among the packer, salt merchant, cooper, drayman, freighter and commission merchant can never be so important to the community as establishments in which the raw material is 15 per cent, and the value conferred on it by labor 85, in many of our factories this being the case.

John M'Ewan.

Human nature is always a study of profound interest. It is presented in the following narrative in a manner seldom witnessed. These details were taken from a letter of M. Waldie, M. D., of Glasgow to his nephew and are doubtless authentic.

"I lodged in the house of a poor shoemaker, by name John M'Ewan. He had no family but his wife, who, like himself, was considerabiy beyond the meridian of life. The couple were very poor, as their house, and everything about their style of living, showed; but a worthier couple, I should have no difficulty in saying were not to be found in the whole city. When I was sitting in my own little cell, busy with my books, late at night, I used to listen with delight to the hymn the two old bodies sung, or rather, I should say, *croon'd* together, before they went to bed. Tune there was almost none; but the low, inarticulate, quiet chaunt, had something so impressive and solemnizing about it, that I missed not melody. John himself was a hard-working man, and, like most of his trade, had acquired a stooping attitude. and a dark, saffron hue of complexion. His close-cut, greasy black hair suited admirably a set of strong, massive, iron features. His brow was seamed with firm, broad-drawn wrinkles, and his large gray eyes seemed to gleam, when he deigned to uplift them with the cold haughty independence of virtuous poverty. John was a rigid Cameronian, indeed; and everything about his person spoke the world-despising pride of his sect. His wife was a quiet, good body, and seemed to live in perpetual adoration of her stern cobler. I had the strictest confidence in their probity, and would no more have thought of locking my chest ere I went out, than if I had been under the roof of an apostle.

"One evening I came home, as usual, from my tutorial trudge, and entered the kitchen where they commonly sat, to warm my hands at the fire, and get my candle lighted. Jean was by hersel' at the fireside, and I sat down by her side for a minute or two. I heard voices in the inner room, and easily recognized the coarse grunt which John M'Ewan condescended, on rare occasions, to set forth as the representative of laughter. The old woman told me that the good man had a friend from the country with him—a farmor who had come from a distance to sell ewes at the market. Jean, indeed, seemed to take some pride in the acquaintance, enlarging upon the great substance, and respectability of the stranger. I was chatting away with her, when he heard some noise from the spence as if a table or a chair had fallen—but we thought nothing of this, and talked on. A minute after, John came from the room, and shutting the door behind him said, "I'm going out for a moment, Jean; Andrew's had ower muckle o' the flesher's whiskey the day, and I maun stap up the close to see after his beast for him. Ye need na gang near him till I come back."

"The cobler said this, for any thing that I could observe, in his usual manner; and walking across the kitchen, went down stairs, as he had said. But imagine, my friend, for I cannot describe the feelings with which, some five minutes after he had disappeared, I, chancing to throw my eyes downwards, perceived a dark flood, creeping broadly, inch by inch across the sanded floor towards the place where I sat. The old woman had her stocking in her hand—I called to her without moving, for I was nailed to my chair: 'See there, what is that?'

"'Andew Bell has coupit our water stoop,' said she rising. I sprang forward and dipt my finger in the stream. 'Blood! Jean, blood!' The The old woman stooped over it, and touched it also; she instantly screamed out, 'Blood, ay, blood!' while I rushed on to the door from below which it was oozing. I tried the handle, and found it was locked—and spurned it off its hinges with one kick of my foot. The instant the timber gave way, the black tide rolled out as if a dam had been breaking up, and I heard my feet plashing in the abomination as I advanced. What a sight within! The man was lying all his length upon the floor; his throat absolutely severed to the spine. The whole blood of the body had run out. The table with, a pewter pot or two, and a bottle upon it, stood close beside him, and two chairs, one half-tumbled down and supported against the other. I rushed instantly out of the house, and cried out in a tone that brought the whole neighborhood around me. They entered the house—Jean had disappeared—there was nothing in it, but the corpse and the blood, which had already found its way to the outer stair-case, making the whole floor one puddle. There was such a clamor of surprise and horror for a little while, that I scarce ly heard one word that was said. A bell in the neighborhood had been set in motion—dozens, scores, hundreds of people were heard rushing from every direction towards the spot.- A fury of execration and alarm' pervaded the very breeze. In a word, I had absolutely lost all possession of myself, until I found mvself grappled from behind, and saw a town's officer pointing the bloody knife towards me. A dozen voices were screaming, "'Tis a Doctor's knife! this is the young doctor that 'bides in the house —this is the man.'

"Of course this restored me to my self possession. I demanded a moment's silence, and said—'It is my knife, and I lodge in the house; but John M'Ewan is the man that has murdered his friend.' 'John M'Ewan!' roared some one in a voice of tenfold horror; 'one elder, John M' Ewan, a murderer! Wretch! wretch! how dare ye blaspheme?' 'Carry me to jail immediately,' said I, as soon as the storm subsided a little, load me with all the chains in Glasgow, but don't neglect to pursue John M'Ewan.' I was instantly locked up in the room with the dead man, while the greater part of the crowd followed one of the officers. Another of them kept watch over me until one of the magistrates of the city arrived. This gentleman, finding that I had been the person who first gave the alarm, and that M'Ewan and his wife were both gone, had little difficulty, I could perceive in doing me justice in his own mind. However, after he had given orders for the pursuit, I told him that as the people about were evidently unsatisfied of my innocence, the best and the kindest thing he could do was to put me forthwith within the walls of his prison; there I should be safe at all events and I had no doubt, if proper exertions were made, the guilty man would not only be found, but found immediately. My person being searched, nothing suspicious, of course, was found upon it; and the good baillie soon had me conveyed under a proper guard to the place of security—where, you may suppose, I did not, after all, spend a very pleasant night. The jail is situated in the heart of the town, where the four principal streets meet; and the glare of hurrying lights, the roar of anxious voices, and the eternal tolling of the alarum-bell—these all reached me through the bars of my cell, and, together with the horrors that I had already witnessed, were more than enough to keep me in no enviable condition.

"Jean was discovered, in the gray of the morning, crouching under one of the trees in the green, and being led immediately before the magistrate, the poor trembling creature confirmed, by what she said, and by what she did not say, the terrible story which I had told.— Some other witnesses having also appeared, who spoke to the facts of Andrew Bell having received a large sum of money in M'Ewan's sight at the market, and been seen walking to the Vennel, arm in arm, with him—the authorities of the place were perfectly satisfied, and I was set free, with many apologies for what I had suffered. But still no word of John M'Ewan.

"It was late in the day ere the first traces of him were found—and such a trace! An old woman had died that night in a cottage not many miles from Glasgow—when she was almost in articulo mortis, a stranger entered the house, to ask a drink of water—an oldish dark man, evidently much fatigued with walking.— This man finding in what great affliction the family was—this man, after drinking a cup of water, knelt down by the bedside, and prayed, a long, an awful, a terrible prayer. The people thought he must be some travelling field preacher. He took the bible into his hands—opened it as if he intended to read aloud—but shut the book abruptly, and took his leave.— This man had been seen by these poor people to walk in the direction of the sea.

"They traced the same dark man to Irvine, and found that he had embarked on board of a vessel which was just getting under sail, for Ireland. The officers immediately hired a small brig, and sailed also. A violent gale arose, and drove them for shelter to the Isle of Arran.— They landed, the second night after they had left Irvine, on that bare and desolate shore— they landed, and behold, the ship they were in pursuit of at the quay! The captain acknowledged at once that a man corresponding to their description had been one of his passengers at Irvine—he had gone ashore but an hour ago. They

searched—they found M'Ewan striding by himself close to the sea-beach, amidst the dashing spray—his bible in his hand. The instant he saw them he said, you need not tell me your errand; I am he you seek; I am John M'Ewan that murdered Andrew Bell! I surrender myself your prisoner. God told me but this moment that you would come and find me;—for I opened his word, and the first text that my eye fell upon was *this*.' He seized the officer by the hand, and laid his finger upon—'See you there?' said he. 'Do you not see the Lord's own blessed decree? *Whoso sheddeth man's blood, by man shall his blood be shed.* And there,' he added, plucking a pocket-book from his bosom, 'there, friends is Andrew Bell's siller —ye'll find the haill o't there, an' be not three half crowns and a sixpence. Seven and thirty pounds was the sum for which I yielded up my soul to the temptation of the prince of the power of the air. Seven and thirty pounds!—Ah! my brethren! call me not an olive until thou see me gathered. I thought that I stood fast, and behold ye all how I am fallen.'

"I saw this singular fanatic tried. He would have pleaded guilty; but, for excellent reasons, the crown advocate wished the whole evidence to be led. John had dressed himself with scrupulous accuracy in the very clothes he wore when he did the deed. The blood of the murdered man was still visible upon the sleeve of his blue coat. When any circumstance of peculiar atrocity was mentioned by a witness, he signified by a solemn shake of his head, his sense of its darkness and its conclusiveness; and when the judge, in addressing him, enlarged upon the horror of his guilt, he standing right before the bench, kept his eye fixed with calm earnestness on his lordship's face, assenting now and then to the propriety of what he said, by exactly that sort of see-saw gesture, which you may have seen escape now and then from a devout listener to a pathetic sermon, or sacramental service. John, in a short speech of his own, expressed his sense of his guilt; but even then he borrowed the language of Scripture, styling himself 'a sinner and the chief of sinners.' Never was such a specimen of that insane pride. The very agony of this man's humiliation had a spice of exultation in it; there was in the most penitent of his lugubrious glances still something that said, or seemed to say, 'Abuse me; spurn me as you will; I loth myself also; but this deed is Satan's.' Indeed he continued to always speak quite gravely of his 'trespass,' his 'backsliding,' his 'sore temptation!'

"I was present also with him during the final scene. His irons had been knocked off ere I entered the cell; and clothed as he was in a most respectable suit of black, and with that fixed and imperturbable solemnity of air and aspect, upon my conscience I think it would have been a difficult matter for a stranger to pick out the murderer among the group of clergyman that surrounded him. In vain did these good men labor to knock away the absurd and impious props upon which the happy fanatic leaned himself. He heard what they said, and instantly said something still stronger himself— but only to shrink back again to his own fastness with redoubled confidence. 'He had *once* been right, and he could not be wrong; he had been permitted to make a sore stumble!' This was his utmost concession.

"What a noble set of nerves had been thrown away here! He was led, sir, out of the damp, dark cellar, in which he had been chained for weeks, and brought at once into the open air. His first step into the open air was upon the scaffold! and what a moment! In general, at least in Scotland, the crowd, assembled upon such occasions, receive the victim of the law with all the solemnity of profoundest silence!—not unfrequently there is even something of the respectful, blended with compassion on that myriad of faces. But here, sir, the moment M'Ewan appeared, he was saluted with one universal shout of horror; a huzza of mingled joy and triumph, and execration and laughter; cats, rats, every filth of the pillory was showered about the gibbet. I was close to his side at that terrific moment, and I laid my finger on his wrist. As I live, there was never a calmer pulse in the world; slow, full, strong: I feel the iron beat of it at this moment.

"There happened to be a slight drizzle of rain at the moment; observing which he turned round and said to the magistrates: 'Dinna come out, dinna come out, your honors, to weet yourselves. Its beginning to rain, and the lads are uncivil at ony rate, poor thoughtless creatures.

"He took his leave of this angry mob in a speech which would not have disgraced a martyr, embracing the stake of glory, and the fatal noose was tied. I observed the brazen firmness of his limbs, after his face was covered.—He flung his handkerchief with an air of semi-benediction, and died like a hero. "

Fancy Trades.

The New York Spirit of the Times has the tallest editor in the lively Porter, and the raciest, drollest, and most mirth-moving correspondents of any juornal in the land. The following is from a letter in the last 'Spirit.'

One evening in particular I was rallying my companion upon his low spirits, and attributing it to long absence from his wife, making as unfavorable a comparison as possible between his situation and my own, a bachelor, when our quondam friend, as usual, joined in. Matrimony, said he, is a fine thing, when you are once in for it, and know what you've got; but its rather ticklish to begin on; you're as likely to make a fancy trade as any, and if I'm goin to make one I want it in horses; for if I'm married I'll have to stand perhaps when I don't want to.

'Yes: but,' said I, 'what do you call a fancy trade?'

Why Captain, a fancy trade is where a man's fancy out jinerals his judgment, and runs away with his brains. I'll tell you a story now, where my fancy ran right straight away with my gumtion to the tune of old hundred.

The last time I was up West I went with the old brown hoss I had of the stage agent, a purty good one, but a little rusty at times. Well, I got to Windham Cattle Show before I see a chance to swap, and for the matter o' that I couldn't see any chance; there was a good many niceish kind of hosses, but nobody seemed to hanker after a trade. Finally I see a countryman leading a black colt—wasn't he a buster! He had the greatest withers ever you see on a hoss, and a set of limbs that would bring tears into a man's eyes. I at's the chap: 'Mister,' says I, 'that's a fust rate colt, if 'twant for them are.' 'Them are what,' says he. ' Law; now do be green,' says I. 'Green,' says he, 'what do you mean by that are?' 'Why, there, man, says

I, 'that'll do with some, but I've been there and staid a week.' 'Why friend,' says he, 'if there's anything out of the way in the hoss, let's know it.' 'Why, do you mean to say that you don't know that colt's got two bone spavins.' 'I deny it,' said he, and his eyes stuck out so you could a hung your hat on 'em.' 'Well, friend,' says I, 'I'll prove this to you; lead your colt over this way where there is a little the soundest horse I ever did see, and we will compare their legs.'—Now that colt was a dreadful made one; his hock jints were deeper than any I have seen, and the upper pints inside the hind leg stuck out clean and handsome I tell you. Well, old Brown's leg was a gunny round thing, like any other old Plug's. 'There,' says I, 'I mean to say that them bones stickin' out like a frog's elbow, on your colt, but when you get him to work, there bound to lame him, for they're nothing more nor less than bone spavins.' 'O, dear,' says he, 'what shall I do?' and he turned as blue as a whetstone. 'Well,' says I. 'there never was a nigger so black but there was some white in his eye, and our case has some bright spots in it yet. Lets find that chap what owns this hoss. I'll help you to trade. We can cut him through and make a good thing out of a bad one.' 'Well, says he, 'you start after him.'

Off I goes to the tavern. for old Jim Dana, a dreadful critter for a trade. 'Jim, says I, 'do yon want to make a trade?' 'I don't want to do anything else.' says Jim. Well 'then,' says I, 'throw away your segar—put your hat square on your head, take that swagger out of your carcass and come and swap my brown horse for me, and I want you to look so much like an honest man that your own wife wouldn't know you.' Well, we got down where the chap was; 'here's the gentleman,' says I, 'what owns the brown hoss and he is willing to make an exchange with you.' 'Very, well,' savs the fellow, 'tell what you'll do.' On this off goes old Jim at half cock. 'I've owned this critter from a colt,' says he, 'I've used him in every way and shape, and he never failed. He aint used to high keepin', but it takes a man's hoss to beat him. Thar he is; look for yourself: sound, kind, and good —eight years old next spring. I'll warrant him in any harness, and when you come to a hill, he's there. I should feel bad to part with him,' and really the old feller looked as if he'd cry. 'Well,' says I, 'how'll you trade?' 'I can't make up my mind,' says old Jim, 'I might trade for $30, how'd you trade?' · 'Offer him $20,' says I, in my covey's ear; 'No,' says he, 'I can't trade short of $20 myself.' 'But,' says I, 'you will trade for twenty?' 'Yes,' says he. I winked tc Jim to close up. 'Well,' says old Jim, 'I shall trade.' We shifted purty quick, I guess, and I never felt safe till I saw his halter on old brown. Just as he was goin' off, he turned round, and says he to me, 'when you put your colt in the wagon, set well back, for he'll kick it all to pieces.' and oh . how he laughed! I've hearn folks laugh and I've hearn them cry, but I never heard anything before or since that come over me as that did. I felt as if I had lived on raw barberries for a week, and exercised myself whetting saws. Old Jim laughed, as though he'd split.— 'Where's that V!' said he, and then he'd laugh, I hired a hoss cart, and put the colt in; he got to kickin' and there he kicked it all to pieces in no time, his hind legs went like a mill race; them ere gambols warnt made for nothin', I tell you; he kicked the cart all to pieces, and I had to pay thirty-seven dollars for it. Well I tho't

I'd make the best of a bad job, so I bought an old cripple for ten dollars to draw my wagon and tied the colt behind, and cuss him he wouldn't go there, but went to pulling back, and broke my new wagon. Well, thinks I, I'll put him up, and try again in the morning; but I hadn't seen the worse yet, for they wouldn't put him up, no how; they said he was glandered and so he was; the chap had blowed powder allum up his nose,so he didn't show, and I was so earnest to pick up a flat I hadn't looked to see anything. And that was the end of my fancy trade.

I gave the colt away after two days, for he wouldn't a fetched me a pint of cider. It-was a good deal for me in the end though, for my school master used to say, that hour's work bred me circumspection. And from that day to this, I have never took a sudden shine to anything without its bringing that colt right afore my eyes. I have never been married, and a gall must manage purty cute and look purty well,to make me sweet,for the black cow's horns show dreadful quick to me on account of the color.

And now, Captain, let's have some hot whiskey punch before we go to roost, and it is your treat, for you are getting your experience mighty fast, *and without paying for it.*

CORRESPONDENCE.

More Pork Stories.

Mr. Cist:

The pork story told in your last paper, of the manner in which some rustic sharper made a city dealer break his contract, when the price of pork had risen in market, reminds me of two other stories which I give as follows—

More than thirty years ago, a large burley man, who dwelt somewhere on the waters of Buck Creek, Ohio, remarkable for his powers of counting a drove, had become famous for his droves of hogs taken over the mountains and sold in Virginia and Maryland. On one occasion he had a large drove in the vicinity of Georgetown, D. C., of which he sold one half to a person there, and as the hogs had to be delivered on the opposite side of the river Potomac, it was agreed they should be divided on Georgetown Bridge. Accordingly, the whole number were driven to the bridge, and as he was a man of energy and despatch, the hogs were put into quick motion and passed over in a hurry. The drover stood at the centre, counting the van of the drove as they hurried by, and when one half had gone past he headed the rest, [whether heading Tyler came from this I do not know-]´ It so fell out that the best runners got through first, and all the heaviest and fattest hogs remained on the drover's side as *cullings*, of course, greatly to his *disadvantage.*

The other story relates to a gentleman with a round good humored face, and portly frame, who dwells in this city without the hand of time making him older to the eye. He

then occupied the store now held by Geo. Conclin, and his next door neighbor was James Reynolds, then a dry goods merchant: he concluded that in addition to selling dry goods, he would deal in pork. He made a contract in writing with some man who dwelt near Brookville, Indiana, and had not been long from Yankee land, to deliver him from one to five hundred good fat hogs, of not less than 200 weight, by a day specified in the contract. Before the day arrived however, the price of hogs had so risen, that the countryman could not procure the hogs to fill the contract, without great loss to himself. So, punctually to the day he placed on a dray a large hog, ready slaughtered and dressed, which he drove to the door of the merchant, and accosting him in the rear of his store, observed that he had brought him the pork according to contract, which he would please to step to the door and receive. Our friend, expecting nothing less than a string of some six or eight wagons along his front, and doubtless exulting in his own mind in the profits which must result, under the circumstances of the case, stepped forward with great alacrity towards the door, when seeing nothing but the dray of which he did not notice the load, turned his eye up and down street by turns to see the approach of the wagons. At last turning to the contractor, he asked, "where are the hogs." "There," said the hoosier, pointing to the dray, is the pork which according to our contract, was to be from one to five hundred hogs. Pork, added he, is rather scarcer than usual in our range, and I have found it therefore, more convenient to deliver you one hog than five hundred. The Porkmerchant finding himself caught, gave in with as good grace as possible, paid for his pork, and dismissed his dealer with much civility, if not cordiality. Being however a practical joker on all oc casions, the misadventure was received with much glee by his neighbors who had long and often suffered in these respects at his hands, and who took care that the story should become known all over town, and lose nothing in the telling.

If any doubt exist as to the truth of this narrative, Captain Stephen Butler who lived in that region in those days could probably furnish evidence in the case.

I think Mr. Editor, the incidents I have given you manifest more wit and talent, if not more fully within the pale of fair dealing than Mr. B. B. who trenched decidedly on the borders of falsehood. Had the lot of the individuals of whom I speak been cast in Wall street N. York, they would no doubt have reached a high standing in the practice of what is called *cornering*.

Yours,   S.

Mr. Cist:--

The tavern bill which you lately published in your paper, under the head of "Fifty
years since," has interested me,and I have some
small criticisms to make, on this antiquarian
matter, which, I think, has been misunderstood.

You say that the bill was incurred by General St. Clair and two other persons. You will
note that this bill was for *Mr.* St. Clair & Co.'
and is dated at Marietta in Oct. 1798. The general court of the territory sat at Marietta in that
month, and *Mr.* St. Clair, the General's son,and
who was then Attorney General of the Territory, was there in attendance on the Court, and
the bill was doubtless for him, and two other
lawyers from Cincinnati. That part of the bill
made out by their host, is in Connecticut currency, of 6 shillings to the dollar, as you may
readily see, and not in Pennsylvania, of 7s, 6d
to the dollar, which did not prevail in that quarter; and the remaining notes were made by that
third person, to whom, as unknown, you attribute all the brandy; for which I excuse you,
as you have reckoned him a military man.

That other person kept the bill, and made
the memo. of his outlay for the whole,and it contains the settlement on returning home, for
you see he "received of St. Clair,at Cincinnati."
The entry of cash, "received of Jacob," shows
the other person to have been one of a familiar
band, and I judge that it was jotted by a brothers's hand. The custom of travellers in those
days to have the bill paid on the road by one
of the company, as treasurer for the whole,who
would settle at the journey's end, is here shad-
owed forth. And the venison ham, the bread,
the last pints of brandy, the cheese, and eke the
victuals were for use on the journey at noon-
tide, and such appliances, as the lawyers, returning from Court, found needful on the dreary
bridle paths, where no houses were found to receive them. I am certain to a common intent
that the affair pertains to a band of pioneer
lawyers; and, with a feeling of jealous reverence for them, strengthened by a belief that one
of the two yet abides in honor among us, I insist that the huge quantities of sack and other
thin potations therein set down, were consumed
by their clients, and other droppers in at their
rooms.

Having thus shown, for the sake of truth, that
the affairs did not pertain to the *military*, but
rather to the *civil* department, and particularly
to the fathers of the Bar, I must, for the honor
of the profession, express my horror at a mistake
by your compositor, who changes "1 qt. brandy," to "19 p. brandy." or one quart to nineteen
pints; and I appeal to the price 3s 6d as proof of
the monstrous aspersion on the elders of our
race. You must, in good sooth, put that printer
under some suitable penance, and make a-
mends as publisher. Think of it! That lawyers should have to travel on horseback from
Marietta to Cincinnati, pack a bushel and a
half of oats, besides their bread and venison,
and have one innocent quart of brandy swelled
to nineteen pints, and published in these days
of total abstinence, post coaches and steamboats! As you dread a bad epitaph yourself,
correct the most horrible mistake!

Yours,

A YOUNGER LAWYER.

Jan. 20, 1845.

The figures were difficult to decipher; so we
put the quantity to suit the profession of the present day. Printer.

Buildings for 1844--in Cincinnati.

I have at length completed the enumeration
of the buildings of 1844, the result of which has
been published ward by ward, as each was finished,and now recapitulate the several returns.

Wards.	Stone.	Bricks.	Frames.	Total.
First.	1.	71.	10.	82.
Second,		97.	5.	102.
Third,		71.	46.	117.
Fourth,		75.	42.	117.
Fifth,		115.	51.	166.
Sixth,		89.	28.	117.
Seventh,		146.	73.	219,
Eighth,		120.	106.	226.
Ninth,	2.	45.	35.	82.
	3.	829.	396.	1228.
Buildings,'43	0.	636.	267.	1003.
Excess in'44.	3.	73.	127.	225.

The aggregate of buildings in 1842,   8542.

do   do   1843,   9545.

do   do   1844, 10773.

This, it will be observed, includes the corporate limits of Cincinnati; there is very little
doubt that in the district between the corporation line, and the base of the hills, on our north,
which is virtually a part of the city, as many as
five hundred buildings have been put up, during
1843 and 1844.

MARRIAGES.

In this city, on Thursday, January the 9th inst, by the
Rev. Mr. Cleaveland, Mr. James Hillhouse to Miss Margaret C. Swinson.

On Thursday the 16th inst, at the Broadway Exchange,
by the Rev. Mr. Kroell. Mr. George Maurer to Mrs.
Christiana Gerhart.

On the 11th inst, by the Rev. Mr. Prescott, Simon Ross
to Miss Margaret G. Smith, of Dundee, Scotland.

On Thursday, the 26th inst, by the Rev. S. W Lynd,
Mr. Hezekiah C. Smith to Miss Anne Coxall.

DEATHS.

In New Orleans, on Saturday, January the 11th, Capt.
John Batchelder, of Cincinnati.

In this city, on Sunday the 12th inst, Mrs. Fanny, wife
of the Rev. James C. White.

On Sunday the 12th inst, Mrs. Margaret Ann, consort of John A. Williams, and daughter of Wm. Jones.

On Friday the 17th inst, Rev. Frederick G. Betts
Pastor of the Presbyterian Church at Clearfield, Penn.

Rites of the Aborigines.

I am indebted for the following interesting sketch of Indian Customs to the "Sidney Aurora," published in the region referred to in the article. As the testimony of an intelligent eye-witness, it is of great value, and throws much light on many long-debated subjects connected with the origin, character, and habits of the Aborigines of our country.

LOWER SANDUSKY, O., 1844.

MR. EDITOR:—Since the epoch of the "Last Sacrifice," we are surrounded by a new race of inhabitants; the almost unprecedented influx of population, which has poured upon us, from the East, and the South, has gathered around us a new generation—so that we of the "olden time," seem now to live in the midst of strangers.

The *Red Man* of the forest has disappeared—the *Pioneer*, shunning the society of the refined and intelligent, has gone in search of the "Ultima Thule," or the "far West," and the *Squatter* has followed his footsteps.

Presuming that the following narration of the Religious Rites of the Aborigines, would not be altogether void of interest to your readers, it is, therefore, respectfully presented.

Yours, &c.

SAM'L CROWELL,

RITES OF THE ABORIGINES.

The SENECAS who roam'd those wilds,
In ages long by-gone;
Are now rejoicing in the chase,
Towards the setting sun.

Their Sacrifices offer'd up,
And Deity appeased—
Their "Father-land" they left in peace,
With their exchange well pleased.

On the first day of February, some fourteen years since, I witnessed an interesting, and to me, a novel, religious ceremony of the Seneca tribe of Indians, then occupying that portion of territory now comprising a part of the counties of Seneca, and Sandusky, Ohio, familiarly known to the inhabitants of this region, as 'the Seneca Reservation.'

The fact that this nation had recently ceded this Reserve to the United States, and were now about to commemorate, *for the last time in this country*, this annual festival, previous to their emigration to the Rocky Mountains, contributed not a little, to add to it an unusual degree of interest.

To those acquainted with the characteristic trait of the Red Men, it is unnecessary to remark, that there is a reservedness attached to them—peculiarly their own; but, especially, when a-bout to celebrate this annual festival, they seem, so far at least as the pale-faces are concerned, to shroud their designs in impenetrable secrecy. And the festival of which I now speak, might have been, as many others of a similar character were, observed by themselves with due solemnity, and without the knowledge or interference of their white neighbors, but that the general poverty and reckless improvidence of the Senecas were proverbial. And those were the causes which awakened the suspicions of the inquisitive Yankees.

In order, therefore, that the approaching festival, as it was intended to be the *last* of those observances here, should not lack in any thing necessary to make it imposing, and impress a permanent recollection of Sandusky, on the mind of their rising race—no effort was spared, and no fatigue regarded, that would tend to promote this object. Thus for some time previous to the period of which I am now speaking, by the unerring aim of the Seneca rifle, the antlers, with the body of many a tall and stately buck, fell prostrate; and in crowds the Indians now came into Lower Sandusky with their venison, and their skins; and the squaws, with their painted baskets and moccasins, not as heretofore, to barter for *necessaries*, but chiefly for *ornaments!*

To the penetrating mind of the merchant, they thus betrayed their object; to-wit: that they were preparing to celebrate their annual festival, or in the vulgar parlance of the day, 'to burn their dogs.'

Inquiry was now on the alert to ascertain the precise period; and to the often repeated interrogatory put by the boys of our village, 'Indian, *when* will you burn your dogs?'—an evasive reply would be given; sometimes saying, 'may be,' (a very common expression with them,) 'two days,'—'may be, three days,'—'may be, one week.' Their object being to baffle the inquirer; so that the further off the intended period was, they would give the shortest time—and vice versa.

The principal Head-men, or Chiefs of the Senecas, were 'GOOD HUNTER,' 'HARD HICKORY,' and 'TALL CHIEF;' there were also some sub or *half* Chiefs; among those of the latter rank, *Benjamin F. Warner*, a white or half-breed, had considerable influence.

In this, as in other nations, civilized as well as savage, though there may be several men of apparent equal rank, yet there usually is *one*, who either by artificial, or universally acknowledged talent, directs in a great measure, the destinies of the nation; and such among the Senecas, was 'HARD HICKORY.'

To a mind of no ordinary grade, he added, from his intercourse with the whites, *a polish of manner*, seldom seen in an Indian. The French language he spoke fluently, and the English, intelligibly. Scrupulously adhering to the costume of his people, and retaining many of their habits, this Chief was much endeared to them; while on the other hand, his urbanity, and for an Indian, he possessed, as already observed, a large share of the *suaviter in modo*—his intelligence, his ardent attachment to the whites—and above all, his strict integrity in business transactions, obtained for him, and deservedly, the respect and confidence of all with whom he traded. Such was the trust the merchants of Lower Sandusky reposed in this Chief, that when an indigent Indian came to ask for goods on a credit, if Hard Hickory would say he would see the sum paid, no more was required. Thus his word passed current with, and current for, the whole nation.

And as in the mind of man there is something intuitive, better known than defined, by which instinctively, as it were, we find in the bosom of another, a response to our own feelings; so in the present case, this noble Indian soon discovered in the late OBED DICKINSON, a merchant of Lower Sandusky, a generous, confiding and elevated mind, whose honorable vibrations beat in unison with his own.

To Mr. D. therefore, he made known the time when they would celebrate their festival, by sacrificing their dogs, &c. &c., and cordially invited him to attend as a *guest*, and if so disposed, he might bring a friend with him.

Correctly supposing that I never had an opportunity of witnessing this religious rite, Mr. D. kindly requested me to accompany him to their Council-House, on Green creek, in that part of this county, included in the present township of Green creek. On giving me the invitation, Mr. D. remarked, that by taking a present in our hand, we would, probably, be made the more welcome. In accordance, therefore, with this suggestion, we took with us a quantity of loaf sugar and tobacco.

It was sometime in the afternoon when we arrived, and immediately thereafter, we were ushered into the Council-House with demonstrations of public joy and marked respect.

As soon as seated, we gave our presents to Hard Hickory, who, raising, held one of them up, and pointing to Mr. D. addressed the Indians in an audible voice, in their own tongue; then holding up the other, he pointed to me, repeating to them what he had before said—this done, he turned to us, and said:

'You stay here long as you want, nobody hurt you.' Confiding in the assurances of this Chief, I hung up my valise, in which were some important papers, for I was then on my way further East, attending to my official duties as Sheriff of this county, and felt perfectly at home.

To the inhabitants of this section of Ohio, a minute description of the Council House, would be deemed unnecessary. Suffice it to say, that its dimensions were, perhaps, sixty by twenty-five feet; a place in the centre for the fire, and corresponding therewith, an aperture was left on the roof for the smoke to ascend. Contiguous to the fire place were two upright posts, four or five feet apart; between these posts, a board, twelve or fifteen inches broad, was firmly fastened; and over this board the skin of a deer was stretched very tight. On a seat near this board, sat a blind Indian with a gourd in his hand, in which were beans or corn—with this he beat time for the dancers. Such was the musician, and such the music.

The dancing had commenced previous to our arrival; and was continued with little intermission, for several successive days and nights. An effort by me to describe their *manner* of dancing would be fruitless. I have witnessed dancing assembles in the populous cities of the east, among the refined classes of society—but having seen nothing like this, I must, therefore, pronounce it *sui generis*. I was strongly solicited by some of the Chiefs to unite with them in the dance: I, however, declined the intended honor—but gave to one of them my cane, as a *proxy*, with which he seemed much delighted. Several of their white neighbors, both male and female, entered the ring.

There was on this occasion a splendid display of ornament. Those who have seen the members of a certain society, in their most prosperous days, march in procession, in honor of their Patron saint, decorated with the badges and insignia of their *Order*, may have some conception of the dress and ornamental decorations of those Head-men, while engaged in the dance.

I will select 'Unum e Pluribus.' Their 'Doctor,' as he was called, wore very long hair, and from the nape of his neck, to the termination of

his cue, there was a continuous line of *pieces of silver*—the upper one being larger than a dollar, and the lower one less than a half dime.

Some of the more inferior Indians were 'stuck o'er with baubles, and hung round with strings.' Many of them wore small bells tied round their ancles; and those who could not afford bells, had deer hoofs in place thereof; these made a jingling sound as they put down their feet in the dance.

The *squaws* also exhibited themselves to the best advantage. Several of them were splendidly attired and decorated. Their dresses were chiefly of *silk*, of various colors, and some of them were of good old fashioned *Queen's gray*. These dresses were not 'cut,' as our fair belles would say, *a la mode*—but they were cut and made after their own fashion: that is; not so long as to conceal the scarlet hose covering of their ancles, their small feet, or their moccasins, which were so ingeniously beaded, and manufactured by their own *olive* hands.

Nor must I omit saying, that the sobriety and correct demeanor of the Indians, and the modest deportment of the squaws, merited the highest commendation.

At the commencement of each dance, or, to borrow our own phraseology, each 'set dance, a chief first arose, and began to sing the word, "YA-WO-HAH!" with a slow, sonorous, and strong *syllabic* emphasis, keeping time with his feet, and advancing round the house; directly, another arose, and then in regular succession, one after the other, rising, and singing the same word, and falling in the rear, until all the *Indians* had joined in the dance; next the *Squaws* at a respectable distance in the rear, in the same manner, by seniority, arose, and united in the dance and the song. Now the step was quicker and the pronunciation more rapid, all singing and all dancing, while *Jim*, the blind musician, struck harder and faster with his gourd, on the undressed deer-skin; thus they continued the same dance for more than one hour, without cessation!

The Indian boys, who did not join in the dance amused themselves the meanwhile discharging heavy loaded muskets through the aperture in the roof the reverberations of which were almost deafening. Taken altogether, to the eye and ear of the stranger, it seemed like *frantic* festivity.

Tall Chief, who was confined to his bed, by indisposition, felt it so much his duty to join in the dance with his people, that he actually left his bed, notwithstanding it was mid winter, came to the Council House, and took part in the dance as long as he was able to stand.

About the 'noon of night,' Hard Hickory invited Mr. D. and myself to accept a bed at his residence; to this proposition we readily assented. Here we were not only hospitably provided for, but entertained in a style which I little anticipated. Even among many of our white inhabitants, at this early day, a *curtained* bed was a species of luxury not often enjoyed—such was the bed we occupied.

Shortly after our arrival at the house of this Chief, Mr. D. retired; not so with our friendly host and myself—while sitting near a clean, brick hearth, before a cheerful fire, Hard Hickory unbosomed himself to me unreservedly.—Mr. D. was asleep and the chief and I were the only persons then in the house.

Hard Hickory told me, among other things, that it was owing chiefly to him, that this feast was now celebrated: that it was in part to appease the anger of the *Good Spirit*, in consequence of *a dream* he lately had; and as an explanation he gave me the following narration:

"He dreamed he was fleeing from an enemy, it was, he supposed, something *supernatural*; perhaps, an *evil spirit*; that, after it had pursued him a long time, and for a great distance, and every effort to escape from it seemed impossible as it was just at his heels, and he almost exhausted; at this perilous juncture, he saw a large water, towards which he made with all his remaining strength, and at the very instant when he expected each bound to be his last, he beheld, to his joy a *canoe* near the shore; this appeared as his last hope; breathless and faint, he threw himself into it, and *of its own accord*, quick as an arrow from the bow, it shot from the shore leaving his pursuer on the beach!"

While relating this circumstance to me, which he did with earnestness, trepidation and alarm, strongly expressed in his countenance, he took from his bosom something neatly and very carefully enclosed, in several distinct folds of buckskin. This he began to unrol, laying each piece by itself, and on opening the last, there was enclosed therein, a Canoe in Miniature!

On handing it to me to look at, he remarked, that no other person save himself and me, had ever seen it, and that, as a memento, he would wear it, as "long as he lived."

It was a piece of light wood, resembling cork, about six inches long, and, as intended, so it was, a perfect model of a canoe.

This chief, being now in a communicative mood, I took the liberty to inquire of him "when they intended to burn their dogs?" for I began to fear I should miss the express object which I came to witness.

After giving me to understand that "the Red men did not care about the pale faces, being present at, nor, if they chose, join in the dance, but burning their dogs was another thing—this was offering sacrifice to, and worshiping the Great Spirit; and while engaged in their *devotions* they objected to the presence and interference of the whites: yet, as I had never been present, and coming as the friend of Mr. D., who was a good man, he would tell me they would burn their dogs *soon* to-morrow morning."

The night being now far advanced, he pointed to the bed and told me to sleep there; but that he must go to the Council House, to the dance, for his people would not like it, if he would stay away, and wishing me, good night, he withdrew.

Anxiety to witness the burnt offering almost deprived me of sleep. Mr. D. and I, therefore, rose early and proceeded directly to the Council House, and though we supposed we were early, the Indians were already in advance of us.

The first object which arrested our attention, was a pair of the canine species, one of each gender suspended on a *cross!* one on either side thereof. These animals had been recently *strangled—not a bone was broken*, nor could a distorted hair be seen! They were of a beautiful *cream* color, except a few dark spots on one, naturally, which same spots were put on the other, artificially, by the devotees. The Indians are very partial in the selection of dogs entirely *white*, for this occasion; and for which they will give almost any price.

Now for part of the decorations to which I have already alluded, and a description of one will suffice for both, for they were *par simles*.

First—A scarlet ribband was tastefully tied just above the nose; and near the eyes another; next round the neck was a white ribband, to which was attached something bulbous, concealed in another white ribbond; this was placed directly under the right ear, and I suppose it was intended as an *amulet*, or charm. Then ribbands were bound round the forelegs, at the knees, and near the feet—these were red and white alternately. Round the body was a profuse decoration—then the hind legs were decorated as the fore ones. Thus were the victims prepared and thus ornamented for the burnt offering.

While minutely making this examination, I was almost unconscious of the collection of a large number of the Indians who were there assembled to offer their sacrifices.

Adjacent to the cross, was a large fire built on a few logs; and though the snow was several inches deep, they had prepared a sufficient quantity of combustible material, removed the snow from the logs, and placed thereon their fire. I have often regretted that I did not see them light this pile. My own opinion is, they did not use the fire from their Council House; be cause I think they would have considered that as *common*, and as this was intended to be a holy service, they, no doubt, for this purpose, struck fire from a flint, this being deemed *sacred*.

It was a clear, beautiful morning, and just as the first rays of the sun were seen in the tops of the towering forest, and its reflections from the snowy surface, the Indians simultaneously formed a semicircle enclosing the cross, each flank resting on the aforesaid pile of logs.

Good Hunter who officiated as High Priest, now appeared, and approached the cross; arrayed in his *pontifical* robes, he looked quite respectable.

The Indians being all assembled—I say *Indians*. (for there was not a *Squaw* present during all this ceremony—I saw two or three pass outside of the semi-circle, but they moved as if desirous of being unobserved,) at a private signal given by the High Priest, two young chiefs sprang up the cross, and each taking off one of the victims, brought it down, and presented it on his arms to the High Priest, who receiving it with great reverence, in like manner advanced to the fire, and with a very grave and solemn air, laid it thereon—and this he did with the other—but to which, whether male or female, he gave the preference, I did not learn. This done, he retired to the cross.

In a devout manner, he now commenced an oration. The tone of his voice was audible and somewhat *chaunting*. At every pause in his discourse, he took from a white cloth he held in his left hand, a portion of dried, odoriferous herbs, which he threw on the fire; this was intended as incense. In the meanwhile his auditory, their eyes on the ground, with grave aspect, and in solemn silence, stood motionless, listening attentively, to every word he uttered.

Thus he proceeded until the victims were entirely consumed, and the incense exhausted, when he concluded his service; their oblation now made, and the *wrath* of the Great Spirit, as they believed, appeared, they again assembled in the Council House, for the purpose of performing a part in their festival, different from any I yet had witnessed. Each Indian as he entered, seated himself on the floor, thus forming a large circle; when one of the old chiefs rose, and with that native dignity which some Indians possess in a great degree, recounted his exploits as a Warrior; told in how many fights he had been the victor; the number of scalps he had taken from his enemies; and what, at the head of his braves, he yet intended to do at the 'Rocky Mountains;' accompanying his narration with energy, warmth, and strong gesticulation; when he ended, he received the unanimous applause of the assembled tribe.

This meed of praise was awarded to the chief by 'three times three,' articulations, which were properly neither nasal, oral, nor guttural, but rather *abdominal*. Indeed I am as unable to describe this kind of utterance, as I am, the step in the dance.

I have seen some whites attempt to imitate the step, and heard them affect the groan or grunt, but it was a mere aping thereof. Thus many others in the circle, old and young, rose in order, and *proforma*, delivered themselves of a speech. Among those was Good Hunter; but he

"Had laid his robes away, His mitre and his vest."

His remarks were not filled with such bombast as some others; but brief, modest, and appropriate: in fine, they were such as became a Priest of one of the lost Ten Tribes of Israel!

After all had spoken who wished to speak, the floor was cleared, and the dance renewed, in which Indian and squaw united, with their wonted hilarity and zeal.

Just as this dance ended, an 'Indian boy ran to me, and with fear strongly depicted in his countenance, caught me by the arm, and drew me to the door, pointing with his other hand towards something he wished me to observe.

I looked in that direction, and saw the *appearance* of an Indian running at full speed to the Council House; in an instant he was in the house, and literally *in the fire*, which he took in his hands, and threw fire coals and hot ashes in various directions, through the house, and apparently all over himself! At his entrance, the young Indians, much alarmed, had all fled to the further end of the house, where they remained crowded, in great dread of this *personification* of the Evil Spirit! After diverting himself with the fire a few moments, at the expense of the young ones, to their no small joy he disappeared. This was an Indian disguised with an hideous false face, having horns on his head, and his hands and feet protected from the effects of the fire. And though not a professed 'Fire King,' he certainly performed his part to admiration.

During the continuance of this festival, the hospitality of the Senecas was unbounded. In the Council House, and at the residence of Tall Chief, were a number of large fat bucks, and fat hogs hanging up, and neatly dressed. Bread also, of both corn and wheat in great abundance.

Large kettles of soup ready prepared, in which maple sugar, profusely added, made a prominent ingredient, thus forming a very agreeable saccharine coalescence. And what contributed still more to heighten the zest—it was all *impune* (Scot free.)

All were invited, and all were made welcome; indeed, a refusal to partake of their bounty, was deemed disrespectful, if not unfriendly.

This afternoon, (Feb. 2d,) I left them enjoying themselves to the fullest extent: and so far as I could perceive, their pleasure was without alloy. They were eating and drinking: but on this occasion, no ardent spirits were permitted—dancing and rejoicing—caring not, and, probably, thinking not of to-morrow.

As I rode from the Council House, I could not but ejaculate with Pope:

"Lo, the poor Indian, whose untutored mind, Sees God in clouds, or hears Him in the wind; His soul proud science never taught to stray, Far as the solar walk or milky way; Yet simple nature TO HIS HOPE has given, Behind the cloud-topt hill an humbler heaven, Some safer world in depth of woods embrace'd Some happier island in the wat'ry waste.

* * * * * * *

And thinks, admitted to that equal sky, His faithful dog, shall bear him company."

A Court Scene in Georgia.

A friend of mine has recently returned from an excursion into the —— circuit of this State He tells me that, while in the county of ——, he strayed into the Court house, and was present at an arraignment of a man by the name of Henry Day, who was charged with attempting to kill his wife, Day was a pale little man, and the wife was a perfect behemoth. The indictment being read, the prisoner was asked to say whether he was "guilty or not guilty." He answered: "there's a mighty chance of lawyer's lies in the papers, but some part is true. I did strike the old lady, but she fit me powerfully first. She can swear equal to little or any thing, and her kicks are awful. I reckon what you say about the devil a moving me is pretty tolerably correct, seeing as how she moved me. I've told you all I know about the circumstances, mister. I gi'n 'Squire Jones there a five dollar bill, and I allow he'll take it out for me." 'Squire Jones then rose and said that he had a point of law to raise in this case which he thought conclusive. It was an established rule of law that man and wife were but one; and he should like to know if a man could be punished for whipping himself; he should be glad to hear what the solicitor general had to say to that. The solicitor general answered that he thought that his brother Jones had carried the maxim a little too far; men had often been punished for beating their wives. If a man were to kill his wife, it would not be suicide.

Here 'Squire Jones interposed, and defied the solicitor general to produce any authority to that effect. The solicitor general looked at "Green and Lumpkin's Georgia Justice" for some minutes, and then observed that he could not find the authorities just then, but he was sure he had seen the principle somewhere, and he called on the judge to sustain him. In the enthusiasm of counsel on the point, they forgot to offer any evidence as to the guilt or innocence of Day in the premises. The Judge, likewise oblivious of the fact, proceeded to charge the jury. He told them that man and wife were one. He remarked, that, in either event, the man was legally bound to suffer; and therefore, come as they would, Day was undoubtedly guilty. He would not decide whether if a man kill his wife it was murder or suicide. He was not prepared to express an opinion on that point, it was a very delicate one, and he had no idea of committing himself. (Some one here observed that he was mighty fond of committing others.) He then called up the bailiff, a tremendous looking cracker, wearing a broad brimmed hat, with crape. (I never saw a man south of latitude thirty-three that did not wear a white hat with crape) and proceeded to admonish him that the jury were very much in the habit of coming in drunk with their verdict, and that, if it happened in this case, he would discharge the prisoner and put the punishment upon him.

The bailiff gave a significant glance at the Judge, and replied that other people besides the jury came into court drunk, when some people were drunk themselves! The jury then retired, and so did my friend; the next day he returned and found matters in *statu quo*, except that Day and his wife had made up, and were discussing the merits of a cold fowl and a quart of beer, and now and then interchanging kisses, despite the frowns and becks of the officers. The Judge, clerk and sheriff had been up all night, and looked wolfish; and the bailiff was seated on his white hat at the door of the jury room, and this indicated that he swallowed the concentrated venom of a thousand wild-cats.— The most awful curses, oaths and sounds preceeded from the jury room; some were roaring like lions, some crying like children, mewing like cats, neighing like horses, &c.

At last a short consultation was held at the jury room, between the foreman and the bailiff, whereupon the latter, putting his hat one sided on his head, came into the court room, and addressed the Judge thus: "Mister, Tom Jakes says the jury can't agree about this man, and if you keep him (that is Tom Jakes,) without grog any more, he'll whip you on sight." The judge appealed to the bar if this was not a contempt of court; and "Green and Lumpkin's Georgia Justice" having been consulted, it was finally decided that, as it was a threat addressed to the Judge as a private individual, and to "whip him on sight," and not on the bench, it was not, under the free and enlightened and democratic principles of Georgia Legislation, a contempt of court. This being settled, the judge directed the bailiff to say to Tom Jakes, the foreman, the jury should agree if they staid there through eternity." The bailiff retired and so did my friend—but he gives it as his opinion, from the frame of mind in which he left all parties, .he jury and bailiff are there still.

The Flower Garden for January.

BY T. WINTER, OF CINCINNATI.

In this department, there will be but little to do this month. Should the weather be open, remove roses and ornamental shrubs, at the same time watch them well to prevent the frost from injuring their roots. It would be advisable to plant no more bulbs in the open ground this season, as the probability is the roots would rot, instead of striking root. Protect your beds of bulbous roots from heavy rains and severe frosts, and your flowers will be the finer in their bloom the coming season. Manure may be strewed over your beds and borders, and in mild weather turn them over to mellow the soil. Dahlias, the last of this month, should be examined, and if mouldy, dried in the sun and re-packed.

THE PARLOR.—If attention be paid to your Camellias at this season, by watering and syringing occasionally, it will be a great benefit, and make their buds swell better, and your plants more vigorous. Exotic plants should be watered with caution, their pots kept clear of decayed leaves, otherwise your plants will get sickly, languish and die. Chrysanthemums should be

cut down, if not done last month, and placed out of the way, their stems being of no ornament after flowering. Hyacinths, Tulips, and Crocuses, may still be potted the early part of this month to flower in the house. Hyacinths, in glasses, must be guarded against frost, and kept in the sun during the day. This department being mostly attended to by ladies, the pleasure derived by them will naturally be some inducement to pay strict attention to their flowers. I would caution them against leaving their glasses in the window on a mild evening, for frequently this month the weather will change twenty or thirty degrees in one night, breaking the glasses and disturb their equanimity, and mar the pleasure anticipated—creating a distaste for flowers, all of which may be avoided with a little trouble.—*Enquirer.*

A Court Martial in 1812.

The following is a literal copy of the original report of a Court Martial, held at Buchanan's Blockhouse, in Darke county, Ohio, soon after the commencement of the last war.

"BUCHANAN'S BLOCK HOUSE, July 8, 1812.

A Court martial ware held agreeabel to genaral orders and proceded to the tryell of W— M— a privet of Capt. B—s companey who stands charged as folows.

1st. For offering to fight a dewel with one or more of the men.

2nd. For profene swaring and blaspheming.

3rd. For cocking his gun, and thretning to shute his fellow soldiers.

4th. For destroying some of the camp equipage.

5th. For disabedience of orders, when the foloing witnisses was examened and declare on oth as folows.

B— S— states that the prisner ofered to take the musill of Mr. Shofes gun in his mouth and to put the musill of his oan gun in Mr, Shofes meuth and fyer and that he did in the most awfull manner swere and blasspheme and swere that hee would sheut the first that would offer to take him or too come neer him and that hee allso bid defyence to all millitarey athority and would not submit to any comand of the oficers the prisent to the 5th charg held giltey.

J— M— states that the prisner ofered to fight Mr, Shofe with their guns and tuk up his gun and swore that hee would sheut him if hee would come neer him and further agrees with the foorgowing witness.

George Shofe states that the prisner tuke said Shofes gun and thretned to sut one of men for betting the droum and afterwards threw the gun on the ground the gun was taken up and found loded and further the witness agrees with the foorgowing witnesses.

N— A— states that the sed prisner when ordered undr gard went up on the left of the Blockhouse and got his gun, and after Mr. Shofe tuke the gun from him and handed hir to sed A— he found the gun loded with pouder an cocked and furthr the witness agrees with the faorgowing witnesses.

J— B— forthermore saeth that the prisner sade hee wood load his gun and Mr. Shofe shold lode his and step five steps and fire nothing more diferent from the foorgowing witness saeth.

G— J— saeth that on the day following that the prisner sade hee disregarded all officers and law.

J— H— states that sed prisner after the gard

were ordered to confinement ran upon the left and got his gun and the sed H— saw him load hir with pouder and aperd to be prepairing to lode hir with ball and furtherer the witnesses sayeth not.

the cort after hering the witnesses and duly daliberating on the testemoney unanemously pronounce him gilty and centace the prisner to be find in the sum of twenty five dollars and be confined for the tarm of twenty days and put on fitege for the same tarm and put on half rations for the last ten days.

President Capt G— B—
Members Capt W— V—
Lieut. J— C— C—
Judg advocat Ensign D— S—

The Commandant of the detachment feels an impression on his mind that the honorable board have acted consistent with their duty in every respect and he feels for the prisner now convicted of the crime herein stated and after considering the foorgowing sentence remits one half of the fine inflicted the other parte of the sentence he concures in and hopes it will be a caution to the prisner and that he will not treate his superiors with contempt or and impunity and at the expiration of his confinement he wil returne to his duty as a faithfull soldier, ordering that the foregoing be read on public parade.

J— H—
July 18th 1812   Lieut Col Com.

[*Dayton Journal.*

Old Times in New Orleans.

A friend has politely furnished us with a venerable file of the New Orleans Gazette, bearing date of the year 1807. We clip the following curious and interestng extract.

Here is an advertisement dated July 23d, 1807 that will create a smile among steamboat captains:

"For Louisville, Kentucky, THE HORSE BOAT, John Brookhart, master. She is completely fitted for the voyage. For freight of a few tons only (having the greater part of her cargo engaged) apply to the master on board, or to

SANDERSON & WHITE.

We are told, by a gentleman who remembers the circumstance well, that the said horse boat used up between a dozen and twenty horses on the tread wheel, before she arrived at Natchez. He never heard of her arrival at Louisville, and is under the impression that the trip was abandoned somewhere in the vicinity of Natchez.— *St. Louis Reveille.*

Early Roads and Pathways of Cincinnati.

In the infancy of the city, there was but little communication maintained between the hill and bottom, so far as keeping roads for wheeled vehicles, and hardly more for horses. Even at a later date, wagons would stall going up Walnut street, opposite to Liverpool's, now Miltenberger's corner. On Main street, from Front to Lower Market street, then many feet below its present grade, from Johnston's store, No. 49, to Lower Market street, boat gunwales were laid as foot ways, part of the distance, and the citizens walked, in very muddy weather, upon the rails of the post and rail fences, which enclosed

the lots of that street. When Pearl street was opened some fifteen years ago, and the building extending from the corner to Dellinger's late store, was putting up, in digging the foundations, a number of pannels of posts and rail fence, the relics of those days, and which had been covered up for probably thirty years, were found and dug up, absolutely sound.— Causeways of logs, generally a foot in diameter, were laid in various parts of Main street, and it was but a few years since, in re-grading Main from Eighth to Ninth streets, that a causeway of such logs were taken up, sound, but water saturated, which extended from near Eighth street, to a spot above Jonathan Pancoast's dwelling, probably 120 feet in distance.

A Leaf from old Records.

Aug. 1, 1803—Associate Judges for the county of Hamilton, met agreeable to law.

Present, Michael Jones,
James Silver,
Luke Foster, Esqs., Judges.

The following certificates for wolves killed were presented, and allowed:

I. Dexter, for 1 wolf under 6 months of age,			1,00
Matthew Coy, 3 wolves, over do	2,00	do	6,00
Jno Vincent, 2 do	do do		do 4,00
D. Endsly & D. Carnagin, 2 do	do do		do 4,00
Jno Vincent, 1 do	do do		do 2,00
Jacob Misner, 2 do	do do		do 4,00
Jno Larrison, 2 do	do do		do 4,00
Luther Ball, 5 do	young, and one old,		7,00
Jos. Thompson, 1 do	do do		do 2,00
Dan. Carnagin, 2 do	do do		do 4,00
			38,00

Account of Abraham Corry, jailer, for the diet, &c., of George Turner, confined in jail, rejected by commissioners, because said George Turner is able to pay his diet, &c., himself.— Also, Abraham Corry's account, for the diet of Archibald M'Clean, confined in jail, not allowed, it being considered the master of said M'-Clean is liable for his jail fees, diet, &c.

Appropriations made.

To prosecuting attorney in Court of Common Pleas, Hamilton co., for one year, $100.

Revolutionary Recollections.—No. 1.

These letters to John Frazer, Esq., of Cincinnati, are from a revolutionary soldier, still living, and on the way to his hundredth year. As may be inferred from their tenor, he is a minister of the gospel, and I may add, on the testimony of the late Gen. Harrison, that he served as army chaplain, during the investment of Fort Meigs, and besides acting in that capacity, in which he acquired the affection and esteem of the troops, all his leisure time was employed in nursing the sick, and providiug such comforts for them as his influence and solicitation could procure.

PLAIN, WOOD COUNTY, O. Sept. 5th, 1839.

JOHN FRAZER, ESQ. :—

I beg leave to trouble you once more with my pension business. If it should be the last time,there would be nothing unexpected, I ought to look for the appointed time daily, yet He who numbereth the days of man, may continue mine a little longer. I think I can submit all to his infinitely wise disposal.

I was able to attend the celebration ot the 4th of July, 1839 ,and state some facts that have not been related in any history of the revolution.— In the spring '76, forepart of April, Patterson's regiment was ordered by Washington, then at New York, to take shipping at Albany, and to proceed, with all possible despatch. for Quebec by Lake George and Lake Champlain. We arrived at Morrell the fore part of May. We soon had information, that a small fort at the Cedar Rapids wasinvested by the Indians, and a small British force—four companies were immediately ordered for their relief, commanded by Major H. Sherburn. The next morning another company of volunteers was ordered, to which I was attached. Sherburn had to cross the outlet of Bacon Lake, had one boat and one canoe. Some time in the forepart of the day,they were attacked by the Indians, and by Foster, a Captain witb about twenty British soldiers. At the first onset, Sherburn drove them; we were then in hearing, but could not reach them. Foster beat a parley, the firing ceased, and he informed Sherburn, that Major Butterfield had surrendered the Fort the evening before; and it would only be a useless waste of lives to contend longer. Sherburn saw that there was no possibility of retreating, and to save his men from a general massacre, surrendered to Foster. Two days after, Arnold, afterwards the traitor, joined our company, with about six hundred men, and boats sufficient to take us all across the Bacon, and two or three pieces of small cannon. The evening after Arnold joined us, just at dark, the Indians fired on our out posts, or sentinels, and made their retreat as fast as they could. We started early in the morning, with men enough only in the boats to man them, and the rest of the men on foot, as fast as the boats could ascend the stream, for the current was pretty strong. We entered the Bacon, sun about two hours high—orders were for every man to prepare for action,and embark on board the boats; Arnold led the van, in a bark canoe, rowed by five Frenchmen. When about half way across the stream, steering to a certain point of the woods, Foster commenced a fire with two small field pieces, and, although we were in close

der, and broadside to his fire, some shot went over us,and some fell short,but none took effect. As we drew near the point of landing, the Indians gave a tremendous yell,and fired—we were too far off; their balls skipped on the water and some of them rattled on the sides of our boats. We sustained no damage. It being near night Arnold thought it best to return, and make our attack in the morning. We set to work to fix our small guns in the bows of our boats. But about midnight, Foster came over in a canoe, with Major Sherburn and Captain M'Kinstrey, who had been wounded in the thigh, during the action. A cartel was entered into, and the prisoners were returned, and hostages on parole.— We then returned to St. Johns,and to Chamblee where we, in five days, saw the red coats; were ordered to retreat as fast as we could to St. Johns; many of us were very feeble by reason of the small-pox but we madegood our retreat from one port to another, until we reached Ticonderoga, and began about the last of June, to build Fort Independence, opposite to the old fort Ticonderoga. Here we tarried until November, when orders came to march for Albany, and from thence to join Washington; reached his camp only two days before Christmas. The rest has been recorded. This campaign, for suffering by hard fatigue, sickness and hunger, exceeded anything that happened through the revolution.

My dear sir, excuse my intruding on your time and patience, to read so long a scrawl, made from the memory of an old, worn out soldier. Early impressions on the mind, when strongly made, are not easily effaced. I thought if I filled the sheet, it might afford a little amusement, and cost no more postage than if the whole was blank.

Yours, most affectionately,
JOSEPH BADGER.

Spirit of Seventy-six.

The following anecdote is extracted from the "Memoirs of Marshal Count de Rochambeau,', who, it will be recollected, was the Commander of the French army which was sent to our aid in the war of the revolution.

I shall here venture to interrupt the regular narrative, says this writer, to relate an anecdote fitting to exemplify the character of the good republicans of Connecticut. In going to this conference the carriage which conveyed Admiral the Chevalier de Ternay and myself, broke down. I sent Fersen, my first aid-de-camp, in search of a wheelwright, who resided at the distance of a mile from the place where the accident happened. Fersen returned to inform me that he had found a man sick of the quartan fever, who had answered that his hat full of guineas would not tempt him to work in the night. I requested the admiral to go with me that we might intreat him together. We told him that General Washington was to arrive that evening at Hartford, for the purpose of conferring with us the next day, and that the object would be defeated, unless he mended our vehicle. "I believe you," said he, "I have read in the newspaper that Washington is to be there this evening to confer with you. I see this is a public matter: your carriage shall be ready at six in the morning." And so it was. On our return from the conference, at Hartford, one of our wheels gave way, nearly at the same spot, and at the same hour; and we were obliged to have recourse to our old friend. "What," said he, "do you want me to work again in the night?" "Alas! yes," was my reply. "Admiral Rodney is arrived and has tripled the enemy's naval forc and we must get back with all speed to Rhode Island, in order to be ready for his attacks." "But," said the wheelwright, "what are you going to do with your six ships against twenty English ships." "It will be a fine day for us, if they attempt to destroy us at our anchorage." "Come," said he, "you are clever fellows; you shall have your carriage at five o'clock in the morning; but before I begin to work, tell me, if there is no harm in the question, are you pleased with Washington, and is he so with ye." We assured him that this was the case. His patriotic feelings were gratified, and he was again as good as his word. Such was the public spirit that animated, not only this worthy mechanic, but almost all the inhabitants of the interior, and particularly the freeholders of Connecticut.

When the British took possession of Philadelphia, one of the soldiers rudely entered a house, and, in highly insulting language, ordered rooms to be prepared for his reception, by a certain hour, at which time he said he would return. The master of the mansion was absent with the American army. His wife, a timid woman, sent for her neighbor, a lady of great spirit and determination, whose husband was also on military duty, in the English army. While these females were engaged in consultation, the intruder entered the door, and the neigbor immediately presented a pistol which she drew from her pocket. "Begone!" said she, "how dare you insult unprotected females? If you advance an inch I will shoot you." The heroine of this little incident still lives to relate it. "The pistol," she concludes, "was given to me by General Mifflin when he marched out of the city, but I had never ventured to load it. I did not tell this however, to the soldier, who precipitately left the room."

The husband of this lady was killed during the war, and she receives his half-pay from the English government. She is in the 87th year of her age, and is obliged to transmit annually, a certificate to England, that she is living and unmarried. Latterly the old lady adds to this latter notification, that she *lives in hopes*.

"The Duke de Lauzun Biron," says the memoir above quoted, "who took the command of these barracks (at Hartford, in Connecticut) rendered himself, by the urbanity of his manners, highly agreeable to the Americans, and succeeded perfectly in whatever business he had to transact either with old Governor Trumbull, or the members of the legislature. A little anecdote will serve to illustrate the Duke's aptitude for social intercourse of every kind. An honest American of the village asked him what trade

his father was of in France. "My father," answered Lauzun, "does nothing: but I have an uncle who is a farrier;" alluding to one of the significations of the word Maréchal in his own language.* "Very well," said the American, shaking him cordially and lustily by the hand, "that is a very good trade."

* In French, the word *Maréchal* means either a marshal or a farrier. Biron, the uncle of Lauzun was a marshal of France.

The Duke de Rochambeau relates another anecdote which is worth transcribing: At the period of the march of the French troops from Cranston, says he, there happened between me, and an American captain of militia, whose habitation I occupied as quarters, an affair pleasantly characteristic of republican freedom. He came to ask from me, before the departure of the troops, a sum of fifteen thousand francs, (three thousand dollars) for wood which the brigade of Soissonnois had burnt on his property. I found the demand exorbitant, and referred him to the Commissary Villemanzy, who was charged with the settlement of all accounts for articles consumed by the army throughout the camp. At the moment of beginning the march the next day, when the roll had been beaten, and the troops were under arms, a man approached me with a very complaisant air, and told me he was not ignorant of the services which I had rendered his country, that he respected me greatly, but that he was obliged to perform his duty. He then served me with a paper and afterwards laid his hand gently upon my shoulder, telling me at the same time that I was his prisoner. "Well, sir," said I, laughing, "take me away if you can." "Not so, your excellency," answered the sheriff: "but I beg of you, now having done my duty to let *me* depart unmolested." I sent the commissary Villemanzy to the house of the American captain, and he found him in a crowd of his countrymen, who were all upbraiding him in the sharpest terms for his proceeding. The commissary agreed with him to submit the matter to arbitration, and the result was that the Captain had to pay the costs, and to content himself with two thousand, instead of fifteen thousand francs.

In the conclusion of this interesting account of the operations of the French army, the Duke adverts to his personal reception and treatment, and relates an anecdote which is not a little singular. I have not mentioned, says he, the multitude of addresses from all the towns and general assemblies of the States of America, presented to me, containing uniformly the warmest acknowledgement of their obligations to France. I will cite but one of these addresses. A deputation from the Quakers of Philadelphia waited on me, in all the simplicity of their costume. "General," said the oldest of them, "it is not on account of thy military qualities that we make thee this visit, these we hold in little esteem: but thou art the friend of mankind, and thy army conducts itself with the utmost order and discipline. It is this which induces us to tender thee our respects."

After the war was over the duke embarked, with the universal benediction of the thirteen States. He states the remarkable fact, that such was the discipline of the army, not a quarrel or a blow between a French and an American soldier occurred during a course of three campaigns.

The Equatorial Telescope.

This long looked for instrument arrived safely by the *Yorktown* last week, and is now in the hands of its owners, the Cincinnati Astronomical Society. There are incidents connected with the receipt of the Telescope, which strikingly demonstrate the absurdity of popular clamor. Captain Halderman had taken it on board at New Orleans, on his previous trip and advanced payment of the bill of charges upon its passage from Europe, and finding by the time he reached the mouth of Cumberland, that the Ohio river would not let him up, he left his freight, the Telescope included, at Smithland, and returned to New Orleans. For so doing he incurred great censure from certain individuals, I think undeservedly. Was it worth while for the sake of getting it up a week earlier or later to jeopardize such an article in careless and irresponsible hands? Besides, had it then been brought up, it would have unquestionably been involved in the destruction by fire of the Cincinnati college in whose upper stories it was designed to be deposited.

What makes the injustice more glaring, the public are indebted to the liberality of Captain Halderman, and Messrs. Kellogg and Kennett, the owners of the Yorktown, that the forty boxes in which this instrument and its appendages, were packed, came *freight free*.

Modern Warehouses.

Such are the improvements of late years in the construction of modern buildings, not dwellings merely, but warehouses, that thorough examination of the premises is often necessary to comprehend the prodigious difference which exists in favor of some of our recent business erections, over their predecessors in the same line. In my lately published statistics of the Fourth ward, allusion was made to the warehouses put up in 1844, in the neighborhood of Walnut and Second streets. I had neither time nor space to say more in that article, and I now avail myself of an interval of leisure to supply, from notes taken on the spot, a statement of one of these buildings as a sample of the rest. I refer to the new Iron and Nail warehouse, owned and occupied by Wm. C. Stewart & Co., on Second, between Main and Walnut streets.

The warehouse fronts on Second street, 46 feet 8 inches, by a depth of 114 feet 8 inches. The stone walls of the basement are 33 inches in thickness, which are succeeded by brick walls—First story, five; second story, four; and third story, three courses thick. In the basement, are eighteen stone pillars, 24 by 66 inches each, which sustain two oak girders, 14 by 16 inches square, the entire length of the building; on these rest the ends of the joints, also of oak, most of which are 13 feet, none more than 16 feet long; and are 16 inches deep, by 2½ inches wide, and hardly six inches apart. The girders are secured together in a novel manner, which I cannot undertake to describe, but which it will be evident to those who examine them, cannot under any degree of strain or pressure, be moved laterally, while fourteen anchors in each story, serve to connect walls, joists and girders together in such a manner that the walls can never become pressed out. On the upper stories, the stone pillars are followed up by oaken uprights 14 by 16 inches square, eighteen of which serve on each floor as supports to the girders above, the girders being throughout the whole building, also 14 by 16 inches square. The cellar and ground floors are of 1½ inch oak plank, and the last descends ten inches in its entire length to facilitate the taking out iron in front, when necessary. The basement story is 8 feet in the clear, the upper stories, respectively, 14½, 11½, 10½, and 9½ feet. The jambs, sills, and lintels of the doors, with the window lintels, are of cast iron. There are six doors in front, two at the side, and one at the rear; the first named, six feet wide, and the others, which are receiving doors, are nine feet square in width and height, exclusive of transom lights above. Through the last three, loaded drays might be driven with ease. The warehouse is lighted with windows front and rear; the sashes being filled with 12 by 18 crown glass. The roof is of No. 26 sheet iron, coated inside with one, and outside with two coats oil paint, to which a third will be added in the spring. The gutters are made entirely of copper. 350,000 brick, and 8,700 square feet of stone, are actually built into the walls.

On the ground floor are two counting rooms, the front 22 by 14 and the rear 17 by 14 feet; a space at the side of this last being taken off for fire proof safe which is built up from the cellar and is 8 feet high on the groundfloor, and occupies a space 6½ by 3½ feet, the walls being 30 inches thick and lined with half inch boiler iron. Space has been left between the boiler iron and walls for a flue to carry off the heated air in case of fire. The doors are double plates of iron and lined with Shawk's patent locks, defy alike fraud and force. The entire materials of the building are of American product and manufacture, the lumber and glass being from Ohio and Western Pennsylvania and the residue are our city manufacture.

Why such a degree of strength should be thus imparted to this building may be comprehended in the fact that there is now actually on the second floor four hundred tons of nails rivets, sad irons &c. and more than one thousand tons of bar, hoop, sheet and boiler iron, on the lower floor, while it is possible they may be required to bear double these weights.

The adjacent leather warehouse of J. W. & W. W. Cooper is built in a proportionally substantial manner and enlarges the entire front to 78 feet.

The building has been examined by persons from New Orleans, Philadelphia and New York, who all concur in opinion, as may be infered from these statistics, that it has not its equal in the United States for convenience of arrangement, solidity of construction and adaptedness to the purpose for which it was built. In point of space, merely, some of the large Cotton warehouses in New Orleans doubtless surpass it, while they are, inferior in every other respect, but it has no superior for size in any other city of the U. States. There are two Warehouses in Pittsburg near the Monongahela bridge, which may be said to approach it. These are fine buildings of 30 feet front by 160 ft. deep, and of course are more than 10 per cent. less in square feet than Messrs Stewart & Co's, to say nothing of the greater importance of front to depth in business buildings.

CORRESPONDENCE.

An Apology for Free Trade in Money.

BY W. SMEAD, BANKER.

Money is undoubtedly an article of commerce and as in every other commodity, its market price varies with the circumstances of plenty and scarcity, supply and demand. Nothing fluctuates more than the interest of money. It is affected by a multitude of causes, commercial, political, and local. In 1837, the best commercial paper in the city of New York, was sold at a discount of 3 per cent. per month; and in 1844 the notes of the same individuals were cashed at 3 per cent. per annum. Interest as fixed by law has differed from age to age. In the dark ages of ignorance and superstition, the smallest compensation taken for the use of money was considered a deadly sin, and the law prohibited all interest under the severest penalties. Under the Romans, in the time of Justinian, the legal rate was 4, 6, 8, and 12 per cent., according to circumstances. In France it has varied from 2 to 10 per cent. It was ten per cent, in England in the time of Henry VII, and has since been reduced to five.

In the United States, the legal rate varies from 5 to 8 per cent., and in some of the States 10, and in others 12 per cent. may be recovered.

It thus appears that legislators have never been able to agree upon any uniform rate of interest, and their laws will uniformly be evaded as often as the market rate for money happens to be higher than the legal rate. The laws of trade founded, as they are, on the law of natures are paramount to legal enactments, and must bo obeyed.

A great demand for money, and a limited supply concurring with unsettled credit, and a general feeling of mistrust will raise the price of money to the highest point. A great supply and small demand with settled credit and firm confidence will sink it to the lowest, and it will vary between these extremes according to the relative proportion of these elements of price. In all times the price will vary, according to the nature of the security, the amount, and the period of payment. Insurers charge from $\frac{1}{4}$ to 6 per cent. or more according to the risk. In lending money, on the same principle, as some persons are extra-hazardous, they should pay extra for the risk. Laws limiting the rate of interest, must proceed on the absurd supposition, that money is always equally abundant, the supply always relatively the same, all men equally honest, punctual, and responsible, and that a small sum borrowed for a single week on personal security, should command no higher rate than a large amount for a term of years on bond and mortgage security. The law has one arbitrary standard for all cases however different. Many fruitless attempts were made in former times, by laws. to regulate the prices of various article of necessity. Since no laws fixing the price of money can be adapted to all circumstances, why not leave it, like all other commodities, to find its level of value? Why not let it regulate itself by free competition? Why leave every other article of commerce to the operation of free trade, and single out this alone for prohibitory enactments. All that the law can do, with either reason or justice is to fix the interest, in cases where no specified rate has been stipulated. Why should not men be left as free to bargain for the use of money as for any other article. Such laws it is pretended, protect the poor and needy against extortion, and secure the weak and credulous against imposition, prevent excessive interest, restrain prodigality, &c. Now in fact, the law actually aggravates the very evils it pretends to mitigate.

It gives to wealth a monopoly in borrowing, over skill and industry, for the lender is confined to the legal rate and prevented from accepting such additional interest as would compensate the risk of lending to a man of small means. It forces the poor man to sacrifice his property, & enables the rich to buy it. In preventing a man from paying 10 per cent. it forces him to lose 50. Under pretence of making money cheaper to him, it makes it dearer; and instead of protecting, it crushes him.

The law interferes with the only contract in

which a man is not liable to imposition. You may cheat him in almost any thing else, but he always comprehends clearly what he is about in borrowing money. The law allows a man to sell every thing but money for the best price he can get. It leaves him at liberty to buy or sell at the most extravagant prices, to make foolish and ruinous bargains, to contract debts with no means of payment; to sacrifice his property, squander his money, and indulge in every species of extravagance and dissipation; in a word, it throws open all the wide avenues of ruin, but carefully closes one of its by-paths. Besides, usury laws are shockingly immoral in their tendency, for they encourage a man to break his contract, reward him for ingratitude, bribe him to be a villain, and hire him to crush the hand held out to help him.

In the present enlightened age, when every man whose mind is elevated by education, above the level of vulgar prejudices, admits that money is a legitimate article of commerce, and that like other commodities, it is always worth what it will sell for, the origin of the prejudice and prohibitory laws against the traffic in it, becomes a subject of curious inquiry.

Money lending has never been a popular employment. The only way to bring it into favor would be, to lend unhesitatingly to all and require payment from none. At the time the money is borrowed, the lender is a friend and benefactor; when payment is enforced, he is an unfeeling oppressor. Refuse a man a loan or force him to pay, and he is apt to complain.— Novelists, poets, and dramatists, have fostered the prejudice by endeavoring to enlist sympathy in favor of the *unfortunate* borrower at the expense of the prosperous lender. Despotic princes, during the middle ages, who were always needy, and always borrowing money to carry on their wars, conceived that by proscribing all interest, they would obtain the use of what money they wanted free of cost. Accordingly, the taking of interest was denounced, and the church prohibited all interest as a mortal sin, and thundered its anathemas against all who dared to receive the smallest compensation for the use of money.

They were shut out from holy communion, rendered incapable of making a will, or of receiving a legacy, and even denied the right of Christian burial. The sole ground of this prohibition was, that Moses had commanded the Jews to take no interest from their brethren, and that Aristotle had discovered no organs of reproduction in coin, and that money therefore ought not to beget money. The philosopher forgot that money would buy houses, and that these would beget money. Armed with this double authority, the church boldly proclaimed

the taking of interest to be contrary to the divine law, natural and revealed; and that it should consequently be regarded with holy horror by every good christian. Now the Mosaic precept was clearly a political, not a moral precept; for although it prohibited the Jews from taking interest from their brethren, it expressly permitted them to take it from others.

During the ages of political thraldom, war was the only honorable pursuit; commerce languished, all lucrative employments were regarded with contempt, as unfit for a christian; and trade was mostly in the hands of the Jews.— When liberty and commerce revived, interest was restored. Up to this time, the term *usury* had been used to signify any rate of interest, great or small. When usury was legalized, it was thought best to give it a new name, and hence it is now called "interest." The prejudices against free trade in money are rapidly wearing away, and are chiefly confined in the present day to the uneducated in the lower walks of life.

It has now become a settled principle in the science of political economy, that all restrictions on the interest of money have uniformly the effect of rendering it dearer. Whenever the market value of money is above the legal rate, usury laws with their penalties, either prevent a man from borrowing at all, or force him to pay an extravagant price; for, in addition to the full value of the money, he must pay the lender for the risk of trusting to his honor and honesty.

The English government has abolished its usury laws, in all cases where money is lent on personal security. The State of Ohio repealed her usury law in 1824, and several States have followed her example.

That usury laws should ever have existed, originating as they have, in ignorance and superstition, will, in the progress of knowlege, become as much a matter of surprise to our posterity, as it is to us that our ancestors should gravely make laws for the prevention of sorcery and witchcraft.

A Parable.
BY PHAZMA.

In a solitary place, among the groves, a child wandered, whithersoever he would.

He believed himself alone, and wist not that one watched him from the thicket, and that the eye of his parent was on him continually; neither did he mark whose hand had opened a way for him thus far.

All things that he saw were new to him, therefore he feared nothing.

He cast himself down in the long grass, and as he lay he sang until his voice of joy rang through the woods.

When he nestled among the flowers a serpent rose from the midst of them, and when the child saw how its burnished coat glittered in the sun like the rainbow, he stretched forth his hand to take it to his bosom:

Then the voice of his parent cried from the thicket, "Beware."

And the child sprung up, and looked above and around, to know whence the voice came;—but when he saw not, he presently remembered it no more.

He watched how a butterfly burst from its shell, and flitted faster than he could pursue, and rose far above his reach.

When he gazed, and could trace its flight no more, his father put forth his hand, and pointed where the butterfly ascended—even into the clouds.

But the child saw not the sign.

A fountain gushed forth amidst the shadows of the trees, and its waters flowed into a deep and quiet pool.

The child kneeled on the brink, and, looking in, he saw his own bright face, and it smiled upon him.

As he stooped yet nearer to meet it, a voice once more said, "Beware."

The child started back, but he saw that a gust ruffled the waters, and he said to himself, "It was but the voice of the breeze,"

And when the broken sunbeams danced on the moving waves, he laughed, and dipped his foot that the waters might again be ruffled—and the coolness was pleasant to him.

The voice was now louder, but he regarded it not, as the winds bore it away.

At length he saw something glittering in the depths of the pool, and he plunged in to reach it.

As he sunk, he cried aloud for help.

Ere the waters had closed over him, his father's hand was stretched out to save him.

And while he yet shivered with chilliness and fear, his father said unto him—,

"Mine eye was upon thee, and thou didst not heed: neither hast thou beheld my sign nor hearkened to my voice. If thou hadst thought on me, I had not been hidden."

Then the child cast himself on his father's bosom, and said:

"Be nigh unto me still, and mine eyes shall wait on thee, and mine ears shall be open unto thy voice for evermore."

The Battle of the Cowpens.

Friday last, the 17th inst., being the anniversary of this battle, one of the most gallant and successful fights, on the side of the Americans, during the whole revolutionary struggle, I have inserted the best account of it, extant.—This, from the pen of a visitor to the battle ground, contains many particulars, new, and of deep interest.

"It may with truth be said, that in no battle of the American revolution, was the contest more unequal, or the victory more signal and complete, than that of the Cowpens. The British army was superior in numbers, in discipline, in arms, and in everything that can constitute an army, save the soul and spirit of the soldier, and the noble daring of the officer. In infantry they were as five to four, and in cavalry as three to one. The American army, under General Morgan, was a retreating detachment, without artillery, without proper arms, and without baggage or

provisions. In the language of a distinguished historian of that period—the earth was their bed, the heavens their covering, and the rivulets which they crossed their only drink.

The battle ground of the Cowpens is in Spartanburgh District, about seventeen miles north of the Court House, and four or five miles from the North Carolina line. The surrounding country is beautiful, and almost a perfect plain, with a fine surrounding growth of tall pines, oak and chestnut. On the memorable 17th of January, 1781, the entire country for miles around the battle ground, was one untouched forest. The inhabitants of the lower part of the District, had been in the habit of driving their cattle into this part of the country, for the purpose of grazing, and had erected pens in the neighborhood, for the purpose of salting and marking them.—Hence the origin of the name of the battle ground. The field of battle, however is about two miles distant from the Cowpens; but inasmuch as there was no nearer known place in the neighborhood, it was called "the battle of the Cowpens." The night previous to the battle, the American army had encamped themselves upon the ground. The position was a favorable one, and lay immediately between the head waters "Suck Creek," and a branch "Buck Creek,' which are not more than two hundred yards apart. The forces under General Morgan were drawn up about daylight, on the bridge extending from one of these springs to the other. These branches, at that time, were well lined with cane and small reeds. General Morgan was retreating into North Carolina, and had determined to give battle on the other side of Broad River; but General Pickens informed him that if they crossed the river, the militia could not be kept together. A large portion of them had joined the army the day previous, and were under no regular discipline. This determined the commander to wait for Tarleton, whose force had been marching all night to overtake the American army, before they could get over Broad River. The North and South Carolina militia, under the command of General Pickens were posted one hundred and fifty, or two hundred yards in advance of the continental troops, under Col. Howard. Col. Brondon's regiment was placed on the left of the road leading from the Union District into North Carolina, and the regiments of Colonels Thomas and Roebuck on the right. They were ordered to stand the fire of the enemy as long as possible, and then retreat, and form again on the right of the continental troops.

About sunrise the British army appeared in sight, and marched within one or two hundred yards of the American lines, and then displayed to the right and left with a corps of cavalry on each wing. General Pickens ordered the militia not to fire, until the enemy came within thirty paces of them. They were also permitted to shelter themselves behind trees, which was at least a prudent, if not a scientific mode of fighting. At the celebration of the anniversary of this battle in 1835, the writer of these sketches was shown by several of the old soldiers, the identical trees from behind which they fired during the engagement. The British, when formed, rushed forward with a shout and a huzza as if in anticipation of an easy victory. The horse of Colonel Brondon was shot down under him, and his regiment immediately fired on the enemy, in violation of their orders to wait until he had approached within thirty paces. The

The regiments of Colonels Thomas and Roebuck soon commenced also a brisk and destructive fire. The enemy then made a charge with fixed bayonets, and the soldiers gave way. The brunt of the battle was now bravely borne by the regular troops, while the militia rallied in the rear and renewed the engagement. Three hundred of the British troops were killed and wounded, and five hundred were taken prisoners. The remnant of Tarleton's cavalry was pursued by Col. Washington, fifteen or twenty miles to Goudelock's, where he was informed the British were out of his reach. This, however, was a false statement, made by Mrs. Goudelock, in order to save the life of her husband, whom Tarleton had just pressed into his service to pilot him across the Pacolet. This good lady supposed that if Colonel Washington overtook the British, an engagement might ensue, and her husband might be killed in the action. She therefore suffered the feelings of a wife to prevail over those of patriotism and morality. For the fact was, that Tarleton has just got out of sight as Washington rode up. Had the American cavalry continued their pursuit fifteen minutes longer, the remnant of the British troops could have been either captured or killed.

The next day after the battle, a portion of the militia were despatched to bury the dead.— Three places of burial are now to be distinctly seen. The largest is near the chimney of a cabin, some hundred yards distant from the battle ground. The second is fifty to one hundred yards distant, and the third on the spot, where the battle took place. One of the soldiers, who assisted at the burying, observed, at the celebration before alluded to, that the dead were to be found in straight lines across the battle ground, and that it gave them a most singular appearance when seen at a distance. The only vestiges of the battle now to be seen, are the trees which have been cut for bullets. Some of these chops are twenty or thirty feet high—an evidence of bad shooting by one or the other of the parties. A great many of the bullets are yet to be found in the trees. The writer saw several that were pewter, and had no doubt been moulded from a spoon or plate. Lead being scarce, some good whig had made the best substitute in his power at the expense of his table, and the convenience of his family. At the time the battle was fought, there was no undergrowth on the ground, and objects might be seen at a great distance through the woods; but since that time, bushes and saplings have sprung up, and destroyed, in a great measure, the beauty of the forest.

American Ingenuity.

Those who can recollect as far back as the commencement of the present century, find in the various improvements in mechanical and manufacturing processes since, the opportunity of noticing many and wonderful changes. A column in a newspaper on this subject cannot cover what would fill a volume to advantage. I shall, therefore, select a single topic—carpenters' tools.

In 1800, the plane bitts, chisels, gimlets, and iron squares, were all miserable articles of English manufacture. To Pennsylvania ingenuity we are indebted for the screw auger, the spiral gimlet, the latter headed with tough durable wood, in lieu of the box handles of the imported article, liable continually to split. We are also indebted to the same State for the present improved pattern of the shingling hatchet.

In 1808, the hardware house in which I was an apprentice, forwarded to England specimens of the spiral gimlet, screw auger, shingling hatchet and modern choping axe, for the purpose of having cheaper articles made of the same patterns. To our great surprise, in due course of time, we learned that they could not be fabricated there. The statement of our correspondent was, that the workmen there could not comprehend how the auger and gimlet were twisted. The fact was, they could fabricate any thing that had ever been made there and improve upon existing fabrics, but they could neither invent like the Americans, nor could they master, in many instances, their inventions. No nation on earth possesses such augers & gimlets as the Americans. The English employ what is termed a pod or barrel auger with a lip at one edge, which takes hold, as our screw, though not so effectually. A carpenter will bore four or five inches with ours while he would bore one with theirs.

As an evidence how slowly mechanical improvements make their way in England, I copy an article in one of their late papers, by which it seems that after it has been in approved use for more than fifty years here, our auger is exhibited in their ship-yards as a novelty:

"Mr. W. Clark, a native of the United States of America, and now a resident at Birmingham, attended at Woolwich dockyard yesterday to afford the master shipwright and the foremen of the shipwrights an opportunity of testing the value and capabilities of a new description of auger for boring wood, constructed in a spiral form, exactly similar in appearance to a corkscrew, which empties itself of the fragments of wood without having occasion to withdraw it from the bore, as is the case with augers on the common principle. It gave great satisfaction, and an opinion was expressed that it would materially abridge manual labor in boring hard woods, as it requires no presure to cause it to take hold, the screw form giving it ample purchase, and it does not appear to be so liable to heat by friction as the others."—*Liverpool Chronicle.*

I notice, also, in one of our Eastern papers, that a cutler at Newark, New Jersey, has received a large order for tailors' shears for the German market, where those of his manufacture are preferred to any of English or their own make.

The Electro Magnetic Light.

Messrs. *Starr and Sanders*, who have been carrying on for the last six months, a series of experiments, the object of which is to simplify their apparatus for producing this new and remarkable light, have at length brought the invention to a practical result.

They have now succeeded in obtaining a steady and intense stream of light, which is produced entirely by the electro magnetic principle. A single effect of this will suffice at present. The *flame* of a burning candle 18 feet from the apparatus, was thrown by broad day light on a plaistered wall three feet off, on which was presented its distinct *shadow*, with fully defined outline. The brilliancy of the light itself was unsupportable as that of the sun to the naked eye.

The proprietors set out on Thursday for the East, where it is their intention to submit the merits of the invention, to special experiment in one of the National light houses, as the most satisfactory test of its general utility.

Relics of the Past.

PITTSBURGH, Dec. 2nd, 1795.

DEAR SIR:—

The hurry of business, while at Mad River, prevented my enclosing you a power of attorney, to transact my business, in my absence. I now write you, and fully signify my approbation to such sales and conveyances of lots, in the town of Cincinnati, as you may think proper, and at such prices as you can agree upon. I would pen the request and authorize you, should I not be at Cincinnati early next Spring, to lease to the best advantage my out lots there. Our journey from Mad River to this place was long and tedious, arising from high waters; some detention on account of the Indians, we were obliged to have a talk with all that fell in our way, and had also a very bushy country to travel through—but have the pleasure to inform you, that a good road may be had from Cincinnati to this place, the distance less than three hundred miles—would be under particular obligations to you, if you would endeavor to prevent the destruction of fences around my out lots. Am, sir,

With due respect and esteem,
Your obedient servant,
ISRAEL LUDLOW.

MR. JOEL WILLIAMS.

NEW BRUNSWICK, April 24th 1791.

Dear ARMSTRONG:—

I am very much obliged to you for your letter of the 19th inst. I am happy to hear that you have your Company so near completed, that they please you so well. I am sure it must give you pleasure to be off so soon, although you are counted a troublesome fellow. Pray how did you make out with only your twenty-five suits?—do lead me into this affair, for I think when mine is done, I am done recruiting. I have got now 14 men here, and Denny has

4 or 6 in New York. These levies has played the mischief with me, and still continue so to do. Capt. Pyatt raised his complement, in and about this town—and now another officer is recruiting here, and others all about the State—however, one consolation is, that perhaps all the fighting will be done before I get out. Denny, on his removal, left several aching hearts about the town, but I imagine he gets those that please him better in New York, if not quite so safe. How does your nunnery come on, and other places? I have not established any such houses here, as yet.

Write me to be sure, before you set out.—Present my compliments, if you please, to Mr. Wade, also Mrs. Nicholas, and all the Conestoga waggon with the appendages.

Believe me to be,
Dear Armstrong, yours friendly,
E. BEATTY.

Capt. ARMSTRONG.

NOTE.—The No. of my Pennsylvania Lottery tickets are, 8491 8492 8493 and 8494; tell me their fate. When are you coming to see me as you promised—I have elegant quarters, and you know the people.

Something in names.

The ferry-boat plying between Louisville and Jeffersonville is owned by Captain John *Shallcross*; a name sufficient to inspire confidence in any ferry-boat—a name equally appropriate for the Captain of a steamboat, and equivalent to go ahead, would be that of the late Secretary of the Treasury, *Forward*.

The Early Steamboats of the West.

I have made out the following list of the first series of steamboats which were built at various points, from N. Albany on the Ohio, to Brownsville, on the Monongahela, for the navigation of the western waters, and their individual history, as far as I can ascertain it.

The first steamboat that ever navigated the Ohio and Mississippi, was the "ORLEANS." She was built at Pittsburgh in 1812, carried 300 tons, had a low presure engine, and was owned by, and constructed for *Fulton & Livingston*, of New York. Started from Pittsburgh in December 1812, and arrived at New Orleans on the 24th of same month, and plied regularly between New Orleans and Natchez, until the 14th July, 1814; when on her trip to the latter place, being opposite Baton Rouge, while lying by at night, and the river falling at the time, she settled on a sharp stump and became wrecked.—Her trips during that period averaged seventeen days. She was abandoned, and her engine with a new copper boiler, made in New York, was put into a new boat in 1818 called the "NEW ORLEANS," which only ran until the spring of

1819, when she also was sunk by a stump on the same side of the river, below Baton Rouge, but was raised by two schooners brought to N. Orleans between them, and there lost totally near the Batture.

The next in the order of time, was the COMET, 145 tons, owned by *Samuel Smith*, also built at Pittsburgh, on French's stern wheel and vibrating cylinder patent, granted in 1809, The *Comet* made a trip to Louisville in the summer of 1813, and reached New Orleans in the spring of 1814, made two voyages to Natchez, and was then sold, and the engine put up in a cotton gin.

Next came the VESUVIUS of 390 tons, built at Pittsburgh, November 1813, by *R. Fulton*, and owned by a company in New York and New Orleans. She started for New Orleans in May 1814, *Frank Ogden* being Captain, and was the first boat that made any effort to reach the falls, having left New Orleans with freight in the early part of July of the same year, but grounded on a sand bar about 700 miles up the Mississippi, on the 14th of July, and lay there till the 3rd of December, when a rise in the river floated her off, and she returned to New Orleans, when she was put in requisition for military service by Gen. Jackson, but in starting up the river for wood, she grounded on the Batture, and became useless to the Government. The succeeding year she plied between New Orleans and Natchez, under the command of *Captain Clement*, who was succeeded by *Captain John DeHart*. In 1816 she took fire, near New Orleans, and burnt to the water's edge, having a valuable cargo on board. The fire communicated from the boilers, which in the first stile of building, were in the hold. The hull was afterwards raised and built upon at New Orleans. After making several trips to Louisville, she was broken up in 1820.

The fourth steamboat was the ENTERPRIZE, of 100 tons, built at Brownsville, Penn., by *Daniel French* on his patent, and owned by a company at that place. She made two voyages to Louisville in the summer of 1814, under command of *Captain J. Gregg*. On the first of December of the same year, she took in a cargo of ordnance stores at Pittsburgh, and started for New Orleans, *Henry M. Shreve* commander. She made the voyage in 14 days, being a quick trip, all circumstances considered, and was then despatched up the river to meet two keels which had been delayed on the passage, laden with small arms. These she met 12 miles above Natchez, took their masters and the cargoes on board, and returned to New Orleans, having been six and a half days absent, in which time she run 624 miles. She was then for some time actively employed transporting troops and supplies for

the army, engaged under Gen. Jackson in the defence of New Orleans. She made one voyage to the Gulf of Mexico as a cartel, one to the rapids of Red River with troops, and nine voyages to Natchez. Set out for Pittsburgh on the 6th of May, and arrived at Shippingport on the 13th, being 25 days out, and proceeded thence to Pittsburgh, being the first steamboat that ever ascended the whole length of the Mississippi and Ohio rivers. A public dinner was given at Louisville to Captain Shreve, for effecting a passage in that space of time, so wonderful and important was it considered. The man who at that dinner would have predicted that, there were those present who would live to see steamboats perform that trip in five days, twenty days less than Shreve's effort, would have been pronounced insane, or at any rate a mere visionary, yet less than a lapse of thirty years has served to accomplish it. She made one more trip down, her Captain being D. Worley; when she was lost in Rock Harbor at Shippingport.

The "ETNA," of 360 tons, was the next one built, owned by the same company as the *Vesuvius*, length, 153 feet, breadth 28 feet, with 9 feet depth of hold. She left for New Orleans under the command of *Captain A. Gale*, and made trips successively to Natchez and Louisville. There being some want of confidence in steam power to ascend the Mississippi with a cargo, above Natchez, she was employed in the summer of 1815, towing ships from the mouths or passes of the Mississippi to New Orleans, the barges then getting freight in preference at eight cts. per lb. from New Orleans to Louisville. In the fall of 1815, the Mississippi being very low, the owners of the *Etna* made another attempt to ascend the river, and put in about 200 tons, for which they charged four and a half cts. per lb. for heavy, and six cts. for light goods. She had very few passengers above Natchez. The dependence was on drift wood, and occasionally lying by two and three days, where settlements were made, *waiting while wood was being cut and hauled*, broke a wrought iron water wheel shaft, near the mouth of the Ohio, and laid by at Henderson, Kentucky, fifteen days trying to weld it, and had at last to end the passage with one wheel to Shippingport in *sixty days*. At Louisville she had two shafts cast. Her next trip down with three hundred tons at one ct. per lb. and a few passengers was made in seven days. The succeeding trip up, under many of the same difficulties, was made in thirty days, breaking the other wrought iron shaft by driftwood in ascending the Ohio.

The sixth, in order of time, was the DESPATCH, *Capt. J. Gregg*; built at Brownsville on French's patent, and owned by the same company with the *Enterprize*. She made several voyages from

Pittsburgh to Louisville and back, and one from the falls to New Orleans and back to Shippingport when she gave out in 1818.

The next were the BUFFALO, 300 tons. and JAMES MONROE, 90 tons, built at Pittsburgh by *B. H. Latrobe*, for a company at New York.— He failed to finish them for want of funds. They were sold by the Sheriff and fell into the hands of *Ithamar Whiting* who finished them with engines—both dull sailers.

The WASHINGTON was the ninth, and the first at Wheeling, Virginia, where she was built under the superintendence of Captain *H. M. Shreve* who was owner in part. The engine was made at Brownsville. This was the first boat with boilers on deck. The *Washington* crossed the falls in September, 1816, went to New Orleans, and returning wintered at Louisville. In March 18-17, she left Shippingport for New Orleans, and made her trip up and down in forty-five days, including detention at New Orleans. This was the trip which was considered to settle the practicability of steamboat navigation in the West.

There are some incidents connected with steamboat navigation on the Western waters worthy of notice. Captain SHREVE referred to already as the Captain of the *Enterprize*, believing the patent granted to Fulton and Livingston, destructive to the interests of the west and unconstitutional in its character, took early measures to test its validity. The ENTERPRIZE reached New Orleans on the 14th December 18-14, and was seized the next day for alleged violation of that patent, and suit commenced against the owners by the New York Company, in an inferior Court, where a verdict was found for the defendants. The case was then removed by writ of error to the Supreme Court of the United States.

Before the question came up before this tribunal, *Shreve* returned to New Orleans with the *Washington*, which was also seized by the company, to whom she was abandoned without opposition by Captain Shreve, who was owner in part. On application however to the Court, on behalf of the Washington and her owners, an order was obtained to hold the company to bail to answer the damages that might arise by the detention of the vessel. The agents of the company in this stage of the business, fearing the downfall of the monopoly which they sought to preserve, directly and through the medium of their att'y, proposed to admit him to an equal share with themselves in all the privileges of the patent right, provided he would so arrange the business in Court as to allow a verdict to be found against him. Had Shreve possessed less firmness or principle than belonged to him, he might have yielded to this tempting bait and thrown back the steamboat operations in the West. for

ten years before another individual of sufficient energy had appeared to contest the patent. It is hardly necessary to add that the Supreme Court finally set the patent aside.

For a share of these facts, I am indebted to Haldeman's Louisville Directory for 1845.

Ingenious Locks.

I notice an extract in a late Enquirer from a New York paper, stating that an ingenious mechanic of that city had invented a lock, which could not be opened even with its own key except by the owner, and had offered 500 dollars to any other person who could accomplish that feat.

This seems surprising, but I can state something of the kind more so. Messrs. *Glenn & M'Gregor* of this city, have a *combination and detector* bank lock, of a construction equally simple and ingenious, the tumbler of which may be so adjusted to its own key, that any person other than the owner making use of that key, would have only one chance in favor of opening it, to four hundred and seventy-nine millions one thousand six hundred chances against his doing so. This renders it next to impossible for any person but the owner to open it.

Exchange Papers.

There are certain rules of propriety which govern my conduct as regards other papers which I expect to govern that of others towards me.

I never send off refuse papers, torn or illegible, to any on my exchange list.

When I copy an original article from my exchange papers, I give due credit for it.

A paper which requires the straining of the eyes to read, I do not desire to receive; and look upon the sending it an imposition. Nor can I afford the time or labor of gathering statistics for others to claim as their own.

If any of my exchanges find themselves dropped hereafter, they will comprehend the cause.

☞ 'Small thanks to you,' said a plaintiff to one of his witnesses for what you have said in this case.' 'Ah,' said the conscious witness, 'but think of what I *didn't* say.'

General Washington.

The following letter from Gen. Washington to W. W. Woodward, bookseller in Philadelphia and now belonging to Dr. C. Woodward, of Cincinnati, is probably his latest manuscript extant, being written within twenty days of his death. As there are numbers who peruse the "Advertiser, who have never seen the autograph of that distinguished patriot and hero, I have added a *fac simile* of his signature, which those familiar with it will acknowledge to be well executed.

MOUNT VERNON, 24th Nov'r 1799.

SIR:—I have been favored with your letter of the 19th inst.

Being well acquainted with Dr. Witherspoon, whilst living, and knowing to his abilities, and shall with pleasure, as far as becoming a subscriber to his works may contribute, promote the success of their publication;—and do authorise you accordingly, to add my name to the sub scription paper which appears to be in existence. I am, Sir,

Your most humble servant,

MR. WM. W. WOODWARD.

Our Aborigines.

PLAIN, WOOD Co., Aug. 25. 1840.

JOHN FRAZER, ESQ:

My Dear Sir—I have lately been very sick—being taken the fore part of July, with a painful dysentery; it suddenly brought me down, so that I was not able to rise from my bed without help—or to have my clothes on for ten days. I thought probably the appointed time to close my earthly existence was at the door; but God's ways are not like our ways, nor his thoughts like our thoughts. He has yet something for me to do,—I hope for the advancement of the Redeemer's kingdom in this region. I am able to ride a few miles; but my recovery is slow; yet for an old wornout man, I am doing as well as could be expected. I hope to be able to go to Perrysburgh the first week in September next.

Be pleased sir, to accept a short historical account of the Wyandot Indians. Having been a resident missionary with them for several years before the late war, and obtained the confidence of the Chiefs—in a familiar conversation with them, and having a good interpreter, I requested them to give me a history of their ancestors as far back as they could. They began with giving a particular account of the country formerly owned by their ancestors. It was the North side of the river St. Lawrence, down to Bacon Lake, and from thence up the Utiwas.—Their name for it was Cunonetoltia. This name, I had heard applied to them, but knew not what it meant. The Senekas owned the opposite side of the river, and the island on which Morel now stands. They were both large tribes, consisting of many thousands. They were blood relations, and I found at this time, they claimed each other as cousins.

A war originated between the two tribes in this way. A man of the Wyandot, wanted a certain woman for his wife; but she objected, and said he was no warrior—he had never taken any scalps. To accomplish his object, he raised a small party, and in their scout fell upon a party of Seneka hunters, killed and scalped a number of them. This precedure began a war between the Nations, that lasted more than 100 years, they supposed more than a hundred winters before the French came to Quebec. They owned that they were the first instigators of the war, and were generally beaten in the contest. Both tribes were greatly worsted by the war. They often made peace, but the first opportunity the Senekas could get an advantage against them, they would destroy all they could, men, women and children. The Wyandots finding they werein danger of being exterminated, concluded to leave their country, and go for the West. With their horses, the whole nation made their escape to the upper lakes, and settled in the vicinity of Green Bay, in several villages—but after a few years the Senekas made up a war party, and followed them to their new settlements, fell on one of their villages, killed a number and returned. Through this long period. they had no instruments of war, but bows and arrows, and the war club. Soon after this the French came to Quebec, and began trading with the Indians, and supplying them with fire arms, and utensils of various kinds. The Senekas having got supplied with guns, and learned the use of them, made out a second war party against the Wyandots—came upon them in the night, fired into their tents, scared them exceedingly—they thought at first it was thunder and lightning. They did not succeed so well as they intended. After a few years they made out a third party, and fell upon one of the Wyandot villages, and took them nearly all. But it so happened at this time, the young men were all gone to war with the Fox tribe, living on the Mississippi. Those few that escaped the massacre of the Senekas, agreed to give up, and go back with them, and become one people, but requested of the Senekas to have two days to collect what they had, and make ready their canoes, and join them on the morning of the third day, at a certain point, where they were to wait for them, and hold a great dance through the night. The Wyandots sent directly to the other two villages, which the Senekas had not disturbed and got all their old men and women, and such as could fight, to consult on what measure to take. They came to the resolution to equip themselves in the best manner they could, and go down in perfect stillness, so near the enemy as to hear them. They found them engaged in a dance, and feasting on two Wyandot men, they had killed, and roasted, as they said for their beef, and as they danced they would shout their victory, and told how good their Wyandot beef was. They continued their dance until the latter part of the night, and being pretty well tired, they all lay down, and soon fell into a sound sleep. A little before day, the Wyandot party fell on them and cut them all off, not one was left to carry back the tidings. This ended the war for a great number of years. Soon after this, the Wyandots got guns from the French traders, and began to grow formidable. The Indians who owned the country where they had resided for a long time proposed to them to go back to their own country. They agreed to return, and having prepared themselves as a war party, they returned: came down to where Detroit now stands, and agreed to settle in two villages, one at the place above mentioned, and the other near where the British fort Malden, now stands.

But previously to making any settlement, they sent out in canoes, the best war party they could make, to go down the Lake some distance, to see if there was an enemy, any where on that side of the water. They went down to Long Point; landed, and sent three men across the point, to see if they would make any discovery; they found a party of Senekas bending their course round the point—they returned with the intelligence to their party. The head Chief ordered his men in each canoe to strike fire, and offer some of their tobacco to the Great Spirit, and prepare for action. The Chief had his son, a small boy, with him; he carried the boy in the bottom of his canoe. He determined to fight his enemy on the water. They put out into the open lake; the Senekas came up; both parties took the best advantage they could, and fought with a determination to conquer or sink in the lakes. At last the Wyandots saw the last man fall in the Seneka party; but they had lost a great proportion of their own men, and were so wounded and cut to pieces, that they could take no advantage of the victory, but only to gain the shore as soon as possible, and leave the canoes of the enemy to float or sink among the waves. This ended the long war between the two tribes, from that day to this:

Respectfully yours, &c.
JOSEPH BADGER.

Interesting Narrative.

For the particulars of the following incidents I am obliged to Mr. Grimes, an elder in the Church of Lower Buffalo. I have hastily penned them, hoping that they might please and profit your readers. What churches now exert themselves as much to sustain the gospel?

Our story will carry the reader back a little more than fifty years. Then all north of the Ohio River was an almost unbroken wilderness, the mysterious red man's home. On the other side a bold and hardy band from beyond the mountains, had built their log cabins and were trying to subdue the wilderness.

To them every hour was full of peril. The Indians would often cross the river, steal their children and horses and kill and scalp any victim who came in their way. They worked in the field with weapons at their side, and on the Sabbath met in the grove or the rude log Church to hear the word of God with their rifles in their hands.

To preach to these settlers, Mr. Joseph Smith a Presbyterian minister had left his parental home east of the mountains. He it was said, was the second minister who had crossed the Monongahela river. He settled in Washington County, Penna., and became the pastor of the Cross Creek and Upper Buffalo congregations, dividing his time between them. He found them a willing and united people, but still unable to pay him a salary which would support his family. He in common with all the early ministers, must cultivate a farm. He purchased one on credit, proposing to pay for it with the salary pledged him by his people.

Years passed away. The pastor was unpaid. Little or no money was in circulation. Wheat was abundant, but there was no market. It could not be sold for more than 12½ cents cash. Even their salt had to be brought across the mountains on pack horses—was worth eight dollars per bushel, and twenty one bushels of wheat were often given for one of salt.

The time came when the last payment must be made, and Mr. Smith was told he must pay or leave his farm. Three years salary was now due from his people.

From the want of this his land, his improvements upon it and his hopes of remaining among a beloved people must be abandoned. The people were called together and the case laid before them. They were greatly moved. Counsel from on high was sought. Plan after plan was proposed and abandoned. The congregations were unable to pay a tithe of their debts and no money could be borrowed.

In despair they adjourned to meet again the following week. In the meantime it was ascertained that a Mr. Moore who owned the only mill in the country, would grind for them wheat on moderate terms. At the next meeting it was resolved to carry their wheat to Mr. Moore's mill. Some gave fifty bushels, some more.— This was carried from 15 to 26 miles on horses to the mill.

In a month, word came that the flour was ready to go to market. Again the people were called together. After an earnest prayer the question was asked, who will run the flour to New Orleans? This was a startling question. The work was perilous in the extreme. Months must pass before the adventurer could hope to return, even though his journey should be fortunate. Nearly all the way was a wilderness. And gloomy tales had been told of the treacherous Indian. More than one boat's crew had gone on that journey and came back no more.

Who then would endure the toil and brave the danger. None volunteered. The young shrunk back, and the middle aged had their excuse. Their last scheme seemed likely to fail. At length a hoary headed man, an elder in the Church, sixty-four years of age arose, and to the astonishment of the assembly said, "Here am I, send me." The deepest feeling at once pervaded the whole assembly. To see their venerated old elder thus devote himself for their good, melted them all to tears. They gathered around old father Smiley to learn that his resolution was indeed taken; that rather than lose their pastor he would brave danger, toil, and even death. After some delay and trouble, two young men were induced by hope of a large reward to go as his assistants.

A day was appointed for starting. The young and old from far and near, from love to father Smiley and their deep interest in the object of his mission, gathered together and with their Minister came down from the church, fifteen miles away to the bank of the river to bid the old man farewell. Then a prayer was offered by their pastor. A parting hymn was sung. Then said the old Scotchman, "untie the cable and let us see what the Lord will do for us." This was done and the boat floated slowly away.

More than nine months passed and no word came back from father Smiley. Many a prayer had been breathed for him, but what had been his fate was unknown. Another Sabbath came. The people came together for worship, and there on his rude bench before the preacher sat father Smiley. After the services the people were requested to meet early in the week to hear the report. All came again. After thanks had been rendered to God for his safe return, father Smiley arose and told his story. That the Lord had prospered his mission. That he had sold his flour for 27 dollars per barrel and then got safely back. He then drew a large purse and poured upon the table a larger pile of gold than most of the spectators had ever seen before. The young men were paid each a hundred dollars. Father Smiley was asked his charge. He meekly replied that he thought he ought to have as much as one of the young men, though he had not done quite as much work. It was immediately proposed to pay him $300. This he refused to receive till the pastor was paid. Upon counting their money there was found enough to pay what was due to Mr. S.—to advance him his salary for the year to come—to reward father Smiley with $300 and then to leave a large dividend for each contributor. Thus their debts were paid, their pastor relieved, and while life lasted he broke for them the bread of life. The bones of both pastor and elder I believe, have long reposed in the same churchyard, but a grateful posterity still tell this pleasing story of the past.

J. W. MILLER.

Presbyterian Advocate.

The Seven Asiatic Churches.

A letter from the the Rev. H. Lindsay, Chaplain to the English Embassy at Constantinople, gives the most recent intelligence respecting the seven Apocalyptic churches. The following extracts from this interesting despatch, will be perused, I am persuaded, with lively emotions, by every christian reader.

From the conversations I had with the Greek Bishop and his clergy, as well as various well informed individuals, I am led to suppose, that, if the population of Smyrna be estimated at 140,000 inhabitants, there are from 15 to 20,000 Greeks, 6,000 Armenians, 5,000 Catholics, 140 Protestants, and 11,000 Jews.

After Smyrna the first place I visited was Ephesus, or rather (as the site is not quite the same) Aiasalick, which consists of about fifteen poor cottages. I found there but three christians, two brothers who keep a small shop, and a gardener. They are all three Greeks, and their ignorance is lamentable indeed. In that place, which was blessed so long with an Apostle's labours, and those of his zealous assistants, are christians who have not so much as heard of that Apostle, or seem only to recognize the name of Paul as one in the calendar of their saints. One of them I found able to read a little, and left with him the New Testament in ancient and modern Greek, which he expressed a strong desire to read, and promised me he would not only study it himself, but lend it to his friends in the neighboring villages.

My next object was to see Laodicea. In the road to this, is Guzelhisar, a large town, with one church, and about 700 christians. In conversing with the priests here, I found them so little acquainted with the Bible, or even the New Testament, in an entire form, that they had no distinct knowledge of the books it contained, beyond the four gospels, but mentioned them indiscriminately, with various idle legends and lives of saints. I have sent thither three copies of the modern Greek testament since my return. About three miles from Laodicea is Denizli, which has been styled, but I am inclined to think erroneously, the ancient Colosse; it is a considerable town, with about 400 christians, Greeks and Armenians, each of whom has a church. I regret, however, to say, that here also the most extravagant tales of miracles, and fabulous accounts of angels, saints and relics, had so usurped the place of the scriptures, as to render it very difficult to separate, in their minds, divine truths from human inventions. I felt, that here that unhappy time was come when men should "turn away their ears from the truth, and be turned unto fables." I had with me some copies of the Gospels in ancient Greek, which I distributed here, as in some other places through which I had passed. Eski-hisar close to which are the remains of ancient Laodi-

156

cea, contains about fifty poor inhabitants, in which number are but two christians, who live together in a small mill: unhappily neither could read; the copy, therefore, of the New Testament which I intended for this church, I left with that of Denizli, the offspring and poor remains of Laodicea and Colosse. The prayers of the mosque are the only prayers which are heard near the ruins of Laodicea, on which the threat seems to have been fully executed, in its utter rejection as a church.

I left it for Philadelphia, now Alahshehr. It was gratifying to find at last some surviving fruits of early zeal; and here, at least, whatever may be lost of the *spirit* of christianity there is still the form of a christian church,—this has been kept from the hour of temptation which came upon all the christian world. There are here about 1000 christians, chiefly Greeks, who, for the most part, speak only Turkish; there are twenty-five places of public worship, five of which are large, regular churches; to these there is a resident bishop, with twenty inferior clergy. A copy of the modern Greek Testament was received by the Bishop, with great thankfulness.

I quitted Alah-shehr, deeply disappointed at the statement I received there of the church of Sardis. I trusted that in its utmost trials, it would not have been suffered to perish utterly, and I heard with surprise, that not a vestige of it remained. With what satisfaction, then, did I find on the plains of Sardis; a small church establishment: the few christians which dwell around modern Sart, were anxious to settle there and erect a church, as they were in the habit of meeting at each other's houses, for the exercise of religion. From this design they were prohibited by Kar 'Osman Oglu, the Turkish governor of the district, and in consequence, about five years ago, they built a church upon the plain, within view of ancient Sardis, and there they maintain a priest. The place has gradually risen into a little village, now called Tartar-Keny; thither the few christians of Sart, who amount to seven, and those in its immediate vicinity, resort for public worship, and form, together a congregation of about forty. There appears then still a remnant, "a few names even in Sardis," which have been preserved. I cannot repeat the expressions of gratitude with which they received a copy of the New Testament in a language with which they were familiar. Several crowded about the priest, to hear it on the spot; and I left them thus engaged.

Ak-hisar, the ancient Thyatira, is said to contain about 30,000 inhabitants, of whom 3000 are christians, all Greek, except about 200 Armenians. There is, however, but one Greek church, and one Armenian. The superior of the Greek church, to whom I presented the Romaic Testament, esteemed it so great a treasure that he earnestly pressed me, if possible, to spare another, that one might be secured to the church, and free from accidents, while the other went around among the people, for their private reading. I have therefore, since my return hither, sent him four copies.

The Church of Pergamos, in respect to numbers, may be said to flourish still in Bergamo.— The town is less than Ak-hisar, but the number of Christians is about as great, the proportion of Armenians to Greeks nearly the same, and each nation also has one church. The Bishop of the district, who occasionally resides there, was at that time absent; and I experienced,

with deep regret, that the resident clergy were totally incapable of estimating the gift I intended for them; I therefore delivered the Testament to the lay vicar of the bishop, at his urgent request, he having assured me, that the bishop would highly prize so valuable an acquisition to the Church; he seemed much pleased that the benighted state of his nation had excited the attention of strangers.

Thus I have left, at least, one copy of the unadulterated word of God, at each of the seven Asiatic churches of the Apocalypse, and I trust they are not utterly thrown away; but whoever may plant, it is God only who can give the increase; and from his goodness, we may hope, they will in due time, bring forth fruit some thirty, some sixty, and some an hundred fold!

CORRESPONDENCE.

Mike Fink.

Mr. Cist:

In your paper of January 22d, there is an article from your pen, entitled "The last of the Girtys," in which you say Morgan Neville has done more than justice to Mike, by classing him with that portion of the keel boat men of his day who were intrusted with the property of others. There is no doubt but that Mike has had charge of many keel boats, with valuable cargoes; and a friend of mine, one of the oldest and most respected of the commanders of steamboats in the Nashville trade, related to me, within the last four days that, in 1819, he was employed to leave Pittsburgh, and go down the Ohio in hunt of Mike and his cargo, which had been detained by some unaccountable delay. At some distance above Wheeling he found the loiterer lying to, in company with another keel, apparently in no hurry to finish the trip. Mike did not greet our envoy in very pleasant style, but kept the fair weather side out, knowing that my friend was able to *hoe his own row*. Mike was determined not to leave good quarters that night, and all went to bed wherever they could. In the night my friend was awakened by some noise or other, and before falling asleep again, he heard Mike say in a low voice, "Well, boys, who's going to *still* to-night?" This question drew his attention, as it was something he did not understand. Watching for some time, he saw Mike take a tin bucket, that had apparently been fixed for the purpose, with a small pipe inserted in its bottom, about the size of a common gimblet. This was taken to a cask of wine or brandy, and a hole made in either cask, the pipe put in, and then a couple of quarts of water turned into the bucket. Then the "still" began to operate, as they drew from the head of the cask until the water in the bucket disappeared.

Thus they obtained the liquor, and the cause of their long detention ascertained. The very casks of wine that Mike drew from, were returned to the merchant in Pittsburgh, more than a year afterwards, having soured.

Thus you see Mike *did* have charge of merchandize, and to considerable extent.

But I did not intend to defend Mike from the charge you have made against him, for in truth, he was all that was "worthless and vile." I intended to tell you an anecdote that occurred about the year 1820, just below the mouth of the Muskingum, in which Mike was prominent. There had several keel boats landed there for the night, it being near the middle of November. After making all fast, Mike was observed, just under the bank, scraping into a heap, the dried beach leaves, which had been blown there during the day, having just fallen, from the effects of the early autumn frosts. To all questions, as to what he was doing, he returned no answer, but continued at his work, until he had piled them up as high as his head. He then separated them, making a sort of an oblong ring, in which he laid down, as if to ascertain whether it was a good bed or not. Getting up he sauntered on board, hunted up his rifle, made great preparations about his priming, and then called in a very impressive manner upon his wife to follow him. Both proceeded up to the pile of leaves, poor "*Peg*" in a terrible flutter, as she had discovered that Mike was in no very amiable humor.

"Get in there and lie down," was the command to Peg, topped off with one of Mike's very choicest oaths.

"Now *Mr.* Fink," (she always mistered him when his blood was up,) "what have I done, I don't know, I'm sure—"

"Get in there and lie down, or I'll shoot you," with another oath, and drawing his rifle up to his shoulder. Poor Peg obeyed, and crawled into the leaf pile, and Mike covered her up with the combustibles. He then took a flour barrel, and split the staves into fine pieces, and lighted them at the fire on board the boat, all the time watching the leaf pile, and swearing he would shoot Peg if she moved. So soon as his splinters began to blaze, he took them into his hand and deliberately set fire, in four different places, to the leaves that surrounded his wife. In an instant, the whole mass was on fire, aided by a fresh wind, which was blowing at the time, while Mike was quietly standing by enjoying the fun. Peg, through fear of Mike, stood it as long as she could; but it soon became too hot, and she made a run for the river, her hair and clothing all on fire. In a few seconds she reached the water, and plunged in, rejoiced to know she had escaped both fire and rifle so well. "There," said Mike, "that'll larn you to be winkin' at them fellers on the other boat."

There are many occasions of this kind, where Mike and Peg were the actors, all going to show that Mike was one of the very lowest of mankind, and entirely destitute of any of the manly qualities which often were to be found among the bargemen of his day. K.

Cincinnati, Feb. 11, 1845.

The Early Steamboats of the West.

Mr. Cist:

Dear Sir—In your paper of this day, you state that, "The first steamboat that ever navigated the Ohio and Mississippi, started from Pittsburgh in 1812." I have seen the same or similar statements published several times, and as I know they are incorrect, will you suffer me to correct them?

In the fall of the year 1811, after the embargo was laid on English vessels, and before the earthquakes of Dec. 1811, my father was residing on the Ohio river, nearly opposite General Harrison's farm at North Bend. The family was one day much surprised, at seeing the young Mr. Weldons running down the river much alarmed, and shouting, "the British are coming down the river," There had of course been a current rumor of a war with that power. All the family immediately ran to the bank.— We saw something, I knew not what, but supposed it was a saw mill from the working of the lever beam, making its slow but solemn progress with the current. We were shortly afterwards informed it was a steamboat. I think it was about an 150 ton boat.

I know I am correct as to the time, for in April 1812, my father sold his farm, and with his family, removed to the Big Bone lick, of which date we have ample proof in the family.

With respect,

P. S. BUSH.

Covington, Feb. 5, 1845.

Scenes at an English Election.

What a scene electioneering is! I shall never forget what I have seen of it. I was prevailed upon to go with a friend to witness his being elected, but it is the last scene of the kind in which I shall ever take a part. There was, however, in it, a mixture of the serio-comic, of the intriguing, of the marvellous, and of the ridiculous. There must certainly be a great charm in being a member of parliament; otherwise, would men condescend and drudge, flatter, fawn, and cajole, stoop to all ranks and to all humours to gain that point? A candidate is the most affable, the most accommodating character in the world; but it cannot be expected, after such rebuffs, that, when chosen, the same painful part should be acted to the end.

The rivalry at the election of which I have spoken, was excessive; and John Bull was more than ordinarily brutal. Yet so supple was one of the candidates, that he considered a stone thrown at him only as a *striking proof* of John's regard, and he "hugged the greasy rogues" as of the maladies incident to man, or restore all their patients to health? Can they always give them even relief?' 'Decidedly not.' "Neither can I provide for all these people. Indeed I don't think that I can provide for any of them; but there is one thing which I can give them, and so can the physician to his patients."—'What is that?' "*Hope!*' I was now quite satisfied with the solidity of his promises.

Ups and Downs of Life.

It is useful as well as interesting to notice the changes for the better or worse, which ten or fifteen years serve to operate in a community.

I know a business man on Main Street refused credit in 1830, for a stove worth twelve dollars. He is now a director in one of the banks, and worth 150,000 dollars at least. Every cent of this has been made in Cincinnati during that period.

I know another business man, also on Main Street, who was refused credit in 1825, by a firm in the drug line, for the amount of *five* dollars. In 1830 that very firm lent that very man *five thousand* dollars upon his unendorsed note.

I know an extensive dealer in the city, now worth 100,000 dollars, and who can command more money on a short notice, for sixty, ninety, or one hundred and twenty days, than almost any man in Cincinnati, to whom I, as clerk for a grocery house here in 1830, sold a hogshead of sugar, with great misgiving and reluctance, under some apprehension of not getting the money when it became due.

I know a man whose credit in 1830, was such that when I trusted him for a keg of saltpetre, my employer told me I might as well have rolled it into the Ohio. Since that period he was worth fifty thousand dollars, then a bankrupt, worth in 1837 one hundred thousand dollars, again a bankrupt in 1841, and now worth twenty thousand dollars.

I know a man good for thirty thousand dollars, who ten years ago exhibited a monkey through the streets of Cincinnati, for a living.

I know a heavy business man—a bank director who sold apples in a basket when a boy through our streets.

I knew one of the first merchants in our city in 1825, who could at that period have bought entire blocks of the city on credit, a director in one of the banks, who within ten years of that period, died insolvent and intemperate.

Another influential man of that day, whose credit was unlimited, being president of one of our insurance companies, and also a bank director, died within five years, insolvent and intemperate.

Another individual who was considered in 1837 worth half a million dollars, has died since, leaving the estate insolvent.

Another individual, of credit equal to all his wants, and worth at one time twelve thousand dollars, and a Judge of the Court, died in our city hospital, and was buried at the public expense. I have seen him once and again presiding at public meetings.

The founder of the Penitentiary system, in Pennsylvania, and well known in that State and elsewhere as a public man, died a pauper in the Commercial Hospital in this city. I have seen him addressing the Legislature of that State, at Harrisburg, and listened to with the attention and deference that would have been paid to John Quincy Adams, or any other public man of this age.

I know a lady, the descendant of a distinguished governor of Massachusetts, who supports herself by her needle, and the niece of a governor of New Jersey still living, who washes for subsistence.

I know a lady, who thirty years ago in the city in which I then lived, was the cynosure of all eyes, one of the most graceful and beautiful of the sex, and moving in the first circles of wealth and fashion, now engaged in drudgery and dependence, at one dollar and fifty cents per week. All these reside in this city.

What are the fictions of romance writers, compared to some of the realities of human life?

Cincinnati in 1812.

The following document speaks for itself. It is one among many evidences of what is familiar enough to thousands yet living, how unprepared the United States was for war, when the country was placed on the 18th June, 1812, in its "armor and attitude." It seems by this document, that hardly more than thirty years ago the mercantile establishments of our city could not produce 200 pairs blankets, for the supply of the 400 volunteers, just entering the public service for the defence of the frontiers.

I suppose Cincinnati at this period, could supply the equipment with blankets for an army of 50,000 men, without rendering it necessary to call on families to part with the article.

A CALL
ON THE
PATRIOTISM OF CINCINNATI.

The situation of our country has compelled the government to resort to precautionary measures of defence. In obedience to its call, 400 men have abandoned the comforts of domestic life, and are here assembled in camp, at the distance of some hundred miles from home, prepared to protect our frontier from the awful effects of *savage* and of *civilized warfare*. But the unprecedented celerity with which they have moved, precluded the possibility of properly equipping them. Many, very many of them, are destitute of BLANKETS; and without those indispensible articles, it will be impossible for them to move to their point of destination.— Citizens of Cincinnati! this appeal is made to though they had been his dearest friends. There were family anecdotes, and private vices, personal defects, and even personal misfortunes, made the broad theme of vulgar clamour, and bandied from side to side in order to annoy the opposite party, I was so ignorant of these matters, that I inveighed against such disgraceful practices, as a dishonour to the representatives of a great nation, and an indelible stain on the people who committed these excesses. But I was informed that it was all according to ancient custom, that a broken head or the receipt of a dead dog in one's face, was only the pot-luck on these occasions; and that elections are the Englishman's carnival, or rather his saturnalia; for, in the former, insults are given and received under the mask, and are of course less gross and degrading; but, in the latter, they are warranted by privilege and usage, and are assumed as it by charter.

One of the candidates became a complete catechumen to his constituents elect; and it was laughable to hear how like a good boy he answered all his catechisers. My friend, however, took it easier; he had represented the city before, and knew the temper of his constituents. The corn bill was thrown in his face, but he swallowed it. The Habeas Corpus Act he took the liberty to parry; and as he had no pension, he got off scot free on those heads. What most astonished me was, that a very proud and a very indolent man should so demean himself for a vote, and bestir himself with such activity in order to accomplish his purpose. His memory too, appeared to me prodigious. He recollected every man's name, his avocation, his weakness, his circumstances, and his interest.—"Ha, Thomas," it was to one, "how well you look! why, you've shaken off your ague!" 'Ees,' says Thomas, 'I've been shaking long enough, but they shan't shake my politics.' "Well done, Thomas! I honor thee; give me thy hand (the dirtiest I ever saw, covered with manure.) Then thou'lt stick to the old Orange interest?" [Thomas] 'Noah—I have had much better offers t'other side. Beside, I think we han't well used by the king's men; dang it, they are too proud; they treads the poor all as well as dirt under their feet.' —"Oh! fie; oh! fie, my dear Thomas." My friend stepped aside with Thomas: what he said to him I don't pretend to know; but thrice they shook hands; and Thomas shook his sides with laughter. He went off grinning, and said, 'Well, ye bid to get the plumper.' He next met an old man, "How sorry I was, friend Barnacle, for the loss of your cattle (this circumstance he had learned a few minutes before.) I wish you had written to me; but I think I have a plan for you. By the by, how many sons have you who are freemen?" 'Four, your honor.' "And how are they doing?"—'Mortal bad; and the young one, I can't do nothing with.' "That's a pity, friend Barnacle. I should think the Blue Coat school would not be a bad thing for the young one; and the two eldest must manage your affairs." '—Ees—' "And I should think that Jack—" 'His name is James, your honor.' "Ah! true—James would make a rare exciseman; he's a keen dog, friend Barnacle." 'Ah! that he be.' "And Bob—" 'Bill, your honor.' "True! how can I be so foolish—Bill would make a good clerk." 'Ees, the lad writes a scholardly hand.' "Well, do you take as much snuff as ever?" 'Ees, your honor, I likes it as well as ever; but its woundy dear.' "Come, give me a pinch, and

I say, my servant shall bring you a pound of rare stuff, which I brought you from town." 'I thank you kindly.' "There, go up to the hustings! take the four boys. All plumpers, I hope." 'Ees.' After which my friend bought a pound of common snuff, and sent it as though he had brought it from London.

Coming to a smart, well-dressed fellow, he said, "Are you out of place?" 'I am, Sir.' "But you have kept your vote?" 'I have, Sir.' "Well, we must get you into place." 'Yes, Sir, I should like a place under government. I am tired of service.' "Surely! well, we must see to that." (The man had been a footman!) Disengaged from him, my friend was attacked by an old woman, who abused him most violently for breach of promise, for voting against the interest of the country, for neglect, and for a long list of sins. His gentleness and adroitness got the better in the end: and after enduring much, he prevailed upon her to allow her son to split his vote betwixt him and the opposite party.

"Honest Mr. Shambles!" exclaimed he next, "Why, you did'nt give me a call when last you came to Smithfield." 'Yes, your honor, I did; but your pert jack-anapes of a French valet almost shut the door in my face, and said as how you was not visible.' "A rascal!" said the member, "I must turn him away, Shambles; he offends every body; he does not know how to discriminate between my real friends, and a parcel of intruders. But I say, that's a mighty pretty woman—your second wife?" 'Tol lol, your honor.' "And what do you think of doing with your heir—a fine lad too—your only son, I think?" 'He is sir. Why I think of making a doctor of him (fine lessons of humanity he must have learned from you, thought I to myself,) but he prefers being a parson; and as I can afford to give him the first of neddycations, it don't matter. He's a bright boy; he'll get on; and I can give him some thousands.'— "Right, my honest friend; and I know a family which has high church interest. But we must not talk of that now, at another time we will. He'll make a capital bishop; he speaks well, don't he?" 'Oh! aye, your honor; he has the gift of the gab; you'll hear him by and by tip 'em a bit of a speech for your side of the question.' "Bravo! but Shambles, why don't you make him a lawyer? I could give him a lift there: I vow, I should not be surprised to see him Lord Chancellor yet." The old butcher was so delighted with this dream of ambition, that he went off resolved to strain every nerve for my friend, and swore, that if his next door neighbor, who had promised his vote for the Blue, as he called it, did not break his word and change sides, he would arrest him for his bill due for meat. We lastly called at a school master's who had seven children. These my friend called Cherubim and Seraphim. Indeed all the elector's children whom he met, were the finest children in the world. In each of their hands he put a guinea. But this was no bribery; for it is clear the poor children had no vote, and the fathers did not see the money given, neither could they be accountable for others. On our road to the hustings, I asked him if he had such extensive interest as to give away all the things which he had led his friends to expect. He answered me in the negative. I inquired what then he could give them? which he answered me by putting the two following questions:—"Can our physicians cure one tenth you—let each family furnish one or more BLAN-KETS, and the requisite number will be easily completed. It is not requested as a boon: the moment your blankets are delivered, you shall receive the full value in money—they are not to be had at the stores. The season of the year is approaching, when each family may without inconvenience part with ONE.

Mothers! Sisters! Wives!—recollect that the men in whose favor this appeal is made, have connections as near and as dear as any which can bind *you* to life. These they have voluntarily abandoned, trusting that the integrity and patriotism of their fellow-citizens will supply every requisite for themselves and their families; and trusting that the same spirit which enabled their fathers to achieve their INDEPENDENCE, will enable their *sons to defend it.* To-morrow arrangements will be made for their reception, and the price paid,

R. J. MEIGS,
Governor of Ohio.
Cincinnati, April 30, 1812.

Cooking Stoves.

How rapid as well as radical are the changes in every department of living, which the last thirty years have made! It may be presumed, within that period, and indeed within half of it, that the modern discoveries in Science and the Arts, with their application to practical purposes, have enabled the community to support in a given bounds, fifty per cent. additional population upon the same resources, by the economy of means and materials on one hand, and the enlarged supply of products on the other.

Take one article as an illustration. Thirty years ago, cooking was universally performed in the chimney, to the great waste of fuel and sacrifice of strength and comfort to our mothers, wives, sisters and daughters, *devoted as they thus were to the flames.* The Cooking Stove was invented. The blessings of millions of suffering women will forever hallow the inventor's name. By this improvement on the old fashioned ten plate stoves, cooking, washing, heating irons, boiling, steaming, &c., are now performed without that exposure of a delicate or feeble female to the scorching fire or stifling smoke of a chimney, which they were once compelled to endure.

But the first Cooking stove was like the first Steam boat, the application of a principle merely, leaving to later projectors the honor as well as benefit of bringing out of the invention by further improvements, the perfection in economy and comfort of which it might be found susceptible.

The latest improvement, perhaps the greatest ever made in these stoves is STRAUB's *Flame encircled oven Cooking Stove.*

This is a stove that claims to combine all that is valuable in the existing Cooking Stoves, with certain improvements peculiar to itself, which unite in a remarkable degree the equalization of

heat throughout the whole baking department, with an economy of fuel which I have noticed in no other article of the kind.

This stove is constructed so as to pass a flue entirely round the oven; the heat being thus used twice, once under, and once over the oven. With an enlarged air chamber through which all the heat must pass, consequently every part of the oven must be heated alike. It is this mode of applying the flame and heat which produces the saving of fuel also.

I regard *Mr. Straub,* as having solved a difficult and long sought problem,—the passing the heat twice round without impairing the necessary draught of the stove. This is effected in the enlargement of the air chamber, which affords increased space for the rarefaction of air and compensates for the usual disadvantage of a circular draught.

I have one of these stoves, a No. 2, in use which I find by reference to dates, burns no more wood in six days than its predecessor, a No. 3 Cincinnati cooking stove did in four. It must be recollected that a No. 2 stove is of a greater capacity by fifty per cent, than a No. 3, and of course, the difference is still greater in favor of Straub's stove than merely the economy of fuel, cooking one third more as it does.

The plates of this stove are thicker than most others, which enables them to retain heat a longer period, as well as to cool more gradually. I deem this a valuable improvement.

Seasoned fuel, fit for stove use, costs four dollars per cord. My annual wood bill heretofore, is for thirteen cords, say fifty-two dollars. The saving in this stove over some of its competitors of the same capacity would therefore pay the price of a new stove for a family of fifteen to twenty persons in two years; and as long as it lasted, prove a yearly saving of eighteen or twenty dollars to its purchaser.

A loaf of wheat or rye bread as it comes freshly baked from this stove, would prove a luxury to millions, who even in our own land, have never tasted a first rate article.

Indian Warfare--Lewis Wetzel No. 3.

Some time after Gen. Harmar had erected a fort at the mouth of the Muskingum river, he employed some white men to go with a flag among the nearest Indian tribes, to prevail with them to come to the fort, and there to conclude a treaty of peace. A large number of Indians came on the general invitation, and encamped on the Muskingum river, a few miles above its mouth. Gen. Harmar issued a proclamation, giving notice that a cessation of arms was mutually agreed upon between the white and red men, till an effort for a treaty of peace should be concluded.

As treaties of peace with Indians had been so frequently violated, but little faith was placed in the stability of such engagements by the frontiersmen; notwithstanding that they were as frequently the aggressors as were the Indians. Half the backwoodsmen of that day had been born in a fort, and grew to manhood as it were, in a siege. The Indian war had continued so long, and was so bloody, that they believed war with them was to continue as long as both survived to fight. With these impressions, as they considered the Indians faithless, it was difficult to inspire confidence in the stability of treaties. While Gen. Harmar was diligently engaged with the Indians, endeavoring to make peace, Lewis Wetzel concluded to go to Fort Harmar, and as the Indians would be passing and repassing between their camp and the fort, would have a fair opportunity of killing one. He associated with himself in this enterprise, a man by the name of Veach Dickerson, who was only a small grade below him in restless daring. As soon as the enterprise was resolved on, they were impatient to put it in execution. The more danger, the more excited and impatient they were to execute their plan. They set off without delay, and arrived at the desired point, and sat themselves down in ambush, near the path leading from the fort to the Indian camp. Shortly after they had concealed themselves by the way-side, they saw an Indian approaching on horse-back, running his horse at full speed. They called to him, but owing to the clatter of the horses feet, he did not hear or heed their call, but kept on at a sweeping gallop. When the Indian had nearly passed, they concluded to give him a shot as he rode. They fired; but as the Indian did not fall, they thought they had missed him. As the alarm would soon be spread that an Indian had been shot at; and as large numbers of them were near at hand, they commenced an immediate retreat to their home As their neighbors knew the object of their expedition, as soon as they returned, they were asked what luck? Wetzel answered, that they

had bad luck--they had seen but one Indian, and he on horseback--that they fired at him as he rode, but he did not fall, but went off scratching his back, as if he had been stung by a yellowjacket." The truth was, they had shot him through the hips and lower part of the belly.— He rode to the fort, and that night expired of his wound.

It was soon rumored to Gen. Harmar, that Lewis Wetzel was the murderer. Gen. Harmar sent a Captain Kingsbury, with a company of men to the Mingo Bottom, with orders to take Wetzel, alive or dead—a useless and impotent order. A company of men could as easily have drawn Beelzebub out of the bottomless pit, as take Lewis Wetzel by force from the Mingo bottom settlement. On the day that Captain Kingsbury arrived, there was a shooting match in the neighborhood, and Lewis was there. As soon as the object of Captain Kingsbury was ascertained, it was resolved to ambush the Captain's barge, and kill him and his company. Happily Major M'Mahan was present to prevent this catastrophe, who prevailed on Wetzel and his friends to suspend the attack, till he would pay Captain Kingsbury a visit, perhaps he would induce him to return without making an attempt to take Wetzel. With a great deal of reluctance they agreed to suspend the attack till Major M'Mahan should return. The resentment and fury of Wetzel and his friends, were boiling and blowing, like the steam from a scape pipe of a steamboat. "A pretty affair this," said they, "to hang a man for killing an Indian when they are killing some of our men almost every day." Major M'Mahan informed Captain Kingsbury of the force and fury of the people, and assured him that if he persisted in the attempt to seize Wetzel, he would have all the settlers in the country upon him; that nothing could save him and his company from massacre but a speedy return. The Captain took his advice, and forthwith returned to Fort Harmar. Wetzel considered the affair now as finally adjusted.

As Lewis was never long stationary, but ranged at will along the river from Fort Pitt to the falls of the Ohio, and was a welcome guest, and perfectly at home wherever he went, shortly after the attempt to seize him by Captain Kingsbury, he got into a canoe, with the intention of proceeding down the Ohio to Kentucky. He had a friend by the name of Hamilton Carr, who had lately settled on the island, near Fort Harmar. Here he stopped with the view of lodging for the night. By some means which never were explained, Gen. Harmar was advised of his being on the island. A guard was sent, who crossed to the island, surrounded Mr. Carr's house, went in, and as Wetzel lay asleep he was seized by numbers; his hands and feet securely bound, and he was hurried into a boat, and from thence placed in a guard-room where he was loaded with irons.

The ignominy of wearing iron handcuffs and hobbles, and being chained down, to a man of his independent and resolute spirit, was more painful than death. Shortly after he was confined, he sent for Gen. Harmar, and requested a visit. The General went. Wetzel admitted without hesitation "that he had shot the Indian." As he did not wish to be hung like a dog, he requested the General to give him up to the Indians, there being a large number of them present. "He might place them all in a circle, with their scalping knives and tomahawks—and give him a tomahawk and place him in the midst of the circle, and then let him and the Indians fight it out the best way they could." The Gen. told him, "that he was an officer appointed by the law, by which he must be governed. As the law did not authorize him to make such a compromise, he could not grant his request."— After a few days longer confinement, he again sent for the General to come and see him; and he did so. Wetzel said "he had never been confined and could not live much longer if he was not permitted some room to walk about in."

The General ordered the officer on guard to knock off his iron fetters, but to leave on his handcuffs, and permit him to walk about on the point at the mouth of the Muskingum; but to be sure and keep a close watch upon him. As soon as they were outside the fort gate, Lewis began to caper about like a wild colt broke loose from the stall.

He would start and run a few yards as if he was about making an escape, then turn round and join the guards. The next start he would run farther, and then stop. In this way he amused the guard for some time, at every start running a little farther. At length he called forth all his strength, resolution and activity, and determined on freedom or an early grave. He gave a sudden spring forward, and bounded off at the top of his speed for the shelter of his beloved woods. His movement was so quick, and so unexpected, that the guard were taken by surprise, and he got nearly a hundred yards before they recovered from their astonishment. They fired, but all missed; they followed in pursuit; but he soon left them out of sight. As he was well acquainted with the country, he made for a dense thicket, about two or three miles from the fort. In the midst of this thicket, he found a tree which had fallen across a log, where the brush was very close. Under this tree he squeezed his body. The brush was so thick that he could not be discovered unless his pur-

suers examined very closely. As soon as his escape was announced, Gen. Harmar started the soldiers and Indians in pursuit. After he laid about two hours in his place of concealment, two Indians came into the thicket, and stood on the same log under which he lay concealed; his heart beat so violently he was afraid they would hear it thumping. He could hear them hallooing in every direction, as they hunted through the brush. At length, as the evening wore away the day, he found himself alone in the friendly thicket. But what should he do? His hands were fastened with iron cuffs and bolts, and he knew of no friend on the same side of the Ohio to whom he could apply for assistance.

He had a friend who had recently put up a cabin on the Virginia side of the Ohio; who he had no doubt would lend him every assistance in his power. But to cross the river was the difficulty. He could not make a raft with his hands bound, and though an excellent swimmer, it would be risquing too much to trust himself to the stream in that disabled condition.— With the most gloomy foreboding of the future, he left the thicket as soon as the shades of night began to gather, and directed his way to the Ohio, by a circuitous route, which brought him to a lonely spot three or four miles below the fort. He made to this place, as he expected guards would be set at every point where he could find a canoe. On the opposite shore he saw an acquaintance, Isaac Wiseman by name, fishing in a canoe. Not daring to call to him, as he could not know whether his enemies were not within sound of his voice, he waved his hat for some time to attract the notice of his friend, having previously induced him to direct his eye that course by a gentle splashing in the water. This brought Wiseman to his assistance, who readily aided his escape. Once on the Virginia shore, he had nothing to fear, as he had well wishers all through the country, who would have shed blood if necessary, for his defence. It was not however, until years had elapsed, and Gen. Harmar returned to Philadelphia, that it became safe for Wiseman to avow the act, such was the weakness of civil authority, and the absolute supremacy of military rule on the frontier. A file and hammer soon released him from the heavy handcuffs. After the night's rest had recruited his energies, he set out for fresh adventures; his friend having supplied him with a rifle, ammunition and blanket. He took a canoe and, went down the river for Kentucky, where he should feel safe from the grasp of Harmar and his myrmidons.

Subsequently to Wetzel's escape, Gen. Harmar removed his head quarters to Fort Washington—Cincinnati. One of his first official acts there was to issue a proclamation, offering considerable rewards, for the apprehension and delivery of Lewis, at the Garrison there. No man, however, was found base or daring enough to attempt this service.

Brother Bailey of the Herald.

Dr. Bailey, the editor of the Herald, has a temperament, so kindly and pleasantly made up, that it is a pity that he should experience any thing else but trouble,—he bears it so gracefully.

His last difficulty was the reception of a letter—but let him tell his own story:

The other evening we received a letter, endorsed "important," on which we had the pleasure of paying postage. We tore it open, somewhat curious to learn the important news. It was from a subscriber, owing about four dollars on our weekly paper, and thus the epistle ran:

"*Dear Sir:—*You have been in the habit since you were away down South, of threatening and bullyragging those that are in arrears to a few dollars for your excellent paper. You learnt it when you were down South, from the slaveholders to their slaves. Bad examples are more easily imbibed than good ones. I came from away down South myself. I understand all the wiles of the slaveholders, for I have been one myself. I will not, I cannot, and I shall not, bear the insults and dictation from any man or set of men. I never did beg my life of man or men, and I hope I never shall. So soon as you shall receive this letter, stop sending your paper to me, for I hope to be able to pay you before very long what I owe you, and then we will be even. Making them that owe a few dollars pay two dollars, and them that do not, one dollar a year, shows justice between the rich and poor. Poverty now a days is nothing but a curse to church and State. Deny it if you can. I have been in the habit of taking newspapers, more or less, the greater part of my life. I never did cheat an editor out of a cent in my life, nor do I intend to cheat you. I never had one before to be bullyragging, dictating and exposing me before. You may have your choice, to stop my paper, at this time, or let me have it for one dollar a year, for I do mean to pay you as soon as I can.

What do christians think of to bring Moses' writings to prove slavery? I thought we were as this time called christians. *   *

You may, if you think proper to continue sending on the paper at one dollar the year, or let it alone, as it suits you best, for I hardly care a straw about it. I want to know if you receive this letter or not.

I am respectfully yours,

JOHN NOEL."

That is what we call the sublimity of independence. Nevertheless, we would remind our friend John Noel, that under both the Jewish and Christian dispensations, men were bound to pay their debts, although St. Paul showed unto them a more excellent way, which was, never to owe any thing.

Of the last paragraph, I would say, it is a problem, whether its humor or good humor is the finest. It is, however, but one specimen among a thousand equally remarkable, of the Dr's characteristic vein of pleasantry.

William Penn.

Mr. Tefft an extensive autograph collector of Savannah, Geo. has recently received from a friend at the North, an original manuscript letter of Wm. Penn, which he regards as one of the most valuable autographs in his collection. Letters written by this distinguished man are extreme rarities at the present day, Mr. Tefft having hitherto never been able to procure more than a bare signature, cut out from some parchment-document. This letter is precious on more than one account,—not only as being a veritable original from the hand of the far-famed Quaker, but as exhibiting the characteristic qualities of the man. We see in it his downright simplicity—his quaintness of style—his remarkable force of mind—his rare mingling together of religious humility with a bold and decided line of policy. The reader may be reminded that Penn, at the date of the letter, was forty-two years of age. Only four years previous, he had purchased, settled, and visited his colonial establishment in America. He had now returned to England, and had taken lodgings near the court of king James II., to exercise his influence with that monarch in behalf of his philanthropic schemes. In this situation it seems he had heard of some unhappy disorders that had disturbed his infant colony in America. The letter before us is chiefly occupied in suggesting measures to suppress them.

Thomas Lloyd, to whom the letter is addressed succeeded William Penn as President of the Colony. He appears to have been an unsalaried officer. Judging from several of Penn's expressions, we should conjecture that he was dissatisfied with Lloyd's want of energy in suppressing the disturbances, though he shrinks from preferring any direct complaint. His mind certainly seems to have wrought up into a sad gust of perplexities and anxieties. But for the letter itself. The orthography, &c. are exactly transcribed.

WORMINGHURST, 17th 9 mo. 1685.

Dear Tho: Lloyd:

Thyn by way of new york is with me, & first I am extremely sorry to hear that Pennsylvania is so Litigious, and brutish. The report reaches this place with yt *disgrace, yt we have lost I am told, 15000 persons this fall, many of ymt men of great estates yt are gone and going for Carolina. O that some one person would in ye zeal of a true Phinias & ye meekness of a Christian spirit together, stand up for our good beginnings, and bring a savour of righteousness over that ill savour. I cared not what I gave such an one, if it were an 100£ or more out of myn own pocket, I would and will do it, if he be to be found, for ye neglect such a care of ye publick might draw on his own affaires. But I hope to be ready in the Spring, my selfe, and I think, with power and resolution to do ye Just thing, lett it fall on whom it will. O thomas, I cannot express to thee ye grief yt is upon me for it. but my private affaires as well as my publick ones, will not let me budge hence yet; tho I desire it with so much zeal, and for yt reason count myself a Prisoner here.

I waite for answer of yt about ye laws; for yt of ye money, I am better satisfied, tho' Quo warrantos at every turn have formerly threatened. I hope some of those yt once feared I had to much powr will now see I have not enough, and yt excess of powr does not ye mischief yt Licentiousness does to a State, for tho ye one oppresses ye pocket, the other turns all to confusion, order and peace with poverty is certainly better. It almost tempts me to deliver up to ye K. (King) and lett a mercenary Gover'r have ye taming of them. O where is fear of god and common decency. pray do wt thou canst to appease or punish such persons, & if in office, out with ym, forthwith. If J. White and P. Robson be of ym, displace them immediately.— *Thom. think not hard of it because of charge in comeing. being and goeing. I will be accountable for yt,* if thou please but to do yt friendly part. lett T. Hor: J. Har: J. Clap, R. Tur: J. Good: T. Sim, see this & who else thou pleasest. If you have any love to me, and desire to see me and myn with you, o prevent these things that you may not add to my exercises. If a few such weithty men mett apart & waited on god for his minde and wisdom & in ye sense & authority of yt, you appeared for ye honour of god, ye reputation of ye governour & credit and prosperity of ye Country, to check such persons, calling ym before you as my ffds (friends;) men of credit with me; & sett your united Shoulder to it, methinks it may be better. to ye Lord I leave you saluting you all in endless Love, being & remaining,

Your true and loving ffriend
Wm. Penn.

Salute me to thy Dr wife, tell her she must remember her name in my busines. also to thy children. give my love to ye ‡Gover'r &c.
P. S.

Ffor Balt. & Sas-quhanagh (Susquehannah) I have not ended, being otherwise stopt too, I waite my time, but doubt not being upon good terms. lett none be brittle about my not being there yet, I come with all ye speed I can; tho I must say, twere better all were in another order first; for these disorders—strike ym back I have had some regard to in staying; which is a sad disappointment to me & ye country. The East Jersey Prop'rs believe thy report about my letter to yee. I am not with ym once in two months. they meet weekly. they are very angry with G. Lowry. Salute me to Frds There away, old Lewis and wife; also to Capt. Berry, I have sent his letters as directed. press about land for me in East Jersey. I shall fall heavy on G. L. if I live, for denying him in my wrong till all be taken up yt is desirable. Speak to G. L. thyself about it, for wt he has done will be overturned (I perceive) by ym here & he served. Vale.
Myn salute yee.

*That. †Them.
‡Who this Governor was, it is difficult to imagine.—The historical records of Pennsylvania mention no presiding officer as being there at this time, except Thomas Lloyd himself. He is designated, however, as "President," and there may have been a magistrate subordinate to him with the title of Governor.—[S. Rose.

I copy the following from the New York Tribune. The idea towards the close of the article, of the hieroglyphics is irresistibly comic:

The Court of Texas.

The advertisement that "Osage City," containing one hundred and twenty six acres of land, one store-house, two dwellings, and sundry out-building, is for sale, reminds us of some incidents related by a gentleman who went to Texas before that renowned empire had acquired its present unparalleled celebrity. At that time the capitol of Texas, Washington, was pretty much in the condition of Osage City, in some respects. Mr. L. the gentleman who gave us the narrative of his adventures, travelled from the coast to the capital of Texas in private conveyance, travelling facilities not being very numerous. He had formed in his mind certain images of what his reception would be at the court of Texas, charged as he was with a petty diplomatic errand, which, however, warranted him to believe that his reception would not be altogether "bare and beggarly," Texas was then younger by several years than at present: her gigantic resources were undeveloped; the fame of her sons had not filled every ear, and the United States had not courted her very valuable alliance, as they have done now, to their shame be it said.

Mr. L——had no particular difficulty in arriving in the vicinity of the capital of Texas. Alive with sanguine expectations as to the beauty of Washington, as his humble equipage entered the city he peeped out, and looked cautiously around. Six small shingled houses greeted his eyes—this was the glory of Texas, the capital of that celebrated empire. This, thought Mr. L. is the suburbs. His doubts were soon dispelled in "thin air;" these six shingled houses constituted the entire domain. Our traveller was set down at the tavern, and forgot his surprise at the diminutive area of the Texan capital over a good supper of "corn-dodgers" and "chicken-fixins." There still floated before him, however, visions of Texas diplomatic corps, the stately American minister, his reception—his excellency would nod, he would endeavor to do something of the same sort—his excellency would scrape and bow, he would follow suit. Such plentiful compliments, such insinuating smiles, such remote and delicate diplomatic insinuations, these things ran in Mr. L——s head, assisted in their flight, perhaps, by copious drinks of "corn" whisky, strong enough to scrape a man's throat like a fish-bone.

Our diplomatist arose next morning with pleasing anticipations of accomplishing the objects of his mission in a manner at once dignified and complete. His first inquiries were for the American minister near the court of Texas; the minister was not then in the city, but resided about six miles out of the metropolis, on the plantation of Col. W. Ah! thought Mr. L. very right in the general, he has retreated to some gentleman's park in the neighborhood to escape from the dissipation of the capitol. Before visiting the minister, Mr. L—— resolved to visit the officers of the cabinet. He sallied forth, therefore, and saw above one door a sign, "Treasury Department."

It was a small one story-house, shingled with what they call "shakes," all over the West and Southwest. Mr. L. approached and knocked,

The secretary was not in. He then tried some of the other offices, but finally discovered the chief clerk of the treasury department, a young man who occupied an apartment by himself, a bed at one end and a table in the middle. This important officer was chiefly remarkable for his intensely green spectacles. On the table in the room, there were three little bundles of paper. One was labelled Galveston, another Matagorda, and another Velasco. These were the archives of the department. Mr. L. after some agreeable conversation with the chief clerk of the treasury department, again took to his vehicle, and drove out to the plantation of Col. W. to visit the American minister. During his drive he endeavored to frame a speech, not very long, but immensely important, just necessary to introduce his subject with becoming gravity. yet not so altogether elevated as to be revolting.

After an agreeable drive, the boy who conducted our diplomatist, stopped at a pair of bars.

"What's this?" said Mr. L.

"This place is the Colonel's," replied the boy; "he's about as wide awake as a bear in a *Jiniary* thaw!"

After taking down the bars and walking through a considerable cow-yard, Mr. L——— approached a double log-house, of an ancient fashion, about the door of which was the usual accumulation of pigs, dogs, hens, and chips. An elderly farmer was seated on a stump, smoking a powerful fragrant pipe.

"Is this Col. W's plantation?" said Mr. L.

"Yes," replied the smoker—puff—puff—puff.

"Is Col. W. at home?" asked Mr. L———.

"Yes! I'm him," was the reply—puff—puff —puff.

"Does the American minister reside here," inquired Mr. L———,

"I reckon," was the reply—puff.

"Will you be so kind as to say that Mr. L. diplomatic agent from the United States would be happy to see the American minister near the court of Texas?" said Mr. L———.

Upon this the elderly farmer slowly screwed himself up off his seat, and poking his head into the door of the log-hut, cried out—"Gineral!"

Soon afterward another elderly gentleman made his appearance at the door, dressed in a picturesque guise, with a pair of pantaloons that were not only seedy, but which had every appearance of having been threshed out.

"Is this Gen. M———?" said Mr. L———, in his most dulcet tones.

"Holler, my old chip," said Col. W———, "he's deafer than a mud turtle with three holes punched through his back."

"Is this General M———?" said Mr. L———. The American minister near the court of Texas, heard the question, and asked Mr. L——— in.— The American minister's suite of chambers comprehended one apartment; one end of this room was covered with an immense American flag, with all its stars and stripes revealed in their original glory; the General's cocked hat and sword hung on a peg; suspended from the rafters were various legs of bacon, some rifles, and bunches of seed corn and red peppers. After a few remarks, the general took up an old felt hat, of a most remarkable size and shape, and holding it up before him, said, "Now ain't that a little the most remarkable *sombrero*, a little the most conscientious flap, a little grain the richest

crack—but never mind the hat, let's go out and look at my pony."

The general slowly marched out, Mr. L. following, and after going through a pair of bars, and across a yard, they came to the one-acre lot, where the pony was imprisoned. The general stopped and directed a look of infinite regard at the pony.

"Now," said the general, "just look at that ar pony, he can't run, nor he can't trot, nor he can't canter, nor he can't walk, but—how he can rack! He'd lick lightning a hundred yards in a mile, and, give it two the start. He'd be perfect pisen to a locomotive with the steam up to bustin' pint, and the screechin' whistle screwed down. Jist walk round and examine the article."

Upon this the general got over the fences, and they approached this racking apparatus with the caution of Minerva; and here let us remark that it is customary to brand the owner's name on the haunches of the horses in that region.

"Look here," said the general, "I've heard a great deal about Gliddon's lectures on hieroglyphics, fresh from some pyramid or other, as if they were stamped in yesterday. I've heard of mystery, but just look at them marks, of all these singular phenetic performances there is the screamer, what shades of brands them are, I'll lay my head there ain't a man among 'em all from Champollion up to Sham the son of Noah, who can decipher the hieroglyphics on that pony's rump!"

Good heaven, thought Mr. L———, have I ventured all this way, on this great diplomatic expedition, to be entertained at the court of Texas by the American minister with disquisitions such as these.

Value of Cincinnati Property in 1845.

The western half of a lot, belonging to Mrs. Hall on Fifth street, east of Elm, was sold a few days since at 200 dollars per front foot, cash down. The property sold is 16½ feet front, by 90 feet deep. I understood that price was offered for the whole lot, but the owner declined selling more than the half, retaining the residue for her residence.

I learn also that the property at the north-east corner of Walnut and Front streets, has been leased to Mr. Merrill at 15 dollars per foot front, facing on Front street, being 6 per cent. per annum on 250 dollars per foot.

What is the world coming to?

One of the most ridiculous propositions in the world, is being treated seriously in the New York papers. It is gravely proposed to make a second story street in Broadway—*id est*, to erect iron pillars at the curb-stone, and on them build a covered railway for cars, as a substitute for the omnibuses that now vex that main artery of old Gotham. What nonsense! We agree heart and pen with the correspondent of the Evening Mirror, when he says:—We are walled in on all sides by private brick and mortar—mother earth is jammed down, suffocated and walked over by corporation stone; and that is enough. Leave New York "*open at the top!*" We have no smell of earth—no sight of green fields—nothing of God's make, as he made it, to look at, but the sky. Leave us the strip of blue, and the small slant of sunshine. Give us a chance to see the stars.

166

CORRESPONDENCE.

Usury Laws.

Mr. Cist:—As the subject of Usury Laws is up before our State Legislature, I will give you my views on this subject.

Competition is the soul of trade, giving life, vigor, and activity to its operation. By causing commodities where scarce to flow in, and where too abundant to flow out, it brings all things to their level of value, and becomes the great regulator of prices. Now the interest of money under a system of free competition, would in like manner regulate itself, and we should never see money continuing abundant in one part of the country at 5 per cent, and scarce in another at 10, any more than we should see flour remaining at $10 per barrel in New Orleans, when it could be had for $5 in Cincinnati.

Usury laws paralyze the trade in money; they destroy competition, and discourage investments. The law of Ohio taxes money at interest, and allows but 6 per cent. to be recovered. The market value of money in this city, ranges from 9 to 12 per cent. and were these rates recoverable, competition would soon bring them down. But the law enables a dishonest man who contracts to pay 12 per cent. first, to defraud the lender out of one half the interest, and then force him to lose the other half in lawyers' fees for collecting. Under these discouragements, Eastern capitalists have refused to lend their money here, and even our own citizens have sought investments in other States, where the law allows the recovery of 10 per cent. Thus capital, ever sensitive, flies from persecution to seek a dwelling place of greater security.

A bill is now before the Ohio Legislature, which, if it becomes a law, will enable any man who may borrow at more than 7 per cent. not only to cheat the lender out of the whole interest, but to subject him to a pecuniary penalty besides.

The law offers a handsome premium for the encouragement of knavery. The honest man gains nothing by it, for he makes it a rule to fulfil his contracts.

As the interest is limited, one man cannot offer a higher rate than another, and the competition will be, not in the rate, but in the strength of the security. Men of great wealth will be accepted, and persons of moderate means rejected. Thus the poor man who cannot give as good security as his wealthy neighbor, and who is prevented by the law from over-bidding him in the rate of interest, and thereby obtaining the preference, is forced to sacrifice his property, and his more fortunate neighbor becomes the purchaser.

If the bill passes, all who have money lent at more than seven per cent. will demand immediate payment. Mortgages will be foreclosed, judgemnts and executions will sweep over the land, and half the State will be up at Sheriff's sale. Buying property at such sales will then become more profitable than money lending.

It is the duty of Government to *enforce the performance* of contracts, instead of *offering a reward for their violation.* The general principles of law, justice, and morality, alike demand their fulfilment when made in good faith, where there is neither fraud nor imposition, nor any undue advantage taken of the weakness or credulity of the contracting party.　　O.

Early Steamboats in the West.—No. 2.

I continue my list of early steamboats, in the order of their being built.

The next boat was the Franklin, of 150 tons, built at Pittsburgh by *Shiras & Cromwell*; engine by George Evans, left that place in December, 1816, was sold at New Orleans, and then put in the New Orleans and St. Louis trade, being the first steamboat that ever made her appearance at St. Louis. Was sunk at St. Genevieve in 1819, while under command of Captain Reed, and on her way to that place.

The Constitution, originally the Oliver Evans, of 75 tons, was the next, and was built by *George Evans*, on his patent; left Pittsburgh also in December 1816 for New Orleans. In April 1817, she burst one of her boilers, near Point Couper, by which eleven persons, principally passengers, lost their lives. This was the first steamboat accident involving the sacrifice of life in the Western waters.

The twelfth in order was the Harriet of 40 tons built at Pittsburgh; owned and constructed by *J. Armstrong*, of Williamsport, Pennsylvania.—She left Pittsburgh in October 1816 for New Orleans; crossed the falls in March 1817, and was the first vessel on the Tennessee river plying between New Orleans and the Muscle Shoals.

The Kentucky of 80 tons was the 14th. She was built at Frankfort Ky. for the Louisville trade, and was owned by *Hanson & Boswell.*

Next was the Pike, of only 25 tons, long, and still a favorite steamboat name. She was built by *J. Prentiss*, of Henderson Ky., plied first between St. Louis and Louisville, afterwards in the Red river trade was lost on a sawyer, in March 1818.

The next was the Gov. Shelby, of 120 tons, built at Louisville by Messrs. *Gray, Gwathmey and Gretsinger.*—Bolton & Watt's engine,—for the Louisville trade.

Next was the New Orleans, of 300 tons, built at Pittsburgh in 1817, by *Fulton & Living-*

ston, for the Natchez trade. Near Baton Rouge, she was sunk and raised again and sunk in N. Orleans in February 1819, about two months after her sinking near Baton Rouge.

The next was the GEORGE MADISON, of 200 tons, built at Pittsburgh in 1818, by Messrs. *Voorhees, Mitchell, Rodgers & Todd,* of Frankfort Ky., for the Louisville trade.

The OHIO, built at New Albany Ind. in 1818, by Messrs. *Shreve & Blair,* for the Louisville trade comes next. This boat of 443 tons was the largest built—up to this period.

Next was the NAPOLEON, of 332 tons, built at Shippingport in 1818, by Messrs. *Shreve, Miller, & Breckenridge,* of Louisville, for that trade.

The next, and the twentieth in order, was the VOLCANO, of 250 tons, built at New Albany in 1818, by *John & Robeson DeHart,* for the Louisville trade.

The GEN. JACKSON, of 200 tons was the next, being built in Pittsburgh in 1818, and owned by *R. Whiting & Gen. Carroll,* of Tennessee, for the Nashville trade.

We come at length to the EAGLE, of 70 tons, as the first boat built at Cincinnati. Sne was owned by *James Berthoud & Son,* of Shippingport Ky., for the Louisville trade. She was built in 1818.

Next was the HECLA, also of 70 tons, built at Cincinnati in 1818; owned by *Honore and Barbaroux,* of Louisville, and employed in that trade.

The HENDERSON, of 85 tons, built the same year at Cincinnati came next. She was owned by Messrs. *Bowens,* of Henderson Ky.; built for the Henderson and Louisville trade.

The JOHNSON, of 90 tons, built at Wheeling in 1818, by George White, and owned by Messrs. *J. & R. Johnson,* of Kentucky; for the Louisville trade, was the next.

The CINCINNATI, of 120 tons, built at Cincinnati in 1818, and owned by Messrs. *Pennywitt & Burns,* of Cincinnati, and Messrs. *Paxton & Co.* of New Albany, is the 26th on the list; built for the Louisville trade.

The next was the EXCHANGE, of 200 tons, built at Louisville in 1819, owned by *David Edwards,* of Jefferson County Ky., for the Louisville trade.

The LOUISIANA, of 45 tons, was the next; she was built at New Orleans in 1818, and owned by *C. Duplissis* of that City, for the Natchez trade.

Next was the JAMES ROSS, of 330 tons, built at Pittsburgh in 1818, and owned by *Whiting & Stackpole,* of that place. This boat made in 1819 the quickest trip then known, being only 16 days from New Orleans to Shippingport, with a cargo of 200 tons.

The FRANKFORT, of 320 tons, built at Pittsburgh in 1818, was the 30th. She was owned by *Voorhees & Mitchell,* of Frankfort Ky.; built for the Louisville trade.

The TAMERLANE, of 320 tons, built at Pittsburgh in 1818, for the Louisville trade was next; and was owned by Messrs. *Boggs & Co.,* N. York.

The CEDAR BRANCH, built at Pittsburgh in 1818, and for the same trade, was owned in Maysville Ky.

The last I name is the EXPERIMENT, of 40 tons, built in Cincinnati, in 1818, which was the next and the first one owned entirely in this city.

It seems that thirty-two boats had to be built, before we could furnish capital and enterprise to own one.

Twistification.

There are *black sheep* in every flock. Not long since, I gave some specimens of Quaker ingenuity in disposing of difficulties. By way of balance, I will state an incident which occurred in a Scotch Irish neighborhood in the West, which I am reminded of in this hog-killing region and period.

A dealer in hogs of this description of people, called on a countryman of his, who was putting up pork some years since, to engage a lot of hogs. The pork packer, after ascertaining the probable weight, and arranging the other features of the bargain, inquired, are they mast or *corn-fed* hogs?" "On ay", replied the contractor, "they are a' corn fed. Sorra the ane else." The contract was closed accordingly; the hogs in due time delivered, and paid for, and it was not discovered until some time after, that they were nothing but mast-fed animals. The packer was of course greatly incensed at the imposition, and when his countryman made his appearance again in town, reproached him bitterly, and asked him how he dared tell him such a lie. "Sorra the lee I tauld ye; I said they were *awcorn-fed* hogs, and so they were. Diel the haet else, they ha fed on but *awcorns*.

I knew some years since an individual in Western Pennsylvania, who possessed this twistifying talent in high perfection. His business, as far as he had one, was that of miller, or more accurately miller's man, and his name was *John Lock.* Many amusing stories of his faculty of *shifting* have been told me of this worthy. I recollect but one.

In that part of the country, a dry season during the summer, is apt to occasion great difficulties in grinding, most of the mills being run by water power. At such periods, the mills in a given neighborhood are beset with crowds gathered from a great distance, as far sometimes as twenty miles. Here every person who brings a grist has to wait his turn, and in this state of things, the careless and improvident are sometimes put to great straits for the purpose of keeping their families in meal or flour. Lock being out of flour and meal, had put a bag of grain one Monday morning on a horse,, and was riding on it to mill, when he passed an acquaintance. "Going to Slippery Rock mill, I suppose" he observed. This was twelve miles off. "No," said Lock, "I am going to Ziegler's." This was a short mile. "More fool you for that," retorted his friend. "I have had a bag there a week, and don't expect it ground till Thursday." "Well," said Lock, "I know *I* shan't wait till Thursday. for I mean to stay and see mine ground." His acquaintance simply laughed at him, and they parted. In about an hour or two however, Lock made his reappearance with the grist.— This excited great curiosity in the village in which he lived, to know how he contrived to get his turn before it was due. He had the telling the story himself, which seemed to do him as much good, if not more, than the time he had gained with the grist.

At the mill he had found Ziegler himself, with *Mike* his miller. "Mr. Ziegler " said Lock, "I am badly off for meal, and have brought you a bag of corn to grind." Ferry well John, but it here, and you shall haf your durn. You know de rule." "Yes." said John, "I have tended mill long enough to know it. But I can't go by rules, and you won't ask me when I tell you my case. *Next Saturday a week will be twelve days* since my family have had a bite of bread about the house." "By sure," said honest Ziegler,"dat ish doo bat," the tears filling in his eyes. "Here Mike but dis pack in te hobber, und let Lock off as soon as bossible." As this was Monday morning, the reader can calculate for himself how long Lock's family had been without bread, and so could Ziegler have done, had he not been put off his guard, by Lock's distressed face.

The Vote on the 24th inst.

On reference to the Mayor's proclamation in this day's "' ADVERTISER," it will be seen that the project of purchasing a lot for city purposes has at length assumed a distinct and tangible shape. One thing I would desire to point out to the voters who are opposed to the purchase of ground for public buildings. They will of course vote *nay*, but let them not neglect to add, "Shires'," "Jones'," "Starr's," or "College," as their preference may be, so that in case the project of purchasing finds a majority to approve it, their vote then will not be lost. This they have the right to do, and it will serve to secure a fuller vote and a more satisfactory result.

As regards the lot itself, there seems to be a great diversity of opinion. Those who are governed by centrality of position merely, will of course prefer the Starr property, while those who desire a scite and building of a description which shall be sufficiently spacious for all time to come, will naturally prefer Shires'.

Relics of. the Past.

Captain John Armstrong, to Gen'l James Wilkinson.

FORT HAMILTON, 27th April, 1792.

DEAR GENERAL:—

My letter of last evening, sent by express, carrying the despatches from Fort Jefferson, I hope arrived safe. If the building ordered to be erected here, should not be finished as soon as you expected, permit me to observe, the fault is not mine. Carpenters were sent forward without tools to work with, or the necessary means of hauling timber. Every exertion in my power has been called forth to complete the business in question. I expect one of the buildings will be finished early next week—which when completed, will contain the provisions already sent forward. Additional ones must be made, and I dread the consequence, as my small command will not enable me to furnish a sufficient party to cover the workmen from the enemy, should they appear in force. When the oxen arrive, I shall proceed to the completion of this business, and use all the industry and precaution in my power. I hope the Steel Carpenters and Armorers tools will be sent forward, as without them your orders cannot be carried into execution. You must be tired of the repeated applications made for them. What is become of my former express? I fear he did not reach you.

I feel for the party under Maj. Shaumburgh. Should those Indians, mentioned in Capt. Shays letter, meet him, his party must be cut off. This is an important suggestion. I wish you might think proper to furnish two good woods-men for this post, who might carry dispatches without confining themselves to the road. I have no such characters in my command.

MARRIAGES.

IN this city, Feb'y 11th, Mr. Daniel J. Morrell, of New York, to Susanna L. daughter of Mr. Powell Stackhouse.

On Thursday, 13th inst, at Pleasant Hill, by the Rev. J. C. White, W. T. Colburn, of this city, to Miss S. E. Thomas, of Pleasant Hill.

On 13th inst, by the Rev. Mr. Thomas, Mr. Edward D. Brannegan to Miss Elizabeth Luck.

On the 13th inst, by the Rev. S. W. Lynd, Mr. Clement Dare to Miss Rebecca Jane Penton.

On the 13th inst., by the Rev. Dr. Brooks, Edmond Pendleton, Esq., of Buchanan, Va., to Cornelia M. Morgan of this city.

DEATHS.

IN this city, on Saturday the 8th inst, Miss. Sarah Agnes Kendall.

In Springfield, on Sunday. Feb'y 9th, Samuel Ayres Sen., of this city.

In this city, on Wednesday, 12th inst, Mr. John Robertson.

On same day, Ephraim Robins, Esq.

On Saturday, 15th inst, Mrs. Harriet D. Jordan.

On Sunday, 16th inst, Mr. George C. Saunders.

On same day, Charles Telford, son of M. R. and Eliza beth W. Taylor.

Indian Warfare--Lewis Wetzel.--No. 2.

The next incident in the history of Lewis was his attaching himself to a body of scouts, which set out in pursuit of Indians. A party of the savages in the spring of 1787 had crossed the Ohio river at what was called the Mingo Bottom, three miles below the present town of Steubenville. Here they killed a family, but as they did not penetrate into the country, and retreated for some reason or other immediately, they made their escape with impunity. This inroad took the settlers by surprize; the Indians not having crossed the Ohio in that neighborhood for the previous twelve or eighteen months, and filled them in their unprotected state with fearful apprehensions.

A subscription was drawn up, headed by those who were in easy circumstances, for the purpose of stimulating the young and active, which pledged more than one hundred dollars as a bounty to the scout who would bring in the first Indian scalp. Maj. M'Mahan, who frequently led the hardy frontier men in those perilous times, soon raised a company of about twenty men, among whom was Lewis Wetzel. They crossed the Ohio, and pursued the Indian trail with unerring tact, till they came to the Muskingum river. There the advance or spies, discovered a party of Indians far superior to their own in number, encamped on the bank of the river. As the Indians had not yet discovered the white men, Major M'Mahan retreated with his party to the top of the hill, where they might consult about their future operations.— The conclusion of the conference was, "that discretion was the better part of valour"; and a hasty retreat was prudently resolved on. While the party were consulting on the propriety of attacking the Indians, Lewis Wetzel sat on a log, with his gun laid across his lap, and his tomahawk in his hand; he took no part in the council. As soon as the resolution was adopted to retreat, it was without delay put in execution, and the party set off, leaving Lewis sitting on a log. Major M'Mahan called to him, and enquired if he was going with them. Lewis answered, "that he was not; that he came out to hunt Indians; they were now found, and he was not going home like a fool, with his finger in his mouth. He would take an Indian scalp or lose his own before he went home."— Arguments were without avail. His stubborn unyielding disposition being such, that he never submitted himself to the control or advice of others, they were compelled to leave him, a solitary being, in the midst of the thick forest, surrounded by vigilant enemies. Notwithstanding that this solitary individual appeared to rush into danger with the fury of a madman, in his disposition was displayed the cunning of a fox; as well as the boldness of a lion.

As soon as his friends had left him, he picked up his blanket, shouldered his rifle, and struck off into a different part of the country, in hope that fortune would place in his way some lone Indian. He kept aloof from the large streams, where large parties of the enemy generally encamped. He prowled through the woods with a noiseless tread, and the keen glance of the eagle, that day and the next evening, when he discovered a smoke curling up from among the bushes. He crept softly to the fire, and found two blankets and a small copper kettle in the camp. He instantly concluded that this was the camp of only two Indians, and that he could kill them both. He concealed himself in the thick brush, but in such a position that he could see the number and motions of the enemy. About sunset, one of the Indians came in and made up the fire, and went to cooking his supper. Shortly after, the other came in, they ate their supper; after which they began to sing, and amuse themselves by telling comic stories, at which they would burst into a roar of laughter. Singing, and telling amusing stories, was the common practice of the white and red men when lying in their hunting camps.

These poor fellows, when enjoying themselves in the utmost glee, little dreamed that the grim monster, death, in the shape of Lewis Wetzel, was about stealing a march upon them. Lewis kept a keen watch on their movements. About 9 or 10 o'clock at night, one of the Indians wrapped his blanket around him, shouldered his rifle, took a chunk of fire in his hand, and left the camp doubtless with the intention of going to watch a deer lick. The fire and smoke would keep off the gnats and musketoes. It is a remarkable fact, that deer are not alarmed at seeing fire, from the circumstance of seeing it so frequently in the fall and winter seasons, when the leaves and grass are dry, and the woods on fire. The absence of the Indian was the cause of vexation and disappointment to our hero, whose trap was so happily set, that he considered his game secure. He still indulged the hope, that the Indian might return to camp before day. In this he was disappointed. There were birds in the woods who chirped and chattered just before break of day; and like the cock, gave notice to the woodsman that day would soon appear. Lewis heard the wooded songsters begin their morning carol, and determined to delay no longer the work of death for the return of the Indian. He walked to the camp with a noiseless step, and found his victim buried in profound slumber, lying upon his side. He drew his butcher knife, and with all his force, impelled by revenge, he sent the blade through his heart. He saia the Indian gave a short quiver, and a convulsive motion, and laid still in his final sleep. He then scalped him, and set off for home. He arrived at the Mingo Bottom only one day after his unsuccessful companions.

He claimed, and as he deserved, received the promised reward.

The Weather--East and West.

An industrious correspondent of the Philadelphia Enquirer, publishes some interesting observations concerning the weather, and the quantity of rain that has fallen in Philadelphia, since the year 1835.

Years,	Rain during some portion of 24 hours,	Rain, the whole or very near the whole of the day,	Total No. of days on which rain fell during the year,	Snow, including very slight falls thereof,	Cloudy days without storming, including days only partially overcast,	Total of cloudy days.	Total number of clear days in the term "clear." The ordinary acceptation of
1835	54	29	83	10	41	134	231
1836	73	27	100	23	32	155	211
1837	73	15	88	30	56	174	191
1838	81	15	96	20	38	154	211
1839	107	14	121	25	76	222	143
1840	76	40	116	27	84	227	139
1841	89	49	138	32	74	244	121
1842	94	44	138	20	51	209	156
1843	86	34	120	32	93	225	140
1844	104	29	133	22	53	208	158

From this it appears that the number of cloudy and stormy days has considerably increased in Philadelphia, although from the following table, it seem that the quantity of rain has scarcely increased at all.

In 1830 there fell 45 inches.

1831	do	43	do
1832	do	39	do
1833	do	48	do
1834	do	34	do
1835	do	39	do
1836	do	42	do
1837	do	39	do
1838	do	45	do
1839	do	43	do
1840	do	49	do
1841	do	55	do
1842	do	48	do
1843	do	49	do
1844	do	46	do

It may be instructive to compare with this, our Cincinnati weather during the same period. I find on reference to meteorological tables kept by Dr. J. Ray, from Jan. 1, 1835 to Dec. 1, 1840, that the average for those six years was clear and fair days 146. Variable days, 114. Cloudy and rainy days, 105. The greatest number of clear or fair days in any one year was 164, and the least 127.. The greatest number of cloudy and rainy was 116, and the least

100, every year during the same series. Average depth of rain 44. 92 inches.

It would appear by this statement, that while there are more rainy days, in a given period in Cincinnati than in Philadelphia, the quantity of rain falling appears to be about the same.

There is a *natural philosophy* among the Pennsylvania Germans, that on an average of years, there is just so much rain, so much dry weather, so much heat, and so much cold in the course of a year. It follows, if you do not get it this year, you have either had it the last, or will have it the next. I confess myself a believer in this philosophy, every day adding evidence to me in its behalf.—

The Anthracite Coal of Pennsylvania.

Statistics appears to many readers, a dry business, and such they undoubtedly are, when they do not set the faculties of the reader at work figuring out results. To state that 1,631,-669 tons of coal have been mined the last year, in Pennsylvania out of the Anthracite field alone without reference to Bituminous coal regions, makes very little distinct impression upon unreflecting minds, who, it is with regret I say it, constitute the mass of newspaper readers. But if we compare, combine and reflect upon this subject, it dilates to vast importance. If we calculate the value of the coal which sells at Philadelphia at $6 per ton, and in New York at 6,50 per ton, we perceive that it produces as an average over twelve millions of dollars annually to the great state in which it is mined. And when we ascertain as we readily may, that the annual produce of the Gold and Silver mines of Peru and Mexico, twenty-two millions of dollars, does not exceed the value of the anthracite and bituminous coal mined each year in Pennsylvia, it serves to give a lively idea of the wealth beneath her soil. For coal is but one item of her mineral resources, limestone, iron, salt and marble abounding in that State.

But it is not the equality in value of the coal of Pennsylvania, with the gold and silver mines of Peru and Mexico, which constitute the more important and interesting features of the subject.

Let us reflect on the amount of industry which this prodigious quantity of mineral fuel puts into employment, for the getting it into market, and actual use. I am not aware of the price of coal at the anthracite mines; but it is easy to perceive, that a large share of its value in New York, Boston, and Philadelphia, must be made up in the cost of transportation, and repeated handling of an article so bulky and heavy. As regards the bituminous coal of the west, one half the cost arises from this source of expense. But if we allow but ten millions dollars on this score, to be divided between the laborers, freighters, wagoners, and coal merchants, it will easily be seen that it is an interest which sustains to double the extent, the industry of a country compared with that of the Peruvian and Mexican mines, in the products of which much value lies in small space, and whose worth is almost as great at the mouth of the mine as when coined into specie.

Bartlett's Commercial College.

We have Colleges in Cincinnati of various descriptions. There are the rival CINCINNATI and WOODWARD Colleges "teaching the young *idlers* how to *shoot;* there are the rival medical Colleges, the OHIO *regular*, on Sixth Street, and the BOTANICO MEDICAL or *Steam*, at the Bazaar, and we have the Law College of Judge Walker, which without making as much disturbance in the community as some of the rest, is doing much to prepare young law students thoroughly for their arduous and responsible profession.— But it may be news io some of my subscribers, as it certainly will be to three-fourths of the citizens at large, that we have also a COMMERCIAL COLLEGE where young accountants are regularly, systematically, and thoroughly trained to the theory and practice of book-keeping, and having passed through the course are examined, and if found duly proficient, receive regular *diplomas*. This is the Commercial college of R. M. Bartlett, at the corner of Main and Fourth streets.

This establishment fell under my notice in my explorations a few weeks since, and I have been led to examine its operations for the purpose of ascertaining whether any system of teaching book-keeping can accomplish what they all profess, to prepare young men for taking charge actually of a set of books, and mastering the whole subject of keeping accounts. I must confess, I have shared largely in the popular notion. that though you may learn all you can from systems of book-keeping, you must begin again when you enter a counting house to keep the books.

What I have seen here and have learned from young men who have been educated by Mr. Bartlett. has satisfied me that this is an unjust prejudice, although it is undoubtedly true, that the system of teaching under most professors of the science has laid a foundation for it. I will give the statistical part of the subject first, for the purpose of rendering apparent, as well as sustaining, the conclusions to which I have come respecting this commercial college.

Mr. R. M. Bartlett, I have learned, has been engaged in this business for the last twelve years, eight years of which he has been established in Cincinnati, During that period twelve hundred students have gone through the colle-

giate course, averaging one hundred to each year. From eight to ten weeks serve for a young man of ordinary capacity to become familiar, theoretically & practically, with the system he teaches. A share of the young men who study here, find employment in this city as book-keepers, but many of them are persons who reside abroad, and come here to qualify themselves for employment at home. Others again, after going through the course here, are sought out by application to Mr. B. for situations elsewhere. Not a few are now keeping books in Pittsburgh, St. Louis, Louisville, Natchez, New Orleans, and Mobile, who studied with Mr. Bartlett. Indeed, individuals from his college are now in heavy houses in Boston, New York and Philadelphia.

The system of Mr. B. is both analytical and synthetical. It is the taking to pieces, as a study, a complicated but exact machine, to contemplate and learn the relation of the several parts to each other and to the machine, and the putting it together to make it operate accurately, and without embarrassment. With this view the student is required to give a reason for every thing he does, to take up an every day transaction and put it through the books to its final close, to shew why one given entry is accurate or any other one incorrect, in short under the severest drilling to render it apparent that he has mastered the theory of Book-keeping as well as reduced it to practice.

I have conversed with several young men who have been taught here, and have now charge of books in various counting rooms here of pork merchants, wholesale dry goods and grocery stores, auction houses, &c, and their testimony is clear, uniform and ample, that they have acquired with Mr. Bartlett, not only the correct system of keeping accounts, but have become prepared to apply it to any set of books which they found opened in the various establishments in which they took desks.

One of these at the age of sixteen was found competent to take charge of the whole counting house operations, and has conducted them to the satisfaction of his employers for several years since. He is yet hardly of legal age, and performs now, what was formerly the work of two persons in the counting room.

Mr. Bartlett is not only engaged in qualifying those whom he has taught from the commencement of their studies, but has frequently been called on to take individuals through their courses who have wasted time and money under incompetent, or merely theoretical teachers. In another column of this day's "Advertiser" will be found certificates from members of firms, or the book-keepers in the various business houses of Cincinnati, which fully corroborate many of the positions I have taken in this article.

CORRESPONDENCE.

Mr.Cist:

CINCINNATI January 31, 1845,

As this is the season for pork cutting it seems an appropriate time to add my contribution to the pork stories which you have lately published.

I remember a case of contracting for pork, which I am disposed to believe from the great similarity in the features of both cases was the truer version of the incidents related by a correspondent in your paper of the 22d inst. At any rate I will tell it as it occurred, and your readers may determine that point for themselves. In the early days of our pork business, a certain produce dealer, to whom I was the next door neighbor, made a contract with a dealer in hogs from the country, for the sale at a given rate, and delivery at Rossville, of a lot of hogs from one to five hundred. The dealer was to receive twenty dollars extra for driving them into Hamilton across the Miami from Rossville. The price of pork rose, and when the period of delivery approached, my friend and neighbor received notice to despatch a person to take charge of the *drove*, on the day named in the contract, as it would be in Hamilton punctually by the time, and added, "Don't forget to send the twenty dollars." Accordingly, he despatched a young man in his employ to engage hands to bring in the *drove*. The Clerk reached Hamilton that night, and while taking breakfast at the Hotel, was called to the door to see the contractor, who had just arrived and was inquiring for him. "So you have brought the hogs, I suppose, where are they?" "In the yard," replied the drover, to which they accordingly repaired.— Here in one corner of the fence lay a dignified porker, "solitary and alone" in his glory, being the impersonation of this important contract.— "Where is the drove," at length asked the impatient clerk, after reconnoitering the yard in all directions. "There," said the other "and tired enough he is—where is my twenty dollars?" "Go to —— with your twenty dollars," profanely exclaimed the clerk, who by this time, discovered he had been sent on a fool's errand; adding, "and take your infernal *drove* with you." "Well" said the drover, very coolly, "you need not take him if you don't wish to. I only wanted to keep my engagement, and found it easier to deliver one than five hundred hogs." The young man I believe, consulted a lawyer on the spot, but obtained no encouragement in the case. If I remember right they compromised the matter by ten dollars being paid for the delivery into Hamilton, of the drove.

I had good reason to know something about this business, the article of agreement having been left in my custody; in those days people not taking the trouble usually, of making copies of an agreement. This contract occupied three sides of a folio sheet, the merchant having drawn it up himself, and made every thing perfectly safe, except the number of the hogs. R.

Human Nature.

When Columbus applied for assistance from the Spanish Crown, to his immortal enterprise—the discovery of America—the attempt was stigmatised as chimerical—when he returned successful, its beneficial results were disputed—and when these became so apparent as to silence all cavil, it was alleged that any one might have made it. These to be sure were the objections of his enemies.

When Fulton proposed to ascend the North River, by steam power, it was first pronounced *visionary*, when accomplished, it could not be *again done*, and when repeatedly done, it could *never* become of any *practical use*. These, wonderful to say, were the cavils and objections of *friends*. Fulton in this respect, fared worse than Columbus.

While the late experiments of *John Starr & J. Milton Sanders*, in our own city respecting the electro magnetic light were progressing, the great body of those who spoke with me on the subject treated it as a humbug. "It had been tried in France and England, and had ended in smoke. So it would here." Well, the young men succeeded, as I suppose. What next! It was ascertained by the very same class of cavilers, that Professor Faraday had discovered it long before, and one of them referred me to the page of one of his publications, in proof. I disdained even to look for it. One of my New York exchanges, I observe, has made the discovery also that it has been *long known* in England.

What a wonderful tissue of inconsistencies is man. "The *wisest, brightest, meanest* thing of earth,"

The Miami Settlements.

Judge Goforth, from whose registers I am favored with copies of extracts, of such incidents as were deemed worthy of transcription, was one of the framers and signers of the original constitution of the State of New York, and an early settler of the west, having reached Columbia on the Little Miami, early in 1790. He was shortly after appointed a justice of the peace for the county of Hamilton, being the first appointed magistrate in that county, and afterwards made one of the Judges of the Territorial Court of the N. W. Territory, being commissioned to that office by *President Washington.*

Extracts from memorandums made by Judge Goforth, in his day book.

1789.

Sep.26 left New York—

Oct. 6 arrived at Norfolk—12th left Norfolk and arrived at Richmond, on 23d. Capitol at Richmond 110 feet long, exclusive of the portico and 80 feet wide.

Nov. 5 left Richmond, and arrived at Norfolk on the

8th. In my passage down I had the curiosity—passing James Island in the day time—to see that settlement—being the first made by the English in North America—now reduced to two farms and part of a steeple being the only remains of the first church and first brick building in North America. Passed thence to Baltimore and Hagarstown and

Dec15 arrived at Magees on the Monongahela

" 18 left to go down the Ohio, floated down about 4 miles, got ou Braddock's lower ford—

" 19 passed Fort Pitt and the Allegheny

" 20 got ashore with the ice 30 miles from Fort Pitt.

1790.

Jan. 2 left our camp and put down the Ohio and on the

.8th arrived at Limestone and thence to Washington which is in 38 degrees some minutes North; and had at that time 119 houses.

" 12th left Washington* on the 12th and arrived on

" 18th at Miami,§

1790.

Jan.23 the first four horses were stolen—by the Indians—

Apl. 4 two of Mills' men were killed.

" 5 a bark canoe passed the town and 5 more horses were stolen.

" 16 Baily and party, returned from pursuing after the Indians.

May 3 Met in the shade to worship.

" 11 A cat fish was taken—four feet long 8 inches between the eyes and weighed 58 pounds.

Judge Symmes arrived on the 2nd of February 1789, as he informed Major Stites, at his own post.

Apl 21 traded with the first Indian,

" 28 Capt. Samondawat—an Indian arrived and traded.

Aug 3 Named the Fort "Miami."

5 Col Henry Lee arrived and 53 volunteers

27 Went to North Bend with Col. Lee.

Sep 3 Capt. Flinn retook the horses.

" 25 Major Stites old Mr. Bealer and myself took the depth of the Ohio River when we found there was 57 feet water in the channel, and that the river was 55 feet lower at that time than it was at that uncommonly high fresh last winter. The water at the high flood was 112 feet.‡

Oct 9 Mr. White set out for the Tiber.

Aug16 Major Doughty went down the River.

1789.

Dec28 Gen'l Harmar past this post down the River.

1790.

Jan 2 The Governor past this post down the River.

" 3 rec'd a line desiring my attendance with others,

4 Attended his Excellency when the Civil and Military officers were nominated.

6 The officers were sworn in.

13 Doctor David Jones preached,

18 Doctor Gano and Thomas Sloo came here

20 the church was constituted—Baptist church at Columbia—

21 Three persons were baptised.

24 called a church meeting and took unanimous to call the Rev'd Stephen Gano to the pastoral charge of the church at Columbia.

Apl 15 General Harmar went on the Campaign past this post,

19 The Gov. went up the River.

Aug30 Worked at clearing the Minister's lot.

2 Mr. Sargent left this post to go up the River together with Judge Turner,

Sep.12 The Mason county militia past this post on their way to Head quarters.

19 200 Militia from Pennsylvania past this post on their way to Cincinnati.

23 the Governor went down to Cincinnati.

25 Major Doughty and Judge Turner also,

30 The main body of the troops marched.

1791.

Jan 2 began to thaw

Mch 1 Indians fired at Lt. Baily's boat

" " Mr. Abel Cook was found dead in the Round Bottom

" 4 Mrs. Bowman was fired at in the night through a crack in the house.

Mch22 Mr. Strong returned from up the River had 24 men killed and wounded on the 19th March.

27 Mr. Plasket arrived—the 24 in the morning fought the Indians just after day

---

* This was Washington, the County Town of Mason County, Kentucky, which it seems had 119 houses before a single dwelling was built in Cincinnati. It probably has no more than 400 houses at this time.

§ Columbia, on the Little Miami.

‡ This seems an unaccountable mistake. The flood of 1832 was but 64 feet above low water, and the highest flood ever known at the settlement of the country was but 12 feet higher,

break, about 8 miles above Scioto—this the same battle mentioned in Hubbles narrative—

July 7 Col Spencer's son taken prisoner

" 14 Francis Beadles Jonathan Coleman a soldier killed

1792.

Jan 7 In the evening Samuel Welch was taken

Nov 2 "last Monday night met at my house to consult on the expediency of founding an Academy—Rev. John Smith, Major Gano Mr. Dunlavy"—afterwards Judge of the Court of Common Pleas—and myself—Wednesday night met at Mr. Reily's school house—Mr. Reily then the teacher was for many years clerk of Butler Common Pleas and Supreme Court—'to digest matters respecting the Academy, the night being bad, and but few people attending post-poned till next night which. was 1st of Nov. met at Mr. Reily's to appoint a committee."

Dec 6 Fell a snow 7 inches on a level

1793.

Sep 24 The first and fourth Sub-Legions march under Gen'l Wayne. The 27th or rather the 30th the Army march.

Marching Orders in Early Times.

The following were given as marching orders to the first military force ever detached to the west. They are very characteristic of the period, and the men who administered public affairs at that date. Nothing can exceed the beauty and clearness of the manuscript.

Harris's ferry on the Susquehanna, referred to in these orders, is the Harrisburg of the present day.

Gen. Henry Knox to Captain John Armstrong.

Sir ;

Your company having been mustered and inspected, and being prepared for marching for the frontiers, you are to commence your march accordingly for Fort Pitt.

Your route will be from hence, to Lancaster, Harris's ferry, on the Susquehannah, Carlisle, Shippensburg, Bedford to Fort Pitt.

You will draw provisions at Lancaster, at Carlisle and Shippensburg from Major Smith or his agent—at Fort Pitt from the contractors.

You will pursue your march with all diligence, consistently with the health of your men.

You will keep a regular journal noticing the weather and distances of each day's march, a copy of which you are to transmit to the war office, and also of the time of your arrival at Fort Pitt.

On your arrival at that place, you will receive further orders from your superior officer.

The expences incident to the march, such as straw, ferriages, and fuel, are to be paid for, and

regular accounts and vouchers are to be obtained for every payment. You have furnished you on this account the sum of ———Fifty ——— dollars for which you are held accountable.

Every officer commanding a detachment of the troops of the United States, or levies, while on the march to the frontiers, will be held responsible, that the conduct of his detachment shall be conformably to the most perfect good order and discipline.

The civil authority is to be held in the highest respect. The inhabitants on the route are to be treated with civility and decency. Any offence against this order is to be punished upon the spot.

No property of any sort is to be taken without a fair purchase and payment.

The troops are to be encamped every evening, and the officers are always to encamp with their companies.

Given at the war office of the U. States, this 26th day of April, 1791.

H. KNOX,
Secretary of War.

Territorial Marriage License.

Arthur St. Clair, Governor of the Territory of the United States, North-west of the Ohio. To all persons who shall see these presents, greeting: Whereas it has signified to me that Stephen Wood and Catharine Freeman, are desirous to be joined together in wedlock, and have requested that the publication of the bans of matrimony by law required, may be dispensed with, and no reason appearing why their request should not be complied with, permission is hereby given, and I do authorize and empower any of the persons by law empowered, to perform the marriage ceremony in cases where publication of the bans has been made, to join together as man and wife, the said Stephen Wood and Catharine Freeman, any want of publication as aforesaid notwithstanding.

In witness whereof the said Governor has hereunto set his hand and seal at Cincinnati, the 24th February, A. D. 1796.

A. St. CLAIR.

Portable Flour Mills.

A visit to Messrs. STEWART & KIMBALL'S machine shop on Second street west of Elm, has put me in possession of some statistics, of general interest, as I suppose.

In this establishment is carried on a great variety of business, and I should judge it to be a remarkable example of what may be accomplished by the energies of twenty-two hands, the number employed within its enclosure. Messrs. *Stewart & Kimball* manufacture here, Carding, spinning, shearing and napping machines, Fuller's stoves and screws, Power looms, Portable

Flour mills, Burton's patent pumps, patent planeing machines, with a variety of articles of minor consequence. These 22 hands produce an annual manufactured value of 29,700 dollars, of which the carding machines and portable mills form four fifths.

Every part of the establishment is worthy of inspection. But I propose to notice the Portable mills only, for the present.

This is an invention, equally simple and ingenious. It proposes to perform in a small compass, with less expense, greater safety and equal efficiency, the work of a merchant mill. If it does not accomplish all this, it is nevertheless a remarkable improvement.

The mill is a square frame with four stout pillars, on which the mill stones, which are of burr blocks, cemented as usual, rest. The whole apparatus forming a cube of about four feet. The upper mill stone is enclosed in a *cast iron case* of suitable weight, which supercedes the usual iron bands, and gives all the power in an equable and steady motion, which is derived in the larger class of mill stones by extra thickness, or height thus rendering them top heavy and producing an inequality of pressure and motion which is obviated here.

The mill stones are 2 to 2 1-2 inches diameter. Owing to the casing referred to, there is at once the proper degree of pressure, and at the same time, elasticity, which furnishes the perfection of grinding; avoiding on the one hand, the irregular motion of a top heavy upper stone, and on the other, the evil of friction and want of spring which results from the old fashioned plan of fastening down the upper mill stone by screws in Portable mills, to say nothing of the greater liability of getting out of order. These mill stones can be run with greater velocity than the large ones, compatibly with safety, the 2 feet making 240, and the 2½ feet 200 revolutions per minute.

The power necessary to drive one of these mills, is not more than that of three horses, or the equivalent water or steam power, with these they will grind 14 to 16 bushels per hour, which is as good a performance as a merchant mill; the quality of the flour being superfine, and passing inspection as such in our markets.

One of the mills is in operation across the Ohio, another at Woods' cotton mills, at Brookville, and a third has been put up lately at the saw mill just over Mill creek, being placed there to accommodate the Storrs and Delhi farmers. These employ respectively, horse, water, and steam power. I cite these locations, because the great mass of these mills go to the west and south-west. Of this article alone, this establishment turns out 80 annually at from 125 to 150 dollars each.

How capricious are all measures of value. In the days when the early pioneers ground all their corn by hand, and were obliged to dispense with the luxury of wheat, from inability to reduce it to flour, one of these Portable mills, would even at its present low price, have bought all Cincinnati, from the canal North, and Sycamore street west.

CORRESPONDENCE.

Usury Laws, No. 2.

Mr. Cist:—

Let us, for illustration, trace the probable effects of limiting the price of other things than money. Suppose that under pretence of moderating the profits of insurers, and preventing people from paying too high premiums, it were decreed that one per cent. and no more, should be demanded. In this case a large proportion of property would remain uninsured—the premium allowed not being sufficient to cover the risk. Now, the charge for insurance varies from ½ to 6 per cent. or more. So, in lending money, one man may be perfectly safe, while the risk alone in lending to another, may amount to more than ten per cent. Is it not fair and just that the lender should be paid for that risk? Restrict the price of Eastern Exchange by law to one per cent. and the moment it happens to be worth more in other markets, no exchange can be had.

Let it be assumed that four dollars per barrel is quite enough, under any circumstances, for flour; and that, as demanding a higher price is taking an undue advantage of the necessitous, let it be prohibited under the severest penalties.

Let the prices of other articles of prime necessity be limited in like manner, and the moment they happen to be worth a much higher price in other places, where free trade prevails, they will leave the country, and the poor will suffer for want of food.

Now, under the operation of usury laws, when money becomes scarce, and continues for a length of time to be worth much more than the legal rate, capitalists refuse to lend. They can make more profitable investments in the purchase of property. Money cannot be obtained—commercial embarrassment begins—the Banks can do nothing—the pressure increases—gloom and despondency prevail—numerous failures follow in rapid succession, and a general feeling of distrust and alarm prevails throughout the whole community. Under these circumstances, men cling to their money. They hug it close and will not let it go.

It is believed that under a system of free trade in money, these evils would be either prevented, or greatly mitigated. Money would fluctuate in price like other things; but like other things could always be had at its market price. A man wants to buy the use of money as he buys the use of a horse—paying the full price for it —and lending would no longer be considered an accommodation.

Why are Bank discounts at 6 per cent. called favors? Why is this selling of money at that price considered a great accommodation? For this simple reason, that 6 per cent. is generally less than the market value, and the difference is a gratuity to the borrower. The merchant, on the contrary, in selling goods at their market value, considers *himself* the favored party, and the money-lender, unrestricted in price, would be placed on the same footing—and the *borrow-er* would be courted for his patronage. O.

Col. Polk.

Much has been said of the *avalanche* of office seekers, which it was reported, had beset for office the President, since his election. We have all heard statements that such had been the influx of visitors on this errand to Columbia, Tenn.; that they had eaten out the place and neighborhood, and that Col. P. had been obliged to take up lodgings in Nashville, to escape his besiegers. All this is untrue.

I have it from *unquestionable* authority, that since it has been ascertained that Mr. P. was elected President, the whole number of applications for this purpose direct and indirect, did not exceed twelve. Of these, three occurred after his departure from Columbia. One at Nashville, one at Louisville, and one at Cincinnati. This modesty on the part of political aspirants, is honorable equally to President Polk and themselves.

It is an act of justice to the two gentlemen, who, as may have been noticed at the reception of Col. P. in this city, whispered something deeply interesting to themselves in the President's ear, to say that neither of them is the applicant from Cincinnati. *Who can he be?*

OBITUARY.

Departed this life on Wednesday, the 29th of January, ult., Capt. ARCHIBALD WOODRUFF, in the 72d year of his age.

The deceased was born in Elizabethtown, N. Jersey, December 25th, 1773, being an immediate descendant of those of the same name who were active patriots in the war of the Revolution, and assisted in converting the British colonies into independent States. The same ardent attachment to liberty, and the same love of country which characterized his ancestors, glowed as fervently in the bosom of the deceased.

His life was one of checquered fortune. He was by profession, a printer, and subsequently joint proprietor and editor of one of the old-

est daily newspapers in the city of New York. Afterwards, about the year 1810, he engaged extensively in the shipping business, from the port of Philadelphia, which afforded him excellent opportunities for visiting most of the kingdoms of Europe, as well as parts of Asia and Africa; and being curious to obtain an intimate knowledge of men and things, he treasured up, by the aid of a most retentive memory, a fund of information highly instructive and entertaining. After a prosperous course of business, he was unlawfully captured by virtue of the famed "Milan Decrees" under the authority of Napoleon Buonaparte, in the year 1813, and compelled, together with one of his sons, to uader-go the painful task of witnessing his valuable vessel and cargo consumed by fire on the high seas, off the coast of France, and to suffer illegal imprisonment within the walls of her dungeons. After an absence of three years from home, and the expenditure of nearly half his fortune, he succeeded in obtaining indemnity from the French government for about 45 per cent. of his claim.

Subsequently he resided in Philadelphia, until the year 1819, when he removed, with his family to Cincinnati, where he has resided until his decease. He was endowed with an extraordinary constitution, having undergone greater exposure by sea and land than ordinarily falls to the lot of man. Whenever he had the means, he was liberal to a fault. His friendships were ardent. His enterprises often exceeded his ability to complete them, but were founded upon sound and intelligent principles. He was a pleasant and interesting writer and sometimes courted the Muses with effect. Some of his nearest relations were among the first settlers of the Miami Valley, and assisted in making the location and survey of Cincinnati. He became early impressed with the growing importance of this city, and had the satisfaction of witnessing its population increase from 8,000 to about 70,000, and the promise of her future greatness. He has left us in a ripe old age, respected by all who knew him.

Some wag says that the only borrowed article he ever returned promptly, was a kiss from a pretty girl's lips. Of course he returned it *on the spot.*

MARRIAGES.

ON Sunday, Feb. 16th, by Isaac Jones, Esq., Mr. SAMUEL C. TURNER, of Cincinnati, to MARY ANN. daughter of Gen. Stephen D. Williamson, of Anderson Township.

On Monday, 18th inst, by the Rev. Dr. Brisbane, Mr. E. G. DYER to Miss MARGARET FERER, both of Columbus, O.

DEATHS.

ON Wednesday, Feb. 19th, Dr. E. W. OLNEY.

On Thursday, 20th inst, MRS. SARAH CAMERON, wife of Mr. Robert Cameron.

On Friday, 21st inst, OLIVER P. RUFFIN, son of the late Major William Ruffin.

CINCINNATI, MARCH, 1845.

Indian Warfare--Lewis Wetzel No. 4.

On his way down, Wetzel landed at Point Pleasant, and following his usual humor, when he had no work among Indians on the carpet, ranged the town for a few days with as much unconcern as if he were on his own farm. Lieutenant Kingsbury, attached to Harmar's own command, happened to be at the mouth of Kanawha at the time, and scouting about while ignorant of Wetzel's presence, met him,—unexpectedly to both parties. Lewis, being generally on the *qui vive*, saw Kingsbury first, and halted with great firmness in the path, leaving to the Lieutenant to decide his own course of procedure, feeling himself prepared and ready, whatever that might be. Kingsbury, a brave man himself, had too much good feeling toward such a gallant spirit as Wetzel, to attempt his injury, if it were even safe to do so. He contented himself with saying, "*Get out of my sight, you Indian killer!*" And Lewis, who was implacable to the savage only, retired slowly and watchfully, as a lion draws off, measuring his steps in the presence of the hunters, being as willing to avoid unnecessarily danger as to seek it, when duty called him to act. He regained his canoe and put off for Limestone, at which place, and Washington the county town, he established his head quarters for some time. Here he engaged on hunting parties, or went out with the scouts after Indians. When not actually engaged in such service, he filled up his leisure hours at shooting matches, foot racing, or wrestling with other hunters. Maj. Fowler who knew him well during this period, described him to me as a general favorite, no less from his personal qualities than for his services.

While engaged in these occupations at Maysville, Lieutenant Lawler of the regular army, who was going down the Ohio to Fort Washington, in what was called a Kentucky boat, full of soldiers, landed at Maysville, and found Wetzel sitting in one of the taverns. Returning to the boat, he ordered out a file of soldiers seized Wetzel and dragged him on board of the boat, and without a moment's delay pushed off, and that same night delivered him to General Harmar at Cincinnati, by whom the prisoner was again put into irons, preparatory to trial, and consequent condemnation, for what Lewis disdained to deny or conceal, the killing of the Indian at Marietta. But Harmar, like St. Clair, although acquainted with the routine of military service, was destitute of the practical good sense, always indispensible in frontier settlements, in which such severe measures

were more likely to rouse the settlers to flame than to intimidate them, and soon found the country around him in arms. The story of Wetzel's captivity, captured and liable to punishment for shooting an Indian merely—spread through the settlements like wild fire, kindling the passions of the frontier men to a high pitch of fury. Petitions for the release of Wetzel came in to Gen. Harmar from all quarters, and all classes of society. To these at first, he paid little attention. At length the settlements along the Ohio, and some even of the back counties began to embody in military array to release the prisoner *vi et armis*. Representations were made to Judge Symmes, which induced him to issue a writ of *habeas corpus* in the case. John Clawson and other hunters of Columbia, who had gone down to attend his trial, went security for Wetzel's good behaviour, and being discharged, he was escorted with great triumph to Columbia and treated at that place to his supper &c. Judge Foster who gave me these last particulars described him at this period—August 26th, 1789—as about 26 years of age, about 5 ft. 9 inches high. He was full breasted, very broad across the shoulders, his arms were large, skin darker than the other brothers, his face heavily pitted with the small pox—his hair of which he was very careful, reached when combed out, to the calves of the legs; his eyes remarkably black, and when excited, sparkling with such a vindictive glance as to indicate plainly it was hardly safe to provoke him to wrath. He was taciturn in mixed company, although the fiddle of the party among his social friends and acquaintances. His morals and habits compared with those of his general associates, and the tone of society in the west of that day, were quite exemplary.

One more of Lewis Wetzel's tragedies, and I am done.

He set off alone, (as was frequently his custom) on an Indian hunt. It was late in the fall of the year, when the Indians were generally scattered in small parties on their hunting grounds. He proceeded somewhere on the waters of the Muskingum river, and found a camp where four Indians had fixed their quarters for a winter hunt. The Indians, unsuspicious of any enemies prowling about them so late in the season, were completely off their guard, keeping neither watch nor sentinels. Wetzel at first hesitated about the propriety of attacking such overwhelming numbers. After some reflection, he concluded to trust to his usual good fortune, and began to meditate upon his plan of attack.

He concluded their first sleep would be the fittest time for him to commence the work of death. About midnight, he thought their senses would be most profoundly wrapped in sleep. He determined to walk to the camp, with his rifle in one hand, and his tomahawk in the other. If any of them should happen to be awake, he could shoot one, and then run off in the darkness of the night, and make his escape; should they be all asleep, he would make the onset with his trusty scalping-knife and tomahawk. Now, reader, imagine that you see him gliding through the darkness with the silent, noiseless motion of an unearthly spirit, seeking mischief, and the keen glance of the fabled Argus, and then you can imagine to your mind Wetzel's silent and stealthy approach upon his sleeping victims.—With calm intrepidity he stood a moment, reflecting on the best plan to make the desperate assault. He set his rifle against a tree, determined to use only his knife and tomahawk; as these would not miss their aim, if properly handled with a well strung arm. What a thrilling, horrible sight! See him leaning forward, with cool self-possession, and eager vengeance, as if he had been the minister of death; he stands a moment, then wielding his towahawk, with the first blow leaves one of them in death's eternal sleep. As quick as lightning, and with tremendous yells, he applies the tomahawk to the second Indian's head, and sent him off, the land of spirits. As the third was rising, confounded and confused with the unexpected attack, at two blows he fell lifeless to the ground. The fourth darted off, naked as he was, into the woods.—Wetzel pursued him some distance, but he finally made his escape. This successful enterprise places our hero, for "deeds of noble daring" without a rival. From the pursuit he returned to the camp, scalped the three Indians, and then returned home. What Ossian said of some of his heroes, might with equal propriety be said of Wetzel—the western "clouds were hung around with ghosts." When he came home, he was asked what luck he had on his expedition? He replied, "Not very good; that he had treed four Indians, and one got away from him; that he had taken but three scalps, after all his pains and fatigue."

Caricatures of the West.

One of the correspondents of the New York Evening Mirror, has presented that periodical with sketches of western customs and modes of life, worked up into a story put into the mouth of Judge Douglass of Illinois, as a specimen of his electioneering among his constituents in the Sucker State. It is just such a view of the West as we find given of the United States generally in the English magazines and journals. I was sorry to see it copied into the Cincinnati Gazette without comment. I have both resided and traveled in Illinois and Missouri, and feel free to pronounce the whole statement, false, and I do not believe Judge D. ever gave it currency. No young *lady* in America, in the wildest part of the frontiers ever manifested the deficiency of respect due to her sex and herself, which that narrative implies. The picture has been drawn by some scribbler who knows nothing of the West.

Washington Fashions.

I do not know that I have told you the *short hand* way of visiting, people have here, and especially the great people. When a new Congressman arrives, he will be astonished at the number of cards he will find on the parlor table for him during a day. The first thought is, well, I have had a great many calls to day. The next, I must have been in when some of them came, and why did not the servants call me? These thoughts will first suggest themselves to a stranger. But upon inquiring, he will find no man has been at his house at all. This is accounted for on the *short hand* principle of visiting, which is this: A man sits in his room writing a letter, as I now am; and, whilst he is at work at home, a negro boy is out leaving his cards to such as he pleases to send them. By and by the compliment is returned, and thus great men visit and are visited without losing time. When one visits another in person and finds him absent, he leaves his card with p. p. in one corner (proper person.) This leaves the inference that he called on business. But the social visits are all made by a negro boy with cards.

As a take off to this cold formality, the Western new members have carried the joke still further; and have large cards with the picture of a splendid dinner table, groaning under the weight of turkies, quails, oysters, pies, wines, &c. &c. engraved upon them. These they send about, and they take admirably well, and rumor says, in former days, this western fashion was introduced into the most fashionable circles of N. Y. Thus, if A sends B a card for a visit, B sends back his for a dinner. This, you see, is saving expense as well as time. Yesterday and to-day, some improvements have been made.—Night before last, at a large party, a lady of excellent talent, worth and beauty, was heard to say she was fond of riding in cabs. So, up to this hour, honorable gentlemen are sending her their cards with the picture of a beautiful cab and horse upon it. To each she sends back her card, which is as much as to say, "I fancy myself riding in a cab with you."

One more observation of the fashions here.—By every man's plate is a glass bowl, about the size of those we eat pudding and milk out of when at home. In each of these, there is about a tumbler of water and a bit of lemon, about the size to make a good whiskey punch. Now what are these for? For nothing but to wet your fingers and lips with, so as to keep them clean and give them a good flavor. Some of our plain republicans will say this is worse than the cards. Not long since, a gentleman, unacquainted with the custom, took his bowl and began to drink; and, not finding it palatable, he called out. "Waiter, curse your lemonade, put some sugar in it." The negro laughed, his neighbors laughed, and finally the whole table was in a roar, and he cleared for the bar-room.

The proportion of New Englanders in the Legislature, though small, is larger than their proportion of countrymen among the constituents. New Englanders representing in all cases but one, the New England settled counties. and some five or six counties besides. The members of the Legislature, from other States of the Union, bear about the same proportion in that body, which the emigrants from those States bear respectively to the whole community. Cne member of German birth is no adequate representation of the large body of naturalized Germans in Ohio. Still the Legislature is as fairly a representation of the various elements of society in this State, as they are of the community i other respects.

Monument of Dr. Webster.

A monument has been erected at New-Haven, to the memory of Dr. Webster. It consists of a lofty shaft of Quincy granite, and rests on a massive block of the same material. Its cost was 400 dollars. The only inscription on the column is "Webster."

One of the New Haven students, fearful the Lexicographer should be mistaken for the statesman, wrote in pencil after the name *Webster—not the Godlike*; him of the *Ark*, not him of the *Lion's den*.

Parlor Organs.

I have already referred to this delightful instrument of music, and to the fact that they are manufactured by Mr. J. Koehnke of our city, in a style of unrivalled beauty and melody. There is one just finished at his establishment intended for Thomas J. Strait, Esq., of Mount Auburn. which is a splendid specimen of the art, well worthy the inspection of those who have any relish for the "concord of sweet sounds." My examination of it a few days since, brings to my recollection what Mr Strait told me in conversation, some twelve months since:

"I was on a visit to Vermont, a few weeks since," said he, "and intended to buy a parlor Organ, which I was told were made in the Eastern cities, first rate articles. I called at the shops in Boston and New York, to see what they could show me. They all fell short of what I supposed a first rate article of parlor Organs ought to be, and I concluded not to buy one; and for the rest of my visit Eastward, and for some time after my return to Cincinnati, dismissed the subject from my thoughts. One day, however, while calling on business, just beyond the corporation line, I heard the sound of an Organ, which I followed to a shanty from which it proceeded, and there I found a German playing on an Organ which he had just finished. I fell into conversation with him, and examined his work, and from what I saw and heard, was satisfied that he could build me the Organ I wanted, and I gave him an order accordingly, for I meant to give him a chance."

The Organ is now finished, and for beauty of construction and finish, and for melodious givings forth, may defy the severest scrutiny. If there be a lover of music among my subscribers, let him visit it before it is taken home to the owner's residence.

Dogs.

The Marietta Intelligencer quotes with approbation, a law enacted in 1662 in the colony of Massachusetts, "that every dog that comes to the meeting after the present day, either of Lord's day, or Lecture day, except it be those dogs that pays for a dog-whipper, the owner of those dogs shall pay six-pence for every time they come to the meeting that doth not pay the dog-whipper." The names of twenty-six men are recorded as agreeing to pay to the Dog-whipper. Five years afterwards another law was enacted of a similar kind. "It was ordered that every dog that comes into the meeting house in time of service shall pay a six-pence for every time he comes."

Dogs create trouble of various kinds in a house of worship. I recollect an example.

Brother —— of the Baptist church many years since, had a fine terrier named *Cato*, who regularly accompanied the family to church, ensconcing himself quietly beneath the seat in time of public service. Whatsoever was the weather, rain or sunshine, intensely warm, or severely cold, Cato never absented himself; in this respect setting an example of punctuality, which the family to which he belonged was far from following. During one period indeed; when a preacher not as acceptable as his predecessor officiated for some months, Brother —— absented himself totally. Not so Cato. As soon as he heard the bell, he would spring up, looking wistfully at the family to see who were going. If he found none of them preparing to set out, he trotted off alone, followed the crowd and couched himself in a most exemplary attitude under the pew seat, where he lay without stirring a limb until the services were through, when he would trot out with the congregation, some of whom were illnatured enough to hint that Cato was a better Christian than his master. So much indeed was said on the subject in and out of the church that Brother —— was at last compelled to remove his membership to another society, for the purpose of removing the scandal.

Poor Cato! I knew him well, he was an extraordinary dog, and his sagacity surpassed any thing I ever saw of the canine species.

Montes, the Hero of the Bull Fights.

Montes is a native of Chiclana, near Cadiz.—He is a man of forty to forty-five years of age, a little above the middle height, of grave aspect and deportment, deliberate in his movements, and of a pale olive complexion. There is nothing remarkable about him, except the quickness and mobility of his eyes. He appears more supple and active than robust, and owes his success as a bull-fighter to his coolness, correct eye, and knowledge of the art, rather than to any muscular strength. As soon as Montes sees a bull, he can judge the character of the beast; whether its attack will be straight forward or accompanied by stratagem; whether it is slow or rapid in its motions; whether its sight is good or otherwise. Thanks to this sort of intuitive perception, he is always ready for an appropriate mode of defence. Nevertheless, as he pushes his temerity to fool-hardiness, he has been often wounded in the course of his career; to one of which accidents a scar upon his cheek bears testimony. Several times he has been carried out of the circus grievously hurt.

The day I saw him, his costume was of the most elegant and costly description, composed of silk of an apple green color, magnificently embroidered with silver. He is very rich, and only continues to frequent the bull-ring from taste and love of excitement, for he has amassed more than fifty thousand dollars: a large sum, if we consider the great expenses which the *Matadores* are put to in dress, and in travelling from one town to another, accompanied by their quadrilla or assistant bull-fighters. One costume often costs fifteen hundred or two thousand francs.

Montes does not content himself, like most matadores, with killing the bull when the signal of death is given. He superintends and directs the combats, and goes to the assistance of those who are in danger. More than one *torero* has owed him his life. Once a bull had overturned a horse and a rider, and after goring the former in a frightful manner, was making violent efforts to get at the latter, who was sheltered under the body of his steed—Montes seized the ferocious beast by the tail, and turned him round three or four times, amidst the frantic applause of the spectators, thus giving time to extricate the fallen man. Sometimes he plants himself in front of the bull, with crossed arms, and fixes his eyes upon those of the animal, which stops suddenly subjugated by the keen and steadfast gaze. Then comes the torrent of applause, shouts, vociferations, screams of delight; a sort of delirium seems to seize the fifteen thousand spectators, who stamp and dance upon their benches in a state of the wildest excitement; every handkerchief is waved, every hat is thrown into the air; while Montes, the only collected person amongst this mad multitude, enjoys his triumph in silence, and bows slightly, with the air of a man capable of much greater things. For such applause as that, I can understand a man's risking his life every minute of the day. It is worth while. Oh! ye golden throated singers, ye fairy footed dancers, ye emperors and poets, who flatter yourselves that you have excited popular enthusiasm, you never heard Montes applauded by a crowded circus.

Occasionally it happens that the spectators themselves beg him to perform some of his feats of address. A pretty girl will call out to him, "Vamos! Senor Montes, vamos, Paquirro" [which is his christian name;] "you who are so gallant, do something for a lady's sake; *una cosita,* some trifling matter." Then Montes puts his foot on the bull's head, and jumps over him; or else shakes his cloak in the animal's face, by a rapid movement envelopes himself in it so far as to form the most graceful drapery, and then by a spring on one side, avoids the rush of the irritated brute.

In spite of Montes's popularity, he received on the day on which I saw him, at Malaga, rather a rough proof of the impartiality of a Spanish public, and of the extent to which it pushes its love of fair play towards beasts as well as men.

A magnificent black bull was turned into the arena, and from the manner in which he made his entrance, the connoisseurs augured great things for him. He united all the qualities desirable in a fighting bull; his horns were long and sharp, his legs small and nervous, promising great activity; his large dewlap, and symmetrical form indicated vast strength. Without a moment's delay he rushed upon the nearest *picador,* and knocked him over, killing his horse with a blow; he then went to the second, whom he treated in like manner, and whom they had scarcely time to lift over the barrier and get out of harm's way.

In less than a quarter of an hour he had killed seven horses; the chulos or footmen were intimidated, and shook their scarlet cloaks at a respectful distance, keeping near the palisades and jumping over as soon as the bull showed signs of approaching them. Montes himself seemed disconcerted, and had once even placed his foot on the sort of ledge which is nailed to the barriers at the height of two feet from the ground, to assist the bull-fighters in leaping over. The spectators shouted with delight, and paid the bull the most flattering compliments. Presently, a new exploit of the animal raised their enthusiasm to the very highest pitch.

The two picadores or horsemen were disabled, but a third appeared, and lowering the point of his lance awaited the bull, which attacked him furiously; and without allowing itself to be turned aside by a thrust in the shoulder, put its head under the horse's belly, with one jerk threw his fore feet on the top of the barrier, and with a second raising its hind quarter, threw him and his rider over the wall into the corridor or passage, between the first and second barriers.

Such a feat as this was unheard of, and it was rewarded by thunders of *bravos.* The bull remained master of the field of battle, which he paraded in triumph, amusing himself for want of better adversaries, with tossing about the carcasses of the dead horses. He had killed them all; the circus-stable was empty. The *banderilleros* remained sitting upon the barriers, not daring to come down and harrass the bull with their banderillas or darts. The spectators, impatient at this inaction, shouted out "*Las banderillas! Las banderillas!*" and "*Fuego al Alcalde!*" —to the fire with the Alcade; because he did not give the order to attack. At last on a sign from the Governor of the town, a banderillero advanced, planted a couple of darts in the neck of the bull, and ran off as fast as he could, but scarcely quick enough, for his arm was grazed, and the sleeve of his jacket rent by the beast's horn. Then, in spite of the hooting of the spectators, the Alcade ordered Montes to despatch the bull, although in opposition to the laws of tauromachia, which require the bull to have received four pair of banderillas before he is left to the sword of the *matador*.

Montes, instead of advancing as usual into the middle of the arena, placed himself at about twenty paces from the barrier, so as to be nearer a refuge in case of accident; he looked very pale, and without indulging in any of those little bits of display, the sort of coquatry of courage, which have procured him the admiration of all Spain, he unfolded his scarlet *muleta* and shook it at the bu l, who at once rushed at him and almost as instantly fell, as if struck by a thunderbolt. One convulsive bound, and the huge animal was dead.

The swoid had entered the forehead and pierced the brain—a thrust which is forbidden by the regulations of the bull-ring. The matador ought to pass his arm between the horns of the beast and stab him in ihe nape of the neck; that being the most dangerous way for the man, and consequently giving the bull a better chance.

Soon as it was ascertained how the bull had been killed, a storm of indignation burst from the spectators; such a hurricane of abuse and hisses as I had never before witnessed. Butcher, assassin, brigand, thief, executioner, were the mildest terms employed. "To the galleys with Montes! To the fire with Montes! To the dogs with him!" But words were soon not enough. Fans, hats, sticks, fragments torn from the benches, water-jurs, every available missile iu short was hurled into the ring. As to Montes, his face was perfectly green with rage, and I noticed that he bit his lips till they bled; although he endeavored to appear unmoved, and remained leaning with an air of affected grace upon his swo·d, from the point of which he had wiped the blood in the sand of the arena.

So frail a thing is popularity. No one would have thought it possible before that day, that so great a favorite and consummate bull-fighter as Montes, would have been punished thus severely for an infraction of a rule, which was doubtless rendered absolutely necessary by the agility, vigor, and extraordinary fury of the animal with which he had to contend. There was another bull to be killed, but it was the Jose Parra, second matador, who despatched it, its death passing almost unnoticed in the midst of the tumult and indignation of the spectators. The fight over, Montes got into a *calesin* with his *quadrilla*, and left the town, shaking the dust from his feet, and swearing by all the saints that he would never return to Malaga.

Profile Likeness of Powers.

We are indebted to NICHOLAS LONGWORTH, Esq., of Cincinnati, who is now in this city, for a beautifully engraved profile likeness of HIRAM POWERS, the great American sculptor. Accompanying it we received the following note:

"MESSRS. EDITORS:—Aware of the interest you have taken in the success of our countrymen Powers, in Italy, I send you his profile, taken in pencil, by P. S. Symmes, Esq., an amateur artist in Cincinnati, a few days before Powers left for Italy. The engraving is by Caston, one of the most promising engravers of Paris. The likeness is admirable, and by comparing it with the profile engravings of Canova, you will discover a strong resemblance. The patronage some of your citizens have extended to Powers, may render his likeness a subject of interest. Yours, truly,

N. LONGWORTH.

St. Charles Hotel, January 18th 1845."

We thank Mr. L. very sincerely for this beautiful present, and shall cherish it accordingly. We never saw the great sculptor, who is now considered the greatest of his day, but the likeness bears all the marks of genius and energy which characterize Powers. The broad brow, the large, glowing eye, the finely chiselled nose, and the compressed, sharply cut lips are replete with intellect and the fire of genius. No one could mistake the likeness for any other than a man of mind, a lover of the pure and beautiful in nature and art. The brilliant success which Hiram Powers has achieved in Italy, gratifying as it is to his countrymen generally, must be peculiarly so to Mr. Longworth. One of his best and earliest friends, that gentleman saw and appreciated, years ago, the talent which was slumbering in the bosom of the young artist. When confidence, advice and friendship were valuable, because most needed, Mr. L. took Powers by the hand, and proved a friend indeed. Mr. L. has lived to see his humble friend mounting, eagle-like, to the highest niche in the temple of fame, the "observed of all observers," and an honor to the land which gave him birth.--*N. O. Tropic.*

Western Lard.

It is matter of great surprise to me why the St. Louis merchants do not ship their mast fed, and otherwise inferior lard to the Cincinnati market. It commands here always 20 or 25 pr. cent higher prices on its face, but 1 suppose the difference would be still greater if we compute the leakage of an article like this liquified in the hold of a steamboat under the temperature of such a place.

I know one lard oil manufacturer alone, whose capacity of producing lard oil if a sufficient supply were afforded him, would require for his year's business 2,000,000 lbs. lard. Most of the inferior lards which are sent from Missouri and Illinois east, and converted into soaps, would pay much better prices if sent to Cincinnati, sold and to the lard oil factories.

MARRIAGES.

AT New Albany, on February 18th, by the Rev. Mr. Saunders, A. M , JOHN LOWRY, of Cincinnati, to Miss EMILY MORECRAFT, of New Albany

In this city, on Thursday the 27th ult., by the Rev. Mr. Walker, Mr. WILLIAM GILMAN, to Miss BULAH ANN STEARNES.

On Sunday, March 2d, by the Rev. John F. Wright, Mr. PAUL F. HAHN to Miss ALICE MANSELL.

DEATHS.

IN this city, Tuesday, Feb. 25th, DENTON DUNN, in the 49th year of his age.

On Wednesday 26th inst, B. FRANKLIN WOOD, aged 23 years.

Same day, Mrs. CORNELIA WIGGINS, wife of Samuel Wiggins.

On Thursday 27th ult., Dr. SAMUEL ADAMS, aged 78 years.

Same day, EDWARD FELIX ASSELINEAU, in the 3rd year of his age.

On Monday, March 3rd, CHARLOTTE E. WOOD, aged 37 years, formerly of Hartford, Ct.

Same day, Mr. JAMES WILDEY, aged 38 years, late librarian of the Young Mens' Librarian Association

Same day, Mr. SIRAH B. LAYMAN,

Harmar's Campaign.

Having gathered a variety of papers, which shed light on the various campaigns of Harmar, St. Clair and Wayne, I feel it a duty imposed on me by that circumstance to compile a fuller and more accurate narrative of those events than I have thus far seen in print. Nor need it at all appear strange, under the existing state of society and condition of things, that much of what is already on record should abound in errors. That both Harmar and St. Clair should mistake the locations of the battle they fought, and that many statements founded on conjecture, should pass current for years in the community to an extent which even yet serves to confuse the truth of history. These things are all easily accounted for, by the wilderness character of the untrodden West, the scattered state of the settlements in the Miami country, the little communication between the respective parts, and the utter absence of newspapers.

I commence with HARMAR's campaign. A column would hardly serve to point out the errors in dates, places, and facts generally, in print, upon this subject. The best mode of correction is to compile the narrative anew, availing myself of unpublished manuscript notes of Capt. John Armstrong, who commanded a company of the United States regulars attached to Harmar's army during that campaign, and whose escape with life in the first battle was so remarkable.

The western frontiers had been for some years say from 1782 to 1788, in a very disturbed state by reciprocal aggressions, of Indians and whites. There does not appear, in the history of those days, however, any systematic and general movement of the Indians for the extirpation of the whites, as was alleged to be the object of their great confederacy of 1782, which dividing into two parties broke, one, upon the upper Ohio settlements, the other on the various Kentucky stations, carrying massacre and captivity so extensively along their course. The irregular and precarious mode of living among the savages forbade the accomplishment of such design, if it had even been their settled purpose; the subsistence of themselves and families being principally derived from the chase, a species of provision which did not permit the laying up extensive and permanent stores, if even their improvident mode of living had permitted the effort. But when they found the settlers entrenching themselves in fort after fort, circumscribing their range and cutting them entirely off from their favorite hunting grounds south of the Ohio, there can be no doubt that a determined hostility sprung up in the minds of the savage, which all the exertions of the American government failed to allay, and soon rendered it appa-

rent that the two races could not live together in amity, where it was the policy of the one to reclaim the country from the hunter, and of the other to keep it a wilderness.

After treaty upon treaty had been made and broken,—and the frontiers had been suffering through this whole period from the tomahawk and the scalping knife, the government, then just going into operation, detached a force of 320 regular troops, enlisted in New Jersey and Pennsylvania for the protection of the frontiers, and devolved the command on Josiah Harmar, who had borne arms as a colonel with credit, during the late revolutionary struggle. A force of 1133 drafted militia from Pennsylvania and Kentucky, was also placed under his orders. The regulars consisted of two battalions, commanded respectively by Majors Wyllys and Doughty, and a company of artillery under Captain Ferguson with three brass pieces of ordnance. Col. Hardin of Ky, was in command of the Militia, in which Cols. Trotter and Paul, Majors Hall and McMillan held subordinate commands. The orders to General Harmar were to march on to the Indian towns adjacent to the lakes, and inflict on them such signal chastisement as should protect the settlements from future depredations.

The whole plan had been devised by Washington himself, who well understood the subject, having prior to the revolution as is well known, learnt much practically of the Indian character, as well as the condition of the west, although it is not easy to conceive why he should have selected such men as Harmar and St. Clair, who were destitute of the training he had himself acquired, and which could have been found on the frontiers of Pennsylvania and Kentucky, in many distinguished Indian fighters, ready for use. The force of circumstances probably biased his judgment, as it served to effect appointments equally exceptionable during the war of 1812, such as those of Hull, Dearborn, Bloomfield and Chandler, men who had outlived their energies, if ever qualified practically for the weighty trust devolving on them.

On the 29th December, 1789, Gen. Harmar arrived at Cincinnati. He had been stationed for some months prior to this at the mouth of Muskingum, waiting at that post for militia force and military supplies from the upper country, and the completion of Fort Washington—which Major Doughty with 146 men from Fort Harmar had been detached to construct. From this period to the 30th September, 1790, he was employed in making every thing ready for the expedition, and on that day all his preparations being made, he started with the regulars, the militia under Col. Hardin having already set out. — continued on p. 184

Punk—great man—Delaware chief."

The army burned all the houses at the different villages, and destroyed about twenty thousand bushels corn, which they discovered in various places where it had been hid by the Indians, a large quantity having been found buried in holes dug for that purpose. In this destruction a variety of property belonging to French traders, was involved. On the 18th, the main body of the troops was moved to Chillicothe, the principal town of the Shawnese, Gen. Harmar having previously detached a party of 180 militia, and 30 regulars in pursuit of the Indians who appeared to have retired westward, across the St. Joseph after the destruction by themselves of the Omee town, Capt. John Armstrong commanding the regulars, and Col. Trotter of the Kentucky militia the entire force. They found and cut off a few Indian stragglers, but did not overtake the main body, being recalled to camp by signal late in the evening. Next morning the same detachment was ordered out anew, and being placed under the command of Col. Hardin, pursued the same route in search of the savages. Finding himself in their neighborhood, he detached Captain Faulkner of the Pennsylvania militia, to form on his left, which he did at such a distance, as to render his company of no service in the approaching engagement. Hardin's command moved forward to what they discovered to be the encampment of the enemy, which was flanked by a morass on each side as well as by one in front, which was crossed with great promptness by the troops, now reduced to less than two hundred, who before they had time to form, received a galling and unexpected fire from a large body of savages. The militia immediately broke and fled, nor could all the exertions of the officers rally them; fifty two of the dispersing being killed in a few minutes. The enemy pursued until major Fountain who had been sent to hunt up Faulkner and his company, returning with them compelled them to retire, and the survivors of the detachment arrived safe in camp.

The regulars under Armstrong bore the brunt of this affair. One sergeant and twenty-one privates being killed on the battle ground, and while endeavoring to maintain their position, were thrown in disorder by the militia running through their lines, flinging away their arms without even firing a shot. The Indians killed in this affair nearly one hundred men.

As regards the force of the savages, Captain Armstrong who was under no temptation to underrate their number, speaks of them as about one hundred in force. Their strength has been stated, but as I think, without any data by Marshall, in his life of Washington at 700. The real strength of the Indians was in a well chosen position, and in the cowardice of the militia, who formed numerically, the principal force opposed to them. This destructive contest was fought near the spot where the Goshen State road now crosses Eel river, about 12 miles west of Fort Wayne. Capt. Armstrong broke through the pursuing Indians and plunged in the deepest of the morasses referred to, where he remained to his chin all night in water, with his head concealed by a tussock of high grass. Here he was compelled to listen to the nocturnal orgies of the Indians, dancing and yelling around the dead bodies of his brave soldiers. As day approached they retired to rest, and Armstrong chilled to the last degree, extricated himself from the swamp, but found himself obliged to kindle a fire in a ravine into which he crawled, having his tinder box, watch and compass still on his person. By the aid of the fire, he recovered his feeling, and the use of his limbs, and at last reached the camp in safety. For some years after, bayonets were found upon this spot in numbers, and bullets have been cut out of the neighboring trees in such quantities as to attest the desperate character of this engagement.

On the 21st the army left Chillicothe on their return to Fort Washington, marching 8 miles, when the scouts, who had been scouring the country, came in and reported that the Indians had re-occupied the "Omee" village, lying in the junction of the St. Joseph and Maumee rivers. Harmar, anxious to efface the stigma resting on the American arms in the affair of the 19th, detached Col. Hardin with orders to surprize the savages, and bring on an engagement. The party under his orders consisted of 300 militia of which three companies were mounted men, with 60 regulars under command of Major Wyllys.

Col. Hardin arrived at the Omee town early on the morning of the 22d. His force had been divided into two parties, the left division of which was to have formed down the St. Mary's and cross at the ford, after which they were to rest until day light, and cross the St. Joseph, and commence an attack on the Indians in front who had encamped out, near the ruins of their town. The right division under Hardin and Wyllys were to proceed to "Harmar's" ford, on the Maumee, where they were to remain until M'Millan's party had reached the river, and commenced the attack which was to be the signal for them to cross the Maumee and attack the Indians in the rear. Owing to the treachery or ignorance of the guides, however, M'Millan's force lost its way in the thickets through which they had to pass, and although travelling all night, did not reach the ford until day light.— As soon as the Indians, who had been encamping about the ruins of their town, discovered

His orders of march and encampment with notes of his progress I shall publish in next number of the "Advertiser" as a separate statement. It is an original article from the pen of an eye witness. The first day's advance was seven miles, and the encampment for the night, was on a branch of Mill creek, course north-east. Eight miles more were made the second day, on a general course of north-west, the army encamping on another branch of Mill creek. On the third day a march of fifteen miles was made, the course generally north, and the encampment on the waters of Muddy creek, a tributary of the Little Miami, within one mile of Col. Hardin's command. The next morning, Col. Hardin, with the militia were overtaken and passed, and halting at Turtle creek one mile further on, the whole army encamped for the night.

On the 14th Oct. the army reached and crossed the Little Miami, on a north-east course moved up it one mile to a branch called Sugar or Caesars creek, near Waynesville, where they encamped, having accomplished nine miles that day. Next day a march of ten miles, still on a north-east course, brought the army to Glade creek, near where Xenia now stands. On the 6th it reached Chillicothe, an old Indian village, now Oldtown, & crossed again the Little Miami, keeping a north-east course, making nine miles that day. Next day the troops crossed Mad river, then called the Pickaway fork of Great Miami, and made nine miles; their course for the first time becoming west of north. On the 8th, pursuing a north-west course, they crossed Honey creek and made seven miles more. On the next day, they followed the same course, and marching ten miles encamped within two miles of the Great Miami. Next day the army crossed the Miami, keeping still a north-west course, and made ten miles more. On the 11th, by a course west of north it passed the ruins of a French trading station, marked on Hutchens' map as the *Tawixtwes*—(Twigtwees.) Encamped after making eleven miles. Next day the army kept a course west of north-west, near Loramie's creek, and across the head waters of the Auglaize. Here they found the remains of a considerable village, some of the houses being still standing; fourteen miles made this day.— On the 13th, marched ten miles, keeping west of north-west, and encamped, being joined by a reinforcement from Cincinnati, with ammunition. Next day, the 14th, Col. Hardin was detached with one company of regulars and six hundred militia, in advance of the main body, and being charged with the destruction of the towns in the forks of the Maumee. On the arrival of this advance party they found the towns abandoned by the Indians, and the principal one burnt. The main body marching on the

14th ten miles, and on the 15th eight more, both days on a north-west course. Next day made nine miles same course, and on the 17th crossing the Maumee river to the Indian village, formed a junction again with Hardin at the Omee (*au Miami Fr.*) village. This was the same town burnt and abandoned by the savages.

At this point of the narrative there is considerable obscurity with names and places which I must explore as I best can. The Indians had seven villages, it seems, clustering about the junction of the St. Mary's and St. Joseph rivers, which, as is well known, form the river Maumee. These were, 1st, the Miami village, so called, after the tribe of that name, corruptly and by contraction *Omee* from *Au Miami*, the designation given it by the French traders, who were here resident in great force. This lay in the fork of the St. Joseph and Maumee. 2nd, a village of the Miamies of 30 houses, Ke Kiogue, now Ft. Wayne—in the fork of the St. Mary's and Maumee. 3d, Chillicothe, a name signifying "town" being a village of the Shawnees, down the Maumee on its north bank and of 58 houses. Opposite this was another of the same tribe of 18 houses. The Delawares had their villages, two on the St. Marys, about three miles from its mouth and opposite each other, with 45 houses together, and the other consisting of 36 houses, on the east side of the St. Joseph's, two or three miles from its mouth.

The day of Harmar's junction with Hardin, two Indians were discovered by a scouting party, as they were crossing a prairie; the scouts pursued them and shot one; the other made his escape. A young man named Johnson, seeing the Indian was not dead, attempted to shoot him again, but his pistol not making fire, the Indian raised his rifle and shot Johnson through the body, which proved fatal. This night the Indians succeeded in driving through the lines between fifty and one hundred horses, and bore them off, to the no small mortification of the whites.

The same day, October 17th, was employed in searching in the hazel thickets for hidden treasure. Much corn was found buried in the earth. On the evening of this day, Captain M'Clure and a Mr. M'Clary fell upon a stratagem peculiar to backwoodsmen. They conveyed a horse a short distance down the river undiscovered, fettered him, unstrapped the bell, and concealed themselves with their rifles. An Indian, attracted by the sound of the bell, came cautiously up, and began to untie him, when M'Clure shot him. The report of the gun alarmed the camp, and brought many of the troops to the place. A young man taken prisoner at Loramies was brought to see the Indian just killed, and pronounced him to be "Captain

Hardin's men, they began to rally for the fight, the alarm spreading, and the Indians rushing in Col. Hardin, discovering that unless he crossed immediately he would be compelled to do it in the face of superior numbers, and expecting every moment to hear the report of M'Millan's men in his rear, gave the order to cross, and by the time two thirds of his force had passed over the battle began. A severe engagement ensued; the desperation of the savages in the contest surpassed any thing previously known, and the greater part throwing down their arms rushed on the bayonets, tomahawk in hand, thus rendering every thing useless but the rifles of the militia, and carrying rapid destruction every where in their advance. While this attack was going on, the rifles of the remaining Indians were fatally employed picking out the officers. Majors Fountain and Wyllys. both valuable officers, fell directly after the battle began, the former pierced with eighteen bullets. Fifty-one of Wyllys' regulars shared his fate, and the other divisions also suffered severely in both killed and wounded.

Major McMillan came up with his force while the battle was raging, but could not turn its tide, although he succeeded in enabling the discomfited troops to retire, which they did in comparatively good order.

The militia behaved well on this memorable day, and received the thanks of Gen. Harmar for their good conduct. What the carnage in this battle was, may be inferred from the return of 180 killed and wounded, not more than half of those engaged in it escaping unhurt. There is no doubt as respects the second battle, whatever was the fact in the first, that the savages outnumbered as well as overpowered Hardin's forces, and the disparity was rendered still greater, by the plan of night attack, which separated M'Millan from the main body when his aid was most needed.

It is alleged by some historians, that the American troops were not defeated, as was proven by their regular retreat, a disorderly flight being the usual concomitant of defeat. But the fact that our troops were obliged to leave the remains of the brave soldiers who fell on that occasion, to become scalped and lie unburied, and their bones bleaching on the ground until Wayne's visit, four years afterwards obtained, them decent burial, scouts the idea.

An affecting incident occurred at the place of crossing the river. A young Indian and his father and brother were crossing, when the ball of a white man passed through his body: he fell. The old man, seeing his boy fall, dropped his rifle and attempted to raise his fallen son, in order to carry him beyond the reach of the white men, when the other son also fell by his side.

He drew them both to the shore, then sat down between them, and with fearless, Roman composure, awaited the approach of the pursuing foe, who came up and killed him also.

If there be any generalship, in thus sending out detachment after detachment to be cut up in detail, then General Harmar deserves that distinction. He put the best face on the matter which the nature of the case permitted, and issued the following orders on the 22nd October, the day of the second battle.

Camp, 8 miles from the ruins of the Maumee towns, 1790.

"The general is exceedingly pleased with the behavior of the militia in the action of this morning. They have laid very many of the enemy dead upon the spot. Although our loss is great, still it is inconsiderable in comparison to the slaughter among the savages. Every account agrees that, upwards of one hundred warriors fell in the battle; it is not more than man for man, and we can afford them two for one. The resolution and firm determined conduct of the militia this morning has effectually retrieved their character in the opinion of the General.— He knows they can and will fight."

It is easy to judge, by the preceeding narrative and orders, what kind of fitness Harmar possesses for the service to which he was called. A general who encamps in the neighborhood of the enemy, with a force large enough to exterminate him, and contents himself with sending out detachments to be destroyed successively, where no adequate reason exists, why the whole force should not have been brought into action, deserves not the name of a military man. Harmar kept two thirds or three fourths of his troops eight miles from the battle ground inactive, and of as little service as if he had left them at Fort Washington. He appeared to be fully consoled for the loss of the brave officers and soldiers who fell by the savage tomahawk and rifle, by the reflection expressed in the general orders that the American troops could afford to lose twice as many men as the Indians. My unfavorable judgment on this subject is supported by that of the actors of that campaign, who still survive.

The celebrated Indian Chief, *Little Turtle*, commanded the savages in both battles, with, Col. Hardin and his troops, as he did afterwards in St. Clair's defeat, as well as bore a conspicuous part in the battle with Gen. Wayne at the Fallen Timbers.

Harmer returned by easy marches to Fort Washington, where he arrived on the 3d November, and which he left soon afterwards for Philadelphia, being succeeded in his military command by St. Clair. He resided in comparative obscurity for some years, on the banks of the

Schuylkill, and died about 1803. I was present at the funeral, which was conducted with great military pomp, his horse being dressed in mourning, and his sword and pistols laid upon his coffin, which was borne on a bier, hearses not being in use in those days.

Revolutionary Recollections.

PLAIN, WOOD COUNTY, April 2d, 1842.

J. FRAZER, Esq.:—

Yours of the 18th of March came to hand the 8th of April. My dear sir, when my pension paper was made out, I was in a very low state of health, having been confined to my room, and most of my time to my bed, for about four months. I am now very low, unable to write but a few lines at a time; but fearing I should not be able to make any communication a few days hence, I thought perhaps a short description of Danbury in Connecticut, would be acceptable. But I am so worn out in body and mind, to do justice to the subject, cannot be expected. However, it has been the will of God, who orders the events of war, and of peace, to prolong my life beyond all who were engaged in the sanguinary contest. O, what millions of the aged, and those who had well entered the varied professional business for life, have gone to their final and invisible abode, since the event, about which I write. But *my appointed time* must be near at hand.

In order to destroy the public stores of Danbury, the British, in the forepart May, 1777, landed about 800 men, with two field-pieces, at a place called Compo; and being aided by a tory party, they were directed along an unfrequented route, and mostly through woods, about 15 miles to the village of Danbury, without alarming the people: but how it went like an electrical shock to every quarter. Altho' many of our young men were then in the army, there soon collected a formidable company of yeomanry. The enemy having effected their design in part, in destroying about 1000 bbls. of pork and flour, and after setting the village on fire, began their retreat on a large road leading to White Plains. As they were entering the village of Ridgfield, General Wooster, with a party of Yankee farmers, directly from the place, fell upon their rear with an alarming effect. They left, it was said, about thirty on the ground. I saw a man stripping some of the dead next morning as they lay on the road. General Wooster received a mortal wound.

They began now to feel themselves in some danger, and took the most direct course to reach their shipping. However, night came on, and they were obliged to encamp, about ten miles from the place of landing. The party I was in,

commanded by Lieut. Hall, an officer of the army, attacked their rear guard just as they began to descend a very stony road into a valley at Wilton meeting-house, from which there were roads in several directions. There was a wall fence on each side of the road, which made them overshoot our men. We soon rushed forward within about eight rods of them, and opened our fire; they stood about three rounds, and ran down the hill. We had five men wounded, one of them mortally. Here the firing ceased for a few moments, and we stood looking to see what course they would take from the Church. They entered with a rolling column into a road leading up a pretty steep ascent, well fenced with wall and bushes on both sides—in about 30 or 40 rods, there was a right-angle completely covered with the fence and bushes. Here General Arnold with a small regular force, with a six-pound piece, had taken a stand. As soon as the enemy had well entered the road, Arnold gave them a shot, that spoke loudly—they were prodigiously startled, and shifted their course with a quick step into a road leading to Compo bridge: but Arnold got the bridge and obliged them to ford with some disadvantage. Here the contest became more severe, and their situation more perilous: but about the setting of the sun, they landed from their shipping two or three hundred fresh troops, which, under the advantage of the night, enabled them to reembark, having suffered the loss of about forty men.

Some things amusing, happen in perilous circumstances. A little before the party overtook their rear, in passing by a farm house, a stout looking fellow set his gun leaning on a pig house, and jumped in to catch some fowls—there were two stout resolute Yankee girls looking out at a window, who saw the fellow jump in, and his gun standing outside; they sprang out, seized his gun, and told him positively, that if he attempted to leave the pen, they would kill him on the spot. They kept him in the pig pen until some of our party released them, and took the fellow into their custody and marched him the other way. The road was strewed in several places with articles of plunder, which they were obliged to throw by.

It seemed to be an object of the enemy, to destroy all they could, even where they had not time to burn. Furniture, for example, as much broken and injured, as their hearty retreat would admit of.

After this severe check, they quit landing parties for plunder in Connecticut.

I think it more probable, this will be my last, than that I shall live, or be able to write again. The invisible realities of another world appear to be near. Here I have lived nearly 86 years; have done much to be accounted for, at the judgment day, when all will stand before the Judgment Seat of Jesus Christ.

Accept, my dear sir, the sincere regards of your aged friend.

JOSEPH BADGER.

August 12, 1842.

Extracts from Judge Goforth's Docket.

1790.

Feby. 2. "Took the oath of allegiance to the United States of America, and the oath of office as a Justice of the Peace, for the County of Hamilton."

Feby. 4. Joseph Gerard took the oath of allegiance to the United States of America, and was qualified as Constable.

Aug. 12. 1790. I received a visit from Esqr. Wells and Mr. Sedam, an officer in the Army who spent most of the day with me, and towards evening as they were going away and I was walking with them to the boat, Esq. Wells introduced a conversation with me respecting the pernicious practice of retailing spirituous liquors to the troops, and informed me that General Harmar wished me to write to Cochran and some others, in order to prevent such mischiefs as were taking place. I observed to the gentleman, that we had more effectual ground to go upon, and that by virtue of a statute of the Territory, a special session might be called, and wished Esq. Wells to meet me on the forepart of the 14th of August for that purpose, at Cincinnati.

Aug. 14. On Saturday 14th, I arrived at Cincinnati with Esq. Gano—waited upon Esq. McMillan who was in a low state of health, but gave me encouragement that he would be able to sit in session. I immediately despatched a messenger to inform Esq. Wells of my arrival, and another to carry the following letter to General Harmar.

Dear Sir:—

It has been intimated to me that the persons sanctioned in May term last, to keep public houses of entertainment for the accommodation of strangers and travelers, have abused that indulgence in a way that must eventually be detrimental to the public service, by debauching the troops under your command with spirituous liquors. I have, therefore, convened a special session on the occasion, which are now met and ready to proceed on that business, and would therefore, thank General Harmar to be so kind as to furnish the session with such evidence as may be an effectual clue to go into a thorough investigation of the matter; and as the session are now convened, your compliance as speedily as may be with conveniency to yourself, will greatly oblige,

Sir, your most obedient humble servant,

WILLIAM GOFORTH.

Hon. Gen. Harmar.

Cincinnati, 14th Aug. 1790.

The court being opened, present William Goforth, William Wells, William McMillan, John S. Gano.

Captain Ferguson, Captain Pratt, Captain Strong, and several other officers appeared agreeable to Gen. Harmar's orders, and informed the court, that in consequence of the troops being debauched by spirituous liquors, punishment had become frequent in the army, and that the men were sickening fast, and that the sickness in the opinion of the Doctors was in a great degree, brought on by excessive hard drinking, and the officers complained of three houses which had retailed to the troops, to wit: Thomas Cochran, Matthew Winton and John Scott. These charges were supported by evidence, and Thomas Cochran, and Matthew Winton, each with a security were bound by their recognizance at the next general quarter sessions of the peace, to be holden at Cincinnati, for the county of Hamilton on the first Tuesday in November next, in the sum of two hundred dollars, and in the mean time to refrain from retailing spirituous liquors to the troops without a written permission from their officers. And John Scott, in the sum of thirty dollars. The Court being adjourned without day.

Chair Factories.

It is not easy in every respect to point out the reasons, why Cincinnati mechanics should excel most others, in cheapness or in quality, in any given article of manufacture, and yet, our superiority over other places is at times, forcibly impressed on me, by what I see almost every day in the factories of this place. I believe the general fact to be that men prepare themselves to better advantage and more thoroughly for carrying on business of this description here, than elsewhere, as a general rule.

Where, for instance, out of Cincinnati, could a building six stories, basement included—as large too as 28 feet by 100 feet—be found, devoted to carrying on the manufacture of chairs. Think what immense space such sized floors must afford for the various operations, particularly as the work is all blocked out in the country, and the sawing and turning all done before the chairs reach the factory. Notwithstanding this, every foot of space throughout the building, not occupied as gangways, is taken up by the manufactured article, in its various stages of fin...

ishing, framing, fitting, veneering, polishing, caning, painting, and varnishing, and by the workmen employed in the establishment.

The factory to which I refer is that of Mr. John Geyer on East Fourth street. A few chair factories in the United States may turn out more work, but nowhere in our republic, are operations in this line so extensively carried on, within the limits of the establishment itself, or conducted so systematically. I hold it a sound axiom in political economy, that our banking facilities and business patronage should be bestowed upon those manufacturing products in which the raw material bought elsewhere, bears the lightest proportion to the cost of labor, in the aggregate value. There are industrial pursuits in Cincinnati, in which the raw material forms 85 per cent. of the manufactured article; as there are others in which almost the entire value of the product, is created by the skill or labor of the artificer. Apply this rule to the manufacture of chairs, and we shall find it a valuable department of productive industry; fifteen per cent being the full proportion of the raw materials.

There are five important establishments in this line of business in Cincinnati; John Geyer, Wm. H. Ross, Jno. Pfaff, Jonathan Mullen, and Robt. Mitchell & Co., besides twelve or fifteen operating on a smaller scale, and in fact in a different line, making low-priced and plain chairs only. In these five establishments, there are one hundred and twenty-five hands employed in the various processes: in the others, perhaps seventy-five more. The aggregate sales of chairs, settees &c. in Cincinnati, for the year 1844 were 120,000 dollars, being a greatly increased extent of goods sold, although at a less price than the sales of 1840, which amounted to 131,000 dollars. The present prices of chairs under the influence of increased skill, improved facilities for manufacture, fall in raw materials and the reduction of business generally to a cash basis, being but two thirds of those of 1840.— Within that period the increase of hands has been at least fifty per cent. Under these circumstances there is no place in the United States where chairs are sold on as favorable terms.

Our market is the entire south and south-west. We also sell extensively to points in the west which manufacture chairs, but fail in competing with us, in some instances in quality, in others in price. It is a striking illustration of the progress of this city in population & wealth, to state that fully one third of the chairs made here are for home use and sale, and that fact leads us to look forward to the period rapidly approaching, when the largest share in this and kindred fabrics will be wanted where made.

It is the capacity of large cities to furnish important home markets after they reach a certain stage of existence which builds them up so rapidly; the home consumption of London for example, being of four times the importance of its foreign export.

There is another interesting feature in our chair manufacture, connected with it, since the last census. I allude to the establishment of ALBRO's *veneering* operations, and the rapidly increasing demand for this article in fancy chairs, which, in connection with what is required for cabinet work, furnishes a market extensively for his veneers, both of foreign and domestic woods of the finer qualities.

CORRESPONDENCE.

Usury Laws. No. 3.

MR. CIST:

If a law were proposed, professedly giving to the wealthy a monopoly of any desirable commodity in general request, driving from the market nine-tenths of the community, in order that the very rich—the favored few—might obtain the article at a low price, while the less wealthy, constituting the great mass of the community were excluded from the dealing in it under heavy penalties, and thereby subjected to the most serious inconveniences, the law would provoke one universal clamor of bitter indignation throughout the whole country, and its infamous advocates would be held up to the merited destitution of their fellow citizens.

Now, usury laws with their penalties, have a decided tendency to give to the rich a monopoly in borrowing. By shutting out competition, the opulent obtain money at a low rate, while the poor are either prevented from borrowing at all, or compelled to pay the lender an extra price to cover the risk of the law. Thus, while the John Jacob Astors of the land obtain money at 5 per cent. smaller men are often compelled to pay 25. O.

Usury Laws, No. 4.

The term usury, derived from the latin *usura*, had originally nothing invidious in its signification. It was the only word used to express what we now mean by "*interest.*" All rates, great or small, were called usury, as the word *rent* is used to denote a consideration given for the use of houses and lands.

In the age of ignorance and despotism, all interest was prohibited under the heaviest penalties. Taking the *least* compensation for the use of *money*, was denounced in the strongest terms. Governments declared it a crime against man. Religion pronounced it an offence against Heaven. The unthinking multitude in these benighted days, regarded usury with religious horror.

The fact that money lending was at this time chiefly in the hands of the Jews, tended greatly to augment the prejudice. It was considered a *Jewish* practice, and the Jews in this intolerant age were regarded as an impious race, accursed of earth and Heaven, and by way of serving the cause of religion, were often plundered and massacred by thousands.

In 1546, under the 8th Henry, usury was, for the first time in England, taken under the protection of the law, and limited to ten per cent.

But so deeply rooted were the prejudices against it among all classes—so effectually had they been taught from their infancy to regard it as an abomination, that the law giving sanction to it, called forth loud murmurs of discontent throughout the whole nation. They became so clamorous in the succeeding reign, that the law was abolished, and the former penalties revived. Under the reign of Elizabeth, usury was restored; not by the old name—not as *usury*, but *"interest,"* which term was now used for the first time. Thus by the substitution of a mere word, the prejudices of men were reconciled.—The law set forth that any rate not exceeding ten per cent. was allowable as *interest*, but that any thing beyond that was usury, which in the preamble to the law was denounced after the old fashion. So much for the magic power of a name.

The prejudice against usury, thus engendered in superstition, and supported by ignorance, is not altogether extinct even in the present day.

Political economists have again and again demonstrated in the clearest terms, the pernicious tendency of all laws restricting the commerce in money. Time after time have they exhibited in the strongest light, the utter fallacy of the grounds on which such laws have been supported.

But error is so wonderfully tenacious of life.—Detect it—drag it forth—strike at it—by well directed blows cripple it, repeat the blows until every mark of animation disappears, yet ere you are aware, the mis-shaped monster is on its legs again, glaring on you in all its original deformity.   O.

Relics of the Past.

Among the many relics of pioneer times in Cincinnati, which are daily swept away in the onward march of improvement, an ancient building which has stood from almost the commencement of our city, at the corner of Butler and Front, has given way to afford space for a new Boiler Yard. The building was of frame, the foundations were of boat gunnels, and much of the other materials made from the plank and other timbers of a flatboat, in which the first settler came from Redstone, now Brownsville, Pa.

On breaking up the building, hardly any of the timbers—being of white and red oak—were decayed. A part indeed was found so far hardened by age as almost to bid defiance to the axe. This ancient structure was put up by Mr. Hezekiah Flint, one of the 47, who by landing at Marietta, became the original settlers on the soil of Ohio, and deceased here, only two years since.

Powers and Kellogg.

The following passages are extracted from a letter lately received from Minor K. Kellogg, by his friends in the United States, which bears date Florence, December 8th, 1844.

"The statue of a Greek slave, by Mr. Powers, has been exhibited in my studio for the last eight days—previous to its departure for London. It is the property of John Grant, Esq. who will take the proper means to let it be seen to advantage in the great metropolis. The Grand Duke and Dutchess have paid their respects to the beautiful slave, and expressed their regret that she was about to leave Florence. The studio was visited by great numbers of the best people—both strangers and Florentines. Indeed the statue seems to attract the attention of all who take any pleasure in examining works of art; and it has become one of the principal attractions, if not the principal one to all who desire to see the best productions of modern sculptors. It is a source of pride to Americans, that their country has had the honor of giving to the world so great a genius as Powers, and an equal source of mortification that it has lacked either the taste, or the liberality, to take into its own possession so lovely a statue. It has fallen to the honor of an Englishman to appreciate and reward Mr. Powers' talents, and this is a source of unaffected delight to the English. Lord Ward has ordered a duplicate of it, and this will also find a home in an English mansion—notwithstanding the aversion of John Bull to the '*holding of slaves.*'

"Powers is still engaged on the statue of Mr Calhoun. It will be a noble work. He has not yet commenced that of Franklin. He is now full of orders, principally from the English. He is well, indeed I think he is in better health than he has been since I have known him."

"The clouds have already passed and the sun of prosperity shines again upon me. I am *full* of commissions, but not so full of *cash*; still there is enough of the latter to keep me for the present—or, until the former shall have been completed. I have been *obliged* to receive orders for copies, a thing which I was in hopes would not befal me again. However, I am most thankful that this means of livelihood was within my reac... u. u ...... of so great a pressure of poverty.

"I have determined that a bottle of champagne shall suffer on account of the news of Gov. Polk's election, and as I cannot kill it all myself, I have a neighbor who works in clay —Powers—who will join me in good wishes for the prosperity of our country under the Polk administration, and forever after. We have no politics among us here, and only make battle for our Republic against the unjust charges which the English are continually making on the subject of repudiation. They are determined to believe that we are all rascals and wish to cheat the world out of their money; there are very few who are generous or just enough to look upon our Government as any thing better than a band of pirates, who are disturbing the peace and happiness of the whole world."

Our Country One Hundred Years Ago.

I continue extracts from *B. Franklin's* Pennsylvania Gazette of 1749, nearly one hundred years since.

ADVERTISEMENTS.

"Edward Downs is removed from his house in Water street to his house in Front street, where Thomas Wells lately lived, and has to sell sundry sorts of European goods, and choice Cheshire Cheese, cheap for ready money."

"Dropt on Sunday, the 31st December last, between the drawbridge and the church, a fashionable silver stay hook, very neatly set with stones in the figure of a *true lover's* knot; whoever finds it, so that the owner may have it again, shall receive ten shillings reward, paid by Robert Warren."

"Ran away the 3d inst, from Samuel Swift of Bustletown, an Irish servant man, named Roger Flanagan, [sandy complexion, short hair, and is used to *tumbling and antic tricks* &c. &c.

N. B. He will probably pass for a chimney sweeper."

Among dry goods articles, I find a string of goods almost impossible now to identify with modern fabrics. Padnasoy, valures, poplin, none so pretties, tandems, pennistones, romals, pistol lawns, hairbines, yard wide garlix, gulix, holland starrits, tammies, camblettees, cushlas, dorsiteens, grassets, durants, ducapes, cheverets, baladine silk, brillions, grandurets, florettas, tabines, saggathies, chinconnes, Lemaners, cherryderries, silveretts, serpentines, paranellas, Paragons, horrations, &c." I presume the oldest survivor cannot tell what these articles were.

It appears by an advertisement of that date that 2 per cent was charged by the vessels sailing for London, on the amount of money remitted from Philadelphia to that city.

"Peter Knowlton, Free fan maker, from London, in Sassafras street, near the Moravian meeting, makes, mends, mounts and setts, wholesale and retail, all sorts of fans and fansticks, and *makes short fans longer*" by piecing I suppose. "He likewise cuts and sells corks of all kinds."

"The charter of the borough of Trenton, being surrendered, and the said surrender accepted by his Excellency, in the following words:

'By his excellency JONATHAN BELCHER, Esq.; Captain General and Governor in chief, in and over his majesty's province of Nova Caesarea, or New Jersey, and territories thereon depending in America, Chancellor and Vice Admiral in the same, &c.

Having perused and considered the within instrument of surrender of the charter for incorporating the town of Trenton, I do therefore in behalf of his most sacred majesty accept the same. Dated at the city of Burlington, in the said province, this ninth day of April, in the twenty-third year of his majesty's reign, 1750.
JONATHAN BELCHER.

Public notice therefore, is hereby given to all persons, to prevent their trouble and attendance upon the fairs, which will not be held as usual."

Force of Ridicule.

An application was lately made to the Legislature of Alabama, for a charter to a Botanico Medical College at Wetumpka, in that State. The Bill for that purpose had gone to its third reading with every prospect of its final passage, when a story told by one of the members, with great gravity and much comic effect, did for it what all the arguments of its apponents failed to accomplish, and gave it its *quietus*.

The Mobile Register gives the narrative thus:

"After Speaker Moore and others had made able speeches in support of the bill, Mr. Morrisett from Monroe, took the floor. You know him. He is an odd *genius*, and withal has good *horse sense*, (as his colleague, Mr. Howard, calls it,) and often speaks to the point and with effect. With an imperturbable gravity, he addressed the House in substance as follows:—"Mr. Speaker, I cannot support this bill, unless I am assured that a *distinguished* acquaintance of mine is made one of the *Professors*. He is what that College wishes to make for us—a *root doctor*, and will suit the place *exactly*. He became a doctor in two hours, and it only cost $20 to complete his education. He bought a book, sir, and read the chapter on fevers, and that was enough. He was sent for to see a sick woman—a *very sick* woman. With his book under his arm, off he went. Her husband and their son John were in the room with the sick woman. The Doctor felt of her wrist and looked in her mouth, and then took off his hat. 'Has you got,' addressing the husband, 'a sorrel sheep?' 'No, I never heard of such a thing in all my life.' 'Well, there *is* such things,' said the doctor very knowingly. 'Has you got then a sorrel horse?' 'Yes,' said

John, quickly, 'I rode him to mill to-day.' 'Well, he must be killed immediately' said the doctor, 'and some *soup* must be made and given to your wife.' The poor woman turned over in her bed. John began to object, and the husband was brought to a stand. Why, doctor, he is the only horse we've got, and he is worth $100, and will not some other soup do as well?' 'No, the book says so, and there is but two questions—will you kill your horse, or let your wife die? Nothing will save her but the soup of a sorrel sheep or a sorrel horse. If you don't believe me I will read it to you.' The doctor took up the book, turned to the chapter on fevers and read as follows:—'Good for fevers—sheep sorrel, or horse sorrel.' 'Why, doctor,' exclaimed husband, wife and son, 'you are mistaken, that don't mean a sorrel sheep, or a sorrel horse; but'—'Well, I know what I am about,' interrupted the doctor, 'that's the way we doctors read it, and we understands it.' Now,' said Mr. Morrisett, with an earnestness and gravity that were in striking contrast with the laughter of the House, 'unless the Hon. Speaker and the friends of this bill will assure me that my sorrel doctor will be one of the Professors, I must vote against the bill.' It is unnecessary to add, that after this blow, the bill never kicked. It was effectually killed.

Air Tight Preservers.

The manufacture of air-tight tin cases for preserving lobsters, oysters, turkeys, and almost any other article of food, is a great business at Eastport, Me. The mode of sealing them up, after the air has been exhausted by an air-pump, is kept a secret—no one being admitted to that part of the establishment.—*N. B. Bulletin.*

We will let out the secret and save the use of the air pump. The case or can containing the substance to be preserved, is set in a vessel of boiling water and made to boil. In this state, while the *steam* excludes *all* the air, (which an air-pump could not well do,) the operator instantly closes the orifice by soldering on a small tin button provided for the purpose. The can is of course removed from the boiling water at the instant of the soldering. Where meats are preserved, they are introduced into the cans before the head is soldered on. It is a small hole in the head which is finally closed while the contents are boiling.

In a similar way fruits may be preserved in bottles without sugar, for an indefinite time. Put them in with water, cause it to boil, and while boiling cork tightly, and then secure the cork with air-tight cement. Green corn, green peas, &c. &c., may be had in winter in absolute freshness and perfection by this process. Those who have never seen it will be surprised to be told that roast meats and soups may be had in perfection five years after their cooking. But such is the fact.—*Emancipator.*

The Hunting Shirt.

The Hunting Shirt, the emblem of the Revolution, is banished from the national military, but still lingers among the hunters and pioneers of the far West. The national costume, properly so called, was adopted in the outset of the Revolution, and was recommended by Washington to his army, in the most eventful period of the War of Independence. It was a favorite garb with many of the line, particularly the gallant Colonel Josiah Parker.

When Morgan's Riflemen, made prisoners at the assault in Quebec in 1775, were returning to the South to be exchanged, the British garrisons on the route beheld with wonder these sons of the mountain and the forest. Their hardy looks, their tall athletic forms, their marching always in Indian file, with the light and noiseless step peculiar to their pursuit of woodland game; but above all, to European eyes, their singular picturesque costume, the Hunting Shirt, with its fringes, the wampum belts, leggins and moccasins, richly worked with the Indian ornaments of beads and porcupine quills of brilliant and varied dyes, the tomahawk and knife; these, with the well known death-dealing of these matchless marksmen, created in the European military a degree of awe and respect for the Hunting Shirt, which lasted with the war of the Revolution.

Washington Fashions.

I do not know that I have told you the *short hand* way of visiting, people have here, and especially the great people. When a new Congressman arrives, he will be astonished at the number of cards he will find on the parlor table for him during a day. The first thought is, well, I have had a great many calls to day. The next, I must have been in when some of them came, and why did not the servants call me? These thoughts will first suggest themselves to a stranger. But upon inquiring, he will find no man has been at his house at all. This is accounted for on the *short hand* principle of visiting, which is this: A man sits in his room writing a letter, as I now am; and, whilst he is at work at home, a negro boy is out leaving his cards to such as he pleases to send them. By and by the compliment is returned, and thus great men visit and are visited without losing time. When one visits another in person and finds him absent, he leaves his card with p. p. in one corner (proper person.) This leaves the inference that he called on business. But the social visits are all made by a negro boy with cards.

As a take off to this cold formality, the Western new members have carried the joke still further; and have large cards with the picture of a splendid dinner table, groaning under the weight of turkies, quails, oysters, pies, wines, &c. &c. engraved upon them. These they send about, and they take admirably well, and rumor says, in former days, this western fashion was introduced into the most fashionable circles of N. Y. Thus, if A sends B a card for a visit, B sends back his for a dinner. This, you see, is saving expense as well as time. Yesterday and to-day, some improvements have been made.—Night before last, at a large party, a lady of excellent talent, worth and beauty, was heard to say she was fond of riding in cabs. So, up to this hour, honorable gentlemen are sending her their cards with the picture of a beautiful cab and horse upon it. To each she sends back her card, which is as much as to say, "I fancy myself riding in a cab with you."

One more observation of the fashions here.— By every man's plate is a glass bowl, about the size of those we eat pudding and milk out of when at home. In each of these, there is about a tumbler of water and a bit of lemon, about the size to make a good whiskey punch. Now what are these for? For nothing but to wet your fingers and lips with, so as to keep them clean and give them a good flavor. Some of our plain republicans will say this is worse than the cards.

Not long since, a gentleman, unacquainted with the custom, took his bowl and began to drink; and, not finding it palatable, he called out, "Waiter, curse your lemonade, put some sugar in it." The negro laughed, his neighbors laughed, and finally the whole table was in a roar, and he cleared for the bar-room.

Scene in a School Room.

'Class in history, step up. Are you ready on the questions?'
'Yeth 'ir.'
'Billy who was the first hunter?'
'Noah.'
'Why?'
'Cause he collected all the beasts and birds and fishes into the ark, so as to save 'em from being drowned.'
'Not exactly, but that will do for you. Harvy Diggs.'
'Yeth, 'ir.'
'Bring up your composition. What subject did I give you?'
'Here it ith, 'ir;' composition on wales and wale fisheries. Wales are a mountanious country in the continent of England. Wale fisheries principally go out from New Bedford and Nantucket round Cape Horner, which is crooked and hard to navigate; the people of Wales are called walemen. and toasted cheese are called Welsh rabbits, ar near as I can remember. There is no more about Wales except whale bones and'——
'Go to your seat, or I'll whale you! Silence! Begin writing class.'
'May I get a drink, thir?'
'No.'
'Well, I swow I can't write any, cause my mouth is so dry.'

The British Pharmocopoeia;

OR, FARMER'S FIRST LESSON IN CHEMISTRY.

A class has been formed at a place down in Hampshire—[Punch does not feel called upon to speak more explicitly]—for the study of Agricultural Chemistry. The plan of instruction is catechetical. The following lesson is founded on the responses, as reported to Punch by his own correspondent, delivered at one of its recent meetings. Mistakes, they say, afford often a valuable lesson. If so, it is hoped that the lesson subjoined will be of great value:—
"Chemistry is keepun" a doctor's shop. An atom is a mossel o' zummit; a bit o' dust or zand loike. The weight of an atom is the heft on un. Light is accordun as it med be; day-light, moon-light, or candle light. Heat is that are as comes out o' the vire."
To the question, "What are the phenomena of heat?" the reply was, "Douan't 'zackly know what you manes, zur."]
"The effect of heat is, rooastun mate, bilin' 'taaters; burnin' your vingers if you gets too cleoase to 't. Lightning is a thunderbolt fallin' out 'o the clouds; a thunderbolt is thing like a clinker. An acid is any sort o' zour stuff like vinegar or varjus. An alkali is a voreign-eerun name vor zummut or other, may be for a pig.—Potash is ashes from under pot. Soda is stuff as washerwomen uses. Ammonia is one o' them fine names as your gentlefolks gives their daaters. If you put zulphuric acid to lime, and makes zulphate o' lime, why, of course, if you

adds it to wuts (oats.) you gets sulphate o' wuts. A simple body means a zimpleton, like Zilly Billy at the Poorus. The laws of Chemical Union is like the laws of any other Union, pretty strictish, and o' coorse every Chemical Union has got a Beadle. Chemical Affinity, Attraction, Cohesion, Composition, Decomposition, Analysis, Synthesis, is a parcel of outlandish gibberish. Justus Liebig is zome Vrenchman."
The foregoing statements, we imagine, exhibit some slight discrepancy with the views of Faraday; but as the agricultural mind expands, its ideas of chemical science will very likely become rather more accurate.

Powers the Sculptor.

We were favored by a friend, yesterday, with the perusal of a letter from Florence, Italy, of a late date which thus makes mention of our native sculptor, Powers:
"Powers is now in a fair way to place himself above want. Commissions are flowing in upon him from right quarters, and of the right kind. He has sold the statue of the Greek Slave to Mr. Grant, and it will go to London in a few weeks to be exhibited in a private manner to the best of society. He has already an order for a duplicate of it from Lord Ward, a very rich nobleman, and there is a talk of another from a person of rank in London. The statue is favorably known in the polite circles of Europe, and few think of passing through Florence without calling to look at "Power's Slave," and all who see it, speak of it in the most rapturous terms. My own opinion is, that Powers is the greatest living sculptor; but as I have always thought so much of his talents, I may be said to be prejudiced. There are others, nevertheless, who think the same thing, and say it, too. It is probable you will have a sight of the works next year, as he intends taking the "Eve," and a duplicate of the "Slave" to America for exhibition. I can promise you a treat in beholding them. Such works of art have never been seen in the New World, for they are not overshadowed, even here, by the fame of the Venus de Medicis in the Tribune.

Transcendentalism.

What has become of our "Cincinnati Dental Surgery College?" Or is the science to flourish here as almost every thing else does best, on its own responsibility.
After all that we hear of transcendental science in Germany or Boston, it is nothing there to transcend dental science in Cincinnati. Professors Kant, Emerson, and Brownson, cannot in this respect, hold candles to Professors Taylor, Cook, and Allen of our City.

DEATHS.

IN this city, on Saturday the 15th inst, JOHN NEWTON ELLIOT, aged 19 years.

On Sunday the 16th inst., WILLIAM T. TRUMAN, aged 36 years.

Same day, GEORGE W BOTTELL, aged 2 years.

Same day, SIMEON B. STURGESS, aged 43 years, of Consumption.

On Monday the 17th inst, ELIZABETH RAMSEY, in the sixth year of her age.

Same day, MARY A. H. RINGOLD, aged 5 years.

Relics of the War of 1812.

Joseph Carpenter, whose name is connected with the following documents, was the publisher of the WESTERN SPY & HAMILTON GAZETTE, the first regularly printed journal, issued in Cincinnati. He commenced its publication, May 28th, 1799. He commanded a company during the war of 1812, and after doing duty in that capacity during the campaign of 1813, under the immediate command of Genl. Harrison, he sunk under the severe privations and sufferings endured under a forced march from Fort St. Mary's, during mid winter, and was buried in this city, with appropriate military honors, and an unprecedented attendance of his fellow citizens at the grave.

CINCINNATI, Dec. 24th, 1816.

I do hereby certify that Captain Joseph Carpenter served under my command a six months tour of duty in the service of the United States, in the year 1813 and 1814, and died on his way from Fort Meigs to Urbana, before he was discharged from the service. And I do further certify, that the said Captain Carpenter commanded his company with high reputation as an officer, and rendered essential service to his country,—and the officer who inspected his company at Fort Winchester, reported to me that they were as well disciplined as any militia he ever saw in service. The muster rolls &c. in the war office, will be further evidence that the said Captain-Joseph Carpenter, was in the service of the United States.

JOHN S. GANO, Major Gen'l,
Commanding 1st. Division Ohio Militia.

FT. WINCHESTER, Feb. 5, 1813.

DEAR SIR:—

Although I sent you a scrap a few days ago, informing you of my arrival at this place. Yet having an opportunity of conveyance as far as Ft. Meigs, which seldom occurs, and believing it would be satisfaction to you, frequently to hear from the numerous posts under your command, that all's well, has induced me to write again.

The Indian Chief of whom I informed you, came to this place, and after some difficulty proceeded on to Dayton, where I am told a great number from different tribes have gone. The total number of Indians in the neighborhood of this place, to whom I have issued flour, is a little upwards of one hundred, including men, wo men and children—more are daily expected.

As the time for which we were ordered out will soon expire, I beg leave to enquire, is any arrangement made or making to relieve us; the anxiety of the men to get home is such, that I fear, unless they arrive previous to that day, or a certainty of it in a day or two after, the garrison will be evacuated, (myself and two or three others excepted)—and there are a very considerable quantity of stores at this place. I am very anxious to hear from you on this subject. I had flattered myself that I should be able to persuade *many* of them to stay a short time, after theexpiration of six months, but I fear, I am almost sure I have deceived myself in that respect. You know yourself, sir, how militia have heretofore acted, and can judge from that how they will act in future. Genl. Harrison, with all his influence, added to the promise of additional pay, could induce them not to stay a day after their times expired, even though (as he called them) they were *"my own Kentuckians."*

Capt. S. Vance of Cincinnati, is with us where he has spent several days, which has made the time pass off very pleasantly; he desires me to make you his compliments. He has sent out a supply of groceries and other articles, which we much needed, and has paid us four months, which enables us to live like nabobs.

Please remember me to Meek and Vance—— and accept, sir, my warmest wishes for your welfare and happiness.

J. CARPENTER, Capt. &c.
GENL. JOHN S. GANO, Com'd O. Militia.

Relics of the Past.

Until within a few days, I was not aware that any enumeration of the buildings in Cincinnati prior to 1815 had been made. The following documents brought me from New Orleans serve to shew that the buildings had been counted at an earlier date, and as seems probable by the statistics of population during the census taking of 1810. There exists no stronger evidence of changes here within 35 years, than the fact that in a community of 388 houses; there were 230 spinning wheels, which, if the number of those buildings were reduced to dwelling houses, would nearly furnish a spinning wheel for each family. *Where are these wheels?* I doubt if there be one in employment, or even existence. *Spinning wheels* are turned to *spinning jennys*, and woolen yarn to *street yarn.*— Indeed there are more pianos in Cincinnati now than there were spinning wheels in 1810, without much being gained to the community by the change, even if we look to the poetry and pictorial bearing alone of the subject, the spinning wheel giving a grace and picturesque outline and effect to female loveliness, which no piano can impart.

But to the documents. This appears to be written out on a card being one of several cards to be used in schools in those primitive days when "geographys" were scarce. These cards or tablets were made out by a schoolmas-

194

ter who once resided here, of the name of Dow, a brother of the famous *Lorenzo,* and equally full of eccentricities. He removed afterwards to New Orleans, in which city he died lately.— The cards were sent to this place as objects of local interest, and are published as such.   *

Cincinnati.

Cincinnati is a flourishing post town in the State of Ohio. It stands on the North Bank of the Ohio river, opposite the mouth of Licking river, 2½ miles South West of Fort Washington; and about 8 miles westerly of Columbia. Both these towns lie between Great and Little Miami rivers. Cincinnati contained about 300 houses in 1810. It is 80 miles North of Frankfort; 90 North West of Lexington, and 770 West by South of Philadelphia. Some persons, a short time since in digging a well, on the hill, in this town, at the depth of 90 feet came to the stump of a tree, the roots of which were so sound that they had to be cut away with an axe: at 94 feet, they came to another, which still bore evident marks of the axe; and on its top, there appeared as if some iron tool had been consumed by rust. Cincinnati lies in North Latitude 39 degrees 22, and West Longitude 86 degrees 44'

You all, well remember Master Thomas Fosdick, who used to live in New London. He is now in Cincinnati on the Ohio. Not long since, he sent a Schedule of the Census taken in that town. The following is a copy of it. The number of

Frame houses,---------------- 242
Log houses, -------------- 55
Brick houses,------------------- 86
Stone houses,------- ---------- 14

Total -------------------- 388 houses.
Number of looms 31—spinning wheels 230. Woolen cloth made the year past, 755 yds. Cotton cloth 2967 yds. Linen cloth 2098 yds. Mixt cloth 685 yds, Total 6480 yds.
Inhabitants under 10 years -------- 387 males
365 females
Over ten and under 16------------ 167 males
142 females
Over 16 and under 26------------- 286 males
241 females
Over 26 and under 45------------- 297 males
217 females
Over 45----------------------------- 106 males
78 females
Whole number of males------ ------------ 1227
Whole number of females---------------- 1043
Whole number of Blacks--------------- 80

Whole number of all------------------- 2340

Salamander Safes.

Charles Urban of our City, who has been manufacturing Lever locks for some time past, at the corner of Western Row and Third streets,

has lately added a new article to the existing variety in our Cincinnati manufactures, namely that of IRON SAFES.

Iron safes are so well known among business men as well as familiarised, and indispensible to their use, that I deem it unnecessary to make a detailed description of these, farther than to say, that they are of the kind termed *Salamanders,* being made on the same principle as well as pattern; as the celebrated WILDER N. York Safes. Indeed Mr. Urban has workmen from that very establishment in his employ.

These Salamander safes are made of stout, wrought bar and plate iron, rivited together in the most substantial manner, and lined with a chemical preparation, which is a non-conductor of heat, and is indestructible by fire. The locks which are on the combination principle, not only defy picking, but cannot be opened, even by their own keys, unless in the owner or maker's own hands.

There is one circumstance respecting safes for mercantile use to which it is proper to advert. It is easy to put iron together in closet form, so as to resemble externally a safe, which at the same time, shall furnish not one particle of protection to its contents in case of fire. There is an article of that very description made in Pittsburgh, for sale in this city. The great fire of 1835 in New York tested this matter to its full extent, by the destruction of every safe except the *Salamander.* And still later at the fire which destroyed the TRIBUNE office a few days ago, one of the Salamander safes in which were lodged, the books of accounts and papers of value in that establishment, maintained its trust with honor, while the forwarding mail books and other papers of less value, which were deposited in the ordinary safe, were found reduced to ashes.

The following testimony of the perfect indestructibility by fire of the composition with which these safes are lined is from Hunt's Merchants' Magazine, May 1843.

"A piece of the composition with which the safes are lined, about six inches square and two in thickness, was laid on a blacksmith's forge, and the full and constant force of the bellows applied to it for the space of about ten minutes, when it was found to have resisted the fire so effectually that we laid our naked hand on it, feeling only a gentle warmth. On turning it over, the part next to the fire did not retain heat enough to burn a card or light a paper; while a bar of iron in the forge about half the time was heated to whiteness. This experiment, simple as it is, must convince every one who may witness it, as it did us at the time, that a safe filled with three or four inches of this material could not be heated through at the burning of a store in any possible situation in which it might be placed.

Some of our first merchants have witnessed similar experiments, and have expressed their entire confidence as to the security of this safe. With these facts in view, we cordially commend the article to the attention of merchants and bankers, and to the State and county authorities throughout the Union, who desire to render secure the valuable papers committed to their charge."[1]

Mr. Urban, I learn, sells his safes at low prices compared with the Eastern article, the smallest size not costing more than 70 dollars.

The SALAMANDER SAFES are for sale, I perceive, at W. & R. P. Resor's, Main st.

Early Records.
Line of March and Encampment of Gen. Harmar's Army.

ORDER OF MARCH.

SPIES AND GUIDES.

ADVANCE COMPANY.

PIONEERS.

McMULLIN'S BATTALION OF MILITIA.

CAVALRY.   CAVALRY.

AMMUNITION.

OFFICERS, BAGGAGE, &c.

FLOUR AND SALT.

CATTLE.

MAJ. PAUL'S PENNSYLVANIA MILITIA.   FLANK.

FLANK.   MAJ. RAY'S BATTALION MILITIA.

HALL'S BATTALION OF MILITIA.

REAR GUARD.

Order of Encampment.

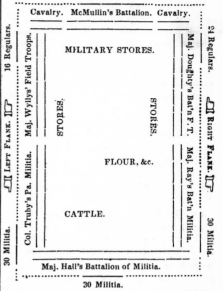

FRONT GUARD. of 30 Militia.

Cavalry. McMullin's Battalion. Cavalry.

16 Regulars. 24 Regulars.

Maj. Wyllys' Field Troops.

Maj. Doughty's Bat'n F. T.

MILITARY STORES.

LEFT FLANK. RIGHT FLANK.

Col. Truby's Pa. Militia. STORES. STORES. Maj. Ray's Bat'n Militia.

30 Militia. 30 Militia.

FLOUR, &c.

CATTLE.

Maj. Hall's Battalion of Militia.

30 Militia.

The daily movements of Harmar's army are recorded in a manuscript journal, kept by Capt. John Armstrong of the regulars as follows.

"September 30, 1790—the army moved from Fort Washington, at half past 10 o'clock, A. M. marched about seven miles, N. E. course—hilly, rich land. Encamped on a branch of Mill creek.

October 15th—took up the line of march at half past 8 o'clock—passed through a level rich country, watered by many small branches, waters of Mill Creek. At 2 o'clock halted one hour; and at 4 o'clock halted for the evening, on small branch of Mill Creek, having marched about eight miles: general course, a little to the westward of North.

October 2d—moved forty-five minutes after 7 o'clock; marched about ten miles a north west course. The first five miles of this day's march was over a dry ridge to a lick; then five miles through a low swampy country to a branch of the waters of the Little Miami, where we halted one hour; and forty-five minutes after 1 o'clock moved on for five miles a N. E., E. and S. E. course, and encamped in a rich and extensive bottom, on Muddy Creek a branch of the Little Miami. This day's march, fifteen miles, and one mile from Col. Hardin's command.

October 3d—the army at 8 o'clock, passed Col. Hardin's camp and halted at Turtle Creek, about ten yards wide, where we were joined by Col. Hardin's command. Here the line of march was formed—two miles.

October 4th—The army moved at half past 9 o'clock—passed through a rich country (some places broken) a N. E. course, and at 3 o'clock crossed the Little Miami, about forty yards wide: moved up it one mile, a north course to a branch called Sugar Creek—encamped nine miles.

October 5th—the army moved from Sugar Creek forty-five minutes after nine o'clock; marched through a level country a N. E. course up the Little Miami, having it often in view. The latter part of this day's march, through low glades, or marshy land. Halted at 5 o'clock on Glade Creek, a very lively clear stream—ten miles.

October 6th—the army moved ten minutes after 9 o'clock. The first five miles the country was brushy and somewhat broken; reached Chillicothe, an old Indian village; re-crossed the Little Miami; at half past one o'clock halted one hour, and encamped at 4 o'clock on a branch—nine miles a N. E. course.

Oct. 7th—the army moved at 10 o'clock; the country brushy four miles, and a little broken until we came on the waters of the Great Miami—passed through several low prairies, and crossed the Pickaway fork or Mad river, which is a clear lively stream, about forty yards wide; the bottom extensive and very rich. Encamped on a small branch one mile from the former; our course the first four miles north, then north-west—nine miles.

Oct. 8th—The army at half past nine o'clock; passed over rich land, in some places a little broken; passed several ponds, and through one small prairie, a N. W. course—seven miles.

Oct. 9th—the army moved at half past nine o'clock; passed through a level rich country, well watered; course N. W.; halted half past 4 o'clock, two miles south of the Great Miami—ten miles.

Oct. 10th—the army moved forty-five minutes after nine o'clock; crossed the Great Miami; at the crossing there is a handsome high prairie on the S. E. side; the river about forty yards wide two miles further, a N. W. course, passed through a large prairie. Halted on a large branch of the Great Miami at half past three o'clock, the country level and rich; the general course, N. W.—ten miles.

Oct. 11—the army moved at half past nine o'clock; marched a north-west course, seven miles to a branch where French traders formerly had a number of trading houses; thence a N. course four miles, to a small branch, and encamped at 5 o'clock. The country we passed over is very rich and level—eleven miles.

Oct. 12th—the army moved at half past nine o'clock; our course a little to the west and north west; crossed a stream at seven miles and a half, running north-east, on which there are several old camps, and much deadened timber, which continues to the river Auglaize, about a

mile. Here has been a considerable village, some houses still standing. This stream is a branch of the Omi [Maumee] river, and is about 20 yards wide. From this village to our encampment our course was a little to the north of west. Rich, level land—fourteen miles.

Oct. 13—the army moved at 10 o'clock; just before they marched, a prisoner was brought in, and Mr. Morgan from Fort Washington joined us; we marched to the west of north-west, four miles to a small stream, through low swampy land; then a course a little to the north of west, passing through several small prairies and open woods to an Indian village on a pretty stream.—Here we were joined by a detachment from Fort Washington, with ammunition—ten miles.

Oct. 14th—At half past ten in the morning, Col. Hardin was detached for the Miami village, with one company of regulars and six hundred Militia, and the army took up its line of march at 11 o'clock; a north-west course; four miles, a small branch—the country level—many places drowned lands in the winter season—ten miles.

Oct. 15th—the army moved at 8 o'clock, north west course two miles, a small branch; then north a little west, crossing a stream, three miles north-west course. The army halted at half past one o'clock, on a branch running west—eight miles.

Oct. 16th—the army moved at forty-five minutes after 8 o'clock, marched nine miles and halted, fifteen minutes after one o'clock. Passed over a level country, not very rich.—Col. Hardin with his command took possession of the Miamitown yesterday, (15th) at 4 o'clock —the Indians having left it just before—nine miles.

Oct. 17th—the army moved at fifteen minutes after 8 o'clock, and at 1 o'clock crossed the Maumee river to the village. The river is about seventy yards wide; a fine transparent stream. The river St. Joseph, which forms the point on which the village stood, is about twenty yards wide; and when the waters are high, navigable a great way up it.

On the 18th, I was detached, with thirty men under the command of Col. Trotter. On the 19th Col. Hardin commanded in lieu of Colonel Trotter; attacked about one hundred Indians, fifteen miles west of the Miami village, and from the dastardly conduct of the militia, the troops were obliged to retreat—I lost one sergeant, and twenty-one out of thirty men of my command. The Indians on this occasion gained a complete victory, having killed in the whole, near one hundred men, which was about their own number. Many of the militia threw away their arms without firing a shot, ran through the federal troops & threw them in disorder. Many of the Indians must have been killed, as I saw my men bayonet many of them. They fought and died hard."

On the morning of the 19th, the main body of the army under Gen. Harmar, having destroyed the Miami village, moved about two miles to a Shawnee village called Chillicothe, where on the 20th, the General published the following order.

"Camp, at Chillicothe, one of the Shawnee towns on the Omee [Maumee] river, October 20th 1790.

The party under the command of Captain Strong, is ordered to burn and destroy every house and wigwam in "this village, together with all the corn, &c., which he can collect. A party of one hundred men, (militia) properly officered, under command of Col. Hardin, is to burn and destroy effectually this afternoon, the Pickaway town with all the corn, &c. which he can find in it and its vicinity.

The cause of the detachment being worsted yesterday, was entirely owing to the shameful, cowardly conduct of the Militia who ran away, and threw down their arms without firing scarcely a single gun. In returning to Fort Washington, if any officer or men shall presume to quit the ranks, or not to march in the form that they are ordered, the General will, most assuredly order the artillery to fire on them. He hopes the check they received yesterday will make them in future obedient to orders."

JOSIAH HARMAR,
Brig. Gen.

LADIES' DEPARTMENT.

The Hydrangea--Hydrangea Hortensea.
BY T. WINTER.

This is another of our universal favorite flowers, which is to be found in the humble dwelling of the poor, as well as the mansion of the wealthy aristocrat. This much esteemed flower was first introduced into the King of England's garden at Kew, about sixty years since, and was imported from China by Sir J. Banks. The flower of this perennial rooted plant in its primitive state, is of azure blue, but cultivation has wrought a change in their colour. It does not fall to our lot to see them of their natural color, which necessarily incapacitates us to judge correctly, if their culture be in reality an improvement or not. The circumstances of its turning blue so seldom makes one of that cast truly desirable. The first I have seen in this country, was at Mr. Jackson's establishment several years since, and no doubt the composition he used, was what is usually found in the ravines in the woods, the free country air combined had the desirable effect in causing his plants to appear so magnificent; this is not attainable with us in this city, consequently no one need expect

to raise flowers of any description to compete with nurserymen in the country. I am inclined to believe that plants raised in the city, will do better with us than those procured from the country. I am more fully convinced of this as I have procured several plants at different times of Mr. Barnard, and with the greatest difficulty, could get them to live, as some would dwindle away and finally die; and I have heard others complain of the same thing. I do not mention this to injure nurserymen in the country, but would feel much pleased in being corrected. If my theory be not correct,—I have tried several compositions to change the color of the hydrangea, but without effect. The hydrangea is one of the few that appears to thrive, even when no care is taken of them, still I would not advise or advocate such looseness in any person that has the least pretention to the culture of flowers. I recollect an anecdote of an nurseryman in London, that was celebrated for selling blue hydrangeas which commanded a great price for several years, but all at once his stock run out, he had none but pink colored ones. It appeared in the sequel, that he had purchased several loads of peat soil with which he potted his plants, little suspecting the effect the quality of soil would produce in his flowers. When the blooming season arrived he was agreeably surprised at the effect; this induced him to keep the balance expressly for that purpose, and so long as any of his soil lasted he could meet all demands. To his mortification he could not find the man he purchased of, neither could he get any soil to produce the same effect. consequently he was like Othello, "his occupation gone." I have no doubt, from the plant being succulent, that soil procured from marshy grounds, dried and sifted would be good. It is said that iron filings will turn the color of the flowers; if such be the case, why would not a yellow sandy loam of redish cast be good, which contains a certain portion of iron? This is easily to be obtained from the brick yards. Turf laid by for a year to rot is a good composition mixed with rotten leaves. In short the plant will grow in almost any soil, but the color is difficult to change.—The hydrangea is of easy culture, and will strike root at any time with the exception of when in a state of rest, this is from the time the leaf begins to drop until the buds swell in the spring. The best time to pot the plants, is the beginning of March, and instead of shaking the soil from the roots as with most plants; take a large knife and cut the roots off, leaving a ball in the centre containing the main body to the size of the large apple, then take your compost and fill the pot, placing the ball with the plant in the centre. I would not advise a large pot, as it would be better in the month of June to shift the plant without disturbing the root into a pot larger. By adopting this plan your plant will become thrifty and bloom more beautifully with a larger head of flowers, a desideratum every way to lovers of good flowers. I would also recommend those plants from their possessing such a desire for water in the summer, to stand them in pans made on purpose, and fill them every day and keep them in the shade for the sun will make them flag. The beginning of October take the plants out of the pans and water them sparingly until the middle of November, then place them in a cellar, and water a little once in two weeks until March, when you may bring them forward to give air, and re-pot them, giving every encouragement to grow, but you must keep them away from the frost. The hydrangea is hardy and will stand out all the winter with a slight protection, but will flower better if kept in the house. Mr. Longworth has a great many planted round his house, and stands the winter with a slight protection, and after a mild winter will flower vigorously. This plant is injured more by the sun than by frost, but will be more judicious in avoiding either. In case your plant should get frosted in the spring through neglect put it in a box and exclude the light until the frost be well out of your plant, then no ill affect will result from it.

Health of Cincinnati.

I have already referred to the fact of the salubrity of Cincinnati as repeatedly illustrated, by ascertaining the proportion of survivors to a given list of names in any document of the past.— The following is a card of invitation to a Ball given at the *Columbian Inn*, where Neff and Brothers, and Thomas H. Minor & Co. are now wholesaling hardware and groceries.

INDEPENDENCE BALL.
—◦✳◦—

The honor of Mrs. S———

COMPANY IS SOLICITED AT A BALL, TO BE HELD AT THE COLUMBIAN INN, ON FRIDAY EVENING NEXT, AT SEVEN O'CLOCK, IN COMMEMORATION OF THE BIRTH DAY OF

AMERICAN INDEPENDENCE.

FRANCIS CARR,		J. C. SHORT,
P. A. SPRIGMAN,	MANAG'RS	T.C.BARKER,
N.LONGWORTH,		W. IRWIN, jr.

June 30------[812.

Of these individuals after the lapse of thirty three years, four out of six of the managers signing this card still survive. As the average age of the survivors is over sixty, this fact speaks well for the temperate habits of these individuals as well as the health of the city.

The Origin of the Indian Tribes.

In my youth, having an ambition to acquire an Indian dialect, I took a few lessons of the Rev. Mr. Heckewelder in the *Lenni Lennape* or Delaware Indian tongue, but was soon driven from my purpose by the abundance of compound words, extending some times, to fifteen or twenty syllables, which seemed a barrier to my eye, no labor could overcome. At that period, I thought this lingual feature peculiar to the aborigines of our country, and attributed it to the fact that their language was undiluted with foreign admixtures. In later life, making some acquaintance with the German, a language which owes less perhaps, to other tongues than any European one, I found the same characteristic. For example, here is a single noun: *Steuerverweigerungsverfassungmaessigbescheinung*, meaning a man who is constitutionally exempt from the payment of taxes, and for a member of a theatrical association, the name of *Marionettenschauspielhausegesellschaftsmitglied*. Also, *Constantinopolitanischerschnupf tabacksdosenverkaeufer*, which stands for seller of a certain species of snuff boxes. Shall we infer from the above that the Indians and Germans have one common origin? If so, the *Dutch* are the *real natives*. I claim, at any rate, to have shed some light on the dark and doubtful question of Indian descent.

Another Pork Story.

MR. CIST:

By way of closing the pork season permit me to narrate a pork story, which I have not yet seen in your paper, although equally authentic with any which have appeared in its columns.

During the pork season a few years since JOHN HADLEY, of Wilmington, Ohio, well known is this market, contracted with a pork dealer in this city to supply him with 200,000 lbs. sides. One half of these, by special engagement, were to be delivered clear of the back bone, an extra price being paid accordingly; nothing was said of the residue, the purchaser of course expecting it would be cut as usual, part with the back bone and part without, as the bone might fall to the one or other side in dividing it. When the meat was delivered, that portion which commanded the extra price was found all right according to contract, but the other lot was made up, not as usual, half with and half without the back bone, but altogether of the other moiety left by the fulfilling of the first part of the contract. Hadley, by this *precious piece of finesse* cleared two or three hundred dollars, the purchaser submitting to the shave rather than carry the case into court.

Cincinnati Fifty Years Ago.

The man is still living, and in the full possession of his faculties, bodily and mental, who stood by surveying the first cellar-digging in Cincinnati. This was the cellar of the first brick house put up here, and which was built by the late Elmore Williams, at the corner of Main and Fifth streets. As one half of the community in that day had never seen a cellar, being emigrants from the farming districts, and the other half were surveying a novelty in Cincinnati, it may readily be conceived, there was no scarcity of onlookers. My informant gives it as his judgment, that the west half of the Wade dwelling on Congress street is the oldest building now standing in Cincinnati, certainly the only one remaining of what were built when he first saw the place. Most of the houses were log cabins, and hardly better, so he phrases it, "than sugar camps at that." The city when he landed, had not five hundred inhabitants. He has lived to behold its increase to 75,000.—Where will the next fifty years find it? The difference between Cincinnati as it now is, and its appearance fifty years ago, will be as nothing compared with the contrast between its present appearance, and its condition fifty years hence.

The Ohio Legislature.

It is known to some persons but not to the community at large, that a list is made at Columbus annually, of the members of the State Legislature, giving their names, post office addresses at home, their birth places, age, years in the state, occupation, and their condition as married or single. By the table for 1844-5, it appears that of the 108 members of both branches which compose that body, 28 are natives of Ohio, 24 of Pennsylvania, 14 of New York, 8 of Virginia, 8 of Connecticut, 5 of Maryland, 5 of Kentucky, 2 of each, Maine, New Hampshire, and New Jersey; 1 of District of Columbia. 104 native Americans. 2 natives of Ireland, 1 of Wales, and 1 of Germany, make up the residue. 62 are farmers, 22 are attornies at law, 6 are merchants, 5 are physicians, 2 are preachers, 2 are millers, and 2 are carpenters; of the residue there is one tanner, one gunsmith, one mill wright, one blacksmith, one printer, one laboror, one inn keeper, one saddler, and one iron founder. The ages vary from 29 to 76, of those not born in the State, most of them have been 25 to 35 years residents, quite a numher, four fifths of their lives. 100 are married men, 7 single, and 1 *engaged to be married.*

The proportion of New Englanders in the Legislature, though small, is larger than their proportion of countrymen among the constituents. New Englanders representing in all cases but one, the New England settled counties, and some five or six counties besides. The members of the Legislature, from other States of the Union, bear about the same proportion in that body, which the emigrants from those States bear respectively to the whole community. One member of German birth is no adequate representation of the large body of naturalized Germans in Ohio. Still the Legislature is as fairly a reptesentation of the various elements of society in this State, as they are of the community in other respects.

Want of Faith.

The defect of our times is the want of *faith.* We live in an age of reality. Every thing is to be accounted for and answered by return of post. The golden currency of enthusiasm has been called in. There is no reverence for any feature of truth behind the veil. Our temper resembles that of the Pundit who inquired of Henry Martyn whether, by embracing the Christian religion, he should behold the Deity in a visible shape. This eagerness to perceive every object without delay and impediment is a characteristic of minds which have not been accustomed to gaze at the luminary of truth, and might be rebuked by a Hebrew legend which we have read. 'You teach,' said the Emperor Trajan to a famous Rabbi, 'that your God is every where, and boast that he resides among your nation. I should like to see him.' 'God's presence is indeed, every where,' the Rabbi replied, 'but he cannot be seen, for no mortal eye can look upon His splendor.' The emperor had the obstinacy of power, and persisted in his demand. 'Well,' answered the Rabbi, 'suppose that we begin by endeavoring to gaze at one of His embassadors.' Trajan assented, and the Rabbi, leading him into the open air, for it was the noon of the day, bade him raise his eyes to the sun, then shining down upon the world in its meridian glory. The emperor made the attempt but relinquished it. 'I cannot,' he said, 'the light dazzles me.' 'If, then,' said the triumphing Rabbi, 'thou art unable to endure the light of one of His creatures, how canst thou expect to behold the unclouded glory of the Creator?' It is a beautiful and touching parable, and teaches humility, not only in religion, but literature and life.

Collecting a Bill.

A gentleman who had gone from New York to Boston to collect some money due him there, was about returning when he found that one bill of $100 had been overlooked. His landlord, who knew the debtor, thought it a doubtful case; but added, that if collectable at all, a tall Yankee, then dunning a lodger in another part of the room, would annoy it out of the man.—Calling him up, he introduced him to the creditor, who showed him the account.

"Wall Squire, 'taint much use trying, I gues. I know that critter. You might as well try to squeeze ile out of Bunker Hill Monument, as to try to collect a debt out of him. But, any how, what'll you give supposin' I do try?"

"Well, sir, the bill is $100. I'll give you—yes, I'll give you half, if you collect it."

"Agreed," replied the collector: "there's no harm in trying, any how."

"Some weeks after, the creditor happened to be in Boston, and in walking up Trenton street, he encountered his very enterprising friend.

"Look here!" said he, "I had considerable luck with that bill of your'n. You see, I stuck to him like a dog to a root, but the first week or two, it was'nt no use, not a bit. If he was home, he was short; if he was'nt home, I could get no satisfaction. By and by, says I, after going sixteen times, I'll fix ye; so I sot down on the door step and sot all day and part of the evening, and I began airly next morning, and about ten o'clock he gin in. He paid me MY HALF, and I gin him up the note!"

Old Times.

At a late Temperance Celebration in Boston, the Rev, Mr. Skinner gave the following statement of the cost of an ordination in Woburn, Mass. We remember some of these festivities, when a meeting house was raised to the top of the flute, violin, and instruments of many strings, and occasionally a sackbut:

"To Mr. Jonathan Poole, Esq., for subsisting the Ministers, messengers and gentlemen, at the time of Mr. Jackson's ordination over the Congregational Church, 1729:

	£.	s.	d.
To 433 dinners, at 2s. 6d a dinner,	54	2	6
To suppers and breakfasts, 179,	8	18	0
To keeping 32 horses 4 days,	3	0	0
To 6¼ barrels cider,	4	11	0
To 2 gallons of brandy and 2 gallons of rum,	1	16	0
To 25 gallons of wine,	9	10	0
To loaf sugar, lime juice and pipes,	1	15	0
	£83	12	6

The Quaker and the Lawyer.

"Friend Broadbrim," said a servant to a rich Quaker, who lived, no matter where, "we have no meat for dinner to-day."

'Why not,' asked the good Quaker.

'Because lawyer Foxcraft's dog stole it, and eat it.'

'Beware, Zephaniah, of bearing false witness against thy neighbor. Art thou sure it was friend Foxcraft's dog?'

'Yea, I saw it with my eyes, and it was Pinch-'om.'

'Upon what evil times have we fallen!' sighed the Quaker, as he wended his way to the lawyer's office. 'Friend Foxcraft,' said he, 'I want to ask thy opinion.'

The lawyer laid down his pen.

'Suppose, friend Foxcraft, that my dog had gone into my neighbor's pantry and stolen therefrom a leg of mutton, what ought I to do?'

"Pay for the mutton—nothing can be clearer.'

'Know, then, friend Foxcraft, that thy dog, Pinch'em, has stolen from my pantry a leg of mutton, of the value of four shillings and 'sixpence, which I paid for it in the market this morning.'

'Well, well, then it's my opinion that I must pay for it:' and having done so, the worthy friend turned to depart.

'Tarry a little,' cried the lawyer; 'thou owest me nine shillings for advice.'

'Then I must pay thee. I have touched pitcher, and been defiled.'

The Letter H in London.

The Humane petition of the letter H to the Inhabitants of London and its Environs.—The memorial of your unfortunate petitioner humbly showeth that, although conspicuous in *h*eraldry, and entitled to the first place in *h*onor, yet he has been by many of you most injuriously treated —spoiled in *h*ealth, driven from *h*ome, and refused a place, not H-only in your *h*ouses, but in every *h*ome, *h*ut or *h*amlet, within your control. You refuse your petitioner *h*elp, and cut *h*im off also from *h*ope, the last resource of the H-unfortunate. Your petitioner is one moment scorched in an H-oven, at the next frozen to death in an H-ice *h*ouse, and is tortured from one H-extremity to H-another. From the *h*ighest *h*ill you precipitate *h*im to the H-earth; you suspend *h*im in the H-air and plunge *h*im in the H-ocean. You relieve *h*im from *h*unger H-only by food which doctors *h*ave forbidden *h*im to approach, such as H-oysters, H-oranges, H-eels, H-apples, &c. &c. while you refuse that which they esteem proper, such as *h*ares, *h*ams, *h*errings, &c. Your petitioner deeply feeling these H-outrages, and the H-ignominy and H-irony to which he is subject, prays you will take him from H-exile and restore *h*im to *h*imself, discard *h*im from your H-eyes and restore *h*im to H-our *h*earts, and your petitioner as in duty bound, will H-ever feel most grateful.

Letter from Dr. W. Goforth.

FORT WASHINGTON, N. W. TER. }
Sept. 3d, 1791. }

"One of the Indian captives lately died at this place,—His Excellency Gov. St. Clair gave liberty to the rest to bury the corpse according to the custom of their nation; the mode is that the body be wrapped in a shroud, over which they put a blanket, a pair of moccasins on the feet, a seven days' ration by the side of the head, with other necessaries. The march from Fort Washington was very solemn; on their arrival at the grave, the corpse was let down, and the relatives immediately retired, an aged matron then descended into the grave, and placed the blanket according to rule, and fixed the provisions in such a manner as she thought would be handy and convenient to her departed friend; casting her eyes about to see if all was right, she found the deceased was barefoot, and inquired why they had omitted the moccasins? The white person who superintended the whole business, informed her that there were no good moccasins in the store, but by the way of amends they had put a sufficiency of leather into the knapsack to make two pairs, at the same time showing her the leather. With this she appeared satisfied, saying that her friend was well acquainted with making them."

"The county of Hamilton lies between the two Miami rivers. Just below the mouth of the Little Miami, is a garrison called Fort Miami; at a small distance below this garrison is the town of Columbia. About six miles from Columbia is the town of Cincinnati, which is the county seat of Hamilton, and here is erected *Fort Washington*, the head quarters of the Federal army. This Fort is pleasantly situated on the banks of the Ohio river. Seven miles below this, is a settlement of eighteen or twenty families called South Bend. About seven miles from this, also on the Ohio river, is the city of Miami, founded by the Hon. John Cleves Symmes. Twelve miles up the Great Miami is the settlement called Dunlap's Station; and twelve miles up the Little Miami, is a settlement called Covalt's Station. The number of militia in these places, according to the best accounts I have received, are—at Columbia, 200; Cincinnati, 150; South Bend, 20; City of Miami, 80; Dunlap's, 15, and at Covalt's, 20.

Bull Fighting in Buenos Ayres.

CINCINNATI, March 14. 1845.

MR. CIST:

I read the description in your last "Advertiser" of *Montes* and his bull fight with great interest, the more so having witnessed in South America, these spectacles so peculiar to Spaniards, both in the old and new worlds.— There are some things narrated in it, however, of which your readers cannot form an accurate idea from the narrative itself, such as the *bandilleras* for instance, and a few inaccuracies like the unfair stroke at the bull who is represented as pierced in the forehead, which is well known to be the last place to strike a blow at a bull to advantage, and is invulnerable to a sword. It is not on the forehead but behind the horns, where his blow must have been struck.— There it would kill instantly.

As it may be interesting to your readers, as well as inspire confidence in the narrative to read a sketch on this subject, drawn up by one of ourselves, I subjoin a few recollections of what I have seen at *Buenos Ayres*, not many years since.

These sports are not now tolerated in any of the South American republics, and their exhibitions was rare, even at the period to which I shall allude. I believe they have also gone into disuse in Spain itself. But at the proclamation of peace between the *Brazilian empire* under the reign of *Don Pedro* and the *Argentine republic* in 1829, amidst the excitement of that period licence was obtained by the people of *Buenos Ayres*, to celebrate the event by a bull fight outside the city, where an enclosure in the approved mode was prepared by digging a ditch a foot wide, in which posts were inserted about 7 feet high, leaning outwards, to which strips of 2 inch plank about 3 inches broad, at perhaps 18 inches apart were fastened as every thing else is done in that country, with strips of hides, where nails or spikes would be employed here. These rails answer a double purpose, serving at the same time to secure the posts to their place, and to afford a species of ladder for the escape of the Toreadors or bull fighters when pressed too closely. The enclosure or circus forms thus an inverted cone in appearance. From the tops of these posts, the seats and boxes constructed for the spectators continue back 30 or 40 feet, rising to the extreme edge of the amphitheatre, some 25 feet, forming in this mode sufficient accommodations for 15,000 or 20,000 spectators. The arena itself is generally from 160 to 175 feet diameter. Its centre is made sufficiently hard and smooth for this particular sport.— Two *reals*, our 25 ct. piece is the charge for a seat, and the seats are usually filled to their utmost capacity, such is the passion of the Span-

iards and their descendants, for this their characteristic national amusement. The whole circle of boxes, and seats are protected from the rays of the sun by appropriate awnings.

The bull being now introduced to the audience through a small door on one side of the circle, raises his head and snuffs the air to ascertain into what new world he has been, as it were by magic, introduced for the first time, scrutinizing the spectators around. Suddenly his eye catches the *picador*, mounted on horse, who has stationed himself within 15 feet of his antagonist. He dashes at him with the speed of lightning, apparently determined to catch the horse on his horns. Notwithstanding the well known skill, and self-possession of the *picador* or pikeman, *Antonio Perez* in this case, such is the vigor and rapidity of the onset, that every one trembles a moment for his safety. With a slight, and at the same time graceful motion of his *picana*, or pike of some fifteen long, and a spike at the end, which gave it something the appearance of a boatman's setting pole, he presses the barbed end against the upper edge of the neck before the withers of the animal, for the purpose of giving a slight deviation in the forward course of the bull, applying at the same instant, spurs to his horse, who springs perhaps ten feet ahead, by which the bull misses the horse three feet or more. Those who know any thing of the habits of this animal will understand all this, in the fact that a bull when he directs his attack at any object, never alters his course, but closes his eyes and drives forward to his purpose, as directly as a bullet from the rifle. When the force of the rush was thus spent, the bull stopped, looking back to see how his adversary had escaped, and evidently enraged in finding his calculations of course and distance had been foiled. The next object that presented itself to his view was the *Toreador*, of which there are four to relieve each other, if necessary, as it sometimes is. This is a man on foot dressed in small clothes or breeches, buttoned below the knees, flesh colored silk stockings, pink slippers, wearing short blue jacket, and fancy colored cap, with a piece three quarters of a yard square of scarlet cloth in his hand, the far corner on the upper side attached to a cane, and the corner opposite held up by his left hand to the edge also of the cane holding it thus immediately in his front. When the bull is within some twenty feet of him, the animal makes his plunge. The *toreador* maintains his position without moving a limb until his opponent is within four feet of him, when he steps nimbly aside without moving the flag or scarlet cloth, which receives and of course yields to the plunge. As soon as the bull passes the object and finds he has missed his antagonist, he turns around and discovers himself faced by another toreador. His purpose and execution take place in the same instant. He rushes to the onset, as though he would sweep his new opponent before him without the possibility of escape. The toreador eludes the blow as before, and as the bull passes he plants a banderilla in his back or side. This is a piece of wood about 30 inches long, two transverse pieces of 18 inches in length crossing each other at right angles to which are attached fireworks, so constructed as to ignite when the barb enters the flesh of the brute, and going off in quick succession, with reports louder than those of a musket. Between agony and affright the animal is soon rendered frantic. A second and a third banderilla were speedily fastened downwards into his back, and by this time, there was no escape for some of the toreadores from the fury of the bull, but by leaping the barricades. After the picador had sustained four distinct attacks from the animal, in which he acquitted himself with great address and coolness, his hat was called for by the audience, and filled with money, as a substantial token of applause.

"Llamar el matador." "Call in the bull slayer," was now the cry of the vast assemblage.— The matador promptly made his appearance being a man of middle stature, stoutly made, and in a dress resembling in some respects that of the toreadores, but of richer materials. He bore the rattan and flag in his left hand, and a two-edged sword in his right. The bull made a plunge at him to toss him in the air, which he met with a slight motion to the left about two feet, and made a thrust with the sword, which entered between the shoulder blade and the ribs, and passing it down in a lateral direction between two ribs, the bull rolled at his feet dead on the instant. His cap was called for, and passed around, and he received his reward amidst the shouts and applause of the delighted multitude.

As soon as this was done, three horsemen appear with lassos which are fastened to the horns of the vanquished brute, and he is dragged out at a gate opposite to that by which he entered, and while the spectators await the appearance of another bull, they are afforded an interval for conversation and criticism on the various incidents of the previous scene, or to take refreshments provided in the adjacent booths.

The next bull that entered the arena was one of a different character. All his desire appeared to be for escape. He made a direct bolt across the arena in an effort to jump the gate opposite to that by which he entered. This was perhaps 6 feet high. At the first bound he lands on top of it, and after a few struggles, has succeeded in clearing it; makes a lane through the alarmed crowd, who have been just engaged in prom-

enading or riding in carriages or on horse, outside the amphitheatre. Fortunately, no person was hurt, the bull keeping on in a straight course, his only object being escape. Four horsemen provided with lassos are in rapid pursuit; he is secured and brought back into the ring amid the shouts of the people. "Matarle el covarde," "kill the coward," and he promptly meets the fate of his predecessor.

On the entrance of the third bull, a young man appeared in the arena in citizen's dress, evidently an amateur as well as a novice at the business. He was received by the spectators with shouts of "Bravo" "tengas corage," "have courage"." He behaved well, receiving and evading the first onset with great address. At the second, he appeared to hesitate as though he wished to leave the ring for a banderilla, the public having called out to him, "banderilla, senor, banderilla," and as he turned for the purpose, the bull made a bolt at him, catching him between the horns under his seat, and tossed him into the air, at least eight feet high, passing along beneath him. He fell to the ground, doubled up, and striking apparently on the shoulders, while the bull had passed to the other side of the circle, the toreadores, ran to his assistance and promptly led him out of the arena. He reappeared in about ten minutes equipped with a flag and a banderilla in his hand which he succeeded in planting in the back of the bull.— This second and successful movement was received with vivas and shouts of "alcanzar su sombrero," "hand your hat," which was passed round among the spectators and promptly filled with paper money, for other nations, besides the United States, have that species of currency, and the Argentine republic among the rest, although it seems to be an universal impression here, that the currency of all South America is gold and silver only.

In the course of a few days, which were devoted to this festival. I saw twenty-one bulls thus brought into that amphitheatre, of which number one only absolutely refused to fight. The combat with each usually lasted about fifteen to twenty minutes. The spectacle commences directly after dinner and lasts until evening, so as to embrace the cooler part of the day.

T

Theological Debate.

One of those public debates which gather immense crowds wherever held, commenced in this city on Monday evening last, the 24th inst., at the Second Advent Tabernacle or Millerite Church, as it is popularly called. The debatants were Rev. N. L. Rice, of the Central Presbyterian and E. M. Pingree of the Universalist Church, and the proposition in debate, "Do the scriptures teach the ultimate holiness and salvation of all men," which Mr. Pingree affirms and Mr. Rice denies.

The Tabernacle is 80 feet square, and although, from its sides being but nine or ten feet high, seems an awkward building, has proved admirably adapted to public speaking. It is at one extremity of the city, and more than a mile from the centre of Cincinnati business, but such was the excitement of the subject, and the reputation of the disputants, that by 7½ o'clock, the period of opening the discussion, the vast space was completely filled, numbers who had not seats, standing during the whole debate. And after the doors and windows had been blocked up with listeners, the roof was mounted and occupied by great numbers, to the danger, as I judge of the roof, which was not built of course with reference to this use of it. Profound order and decorum governed the debate which lasted nearly three hours. Judge Coffin, Wm. Green, and Henry Starr, Esqrs., are the moderators. The debatants treated each other with great courtesy, and the discussion itself, it is almost needless to add, was conducted with marked ability. It is expected to last during the evenings of eight days, and will no doubt, maintain to the last the interest it has already inspired.

The Egeria.

Years ago, and before the Cincinnati artists had built up a name for this city in the world of art, the favorite hope and purpose of some of our citizens was an *Academy of Fine Arts* here. Every new triumph of our young artists, gives fresh vigor to that hope and purpose, and I cannot doubt that our city, after sending her sons to the banks of the Arno and the Tiber, to study those beautiful visions of fancy, which have been embodied into form by a Praxiteles, a Lysippus, a Phidias, a Michael Angelo, and scores of names which will endure as long as the world lasts, and after furnishing New Orleans, Boston, New York and Philadelphia with artists in portrait and landscape painting of merit sufficient to supercede their own, will in less than ten years erect a temple of the Arts in which shall be enshrined from time to time, the various *chef d'oeuvres*, which our sons shall execute.

We have two busts from the classic chisel of Powers already in our city. One of Judge Burnet, the other a fancy piece belonging to Mr. N. Longworth. These would make an admirable commencement. Last Saturday, the *Egeria*, by Nathan F. Baker reached our city from Rome, a tribute of acknowledgement to Professor O. M. Mitchell for past kindness. This is a bust of the nymph, who was the presiding genius of the fountains and grottos in the vale of Italy,

which bears her nature. Egeria, was the tutelary goddess or nymph, to Numa the Roman legislator, and such was her reputation for wisdom, that he consulted her on all occasions before he framed and published those institutions which he confered on the Romans. The statue in a recumbent posture at the fountain of Egeria, is a headless trunk. Whether it was designed to represent a male or female figure is matter of doubt, and I believe Mr. Baker to be the first artist who has embodied classic mythology in this case, and from the creation of his own fine fancy, given us in this western world, a specimen of the nymphs of antiquity. His full length statue, of this same subject, is in his studio at Rome nearly finished, and represents Egeria as a water nymph with the urn or pitcher of antiquity at her side. The Egeria, which has reached Cincinnati, as already stated, is a *bust* merely, and is designed and well calculated to give some idea of the statue itself. I am no artist, and cannot speak of this charming specimen of art by rules, but it pleases me greatly, and I believe it will gratify all who have taste for beauty, in any of its varied forms.

The Egeria, is at the dwelling house of Mr. J. Baker, at the corner of Walnut and Fourth sts. where it will remain a few days, for the inspection of the public. It will, I am persuaded, fulfil all the expectations raised by the sculptor's earlier performances, before he left home. I understand from Mr. Baker, that he will be happy to afford his fellow citizens, the opportunity of calling at his dwelling to see this bust.

Heroes of Tippecanoe.

After the battle of Tippecanoe, and in the anticipation of the war with Great Britain, impending at the time, the 4th Reg't. U. S. troops marched from Vincennes Ind., via: Louisville, and Frankfort to Newport, Kentucky, where they arrived on the 1st day of June, 1812. The remnant of that corps adjudged fit for service in the Northern Campaign, amounting to above 300 men, crossed the Ohio for the frontiers, and on their arrival at Cincinnati, the commanding officer, Lt. Col. Miller received the following address. While crossing, they were saluted with discharges from an artillery company stationed on the river bank, which were acknowledged by the music of the regiment, and when they ascended the bank, a general shout and three cheers expressed the sense entertained by our citizens of their soldierly behavior in that battle, when their cool collected conduct, saved the body of the American troops, by giving them time to form in efficient order for defence, against the tremendous onset of their savage assailants. On Main street near 5th; a triumphal arch had been erected, decorated with floral ornaments, and enscribed, "To the heroes of Tippecanoe." Here they were again saluted by artillery; and having marched about five miles out to encamp, they were there supplied with bread, beef and whiskey; as a contribution from the citizens, and the next morning proceeded on their march to the lines.

To LIEUT. COL. MILLER:
Commanding the Fourth Regiment of the U. S. Army.

SIR:

The citizens of Cincinnati, impressed with a sense of the important service performed by the brave regiment (under the command of Col. Boyd at the battle of Tippecanoe) since their departure from us the last summer; sensible too of the great fatigues and privations which must have been experienced, most cordially salute you and each of the officers and soldiers under your command, on your return with your regiment, covered with glory. We cannot suffer you to pass us without presenting this tribute of our respect to the BRAVE. Your memories will live so long as we live, and will never be effaced from the annals of the western world.

As you pass to the northward at the call of your country, we are confident it will be but to gather fresh laurels. Our sons! will be by your side, composing the Militia of this State, destined on that service, and now encamped at the general rendezvous. Teach them the art to *conquer*—we will vouch for their *spirit*. On your tried and brave troops, much reliance is placed, and we confidently expect to hear a good account of the expedition.

Accept for yourself, and for the officers and soldiers under your command, this small tribute of respect, from the inhabitants of Cincinnati, and their warmest wishes for your personal welfare, as well as for that of every individual, of the HEROES whom you lead.

Cincinnati, June 3, 1812.

A Lady's Age.

One of these *hidden mysteries* of nature which baffle human calculations and scrutiny, is that intangible, unascertainable fact, *a lady's age.*— When a lady gets beyond twenty-five, she becomes what the French call of "a certain age," which I would correct by the phrase "an *uncertain* age, for I defy a census taker, or even a chancery examination, which is said to be the most searching process in nature to ascertain the exact number of years in the case.

Take the following example:

"In the course of the memorable trial of Lord Baltimore, at Kingston, in March, 1768, his lordship cross-examined the prosecutrix, Sarah Woodcock, when the following questions and answers occurred:

Lord Baltimore.—How old are you?
Sarah Woodcock.—I am twenty-seven.
Baltimore.—Will you swear you are no older?
Sarah.—I will swear that I am twenty-eight.
Baltimore.—Will you swear that you are no older?
Sarah.—I will swear that I am that.
Baltimore.—Will you swear that you are no older.
Sarah.—I do not know that I need to tell. I am twenty-nine, and that is my age; I cannot exactly tell.
Baltimore.—To the best of your belief, how old are you?
Sarah.—I believe I am thirty next July; I cannot be sure of that, whether I am or not."

I will add my own experience in the discharge of my duties as Census taker in 1840. In the prosecution of my employment I called on a lady in the higher walks of society, considerably beyond the meridian of life, and made the usual enquiries. 'How old is Mr. D——,' the husband. 'Sixty-one.' 'And your oldest son.' 'Twenty-seven.' 'And the next.' 'Twenty one.' 'And what shall I put you down?' 'I do not know my age exactly, but it is about thirty.' 'Did I understand you, madam, to say that your eldest son was twenty-seven?' 'Yes.' 'You must surely then be more than thirty.' She saw the *fix.* 'Well sir,' replied she quite pettishly, 'I told you I did not know exactly, it may be thirty-one or thirty-two; I am positive it is no more.' It was obviously useless to press the subject any longer.

How extensively this feeling operated may be judged by my returns of the Fifth Ward, to which I refer as a sample. Under fourteen years of age, and over twenty-five, forming two classes, there were two hundred and seventy-six males more than females, although in the intermediate class from fourteen to twenty-five, there was an excess of one hundred and seven females over the number of males.

At one house where I called, and was acquainted, I found the entire family, the parents excepted, in the parlor. Before I had time to announce my business, the oldest daughter exclaimed, "I know what you have come for, but you shant get a word out of me about *my* age, I am determined." "Well, says I, I'll bet you a big apple on that." "Done," said she. taking her seat very triumphantly. Instead of asking her the question she expected, I asked and put down in the proper column the age of the parents, and then inquired, how many boys are there under five? between five and ten? and then—girls between five and ten? between ten and fifteen? After recording the ages as given me thus far in the proper columns—and now, said I, Jane and Eliza I suppose, are between fifteen and twenty? Yes, said she, drawing a long breath. And you I suppose are 20? Yes. Another long breath. Very well, I observed, you are not thirty I know, and I have now got all I want out of you. I guessed when I began you would not find the operation as severe as pulling teeth, which you thought it next thing to! A charming smile paid me for my politeness, and we parted the best of friends.

Grindstone Sales.

I copy the following from the Boston Times.

"There is a certain merchant in one of our neighboring towns, a hardware dealer, who is a very shrewd and thrifty trader. Not long ago he had occasion to take into his employ a new clerk. The young man having been with him but about a week, was not thoroughly versed in his duty, when one day a person called for an article which the merchant did not happen to have in his store. The boy knew this, and therefore when the question was asked, have you got so and so, he replied in the negative, and the customer passed out. Whereupon the merchant took his assistant "to do," in the following words:

"Henry, never tell a person you have not got what they call for, but bring them, if you have not got the article they require, the next nearest thing to it that you have got. Ten to one they will take it."

Henry was a good boy, and always did as his employer instructed him. The next day a person, a stranger in the town, called in and asked if they had any cheese for sale. Now the boy could not say no; that was contrary to his directions. After scratching his head for a moment, a thought struck him, and proceeding to the back part of the store, he rolled out a moderate sized *grindstone*, as the thing *next nearest* to a cheese! Now, singular enough, though the man had called for a cheese, he was in want also of a grindstone, and this one suiting his fancy, he took it! Nothing was said by the employer until the customer had got the stone in his cart and driven off. Then stepping up 'to Henry, he said, you may see my boy how well the principle works! You have done well, and I will present you with a new suit of clothes as an encouragement for your promptness."

Henry sported a new "fit" the next Sunday."

This reminds me of a story, I have heard told of Michael Gundacker, who figured in Lancaster as a storekeeper, some forty or fifty years since. He was a very illiterate man, having sprung from very obscure beginnings, and as he could hardly write, and employed no clerk until late in life, was accustomed to make his charges in various hieroglyphics, intelligible to no one but himself. One day in settling with a customer, who had a running account, and reading off the items, he called out, "a cheese 18 shillings— 2,40 cts.—I never bought a cheese in my life,' said the other. By sure you dit. The customer again denied it flatly, and a quarrel might have ensued, had not Gundacker suggested "may pe it wash a grindstone." By George! said

the customer, I recollect I had a grindstone of you about that time. Dat ish it, grunted Mike, unt I forgot to put a hole in de mittle."

Ship Building at Marietta.

The frequent inquiries that have recently been made as to the number and tonnage of vessels built at this place in olden time, have induced us to copy the following memorandum, which we prepared and published four years ago.

1800.	Names.	Ton.	Builder.	Owner.
Brig	St. Clair	110	S. Devol.	C.Green & Co.
1801.				[& Co.
Ship	Muskingum	230	J. Devol.	B. I. Gilman
Brig	Eliza Green	126	J. Devol.	C. Green.
1802.				
Brig	Dominic	100	S. Crispen.	D. Woodridge.
Schr.	Indiana	75	G. Shreve.	E. W. Tupper.
Brig	Marietta	150	J. Whitney.	Abner Lord.
Brig	Mary Avery	150	D. Schalinger	Gunn & Avery.
1803.				
Schr.	Whitney	75	J. Whitney.	Abner Lord.
Schr.	McGrath	75	J. Whitney.	Abner Lord.
Brig	Orlando	150	J. Baker.	E. W. Tupper.
1804.				
Ship	Temperance	230	J. Whitney.	Abner Lord.
Brig	Ohio	150	Devol & Mc-Farland.	Mills & Frazer.
1805.				
Brig	Perseverance	160	J. Whitney.	B. I. Gilman.
1806.				[& Co.
Ship	Rufus King	300	J. Whitney.	B. I. Gilman
Ship	J. Atkinson	320	W. McGrath.	A. Lord.
Ship	Tuscorora	320	W. McGrath.	M. Jones.
Brig	Soph. Green	100	A. Miller.	C. Green.
Two Gun Boats		75	J. Barker.	E. W. Tupper.
1807.				
Ship	Francis	350	J. Whitney.	B.I.Gilman.
Snip	Rob't. Hall	300	J. Whitney.	B,I.Gilman.
Brig	Ruf. Putnam	300	W. McGrath.	A. Lord.
Brig	Collatta	140	W. McGrath.	A. Lord.
1808.				[D.Woodbridge.
Schr.	Bell	100	J. Whitney.	B. I.Gilman &
1009.				
Schr.	Adventurer	60	J. Whitney.	J. Whitney.
1812.				
Sch.	Maria	75	J. Whitney.	B. 1. Gilman.

7 Ships; 11 Brigs ; 6 Schooners; 2 Gun Boats.

There were then no facilities for towing vessels to the ocean, and no canal to enable them to pass the falls. Two of the ships built in 1806 were injured in passing the falls, and at about the same time one had to lay by several months before she could pass them, on account of low water. These facts very much disheartened those engaged in the enterprise, and finally the embargo preceeding the war put an end to it.— The barque Muskingum—250 tons burden—is the first fruit of the resumed enterprise,—which we trust may be prosecuted with success.

Steamboats have been built here and in Harmar, every year since 1821. The total number built since that time is thirty-eight. Their aggregate burden is 6285 tons.—*Mar. Intel.*

Our Municipal Elections.

There will be ample room for choice, doubtless, for the citizens of Cincinnati, in selecting candidates to fill the various local offices at the Spring elections. Four regularly nominated sets of tickets will be offered by as many parties. The whigs, democrats, native Americans, and liberty parties, besides volunteers who will nominate themselves beyond all boubt. If my voice could be heard in the din of the approaching battle, I should plead for my *ism* which is Anti-hucksterism. Let no man receive a vote for councilman who is friendly to the licensing hucksters to sell-butter, eggs or poultry.

Many people appear puzzled as to the propriety of giving or withholding these licences. A few remarks will, I think, set these doubts at rest.

The articles to which I have referred, injure in flavor, if not in soundness, by keeping. If then, a class of people be permitted to exist, who can offer the same article for a week or more for sale, under circumstances which render them independent of their customers, the equality of dealing, which has existed heretofore between the country producer and the city consumer is destroyed. While the farmer was compelled, as it were, to sell what the purchaser was compelled to buy during the day in which the article was brought into market, a proper state of things existed. But if the huckster anticipates the purchaser, and compels him to buy of him at second hand, stale or spoiled, or re-manufactured provisions, all the ends of a public market are defeated, the more so, because, we cannot even go to grocery stores to buy of responsible men, those articles which are now monopolised by the hucksters.

Another simple principle on this subject, will commend itself to the judgment of all. If we must buy of hucksters what we formerly bought direct from persons attending market, are we not compelled to supply the means of living to a useless class, the expenses of maintaining whose families are clearly and distinctly paid out of our pockets, besides large sums on the score of profits.

There are some hundred and fifty hucksters and the expense of supporting these with their families, will average to men of small property, a sum equal to their county taxes. What must it be accordingly, to renters?

I hope these fellows will be swept from our markets, and their apologists and patrons from the Council board

The Wise Men of the East.

Innumerable are the stories "going the grand rounds" of the American press, in which the ignorance of the West is set forth in bold relief. I am aware that the sun rises in the east metaphorically as well as literally, and we must expect most light where it first appears. But there are dark spots *east* as well as *west*, of which the following are instances. There is this difference however in the cases. What is said of the west is usually given without specifications of individuals referred to, or the testimony on which it rests, while here we have the names of persons, and the authority which states the facts.

"The reporter of the *Boston Courier* says, that Dr. GARDNER, Chairman of the Committee

on Education. in the Senate, informed that body that LOUIS PHILLIPPE, was the son of Napoleon. At another time, while debating certain resolutions on Agriculture, which he had introduced, he asserted that the duty on *soft soap* was fifty cents a pound. Several gentlemen corrected him, saying it was fifty cents a barrel. Dr. Gardner would not stay corrected, but read from the tariff the provision, fifty cts. per bbl. "Now," said the Doctor, "if *bbl.* does not mean *pound*, I will thank some gentleman to tell me what it does mean!"

☞ A correspondent of the Boston Atlas says that Manly B. Townsend, formerly Senator in Maine, was so much of an ass that upon his reaching the Capitol, he could not distinguish between the State House and the United States Arsenal, but actually went into the latter building and claimed his seat, and upon signing the papers presented to him by the commander, found himself regularly enlisted for seven years in the United States Army!

Building in Cincinnati.

Statistics are like other things which go the rounds, accumulating like a rolling ball of snow in their progress.

Not long since, I obtained at our brickyards the amount of bricks manufactured in 1844 for the consumption of Cincinnati. It was given me carefully, and I believe accurately, amounting to 80,000,000. As I had been accused,—anonymously however—of overrating the number of buildings put up annually here, I was not only careful to ascertain as correctly as possible the quantity of brick made here, but hesitated to publish the result, so largely exceeding the product of former years. On deducting however, what was judged to be the consumption of brick for paving side walks, building foundations, cisterns &c, and dividing the surplus by the number of buildings erected, it appeared to me to be about reasonable, and I published it accordingly.

I have since seen 225,000,000 bricks given in one, and 350,000,000 in another of our city papers as the manufacture and consumption of 1844. The most amusing feature in these statements being, that this last was made in the same print which gave currency to the charge against me of exaggeration in the number of the houses built in Cincinnati during the same period.—Making due deductions for other purposes of ten per cent., the quantity last alluded to, would suffice for 4500 buildings estimating each to require on an average seventy thousand bricks—a high average—or 5250, if we allow sixty thousand bricks to a house, which I deem a fair average. Many of our erections being houses of moderate size, requiring not more than from thirty to fifty thousand bricks to a building.

Military Order.

During the troubles which grew out of the conflicting claims of Connecticut and Pennsylvania to land title as well as sovereignty to that part of Pennsylvania, lying between the 41st and 42nd degree north latitude, a state of lawless violence existed, of which the following document illustrates a slight portion merely.

The order is endorsed, "these people disarmed, and their arms deposited in the State Magazine." Such documents as these are valuable, as materials to form what does not yet exist, a full and accurate history of the State of Pennsylvania.

Sir:

In consequence of reports, that a number of the Connecticut claimants at Abram's Plains appeared under arms, and ordered a number of the good and peaceable citizens of this State, from their settlements, and are preventing others from settling on their lands, to the great terror of these persons.

You will therefore proceed with fifteen men to Abram's Plains, and disarm all the Connecticut settlers in that neighborhood until further inquiry can be made into their conduct.

Should they behave peaceably, and discover a good disposition to the interests of this State, and its citizens, every security is to be given to their persons and prosperity. But in case of opposition, your own prudence must direct your measures, avoiding if possible the effusion of blood.

I am your ob't. serv't.,
J. MOORE.

CAPTAIN ARMSTRONG.
Fort Dickinson, May 11, 1784.

Relics of the Past.

Lieutenant Jno. Armstrong to Col. J. Harmar.
FORT PITT, March 12, 1784.

Sir:

A Mr. Leith, a man in David Duncan's employ, arrived at this place on the 6th June, from an Indian town on the Muskingum, twenty miles above the Tuscaraway, one hundred and forty from the mouth of the river. The accounts brought by him were as follows. The Delawares came to his camp, observed that several parties were gone to war—that he belonged to that family, and that if he would come and live with them he & his property should be safe. That a party consisting of 100 warriors who had marched against the settlement of Kentucky—had brought off several scalps. with the loss of a principal Chief, called the Black Wolf, and five of his party, who were killed by a party of whites, who pursued them. That a large party were then preparing to revenge the loss of their brethren. Mr Leith and Mr. Robbins, a partner of D. Duncan's, on consultation, thought best

to consult Duncan respecting the removal of their property, which was by the latter directed to be brought to this place. Mr. Leith set out immediately for his camp; when he arrived there the friendly Indians were much alarmed for the safety of Leith and Robbins. As a Mr. Dawson and McClane who had, during the late war, lived and traded among the Indians under British protection, had been plundered of a cargo of goods which they took from Wheeling on this river some time since, and had arrived at Young Woman's Creek, four of the men in their employ were killed. The Delawares and Wyandots took charge of Mr. Duncan's property, and directed Lieth and Robbins to proceed to the commanding officers, and give the necessary information. They arrived at McIntosh some time yesterday, and this day Mr. Leith arrived at this place; the former, it is said, proceeds to the Salt Licks on Beaver, in order to bring off some traders that are at that place.

Inclosed you have a letter from Capt. Hart to Major Wyllys, which in his absence, I was directed to open. It is now reduced to a certainty that an Indian war is inevitable.

I would wish to observe, that some of the inhabitants of this State have contracted with some persons at Detroit to furnish large supplies of bacon and flour; and that in a few days, not less than seventeen thousand weight will be transported for that place, as much of it is already purchased and packed. In the present situation of affairs the suffering provision to go to that country, appears impolitic, but neither the civil or military are authorized to prevent a traffic of this kind.

Your ob't servant,
JNO. ARMSTRONG.

PHILADELPHIA, March 16th, 1786.

Sir:

I have the pleasure to acknowledge the receipt of your several letters. Mr. Nicholson's intelligence I observe bodes no good, and we may expect some disturbance with the Indians unless the commissioners at the Miami exert their persuasive talents to prevent it. I am very anxious to hear the result of that treaty.— As to the circumstance of citizens and soldiers intermixing in the garrison, it is in my opinion unmilitary, nevertheless I would have you not to proceed so hastily in removing them. The good will of the inhabitants is an object worthy your attention to gain. Many abuses I make no doubt, have been committed respecting the public property, previous to the corps taking charge of them, but must observe that, report should be made to Major Wyllys, the senior officer, who will certainly pay attention thereto. We are now recruiting, and I expect to leave this city about the middle of next month for the westward. I shall again proceed to New York in the course of a few days, and hope to be able to bring along with me what I am sure must be very acceptable to both officers and men, viz: a little *ready money.* The books and lines I shall purchase and bring with me. I thank you for the different intelligences you have transmitted me respecting the Indians. I wish you to have my bedding aired as I am fearful many articles will spoil, being so long from the sun. Be pleased to present my compliments to all acquaintance.

I am sir, with esteem,
your very humble servant.
JOS. HARMAR.

Lt. Jno. Armstrong.

Friendly Sons of St. Patrick.

We are indebted to a friend for a duodecimo volume of 112 pages containing a "brief account of the society of the Friendly sons of St. Patrick, with biographical notices of some of the members and extracts from the minutes." Prepared and published by order of the Hibernian Society.

This is one of those volumes that occasionally spring up in our way, to shew how much, *patriotism and public good owe to social intercourse.*— The Society of the Friendly Sons of St. Patrick, was organized in the city of Philadelphia, in the year 1771, for social and convivial objects, of natives, or descendants of natives of Ireland.— The liberty of electing 10 honorary members, without the qualification of Irish descent, was reserved. In the list of members are found the names of many distinguished men of that period. The author of the volume gives a brief biographical sketch of the members ordinary, and it would seem that nearly every one was subsequently found playing an important part in the revolutionary war, which commenced a few years after the organization of the society. In the course of the revolutionary war, many distinguished officers were admitted to membership on the ground of the Irish blood in their veins. Gen. Washington was proposed, but when they would have selected him, it was found that he was not of Irish descent, by either father or mother. Here was a dilemma, which it took an Irishman to escape from. Instead of hunting up distant possibilities of relationship, a member proposed, and it was unanimously agreed to *adopt* Gen. Washington as a son of St. Patrick. Paternity was never more honored or enviable.

General Washington replied to the letter of the President; George Campbell, Esq., father of our esteemed townsman of that name; that he accepted with singular pleasure the ensign of so worthy a fraternity as that of the sons of St. Patrick in this city—a society distinguished for the firm adherence of its members to the glorious cause in which we are embarked. And the *country's father accepted of a splendid dinner on the occasion, and gave a dinner in return* at the city tavern.

Very many of the society were officers and members of the first Troop, at its formation, and there seems to be a hint, that that "ancient and honorable corps" owes its existence to the sons of St. Patrick; or at least, that the credit of its origin is to be divided between that society and the fine old "Hunting Club."

We cannot forbear to notice one anecdote set forth. In 1780. General Washington was compelled to appeal to individuals for aid in order to avoid the establishment of a bank, for the supply of the army with provisions. *The sum of £300,000 was needed, and of this the members of the society of the Friendly Sons of St. Patrick subscribed as follows:*

Robert Morris, £10,000; Blair McClenachan, £10,000; Wm. Bingham, £2,000; J. M. Nesbit & Co., £5,000; Richard Peters, £5,000; Samuel Meredith, £5,000; James Mease, £5,000; Thos. Barclay, £5,000; Hugh Shell, £5,000; John Dunlap, £5,000; John Nixon, £5,000; Geo. Campbell, £2,000; John Mease, £4,000; Bunner, Murray, & Co, £6,000; John Patton £2,000; Benj. Fuller, £2,000; George Meade & Co, £2,000; Jno. Donaldson, £2,000; Henry Hill, 5,000; Kean & Nichols, £4,000; James Caldwell, £2,000; Samuel Caldwell, £1,000; John Shee, £1,000; Sharp Delany. £1,000; Tench Francis, £5,000.

Old Times.

At a late Temperance Celebration in Boston, the Rev, Mr. Skinner gave the following statement of the cost of an ordination in Woburn, Mass. We remember some of these festivities, when a meeting house was raised to the top of the flute, violin, and instruments of many strings, and occasionally a sackbut:

"To Mr. Jonathan Poole, Esq., for subsisting the Ministers, messengers and gentlemen, at the time of Mr. Jackson's ordination over the Congregational Church, 1729:

	£.	s.	d.
To 433 dinners, at 2s. 6d a dinner,	54	2	6
To suppers and breakfasts, 179,	8	18	0
To keeping 32 horses 4 days,	3	0	0
To 6½ barrels cider,	4	11	0
To 2 gallons of brandy and 2 gallons of rum,	1	16	0
To 25 gallons of wine,	9	10	0
To loaf sugar, lime juice and pipes,	1	15	0
	£83	12	6

Our Early Settlers.

How would it impress the stranger, who without any distinct knowledge of its early history, beholds Cincinnati, a flourishing city of eleven thousand buildings, and seventy-five thousand inhabitants, to learn that all this is the creation of little more than half a century, and how would that impression be rendered more vivid, if he were told as he might be with truth, that the individuals are still living in the neighborhood, who killed Buffalo and Bear for the supply of the first body of settlers who landed here and who ranged and hunted through Cincinnati when there was not even a cow path in the forest. Still more that persons are living, engaged in chopping wood and tilling the soil who did these things, and one of them Major Fowler of whom I have spoken heretofore, is as able to pick a squirrel off a tree at a hundred yards now as he did when the whole country north of the Ohio was an unbroken forest.

Among the individuals, that I am raking up from the dead, as it were, I have just made the acquaintance of Mr. E. E. Williams, the particulars of whose long and eventful life I shall compile from his own lips for the Advertiser. Mr. W. is 75 years of age, and as is the case also with Major Fowler who is 81, can even yet walk some of our city dandies to death. His mind is equally vigorous with his body. Mr. W. is one of three, if not more, still living, who participated with Daniel Boone, Kenton and others in the border warfare which Kentucky waged with the relentless savage. Of course, he was comparatively a boy at the time, but in those days as soon as a youth could steady a rifle to his shoulder, he was expected to perform a man's duty.

Mr. Williams was originally the owner of all that valuable property at the corner of Main and Front streets, facing 100 feet on front and 200 on Main street, extending from Worthington Shillito & Co's. grocery store south to Front, and thence Place Traber & Co's. store, west to Main street, and became so under these circumstances. The lot in question was taken up by *Henry Lindsey*, who after holding it a year or more. disposed of it to a young man for a job of work, whose name Mr. Williams has forgot.— The second owner, having a desire to revisit his former home in New Jersey, and being unwilling to trust himself through the wilderness without a horse, begged Mr. Williams with whom he was acquainted, the latter then residing at the point of the junction of the Licking

and the Ohio, to take his lot in payment for a horse, saddle and bridle of his, valued at sixty-five dollars. After much importunity and principally with the view of accommodating a neighbor, Mr. Williams consented, and after holding the property a few days disposed of it again for another horse and equipments, by which he supposed he made ten dollars, perhaps. This lot not long afterwards fell into the hands of Col. Gibson, who offered it for one hundred dollars to Major Bush of Boone county in 1793. So slight was the advance for years to property in Cincinnati. This lot, probably at this time the most valuable in the city, estimating the rent at 6 per cent. of its value, is now worth 337,400 dollars. Where else in the world is the property which in 54 years has risen from four dollars to such a value?

Building in Cincinnati for 1845.

Notwithstanding an erection of 1228 buildings, principally dwelling houses for the past year, the wants of our enlarging population are such that there is just as much difficulty as ever to procure dwelling places for incomers. Not merely are houses taken as fast as they are built, but many are actually engaged for rent, as soon as the digging of a cellar affords evidence that a new dwelling is about to be built. By present indications, I should judge the number of buildings to be put up in 1845 in Cincinnati and its northern suburb, will not fall short of 1500.

One of the most striking features of city improvement, is the uncommon number of public buildings, contemplated or contracted for, and to be put up during this year, some of which have been already commenced, and a few finished or nearly so.

I will begin with edifices for religious perposes. A Roman Catholic chapel has been put up on Vine, immediately north of Liberty street, and another will be commenced in the neighborhood of Pace's saw mill, in the Third ward, as soon as the precise location can be determined on. Four Presbyterian houses of worship are contracted for, as follows: one on the scite of the present Tabernacle, on Betts street; one for Dr. Beecher's congregation on Seventh, east of John street; one for the Central Presbyterian Church, on Fifth between Plum and Western Row. and one for the Third Presbyterian Church, at the corner of John and Fourth streets.

The *Anti-Slavery Baptists*, under the care of Dr. Brisbane, are erecting an edifice on College street, and the *Christian Disciples* are about to do the same on Third between Elm and Race streets. Our Methodist friends whose zeal in the cause of church extension transcends that of all other denominations, have already completed and dedicated for worship the *Maley Chapel* just outside of our corporation line, to the north-west, and are commencing two new Chapels, one on Catharine west of Fulton street, and another in the south-west region of Cincinnati.

So much for houses of worship. Of other public buildings erecting, there are the *Odd fellows and Masonic Halls*, on the opposite corner of Walnut and Third streets. The friends of Temperance are about to put up a spacious hall for their meetings, at the corner of Race and Seventh streets, and the *Cincinnati College* lately destroyed by fire will be re-built in a style worthy of its importance with as little delay as possible. It is expected to cost 35,000 dollars.— Several of these churches, and all those other buildings will form distinguished ornaments to our city. The College and some of these Halls being designed to exhibit fronts of Dayton marble.

Here are fifteen public buildings therefore in progress, to be commenced, and with the exception of the College, calculated to be finished in the current year. This is equal to the aggregate of public buildings here for 1840, 1841, 1842, 1843, and 1844, to say nothing of the more substantial character, and the greater magnitude of the edifices.

While on this subject, some late changes in ownership of existing buildings may be noticed as subjects of public interest. The True Weslyan Chapel on Ninth street has been bought by the English Lutheran congregation in charge of Rev. Mr. Reck, and the Third Presbyterian Church will soon be occupied as well as owned by a German Protestant Society.

The spacious and massy Cathedral on Plum street will be rendered fit for occupation, I understand, in the course of the present year, although some time must elapse yet before the tower will be completed so as to finish the edifice.

Relics of the Past.

Capt. Armstrong to Gen. St. Clair and Lady.

FORT HAMILTON, March 17, 1792.

DEAR GENERAL:

Col. Wilkinson left this place at 10 o'clock yesterday with about two hundred men, with the intention of establishing an intermediate post between this and Fort Jefferson now under the command of Captain Strong.— On the 15th my runners returned from the place appointed for the exchange of letters, and having waited two hours after the appointed time of meeting, returned without any information

from Jefferson. As Captain Strong is a punctual officer, some accident must have happened to his express—my young men discovered fresh tracks of horses in several places on the road as many as five in a body, the enemy must therefore be watching the trace, and perhaps concerting a plan of attack on our advanced posts. A small party leave this Garrison every morning before day, and reconnoitres the neighboring woods. They have not as yet discovered any signs of Indians. This Garrison is now in a perfect state of defence, and for its greater safety, I have commenced sinking a well.

I beg leave also to observe that due attention is paid to the exercise and discipline of the men, &c.

* * * * * * *

I hope, madam, this letter, although out of the line of etiquette will not give offence.

Unacquainted with the etiquette of addressing a lady, I have hopes, the language of my profession will not be offensive to the companion of a brother officer. Be pleased therefore, madam, to accept the thanks of my family, *alias the mess*, for your polite attention in sending us garden seeds, &c., and should we be honored by a visit from the donor, the flowers shall be taught to smile at her approach, and droop as she retires. We beg you to accept in return a few venison hams, which will be delivered you by Mr. Hartshorne, they will require a little more pickle and some nitre

JNO. ARMSTRONG.

JNO. ARMSTRONG, Esq.

Capt. Com'dt. Fort Hamilton,

SIR :

The public service requires that a second flat or boat, for the transportation of horses be built with the utmost despatch at this post, to facilitate the passage of the river. You will therefore be pleased to take the necessary measures with your usual promptitude, and believe me with respect and attachment, sir,

Your most ob't. humble servant,

J. WILKINSON,

Lt. Col. Com'dt. 2d U. S. Reg't., Commanding Ft. Washington and dependencies.

FORT HAMILTON, Feb. 5th, 1792.

JNO. ARMSTRONG, Esq.

Capt. Com'dt. Fort Hamilton.

DEAR SIR :

Please forward the enclosed express, and if Mr. Elliott gives you notice, that his boats are ascending the Miami, you will detach a Sergeant and 12 men to meet them at Dunlap's station, and escort them to the post under your command. Every thing is safe here, and Charley may kiss my foot. I built upon a square of 120 feet, a foursided polygon with regular Bastions—the Bastions will be completed in two hours. the work substantial and rather handsome. The area covered yesterday morning by immense oaks, poplars and beeches, is now clear for parade. Adieu.

I am your most obedient servant,

J. WILKINSON,
Lt. Col. Com'dt.

CAMP, March 19th, 1792.

Poetry.

CHERISH THY FRIENDS.

BY L. J. CIST.

Oh! cherish, in thine heart of hearts,
  The friends thou'st loved and tried;
Those who have stood from childhood up
  Still faithful at thy side:
Thy chosen 'brothers of the soul'—
  The trusted and the true;
Cherish them! if thou many hast—
  Yet more, hast thou but few!

CHERISH THY FRIENDS.—Oh! never let
  A light and hasty word,—
An idle jest, misunderstood.—
  Some phrase, perchance half heard,—
Or fancied slight, offence ne'er dreamed,
  Thy kindly feelings change;
And never let the evil tongued
  Thy friend from thee estrange!

Ah many a careless look is made
  To bear a wrong intent!
And many a thoughtless word construed
  To mean what ne'er it meant!
And there are ever those, are quick
  Occasion fair, to take,
By mischief bearing words, the links
  Of Friendship's chain to break.

CHERISH THY FRIENDS! If e'en, perchance
  By passion led astray,
Thy friend shall give thee just offence,
  Still cast him not away!
Deal kindly with him!—So shall yet
  His soul to thee return;
And friendship's flame rekindled, long
  As with new light shall burn.

To err is but the mortal lot,
  To pardon the Divine!
Can'st thou forgive not?—then is naught
  Of the true God-like thine!
And thou—if thou art conscious, just
  Offence thou'st given a friend,
Let no false pride prevent thy soul
  From making just amend!

This world is but a weary world,
  And friends at best but few;
But what were earth had we not some—
  The trusted and the true?
Oh! thou who hast a friend approved,
  Till life's last sands shall roll,
Grapple thou, "as with hooks of steel,"
  That friend unto thy soul!

A Game of Chess with Napoleon.

* * * When I was a petty clerk at Rothschilds, the narrowness of my finances allowed me to indulge in no amusement but chess, and as a constant habitue of the Cafe de la Regence, I had attained a certain degree of force, that is to say, a first rate player could only give me the advantages of a couple of pieces. It is necessary I should premise all this, before I come to my encounter with the emperor. I gave, then, all my leisure time to chess; but to conceal the poverty of my appointments, maintained the most rigid secrecy at the Regence, as to who or what I was, and was universally supposed to be living on my means—a mere Paris flaneur. Do not lose sight of this fact. Well, I bore my condition cheerfully, practised the most rigid economy as to ways and means, and sat early and late at my desk, during business hours; existing on the present, living on the future; watching the opportunity to better my hard fate, by seizing that critical moment (should it present itself,) which they say Fortune offers once, at least, in the life of every man.

On the 5th of March, in the year 1815, we were at our posts in the evening, making up the monthly mail for Constantinople. It was late—between eight and nine o'clock. I was rocking on my hard wooden stool as usual, scribbling away for dear life, in company with some nine or ten other clerks, all of superior grade in the office, when the door flew open, and our chief, Rothschild, stood before us, with a face as pale as a pretty woman's when the doctor says her aged husband will recover!

Every sound was hushed, every stool ceased to rock, every pen was stopped scratching.—Something important had evidently happened—some dire event "big with the fate of Cato and of Rome." Mexico was engulfed by an earthquake, or Peru was washed to powder by a tornado. Rothschild spoke, and his voice quivered. "Gentlemen," said he, "though I opened not the black book, I could not prevent others, many hours, from unfolding its leaves. France is no longer France! The whirlwind has smitten her! The thunder cloud has burst upon our happy shores! I may be announcing to you the ruin of the house of Rothschild and Brothers!"

Ruin and Rothschild! The association of terms appeared too ridiculous. We thought the governor mad!

"Gentlemen," resumed the mighty Israelite, "hear me out, and appreciate the magnitude of the communication. Napoleon Bonaparte has left Elba, has landed in France, the army join him, and his eagles are flying to Paris with lightning speed. I come now from the Tuilleries. Louis XVIII., by the grace of God, will be off for Flanders in a few days as fast as his fat will let him. The ministers are drawing up a bombastic proclamation to issue to-morrow to the people, but I foresee their downfall is assured. The folly of the Bourbons again breaks the peace of Europe, and France is about to plunge anew into a thirty years' war!"

"Hurrah!" shouted two or three clerks, staunch Bonapartists.

"Forgive, me, my dear sir," cried one of them to Rothschild, "forgive the interuption, but this cannot touch the house. Be yourself. This alarm is surely premature.—Hurrah! the emperor must have money. He will want a loan,—

We shall have the crown jewels, worth fourteen millions of gold, in pledge; and the fat citizens of Paris, who swear by the house of Rothschild, will furnish the cash! Hurrah, then! Vive l'Empereur!—A basles Bourbons! Vive Napoleon!"

"Sir," replied Rothschild, sternly; "sir, you are a fool! and you talk like the fool you are! The emperor must have money instantly, too true! But Louis is even now packing up the crown jewels, in case he is obliged to fly to Ghent; trust the old fox for that, and all his private treasures to boot. The emperor can offer no guarantee capable of being quickly realised. He will tender me his note of hand—bah! and the Congress of Vienna still sitting! and the armies of the allies not disbanded! and the Russians in Germany, and the Cossacks of the Don, in sunny Europe, like vultures, eager to whet their filthy beaks in the dearest blood of France! Sir, you talk like a child! Do you forget our cash operation of last week? Do you remember that in our vaults lie five millions of gold Napoleons! and doubtless, Talleyrand and Fouche will try to make their peace with Bonaparte, by advising that this sum should be seized as a forced loan. Five millions!"

"The allied armies will dissolve like snow beneath the sun of June!" retorted the Bonapartist clerk.

"Never!" cried D——, emphatically; "Napoleon has laid too many obligations upon Russia and Austria. They groan beneath the weight of his favors. Benefit a scoundrel, and be sure he flies at your throat when he can!"

"Yes," continued Rothschild. "five millions in gold, one hundred millions of francs! My brain reels—the house must go! Nothing but a miracle can save us. Five millions."

"But, asked the imperialist clerk, "can we not hide the gold?—can we not send it away!"

"And what can we do with it?" impetuously interrupted Rothschild. "Where can we hide it, that its place of concealment will not be known? The barriers are closed sir, and no person may leave Paris. The moment Napoleon sets foot in the Tuilleries, I shall be summoned thither. and this gold will be demanded as a loan. A loan indeed?"

"But perhaps, Lafitte——"

"Lafitte the devil, sir! To Lafitte's house I shall be politely invited to send the money.— I must give up this vast sum, or perhaps be tried by a court martial and shot for petty treason! Think you Bonaparte comes this time to play anything but the game of life and death? Do we not know the man? Remember the active part I have taken in arranging the affairs of these Bourbons, and think not my exertions in their cause can ever be overlooked, *except by themselves.* A hundred millions! Oh, brother my dear brother! of all men on earth, you alone could save me by your counsel; and I am in Paris, and you are in London!"

"The emperor cannot be here yet, why not send to your brother?" asked the imperialist.

"The barriers are, I repeat, closed and guarded by the artillery with loaded guns. I applied myself for a passport, and was refused. The gratitude of kings! I was refused this by the Bourbons, who wish naturally to delay the heavy tidings of lament for France, until their own personal safety is insured. The peasants love Napoleon, and might arrest them. A hundred millions!"

"And no one can then leave Paris? This is

really so!" ejaculated the Bonapartist, beginning himself to tremble for the safety of his idol, *the house.*

"Such is literally the case. None may pass but one courier for each ambassador. The messenger of the English Embassy this moment leaves with despatches for the Court of St. James. I have spoken with him, and offered him £500 to bear a letter to my brother, and the man refuses! The post, too, is stopped, or will stop. Five millions of gold!"

"The English courier is a German named Schmidt, is he not?" queried the Bonapartist clerk, by way of saying something.

"He is, may he break his neck on the road! The moment he communicates his news in London, the British funds fall ten per cent., as they will do here to-morrow morning, and in both cities we hold consols to an immense amount. Oh, for some heaven-inspired idea to circumvent this fellow Schmidt! But I talk as a child!—my brain reels! Five millions of Napoleons in our cellars! Oh, my brother, why cannot the spirits of our father arise and stand before you to-morrow in London, ere the arrival of this courier?"

The climax had arrived. Rothschild's heart was full. He sunk into a chair, and hid his face in his hands. The deep silence of profound consternation prevailed throughout the office.

Now whatever was the feeling of my fellow clerks I cannot convey to you the slightest idea of the revolution which had sprung up in my breast during the foregoing conversation. I had not spoken, but eagerly watched and devoured every word, every look of the several speakers. I was like the Pythoness of Delphi when the inspiration of her god, my 'Magnus Apollo' being my poor 1500 franc salary. Never was there a more burning genius of inspiration for an enterprising man than an income limited to 1500 francs! My frame dilated like that of Ulysses in Homer, when breathed on by the sage Minerva; or to pair my Greek with a Latin smile, I might be likened to Curtius, resolved to save Rome by leaping into the gulf; only, as an improvement upon this latter hero, I fancied I could take the plunge without breaking my neck! Any how, I jumped up, kicked my wooden stool away, and presented myself before Rothschild.

"If being in London three hours before the English courier may advantage the house, cried I, here do I undertake the task, or will forfeit life. Give me some token of credence to hand your brother, sir, gold for my expenses on the road, and trust to me?"

"What mean you? Are you mad?" said Rothschild, surprised, while my fellow-clerks began to mutter at my pretensions.

"I have my plan," returned I. "Oh, do but trust me! I am acquainted with this courier—with Schmidt. I have a hold on him—a certain hold, believe me! Though I am but the junior here, I will travel with Schmidt, ay, in his very carriage, and will win the race, though I should be guillotined afterwards for strangling him by the way! Time, flies, sir—trust me—say I may go!"

Rothschild hesitated.

"Is he trustworthy?" asked he of the head clerk, with whom I was luckily a favorite, because I was in the habit of mending his pens, and taking his seven children *bonbons* on New Year's day.

"Wolverpenden," answered the head clerk, "is as steady as time. He is prudent and clever. I would trust him with my children—and wife too!"

There was a little time for parley. Great men decide quickly. The truth was, I presented myself as a *pis aller*, a sort of forlorn hope.— Even if I went over to the enemy, nothing could be lost, matters were evidently at their worst & the critical moment all but on the wane. Mr. R, resolved to trust me. He took from his finger the carbuncle I now wear, the stone cost 50,-000 francs in Levant, and placed it in my hand.

"Show this ring to my brother," said he; "he knows it well; and stay—quick—give me the ink!" Snatching up a piece of paper, our chief wrote in the Hebrew character, "Believe the bearer!" "Put that in his hands," said he, "what your plan is I know not. You have *carte blanche*. Explain all to my brother. He is the genius of the family. The fortunes of the house of Rothschild are in your keeping. Be thou, as David says, 'a dove for innocence, but a very serpent in guile. The courier starts at the stroke of ten. It wants twelve minutes."

"He goes, of course, from the house of the embassy?" asked I, clapping on my hat, snatching a cloak from the wall, and pocketing a heavy bag of gold all in a breath.

"He does—he does—away with you—away!" and Rothschild literally pushed me out at the door, amid the varied exclamations of the clerks, I took the step stair-fall at half a dozen bounds, and in half a dozen more found myself in the Place du Palais Royal.

Through life we find that to narrate important events frequently consumes more time than their realization. That it was with me at this moment, and I must hazard weakening the interest of my narrative to state here the grounds of my calculation. In almost every thing runs an under current, not seen by the world.— Schmidt and I were bound together by but a silken thread, and yet on that I reckoned. We were both frequenters of the Cafe de la Regence, and constantly in the habit of playing chess together.

Nobody but a chess player can appreciate the strong tie of brotherhood, which links its amateurs. When men spend much time together, they ebcome accustomed to each other, like horses used to run in the same coach. For a fellow chess-player a man will do that which he would refuse his father and mother. The habit of breathing the same air and looking at the same chess-board creates a friendship to which that of Damon and Pythias was mere 'How d'ye do?' It was upon this that I reckoned. Schmidt and I had played thousands of chess-games together, and barely exchanged three words. He no more suspected me of being a banker's clerk than of being the King of the Sandwich Islands. We had mostly singled out each other as antagonists, because pretty nearly matched; and Schmidt loved me the more, as I know, because it was not every man that could play with him.

Schmidt was the slowest chess-player I have ever seen. He has been known to sit three quarters of an hour on a move, his head covered by his hands, and then to be discovered fast asleep! In every thing he was the same. Correct as the sun; but a slow sort of person, for all that. Schmidt was the kind of a man who, meeting you in a pouring rain, says, 'What a wet day is this!" A wholesale dealer in prosy truisms, and nothing brighter; and yet covered all over with a portly assumption of consequence, which famously dusted the eyes of the vulgar. I had ever been a judge of physiognomy, and knew my man. How many Schmidts there are in the world!

The English embassy at this time occupied a hotel adjoining the Cafe de la Regence, at the door of which latter temple of fame I planted myself in a careless looking attitude, with my pulse beating like a sledge hammer. The night was dark above, but bright below, shining forth in all the glory of lamp light. At the *porte cochee* of the British envoy's hotel stood a light travelling carriage. I was in the nick of time.— Schmidt was ready, enveloped in a heavy *redingote*. Five horses were being caparisoned for the journey. I went up to the carriage, and addressed my chess friend:—

"How's this, Schmidt? no chess to-night?— I've been looking for you in the Regence!"

"Chess! no indeed, I've other fish to fry.— Have you not heard the news? It's no secret. Bonaparte has landed from Elba on the coast of France. Paris will ring with tidings in an hour or two. I'm off this moment for London with despatches."

"I don't envy you the journey!" said I— "What a bore! shut up in that machine all night; not even a pretty girl to keep you company!"

"But duty, you know!" said Schmidt, with a smile.

"Duty, indeed! but perhaps, you light up, *en grand seigneur*, and read all the way? To be sure you can study our new gambit!"

"What a pity you can't go with me!" responded Schmidt, in the pride of five horses and a carriage all to himself. "What a pity you can't go with me; we'd play chess all the way!"

My heart leaped to my mouth. The trout was gorging the bait. Schmidt had drawn the marked card!

"Don't invite me twice!" said I, laughing, "for I am in a very lazy humor, and no one earthly thing to do in Paris for the next few days." This was true enough.

"Come along, my dear fellow?" replied Schmidt, "make the jest earnest. I've a famous night lamp, and am in no humor to sleep. I must drop you on the frontiers, because I dare not let the authorities of Calais or Boulogne see that I have a companion, lest I should be suspected of stock jobbing, but I'll pick you up on my return. Now are the horses ready, there?"

"Do you really mean what you say, Schmidt?" "Indeed I do?"

"Then I'll tell you what, said I, 'I'm your man, and famous fun we'll have!"

I darted into the Cafe de la Regence, snatched up the first chess equipage that came to hand, and stood in a moment again by the side of my friend. The postilions were on their saddles, in we leaped, bang went the door, round went the wheels, and away bounded our light calash at the rate of ten French miles an hour!

"Ciel!" said Schmidt with a grin, "what a joke this is! We shall have something in the chess way to talk about for the next hundred and fifty years!"

"We shall indeed!" replied I. For a moment we were stopped at the barrier St. Denis, and here I became sensible of the truth of Rothschild's reasoning. The gates were closed, and a heavy force of horse and foot drawn up by the portals. My friend's passport was strictly scanned, and we learned that no other carriage could pass that night, the order being special. I may here say, that throughout the route, thanks to the telegraph, our horses were always changed at the various posts houses with lightning speed.

"Good night, gentlemen!" cried the officer on guard, and away he went through the barriers, dashing over stone and sand, rut and road, like the chariot of Phaeton running away with its master. I looked back on Paris for the last time. *"Aux grands hommes, la patrie reconnissante!"* thought I. Should I succeed, the Rothschilds will at least bury me in the Church of St. Genevive!

Now, at this point, my friends, the chess board, I consider, was in reality placed between Napoleon and myself, its type only being the chequered piece of wood on which Schmidt, poor fellow! was setting up the chess-men. By the by, if you ever play chess in a carriage, and for want of the men being pegged at their feet, you cannot make them stand, wet the board with a little *vin de Grave*, as we did, and you'll find no difficulty.

Yes, Napoleon and I were about to play a game at chess, and, although he might be said to have taken the first move, his attack was necessarily clogged by so much incumbrance, that our chances at least became equal. "To beat the emperor," thought I, "all must be risked in a rapid attack, which shall countermine his plans. The position must not be suffered to grow too intricate. My first stroke must be successful, or I may as well throw up the game at once. Nothing, however, can be done for some hours; so *voyons!* there's a Providence for the virtuous."

Imagine for yourselves the details I am compelled to omit. We played chess all night, talked, laughed, and enjoyed ourselves. We supped *en route* in the carriage; and, as my courteous antagonist was deeply engaged in discussing the relative merits of a *Perigord pate* and a bottle of old Markbrunner, I could but sigh that time had been denied me to put a vial of laudanum in my pocket. Schmidt should have slept so soundly!

Time wore on. "Shall I pitch him out by main force?" reflected your humble servant.— "Shall I decoy him forth, leave him like one of the babes in the wood to the care of the redbreasts, assume his name, and dash on alone?" Too hazardous. I must take care not to find my way into that dirty old gaol at Calais, where the starving debtors are so everlastingly fishing for charitable pence with red woolen nightcaps. The Code Napoleon does not allow of robbery with premeditated violence. More the pity! and then, probably, if alone, I could not procure horses. Shall I tell Schmidt the whole truth, and throw myself on his friendship? No; I should be checked and checkmated. We have rattled through Abbeville, we are even passing Montreuil, and I am just where I was. But stop! a thought lights up my brain. Will it do?

Luckily my adversary was, as I have said, the slowest of all slow chess players—heavy, sleek and sleepy. This gave me the more time to ruminate while he concocted his views upon the chequered field, and my scheme, such as it was, became at length matured. While Schmidt the innocent, with his fishy eyes was poking over the board, how little he thought upon the real subject of my meditations. At this moment some persons would liken Schmidt to the Indi-

an traveller, laughing in the fullness of his joy, while the Thug, his companion, makes ready the fatal scarf wherewith to strangle him; others would compare him to a calf grazing in a butcher's field. You may compare him to what you will.

'Do you cross from Calais or Boulogne? Schmidt?—Check to your king!'

'Check? I shall interpose the rook.—Oh! through the Anglomania of the Bourbons, our embassy has worked the telegraph double duty, and at both ports a fast sailing boat awaits me, —I think I shall win this game. Your queen seems to me not upon roses. If the wind hold strong south-west as now, I shall prefer crossing from Boulonge.'

By this time we had reached that little village, I forget the name of the dog-hole, seven miles on the Paris side of Boulogne. It was half past four in the afternoon, and we had eaten nothing since our scanty breakfast of bread, butter, and *cafe au lait*, at eight in the morning. Chess, chess, still had our chess gone on. I knew Schmidt was of the gourmand order, and now or never must the buffalo be taken in the lasso; I easily prevailed upon him to alight at the little inn of the village, which was also the post house, for a quarter of an hour, to snatch a hot dinner, which I assured him, was far better than his dining at Boulogne and crossing the sea on a full stomach; so, chess-board in hand, away went Schmidt the simple into a dark little back room to study his coming move while dinner was dishing. 'Now or never!' I say, was my battle cry. I rushed out, and demanded, what think you? a blacksmith! I was gazing on our carriage when the man stood before me. No one was within hearing.

'What a curious thing is a carriage like this, friend?' said I, musingly.

'It is!' responded he, in a tone which seemed to say, "Have you come from Paris to tell me that?'

'A strange wilderness of wheels and springs, wood and iron. Now what would follow if that large screw there were taken out? Answer me promptly?'

'What should follow? Why, the coach would go on very well for a few hundred yards, and then would overturn with a crash, and smash all to shivers!'

'Hum!' said I; 'and the traveller would doubless go to *shivers*, as you call it, also! And what if only that tiny screw there were drawn?'

'The body of the vehicle would equally fall upon the hind axle, but without material consequences; causing, however, some inevitable delay.'

'Are you the blacksmith always in attendance here? I mean, if this carriage overturned in decending yonder hill, would it fall to your lot to right it?'

'It would!' and the Frenchman's eye sparkled with intelligence. I could have hugged the swarty man to my bosom. I love a blacksmith!

'Here are ten Napoleons,' said I; 'give me out that little screw; I have a fancy for it.' And the screw was in my hand.

'And now,' continued I, 'here are ten other Napoleons. I *hope* no incident will happen to us as we leave the village; but should the carriage overturn, have it brought back here to repair, and take a couple of hours to finish the job in, that you may be sure the job is done properly, you know. And remember, O most virtuous of blacksmiths, that a man who earns twenty Napoleons so lightly has two ears, but only one tongue."

'Assez, assez, mon maitre!' grinned Vulcan, emphatically; 'je compends; soyez tranquille! Allez donc!'

I pocketed the precious screw and rushed in to dinner while the horses were putting to.—Schmidt was so tranquil, I felt provoked I had such a lamb to deal with. I intend that screw to go down in my family as an heir-loom.

We left the inn at full gallop. A very small quantity of pace like ours proved a dose. The body of the carriage dropped gently into "a critical position," The postilions pulled up.

'We are overset,' cried I.

'God forbid!' said Schmidt; "say it's the English courier!" The man was so deep in his dear chess. 'What's to be done?' cried he, coming to his senses.

I had already sprung out.

'There seems little the matter, Schmidt.—Back the carriage to the inn, and all will be right again in a twinkling.'

So said so done. My friend the blacksmith assured us he would pay all damage directly; and, while he began to hammer away like a Cyclops forging thunderbolts, we philosophers coolly resumed our chess in the inn parlor.—The position of the game was now highly critical, both for me and Napoleon, and also for me and Schmidt. My latter adversary was decidedly under a mate, and his coming move I felt must occupy twenty heavenly minutes! Surely his guardian angel must have just now been taking his siesta!

I left the room and darted to the stable. A groom was busy at his work.

'Have you got a saddle horse ready for the road?'

'Yes, sir, we've a famous trotting pony—won the prize last——'

'Enough! I am sent on in advance. Tell the landlord my friend within settles all. Give me the bridle!'

I mounted my Bucephalus, and galloped off like the wind.

'Boulogne!' cried I, aloud, as I raced through the village in a state of ungovernable excitement. I was playing the great game with a vengeance. If that horse yet lives, be sure he recollects me.

I rattled into Boulogne. the St. Pelage of Great Britain, and the very gendarmerie quailed before me at the gates. In a minute more I had alighted at the water side. The soldiers shouted behind for my passport. I threw them some gold, which, as none of their officers happened to be in sight, they were vulgar enough to pick up from the beach. I cast my eyes around. It was six o'clock, and the scene was deeply interesting.

The breeze had set in well from the west.—The evening was cold, but bright; the air slightly frosty. The sun yet shone, and lighted up the harbor, tinging the far-off waves with ten thousand different shades of emerald hue. It was known already that Napoleon had escaped from his prison house, and was marching on Paris; and the English residents were flying from France like sheep before the wolf. A golden harvest was reaping on this narrow sea, and I was hailed in a moment by several bronzed fishermen, with offers of service and vaunts of superior qualities of their several respective vessels. I selected at a glance a stout, trim looking boat, and leaped on board, leaving my horse to his meditations. I hope, for the hospitality of Boulogne, he was taken care of.

'For Dover!' cried I to the master of the boat, 'My pay is five guineas a man, I must have eight men on board in case it comes on to blow. Be smart, fellows, and away!'

The men were active as eels. The police were about to detain me with some infernal jargon about my passport again.

'Cut off!' cried I, eagerly.

My captain (if I may so term a Breton sailor, half smuggler, half fisherman,) severed the rope which held us to the pier head, our heavy brown sails were flung to the wind, and we were sweeping across the waters.

We dashed under the bows of a large English built packet, straining at her lashings like mad, ready to kick off in ten seconds. Her sails were flying abroad, and several stout hands were at the tacks, ready to sheet them home. The captain was reading the very stones and windows of the town, impatiently, through a glass. The mob of idle spectators were so busily engaged watching his proceedings, I was hardly noticed.

'A nice craft, that!'

'Yes, sir; waiting for the English courier.—If he don't make haste she'll lose her tide.'

'I should be sorry for that,' said I. 'Give her a wide berth, and go ahead.'

And we did go ahead. I have crossed Calais Straits many times, but not under such exciting circumstances. Every bit of canvass we could stretch was spread, and the billows washed our deck from stem to stern. The men were on their mettle, and the little vessel answered gloriously to the call, shaking herself after each wash like a wild duck, and dipping her wings again to kiss the briny waters. In one moment I verily thought we should have been swamped. My fellows themselves hesitated and seemed inclined to take in sail.

'Carry on!' cried our Captain.

A little more washing and we were in comparatively smooth water under the chalk cliffs of Albion. By half past nine I had left Dover, and was tearing away on the London road behind fleet horses. Canterbury and Rochester were won and lost. I took the direction of London, and my carriage pulled up before the gates of Rothschild's villa at 5 o'clock in the morning. I had come from Paris in thirty hours.

The inmates must have thought I had come to take the mansion by storm, so powerful was my appeals to the great bell, as I stood at the gate in the early sunbeams of the morning.—In five minutes more, I found myself by the conjugal bed of Rothschild. God knows how I got there.

Assuredly the Rothschilds received me as they had never done visiter before, sitting up both in bed, side by side, rubbing their eyes, as just awakened from a dead sleep. I had made my entry vi et armis, and, by the time Rothschild was fully wakened up, had handed in my credentials. Without pausing a moment in my hitherto successful career, I rapidly explained the circumstances of the case, and minutely detailed the situation of our Paris house. What words I used I cannot remember. I had not slept for two days and nights, and my brain began to reel for want of rest

'Go into my dressing room there,' said Rothschild, with the most imperturbable sang froid. 'Do me the favor to open the shutters, and in three minutes I will be with you.'

I retired mechanically; a heavy load seemed already moved from my chest. Its every tone of the great man's voice was something more than authority; there was genius, talent and power. I felt that our position was fully understood, and so profound was my confidence in the king of London merchants, I already felt assured we should find relief in his counsels.— How extraordinary that so much effect should have been produced by half a dozen common-place words!

I threw myself upon a sofa. Rothschild joined me. He wore a scarlet night-cap, and enveloped in the blanket he had hastily dragged off the bed, he looked, with his grisly beard and massive throat, like a chief of the Cherokee Indians about to give the war whoop. But I thought at the moment of neither nightcap nor blanket, I thought only of Napoleon Bonaparte on the one hand, and Rothschild on the other; and I would have staked my life on the latter, simply because he seemed master of himself.— It is so easy to govern others!

Rothschild was grand, he was sublime! Startled abruptly from his sleep, informed that the whole fortunes of his house were trembling in the balance, that the mighty European edifice he had for so many years been laboring to establish was tottering in the wind—that name, fame, and fortune, were being rent asunder, he was still Rothschild. He was the lion of the desert awakened to battle by the jungle tiger of the East, and rushing at once to the desperate conflict. Only, be it remembered, that lions of the desert seldom appear in flannel, even in the Zoological Gardens.

Rothschild spoke, and in the same quiet tones which he could have ordered his maitre d' hotel to get him a cutlet.

'Return to France,' said he—'to my brother with all speed. Spare no exertions at all hazards to be in Paris a little time before Napoleon enters, and all will go well. Your services in this affair will not be forgotten by our house. To thank you here were waste of time. Now mark my words! I have no faith in the Napoleon dynasty. The emperor has returned too soon.— The army will declare in his favor, but the nation, torn by war, will not stand by him. The natural cry of France is, 'Peace, peace! that we may heal up our wounds.' The emperor may win a battle, but he must fall before numbers, and his fall this time will be forever. I give him a hundred days reign, and no more. Very well. If I believed in the endurance of Napoleon, I should say, '*Make a friend of him*—lend him this gold;' but as it is, the bullion must be preserved. I know the Bourbons. If the emperor borrow the gold, even in the name of the government, and pawn the palaces of Fontainbleau and the Louvre for the amount, the others are capable of disavowing the transaction. And although the absolute loss of this sum would not of itself shake us, yet the credit of our name would be severely damaged; a run upon our branch houses would inevitably follow, and we should be compelled to stop payment before we could realize our assets. And yet true policy forbids our now directly affronting the Emperor. How then to act? The problem to be solved is this,—to keep the gold out of his hands, and yet to remain friends with him. And thus would I have my brothers proceed. Treasure up my every word, sir, and digest it en route. All paper money in France will now be depreciated. Any premium will be given for gold to hoard during the crisis. We have undue bills to the amount of millions and millions flying about in Paris. I pray you mark this; sir. Seek out the holders of our paper, call it all in, and pay it off in gold. The money market will be so pressed that even our name will be at a discount.— Work out this scheme, and watch the result.— Every holder to a note of hand will be glad to allow ten per cent. discount for gold. Call in all. Leave not a rag of paper in any house in Paris with name thereon as acceptors. Should it chance that even then you do not find bills enough come into absorb the gold, let my brother extend the operation, and discount equally the flying bills of the three Paris houses, marked in his memorandum book as A, B, C. Never mind whether the bills have two, four, or six months to run. I say pay off all. Ferret them out from every corner of Paris. Lock your paper in your desk, and the ship will ride out the storm. How like you the plan, sir? Ha! The bills will be useless to Napoleon. Gold alone will meet his views, and he must get it through those houses who have been in the secret of his return. Meanwhile, bid my brother to be foremost at the Tuilleries levees, and profuse is his assurance of devotion to the emperor, with regret that he has no gold.'

Rothschild paused, as if to demand my applause for his plan. I saw it all, the riddle was solved. Success was all but certain. Check to Napoleon! and probably checkmate; for other blows are yet in reserve for him! Rothschild resumed, with the gravity of a veteran commanding in a battery with the bullets flying around him,—

'Tell my brother, moreover, to operate on the French funds for a rise, the moment they recover from their first depression. Operate largely, and in the certainty that the Bourbon star will shine again, in less than four months, brighter, and more enduring from this dark cloud having passed away. Remind my brother, however, to operate against the emperor; only through third parties, and to beware; for Napoleon will owe us a grudge for present proceedings, though at first he will be too eager to court public opinion to dare to seek revenge on our house. And now, away with you, sir, on the wings of the wind; but, hold! what is the earliest hour at which the courier of the English embassy can be at the Foreign Office here?'

'I should say, eight or nine.'

'Ha!' said Rothschild, then stop yet a moment. Thy coming is, indeed, a God-send!'

Seating himself, Rothschild hastily wrote and sealed a short note, addressed to Lord Castlereagh.

'Leave London by Westminster, and hand in this note as you pass Downing street (of course you know London,) to be delivered as early as possible. Lord Castlereagh comes punctually to business at 9 o'clock, and will find it on his desk. It is right that I should briefly acquaint his lordship with the outbreak of Napoleon.'

'But,' remarked I (child as I was, compared with Rothschild,) 'would you not prefer my leaving it at his lordship's private residence; in which case he will get it at least two hours sooner?'

'Content yourself, young man,' returned the chief, a grim smile; 'obey orders without reasoning upon them. Ahem! he might not like to be disturbed so early. Besides, how do we know he is at home? There; I date my envelope, half past five A. M. Can man do more?

And now away, sir. We shall soon meet again. Return by Calais. The Boulognois might lay hold of you."

"But allow me to remark, one difficulty remains," observed I. "I have no passport."

"Oh, I can remedy that in a moment. The English government allow me to keep a few blanks for emergencies."

With Rothschild, to will and to do appeared to be the same thing. He filled me up a passport ready signed, describing me as one 'especial mission;' and we parted with a cordial squeeze of the hand. I can truly say, I neither ate nor drank in or near the British metropolis.

"How shall we drive, sir?" asked the postboy, as we crossed Westminister Bridge.

"Drive," said I, "as if the devil were after us!" Luck was on my side throughout this eventful chess game; for such I contend it was in the highest signification of the word. Life is chess on a grand scale, and chess is an emblem of life, with its hopes and its fears, its losses and its gains; only, in chess, if you lose one game through a false move, you can set up the pieces and play another. My chances of checkmating the emperor now increased hourly. The ball was at my foot. It may be said, the greater share of the laurel-branch ought to be Rothschild's. Never mind, I was not puffed up with pride. Could I have a more worthy partner than the mighty monarch of European finance. It was king against Kaisar, and mine own was at least the hand that moved the pieces.

Fate was constant throughout my journey. I reached Dover and Calais without an accident, and reeled into our Paris counting house, more dead than alive, soon after noon, on the 8th day of March. I need not say how delighted was our French Rothschild at the counsel I brought. All hands went immediately to work to carry out the scheme. As for me, I went to bed.

Rothschild's behavior was perfect. He made me keep the ring I wore, and thus I gained my carbuncle. More valuable orders of merit have been given by monarchs for services of inferior value.

To make my narrative complete, I must here trouble you with a chapter of dates.

Bonaparte had landed in France on March 1, and the news came to the Tuilleries, as I have said, by the Lyons telegraph, on the 5th. On the 6th, Louis le Desire, issued his first proclamation, and ran away from Paris, his loved city, on the 19th. March 12, the emperor entered Lyons, left that city next day; was at Fontainbleau on the 20th; and came into Paris on the same day at nine o'clock at night. Le petit Caporal had covered two hundred French leagues, partly hostile, in twenty days; not bad work, considering a part of the journey was performed on foot, that armies were to be conquered and municipal authorities harangued, en route, in every town. On my part, (for as I am playing chess with the emperor, I may here contrast my doings with his,) I had left Paris on the night of the 5th of March, and was back at my post on the 8th. We were, morally speaking, assured of at least a clear week, even should the troope sent to oppose the emperor, unite themselves to his cause. A good deal may be done in a week!

The success of the house of Rothschild was complete; and Napoleon, as far as our game went, was irrevocably checkmated. All our gold was paid away; barely a single twenty franc piece remained in our treasure vaults.—

We stood upon our bills and waited the event.

On the 21st of March, the emperor had a grand levee at the palace of the Tuilleries, to which our chief went, though with a trembling heart. Bonaparte looked at him from head to foot, with any thing but a pleasant expression of countenance, and turned on his heel with this one significant phrase, "I see there are two Napoleons in Europe."

The courtiers stared at each other, but could not read the riddle. Our Rothschild saw that his counter-plot was known, and appreciated, though not perhaps gratefully! During the hundred days' reign—that meteor flash of regained power—the emperor took no further notice of the matter, but subsequently alluded to it at St. Helena, in his conversations with Las Cases. He then laughed at the trick, and owned we had completely foiled him. A Napoleon to confess himself beaten is twice vanquished.

And now, in the manner that emperors count over their spoils, let me briefly sum up the gains of the Rothschilds. The net is thrown into the waters, and drawn to land; let us tell over the fish taken.

Firstly, you will take notice that, in our exchange of gold for paper—hailed at the same time like the changing of the new lamps for old in the Arabian tale of Aladdin—in this exchange, I say, we cleared a profit of ten per cent., making ten millions of francs nett of itself. The emperor lost Waterloo—commerce was restored—oil was poured upon the waters—the Bourbons crept forth from their holes, like mice when the cat is out of sight. Gold became a dead weight—bills were in requisition for remittal to foreign countries—the bullion all came back to our vaults—and we favored our friends, by charging them only 5 to 8 per cent. premium for taking the cumbersome metal off their hands.

The Bourbons were not ungrateful. With an incomparable degree of adroitness, Rothschild made them see that we had been instrumental in crippling the resources of the emperor! Thus goes the world. In return for our fidelity to the fleur de-lis, we were permitted to suck some of its sweetest honey. And the records of French finance yet ring with our gains upon the Bourse, through our buyings and sellings of stocks upon this occasion.

On the morning I bore the news to England, Rothschild went down to the Stock Exchange of the British metropolis, at 9'clock. He was always a punctual man. At this very time, Schmidt was about to open his budget to his employers at Westminster. Acting through agents, Rothschild operated in the bonds to an enormous amount for an anticipated fall. His brokers did all this while the great man was quietly reading the Times newspaper. I will not dwell upon the results in figures. The crop was enormous! At 10 A. M. the news came at the Stock Exchange from the government Home Office, and the thing was blown.— It was the interest of Rothschild's brokers to keep the secret, and they did so. In the course of the same day, Lord Castlereagh forwarded to the illustrious Rothschild an autograph letter from the Prince Regent, thanking him for his personal attention, as well as for his disinterested conduct, in placing his own private information at the service of the government, before the arrival of their own courier! Now it is all over, I look back with astonishment.

STATUE OF CINCINNATUS.

MODELED BY NATHAN F. BAKER--ROME, 1844.

Nathan F. Baker, one ot our Cincinnati artists, who has been for the last two years or more
engaged at Rome and Florence in the pursuit of
his art, has finished the model in plaster of a
statue of Cincinnatus, the illustrious Roman
Dictator with whose name that of our city is in-
separably connected. Mr. B. is a young artist
in the double sense of age and practice, and if
an apology may be needed for that ambition
which has prompted him in the second or third
year of his pursuit of the Fine Arts to finish a
statue, it may be offered in the beautiful specimen of his capacity for such undertakings which
is supplied by the bust of Egeria, to which I
referred in my last. Mr. Baker was encouraged
by some of the lovers of the Fine Arts in Cin-

cinnati to undertake this enterprise, under their expectation that the city which bears the name of the subject, and is the birth place of the artist, would subscribe the necessary amount to obtain the statue in marble of *Cincinnatus* as an appropriate embellishment of some of our public rooms, the new College for example.

Almost every one can understand how imperfectly an idea of a statue, large as life can be afforded by an engraving of the size and the material which heads this article. It will serve however to give some idea of its design and effect. The following note is from the pen of the artist himself, written before the completion of the model and describing the sketch he sent.

"The drawing which I send you is taken from the unfinished statue which I am now working at. I have represented Cincinnatus in the attitude of a mediator, when he was called for the first time to act in a public capacity, and have endeavored to give the action of the speaker when before the Roman citizens. I consider, however, that the statue will express equally the first position as the last, although he was at that time acting more in the character of a warrior than the mild and stern judge between the parties who threatened to overthrow the existing Republic. I have dressed him simply in the Roman toga, which was worn by all classes of his time with but little distinction. The plough I have merely indicated in the sketch, and will take an excursion into the country to see the form of the common plough which has preserved the same shape with but little change to the present time."

What the ability of Mr. Baker for such a performance is, may be inferred, even beyond the *Egeria,* by the following testimonies, which I have selected from a number of others, because the writers are of ourselves. A letter from a Cincinnatian abroad to his correspondent here, says, "Baker I see often, he is a fine fellow, and has great talent." Another of our citizens writes as follows:

"By the way, Baker, a young Cincinnati artist, in Rome, has modelled a Cincinnatus very highly spoken of by the artists there, and which will be, I doubt not, an excellent thing. He would like to have a commission for it, and I think the city would do very well to give him one, or if the city will not, perhaps a private gentleman would. If you have an opportunity to say to any one of the lovers of the Fine Arts, that is the case do so, and say also it is very much praised by all who have seen it. I feel an interest in Baker's success, and now is the time to encourage his efforts."

The following is an extract from a letter received here by the last packet, written by another of our citizens traveling in Europe.

"I have conversed with Mr. Powers at Florence, and with as many persons acquainted with Mr. Baker as I knew, and all concur in awarding him decided talent and capable of attaining great excellence in his art. The statue he has modeled pleases me much, and has been

generally admired. I feel my deficiency in the rules of art too much to pronounce a judgment upon it—I can only say *I like it.* Should our friends of the Queen City think proper to give him the order, I have full confidence in their getting a statue of the great Roman that will give satisfaction and reflect credit on our young citizen and countryman. If a subscription for that purpose be got up, you can put my name down for fifty dollars."

An effort will be made as I learn, by some of the admirers of the Fine Arts to bring this subject before our community, and I trust a liberal subscription will enable Cincinnati to possess a work which shall forever associate *Roman patriotism with American genius.*

A Panther Adventure.

It is much to be regretted that the great mass of personal adventures, with which the life of the pioneers in the west is known to have abounded, has accompanied the actors in those scenes to the oblivion of the grave. And yet we could expect nothing else. The privations and sufferings of the wilderness, the dangers and escapes in conflicts with savage beasts, and equally savage Indians were such every day occurrences, as to be considered hardly worth repeating, still less recording, and many a spirit-stirring incident and adventure is now forever lost.

Here and there however, may be found some rough pineknot survivor, who in the evening of life can look back to the scuffles with Indians, or conflicts with wild beasts with an interest of which he felt nothing at the time, the more so when he finds a stranger like myself, ready and desirous to take the narrative from his own lips.

Mr. E. E. Williams, to whom I refered in my last has furnished me with some interesting notes of pioneer adventures. He has been an old hunter, supplying not only his own family, but the settlements in which he lived—Cincinnati among the rest,—with venison and bear meat. He killed the last buffalo seen in Kentucky. At the age of 75 his bodily and mental powers are unimpaired. He owns a farm in the rear of Covington Ky., and last Friday a week, as his day's work, *split over an hundred rails.*

"Well," said this old veteran, after finishing his statistics of Indian warfare, and in reply to other questions, let me tell you a story or two of bears and panthers.

I was living on a branch of Bigbone, called Panther Run, from the circumstance to this day. It was the year after I had been out with Gen. Wayne. I had left home for a deer hunt, with rifle, tomahawk, and butcher knife in my belt as customary, and scouring about the woods, I come to a thick piece of brush, in short, a perfect thicket of hoop-poles. I discovered some dreadful growling and scuffling was going on, by the sound appearantly within a hundred yards or so. I crept as cautiously and silently as possible through the thicket, and kept on until I found myself within perhaps twenty steps of two very large male panthers, who were making a desperate fight, screaming, spitting and yelling like a couple of ram cats, only much louder, as you may guess. At last one of them seemed to have absolutely killed the other, for he lay quite motionless. This was what I had been waiting for, and while the other was swinging back and forwards over him in triumph, I blazed away, but owing to that kind of motion, I shot him through the bulge of the ribs, a little too far back to kill him instantly.— They are a very hard animal to kill, any how. But he made one prodigious bound through the brush, and cleared himself out of my sight, the ground where we were being quite broken as well as sideling. I then walked up to the other, mistrusting nothing, and was within a yard of him, when he made one spring to his feet and fastened on my left shoulder with his teeth and claws, where he inflicted several deep wounds. I was uncommonly active as well as stout in those days, and feared neither man nor mortal in a scuffle, but I had hard work to keep my feet under the weight of such a beast. I had my knife out in an instant, and put it into him as fast as possible for dear life. So we tusseled away, and the ground being sideling and steep at that, which increased my trouble to keep from falling; we gradually worked down hill till I was forced against a large log, and we both came to the ground, I inside and the panther outside of it, he still keeping hold, although evidently weakening under the repeated digs and rips he was getting. I kept on knifing away till I found his hold slackening, and he let go at last to my great rejoicing. I got to my feet, made for my rifle which I had dropped early in the scuffle, got it and ran home; I gathered the neighbors with their dogs, and on returning found the panthers not more than fifteen rods apart; the one I had knifed dying, and the one I had shot making an effort to climb a tree to the height of 8 or 10 feet when he fell and was speedily despatched. Next day 1 stripped them of their skins, which I sold to a saddler at Lexington for two dollars a piece. You may depend, I never got into such a grip again with a panther.

Street Paving.

I observe that the pavement on Main street from Fifth to Seventh, is in process of macadamization,—a great and obvious improvement, calculated to rid us of the holes and ruts which have so long disgraced that great thoroughfare. It will however prove matter of regret, I judge, that this improvement has been made on the ex-

isting bed of the street, whereas the whole pavement should have been taken up and the metal laid upon an even surface of earth if a permanent job is expected as the result. This procedure is the less excusable when the part of this block from Sixth to Seventh street was paved in the very manner to which I object.— If the present improvement shall not be more thoroughly and carefully done, there may be danger that it will form an objection to the whole principle of macadamizing as applied to our streets.

Relics of the Past.

FORT WASHINGTON, March 26, 1792.

SIR:

To the Corporal and eight which accompanies the Convoy that leaves this post today, and the Sergeant and twelve, which returned with McCleland to Fort St. Clair, you will be pleased to add a subaltern, two non-commissioned officers and ten privates—to form an escort for the protection of the brigade which accompanies this letter, and those of McCleland and Tate, which are to be reloaded and return from your post with all possible despatch to Fort St. Clair; as this movement will be critical, the officer must be extremely cautious, and to that end I must request you to give him necessary instructions. When the convoy returns, you will direct the whole of the horses, and of the detachment belonging to this garrison, to proceed to this post.

Mr. Elliott positively refuses to construct Magazines for the reception of the Army provisions, at our out posts, and as a contest would greatly injure the service, and might possibly ruin the depending campaign, I shall make the provision, with an immediate and pointed reference of the subject, to the president of the United States.— You will therefore lose not one moment, in constructing stores, either within your fortress or immediately under its protection, for the reception of eight hundred or one thousand barrels; and in the mean time you are by every means in the compass of your power, to keep from damage by weather, the flour and other provisions, which have been or may be deposited under your command; keeping exact accounts and estimates of every expense which may occur in this business. And to enable you to proceed rapidly, I shall send out a pair of oxen, and a mechanic or two very shortly.

With due consideration,

I have the honor to be, sir,

Your most obedient servant,

J. WILKINSON.

JNO. ARMSTRONG,

Capt. 1st Reg't. U.S. Com't, Ft. Hamilton.

COMMUNICATIONS.

Citizens' Bank. No. 1.

MR. CIST:—The proprietors of this Bank beg leave through your columns to make known some of the leading features of its plan and operations.

The Bank is calculated to supply wants unprovided for in other monied institutions. For a small compensation, it is always ready to make such loans as are gratuitously obtained from neighbors. It is not proposed to supply facilities for the regular transaction of business, but to furnish money for a few days where it is wanted on the spur of the occasion, for some special purpose. Such loans give a man time to realize his resources, or make more permanent arrangements.

Take a few examples by way of illustration: A man expects money to meet a payment where his credit is at stake, but is disappointed. An unexpected but pressing demand comes upon him; he is unprepared for it. A profitable speculation offers, or an article needed for immediate use in his business, may be had for cash much below its real value, but for the want of a little ready money he loses the bargain; or for want of present means, he may incur a serious loss in being forced to sell property at a ruinous sacrifice, which might in a short time command a fair price.

CITIZENS' BANK, NO 2.

MR CIST.—The utility of this Bank is already felt and appreciated by a large portion of our most respectable citizens.

It receives money on deposit, payable with interest on demand, and thereby attracts the scattered, hoarded, and unemployed capital of the city to its vault, whence, as from a reservoir, it is distributed among the active and industrious portion of the community.

Already the Bank numbers nearly three hundred depositors, and among them are many of our oldest and wealthiest citizens. Hundreds of our thrifty merchants, mechanics and manufacturers resort to this Bank for temporary loans, rather than borrow from their neighbors. They esteem it a great convenience to be enabled, at a trifling expense, to obtain money at all times, for short periods, without being required to pay for it a moment longer than it is needed.

CITIZENS BANK, NO. 3.

MR. CIST:

As this Bank is always provided with the means of furnishing temporary loans at a moment's notice, it may be relied on as an unfailing resource in all emergencies.

A man having money to pay within a short period, or having claims falling due against him during his absence from the city, and wishing to guard against accidents, may make a conditional provision for the sum that may be wanted, which, if not needed costs him nothing; thus giving him all the advantage of a reserve fund for contingencies, free of expense.

Persons of ample means and undoubted responsibilitiy, may obtain money on their individual obligations; or a man may obtain a loan by adding a good name to his note, or by depositing as collateral security any good note or claim he may hold, or anything. in short, that will secure the payment of the debt. Borrowers will not be required to pay for money lorger than it is needed.

Human Nature.

Gnothe seauton. Know thyself;—was the sublime lesson which one of the ancient philosophers spent a life time in inculcating on his disciples, & reducing to practice in his own case. Burns, in a couplet which his genius has rendered immortal, exclaims,

"Oh would some power the giftie gie us,
"To see ourselves as others see us "

and a wiser either than the ancient sage or modern bard says, "Let not any man think more highly of himself than he ought to think," but the world still goes on, despising or neglecting the pursuit of self-knowledge, though of greater importance than any other worldly knowledge, being the foundation of all the rest.

I have met in my life time with many illustrations of this subject, of various characters.—Let me specify a few.

Travelling once in the Western Reserve, many years since, I put up at a public house at the town of Canfield, Trumbull county. The township election had been that day held; the votes were just counted off, and the result declared, it seems, a short time before I reached the house. The candidates successful and otherwise, were regaling themselves and others with potations at the bar, and the bar-room was a perfect babel of sounds. My horse had been attended to, and I seated myself on one of the benches, waiting till supper should be made ready for me and my fellow travellers. In the crowd was an unsuccessful aspirant for office, named Jacob Humiston, who believed and spared no pains to convince those who chose to listen to him, that he had been cheated out of his election. He succeeded by dint of brazen lungs in obtaining a hearing amidst the discordant sounds, and made a speech of which I recollect at this lapse of time, the peroration merely.—"He had run for Constable, he had got votes enough to elect him, there was no doubt of that, how he had been swindled out of the election he could not say, but he meant to find out, and when he did"—Here he made an awful and significant pause,—"all Canfield should hear of it---Trumbull county should hear of it---the Reserve should hear of it---the whole State should hear of it---the United States should hear of it,"---and rising in tone and energy at every step in the climax, finished by declaring "the whole world should hear of it!"

But what was this compared to the case of a constable I knew in Pennsylvania. He had served a legal precept of some sort on a particular friend of his, greatly his superior in strength, who being particularly drunk at the time, rebelled against the law and its myrmidon, seizing the officer and shaking him as though he meant to shake him to pieces. The parties meeting a few days after, Jim. the offender, was profuse in his apologies. "You know Jake, says he, I would not have served you so if I had been duly sober, it was all the devilish whiskey did it. The official at last mollified and relented under Jim's expostulations. "As to the sh aking" said Jake, "I don't bear any malice, I don't vally it a cent on my own account, but as an officer, recollect next time Jim, whoever *shakes me, shakes the commonwealth.*"

I have only one incident more to relate on this subject. A few weeks since I met an acquaintance residing across the canal, a German who makes *sour kraut,* very extensively. As he approached, I saw something was wrong by his countenance. ''What's de reason you not but me town in your *correctory.*'' I could not tell, I said, was he not down? ''No,'' he replied angrily, "your *correctory* is not one cent wert to peeples. How dey know where he kits *sour kraut?*"

Fire Engine Building.

The value of preparation, was probably never more strikingly demonstrated than at the late fire at Madison. An elegant church and other valuable buildings were subjected to destruction simply for want of sufficient fire apparatus, and property to the value of 75,000 dollars destroyed which might have been saved by the expenditure of fourteen hundred dollars, not two per cent. of that amount for the purchase of a first-rate Engine and Hose appurtenances. There was a supply of water in a public cistern, within two hundred and fifty feet of the devoted buildings, which sufficed by means of buckets to keep the fire under for fifteen minutes.

Our Madison neighbors have learned wisdom by experience, and have given orders to Messrs. Paddack & Campbell, our principal Fire Engine builders, for an Engine of the largest class, and sixteen hundred feet of Hose.

I trust the lessons taught at such a price lately to Madison and Zanesville may not be lost upon other places which are now inadequately protected from fire, and that they will see their true policy to disburse a few hundreds, as they desire to escape the loss of thousands or hundreds of thousands.

By way of contrast, I would refer to the fact, that Cincinnati with over an hundred fires during the past twelve months has sustained hardly greater loss than Madison at this single fire, and express my conviction, that had we been as destitute of protection from the devouring element as that city, our losses on this account must have been reckoned by *millions.*

Buckeye Mayors.

Within the last two years, Cincinnati has advanced to what may be termed an era in her political existence, in being able to furnish in two individuals, natives of this county, and of mature age, rival candidates for the mayoralty of the city. This was the case at the election of 1843, and again the case at our late election, Henry E. Spencer and Henry Morse being opposed to each other at both periods.

Relics of the Past.

Capt. John Armstrong to Gen. J. Wilkinson.

Fort Hamilton, April 26th, 1792.

Dear General:

An express is this moment arrived from Fort Jefferson—the despatches accompanying this will give you the news of that place.

I have only to add, although the enemy are in the neighborhood of this post, I have as yet evaded the execution of their designs—and that with the assistance of Capt. Ford's horse, have, and will on to-morrow have timber enough in the Garrison to finish one of the buildings mentioned in my last—it will contain all the flour now exposed, and what is on board the boats now coming up—I wish they may arrive safe.

The express did not touch at St. Clair.

I have the honor to be with respect,

your obedient servant,

JOHN ARMSTRONG,

Capt. 1st Reg't. U. S.

Fort Hamilton, May 9th, 1792.

Dear General:

The express from St. Clair arrived this morning about 7 o'clock—Sergeant Brooks who brought the dispatches says he saw and was within two rods of an Indian about half a mile from this post. The savage was endeavoring to shoot a deer with an arrow, and on discovering the party gave a yell, which was answered at no great distance by three or four others. A raft on which three or four might have crossed the river floated past the fort about 2 o'clock. The horse on which McDonald was sent express on the 23d of April, has returned to the garrison, his rider must therefore have been killed.

There being no noncommissioned officer with those men of Capt. Kersey's company, if there was no impropriety in the request I should wish one to join the command.

JOHN ARMSTRONG.
Capt. Commandant.

Gen. J. Wilkinson to Capt. J. Armstrong.
Fort Washington, May 11th, 1792.

DEAR SIR:

Your letter of the 8th came to hand in due season, I thank you for the precautions taken for the security of the convoy to St. Clair —*I* love a man who thinks, too few do so, and none else should command. All the tools which can be procured here, will be delivered you by Capt. Peters, *I* mean of those you have required. The balance of Kersey's company one Sergeant and 3 privates will join you with this escort; you may make the exchange proposed for a man at Dunlap's, station, but must send an orderly good soldier to take the place of the sawyer.

Your monthly rations are in future to be regulated by the enclosed form, and they must be delivered at this post, (as practicable) on the 4th of each successive month. The Couriers will in future leave Jefferson on the 1st day of the month, and every twelve or fifteen days after. You may rest satisfied that the command of Fort Hamilton, shall not be changed whilst *I* have influence in any instance, until some general movement takes place—"Let him who wins wear, He who woos enjoy," will, *I* believe be the motto of my colors. Mr. Hartshorn must be here by the 25th to take command of the horse; Hamilton will be up by the same day *I* expect. *I* rest much upon the enterprize and perseverance of these young men, *I* hope they may distinguish themselves. *I* will furnish you another officer the moment the state of this garrison permits.

For the safety of our communications, to save the troops, to assist in guarding the cattle, and for the purpose of scouting and reconnoitring, *I* have determined to annex to each of the out posts, two confidential woodsmen, to be subject to the orders of the respective commandants, agreeably [to the enclosed article. The whole party are to accompany the convoy out, and on Capt. Peters' return, Resin Baily and Joseph Shepherd, are in the first instance, to be stationed with you; but to proportion the duty of these men fairly, there must be a rotation. The party then which leaves Fort Jefferson, will deliver the dispatches from that post and St. Clair to you, your men are to run with them to this post,

and on their return, are to go forward to St. Clair where they will continue, and the party at St. Clair, will carry forward the dispatches to Jefferson, where they will take post, until remanded by Maj. Strong, and will proceed in this manner until other regulations may be deemed expedient—nevertheless on extraordinary occasions, extraordinary messengers are to be dispatched.

You will receive by this escort ten fat Bullocks, which are to be killed and issued, before you touch a ration of the bacon, other than what may be necessary to your own mess.--- The grazing of these cattle, and saving the guard harmless, will I know be extremely hazardous, but rely on your genius and resource.— The cattle must be penned inside the walls of the garrison every night—should any men desert you,[the scouts are to take the track, pursue, overtake, and make prisoners of them, and for every one so apprehended, and brought back, you may engage them twenty dollars. If the deserter is discovered making for the enemy, it will be well for the scout to shoot him and bring his head to you, for which allow forty dollars. One head lopped off in this way and set upon a pole on the parade might do lasting good in the way of deterring others.

Yours respectfully,
J. WILKINSON.

CAPT. JNO. ARMSTRONG, Ft. Hamilton.

Original Masonic Lodge.

The Nova Caesarea Harmony Lodge of this city still subsisting, was the first Masonic Lodge ever established here. Its charter was received from the Grand Lodge of New Jersey, and bore date Sept. 8, 1791. The officers appointed were *Dr. William Burnet* master, John S. Ludlow Senior Warden, *Dr. Calvin Morrell* Junior Warden. Owing to the absence of Dr. Burnet the lodge was not organized until Dec. 27th., 1794, when the following officers were elected. *Edward Day* master, *Dr. Calvin Morrell* Senior Warden, *Gen. John S. Gano* Junior Warden.

The following original document makes its appearance for the first time. It seems to have been a part of the proceedings connected with their organization.

The petition of sundry ancient York Masons residing in the Territory north-west of the river Ohio, humbly sheweth—

That your petitioners are extremely desirous to organize themselves into a Lodge of free and associated Masons.

For which purpose they solicit your warrant to be holden in Cincinnati, Hamilton county aforesaid.

They beg leave to offer Edward Day as Master, John S. Gano, as Senior Warden, and Calvin Morrell, as Junior Warden.

Brother Edward Day, one of your petitioners is known to your Right Worshipful Lodge as Junior Warden of No. 35. Joppa, Maryland when it was first established under your jurisdiction, and has since advanced the chair.

Brother John S. Gano will pay for this charter on demand, and will receive your communications and instructions.

Brothers Elias Wallen, John Allen and Isaac Guion, are well known to be Past Masters of good repute. You will be pleased to appoint one of them or more to instal the officers or obviate this difficulty in any other manner which your wisdom may think meet, and your petitioners as in duty bound shall ever pray.

EDWARD DAY.
Elias Wallin,
Ezra Fitz Freeman,
James Brady,
Calvin Morrell,
Pat Dickey,
John Allen,
Ephraim Kibbey,
John S. Gano,
Nathaniel Stokes,
Wm. Stanley.

Cincinnati, March 17th, A. L. 5795.

The Sea-Boy's Farewell.

Wait, wait ye Winds! till I repeat
A parting signal to the fleet
  Whose station is at home;
Then waft the sea-boy's simple prayer,
And let it oft be whispered there,
  While in far climes I roam.

Farewell to FATHER! reverend hulk
In spite of metal, spite of bulk,
  Soon may his cable slip;
Yet while the parting tear is moist,
The flag of gratitude I'll hoist,
  In duty to the ship.

Farewell to MOTHER! 'first-class' she!
Who launched me on life's stormy sea,
  And rigged me, fore and aft;
May Providence her timbers spare,
And keep her hull in good repair,
  To tow the smaller craft.

Farewell to SISTER! lovely yacht!
Though whether she be manned or not,
  I cannot now foresee;
May some good ship a tender prove,
Well found in stores of truth and love,
  And take her under lee.

Farewell to GEORGE! the jolly boat!
And all the little craft afloat
  In home's delightful bay;
When they arrive at sailing age,
May Wisdom give the weather-guage,
  And guide them on their way.

Farewell to all on life's rude main!
Perhaps we ne'er shall meet again,
  Through stress of stormy weather;
But summoned by the board above,
We'll harbor in the port of Love,
  And all be moored together!

Early Navigation of Lake Erie.

The first vessel navigation on Lake Erie, under the American flag, was the sloop Detroit, purchased by the government of the British North West Company, in 1796. She was about 70 tons burthen, but was old and scarcely sea worthy when purchased, and soon after was condemned and laid up at the river Rogue. In the same year, '96, a small schooner called the Erie Packet was built in Canada, to run before Fort Erie and Presque Isle. She was lost in '98 by drifting out of the Erie harbor. In 1797, the schooner Wilkinson, of 80 tons, was built at Detroit by Abbott and Conelly, and sailed for two years by Conelly as master. In 1810, she was thoroughly repaired and her name changed to the Amelia; and in 1812 was purchased by the government and armed, and had the honor of belonging to Commodore Perry's squadron, and of participating in his glorious victory. The Good Intent, of 35 tons, was built by Capt. Lee, in 1799, and navigated the Lake till 1806, when she run on the Point Abino, and was lost, together with her cargo and crew. The same year, '98, the brig Adams and schr. Tracy were built by the government. The former was captured by the British the first year of the war, afterwards re-taken at Fort Erie and run upon Squaw Island and burnt. The latter was sold to Porter, Barton & Co., and afterwards lost on the reef near Fort Erie. In 1805, the War Department, possessing, as it would seem, no very accurate notion of our localities, directed the commanding officer at Fort Niagara to construct at that post, a vessel of size to transport the Indian presents from Niagara to Fort Wayne. The commanding officer anticipating some difficulty in navigating up the Falls, ventured to depart so far from his instructions as to cause the vessel to be built at Black Rock. She was called the Nancy, and was of about 50 tons burthen. The Contractor, a fine vessel of about 80 tons burthen, was built at Black Rock, in 1806, by Porter, Barton & Co., and was sold to the government in 1812. The Catharine, another fine schooner, was built by Sheldon Thompson and others, at Black Rock, in 1808. Several other vessels were built about this time at different places on the lake, but our recollection does not serve to give their names.

MARRIED,

ON the 9th inst, by the Rev. A. Lowrey, Mr. JOHN TOWNSEND to Miss CATHARINE S., daughter of D. C. Cassat.

On Thursday the 10th inst, by the Rev. Dr. Brooke, McLEAN J. BLAIR to Miss CAROLINE S. WALKER, daughter of W. M. Walker, Esq.

Same day, by Rev. N. L. Rice, Mr. L. P. SHERMAN to Miss MARY A. GITCHELL.

On Monday the 14th inst, by the Rev. James E. Wilson, Mr. JAMES ILEF to Miss MARTHA ANN REAGIN.

DEATHS.

ON Saturday, March 29th, Mrs. MARY ANN, consort of John Ewing.

On Thursday morning, 10th inst, MARY ASHTON, daughter of Dr. W. I. and Mary E. Madeira. Aged 2 years 10 months.

On Friday the 11th inst, MARY F., daughter of Wm. and Jane E. Meguier, aged 11 months 24 days.

Same day, ROBERT W. HARBESON, formerly of Free port, Pa.

On Saturday 12th inst, JOHN WHITAKER, aged 55 years, formerly of Bradford, Yorkshire, Eng.

Annals of the Late War.

Such was the want of preparation on our part for the war which was declared by the United States against Great Britain in 1812, that by the time it had been waged a twelvemonth, the Government found itself destitute alike of funds and credit. The public chest was empty, the Treasury notes issued for the exigencies of the times were obliged to be sold at a ruinous discount, and many of our military and naval operations throughout the whole land, were carried into effect by pledges of individuals who obtained on their own credit, the necessary supplies of provisions and money, when that of the government was unavailable. The following documents form one chapter on this subject.

Chillicothe, Aug. 5th, 1812.
MAJ. GEN. GANO,

Sir—You will immediately march 300' men from your division, under the command of a Major—furnish them with a blanket and knapsack, arms and ammunition. Capt. Sutton will march them to Urbana, at which place I hope to see them. Volunteers under the law of Ohio will be preferred. I trust you will use every exertion to cause a compliance with the requisition.

Your ob't. serv't.,
R. J. MEIGS.

incinnati, Aug. 20th, 1812.
R. J. MEIGS,

Sir—Since I received your letter of the 5th inst., I have exerted every nerve. night and day to send the arms out to Urbana, and get the detachment from this place on the march. I have had innumerable obstacles to contend with and surmount, we knew nothing of before. There was no paymaster agent here that is Taylor's agent, and objections to every thing; I then had to set all my wits to work, and friends a few, assisted. I had to get Maj. Barr to join me to put in our note in Bank for $3500, payable in 10 days, which is all we could raise, and the bills on Government will not command the cash here, there are so many drawn they cannot be accommodated—I have sent to Urbana to Judge Reynolds, (you did not direct who) 500 stand of arms and 400 cartridge boxes, and belts as I could get. I have also sent ammunition, which you did not direct, and have sent camp kettles, &c. &c. The bills sent to Judge Reynolds to be delivered on your order. I have six as good companies as I have seen in the State—four have marched from here yesterday to join two others at Lebanon, where they will elect their Major. I found it impossible to attend to your request in meeting you and organize this detachment. I have appointed a Reg't. Quartermaster—he is very capable and very attentive, and the United States Assistant Deputy

Quarter Master approves—and he is the principal assistance I have had, for I have done all without an Aid de camp, you may therefore judge of my situation—since the rendezvous here my house has been almost like a barracks, —Having no particular order on the Assistant Deputy Quarter Master, Lt. Bryson, or the contractor for supplies for this detachment, I have taken the responsibility on myself, but have not drawn (*for it could not be had*,) what was actually necessary. You will please, if it meets your approbation, to sanction what I have done for those troops, and give an authority for the Deputy paymaster or his agent to pay the troops the advance the law allows, and refund the money I have advanced to the troops, that it may be returned to the Bank. The detachment is as follows: Capt. Jenkinson with his company of artillery, fitted completely with muskets,&c. &c. Lebanon light infantry, in exactly the same uniform, as Mansfield's company—four companies of riflemen completely equipt, one company one hundred strong, all can instantly fix bayonets to their rifles, the others, every man a tomahawk and knife—the whole are volunteers, except the light infantry of Lebanon. They have not yet received any advance for I could not draw sufficient; I have had complete muster pay and receipt rolls made out and signed as far as we have gone. We advanced one month's pay to the officers, and ten dollars to each man which has taken a larger sum than we received from Bank, to wit: $3500—Captain Torrence and Carr drew the money and paid the men under the direction and assistance of Captain Adams of the fourth regiment. whom I got to assist, that it should be regular and pass. The Kentucky troops begin to arrive at Newport—1 think it will be several days before they leave this; I wish our detachment to be ahead of them, therefore marched them for Lebanon yesterday. If it was not for the obstacle of the pay being wanting, they might proceed on in advance as fast as possible; I am very anxious to push them on, and have been from the first, for I am convinced they are wanting, and a better set of Militia, and a more orderly, I never saw collected, and I believe will *fight*. *I* sent more ammunition to Urbana than *I* contemplated for that number of muskets. The rifle powder sent by mistake, which can be rectified when they get to Urbana—I expect to be there by the middle of next week, and if you have not left Piqua, *I* shall endeavor to see you before my return. The bearer will receive your answer, and any communication you may think proper to make. From accounts, McArthur is gathering laurels. God send them success.

Yours with sentiments of respect and esteem,
JOHN S. GANO.

Sent this by Capt. Cox, express of Clinton Co., to whom *I* paid cash $3, and he is to meet me at Lebanon.

Cincinnati, Aug. 14th, 1812.

The Governor of the State of Ohio has given orders to Gen. Gano to have 300 men, properly officered, from his division, to convene in the shortest time possible, and have them march to Detroit to join Gen. Hull's army and escort provision &c. for the army. And the paymaster's agent being absent, and the men very anxious to receive their pay to provide themselves necessaries, the paymaster and receipt rolls are ready and will be sufficient vouchers for the payment. If the Miami Exporting Company or any persons will advance the pay we will jointly and severally hold ourselves bound for the amount. There will be 350 men from the 1st division in this detachment, the advance pay as to the amount per month is stated in our advertisement in the papers.

JOHN S. GANO,
Commander 1st Div'n. O. Militia.
WM. BARR,

To the President and Directors of the Miami Exporting Company Bank, Cincinnati.
$3,500.

Ten days after date we or either of us promise to deliver to the President and Directors of the Miami Exporting Company, James Taylor's check on the Cashier of the said company, for three thousand five hundred dollars, or on failure of delivering the said check as stipulated therein, we or either of us promise to pay, at the expiration of the term aforesaid, to the President and Directors aforesaid at their office in Cincinnati three thousand five hundred dollars, value received.

The Pittsburgh Fire.

This is the severest calamity in this line, that has ever visited the United States. In the great New York fire of 1835, probably merchandise to as great value was consumed, but the number of dwellings and the amount of personal property in that case was far short of what was involved in this wide spread devastation.

Some idea may be formed by our citizens of the extent of the city which suffered, as well as the region in which it took place, by taking all that space which would be marked out by following Walnut street in Cincinnati to Third, along Third both sides to Main, along Main to Fourth, Fourth to Sycamore, Sycamore to Fifth, Fifth to Deer creek, and then following a line more than half a mile east, and including all that lies between these bounds and the river.— This gives an accurate idea, not only of the space and region, but of the business character of the burnt district.

In view of the fact that such extensive conflagrations as those at New York in 1835, and Pittsburgh now, leave the sufferers unprotected by the insurances made at home, it becomes matter of serious consideration for the community, whether insurance from fire should not always be effected at other cities than those in which the property lies.

Those who were insured in New York at the period of the fire of 1835 lost all in the insolvency of the N. Y. Insurance Companies, which resulted from that event. Those who were insured in Boston were safe. So it will be found now, as respects Pittsburgh, all the insurance recoverable there, will be that effected at foreign offices.

Bear Adventure.

I published last week a panther fight in which my old pioneer friend Williams was engaged some fifty years ago. One or two adventures with bears, which occurred to him about the same time, will serve at once to diversify this narrative, and afford additional light on the modes of living, in early days of the West. I give the story almost in his own words.

"My wife was lying at home in her confinement with her second child, and to lighten our cares, the older one about two years of age had been taken home to her grandmother's, who lived a matter of two miles off. When my wife was able to be stirring about once more, I went over to fetch the little one, and was returning with it in my arms when it began to cry, and I was so busy trying to quiet it, that I hardly noticed at first the sound of steps and a savage growling behind me. Turning my head around, I saw a great he bear, one of the largest I ever saw. He was then within a rod of me. As I turned, my dog, a large and powerful brute, part bull, part grey hound, turned also; and springing at the bear seized him by the hind leg, to check his progress and favor my escape. I made tracks with all the speed I could. The bear would turn on the dog, when the dog would break his hold, and the bear put off again after me. Again the dog would lay hold, and the bear again turn on him compelling him to let go. In this way I was gaining on him, although excessively tired, being obliged to carry the child at arms length, and a very heavy one it was. The child cried the more from being held in so awkward a position, which made the bear more and more savage on my tracks. At last I came in where a path led off through the brush to my home, and the bear being intent on keeping off the dog, passed it without notice and I got home safe. I gave the child to its mother, and taking my rifle down, started out after the old *cuss.* I had hardly got to the road when I met my dog *Tory*, as I called him, breathless and bloody, having received some pretty severe bruises from the bear. He refused to follow me, and I was obliged to give up the bear hunt for that time.

Some time afterwards one of the neighbors reporting he had seen the bear fasten on a large hog, a constant lookout was kept for him in the settlement. I was out one evening after deer, when I discovered by the smell that carrion was in the neighborhood; I watched the crows to see where they would light, and as I got nearer I heard the bear growl, having been absent for water, and on his way back to the carcass. As soon as I saw him I took aim and fired, hit him on the skull, tore off a large stripe over the eye brow, and while he lay stunned ran up to him within a few feet, fired again and killed him on the spot. This bear had been a nuisance to the neighborhood for three years, having killed in that space of time between 75 and 100 head of hogs, big and little, besides other domestic animals, some fine calves among the rest.

At another time I was out hunting one day, and came on the tracks of a large bear. A light snow on the ground enabled me to follow it up readily, which I did for half a mile to a large oak, up which at about thirty-five feet high there was a hole sizeable enough to let the bear in. As it was winter I knew that it would stay there some time if undisturbed, and went home to gather some of the neighbors for the hunt. So a few days after I got two of them, Alexander Herrington and Richard Shorit with their dogs. One of the men had a rifle and the other an axe. We found the tree too large and otherwise difficult to climb, being the 35 feet without a limb, and we concluded finally to fell a small beech tree against it, by which we could climb up to the hole. This was accordingly done, and it lodged safely against the oak. I built a fire to make chunks to throw in the hole, and proposed to the men to go up and get the bear out, which they both refused to attempt. I was unwilling to go up myself having no confidence in their knowledge of hunting, and feared they would miss the bear, but seeing there was no other way I took off my moccasins for fear of slipping, and tying a string to a chunk of fire, I gave my rifle to Herrington and climbed the beech which lay very steep against the hollow tree. When I got to the hole I looked in very cautiously, and after waving the chunk backwards and forwards in the air, to make it burn, held it there as a light, to judge the depth of the bear's retreat. Seeing nothing however, I dropped the chunk, which by the sound appeared to fall twelve or fifteen feet before I heard it strike. Presently the bear started up with a

grunt like an old sow roused from her lair, and growling awfully, clambered up, snorting at a great rate, while I let myself down as fast as possible on the tree by which I came up. The bear, on getting to the hole, began to poke her head in every direction to ascertain who and how many were disturbing her. I called out to Shorit to shoot her in the sticking place, but he having no experience hit her on the nose which only enraged her the more, and down she came butt foremost winding the tree round like a squirrel, and nearly as fast, letting go her hold when within a few feet of the earth. As soon as she came to the ground, two of the dogs seized her, but she soon crippled both. Herrington had run off with my rifle as soon as she began to come down. I had to run some distance before I could get it out of his hands, and when I did, the priming had got wet by his carelessness, and the gun would not go off. I then seized a dead limb by way of handspike and banged away at the bear to make her let go one of the dogs which she was killing as fast as possible. Two or three blows made her let go. The creature was so fat and cramped up in the tree that she could hardly move over the ground at first, and giving the crippled dogs to the others to carry home, seven or eight miles, I run to where I had hung my powder horn, and after wiping out the damp powder, and priming afresh, I put on my moccasins and set out after the bear, which had by this time got considerable of a start. I run it ten or twelve miles, before I caught up, which I did, by finding the bear which was fat and heavy, had taken to a large hollow beech tree to rest herself where she lay in the crotch. One crack of the rifle brought her down lifeless. I then butchered her, took the entrails out and left the bear on its belly, spreading out the legs, well knowing that in this position, nothing in the shape of wild beasts would molest it in the woods. I went home very tired. Next morning my brother and I took horses on which we carried the carcass home. It weighed three hundred and eighty-seven pounds when dressed.

I have killed in the course of my hunting scrapes rising of twenty bears, of which these were the two largest.

The next time I saw Herrington and Shorit, I told them never to go hunting with me or I might be tempted to serve them as I had done the bear, and upbraided them with their cowardice, which might have cost me my life. Shorit was from Pomfret, Connecticut, the neighborhood where Putnam killed the wolf, and excused himself by saying, he would far rather have gone in after that wolf, than risk the hug of a bear thirty or forty feet from the ground.

Relics of the Past.

Fort Washington, Dec. 2nd, 1791.

Sir:

I received your favour of the 29th, since which Mr. Hodgdon has been endeavoring to procure a boat, which would have been the best and easiest way of sending money to your post, but by some accident or other he has been constantly disappointed, and now they go on horseback. I hope the little delay may not have been very inconvenient—that the men sent for your trunk be met with. Could Mr. Hartshorne have gone by water, it would have been easier and safer for them to have taken that route also—they will return with him except the armourer who is wanted here.

Should you have an opportunity to send to Fort Jefferson be pleased to forward the enclosed letter, but I little expect that you will, before the escort goes with provision in about a week hence.

The old contractors have a large quantity of flour at Fort Hamilton, and the new ones are also sending forward a considerable supply.—What will be done for store houses I know not—is it not possible yet to raise a building for the purpose—if it can be done you will not think much of the trouble I know, and tho' you may have some just prejudices against the persons of the men who have the control at present—they are in some sense public servants, and in the posts have a right to have the provisions they buy in, secured from damage. At the same time it would be very hard on the old contractors to have what was laid in by them, in the just expectation that it would be wanted, turned out to destruction at a season when they cannot remove it to a place of safety. Do what you can to accommodate both.

I am sir,
your humble ser'vt.,
A. ST. CLAIR.
Capt. Armstrong.

Fort Steuben at the Falls of Ohio.

It is within my recollection, that when the present century commenced, the great mass of the writing paper consumed in the United States was of English manufacture. It was made entirely of linen rags, and compared with what is now used, a coarse and thick article, and rough in surface. I have a specimen in the subjoined letter, in which the *water mark* or stamp is G R, surmounted with a crown. When I examine the texture and substance of the letter which has been written more than half a century, and the creases of which have not injured in the slightest degree its strength, I feel disposed to wonder how much more careful handling among posterity the cotton fabric paper of our time will require.

I publish this letter simply as a testimony of the name in 1790 of the Fort at the Falls of Ohio, now Jeffersonville Ind. The station at that place had borne originally the name, Fort Finney.

Fort Washington, Jan. 12th, 1790.

Dear Sir:

I find by a letter of Mr. Robt. Moore, in whose hands I left your two notes for £72, 1,3 to D. Britt & Co—that they have not yet been paid, I will thank you to send, either to me or Mr. Robt. Moore, near Philadelphia, Captain Beatty's orders, that these notes may be settled out of the first or second instalment for the pay of the regiment.

I enclose you a state of your account with D. Britt & Co., at Pittsburgh, by which you will find that a number of articles have been omitted in the account I settled with you at Fort Vincennes. Please examine the same and inform me if any errors.

I am sir, yours,
D. BRITT.
Capt. Armstrong.
Fort Steuben, Rapids of Ohio.

Valuable Hint.

I copy the following article from the Boston Chronicle.

There is no reason why a manure of such concentrated strength, and of course cheap transportation might not be advantageously made in Cincinnati, where the raw material abounds, and charcoal could be procured at a low price, while blood is suffered to run absolutely to waste.—Probably also the charcoal which is thrown out by the whiskey rectifiers might be used to advantage. It will cost nothing to make an experiment, which I doubt not will be attended with complete success.

"The guano mania, by which whole islands are being transported across oceans, and sold out by the pound, has excited great attention to the subject of manures. As to guano itself, it is of exceedingly variable value, and in its best quality is inferior to manures which may be procured at less expense, This had been scientifically proved on the model farms of France, before the rage commenced.

The best sugar manufactories of France have given rise to a species of manure which is little if at all known in this country, and which we think our agriculture might avail itself of to great advantage. In the clarification of sugar, blood and animal carbon are used. The carbon charged with the animal matter and impurities of the sugar, was at first thrown away as useless. But it was ere long observed, by the sharpsighted French, that the vegetation about the heaps where it lay, was exceedingly luxuriant and prolific. It was directly proved to be a valuable manure, and commanded such a price as to form a considerable portion of the income of the beet sugar manufactories, and in fact to insure the permanence of that branch of national industry.

By careful experiment it was discovered that the stimulating effect on vegetation was not due in any degree to the residuum of sugar contained in the *noir animal*, as the substance is called, nor to the carbon or blood alone, but to the proper combination of the two last. From this grew a new business of manufacturing manure, called *noir animalise*. This is an intimate mixture of carbon, the charcoal of wood, peat, straw, &c., and blood, butcher's offal, dead carcasses, or other animal matter. The mixture is made as perfect as possible, when the charcoal is in its driest state; it is then perfectly dried and sold in a powdered or granulated form.

This manure produces the most extraordinary effects upon the fructification of plants, especially the grains. Being sowed along with the seed, the charcoal has the effect so to retard the decomposition of the animal matter, that it proceeds at about an even pace with the development of the plant, and is about at its height, while the fructification takes place, instead of having exhausted itself in the production of leaves, as is too much the case with other manures. By the use of this manure in France, it appears that the wheat crops have been increased nearly one third on an average in the districts where it is used: taking into view the expense, the results are considerably more satisfactory than those of any other manure, guano not excepted.

It is manufactured on an immense scale near the slaughter-houses of Paris, and thus benefits not only the agriculture of the country but the health of the city. Why could not the same thing be done in this country, where immense quantities of animal matter are now wasted, and where charcoal is probably cheaper than in France? Why should not even our western farmers avail themselves of such an aid, if they can add a third to their crop without adding a third to their expenses? Those who would try this manure have only to pour upon dry pulverised charcoal, recently heated, as much blood as it will absorb, and they have the manure.— There is no danger of sowing or planting the seed immediately upon it. The closer the contact the better. It is excellent for all sorts of garden and house plants."

The First Court in Ohio.

The first court held northwest of the river Ohio, under the forms of civil jurisprudence, was opened at Campus Martius, (Marietta,) September 2d, 1788.

It will be remembered that on the preceeding 7th of April, Gen. Rufus Putnam, with 47 men had landed and commenced the first settlemen, in what is now the State of Ohio. Gen. Harmar, with his regulars, occupied Fort Harmar. Gov. St. Clair, and also Gen. Samuel Holden Parsons and Gen. James Mitchell Varnum, Judges of the Supreme Court, arrived in July. The Governor and Judges had been employed from their arrival in examining and adopting such of the statutes of the States, as in their opinion would be appropriate to the situation of this new colony. The Government had made appointments of civil officers for the administration of justice, and to carry into effect the laws adopted. Some idea may be obtained of the character of the early settlers of Ohio, by describing the order with which this important event, the establishment of civil authority and the laws, was conducted. From a manuscript written by an eye witness, now in my possession,

I have obtained the substance of the following. The procession was formed at the Point (where most of the settlers resided,) in the following order:—1st. The High Sheriff, with his drawn sword; 2d, the Citizens; 3d, the Officers of the Garrison at Fort Harmar; 4th, the members of the Bar; 5th, the Supreme Judges; 6th, the Governor and Clergyman; 7th, the newly appointed Judges of the Court of Common Pleas, General RUFUS PUTNAM and BENJ. TUPPER.

They marched up a path that had been cut and cleared through the forest to Campus Martius Hall, [Stockade,] when the whole countermarched, and the Judges Putnam and Tupper, took their seats. The Clergyman, Rev. Dr. Cutter, then invoked the divine blessing. The Sheriff, Col. Ebenezer Sproat, (one of nature's nobles) proclaimed with his solemn "O Yes," that "a court is opened for the administration of even-handed justice to the poor and the rich, to the guilty and the innocent, without respect of persons, none to be punished without a trial by their peers, and then in pursuance of the laws and evidence in the case. Although this scene was exhibited thus early in the settlement of the State, few ever equaled it in the dignity and exalted character of its principal participators. Many of them belong to the history of our country, in the darkest as well as the most splendid periods of the Revolutionary war. To witness this spectacle, a large body of Indians was collected, from the most powerful tribes then occupying the almost entire West. They had assembled for the purpose of making a treaty.— Whether any of them entered the Hall of Justice, or what were their impressions, we are not told.

A Fragment of Recollections.

The first approach of actual settlement or population, to the Ohio river, followed in Braddock's trace, from Fort Cumberland to Red Stone Old Fort. And from Red Stone to Wheeling, Buffalo, Cross creek on one hand—to Pittsburgh on another, and on a third, up to the Monongahela in the line of Morgantown and Clarksburg. The settlements advanced most rapidly and most directly through the tract of country that now constitutes Washington county, Pennsylvania, to the Ohio, in the compass from Wheeling to Brown's Island or Holliday's cove, Fifty years ago this tract of country sustained a numerous population, and was to a considerable extent improved. There were open farms, bearing orchards, substantial houses of hewn logs, with shingle roofs, and stone chimnies. And there were occasional school houses sparsely scattered through the settlements, in which urchins were taught their *A B abs*, and the spelling and reading lessons of Dilworth's spelling book. The inhabitants were of the same men who slaughtered the Moravian Indians, and among them there was as yet no place of public worship, no ministers of the Gospel.

It is fifty years ago—nay, in exact accuracy, it is fifty eight years ago, since a first movement was made among these people to found a place of public worship.

In the month of June, 1787, an arrangement was completed for organizing a religious congregation thirty miles in advance of any existing organization. Preparations was made in the depths of the forest. A rough wooden erection was constructed, as a pulpit, and felled timbers were arranged for seats. Thursday was the day of the week selected for the first meet-ing, and the sun never shone upon a more gen-ial day in the month of June. For miles around the whole population was collected together.— The minister came to make his trial sermon.— A young licentiate with his young wife in com-pany.

In the tract of country I have described, the Presbyterian clergy were the religious pioneers. At that day, their most western location was east of the new towns of Washington and Can-onsburgh. JAMES McMILLEN, ROBERT PATTER-SON, JOSEPH SMITH. If there was another, I do not remember him. Young men studied divin-ity in the private establishments of these pio-neers. More than this, they acquired all the elements of such education as they possessed, in those same family establishments. From these beginnings the college at Canonsburgh arose. The founders were the clergymen I named and their few friends and associates.

The minister who presented himself to make his trial sermon, was the pupil and son-in-law of the Rev. Joseph Smith. The Rev. James Hughes has since been well known as a faith-ful and unpretending preacher of the Gospel, in the Presbyterian Church-

The School-mistress Abroad.

'Now close your book, Bob,' said the mother, 'and Alec give me yours. Put your hands down, turn from the fire, and look up at me, dears,' 'What is the capital of Russia?'

'The Birman empire,' said Alec, with unhes-itating confidence.

'The Baltic sea,' cried Bob quickly, emulous and ardent.

'Wait—not so fast, let me see, my dears, which of you is right.'

'Mrs. Thompson appealed immediately to her book, after a long private communication with which, she emphatically pronounced them both wrong.

'Give us a chance, mother,' said Bob, in a wheedling tone, (Bob knew his mother's weak-ness,) 'them's such hard words, I don't know how it is, but I never can remember them.— Just tell us half the syllable—oh, do now, please!"

"Oh, I know now!" cried Alec, "it's some-thing with a G in it."

"Think of the apostles, dears. What are the names of the apostles!"

"Why, there's Moses," began Bob, counting on his fingers' "and there's Sammywell, and there's Aaron, and————."

"Stop, my dear," said Mrs. Thompson, you must begin again. I said who was Peter—'tis not that—who was an apostle?"

"Oh, I know now!" cried Alec again—(Alec was the bright boy of the family,) It's Peter,— Peter's the capital of Russia."

"No, not quite, my dear, try again."

"Paul," half murmured Robert, with a reck-less hope of proving right.

"No, Peter's right, but there's something else. What has your father been taking down the beds for?"

There was a solemn silence, and three indus-trious sisters blushed the slightest blush that could be raised on a maiden's cheek.

"To rub that snuff off the walls," said the ready Alec.

"Yes, but what was it to kill!" asked the in-structress.

"The fleas," said Bob.

"Worse than that, dear."

"Oh, I know now," shrieked Alec for the third time; "Petersbug's the capitol of Russia."

Primitve Times.

Our neighbors in the west—(say 600 or 700 miles distant, and this of course does not in-clude the great west, which is somewhere in the neighborhood of sundown, nor the Far West, which is towards sunrise of to-morrow)—our neighbors in the West, we say, were formerly blessed with the large church of out-doors—but the Gospel had no better quarters than the Law.

'Mr. Sheriff,' said the Judge, who was seated on a stump, 'have you empaneled the Jury?'

'Nearly, sir. I have eleven of them secured in the ravine, tied with a grape vine; and the constables are running down the twelfth.'

—So goes an anecdote of thirty years ago in Ohio—which is now No. 3 of the confederacy, and will probably be only second to New York in the census of 1850.

—Whoever has reached the twenties, can re-member how far Ohio was distant when he was a boy. We marvelled that any should think of going so far away. And yet the settlers soon surrounded themselves with attractions, and home proved the centre of the universe to each family of the content and industrious. Is there not instruction in the remark of the borderer's wife? She and all hers were located on a pra-irie somewhere in the depths of the Great West. A cosmopolite and amateur hunter saw her cab-in and entered. In the course of conversation she inquired where he came from?

'My home is in Boston,' said he.

'Where is Boston, I pray?'

It is little short of two thousand miles towards sunrise,' was the answer.

'La me!' said the simple-hearted, home-lov-ing woman—'La me! I wonder how any body can live so far away!'

—O brother—O sister! consider, and be wise. Is home the centre of the Universe to thee? If it be, thy soul hath attained the blessedness of primitime times, ere fashion and shame perver-ted the true uses of Life.

CITIZENS' BANK, NO. 4.

MR. CIST.—The rates at this Bank will not be thought excessive when it is considered that a loan may be obtained for a single day, if re-quired, and that the price in many cases barely compensates the labor alone of the transaction, and further, that a liberal deduction is always made when large sums are borrowed for a month or longer.

$50, for example, is wanted for a single day: here it is necessary to count the money twice, draw up a note, enter the transaction in several books—and all for the sum of 6¼ cents; for the Bank never in any case, however small the loan, charges more than one-eighth of one per cent. per day, even for the shortest periods.—Again it should be borne in mind that the Bank seeks no profit from the issue of Bills for circulation, and that it pays interest on all its deposites.— That to be ready for the demands of borrowers and depositors, it is obliged to keep on hand at all times a large sum of money unemployed.—Besides, that it is not only subject to the usual expenses of a Banking house for rent, salaries, &c. but compelled to pay $400 annually to the City Government, for its privileges, and a heavy additional tax to the State.

Now, where a business is attended with all the labor and expense of ordinary trade, it is but just that it should command the profits of trade.

It is only where money is wanted for short periods, that it can be borrowed to advantage from this Bank. A man may pay $1 per day for the use of a $50 horse; or 6¼ cents per day for the temporary use of $50. He may pay 50 cents for a meal at a tavern, or 50 cents for a loan of $400 for a day. But as no one would think of hiring a horse for a year at one dollar per day, or of remaining at a tavern during a like period at two dollars per day, so no man in his senses would think of borrowing money for long periods at one-eighth of one per cent. per day.

Living by Faith.

Rev. E. N. Sawtell, it will be recollected lectured not long since at the First and Second Presbyterian Churches of Cincinnati on the religious state of France and Italy. I am not aware in what official capacity he appeared before the Presbyterian Churches here, I presume however as an agent to some of the religious societies in New York.

In 1836 and 37, if not later he was employed by the Seaman's Friend Society to occupy the pulpit of their Chapel at Havre, France. It was during that period, and while struggling with the financial embarrassments which he shared with his employers in America during that gloomy business period, that he wrote the following letter, in which it is impossible to say whether wit and humor, or pious confidence and cheerfulness abound most.

"HAVRE, June 8, 1837.

"You are indeed putting my faith to the test. My spirit sunk within me at getting no remittance by the Utica. Obtain funds here is entirely out of the question, for the prevailing opinion is, that all America has failed, from General Jackson down to the shoe-black. In my letter, by Mr. Stoddard, I more than intimated that I must leave, and return to America, and yet how to do it, in the present embarrassed state of the chapel, is a thing that quite puzzles me. My situation is unlike that of a broken merchant, who may, perhaps, out of the fragments of a vast estate, line his pockets with something to feed his family. For me to *stop payment*, is to *stop eating*—and I need not tell you what would be my next *stoppage* in this *stopping process*, in all probability it would be that of *breathing*—quite a serious failure *that*, particularly to a public speaker. Several little occurrences, however, have of late transpired, which encourage me

to hope, that in angling about I may yet catch a fish with money in his mouth.

A few days ago a handcart stopped at my door loaded with chickens, ducks, fish, a turkey, a calf's head and feet; indeed,for variety, it bore no small resemblance to Peter's sheet, and I strongly suspect, that the same hand that let down the sheet had something to do in this matter. It appears that on the arrival of the Utica, their fresh provisions, which are packed in ice, must be disposed of, and, in their disposal, the officers kindly remembered their chaplain. They have ever manifested a deep interest in the cause of the chapel since I have been here. The Lord be praised, and a thousand thanks to them.

For many months my wardrobe had given ocular demonstration of hard times, and seemed strongly to sympathize with the deranged state of the commercial world. When it became entirely unable to meet its demands, I went to the tailor, was measured for a new suit, without even the courage to ask him to wait for his pay, or the honesty to tell him he was running a risk. It seems, however, that the American captains, (an increased number of whom, I rejoice to say, attended the chapel) had been noticing the same thing, to wit, that the parson's outer-man. to say nothing of the inner, needed a reformation, and intimated to some of my friends, that they would make an attempt upon my person, if they were certain that I would take no offence; being assured that I considered the servant not above his Lord, they very soon called on me, and intimated their wishes, that I would get me a suit of clothes, and they had the money to pay for them. I told them that I was expecting a suit sent in, and had feared they would come before I was prepared to pay for them. Just as they began to count out the money, in came the tailor with the clothes. Surely, thought I, "I need to take no thought for my life, what I shall eat, nor for my body what I shall put on." But, like the Jews of old, who could murmur with the flesh between their teeth I soon forgot it—for I was owing several hundred francs of borrowed money, which must be paid on a certain day in the following week, clouds thickened and darkened around me to such a degree, that I lost all faith, and my mind was not a little troubled in my preparations for the Sabbath, and on my way to the chapel, I felt as though a covering of sackcloth would suit me better than my new coat. I found, however, the chapel full of people, and many I knew to be Americans. I noticed in particular, one keen, black-eyed gentleman, who listened just as though he loved the truth. After preaching, he sought an introduction. walked home with me, and called to see me on Monday. I showed him your letter by the Utica; he went out, but returned with a hundred dollars, which he put in my hands, saying, "If the winds change so as to detain the vessel, I shall have to call for this to pay my tavern bill;" but he who holds the winds in his fist did not suffer it to change, and that debt, about which I was so faithless and unbelieving, is paid.

Coleman and his Attachment.

I do not recollect in the fictions of Johnson, or the more scrupulous narrative of Gibbon, a more striking instance of the vanity of human wishes, and the uncertainty of human calculations than the decease of COLEMAN, of the Eolian attachment of which a late mail has brought us tidings. After buffeting the world for years, friendless and insignificant, prospects of honor and profit open on him, such as offer themselves to few men for acceptance. He realises an hundred thousand dollars in the United States, and half a million in Europe from his ingenuity, and just as he is casting about to see where he shall invest his accumulating riches, he is swept from the stage of existence. "What shadows we are and what shadows we pursue!"

Sitting for a Portrait.

This is the title of a most amusing article in the February number of Blackwood's Magazine which we commend to the attention of artists as well as sitters, the latter of whom may gain some hints from it as regards posture, attitude, modes of concealing defects, &c., whilst the former may see some of the accessaries of their profession sketched to perfection. The article, too, is illustrated by some humorous anecdotes of which we select the following.

I will tell you what happened to a painter my acquaintance. A dentist sat to him two of days—the painter worked away very hard—looked at the picture then at the sitter. 'Why, sir,' said he, 'I find I have been all wrong —what can it be? Why, sir, your mouth is not at all like what it was yesterday.' 'Ah! I will tell you vat it ees,' replied the French dentist; 'ah! good—my mouse is not the same—yesterday I did have my jaw in, but I did lend it out to a lady this day.'

Painters generally discover the vanity of their sitters; they seldom fail to observe the pains they take to conceal any little defects or even great deformities. The annexed is an illustration:

I happened to call some time since, upon a painter with whom I was on intimate terms· I found him in a roar of laughter, and quite alone, 'What is the matter?' said I. 'Matter!' replied he; 'why, here has been Mr. B. sitting to me these four days following; at last, about half an hour ago, he, sitting in in that chair puts up his hand to me, thus, with 'Stop a moment, Mr. painter; I don't know whether you have noticed it or not, but it is right that I should tell you that *I have a slight* cast in my eye.'

You know Mr. B. a worthy good man, but he has the very worst gimlet eye I ever beheld.' Thought his defect wondrously exagerated, when, for the first time, he saw it on canvass; and perhaps all his family noticed it there, whom custom had reconciled into but little observation of it, and the painter was considered no friend of the family. Do you remember how a foolish man lost a considerable sum of money once, by forgetting this human propensity? He had lost some money to little K—— of Bath, the deformed gambler—and being nettled at his loss, thought to pique the winner. 'I'll wager,' said he, '£50, I'll point out the worst leg in the company.' 'Done,' said K—— to his astonishment. 'The man does not know himself' thought he, for there sat K—— crouched up all shapes by the fireside. The wagerer, to win his bet, at once cried, 'Why, that,' pointing to K——'s leg, which was extended towards the

grate, 'No,' said K——, quietly unfolding the other from beneath the chair, and showing it. 'that's worse.' By which you may learn the fact—that every man puts his best leg foremost.

* * * * * *

All sitters expect to be flattered. Take, for instance, the following scene, which was related to me by a miniature painter: A man upward of forty years of age, had been sitting to him—one of as little pretensions as you can well imagine; you would have thought it impossible that he could have had any homœpathic proportion of vanity—of personal vanity at least; but it turned out otherwise. 'Well, sir,' said the painter, 'that will do—I think I have been verv fortunate in your likeness.' The man looks at it, and says nothing, puts on an expression of disappointment. 'What! don't you think it like sir?' says the artist. 'Why—ve—ee—s, it is li—i—ke—but——' 'But what sir? I think it is like?' 'Why, I'd rather you should find it out yourself. Have the goodness to look at me.'— And here my friend the painter declared, that he put on a most detestably affected grin of amiability. 'Well, sir, upon my word, I don't see any fault at all; it seems to me as like as it can be; I wish you'd be so good as to tell me what you mean.' 'Oh, sir, I'd rather not—I'd rather you should find it out yourself, look again.' 'I can't see any difference, sir; so if you don't tell me it can't be altered.' 'Well, then, with reluctance, if I must tell you, I don't think you have given my *sweet expression about the eyes.*'

Our last anecdote shows the importance of a painter's never forgetting *the characteristics* of his sitter:

A painter, the other day, as I am assured, in a country town, made a great mistake in a characteristic, and it was discovered by a country farmer. It was the portrait of a lawyer—an attorney, who, from humble beginnings, had made a good deal of money, and enlarged, thereby, his pretensions, but some how or other not very much enlarged his respectability.

To his pretensions was added that of having his portrait put up in the parlor, as large as life. There it is, very flashy and very true—one hand in his breast, the other in his small clothes' pocket. It is market day—the country clients are called in—opinions are passed—the family present, and all complimentary—such as, 'Never saw such a likeness in the course of all my born days. As like 'um as he can stare.' 'Well, sure enough, there he is.' But at last—there is one dissentient! ''Tan't like—not very—no 'tain't,' said a heavy, middle-aged farmer, with rather a dry look, too, about his mouth, and a moist one at the corner of his eye, and who knew the attorney well. All were upon him. 'Not like! how not like? Say where is it not like?' 'Why, don't you see,' said the man, 'he's got his hand in his breeches pocket. It would be as like again if he had his hand in any other body's pocket.' The family portrait was removed, especially as, after this, many come on purpose to see it; and so the attorney was lowered a peg, and the farmer obtained the reputation of a connoisseur.

MARRIAGES.

On Thursday evening, the 17th inst., by the Rev. E. W. Sebon, Mr. ALFRED MILLER to Miss SUSANNAH GASKILL, all of this city.

Sunday, April 20th, by Elder Wm. P. Stratton, Mr. STEPHEN S AYRES to Miss ELIZABETH AYRES.

Relics of the Past!

There are two references in the annexed letter of Gen. Wilkinson, which need explanation. The "God of war" refers to Gen. Knox, then Secretary of the War Department, always deemed unfriendly to the settlement of the West, for private and mercenary reasons. The "Gaines" alluded to is Gen. Edmund P. Gaines, whose promotion from Ensign to Lieutenant it announces, and whose continuance in the army for nearly sixty years is without a parallel in the United States service, and has few examples in European military registers.

Gen. J. Wilkinson to Capt. John Armstrong.

Fort Washington, April 29th, 1792.

DEAR SIR:

All your letters except those by Mc-Daniel have come safe to hand; I fear these have taken the back track, as we have not seen or heard of the man. Please to forward me a duplicate of your letters by him.

You will find from the enclosed list, that little Hodgdon, altho' always deficient, has not been so much so as you expect—the articles receipted for by Shaumburgh were expressly for your garrison, and exclusive of those intended for Jefferson. The articles which remain unsupplied, will be furnished by the next escort as far as they can be procured, and you must write to Lt. Shaumburgh to return you the articles which he improperly carried forward, or such part as may be handily conveyed by your expresses—viz: the chalk lines, gimlets, stone, compass, saw and chisel. You cannot be too cautious, for I fear it will be impossible with all your vigilance, to preserve every man's hair a month longer—you have to combat an enterprising, subtle, persevering enemy, who to gain an advantage would think it no hardship to creep a mile upon his belly over a bed of thorns.

Your regiment is broken all to pieces by promotion, you are now second Captain, and if the God of war was not unfriendly to you, you should soon be a major. The organization and discipline of the army. is to undergo a great reform. The particulars have not yet been transmitted to me—but I am told, it is to be stiled the American Legion, commanded by a Major general, and divided into four sub legions, to be commanded by Brigadiers. I infer that the inferior corps will be battalions commanded by majors, and that regiments are to be done away, as we are to have no more Lt. Colonels. Ziegler's resignation was accepted, and he struck off the rolls the 5th of March, long before he had offered his commission to me. Subordination and sobriety are circumstances which the President is determined to enforce at all hazards.

I wish you to congratulate Gaines for me or his promotion, and tell him that it will depend upon himself, in a great degree, when he may be a Captain. My friendship will depend entirely upon his continuing the sober man, I formerly knew him to be. I feel some anxiety for Elliott's last convoy by the river—should it arrive safe, you will return the escort under cover of the night to this place. The season approaches when we must not trifle with the enemy. Adieu.

I am with sincere regard, yours,

JAS. WILKINSON,
Lt. Col. Commandant.

N. B. You will make up and sign the abstracts of the contractor, in as strict conformity to the order of the 18th Feb. as may be, and in future are to observe it exactly; to this end all detachments and parties passing you, must specify in their returns, the respective corps and companies to which they appertain.　　J. W.

CAPT. JNO. ARMSTRONG.

Capt. John Armstrong to Gen. J. Wilkinson.

FORT HAMILTON, 16th May, 1792.

MY DEAR FRIEND:

Your letters of the 29th of April, and 11th May, come duly to hand. Capt. Peters with his convoy marched this morning; and I am extremely happy you mentioned the circumstance of the troops returning from St. Clair being detained on the opposite shore all night, as it gives me an opportunity of communicating to you the cause why they were so detained, and trust my motives will justify the measure, and convince you that in doing so, I did my duty. Those troops arrived at sunset. The large flat being rendered useless by a neglect in the men of Lt. Shaumburgh's command. The river was high. Having the small flat only to effect the crossing, it would have taken the greater part of the night: and from the height of the water and darkness of the weather, I conceived would be attended with much danger, and perhaps the loss of several lives.

I sincerely thank you for your friendly advice, respecting the exercise of the law martial against a citizen, and shall adhere strictly thereto.

Sure I am the circumstance of having confined one of the contractor's men must have been improperly and partially represented to you. Contempt of an order of the commanding officer of a post, would be unjustifiable in a citizen—much more so in one that is in some measure connected with the army and agreeable to the customs established in the last war, subject to be punished by martial law. See sect. 13, art. 23rd, of the articles of war. Men employed by the contractor as an Q. M., are indulged

..a an idea that they were not subject to the law martial, figure to yourself what would be the situation of an officer commanding one of our recruits. That they are subject thereto, I never heard disputed. Should those characters be impressed with a different idea and supported therein, fatal would be the consequences produced in an army. I shall at all times give a negative to the establishment of so bad a precedent.

In the return you inclosed from the Quarter Master, he has committed an error—the company book mentioned therein it seems was intended for, and is appropriated with the wafers, quills, and greater part of the paper to the use of his department.

The oil stone is also missing. My surveyors remain idle for want of files. On further inquiry, I find the surveyor mentioned in my last, is at Covault's station, instead of Dunlap's. I wish you could for a time spare me the cooper belonging to Capt. Kersey's Company, and now at Fort Washington, to be employed in making canteens. I have a quantity of cedar collected for that purpose.

A part of each of the unfinished buildings in the Bastions, is raised two stories high, and may hereafter be converted into soldiers' barracks and officers' quarters. I intend finishing the upper story in each, so that when you honor us with a visit, a cool, comfortable room will be at your service. The articles mentioned in the inclosed returns are actually wanted, and I hope you will think proper to order them furnished.

Capt. Peters' detachment marched yesterday morning, and in the evening the savages tomahawked a man, employed by the quarter master to drive the public team, about four hundred yards from the fort, where he had strolled without arms, and contrary to the order of 5th April. It appears that the fellow was sitting down at the root of a tree, and perhaps asleep.

I employ as a guard to the cattle a non-commissioned officer, and eight who have orders to confine themselves to some thicket near the drove, and be seen as seldom as possible. Permit me here to observe the contractor ought to have one or two men to drive the bullocks, covered by the guard. Your orders respecting the bacon &c. shall be strictly attended to. I have signed the abstracts up to the 1st of May, and confess to you, I can't see any way of executing them agreeable to the copy from the war office. You will please to observe there is no column for artificers, wagoners, pack-horsemen, or for any extra rations whatever. I would thank you to point out the mode of bringing those in with a strict uniform one to the returns sent forward refered into your orders. I kept no copy of my letter by McDonald, or it contained nothing material. Our regiment is broken indeed, and not benefited much by the commanding officers being at so great a distance, who, I presume; would reduce some companies to fill others, and send the supernumerary officers on the recruiting service.

Those woodsmen you have been pleased to direct for each post will be the means of saving many of our best men, who are generally employed on the service undertaken by them.—Your partizan corps will have much in their power, and I trust do honor to themselves—it is the handsomest command in the army. I am sorry the God of war has formed any unjust prejudices against me. I will not suffer him to do me injustice and ask no favors. The person who made the representation to you, must be young in service, and possessed of more passion than judgment, to have crossed the troop and left near a hundred horses without a guard, would, in my opinion, have been very improper.

Yours respectfully,
JOHN ARMSTRONG.
Capt. Commandant.

Ship Building on the Ohio.

It appears to be a general impression on the public mind, that the Barque "Muskingum," which was built at Marietta, and was loaded a few weeks since at Cincinnati for Liverpool, is the first vessel built upon our western waters for crossing the broad Atlantic. This is a great mistake, as is well known to hundreds.

The Brig "General Butler," was built in Pittsburgh in 1810 by Gen. James O'Hara of that place. It was loaded with flour for Liverpool, to which port Wm. O'Hara sailed as supercargo. After unloading at Liverpool, she cleared for Philadelphia, and was supposed to have foundered at sea, as she never reached that port.

Still earlier, and about the year 1806, a ship named the *Western Trader*, was also built. She was commanded by Capt. John Brevoort, under whose superintendence she was fitted out. This vessel was cleared for Marseilles, France, where she arrived safely, but on the production of her papers at the customhouse, they were pronounced false, no such port in the world as Pittsburgh being known at Marseilles.

A map of the United States, however, being produced, Capt. Brevoort pointing out the mouth of the Mississippi, traced with his finger its course up to the junction of that stream with the Ohio, and followed the latter river on the map one thousand miles to the junction of the Monongahela and Alleghany, at which spot, he pointed out his port of departure to the great astonishment of the French *douaniers.*

The rigging, cables, anchors, sails, &c of the *Western Trader* had been hauled across the Alleghany mountains. Those who recollect the condition of the road from Philadelphia to Pittsburgh, even after it became a stage route, and as late as 1814, will comprehend what an enterprise this must have been at that date. The crew were also engaged at the east. The *Western Trader* returned to Philadelphia, from which port she made several voyages, and was shut up there during the general embargo, which preceded the war of 1812. Much of her timbers were black walnut, and the vessel decayed in a few years.

The facts in the case of the *Western Trader* were given by HENRY CLAY, substantially in these terms, on the floor of Congress in his speech on the imprisonment of American sailors.

Poetry.

WOMAN'S SPHERE.
INSCRIBED TO MISS. A. B.

BY L. J. CIST.

" She filled her woman's sphere on earth."

"HER woman's sphere!"—and tell us, thou
To whom our heart in reverence bow—
  Thou who so well dost fill it here—
Say how could nobler sphere be given
This side the white-robed choirs of heaven
  Than, rightly filled, is "woman's sphere?"

Where lieth woman's sphere?—Not there,
Where strife and fierce contentions are;
  Not in the bloody battle field,
With sword and helmet, lance and shield;
Not in the wild and angry crowd,
Mid threat'nings high, and clamors loud;
Not in the halls of rude debate
And legislation, is *her* seat;
Nor yet in scenes of weak display—
Of vanity, with its array
Of pride and selfishness—not *here*,
Lieth *true hearted* "WOMAN'S SPHERE!"

What then *is* "woman's sphere?"—The sweet
  And quiet precincts of her home;
Home!—where the blest affections meet,
  Where strife and hatred may not come!
Home—sweetest word in mother-tongue,
Long since in verse undying sung!
Home—of her holiest hopes the shrine,
Around which all her heart-strings twine!
There, loved and loving—safe from fear,
Lies ever woman's noblest sphere.
There hers the mighty power to wield,
To which the warrior's lance and shield,
Helmet and sword are powerless—
The God-like gift to save and bless!
To save the erring from his sin,
And back to paths of virtue win;
To bless—in every stage of life,
As MOTHER—DAUGHTER—SISTER—WIFE!

As MOTHER! Sweet and holy tie,
First known, best loved in infancy!
From her own vital breath we draw,
Her gentle looks our infant law;
Her love our refuge in alarm;
Her watchful care our shield from harm;
Her lessons the first precepts given

To form for earth and fit for heaven;
Her love—unselfish, ever known
To seek our interests, not her own—
Through all this changing scene extends:
With life begun—with death but ends!

As DAUGHTER!—'Tis upon her laid
To be the aged mothers aid;
In one the varied ties to blend
Of child, companion, helper, friend;
Repay in thousand gentle ways,
The love that crowned her childish days;
From thousand cares of age to save
And smooth life's pathway to the grave:
And Heaven's benignest gifts are shed,
Ever on such a daughter's head!

As SISTER!—He who doth not prove
  Her kindness, cannot know its worth!
How all unselfish that pure love
  That in a sister's heart hath birth!
Playmate! companion up from youth!
  Gentle and sympathizing friend!
Whose lips like hers, with faithful truth,
  So well can kind persuasion blend?
Thou who hast such—that long on earth
  She may be spared thee, kneel and pray!
Such too had I—nor knew her worth,
  Till she was called from earth away!
A pious sister! who can tell
  How oft to her it may be given,
To save a brother's feet from hell—
  To lead his wandering steps to heaven!

But more than all 'tis hers, as WIFE!
  To wield her mightiest influence still
To check and temper manhood's strife,
  And mould his purpose to her will:
For where is he who does not feel
That he could easier burst through steel.
Than wound that fond and faithful heart,
Of his *own more than self*, a part—
Or spurn the gentle thraldom known
To seek *his* happiness alone!

O! woman hath, in every phase,
  Controlling influence o'er our ways;
But chief. as man's companion high
  'Tis hers to guide his destiny:
And from that day our parents erst
  Were driven from Eden's blissful shade—
When both had fallen—yet woman *first*,
  Man by *her* weakness then betrayed—
All potent still, for good or ill,
Hath been the force of woman's will.
And mightier, with each added year,
Grows WOMAN'S POWER in WOMAN'S SPHERE!

The Fire at Pittsburgh.

Great calamities, serve to develope the worst as well as the best principles of human nature. The late fire at Pittsburgh, brought into exercise to a great extent, a system of plundering, which has filled the jail of that city with depredators on property.

It is pleasant to turn to the brighter side of the picture. Contributions of the most liberal character have been poured in for the relief of the sufferers from those who have escaped the visitation, both abroad and at home. Among these, the unsolicited gift of several hundred dollars, the accumulated savings for years of a young woman, at service in the family of Rev. Dr. Herron, shines conspicuous. It is the widow's two mites, among the offerings at the treasury by the rich. *It was her all.* And the same judge who characterised that gift, as being of more value than all the rest, will no doubt regard this self-sacrificing contribution as a higher exercise of benevolence than that of individuals, who may give thousands out of their abundance.

Diagram.

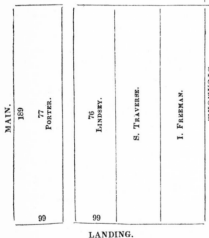

The lot you speak of in your paper of April 2nd was one of the *thirty* in-lots subjected to on the 7th January, 1789, and was drawn by *John Porter*—as was the adjoining one on the east by *Henry Lindsay*, who I believe is still living above New Richmond, Ohio. The lot on the corner of Main and Front was conveyed to Col. Thomas Gibson by Judge Symmes 19 April, 1798, in consideration of $

The east half of the lot 76 lying east of the alley, was conveyed to D. Achison 20 Dec., 1797, and the West half to J. & A. Hunt 30 Sep. 1796, in consideration of $2.

Mr. C. Cist.

Yours,   F.

Attack on Bryant's Station.

Sixty-three years ago, almost, a cloud of savage hostility, long threatened, burst upon this station, at that time one of the most important in Kentucky, under the following circumstances.

The border war between the whites and Indians, had for many years prior to 1782 been waged by small parties, at least so far as the aborigines were concerned. This best suited the temper and mode of life of the savages, whose supplies for themselves and families lasted usually but for a few days, and constantly required replenishing. It accorded, besides, little with their character and spirit to assemble in large masses, which are moved slowly, and must always depend for success upon a thorough and prolonged co-operation of its various elements. But as fort by fort become established in the country north of the Ohio, and the whites were steadily spreading over Kentucky, it soon became apparent to the Indians that they must either prepare to abandon their favorite hunting grounds south of the Ohio, or by one concentrated and general effort to drive the whites from these settlements.

Accordingly, early in August, 1782, a grand council of the savages was held at Chillicothe, the great head quarters of the Shawanese, a few miles from the present town of Xenia, at which besides that tribe, the Wyandots, Mingoes, Ottowas, Potowotamies, Miamies, and less important bands of Indians assisted or were represented. Girty and M'Kee, the one a renegade white, the other a British agent were present, and actively engaged in fanning to a flame the hostile feeling of the savages toward their pioneer neighbors. It was urged by these men who were more bitter enemies to the whites than the Indians themselves, that the American war was now over, and the whole forces of Western Pennsylvania and Virginia, were ready to be let loose to crush them at once. They were reminded of the gradual encroachments of the whites, of the beauty of Kentucky, and its value to them as an hunting ground. They were warned that they must combine their scattered strength if they did not mean to be driven from the wigwams they and their fathers had occupied for thousands of moons past, and if they were not beforehand in striking a blow at the whites, they would soon be deprived of every means of buying blankets to warm their bodies, and rum to cheer their souls. Such was the inflammatory harangue of Simon Girty. It fell like turpentine poured upon coals of fire. The council resolved to gather the whole disposable force of the tribes which as far as it could be assembled for immediate service, was not far from one thousand warriors. Of these it was determined that six hundred should make an irruption into the Kentucky settlements, while the rest were to follow the route higher up the river Ohio, which should enable them to fall upon the various settlements in the region of Wheeling, Virginia. These movements were accordingly carried into effect.

I shall confine my narrative to the detachment which moved against the Kentucky settlers, and which having reached Bryant's station on the 15th August, 1782, placed themselves in ambush around it, ready to take whatever advantage might present itself, not doubting their ability to take it by storm on the first assault. The lapse of sixty-three years, has laid in the dark and silent grave, nearly all the actors in that memorable attack, but there are three or four Kentuckians who still survive, all in the full vigor of mind and body, and it is from the statements of one of those whose voices rise, whose eye kindles, and whose tongue becomes eloquent on this subject that I compile my narrative, incorporating with it well attested circumstances recorded elsewhere, which in the nature of the case were to him unknown. Mr. Ellison E. Williams, my informant, was born in Surry county, N. C. on the 19th April, 1770. He is of course now seventy-five years of age. His father settled at Bryant's station, having planted a crop of corn that same spring, and in the autumn removed his family out to Kentucky. When the attack was made, young Williams was over twelve years of age, a period of life when labor was expected from and performed by the boys of those days, which in modern times would hardly be devolved upon youths of eighteen or nineteen.

A brief description of the fort will render the narrative more easy to comprehend.

Bryant's station had been settled by William Bryant, brother-in-law to Daniel Boone, and was about 5 miles distant from Lexington on the present road from Maysville to that city, and on the South bank of Elkhorn. Bryant, who was well fitted to take charge of the interest of this settlement, had been unfortunately surprised and killed by Indians near the mouth of Cane Run. Many of the original settlers had returned to North Carolina, and a new set from Virginia, among whom was Robert Johnson, father of Col. R. M. Johnson, late Vice President of the United States, occupied their places. These were far from being familiar with the character of the Indians, and the danger to which their inexperience exposed them on this account.— The fort itself contained about forty cabins placed in parallel lines, connected by strong palisades, and garrisoned by forty or fifty men. It was a parallelogram of thirty rods in length by twenty in breadth, forming an enclosure of nearly four acres, which was protected by digging a trench four or five feet deep in which strong and heavy pickets were planted by ramming the earth well down against them. These were twelve feet out of the ground, being formed of hard durable timber, at least a foot in diameter. Such a wall it must be obvious defied climbing or leaping, and indeed any means of attack, cannon excepted. At the angles were small squares or block houses, which projected beyond the palisades, and served to impart additional strength at the corners, as well as permitted the besieged to pour a raking fire across the advanced party of the assailants. Two folding gates in front and rear, swinging on prodigious wooden hinges sufficient for the passage in and out of men or wagons in times of security. These were of couse provided with suitable bars.

This was the state of things as respects the means of defence at Bryant's station on the morning of the 16th August, 1782 while the savages lay concealed in the thick weeds around it, which in those days grew so abundantly and tall, as would have sufficed to hide mounted horsemen. They waited for daylight, and the opening of the gates for the garrison to get water for the day's supply from an adjacent spring before they should commence the work of carnage.

It seems that the garrison here were rather taken off their guard. Some of the palisade work had not been secured as permanently as possible, and the original party which built the fort had been tempted in the hurry of constructing, and their fewness of hands to restrict its extent, so as not to include a spring of water within its limits. Great as were these disadvantages, they were on the eve of exposure to a still greater one, for had the attack been delayed a few hours, the garrison would have been found disabled by sending off a reinforcement to a neighboring station—Holder's settlement—on an unfounded alarm that it was attacked by a party of savages. As it was, no sooner had a few of the men made their appearance outside of the gate than they were fired on, and compelled to regain the inside.

According to custom, the Indians resorted to stratagem for success. A detachment of one hundred warriors attacked the south-east angle of the station, calculating to draw the entire body of the besieged to that quarter to repel the attack, and thus enable the residue of the assailants five hundred strong, who were on the opposite side, to take advantage of its unprotected situation, when the whole force of the defence should be drawn off to resist the assault at the south-east. Their purpose however was comprehended inside, and instead of returning the fire at the smaller party, they secretly despatched an express to Lexington for assistance, and began to repair the palisades, and otherwise to put themselves in the best possible posture of defence. They were aware that the Indians were posted near the spring, but believing they were not disposed at this stage of the siege, to unmask a fire in that direction upon any small party, the women were sent to bring in water for the use of the garrison. The event fulfilled their expectations. The Indians forbore to fire, being unwilling, as it appeared, that their presence in that direction should become known at that moment.

When an ample supply of water had been thus obtained, and the neglected defences completed, a party of thirteen men sallied out in the direction in which the assault had been made.— They were fired on by the savages, and driven again within the palisades, but without sustaining any loss of life. Immediately the five hundred on the opposite side, rushed to the assault of what they deemed the unprotected side of the fort, without entertaining any doubts of their success. A well directed fire, however, put them promptly to flight. Some of the more daring and desperate approached near enough with burning arrows to fire the houses, one or two of which were burned, but a favorable wind drove the flames away from the mass of the buildings, and the station escaped the danger threatened from this source. A second assault from the great body of the Indians, was repelled with the same vigor and success with the first.

Disappointed of their object thus far, the assailants retreated, and concealed themselves under the bank of the creek to await and intercept the arrival of the assistance which they were well aware was on its way from Lexington. The express from Bryant's station reached that town without difficulty, but found its male inhabitants had left there, to aid in the defence of Holder's station, which was reported to be attacked, as already stated. Following their route, he overtook them at Boonesborough, and sixteen mounted men, with thirty on foot immediately retraced their steps for the relief of the besieged at Bryant's. When this re-enforcement approached the fort, the firing had entirely ceased, no enemy was visible, and the party advanced in reckless confidence, that it was either a false alarm, or that the Indians had abandoned the siege. Their avenue to the garrison was a lane between two cornfields, which growing rank and thick formed an effectual hiding place to the Indians even at the distance of a few yards. The line of ambush extended on both sides nearly six hundred yards. Providentially it was in the heat of midsummer, and dry accordingly, and the approach of the horsemen raised a cloud of dust so thick as to compel the enemy to fire at random, and the whites happily escaped without losing a man. The footmen on hearing the firing in front, dispersed amidst the corn, in hopes of reaching the garrison unobserved. Here they were intercepted by the savages who threw themselves between them and the fort, and but for the luxuriant growth of corn they must all have been shot down. As it was two men were killed and four wounded of the party on foot before it succeeded in making its way into the fort.

Thus reinforced, the garrison felt assured of safety, while in the same measure the assailing party began to despair of success.

One expedient remained, which was resorted to for the purpose of intimidating the brave spirits who were gathered for the defence of their wives and little ones. As the shades of evening approached, Girty who commanded the party, addressed the inmates of the fort. Mounting a stump from which he could be distinctly heard, with a demand for the surrender of the place, he assured the garrison that a reinforcement with cannon would arrive that night, that the station must fall, that he could assure them of protection if they surrendered, but could not restrain the Indians if they carried the fort by storm; adding, he supposed they knew who it was that thus addressed them. A young man, named Reynolds, fearing the effect which the threat of cannon might have on the minds of the defending party, with the fate of Martin's and Ruddle's stations fresh in their memories, left no opportunity for conference, by replying instantly, that he knew him well, and held him in such contempt that he had called a good for nothing dog he had by the name of Simon Girty. "Know you!" added he, "we all know you, for a renegade cowardly villain, that delights in murdering women and children. Wait till morning and you will find on what side the reinforcements are. We expect to leave not one of your cowardly souls alive, and if *you* are caught our women shall whip you to death with hickory switches. Clear out, you cut throat villain." Some of the Kentuckians shouted out, "Shoot the d— rascal!" and Girty was glad to retreat out of the range of their rifles lest some one of the garrison might be tempted to adopt the advice.

Before morning, however, the whole force of savages decamped, taking the route to the Blue-licks, where three days afterwards, they decoyed the whites into the disastrous ambush and battle of that name.

Before retiring they wreaked that injury which they could not inflict upon the garrison, upon the cattle and other domestic animals belonging to its inmates, wantonly slaughtering all within their reach.

My friend Williams, then but twelve years of age, was stationed with others, as young as himself, and even younger, to the number of twelve or fifteen on the roof of the cabins to get hold and throw off the arrows which the Indians were shooting there. The bullets occasionally whistled by them, but did no harm. Col. Cave Johnson and Maj. Craig of Boone county, Kentucky, are the only survivers within his knowledge of the men engaged in that memorable defence. Col. Johnson is ninety-one years of age, and the Major is probably eight years younger. A few vears must consign these gallant relics of the past to the grave, and the early history of Kentucky cease from the living lips of its early pioneers.

Improvement in Tanning.

A new process in tanning, which converts skins and hides into leather in a few days or weeks, has been lately discovered and put into operation at Dayton, by Mr. Simon Snyder o that place. It is easy to comprehend what a revolution this must produce in leather, one of the heaviest and most expensive raw materials in manufactures.

The following letter on the subject speaks for itself. It is from Mr. Schenck, member of Congress from the Dayton district, to Mr. John H. Wood of our city.

DAYTON, April 13th, 1845.

DEAR SIR:—

My absence from home the past week has prevented an earlier reply to your letter inquiring as to Mr. Snyder's Patent for the improved method of tanning.

There has been published in the newspapers a fuller account of the discovery or invention, than I have time to attempt. The principle of the system, is the speedy and thorough penetration of the hide or skins by the tanning, by means of punctures or perforations made in a certain stage in the ordinary process. But any person wanting to purchase a right should come here and examine for himself and to his own thorough satisfaction. An opportunity will be given to see the operation in all its stages. Many a scoffer or doubter of this *paradoxical* plan of making good sound impervious leather by first filling it with holes, has become a convert from the evidences of his own senses; and that is the proof we offer.

There is now at Mr. R. Green's shop in this city, some beautiful leather manufactured by this new process.

Respectfully yours,
ROBT. C. SCHENCK.

MR. JOHN H. WOOD, Cincinnati.

Brass and Iron Moulders' Society.

This society instituted for the benefit of tho operatives which confer their name upon it, held its anniversary Wednesday last at the assembly rooms, Pearl street, commemorating it with an oration by one of themselves, and a supper which the members partook with several invited guests, principally of the bar and the press. Every thing went off pleasantly, and it might be a mooted question whether more good things were said or *swallowed* in the course of a four hour's session at the table.

Among the speakers were Messrs. Collins, C. H. & J. Brough, Campbell of the bar and the press, and Messrs. R. C. Philips and Gatchell of the craft. A continued corruscation and scintillation of wit like summer lightning, and New Jersey champaigne was kept up from the delivery of the oration until the hour of adjournment. Among these the reference to the Messrs. Broughs, *brothers* thus far through life, and now *brothers in law*, alluding to the admission to the bar that morning of Mr. J. Brough, Mr. B's. own spicy caricature of his legal examination, and above all, Mr. Phillips after expressing his inability to do justice to the bar in his remarks. being desired to say what he could in good conscience in their favor, drily remarking, *That* WAS the difficulty. This sarcasm was received with a roar of laughter, in which all—lawyers included joined, that shook, in a sense, the building "from floor to canopy."

The oration by Mr. John Goodin, one of the society was apt and appropriate, full of sound thought and manly spirit, and was itself the best illustration of the value of such associations in stimulating their members in the great pursuit of mental and moral improvement. I copy Mr. B's. examination, as alluded to in the Enquirer of Saturday last.

Fancy Names.

Few things are more remarkable as well as universal, than the tendency to supply fancy or nick names to individuals or States, unless it be the tenacity with which these appellations adhere, and the extent to which they displace tho proper title. I have known individuals who have been so long and so generally known by nick names, as to be at times unconscious who was meant, when called by their true names. I saw an instance of this one day in a court house, where the sheriff called repeatedly the name of a person present, bearing a fancy name, that was not made aware he was referred to, until reminded of it by an acquaintance. *Mad Anthony* and *Old Hickory*, are names more familiar to the community at large than those of Genl's. Wayne and Jackson who were hardly known by any other appellations than these in the region of their exploits. *John Bull*, the world over is the designation of England, as *Jean Crapeau* is that of France.

I have compiled the *flash* or *fancy* names of the States, or rather of the inhabitants of our respective State sovereignties, known as the U. States of America. I' believe it to be the only *complete* list ever published.

The inhabitants of	
Maine, are called	Foxes.
New Hampshire,	Granite boys.
Massachusetts,	Bay Staters.
Vermont,	Green Mount'n boys.
Rhode Island,	Gun Flints.
Connecticut,	Wooden Nutmegs.
New York,	Knickerbockers.
New Jersey,	Clam-catchers.
Pennsylvania,	Leatherheads.
Delaware,	Muskrats.
Maryland,	Craw-thumpers,
Virginia,	Beagles.
N. Carolina.	Tar-boilers.
S. Carolina,	Weasels.
Georgia,	Buzzards.
Louisiana,	Cre-*owls*.
Alabama,	Lizards.
Kentucky,	Corn-crackers.
Tennessee,	Cotton-manies.
Ohio,	Buckeyes,
Indiana,	Hoosiers.
Illinois,	Suckers.
Missouri,	Pewks.
Mississippi,	Tadpoles.*
Arkansas,	Gophers.
Michigan,	Wolverines.
Florida,	Fly up the Creeks.
Wisconsin,	Badgers.
Iowa,	Hawkeyes.
N W. Territory,	Prairie Dogs.
Oregon,	Hard Cases.

Cents or Coppers are generally known in the West as, "Cincinnati Bullion."

*This name is especially appropriate, as among a certain class in the eastern cities, an abbreviation of it, *id est*, the word *Tad*, is applied to *one who don't nor won't pay*.

A Legal Examination.

We know not how many neophites have been examined and admitted to the bar during the present week, in the Supreme Court. A friend spoke the other day of the number of twenty-five or thirty, but he has become tired and quit counting since. The idea must prevail, we fancy, that the practice of law is immensely profitable, or immensely honorable; and which of these notions is the greater mistake, the deponent saith not.

The quizzing of applicants by the committee of examination, we understand, has been such as thoroughly to test their capacity and qualifications. One case, however, we have heard of, in which the questioning was altogether brief and unique,—whether because there was no time for further inquiry, or because of the confidence felt that the applicant would answer all the questions that might be asked as well as he answered those which were, we shall not attempt to say. The course of examination was thus,—the parties sitting upon a rail in the shade of the Court House:

"Suppose you don't know what *law* is?"
"No."
"Have you any notion about Equity?"
"Can't tell; have heard said, law was mystification, and equity, simple justice, but have my doubts?"
"Can one man make a riot?"
"S'pose he can, if he has enough to help' him?"
"That 'll do;—I've examined you on each of the three subjects of Law, Equity and Criminal Jurisprudence, and shall certify to the Court that you are fully qualified. You may go in and be sworn."

Living Man-traps.

Over the garden fence of a ladies' seminary, in the neighborhood of London, there is painted in large characters—

"*Man-traps* set on these premises." A wag, who was passing, chalked beneath the notice—"*Vir Gins* " Whereupon he was taken before a magistrate by a police officer. Being put upon his defence for thus defacing the wall of a respectable establishment, he argued "that *Vir* was the Latin for *Man*, and *Gin* the English for *Trap; ergo*, that *Virgin* was only another word for *Man-trap*; though the fact might be that it was a highly inappropriate term, and ought not to be used." The magi was posed, and the man was sent about his business, with a hint to beware lest he should be caught in his own description of trap, as he might expect no mercy if he were.

Proportion of Alchohol in Wines, &c.

Marsala,	25 p. ct.	Syracuse,	25 p. ct.
Madeira,	22 "	Sauterne,	14 "
Sherry,	19 "	Burgundy,	14 "
Teneriffe,	10 "	Rhine,	12 "
Lachryma Christi,	10 "	Champagne,	12 "
Constantia	19 "	Red Hermitage	12 "
Lisbon	18 "	Vin de Grave	12 "
Malaga	18 "	Frontignac	12 "
Red Madeira	20 "	Currant Wine	11 "
Cape "	20 "	Orange "	11 "
Cape Muscat	19 "	Tokay	9 "
Grape Wine	18 "	Cider	9 "
Vidonia	10 "	Perry	9 "
Metheglin	7 "	Wht. H'mitage	17 "
Roussillon	18 "	Ale	6 "
Claret	15 "	Strong Beer	6 "
Schiras	15 "	London Porter	4 "
Brandy	53 "	Rum	53 "
Gin	51 "	Whiskey	54 "

MARRIAGES.

On the 18th inst. by the Rev. G. W. Walker. Wm. H. Thompson to Harriet N., daughter of Dr. J. Dart.

On Tuesday, 22d inst. by the Rev. J. H. Perkins, Dr. A. Addams, of Dresden, O, to Miss Catharine A. Moffett, of this city.

On the 24th inst. by Rev. A. Drury, Jacob Burnet Jr to Miss Mary S. daughter of the Rev. Dr. Lynd.

On the 27th inst. by Rev. J. W. Hopkins, Henry W Wayman of Covington, Ky , to Elizabeth Rogers, of this city.

DEATHS.

On Sunday. April 20th, at 9 o'clock, Maria Clark, daughter of Thos. H. Minor, aged 2 years, 1 mo.

On the 25th inst. Mrs. Louisa M. Ernst, in the 33rd year of her age.

On the 28th inst, Henriztta, only daughter of Chas W. and Lydia A. Bunker. aged 18 months and 8 days.

CINCINNATI MISCELLANY.

CINCINNATI, MAY, 1845.

CORRESPONDENCE.

Another Bear Adventure.

MR. CIST:

As you appear somewhat inclined to amuse your readers occasionally with a panther or bear story, I take the liberty to send you one as related by one of our company at one of our "bivouacs," on our route to Santa Fee, after our sentinels had been placed on the first watch.

In the early settlement of St. Louis, a widow lady by the name of Atkinson, with her daughter, an only child, aged about sixteen, resided somewhere near where the St. Louis water works now stand. On one occasion, some little while after having retired for the night, she became startled by an unusual noise among the domestic animals. She jumped out of bed, took down her rifle, examined the priming, and cautiously opening the door stepped out, and took a survey around the house and negro hut, but could discover nothing. She then returned into the house and set her rifle down. Her daughter by this time had got up and struck a light, assuring her mother, (for as old Tim Watkins the narrator said, "the gals did'nt call their Mothers Ma in those days,") there was some strange animal about the 'diggins' for she heard it "fussing" around whilst her mother was out. They sat thus in conversation sometime, when the mother determined to go down to the negro hut, and wake up her negro man Dan. She started, aroused him and told him to come with her to the house, take the rifle, run round the place, brush up a little, and see if there was any thing about." They started for the house, and when about half way from Dan's hut, Mrs. Atkinson was seized in the fraternal "hug" of a huge "bar." The negro immediately commenced operations on Bruin's head and sides, which somewhat astonished his bearship, for the fists and heels of Dan used by a kind of perpetual motion rapidity, was no light affair. So fully satisfied of this fact was Bruin, that he ungallantly dropped the lady whom he had but just began to squeeze so affectionately and turned upon Dan, who kept up a running "skrimage" until he reached his own hut, where he very unceremoniously "slam'd" the door in Bruin's face, who thereupon turned round to bestow proper attention to Mrs. Atkinson, who by this time had nearly reached the house. Bruin hurried on with the intention no doubt of renewing his interesting "hug," for just as Mrs. A. opened the door the bear stretched forth his "arm," and seizing a part of the lady's dress, drew her towards him, when alas, for Bruin, at this critical moment the click of a gun lock was heard, the sharp crack of the rifle followed, and the "Bar" doubled up and rolled over in his last dying struggle. Mrs. A's daughter, a girl of sixteen summers, with the courage and heart of a pioneer's daughter, had shot the bear and saved her mother's life. These, sir, are the kind of girls and women who accompany our frontier settlers, and are always ready to look danger in the face, and who are prepared to give a good account of it when it does come, whether in the form of a bear or an Indian. I have another of old Tim Watkins' tales about some Indians and a female heroine, which at some leisure moment I may possibly give you; if this meets your approbation.

Yours &c.

G. REDDING.

Early History of Hamilton County.

MR. CIST,

DEAR SIR: Your chapters on the early history of Cincinnati have ended—may I rather say rested—with the landing of the first settlers, and the establishment of the town. When you resume the story, you may have occasion to note the organization of the county—towards which I give you these notes.

On the 2d Jan. 1790, Gen. St. Clair arrived at Fort Washington in the purchase of Judge Symmes, and on the 4th established the county of Hamilton with the following limits: "Beginning on the bank of the Ohio river, at the confluence of the Little Miami river, and down the said Ohio river to the mouth of the Big Miami, and up said Miami to the Standing Stone forks or branch of said river; and thence with a line to be drawn due east to the Little Miami, and down said Little Miami river to the place of beginning."

On the same day, commissions for the county courts of common pleas, and general quarter sessions of the peace, for said county, were granted by the Governor. And Wm. Goforth, Wm. Wells, and Wm. McMillan were appointed Judges of the court of common pleas, and justices of the court of general quarter sessions of the peace. They were also appointed and commissioned as justices of the peace, and quorum in said court. Jacob Topping, Benjamin Stites and J. Stites Gano, were also appointed justices of the peace of the county. J. Brown *Gent.* was appointed and commissioned as Sheriff during the Governor's pleasure. Israel Ludlow Esq., prothonotary to the court of common pleas, and clerk of the court of general quarter sessions of the peace of the county.

The Governor also made the followin~

..g military appointments, viz: Israel Ludlow, James Flinn, John Stites Gano and Gershom Gard, captains—Francis Kennedy, John Ferris, Luke Foster, and Brice Virgin, lieutenants—Scott Traverse, Ephraim Kibby, Elijah Stites, and John Dunlap, ensigns—all in the first regiment of militia of the county of Hamilton.

The civil and military powers were thus organized, and the government brought to act for the protection of the people.

On the 1st Dec., Scott Traverse, was appointed lieutenant in place of Kennedy resigned, and Robert Benham an ensign, vice Traverse promoted, both in the company of Capt. Ludlow.

On the 24th May, 1791, William Burnet was appointed Register of deeds in said county.

On the 10th Dec., 1791, Oliver Spencer was appointed Lt. Colonel, Brice Virgin a captain, Daniel Griffin a lieutenant, and John Bowman an ensign.

On the 14th Dec., George McCullum was appointed a justice of the peace.

On the 18th Feb. 1792, the Secretary of the Territory, then at Cincinnati, and in the absence of Governor St. Clair, acting as Governor, issued the following proclamation.

"To all persons to whom these presents shall come greeting:—

Whereas it has been represented to me that it is necessary for the public interests, and the convenience of the inhabitants of the county of Hamilton, that a ferry should be established over the river Ohio, nearly opposite the mouth of Licking in the commonwealth of Virginia, and Mr. Robert Benham having requested permission to erect and keep said ferry:

Now, know ye, that having duly considered of the said representation and request, I have thought it proper to grant the same, and by these presents do empower the said Robert Benham of the county of Hamilton, to erect and keep a ferry over the Ohio river, from the landing place in the vicinity of his house lot, which is nearly opposite the mouth of Licking, to both points of the said *rivulet* upon the Virginia shore; and to ask, demand, recover and receive as a compensation

For every single person that he may
transport over the said ferry, 6 cents.
For a man and horse, 18 "
For a waggon and team, 100 "
For horned cattle per head, 18 "
For hogs, each, 6 "

until those rates shall be altered by law or future instructions from the Governor of this territory.

And he is hereby required to provide good and sufficient flats or boats for the purpose, and to give due attention to the same according to right and common usage, and to govern himself

in the premises by all such laws as hereafter may be adopted for the regulation of ferries, as soon as such laws shall be published in the Territory.

Given under my hand and seal at Cincinnati, in the county of Hamilton, this eighteenth day of February, in the year of our Lord, one thousand seven hundred and ninety-two, and of the independence of the United States the sixteenth—and to continue in force during the pleasure of the Governor of the Territory.

WINTHROP SARGENT.

Yours respectfully, J.

CINCINNATI, April 22, 1845.

Miner K. Kellogg.

It is some time since I have been able to furnish tidings of this artist's *locale*, and presuming the subject will interest not only his circle of acquaintances and friends here, but gratify numbers who feel deeply for the welfare of those who like Powers and Kellogg, are fine specimens of Cincinnati artists, as well for professional talent as in personal character, I make extracts from his last letter, dated Constantinople, Feb. 27, 1845. It was received here after a circuitous passage via Smyrna, Malta and Marseilles to the United States in less than fifty days from its date. I can recollect when fifty days' old news from London, were considered late advices, even in Philadelphia.

He left Florence in December, stopping in Naples eight days, coasted along the Calabrian shores, visiting Messina, Catania and Syracuse, and after remaining eight days at Malta, and calling at Syra on the passage to make repairs to the steamboat in which he travelled, made the continent once more at Smyrna, plying his pencil with great industry the whole voyage. He reached Constantinople on the 17th January, where he was received with great kindness, although in a land of strangers, and found his letters a passport to the best society there—I presume he is speaking of the European residents. He adds,

"Last night I attended the meeting of a few friends at the house of Mr. Goodell, the American Missionary here. Dr. Joseph Wolff was present and gave an account of his late journey into Persia, in search of Messrs. Stoddard and Connally—who had been murdered some time since. Mr. Wolff is a singular creature, that's certain, and entertained us over two hours in the recital of his adventures. I cannot give you any more than a general idea of what he said—but he intends calling at my studio soon, when I shall have a talk with him myself, which I may tell you of some future time. He entered Bokhara dressed in his canonicals, with his open bible in his right hand, followed by hundreds of people, who took him for some wonderful *Dervish*, or teacher of the Koran, proclaiming in a loud voice, that he had been sent by all Europe to enquire after the above persons, and if he could find them, to take them back home with him. After great difficulty he obtained an audience of the King, a savage pompous looking man, and after asking him the reason of the death of those Englishmen, was told that Stoddard did not bow when he come into his presence, and on attempting to force him to do so, he drew his sword. Wolff told him *he* was not that kind of a man, and would bow twenty times, and immediately suiting the action to the word, prostrated himself, and would have kept good his promise, when the King burst into a fit of laughter, and put a stop to his obeisances. He soon became in danger of being put to death by the military chief of the King's Stores, and escaping from his garden by a water hole, besmeared his face with mud, and doffed his professional habiliments in order to escape detection and pursuit. *Nakedness*, as he expressed it "being about the best disguise he could assume." He fled into a small house where he remained secreted two days, when the woman of the house wished to entrap him into marriage, or as he thought, intended to betray him into violent hands—but he turned on the woman and gave her jesse, in other words gave her as a mittimus "Go to ——— woman."

All his thoughts were directed to getting away faster than he came to the city; that he did get away, and with his head on his shoulders, I can truly affirm for I saw him last night. As this is the very latest tidings of the learned Rabbi and enthusiast you will receive in America, that is, since his return to Constantinople on his way to England, the above may amuse some who know him by report. You can stick it in the papers if you please."

Wolff is equally remarkable in getting in or out of a scrape. He has already passed safely through such imminent perils during his past life as would furnish a mussulman, with illustrations of his great truth. "*It is written in the book*, you cannot take such a man's life."

Kellogg's letter is pierced with incisions and fumigated with various odors as a preventive to transmitting the plague. Among these, that of vinegar predominates. Happy America! which has never known by fatal experience, this dreadful epidemic.

Patent Bedsteads.

In the first stages of manufacturing operations all the articles in a particular line of business, however various in character and materials are usually made in the same establishment. A cabinet workshop, for instance originally

makes every description of furniture. As business enlarges, it is found a more convenient as well as efficient and economical process to direct labor to a less variety of objects. A part of the craft devote themselves to plain work, a part to fancy articles. One establishment makes sofas alone, another confines itself to bedsteads. These again subdivide the business into fine or costly articles for home consumption, and low priced ones made by labor-saving machinery for foreign markets. In this way every year adds to the division of labor and the consequent increase of skill and the exercise of ingenuity which results from concentrating the inventive or corrective faculties of the mind on a single object.

Mr. HENRY BOYD, who manufactures extensively *swelled rail bedsteads*, for which he holds a patent, at the corner of Broadway and Eighth streets, began his operations in 1839. I was one of his first customers, and found those of his make so much better than what I already had, that I sent these last off to auction and replaced them with others from Boyd's factory.

Such was his success from his commencement, that many cabinet makers left off making bed steads, advising their customers frankly, to buy Boyd's; and others of a lower tone of morality set about imitating them as nearly as they could, without rendering themselves amenable to the laws. These, like counterfeits of other kinds bore more or less resemblance to the original; but were of no actual value.

The peculiar merit and distinctive character of his article of Bedsteads are, that he dispenses with the moveable iron screw, whose power of holding the rails of the bed stead to the posts is always inadequate to the regular strain upon it, and thereby soon gives way, rendering the bedstead shackling and affording inlets and concealments to bed bugs. A further nuisance is, that in the taking bedsteads to pieces for cleansing, thus rendered necessary, the screws become bent or mislaid, or at any rate, lose their proper fit in change of places, and a series of inconviences result, which always render the annual or semi-annual taking to pieces and putting up again of bedsteads, one of the house keepers '*miseries of human life.*'

All this is avoided here by the adoption of a different principle of putting bedsteads together, which fits them close and keeps them so, and renders it unnecessary even to take them apart. I have had these bed steads for six years, and they are as perfect as they were when bought.

The materials of these bed steads are sycamore, maple, cherry, black-walnut and mahogany; and although our city furnishes a home market extensively, numbers are bought here and sent to the South. Boyd's average manufacture for the last six years, is one thousand per annum. He has ten hands in his establishment.

Proprieties of Business Life.

Many of the evidences of the rapid growth of our city, and the increasing value of property, are of the most pleasant kind. Some few are otherwise. Such is the scarcity of store rooms and ware houses within the business region of Cincinnati, that instances are becoming frequent of persons about to open new establishments, applying to landlords for stands already occupied, and tempting them with one or two hundred dollars extra rent. Where a building is vacant, it is undoubtedly open for any competition the owner may create, but when rented and found to be a good stand, the offer by a stranger of higher rent, only serves to advance the price to the existing occupant, who will always be induced to submit to an increase of rent rather than subject himself to the inconveniences of moving, and creating a new business elsewhere. Some people have a very low standing of morality on these subjects, who would scruple directly to cheat another out of a cent. I regard, however, the decoying a servant girl away from her place, or the taking of a dwelling house or store from its tenant, by renting it without his knowledge as *stealing*, in the absolute sense of the term, and if I had the name of an individual who in a recent case, made an attempt in the line last referred to, I would place it on record in the Advertiser as a *terror for evil doers*.

Cincinnati Directory for 1845.

Two years have elapsed since I published the last *general* directory which has appeared. A *business* directory was got up for 1844, and another is getting up now, which are well enough in their proper sphere, but a register of names in which the whole population shall be fully and accurately recorded, is of vastly greater consequence. The business man or any other influential member of the community, may be readily found on inquiry, but the great mass, who have no signs up, and are to be sought only at their dwellings, can only have their residence ascertained by a directory. I have, naturally enough, been applied to by numbers to know what is doing to get up such a directory for 18-45, and will now say that if any *competent* person of the hundreds who are here seeking employment, will undertake this business, I will give them all the aid in my power to carry it into effect. By competency, I mean a person who will give the necessary time and labor, as well as possess certain business aptitudes. A directory is not worth much unless it is both full and exact.

I do not consider a man rendered unfit for the work by being a stranger to the place, if otherwise qualified; and if such person will apply to me it will give me great pleasure to put him in the track of making a few hundred dollars in such employment.

Spirit of the Age.

This is the age of poetical excitement. Poetry fills the camp, the grove, constitutes a large share of patent medicine notices, and as may be seen in the specimen below, begins to form directions to, as well as contents of, letters.

The following inscription was found on a letter which passed through New York city having been mailed at a town in New Jersey.

> To the State of Ohio,
> Where the land is not barren,
> To Goshen Post Office,
> In the county of Warren,
> In the township of Salem,
> Where hardy boys grow,
> And the little Miami
> Adjoining does flow:
> So please, Mr. P. M.,
> Send me along,
> In haste and great care,
> To Isaac Armstrong.

For Cist's Advertiser.
Reminiscences of Olden Time in Virginia and Ohio.
BY HORATIO G. JONES, JR.

Leverington, Pa.

Although a stranger in "the Queen City of the West," yet I feel a great interest in every thing relating to its early history or that of any of the towns of this young but thrifty State.— I regard the man who collects and preserves such information as one upon whom in future time, will redound much honor, because materials apparently worthless, are oftentimes the very means by which the historian is enabled to elucidate some early, disputed fact.

Through the kindness of Col. Augustus Stone, of Marietta, I have learned that Dr. S. P. Hildreth, is engaged in collecting materials towards writing a general history of the State of Ohio, and is much in need of information concerning the numerous small towns settled anterior to our independence as a nation.

Now I have in my possession, a Journal kept by a traveller who passed through the southern and south-eastern part of Ohio, in the year 1772! He made the tour from Fort Pitt *in a canoe*, and travelled pretty extensively among the Delaware and Shawanese Indians, having ascended the Little Kanawha, the Muskingum and other streams. He was the grandfather of the writer of this article, and in after years was well known as an ardent friend to American freedom—having served in the revolution as a chaplain, and also in the Indian wars under General Anthony Wayne, and in the late war on the Lakes. At present I shall make but a few short extracts; but should they meet with a favorable reception I will continue to lay before the intelligent public tho whole of the Journal.

Extract from a Journal made by the Rev. David Jones, of Freehold, N. J. in the years of 1772 and 1773.

"I left Fort Pitt on Tuesday June 9th 1772, in company with George Rogers Clark, a young gentleman from Virginia, who with several others inclined to make a tour in this new world. We travelled by water in a canoe, and as I labored none, I had an opportunity of making my remarks on the many creeks which empty into Ohio, as also the courses of the said river. From Fort Pitt it runs for 16 miles near a north west course, then it turns near north about 14 miles, then it makes a great bend for above 20 miles, running a little south of west. Thence for 20 miles south east to the place called the Mingo Town,* where some of that nation reside; but as they have a name of plundering canoes, we passed them quietly as possible, and were so happy as not to be discovered by any of them. From this town the river runs west of south for 30 miles to Grave Creek.

Here I met my interpreter, who came across the country from the waters of the Monongahela †and with him some Indians, with whom I conversed. It was in the night when we came; instead of feathers, my bed was gravel stones, by the river side. *From Fort Pitt to this place we were only in one place where white people live.* Our lodging was on the banks of the river, which at first seemed not to suit me, but afterwards it became more natural.

Saturday, June 13. We concluded to move down to a creek, called by the Indians Caapteenin.‡ This comes from the west side of the Ohio, and is from Newcomerstown, which is the chief town of the Delaware Indians, about 75 E. S. E. We encamped on the east side of the Ohio opposite to the mouth of Caapteenin. We went over and conversed with the Indians and in the evening some came over to us. Mr. Owens§ was well acquainted with them and let them know what sort of a man I was. They all seemed to show respect to me, even

*Supposed to be the present Steubenville! How great the change!

†In a previous part of the work, he says, "The proper Indian name of this river, is. Mehmonawonsgehelak, which signifies, falling-in-bank-river; as it is common for the river's bank's from the richness of the soil, to break and tumble down into the stream."

‡Caapteenin is the present Captina.

§David Owens was his interpreter, whom he employed at £5, per month.

afterwards when some were drunk, they were not rude to me, but would take hold of my hand and say, "you be minsta." We remained here over the Sabbath and in the evening I instructed what Indians came over. The man of most sense and consideration in this place is called Frank Stephens. I asked him before the others, if he believed that after death there was a state of eternal happiness or misery? He said this he believed and looked on God as the giver of all good things. If he killed a deer, he thought God gave him that good luck. He paid great attention to what I said, while I spoke of God and of the Scriptures which he gave us. He said that he believed that Indians long ago, knew how to worship God, but as they had no writings, they had lost all knowledge of Him; yet sometimes some of them tried to worship Him, but did not know whether their services were pleasing to Him. I told him that good people among the white folks, used to pray to God before they went to sleep, and that I was going to pray and would pray for him, and though he could not know what I said, maybe God would give him good thoughts while I was speaking. With this we all arose up to pray, and the Indians arose likewise. I spoke with a solemn heart and voice to God. I was informed that all the time, the Indians looked very seriously at me. When I ended, Frank told my interpreter that my voice affected his heart, and he thought I spoke the way our Saviour did when he was on earth. 'Tis likely this Indian had heard of our Saviour from the Moravians or their Indians. Here I expected an answer by my ambassador, whom I had sent to the chief town of the Delawares; but a trader having brought rum, there was no prospect of doing any service at this time by any longer continuance, and my ambassador delaying his return, we concluded to go down to the little Kanawha to view the land.

This was near 70 miles below, and from Grave Creek to the Kanawha the river Ohio may be said to run S. W. but it is very crooked, turning to many points of the compass.

Tuesday 16th. Set out for the Little Kanawha, and in the evening on Thursday the 18th, we arrived at the Kanawha; it comes from the east, and is near 150 yards wide at the mouth.— We went up this stream about 10 miles, and out on every side to view the land and to obtain provisions. My interpreter killed several deer, and a stately buffalo bull. The land is good, but not equal to the land nearer to Fort Pitt.— It is not well watered about the Kanawha, and consequently not the most promising for health. Here we have pine hills, but they do not appear too poor to raise good wheat. Having satisfied ourselves with a view of this part of the country, we set out for Caapteenin again, and arrived safe Tuesday, June 30th. Here an Indian was sent to me from the Delaware's Town, who informed me that all of their council were not at home, that they were considering the matter, and that I should soon hear from them. Had I known them as well then as I do now, I would have understood their answer better than I did then. Being rather unwell we moved up to Grave Creek, and then left our canoes and crossed the country to Ten-mile creek which empties into the Monongahela. I suppose the way we travelled, it was between 50 and 60 miles before we came to the house of David Owens. Tuesday, July 14. Set out for Fort Pitt on horseback in company with Mr. Clark, Mr. Higgins and Mr. Owens my interpreter; but as it was some time before the Indians could be at Fort Pitt, we took another tour down to Ohio across the waste wilderness, and on the Sabbath, I preached to about 15 white people, who met in a cabin near a creek called Wheeling. Monday July 20. Set out for Fort Pitt. We had a small path called Catfish's road, which led us through the middle of the land between Ohio and Monongahela; so that I had the pleasure of seeing a large extent of good land, but very few inhabitants. The land is uneven, but the greater part can be settled. Wednesday, July 22d, came to Fort Pitt, and conversed with several principal Indians of different nations. I found that it was some time before I might expect any further knowledge of their minds respecting my visit; therefore I wrote another letter to the Delaware King aud chiefs of the nation. This letter was interpreted to one of the chiefs of the Delawares, and with it I sent a belt of wampum, which, I was informed he delivered with care; but him I saw not in my second visit. Parted from my friends here and reached home the 20th day of August.

First Mill in Hamilton County.

The first settlers here suffered greatly for provisions before the crops of their second year produced food in abundance, subsisting on short allowance of corn, which was pounded or ground into hommony in handmills. They were thankful in those days if they could only procure corn enough. Many of the families at Columbia subsisted on the roots of the bear grass. Mr. Jesse Coleman still surviving, and residing in this county, tells me that he has repeatedly had nothing more *for three days subsistence than a pint of parched corn.* He was then six years of age.

Mr. C. says the first mill in Hamilton county was constructed by his father, Mr. N. Coleman, at Columbia, who made fas:' .o flat boats, side by side, the water wheel being put up between both. The grindstones with the grain and flour were in the one boat, and the machinery in the other. Up to this time the grinding through the whole country was by handmills. The change in fifty years to the grinding annually in Hamilton county of 250,000 bbls. superfine flour, to say nothing of the hundreds of thousands of bushels corn meal, ground in the same bounds, has no parallel even in the extravagant fictions of the Arabian Nights Entertainments.

Lotteries in Ohio.

I have been under the impression that Lotteries in every shape were prohibited by the laws of this State. The following advertisement—one only of three or four of the same nature—which I condense and copy from the Wayne Co. (O.) Standard, would seem to indicate a mistake on this subject on my part. I publish it as traits of the times. As such is will be of value for future reference.

LOTTERY!!!

Grand distribution of real and personal property, by way of Lottery, to be drawn in Wooster on the 6th of June, 1845.—Capital $6,816.

The subscriber, desirous of settling up his business preparatory to his anticipated removal to Oregon, offers his real and part of his personal property, to the public, by way of Lottery, as follows: The North West Quarter of Section 24, in Township 20, and Range 14.

GRAND SCHEME.—REAL ESTATE.

First prize, Dwelling-house and 20 acres of land,	$1,200 00
2nd do. Saw Mill and 10 acres of land,	1,200 00
3d to 28th 5 acres of land in lots of $120 to $150	3,363 00
29th to 32nd 1½ acres, each at $50,	200 00

PERSONAL PROPERTY:

One prize—sorrel mare,	$85 00
One do black filly,	60 00
One do a two horse wagon nearly new,	50 00
One do eight day brass clock,	40 00
One do large rotary cooking stove,	35 00
One do large black ox,	25 00
One do red ox, large and beautiful,	25 00
One do silver watch,	13 00
One do room-heater and pipe,	12 00
One do eight head of sheep at $1 50 each,	12 00
One do box stove and pipe,	12 00
One do silver watch,	12 00
One do steer, 2 years old, black, (white face,)	10 00
One do steer, 1 year old,	6 00
One do wind-mill and cutting box,	6 00
One do plow,	7 00
One do harrow and double and single tree,	6 00

CASH:

Twenty-five cash prizes, $1,			25 00
Fifty	do	do 75 cents,	37 50
Seventy-five do		do 50 "	37 50
One hundred do		do 87½ "	37 50
Twelve hundred	do	do 25 "	300 00
1502 prizes.			$6,816 00

The above property will be disposed of as indicated in the foregoing scheme, in 2272 chances, at three dollars each. The personal property will be kept in good condition and delivered to the drawers thereof on demand. A good and sufficient title for the landed property will be made to the holders of the fortunate chances in the above scheme, within two days from the drawing.

Possession of the house reserved until the first of October, 1845.

Grain in the ground reserved.

LAZARUS PLUMER.

Chester tp. March 13, 1845.

Building Architects.

In that simplification of business which tends both to economy and efficiency, house building in Cincinnati is now generally bid for, in its various departments of stone and brick masonry, carpenter work, plaistering and painting, a professional builder receiving the contracts and superintending their execution. The saving of money as well as of trouble in this mode, is so great that the charge of the superintendent would not probably equal one fourth its amount. But not only is economy consulted, but time gained, and nothing in the shape of money expenditure is left to conjecture. Accordingly, all buildings of any importance are now let in this mode.

A case or two of actual occurrence may illustrate the system.

MR. SENECA PALMER, engaged as superintendent to the building of the Central Presbyterian Church, now putting up on Fifth street, made out his estimates for that edifice, amounting in the aggregate to 7815,83cts. When the proposals, in case contracts were actually completed at 7776, 65cts, varying only 29 dollars 18 cts, and falling so far short of the estimate.

But I have a still more striking example of the accuracy attainable in this mode.

Col. A. Dudley is building a dwelling house on Sixth street, under contract. The estimate of Mr. Palmer for the carpenter work, nails and lumber inclusive, was 1931 dollars 39 cts. The bids were as follows.

No. 1	2000
" 2	2000
" 3	1936
" 4	1881
" 5	1850

$9667 averaging 1931 dollars 40c.

I have given these particulars because individuals *wise in their own conceit*, say that actual expenditure always exceeds any estimate, and that you must add fifty per cent to estimates when you go to build. By *estimates*, they mean what I should call GUESSES. In cases like those I refer to, we have the actual cost when we complete the contract.

The Baltimore and Ohio Rail Road.

Ever since it has become manifest in our Eastern cities, that their internal rather than their foreign commerce, has been the main element of their growth and prosperity, there has been a constant rivalry in efforts between New York, Boston, Philadelphia and Baltimore to engross the trade of the West.

Our shortest, and in many other respects, most desirable route to the Atlantic, leads to Baltimore, and a rail road, as is well known, has been constructed from that city as far west as Cumberland, Md., fully one third of the distance to this city. This was intended to strike the Ohio river at Wheeling, and would have served to connect by water communication with us until a line of rail road should continue from the Ohio side through the State. But the State of Pennsylvania is unwilling to grant the *right of way* through her territory unless under very oppressive exactions, if at all; the Legislature of that State having lately adjourned, after postponing indefinitely, a measure relied on to accomplish the object. The Baltimore and Ohio rail road company in the progress of their operations, discovered what they ought to have ascertained before they commenced them, that a direct road can be made from Cumberland to Parkersburg, 80 miles lower down on the Ohio than Wheeling, and only ten miles further from Cumberland than that place; and are now unwilling to make Wheeling the terminus, encumbered as they would be by the expense of a lateral road to Pittsburgh, and other oppressive impositions as the price of right of way through Pennsylvania.

In the meantime the Wheeling interest has succeeded in the Virginia Legislature to make its termination there, an absolute condition to the concurrence of Virginia, and in these complicated difficulties of the case, the enterprise stands still. Now there is no doubt that the company are right in abandoning the Wheeling route, but they are wrong in waiting,—as it seems they are—on a change of sentiment in the Virginia Legislature to accomplish their objects. In the present position of the case, it will take at least two years to effect that change. Eastern Virginia will do nothing for Western Virginia, the two sections being as much seperated in interest and feeling as if they were seperate States, and the reason why Parkersburg should terminate the route, would probably be the very one to defeat the measure in the capitol at Richmond, namely, the building of the West into importance.

While this state of things exists, Boston with her immense means, and vigorous enterprise, has been for the last two or three years preparing to thrust her sickle into the great harvest.

Her first move was to intersect the New York rail road at Albany, so as to give her a communication with Buffalo. What next? She has just loaned 500,000 dollars for the completion of the *Little Miami and Mad River rail road* from Cincinnati to Sandusky. When that shall have been completed, and the present year will see i nearly done, what remains? A rail road along the lakeshore, from Sandusky to Buffalo of less than 260 miles. This will not take long to complete, and *where then will be Philadelphia and Baltimore,* as far as regards western trade, the breath of life to those cities? I say Philadelphia and Baltimore, for owing to their proximity and facility of water communication, I consider their interest in this matter one and indivisible. As respects that trade they are now sleeping on a mine of gunpowder, ready to explode before they are aware. If something be not done at once, Boston will distance them forever in the great commercial race. The increase of that city since 1840, merely in the anticipation of her Western trade has been greater than that of any other place of equal magnitude in the United States. What will it be when she actually absorbs the trade of the great valleys of the lower Ohio and central Mississippi? In 1842, the number of buildings put up in Boston was 776, in 1843, 1117; and in 1844, 2145! What will it be in 1845? What will it be in 1846 when rail roads shall have connected Cincinnati and Boston?— Let Philadelphia and Baltimore *look to it.* Statistics like these are surer omens of coming events than the flight of birds.

What resource or remedy is left? Does any exist? I think so, and shall point it out in my next.

Sagacity of the Horse.

Two or three years ago, a remarkable narrative of a horse named John, written by his owner in one of our western cities, Nashville I believe, went the rounds of the periodical press. It is too long for me to copy, and most of my readers will recollect it when I extract two or three of its leading features.

"A few months since, I sent him from my house across the country to the Spring hill road, and up that road a distance of a mile to the house of a friend, although he had not been there for more than a year. I have often sent him such errands. I have only to go with him and show him a place and he never forgets it.— He is perfectly under command of my voice. I speak to him as to a servant, and that he understands what I say is proved from the; fact that he obeys me."

The writer goes on to say, that having left his stable door open according to his usual practice, the horse on one occasion came to the kitch-en door and made a loud knocking with the point of his hoofs. "From what I knew of the sagacity of the animal I judged he had not been fed, and calling up the servant, accused him of the neglect. He denied the charge. I did not believe him, but could say no more. The same thing happening several times, I as often called up the servant taxing him with neglecting the horse. He still asserted he had been fed. One day going by the kitchen door, I heard the old negro talking to the kitchen servants, laughing heartily and repeating, "John won't lie and master knows it," a laugh. "He believes John and won't believe me," another laugh. "I won't tell any more lies about feeding John."

These things and much more of the same character are very remarkable, and leave us in doubt how far the faculty of instinct is developed or understood.

I have now to add a brief statement of what is within my own knowledge, or has fallen under my own notice.

Many of my readers, who remember Philadelphia thirty years ago, will recollect Cope the butcher, who kept a stall on Market just above Third street, and in his own case, finely illustrated Dr. Johnson's mock heroic "Who slays fat oxen, should himself be fat." He resided in Spring-garden, and his slaughter house was on the same premises.

Cope had a horse remarkable for his intelligence. I have known the owner on reaching home with a large drove of bullocks, which he had driven to the gateway of the slaughter yard, to alight, secure the reins tight to the saddle, and after opening the gate to the house, leave it to the horse to drive the cattle in, which was always done as carefully and judiciously as if the rider had been present. On one occasion, I recollect, a large bullock broke away from a dozen, left under these circumstances at the gate. After running six or seven squares, pursued by the horse who was fast overtaking him, he sprang across the side walk over a board yard fence, where he was followed by the horse who succeeded in heading him at the opposite side of the lot, turned him back and made him jump out where he sprang over, and followed him home to the slaughter yard, where he shut him up, the gate closing with a pully.

There is a horse belonging to a respectable butcher here, who can drive cattle home also, but whose most remarkable trait is antipathy to strange dogs, no one of which he will suffer to remain on his master's premises, if within his reach, biting and chasing them away. His master can set him on a dog at any time by a certain signal, which he readily understands.

Are these things the result of training, or are there instincts in the brute creation yet undeveloped and unknown?

White Lead Factories.

It is but a few years since, that the Cincinnati market was extensively supplied from Pittsburgh, and still further East, with White Lead, Chrome Yellow, Chrome Green, Paris Green, &c. In these articles, however, as in many other manufactured in this place, the tide has turned, and we are now supplying home, and distant regular customers with white lead of purity and tint which cannot be surpassed anywhere—and we shall be prepared as our operations enlarge, to furnish this article, as we now do many others to advantage, in the markets whence we formerly derived our supplies. The magnitude of this interest in the home market may be inferred from the fact, that we are annually putting up twelve to fifteen hundred houses in this city, and its northern suburbs, whose finishing must necessarily consume an immense amount of paint.

For the benefit of those readers, numbering thousands in every community, who are ignorant not only of *what* this beautiful pigment, white lead, is made, but *how* it is made, it may be briefly stated that the raw material is piglead, which being run into thin and narrow sheets of about seven inches breadth, and two feet in length, are loosely rolled and placed in crocks so made for the purpose as to let the lead rest on projections one third of the way up. These have been previously filled to that height with vinegar, and placed in squares upon horse-manure in suitable houses, provided for that purpose.

Here the carbon developed under the process of heat combines with the lead corroded by the action of the vinegar, and becomes *carbonate of lead.* It is then taken to be ground and washed. In these processes it is seperated from impure parts, and foreign ingredients, pumped up and run into boxes on a drying floor, after which it is again ground with oil, which is the last preparation to render it fit for use. It is then packed into kegs ordinarily of 25 lbs. each, and branded for market. A small proportion is put up dry.

The Emerald Green is a new article intended to supercede the Chrome Green, which has been so extensively used for shutters and blinds, but found to become dingy in the lapse of a few years. It is the arseniate of copper in chemistry, applied to practical purposes.

A few statistics on this subject will serve, however, to give a better notion of the extent of this manufacture, than any general remarks.— Some notes made not long since at the white lead factories of R. Conkling, & Co., and E. & S. J. Conkling on Court street, east of Broadway, will serve as a basis to the statement which closes this article. The first named firm is an old establishment, on the south side of Court street in which the individuals last alluded to were brought up to the business. Their factory which is of recent erection, and embracing all the modern improvements, is nearly opposite the old concern, being on the scite of Jesse Hunt's tan yard, the beginning of all things in that line in Cincinnati. These two establishments consume in their processes annually, 1,200,000 lbs. lead, 600 barrels flaxseed oil, and 2500 bbls. vinegar, which last article is made on the premises. They also manufacture their own kegs by machinery—employing some fifty hands in the various business departments. Superior Emerald, Green and Chrome Yellow are also made here. There are two other important factories in Cincinnati besides, Messrs. McLenan & Co., and T. Hills & Co., also long and favorably known in the market, to whose operations doubtless many of these remarks apply with equal force.

These four establishments are prepared to supply any amount of white lead which may be needed in this market, and are actually making at present as follows:

R. Conkling & Co. per. week		900
E. & S. J. Conkling, do		600
B. McLenan & Co., do		300
T. Hills & Co., do		600
		2400 kegs.

In 1840 the manufacture of white lead here in three establishments was 900 kegs per week. This was increased in 1844 to 1500, and now to 2400 kegs weekly, being the largest manufacture of white lead in the West.

I referred to Hunt's tan yard as an antiquity, but we may go farther back here to the past.— The original great Elm, a superb tree, at least an hundred and fifty years old, still canopies as it then did, the well known spring, at which the aborigines drank in their expeditions to Kentucky, long before a white man was settled here.

Relics of the Past.

Capt. John Armstrong to Gen. James Wilkinson.
DEAR SIR:

Bailey and Clawson left this on the night of the 7th, which was the evening of the day they arrived. They report two miles on the other side the 17 Mile Creek, about half past 5 o'clock, P. M., they saw three Indians standing in the road with their faces towards St. Clair and about 150 yards in their front—they took to the left of the road in order to make the fort for which they were bound; a foot from the road in crossing a branch, they saw two watching a lick—in running down the bank their belts broke, and they lost their packets—after which at a little distance, they saw two more Indians, who pursued them. They say they heard the savages in pursuit until yesterday 10 o'clock, when they struck a creek, the centre of which they took, and kept it until they struck the river— I suppose ten miles.

Yours with great respect,

JNO. ARMSTRONG.

Ft. Hamilton, June 11 1792.

Fort Washington, June 11th, 1792.

DEAR SIR:—I this morning received your letter of last evening, and regret the accident whch has befallen my last dispatches, though I think it is fifty to one, the enemy have not got them, for it is probable they were not in view when the papers were dropped, and if they were, their attention would have been too much engaged to regard the pacquet.

By this conveyance you will receive the Iron, Hemp, and two Scythes, & I have ordered Hodgdon to send out the Window Glass and every other article which has not been heretofore furnished, and to strengthen your Garrison, I send you the fragment of Pratt's co. at this place.

One half the Scythes fairly assorted, must be sent forwarded to Fort Jefferson, and I must flatter myself, that you will employ your utmost exertions to procure the largest quantity of Hay profitable, in your neighbourhood. This is indeed an object of great magnitude. When the grass is finally secured, it is my purpose to throw a small quantity of salt among it, in order to render it palatable and nutritious. In this momentous business, you shall command every requisite aid, and must duly notify me of every want.

The Lieutenants stationed with you and at St. Clair, are to accompany Lieut. Hartshorn to Fort Jefferson, where they are to continue for the security of the Bullock and Grass Guards at the Post. The regular transport of provisions which we are now about to commence will furnish frequent opportunities of writing, and as the Horse will make their Head Quarters with you, you can at any time employ a party to come on to this post. I expect one hundred mounted rifle-men from Kentucky in six or seven days, engaged for three months, to ply on the communication to Jefferson.

With much esteem, I am dear sir, yours sincerely,

JAS. WILKINSON,

Brig. General.

N, B. You must consider the order restraining the movements of the commanding officers of Posts, as done away, and are to exercise your discretion. The Cavalry is to receive your orders after they return from Jefferson.

J. W.

Capt. JOHN ARMSTRONG.

Enlistments and Discharges.

I Arthur Conway do acknowledge myself to be fairly and truly inlisted in the service of the United States of America, and in the first United States Regiment. To serve as a Soldier for the term of three years, unless sooner discharged; and to be obedient to the orders of Congress and the officers set over me; agreable to the establishment of Congress, passed the thirteenth of April, 1789—as witness thereof I have set my hand, this 22d day of February 1794.

Witness   ARTHUR CONWAY.

Adam Yohe.

Certificate.

This may certify that Casper Sheets, late a soldier in my Comp'y. was appointed Corporal 1st day of April, 1788, and was reduc'd the 17th of Sept. 1790.

D. STRONG,

Capt. 1st U. S. Regt.

Fort Washington, May 13th, 1791.

By *Josiah Harmar Esq. Brigadier General in the service of the United States of America, and commanding the troops in the Western Department.*

These are to certify, that the bearer hereof, Casper Sheets, private soldier in Capt. David Strong's company, and in the first regiment having faithfully served the United States for the term of two years, eight months and three days, and not inclining to re-enlist upon the establishment of the 30th April, 1790, he is hereby honorably discharged the service.

Given at Head Quarters, at Fort Washington this 4th day of December, 1790.

Attest.

JOS. HARMAR,

Brigadier General.

WM. PETERS, Lieut., Acting Adj't.

Baltimore and Ohio Rail Road--No. 2.

In my last article on this subject, after alluding to the difficulties in which the Baltimore and Ohio Rail Road Company had plunged themselves by doing first what they ought to have done last—deciding on the route; and doing at last what they should have done first, ascertain by survey, that Parkersburg was preferable to Wheeling in directness of course for rail road purposes, I proposed to suggest means by which to accomplish the desired object, a termination of the route to the Ohio river at the proper points.

I propose then, that in place of wasting time as well as jeopardizing success, by farther applications to the Legislature of Virginia, that direct personal negotiation along the entire line from Cumberland to Parkersburg be opened by the company to obtain from the owners of property the right of way by grant or sale.

I know that such a proposition will grate harshly on the ears of corporate institutions, who have been in the habit, under the operation of charters, to run roads without any regard to the feelings, convenience, or interest of those whose landed property they cross. But I have no doubt, every purpose sought to be accomplished, can be obtained as readily, and as cheaply in this as in any other mode. I am assured that the right of way along that route, would in most cases be given gratuitously, and if, which is probable, a few mercenary individuals would desire to fill their pockets by taking advantage of the necessity of the case, and exact unreasonable prices for land needed by the company; I feel confident still, that by this course of proceeding, the rail road company will not be paying higher in the whole, than it would cost them, under the damages which they must pay in taking land compulsorily along the whole line.

But it may be alleged, there would be individuals who will withhold their lands through caprice, or a determination to extort a price from the rail road company, which it ought not or could not pay. Such cases when they occur, may be safely left to the omnipotent influence of public sentiment. There is no man in any community, so independent of his neighbors, as to stand out for any personal advantage, to the sacrifice of the entire interests of that community, and if he were to attempt it, the united voice and action of the public would speedily bring him to reasonable terms.

Let the Baltimore and Ohio rail road company adopt this course, the only course in my judgment which they have left, if they mean to act in time to accomplish their object. Let the entire rail road from Boston and New York to Cincinnati be completed, and Philadelphia and Baltimore will, when it is too late, find that they have undervalued the importance of Western trade, and misunderstood the sources of their past growth and commercial importance.

Christ Healing the Sick.

This picture has been in process of exhibition for a few days past at the Unitarian Church in this city, and will remain for that purpose two or three weeks. I make no pretensions to connoisseurship in these things, and leave the analysis of its merits to others. Every one I think, after seeing it, will receive a more distinct as well as vivid impression of the sad and varied catalogue of human suffering which the kind Saviour was so often called on to relieve.

There appears some doubt in the community as to its being from the crayon and brush of WEST. I suppose that there are three pictures on this subject by WEST, of which in 1811, one was in the Royal Chapel at Windsor, one in the Pennsylvania Hospital, and one in the Royal Gallery. The last is the original of which the others are copies by WEST, and the one now exhibited is the first named. The Port Folio of 1811 contains a list of West's paintings which embraces these three on the same subject. As to his death of Gen. Wolfe, his *sixth* copy of it, is in the same list. If it has merit enough to pass for a painting of Benjamin West's, it must have merit enough to be admired for its own sake.

CORRESPONDENCE.

CINCINNATI, May 3d, 1845.

MR. CIST:

It may be interesting to some of your readers to obtain a few statistics, reminiscences and observations, (not generally known) respecting God's ancient people, the Israelites, who are dispersed throughout the world, and whose settlement in this country, especially in the West, is but recent. An individual of that nation who arrived in this city in March 1817, found himself an isolated being, having none of his faith to communicate with. But having communicated to his brethren abroad that the Lord of Hosts had provided another peaceful and happy asylum for his dispersed people;--they soon began to emigrate to this beautiful city, and to spread themselves abroad over the delightful regions of the West; and wherever they locate themselves, become excellent members of society, forming friendship with their christian brethren, conforming to, and sustaining the institutions of the country. It is a well known fact in history, that wherever the Jews congregate, and are well received, that country or city becomes happy and prosperous in all its undertakings. One proof of this is, that the first congregation founded in the West, was in Cincinnati, where they have now increased to about three hundred families. When the person above mentioned arrived in this city there were only 5,000 inhabitants, what is it now? No other city in the West has been able to compete with it! The citizens have always been friendly to the Israelites, and assisted them liberally in 1835 towards erecting their Synagogue, when they were but few in number. A Jew has always gratitude, he never forgets a benefit conferred on him;—it is characteristic of them as a body, that they always maintain their own poor; charity being one of the main pillars of their religious institutions—their hands and hearts are always open to relieve the distresses of their fellow creatures. As an instance of this, as soon as the disastrous conflagration at Pittsburgh was known, meetings were summoned of their several institutions and societies, committees were appointed to make collections, and the following sums have been remitted to Pittsburgh.

Holy Congregation, Children of Israel,	$100 00
Hebrew Beneficent Society, (remitted separately,)	50 00
Hebrew Gentlemen's Benevolent Society,	25 00
Hebrew Lady's Benevolent Society,	30 00
Hebrew German Lady's Benevolent Society,	25 00
Hebrew Individuals (through the Committees,)	134 25
	$354 25

Besides this amount something like two hundred dollars was collected from individuals of the Jewish persuasion by the several ward committees. In my next I will continue this article with respect to their locations in several portions of the United States, and if my remarks should draw the attention of your readers, will extend my researches to the whole nation dispersed throughout the world.

J.

Facts for Physiologists.

In looking over the Kentucky legislative documents, we were struck with the following facts, found in the Second Auditor's report. (Legislative Documents, 1844-5.) From a tabular statement showing the whole number of idiots in the State supported at the public expense, we find the following facts, showing clearly that idiocy is a family misfortune.

In Adair county, we find four idiots, three of them one family name, viz: Joseph Frankums, Fielding Frankums, Hiram Frankums.

Boyle—Edward Jones, Richard Jones.
Bracken—Catharine Davis, William Davis.
Bath—Elizabeth Coffer, James Coffer.
Cumberland—John T. Scott, Parmelia Scott.
Fayette—Sally Yates, Lucy Yates.
Fleming—John Swin, Isaac Swin, Robert Kissick, Nancy Kissick.
Grant—Mahala Thornhill, Priscilla Thornhill, John Thornhill, Betsy Thornhill.
Hardin—George Arvin, Mary Arvin.
Henry—Mary Sutherland, Elizabeth Sutherland, Charles Kidwell, Mahala Kidwell.
Jessamine—Elizabeth Harbough, Lewis Harbough, Mary Harbough, James Hunter, Squire Hunter, Joseph Hunter, Davison Hunter, Asher Hunter, Sidney Hunter.
Letcher—Lincoln Croft, James Croft.
Livingston—James Caldwell, Joseph Caldwell, David Caldwell.
Madison—Lucy Gentry, John Gentry, Betsey Gentry.
Mercer—Minerva Norvell, Martha Norvell, Lydia Anderson, Jane Anderson, Mary Sanders, Sarah Sanders, Nancy Uptigrove, John S. Uptigrove, Jane Uptigrove, James Vandevere, Abram Vandevere.
Morgan—Silas Ratliff, Jeremiah Ratliff.
Nicholas—Aris Wiggins, Sarah Wiggins, John Wiggins, Jefferson Wiggins.
Ohio—Martha Davis, Valentine Davis, Cook avis, Charles W. Davis.

Perry—Samuel Ellis, Polly Ellis, Jacob Ellis.
Pike—Isaac Taylor, Mary Ann Taylor.
Scott—Charles Riley, Lydia Riley, Cynthia Lindsey, James Lindsey.
Wayne—Lucinda Coyle, Lavina Coyle, Stephen Coyle, James Green, William Green.
Whitley—Francis Powers, John Powers, Thos. Veatch, Marion Veatch, Barbary Yancy, Sally Yancy.
Washington—Nancy Montgomery, Lucy Montgomery.

There are 415 idiots supported at the public expense in the State—Mercer county has the most of any one county, 23; Whitley, the greatest number in proportion to population, 16. The facts here stated prove that idiocy is a family disease, but from what cause it originates we are not prepared to say, and should like to have the science in explanation by some one versed in physiology.—*Kentucky Yeoman.*

For Cist's Advertiser.

Reminiscences of Olden Time in Virginia and Ohio.

BY HORATIO G. JONES, JR.

Leverington, Pa.

Extracts from the Journal of Rev. David Jones—Communicated by Horatio G. Jones jr., Leverington, Pa.

Oct. 26th, 1772, I left my house and family. For the convenience of carrying provisions and as a defence against storms I went this time in a covered wagon, but the carriage rendered the journey less expeditious. We travelled so slow and could make so little way over the Allegheny Mountains, that we did not arrive at Redstone till Nov. 17th. A few days before me the Rev. John Davis arrived here and intended to go with me to Ohio. When we came to the house of my interpreter, I found that, some time before our arrival, he had, in company with a number of Delaware Indians, gone far down the Ohio, but left word that I might find him about the Shawanese towns, or somewhere along the Ohio. In hopes of finding him, Mr. Davis and I, in company with some others set out for the river Ohio, but by stormy weather, and high waters, our journey was so retarded that we did not arrive there, until Wednesday, Dec. 2d, when we came to the house of Dr. James McMeehan, who formerly lived a neighbor to Mr. Davis. The heart of poor Mr. Davis was filled with joy to see his old acquaintance, and the river Ohio, after such a tedious journey: but dear man! his time was short, for on the 13th of the said month, he departed this life, and left me his remains to commit to the earth. Mr. D. was a great scholar, possessed a good judgment and very retentive memory. He told me, the reason why he left Boston was, because he abhorred a dependant life and popularity; that if God continued him, he intended to settle in this new country and preach the gospel of our Saviour freely. The remains of this worthy man are interred near a brook, at the north end of the level land, that lies adjacent to Grave creek. About 16 feet north of his grave stands a large black oak tree; on this, with my tomahawk, I cut the day of the month, and date of the year, with Mr. Davis' name. This is all the monument that I left there, but Dr. McMeehan intended a tomb for him. *He was the first* white man that departed his life in this part of the country, but before I came away a child was laid by him.

Not finding my interpreter, I had thought of returning home, but while I ruminated on the subject, a canoe came along, bound for the Shawanese town. This canoe belonged to Mr. John Irwin, an Indian trader, with whom I was acquainted. She was 60 feet long, and at least 3 feet wide, was fitted out with 6 hands and very deeply laden. The principal hand was Mr. James Kelly, who was very kind and offered to take me along. I concluded to go, thinking that travelling by water might be conducive to my health, and in hopes of meeting my interpreter. In the morning, and on the 27th of Dec., parting with my brother and other friends, committing the event to Providence, I started on my voyage to the Shawanese Indians. The day was cold, and as it snowed at times, it was uncomfortable travelling, but I kept myself lapped up in my blankets, so that I was preserved from receiving any damage by the severity of the season. We encamped at night on the west side of the Ohio, and by the help of a good fire, slept comfortably, at least more so, than could be imagined by those who are strangers to this way of lodging.

Monday 28th. The wind blew from the south; which made the river so rough that we were obliged to lay ashore a great part of the day.— I am informed by the traders, that the wind almost universally blows up the Ohio, especially in the winter season. Indeed I never remember to have seen it otherwise, and if this continues to be the case, it must be of great use to the trade up this river. In the evening Mr. Kelly concluded that as the wind had abated, it was his duty to continue at their oars all night: therefore we set out and by morning we were, as I suppose, about 8 miles below the little Kanawha. This night proved severely cold, and my lodging was not only uncomfortable but also very dangerous, for the canoe was loaded 18 inches above its sides, and there was no berth for me, so that I had to lie on the loading.— Though I was well furnished with blankets, I was afraid my feet would have been frozen: it may be well thought, that my sleep was unpleasant. My danger was so great, that if I moved in my sleep, the bottom of the Ohio must

have been my bed. This brought many thoughts into my mind what would be the event, but believing that God was able to keep me from dreaming, or starting in my sleep, I committed all into His hand and slept without fear, and in the morning found myself safely preserved through the care of Him whose tender mercies are over the works of His hands. Here on the east side of the Ohio, the country appears level and good, but I was not out on it.

Tuesday, Dec. 29th., we traveled but very little by reason of contrary winds. Wednesday 30th. The morning being pleasant, we set out for the great Kanawha. We passed Hockhocking which is a pretty large creek, coming in from the west side of the Ohio. Several creeks came in from the east side, but as we rowed all night, I had not an opportunity of making my remarks on each; but the land in general, while I had daylight, appeared level and good. About day break we passed the mouth of the Great Kanawha. This is a great river that comes from the borders of Virginia, and appears about 300 yards wide at the mouth. The land about this river, I am informed is very good, & it is thought that the seat of government will be on its banks. I am of the opinion that the great Guiandotte will be found the best place for the metropolis. The great Kanawha, according to Mr. Hutchins, is 226 miles below Fort Pitt. This morning we put ashore and took breakfast of chocolate, using rum as an ingredient instead of milk, it is deemed very useful here in the wilderness where flesh was our chief provisions; therefore it was common for us afterwards to continue the practice, though I could scarcely be persuaded at first to make a trial of it. Thursday 31st. After breakfast we set out for the Great Guiandotte. The river Ohio bears in general S. W. and a little more westerly, but it is in many places very crooked. This day we had pleasant weather and travelled a great distance, so that the next day—being the 1st of January, 1773, we passed the mouth of the Great Guiandotte. This is a very large creek, coming from Clinch Mountain, which separates it from Holston river and lies, I apprehend, west of the south part of Virginia, or west of the north part of North Carolina. This creek appears to be large enough to be navigable for canoes and small craft for a great distance up it. The land appears charming and level, covered with fine timber, and as I am informed abounds with extraordinary springs, especially about the branches that form this creek. This is an extraordinary country for pasturage, so that cattle without any further supply, than what is common in the woods, will be good beeves all winter. *Here we have the greatest abundance of buffaloes,* which are a species of cattle as I apprehend, left her;

by the former inhabitants,* for it is most evident that this country has once been inhabited by some people that had the use of iron. Up some of these creeks, I have been told, by sundry persons, that there is a pair of mill stones, where in former ages a mill has stood. The bank of the Ohio, below the mouth of this creek seems near 100 feet higher than the water in ordinary times, so that here is the best place for a town that I saw on the river Ohio, as it will always be safe from floods of water, and will be easy for this new Province to transport its produce down the stream. There is another creek as large, or nearly so, about 13 miles below, called Great Sandy creek. On the heads of these creeks I am informed, is the most beautiful and fertile country to be settled, that is any where in this new Province, and I recommend it to all who design to emigrate to this new world, as most agreeable in all respects. The latitude must be in the end of 38 deg., or in the beginning of 39 deg. very convenient to this, are the most famous salt springs, which are a peculiar favour of God. I have also seen in this country, what the people call alum mines, though they rather appear to me, as a mixture of vitriol and alum. Throughout this country, we have a very great abundance of stone coal, which I have often seen burn freely. The smiths about Redstone use no other sort of coal in their shops, and find that it answers remarkably well, This one article, must be of great advantage to this country, in process of time. Another advantage which it enjoys is abundance of lime stone, with excellent quaries of free stone, fit to erect the best of buildings.

Saturday, January 2d, it rained so that we were obliged to remain in camp, and notwithstanding we took all care to stretch our blankets, the rain was so great, that Mr. Kelly and myself were soaking wet in water, in our bed thro' the night, yet I was not sensible of any danger.

Sabbath 3d, it continued rainy, so that we remained in the same place.

Monday 4th. Set out for the river Sciota, and about the middle of the day, we came to the mouth of this river, on which the Shawanese now live. This river is better than 200 yards wide at the mouth, and was then very deep, owing to the late rains. The mouth of this river is the end of the new Province that is expected to take place. For some miles before we came to the mouth of this river, there appears an impassable mountain on the east side of the Ohio, coming close to the edge of the river, opposite the mouth of the Sciota. There is a way to pass over, rather below the Sciota, and I was

* It is rather remarkable, that W. C. Bryant in one of his late poems, hazards the same conjecture.

informed by an old Trader, who had been often there, that after you pass east 13 miles you will come to a famous level land of fine springs, and the best pasturage. This must be connected with or part of the land, which I described above on the branches of Sandy Creek and Guiandott. This river is not called Sciota by the Shawanese, but yet something which sounds a little like this is used, as one name. I remember the name which they give it signifies *hairy river*. The Indians tell us that when the first of them came to live on this river, the deer were so plenty that as they came to drink in the river, in the spring of the year, their hair was cast off in such abundance that the river appeared full of hair; hence this name was given to it.

The Cincinnati Observatory.

After the many stripes inflicted on our astronomical society and the *astronomer royal*, at home and abroad, especially the merciless ones laid on at Louisville, it will doubtless, be pouring in oil and wine to republish the following article from the N. O. Bulletin.

American Science and Enterprise.

I perceive that the Cincinnati Telescope is now mounted, and the Observatory opened.— Well done, the Queen City! What city comes next? "Don't all speak at once." Now stand aside ye moons, and planets, and common stars! Let the Buckeyes have a peep, just a little beyond an infinite distance, and describe a few thousand constellations of suns, whose light grows tired and cannot reach here, and which never could have been known but for the Buckeye Telescope.

It sounds curiously to us, and still more so to people across the water; but I must tell you the short history of this great Telescope.

ORMSBY M. MITCHELL, the Astromomer elect of the Observatory, a native of this glorious valley, and a distinguished graduate of the Military Academy at West Point—one in whom the American blood seems more highly concentrathed than Stillman's sarsaparilla—had been some years Professor of Mathematics in Cincinnati College, and was delivering a few popular lectures on astronomy in that city, in the spring of 1843. Public interest was aroused by the profoundness and eloquence of this man of fire, when he conceived the idea of an Astronomical Society, and a "*light-house of the skies*," in that city. No sooner thought than embarked in—he took a paper in his hand and ranged that city on his visionary scheme; and at the end of a few weeks his *Astronomical Society* numbered near four hundred members, all elected by subscribing twenty-five dollars each, and composed of all possible vocations of society—draymen, butchers, carpenters, boatmen, merchants, doctors, lawyers and gentlemen.

In three months from that date, if you could have peeped into that room of eternal silence—the *computation* room of the Greenwich Royal Observatory—you might have seen the fire of an American eye- pouring over the tables of figures, and running up lines of algebraic symbols—an assistant, *pro tempore*, to Mr. AIRY, the Astronomer Royal, and one of the most illustrious men of the age. In two short weeks, in fact, Prof. MITCHELL had mastered the Cyclopædia of Observatory labors, in a relation never before granted to an American; and thence repaired to Paris, where his letters secured him the attentions of ARAGO, and the facilities of the Royal Observatory. Thence he repaired to Germany, whither he was bound for the apparatus of his Buckeye Observatory. FRAEUNHOFFER, who constructed the great Dorpat instrument, alone could satisfy him; and no common instrument, such as graced common European Observatories, would suit one who came from the land ot superlatives. Ten thousand dollars was more than the whole heterogeneous Buckeye Society had subscribed; but that was the price of the greatest telescope, just about to be constructed, and like an American, nothing less would satisfy him; and so he contracted for it. The mechanicians stared, and philosophers thought him a madman, that he should tell of an Astronomical Society of four hundred members, in the wilds of Western America, contracting for the greatest telescope, that of Dorpat excepted, that had ever been mounted.

In September of the same season he made his report to the said *Society*, and to half the people of Cincinnati, who heartily applauded his extravagance and ubiquity, and soon ran up the lists of the society to six or seven hundred members.

Men are ever ready to be liberal, when the great work has been already done despite the want of means. Every body would now be a member.

A large lot of ground was tendered, on the highest of the tall summits around the Queen City, by that substantial friend of native genius, Mr. LONGWORTH, the early patron of POWERS; and now, upon that eminence of four hundred feet, stands a large stone edifice, and upon its top that huge instrument, the eye of astronomical science, is wheeled to the heavens by that same daring spirit, whose phantasy was sneered at by his neighbors, when first conceived, and whose crazy story was laughed at in the Royal lighthouses of European skies. Three cheers for American extravagance! Nine cheers for ORMSBY M. MITCHELL!

The city of Boston, I believe, has lately made a movement somewhat similar, but as for us, we must be satisfied with our schools, and lyceums, and libraries. An Observatory can never be successfully conducted here, for a want of firmness in our foundation—perfect quiescence being absolutely necessary for such purposes—unless our city pride could be extended to the other side of the lake for this department of science.

Organ Building.

I learn from my friend Koenke, that orders for organs are pouring in on him from all quarters. He has contracted within a few weeks for an organ at Lancaster Ohio, at 500 dollars. Two organs for Memphis at 2000 and 800 dollars respectively. One for New Orleans at 875. Two for St. Louis at 800 and 3500. He is now engaged on a fine parlor organ which ranges from C C to F, being an octave higher than any instrument of the kind in the United States, and an experiment for which the community is indebted to the ingenuity of Mr. K.

I feel deeply gratified in stating these facts, which indicate not less the increasing demand in this market for an important manufacture of Cincinnati, than the general satisfaction given by Mr. Koenke's organs, which are unsurpassed any where in power and sweetness.

Organ building here is what our more important manufactures once were; the beginnings of operations, which are to expand and enlarge to the supply of half the United States.

Early Drought.

We are experiencing a degree of drought unusual in this country, even during summer, and extremely rare for the spring season. During the last sixty days, but two showers have fallen around us. These have not sufficed much more than to penetrate the earth's surface. Mr. D. Lapham writes in from the country, that the "oldest inhabitant" does not recollect such a drought. The *oldest inhabitant* has a short memory. The early part of the year 1806, in the Miami country was characterised by just such weather as the present, with the aggravation that from the 10th of March to the 28th August not a drop of rain fell throughout the whole region, and had the country been as extensively opened, at that day as at present, serious and permanent injury to the soil must have resulted, for as is well known to intelligent farmers, the aridity of summer heats is more exhausting to land than the cultivation of a crop, which while it draws nourishment from the soil, to a great extent, shields it from the burning influences of the solar rays.

Pioneers of Cincinnati.

The following list comprehends the names so far as I have been able to obtain them with the dates of their arrival here of those of our early settlers who have been here from the commencement of the present century.

1796 Jacob Burnet,	1798 Hugh Moore,
Isaac Burton,	Samuel Newell
William Burke.	Ebenezer Pruden.
1804 Ephraim Carter,	1804 Jona. Pancoast,
James Crawford,	Jos. Perry.
William Crippen,	1802 Sam'l. Perry,
Henry Craven,	Wm. Pierson.
1800 Daniel Drake,	1804 Jos. Pancoast,
Jno. B. Enness,	Robt. Richardson.
Edward Dodson.	1790 John Riddle,
1800 Charles Faran.	Christop'r. Smith.
1790 Jas. Ferguson.	1802 Ethan Stone.
1790 Mrs. Mary Gano.	1796 Sam'l. Stitt,
1794 Dan'l. Gano.	Wm. Saunders.
1792 Asa Holcomb.	1804 P. S. Symmes,
1803 Caspar Hopple,	Benj. Smith,
Andrew Johnston.	P. A. Sprigman.
1798 David Kautz,	G. P. Torrence.
Wm. Legg.	1800 A. Valentine,

Nich. Longworth.	Stephen Wheeler,	
1794 Jonathan Lyon.	John Wood,	
1804 Benjamin Mason.	J. L. Wilson,	
1797 John Mahard.	Caleb Williams.	
1795 Jonah Martin.	1790 Mrs. H. Wallace.	
1804 Peter McNicoll,	1801 Robt. Wallace,	
Adam Moore,	John Whetsone.	
Wm. Moody.	1794 Griffin Yeatman.	

As I intend to correct this line as far as opportunity permits, I shall feel obliged to those who can present me the necessary information to do so.

Hopple's Row.

The increase of business in Cincinnati compels it to radiate from its former centres. Blocks of business stands are forming, East, West and North of the existing commercial regions. Thus some thirty large ware and store houses have been, or are just about to be erected on Walnut, between Water and Second streets. Commerce is finding vent down Second, Third and Front streets to the west, and up Second and Third streets to the east. That fine block known by the name of Hopple's row, and which has hardly been a year built, is now occupied with Lace and Dry Goods stores, Drug shops, Carpet warehouses, &c, in which goods are offered wholesale to as good advantage as in any other part of the city. Among these the Dry Goods store of Baird & Schuyler's may be especially alluded to, as a fine establishment.

These are the occupants of the lower buildings; up stairs is a perfect den of *wipers* in the shape of lawyers and editors.

Prince Albert at Fault.

On the occasion of her Majesty's recent visit to Scotland, the Prince was taking a turn upon the deck of the royal yacht; and on approaching the caboose, or cooking house, the olfactory nerves of his Royal Highness were sensibly affected by the "sweet smelling savor" emerging from the boiling cauldron. "What is in the pote?" asked the Royal Consort of the Queen. "Eh, surr, do you no ken it's the hoodge poodge!" was the reply of the sturdy Caledonian. "De hoodge poodge!" exclaimed the Prince; "what is him made with?" "Why, man?" said the chief de cuisine, ignorant of the rank of his interrogator; 'aw'll be telling you enough; there's toorneps intelt, and there carrets intelt, and there's mooten intelt, and there's water intelt, and there's——." "Yah, yah," interrupted the Prince, "but what ess inelt?" "Am aw no tellin ye a' the time?" said the gastronomic artist; "there's toorneps intelt;" and again repeating the category of ingredients, he was a second time stopped by the Prince, who was perplexed to know the meaning of "intelt." The Scot, losing all patience, exclaimed, "ye daft gowk, if ye canna understan' me, maybe ye'd like to put your nose intelt." The Prince, somewhat disconcerted, lighted his meerschaum, walked aft, descended into the saloon cabin, and requested his secretary to refer to the latest edition of the Scottish dictionary, in order to find out "what was intelt."

OBITUARY.

It is not possible for an editor at all times to present appropriate notices of the deaths of individuals whose relation to the community seem to demand some thing more than a bare register of the fact. He has neither time nor opportunity in many cases to gather the necessary or instructive facts in the case.

CHARLES TATEM, who deceased on the 29th ult., in the 73rd year of his age, was born at Gosport, Va., and was brought up to the blacksmith business, at Wilmington, Delaware. After serving the usual apprentice-ship, he commenced in that line on his own account, and such was the wide spread reputation for skill and ingenuity, he established for himself, that he filled orders for work of certain descriptions, not only throughout the continent, but even from France. In 1818, he emigrated to Cincinnati, where he established himself by buying out a firm—the Hodgsons—who had a foundery in the rear of the present Universalist Church, on Walnut street.— Here he commenced a business which enlarging with the increasing importance of Cincinnati, became, with one or two other establishments, the means of directing to this market that immense amount of steam boat building, and steam engine, and sugar mill business, for the Southern markets which now form such heavy elements in our manufactory statistics.

In 1827 his operations had become so much increased as to require him to add a new foundery which was put up on Plum, between 2nd and 3rd streets, and is now occupied by the Messrs. Resor. Here the business was carried on for years until he saw fit under the increasing pressure of age, to relinquish active employment.

He lived to see the City of his adoption enlarge from an extent of 1890 houses to 12,000; from a population of 9602 to 80,000; and the products of manufactured industry, in iron alone, from some fifty thousand dollars per annum to two and an half millions at the lowest estimate.

Charles Tatem was a man of singularly high minded and honorable feeling and conduct, active in every benevolent enterprise, and enjoying the esteem of the whole community. He was repeatedly nominated for public employment--in the last case for the Senate of the State of Ohio—but always declined, prefering private life.

DEATHS.

On Tuesday the 29th ult, AMELIA ELIZABETH, daughter of Luke Kent, aged 7 years and 9 months.

Friday the 2nd inst, MARY CHASE, infant daughter of Wm. P. Steele, Esqr.

Saturday the 3rd inst, JULIA F. HOLMES, aged 9 years.

Sunday the 4th inst, WILLIAM HENRY, son of Edward and G. and Jane Drake, aged 3 years 11 months 7 days.

Same day, LAURA JANZ, daughter of Geo. and Eliza beth Mendenhall, aged 2 years.

Thursday the 1st inst, of Dropsy, ELIZABETH, relict of the late RICHARD BERESFORD, in the 81 year of her age.

MARRIAGES.

On Sunday 20th ult, by the Rev. Mr. Wilson, JOHN WALKER to Miss ISABELLA WEIR.

Thursday the 22nd ult, by the Rev. Geo. W. Maley, Mr. JAMES HILL, of Madison Ia., to Miss MARY ANN TAYLOR of this city.

Wednesday the 23rd ult. by Mark P. Taylor, Esqr. Mr. BENONI NICHOLS to Miss KEZIAH COPELAND.

Thursday the 24th ult, at Waynesville, WILLIAM G KINSEY of Cincinnati, to ANN, daughter of Thos. Evans, of Warren County.

Thursday the 1st May, by the Rev. Mr. Gillaspie, Mr MACAULEY AKIN, of Louisville, Ky., to Miss CHLOE P MIX of this city.

Sunday the 4th inst, by Elder James Challen, Mr. WM SMITH to Miss LOUISA M. McDONOGH.

Jerk Beef in Buenos Ayres.

Cincinnati, April 26th, 1845.

Mr. Cist:

Sir—A few days since you expressed a wish to have me give you a description of taking cattle and making "Jerk Beef" in Buenos Ayres, for the different markets on the coast of Brazil, and the West India Islands.

The cattle are driven from the country in numbers from two hundred to a thousand, to the *mataderos* or slaughter yards, where they are put in large fields, enclosed by ditches nine feet wide at top, and seven feet deep, tapered to a foot in width at the bottom, with the earth deposited on the outside. This is the only species of inclosure that can be made in the country, as there is no timber to be had sufficient for fencing or stone for walls. This ditch costing twenty dollars for every hundred feet, or about three hundred dollars to enclose a four acre lot.

Near this enclosure there is a pen or yard in a circular form, made by inserting posts in the ground side by side, and close together, secured by strips in a horizontal direction, laced to the posts with thongs of raw-hide. These enclosures have to be made strong and secure, the cattle being in quite a wild state, as they are fresh from the *pampas*, and on the approach of a man they crowd with great force against the side of the pen.

The entrance to this "*Coral*" is about fifteen feet wide and stopped by two poles of the palm tree placed across the opening as bars. There are generally from 25 to 30 men engaged in killing and salting the beef, including all the branches connected with the business.

Seven men are generally employed in killing—two on horse back, with each a *lazo*, and one of them has in his hand an instrument made in the shape of a crescent attached to a handle with the concave edge at the extremity. One of the mounted men enters the pen, separates a bullock from the herd, the keeper standing out of sight and lets him sally forth with the horseman after him at full speed, with his lazo attached to an iron ring made fast to the girth of the horse on the right side immediately behind the leg of the rider. The lazo is about 75 feet long with an iron ring about 2 inches in diameter at its extreme end, and with this the noose is formed, the lazo is platted round a strip of raw-hide in the centre and with four strands on the outside about 3-16 of an inch in width, with the hair shaved off and the thongs brought to an equal thickness before platting. These strips are rubbed in the hands three or four days to prevent them from becoming hard. Strips thus prepared, are platted around the center part and form a cord about ½ inch in diameter when fin-

ished. The noose is opened to about ten feet in diameter, which would bring the ring at the right hand, the "standing part," and the part forming the noose is drawn through the hand until the ring is in the centre of the opening; this makes one side of the noose heavier than the other; the balance of the lazo being in a small coil in the left hand, swinging it around in a horizontal direction over his head, the hand being back up when in front, and palm up when at the back part of the hand. Thus you will perceive the lazo does not turn over. The speed of the horse increases the velocity of the lazo until he approaches to within a proper distance, when the noose is let go through the air and falls upon the bullock with probably just space enough to encompass the horns and secure the prey.

This part of catching the animal is probably performed in 15 to 20 seconds. The second horseman approaches and cuts the ham strings of the bullock; but the method generally practised is for the other "Gaucho" or Ensayador to follow the bullock as he is fast by the head.—He runs round the first horseman sideways and throwing his lazo over the hips or hinder parts of the bullock, catches him by both hind legs; thus with the animal fast with two lazos, the horsemen move in opposite directions with a slight curvature from a right line, the bullock falls, the killer approaches and dispatches him at once; four men come up and the skin is taken off, all in about 5 minutes from the time he left the "Coral," being cut in quarters and removed on wheelbarrows to the "Saladero" the part of the establishment for "dissecting" and salting. This is a collection of four buildings, of from 100 to 150 feet long and 35 feet wide, made of poles and thatched with a kind of wild flag. like those used by coopers for making tight joints near the croze of a barrel, presenting to the view a shed standing on poles with a fork at the top, and the bottom end in the ground, open at the sides and ends. In the centre of this are vats built of brick about a foot deep, eight feet wide and from fifteen to twenty feet long, lined with cement, in these is first sprinkled salt and then a layer of beef, then salt and another layer of beef, this they continue until the pile is 8 or 10 feet high. On either side are poles suspended with large tenter hooks in them, to hang the quarters of beef on. The bones are all taken out, the meat cut into strips about 10 inches wide 3-8 of an inch thick, salted about 24 hours and then exposed to the sun to dry, and when thoroughly dry it is ready for shipping. The bones are saved and shipped to England and the United States for buttons, knife handles, tooth brushes, &c.

The number of bullocks killed per day at each of these "Saladeros," varies from 150 to 300, according to the number of men employed.

T.

Bathing.

With all the advance in civilization and improvement which characterizes the Anglo-american race, it may be well doubted if we have not left it to those we stigmatise as barbarians, or at least semi-civilized, habits and customs which we ought to have carried with us along the tide of time and improvement. Among these may be named the use of the bath, which enters so largely into the modes of living in three fourths of the globe. I know no reason it should be neglected in the United States to the extent it is, but our national characteristic, to sacrifice or undervalue every thing which withdraws us from "*the one great idea*" of making money. We have not *time* to bathe!

It is true that time is money, but is it not also true in the same sense, and indeed to a greater gdeeer that *health* is money. There are few will dispute this. Well then, I tell my fellow citizens, that the man who goes without bathing from week to week during any period of the year, is injuring his health, and laying foundations for disease, and that the man who does so during the heats of summer is absolutely committing suicide. This is strong language, but I can render its truth apparent, by a few facts—equally important and interesting—with which I have lately made myself acquainted, and which are indisputable.

1st. MM. Lavoisier and Seguin, French physicians, by way of experiment, for thirty years, weighed themselves, their food and their excretions, and ascertained in a most conclusive manner, that five-eighths of what they ate, passed off by the pores of the skin. Another series of experiments, demonstrated that the weight of what was thus discharged, was twenty ounces every twenty-four hours, being greater than the united excretions of both the kidneys and bowels.

2nd. Concentrated animal effluvia forms a very energetic poison, and late medical observations render it certain that malaria, the plague, spasmodic cholera, and other epidemics, are absorbed by the skin.

3rd. By the agency of absorption, substances placed in contact with the skin, are taken up and carried into the general circulation. This is demonstrable in the process of vaccination, and by the mercurial preparations, which, rubbed on the skin are absorbed, and affect the patient precisely as when swallowed. The effect of poison from the bite of rabid animals, and wounds received in dissections, which are familiar occurrences, are referable to the same principle.

It results from all this—and I have barely glanced at the more important points—that those who suffer themselves to go from day to day, and week to week without purification of the skin by bathing furnish a ready, cause for various complaints, and are exposing themselves to dangerous and fatal consequences.

I need only advert to the benefit derived from frequent ablutions by those—even in our own country—whose bodily purification is part of their religious ritual. Still further; in none of my reading and reference to travel in the Levant, or any where, in which bathing is a regular and frequent habit, can I find any notice of the existence of rheumatism. One writer, who travelled extensively in Turkey, and resided there many years—Slade, expressly says, he he never saw nor heard of a case of rheumatism throughout the East.

Besides the direct attack of disease invited by the neglect to which I allude, there can be little doubt that the general debility which is so prevalent in summer is ascribable to the same cause.

Bathe! then, bathe! The bath house is the true *Hygeian Fountain*, where Health presides, and *Woodruff* at the ARCADE on Sycamore, opposite the National theatre, is the priest who officiates at the shrine. A trifle of expense in these ablutions will save days and nights of suffering, and dollars upon dollars in physician's bills.

Public Meetings in Cincinnati.

On Thursday the 15th inst. the General Assembly of the Presbyterian church holds its annual meeting, and for the first time in Cincinnati. This is a delegation from the whole Presbyterian church in the United States, and will probable be composed of rising 250 members. Several of those who have never been in the west, will probably bring their families, or at least their wives. In addition, there will be numbers present on that occasion, of those who have business to transact with the assembly, and of those who will be attracted from the neighboring counties, and adjacent States, by a desire to witness what they have never seen, the supreme ecclesiastical court of the church to which they belong. Under these circumstances, I look for a temporary addition to our population of more than a thousand adults. There are several important questions that will come up for discussion, and settlement, which must give considerable interest to its meetings. Of these are

1. The Elder question.
2. The validity of baptism in the papal church.
3. The removal of the Board of Domestic

Missions to the west.

4. The marriage question.
5. The abolition question.

The list of members, so far as I have examined it, enrolls a full share of the weight of talent, learning, and experience belonging to that denomination of Christians; and I think it probable that our citizens and their guests may make interesting and profitable acquaintance with each other.

By the time the Assembly shall have adjourned, a still larger body will convene in Cincinnati, as "the *friends of Constitutional Liberty*," on Wednesday the 11th June. It is understood that the Second Advent Tabernacle, corner of John and Seventh sts. will be the place of meeting; and there is little doubt, from arrangements already made, that it will be as crowded an assemblage as filled and overflowed that building, during the late Theological debate. Most of the eminent Liberty men of other States will no doubt be present. And as that party commands its full share of the speaking talent of the community, many interesting addresses may be expected.

Burr's Expedition.

At this distance of time, we can smile at the excitement produced throughout the whole west, by the chimerical expedition of Burr, Blennerhassett and others. In that day however, the whole subject was clothed in so much mystery, that no one could ascertain the extent of the preparations or resources for doing mischief, and the whole Ohio and Mississippi valley was on the *qui vive* for the explosion threatened by these movements.

The letters which follow are worthy preservation, as part of the documentary history of that enterprise, the main objects of which the public at large are to this day as ignorant of as they were forty years since. The Major Riddle alluded to is *John Riddle*, of this place, one of the few survivors of our early pioneers; and as regards length of residence as well as age may be considered the patriarch of Cincinnati. *Tiffin* it seems was Governor of Ohio at that period, as was *Gano* the commanding officer of the Ohio militia in this section of country.

Chillicothe, Dec. 17th, 1806.
HIS EXCELLENCY GEN. GANO:

Dear Sir—I received yours per mail—the moment I received the information I attended at the Collector's office, and found that John Carlisle Esq., had assumed payment for one tract, and that previous to his receiving your information, two tracts, part of them had been sold for the tax—but since Mr. Carlisle has compromised, the particulars I presume the squire has informed you of per mail. You I presume, are

master of any information that is of any great consequence. I am informed that the people of Cincinnati discover great patriotism—I am pleased to hear it—it is what every man ought to do who is a friend to his country.

I hope to hear by next mail, that those boats which have been built in consequence of the nefarious scheme, that there appears but too good reason to believe are on foot, will be taken; and those fellows who have designs of attempting the destruction of our government—if such there be, may be brought to meet condign punishment. It behooves every friend of liberty to be active—and willingly would I sacrifice my life and little property in support of the Union of the United States; for I am led firmly to believe, that if ever a separation take place—that then we may bid adieu to that liberty that is necessary to the promotion of national happiness. The piece of ordnance consider under the control of you and his honor Judge Nimmo. I have a swivel that lays at home in my cellar that may be useful; if so, call on Mrs. McFarland and ask her to let you have it. Any thing I can do to aid the government, be it ever so little shall with pleasure be contributed.

Accept sir, the high assurances of my respect,
And believe me your excellency's
Obedient servant,
WM. McFARLAND.

Chillicothe, Dec., 14th, 1806.
DEAR SIR:

I have just received a communication from the Secretary of war of the United States, a copy of which I herewith enclose to you. I have also just received a letter from Judge Meigs, of Marietta, informing me that he has arrested ten Batteaux, forty feet long each, with stores &c. on the Muskingum as they were descending the river, and that four more remaining on the stocks will be arrested, that Comfort Tyler was lying with a number of fast running boats at Blannerhassett's Island, and about 50 men armed, &c. &c.

I have sent this off as soon as I could obtain an express and get my letters wrote, authorizing you to raise immediately two companies of volunteer militia, agreeably with the letter of the Secretary of war to me, each company composed of one Major, one Captain, one Lieutenant, and one ensign, and sixty non-commissioned officers, privates and musicians. I delegate the power to you to appoint these officers, and to direct that the instructions given in the Secretary's letter to me be complied with—and due returns &c. be made. You will observe they will be under the pay &c., of the United States. I have ordered one company to be raised at Marietta, as the boats are arrested there, for the purpose of keeping them secure—and have directed these two companies to be raised at Cincinnati, that my instructions to you of the 10th inst., may be most certainly put into effect. I have only to repeat, that I wish the orders there given to be most strictly attended to, and not suffer a boat to pass unexamined and arrested, if suspicion in the least degree be attached thereto.

Blannerhassett and Comfort Tyler have made their escape, but Col. Phelps, of Virginia with a party of men are after them.

In haste, I remain dear sir,

Yours, &c. &c.

EDWARD TIFFIN.

Gen. J. S. Gano.

Chillicothe, Jan. 8th, 1807.

DEAR SIR:

I received by the mail yours of the 28th ultimo, and by Mr. Goforth yours of the 2nd. inst. I was in hopes ere this to have received further instructions from the Secretary of war, but herein I am disappointed; when I first ordered out a detachment of our militia on duty at Cincinnati; it was for the express purpose of endeavoring to arrest Comfort Tyler and Blannerhassett's boats, part of which was represented to be armed, and in a situation to make a resistance—as well as any others which might be descending the Ohio with hostile views. Part of this object was accomplished by our troops at Marietta who have taken fourteen boats and secured them,—the other part of the object failed, as Tyler had passed Cincinnati before you were in a situation to arrest them. Had I not received orders from the Secretary of war to raise men which would be paid by the United States, I should not have felt justified after these occurrences to have either subjected this State to the expense, or our citizens to the burthen of being drafted on further duty.

I believe I have got pretty correct information, that from the vigilance of the general government in providing to secure some boats that are said to be built up the Alleghany river with hostile views, and the stationing of troops at different points on the Ohio, as well as the precautions I have taken at Steubenville, at Marietta and elsewhere—that all who were engaged in the enterprize above us, gave it out—and that no armed boats will either get leave, or dare to descend the Ohio. Under this state of things, and not knowing that the Secretary of war will agree to pay any men but who are regularly enrolled under the orders I gave for enlisting two companies of volunteer militia, I have to repeat the directions I gave two weeks ago, for you not to draft any more of our citizens on duty.

I shall write to Major Riddle, who I understand you have appointed to the command of these troops, how to act, &c. You observe Capt. Perry has enlisted 30 men, and Capt. Carpenter 15. I hope they will get their companies complete—and these men who are raised under the authority, and in the pay of the United States, will be sufficient for any service that can be required of them; it is quite unnecessary to harrass men when we are certain no hostile boats are to come down, or to have more out than is necessary to bring to any who may be suspected for examination.

I shall therefore give the necessary orders to Major Riddle, and I beg you to accept my thanks for your kind and patriotic exertions during the late occurrences, and am with great respect and regard,

Yours &c.,

EDWARD TIFFIN.

GEN. GANO.

P. S. Gen. Buell enlisted his men for three months unless sooner discharged, and his quota complete in a day and a half.

A Deep Bite.

At this season of assessing the property and business taxes of Cincinnati, I am reminded of an incident in the operation of past years here. Jonathan Pancoast, an old citizen, although at that period not so well known among the active business men in Cincinnati, as he deserved to be, had been appointed assessor, and one of the first individuals he called on was an extensive wholesale dealer in drygoods, who bore as many names as he had feet to his height, *Gustavus Vasa Hannibal D————*. What illustrious names were here thrown away on a merchant, which should have graced a general's commission at least! Pancoast entered the warehouse with the air and appearance of a country storekeeper, and glancing around the piles of dry goods that reached from the ceiling to the floor and on the shelves, at length remarked, "A pretty smart chance of goods you seem to have here. I suppose a man could suit himself in your store with every thing he might want." "Yes," said the merchant, who mistook his visiter for a buyer from the country, "We can suit a customer here with all he needs—but walk up stairs if you want to see a fine stock of goods." So taking his visiter up one two & three pair of stairs, through rooms filled up with merchandize.—"There" said he, "is'nt there a pile for you to pick among." "I should think there was," replied Pancoast, "and I suppose there can't be less than eight or nine thousand dollars worth of goods." "Eight or nine!" exclaimed the merchant in a contemptuous tone, "There is sixty or seventy thousand dollars worth, at least!"—"Very well," said the assessor, taking a large roll of paper from one of his coat pockets, "that will do," and while the undeceived salesman stood petrified with astonishment, and chagrin at his own folly, made his entry, "*G. V. H. D. dry goods merchant, value of stock* 60,000 *dollars!*" This swell cost the unfortunate merchant all of 300 dollars extra taxes.

A Legend of Cincinnati.

Most of my readers are familiar with the narrative of the late Oliver M. Spencer, and have read in various shapes the account of his capture by Indians between Cincinnati and Columbia, while on his way home to the latter settlement in July, 1792. There is a legend connected with that event very current among the early settlers which refers to an incident connected with that narrative, to wit, the escape from those Indians of Mrs. Mary Coleman, by her floating down to Cincinnati, supported by her clothes which are stated to have buoyed her up all the way, from the scene of those events a distance of four miles.

A late visit to Montgomery in this county has given me an opportunity to enquire of *Mr. Jesse Coleman*, son of the lady named, and who at the period referred to, was a boy old enough to know something of the circumstances. He is now considerably over sixty, and his intellects are clear and strong. He gave me the following statement, which he has repeatedly heard made by his mother, by which it appears that the distance she thus floated was not more than a mile, and affords some interesting particulars I had never known.

The scenery of the Ohio between Columbia and Cincinnati was in those days truly romantic; scarcely a tree had been cut on either side, between the mouth of Crawfish and that of Deer creek, a distance of more than four miles. The sand bar now extending from its left bank, opposite to a sportsman's Hall, was then a small island, between which and the Kentucky shore was a narrow channel, with sufficient depth of water for the passage of boats. The upper and lower points of this island were bare, but its centre, embracing about four acres, was covered with small cotton wood, and surrounded by willows extending along its sides almost down to the water's edge. The right bank of the river crowned with its lofty hills, now gradually ascending, and now rising abruptly to their summits, and forming a vast amphitheatre, was from Columbia, extending down about two miles, very steep, and covered with trees quite down to the beach. From thence, nearly opposite the foot of the island, its ascent became more gradual, and for two miles farther down, bordering the tall trees with which it was covered was a thick growth of willows, through which in many places it was difficult to penetrate. Be-

low this, the beach was wide and stony, with only here and there a small tuft of willows, while the wood on the side and on the top of the bank was more open. Not far from this bank and near the line of the present turnpike, was a narrow road leading from Columbia to Cincinnati, just wide enough for the passage of a wagon, which, winding round the point of the hill above Deer creek, descended northwardly about four hundred feet, and crossing that creek, and in a southerly direction ascending gradually its western bank, led along the ground, now Symmes street, directly toward Fort Washington, and diverging at the intersection of Lawrence street to the right and left of the Fort, entered the town.

The river between Columbia and Cincinnati is thus minutely described, not only to give an idea of the former appearances to those who have come to reside here since, but also to explain the statement which Mr. C. give me.

Spencer, as he tells us in his own narrative, had got on board a canoe at the bank in front of Fort Washington, which was just ready to put off from the shore on the afternoon of the 7th July. It was a small craft, and hardly fit to accommodate the party, which thus consisted of a Mr. Jacob Light, a Mr. Clayton, Mrs. Coleman, young Spencer, a boy of 13, and one of the garrison soldiers, which last individual being much intoxicated, lurched from one side of the canoe to the other, and finally by the time they had got up a short distance above Deer Creek, tumbled out, nearly oversetting the whole party. He then reached the shore, the water not being very deep at the spot. Spencer did not know how to swim, and had become afraid to continue in the canoe, and was therefore as his own request put on shore, where they left the soldier, and the party in the boat and Spencer on shore, proceeded side by side. Light propelled the boat forward with a pole, while Clayton sat at the stern with a paddle which he sometimes used as an oar, and sometimes as a rudder, and Mrs Coleman a woman of fifty years, sat in the middle of the boat. One mile above Deer creek, a party of market people with a woman and child, on board a canoe, passed them on their way to Cincinnati. Light and the others had rounded the point of a small cove less than a mile below the foot of the island, and proceeded a few hundred yards along the close willows here bordering the beach, at about two rods distance from the water, when Clayton looking back, discovered the drunken man staggering along the shore, and remarked that he would be "*bait for Indians.*" Hardly had he passed the remark when two rifle shots from the rear of the willows struck Light and his comrade, causing the latter to fall towards the shore, and wounding the other by the ball glancing from the oar.— The two Indians who had fired instantly rushed from their concealment, to scalp the dead, and impede the escape of the living. Clayton was scalped, and Spencer in spite of all his efforts to get off, was made prisoner, but Light soon swam out of reach of his pursuers, and Mrs. Coleman who had also jumped out, preferring to be drowned to falling into the hands of Indians, and floated some distance off. The Indians would probably have reloaded and fired, but the report of their rifles brought persons to the opposite shore, and fearing to create further alarm, they decamped with their young prisoner in haste, saying "squaw must drown." Light had first made for the Kentucky shore, but finding himself drifting under all the exertions he could make in his crippled state, directed his way out on the Ohio side. Mrs. Coleman followed as well as she could by the use of her hands as paddles, and they both got to shore some distance below the scene of their events. Light had barely got out when he fell, so much exhausted that he could not speak, but after vomiting blood at length came to. Mrs. Coleman floated nearly a mile, and when she reached the shore, walked down the path to Cincinnati, crossed Deer creek at its mouth, holding on to the willows which overhung its banks—the water there in those days flowing in a narrow current that might almost be cleared by a spring from one bank to the other. She went direct to Captain Thorp at the artificer's yard, with whose lady she was acquainted, and from whom she obtained a change of clothes, and rested a day or two to overcome her fatigue.

Mrs. Coleman, deceased six years since at a very advanced age, at Versailles, Ripley county, Indiana.

Literary Notice.

I adverted a few weeks back to the *Pictorial History of the World*, by John Frost L. L. D., writing out a notice of the character of the first number. Nos. 2 and 3 are now both on my table.

Egypt, Ethiopia, Babylonia, Assyria, Asia Minor and Syria, form subjects of the three earlier numbers published. Nothing can be treated more judiciously than the early history of these regions, objects of the deepest interest, to the reader alike of classic and sacred literature. I have already spoken of the typography, engraving, and paper of this publication. They are perfect of the kind.

I observe also by a circular handed me on the subject, that the Ohio Dental College has been organized; and that lectures will be delivered in the Institution on the first Monday of November ensuing, the session to continue four months. It speaks well for the west that this is the only college of Dental Surgery in the United States, that of Baltimore excepted. We leave *transcendental science* to the Bostonians, intending ourselves to *transcend dental science* as it exists in any part of the republic.

A Chapter on Names.

These are in every measure of oddity and variety throughout the United States, and in many respects illustrate the character of our respective communities. A man in Baltimore bears the name of Origen L. Herring. He goes by no other name than *Original* Herring. This name in turn naturally reminds us of Preserved Fish, of New York City, who ought to have been called Pickled Fish, on the dictionary principle that to pickle is to preserve.

I have heard of a man who had vowed to name his first child Thomas Jefferson, of course he calculated on a boy, but his first born was a female. He kept his oath however, and the lady bearing this unfeminine appellation is still living, and called by her little nephew and niece, *Aunt Jiffy.*

Another individual, a Mr. New, had his first born baptised something, and the next nothing. These were of course—the first, *Something New,* and the second, *Nothing New.* An auctioneer in N. Orleans called his first daughters who were twins, *Ibid* and *Ditto.* His three boys who followed, were *A Lot, One More* and *The Last.* What name he could give his sixth, if he should have had one after this I, cannot conjecture.

A man by the name of Stickney up the Great Miami, determined on a succession of numbers as names for his children, and actually had them baptised, One Stickney, Two Stickney, and so on to the babe at the breast who was called Nine Stickney.

I knew a storekeeper in Pennsylvania who promised one of his customers, a married woman, half a dozen frock patterns for her infant baby if she would allow him to give the name, adding, as he was considered little better than an infidel, it should be a Scripture name. The banter was accepted, and the name handed in accordingly *Mahershallalhashbaz.* He had named it thus, expecting that the dresses would be given up rather than taken encumbered with such a name. But the mother kept the name and the clothes too.

The following is an actual list of names in one neighborhood in Georgia. Drusilla Narcissus Baker, William Green Marion Stibbs, Peggy Caroline Amanda Steele, Matilda Polly Araminta Jacobs, David Thomas Jasper Jackson, Rebecca Tabitha Jane Armor, Violet Delilah Clementine Bell, Abraham Orlando Symmachus Jones, Miranda Delia Sally Williams. Enough for one dose.

Modern Traveling.

Dr. Brisbane now travelling eastward, gives the following table of travelling expenses from Cincinnati.

Passage to Wheeling, steamboat,	$5
Wheeling to Philadelphia,	13
Philadelphia to New York,	4
New York to Boston,	3 50
Seven meals,	3 50
Porter's fees,	1 00
	30 00

Tour five days eighteen hours.

Let our rail road once be completed via. Sandusky and Buffalo to Boston, and we ean be taken on to the last named place in 50 hours and at an expense not exceeding ten dollars. I remember when the eastern practicable route hence to Philadelphia alone cost the traveller twelve days and an outlay of fifty dollars.

Ingenuity of Germans.

There is in many minds a prejudice against the German nation, on account of the stupidity unjustly laid to its charge. On examining the subject I find the following inventions have ori. ginated in Germany.

A. D.
350 Saw Mills
898 Sun Dial
996 Fulling Mills
1070 Tillage of hops
1100 Wind Mills
Oil Painting
1270 *Spectacles*
1300 Paper of linen rags
1312 Organs
1318 Gun powder
Cannons
1350 Wire making
1330 Hats
1379 Pins
1389 Grist mills
1423 Wood engravings
1436 Printing
1439 Printing press
1440 Copperplate engraving
1450 Printing ink
1452 Cast types
1487 Chiming of bells
1500 Watches
Letter posts or mails
Etching
1500 Bolting apparatus
1527 Gun locks
1535 Spinning wheels
1546 Almanacs
Stoves
Sealing wax
1590 Telescopes
1610 Wooden bellows
1620 Microscopes
1638 Thermometers
1643 Mezzotint engraving
1650 Air pumps
1652 Electrical machines
1656 Pendulum clocks
1690 Clarionet
1700 White china ware

1707 Prussian blue
1709 Stereotyping
1715 Mercurial thermometer
1717 Piano Fortes
1738 Solar microscope
1753 The gamut
1796 Lithography.

Besides these are several German inventions of which I cannot ascertain the date—such as door locks and latches, the modern screw auger, and gimlet, the cradle for harvesting, &c. &c.

Surely a nation which has made such contributions to the interests of literature and the arts must occupy a high rank in intellect and ingenuity.

Western Heroines.

CINCINNATI, May 12th, 1845.

Mr. CIST:

As opportunity now offers I will proceed to redeem my promise by giving you another of "Old Tim Watkins'" tales. On the Illinois river. near two hundred miles from its junction with the Mississippi, there lived at the time I write of an old pioneer, known in those days as "Old Parker the squatter." His family consisted of a wife and three children, the oldest a boy of nineteen, a girl of seventeen, and the youngest a boy of fourteen. At the time of which we write, Parker and his oldest boy had gone in company with three Indians on a hunt, expecting to be absent some five or six days.— The third day after the departure, one of the Indians returned to Parker's house, came in and sat himself down by the fire, lit his pipe and commenced smoking in silence. Mrs. Parker thought nothing of this, as it was no uncommon thing for one or sometimes more of a party of Indians to return abruptly from a hunt, at some sign they might consider ominous of bad luck, and in such instances were not very communicative. But at last the Indian broke silence with "ugh, old Parker die." This exclamation immediately drew Mrs. Parker's tatention, who directly enquired of the Indian, what's the matter with Parker? The Indian responded Parker sick, tree fell on him, you go he die. Mrs. Parker then asked the Indian if Parker sent for her, and where he was? The replies of the Indian somewhat aroused her suspicions. She however came to the conclusion to send her son with the Indian to see what was the matter. The boy and Indian started. That night passed, and the next day too, and neither the boy or Indian returned. This confirmed Mrs. Parker in her opinion that there was foul play on the part of the Indians. So she and her daughter went to work and barricaded the door and windows in the best way they could. The youngest boy's rifle was the only one left, he not having taken it with him when he went to see after his father. The old lady took the rifle, the daughter the axe, and thus armed they determined to watch through the night and defend themselves if necessary. They had not long to wait after night fall, for shortly after that some one commenced knocking at the door, crying out mother! mother! but Mrs. Parker thought the voice was not exactly like that of her son—in order to ascertain the fact, she said "Jake where are the Indians?" The reply which was "um gone," satisfied her on that point. She then said as if speaking to her son, put your ear to the latch-hole of the door I want to tell you something before I open the door. The head was placed at the latch-hole, and the old lady fired her rifle through the same spot and killed an Indian. She stepped back from the door instantly, and it was well she did so, for quicker than I have penned the last two words two rifle bullets came crashing through the door. The old lady then said to her daughter, thank God there is but two, I must have killed the one at the door—they must be the three who went on the hunt with your father. If we can only kill or cripple another one of them, we will be safe; now we must both be still after they fire again, and they will then break the door down, and I may be able to shoot another one; but if I miss them when getting in you must use the axe.— The daughter equally courageous with her mother assured her she would, Soon after this conversation two more rifle bullets came crashing through the window. A death-like stillness ensued for about five minutes, when two more balls in quick succession were fired through the door, then followed a tremendous punching with a log, the door gave way, and with a fiendish yell an Indian was about to spring in when the unerring rifle fired by the gallant old lady stretched his lifeless body across the threshold of the door. The remaining, or more properly surviving Indian fired at random and ron doing no injury. "Now" said the old heroine to her undaunted daughter "we must leave." Accordingly with the rifle and the axe, they went to the iver, took the canoe, and without a mouthful of provision except one wild duck and two blackbirds which the mother shot, and which were eaten raw, did these two courageous hearts in six days arrive among the old French settlers at St. Louis. A party of about a dozen men crossed over into Illinois—and after an unsuccessful search returned without finding either Parker or his boys. They were never found. There are yet some of the old settlers in the neighborhood of Peoria who still point out the spot where "old Parker the squatter" lived.

Respectfully,

G. REDDING.

Relics of the Past.

FORT WASHINGTON, May 4th, 1792.

SIR:

A disappointment on the part of the Contractor, prevents my despatching the heavy escort so soon as my last letter mentioned, and the party which now goes on, is to endeavor to join Fort St. Clair under cover of night. They are to halt with you the day they may arrive, and you are to cross thence over the river, on the evening of that day after sun-set, taking the necessary precaution to prevent the enemy from discovering their numbers. You will give the Corporal orders to reach St. Clair, in the course of the night on which you despatch him. His safety and the safety of the little convoy, depend on the strict observance of this order. Captain Peters, with the efficient escort, waits the arrival of a drove of bullocks, which have been injudiciously halted at Craig's, and will not reach this place until the 8th inst,—by him you will receive a volume, from

Yours sincerely,

JAS. WILKINSON,
Lieut. Col. Com'dt.

JNO. ARMSTRONG, ESQ. Capt. Com'dt.

P. S. I expect to break an ensign here tomorrow, he is under trial.

FT. HAMILTON, May 7, 1792.

LT. COL. JAMES WILKINSON,

Dr. Sir—on the evening of the 5th inst. your letter was handed me by the Corporal conducting the escort. As Indians had shown themselves on the the opposite shore for three succeeding days, I detained the escort until the evening of the 6th, and in the interim detached Lt. Gaines with 20 men, five miles on the road leading to St. Clair with directions to re-cross Joseph's creek, and to form in ambuscade, until the small party pass him—which promises an ample reward; if there was nothing improper in the request, I would solicit their continuance here until the opening of the campaign.

Yours,

JNO. ARMSTRONG,
Capt. 1st Regt. U. S. A.

MARRIAGES.

On Friday 11th ult., Miss MARY E. SHERWOOD, daughter of Mrs. Ann S. and step-daughter of S. W. Davis, to Mr. WILLIAM L. THOMAS.

At Baltimore on the 29th ult. by the Rev. Mr. Trapnell, Mr. LEWIS A. HOWSER, to MARY ANN BURDICK, of Wheeling.

On Sunday evening, 4th inst. by the Rev. Mr. Lynd, Mr. JACOB HOFFNER to Miss FRANCIS A. SMITH—all of this city.

On Tuesday, 6th inst. Mr. GEORGE MELLUS, of N. Orleans, La., to Miss SUSANNAH BATES, of this city.

DEATHS.

On Thursday, 8th inst. Mrs. ELIZABETH ANN SMITH

Monday, 12th inst. Hon. WILLIAM MILLER, aged 83.

Journal of Rev. David Jones.

COMMUNICATED BY HORATIO G. JONES JR., LEVERINGTON, PA.,

We encamped on the east side of this [the Scioto] river, at a place called Red Bank, and indeed this was the first place that we could encamp with safety, for in floods the waters of the Ohio and Scioto spread over the low land at the mouth of the latter. For about one mile or more, the two rivers were near the same course, and are not far apart. The mouth of this river, according to Mr. Hutchins, is in lat. 28 deg. 22, and he calculated it only 366 miles, as the river runs from Fort Pitt, but it is accounted 400 by the traders, and I am persuaded it will be found good measure. I am informed this river has its source towards Lake Erie, and that there is but a very small land passage between this river and the streams that empty into that lake. The Scioto is very crooked but not rapid, so that men with canoes can stem the current to the head. Tuesday June 5th, I went out and killed some turkeys, and the men rowed up the canoe 6 or 7 miles and were obliged to encamp, because of the depth of the water. Wednesday 6th, moved but slowly, and spent some time in fitting poles of pawpawwood, which is very plenty here and very light, so that it is used chiefly for canoe poles; we encamped on the west side of the river. It rained very hard, so that our lodging was not the best. Thursday 7th. As the canoe was polled up the stream, I chose for the advantage of killing game, to walk on land; but mistaking the way that the river turned, I lost myself on the finest and largest walnut bottom that my eyes ever beheld. The sun did not shine, and after some time I perceived that I was lost, and what added to my surprise on the occasion, was that it drew near night. After ruminating on my case with some degree of disquietude, and reflecting on the course that I came, I thought I knew which way the west was, and therefore ran over many bad places, and at last saw the top of a very high hill, which I apprehended would afford me a prospect of the river. To this I made with all speed, and before I ascended it far, I saw the river; this was pleasing, but I knew not whether the canoe was above or below me. However I first went up the river, and both whistled and halloed, but finding no answer, I turned down again and went many miles back until I was sure they were above me. Thereupon I retraced my steps, and was marching up the stream, expecting nothing else than to be left in the wilderness, with but little ammuniiton. While many thoughts arose in my mind, I heard them fire for me at their camp. I supposed they were three miles above me, and began to run firing as I went, but as the wind blew towards me, they never heard the report of

my gun, though I heard theirs every shot. I ran as fast as I could in the night, they continuing to fire. At last I arrived safe and was received with great joy by all; for they were more distressed about me, than I was myself. This day we passed a large creek on the west side of the Scioto, and several small ones on the east side.

Friday 8th, passed some miles up the river and encamped on the west side. Saturday 9th, we overtook Mr. William Butler and his canoes. He had met with an accident and got some of his goods wet, which retarded his progress, so that we came up to him, though he had set out several days before us. We went in company with him past a place where some very unruly Indians were, who had been violent to Mr. B. though he sustained no great damage. Our crew knew the disposition of Indians better than I; therefore as their greatest safety, they made themselves nearly half drunk, and made a great bustle, so that the Indians were afraid to molest us, as we were afterwards informed; for Indians are extremely afraid of any one when intoxicated, because such are looked upon as mad, and among themselves, in such a condition, they are always for killing each other. Encamped this night near the crossings of the river and rested safely. Sunday 10th, we moved up to a place known by the name of Kuskuskis—sometimes it is called Kuskuskis Cabins. This is the common place to disload part of the canoes, and carry the goods from here to some of the towns on pack-horses; but they can come much nearer, though it is with considerable labor. as the bend of the river makes the distance much farther. Here some Indians encamped near us, who were going to Pickaweke, an Indian town on Deer creek. Monday 11, Mr. Butler and Mr. Nailor concluded to take part of their load by land, their horses being brought by hands employed for that purpose. I was very desirous to leave the canoe, and therefore requested Mr. Butler and Mr. Kelly to intercede for me to the Indian who was going to Pickaweke, that he would hire me a horse to ride to the town. The gentlemen were very kind, and by many good words and good treatment I got a horse; so we set out about 10 o'clock and came that night to Paint Creek, which is considered about 14 miles from Kuskuskis, and I think the last part of the way was due north. The Indian name of this creek is *Alamoncetheepeera*, and is so called from some kind of paint that is found there. This creek comes from the west and empties into the Scioto, near where we encamped. The water is exceedingly clear and beautiful, demonstrating that it has its rise from excellent springs. On branches of this creek, are situated some chief towns of the Shawanese, of which I shal speak hereafter. Tuesday 12th. After taking breakfast with Messrs. Butler and Nailor, I set out for Pickaweke, in company with my Indian friend (whose name was Cuttleway,) his wife and some other Indians. It may well be supposed that my journey was lonesome, for I knew not one word of the Shawanese language, and my fellow traveller knew not one word of English; so that we could converse little more than the horses on which which we rode. The day was cold and we rode fast, so that about 2 o'clock, we came to the town. When we came within one mile of it, my friend displaced part of his load, and leaving the women behind, he made signs for me to ride on with him. I apprehend the reason of his conduct, was lest he might be molested by drunken Indians, for when intoxicated their abuses to white people are unlimited. As I drew near the town many thoughts arose in my mind as to what I should do, for I knew not whether there was one white man in the place, but my anxiety was soon removed by seeing Joseph Nicholas, with whom I was acquainted at Fort Pitt. He received me very kindly, and entertained me with such refreshments as the situation afforded. While we were refreshing ourselves, Mr. John Irwine came in and invited me to his habitation. Mr. Irwine resides chiefly in a small town, called by the English Blue Jacket's Town—an Indian of that name residing there; but before I speak of it I shall describe Pickaweke. This town is situated south of a brook that empties into Deer Creek. It is named from a nation of Indians called Picks, some of them being the first settlers, and it signifies the place of the Picks. Now, its population is about one hundred souls, being a mixture of Shawanese and other tribes, so that it is called a Shawanese town. It is a remarkable town for robbers and villains, and yet it pretends to have its chief men, who are indeed the veriest scoundrels, being guilty of theft and robbery. Leaving this town I went home with Mr. Irwine, whose civilities to me during all our acquaintance. were very marked. Blue Jacket's Town is on Deer Creek, about 3 miles west and by north, from Pickaweke. It is situated south-west of a large plain and east of the creek, which is a clear and beautiful stream, appearing useful for mills, and beautiful for the inhabitants. The buildings are of logs, and their number is about 12. It is a quiet and peaceable place. In this town *Kishshinottisthee* lives, who is called a king, and is one of the head men of this nation. In English his name signified Hardman. Wednesday 13th. Mr. Irwine invited the king and some of his friends to take breakfast with me. He had informed the king, that I was no trader but was a good man, whose employment among white people was to speak of heavenly matters, and came with that view to see my brothers—the Indians. This nation never saw a minister, except a chance one at some Fort; so that they have no prepossessions, but such as are natural. When the king came, he met me with all appearance of friendship, and respectfully gave me the right hand of fellowship, with some kind of obeisance, and ordered the others to do the same. When breakfast, which consisted of fat buffalo meat, beaver tails and chocolate, was ready, I acknowledged the goodness of God in a solemn manner, and desired Mr. J. to let the king know the meaning of my proceedings; he did so, and told me that the king well approved of it. The king desired to know my business among them, seeing that I did not trade. I informed him that I could not perfectly tell him at present, because I could not speak his language, and had not yet got an interpreter who could rightly speak for me, but expected to get one soon, when he should fully know my errand. At present I told him only a little respecting divine things, as Mr. J. could not interpret very well, except on common affairs, not having traded long, in this nation. *Kishshinottisthee* is indeed a man of good sense, and ever remained my hearty friend. If he could have had his will, I would have instructed them in the knowledge of God; he was however but one, and the Indians at Chillicothe were unanimously against him. While I remained here I went to see the king in his own dwelling, he always received me kindly, and treated me with hickory nuts (of which their food consists in part,) being much superior to any of the kind in the east. He is neither distinguished in apparel or dwelling, his house being one of the least in town, being about 14 feet by 12. While here I was very unwell, one day—and the queen was so kind as to bring me, what she thought light food for my stomach. The present consisted of dried pumpkins boiled, and bear's grease, of which I ate a little, rather out of politeness than from any appetite. About this time it snowed 6 inches deep, and seemed as cold as winter commonly is at Philadelphia, though I am of the opinion that it is nearly 2 degs. south. Before I moved from this town, Capt. McKee arrived from Fort Pitt, in company with Major Smallman. Mr. McKee is agent for this department of Indians. I acquainted him with my design and he appeared very well pleased and promised to do any thing in his power, that might be of service to make my journey prosperous.— Of him I enquired about an interpreter, for the Indians told me that my old one—David Owens, was away below the Falls, towards the Wabash river. Mr. McKee recommended one whose name was Cœsar, who is a foreigner, and understands something about religion, and therefore would be the best interpreter on that subject. We parted in expectation of seeing each other at Chillicothe. I was unwilling to leave this town, before I had the assistance of an interpreter, but being disappointed I concluded to remove to the chief town. Accordingly on Friday 22d, Mr. Irwine and I came to Chillicothe, far in this town Mr. I. kept an assortment of goods, and for that purpose had rented a house from an Indian whose name was *Wappeemonee-to*. We went to see Mr. Moses Henry a gunsmith and trader from Lancaster. This gentleman has lived for some years in this town, and is lawfully married to a white woman. who was taken captive so young, that she speaks the language as well as an Indian. She is a daughter of Major Collins, who formerly lived on the south branch of the Potomac, but latterly on the Ohio, near the little Kanawha. Mr. Henry lives very comfortably, and was as kind to me as a man could be. Soon after I came to this town I dieted altogether with Mr. H. but slept on my blankets at Mr. Irwine's. Chillicothe is the chief town of the Shawanese nation, and is situated north of a large plain adjacent to a branch of Paint creek. This plain is their corn-field which supplies all the town. Their buildings are in no regular form, as every man erects his house just as fancy leads him. North of this town are the remains of an old fortification, the area of which may be 15 acres. It lies nearly four square and appears to have had gates at each corner, and likewise in the middle. From the west middle gate there went an entrenchment including about 10 acres, which seemed designed to defend the Fort on all quarters. Mr. Irwine told me that there is one exactly resembling this on the river Scioto, but the banks of that are much higher, for if men ride on horse-back with the bank between them, they cannot see each other. 'Tis evident to all travellers that this country has formerly been inhabited by a people, who had the use of tools, for such entrenchments could not otherwise have been made; but of this part of antiquity, it is likely, we shall ever remain ignorant. Saturday 23, in company with Mr. I. went to see Capt. McKee, who lives about 3 miles west and by north, from Chillicothe in a small town called *Wockachalli*, which signifies Crooked Nose's place. Here the Indian relatives of the Captain lives. The town seems quite new, and not much ground is cleared; it is situated east of a creek which must be a branch of Paint creek. The Indians who live here have a great number of the best horses in the nation, and cattle also, so that they live chiefly by stock. Capt. McKee was very courteous and still promised well.

Relics of the Past.

I have been led to the publication of the following letters from the fact that they convey a lively idea of the political feeling produced by the presidential election of 1801, and which has never been surpassed in intensity since. Gen. Gano's letter affords some interesting views on lawyers and marriage, which are just as true now as they were forty years ago. It seems also that our predecessors have been as much annoyed by incendiaries as ourselves.

CINCINNATI, April 3d, 1803.

DEAR SIR:

Yours of February last came to hand this week, for which please to accept my thanks—it has not been for the want of esteem that you have not had a line before this from me, but the great revolution and change in our government, and politics has left every thing respecting offices &c. &c., at an uncertain and precarious issue, and what effect it will have on the minds of the people at present I cannot inform you, and have delayed writing on that account; but as our legislature is now in session, and have a number of important appointments to make, it will soon be known, when the new government comes into full operation, whether the change will be of advantage or not. I am in hopes it will encourage population and add to the prosperity and happiness of the people of our new State. The base conduct of the Spaniards on the Mississippi has injured the western country very much in their commerce this season, though there has been considerable shipments of flour and pork from this place, notwithstanding the uncertainty of the market. I am pleased with your having undertook the study of the law, and have no doubt but you will find it of great service to you whether you practice it or not. We may look round and see the most popular men in the State, and in society, have been of that profession; that alone ought to be an inducement for you to persevere. Many other motives can be mentioned; we find them generally rich after a few years application to business—they have advantage in trade, and making contracts &c. I cannot till I see the Judiciary Law inform you, how the practice of law will be affected by the change of government; I will then write you my opinion more particularly on that subject, from the P. S. &c.

In your letter I find you are still anticipating something in the hymenial order. It is certainly a very desirable object in this life, but it sometimes strews our path with thorns, thistles, briars, rocks, mountains, valleys, &c., and make our passage more difficult than the road from Providence to Hillsdale. Do not understand me as wishing to discourage you, for as many or more happy effects may be produced by it, and it may make the passage through life as serene as a May morning in a garden of flowers, and delightful plants where all nature appears designed to make us happy, and you press on with the current of bliss in the enjoyment of the greatest felicity that can be in the possession of mortals—my pen and tongue cannot describe it justly. *So much for that.* We have been greatly distressed in my family, and neighborhood, lately by fire—we have had three fires in quick succession, and the farthest not 100 yards from my dwelling; and it appears as if it was nothing but the kind interposition of providence in directing the wind, that saved my buildings. We are obliged to keep a night-watch, as the incendiary cannot be discovered, though we do not feel safe at night. There is a man imprisoned on suspicion; but I cannot allow myself to think he is so base as to be guilty.

We have no news interesting except what I have related, I therefore close, as I think you must be tired by this time with reading this scrawl. John and the rest of the family desires love and compliments to my brother and family. And believe me to be with much esteem,

Your friend and humble servant.
JOHN S. GANO.
MR. JOHN HOLROYD, Providence.

PROVIDENCE, June 9th., 1803.

Respected Sir:

Yours of April 3rd came duly to hand, and should have been answered before, but that I was induced to wait till this opportunity; knowing this to be safer than trusting to the *giddy flights of an infatuated satelite of J——n.* The bearer of this is a cousin of mine, who intends, if he is suited with the country, to settle in Cincinnati. His companion is a young man who is master of the ropemaking business, and intends to set up that business in your country if he finds it will suit. My cousin lost his parents while young, since which time he has lived with my father, and seems as near to me as any of my brothers. You will find both them upright, honest and industrious men. If they should succeed in their undertaking, I think they will be very useful to your part of the country. A recommendation from me is unnecessary, as I make no doubt your brother will do them justice, and all that lies in his power to make them agreeable to you. However any attention you will please to bestow on them, will be gratefully acknowledged by me. I was much pleased in perusing your favor to find sentiments perfectly agreeing with mine. I believe, if the subject of matrimony was more seriously considered, before entered into thousands, would have been free from the difficulties in which

they are now involved. I am happy in saying, however anxious I may be to be married, yet to plunge myself and her I love into poverty and wretchedness, would be the height of folly and extravagance. I believe I have chosen a profession, which, by diligence, honesty and punctuality on my part, will not fail of enabling me to obtain a livelihood. I feel a great degree of pleasure in striking upon the profession I have chosen, and much more since you have favored me with your sentiments upon that subject.— But the profession of the law, is not now very profitable in this place, (except to a few characters.) I wish very much to settle in your country, and I hope my wishes will be gratified, after I have finished my studies, which will be in a year from next September.

Politics are about the same as when you was here, but I think appearances are more in favor of the federal party. I think the time is not far distant, when democrats shall hide their heads in shame and blush at their folly and wickedness. When federalism shall shine resplendent as the sun, and this country shall once more become as happy and respected as when under the wise and politic reign of the sage and hero of *Mount Vernon.* Business is very dull, every one complaining there is nothing due— the want of money is the cry. *The wise policy of our present rulers* cannot save us from the cruel hand of pinching poverty; and I fear, will not protect us from the merciless and bloodthirsty Spaniards: Secure with *Sally,* in the cabin at Monticello, the *Hero of Carter's Mountain* fears no storm while his retreat can be effected. We have had the honor of a visit from the President's *giddy man.* His arrival in town was announced in a paper, stiled the Phœnix, under the guidance of a host of democratic desperadoes. Enclosed is a piece of our newspaper, containing proposals for the life of the detestable Arthur Fenner, Governor of this State. I think it will afford you much amusement.— You will there see some of his numerous crimes portrayed in colors no way exaggerated. I hope it will not be long before I shall receive a line from you. My respects to John and your family, though a stranger to them.

I am with sentiments of esteem,
Your friend and humble servant,
JOHN HOLROYD.
Col. JOHN S. GANO.

Jones' Patent Changeable Locks.

As the late fire at Pittsburgh has demonstrated that while there are many FIRE SAFES absolutely worthless and *unsafe*, so daily experience serves to show that there are many locks termed *thief detectors* which not only fail to *detect* thieves but to defy picklocks.

Mr. H. C. Jones of Newark, New Jersey, is the Patentee as well as manufacturer of this truly ingenious piece of mechanism, which in addition to the usual safeguards to bank-vault door locks, possesses peculiar protective features of its own. These will be understood in some measure by the description of it which follows, and a personal inspection of the article which is left for sale at Isaac Young's, No. 100 Main street, will serve to explain and illustrate this statement. The lock is of great strength, exact construction, and convenient size, and the bolt which is secured inside of it by a proper staple, when it is shut is of equal thickness inside and outside of the lock in this respect defying the power of violence. It has six tumblers and duplicate keys, with twelve moveable bitts made of cast steel, as are also the tumblers.

Each tumbler has a distinct and separate groove in which to rise and fall, whereby two distinct setts of bitts—six at a time, may be made to operate on either of the grooves. The bitts of one sett being numbered from 1 to 6, and those of the other from 10 to 60. Each tumbler is so numbered as to correspond with its appropriate bitt, so that the bitts to the key may be changed in a minute, in the event of losing one of the keys, so as to prevent the lock being opened with the missing key. It must be obvious by this statement, that when the owner has received his lock, he is protected from the power of any one, even the maker, to open it. And it is the only lock in the world, which even the man that made it cannot pick. But this lock has a farther security. If the maker or any other person becoming possessed of a duplicate key, were to attempt unlocking it with a different bitt from that which aided in locking it, the key would derange the tumbler, throwing it into a cog or tooth so as to prevent even the proper key from opening it until its reacting motion should accomplish it, and put the owner on his guard by affording him evidence that the lock had been tampered with. The tumblers are protected from friction by washers, so that no amount of use can ever put them out of fit to the proper keys. Each tumbler has its appropriate recurved elliptical spring, so ingeniously contrived as to distribute the pressure equally along its length, and which is made of wrought brass rolled out under the pressure of rollers an half ton weight each, which completely closes the pores of the metal and gives it the elasticity and durability of steel without subjecting it to the influence of dampness so prejudicial to this last substance.

The tumblers of the lock, after it is locked, fall down to a level, which renders it impossible to take an impression for making a false key.—

The bolt of the lock is secured independently of the main tumbler by a cog or tooth held by a cam or lever, to be relieved only by a revolving eccentric, passed around by the proper key with a pin or projection at the bottom of the key, requiring it to carry the cog to an elevation so exact that a thickness of tissue paper would intercept its passage. This cog is susceptible of being raised higher than its proper key will carry it, which being done, the bolt will not pass back, although each and every tumbler be raised to its proper elevation to pass it through its groove. This eccentric with its peculiar arrangements is entirely a new feature in this lock rendering it different in these respects from all others, foreign or home made. If any instrument in the shape of a key is introduced into the key-hole, it cannot be turned round to act on the bolt without covering the key-hole below, which prevents the insertion of any other instrument to aid in picking the lock. An additional guard against picking it, is found in the arrangement, that when the tumblers fall to the level in front of the stud or stump of the lock, the stump is secured at each end, so as to prevent the forcing of the bolt by any instrument inserted at the key-hole. Nor can it be picked by the aid of pressure as in ordinary cases, there being teeth on the edge of the tumbler corresponding to teeth in the face of the stump which shut in each other. The tumblers and bitts are arranged on the principle of combination and permutation, making the chance of the picklock to open it after he has got hold of the lost key as one possibility out of 134,217,728 trials.— These, a life time, if devoted to the employment, would not furnish leisure to effect. The combination and permutation powers are 22 in number, nearly that of the English alphabet, and some idea of the almost infinite variety attainable here, may be formed by reminding my readers of the fact, that millions upon millions of pages have been written and printed, no two of which are alike.

This lock took the first premium at the fair of the American Institute held last fall, being exposed on the table there for three weeks, with a placard, offering 500 dollars to any person who should open it with its own key, left there for the purpose.

This safety lock has been already introduced into many of the principal stores, banks and broker's offices at the east, and into a few of the banks of our own State.

We can all comprehend the importance of firstrate engraving as a means of protecting the banks, and through them the community from counterfeits. Not less important is a safety lock, which is protecting alike for the benefit of the bank and the bill holder, the funds required for the redemption of the notes which constitute our currency.

This lock commends itself to public favor as an American invention, being designed to supercede CHUBB's thief detector, a foreign article heretofore relied on by the banks. What protection these afford may be judged by the fact of which *I* saw the certificate, by the Town Council, Newark, N. J., that Mr. Jones set one of his boys to pick it, which he accomplished successfully *in eight minutes.* But Chubb's day of security is past. *I* observe even Mrs. Caudle, in her last lecture speaks in terms of unbounded contempt of it, as having failed to afford the protection it promises.

One convenience may arise to a certain species of banks from the use of this particular lock, of great value. The lock being safe alike from force or fraud, and not susceptible of being picked, all they need when they wish to suspend specie payments, is to discover *that they have lost the key of the vault.*

The Metroscope.

A very ingenious instrument, called a METROSCOPE, which has been lately invented for the purpose of taking the measure of the human head so as to furnish an exact fit of hats in every individual case, has just made its appearance here. Most persons appear to think that variations in men's heads consist only in the difference of size. Those who are of that opinion will be undeceived by calling at Dodd's hat store on Main below Fourth street, where they may see more than an hundred patterns, taken from the heads of citizens well known here, of every conceivable variety in form, and no two alike. They will find as great diversity in size, shape and features to the human head as exists in the human face. Indeed the outlines are so strange, and at the same time so characteristic, that *I* fully expect *craniometrology,* or the philosophy of head-measurement will soon rank with Mesmerism, Phrenology, Etherology and other occult sciences of the age. Be this as it may, it is wonderful what a degree of luxury and comfort belongs to hats made on these models. These are attained by following the sinuosities and indentations around the head, and conforming the hat in its fit accordingly. And a customer by once getting his measure taken, has his pattern card placed on file, and can at any future time, by ordering a hat, be certain of as perfect a fit as if he were present. *I* apprehend most of the complaints made of headache by exposure to the sun will be obviated by the use of this kind of hats, which by dividing the pressure in perfect equality over the entire head, renders the weight on the parts usually affected comparatively nothing. *If any* one is inclined to suppose too much consequence attached to this, I would seriously ask, what is it that enables us to bear tons in weight of atmospheric pressure upon our persons, but the circumstance that it is equally distributed over the whole body exposed to its influence?

Sheriff's Sales of Property.

Persons at a distance who read or hear statements of the rise of value to property in Cincinnati, are disposed in many instances to regard them as based on fictitious estimates. *I* have therefore annexed a memorandum of prices obtained at Sheriff's sale, on Monday the 19th, on a certain property at the north-east corner of Vine and 4th streets, with the appraised value, and prices which brought.

Nos.	Appraisement.	Actual Sale.
1	4,800	6,000
2	5,200	5,550
3	5,000	5,225
4	4.500	4,250
5	13,000	11,200
6	4,230	4,150
7	4,230	4,250
8	9,400	7,600

It is a singular fact that the reason why the last lot fell so far short of the appraisement was *that it had two brick houses on it.* The naked lots averaged almost 200 dollars per front foot. Those with the houses on them brought the same price. This indicates the constantly improving value of open lots as compared with property ready for renting.

The history of this property is curious. Forty-five years since it was part of a cornfield of four acres, which might then have been bought at one hundred dollars per acre. *In* 1802, Ethan Stone bought a portion of that field or block 250 feet on Vine by 200 feet on Fourth, including the property referred to for 220 dollars, little more than the price per foot at the late sale. Estimating his whole purchase at the value set on it by actual sale at the Court house, this property has advanced in value in forty-three years from 220 dollars to 62,250 dollars. And this it must be recollected, does not include any value conferred on it by improvements.

The Last Tree.

Those who remember the original line of the river bank between Main street and Broadway as far back as the commencement of the present century, need hardly be reminded of an ancient black-walnut tree which survived the destruction by the axe, or by natural causes, of its cotemporaries which were found here in great numbers from Western Row to Broadway, and from the brow of the river bank to the swamp which stretched from Columbia street to the foot of the hill, and was in fact the only aborigine of the kind in the first plat of Cincinnati.

This tree stood where at a point or angle which would intersect lines drawn from Huddart's tin ware shop on Main street and south from the Cincinnati Insurance Company office. It was nearly four feet in diameter. The top of the main trunk was dead, and had been perforated by woodpeckers into holes in which the martens had built their nests. In June 1807, this tre was lightning struck, and the top being dry as well as dead it took fire and burned with great rapidity, which rendered it necessary to cut the tree down to prevent further mischief or injury to a salt shed 50 feet by 16 which occupied ground to its north. At the corner of the landing, and what was then a corner of Main and Front streets, stood a two story brick building in which Henry Weaver, one of the early merchants of Cincinnati carried on business, the upper part unfinished at first, and afterwards occupied for a council chamber by those conscript fathers of the city who first sat in that capacity to legislate for public interests. This was a building of about 25 feet square. Immediately east of it was a frame tenement 1½ story high, occupied as a provision store. The whole space on Front street to perhaps 150 feet east of the line of Main street, and south as far as along the line of the salt shed was enclosed in a worm fence as late as 1806 and perhaps later. During this period the title to the public landing was in litigation between Joel Williams and the city of Cincinnati, and this occupation of the premises was kept up in behalf of Williams. After a protracted controversy the title was adjudged to be in the city, and the Sheriff, Goforth, put the municipal authorities in formal possession of it by offering them a spade full of earth, thus delivering a part for the whole.

The frame buildings refered to, were built of plank taken from the first bridge built over the mouth of Mill creek, when that bridge gave way, under circumstances which shall form hereafter the basis of another article of pioneer history.

Short Articles.

Brevity, condensation, pith and marrow, nuts without shell, are in demand now-a-days. Most readers are discouraged at the bare sight of a long article. Reporters dread long speeches, children long remarks, and people long sermons.

It would seem at first that ever body is fully impressed with the solemn truth, "The time is short:" "whatsoever is to be done must be done quickly." And whether it be that God may be the more glorified or themselves the better gratified, so it is that every body is in a hurry—every thing must be done with dispatch—journeys of hundreds of miles must be compressed by steam into the space of a few hours—tidings communicated from city to city by something "swifter than a post." And the minds and hearts of men must be impressed, if at all, by Daguerreotype process.

Thereforefore let the press be admonished.— Editors take heed—writers, condense and be brief, or you will spend your breath for nought. Are you too la·y or too hurried to allow you to condense' then do not write at all—you will exclude many better writers from the columns ot the journal which you occupy. I do not wish the room, but others may.

Statesmen, be not so lavish of your words.— Long speeches are tedious. They indicate vanity on your part, and cause vexation of spirit to others. You may speak, speak well, speak to the point, but then stop! Superintendents and teachers in Sabbath schools and school committees, when you address children be brief. It will cost you much effort to address children profitably—make your preparation therefore beforehand; if you do not, you had better say nothing. For you will weary young hearts that are longing for release, and do them more hurt than good.

Preachers, make your sermons short. Firstly, secondly, sixteenthly, lastly, finally, in conclusion, and once more, will tire your hearers all out. Your congregations are not composed of Jobs. They will not endure it—they will not be edified by your preaching, because they will slumber before you come to the point. Paul himself could not keep all his hearers awake during a long sermon. Therefore be brief.— Take time to condense. Study the Proverbs. See the conclusion of the wise Preacher. How brief, how comprehensive, like a nail in a sure place. Three reasons for brevity and condensation.

Short articles if printed will be read. It will not take much time or cost much labor to gratify curiosity by reading them, and they are read. But multitudes have neither time nor inclination for reading long articles. Many therefore read the review of a work and content themselves without reading the work—for the review is much the shortest, or should be.

Let the preacher announce from the desk that he shall consider his subject under sixteen grand divisions, apply it in seven important points, and close with some pertinent remarks, natural reflections, and a brief exhortation, and I have heard enough. The prospect tires me. A long prayer at its commencement leads my heart upward to God, and kindles the fire of devotion in my bosom, but my heart returns, and the fire is extinguished by the time the prayer is done, Christ's prayers are not too long for me. But it wearies me to hear Christians use vain repetitions as the heathens do, in order to lengthen out their prayers.

Short articles will be remembered. Men always admire brevity of speech, whether spoken or written. When the Spartan mother gave her son the battle shield, saying, "This, or upon this," could that son forget the patriotic lesson thus impressed? No—in the din of battle it rung in his ears—it nerved his arm in the hour of conflict. Look at the parables of Christ—none of them are long—all of them are easily remembered. And is it not partly at least on account of their brevity? The impression of a brief article is apt to be distinct upon the memory. It must be apparent to all that memory grasps most easily and retains most permanently, brief articles, sententiously expressed.

Short articles, other things being equal, will do most good. This is evident from the fact that they will be read and remembered. But this is not all. If one hears a short sermon and it closes too soon, he will reflect upon it when it is done, prosecuting the subject in his own mind. If he reuds a short article and wishes it had been longer, he will naturally read it again. Its brevity furnishes his own mind something to do to supply what is wanting. He involuntarily attempts to do this. The powers of his intellect are excited to action. An impulse and a direction is given to his own thoughts. And to me it seems by no means the least benefit of brief and weighty articles, from the pulpit or the press, that they excite and direct the energies of the mind without wearying, serving as a projectile force to one's own thoughts.

Pioneers of Cincinnati.

The following list comprehends the names so far as I have been able to obtain them with the dates of their arrival here of those of our early settlers who have been here from the commence ment of the present century.

1796 Jacob Burnet,	1798 Hugh Moore,
Isaac Burton,	Samuel Newell,
William Burke.	Ebenezer Pruden.
1804 Ephraim Carter,	1804 Jona. Pancoast,
James Crawford,	Jos. Perry.
William Crippen,	1802 Sam'l. Perry,
Henry Craven,	Wm. Pierson.
1800 Daniel Drake,	1804 Jos. Pancoast,
Jno. B. Enness,	Robt. Richardson.
Edward Dodson,	1790 John Riddle,
1800 Charles Faran.	Christop'r. Smith.
1790 Jas. Ferguson.	1802 Ethan Stone.
1790 Mrs. Mary Gano.	1796 Sam'l. Stitt,
1794 Dan'l. Gano,	Wm. Saunders.
1792 Asa Holcomb.	1804 P. S. Symmes,
1804 Caspar Hopple,	Benj. Smith,
Andrew Johnston.	P. A. Sprigman.
1798 David Kautz,	G. P. Torrence,
Wm. Legg.	1800 A. Valentine,
Nich. Longworth.	Stephen Wheeler,
1794 Jonathan Lyon.	John Wood,
1804 Benjamin Mason.	J. L. Wilson,
1797 John Mahard.	Caleb Williams.
1795 Jonah Martin.	1790 Mrs. H. Wallace.
1804 Peter McNicoll,	1801 Robt. Wallace,
Adam Moore,	John Whetsone.
Wm. Moody.	1794 Griffin Yeatman.

As I intend to correct this line as far as opportunity permits, I shall feel obliged to those who can present me the necessary information to do so.

Newspaper Paragraphs.

The mischief which may result from the practice of hastily making up articles for newspapers, is forcibly illustrated by the following incident, which is derived from the most authentic source.

"When Baron Humboldt sailed from Europe in 1799, to prosecute his scientifiic inquiries in the new world, he agreed with the commander of the exploring expedition about to be sent by the French Government into the Pacific, that if he should take the route by Cape Horne, he would join him at Chili or Peru, or at any port where the vessels would touch. At Cuba, Humboldt saw in an *American newspaper*, that the expedition had sailed from Havre, and also, that *it would make the circuit of the Globe from east to west.* The last was a gratuitous supposition, but in reliancé upon the correctness of the information, Humboldt and Bonpland, his associate, hired a small vessel to transport them to Porto Bello, on the Spanish main, and crossed the isthmus to the Pacific, and it was not until after a journey of eight hundred leagues, that they found at Quito they had been deceived by the American journalist."

Family Government.

The following is not new, but it is both good and true. Parents, whose children 'tease them to death,' commit suicide, being themselves the cause of the teasing.

Child.—Mother, I want a piece of cake.

Mother.—I havn't got any; it's all gone.

C.—I know there's some up in the cupboard: I saw it when you opened the door.

M.—Well, you don't need any now——cake hurts children.

C.—No it don't (whining) I do want a piece; mother, mayn't I have a piece?

M.—Be still, I can't get up now, I'm so busy.

C.—(still crying) I want a piece of cake.

M.—Rising hastily, and reaching a piece; there, take that and hold your tongue! Eat it up quick. I hear Ben coming.——Now don't tell Ben you've had any.

(*Ben enters.*)

C.—I have had a piece of cake; you can't have any.

Ben.—Yes I will; mother, give me a piece.

M.—There, take it, it seems as if I never could keep a bit of any thing in the house. You see, sir, if you get any more.

(Another room.)

C.—I've had a piece of cake!

Young Sister.—Oh, I want some too.

C.—Well, you bawl, and mother'll give you a piece; I did.

MARRIAGES.

IN Henry Co., Missouri, on the 8th ult., Dr. J. EMERY of Paris, Mo., to Miss ELIZABETH B. DANA, of Harmar, Ohio.

ON Thursday 15th inst., by the Rev. Geo. W. Maley, Mr. MILTON J. WOODWARD to Miss SARAH GILDERS-LIEVE, of Covington, Ky.

Same day, by the J. T. Brooke. Wm. H. THOMPSON to LAURA GRAHAM, neice of T. H. Yeatman, Esqr.

Same day, by Rev. Dr. Thompson, JOHN FRAZER Esqr. to Miss ROSANNA B., daughter of Calvin Fletcher.

I have to make my acknowledgements to my friend FRAZER, who "lapt in Elysium," and placed under circumstances that might have led a man to forget even taking up a note in bank, remembered his friend the editor. The Pound cake was moistened with Adam's ale of my own providing, and was easier for me to take than any of Dr. Ridgely's proscriptions for ten years past. My best wishes and sincere prayers for the happiness of the new married couple, will be theirs for life.

THE

CINCINNATI MISCELLANY,

OR

ANTIQUITIES OF THE WEST:

AND

PIONEER HISTORY AND GENERAL AND LOCAL STATISTICS.

COMPILED FROM THE

WESTERN GENERAL ADVERTISER,

FROM APRIL 1st, 1845, TO APRIL 1st, 1846.

BY CHARLES CIST.

VOLUME II.

CINCINNATI:

ROBINSON & JONES, 109 MAIN STREET.

1846.

PREFACE.

THE editor and publisher of "Cist's Advertiser," at the instance of his friends and subscribers, nearly a year since issued a volume compiled of various historical and statistical sketches, which made their appearance originally in his columns. Of these but a small edition was sold, the editor's other engagements not permitting him the opportunity of offering it personally to his subscribers and others.

A new volume is now presented, which, like the former, comprehends many valuable records, both of the past and the present, which will derive still higher interst in the lapse of time, and as subjects of reference in future years.

There is no individual in Cincinnati, expecting to make it his permanent residence, whose gratification and interest it will not be to preserve the information thus afforded, as a means of retracing the past, and thus affording him a source of rich enjoyment in the decline of life, when such gratifications have become few and faint.

CINCINNATI MISCELLANY.

CINCINNATI' JUNE, 1845.

No postponement on account of the Weather.

I observe the following, which forms a regular advertisement in a Hickman (Ky.) newspaper, and put it on record as a trait of the region and the times:

"NOTICE.—The funeral of *Mr. Nicholas J. Poindexter,* having been postponed on account of the inclement weather, will take place near Totten's Mill, on the 26th April next. The public are invited.

Ear for Music.

The band of an English Ambassador at Constantinople, once performed a concert for the entertainment of the sultan and his court. At its conclusion his Highness was asked which of the pieces he prefered. He replied, the first, which was recommenced, but stopped, as not being the right one. Others were tried with as little success, until at length the band, almost in despair of discovering the favourite air, began *tuning* their instruments, when his Highness exclaimed, " Inshallah, Heaven be praised, that is it!"

Sentimentality.

The French carry *sentiment* farther than any other people in the world—in fact they carry it into every thing. The remains of *Bichat,* one of the most distinguished physiologists and medical writers of France, after having reposed forty-three years in the old Catherine Cemetery at *Paris,* have been lately removed with great pomp and ceremony to *Pere Lachaise.* But on exhuming the remains, lo and behold! the skeleton was found *without a head!* The grave digger supposed he had mistaken the grave of the celebrated professor for that of some decapitated malefactor, but the circumstance served to identify the skeleton as that of the professor; for when Bichat died, his loss caused his friend, Prof. Roux, so much grief, that he procured its amputation to preserve it as a souvenir. The latter was now called upon for the head, and it was finally restored and intered with the body, *in situ.*

The son of the celebrated *Broussais,* also, for the purpose of preserving a vivid remembrance of his father, had his head cut off, and it now forms a mantel decoration in his study. *Buffon,* almost inconsolable for the loss of his wife, allayed his grief in the occupation of dissecting her body as a labour of love! This is an indisputable fact.

Of what individuals but Frenchmen could such traits of sentimentality be, with truth, recorded?

" Doctor," said a wag to his medical adviser one day " isn't there such a disease as the *shingles?*" " Yes, to be sure," replied Galen.— " Then I've got it, for certain," said the patient, " for the *roof* of my mouth has broken out in a dozen places!"

First born male Child of Ohio.

The question has been repeatedly asked—who is the oldest white male born in Ohio, and still living?

The Marietta Intelligencer gives *Judge Joseph Barker,* son of Col. Joseph Barker, who was born at *Belpre,* as having long borne the reputation of the oldest native, if not the " oldest inhabitant" of the State; and adds, that *Lester G. Converse,* of *Marietta,* has a better title to the distinction in being born at *Waterford,* in Washington county, on the 14th February, 1790.

I cannot find any individual living who was a native of Cincinnati at an earlier date than May, 1793, which was the birth day of *David R. Kemper,* who was born on Sycamore street, Cincinnati, opposite Christopher Smith's present residence.

I am able, however, to furnish the names of the first born who survive to this day, both of males and females. They are probably also the first born male and female in Ohio, among the living or the dead. These are *Christian F. Senseman* and *Mary Heckewelder,* the children of Moravian Missionaries, who were born in 1781, at *Gnadenhutten,* on the Tuscarawas, now residing both in the same county in Pennsylvania; one at *Nazareth,* the other at *Bethlehem.* They were born within a day of each other.

While on this subject, let me state a singular fact. Although our city is but fifty-seven years of age, we have as residents a lady who with her son and granddaughter are all born within four miles of Cincinnati, the last two being born in the city itself.

The granddaughter is thirteen years of age. Of course then as far back as 1833, we had individuals of the third generation born here. The great grandmother, one of the early pioneers, is also yet alive. This is a state of case probably unparalleled in Ohio, or indeed in any settlement no older than our state.

Chancery Delays.

Soon after Mr. Jekyll was called to the bar, a strange solicitor coming up to him in Westminster Hall, begged him to step into the court of chancery to make a motion, of course, and gave him a fee. The young barister looking pleased, but a little surprised, the solicitor said to him, " I thought you had a sort of right, sir, to this motion; for the bill was drawn by Sir Joseph Jekyll, your great-grand-uncle, in the reign of Queen Anne."—*Lord Campbell's " Lives of the Chancellors."*

Early Maps of Cincinnati.

Streets.—West of the Section line separating Section 24 from the rest of the city, there was not a street laid out at the date of 1815. That line followed a due north course from a point at the river Ohio, about half way between Mill and Smith streets, crossing Fifth street just east of the mound which lately stood there, and Western Row about two hundred yards south of the Corporation line. Plum, Race and Walnut streets extended no farther north than Seventh street, and Sycamore was not opened beyond the present line of the Miami Canal. From Walnut street west as far as Western Row not a street was opened north of Seventh st., nor from Main street east, beyond the bank of the canal already refered to. It was the same case with respect to Broadway from Fifth street to the Corporation line in the same direction. Court street, west of Main, was called *St. Clair* street, and Ninth street to its whole length, at that time, was laid out as *Wayne* street. Eighth street, east of Main, was called *New Market* street.

Public Buildings.—Of churches there were only—the Presbyterian Church which preceded the present building, on Main street; the Methodist Church on Fifth, where the Wesley Chapel has since been built; a Baptist Church on Sixth street, west of Walnut, on the scite of what is now a German Church, corner of Lodge street; and the Friends' frame meeting house, on Fifth, below Western Row. Of all these the last only remains on its original scite; the Presbyterian Church having been removed to Vine, below Fifth, where it still stands under the name of Burke's Church, and the others having been since removed to make way for their successors. The scite of the present Cincinnati College, on Walnut street, at that date was occupied by the Lan-

caster Seminary. Young as was the place it furnished business for three banks—the *Bank of Cincinnati* was on Main, west side, and north of Fifth st.; the *Farmers' and Mechanics' Bank*, on Main, west side, between Front and Second streets; and the *Miami Exporting Company* on the spot now occupied by W. G. Breese's store, facing the public landing. These, with the Court House and Jail, which stand now where they then stood, made up the public buildings for 1815. The brewery, corner of Symmes and Pike streets; another, corner of Race and Water streets; a potash factory on Front street, immediately east of Deer Creek; Gulick's sugar refinery on Arch street; a glass house at the foot of Smith street; a steam saw mill at the mouth of Mill street; and the great steam mill on the river bank, half way between Ludlow street and Broadway, constituted in 1815, the entire manufactories of the place.

Markets.—Besides Lower Market, which occupied the block from Main to Sycamore, as well as that from Sycamore to Broadway, in the street of that name, and Upper Market, which stood on Fifth between Main and Walnut streets, there was ground vacated for markets, which having been found unsuitable for the purpose, was never occupied for that use. One of these embraces the front of Sycamore street on both sides from a short distance north of Seventh, to the corner of Ninth street. Another is on McFarland street, west of Elm, forming a square of two hundred feet in the centre of the block. A slight examination of these places where the dwellings have been built back from their line of the respective streets, will point out at once the space dedicated for this purpose.

They who will abandon a friend for one error, know but little of human character, and prove that their hearts are as cold as their judgments are weak.

Patronymics.

No man thinks his own name a strange or odd one, however much so it may be to others. We are so familiar with the names of John Taylor, or John Miller, or John Carpenter, or John Baker, that we have lost all sense of the oddity of a surname which signifies simply, in the original, who bore it, his occupation or employment.

The Cherokees, in Arkansas, having adopted most of the customs of the whites, their aboriginal names are now translated into the English language, furnishing a series of names which seem very singular to our eyes and ears. Of four individuals arrested under a charge of murder near *Tahlequah* lately, the names are *Squirrel, John Potatoe, Wm. Wicked* and *Thomas*

Muskrat. The chief justice in the *Going Snake* district, is *Jesse Bushyhead.*

Church Organs.

The lovers of music should witness the performance of an organ made by Mr. *John Koehnke,* of our city, for *Zion Church,* on Columbia near Vine street, in which building it is now put up. It is wonderful that organs made by *Erben* and others are brought from the East, when at less expense a far superior article can be obtained of Cincinnati manufacture. I fearlessly challenge comparison here between those made by Erben and the organ here refered to. There are few finer instruments of the kind and size any where.

The Cincinnati Historical Society.

It is desirable that files of periodicals now in existence, or that were once published here, should be placed for preservation in the library of this society. Even single numbers, where files cannot be presented, will be acceptable.

The following prints have been deposited with Mr. Randall, Librarian of the Society, as a commencement:

1. The Western Washingtonian.
2. The Daily Commercial.
3. Orthodox Preacher.
4. Reformist.
5. Licht Freund.
6. Christliche Apologete.
7. Western Medical Reformer
8. Youth's Visiter.
9. Christmas Guest.
10. Artist and Artisan.
11. Western General Advertiser.
12. Cincinnati Miscellany.

I trust that our city press will make up files for this commendable purpose.

An Apt Scholar.

An old chap in Connecticut who was one of the most niggardly men known in that part of the country, carried on the blacksmithing business very extensively; and, as is generally the case in that State, boarded all of his own hands. And to show he envied the men what they eat, he would have a bowl of bean soup dished up for himself to cool, while that for the hands was served up in a large pan just from the boiling pot. This old fellow had an apprentice who was rather unlucky among the hot irons, frequently burning his fingers. The old man scolded him severely one day for being so careless.

"How can I tell," said the boy, "if they are hot unless they are red?"

"Never touch any thing again till you spit on it; if it don't hiss it wont burn."

In a day or two the old man sent the boy in to see if his soup was cool. The boy went in—spit in the bowl; of course the soup did not hiss. He went back and told the boss all was right.

"Dinner!" cried he.

All hands run; down sat the old man at the head of the table; and in went a large spoonful of the boiling hot soup to his mouth.

"Good Heavens!" cried the old man, in the greatest rage, "what did you tell me that lie for? you young rascal!"

"I did not lie," said the boy, very innocently, "You told me I should spit on any thing to try if it was hot; so I spit in your bowl, and the soup did not hiss, so I supposed it was cool."

Judge of the effect on the jours. That boy never was in want of friends among the journeymen.

From the St. Louis Reveille.

A Desperate Adventure.

[The following adventure of two men, one of them a *St. Louis Boy*, has been sent us, with a request to publish. The incident is one of those which gave such wild interest to the homeward journey of Lieut. Fremont.—Eds.]

While encamped on the 24th of April, at a spring near the Spanish Trail, we were surprised by the sudden appearance among us of two Mexicans; a man and a boy—the name of the man was Andreas Fuentas, and that of the boy (a handsome lad eleven years old) Pablo Hernandez. With a cavalcade of about thirty horses, they had come out from Puebla de los Angelos, near the Pacific; had lost half their animals, stolen by Indians, and now sought my camp for raid. Carson and Godey, two of my men, volunteered to pursue them, with the Mexican; and, well mounted, the three set off on the trail. In the evening Fuentas returned, his horse having failed; but Carson and Godey had continued the pursuit.

In the afternoon of the next day, a war whoop was heard, such as Indians make when returning from a victorious enterprise; and soon Carson and Godey appeared driving before them a band of horses, recognised by Fuentas to be a part of those they had lost. Two bloody scalps, dangling from the end of Godey's gun, announced that they had overtaken the Indians as well as the horses. They had continued the pursuit alone after Fuentas left them, and towards nightfall entered the mountains into which the trail led. After sunset the moon gave light, and they followed the trail by moonlight until late in the night, when it entered a narrow defile, and was difficult to follow. Here they lay from midnight till morning. At daylight they resumed the pursuit, and at sunrise discovered the horses; and immediately dismounting and tying up their own, they crept cautiously to a rising ground which intervened, from the crest of which they perceived the encampment of four lodges close by. They proceeded quietly, and had got within thirty or forty yards of their object, when a movement among the horses discovered them to the Indians. Giving the war shout they instantly charged in the camp, regardless of the numbers which the *four* lodges might contain. The Indians received them with a flight of arrows, shot from their long bows, one of which passed through Godey's shirt collar, barely missing the neck. Our men fired their rifles upon a steady aim, and rushed in. Two Indians were stretched upon the ground, fatally pierced with bullets; the rest fled, except a lad, who was captured. The scalps of the fallen were instantly stripped off, but in the process, one of them, who had two balls through his body, sprung to his feet, the blood streaming from his skinned head, and uttered a hideous howl. The frightful spectacle appalled the stout hearts of our men; but they did what humanity required, and quickly terminated the agonies of the gory savage. They were now masters of the camp, which was a pretty little recess in the mountain, with a fine spring, and apparently safe from all invasion. Great preparations had been made for feasting a large party, for it was a very proper place for a rendezvous, and for the celebration of such orgies as robbers of the desert would delight in. Several of the horses had been killed, skinned, and cut up—for the Indians living in the mountains, and only coming into the plains to rob and murder, make no other use of horses than to eat them. Large earthen vessels were on the fire, boiling and stewing the horse beef; and several baskets containing fifty or sixty pairs of moccasins, indicated the presence or expectation of a large party. They released the boy who had given strong evidence of the stoicism, or something else of the savage character, by commencing his breakfast upon a horse's head as soon as he found he was not to be killed, but only tied as a prisoner.

Their object accomplished, our men gathered up all the surviving horses, fifteen in number, returned upon their trail, and rejoined us at our camp in the afternoon of the same day. They had rode about one hundred miles in the pursuit and return, and all in thirty hours. The time, place, object and numbers considered, this expedition of Carson and Godey may be considered among the boldest and most disinterested which the annals of western adventure, so full of daring deeds, can present. Two men, in a savage wilderness, pursue day and night an unknown body of Indians into the defiles of an unknown mountain—attack them on sight without counting numbers—and defeat them in an instant—and for what?—to punish the robbers of the desert, and revenge the wrongs of Mexicans whom they did not know. I repeat it was Carson and Godey who did this—the former an *American*, born in Boonslick county, Missouri; the latter a Frenchman, born in St. Louis—and both trained to western enterprise from early life.

Fine Feelings.

We knew a blunt old fellow in the State of Maine, who sometimes hit the nail on the head more pat than the philosophers. He once heard a man much praised for his "*good feelings.*" Every body joined, and said the man was possessed of excellent feelings.

"What has he done?" asked our old genius.

"Oh! in every thing he is a man of fine benevolent feelings," was the reply.

"What has he done?" cried the old fellow, again.

By this time the company thought it necessary to show some of their favourite's *doings.* They began to cast about in their minds, but the old man still shouted, "what has he *done?*" They owned that they could not name any thing in particular.

"Yet," answered the cynic, "you say that the man has good feelings—fine feelings—benevolent feelings. Now, gentlemen, let me tell you that there are people in this world who get a good name simply on account of their feelings. You can't tell one generous action that they ever performed in their lives, but they can look and talk most benevolently. I know a man in this town that you would all call a surly, tough and un-

amiable man, and yet he has done more *acts* of kindness in this country than all of you put together. You may judge people's actions by their feelings, but I judge people's feelings by their actions."

Superstitions of the Sea.

The author of the "Naval Sketch Book" gives the following as the origin of the prevalent notion among sailors that the appearance of the birds known as "Mother Carey's Chickens," is the precursor of a storm:

"The 'Tiger,' an outward bound East-Indiaman, had one continued gale, without intermission, till she got to the Cape of Good Hope, by which time she was almost a wreck: that off this Cape in particular, she was nearly foundered: that in the height of the gale were seen a number of ominous birds screaming about in the lightning's blaze, and some of them of monstrous shape and size: that among the passengers was a woman called 'Mother Carey,' who always seemed to smile when she looked upon these foulweather birds, upon which it was concluded that she was a witch: that she had conjured them up from the Red Sea, and that they never would have a prosperous voyage whilst she remained on board; and, finally, that just as they were debating about it, she sprung overboard and went down in a flame, when the birds, (ever after called '*Mother Carey's Chickens*,') vanished in a moment, and left the Tiger to pursue her voyage in peace."

"The Stars and Stripes."

A correspondent of the New Bedford Mercury has picked up the following interesting scrap of history:

1783. "On the 3d of February, the ship Bedford, Capt. Moores, belonging to the Massachusetts, arrived in the Downs, passed Gravesend the 4th, and was reported at the Custom House the 6th. She was not allowed regular entry until some consultation had taken place between the Commissioners of the Customs and the Lords of the Council, on account of the many acts of Parliament yet in force against the *rebels of America.* She was loaded with *five hundred and eighty-seven butts of whale oil,* manned wholly with American seamen, and belonged to the island of Nantucket, in Massachusetts. The vessel lay at Horsley Down, a little below the Tower, *and was the first which displayed the Thirteen Stripes of America in any British port.*"—*Barnard's History of England, page* 705.

Brevity.

It is a common idea that the most laconic military despatch ever issued, was that sent by Cæsar to the Horse Guards at Rome, containing the three memorable words, "*Veni, vidi, vici,*" and perhaps until our own day, no like instance of brevity has been found. The despatch of Sir Charles Napier, after the capture of Scinde, to Lord Ellenborough, both for brevity and truth, is, however, far beyond it. The despatch consisted of one emphatic word—"*Peccavi.*" "I have Scinde," (*sinned.*)

Jesse and Elias Hughes--No. 1.

Day by day the gallant band who settled the west at the peril of their lives, are disappearing from the theatre of human life, and a few brief years must sweep the survivors to that bourne from which no traveller returns.

Among these heroic spirits two brothers, Jesse and Elias Hughes figured in the frontier wars of Western Virginia. They were both remarkable men, As early as 1774, Elias bore arms at the age of 18, and was doubtless at the period of his death, which occurred as lately as the 22d of last March, the last survivor of the memorable battle of Point Pleasant, on the 10th October, 1774. This was the hardest fight ever sustained with the Indians, it having lasted from early in the morning till near night, several persons perishing from exhaustion in the course of the day.

Thomas Hughes, the head of the family had emigrated from the south branch of the Potomac, and established himself with his wife and children at Clarksburg, Harrison county, on the head waters of the Monongahela, at that period on the frontiers of the white settlements. In this region, periodically invaded by Indians, the brothers, Jesse and Elias served their apprenticeship to border warfare.

In 1777, Jesse, who was twenty-two, and Elias twenty years of age, attached themselves to a company of spies or rangers, raised by Capt. James Booth for the protection of the settlements. At one time the brothers being out on a scout, they examined the localities of the enemy near the steep bank of a run, made a smoke of rotten wood to keep off the gnats, and lay down upon their arms for the night, their moccasins tied to the breech of their guns. Sometime after, hearing something like the snapping of a stick, and looking in the direction, they saw at a distance three Indians approaching. Instantly the young men sprang to their feet, leaped down the bank and over the run. The Indians in pursuit, not knowing the place so well, fell down the bank. The whites hearing the plash, stopped an instant, put on their moccasins, raised a yell and put off at full speed, leaving the Indians to take care of themselves.

In the middle of June three women went out from West's fort to gather greens in an adjoining field, and while thus engaged were fired on by one individual of a party of four Indians.— The ball passed through the bonnet of a Mrs. Hacker, who screamed, and with the others ran towards the fort. An Indian having in his hand a long staff mounted with a spear, pursuing closely after them, thrust it with so much violence at a Mrs. Freeman, another of the women that,

entering her back just below the shoulder, it came out at her left breast. With his tomahawk, he cleft the upper part of the head, and carried it off to save the scalp.

The screams of the women alarmed the men in the fort, and seizing their rifles they ran out just as Mrs Freeman fell, a few shots were fired at the Indian while he was tugging away at the scalp, but without effect, except so far as to warn the men outside of the fort that danger was at hand, and they quickly came in. Among these were Jesse Hughes, and a comrade named John Schoolcraft, who, while they were getting in, discovered two Indians standing by the fence, and looking so intently towards the men at the fort as not to perceive any one else. Hughes and Schoolcraft being unarmed—having left their guns in the fort—stepped to one side and made their way in safely. Hughes, his brother and four others, armed themselves and went out to bring in the dead body, and while Jesse was pointing out to the rest of the party how near he had approached the Indians before noticing them, one of the Indians made a howl like a wolf, and the whole party moved off in the direction whence the sound proceeded until supposing themselves near the spot, and stopping in a suitable place, Jesse howled also. He was answered, and two Indians were soon seen advancing. An opportunity offering, Elias Hughes shot one and the other took to flight.— Being pursued by the whites, he took shelter in a thicket of brush, and while they were proceeding to intercept him at his coming out, he returned [the way he entered and made his escape. The wounded Indian also got off. In their pursuit of the others, the party passed by where the wounded man lay, and one of the men was for stopping and finishing him, but Hughes called out "he is safe! let us have the others," and they all pressed forward into the thicket. On their return the savage was gone, and although his free bleeding enabled them to pursue his track readily for a while, a heavy shower of rain falling while they were in pursuit, all traces of him were finally lost.

On the 16th June, Capt. Booth, who being an well educated man, as well as an efficient leader in scouting parties, being at work in his field, was surprised and shot by the savages. Jesse Hughes by common consent succeeded to his post.

In 1780 West's fort was again visited by the Indians. The frequent incursions of the sagages during the year 1778, had led the inhabitants to desert their homes and shelter themselves in places of greater security; but being unwilling to give up the improvements which they had already made, and commence anew in the woods; some few families returned to their farms during the winter, and on the approach of spring moved into forts. In this case, the settlers had been in only a short time, when the enemy made his appearance, and continued to invest the fort for some time. Ignorant when to expect relief, the feeble band shut up there were becoming desperate when Jesse Hughes resolved at all hazards to obtain assistance from abroad. Leaving the fort at night, he eluded their sentinels, and made his way to the Buchannan fort. Here he prevailed on a party of the men to accompany them to West's and relieve those who had been so long shut up there. They arrived before day, and on consultation, it was thought advisable to abandon the place once more and remove to Buchannan fort. On their way the Indians resorted to every artifice to separate the party so as to cut them up in detachments, but to no purpose. All their stratagems were frustrated, and the entire body reached the fort in safety.

In March 1781, a party of Indians surprised the inhabitants on Leading creek, Tygart's Valley, nearly depopulating the settlement. Among others they killed Alexander Roney, Mrs. Dougherty, and carried away Mrs. Roney and son, and Mr. Dougherty prisoners. On receipt of these tidings at Clarksburg, a party was promptly made up to chastise the savages, and if possible, rescue the prisoners, and pursuit being immediately made, the advance of the party discovered the Indians on a branch of Hughes' river. Col. Lowther and the brothers, Jesse and Elias Hughes led the pursuing force. It was concluded to leave the Hughes' watch the enemy, while the residue of the party retired a short distance to rest, with the design to attack them in the morning. As soon as day dawned, on a preconcerted signal being made, the whites crawled through the brush, and a general fire was poured in on the Indians of whom one only made his escape. Young Roney unfortunately lay sleeping in the bosom of one of the Indians, and the same bullet that passed through the head of the savage deprived the boy of life. Mrs. Roney, ignorant of the fate of her son, and in the prospect of deliverance, losing the recollection of the recent murder of her husband, ran to the whites repeating, "I am Aleck Roney's wife of the Valley, I am Aleck Roney's wife of the Valley, and a pretty little woman, too if I was well dressed." Dougherty who was tied down and unable to move, was discovered by the whites as they rushed into the camp. Fearing that he was one of the enemy and might do them injury as they advanced, one of the

party stopping, demanded who he was. Benumbed with cold, and discomposed by the firing, he could not make himself known or understood. The white man raised his gun, directing it towards him and called out that if he did not say who he was, he would put a ball through him, be he white man or Indian. Fears supplying him with energy, he exclaimed at last, "J——, am I to be killed by white people at last." Col. Lowther then recognized him and saved his life. The plunder recovered on this occasion was so abundant as to divide fourteen pounds seventeen shillings and six pence—nearly forty dollars to each of the recaptors.

In September, 1785, a party of Indians who had been stealing horses near Clarksburg were followed by a company raised on the spot out of the border warriors, commanded as before by Lowther, and the brothers Hughes, Jesse and Elias. On the 3d night after starting, the whites and Indians unknown to the fact had encamped within a short distance of each other. In the morning the pursuers divided taking two different routes. Elias Hughes and his party discovered the Indians by the smoke of their fires, and creeping cautiously up through the brush were enabled to get near enough for Hughes to shoot, when one of the savages fell and the residue took to flight. One of the Indians passing near where Col. Lowther stood, was fired at by him as he ran, and killed on the spot. The horses and other plunder regained from the savages were taken home by the whites who were however waylaid on the route, and one of their number, John Barnet, so badly wounded, that he died before reaching home.

At another time Elias Hughes and his men discovering a party of Indians, fired upon them. The Indians ran in different directions. Hughes made after one, and was gaining upon him fast, in a bottom piece of land in which were no trees, when the Indian turned quickly about with loaded gun uplifted. Hughes' gun was empty and there were no trees to spring behind. But instantly springing obliquely to the right and left, with a bound and out stretched arm, he flirted the muzzle of the Indian's gun to one side, and the next moment had his long knife in him up to the hilt.

On the 5th December of the same year, the Indians made another inroad into these devoted regions, and marking their progress with blood and plunder, massacred several of the men and women and carried off some prisoners, a daughter of Jesse Hughes among the the rest. She remained in captivity a year, when she was ransomed by her father.

In September 1789, Jesse being one of a party

of drovers who were taking cattle into Marietta for the supply of the settlers there, the company encamped for the night, when within a few miles of the river Ohio. In the morning while dressing they were alarmed by a discharge of guns which killed one and wounded another of the drovers. The most of the party escaped by flight. Nicholas Carpenter and his son, who had hid in a pond of water, were discovered, tomahawked and scalped. George Leggett, another of the drovers was never heard of afterwards, having doubtless lost his life there. Hughes himself, although taken at great disadvantage, effected his escape. He wore long leggings, and when the firing commenced, they were fastened to his belt, but were hanging loose below. Although an active runner he found his pursuers were gaining on him, and that his safety depended in getting rid of these incumbrances. In as brief a space of time as possible, he halted, stepping on the lower part of the leggings and broke the strings attaching them to the belt, which he had no time to untie or even to get out his knife and cut. As little time as this cost, it was at the hazard of his life. One of the Indians approached and flung a tomahawk at him, which however, only grazed his head.— Once disencumbered of the leggings, he soon made his escape.

On one occasion during this period of danger, which kept such men as the Hughes' in constant employment Jesse, observed a lad, intently engaged, fixing his rifle. ''Jim,'' said he, ''what are you doing there?'' ''I am going to shoot a gobbler that I hear on the hill side,'' said Jim. I hear no turkey'' replied Hughes. ''Listen,'' said Jim. ''there—don't your hear it; listen again.'' ''Well'' said Hughes, after hearing it repeated, ''I'll go and kill it.'' ''No you won't,'' exclaimed the lad, ''it is my turkey; I heard it first.'' ''Well,'' said Hughes ''you know I am the best marksman, and besides I don't want the turkey; you may have it.'' Jim then acquiescing, Hughes went out, with his own rifle from the side of the fort which was furthest from the supposed turkey, and skirting a ravine came in on the rear, and as he expected, discovered an Indian who was seated on a chesnut stump; surrounded and partly hid by sprouts, gobbling at intervals and watching in the direction of the fort, to see whom he would be able to decoy out. Hughes crept up behind him, and the first notice given the savage of his presence, was a shot which deprived him of life. He took off the scalp and went into the fort where Jim was waiting for the prize. ''There now,'' said the lad. ''you have let the turkey go; I should have killed it if I had gone.'' ''No,''

said Hughes, ''I did not let it go,'' and taking out the scalp & throwing it down, ''There take your turkey, Jim, I don't want it.'' The lad was overcome and nearly fainted in view of the narrow escape he had made.

In 1790 the hostilities of the Indians had been reduced to stealing horses, merely. The Ohio above Marietta was their crossing place to Clarksburg, the route from that river being through a dense forest. All was quiet in the settlements, as they had been for some time without alarms on the score of Indians. One night a man who had a horse in an enclosure, heard the fence fall: he jumped up and ran out and saw an Indian spring on the horse and dash off. An hour or two sufficed to rouse the neighborhood, and a company of twenty-five or thirty persons agreed to assemble and start by daylight. They took a circle around the settlement, and soon struck the trail of ten or twelve horses, ridden off, as they judged probable, by the same number of Indians. The captain called a halt for consultation. Jesse Hughes who was one of the party was opposed to following their trace, alleging he could pilot them a nearer way to the Ohio, where they would be able to intercept their retreat. A majority, including the captain advocated pursuit. Hughes then insisted that the Indians would waylay their trail, in order to know if they were followed, and could choose spots where they would be able to shoot two or three of the whites, and put their own friends upon their guard, and that the savages once alarmed would keep the start they had already got. These arguments appearing to shake the purpose of the party, the commander, jealous of Hughes' influence, broke up the council, calling on the men to follow him, and let all cowards go home. He dashed on then, the men all following him. Hughes felt the insult keenly, but kept on with the rest.— They had not proceeded many miles till the trail went down a drain, where the ridge on one side was very steep, with a ledge of rocks for a considerable distance. On the top of the cliff, two Indians lay in ambush, and when the company got opposite, they made some noise which induced the men to halt; that instant two of the company were shot and mortally wounded.— Before any of them could ride round and ascend the cliff, the Indians were out of reach and sight.

The party of whites then agreed that Hughes was in the right, and although fearful they were too late, changed their route to intercept them at the crossing place. They gave the wounded men in charge of some of their numbers, and making a desperate push, reached the Ohio river next day about an hour after the savages had crossed it. The water was yet muddy with the horses trails, and the rafts the Indians had crossed on, were yet floating on the opposite shore. The company were then unanimous for abandoning all pursuit. Hughes had now full satisfaction for the insult. It seemed, he said, as if they were going to prove the captain's words and show who were the cowards. As for himself, he said he would cross with as many as were willing, half their party, being as he supposed, enough to take the enemy's scalps. They all refused. He then said if but one man would cross with him he would keep on, but still no one would consent. He then said he would go by himself and take a scalp or leave his own.

After his party had got out of sight, Hughes made his way up the river three or four miles, keeping out of view from the other shore, as he supposed the Indians were watching to see if the party would cross. He then made a raft and crossed the river, and encamped for the night. He struck their trail next day, and pursuing it very cautiously some ten miles from the river found their camp. There was but one Indian in it, the rest being out hunting. In order to pass his time pleasantly, he had made a sort of fiddle out of bones, and was sitting at ease singing and playing. Hughes crept up and shot him. He then took his scalp and made his way home. This is the last I have been able to learn of Jesse Hughes, except that he survived many years, and died not long since.

After Gen. Wayne's treaty, Elias Hughes and family settled upon the waters of the Licking in Ohio. The Indians having, at an early day, killed a young woman whom he highly esteemed, and subsequently his father, the return of peace did not eradicate his antipathy to the race. In the month of April, 1800, two Indians, having collected a quantity of fur on the Rocky Fork of Licking, proceeded to the Bowling Green, stole three horses and put off for Sandusky.— The next morning Hughes, Ratliff and Bland, going out for the horses and not finding them, did not return to apprise their families; but continued upon the trail, and at night discovering the Indians' fire on Granny's creek, some few miles N. W. of where Mt. Vernon stands, lay down for the night, and the next morning walked up to the Indians as they were cooking their morning repast. At first the Indians looked somewhat embarrassed, proposed restoration of the horses, and giving part of their furs by way of conciliation, from which the whites did not dissent, but were thinking of the whole of their furs and the future safety of the horses.

It being a damp morning; it was proposed to shoot off all their guns and put in fresh loads.— A mark was made; Hughes raised his gun ostensibly to shoot, which attracted the attention of the Indians to the mark and was a signal.— Ratliff downed one, Bland's gun flashed, but Hughes turning quickly round, emptied his gun in the other Indian's head, setting fire at the same time to the handkerchief around it. On returning they kept their expedition a secret for some time.

Hughes' memory failed him considerably the last three or four years. Previously his eye sight failed him entirely, but partially returned again. With patience he waited his approaching end, firmly believing that his Redeemer lived, and that through Him he should enjoy the life to come.

His decease occurred, as I have stated, on the 22nd last March. With him doubtless disappeared the last survivor of those who bore a part in the memorable battle of Point Pleasant, at the mouth of Kanawha, seventy-one years since. The body was attended to the grave with every demonstration of the respect due to his past services, by several military corps, and a concourse of his fellow citizens.

The General Assembly of the Presbyterian Church.

This body composed of the delegates of the Presbyterian churches in the United States, met for the first time in Cincinnati, and for the second time in the west, on Thursday last. There are nearly two hundred on the rolls, who are constituted in about equal proportions of ministers and ruling elders. They are generally fine looking men, with much less of the rigid Scotch and Scotch Irish cast of features than might be expected from the great element of their descent.

An impression appears to prevail that this body is selected from the church at large, out of its strongest members. This is a great mistake. Each Presbytery, according to its number, sends one or more ministers, and as many lay representatives, and the usual practice is to delegate them in turn, varying in particular cases to suit the convenience of members. The presumption therefore is, that each general assembly is a fair representation—and no more, of the talent and weight of character of the denomination at large. Neither is the title D. D. appended to the names of the ministers, any evidence of the greater weight of influence, talent, knowledge or piety of him who holds it as compared with the rest. It is conferred not by the church but by the various colleges of learning throughout the land, and as a general rule, it is doubtless the fact that those who bestow degree most freely, are least qualified to judge on the subject.— One of the *Doctorates* in the Synod of Cincinnati was lately confered on one of the members by Augusta college, Ky. He had probably graduated there. *I* could find fifty ministers of others in the same denomination better entitled to pre-eminence in knowledge, judgment, and pulpit abilities. *If* these distinctions are to be confered, they ought to be bestowed by the General Assembly; but the whole system is at variance with that parity of presbyters which forms a fundamental doctrine in the church order and government of Presbyterians.

Various questions of deep interest to that church are fairly before the assembly, and some of them have been discussed, at length. The debates are public and appear to command a crowd of auditors.

The Indian Trail.

"The Indians have attacked Mr. Stuart's house, burnt it, and carried his family into captivity!" were the first words of a breathless woodman. as he rushed into a block-house of a village in Western New York, during one of the early border wars. "Up, up—a dozen men should have been on the trail two hours ago," "God help us!" said one of the group, a bold, frank forester, and with a face whiter than ashes, he leaned against the wall gasping for breath, Every eye was turned on him with sympathy, for he and Mr, Stuart's only daughter, a lovely girl of seventeen were to be married in a few days,

The bereaved father was universally respected. He was a man of great benevolence of heart, and of some property, and resided on a mill seat he owned about two miles from the village.— His family consisted of his eldest daughter and three children. He had been from home, so the runner said, when his house was attacked, nor had his neighbors any intimation of the catastrophe until the light of the burning tenements awakened the suspicions of a settler, who was a mile nearer the village than Mr. Stuart, and who proceeded towards the flames, found the house and mills in ruins, and recognized the feet of females and children on the trail of Indians. He hurried instantly to the fort, and was the individual who now stood breathlessly narrating the events which we in fewer words have detailed.

The alarm spread through the village like a fire spreads in a swamp after a drought, and before the speaker had finished his story, the little block-house was filled with eager and sympathizing faces. Several of the inhabitants had brought their rifles, and others now hurried home to arm themselves. The young men of the settlement gathered, to a man, around Henry Leper, the betrothed husband of Mary Stuart; and though few words were spoken, the earnest grasp of the hand, and the accompanying looks, assured him that his friends keenly felt for him, and were ready to follow him to the world's end. That party was about to set forth, when a man was seen hurriedly running up the road from the direction of the desolated home.

"It is Mr. Stuart!" said one of the oldest of the group, "stand back, and let him come in."

The men parted right and left from the door-way, and immediately the father entered, the neighbors bowing respectfully to him as he passed. He scarcely returned their salutation, but advancing directly to his intended son-in-law, the two mutually fell into each other's arms. The spectators, not wishing to intrude on the privacy of their grief, turned their faces away with that instinctive delicacy which is nowhere to be found more often than among those who are thought to be rude borderers; but they heard sobs and they knew that the heart of the usually collected Mr. Stuart must be fearfully agitated.

"My friends," said he, at length—"this is kind, I see you know my loss, and are ready to march with me! God bless you! He could say no more, for he was choked with emotion.

"Stay back, father," said young Leper, using for the first time a name which in that moment of desolation carried sweet comfort to the parent's heart "you cannot bear the fatigue as well as me—death only will prevent us from bringing back Mary."

"I know it—I know it, my son—but cannot stay here in suspense. No, I will go with you. I have to-day the strength of a dozen men!"

The fathers who were there nodded in assent, and nothing further was said, but immediately the party, as if by one impulse, set forth.

There was no difficulty in finding the trail of the Indians, along which the pursuers advanced with a speed incredible to those unused to forest life, and the result of long and severe discipline. But rapid as their march was, hour after hour elapsed without any signs of savages, though evidence that they passed the route a while before was continually met. The sun rose high above the heavens until he stood above the tree tops, then he began slowly to decline, and at length his slant beams could scarcely penetrate the forest; yet there was no appearance of the Indians, and the hearts of the pursuers began to despond. Already the pursuits was useless, for the boundaries of the settlers' district had long been passed; they were in the very heart of the savages' country; and by this time the Indians had probably reached their village. Yet, when the older men, who alone would venture to suggest a return, looked at the father or the intended son-in-law, young Leper, they could only utter the words which would carry despair to two almost breaking hearts, and so the march was contined. But night drew on, and one of the elders spoke:

"There seems to be no hope," he said, stoping and resting his rifle on the ground, "we are far from our families. What would become of the village if attacked in our absence?"

This was a question that went to every heart, and by one consent the party stopped, and many, especially of the older ones, took a step or two involuntarily homewards. The father and young Leper looked at each other in mute despair.

"You are right, Jenkins," said the young man, at length. "It is selfish in us to lead you so far away from home on"—aud here for an instant he choked—"on perhaps a fruitless errand. Go back; we thank you for having come so far. But as for me, my way lies ahead, even if it leads into the very heart of an Indian village."

"And I will follow you!" "And I!" exclaimed a dozen voices; for daring, in moments like these, carried the day against cooler counsels, and the young to a man, sprang to Leper's side. Even the old men were affected by the contagion. They were torn by conflicting emotions, now thinking of their wives and little ones behind, and now reminded of the suffering captives before. They still fluctuated, when one of the young men exclaimed in a low voice—"See! there they are!" and as he spoke he pointed to a thin column of light ascending in the twilight above the tree tops, from the bottom of the valley lying immediately beyond them.

"On them, on," said Jenkins, now the first to move ahead; "but silently, for the slightest noise will ruin our hopes."

Oh, how the father's heart thrilled at these words! The evident belief of his neighbors in the uselessness of further pursuits, had wrung his heart and with Leper he had resolved to go unaided, though meantime he had watched with intense anxiety the proceedings of the councils, for he knew that two men, or even a dozen, would probably be insufficient to rescue the captives. But when his eyes caught the distant light, hope rushed wildly back over his heart. With the next minute he was foremost in the line of pursuers, apparently the coolest and most cautious of all.

With a noiseless tread the borderers proceeded until they were within a few yards of the encamped Indians, whom they discovered through the avenue of trees, as the fire flashed up, when a fresh brand was thrown upon it.— Stealthily creeping forward a few paces further, they discerned the captive girl with her two little brothers and three sisters, bound, a short distance from the group; and at the sight, the fear of the father lest some of his little ones, unable to keep up in the hasty flight, had been tomahawked, gave way to a thrill of indescribable joy. He and Jenkins were now by common consent looked on as the leaders of the party. He paused to count the group.

"Twenty-five in all," he said, in a low whisper. "We can take off a third at least with one fire, and then rush in on them," and he looked to Jenkins who nodded approvingly.

In hurried whispering the plan of attack was regulated, each having an Indian assigned to his rifle. During this brief pause every heart trembled lest the accidental crackling of a twig or a tone spoken unadvisedly above a whisper should attract the attention of the savages. Suddenly, before all was arranged, one of them sprung to his feet, and looked suspiciously in the direction of our little party. At the same instant, another sprung toward the prisoners, and with eyes fixed on the thicket where the pursuers lay, held his tomahawk above the startled girl, as if to strike the instant any demonstrations of hostilities should appear.

The children clung to their sisters, side with stifled cries. The moment was critical; if the proximity of the pursuers was suspected their discovery would be the result. To wait until each man had his victim assigned him, might prove ruinous; to fire prematurely might be equally so. But Leper forgot every consideration in the peril of Mary, and almost at the instant when the occurrences we have related were taking place, took aim at the savage standing over his betrothed, and fired. The Indian fell dead.

Immediately a yell rang through the forest—the savages leaped to their arms, a few dashed into the thicket, others rushed on the prisoners, the most sagacious retreating behind trees. But on that whoop a dozen rifles rang in the air, and half a score of the assailed fell to the earth, while the borderers, breaking from the thicket, with uplifted tomahawks, came to the rescue.— A wild hand-to-hand conflict ensued, in which nothing could be seen except the figures of the combatants, rolling together among the whirling leaves; nothing heard but angry shouts, and the groans of the wounded and dying. In a few minutes the borderers were victorious.

Leper had been the first to enter the field.— Two stout savages dashed at him with swinging tomahawks, but the knife of Leper found the heart of one, and the other fell stunned by a blow from the but end of his father's rifle, who followed his intended son-in-law a step or two behind. A second's delay would have been too late.

Fortunately none of the assailants were killed, though several were seriously wounded.— The suddenness of the attack may account for the comparative immunity which they enjoyed.

How shall we describe the gratitude and joy with which the father kissed his rescued children? How shall we tell the rapture with which Leper clasped his affianced bride to his bosom? We feel our incapacity for the task and drop a veil over emotions too holy for exposure. But many a stout borderer wept at the sight.

Soda Water Factory, Steam Putty, &c.

One of the summer luxuries of large towns and cities, great and little, is Soda Water. Of this the consumption in many places, is inconceivable to those who forget how extensively and frequently, men need, or fancy they need the refreshing influence of cooling draughts,— There are two soda water manufacturers in Cincinnati, where the article is made, and the fountains charged fit for use: My notes refer however only to that of J. S. Glascoe, the more important of the two establishments.

Soda water is made by impregnating water with carbonic acid gas, in the proportion of 5 parts in bulk of one, to twelve of the other, the gas in a fountain of the capacity of 17 gallons, being condensed into a volume of one twelfth its natural space. It is the expansion of that gas when discharged for use, which creates the effervescence in the tumbler, and the pungency of the soda water when drained at a draught.

The following is the process of manufacture. The gas is generated in a strong leaden vessel by the action of diluted sulphuric acid on marble dust—carbonate of lime. It is passed into two gasometers holding 75 gallons each, and thence forced by steam power acting on three air pumps into the fountain, compressing ninety five gallons of carbonic acid gas into the space of seven gallons in the course of three minutes.

A safety valve is in connection with the machine which indicates a pressure of 85 lbs to the square inch in the fountain. I learn that *Mr. Glascoe* fills fountains for Maysville, Covington and Frankfort, Kentucky; Lawrenceburg and Rising Sun, Indiana; and Dayton, Ohio, as well as great numbers in our city. As only one dollar for each filling is charged by him, the old method of filling by hand, equally inconvenient and dangerous, has been generally abandoned. He tells me he filled last year more than 1100 fountains, the number of which he expects will reach this year to 1500.

Mr. Glascoe also manufactures putty by steam power, producing at the rate of four hundred thousand pounds per annum, equal to 8.000 kegs of 50 pounds each. In this process he has been enabled to reduce the price from 12½ to 4 cts. extending his sales in all directions to a distance which controls the markets of the west, the south-west, and the region along the lakes to the north. This is effected by machinery which crushes the whiting, previously dried by hot air, under a huge roller of 1200 lbs., the mass being turned up again under the action of plough sheares, so that no part of it escapes pulverising. The oil being then poured in on the mass, the process of grinding and crushing is renewed and carried on until the entire mass is thoroughly mixed and rendered fit for immediate service.

The whole process is well worth a visit to the manufactory.

Modern Buildings.

The progress of the arts as well as of wealth and cultivated taste, is introducing improvements in house building, of which our predecessors had no conception. We of Cincinnati, cannot of course build houses which shall compare in luxury and extravagance, with some of the palaces in Boston, New York, and Philadelphia. Still, we are erecting houses as fine as any people ought to build, and some equal in substantial and simple elegauce, to those found anywhere. One of the latest of these is that of J. M. Niles, on Eighth, between Walnut and Vine streets. The mouldings, stucco work, &c., of the parlors are very rich, indeed.

In another class of these buildings, such as Messrs. Parkhurst, Probasco, S. S. Smith, on Fourth street, bath houses and other conveniences are introduced to great extent. In Mr. Probasco's the doors are all made in the style of cabinet work, and of our richest and most beautiful native woods. This is the introduction, or rather the revival of a highly ornate feature in architecture. I say revival, the oldest house in this city—Mr. Wade's, on Congress street —being built in this style. All the wood-work except the floors being of black-walnut, a wood whose beauties cannot be duly appreciated until the lapse of time has brought them out to view.

Relics of the Past!

Ft. Hamilton, June 21st, 1792.

Dear General:

Agreeable to the directions contained in your letter of the 11th inst, five of the scythes were sent forward to Major Strong, and with the remaining six I commenced work on Monday, and have already cured five cocks of hay, which in my opinion, is little inferior to timothy. It is so warm on the Prairie that it is cut, cured, and cocked the same day; consequently can lose none of its juices. An additional number of scythes will be necessary, in order to procure the quantity you want. I can find no sand as a substitute for whetstones—perhaps some might be procured among the citizens. One, two or three, if more cannot be had, would be a great relief. The window glass, iron and hemp came forward, but not of the other articles wrote for.

I have allowed the mowers one and a half rations per day, and both them and the hay-makers, half a pint of whiskey each. This I hope will meet your approbation. I have also promised to use my endeavors to procure them extra wages. As the contract price of whiskey is about 16 shillings per gallon, and this extra liquor cannot be considered as part of the ration; would it not be well to furnish it as well as the salt in the Quarter Master Department. I am sure you will conceive that men laboring hard in the hot sun require an extra allowance, and it may be brought here at 15s, cost and carriage. Lt. Hartshorn returned last evening with his command, and will no doubt report to you. He is of opinion there is a camp of Indians not far distant from this, on the west side of the river. I shall employ his cavalry as a covering party to the hay makers, &c., which will make the duty of the infantry lighter—the many objects we have to attend to makes their duty very hard.— The want of camp kettles to cook their meat in is a great inconvenience. Inclosed you have a return for articles we cannot well do without. The want of clothing for the men is also a subject of complaint. I am told there are a number of pairs of linen overalls in store at head quarters. I wish you would think proper to send them here, with some shirts to cover our nakedness. Indeed I should feel much relieved by a visit from you. Permit me here to suggest the necessity of furnishing grass hooks for the horse, and indeed the contractor's men ought to have them also.

The officers of the 2d regiment contend with me for rank, and I believe are about to make a representation to the President on the subject. As I filled Captain Mercer's vacancy, and was myself the bearer of his commission, and being appointed by a different act of Congress, I feel no uneasiness with respect to their claims. But the want of my commission may be some inconvenience. I addressed Gen. Knox on this subject in March last—having received no answer, I fear from the multiplicity of business in your office at that time he overlooked my request, and have therefore to solicit your influence with him for a copy of my commission to support my claims.

Respectfully yours,
JNO. ARMSTRONG,
Capt. Commandant.

GEN. JAS. WILKINSON.

FORT WASHINGTON, July 6th, 1792.

DEAR SIR:

I have only time to tell you that you must forward by the convoy, if it has not reached, the enclosed letter, or if it has, by two of your runners—it being of moment. Keep a good lookout for "poor Jack" or Charley may burn the hay. Adieu.

Yours, &c.

JAS. WILKINSON, B. Gen'l.

N. B. I send a nag for your particular attention. She is my favorite, and is very poor.

J. W.

J. ARMSTRONG, Esq., Capt. Com'dt.

Ferocity of a Bear.

The following remarkable instance of ferocity in a bear is related as having occurred at Bridgeport, Maine, nearly forty years ago. It is seldom that the black bear manifests so much ferocity when met with in the forest of New England. This one, however, was accompanied by her cubs, and her courage and rage were stimulated by the love of her offspring:

"Benjamin Foster, son of Maj. Asahel Foster, of Bridgeton, being on his way through a thicket of woods, was suddenly alarmed by the growling of a bear. He soon discovered an old she bear and two cubs. The old one immediately made towards him, growling, and very fierce. He immediately took to the first tree he could find, which was about nine inches diameter, and about twenty feet to the first limbs; this he ascended with all possible speed, and having reached the limbs, he called to the nearest neighbor, who lived about a quarter of a mile distant, for help. The bear, on hearing his cries, retreated from the tree and hallooed also, which she repeated as often as he called for help.

The bear then returned to the tree and climbed up nearly to the first limbs, but losing her hold she fell to the ground; this enraged her,

and she again ascended the tree with greater velocity, and overtook him at the lenght of about thirty feet, when she seized him one foot, but the shoe coming off she fell to the ground; recovering, she ascended the tree a third time, and took off the other shoe, he constantly calling for help and finding none. He had now ascended the tree as far as was safe for him to venture, the bear constantly tearing his feet with her teeth, until they became a most shocking spectacle.

The bear at length fastened her jaws so powerfully to one of his heels as to cause the limbs by which he held to break, and he fell to the ground, the bear falling at the same time on the other side of the tree; and notwithstanding his feet was in this mangled condition, he escaped to the nearest house and arrived safe. The distance from the ground by measurement, from whence the young man fell, was 48 feet It is supposed that his repeated and eager cries for help tended to increase the rage and fury of the bear, which had her whelps with her.

Governors of the States.

States	Governors.		T'm exp.
Maine,		Hugh J Anderson,	Jan 1846
New Hampshire,		John H Steele,	June 1845
Massachusetts,	*	George N Briggs,	Jan 1846
Rhode Island,	*	James Fenner,	May 1845
Connecticut,	*	Roger S Baldwin,	May 1845
Vermont,	*	William Slade,	Oct 1845
New York,		Silas Wright,	Jan 1847*
New Jersey,	*	Charles C Stratton,	Jan 1848
Pennsylvania,		Francis R Shunk,	Jan 1848
Delaware,	*	Thomas Stockton,	Jan 1849
Maryland,	*	Thomas J Pratt,	Jan 1848
Virginia,		James McDowell,	May 1846
North Carolina,	*	William A Graham,	Jan 1845
South Carolina,		William Aiken,	Dec 1845
Georgia,	*	Geo. W Crawford,	Jan 1847
Alabama,		Benj'n Fitzpatrick,	Dec 1845
Mississippi,		Albert G Brown,	Jan 1846
Louisiana,		Alexander Mouton,	Jan 1847
Ohio,	*	Mordecai Bartley,	Dec 1846
Kentucky,	*	William Owsley,	Sept 1848
Tennessee,	*	James C Jones,	Oct 1847
Indiana,		Thos J Whitcomb,	Dec 1846
Illinois,		Thomas Ford,	Dec 1846
Michigan,		John S Barry,	Jan 1846
Missouri,		John C Edwards,	Nov 1849
Arkansas,		Thomas Drew,	Nov 1848
	TERRITORIES.		
Florida,		John Branch,	Aug 1847
Iowa,		John Chambers,	Mar 1847
Wisconsin,		Henry Dodge,	July 1847

*Whigs 12; Democrats 17.

MARRIAGES.

ON Tuesday, May 8th, by the Rev. D. Shepardson, Mr. JAMES M. SMITH to Miss JANE POINIER.

Thursday, May 22d, by Rev. F. Beecher, Dr FREDERICK H. BANKS of New Orleans, to Miss VIRINDA WIGGINS.

Sunday, 25th inst. by Rev. J. W. HOPKINS, Mr. JOHN CLARKE to Miss SUSAN HAYMON.

DEATHS.

ON Tuesday, 13th inst, HEMSLEY A. son of Andrew M. and Elizabeth Springer—aged 3 years.

Tuesday, 20th inst. SARAH, consort of N. T. Horton.

Wednesday, 21st inst, ALBERT, son of John and Maria Sherer—aged 1 year, 11 months.

Value of Property here.

I am asked sometimes, why I do not publish regularly the sales of real estate as they occur, by way of evidence abroad to capitalists of the increasing value of property in Cincinnati.

To this the reply may be made, that our city dailies keep the community advised of such statistics to better advantage than a weekly publication permits me. There is however a reason more forcible in the case. It is difficult to impress persons resident elsewhere, with the fact that these ordinary sales are any thing else than heated speculations which must burst as bubbles. They cannot understand why money for which it is difficult to obtain 6 per cent in our atlantic cities should produce 10 to 15 per cent invested here in real estate, and they never will, until they become residents here, and observe with their own eyes the elements of our prosperity.

For these reasons, it is occasionally only, that I touch on the subject. Lately I gave prices of property sold at sheriff's sale, feeling that such a feature in its disposal, must remove all distrust as to its true value. And I will now add a remarkable example, strictly authentic, of the perfect safety and great productiveness of judicious purchases in real estate here.

In the year 1839—only six years since, James Wise and Thomas Bateman purchased a block or square of the Betts' property, at $3 33 cents per foot front. In a year or two they made sales of a part successively for 7, 10, 12 and 14 dollars. For the whole of the residue, *they have since refused thirty dollars* per front ft. Just such speculations offer now as formerly, the only difference being that it takes in later days, larger investments to produce the same profits.

Veneers.

This article has been extensively imported from the Atlantic cities heretofore, for our market, both for use and for sale. For the benefit of multitudes who purchase the finer qualities of furniture, ignorant that the outside wood is a *veneer* or facing upon some other, which is either cheaper or stronger, or perhaps both, it may be not impertinent to state that most of what they buy is of this description. In this there is however no deception, they being supplied with an article of furniture equally good, if not better, and much cheaper, than if made solid. The *veneers* brought to this market are Mahogany, Rose, and Zebra, of foreign woods, and Black Walnut and Curled Maple of domestic growth, much the larger share being of the first class. Not less than fifteen to twenty thousand dollars in value of them have been annually sold or used here.

In those revolutions of manufactures which are constantly occurring, Cincinnati is now becoming the head quarters to the west for the supply of this article. Mr. Henry Albro, at the intersection of Symmes street and the Canal, has had in operation, for the last two years, a veneering saw, and is turning out every description of veneering from foreign and domestic woods that may be required. He has already effected a reduction of 25 per cent. in prices and is preparing the way to supply our own and foreign markets with native woods of unrivaled beauty in surface and figure.

There are no finer ornamental woods in the world for furniture, than those of American growth, the black-walnut, cherry and curled maple, for example. Fashion has heretofore patronized those of foreign countries, on the principle which governs thousands, that nothing is valuable but what is "far sought and dearly bought." But fashion, like all despots, has her caprices, and the Rose and Zebra and Mahogany are evidently declining in favor; and as our native growth appears winning its way into use into England and France, and challenges the admiration of foreigners, it will command a preference eventually in the domestic as well as the foreign market.

But our American woods are not only equal to any of Foreign growth, but the various western articles are superior for cabinet ware to the corresponding kinds east of the mountains.— This is no doubt owing to the greater rapidity of growth incident to our more fertile soil and milder climate.

As a specimen of the value of western timber for these purposes, it may be stated that black-walnut forks have been sent from St. Louis to the eastern cities, sawed into veneers, and sent back and sold in that shape for 12½ cents per superficial foot. These veneers are so thin that it takes thirty-two to make an inch in thickness, they being not as thick as pasteboards, and the same log which furnishes boards of a given size, will saw into veneers fifteen fold.— Specimens of black-walnut, plain and curled, sawed here and worked up into chair-backs, cabinet furniture, and piano frames, may be seen at Geyer's, Pfaff's and Ross' chair factories, M'Alpin's cabinet ware rooms, & Britting's piano factory, which cannot be surpassed any where. Mr. Albro has received an order for veneers of select western woods, to send to the Boston market, a portion of which is designed for shipment to London and Liverpool, by way of testing the demand there. Of that demand there can be no doubt, for it will prove not only one of the most elegant materials for use there, but among the cheapest of veneers, the duty under the late Tariff being but 25 shillings per 50 cubic feet—about 25 cts. on 500 veneers of the usual size, a rate which renders the impost merely nominal.

The parts of trees adapted to ornamental purposes are the forks or crotches, curls, warts, and other excrescences, which, valuable as they are for this purpose, are fit for nothing else. As these have heretofore been sawed into boards, in which shape they are not one fifteenth part as productive as in veneers. an inadequate supply only has been furnished by the saw mills. But the increased supply created by their multiplication into veneers, will not only provide for our domestic markets, but furnish an extensive sale abroad in Europe, and our atlantic cities.

The domestic woods, thus far sawed at Albro's are black walnut, curled maple, cherry, sugar tree, oak, ash and apple, which afford when sawed up, an infinite variety of curls, dottings, waves, streaks and other fancy figures, some being of the most graceful and others of the most grotesque appearance. These are furnished at the mill, at a price as low as from three to six cents, per superficial foot, and of first rate specimens. They also saw for the owners of the logs if desired, *and as low as at 125 to 150 cents per 100 feet.* It is easy to conceive the increased demand and use, which this reduction in prices must create. Nor is it less obvious that hereafter the entire veneer supply of the West will be sawed *in the West.* Independently of its own growth of woods, which, wherever it can be done, will be cut up on the spot, the foreign woods from Hayti, Campeachy, Honduras and other places can be imported at as little expense into Cincinnati or any other place in the West, of steamboat access, as into any of the Atlantic cities, The freight from New Orleans, which is the butt end of the expense, is only 18 cents per cwt,, and must become even less as the demand enlarges. Besides, the finest veneers made east, are laid aside on the spot, for the piano and finer descriptions of furniture trade, and our workmen here will not be satisfied with any thing short of a first rate article when within their reach.

Mr. Albro's establishment was built by Mr. Ferdinand Walters, who possessed an equal interest in it. Mr. W. has the reputation of being one of the most ingenious machinists in the United States, and certainly there are many evidences of it on the premises, the machinery being greatly simplified as well as improved; one lever here serving to run the carriage back and forwards, while on most of these saw mills, two, and even three are requisite. Nor must it be

supposed that it requires no more skill or judgment in these than in the ordinary saw-mills, for eight or ten years in attending a veneering saw, is preparation little enough for the employment.

The veneering saw is 4½ feet in diameter, and is driven with such power and velocity as to make 400 revolutions in a minute. It has the capacity to cut two thousand feet per day, but such is the severity of its service that more than half the time is occupied in sharpening it.

Mr. Albro is about to add a chair top and a scroll saw for preparing all sorts of scroll work, and sawing mahogany and other valuable woods into every needed variety of form and shape.

Any intelligent man, who will sit down and reflect a few minutes, on the extent and comparative unproductiveness of our American forests, devoted hitherto merely to furnishing firewood and pearl ash, will discern that it is hardly possible, in a pecuniary sense, to overrate the importance of furnishing countries like England and France, with their supply of ornamental woods.

What the additional advantage of veneering upon our Western timber will prove, may be judged by the fact, that a *single log* of Massanilla mahogany was sold at auction, in New York, not long since, for $502 17 cents, or $1 32 cents per superficial foot.

Relics of the Last War.
Fort Hamilton, Aug. 17th, 1812.

Sir:

Capt. Collins has agreed to meet the detachment at Lebanon as you wished. I promised to them payment of his company about 10 o'clock. He has really one of the finest companies I ever saw; somewhere about 100 strong; they are a fine cheerful set of fellows as can be well placed in exercise—whatever is offered them they are ready and willing to march when and where they are wanted. I expect to be in Cincinnati to-morrow. They have some tents and are preparing more. They expect orders from you for marching.

I am sir respectfully,
Your ob't, servant,
GEO. P. TORRENCE.
Maj. Gen. J. S. Gano.

Marietta, June 24th, 1812.
Maj. Gen. Gano:

Sir—The Secretary at war had authorized me to draw from the Arsenal at Newport fifteen hundred stand of arms—I request you to receive them from Major Martin, together with as many cartouch boxes. Inspect them thoroughly before you receive them. Let them be taken to Cincinnati and safely deposited in some place where they will not be likely to be endangered by fire. They are for the use of Ohio militia.— Please write me whether there are any tents, camp kettles, sabres and pistols &c. &c. in the Arsenal—as I am recently called upon by the Secretary at war to establish a military post at Sandusky.

The expenses of inspection, transportation, &c., you will please to charge the State of Ohio and I will cause payment to be made.

If Maj. Martin will not deliver them subject to inspection, you will receive them in boxes as they are. New arms have lately gone to the Arsenal—if better than the old ones take them—get the best you can.

Address me at Chillicothe.

With esteem and friendship yours,
R. J. MEIGS, of Ohio.

June 30th, 1812, received on this letter fifteen hundred stands of arms without inspection, and four hundred cartridge boxes. Capt. Jenkinson, Capt. Carpenter and Lt. Ramsey, present.

Chillicothe, Aug. 16th, 1812.

GEN. GANO:

You have before this seen Capt. Sutton, from the Army. Muskets and bayonets are preferred in the army to rifles, even against Indians. Many of the muskets want great repairs, and I have not enough for the present requisition. I wish you to send without delay, as many boxes of muskets and cartouch boxes, and tents, and camp kettles as will be enough for 500 men to Urbana. I do not wish in supplying the new requisition, to take the arms &c., which you have for your division, and I enclose an order for what I want. I am putting you to some trouble, but it cannot be helped. Please keep an account of postage, expenses, &c. &c. I will adjust this after the Piqua council is over. I should have spent a few days with you, but the new call prevents me.

I should be pleased to see you at Piqua—if you do not come, write to me there. I am afraid Hull is too slow. The terror the army impressed on its first arrival in Canada, is greatly diminished.

One waggon will carry all the arms &c. which I require.

I am sir,
Your ob't. serv't.
R. J. MEIGS.

URBANA, Aug. 25th, 1812.

Gen. GANO.

Or the commandant of the militia of Ohio in the town of Cincinnati:

SIR:

You will without any delay, send by a two horse light wagon, the six-pounder piece of artillery at Cincinnati to this place by day and night.

You will also send me one large and full wagon load of six-pounder balls, and powder, for which purpose I send an order on the United States Military Storekeeper at Newport.

Your ob't. serv't.
R. J. MEIGS,
Gov. of Ohio.

300 balls and 500 lbs. powder sent on the within to Urbana.

Pioneer Libraries.

The records of the past in the great west are always interesting waymarks of its progress.— Beyond this, they frequently serve to shew our obligations to the noble race of men who have subdued it for our use.

I trust my readers will find the following notices of the first Library formed in Athens county in our State, and its happy results, as interesting as it appears to me. I condense it from the proceedings of the Washington county school association, published in the Marietta Intelligencer of the 22d ult. A discussion arising in that body on the establishment of libraries in each township of the county, Judge Cutler made the following statement.

"A settlement was commenced in Athens County about the year 1799 in the midst of a broad wilderness. But few families commenced it, and they were twenty miles removed from all intercourse with the settlement in this county. They were alone. They were at first only three families. In a little time another settlement was formed on Sunday creek. One settler, Squire True, came to the Eastern settlement to consult about making a road from one settlement to the other. All collected; and some one after describing their solitary condition, and stating that there was but one newspaper taken, coming only once in two months, and but very few books, suggested the plan of procuring a library. All were agreed. The next question was, how shall we get it? We have no money. Esq. Brown was at that time on a visit, preparing to move to Sunday creek. Esq. True said that he could show them how a library could be obtained. They could do it by catching *Coons*, if Esq. Brown would agree to take and sell them and lay out the money for books.— The plan was resolved on; the coons were abundant; the boys could catch 8 or 10 apiece. The skins were taken to Boston and sold for fifty dollars. Two eminent men were asked to select the books. Their choice was excellent. And now for the history of that library, It was increased. The settlement increased; the children increased. All had access to that library,

Some fifty young men, now scattered about over the West, gained information from that library. Some are distinguished lawyers, some wealthy merchants, some professors in colleges, some Judges of court, and one became *Thomas Ewing*. Another settlement, containing about the same number of young men, without these advantages, presented in the result a very different aspect. Only a ridge separated the two settlements. Of the latter only a few rose even to mediocrity of circumstances. Their history has been stained by crime. Murder and robbery have been committed among them. Of late the library has been divided between the settlements on Federal creek and Sunday creek. The Federal creek division contains about 400. From the commencement, the library has been a good one. There has also been a library at Belpre, called the Putnam Library, which afforded vast benefit to the young men of Belpre, and as a consequence, a most respectable settlement has been built up there. We should commence with the mind while it is tender. Children, if not engaged in something beneficial, will be in mischief. There should be a good foundation laid in season.

Mr. Wm. P. Cutler gave his experience and recollections, which were that books were exceedingly uninteresting to him, until he drew a book from the coon-skin library, which gave him a taste for reading. Sabbath School books carry forward children in the work of education, and sometimes quite as much as the instruction of the day school. Was of the opinion that diffusing libraries was a cheaper as well as more efficient mode of educating those who had once learned to read, than schools. On this point he gave facts and statistics for which I have not space in my columns.

Judge Cutler resumed.—In 1800 a family from Vermont came into this State very poor. The father was intemperate, but industrious. He was a shareholder in the coon-skin library. The family never had any opportunities for education, but the boys were excellent at catching coons, and caught a fine parcel, took a share in the library and got books. One boy was found to possess a mathematical mind superior to almost any in this country. He went to Athens and proved himself very remarkable as a mathematical scholar. He is now dead. He left a property estimated at $500,000, and a high character. The young persons who drew from that coon-skin library, acquired millions which they probably would not have obtained without the instruction derived therefrom.

Mr. Slocumb, a teacher testifies as follows.—His opportunities for instruction were very limited. At 15 or 16 could write his name and read, when the tall words did not happen too often.—For a few months in the winter season we had such schools as we could get. Was accustomed to see boys go on the ice to skate; got him a pair, put them on and started off. His feet outstripped his head which fell on the ice.—Before getting up, he pulled off his skates—and that was his last skating. Resolved to employ his evenings in reading. The first book happened to be very interesting. After labor done in the day time he spent his evenings and early mornings in reading. Whatever proficiency he had made in teaching was the effect of that fall on the ice. When teaching school in Harmar, two lads come under his instruction about the same time, with equal capacities. One boy was allowed to run abroad on the Sabbath; the other was kept. Many years after, within five days, the first was hanged, and the second, ordained as a Presbyterian preacher. The latter having his Sabbaths to spend at home, acquired a taste for reading. The latter when in school was the more mischievous of the two.

Cake and Candy Factories.

One of the wonders suggested by many descriptions of our city business is, how can most of these persons pay such extravagant rents as they do out of such *picayune* operations as they appear to carry on? This difficulty has presented itself to me frequently, as I suppose it has also to others. Taking the census of 1840, and many of my statistical examinations since, have set me right on this score, and made it apparent that individuals were piling away three, five and even ten thousand dollars per annum, out of a business which did not appear to me likely to pay expenses.

One of these businesses thus underrated by me was that of cake and candy manufacturing.—I supposed in the eight or ten establishments of this sort, there might be perhaps as many thousand dollars worth of products sold. On this it must be obvious, nothing more in the shape of profit could be made than to support the families of those engaged in them. Yet many of them paid high rents, and had other expenses to meet.

When I took the census, I found that there were twelve persons engaged in this business, and the yearly value made by themselves and hands amounted to 54,000 dollars. The value produced at this time in the general preduction of prices, is but 40,000 dollars, and the quantity made, & nett profits are about the same as five years since. 24 hands are employed as assistants.

I take the case of Mr. E. HARWOOD on Fift street to illustrate this business. His differs from the rest in this respect, that while individuals produce more than he does in particular branches of Confectionary and fancy baking, he manufactures a more general assortment than any of the others. Besides the almost infinite variety of cakes and candies usually made, he makes lozenges of every description, Jujube paste of various flavors; wedding cake ornaments, and fancy work of all sorts.

One interesting feature of this business is the supply of wedding cake &c. for wedding occasions. These are furnished to an extent of which I was not aware. One bill, the highest supplied this season amounting to as much as one hundred and sixty-three dollars. Another, one of our longest established cabinet makers ordered to the value of one hundred, as did one of our *arbiters of fashion* in a different line, to the same value. It is well that these expenses are not ordinarily incurred oftener than once in a lifetime, a few such drafts on his purse, sufficing to strip a man of ordinary resources.

I have the testimony of eastern men, that they have nothing in New York, Boston, or Philadelphia, to surpass in taste, elegance or quality, the finer specimens supplied wedding parties by either Harwood or Burnett.

Strawberry Statistics.

This is almost the only article which, between the action of drought and cold weather, has not failed in our market supplies this spring.

It has been repeatedly stated that 4000 quarts per day are sold during the season of strawberries in our markets. As I have understood, this is considered abroad incredible. I examined the strawberry stands at Lower Market street last Saturday, and found one hundred and sixteen cases, averaging thirty-five boxes of one quart each to the case, being a total of four thousand and sixty quarts. The quantity offered at Canal Market, and at various stands through the city, would easily increase the aggregate to 5000 quarts. These are sold at present from 5 to 6 cents per quart, according to quality, the price of the article averaging 8 cts. throughout their entire period of sale.

A four-horse waggon drove up on Friday last to Fifth street market with *two tons strawberries!* Most of this delicious fruit is cultivated in adjacent Kentucky, where patches of from five to ten acres are frequent. Two of the Strawberry gardens are eighteen and twenty acres, and one of them reaches to thirty acres in extent, there being at least one hundred and forty acres devoted to the culture of this article.

Poisons and their Antidotes.

I notice in one of my exchanges a case of loss of life, by a mistake of Sal petre for Epsom Salts. The following table serves to show what abundant means are supplied as antidotes to poison in mistakes of the sort. It is indeed remarkable how many of them may be handed from the tables or cupboards of almost every family in the land. It seems providential, that remedies so simple, and at the same time so readily obtained at the instant of need should be found almost every where, Pearlash, vinegar, sweet oil, green tea, whites of eggs, sugar, milk, molasses, tobacco, chalk, lime, and salt, constituting the great mass.

POISONS.	TREATMENT.
ACIDS: *Vitriol, Aqua Fortis,*	Potash or Pearlash, dissolved in water: or magnesia; copious draughts of warm water or flax seed tea.
ALKALIES. *Potash, Soda, &c.*	Vinegar,—large quantities of Sweet Oil.
ANTIMONY:— *Tartar Emetic.*	Strong decoction of green tea, or of Peruvian bark, or red oak bark. Abundance of warm water, or flax seed tea to promote vomiting.
ARSENIC.	Hydrated per-oxide of Iron; otherwise thirty grains white Vitriol, as emetic; great quantities white of eggs with milk, tobacco smoked largely in a pipe. Solution of Epsom Salts, or of Glauber Salts.
COPPER: *Blue Vitriol.*	Brown Sugar; white of egg with milk; molasses.
LAUDANUM:	Stomach pump: otherwise 30 grains white vitriol; promote vomiting.
SUGAR OF LEAD.	Epsom or Glauber Salts; otherwise thirty grains white vitriol.
MERCURY: *Corrosive Sublimate.*	Very large quantities of white of eggs, or Flour mixed with water and milk.
SAL PETRE.	Produce vomiting with large draughts of warm water and Flax seed tea.
ESSENTIAL SALT OF LEMONS.	Chalk and water, or lime in water. No drinks to produce vomiting; mind this last.
LUNAR CAUSTIC.	Strong salt and water in large quantities; much flax-seed tea, or milk and water.
WHITE VITRIOL.	Large quantities of milk ;

white of eggs; warm drinks.

HEMLOCK, STRAMONIUM, &c. 30 grains white vitriol as emetic; use stomach pump; after these, coffee, lemonade or vinegar and water.

The dose of white vitriol named is for an adult. The stomach pump must be used by a physician.

Send for a physician instantly; in the meantime use the remedies directed as they may be accessible. Use them most promptly.

Hamilton and Burr.

Our thanks are due, and cordially tendered to the correspondent from whom we derive the subjoined interesting communication: "I send you," he writes, "an original anecdote of Gen. Hamilton and Colonel Burr, which you may rely upon as authentic. It was related to a party of gentlemen, of whom I was one, by the late Judge Rowan, of Kentucky, in his life time at different periods, a distinguished member of both houses of Congress, from that state; and celebrated in the western country as the first criminal lawyer of his day—not even excepting Mr. Clay himself. At the time of the relation, in the winter of 1840, he had passed his eightieth year, but he had retained his eminent colloquial faculties unimpaired; and he told the story with an emphasis and manner peculiarly his own. He remarked that he retained in his memory the exact words of the parties, and that he was the only living recipient of them. But four persons, up to that moment, had ever had cognizance of the circumstance; these were, General Hamilton, Colonel Burr, their mutual friend General D****, and himself. He had his information from General D****, and he was pledged to secrecy during his life time. The injunction of secrecy was now removed, by the recent death of his friend, and he felt at liberty to speak. He had been silent for forty years; he was a young man when he heard the anecdote; he was an old man now, when proposing to relate it for the first time, "Gentlemen," said he "this one circumstance filled up, in my mind, the outlines of the character of these two celebrated men; I want no other history of them. You may write ponderous tomes, eulogistic of the one and denunciatory of the other; but I have a fact in my head, and it is the centre of my opinion. Colonel Burr, when arraigned for his trial, did me the very great honor to invite me to become his counsel and advocate, but I remembered the fact, and refused.

"It was at that period in our history when the Confederation, having cast off the iron hoop of war, seemed to have no other bond of strength. Men's minds were unsettled; there was no gravitation of principle; no unity of purpose; no centre of motion. Patriotism had expended its enthusiasm; liberty had lost its vitality, and forbearance its subordination. Burr believed that the staggering elements would fall in confusion, writhe for a season in anarchy, and emerge in monarchy. He believed that the fermentation, if allowed to take its course, would froth and effervesce, and rectify, by crystalizing the desire to put Washington on the throne. He thought however, that there was a shorter way to 'stability' by intrigue; by the conjunction of adverse influences; a way less sinuous to his own advancement. He believed that there was no man without his price, while his acute discernment told him that Hamilton's was a character which even his own partizans would turn to in despair, and prefer it to his, in testing an experiment or trying a theory. He had a proposition to make to General Hamilton; it was patriotic or it was traitorous; it was full of meaning, overreaching the words, balancing the ambiguity nicely, but searching enough to find the weakness, had it existed. He knew he would be understood without being committed; answered without being betrayed. There was treason in it; but it was in the occasion, the manner, the words, if you please, and yet it was no where, if he chose to disclaim it! He had a proposition to make, but he would not write it down! Mark the man: he could not be prevailed on to put it upon paper. He gave his friend the words, and the emphasis, & made him repeat both, until they told right to his own ear. These were the exact terms:

"'Colonel Burr presents his compliments to General Hamilton: Will General H. seize the present opportunity to give a *stable* government to his country, and *provide for his friends?*'

"'General Hamilton did not hesitate a moment: this was his answer:—

"'General Hamilton presents in return, his compliments to Colonel Burr: Colonel B. thinks General H. ambitious: he is right; General H. is one of the most ambitious of men, but his *whole* ambition is to deserve well of his country.'

"There is an answer," continued the narrator, "which would have deified a Roman; there is the *first* of the offences which he expiated at Weehawken.

CORRESPONDENCE.

One of the Cincinnati Pioneers.

Butler Co., State of Ohio, May 31, 1845.

MR. CHARLES CIST:

Dear Sir—In your paper of the 7th inst. I see a list of the names of the early pioneers of the city of Cincinnati—among them I see four as far back as 1790; that is John Riddle, James Ferguson, Mrs. Wallace and Mrs. Gano. When I was about 17 years of age Mr. James Burnes and myself from Washington co., Pennsylvania, landed at Cincinnati, between the 1st and 10th of April, 1789. We continued there until the second week in June. Mr. Burnes purchased one in and out lot—he cleared one acre of ground, and planted it in corn and moved there the next spring. There was but four families there when we landed. Mr. McHenry had a large family, two sons and two daughters, young men and young women. I expect some of them live in Hamilton county. They lived a number of years where the Hamilton road crossed Mill creek, perhaps 4 or 5 miles from the city. A Mr. Kennedy had a small family. A Mr. Dement had a small family. A Mr. Ross had a small family. Mr. McMillin, John Vance, David Logan, Mr. Reeves, Hardesty, Van Eaton, and McConnell, all lived in one shanty, being perhaps the first that was ever put up in the place, as nearly all of them had been out with the surveyors, surveying Symmes' purchase, and were there when the town was laid out, and all had lots in it. I returned then as a volunteer in September 1790 on Harmar's campaign. Harmar's army marched from there the last week in September for the Indian towns, near where Fort Wayne was afterwards built. I served through that campaign, returned with the troops to Cincinnati, and tarried there that winter, and until December, 1791. I was a volunteer in St. Clair's defeat on the 4th of November 1791. That winter after Harmar's campaign that I was at Cincinnati, I recollect Mr. Riddle was there—Mr. Ferguson I think was there—if it is the same, he married a Miss Reeder—Mrs. Wallace was there—her maiden name was Sayre—Col. Wallace and she were married in 92 or 93. I do not recollect any of the name of Gano—there are of that name who lived at Columbia.

I expect if live to be in the city in the course of a month, when I expect to give you a call.

THOMAS IRWIN.

Professional Ideas and Feelings.

It is inconceivable how thoroughly habit imbues men with a professional spirit. A few instances will suffice to establish this point.

Brindley, the celebrated Engineer, on an examination before the House of Commons, made a remark which implied his very low estimate of river navigation. A member of the committee which was taking his testimony became quite restive, and at last exclaimed. Mr. Brindley, for what purpose do you suppose rivers were made? *To feed canals*, was the characteristic reply.

An auctioneer in New Orleans, had five children which he named *Ibid. Ditto, A lot, One More and The Last*. The man was obviously insensible of the ridiculous character of such patronymics, and decided on them with the same motive, that he would strike off an invoice of goods under the hammer, the whole choice springing from business association of ideas.

An instance of professional feeling of a different kind is the following.

A brave veteran officer during the war of 1812 reconnoitering a battery considered impregnable and which it was necessary to storm, answered the engineers who were dissuading him from the attempt: "Gentlemen, you may think what you please; all I know is that the American flag must be hoisted on the ramparts to-morrow morning, *for I have the orders in my pocket.*" In this case the simple feeling uppermost was "I must obey orders." It never seemed to enter his mind that the attempt might prove impracticable.

Here is one case *sui generis.*

Favart, a French author wrote to a friend in London: "Buffon, the great naturalist, has just lost his wife. He would be inconsolable at the event were it not for the pleasure he anticipates in dissecting her.

Horne Tooke, on his death bed, was asked by one of his friends. How do you do. Do! said the grammarian, tortured probably more by the bad English than by his own pains, I don't *do* at all—I *suffer.*

Some of my readers have seen a grammar of the Latin language, by James Ross, of Philadelphia. Never was a man more wrapt up in his studies than Ross. A man who did not understand Greek or Latin, and that critically, was in his eyes, of no use in society. Business called him once to Harrisburg, and to occupy a few minutes while waiting for the individual he came to see, he strolled into the court house. A murder case was before the jury, the evidence was all through, and the prosecuting attorney had closed his speech, in which he had happened to observe that such and such was the general rule of law on a particular point then in issue. The counsel for prisoner adverting to this remark admitted the rule, but added, It is well known there is no general rule without an exception.—This was too much for Ross. He had stood unmoved, the most pathetic appeals to public sympathy, but that a proposition like this should be asserted in open court was absolutely shocking. "Begging the counsel's pardon," said he "that is not true, all Greek nouns ending in, *os* are of the masculine gender. There is one universal rule and admits of no exception." The surprise of the court, and the irrepressible laughter of the auditory may be more readily imagined than described.

Perhaps the most striking example of the kind, is an anecdote recorded of an Oxfordshire jailor, who accosted a prisoner condemned to the gallows, thus—my good friend I have a little favor to ask, which, from your obliging disposition, I think you will hardly refuse. You are ordered for execution on Friday a week. I have a particular engagement on that day; if it makes no difference to you, suppose we say next Friday instead!!!

Things in England.

In the Davenport Gazette of the 5th ult., I observe an interesting letter to the editor from his brother, *J. Milton Sanders*, now in Europe on the "*Magnetic Light*" business. It is too long to transcribe for my columns. I subjoin however, one or two brief extracts which will interest us of Cincinnati. His own observations of the destitutions and sufferings of the poor in England, are not at all in accordance with the notions on that subject, in the United States.

"What strikes an American upon visiting this country, is the solidity with which every thing is built. The English appear to have long ago tried all our present experiments, and, like wise men, they have ascertained that the only cheap way to build a thing is to spare no expense, but to construct it from the solid iron or marble, and in a manner that ages may make no impression upon it. We are paving our streets with small stones, or else trying experiments with other materials. The streets here are composed of huge blocks of marble sunk in the ground. Every street is like a floor, and every pavement like Platt Evens', only instead of free stone, they here have granite or marble. The docks are built to last for centuries, as also the Assizes Court, a building partly finished, and which when completed, will be one of the most magnificent structures in the world. It was begun in 1838, and will require at least half a dozen years more labor to finish it. Our buildings, however, magnificent or vast, must be driven forward with lightning rapidity, even if they do totter in a dozen years, but there they take things more coolly—they have worn off their youthful ardor, and like a full grown man, they build—not for present comfort and gratification alone, but for the present and future also. Every thing here that you look at is *solid*. Marble seems used altogether for purposes where we use wood, and where we constantly employ the carpenter, the English employ the iron founder or the stone-cutter.

· So far as I have seen and read since I have been here, *I* am inclined to think that the accounts we get of the starvation and misery of the poor, is altogether exaggerated. The population here is more dense than in our country, therefore we must look for more poor people, and consequently more destitution. But, thus far, I have seen but three or four children—and no grown persons—barefooted, and none dressed worse than you will find them in New York.— The poor here mostly wear rough shoes with thick wooded soles, and are dressed in corderoy, or some fabric similar to it. I scarcely or never take up a newspaper but I see some article relative to assisting the poor, and speaking of their destitution, of the cold weather, and of the necessity of doing something for their relief. There are twenty-seven benevolent societies and institutions in this city, and I understand that they do a vast amount of good.

There is a marked difference between our poor people and those here, in respect to education. Here the poor are very ignorant, while ours can, with few exceptions, read and write.

There is considerable difference between the English and American in appearance as in every thing else. The English all look alike. They have fair skin, flush faces, and the same cast of features; and with some exceptions, they do not appear naturally to possess the mental vigor of our countrymen. This may be a mistaken idea, but still I gained it by what I conceive to be close observation. So far as I have seen, the English are also a polite, obliging people. They treat you with attention, are gentlemanly in their address, and prove that they are an enlightened people.

I have seen more drunkenness here than I would see at home in a month; and who could anticipate any thing else when you encounter a "Gin Palace" at every turn of a corner? Here they drink the liquor pure, not mix it into 'Ju-leps,' 'Cocktails,' 'Slings,' etc. as we do; still with all of this, the more I see of the English, the more I am convinced of the distorted caricatures Charles Dickens has drawn, and which pass with us for genuine and highly wrought sketches. Dickens' sketches of us are equally truthful as those drawn by his own people, and therefore you may judge how well he paints.

The First Lion.

A writer in the N. Y. Commercial gives the following account of the first lion introduced into the U. States:

"The first lion that appeared in this country made his *début* in the year 1798. He came to New York in a French Brig belonging to the Island of Gaudaloupe, which had made a voyage to Africa for slaves, and, having landed them at Charleston, South Carolina, proceeded to New York to obtain an outward cargo of calicoes, beads, New England rum and tobacco, for the Congo market.

"The lion was a small young whelp, not more than six months old, and was brought as a pet by the commander of the French slaver.. While the brig was in New York, the lion became troublesome and mischievous, and the Frenchman, weary of him, sold him to a man who was a servant in a hotel situated where the old Tontine now stands. This man, whose name *I* think was Gold, paid ten dollars for the whelp, took him home and caged him till he was a year old, when he commenced exhibiting him. A lion in that lionless age, was a downright wonder, and every body was anxious to say, 'I have absolutely seen a sartin live lion.'

"Mr. Gold, the owner of the animal, without the aid of the puffs of the press, soon became a lion himself, in consequence of his association; and the two lions were objects of universal curiosity. Mr. Gold was not unapprised of the fact, and made the most of it.

To obtain admittance to the lions, the curious had to pay *one dollar*, and that fee was deemed dog cheap by the admirers of the wonders of animated nature. Mr. Gold remained proprietor of the 'only lion there was in the U. States' till the year 1820, when he sold out for the sum of one thousand dollars, and with deep regret parted with the author of his fortune and his fame, his majesty the king of the beasts.

"I met this Mr. Gold in the year 1832, and these facts from his mouth. He was then an old man, possessed of a large fortune, all of which came through the lion; and he told me that before he sold the animal, he had produced him upward of thirty thousand dollars. He never exhibited him for less than one dollar 'the sight.'

"Those were old and happy days; the men of that era about which Mr. Thomas Ritchie likes to talk, when Mr. Jefferson wore red plush breeches, and old John Adams and Timothy Pickering insisted that every man of taste and fashion should wear a cocked hat and periwig. But—

Old times have changed; old manners gone— A stranger fills the Stuarts' throne.

"And now you can see a whole army of lions, tigers, leopards, zebras, elephants, rhinoceroses, and one-third of the whole animal world, by paying the very small sum of twenty-five cents."

Cincinnati in 1876.

The following article was written for the carrier of the "Advertiser" for last New Years day, and was designed, as appears on its face, to furnish a picture of Cincinnati, so far as it is sketched, thirty years hence. Some of the anticipations may appear extravagant, but the reality when that period shall arrive, will be found in advance of present conjecture. In one respect, what was fancy six months since, is now reality. I allude to Texas forming a part of our republic. And I am induced to publish these speculations now, in the fear, that if I put them aside for any length of time, what is now prophecy will probably lose its interest by becoming history.

I have no doubt that in less than thirty years, the hourly issues of newspapers referred to here, will supercede the immense sheets which now constitute some of our most important dailies.

THE CINCINNATI ROCKET.

JANUARY 1st, 1876, 10 o'clock issue.

The New Custom House.

We learn on undoubted authority, that the commissioners appointed for that purpose by the President, have selected as a scite for the new Custom House, that desirable location now occupied by the row of dry good stores stretching from Tate Willoughby & Co. to Norton, Brothers & Co., embracing a front of 150 feet on Pearl street, and nearly central to the block from Walnut to Vine street. As this lot has been purchased through to Third street, there will be ample space for the splendid edifice, with its appropriate offices for the various deputies connected with the department, which the already heavy and rapidly increasing importations to this port require. We learn that Mr. J. Longworth, the owner of the premises is to receive 750,000 dollars for the property. We consider that sum not much more than the value of the mere ground, and allows him hardly any thing for the substantial warehouses erected not more than fifteen years ago, leaving nothing for the Third street improvements, which in truth ought to have been pulled down twenty years since.

Our City Hall.

The city hall is now rapidly advancing to completion, and will when finished, form one of the most magnificent structures in our magnificent city. Its transcendant elevation, which will enable it to overtop even the new Custom house, about to be built just south of it, must display its glories, and render it an object of admiration to the thousands upon thousands who pass every week up and down the beautiful riv-

er which washes our proud city's feet. We understand that it will be ready for occupation on the 15th inst., just six weeks from the period when the foundation stone was laid. We defy any city in our widespread republic, to surpass this specimen of industry and activity, as we also challenge its equal in elegance of design, and symmetry of proportions. Some of our older citizens whose recollections go back far enough, remember it as a place of public amusement in 1845, under the name of Shires' gardens.

Members of Congress.

On the steamboat Texas just landed at our wharves from Galveston, came passengers, the Hons. Wm. Burnet, and J. L. Williams, Senators elect from Brazoria, the State lately added to one great National Confederacy and forming its sixty fifth Star. Mr. B. is a son of the late D. S. Burnet in the early days of Texas its Vice President. Col. Williams is an emigrant from Arkansas, who has however been a citizen of that State for twenty-five years. They will go in the 12 o'clock cars to Washington, which will enable them to see a delightful country for the first time, and also to reach that city by day-light.

The Philadelphia Fire.

The 9 o'clock cars from Philadelphia of this morning, bring no further particulars of the calamitous fire which has desolated that fair and flourishing city. We are promised all the details by our correspondent there, which will doubtless reach us by the 12 o'clock line, and we shall lay them before our readers in the 10 o'clock issue of to day, The train this morning reached the depot in the unprecedented period of four hours and fifty minutes, being at least twenty minutes shorter passage than ever known before. The past generation thought, when they had carried steam on rail roads to sixty miles an hour, the *Ultima Thule* of progress had been reached; what would they have thought of being swept forward at the rate of one hundred and twenty miles per hour by atmospheric pressure? We do not despair, in view of the late important discoveries in chemistry, which we announced in our 8 o'clock issue, of a speed of 200 or even 250 miles per hour, being brought within reach of our enterprising citizens. We recommend Locke's line as affording the best accommodations to persons travelling this route.

Main Street Grade.

We have received a communication signed *Publius*, denouncing the project on foot in the City Councils, for making a new and strait grade from the corner of Main and Front, to strike the present grade at Jackson place, formerly Court square, the old City Court House, once occupying the West end of that square. We are obliged to decline publishing the article, our restricted limits precluding it.

Centennial Anniversary of Independence.

Throughout the whole length and breadth of the land, but one spirit appears to animate the American people in reference to the approaching Centenary of our National Independence, which occurs on the 4th July of the present year. There is no doubt, judging by the general interest the subject has already elicited, that the festivities and spectacles of every description that are arranging for that day, will be on a scale worthy of the greatest empire in the world. We know of nothing determined here, as a part of the exercises or exhibitions for that occasion, except that the directors of our Academy of Fine Arts, have resolved to throw open the doors of its great rotunda to the public, on that day, free of expense. We can conceive of nothing more appropriate. No American can contemplate the sublime works of Powers, or the series of our early Presidents and Statesmen from the pencil of Kellogg, with other works of other Cincinnati artists without a thrill of rejoicing in the glories of the land which gave him birth.

An Old Pioneer.

On Christmas last, we started down to pay our respects to Jonah Martin Esq., the patriarch of our city, and the last survivor of the pioneers. Mr. M. is now in his eighty-seventh year, and in the possession of better health than he has had for many years. He is a noble relic of the past. It is wonderful to think of a man in the enjoyment of an existence which may last for a dozen years yet, and lost as it were among the 675,000 inhabitants of our populous city whose recollections go back to the period of 1795, when he personally knew every man, woman and child which then made up its inhabitants, then numbering only 500 persons. We understand he attributes his vigorous health, to the early abstinence from spirituous liquors, which characterised his habits at the period in the early part of the present century, when it was the fashion for almost every one to sacrifice on the altars of Bacchus.

Street Paving.

One of the great improvements of the age, we regard Stevens' system of paving streets.— A specimen of this may be found on Fourth st.,

extending from Main to Sycamore. It consists of a chemical preparation, which in its fluid state, passes over and through a layer of six or eight inches deep of tan bark or sawdust, and hardens to a degree which keeps the whole pavement perfectly elastic, while the surface is smooth enough to pass the water during and after rains immediately into the gutters. Nothing can be more delightful than the noiseless revolution of carriage wheels over such surfaces. It is like rolling over an unbroken sward, or rather over carpeting. Mr. S. deserves the thanks of the community he has delivered from the nuisance of noise, filth. jolting and dust, to which we have been for years subjected under the old system of paving our streets.

Course of Trade.

Our rail road reporter has registered yesterday by the Transportation Car line to Boston, via. the Lakes, two hundred and fifty bales 4-4 cotton sheeting, as a consignment to the Boston market. At the value there—seven cents, they will bear transportation, and nett a fair profit to the forwarders, Messrs. Sprague and Adams of the Globe mills of this city. We learn that it is the calculation of these gentlemen to enlarge their operations the ensuing spring, so as to embrace the manufacture of fancy prints for the Eastern markets, which we have already three or four factories engaged in making, who expect to find a market for their surplus articles in the Chinese and India markets, now thrown open the commerce of all nations.

Early Bridges over Mill and Deer Creeks.

At the commencement of the present century, there was a floating bridge across Mill creek at its mouth, and a ferry kept along side, which became the dependence for crossing when the high waters rendered the bridge useless. They were both in charge of a man named White, who probably owned the ferry. Between the two he carried on quite a profitable business.— In the spring of 1807 or 8, a rise in the Ohio unmoored one of Jefferson's gunboats, which was built at the mouth of Crawfish creek, just above Fulton, and had been fastened by a grape vine cable, my friend Salisbury not having then opened his assortment of Manilla rope. As she floated by the then village of Cincinnati, every canoe here was put in requisition, and with some difficulty the vessel was towed into Mill Creek, and secured beneath the bridge already referred to. The river continuing to rise, Mill Creek was backed up, as it has since been, several miles, with the effect to use the boat as a lever to lift the bridge from its moorings, the string pieces and all above giving way, and likely to float off in detached parts. To prevent this as far as possible, White stripped the bridge of its plank, when away went the craft, and with it a considerable portion of the bridge timbers. — These plank afterwards formed the floor of the first warehouse built in Cincinnati.

At that period, the only bridge across Deer Creek, was one with a descent at each end, less than one-fourth in height compared with those now built over it, and built of a single string piece from bank to bank. This was protected from freshets by piling loads of stone on the edges, for thirty feet or more each way from the banks. The ravine in 1800 was not more than 12 feet across, and overhung with evergreen and water willows.

At a later date, that is to say, during the great flood of 1832, the bridge over Mill Creek was raised as in 1807, by the pressure of the waters, but being substantially built, floated off entire, keeping company down the Ohio, with a Methodist meeting house which was carried out of the Muskingum. The bridge lodged at the head of an Island, 6 miles above Louisville, and was soon after brought up to reoccupy its original position. This was effected, after a vain effort to tow it back entire by steamboat, by taking it to pieces and loading it into a flatboat. This was the bridge destroyed by fire at a later date.

Relics of the Past.

Capt. Jno. Armstrong to Gen. Jas. Wilkinson.

DEAR GENERAL:

I feel myself in some measure relieved from the visit you have paid this post. As the important duties imposed on my command, have come within your own observation, any remarks with respect to my apprehensions from the enemy become unnecessary. Every force you may please to put under my command, shall be employed to the utmost advantage, my abilities and exertions may be adequate to.

Securing the hay appears to be an object of great attention, perhaps one or more public teams may be had at head quarters—the use of them here would effect your wish. Fifty pairs of shoes, if more cannot be spared, would be a great relief. Ten cartridge and ten bayonet belts also would enable me to parade my company in uniform. To serve me in this instance I well know would give you pleasure. I well know they are in store, but perhaps claimed by some officers who have not men to wear them. Ten men will complete my company, perhaps you may think proper to increase my command by sending them forward. The whipsaw I have received is not calculated for my wants—perhaps a better one might be procured. The

scythes are subject to be broken, and some of them being good for naught, more may be thought necessary. The whipsaw, file, and whetstones as soon as they can be had, will serve to forward the business you have ordered.

Two or more non-commissioned officers would add to the safety of my small parties.

Yours with respect,
JOHN ARMSTRONG.
July 1st, 1792.

FT. HAMILTON, July 8th, 1792, half past 12 o'clock, P. M.

DEAR SIR:

Your letter by express was this moment handed me—I am truly sorry for the misfortune of Col. Spencer's family, and much obliged to you for the early information and advice. The convoy moved this morning, at which time the spies were detached in the direction mentioned in my letter of yesterday. If they discover no fresh tracks they will not return. Be assured every exertion on my part will be made, not only to save my men, but to procure as much hay as possible. The weather for some days past has been unfavorable to our hay parties. The horse will be detached for you the moment Capt. Peters arrives.

Yours with due respect,
JNO. ARMSTRONG.
Gen. JAMES WILKINSON.

Gen. James Wilkinson to Capt. Jno. Armstrong

FORT WASHINGTON, July 10th, 1792.

DEAR SIR:

I send you by Capt. Peters ten gallons port wine, and 5 galls. brandy which please accept.

The waggons are hired at 20s. per day and found—you know how to get the penny worth out of them—drive late and early, and make short halts—at the same time keep your scythes steadily at work. We shall soon complete the 300 tons, and the sooner the safer and better.— I wish you to send me an escort of 20 horse on Friday, that I may join you.

Last night I received an express from Maj. Gen. Wayne, the purport solely to prohibit offensive operations, on our part. This express costs the public 100 dollars, for what? The shoes and belts are sent to you. Mr. Miller is to do duty whilst he continues with you.

In haste, I am yours &c.
JAS. WILKINSON, B. Gen'l.
J. ARMSTRONG, Esq., Capt. Com'dt.

FT. HAMILTON, July 14, 1792, 8 o'clock P.M.

DEAR GENERAL:

Your letter of this morning by Serj't. Armstrong came duly to hand. I send you the two men mentioned therein, as also a letter to

Col. Johnston on private business, which I will ask you to forward by your express. My hay and bullocks are safe, and I conceive much more exposed when grazing than in the pen.— Capt. Peters' company will on to-morrow encamp on the parade, as well as the men of Lt. Hartshorn's troops. I am willing to believe were you here they would be permitted to remain on the ground they at present occupy.

Believe me sir, I am conscious of our exposed situation, and well know we have been reconnoitred by the enemy; who will probably with three hundred attempt a stroke at this post —I mean the haymakers. In two days more I shall have all my hay home. And Mr. Miller who has been particularly useful to me, and a judge of the quantity, says there will be an hundred and fifty tons. This is more than I calculated on. The remaining 150 can easily be procured, and as much more if wanted, and workmen, guards, &c. can be furnished. Two or more carpenters are wanted to assist Ward.

With due respect,

JNO. ARMSTRONG,

Gen. JAMES WILKINSON.

Orthography.

The following order for goods on a business house here by its customer at Dayton, is a specimen of the literature of the period and region which gave it birth. If the schoolmaster was abroad at that date, he had not got far west.

Dayton, Dec. 6th, 1813.

Messrs. YATEMAN & ANDERSON,

Gentilmen—You will pleas let Mr. vancleve have the barril of Coffy and a Blige aus,   SMITH EAKER.

N. B. Pleas to let aus no if a half tun of shugger kittle Can Be had and at wat prise—By the Bare. if you can purchis 4 Dizen Duch Aulmacks and send them by the Bare you will much a Blige aus.

Value of Property.

A sale of property yesterday on Vine street just over the corporation line, presents some interesting facts. It was taken at Sheriff's sale in 1830 by the late owner, resident in Philadelphia to secure a debt, at 5 dollars 33cts., being two thirds its appraised value. In 1833 during the palmy days of the United States Bank, the purchaser disposed to invest the proceeds in the stock of that institution, authorised his agent here to sell it for what it would fetch, even if not more than it had cost in 1830. The agent dissuaded his principal from doing so, asserting he could make no other investment of money so much to his advantage, and that if he would keep it ten or twelve years, it would sell for more than thirty dollars per front foot. It was accordingly retained, and offered for the first time yesterday at public sale, when it brought the average price per foot of thirty-six dollars fifty cents.

The front was 280 feet, and the property which cost in 1830 fifteen hundred dollars, has within 15 years produced over ten thousand dollars.

Quere, what would the fifteen hundred dollars have produced the owner if he had put it into United States Bank stock? It would have bought less than ten shares which have since sold as low as three dollars per share.

A Disappointment.

My friend Dick B——, who never buys any thing for cash which he can obtain on credit was passing by a tailor's shop on Main street, where the firm of —— & —— *take measure on a large* and a sliding *scale,* when glancing at the wall he beheld the significant words, WE TRUST, and was about to negotiate for a new suit, when approaching nearer and reading on, to the smaller letters below, he found the whole read as follows: *We trust* no one will ask credit, who is not prepared to give us accepted orders on a wholesale dry goods store, or ready money. Dick evaporated on the spot.

Early Militia Parade.

CINCINNATI, Sep. 24th, 1798.

General Orders.

The Secretary of the Territory, now vested with all the powers of Governor and Commander in Chief of the same—will on Tuesday the 25th instant, review the first battalion of the militia of Hamilton county. The battalion is to be formed for this purpose at 3 o'clock, on some convenient spot of ground near to Major Ludlow's.

Arthur St. Clair Jr. and Jacob Burnet Esqs., will act as aids de camp to the Commander in Chief on this occasion, and are to be respected and obeyed accordingly.

WM. HENRY HARRISON,
Commander in Chief
Militia N. W. Territory.

Will Col. Gano please to fill up the blank in the above order with the hour which he may think most convenient, and let me know the one fixed on.   W. H. H.

Lt. COL. J. S. GANO,
Commander First Battalion Hamilton county Militia.

The Battle of Waterloo.

Among other things in a volume recently published in Eugland, entitled "The Iron Duke," and consisting mainly of sayings and doings of his Grace of Wellington, is the following laconic letter, written by the Duke to Marshal BERESFORD, giving an account of the Waterloo affair soon after it took place:

"You will have heard of our battle of the 18th. Never did I see such a pounding match. Both were what the boxers call 'gluttons.' Napoleon did not manœuvre at all. He just moved forward in the old style, in columns, and was driven off in the old style. The only difference was that he mixed cavalry with his infantry, and supported both with an enormous quantity of artillery.

"I had the infantry for some time in squares, and we had the French cavalry walking about as if they had been our own. I never saw the British infantry behave so well.".

Shed not a Tear.

Shed not a tear, o'er your friends early bier,
　　When I am gone.
Smile when the slow tolling bell you shall hear.
Weep not for me, when you stand round my
　　grave;
Think who has died his beloved to save:
Think of the crown all the ransomed shall have,
　　When I am gone.

Plant ye a tree, which may wave over me,,
　　When I am gone.
Sing ye a hymn when my grave ye shall see,
Come at the close of a bright summer's day,
Come when the sun sheds its last lingering ray,
Come and rejoice that I thus past away—
　　When I am gone.

Plant ye a rose that may bloom o'er my head,
　　When I am gone.
Breathe not a sigh for the blest early dead,
Praise ye the Lord, that I am freed from all care:
Serve ye the Lord, that my bliss ye may share;
Look up on high and believe I am there,
　　When I am gone.

Good Breeding.

To be thoroughly well bred, requires education, early training, and real goodness of heart.

To those who have not had and have not now these advantages, some hints may be offered, so far as personal behaviour is concerned, and when we enumerate some of the transgressions against good manners, we will perceive they are more common than we might have supposed. Among them, says a good critic is "loud and harsh speaking, making noises in eating or drinking, leaning awkwardly while sitting, rattling knives and forks when at table, starting up suddenly and rushing unceremoniously out of a room, tossing any thing away with indifference or contempt, receiving any thing without thanking the giver, standing in the way of any one when there is little room to pass, (a grievous practice in this city,) stepping before any one who is looking at any object particularly, pushing or jostling any one without apologizing, taking possession of a seat that belongs to another, intruding opinions where they are not sought, or where they give offence,

leaving acquaintances in the street or in a private circle without bidding them good bye or courteously saluting them, slapping any one familiarly on the shoulder, interrupting a person who is in conversation, telling long, tedious, or humdrum stories, whispering in company, making remarks on the dress of those about you or upon things in the room where you are, flatly contradicting a person—using slang phrases, (a very common habit,) interlarding our speech with foreign phrases, (well hit off in the new comedy of Fashion,) repeating the words, says she, you know, and you understand, helping yourself first at the table, using a fork as a toothpick, scratching the head, putting the fingers in the ears, cleaning or paring the nails before company, mentioning the price of any thing when it is offered to a guest, asking questions which give pain, and neglecting to answer letters."

Clerical Witness.

The London Herald has a rich report of a breach of promise case. The plaintiff was the daughter of a clergyman; the defendant, a captain of one of her Majesty's regiments. One of the witnesses for the plaintiff was Rev. Lucius George, who testified that the gallant Captain was a constant visitor in the young lady's family, and was with her in her walks and drives. So marked were the attentions as to attract the "decided notice" of the witness. One day, the latter met Capt. O'Brien at the bar of a hotel, at Cove, the place of the lady's residence, and asked him what brought him there? The latter, in reply, wished to have a talk with the Rev. witness. It seems that O'Brien wished to have some doubts cleared up touching the creed of the girl's father. He had heard, that, though he was a clergyman of the established church, yet he was a papist at heart. During the talk, the Captain partook brandy and water freely; the clergyman, however, declined. At this point the counsel for O'Brien thus cross examined the witness:—

"Cross examined by Mr. Freeman—When did the conversation take place in Cove?—About the beginning of July.

At what time of the day was it?—about half-past 10 o'clock at night, when I went to get a candle to go to bed.

Well, I suppose with the help of the brandy punch you changed his opinion? I did not take any of it; (laughter.)

Well, but he took two tumblers of brandy punch before he spoke to you on the subject? Not it; he only took one tumbler—but he came up to the mark afterwards.

Yes, he came up to the mark, as you call it. You have the misfortune, like myself, to be a bachelor? I have, if it be a misfortune, (laughter.)

But I wish to have your opinion on it? I would sooner you gave me your own; (laughter.)

Then my opinion is that it is a most miserable state, (laughter.)

Mr. Bennett—then I advise you to try matrimony, (great laughter.)

Mr. Freeman—I believe you are a pretty pleasant companion to the ladies!

Mr. George—I am very glad you think so. Now, are you not a very pleasant man? Why you may say so if you think proper, (laughter.)

Now, did you ever pay attention to a nice young lady in your life? Really, *I* do not 'see what this has to do with Miss Forrest, (laughter.)

Come now did you ever pay attention to a young lady? My lord, are these the usual questions a witness is subject to in the chair.

Mr. Freman—When we have such a witness and such evidence, they are. Now did you ever sit next a girl? I don't think it necessary to answer such a question, (laughter.) It I saw any object but to annoy a person I would answer it.

I assure you I have no wish to annoy you. and if I have done so *I* humbly beg your pardon, but I must put the question and ask you, did you ever sit near a nice girl at dinner? I have no doubt but I did, [laughter.]

And did you not pay her those nice and gentle attentions? I suppose *I* have; but what has this to do with the matter? However, I did not come here to give an account of every transaction of my life, [laughter.]

Court—I may as well relieve you of your embarrassment by telling you the object of these questions. You have sworn that you saw him pay attentions to the lady, and Mr. Freeman wishes to know what your notion of attention is.

Mr. Freeman—I do not wish to give you the slightest offence, and you need not have called on the court for protection.

Mr. George—Then I will answer you with pleasure; but I did not see what reference the question had to the matter. I will now bow to the decision of the Court.

Mr. Freeman—Now, don't criminate yourself, [laughter.]

Washington Officials.

In all countries, and under every form of Government, there is a power behind the throne greater than the throne itself. Do you see that boy? said one of the illustrious ministers of France. He is the arbiter of the destinies of Europe. How so? you ask. I will tell you; he governs his mother, his mother governs me, *I* govern the king my master, and my gracious sovereign governs the whole continent.

Among those of my readers who have visited Washington during the administration of Gen. Jackson, there are individuals who well recollect *Jemmy Duffy*, one of the officials of the White House. *I* never could make out Jemmy's office exactly, but a very important part of his functions was to stave off a gang of people who had no business with *Old Hickory*, yet who would have absorbed his whole time to the exclusion of his appropriate duties, but for the guardian care of *Duffy*, whose intuitive knowledge taught him who among the crowds of Goths and Vandals in the shape of office seekers and loafers, besetting the Capitol, had a claim to be admitted to an audience. It may be readily supposed Jemmy had no sinecure, and that he made ample use of his discretionary

powers. "Faith" said Jemmy, on one occasion, "they do say I am *a thought* rough, and may be its *thrue*, but I don't know how long I may *howld* my office, and while I do reign, I *mane* to reign."

When General Jackson left the white house Mr. Duffy left the premises also. "There niver was but one ould Hickory in the world, and no man could be his aqual, and afther being his right hand man for eight years, its not meself that shall keep the doors for the nixt one." So Jemmy abdicated, and Martin Dunnavan succeeded him during the administration of Mr. Van Buren. He also proved well suited for his employment and continued in office until the ides of March, 1841, when; Gen. Harrison came on to take possession of the White House. The palace had been duly vacated by its late tenant, and Dunnavan stood at the door ready to receive the new President, and deliver up the keys of the house. As Harrison entered the dwelling. Martin put his best leg foremost, in the attitude of delivering up his trust. And who are you? said the President. Plaze your honor's worship and glory, my name is Dunnavan, I am the last of the Martins, and *will* I go too? Why, said the kind hearted old man, with a smile, we have a saying in our part of the country, that it is ill luck to drive the martins away from the house, so *I* think you had better stay, Dunnavan.

Whether Martin remained under Tyler, and continues under Polk, I never distinctly learnt, but believe to be the fact. *If* so he has done the honors for four Presidents, in little more than as many years.

St. Clair's Defeat.

I am indebted for the following letter to Judge Matson, of North Bend. The Judge has been a resident of Hamilton county for fifty-four years, and an accurate and intelligent observer of cotemporary events, as well as a sharer in the toils, privations and dangers of western pioneer life. He has promised me further interesting notices, on subjects kindred to the present.

"In the month of January, 1792, Gen. Wilkinson being about to set out to St. Clair's battle ground to bury the dead who had been left there in the disastrous action of the 4th November preceding, and bring off valuable public property, reported to be still on the spot, made a call for volunteers to strengthen his force which amounted to merely two hundred regulars.— Some one hundred and fifty men or more from various parts of the county, rendezvoused in Cincinnati. The volunteers from North Bend of which *I* was one, were under the command of Capt. Brice Virgin, and we left that place—some mounted, but principally on foot, being promised horses from among those belonging to the United States, which were kept across the river, in Kentucky where Newport now is. There was the heaviest snow on the ground ever known within the memory of the whites, which on the day before we started was increased to two feet in depth. The Ohio had been frozen, and so thick was the ice at Cincinnati that all our efforts to open a channel for the flats to bring over the horses proved abortive, and they had to be taken up and crossed above the mouth of the Little Miami, where the ice was found strong enough to bear their weight. As soon as we could be made ready, which was on the 25th, the regulars and volunteers set out, the late Gen. Harrison, then an ensign, and lately arrived, being one of the officers. We took the old trace, opened by Gen. St. Clair. The first night we encamped on the hill, near what is now Cary's Academy, this side Mt. Pleasant, and the next arrived at Fort Hamilton. Left Hamilton pretty late in the day, and encamped that night at Seven Mile creek, and next day reached Fort Jefferson, then the outside post. Capt. Shaylor was in command there.

Here Gen. Wilkinson issued a general order to the effect that the severity of the season had compelled him to abandon one object of the expedition, the destruction of an Indian town fifteen miles below, on a branch of the Wabash, that he would send back the regulars to Fort Washington, and that the mounted men would proceed to the battle ground, with the public sleds to bring off such of the artillery and other property as might be recovered. We encamped next night, eight miles this side of the field of battle, which last spot we reached the succeeding morning at 11 o'clock.

On this day's march, and when we were about half way to the battle field, we arrived where the pursuit had ceased, and on counting the number of dead bodies which appeared to have been dragged and mutilated by wild beasts, I made it seventy-eight, between that spot and the battle ground. No doubt there were many more, who finding themselves disabled, crawled into the woods and perished there.

We were ordered to encamp directly where the artillery &c. had been left, I suppose with the view of beating down the snow to facilitate finding what we were in search of. · Here we found the artillery dismounted, except one piece, a six-pounder. Some of the carriages had been destroyed as far as they could be with fire. We brought off that piece and two carriages with the irons of the rest, together with several muskets. We previously buried the dead by the fatigue parties digging a large pit, into which

as many of the dead were thrown as it would contain. We had not a sufficiency of spades &c. to do justice to the undertaking, and left great numbers unburied, as we worked little more than the residue of that day. The men had been all scalped, and so far as their clothing was of much value, all stripped. Hardly one could be identified, the bodies being blackened by frost and exposure, although there did not appear any signs of decay, the winter having set in early, and proving very severe. One corpse was judged by Gen. Gano and others to have been that of Gen. Richard Butler. They had noticed the spot where he fell during the action, and entertained little doubt as to his identity. He lay in the thickest of the carnage the bodies on one side actually lying across each other in some instances. The pile in the pit was so numerous that it raised quite a mound of earth above the surface of the ground, when we covered it up, The main body had been encamped on a large open flat, and the advanced corps of Kentuckians occupied timbered ground in front, from which they were driven in by a general assault of the savages, who then occupied sheltered ground to pour in a destructive fire on the Americans. Two ravines, one on each side of the main encampment, put down to the creek which were also occupied by the Indians who were thus enabled to creep under shelter of the edges to attack their enemies.

We then travelled to Cincinnati where the public horses were given up, and the troops dispersed home, many of the volunteers being frost bitten on the route.

Most of the pieces of artillery had been carried off, and of course escaped our search at the time. Several were afterwards found in the bed of the creek. One piece, a six-pounder, was ploughed up a number of years after, on the battle ground, by some person who occupied the field, and taken down to Cincinnati and sold for sixty dollars to a Capt. Joseph Jenkinson who commanded a volunteer artillery corps in the place. I suppose it to be the same piece which Governor Meigs ordered to Urbana in 1812, in the letter you published lately in the "Advertiser" Perhaps some of your readers can shed light on this part of the subject.

Yours,

J. MATSON.

North Bend, June 16th, 1845.

Infirmity of Purpose.

Cruel as the spectacle may appear, yet one may derive a moral lesson even at a Spanish Bull Fight. The *Plaza de Toros*, with its fierce encounters and ghastly wounds, is not perhaps, exactly the place at which one would reason to learn philosophy; but still the reflecting observer cannot fail to see that the reason why the bull, with his untamed strength and desperate courage, does not. triumph completely over his puny foes, is because he lacks a determined purpose. The mounted *picadore* (lancer) goes down horse and man, before the impetuous charge of the infuriated bull—the horse is pierced through and through, and the rider lies helpless and crushed beneath his struggling steed. One would suppose, indeed that there was no hope, and that another thrust from those blood-stained horns must silence the foe forever. But it is rarely so. As the Bull gathers strength for a fresh attack upon the prostrate mass before him, an *espad*—a little fellow, attired like the Figaro of the stage—adroitly intervenes, flashing a scarlet mantle before the dazzled eyes of the raging creature. Cunning combats against force—the impetuous monarch of the Andalusian plains hesitates irresolute, and then dashes after the new annoyance, leaving the bruised *picadore* to the rescuing care of the attendants. And it is upon this principle that the combat is mainly conducted. When any one of the quadrilla of bull fighters is too hard pressed, another calls off the attention of the bull by ready interference, and thus, while many horses perish, but few of the biped combatants are slain.

The bull lacks a determined purpose—he has power enough and more than enough; but he suffers his attention to be distracted by a multiplicity of objects; and it is often even so with men. An iron will must triumph over obstacles; but if we lack perseverance and concentrativeness, running first to the right hand and then to the left, after any thing that may catch the eye or please the fancy, the probabilities are that we shall fail in every endeavour. It is the faculty of having a determined purpose, fixed and inflexible, which for the most part constitutes greatness among men. They pursue a straight line, and are not to be called off by the flitting by of gaudy colours: and in every pursuit, this is the main element of success. Mark out your object then—do you seek fame or fortune—would you excel in science or gather renown in literature—have you a thirst for distinction—would you traverse distant lands? No matter what your intend, set it clear before you and press onward towards it unfalteringly. This is the grand secret of a triumphant life; and it will be found that many of those who stumble and fall down by the wayside, are like the bull of the *Plaza de Toros*, deluded victims to idle streamers and flaunting flags.

Habits of Sheep.

Dr. Anderson relates the subjoined anecdote, which shows how perseveringly these animals will follow their leader, an amusing fact in illustration of natural history,

"A butcher's boy was driving about twenty fat wethers through the town of Liverpool, but they ran down a street along which he did not want them to go. He observed a scavenger at work with his broom a little way before them, and called loudly for him to stop the sheep.— The man did accordingly what he could to turn them back, running from side to side, and flourishing his broom with great dexterity; but the sheep much agitated pressed onward; and at last one of them came right up to the man, who fearing it might jump over his head, while he was stooping, grasped the broomstick in both hands.

and held it over his head. He stood for a few seconds in this position, when the sheep made a spring and jumped fairly over him without touching the broom. The first had no sooner cleared his impediment than another and another, in so quick succession, that the man, perfectly confounded, seemed to lose all recollection, and stood in the same attitude till the whole jumped over him: not one of them attempted to pass on either side, though the street was quite clear."

Shoulder Arms!

An unexpectedly touching scene was presented to the French Academy of Sciences very lately. The new invention of Van Petersen was to be exhibited—an artificial arm, by which, if the wearer has but a third of the shoulder remaining, he can pick up a pin, lift a glass of wine to his lips, hold a newspaper, etc. A committee had been appointed by the academy to decide on its merits, and an old soldier from the Hospital of Invalids was the subject of experiment. He had been for many years deprived of both arms at the shoulder, and when the substitutes were attached, he performed all that was set down by the inventor, with the greatest ease—taking a glass of wine, etc. But half an hour of these restored functions had moved the heart to the old militaire. As the arms were detached, his breast heaved with emotion difficult to be suppressed—'harder to bear," he murmured, "than the first loss, when he did not know their value." The Academy sat a few moments in breathless silence, all present evidently affected.

"Well!" exclaimed M. Arago, at last, "has no one any thing to propose? Are we to let this brave old man go back mutilated, when we can relieve him? How much do they cost?" "Five hundred francs each!"

"Ah! it would be costly to re-furnish all the maimed soldiers of the Hospital, but the others have not been reminded of their loss. We will subscribe the thousand francs for this one."

The proposition was received with acclamation, and the veteran walked away gesticulating with new arms.

Pharmacy in Questions and Answers.

What is Pharmacy? The science of concealing how little can be done to assist nature.

What is the best method to procure bark?— Throw physic to the dogs.

When may a cold be said to be caught?— When your nose runs after it.

What would you call a slight attack of the fever and ague? No great shakes.

What is phlebotomy? Skilful bleeding.

State the most effectual time to bleed. The moment your patient becomes convalescent, then put in your bill; delay is dangerous, and health ungrateful.

What would you call a violent outbreak?— Rash!

What is the usual result of affection of the heart? Increase of *sighs*.

Can the patient get assistance? Yes. How? By ringing the *belle*.

How is the heart enlarged? At the expense of the corporation.

Where is the best place to examine diseases? At a magistrate's office.

Why? Because there they lodge all complaints.

First Settlement on the Miami.

The impression that John Cleves Symmes, and those who purchased from him were the first settlers on the banks of the Miami, has extended so generally as to leave no doubt of the fact in the public mind. It will probable therefore surprise the community as it did me to learn that in 1785, sixty years ago and four years prior to the landing of Symmes, the whole Miami bottom was explored as far up as Hamilton and openings made at the best spots for the purpose of establishing pre-emption rights, by a party from Washington county, Pennsylvania. One of the company, John Hindman is yet living and resides a few miles from Hillsborough Ohio. I add his narrative as given to me in his own words.

"My father, John Hindman was a native and resident of Lancaster county, Pennsylvania, where I was born in 1760, and at the age of 20 left that neighborhood for Washington county, where I remained four years. In the month of March, 1785, I left the State of Pennsylvania, taking water at the mouth of Buffalo creek with a party, consisting of William West, John Simons, John Seft, and old Mr. Carlin and their families. We reached Limestone point, now Maysville, in safety, where we laid by two weeks. The next landing we made was at the mouth of the Big Miami. We were the first company that had landed at that place. The Indians had left two or three days before we landed. We found two Indians buried as they were laid on the ground. a pen of poles built around them, and a new blanket spread over each one. The first we found was near the bank of the Ohio, and the second near the mouth of White Water. Soon after we landed, the Ohio raised so as to overflow all the bottoms at the mouth of the Big Miami. We went over therefore to the Kentucky side, and cleared thirty or forty acres on a claim of a man by the name of Tanner, whose son was killed by the Indians some time afterwards on a creek which now bears his name. Some time in May or June we started to go up the Big Miami, to make what we called improvements, so as to secure a portion of the lands which we selected out of the best and broadest bottoms between the mouth of the river and where Hamilton now stands.— We started a north course and came to White Water, supposing it to be the Miami; we proceeded up the creek, but Joseph Robinson who started from the mouth of the Miami with our party, and who knew something of the country from having been taken prisoner with Col. Laughery and carried through it, giving it as his opinion, that we were not at the main river,

we made a raft and crossed the stream, having the misfortune to lose all our guns in the passage. We proceeded up to where Hamilton now is, and made improvements wherever we found bottoms finer than the rest, all the way down to the mouth of the Miami. I then went up the Ohio again to Buffalo, but returned the same fall, and found Gens. Clarke, Butler, and Parsons at the mouth of the Big Miami, as commissioners to treat with the Indians. Major Finney was there also. I was in company with Symmes when he was engaged in taking the meanders of the Miami river at the time John Filson was killed by the Indians."

Kentucky.

Kentucky has a State character *sui generis.*— When we cross the Ohio river from Cincinnati, a people is found of temperament, habits, pursuits and taste, as different from the population of Ohio as can be found, if we were to travel five hundred miles in any other direction. In early days the Kentuckian was half horse, half alligator, and a slight sprinkle of the snapping turtle. Now he is *all horse.* He realises the fable of the centaur, being inseparable from his steed. Every man there ought to receive the given name of Philip ———, a lover of horses. Accordingly wherever one of our citizens travels through Kentucky, horse-bills and advertisements of races are apt to attract his notice.

Apropos of races. The Oakland races near Louisville *came off,* in jockey phrase, last week. This leads me to notice another characteristic trait of these people.

It is well known that Rev. N. L. Rice now of our city, held a public theological debate last year at Lexington, Ky., with a distinguished opponent, Alexander Campbell, of Bethany. That such a discussion should attracts crowds will not surprise those who recollect the dense masses which blocked up the Tabernacle a few weeks since during the debate between Messrs. Rice and Pingree, but I suspect no where else than in Kentucky, could the *sporting fraternity* have found in such controversies, materials for the *long odds.* Bets were made on the speed and bottom of the debatants, as they would have been at the race ground, begining with three to one on Campbell, the odds equalizing in the progress of the debate, and finally two to one that Rice would drive his opponent out of the field in the course of debate. As the judges who presided there were not authorized to decide, and popular vote was taken on the merits of the debate, I presume the shareholder in each case was allowed to determine which had won or lost, in the exercise of his own personal judgment.

That debate was conducted with ability on both sides, no doubt. I never heard Mr· Campbell make a public address, but his reputation is established in the whole west. Mr. Rice, although comparatively young in years, is, as is well known, of great intellectual power, and otherwise admirably qualified for oral discussion, and as he was a Kentuckian, and the debate held on the soil of the State, it is probable much State pride and feeling was excited in the breasts of many, who cared little for the subjects in dispute. This feeling was exhibited afterwards, in a shape which could hardly have been shown any where else. One of the running horses at the Oakland races I have referred to, bore the name of *Nathan L. Rice*, in honor of the champion of Kentucky. He was, indeed, beaten with great ease, which is more than can ever have been said of his name-sake. The name was at any rate as much out of character for the horse, as the race ground would have been for the man.

CORRESPONDENCE.

The Mammoth Cave--No. I.

Mr. Cist:

The natural curiosities of our country are many and wonderful, and each day, almost, brings with it some new discovery. The falls of the great Niagara, our burning and hot springs, the Natural Bridge of Virginia, as well as our caverns and grottoes, have their visiters in countless numbers, seeking the gratification of a laudable curiosity, or to regain lost health. The most singular and most wonderful of all, is allowed to rest, nearly in its original beauty and grandeur, scarcely attracting a tithe of the great stream of travels, that courses yearly from one end of our Union to the other. I would call the attention of those who desire to have their curiosity satisfied, or knowledge added to, to the Mammoth cave of Kentucky. It is within two days travel of Cincinnati, being 95 miles south and west of Louisville, in Edmonson county, Ky., one fourth of a mile from Green river. There is a steamboat running regularly past the Cave, affording every facility to travellers. Upon their arrival they will find the "Cave House" to be neat and clean, with fine piazzas for promenading, and a table sufficiently well supplied to satisfy the palate of the most dainty. The surface of the country, in the region of the Cave is peculiarly diversified, and will attract the attention of the naturalist in an eminent degree. But the external of the country, however singular it may be, yields in interest, to the internal of the Cave, which all visiters are anxious to enter the moment of their arrival. At least I found it so with myself. Five of us, with the guide in advance, left the house for the entrance, which is in a little ravine called "Cave Hollow,"

and is 200 feet above Green river, and 100 feet below the general level of the table land above. It is thickly shaded by forest trees, that serve as a sort of screen, to hide the mouth which is yawning to receive you. Turning short round a mass of rock, you stand instantly in the very breath of the cave, which is steadily passing out, condensing as it strikes you. In summer you experience a chilly damp, and feel as if you were entering some long-shut-up and uninhabited old house. The thermometer, in the heat of summer varies some 30 degrees, by being raised or lowered at this point some five or six feet. Fifty feet below, and at an angle of 30 degrees from where you stand, you see, in the dim light of the Cavern, a large hopper, capable of holding 20 cart loads, which was used during and previous to the last war, for leaching the earth of the Cave, by the saltpetre workers. You become used to the chill in a few moments, and start down the steps, which lead around the side of the immense opening—at the bottom you find level and good walking, and after advancing a few rods, your torches become of use.— About a hundred yards from the entrance, at the "narrows," you come to a door, above which a rude Æolian harp is fixed, that is forever "discoursing sweet sounds," as the cool air of the Cave is constantly rushing out to the warmer atmosphere above, with a current of four miles per hour. Near this place and beyond, the tracks of oxen and carts remains as perfect as when made 30 years ago, and being protected from heat and frost, drought and rain, why should they change in a thousand years? You now gradually descend until the Cave opens out into immense proportions, and you come to the first branch, called after the ornithologist, Audubon, being the only place where *birds* of any kind have ever been found, and they were *bats*. At this point is what is called the Grand Dome, being 80 feet high, and near a hundred feet in diameter. We lit it so as to have a fine view, with Bengal lights, when we stood enchained by wonder and admiration. "Gothic Avenue," next received us after climbing up a long flight of steps, running out and up, from the side of the main Cave. The purity of the air is now felt by all; the chill has now left us, and the thermometer stands at 57, never varying either winter or summer. Our curiosity was now ravenous, and we proceeded to gratify it at all hazards. Forward was the order for the time, each one seeing something to wonder at, and exclaim about. "Stalagmite Hall," is the first place of great interest in this avenue. It is a spacious enlargement of the Cavern, the roof of which is curiously supported by columns of all shapes and dimensions; being formed by the stalagmite ascending, and the stalactite descending, until they meet, and form a single piece. They are sometimes in rows, and sometimes isolated, producing a most singularly beautiful effect, as all beyond the reach of our lights was in utter darkness, and left the imagination free as air, to fill up the distance in whatever manner the intense excitement of the moment could conjure up. A few hundred yards farther on, we stopped and refreshed ourselves at a sulphur spring, which lay directly in our path. All this distance we had fine walking, and we began *now* to act more like boys just let loose from school than any thing else. Certain it is we were not sober and sedate men, for we ran, jumped, hollowed, screamed, and laughed as if we were mad!—Dr. Croghan, the proprietor of the Cave, explained all this, for I was anxious to know why our desire to jump, run, and laugh, *could not without some exertion be repressed.* He said, that the carbon of the blood, that principle which is so abundant in the upper air, and which when the blood is nearly saturated with it, produces that dull and lethargic feeling often experienced, was continually being extracted by the pure air of the Cave when breathed into the lungs; and as a consequence, your blood was coursing through your veins, red and limpid, and as volatile as quick-silver. Elastic to a wonderful degree in every muscle, and buoyant in feeling from the novelty of our situation it is not to be wondered at, that we made boys of ourselves for the time. "Devil's Arm Chair" and "Elephant's Head," formed out of the Stalagmite were the next curiosities. 'Haunted Chamber" is a place where two mummies were found in a high state of preservation. The Indians no doubt, have penetrated into this Cavern to a greater distance than we might expect, as there are sundry indications, in other avenues. It is said, there is no principle of decay in the Cave, as the temperature is so uniformly at one point, and so dry. "Lover's Leap," next arrests your footsteps, after getting down which, you find your way through a fissure in the rock, and come into a lower cavern, containing what is termed the "Gothic Chapel," one of the most beautiful places we had yet seen. Talk about the abbeys and pillared halls of the old world! they are nothing to this specimen, in the backwoods of the new. Here is a temple, older than any built with hands, and of an architecture so unique, that it has not to this day, received its appropriate name. A more original pulpit cannot be conceived. It is of the most singular shape, just large enough to hold a man, and is formed about the centre of this part of the Cave, by the drippings from the roof, which is supported on each side by double rows of columns, leaving it in a half circle, and forming a sort of an amphitheatre, as it were, for the audience. Long did we stop here, and admire the ever varying changes produced by each different disposition of our lamps. We left however, and went on still farther to the "Cinder-pile," a very appropriate name for the spot, as the formation

here, resembles remarkably, the pile of cinders thrown from a blacksmith's forge. We were now four miles from the entrance, and had to retrace our steps, to the main Cave, our curiosity wonderfully excited by promises made by our guide of what we should see on the morrow.— We had been in the Cave over six hours, which had flown by, as so many minutes. We found a good supper ready for us, and very comfortable quarters in the "Cave House." The couch soon received my tired limbs, and slumber came, bringing with it the wildest dreams imaginable. The caverns presented by the excited imagination, were of the most fantastic shape, and perpetually changing. Daylight at last peeped in at my windows and with alacrity I arose, that I might be ready for my under-ground journey.— I found five or six of the gentlemen belonging to our party already on the piazza, preparing for the descent. The guide came at length, with a lamp for each, and a gallon can of oil slung upon his back. As this was to be a long journey, our host had, with commendable care, paid attention to the antcipated wants of seven or eight men, who, no doubt, might be hungry during the day.   K.

Seats of Government in Ohio.

It seems by the following letter, that the Ohio Legislature held its session of 1810–11, at Zanesville, and that they were then about to determine on a permanent scite for the capital of the State.

Zanesville, Jan. 3d, 1811.

Sir:

I received yours of the 25th ult., since which nothing of importance has transpired, though business is going on more briskly now, but there is too much argument; six lawyers in the house of Representatives, and two practicing lawyers in the Senate. This day the seat of government comes on the carpet in the House of Representatives. Sell's farm, which is the place the Commissioners reported, twelve miles above Franklinton, on the west side of the Scioto is most spoken of; but there is Worthington, Franklinton, Zanesville, a place in Delaware, not far from Bixbie's; but this latter place is supposed too much north—it is difficult to say where it will rest yet. Very little is yet said of the resolution, but its friends I fear are the majority. If so, as they are in the habit of sweeping, they may sweep away with it, but *I* find there is no telling how a question will be determined until it is tried.

I cannot tell when an adjournment will take place, but I do not expect to be at home before the last of the month.

Remember me to my old friend Capt. Carpenter. Capt. Hubbell ate breakfast with me on Monday last, and was on his road to Washington—I think he started on with Worthington.

Please remember me to the family.

Yours,
AARON GOFORTH.

Adventure at Higgins' Block-House.

I give the following narrative from notes of a statement made me a few weeks since, by Mr. E. E. Williams, of Covington, Ky.; probably the only survivor among the actors in the events which he records.

After the battle of the *Blue Licks.* and in 1786 our family removed to Higgins' block-house on Licking river, 1½ miles above Cynthiana. Between those periods my father had been shot by the Indians, and my mother married Samuel Van Hook, who had been one of the party engaged in the defence at Ruddle's station, in 17-80, and on its surrender was carried with the rest of the prisoners to Detroit.

Higgins' Fort, or block-house, had been built at the bank of Licking, on precipitous rocks, at least thirty feet high, which served to protect us on every side but one. On the morning of the 12th June, at day light, the fort which consisted of six or seven houses, was attacked by a party of Indians, fifteen to twenty in number. There was a cabin outside below the fort where William McCombs resided, although absent at the time. His son Andrew and a man hired in the family, named Joseph McFall, on making their appearance at the door to wash themselves were both shot down, McCombs through the knee, and McFall in the pit of the stomach. McFall ran to the block-house, and McCombs fell, unable to support himself longer, just after opening the door of his cabin, and was dragged in by his sisters, who barricaded the door instantly. On the level and upon the only accessible side, there was a cornfield, and the season being favorable, and the soil rich as well as new, the corn was more than breast high. Here the main body of the Indians lay concealed, while three or four who made the attack attempted thereby to decoy the whites outside of their defences. Failing in this they set fire to an old fence and corn-crib, and two stables, both long enough built to be thoroughly combustible.— These had previously protected their approach in that direction. Capt. Asa Reese was in command of our little Fort. "Boys," said he, "some of you must run over to Hinkston's or Harrison's." These were 1½ and 2 miles off, but in different directions. Every man declined. I objected, alleging as my reason, that he would give up the fort before I could bring relief, but on his assurance that he would hold out, I agreed to go. *I* jumped off the bank through the thicket of trees which broke my fall while they scratched my face and limbs. I got to the ground with a limb clenched in my hands, which I had grasped unawares in getting through. I recovered from the jar, in less than a minute, crossed

the Licking, and ran up a cow-path on the opposite side which the cows from one of those forts had beat down in their visits for water. As soon as I had gained the bank, I shouted, to assure my friends of my safety, and to discourage the enemy. In less than an hour I was back with a relief of ten horsemen, well armed, and driving in full chisel, after the Indians. But they had decamped immediately upon hearing my signal, well knowing what it meant, and it was deemed imprudent to pursue them with so weak a party, the whole force in Higgins' block-house hardly sufficing to guard the women and children there. McFall, from whom the bullet could not be extracted, lingered two days and two nights in great pain, when he died, as did Combs on the ninth day, mortification then taking place.

From Higgins' station, we moved in the fall of 1791 to Covington, or rather the mouth of Licking, building a cabin about twenty rods below the point. This was the first house put up in what is now Covington.

Before this however, and in the fall of 1790, *I* had volunteered in Harmar's expedition, and was on my road, when my horse descending a piece of hill ground got one foot entangled among the roots of a tree, and in his efforts to extricate himself, fell and broke his leg. In the fall I was so much hurt as to confine me to bed for two weeks, before I could again walk.— Next year my brother James and myself volunteered with St. Clair among the troops from Kentucky, and continued with him till the defeat. I assisted in building Forts Hamilton and Jefferson and Greenville. I was not in the battle, being detached with the troops under Maj. Hamtramck, back to Fort Hamilton to escort on the provisions, clothing, &c., of which the army stood in want, When we had nearly reached on our return, the place where we had left the army, we met the flying stragglers. I then returned to Kentucky. Wayne sent on troops in 1792, and came on himself in 1793, and encamped his entire force at "*Hobson's Choice*," a strip of dry ground above Mill creek, reaching at its upper range somewhere about the present Gas works, and started thence about the first of August. James and I were sent for as old Indian fighters, and a corps of about 65 scouts was formed and put under the command of Captain Ephraim Kibby, of Columbia. We moved on the line of forts already constructed, built Fort Recovery—St. Clair's battle ground,—Fort Wayne in the forks of Maumee, and Fort Defiance on the Auglaise. We then went on to the rapids of the Maumee, where Wayne defeated the Indians. Here again I escaped the battle, although less danger was incurred in it than usual in Indian fights, the regulars having driven the enemy with such spirit, and at such a rate, that the volunteers, and especially the mounted men who were compelled to take an extensive circuit to get round the fallen timbers where the charge was made, were not able to overtake either the pursuers or pursued, who were driven two miles on a run at the point of the bayonet. Capt. Kibby's company had been detached across the river to scour the woods, and rouse the Indians, who were supposed to be concealed on that side, and likely to endanger the rear of the American troops, as they could easily have crossed by wading the ripple above the rapids. It appeared however, that there were none at that place. I returned home being regularly discharged. There was hardly any money in circulation. A few of the officers drew enough to pay their expenses home, but the private soldiers and volunteers did not get their pay for many months afterwards.

Mill Creek Bridge in 1798.

In one of my lat numbers I published a history of the early Mill and Deer Creek bridges. The following subscription paper drawn up by John Cleves Symmes, supplies a chasm in the early records of Cincinnati. Of the individuals, signing the subscription, Judge Burnet and Griffin Yeatman of our City, alone survive.

Hamilton County, April 10th, 1798.

We the under-written subscribers, whose names are hereunto affixed, do promise to pay to Thomas Gibson, George Cullum, John Matson, Sen., and William H. Harrison, Esqs., or to the order of any three of them, the several sums annexed to our names for the express and sole purpose of forming and erecting a bridge over Mill creek at its mouth, either of stone or wood, on pillars or bents, so high as to be level with the top of the adjacent banks, and twelve feet wide, covered with three-inch plank, and so strong that waggons with three tons weight may be safely drove over the same, and so durable that the undertaker shall warrant the bridge to continue, and be kept in repair for passing loaded waggons, seven years after the bridge is finished.

The great advantage of this bridge, as well for supplies going to market, as to the merchants, tradesmen, and other inhabitants of Cincinnati, as for travellers in general, need no illustration.

One year from the date hereof is allowed to fill this subscription, and contract with an undertaker to build the said bridge, which if not begun within the year. this present subscription shall be void.

Subscriber's Names.

John Cleves Symmes, One hundred dollars.

Thomas Gibson, Forty dollars.
Wm. H. Harrison, Forty dollars.
Corn's. R Sedam, Forty dollars.
Israel Ludlow, Seventy dollars.
Joel Williams, Thirty dollars.
Wm, Ramsay, Five dollars.
Samuel Dick, Seven dollars.
Smith & Findlav, Ten dollars.
George Fithian, Three dollars.
J. Clarke, Five dollars.
Andrew Park, Three dollars.
Culbertson Park, Three dollars.
Stephen Wood, Ten dollars.
David Snodgrass, Two dollars.
Aaron Reeder, Three dollars.
Burt & Newman, Five dollars.
Griffin Yeatman, Five dollars.
J. Sellman, Five dollars.
Benjamin Stites, Eight dollars.
Thomas Goudy, One dollar.
George Gordon, Three dollars.
A. St. Clair. jun., Five dollars.
Wm. McMillan, Two dollars.
J. & Abijah Hunt, Twenty dollars.
Jacob Burnet, Five dollars.
Joseph Prince, Three dollars.

*Twenty dollars in addition to Wm. Ludlow's subscription, subscribed for him by Wm. H Harrison at Mr. Ludlow's consent.

Great Men not always wise,

John Quincy Adams, having received a volume of Scott's Commentary on the Bible from the publisher at Philadelphia, in reply said:—

"With my sincere thanks for your kind attention, I must pray you consider me a subscriber for the book, and, to save the trouble of repeated payments, enclose a check for the whole subscription—a general principle of propriety interdicting my acceptance of articles of value while I am in the public service."

Mr. Adams does not seem to perceive that by such a course, he is opening wide the door for his becoming an unwilling purchaser of not only books of every description, but various other kinds of goods. He will find his card, or I greatly mistake, an open letter or authority for every book publisher to draw on him for the value of one copy of any publication he makes. Nor will this prove the only article he will thus be compelled to buy.

Mr. Clay, on the contrary, has more knowledge of the world, that is to say of human nature. Witness his late correspondence with Orlando Fish, of New York.

"Epistolary.—Punch will have to knock under to Orlando Fish. The following correspondence is a curiosity:

"*Dear Sir:* Deprived as we are doomed to be, of the pleasure of having yourself at *our* head for a few ensuing years, will you allow us the minor pleasure of having ourself at *yours*, for a brief period, by accepting this Hat? and may it afford you, sir, what you have so zealously labored to secure to us—Protection.

Very respectfully your ob't servant,
ORLANDO FISH.

Hon. HENRY CLAY.

REPLY.

ASHLAND, 29th Jan., 1845.

My Dear Sir: I offer many and cordial thanks for the Hat which you have kindly presented to me, and for the note which accompanied it. The Hat might have "protected" a better or wiser head than mine, but no head was ever covered by a better or more elegant Hat.

Most truly, I am your friend and
obedient servant,
H. CLAY.

ORLANDO FISH, Esq.

Had Mr. Clay paid for the hat, he would have been supplied with hats sufficient, and more than sufficient to last his natural lifetime. He treated the subject like a man of sense. Mr. Adams is a learned man, learned rather than wise. If he had been more piactical in his knowledge, he must have perceived that he laid himself under no more obligation by accepting the commentaries than Henry Clay was under to Orlando Fish for the beaver. The publisher and the manufacturer could make more money out of the names of John Q. Adams and Henry Clay, than they could have obtained by the direct payment of their articles of which they made presents. These things are tricks of the trade, perfectly understood in the business world.

Territorial Marriage Licences.

The following document, among the papers of Col. Thomas Gibson, who solemnized the marriage referred to, relates to the lady whose brief history may be found in the last Advertiser. It is one of those remarkable coincidences which baffle all calculation and probability, that my narrative had hardly gone to press, when this licence came to light.

BY HIS EXCELLENCY,

ARTHUR ST. CLAIR, ESQ., *Governor of the Territory of the United States North West of the Ohio.*

PERMISSION of *MARRIAGE* is given to *John Downs* and *Lucy Virgin,* both of Hamilton county, and the honorable the Judges of the Territory aforesaid, the Justices of the Courts of Common Pleas, or any of them, or any other person authorized by the Statutes of the Territory aforesaid to solemnize *MARRIAGES,* are hereby empowered, upon application to them made by the parties aforesaid. to join them together as *HUSBAND* and *WIFE*.

GIVEN under my hand and seal at Cincinnati the twentieth day of September, in the year of our Lord, one thousand eight hundred.
ARTHUR ST. CLAIR.

Relics of the Last War.

CINCINNATI, Feb. 14th, 1813.

DEAR SIR:

I have the pleasure to inform you that the detachment of militia has marched for Dayton in good health and spirits. The batallion from my division will consist of five companies, between three and four hundred strong.— I have had uncommon difficulties to encounter in organizing and marching them, the Brigade Major having notified me of his resignation at a time when his services was most wanted, and Gen. Findlay not having official notice of his exchange, and Brigadier General Wingate, Col. Mills, and Major Kain never joining until yesterday, so you may judge of my situation, having the sick, lame, lazy, and worst of all, the ignorant, to attend to, and had not Mr. Thompson taken some part of the arrangement off my hands in the Quarter Master department, I could not have got them on the march so soon. They are now completely equipt—I made them purchase blankets &c. with their advance pay, and have several engaged that I have hired to make up cartridges, as we could get none at the Arsenal. I shall send a load of ammunition to Dayton on Tuesday—have kept a guard for that purpose. The cartridges made are the best I have ever seen. I got buckshot moulds made, and as I got them for eight dollars, which is very cheap, I shall not put them in Bryson's account as they are very useful for the State, some 9 and some 12 buckshot in each cartridge, and by experiment, I find they will answer much better than ball cartridges; though I have had some of them made—I have them put up in dozens, and completely packed—about 60 dozen in each tight keg, that will not admit the wet to injure the ammunition. I have sir, been indefatigable in my exertions on this occasion, and hope my transactions will meet your approbation. I send a greater supply of unfixed ammunition than the detachment will require, which will be wanted in advance as I presume, and knowing the difficulty of obtaining buckshot, I will order the man to go on casting a quantity, that by giving a short notice, may be forwarded to your order to any point on the frontiers. We have a rumor in town that Gen. Harrison has had an engagement and been victorious, God grant it may be true. I am sir in very great haste, which will apologise for this confused scrawl.

From your most ob't. humble ser'vt.
JOHN S. GANO.

His Ex. Gov MEIGS.

St. *Marys,* May 28th, 1813.

Maj. Gen. J. S. GANO.

Sir—A company of riflemen, under the

command of Captain David E. Hendricks from the division under the command of Major Gen. Whiteman has recently been ordered to this place, and perhaps they never could have rendered more essential services than at this time as there is not a man for duty here. I expect a part of said company here to day. The Captain came in last evening. He states that the company is extremely reluctant to come on without assurance of receiving one month's pay; I have promised they should be paid one month's wages in advance, and notwithstanding, you may consider it as not coming within your jurisdiction, yet under existing circumstances, I thought it my duty to call on you to intercede with the District Paymaster, to send on the money with Captain Hendricks. I hope you will use every exertion with Mr. Hunt or Mr. Taylor, (as the case may be,) I have wrote to Mr. Hunt on the occasion. The money may be enclosed to me, I will make any arrangement he may direct, or he may authorise any other person that may seem just to him. Paymaster Smith has gone to the Rapids, and will be gone a considerable time before he can return. Something is necessary to be done, or I shall have command of a garrison without an individual to do duty, myself and staff excepted.

The water taking a rise in the St. Mary's and Auglaize, and believing it indispensibly necessary, that the provision should descend the river the first opportunity, as we cannot expect another flood, I sent every man on with the boats from this post, and left but a Sergeant's command at Amanda. You may therefore judge our situation. We have no news only what you must have heard. Please write me when convenient. And permit me to close with my best wishes for your welfare &c.,

JOHN WINGATE,
Brigadier General.

Cincinnati, May 31st, 1813.

DEAR GENERAL:

I received your letter by Capt. Hendricks and immediately attended to your request. I called on Mr. Hunt who informed me he was instructed by the Secretary of war to make no payments in advance. I then called on Gen. Harrison, who informed me he wished to accommodate the men, I then proposed if he would sanction it I would make the advance, which he said he would, and I send by Capt. David E. Hendricks five hundred dollars, which you will please to have paid out on regular muster pay, and receipt rolls in the name of your pay master Smith, as I have thought best to attach them to Col. Mills' regiment. Out of the five hundred dollars I have given Capt. Hendricks forty for his

own use, which he will account for in his pay. The better way will be to pay one month's pay and have all the rolls complete for the month; it will save trouble.

I am sir, in great haste,
Your friend and humble serv't.
JOHN S. GANO.
Gen. JOHN WINGATE.

Franklinton, Sept. 26th, 1813.

DEAR GENERAL:

I have the honor to report myself to you as Maj. Gen. Commandant of the Ohio Militia in service, under your command. I have ordered two companies of upwards of eighty to St. Mary's. The one commanded by Capt. Joseph Carpenter, I presume Major Whistler took on to Fort Wayne, and Capt. Titus' company ordered to report to, and receive orders from the commanding officer at St. Mary's. I have in addition, a regiment commanded by Col. Delong on their march to Seneca, and ordered one hundred men properly officered to Fort Meigs, from his regiment, which is about 800 strong. I have one regiment from my division here of 8 companies, and 600 strong, though some are about to be detailed or engaged in the Quarter Master's employment. I have a regiment here upwards of 600 strong—they will march to-morrow for Seneca. Unless I receive your orders to the contrary, I will leave this on Wednesday morning for that place, with my staff which is small, Maj. A. A. Meek, aid, and Maj. Joseph Vance, and await your orders. The Governor considered Fort Findlay as a post of no importance, as the stores have been removed—though I will send a small detachment from Upper Sandusky on my arrival there as I think it of importance to keep open that communication. I shall be happy to hear from you and receive your orders which shall be promptly obeyed at all times.— I only regret I could not be with the first to cross into Canada with you.

I am sir, yours
with respect and esteem,
JOHN S. GANO,
Maj. Gen. Com'dt. O. Militia,
Gen. WM. H. HARRISON.

Felix G. M'Connell.

With much of the manner of Crockett, he is by far his superior in intellect. I would place implicit confidence in his judgment. Some of his colleagues have informed me that in his section of country he is invincible before the people, and respected by all who know him. Many anecdotes, which I cannot write out, have been related pertaining to his canvass for Congress, in which he was opposed by a Whig gentleman of great ability as speaker. Let me tell one, although it loses its force when put on paper. At a great gathering of the people of his district on the 4th of July last, to hear the competitors for Congress express their views, his opponent, after discussing various points of political moment, concluded his address with an eloquent appeal to the ladies, hundreds of whom, from all parts of the district, had assembled upon the occasion. The concluding part of his opponent's speech seemed to strike home, which McConnell, who was watching its effects, instantly perceived. When he took the stump, after replying to the prominent political allusion of his competitor, he haid it was not in him to do injustice to any one; but as the gentleman had alluded to that tender passion called love, he must say comparatively with himself he knew no more about it than did an old aunt he had in North Carolina, who lived to the age of 150, and after all died an old maid "I grant," said McConnell, "that my Whig friend is a fine looking man, just forty, and not yet married—look at him ladies, and assure yourselves I do him no discredit. But I do say that men must be judged by their acts—a fine looking man just forty, and not yet married! Look at that picture," pointing down upon his competitor, "and now look at this!" (Here the speaker drew himself to his full length, and running both hands through his fine bushy beard, gazed around and around upon the audience, and continued.) "I am, I think, a pretty considerable good looking man for my age and inches, and I have one of the best and prettiest little wives, a straight and strict member of the Methodist persuasion, that this or any other country ever produced. And why did I get her? Because I possessed that passion which my more polished friend rubbed out years ago—yes, years ago—four hundred and sixty moons have shone upon him and yet unmarried! When I discovered that the consent of her father could not be obtained—and he, by-the by, was a good old fellow, although a Whig—like a man, I entered beneath the roof of her parents, and like a man, I bore her upon my shoulders from the house to the bridal altar, chased by dogs howling, barking and biting, to the portals of the Church. A happy wife, three little McConnels, and an easy conscience, are the fruits of the tender passion as I possessed it. If he can say as much, Felix Grundy McConnell backs out from the canvass —if not, let him forever hold his peace." My informant says, nothing could have been more effective—the ladies waived their white 'kerchiefs in very ecstacy of delight—the men shouted and stamped as men never shouted and stamped before—and the county gave the eccentric McConnell an overwhelming majority.

The Bright Side of Human Nature.

In a letter published in the Lynn [Mass.] Pioneer, giving a description of the fire in Pittsburgh, we find the following passage:

"The big church below me kept the flames in check, and not until the buildings beyond me had done their worst did my house take fire. I was sitting upon a trunk, my wife beside me, and Jesse behind us in the open cross street a little east of our house, when four or five of the mass came to me and asked where my house was. I pointed to it, and accordingly they went to work and cleared every room in that house, bringing out every thing, I believe, that it contained, the kitchen furniture only excepted; they brought out every bedstead, every bureau; they brought my lipsalve, my tooth brush, all my books and papers, every straggling pamphlet and newspaper; and, finally, pulled my sign off the window-shutter. Nor did they stop at this; but they procured a dearborn wagon, and never stopped till they had carried every article to a place of safety, taking glasses and breakable ar ticles in their hands. I do not know the name of one of them. Two black girls of fourteen or fifteen years of age carried out a good furniture wagon load of articles, taking them up to the new court-house and watching them till they were finally removed, and all refused not only compensation or wages, but they refused to accept presents. To one man I presented a mantle clock, because I believed it could not be saved but by being carefully carried to the country. He took it away. Yesterday I left my office door open; and, when I came back, the clock was on the mantlepiece keeping time and exactly right. My goods were carried to six or seven different places upon the hill above the town; they have all been returned to me I believe. and all that I have paid for trouble taken was two dollars to the wagoner. Yesterday a colored woman brought home our first washing of white clothes since the fire, and begged that we would accept the trifling favor from her, because we had done so much for 'her kind of people.' Mrs. E. saw a bundle of her clothes upon a cart on the evening of the fire as she was going up on the hill; she took hold of it, and the cart went on, leaving the heavy bundle on the road with her. Two little ragamuffin boys, less than twelve years old, came to her assistance, and carried it a great way to the house of an acquaintance; when she took out her purse to pay them there was not a cent in it. It was a hand some bead purse; she offered it to them. 'No, indeed,' said one of them, 'we'd be ashamed to take any thing from you at such a time as this.' There were their regular alley blackguards."

Long and Short.

An amusing anecdote is related of the late Sir Charles Williams, who for many years traveled the western circuit, and had a full share of business. Being a diminutive man, he presented a striking contrast to another counsellor Williams, who went the same circuit, and who was a very tall person. It happened, on one occasion, at Exeter, that some irregularity among the counsel called for the interference of the Judge, to whom the persons of the two barristers were unknown out of court. Mr. Williams the little was addressing the court, when the judge requested him to stand.

"My lord, I am standing," exclaimed the astonished counsel.

"Then," continued his lordship, addressing the other, "Mr. ohn Williams, I will thank you to sit, sir."

"My lord, I am sitting," said Mr. Williams the tall.

Wonders of Art.

Some time since I referred to a master piece of name punching, bearing in circular form, the stamp, "7th Annual Fair of the Ohio Mechanic's Institute," which was so minute that four of these circles could be laid upon a dime. Every letter was distinctly formed, duly proportioned, and visible to the naked eye. This piece of work was executed by Mr. Sheppard of the firm of Sheppard & Davies, gold pen manufacturers, Main between 7th and 8th streets, and was exhibited at the last fair of the Institute. *I* thought the performance wonderful, and did not suppose it could be surpassed as a piece of delicate and accurate engraving.

What will my readers think of an engraved circle so small that it covers no more space than the wreath circle of a half dime, and yet presents in that space a well defined copy of "The Lord's prayer, and the ten commandments" with their respective titles? This was executed in the establishment of Toppan, Carpenter & Co., and handed me by Mr. C. A. Jewett, who has charge of their branch in Cincinnati. It may be seen at my office by the curious in such matters.

The First Church in Cincinnati.

The original proprietors of Cincinnati, when they laid out the town, dedicated four in-lots, numbered 100, 115, 139, and 140, for the use of a church, grave yard, and school; this was in 1789. *In that year the property* was occupied as a burial ground. In 1790, Rev. David Rice of Kentucky, a Presbyterian Clergyman, came to Cincinnati and organized a Presbyterian Society, which has continued ever since, and is now represented by the First Presbyterian Society of Cincinnati.

In 1791, a number of the inhabitants, formed themselves into a company, to escort the Rev. James Kemper from beyond the Kentucky River to Cincinnati; they accompanied him hither and on his arrival, a subscription was set on foot to build a meeting house. Before this time the trees upon a portion of the lot, at the corner of Fourth and Main streets, had been partially cleared, and within a small circle, seated upon the logs—the people met for worship, in the open air, with their rifles by their sides. In 1792, the meeting house was erected, and the whole four lots were enclosed with a post and rail fence. The timber for the building was taken from the spot upon which it was erected.

The subscription paper for the erection of the Church is still in existence—it is dated January 16th, 1792. It is headed as follows:

"We the subscribers, for the purpose of erecting a house of public worship, in the village of Cincinnati, to the uses of the Presbyterian denomination, do severally bind ourselves, and executors, firmly, and by these presents, the several sums of money, and commutations in labor, respectively annexed to our names, to be paid to John Ludlow, Jacob Reeder, James Lyon, Moses Miller, John Thorpe, and Wm. McMillen, or either of them, their heirs or administrators, trustees appointed for the business of superintending the building aforesaid, payments to be made as follows:

One third part of our several subscriptions, to be paid so soon as the timbers requisite for the aforesaid building may be collected on the ground, where the said house is to be built.—Another third, when the said house is framed and raised. And the other third part, when the aforesaid house may be under cover, and weather boarded.

In witness whereof, we have hereunto subscribed our names, on the day affixed to our names."

Here follow the names of the subcsribers, which are given, that we may cherish the memory of the generous dead, and furnish an example to the living.

John Ludlow	Isaac Felty
Jacob Reeder	James Wallace
James Lyon	Robert Caldwell
Moses Miller	Jona Davies
John Thorpe	Thomas Ellis
Wm. McMillen	Daniel Shoemaker
John B Smith	John Blanchard
David E Wade	Benjamin Jennings
James Brady	Jno Gaston
Joel Williams	Jonas Seaman
Levi Woodward	Reuben Roe
Wm. Woodward	John Cummins
Jeremiah Ludlow	Elliott & Williams
James Dement	Thomas McGrath
Richard Benham	James Bury
John Cutter	Thomas Gibson
Joseph Lloyd	Henry Taylor
Nehemiah Hunt	Elias Waldron
Cornelius Miller	Thos. Cochran
Abram Bosten	James Richards
Gabriel Cox	John Bartle
Samuel Pierson	J Mercer
Daniel Bates	H Wilson
Benj. Fitzgerald	Wm. Miller
James Kemper	James Reynolds
Isaac Bates	Thomas Brown
John Adams	Matthew Deary
Wm. Miner	James McKnight
James Miller	John Darrah
Seth Cutter	Samuel Martin
S Miller	Dan'l. C Cooper
John Lyon	Moses Jones
James McKane	Francis Kennedy
William Harrison	Israel Ludlow
Margaret Rusk	J Gilbreath
Benjamin Valentine	James Wilkinson
Asa Peck	Winthrop Sargeant
Robert Hind	Richard Allison
Robert Benham	Mahlon Ford
Samuel Dick	John Wade
Joseph Shaw	M McDonogh

Samuel Kitchell J Mentzies
Matthias Brant Joshua Shaylor
Samuel Williams Wm. Peters
Jabesh Wilson James Kremer
David Logan W M Mills
James Lowry H Marks
David Long Matthew Winton
Alex. McCoy Ezekiel Sayre
Joseph Spencer Samuel Gilman
David Hole W Elwes
James Blackburn John Dixon
James Cunningham Daniel Hole

On the 11th June, 1794, another subscription was circulated for the purpose of further finishing the Presbyterian meeting house in Cincinnati, and also for paling the door yard and fencing in the burying ground, to be paid to the same persons named as Trustees.

To this paper, in addition to those who had already subscribed to build the meeting house, and who again contributed to its completion, we find the names of

Ezra F Freeman Jno Brown
David Zeigler Joseph Prince
C Avery Andrew Park
Oliver Ormsby John Riddle
Job Gard Patrick Dickey
Robert Mitchell A Hunt & Co.
Martin Baum Peter Kemper
G Yeatman

When the property was dedicated by the proprietors, they held the equitable title only; the government held the legal estate, but had contracted with John Cleves Symmes, to convey to him a large tract of land which included the town plat of Cincinnati; the proprietors claimed under Symmes. In 1794, the President of the United States issued a patent to Symmes, who was thus invested with the legal estate; and afterwards on the 28th December 1797, conveyed the lots to Moses Miller, John Thorpe, John Ludlow, James Lyon, Wm. McMillen, David E. Wade and Jacob Reeder, Trustees for the Presbyterian Congregation of Cincinnati. The title thus conferred, has been fully confirmed by the Supreme Court of Ohio in Bank, in 1838–39, in their decision in the case of the city of Cincinnati against the 1st Presbyterian Church.

In the list of subscribers for building the meeting house, we may notice *James Wilkinson*, then a Colonel in the army, and commandant of Fort Washington, and the Gen. Wilkinson of later American history.

Winthrop Sargeant Adjt. Gen. of the North Western Army, afterwards Secretary of the N. W. Territory and subsequently Gov. of Mississippi.

Richard Allison, Surgeon Genl. of St. Clair and Wayne's armies. Mahlon Ford, a Captain in the regular service, and who was afterwards dreadfully wounded in St. Clair's defeat.

Captain Shaylor and Peters, officers in St. Clair's

army, John Thorpe, Superintendent of artificers.

Mr. Elliott, one of the partners of Elliott and Williams government contractors, was the father of Commodore Elliott, of the U. S. Navy, and was killed between Springdale and Hamilton by the Indians in 1794. His body was interred near the corner of Main and Fourth sts., in the Presbyterian burial ground, and was removed some years since to the Cemetery beyond the canal, where his son has erected a handsome monument to his memory.

Relics of the Past.

FORT WASHINGTON, July 10th, 1792.
DEAR SIR:

I will thank you to spare the rifle horse, as much as may consist with due caution. They have a hard tour before them, and I wish to have the horses in vigor.

Yours,
  JAS. WILKINSON,
   Brigadier General.
JNO. ARMSTRONG,
Com'dt. Ft. Hamilton.

N. B. 1 have expected Ashton some days with three hundred men, but have given him up.— He means to resign, poor Smith is dying—Freeman killed—what then? J. W.
Capt. JOHN ARMSTRONG.

Fort Washington, July 14th, 1792.
DEAR SIR:

I have this moment received your letter by Serj't. Policy, and send out Ser'jt. Armstrong and a party of the horses for the two prisoners, who have escaped from the enemy. You will mount them on two of the Quarter Master's best horses, and let them move under cover of the night. *I* cannot leave this post until I take their examination and transmit it to the Sec'y. of war, and therefore the sooner they arrive the better.

Should the enemy attempt to *pull down* your *bullock pen*, or to fire your hay, during the season of darkness, Capt. Peters and a Sub, are to sortie with fifty men, and with or without flints, as you may judge proper. The gates to be instantly shut, and your works manned in the most defensive manner your force may admit. I go upon the possibility that circumstances may induce you to have his command, some where or some how within your walls.

Capt. Barbee is not to move before he receives further orders, but is daily to keep out light reconnoitring parties, on foot or horseback, in every direction.

My respects to Barbee.
In haste, yours,
  JAS. WILKINSON,
  'Brig. Gen. Commanding.
JNO. ARMSTRONG,
Capt. Com'dt. Ft. Hamilton.

Fort Hamilton, July 17th, 1792.

BRIG. GEN. JAS. WILKINSON.

DEAR GENERAL:

Your letter of yesterday came duly to hand. The distressed situation of the settlers on the Little Miami, and in short every where on the frontiers calls loudly for the aid of Government. Is it not probable that you may be authorized to call into service from Kentucky, a body of horse sufficient to justify an enterprize against some of the Indian towns. Perhaps that on Auglaize river, or at its mouth. The savages are certainly very poor, and the destroying their cornfields would make them more so. This in my opinion would have a better tendency to bring about a peace, than to expend —— dollars in presents at a treaty. Some of Capt. Barbee's men being sick and their horses lame, the greater part of the infantry being on fatigue, was I to detach any part of the former, who are employed for the safety of the workmen, the objects you have in view could not be accomplished in due season; and indeed with all my exertions, unless additional workmen are sent forward, it will be winter before the house I have began will be finished. Two carpenters, two sawyers, with whipsaw files could be employed to public advantage.

Enclosed you have a return of Captain Barbee's troops, who are daily employed as patroles. With me there is no doubt but the enemy are contemplating a stroke at our advanced posts; if intended against this place and St. Clair, policy would justify the peaceable disposition they have shown towards both, as it might in their opinion throw us off our guard, but be assured I shall leave as little to chance as our situation will admit of.

Enclosed you have an account against those spies for articles furnished by Mr. Ewing for the payment for which I am held responsible. Please to direct the stoppages to be made and paid to Mr. Bunton, in behalf of the contractor. All is well here. Yours,

JOHN ARMSTRONG.

Fort Washington, July 19th, 1792.

DEAR SIR:

Mr. Hartshorn has this day returned from Columbia, and I expect to leave this post [if nothing material intervenes] on the 2d, with 68 fresh pack horses; in the meantime, you will be pleased to send back all the hired teams you can spare, as they are expensive, under an escort of infantry, taken from your garrison—say 20 or 25 men. I gave the horse, the riflemen, and Capt. Peters' company, for a march forwards, and shall take from you all but two of your

scythes—this may happen about the 24th; in the meantime make hay.

Yours,

JAS. WILKINSON.

J. ARMSTRONG, Capt. Com'dt.

Scenery around Cincinnati.

In the neighborhood of this city, we have every variety of scenery, picturesque, wild or magnificent, where nature and art have vied with each other in the exhibition of their respective charms. Of these, various instances will occur to my readers; it is natural scenery, simply, I am about to describe.

There is a tract of seventy acres just this side of Columbia, in the rear of, and overtopping what is called Sportsman's Hall, a mile or two above Fulton, which embraces, in that part of it adjacent to the river, every thing to interest and gratify the man of taste. Of this tract some ten acres forms a perfect circle, except where a narrow tongue of land connects it with the adjacent country. Opposite this tongue the circle of the tract strikes the Ohio bottom, beyond which the river itself sweeps in a graceful curvature, which presents circle touching circle, and affords from the spot to which I refer, a view which can be taken at one glance to the right and left, four miles up the current of the Ohio, and down as far as the lower part of Covington, being in range 10 miles and an half. In this glance, frequently four or five steamboats at a time serve to grace and enliven the scene. Stepping forward to the edge of the circle, the whole scope of that magnificent clearing, Turkey Bottom, is visible to the east, while immediately in front, the highly cultivated farms and extensive uncleared timbered land of Kentucky lies before the spectator.

The circle to which I refer is elevated abruptly, perhaps 210 feet from the bottom land, which skirts its entire edge, the surface rolling gently and gracefully on every side. And what I admire as much as any other feature of this charming spot, is the native forest, which cleared of its undergrowth, exhibits a grove of sugar trees of the noblest class. The proprietor, I. D. Wheeler, of the firm of I. D. Wheeler & Co. has on this place erected a cottage edifice of great simplicity, and in perfect keeping with the whole scene, where he passes the hours abstracted from business pursuits. I was reminded by the spot, of Robinson Crusoe and his island, not merely in its isolation, but the tameness of the birds, squirrels, and rabbits which rove the scene, fearless of guns, which are never permitted to be fired on the premises.

I regret to add that there is one thing wanting to complete the magic of the scene. What that is may be conjectured, when I state as I am bound in candor to acknowledge, that Mr. Wheeler abides there in single blessedness. As the beauty of the scene brings visitors daily in numbers, it is to be hoped, that some of the forms of loveliness, which press the velvet carpets on his lawn with steps so light as to leave hardly an impression there, may be persuaded to take up an abode, and become the guardian genius of so sweet a spot, which only needs an Eve to complete its attractions. Even Eden was a desert and a solitude while Adam was alone. What lady will take the hint?

Cat Latin.
FELIS ET MURES.
A FABLE.

Felis sedit by a hole,
Intenti she cum omni soul—
Prendere rats;
Mice cucurrerunt over the floor,
In numero duo, tres, or more—
Obliti cats.

Felis saw them oculis,
I'll have them, inquit she, I guess—
Dum ludunt,
Tunc illa crept toward the group,
Habeam, dixit, good rat soup—
Pingues sunt.

Mice continued all ludere
Intenti they in ludum vere—
Gaudenter:
Tunc rushed the felis into them;
Et tore them omnes limb from limb—
Violenter.

MORAL.

Mures omnes nunc be shy,
Et aurem præbe mihi—
Benigne,
Sic hoc facis—"verbum sat,"
Avoid a devilish big Tom cat—
Studiose!

DEATHS.

On Monday, June 30th, Mrs. HULDAH GAZLAY MILLS, wife of Rev. Thornton A. Mills, in the 30th year of her age.

On Monday, June 30th, at 11 o'clock A. M., NAPOLEON B. MOSBY.

Planing Machines.

This is a part of the labor-saving apparatus of modern days, which threatens to change the face of mechanical employment. The planing machine however,, takes from manual labor its severest as well as most unprofitable drudgery; the ripping up and planing out flooring boards. In the putting up annually, for this city and suburbs 1500 houses, an immense amount of this article is needed, certainly not less than five millions of feet. Accordingly there are twelve planing machines operating in Cincinnati, principally on *Woodworth's patent.* There are three or four however, which run on the *concave* system with *Conical spring rollers or slides*, being *Bicknell's patent*, a Cincinnati invention which cuts 25 pr. cent per day more than the other, and what is of more importance to the purchaser, supplies an article of perfect joint and surface superior in smoothness to any other wrought by machinery.

Messrs J. H. Story & Co. have just put their planing machine in operation, which is one of Bicknell's patent, in a newly erected building constructed expressly for the purpose, on Third below John street. The floor of the establishment is made of brick, and the shavings are consumed as fast as made, serving to put and keep the Engine in motion. Messrs. Story & Co. are practical carpenters, whose workshop occupies the upper story of the building, and as such offer special advantages to builders in their knowledge of what kind of article suits for brother carpenters, both as respects materials and work.

The value of flooring boards made at these twelve machines amounts to 120,000 dollars annually; the average price being equal to $2 40 cts per M feet.

CORRESPONDENCE.
Mammoth Cave--No. 2.

Mr. CIST:

In my last number I closed by a description of our party of eight, with their preparations, for their journey to be undertaken, intending to find our way as far into the Cave as any who had preceded us: It is better for visiters to associate some six or eight together, that they may have the benefit of a combination of lights, as each person carries a lamp, suspended by an iron wire bale. Great care should be taken in crossing the rivers, not to get all your lights in one boat at a time, as an accident, such as up-setting your frail craft, would leave you in darkness visible, and no means that I am aware of would give you any clue to the shore. For who can swim in perfect darkness, in a strait line? And should you be fortunate enough so to do, the hirsute horrors of a perpendicular rock, springing directly up from the water, might be the barrier to safety, instead of the gentle and sandy declivity, of the point of departure. In our eagerness to cross the rivers, we did not think of danger, until we were afloat, and all our flambeaux, placed upon a little spot in the prow of our tottering bark.

But let us start on our journey. Equipped as

I have mentioned, we soon entered the mouth of the ever-breathing Cavern. The enchanting strains of the Eolian Harp greeted our ears, passing which, we lost the last remnant of the light above. Leaving "Gothic" and "Audubon" avenues on our right, we continued our journey in what is termed the "Main" Cave, until we came to a small house, or box, rather, as it had no roof, and but one apartment. It was occupied by a Dr. Mitchell, who had been its inhabitant near four months, hoping to cure an affection of the lungs. He had improved somewhat, but I am satisfied, no permanent *cure* can be effected by this mode of living.

A little distance beyond the house, there is a large rock which has fallen from the roof, very much resembling the hull of a steamboat. Behind this rock, you descend through an opening as it were under the wall of the Cave, called the "Dog Hole." As unpromising as this may sound, and as difficult as may be the entrance, it is the vestibule of one of the most interesting and wonderful avenues, amongst the one hundred and sixty-nine already discovered. Descending in your journey, you arrive at the "Side Saddle" pit, "Minerva's" dome, and next the "Bottomless Pit." This is a curious point. The dome, is merely the "pit," extending up through the roof, say twelve or fifteen feet in diameter.— From the top of the dome, to the bottom of the pit, which are exactly opposite, it is very near 300 feet. The pit has very much the appearance of an old well, the sides being perpendicular. The pit is directly in your path, and there could be no further progress, were it not that the proprietor has throw a temporary bridge across it, with a railing upon one side, and that a very frail one. That we might have a good view of it, the guide saturated a newspaper with oil from his can, set it on fire, and dropped the blazing envoy into the pit. The illumination was beautiful, showing every fissure in the walls of this immense shaft.

Leaving the pit, it is no great distance to the winding way. This, in some places is not more than four feet high, the top half of which, is from three to five feet in width, while the lower half is not more than 18 inches. It is very crooked, and your entrance into the "Relief Chamber," allows you to straighten up and expand, much to your comfort. Next you come into the River Hall, which traversing some distance, and descending a ladder, you come to the first river,—the river "Styx." This is four miles from the mouth of the Cave. The river has a sandy margin, and I should suppose was nearly fifty yards in width, without any apparent current, as it was said to be very low, five or six

feet in depth, and transparent as air A few steps further on, is "Red River," a little wider, and about as deep as the "Styx." One fourth of a mile from this, is the "Echo" River, the deepest and widest of the three, being about 10 feet in depth, and a quarter of a mile in width. In several places we discovered a slow current. It has been ascertained that the surface of this river, is nearly upon a level with the surface of Green river, which passes the Cave House but a short distance from the lawn. It must of course flow into Green River, as they usually rise and fall together. This point is five miles from the entrance. Five miles! It is a long distance from the light of the glorious sun. Miniature rivers and mountains, vales and cliffs had been passed, that had never in all previous time drank in the light, of aught save our torches, while their relations and namesakes above had been revelling in the sun's rays for countless ages. But then the distance yet to be made is before us, with all the jewels of this rich casket yet to be seen, and we must enter our boat, and shove out into the darkness beyond. The transparency of the water is astonishing, as we could see the sand and pebbles by the light of our lamps, as plainly as if in air. The guide told us the water was very low, and we found that we had almost to prostrate ourselves in the boat, that we might pass under the roof, which appears like an arch sprung from one side of the Cave to the other. This was soon after leaving the shore. One Fourth of July, some three or four years since, a party of two ladies and two gentlemen, with the guide, crossed the river, which was then slightly rising, and made a visit of some six or eight hours. They enjoyed themselves. as all do, who see the wonders of the Cave beyond the rivers, little thinking of the danger, which they had left behind, and which was increasing each moment of their stay. Upon their return, they were amazed and stupified to find the water had risen some 4 or 5 feet, in their absence. Consternation seized upon them for a time, as visions of starvation, in utter darkness flashed upon their minds. They gave themselves up for lost. They knew not when the water would fall, or whether they could repass the low and arched portion of the roof spoken of above. They resolved however to try, and that quickly, as each fleeting moment added to the fast rising flood, and a little delay might cut them off forever from the cheerful light of day, and anxious friends without. They stepped into the small and tottling flat boat with beating hearts—they pushed boldly out, the guide in the bow. In a little time they see the dreaded arch by the light of their torches, and instantly feel the descending roof with their hands. All now lay down on their backs in the sand and water which was at the bottom of this craft, and succeeded in squeezing themselves, and their cockle-shell of a boat through the opening left by the still rising water. One hour longer, and their egress would have been utterly stopped!— On their arrival at the mouth, they found there had been a tremendous fall of rain, which had suddenly raised Green River, as much as it had its counterpart in the Cave.   K.

Mammoth Cave--No. 3.

Mr. Cist:

About half way across the river the cavern expands into mammoth proportions, and the number of chambers and recesses above are innumerable. Here is the remarkable echo which gives its name to the river. A slight stroke of the oar upon the frail boat, is repeated millions of times, receding at each successive echo, until the sound dies away in the most distant chambers above you, assuming the melting tones of the wind harp. The ear is never surfeited with this musical echo, and all the different noises we could conjure up, were tried over and over again with the same harmonious effect. The most bewitching melody, is returned to the expectant ear, from the musical apartments above, whatever may be the cause. A pistol was discharged, and thunder burst upon us, as grand and startling as any ever heard above; always, however giving us a strain of sweet melody as it left us. Simple and disconnected sounds suit this place the best. Ole Bull might play one of his most ravishing airs here, and it would be a jumble of discords on its return. One plain, distinct cause will give back a most beautiful effect, as each portion of the cavern has time to articulate, and send to you its own echo, in its own form. This will be soon discovered by the visiter. During our voyage, we saw many of the eyeless fish, floating in the clear water, without any apparent concern for their safety. With a scoop net we caught several, and examined them closely. They are white, about four to six inches in length, and entirely destitute of eyes. They are a new species, wonderfully suited to their dark and silent abode, being so constituted as to possess an external covering, whose sense of touch, is peculiarly delicate, enabling it to perceive the slightest impulse given to the water, and from whence it proceeds. I had sent to me, by a friend who is travelling upon the continent of Europe, a short time after my visit to the Mammoth Cave, a bottle, containing a fish in fine preservation, from the celebrated Grotto of Adelsberg, at the head of the Adriatic, Austria.

This fish is also without eyes, but is very different in its conformation, from the fish of the Kentucky Cavern. The "Proteo" of the Grotto of Adelsberg, is nearly six inches in length, very much the shape of an eel, having the same character about the head and tail. The color is of an ashy grey on the back, running into a dirty white underneath. It has no fins. The tail is flatened, and answers all the purposes of an oar for sculling. About an inch from the point of the nose, there extends from its body, on each side, an arm, of half an inch in length, the end of which is garnished with three fingers or claws. It has two exactly similar appendages, one third of its length from the tail. These arms, or legs, indicate that it walks upon the bottom of the stream which runs through the Austrian Grotto. The fish of our great Cave bears a strong resemblance to the catfish of our rivers, but has no thorns for its defence, its delicate sense of touch answering in the place of all warlike weapons.

Leaving the river, we pursued our journey, and at some distance from the river, a sharp angle of the wall of the Cave presented to us, the rudder, pink stern, after bulwarks, and wheelhouse of a large steam ship. Farther on "Mary's Vineyard" is reached, through a hole in the roof, by the aid of a ladder. Here met our eyes, the beautiful Stalagmite formation, in the shape of bunches of grapes. They are formed by the dropping of water, impregnated with lime. The water upon its striking, flies off in spray, and thus forms the globule, which looks much like a half-ripe grape. Beautiful stalactites, are immediately above, suspended from the roof. Two miles from the "Vineyard" you are ushered into "Cleaveland's Cabinet." Here let the scientific, as well as the enthusiastic stop—look—admire—and wonder. This portion of the Cave cannot be described. No person will ever have an adequate idea of it, unless he sees it.

Conceive, if you can, yourself standing under an arch, some twenty feet in height, and fifty in width, encrusted with a thick coating of frost, which is protruding in all directions, buds, vine-tendrils, rosettes, sun-flowers, cactus leaves,—every thing from the most exquisite and perfect lily to the elegance and taste, of the most elaborate Corinthian Capital, fashioned from a material the most delicate; and all of a pearly white; and you may have some conception of this unique Cabinet. At some points the roof is entirely studded with snow-balls, which have, apparently, been frozen there, and present innumerable facets to your lamps, wherein the light is reflected, with sparkling brilliancy, as if from millions of diamonds. Sulphate of Soda, as pure as it can be is under your feet, in piles. Every turn you make, presents some new and beautiful vegetable form, of the utmost delicacy. All are very fragile, and many visiters destroy them with the most wanton carelessness. They do not think that any curious traveler will ever come after them. As these specimens of *Fibrous Gypsum* are entirely unique, being very probably without a parallel in the world, and have been thousands of years in arriving at their present wonderful state, the barbarity, and idiotic gratification, of a stupid and ignorant visiter may be conceived. A most shameful course taken to disfigure, the beauty of this chaste ceiling, and apparently very popular, is to make the initials of the name, upon its white surface, by the smoke of the lamp. Hundreds of such efforts are visible in all parts of the Cave, but especially here. The guide should be instructed to report every visiter to Dr. Croghan, who is guilty of such shameless conduct, and payment should be exacted for spoliation of property.

A gentleman of our city, of scientific attainments, has given the name of Oolophylites; or *Curled Leaf Stones*, to the fibrous gypsum formations, of "Cleaveland's Cabinet." After leaving the Cabinet, which is near a mile in length. you are arrested by the "Rocky Mountains"—truly and appropriately named, as any who may ever cross them, will surely acknowledge. Gloom of a peculiar nature, characterizes this spot above *all* others. Pen and pencil, will both *fail*, in giving the *slightest* idea of the magnitude and grandeur of this awful place. We lit our Bengal lights, and were silent with awe.

Still further on, and thirteen long and weary miles from the entrance, we came to the *gem* of this whole cavern. It is named "Serena's Bower." This beautiful spot is guarded by an aperture, which is very difficult to enter. The interior of the Bower is a fit ending to so vast a Cavern, amply repaying the determined explorer for his energy in reaching it.

It is small and deep, bottom, roof and sides being entirely covered with stalactite formations. From the ceiling, the stalactites join on the sides, and run down to, and form the very floor of this *most* beautiful grotto. The roof is shaped much like an umbrella. The idea that strikes you is, as if from a common centre in the roof, the long hair from the heads of an hundred females had been let down, and that it had been dropped from that centre in the most graceful manner imaginable to the walls, down which it flows in most grotesque confusion, forming miniature grottoes, surrounded with fan-like pillars; and when illuminated interiorly, producing a most

exquisite picture. This is a Fairy realm, and this the abode of their Queen.

In the side of the Bower, and about three feet from the floor, is a basin of the most limpid water; around the edge of which, the most curiously shaped pillars, form as it were, a fence for its protection. Hanging a lamp inside of the columns, and above the water, it illuminated this magic fountain, and drew from each one present, an acclamation of wonder and delight. We sat down, and quietly feasted our eyes, with the rare and exquisite beauties of this lovely spot. We had been over six hours, constantly traveling and wondering; and were now much impressed with our utter exclusion from our fellow beings.

Six hours longer, and we were again within sight of the heavens, with the sun, red and low in the west.   K.

Governors of the States.

States	Governors.	T'm exp.
Maine,	Hugh J Anderson,	Jan 1846
New Hampshire,	John H Steele,	June 1845
Massachusetts,	*George N Briggs,	Jan 1846
Rhode Island,	*James Fenner,	May 1845
Connecticut,	*Roger S Baldwin,	May 1845
Vermont,	*William Slade,	Oct 1845
New York,	Silas Wright,	Jan 1847
New Jersey,	*Charles C Stratton,	Jan 1848
Pennsylvania,	Francis R Shunk,	Jan 1848
Delaware,	*Thomas Stockton,	Jan 1849
Maryland,	*Thomas J Pratt,	Jan 1848
Virginia,	James McDowell,	May 1846
North Carolina,	*William A Graham,	Jan 1845
South Carolina,	William Aiken,	Dec 1845
Georgia,	*Geo. W Crawford,	Jan 1847
Alabama,	Benj'n Fitzpatrick,	Dec 1845
Mississippi,	Albert G Brown,	Jan 1846
Louisiana,	Alexander Mouton,	Jan 1847
Ohio,	*Mordecai Bartley,	Dec 1846
Kentucky,	*William Owsley,	Sept 1848
Tennessee,	*James C Jones,	Oct 1847
Indiana,	Thos J Whitcomb,	Dec 1846
Illinois,	Thomas Ford,	Dec 1846
Michigan,	John S Barry,	Jan 1846
Missouri,	John C Edwards,	Nov 1849
Arkansas,	Thomas Drew,	Nov 1848
	TERRITORIES.	
Florida,	John Branch,	Aug 1847
Iowa,	John Chambers,	Mar 1847
Wisconsin,	Henry Dodge,	July 1847

*Whigs 12; Democrats 17.

Washington Officials.

Cincinnati, June 20th, 1845.

MR. CHARLES CIST:

Dear Sir—I read the notice of Martin Dunnavan in yours of the 18th with much interest, as an evidence of which I add my own recollections of *Martin*.

I saw him at his post on a visit I made to Washington in 1843, and again in 1845, and can therefore vouch the fact that he continued under both the Tyler and Polk dynasties, after having served under both Van Buren and Harrison.

When I saw him in 1843, it was in company with Mrs. L—— and other ladies. "Oh!" said Martin to Mrs. L., who was remarking the faded and soiled condition of the furniture and upholstery, "things do look very shabby here indade. When we gave the last party to Lord Ashburton, I pledge you my honor there was hardly lights enough for the party to see each other's faces. It's aaltered times here now. But we shall see better days soon I hope." Then sinking his voice and looking round, as if afraid of its echo. "I hope your ladyship is a ginuine dimocrat. "Surely, Martin, and so is all the party." "There," said Martin, "I knew yees well enough, that you would not betray me."

When I saw him in 1845 he reminded me of this scene. "I towld you," said he "things would all come round again."

I feel it but justice to Martin to vindicate him from the imputation to which his continued service under the last four Presidents might subject him, of being a successor of the vicar of Bray.

An early settler.

One of my subscribers who has recently returned from a business trip to the neighborhood of Greenupsburg, says:

"Among many objects of interest to me in my visit to the neighborhood, was an old lady, Mrs. Lucy Downs, at whose table I sat with her self, her daughter, grand daughter, and great grand daughter. By this you may readily suppose she is a relic of the past. She was the daughter of Jeremiah and Lucy Virgin, and the sister of Brice Virgin, a name well known to our early settlers She was born September 17, 1769, in what is now Fayette county, near Beesontown—since Uniontown, being the first child of American parents born on this side of the Allegheny mountains; and is therefore an impersonation of the great west. She says she removed in 1790 to Limestone and thence in 1792 to Cincinnati, where she was married to Mr. John Downs. They returned to Pennsylvania and finally settled in Greenup county, Kentucky. Her residence is at Oldtown in that county. She distinctly recollects seeing Gen. Washington at her father's, and a neighbor's house when she was between four and five years of age. He was then engaged surveying lands in what is now called "Washington's bottom," from that circumstance. The old lady enjoys good health and walks quite erect.

Old town, her place of residence, is alleged in the neighborhood to have been an Indian village in early times. There are old residents who have been there 45 and 50 years, who always considered it such, by what they learned from the first settlers. It is certain that tomahawks, flints, pipes and other Indian appendages have been picked up for years and are still found, although in less numbers.

I have learned from other sources that there was an Indian village also in the southern part of the State. I should be glad if some of your correspondents who are familiar with the subject, could determine these facts. It is well known to be the received opinion that Ohio and Indiana were the dwelling places for the Indian tribes, to whom Kentucky was hunting grounds and battle fields. I had no other opinion prior to this visit of mine to Greenup county."

Planing Machines.

I have referred two or three times to the subject of planing machines, as of vast importance to the house building interest, divesting the journeyman carpenter of the most laborious and unprofitable part of his business—ripping out rough boards and dressing their surfaces.

Mr. B. Bicknell, a highly ingenious mechanic here, has greatly improved as well as simplified the old fashioned Woodworth's planing machine, and as a consequence has been annoyed and persecuted with suits from individuals holding under that patent. It is with great pleasure I learn, therefore, that the suit brought in he Kentucky district Court at Frankfort, to test the validity of his right to make and sell "Bicknell's Concave or Conical planing machine," brought by the rival establishment, has just been decided in favor of the Cincinnati inventor.— Judge Munroe held, "That Bicknell's was no infringement of Woodworth's patent, even if Woodworth's could be sustained, either for a combination or improvement;" that it did not use the carriage claimed by Woodworth: that it did not use his planing wheel, either horizontal or vertical; and that Bicknell's planing wheel is differently applied to the boards, which gave it a greater capacity to plane the surface, and that the cutter wheels, used for tonguing and grooving were not the same described by Woodworth; Bicknell's having cutters to give a smooth edge to the plank, which Woodworth's had not.

There are now four of Bicknell's machines in operation here, to wit: T. Bateman & Co., J. H. Story & Co., Thompson and Mitchell, Worcester & Co., and a fifth belonging to Bicknell and Jenkins, is about to be put up, at the intersection of Race street with the Miami canal.— This will make when completed, 13 establishments of the sort, which will cut this season over five millions of feet of flooring boards, which at twenty-four dollars per M, the current average price is a product of 120 000 dollars.

Revolutionary Patriotism.

Instances of heroic devotion to the liberties and independence of the United States during our revolutionary struggle. were of constant occurrence. I publish the following authentic narrative of the life of CHRISTOPHER LUDWICK, who resided during my boyish days in the Northern Liberties, of Phila. and whose grave and venerable appearance always filled up in my youthful fancy, the picture of one of the ancient patriarchs. His history and example point out what men, comparatively obscure, may accomplish for the public welfare where the spirit of doing so exists.

Christopher Ludwick was born on the 17th of October, 1720, at Giessen in Hesse Darmstadt, in the circle of the Upper Rhine, in Germany. His father was a baker, in which business the son was instructed as soon as he was able to work. At fourteen years of age he was sent to a free school, where he was taught to read and write, and the common rules of arithmetic. He was carefully instructed at the same time in the principles of the christian religion as held by the Lutherans. Of this school he always retained a grateful remembrance. At seventeen years of age he enlisted as a private soldier in tho army of the Emperor of Germany, and bore his part in the war carried on by the Austrians against the Turks, between the years 1737 and 1740. At the close of the war in Turkey, he set off with one hundred men for Vienna. Their march was through a dreary country, and in extremely coid weather. Seventy-five of his companions perished on the way. He spent seven months in Vienna. The incident that made the deepest impression on his mind while he remained in that city, was the public execution of the commissary-general of the Austrian army, for fraud and peculation.

From Vienna he went to Prague, where he endured all the distresses of a seventeen weeks' siege. After its surrender to the French arms in 1741, he enlisted as a soldier in the army of the king of Prussia.--Upon the return of peace he went to London, where he entered himself as baker on board the Duke of Cumberland East Indiaman, and went to the East Indies under the command of Admiral Boscawen. He spent three years and a half in different parts of that country. In 1745 he returned to London, where he received in wages for his services one hundred and eleven guineas and an English crown.

With this sum of money in his pocket he set off for Germany to visit his father, who he found had died during his absence in India, and had left him his whole estate consisting of a small freehold, which he immediately sold for five hundred guilders. With this money, and part of his wages, he returned to London, where he remained several months, enjoying the pleasures of that great city. After spending his last shilling at the places of public resort in the neighborhood of London, he went to sea, and passed the years between 1745 and 1752 in successive voyages from London to Holland, Ireland, and the West Indies, as a common sailor. In these voyages he saved 25 pounds sterling; with which he bought a quantity of ready made clothes, and embarked with them for Philadelphia, where he arrived in 1753. He sold these clothes for a profit of three hundred per cent, and with the proceeds returned to London. Here he spent nine months in learning the Confectionary business, and the making of gingerbread.— In the year 1754 he returned to Philadelphia with a number of gingerbread prints; and immediately set up his business of family and gingerbread baker.

In the year 1774 he felt, with the great majority of the people of America. the impulse of that spirit of liberty, which led them to oppose, first by petitions and afterwards by arms, the attempts of Great Britain to subjugate the American colonies. He possessed nine houses in Philadelphia, a farm near Germantown, and three thousand five hundred pounds, Pennsylvania currency, at interest, all of which he staked with his life, in the cause of his country. He was elected successively, a member of all the committees and conventions which conducted the affairs of the revolution, in Pennsylvania, in 1774, 1775 and 1780. His principles and conduct were alike firm, under the most difficult and alarming events of those memorable years. In one of the conventions in which he was a member, it was proposed by General Mifflin to open a private subscription for purchasing fire-arms. To this motion some persons objected the difficulty of obtaining, by such a measure, the sum that was required. Upon this Mr. Ludwick rose and addressed the chair in the following laconic speech, which he delivered in broken English, but in a clear and firm voice: "Mr. President, I am but a poor gingerbread baker, but put down my name for two hundred pounds.' The debate was closed with this speech, and the motion was carried unanimously in the affirmative.

In the spring of 1777 he was appointed superintendent of bakers. and director of baking in the army of the United States. When his commission was delivered to him by a Committee of Congress, they proposed that for every pound of flour he should furnish the army with a pound of bread. "No, gentlemen," said he, "I will not accept of your commission upon any such terms; Christopher Ludwick does not want to get rich by the war; he has money enough. I will furnish one hundred and thirty-five lbs. of bread for every hundred weight of flour you put into my hands." The committee were strangers to the increase of weight which flour acquires by its manufacture into bread. From this time there were no complaints of the bad quality of bread in the army, nor was there a moment in which the movements of the army, or of any part of it, were delayed from the want of that necessary article of food. After the capitulation of Lord Cornwallis, he baked six thousand pounds of bread for his army by order of General Washington.

At the close of the war he returned and settled on his farm near Germantown. His house had been plundered of every article of furniture, plate and wearing apparel; by the British army on their march to Philadelphia. As he had no more cash than was sufficient to satisfy the demands of the market, he suffered a good deal from the want of many of the conveniences of life. He slept six weeks between blankets, rather than contract a single debt by replacing his sheets. He was alike averse to borrowing money; for such had always been the accommodation of his manner of living to his ready cash, that he never but once was, without as much as was equal to the necessaries of life, and that was in Berlin, where he received a gratuity of two-pence from a stranger, to purchase a mug of beer.

He died on the evening of the 17th of June 1800, in the 80th year of his age.

The following is an extract from his will.

"As I have, ever since I have arrived at years of discretion; seen the benefit and advantage that arise to the community by the education and instruction of poor children, and have earnestly desired that an institution could be established in this city or liberties, for the education of poor children of all denominations gratis, without any exception to country, extraction or religious principles of their parents or friends, and as the residue and remainder of my estate will, in my opinion, amount to upwards of three thousand pounds specie, I am willing that the same shall be a mite or contribution towards such institution, and flatter myself that many others will add and contribute to the fund for so laud-able a purpose. And therefore I do will, devise and direct that all the residue and remainder of estate: real and personal, whatsoever and wheresoever, not hereinbefore otherwise disposed of, shall be appropriated as and towards a fund, for the schooling and educating gratis of poor children of all denominations in the city and liberties of Philadelphia, without any exceptions to the country, extraction, or religious principles of their parents or friends."

In every stage and situation of life, Mr. Ludwick appeared to be, more or less. under the influence of the doctrines and precepts of christianity. Part of this influence, it has been said, was derived from his education. But it much increased by the following circumstance. His father inherited from his grandfather a piece of silver of the size of a French crown, on one side of which is marked in bas relief, a representation of John baptizing our Saviour, with the following words in its exergue, in the German language: "The blood of Christ cleanseth from all sin." 1 John i. 7. On the other side was the representation of a new born infant, lying in an open field, with the following words in its exergue: "I said unto thee when thou wast in thy blood, live." Ezekiel xvi. 6. This piece of silver Mr. Ludwick carried in his pocket, in all his voyages and travels in Europe, Asia and America. It was closely associated in his mind with the respect and affection he bore for his ancestors, and with a belief of his interest in the blessings of the Gospel. In looking at it in all his difficulties and dangers, he found animation and courage. In order to ensure its safety and perpetuity, he had it fixed a few years ago in the lid of a silver tankard, in the front of which he had engraved the following device: a Bible, a plough and a sword; and under it the following motto: "May the religion, industry and courage of a German parent, be the inheritance of his children."

The Pardoning Power.

On the assumption by Thomas W. Bartley of the office of Governor of Ohio, which devolved on him by the appointment of Wilson Shannon, Minister to Mexico, a rule was introduced by him in relation to applications for the pardon of convicts in the State Penitentiary, that previous notice must be given in the public prints to the community, of which the culprit had heretofore made a part, that such application would be made. I objected to the rule at the time as unfair, impolitic and divesting the Governor of responsibility, which alone belonged to him.—That it was both, might be found in the facts, that while the friends and relations of the convict would always be actively engaged in getting him out, the keeping him in lay, in the neglected province of no body's, or perhaps every body's business. I alleged from what I had seen in service as a juror, that it was generally difficult to obtain a conviction, impossible without the clearest evidence, and that the whole responsibility of judging whether the executive clemency ought to be exercised, was thus left entirely to a mass of signatures, of which it was impossible to judge what representations had been made to obtain them. As I expected, the rule has been made a means of getting men out of the penitentiary, in whose presence no man in society is safe. In the case lately, of two persons who were convicted of murder, pardons were issued, when the fact was, that a larger number of signatures was obtained to a remonstrance than were signed to the application for release. As matters now stand, our criminal court trials and convictions are a perfect mockery. For my individual share, I shall hereafter vote for no man for Governor of Ohio, who acts under any such rule, or disturbs the verdict of a jury where fresh evidence has not come to light subsequently to the trial. I believe that every man who signs such petitions, or votes in Governors who pardon convicts of whose guilt there can be no doubt, is taking a sure course to establish Lynch law in this community, In proportion as it becomes evident that the ordinary course of justice is uncertain or defective, will individual feeling interpose as the avenger of its own wrongs.

City Officers.

Cincinnati had a town charter as far back as forty-three years, This was given by the Territorial Legislature, Jan. 1st, 1802. The government of the place was put into the hands of seven trustees or members of town council, with a President, Recorder, Collector or Clerk, and Marshal.

The early records are imperfect, and such as have been preserved, do not present a full list of public officers. Those which are on record from 1802 to 1815, at which date a new charter was confered on the town of Cincinnati are as follows:

PRESIDENTS.
David Zeigler, 1802, and 1803.
Joseph Prince, 1804.
James Findlay, 1805, 1806, 1810 and 1811.
Martin Baum, 1807 and 1812.
Daniel Symmes, 1808 and 1809.
Wm. Stanley, 1813.
Samuel W. Davies, 1814.

RECORDERS.
Jacob Burnet, 1802 and 1812.
Charles Kilgour, 1803.
Aaron Goforth, 1805 to 1809.
James Andrews, 1810 and 1811.
Samuel W. Davies, 1813.
Griffin Yeatman, 1814.

CLERKS.
John Reily, 1802.
Wm. McFarland, 1813.
Matthew Nimmo, 1804.
Griffin Yeatman, 1805 and 1806.
John Mahard, 1807.

Until 1813, the Council does not appear to have preserved regular minutes of proceedings, or to have held its meetings at any fixed place. In 1813 and 1814, that body met at the Columbian Inn—the present Neff & Brothers corner of Main and Second streets.

In 1815, the town received an act of incorporation from the Legislature of Ohio. The council met at the house of Samuel McHenry. Wm. Corry, Mayor and President; Oliver M. Spencer, Recorder; Wm. Ruffin, Clerk; David Kilgour, Treasurer; and James Chambers, Marshal.

By the charter of 1815, the Mayor was elected by the Trustees out of their own number.— On the 14th April, 1817, the board met at the Council chamber, the upper floor of a building which then stood on the public landing, just east of Main street, and opposite Bonte's cordage store. Wm. Corry was Mayor for 1815, 18-16, 1817 and 1818; and O. M. Spencer Recorder for 1815 and 1816; and Martin Baum for 1818. Wm. Ruffin Clerk in 1815, Geo. P. Torrence in 1816, and Jesse Embree in 1817 and 1818.— David Kilgour was Treasurer for 1815 and 1816, as was Jacob Wheeler for 1817 and 1818. Jas. Chambers held the office of Marshal during these four years.

In 1819 the city was created, and divided into four wards. Up to this time the voting for the whole city was done at the Mayor's office. The Mayor was elected by the city at this date. Isaac G. Burnet held that office from 1819 to 1830, of which periods, from 1827 was by popular election. The successive Presidents of council from 1819 to 1834, were Jesse Hunt, Wm. Oliver, Samuel Perry, Calvin Fletcher, Lewis Howell, Dan Stone, E. S. Haines, & N. G. Pendleton. Recorders during the same period, Wm. Oliver, Sam'l. Perry, Thomas Henderson, Chas. Tatem, Oliver Lovell, Samuel R. Miller, and Ebenezer Hinman. Clerks, Rich. L. Coleman, Wm. Phillips, Wm. Ruffin. Thomas Tucker. Daniel Roe, John Gibson. John T. Jones and Charles Satterly, who still holds the post. Treasurers, Jacob Wheeler, Richard L. Coleman, Stephen McFarland, James Comly, & Samuel Scott. Marshals, Samuel R. Miller, John C. Avery, Wm. C. Anderson, Zebulon Byington, Wm. Doty, and Jesse Justice.

In 1831, Elisha Hotchkiss was elected Mayor, and in 1833 Samuel W. Davies to the same office, who held it by successive elections until 1843, when Henry E. Spencer became its incumbent.

The new Route East.

I had the pleasure on Monday, of seeing Mr. Winter, of the "Chemical Dioramas," who is just in from the Lakes, and have taken the following minutes from him on that. interesting subject—travelling on the newly opened route via Toledo to the East.

Mr. W. says he came through from Toledo by the Canal,247 miles, to our city,in 56 hours. Ex penses from Rochester to Cin'ti,as follows. Rochester to Buffalo, by Canal boat 100 feet long and cabins to match, $2 Buffalo to Toledo by steamboat Indiana, $6   Canal boat to Cincinnati, $7 50cts. Total from Rochester, $15 50cts.— If we add $2¼ from Rochester to Albany, and 50cts from Albany to New York, we have the aggregate expense from Cincinnati to New York, $18 50cts. Canal and steamboats, and rail road departures daily on the whole route.— Mr. W. who has been travelling of late years, all over the United States, gives this route eastward the preference for convenience and comfort over all others. Its speed and cheapness commend it equally to public notice and support.

Cincinnati Historical Society.

This Society has just issued a circular explaining its object, and inviting the co-operation of all who take any interest in collecting and preserving the various documents which are scattered through the community, shedding light on the early history, biography and antiquities of the west.

There must be much, within the reach of individuals, owned by them for which they cannot obtain as safe a depository as the society offers in its shelves and closets, much, that if not soon secured, must inevitably perish in the varied dangers to which it is exposed. I trust that the call of this Society will meet a ready and liberal response.

Building in Cincinnati.

The Louisville Courier of the 21st ult., offers a challenge by James S. Speed, bricklayer, on behalf of himself and brother-master bricklayers of that city, I presume, that they will lay more bricks there this season than any individual or firm in this city; and offer to bet a suit of the best that can be made in either city on the result. I am opposed to betting, and shall do nothing to secure them a bet here, the more so that I am conscious they would lose it, if made. I prefer stating facts to set Mr. Speed right, and refer him to any friend of his in Cincinnati; to verify the statement.

Mr. Lewis Todhunter, bricklayer, of our city, has now on hand, in various stages of erection,

nineteen buildings, in behalf of which bricks to the amount of 2,500,000 have been purchased or contracted for. Mr. John N. Ridgway has buildings, in progress and under contract, which will require 2,500,000 more.   From the 15th March to the 10th June; a period of but three and a half months, he has actually laid 1.500,000 of these, and the residue will be put into the walls by September.   Mr. Todhunter's engagements will also be completed by the same period, and there can be little doubt, judging by last year's work, that a million more bricks will be laid by these individuals before the year expires.— Here then will be six millions brick laid by these two alone. Will Mr. Speed say that he and his brother will lay in Louisville an equal quantity? When he does so I will furnish him with evidence that we have laid last year 80,000,000 brick, in and adjacent to Cincinnati, and there is every reason to believe we shall equal that amount this.

Our Common Schools.

I have said nothing on the subject of the late examination of our public schools, not that they do not interest me greatly,but because a weekly publication like mine, is not the proper vehicle for the record of matters occuring day by day successively, and because I have not room, consistently with other subjects requiring my notice, to do justice to our schools. By what I saw and what I learned, these institutions, popular in a double sense, are maintaining, and in some respects advancing their well earned reputation of past years. The public exhibitions, which on Tuesday last, crowned the labors of the past year, and brought the school sessions to a close for the summer vacation were crowded with deeply interested and admiring auditors and spectators. At the first district school, the following valedictory was sung by the scholars with marked effect.

A Parting Song.

Written for the Children of the First District Common School, Cincinnati; and sung at the Close of the Exhibition in that School, Friday, June 27th, 1845.

TUNE—Lucy Neal.

We meet, a band of children young,
  And on this happy day
We join together in a song,
  With voices light and gay;
No servile subjects of a King—
  No slavish tyrant's tools—
We freely meet, and freely sing
  Our noble COMMON SCHOOLS!
Oh! the Common Schools,
  Oh! the Common Schools;

The pride of Cincinnati fair,
Are these, her Common Schools!

From day to day, throughout the year,
With faithful mind and heart,
Our teachers kindly meet us here,
Instruction to impart:
And this our sole tuition fee—
Obedience to the rules;
For still to all alike are free
Our noble COMMON SCHOOLS!
Oh! the Common Schools, &c.

And while we join the good to praise
That on our lot attends,
To God our thankful hearts we raise,
Who gives us home and friends:
We bless him for the gift of mind,
With all that gift controls;
For parents, friends, and teachers kind,
And for our COMMON SCHOOLS!
Oh! the Common Schools, &c.

And now we part!—and all below
May never meet again;
For Life's a stage on which, we know,
Is many a changing scene:
But may each one around we see,
Life's lesson so improve,
That we shall all admitted be
To that great school above!
Oh! the Common Schools,
Oh! the Common Schools;
The pride of Cincinnati fair
Are still her Common Schools!.

L. J. C.

Cincinnati Fifty Years Ago--No. 1.

It will be recollected that Wayne's treaty with the Indians was made in 1795. This gave a wonderful impulse to the growth of the whole west, especially to the region in the neighborhood of Cincinnati. I propose to sketch as accurately as possible, the appearance and condition of our city at that period, as that of a village of a few hundred inhabitants. At that date, the residents, men, women, and children, were all personally known to each other.

I shall make my statements from notes taken down from the lips of the early settlers here.

The river Ohio was a bluff bank, and the trees in front of the city had been partially cleared.

Two or three coves at various points between Main and Lawrence streets, afforded landing places for boats. One of these known by the name of Yeatman's Cove, from the circumstance that our old fellow citizen, Griffin Yeatman kept tavern at the head of it, indented the bank at the foot of Sycamore street. Here the river was let in as far up nearly, as the line of Front street.

Another cove afforded a landing, as well as protection or boats just above Ludlow street; this was called Dorsey's cove. Another still higher up, projected from the river not far below Deer Creek. The shore fell off to Second or Columbia street, Water street being then higher than Front. An extensive swamp filled up the ground rearwards until it struck the base of the hill.

I shall complete the residue of this number from notes taken down by me, two or three years since, as the recollection of the oldest settler in Ohio. He has since deceased.

Emigrants came down in every sort of craft. I came down in a flat, loaded with corn, and landed in Cincinnati, April 7th 1794, precisely six years from my first landing at Marietta, April 7th, 1788, having been one of the original 49 who made the first settlement in Ohio. The oldest building now in the city, is Liverpool's old log cabin, corner of Walnut and Front street. It was one of the original cabins.*— There was a pond at the corner of Main and Fifth streets, which extended into the southwest corner—Burdsal's—of that block, a considerable distance. This was overgrown with alderbushes, and occupied by frogs. Main street above Fifth had to be causewayed with logs to pass it. I bought a lot of James Lyon, in 17-94—100 ft. by 200, on Walnut below Fourth for 150 dollars, and the corner of Fourth and Walnut the same size, three years afterwards, for a stud horse valued at 400 dollars. I cultivated the square opposite the Cincinnati College from 1795 to 1800, as a corn field. I was offered the corner lot of Main and 4th, 100 ft. on Main by 200 on Fourth street—the Harrison drug store corner—in 1796 for 250 dollars. The same year, Francis Menessier, of Gallipolis, bought the lot 100 feet on Main, and 200 feet on Third Street—where the Trust Company Bank stands, for an old saddle, not as good as can now be bought for ten dollars. Governor St. Clair bought 60 acres at 50 dollars per acre. This included that part of the city from the Canal to Mrs. Mercer's line, and from Main to Plumb streets. The wagons used frequently to mire in getting to the hill. I have helped to get them out at Liverpool's corner, and on Main street opposite Jonathan Pancoast's, where we had to pry them out with rails. Corn sold at 37½ cents per bushel, Pork at 50 to 75 cts. per 100 lbs. When it rose to one dollar every body said it would not keep that price. Wheat flour, 75 to 100 cts. per 100 lbs. Wild Turkeys 12½ to 25cts. each, according to quality. I have known wild turkeys shot, that were so fat that they would burst in falling. Rifle powder sold at 100 to 150 cts. per lb. Salt 6 to 7 dollars per bushel. I bought at those prices rock salt from M'Cullagh, who kept store on Main where Lawson's copper smith establishment now is. I was offered Conn's lot at the corner of Main and Lower Market street, 100 by 200, for 250 dollars, payable in carpenter work. St. Clair's house on Main street is the oldest permanent dwelling, & Hopple's on Lower Market street, the oldest building for business purposes in Cincinnati.

*Taken down in 1844.

Boston Wit.

The Bostonians, stimulated in water as well as railroads by New York City, have been for several months agitated by the question of introducing water from abroad for the supply of the article to that city. Handbills, addresses, pamphlets, and even caricatures on the subject abound. The following appears in the "Boston Courier" on the subject.

Examination of a Candidate for Water Commissioner.

"*Mark me,—now will I raise the waters,*"—MERCHANT OF VENICE.

Q.—Are you in favor of pure soft water?
Ar—I am in favor of whatsoever things are pure.
Q.—What water can be brought into the city successfully?
A.—Any that will run down hill.
Q.—But suppose the case of Taunton?
A.—It might be reinforced.
Q.—Do the people of Boston lack water?
A.—I know many who cannot boast of clean hands.
Q.—Where is the want chiefly felt?
A.—Among the "great unwashed·"
Q.—How many straddling bugs to the bucket full does the water of Long Pond contain?
A.—Just enough to make it a lively drink.
Q.—What do you think of the tadpoles in Mother Brook?
A.—That they may turn to croakers in time.
Q.—What animalculæ are to be discovered in the water of the Boston wells?
A.—Chiefly dead cats.
Q.—Are they numerous?
A.—Almost as numerous as the pamphlets on the water question.·
Q.—What proportion of a cat would a chemical analysis of the Boston water exhibit?
A.—I cannot say, but it is estimated that their united tails would reach the length of the proposed aqueduct.
Q.—Do you think a single-catted well affords water superior to one pretty well "stodged" with those animals?
A.—In general, I think it is not desirable that water for nice drinking should taste too strongly of cat.
Q.—Can you explain the reason why the water in Charles river is less catty now than formerly.
A.—It is supposed to have some connection with the increased manufacture of sausages.

Q.—What is your definition of "hard drinking?
A.—Sitting on a rock and swallowing cold water.
Q.—What corporation bids the fairest to bring a certain and constant supply of water into the city?
A.—A corporation of milk men.

The Harvest.

The farmers in the west are in the midst of a harvest, which is equal in abundance and quality to the finest they have ever gathered into their barns. The early hay has been comparatively a failure, but the second crop, as such, is superior to any thing previously known.

What is most remarkable in this, is that two or three weeks since, there was a general, indeed, universal impression, that the crops this year would prove a failure, in some regions utterly so. Such was the effect of the dry and parching weather, through March, April and May, that hay rose in the Cincinnati markets to twenty dollars per ton. Every description of feed for horses and cattle threatened to become exhausted, and probabilities of partial famine, and extreme pecuniary pressure became matter of gloomy foreboding. Two or three weeks of copious rainy weather, have changed the whole face of things, and increased our faith in the glorious promise, that seed time and harvest should not fail on the earth as long as it stands. I am glad to find that individuals who had bought up certain necessaries of life extensively, as objects of speculation, have been taught a valuable lesson on this score.

Bank Note Engraving.

A variety of Banks are now organizing throughout this State, and if we derive no other benefit from their issues, two points at any rate will be gained by the community. The banishment of the ragged and greasy notes now in circulation, and the establishment of a currency behind which we can look to the credit of the State, so far at least as to the value of bonds on which these issues are based. The engraving is doing and about to be done by *Rawdon, Wright & Hatch*, and *Toppan, Carpenter & Co.*, two engraving houses in Cincinnati.

It is the design of these banks to furnish portraits of the successive Governors of Ohio, as decorations for the three and one dollar issues.—Of these, I have seen those of Gov's. MORROW, VANCE and CORWIN, at the office of Messrs. Toppan, Carpenter and Co., and at Messrs. Rawdon, Wright, & Hatch, the portraits of Gov's. TIFFIN, M'ARTHUR and WORTHINGTON.

These are fine specimens of the proficiency to which Bank note Engraving has been brought in the West, and evidences that Ohio is able to supply these as well as other wants, out of her own resources.

Wayne's expedition in 1793.

The following diary appears to have been kept by an officer belonging to the legionary corps of Gen. Wayne. Aside from the freshness of this species of narration, written down on the spur of the moment, which in the hands of an intelligent writer is sure to interest, there are some incidental remarks worthy of notice.

The first is, that distances are described by the 'five mile spring,' 'seventeen mile' and 'twenty-nine mile tree,' which serves to point out the little improvement which the Miami country at that period afforded, as way marks on the march. But the letter is especially valuable, as a testimony from beginning to end of the untiring vigilance, and press-forward spirit of ANTHONY WAYNE, which afforded a presage from the first day's march, of his peculiar fitness for the hazardous and responsible service on which he was detached by government.

Camp S. W. Branch Miami, Oct. 22d. 1793.
DEAR SIR:

Agreeably to promise I have seized the first opportunity of writing you, and to be methodical in the business, I shall give it to you by way of journal.

7th Oct. our first day's march was great, considering that the army had not got properly in their geers—I think it was about 10 miles. Our second, 8th, was greater, it reached Fort Hamilton. Many of the men were exceedingly fatigued, and it was pretty generally believed, hard marching—the General thought otherwise, and it must be so. 9th, our third day's march, was to the five-mile spring, advance of Hamilton. Observe, we fortified our camp every night and were very vigilant, or ought to be so, 10th, our fourth day's march, we encamped about the 17 mile tree, and nothing extraordinary happened, excepting that our line of march extended for near five miles, owing to the rapidity of the marching, and the badness of the roads for our transportation, superadding the straggling soldiers, worn down with fatigue and sickness, brought up by the rear guard whom they retarded considerably.

11th, we proceeded on to the 29 mile tree, fortified as usual, and occupied a fine commanding ground, and nothing of consequence happened here. 12th, the roads were very bad, and some of our waggons broke down, but as the General's orders declared there should be no interstices, the line of march, was not impeded,

and we made say ten miles, this day. 13th we advanced by tolerable quick movements, until we came within a mile or so of Fort Jefferson, and this day furnished a good deal of sport, for as the devil would have it, Col. Hamtramck was manœuvreing his troops, and had a sham fight, which was construed by the whole army, as an attack upon our advanced guards or flankers—it really frightened a good many, but we all said, let them come, or, we are ready for them. We had marched hard this day, and I think not so well prepared; however it was at length discovered to be a sham fight, and every body knew it then. Oh, it was Hamtramck's usual practice! said they; but it was all in my eye—they never thought of Hamtramck. 14th, we marched past Fort Jefferson without even desiring to look at it; indeed some of us turned our heads the other way with disdain; and it has been threatened (as report says) to be demolished entirely. This day's march brought us to where *I* am now sitting, writing to my friend. We fortified our encampment very strong and feel very secure. 15th, the waggons were sent back to Fort St. Clair for stores, provisions, &c. and an escort of two subaltern, and between 80 and 90 men; and nothing happened extra this day. 16th, the devil to pay, Col. Blue, with near 20 of the cavalry went out to graze the horses of the troops, and after some time Blue discovered something crawling in the grass, which he at first thought was turkeys, but immediately found them to be two *Indians*, and ordered a charge; himself, two serjeants and a private charged, the rest ran away; the consequence was, the two Indians killed the two Serjeants—Blue and the private escaped. The leader of the rascals who behaved so cowardly was immediately tried and condemned, but pardoned the next day.— 17th, Lt. Lowry, Ensign, formerly Dr. Boyd with the escort of 90 men, guarding the wagons, were attacked by a party of thirty or forty Indians who rushed on with savage fury and yells which panic struck the whole party (excepting the two officers, and about 15 or 20 men, who fell a sacrifice to savage barbarity,) and they all fled, and have been coming into Fort St. Clair by twos and threes ever since. The Indians plundered the waggons, and carried off with them sixty-four of the best waggon horses in the army, killing six horses at the waggons in this defeat. Mr. Hunt has been a considerable loser; his wagon was plundered also. Col. Adair pursued the Indians, and found several horses dead, which he supposed had been tired and they killed them, a proof that their flight was very rapid. In this attack we have lost two promising, worthy and brave officers, and about twenty men, mostly of Capt. Shaylor's company for his and Capt. Prior's formed the escort, and are both now rather in disgrace.

We have been led to believe that this place would have been made the grand deposit until this day; we now learn that there will be a *forward move* in the course of ten days, nine miles further into the Indian country, to a place called Still Water; the reason I can't surmise, but they say, they are very cogent ones, *I* have no business to pry, but if I should accidentally find it out. you shall be informed. In the meantime, Believe me to be very sincerely,

your friend,
JNO: M. SCOTT.

Mill Creek Bridges.

MR. CIST:

Dear Sir—When I first knew Mill creek, and until the year 1822, the bed of that stream was not more than half of what it is at present. The creek banks, especially on the east side, were much bolder, and the creek extended further into the river than at present. Mill creek was deep and miry in that neighborhood, and we were compelled to cross at a ford about half a mile up. Even at this distance, so subject was the creek to back water, that many lives were lost in early days, at such times, of those who rode or drove in, ignorant of the depth.— The first effort towards a bridge was made in 1798, by Symmes and others, which failed for want of funds. In 1806, exertions were again made to put a bridge across, by subscription.— One Parker was the architect, who built it of yellow poplar which grew on the Mill Creek bottoms. This was a fragile affair which might have lasted a few years, if it had not been carried away by a flood in December, 1808. It cost about 700 dollars. This was the bridge alluded to in yours of the 11th inst. *I* knew Francis White very well. He was suspected by the neighbors of securing the gun boat under the bridge with the design of carrying it away, in the expectation of making money by the ferry he kept. *In* 1811 a new bridge was put up by Ethan Stone, under authority from the Legislature and of course was subject to toll. This remained eleven years, and was carried off in 18-22 by the greatest freshet ever known on that stream before or since. Mill creek had been swollen by heavy rains at the head waters in the course of one night, and such was the effect at the mouth, that by morning the bridge and an immense pile of masonry in the shape of abutments had disappeared, and the creek doubled in width to its present size. Such was the violence of the freshet, that it tore out of root two sycamore trees, adjacent to the bridge, of the largest description. Muddy creek which

puts into the Ohio, two miles above North Bend, was equally swelled, and on this occasion more than an acre of Judge Short's orchard was swept away, on the highest bank between the Great and Little Miamis. The river Ohio was then as low as it has been any time this season, which increased the power and injury of this freshet. As an evidence how much narrower the mouth of Mill creek has been. it may be stated that the bridge put up in 1811 was but one hundred and twenty feet in length. By virtue of the same authority, Mr. Stone again put up a bridge; this time built with arches, which the county purchased out of his hands, and made a free bridge. This was the one carried off by the great flood of 1832, brought back from near Louisville, and afterwards destroyed by fire three years since.

Yours respectfully,
J. MATSON.
North Bend, June 29th, 1845.

Churches in Cincinnati.

A correspondent corrects my last list of Churches, by stating that the church on College street, put down as under the pastoral care of Dr. Brisbane, is in reality a Welsh Calvinistic Methodist church, in charge of Rev. Edward Jones, which worships in Harrison street, having sold the house, now and formerly occupied by them for religious purposes, to the "Colored Disciples Church."

It is believed that this Welsh church applied for admission into the Presbyterian church general, by making an application to that effect to the late Gen'l Assembly, sitting in Cincinnati, and that their application was granted, although no public recognition of the fact has been made.

Dr. Brisbane's congregation, since they left their late church edifice, occupy the Doctor's parlors, which has been furnished with seats for that purpose.

MARRIAGES.

In this city, on Sunday the 13th inst., by Mark P. Taylor, Esq., by Mr. WILLIAM ALLEN to Miss MARY LOUISA WILCOX.

On Tuesday the 8th inst., by the Rev. D. Sheppardson, Mr. ANDREW GALLY to Miss CHARLOTTE FOUNTAIN.

On Wednesday the 9th inst, by Elder Wm. P. Stratton, Mr. JOSEPH T. VANSANT to Miss PHEBE DAVIS.

DEATHS.

At Bedford Springs, Pa., on the 3d inst, JAMES F. CONOVER, Esq., president of Cin. Gas Co.

In this city, on Monday the 7th inst. SARAH AMANDA, youngest daughter of Allen Goodrich and Harriet Elliot Kellogg; aged one year and eight months.

On Wednesday the 9th inst, CAROLINE VICTORIA, eldest daughter of John and Mary Bailey; aged 7 years.

On Thursday the 10th inst, Mrs. MARY CLARK, wife of John Clark, late of East Kensington, Pa.

Documents of last War.

ORDERS, CINCINNATI, Sept. 16th, 1813.

COL. HENRY ZUMALT:

Sir--You will on the receipt of this, march your regiment with as much expedition as possible to Dayton, and from thence to Franklinton, and report yourself to the commander in Chief or your superior officer, and obey such orders as you may receive as to the further march and disposition of the regiment under your command. The two companies from Lebanon, and the two companies from Hamilton, you must order to march, and join you at Dayton. The procuring music is essential, and the commander in chief has informed me some extra pay will be allowed if you can procure it--you will march this evening if possible. Two months pay will be advanced as soon as it can be procured, therefore the pay-master must be furnished with the muster rolls, that he may follow with the money. The Qrms &c. on your march will see that you are furnished with every necessary for men on march.

Attest   J. S. GANO,

Maj. Gen. Com'dt. 1st Div. O. Mi.

D. WADE, Aid.

This day gave an order on Maj. Morton for 50 stands of arms and accoutrements for Zumalt's regiment.

Extracts from a letter dated Sept. 18th, 1813, from Gen. Harrison to Gov. Meigs.

"Be pleased to send a full company of one hundred men to Fort Meigs—thirty or forty will do for Lower Sandusky."

"I am informed that the term of the Garrison at Fort Findlay, will expire on the 22d inst. will you be pleased to order there twenty or thirty men."

ROBT. C. BARTON,

Aiddecamp.

Rec'd. the 24th.

Franklinton, Sept. 22d, 1813.

FRANKLINTON, Sept. 28th, 1813.

DEAR GENERAL:

I have to inform you the regiment from the first division left here yesterday for Sandusky, and from thence to Seneca, without receiving their advance pay as promised them. I was obliged to apply to the Quarter Master, at this place for some shoes, socks and blankets for them which I procured, on a statement made, and becoming responsible to that department, that I would procure your sanction—69 pair shoes--26 pair socks, and 68 blankets, which the men have receipted for as part of their pay, and will be deducted. I expect to leave this day for Sandusky, from which place I will again write you.

I am happy to inform you I have prevailed on Major J. Lawrence Lewis, a gentleman, and an excellent disciplinarian, to act as Brigade Major and Inspector to the Ohio troops. He certainly will be an acquisition to us, and to the service, and is very highly recommended by Gov. Meigs, and the first characters in the State. I have ordered a detachment to Fort Findlay, and there is also a company at Manares Blockhouse, &c. I have had no accurate return of the Ohio militia in service, except Col. Zumalt's regiment, which is near eight hundred strong, and Col. Delong's, which is about the same, though a number has been detached to the Quarter Master, and artificer's department; and I have had to leave some sick. The men that have marched are fine, robust, healthy men; and if they had some pay to purchase necessaries, say they will be willing to march to any place where ordered. I have been obliged to be very rigid with the officers and men, and I find both want drilling--and that will never make some men officers. Any orders you may have to communicate relative to the Ohio commission shall be immediately attended to by your most Ob't. humble serv't.

JOHN S. GANO,

Maj. Gen. Com'dt. O. Mil. in service.

HEADQUARTERS, SANDWICH,
CANADA, Oct. 1st. 1813.

SIR:

Your dispatch of the 26th inst., was received last evening. You will leave a company at Upper Sandusky, and march all the rest of your command to Lower Sandusky, where also you will leave a company. With the balance of your command you will proceed to Fort Meigs. You will be pleased to give Capt. Oliver, the commissary, every assistance in your power to get the provisions for the army. Upon your arrival at Fort Meigs, you will leave there about twenty effective men, and with the balance proceed to this place with the drove of cattle which is coming on for the use of the army.

Yours respectfully,

WM. HENRY HARRISON.

Col. DELONG, Com'dg. a Det. of O. Mi'a,

A true copy, A. A. MEEK.

Growth of our cities.

I have been waiting to get the house building for 1844 in our principal cities, that I might compare their relative growth, and now present the results.

The number of houses put up in 1844, was in

Philadelphia,	1512
New York,	1213
Boston,	1625
Cincinnati,	1228

Assuming the existing population as a basis, to keep up the Cincinnati ratio of improvement, Philadelphia should have put up 2763, N, York 4052, and Boston 2149. In other words, to equal our growth, Philadelphia should have increased 80, New York 230, and Boston 32 por cent, more than they have during the year referred to.

The actual increase of buildings in these cities brought to a scale common to them all, points out the present growth of New York 4, Philadelphia 7, Boston 10, and Cincinnati 13 per cent. annually, calculating on the existing condition of those cities, respectively.

March of Mind.

We are apt to boast of the refinement and intelligence of the nineteenth century. What with Phrenology, Etherology, and Clairvoyance, we seem retrograding to the dark ages, and it may be within the chapter of possibilities, that we shall yet revive "witch craft" panics. What is there in the superstitions of the past to surpass the following?

SALES' CELEBRATED MAD-STONE, *A well tried and sure preventive to HYDRO-PHOBIA, from the bites of Mad-dogs and other rabid animals.*

THIS justly celebrated Mad-Stone, so long the property of the late Humphrey Sale, of Caroline county, Virginia, in whose hands it proved so successful in preventing that dreadful disease, the HYDROPHOBIA, in hundreds of cases, of persons who had been so unfortunate as to be bitten by Mad-dogs, or other mad animals, is now the property of the subscriber, who has it in his possession, and who resides at CHERRY GROVE, in the lower end of Caroline county, three miles from Sparta, and on the road leading from Port Royal to Newtown.

The subscriber begs leave to assure the pulic, that the good qualities and virtues of this Stone, in preventing bad effects from the bites and wounds made by Mad-dogs and other rabid and venomous animals and reptiles, have been so frequently and fully proven to the satisfaction of the community at large, that he deems it only necessary for him to say, that it is with the greatest confidence he recommends it to public patronage.

The terms of application of the Stone, are, for every patient Fifty Dollars, and Board, with the kindest attention given, free of charge.

He would also inform persons residing at a distance, who may require the services of the Mad-Stone, that his residence is about 12 miles from Milford Depot, on the Richmond and Fredericksburg railroad, and about the same distance from Port Royal, on the Rappahannock river, where a steamboat passes twice a week

SAMUEL ANDERSON.

'Tommy, my son, what is longitude?'
'A clothes line, daddy.'
'Prove it, my son.'
'Because it stretches from pole to pole.'

Value of a Lawyer's Opinion.

Cities, like men, have their peculiar characteristics. Industrious, maritime, wise or frivolous, they reveal by their physiognomy the nature of their inhabitants. Every thing that strikes your eye will be a revelation of the fates of the citizens, the history of each class of population will be found, so to speak, written in the streets.

One is especially struck with the truth of this remark, on visiting Rennes; on seeing its grand edifices and magisterial mein; its magnificent squares, with grass springing up between the paving stones; promenades traversed at long intervals by thoughtful students.

It happened that a farmer named Bernard, having come to market at Rennes, took it into his head, when his business was accomplished and there were a few hours of leisure, that it would be a capital use of that spare time to consult a lawyer. He had often heard people speak of M. Portier de la Germandie, whose reputation was so great that the people thought a suit already gained if he undertook it. Bernard asked for his address, and went immediately to his office in St. George street.

The clients were numerous, and Bernard had to wait for a long time. At length his turn came and he was introduced. M. Portier de la Germandie pointed him a chair, laid his spectacles upon his table, and asked what brought him there.

"Pon my word, Squire,' said the farmer, twirling his hat round, 'I heard so much talk about you, that finding myself at leisure in Rennes, I thought I would take advantage of the circumstance and come and get an *opinion* of you.'

'I thank you for your confidence, my friend,' said M. de la Germandie, 'but you, of course, have a law suit.'

'A law suit! a law suit, indeed!! I hold them in utter abomination; and more than that Peter Bernard never had a dispute with any man living.'

'Then you wish to settle some estate, or divide the property among the family.'

'Beg pardon, Squire, my family and I never had any property to divide: we eat from the same dish, as the saying is.'

'It is about some contract for the purchase or sale of something.'

'Not at all; I am not rich enough to purchase any thing, nor so poor as to sell what I have.'

'What, then, do you want of me?' asked the astonished lawyer.

'What do I want? Why, I told you at first, Squire, I came for an *opinion* for which I will pay of course, as I am in Rennes now at leisure, and it is necessary to profit by the circumstance.'

M. de la Germandie took pen and paper, and asked the countryman his name.

'Peter Bernard,' answered he; happy indeed that he had succeeded in making himself understood.

'Your age?'
'Thirty years or thereabout.'
'Your profession?'
'My profession? Oh, ah, yes—that is what I am. Oh, I am a farmer.'

The lawyer wrote two lines, folded up the paper and gave it to the client.

'Is it done already?' said Bernard. 'Very well, that's right. There is no time to get rusty here, as they say. How much do you charge for this opinion, Squire?'

'Three francs.'

Bernard paid without disputing, made a grand scrape with his foot; and went out delighted with having profited by the occasion.'

When he arrived at home, it was already four o'clock. The jaunt had fatigued him, and he went into the house for repose.

Meantime, his grass had been cut four days, and was completely dried, and one of his lads came to ask whether he should get it in at once.

'Not this evening,' said Mrs. Bernard, who had just joined her husband; 'it would be too bad to set the people to work at so late an hour when the hay can be got in to-morrow just as well.'

The lad urged that there might be a change of weather, that every thing was in order, and the people were doing nothing.

Mrs. Bernard said the wind seemed to be in the right quarter for fair weather, and they would not get the work done before dark that night.

Bernard listened gravely to these *advocates* without knowing how to decide between them, when he suddenly recollected the paper he had received from the lawyer.

'Stop a minute,' cried he, 'I have got an *opinion*. It is from a famous lawyer, and cost me three francs. This will settle the matter. Here, Therese, come tell us what it says; you can read all kinds of writing, even a lawyer's.

Mrs. Bernard took the paper, and with some little difficulty read these lines:—

'Never put off until to-morrow what you can do to-day.'

'That's it,' said Bernard, as if he had received sudden light upon the subject. 'Make haste with the wagon, the girls and the boys, and let us get the hay in.'

His wife offered some more objections, but Bernard declared that he was not going to pay three francs for an opinion, and then not follow it; so he set the example, and led all hands to the field, and they did not return to the house until all the hay was in the barn.

The event seemed to prove the sagacity of Bernard's movements, for the weather changed in the night. A terrible storm came on, and the next morning the streams had overflowed their banks, and swept off every particle of new mown grass. The hay harvest of every other farmer in the neighborhood was utterly destroyed.— Bernard alone saved his hay.

The first experiment gave him such confidence in the *opinion* of the lawyer, that ever after he adopted it as a rule of conduct, and became—thanks to his order and diligence—one of the richest farmers in the country. He never forgot the service which M. de la Germandie had rendered him, and he brought every year to that lawyer, a pair of good fat chickens; and he was in the habit of saying to his neighbors, when they were talking of the lawyers, that next to the commands of God and the church, the most profitable thing to the world was a lawyer's OPINION.

New Mayor of New York.

The New Mirror gives the following republican anecdote of the new municipal first magistrate.

"Mr. Havemayer was educated at Columbia College, where he took his degree with great credit to himself. The day after his release from Alma Mater, he was standing with his father, on the steps of the sugar bakery, and the old gentleman took the opportunity to inquire into his choice of a profession, 'I suppose, now you have finished your education," said he, "you will be a lawyer or a physician?" "Neither!" said the son. "And what then?" exclaimed the father, a little surprised at his son's decision.—'In the first place, sir, I'll drive that cart!' was the firm reply, and when I have been through all the subordinate steps of your business, I'll share in the direction of it, with your leave?' He "suited the action to the word," for calling to the man who was about leaving the door with a load, he jumped upon the cart, took the reins and commenced his apprenticeship.— He *drove cart for a year*, and rose gradually, through all the stations of his father's employ, till he finally became a partner, and an able one, in the business.

Science of Sounds.

The following hints will be of much utility to some of our readers,—and especially to those whose duty calls them to speak often in public.

"It is a curious fact in the history of sounds, that the loudest noises perish almost on the spot where they are produced, whereas musical tones will be heard at a great distance. Thus if we approach within a mile or two of a town or village in which a fair is held, we may hear very faintly the clamor of the multitude, but most distinctly the organs and other musical instruments which are played for their amusement. If a Cremona violin, Amati, be played by the side of a modern, the latter will sound much the louder of the two, but the sweet brilliant tone of the Amati will be heard at a distance the other cannot reach. Doctor Young, on the authority of Durham, states, that at Gibraltar the human voice was heard at the distance of ten miles. It is a well known fact, that the human voice is heard at a greater distance than that of any other animal. Thus, when the cottager in the woods, or in an open plain, wishes to call her husband, who is working at a distance, she does not shout but pitches her voice to a musical key, which she knows from habit, and by that means reaches his ear.—The loudest roar of the largest lion could not penetrate so far. "This property of music in the human voice," says the author, "is strikingly shown in the cathedral abroad.— Here the mass is entirely performed in musical sounds, and becomes audible to every devotee, however placed in the remotest part of the church; whereas, if the same service had been read, the sounds would not have travelled beyond the precincts of the choir." Those orators who are heard in large assemblies most distinctly, are those who, in modulating the voice, render it most musical. Loud speakers are seldom heard to advantage. Burke's voice is said to have been a sort of a lofty cry. which tended, as much as the formality of his discourses in the house of Commons, to send the members to their dinner. Chatham's lowest whisper was distinctly heard, "his middle tone was sweet, rich and beautifully varied;" says a writer describing the orator, "when he raised his voice to its high pitch, the house was completely filled with the volume of sounds; and the effect was awful, except when he wished to cheer and animate; and then he had a spirit-stirring note, which was perfectly irresistible. The terrible, however, was his peculiar power. Then the house sunk before him; still he was dignified, and wonderful as was his eloquence, it was attended with this important effect, that it possessed every one with a conviction that there was something in him finer even than his words; that the man was infinitely greater than the orator."

Fancy Drinks.

The following are ONLY a few of the fancy drinks manufactured at Concert Hall, Boston:—Clay and Huysen, Polk and Dallas, Race Horse, Ching Ching. Tog. Rappee. Tip and Ty, Fiscal Agent, I. O. U., Tippena Pecco, Morai Suasion, Vox Populi, Ne Plus Ultra, Shambro, Pig and Whistle, Silver top, Poor Man's Punco. Split Ticket. Deacon, Exchange, Stone Wall, Virginia Fence, Floater, Shifter.

Who says that Boston, with all its boasted temperance, cant come the "fancy touches" in the spirituous way, over all other cities.

Irish Friars.

In Ireland a warming pan is called a friar.—Not many years ago, an unsophisticated girl took service in a hotel in the town of ———— Poor thing—she had never heard of a warming pan in her life, though she regularly confessed to a friar once a year.

It so happened, on a cold and drizzly night, that a priest took lodgings in the inn. He had travelled far, and being weary, retired at an early hour Soon after, the mistress of the house called the servant girl.

'Betty, put the friar into No. 6.'

Up went Betty to the poor priest.

'Your reverence must go into No. 6, my mistress says.'

'How, what?' asked he, annoyed at being disturbed.

'Your reverence must go into No. 6.'

There was no help for it, and the priest arose donned a dressing gown and went into No. 6. In about fifteen minutes the mistress called to Betty,

'Put the friar into No. 4.'

Betty said something about disturbing his reverence, which her mistress did not understand. So she told the girl, in a sharp voice to do always as she was directed, and she would always do right. Up went Betty, and the unhappy priest, despite his angry protestations, was obliged to turn out of No. 6, and go into No. 4.— But a little time elapsed ere the girl was told to put the friar into No. 8, and the poor priest thinking that every body was mad in the house, and sturdily resolved to quit it on the next morning, crept into the damp sheets of No. 8. But he was to enjoy no peace there. Betty was again directed to put the friar into No. 3, and with tears in her eyes she obeyed. In about an hour, the landlady concluded to go to bed herself, and the friar was ordered into her room.—Wondering what it all mean Betty. t roused up the priest and told him that he must go into No. 11. The monk crossed himself, counted his beads, and went into No. 11. It so happened that the husband of the landlady was troubled with the greeneyed monster. Going up to bed,

therefore, before his wife, his suspicions were confirmed by seeing between his own sheets, a man sound asleep. To rouse the sleeper and kick him into the street was the work of a moment; nor was the mistake explained till the next day, when the priest informed the innkeeper what outrages had been committed upon him, and he learned to his amazement, that he had been serving the whole night as a warming pan.

Hiram Powers.

Late letters from Hiram Powers to his friends in Cincinnati, afford us some interesting information of that distinguished artist's progress and prospects.

Since the exhibition of his GREEK CAPTIVE at Pall mall, which was attended by the whole world of fashion and influence in society, Mr. Powers has received three orders for duplicates of that statue. He has also an order for a duplicate of the EVE, the original being destined for this country, which it will no doubt reach by spring, in company with copies of the Greek Slave, Fisher boy, &c. These may be expected in Boston by June next. Lord Francis Egerton, the owner of the well known Stafford gallery of Sculpture and paintings, has transmitted Mr. P. an order for a work from his chisel, giving the artist a carte blanche as to the subject.

The high eminence and distinguished success of Powers, reflect great credit on the judgment of his early friends, and the discriminating liberality of one of our citizens, who afforded him the means of establishing himself in Italy, where surrounded by all that is excellent in Art, ancient or modern, his wonderful productions are creating an era in Sculpture.

Property Investments in Cincinnati.

As the central parts of our city fill up, its outside is of necessity taken up for improvements; and garden, and even farming lots are becoming rapidly absorbed in the demands for building purposes which are growing out of our constantly increasing population and business. On monday morning the owner of a three acre lot on Eighth street, near Mill creek who purchased it in 1829, at $700 per acre, was offered, forty thousand dollars for the premises! After reflecting an hour or two, he refused it.

On Friday last, a kitchen garden property of sixteen acres just across Mill creek, exchanged owners, at the price of 22,000 dollars, one half cash down—the residue one and two year payments. The purchasers in this case have bought it as an investment, having heretofore never laid out money in property. I state this to indicate that these prices are not speculative values. In connexion with these facts, it may be well to remark that Eighth st. is now paved, or in process of paving from Main street west, *more than two miles,* and will require and maintain a communication to Delhi, Greene, and other townships which must constitute it shortly one of the main avenues of Cincinnati.

Wm. Penn and John Cleves Symmes.

These men were wonderfully alike in some things, while greatly dissimilar in others. The same intelligent views of dealing with their savage neighbors, actuated both. It is true that Symmes cannot compare with Penn in the enlarged benevolence which shut out the sale of rum to the aborigines, but it must be recollected that Penn had been enlightened on that subject before he left his native country, and that Symmes merely conformed to the almost universal practice of the region and the age in which he lived. Both were men of comprehensive views, who looked to and lived for the future, conscious that they were laying foundations for commonwealths of greater consequence than the States they left. Wm. Penn when about taking possession of his new purchase, directed this letter to his Indian neighbors. Its authenticity may be relied on.

ENGLAND, 2mo. 21st, 1682.

The Great God, who is in the power and wisdom that made you and me, incline your hearts to righteousness, love and peace. This I send you to assure you of my love, and to desire you to love my friends: and when the Great God brings me among you, I intend to order all things in such manner, that we may all live in love and peace, one with another, which I hope the Great God will incline both you and me to do. I seek nothing but the honor of his name, and that we who are his workmanship, may do that which is well pleasing to him. The man which delivers this unto you,is my special friend, sober, wise and loving, and you may believe him. I have already taken care that none of my people wrong you; by good laws I have provided for that purpose; nor will I ever allow any of my people to sell *rumme* to make your people drunk. If any thing should be out of order, expect when I come it shall be mended, and I will bring you some things of our country that are useful and pleasant to you.

So I rest in the love of our God that made us. I am your loving friend,

WM. PENN.

I read this letter to the Indians by an interpreter, the 6th mo, 1682.

THO. HOLM.

After SYMMES had completed his contract with the United States for the Miami purchase he despatched the following letter, from Lime-stone, now Maysville, Ky., to the Indians in possession of the territory.

"Brothers of the Wyandots and Shawanese! Hearken to your brother, who is coming to live at the Great Miami. He was on the Great Miami last summer, while the Deer was yet red, and met with one of your camps; he did no harm to any thing which you had in your camp; he held back his young men from hurting you or your horses, and would not let them take your skins or meat, though your brothers were very hungry. All this he did, because he was your brother, and would live in peace with the Red people. If the Red people will live in friend ship with him, and his young men who came from the great Salt ocean, to plant corn and built Cabins on the land between the Great and Little Miami, then the White and Red people shall all be brothers and live together, and we will buy your Furs and Skins, and sell you Blankets and Rifles, and Powder and Lead and Rum, and every thing that our Red Brothers may want in hunting and in their towns.

Brothers! A treaty is holding at Muskingum Great men from the thirteen fires are there, to meet the Chiefs and head men of all the nations of the Red people. May the Great spirit direct all their councils for peace! But the great men and the wise men of the Red and White people cannot keep peace and friendship long, unless we, who are their sons and warriors, will also bury the hatchet and live in peace.s

Brothers! I send you a string of white beads, and write to you with my own hand, that you may believe what I say. I am your brother, and will be kind to you while you remain in peace. Farewell!

JNO. C. SYMMES.
January the 3d, 1789.

The Western Farmer and Gardener.

This is a periodical, devoted, as its title purports to the cause of the cultivation of the soil, that grand and sole basis of worldly prosperity to the whole community. It is now in its fifth volume, struggling along through the precarious and inadequate support which almost every publication beyond a newspaper seems doomed to, in this banknote world of ours.

The Farmer & Gardener is however, a work of great merit, and of peculiar value, as a register of observations and facts communicated by many of its intelligent subscribers. It is embellished monthly with lithographs of our best fruits and fairest flowers, and at two dollars per annum, affords the cheapest vehicle of communicating or obtaining much interesting matter of great interest to the Farmer and Horticulturist The names of those who are engaged contributing original articles from time to time as may be seen by looking them over, are such as would confer credit upon any periodical of the kind, while they inspire confidence in the views they express, or facts they communicate.

The Jewish Pilgrim at Jerusalem.

Are these the ancient, holy hills,
   Where Angels walked of old?
Is this the land our story fills
   With glory yet not cold?
For I have passed through many a shrine,
   O'er many a land and sea,
But still, Oh! promised Palestine,
   My dreams have been of thee.

I see thy mountain cedars green,
   Thy vallies fresh and fair;
With summers bright as they have been
   When Israel's home was there:
Tho' o'er thee sword and time have passed,
   And cross and crescent shone,
And heavily the chain hath pressed—
   Yet still thou art our own:

Thine are the wandering race that go
   Unblessed through every land,
Whose blood hath stained the polar snow,
   And quenched the desert sand!
And thine the homeless hearts that turn
   From all Earth's shrines to thee,
With their lone faith for ages bourne
   In sleepless memory.

For thrones are swept and nations gone
   Before the march of time.
And where the ocean rolled alone
   Are forests in their prime;
Since Gentile plowshare marred the brow
   Of Zion's holy hill—
Where are the Roman eagles now?
   Yet Judah wanders still.

And hath she wandered thus in vain
   A pilgrim of the past?
No! long deferred her hope has been,
   But it shall come at last;
For in her wastes a voice I hear,
   As from some prophet's urn,
It bids the nations build not there,
   For Jacob shall return.

Oh! lost and loved Jerusalem!
   Thy pilgrim may not stay
To see the glad earth's harvest home
   In thy redeeming day;
And now resigned in faith and trust,
   I seek a nameless tomb;
At least beneath thy hallowed dust—
   Oh! give the wanderer room!

A Legend of Kentucky.

NORTH BEND, July 12th, 1845.

MR. CIST:

Your friend *John Hindman* is in error, alleging that Tanner's Creek, Indiana, derived its name from young Tanner being killed by the Indians on its waters. Tanner was not killed at all, although doubtless believed to be by the neighborhood, at the time Hindman left the Great Miami, which was soon after Tanner had been carried away by the savages. I knew the whole family well—the old man Tanner being the first clergyman, I ever heard preach at North Bend, and for some time the only one.

Tanner the father, owned the land, where Petersburg, Kentucky, is now built, and resided on it, being about three miles below the Miami, and opposite the creek which derived its name as the station also did, from Tanner who was the principal man settled there. Hogan, Tanner's son-in-law, who lived with him, and was a first-rate hunter, gave name to the creek just above Aurora.

In May, 1790 *John Tanner*, the youngest boy, and nine years of age, was out in the woods gathering walnuts, which had been lying over from the previous season among the leaves, when he was made prisoner by a party of Indians, and carried to the *Shawnese* towns, in the first place, and afterwards taken away to the head waters of the Mississippi. Nothing was heard of him by his friends for 24 years, except that in 1791, the next year, a party of Indians, composed partly of the same individuals, prowling in the neighborhood, captured *Edward Tanner*, a brother of John, and nearly fifteen years old. After travelling two days journey in the wilderness. the boy appearing contented, and supposing that he would be discouraged from attempting to make his escape, at such a distance from home, his captors relaxed their vigilance, and the boy watching his opportunity regained his liberty, being obliged in the hurry to leave his hat, which was of undyed wool, behind, and which the Indians carried to their home. They had told him on their way out, that they had carried a boy off from the same place the year before. John Tanner recognized the hat as soon as he saw it as his brother's.

Nothing was known of John, as already stated, for many years, although Edward attended the various treaties for successive years, and travelled to distant points, even west of the Mississippi. The Indians with whom John was domesticated, had been for years settled on the Upper Mississippi, and traded with the Hudson Bay Company, which of course baffled the search thus made. In 1798, the Tanner family left

Kentucky for *New Madrid,* where old Tanner died, after marrying in the mean time a third wife.

In 1817, soon after the close of the war, Tanner, who by this time had married an Indian wife, and had six children by her, with a view of learning something about his relations, and expecting to receive a share of the family property came down the chain of lakes to Detroit, and there reported himself to Gov. Cass, as an Indian captive, taken from opposite the mouth of Big Miami, in Kentucky, in 1790. He gave the family name as Taylor, which was as near as he could recollect or probably articulate it. Cass gave notice of the fact through the medium of the press, adding that the individual would be present at a treaty to be held with the *I*ndians at St. Mary's, formerly *Girty's town,* and now the county seat of Mercer County, Ohio. The Tanner family had removed years since to New Madrid, and with the exception of Edward Tanner, was composed of the widow and children, born of the later marriages, since John's capture. But a nephew by marriage of the young men named Merritt, who lived where *Rising Sun* has since been built, having seen the notice, was firmly persuaded, that the individual, although improperly named, was his long lost and long sought uncle Tanner, and under that conviction went to the treaty ground, and found the case as he supposed it to be. The two started off for the Miami region together. Tanner, although in feeble health, having fever and ague at the time, was with difficulty persuaded to sleep in the cabins which they found on the route, preferring to camp out, and to gratify him, one fine night, Merritt, having selected a suitable spot for repose, went to a neighboring house, got coals, and attempted to kindle a fire, which as the leaves and brush were wet, burned with difficulty. Tanner who had become thoroughly Indian during his long residence among them, now got up in a pet, kicked the fire to pieces, and flashing powder from his rifle made his own fire, remarking, White man's fire *no good.* Indian fire, *good!* They stopped all night at my house on their way to the lower country, and there I obtained these particulars. When they reached New Madrid, it so happened that Edward was out on one of his excursions to hunt up his brother, and John after waiting a few days, became impatient to get back, and left for home without even seeing his brother, who had sought him so anxiously for years. Soon after reaching his Indian home, Tanner had a quarrel with an Indian and was badly shot, but after lingering a great while, recovered so far as to set out with Col. Long, and a party who were

on their way to Detroit. His strength gave way on the journey, and they were obliged to leave him on the road. He finally recovered and was employed by the United States authorities as interpreter among the Indians at the Sault St. Marie at the outlet of Lake Superior, which is the last I heard of him.

Tanner's life was published years ago, but I never saw a copy of it, and do not know whether it is now extant.

Respectfully yours,

J. MATSON.

Problem in Physics.

Every miller is familiar with the fact, that the velocity of water wheels is greater by night than by day, and that, of course, he can grind in the same proportion more, in an equal period between sun-set and daylight, than from daylight to sun-set. At a saw mill, also, a greater quantity of lumber can be cut by night than by day, in the same number of hours. So a flat or keel boat floats further in an equal space of time by night than by day. And there are many more facts of the same class, well attested, which present an interesting problem in natural philosophy. I can conceive of but two causes to produce these results; and they do not, even unitedly, seem to me sufficient to account for the effect. The first is, that water, at a temperature of 60 deg., weighs 61 lbs. per cubic foot, while at 40 degrees, it weighs 62 lbs. If these temperatures represent the ordinary difference between day and night, the specific gravity of the water is 1-62nd part greater by night than by day, and the same ratio will indicate the difference of power applied to the wheels during the same periods.

Another and weightier cause, is that vapors held suspended in the upper regions of the atmosphere by day, descend by night, and rest upon the water, and by their weight and density, increase the action of the water, in the same degree of difference that exists between air heated by the noon day sun, and the same air chilled by the dews of night.

I have said that a boat will float further in the same number of hours by night than by day, but the fact on this point of the subject, as determined by my own experience, is, that a keel boat will *float* as far in the twelve hours of night as she can be *rowed* during the twelve hours of day. I came down the Ohio in 1826, on a keel boat, during an uncommon rise, and the last two days of our passage to Cincinnati, we rowed forty-eight miles each day, and floated forty-eight miles each night, commencing both periods from six o'clock, and of course, allowing to each twelve hours.

I should feel gratified to receive a better solution of the problem involved in the case, than I am conscious, is furnished in this article.

A Law Student in Alabama.

An exchange says, that Mr. C., who studied law in the office of a senior member of the bar in some town of some State, emigrated to Alabama for his examination.

'Judge P.,' said Mr. C's. friend, 'is now in the village; will you go and stand your examination.

Of course C. consented. He had been several days anxiously waiting for the Judge at the ——Exchange, alias grocery,——alias doggery. After the formality of an introduction, the Judge said:

'Well, Mr. C., you want to be examined for admittance to the bar.'

'Yes, sir.'

'Well, sir, let's take something to drink—Barkeeper, give us two juleps.'

'Mr. C., can you swim?'

'Yes sir, I can,' said C., greatly surprised.

'Well, sir, let's take another drink—barkeeper, two cocktails.'

The cocktails vanished, and the Judge said—

'Mr. C. have you got a horse?'

'Certainly sir,' said C.

'Very good,' said the Judge, as soberly as though charging a Grand Jury. 'Mr. C., if you please, we'll take a drink. Barkeeper, two toddies.'

The toddies disappeared, and C. owns he began to feel rather queer.

'Mr. C.' said the Judge, 'can your horse swim?'

'Yes, sir,' he can—'for I have tried him from necessity.'

'Then sir,' said the Judge with increased gravity, 'your horse can swim—and you can swim, and by ——, I think you are well qualified for an Alabama lawyer. Give me your commission, and I will sign it. Meanwhile, barkeeper, give us two punches for my friend Mr, C, and myself.

Mr. C.,' continued the Judge, 'I drink success to your admission to the Alabama bar.'

Powers of Music.

In the "Gossip with Readers and Correspondents" we find the following illustration on the power of music.

'Oblige us, reader, by confessing that the following anecdote forcibly illustrates the power of simple, plaintive music, a theme upon which we have often dwelt in these pages. Would that we could relate it to you in the inimitable manner of our friend B——: if we could, by the by, the manner would'nt be inimitable:—Some years since, a well-known military gentleman and musical amateur of Philadelphia, being on a visit to his numerous friends in New York, was delighted to encounter here the band of the far-famed Frank Johnson. He forthwith engaged the 'colored troupe' to accompany him, together with two or three vocalists, on the following evening, on a serenading tour to the residences of his distinguished friends, in various quarters of the town. They every where met with the most rapturous reception, and were often invited in, to partake of the hospitalities of the families whom they serenaded. Between two

and three o'clock in the morning, they arrived opposite to the residence (as they supposed) of a most lovely lady, to whom the leader of the serenade movement had well nigh lost his heart, upon a very casual acquaintance. Here was poured forth the wealth of their instrumental and vocal powers. But not the slightest sign of appreciation or approbation was manifested; all was silence; no outward blind rattled, no inner curtain rustled. At length, while the prime mover of the entertainment was singing in a most tender style the closing stanza of 'Home, sweet Home,' a light suddenly gleamed through the fan-lights of the entry; steps were heard approaching; the door was unbolted, and a cadaverous 'male human,' in night gown and night cap, the latter surmounted by a broad brimmed Quaker hat, stepped out upon the door stone, and holding the candle above his head, that he might better survey the rather 'mixed' company of performers, addressed the last singer with: 'Friend, there seems to think there is no place like home—like thy 'sweet, sweet home,' I think thee said: now, *why doesn't thee go to thy home?* Thee surely is not wanted *here*—neither thee nor thy friends!" and the door was closed behind the speaker. Perhaps no wetter blanket ever enveloped a 'water-cure subject at Graffenburgh,' than was felt to come down upon that corps of musicians and their employer, when the white skirts of that vanishing Quaker disappeared along the hall.

CHARACTERISTIC.—The Pittsburg Chronicle, whose editor has just returned to the city, after an absence of a month, notices the new buildings and the increased business in the same squares where smoke still ascends from the smouldering ruins. It says, Our people are like their own steam engines—*the more fire that is applied to them the faster they work.* Their energy and perseverance is like their iron—it was not made to be burnt."

Cincinnati Fifty Years Ago.

It seems wonderful at this brief lapse of time, to contemplate the rise of property in our city. Major Ferguson, who fell in St. Clair's defeat in 1791, a short time before bought lot No. 13, on the original town plat, for *eleven* dollars. This is the property one hundred feet front on Broadway, by two hundred feet on Fourth street, being the south-west corner of those streets. The property, if divested of improvements, would now command at Sheriff's sale, twenty thousand dollars.

At this time there was but one frame dwelling in Cincinnati, which belonged to Israel Ludlow, and stood at the lower end of Main street. The room in front was occupied as a store. Matthew Winton kept tavern on Front st., nearly opposite to David E. Wade, rather to the west. Ezekiel Sayre exactly opposite Wade. John Bartle kept the first store in Cincinnati.— This was the scite of the present Cincinnati Hotel and a hipped roof frame house. A German named Bicket had a dram shop opposite Plum s treet, between Front street and the river bank. John S. Wallace, resided on Front street, below Race. Joel Williams kept tavern at Latham's corner. There was a great flood in 1792, which flooded the entire bottom to the depth of five feet. The original timber on the town plat was beseech, sugar tree and walnut, with poplar on some spots, many of the trees of large growth.— The improvements went gradually up Main and Sycamore streets towards the hill, which was so steep, the ascent was almost too much for a horse. Corn was raised here in 1790 and 1791. The men worked in companies, and kept a guard on the lookout. In a large field up Western Row, John S. Wallace and several others were shot at by Indians. The party fired back, and drove off the savages, who left fifteen blankets on the field, but succeeded in carrying off the horses belonging to the party, which were in the enclosure. The Indians were still more troublesome in 1792, although their mischief was confined to destroying cattle, and conveying off horses. They shot three arrows into a large ox, with such force as to make marks on the opposite side. The arrows had stone heads. Provisions were very scarce and dear on the first settlement. I saw ten dollars given for a barrel of flour, and eight dollars for a bushel salt. Our meat was got principally from the woods, A great share of the hunting was done in Kentucky, where the game was more abundant, and less danger of being surprised by the Indians. My husband killed two bears and an elk, as late as 1794. The game was so abundant as to form the principal support of the army at Fort Wash-ington. Turkeys were so plentiful that their breasts were salted down, smoked, and chipped for the table as dried beef in later days.

Antiquities.

A few years since Mr. E. Chidester of Canfield, Trumbull county, in this State, in felling an oak tree on his father's farm, discovered un doubted marks of an axe, which by the later growth of the timber, as indicated by its annual circles must have been impressed on it some two hundred years since. This remarkable circumstance attracted many visiters and close scrutiny, but the opinion was universal, that the tree had been cut into, centuries before. The incision had been made, apparently when the tree was fifteen inches diameter, doubtless with the view of cutting it down, as the chip had gone to the centre, when a small hollow appearing at the heart of it, the tree had been abandoned. The entire space cut away was filled with new and solid wood in which was distinctly preserved, each stroke of the instrument. Nothing peculiar was observed until the tree fell, when the appearance of a stump within a stump was observed in the northerly half, which was the side on which the cutting had been made. The butt was afterwards split into firewood, of which several pieces, plainly establishing the above facts, were kept for considerable length of time. Outside of the old scar one hundred and sixty concentric circles of growth in sound wood were apparent. The tree had been dead some years, and the sap and the parts adjacent, were so far decayed as to prevent a certain count— perhaps 15 or 20 should be added. This, with the time the tree had been dead, being over five years, gives at least 180 years back, or the year 1660, as the date of this visit from civilized men to Northern Ohio. Whether these are the relics of the French, Spanish, or English explorers, is a question for antiquarians to discuss, although the origin is probably shrouded forever in impenetrable darkness.

In connection with this remarkable circumstance, I will add the statement of one of the oldest settlers here who records what fell under her own notice at the time. I have it direct from her own lips.

"*In* 1791, an old poplar tree nearly seven feet feet in diameter, was cut down in the process of clearing, going on in those early days. It stood some distance west of where Powell's foundry is built. On chopping eighteen or twenty inches from the outside, the chopper came to where it had been before cut, and grown over solid again, the old mark being full broader than one made by a common axe. I found an old chip there which had not been cleaned out, and looked much discolored. Judging by the circles of the tree, the first chopping must have been done more than one hundred years since, say in the neighborhood of the year 1680."

Doouments of last War.

HEAD QUARTERS, OHIO MILITIA,
LOWER SANDUSKY, Oct. 6th, 1813.

DEAR GENERAL:

I have the honor to inform you by Major Vance, that I arrived here yesterday with the 2nd regiment; the 1st will be here from Seneca to-day; the 3rd is on the left and centre lines of communication. These two regiments are considerably reduced, having detached one company at Upper Sandusky, two companies to Fort Meigs, and three small companies to Detroit, who start to day as an escort to the beef cattle. And there is a number engaged in the employ of the Quarter Master, by special request of Col. Bartlet, and a number sick. The effective force in the two regiments at this place, is about one thousand. The garrison here will be relieved as the Chilicothe Guard's time has nearly expired. I found the garrison of Upper Sandusky in a dirty miserable state. I have ordered the company of militia there to build a small hospital, to cleanse the fort and put the rooms in repair, with safe and comfortable fire places, which must be done at this post. If you think proper, I am anxious to receive your orders to know how the troops are to be disposed of. We are all willing to cross into Canada or go to Detroit, or where you may think proper. The men are very orderly good militia, and willing to do their duty, but are badly clothed for the winter in this northerly climate, on account of their not receiving the pay that was promised in advance, which was attended with great murmuring and complaint. Many were not able to buy a blanket or pair of shoes, and actually marched from the neighborhood of Cincinnati to Franklinton, without shoes, blankets, tents, or camp kettles. I there got a partial supply, and some companies marched to Seneca without more than two tents, and 2 camp kettles to a company. They are all now supplied with camp equipage, so that they are more comfortable. Brigade Major Lewis I expect up to day, and will have the two regiments again inspected and make report.— Major Vance, one of my aids, can give you every information in detail, whom I highly recommend to your excellency, and beg that he may be despatched back as soon as practicable.

I am sir, with great respect and esteem,
Your humble servant,
JOHN S. GANO.
Maj. Gen. Com'dt. O. Mil. in service.
GEN. WM. H. HARRISON, Detroit.

HEAD QUARTERS, DETROIT Oct. 12th, 1813.
DEAR SIR:

Your favors by Major Vance were duly received. He will return by water as soon as the wind is fair for him, I will give you further instructions. In the mean time, you will be pleased to send a detachment to repair and open the road to portage on Lake Erie. One or two bridges must be built or the road will be impassable for waggons. If there should be any old boats at Sandusky, please to repair them for the purpose of transporting all the provisions and clothing at Sandusky down to the portage on the bay, and give to the Quarter Master and Commissary all the assistance in your power. If Capt. Oliver is yet at Sandusky; tell him that it is important that all the salt provisions which may be at Fort Meigs, should be immediately sent to this place.

Yours with great respect,
WM. HENRY HARRISON.
MAJ. GEN. JOHN S. GANO.
Lower Sandusky.

HEAD QUARTERS, DETROIT, Oct. 14, 1813.
SIR:

You will furnish Lt. Col. Croghan, with two of your smallest companies, amounting in the whole to not less than one hundred men, for the purpose of a guard to the prisoners under his direction to Chillicothe. Upon the arrival of these companies at Chillicothe, they will be discharged.

I am very respectfully,
your humble servant,
WM. HENRY HARRISON.
MAJ. GEN. JOHN S. GANO.
Lower Sandusky.

UPPER SANDUSKY, Oct. 12th, 1813.
DEAR SIR:

The large quantity of commissary stores now at McArthur, for which I am required to furnish immediate transportation, requires that considerable repairs should be made on the road to enable me to comply with the requisition. I do not feel myself authorized without special instructions from a superior officer to employ men for this purpose, the less so as it has been the custom generally to have the roads and bridges repaired by the troops in service. The object of this is to know, if it be practicable to obtain a detachment from your command to open the road and repair the bridges between this and Lower Sandusky. A bridge will be necessary across Wolf creek, between Seneca and Lower Sandusky, and a number of smaller ones between here and that post. Capt. Welsh is now engaged in erecting one across Tymochtee. He is at work under an order of Gov. Meigs. I find it impossible for the teams to get on until h e road is opened wider, and the bad place bridged. Will you have the goodness sir, to inform me if you can give me any aid in this business—repairs must be made on it, and this appeared to me the most proper mode.

I am sir, with much respect.

your most ob't. serv't.,

B. HUGHES, A. D. Q. M. G.

Maj.Gen.J. S. GANO, L. Sandusky.

Bicknell's Patent Planing Machine.

I feel highly gratified in learning that the U. States District Court, at its late session at Columbus, decided the case of Brooks & Morris vs. Bicknell & Jenkins, in favor of the defendants, ruling that the invention of Bicknell's was no infringement of Woodworth's patent, and leaving it free for the public to *rule*, as it undoubtedly will, that Bicknell's *buckeye* invention is vastly superior in merit to that of his New York competitor. The case has resulted, as I said in one of the early numbers of this paper, that it must. It is gratifying to find that all the array of influence enlisted on the part of the plaintiff failed to crush the ingenious and public spirited inventor of this valuable improvement.

Sugar Mills and Engines for Louisiana.

I had occasion to refer last week to a notice in the Pittsburgh "Spirit of the Age," on the subject of the manufacture of sugar mills &c. for the southern markets. For want of time, and yet more, owing to the incompleteness of my information at the moment, the correction I made was neither explicit nor minute enough to do our Cincinnati mechanic establishments justice. I will now upon undoubted authority go into specifications.

The Pittsburgh article stated, as an evidence of the thriving condition of the foundries and machine shops of that place, that seven sugar mills and engines had been made at one establishment, and five at another there during this season.

Let us contrast our city manufactures in this line with these results. Messrs. Niles, & Co., have put up twenty-five; David Griffey, eight; James Goodloe, seven; Anthony Harkness, six, of these Sugar Mills and Engines this season. J. Holabird and Bevan, Scott & Co., who have just engaged in the business have, put up one each, making forty-eight manufactured in Cincinnati to twelve in Pittsburgh.

This difference, great though it be, does not cover the whole case. *All the larger class* of Sugar Mills and Engines for Louisiana are made in Cincinnati. These cost from four to seven thousand dollars, and will average all of five thousand dollars each. The article supplied from Pittsburgh, is of the second class, and for

second rate sugar estates, costing thirty-five hundred dollars.

Let me exhibit the difference in figures.

12 Mills and Engines made at Pittsburgh, 3500   42,000

48 do   do   do at Cincinnati, 240,000

There is a large amount besides of repairing and refitting Mills and Engines for Louisiana, done here, of which this season's bills will exceed 30,000 dollars, making an aggregate of 270,000. It is an under estimate, to say that twelve more will be built in the course of the current year, at least ten of that number being already under contract.

I have been thus at once, full and minute on this subject, because an impression prevails abroad, that our manufacturing interest is of less weight than that of Pittsburgh, and in fact many of our own citizens are ignorant of the real state of facts. Abstract the rolling mills, glass and cotton yarn factories of Pittsburgh from the manufacturing comparison, and in every other description of mechanical industry and product, Cincinnati is far in advance of that place.

Documents relative of War of 1812.

HEADQUARTERS, OHIO MILITIA,
Lower Sandusky. Oct. 15th.

His Excellency Gen. HARRISON:

Sir—*I* dispatched my acting brigade, Major Vance to you for orders on the 6th inst.—he has not returned. *I* have made several details of detachments since he left this. I have furnished the Quarter Master and Commissary with a number of men for extra duty, and have sent a company to Fort Findlay—I will send another detachment with beef cattle to Detroit as soon as they can be collected in sufficient numbers for an escort. I have directed the commandants at the different posts on the left centre and right lines of communication, to afford every assistance to the Quarter Master and Commissaries in protecting the public stores, and escorting provisions &c., and have rendered considerable service with the waggons *I* brought on to those departments, and have twelve now loading with provisions for the Kentucky troops at Portage. If you calculate on retaining the Ohio troops, I will be much obliged by your informing me of their probable destination, as I wish to make some arrangements for my winter qrs. &c.; and if to be discharged, the sooner I am to be informed the better. I will always take pleasure in rendering my country and yourself all the service in my power, and most sincerely congratulate you upon your glorious victories and success.

With respect, &c.,

J.S. GANO.

10 o'clock P. M. I this moment received yours

of the 12th inst., and have in some measure anticipated your orders by sending on a detachment to repair the road to portage, which I expect them to complete to-morrow, and have had a detachment at work on the road between McArthur and Upper Sandusky, and are building a bridge across Tymochtee &c.

Head Quarters, Detroit, Oct. 16th, 1813.
DEAR SIR:

· You will take the command of all the posts upon the frontier of the State of Ohio.— You can establish your quarters at Fort Meigs, Lower or Upper Sandusky. You will afford all the security possible to the frontiers as well by repelling any invasion of the savages as by preventing any depredation upon them.

You will as expeditiously as possible, order to this place such a number of men from your command, with a due proportion of officers, as added to the number already sent, will make five hundred men. It is all important that beef cattle should be forwarded to this place with as much expedition as possible—you will use every exertion to forward them, and take care that they are furnished with suitable escorts from the troops under your command.

I am with great regard,
your humble servant,
WM. HENRY HARRISON.
Major Gen. JOHN S. GANO,
L. Sandusky.

Head Quarters, Buffalo, Oct. 25th, 1813.
DEAR SIR:

I arrived here yesterday with a detachment of the army, and will proceed immediately to Fort George. Nothing of consequence had taken place, when the last accounts came from Gen. Wilkinson's army. He has certainly however, before this, entered Canada at the head of a very large force which he had assembled at, and in the neighborhood of, Sackett's Harbour.

There was a man by the name of Crandall, in custody at Lower Sandusky, on suspicion of being a spy—there is no positive proof against him; be pleased therefore to release him. I will thank you also to deliver the three Mingo or Delaware Indians which you have in your possession to the Delaware Chief, Anderson, who has promised to to be responsible for their good behaviour. Indeed I believe that they never intended any harm. If Anderson has returned home, you can send them to him, or to Mr. Johnston at Piqua.

Yours very respectfully,
WM. HENRY HARRISON.
Major Gen. GANO.

Upper Sandusky, Nov. 4th, 1813.
SIR:

Major Thompson informed me this morning, that you were much in want of forage at Lower Sandusky. I expected a supply would have been sent from Cleaveland some time since, and am astonished that it has not come on. Capt. Reed, the Quarter Master at that post, wrote me about the 15th ult., that he would in a few days send on a supply. I have not at this time one team to command, all the public teams fit for service, being in advance. Four private teams came in this morning with oats; I offered them two dollars per bushel to go on to Lower Sandusky, but they refused; I would have impressed them, but they were so poor and weak they would not have been able to get through. The fact is the roads are impassable for loaded waggons. A brigade of ox-teams were about six days getting from here to Fort Ball, where finding it impracticable to proceed, they deposited their load and returned, after having left a number of their oxen on the way, and this not in consequence of mismanagement or neglect of the wagon master, but in consequence of the extreme badness of the roads, and the worn out situation of his oxen.

Capt. Catterlin favored me with a copy of your general order of the 16th ult, relative to having the roads repaired by the troops, stationed at the different Garrisons, which I enclosed to the commanding officer at Fort McArthur, at the same time urging the necessity of his detailing a part of his company to open the road from that to this post immediately. Mr. Smith, the commander at that post wrote me, that the Captain and Lieutenant, and a number of the men had gone home sick, and that the ensign, did not think proper to comply with the requisition. This information I requested Capt. Oliver to give you.

By the first wagons I will send you a small supply of grain, if you should not get it from Cleveland, every exertion has been made to get a stock on hand here for the winter, but the heavy draft made on it by Gov. Shelby has left us but little; it was always contemplated to supply the post at Lower Sandusky from the settlements on the Lake.

I will send the blacksmith (Piatt) on to-morrow or the day after. The flour &c. left at Fort Ball shall be taken on as soon as teams can be had to do it. Major Thompson informs me that the commandant at Seneca has sent a corporal and six men to guard it until it can be removed.

With great respect, Your obedient servant,
B. HUGHES,
Maj. Gen. J. S. GANO,
Lower Sandusky.

A Legend of Kentucky.

Sixty-three years have passed away since the disastrous battle of the Blue Licks, where Kentucky valor was betrayed by its characteristic impetuosity into the ambush of the savages, and the most gallant settlers of the west, became the victims of Indian barbarity. Hardly a family in the settlements escaped the loss of one or more valuable members. Cols. Todd and Trigg, Lieutenant Boone—son of Daniel Boone, and more lamented than any other one, the noble spirited Capt. Harland, with numbers of less note, fell in that bloody field. No adequate idea can now be formed of the grief and despondency which followed the catastrophe of that unfortunate day.

On the long roll of the reported slain were the names of a few, who had in fact been captured, and after surviving the ordeal of the gauntlet had been permitted to live as captives. Among these was an excellent husband and father, who, with eleven other captives, had been taken by a tribe, painted black, as the signal of torture and death to all. The night after the battle these twelve prisoners were stripped and placed in a line on a log, he to whom we have specially alluded being at one extremity of the devoted row.

The cruel captors, then beginning at the other end, slaughtered eleven, one by one,; but when they came to the only survivor, though they raised him up also and drew their bloody knives to strike under each uplifted arm, they paused, and after a long powwow, spared his life—why, he never knew. For about one year none of his friends, excepting his faithful wife, doubted his death; she, hoping against reason, still insisted that he lived and would return to her. Wooed by another, she from time to time postponed the nuptials, declaring that she could not divest herself of the belief that her husband survived. Her expostulating friends finally succeeded in their efforts to stifle her affectionate instinct; she reluctantly yielded, and the nuptial day was fixed. But just before it dawned, the crack of a rifle was heard near her lonely cabin; at the familiar sound she leaped out like a liberated fawn, ejaculating as she sprang, "*that John's gun!*" It was John's gun, sure enough, and in an instant she was once more in her lost husband's arms. But nine years afterwards, that same husband fell in "St. Clair's defeat," and the same disappointed but persevering lover renewed his suit, and at last the widow became his wife.

Total abstinence testimony.

Indisputable and valuable as are the direct benefits of the modern Temperance movement, the indirect effects are hardly less so. It is not merely that confirmed inebriates have been rescued from wretchedness and disgrace, and their families saved from want, but individuals are in various ways withdrawn from the fascinating influence of convivality before habitual drinking has created an appetite which can no longer be restrained within bounds. Fifty years ago, it was as much a matter of course to invite a guest to take a glass of wine, or brandy, or whisky, as to offer a plate at the dinner table. The following document from the pen of WILLIAM EATON, in early life a subaltern in Wayne's army, and holding in later years, a General's commission in the United States service, affords a striking because a condensed view of the effects of such customs.

AN INSTRUCTIVE RECORD.—In August, 1793, a court martial was convened on the spot where Cincinnati now stands, by order of General St. Clair, for the trial of one ensign Morgan; who was found guilty and cashiered. Three years thereafter, the late Gen. WM. EATON, (a member of the court,) then consul to Tunis, thus recorded the fate of his associates:

Brig. Gen. POSEY	Resigned and dead.
Major D.	" " "
" H.	Damned by brandy.
Capt. P.	Dead per do.
" P.	Dead.
" EATON,	At Tunis.
" P.	Damned by brandy.
" M.	Dead.
" F.	Dead.
" P.	Dead.
" J.	Damned by brandy.
" C.	Killed.

Eaton's own fate, although delayed, was sealed by the same habits. He died in 1811, confirmed in intemperance.

Among orders filed away in 1792, by a merchant of that period, and now lying on my table, the whole number being twelve, ten are for spirituous liquors, as follows: "Twenty Gallons whiskey,—half a gallon cogneac—ten gallons whiskey—three gallons whiskey—one gallon madeira—two gallons cogneac—whiskey—whiskey—whiskey—whiskey. These were all for officers in the United States army. Some of whose initials correspond with Eaton's list.

Howard, the Philanthropist.

He was a singular being in many of the common habits of life; he bathed daily in cold water; and both on rising and going to bed swathed himself in coarse towels, wet with the coldest water; in that state he remained half an hour or more, and then threw them off, freshened and invigorated as he said, beyond measure. He never put on a great coat in the coldest countries; nor was he ever a minute under or over the time of an appointment for 26 years. He never continued at a place, or with a person a single day beyond the period prefixed for going, in his life; and he had not, for the last ten years of his experience, ate any fish, flesh or fowl, nor sat down to his simple fare of tea, milk, and rusks, all that time. His journeys were continued from prison to prison; from one group of wretched beings to another, night and day; and when he could not go in a carriage he would walk. Such a thing as an abstraction was out of the question.

Some days after his first return from an attempt to mitigate the plague at Constantinople, he favored me with a morning visit to London. The weather was so very terrific, that I had forgot his inveterate exactness, and had yielded up the hope of expecting him. Twelve at noon was the hour, and exactly as the clock struck, he entered my room; the wet—for it rained in torrents, dripping from every part of his dress, like water from a sheep just landed from its washing. He would not have attended to his situation, having sat himself down with the utmost composure, and began conversation, had I not made an offer of dry clothes. 'Yes,' said he, smiling, 'I had my fears, as I knocked at your door, that we should go over the old business of apprehension about a little rain water, which though it does not run off my back as it does that of a duck, does me as little injury, and after a long drought is scarcely less refreshing.— The coat that I have on has been as often wetted through as any duck's in the world, and indeed gets no other cleaning. I assure you, a good soaking shower is the best brush for broadcloth. You, like the rest of my friends, throw away your pity upon my supposed hardships, with just as much reason as you commiserate the common beggars, who being familiar with storms, necessity, and nakedness, are a thousand times (so forcible is habit) less to be compassionated than the sons and daughters of ease and luxury, who, accustomed to all the enfeebling refinements of feathers by night and fires by day, are taught to shiver at a breeze. All this is the work of art, my good friend; nature is intrepid, hardy, and adventurous; but it is a practice to spoil her with indulgences from the moment we come into the world. A soft dress and soft cradle begin our education in luxury, and we do not grow more manly the more we are gratified; on the contrary, our feet must be wrapt in wool or silk, we must tread upon carpets, breathe, as it were, in fire, and fear the least change in the weather. 'You smile,' said Mr. Howard, after a pause, 'but I am a living instance of the truth I insist on. A more puny youngster than myself was never seen. If I wet my feet I was sure to take a cold. I could not put on my shirt without its being aired. To be serious, I am convinced *that what emasculates the body debilitates the mind*, and renders both unfit for those exertions which are of such use to us social beings. I therefore entered upon a reform of my constitution, and have succeeded in such a degree that I have neither had a cough, cold, the vapors, nor any more alarming disorder, since I surmounted the seasoning. Formerly mulled wines, and spirits, and great fires, were to comfort me, and to keep out the cold, as it is called; the perils of the day were to be baffled by something taken hot on going to

bed, and before I pursued my journey the next morning, *a dram* was to be swallowed to fortify the stomach! 'Believe me,' said Mr. Howard, 'we are too apt to *invert the remedies which we ought to prescribe for ourselves*. Thus we are forever giving *hot* things when we should administer *cold*. We bathe in hot instead of cold water, we use a dry bandage when we should use a wet one, and we increase our food and clothing, when we should, by degrees, diminish both.' 'If we would trust more to nature, and suffer her to apply her own remedies to cure her own diseases, the formidable catalogue of maladies would be reduced to one-half, at least, of their present number.'—*Pratt's Gleanings.*

☞ The Rev. Sydney Smith had a talent for dressing salad as well as repudiators. See his poetical recipe, so put:

Recipe for Dressing Salad.
BY THE REV. SYDNEY SMITH.

Two large potatoes passed through kitchen sieve,
Smoothness and softness to the salad give;
Of mordant mustard add a single spoon—
Distrust the condiment that bites too soon—
But deem it not, thou man of herbs, a fault,
To add a double quantity of salt;
Four times the spoon with oil of Lucca crown,
And twice with vinegar procured from town;
True flavor needs it, and your poet begs,
The pounded yellow of two well boiled eggs.
Let onions' atoms lurk within the bowl,
And, lastly, in the flavored compound toss
A magic spoonful of anchovy sauce,
O! great and glorious: O! herbacious treat!
'Twould tempt the dying anchorite to eat.
Back to the world he'd turn his weary soul,
And plunge his fingers in the salad bowl.

Lightning Rods.

As the summer advances, I feel it my duty to call public attention to providing lightning rods to our various buildings, public and private.— Probably there are not one in twenty of the edifices in Cincinnati protected by these important preservatives.

This may be ascribed partly to the general disposition in mankind to undervalue dangers which are not immediately at hand, and to neglect, therefore, proper precautionary measures, but is principally owing to the fact, that there has hitherto been no person here engaged in the manufacture, and putting up of electric rods as a distinct business. Mr. J. SPRATT, I observe by his advertisement to that effect, has gone into that business, and puts up conductors at the extremely low price of ten cents per running foot, which will enable most persons to have themselves protected from lightning, at an expense not exceeding five dollars to a building. *Mr. Spratt* has abandoned the insecure and inefficient plan of linking iron joints, and connects his rods by screwing one length into another which preserves the connecting parts, from *oxydation*, and the building from the injury which must result from that circumstance.

Marriage Licenses.

A statement of Marriage Licences issued by Arthur St. Clair, Gov. to wit.

1795.

Nov. 14th, Isaac Bates and Nancy Duvall.
" 16th, John Smith and Phebe Van Nuys.

1796.

Feb. 9th, Robt. Mitchell and Frances Cox.
" 21st, Miles Morfoot and Mary Alter.
" 22nd, Wm. Sloan and Elizabeth Pricket·
" 24th, Stephen Wood and Cath. Freeman.
" 25th, Ian Gregarach and Temperance Young.

April 10th, Daniel Symmes, Esq. and Elizabeth Oliver.

May 9th, Nichs. Johnston and Sarah Ferris.
·· 10th, Geo. Morfoot and Ruth Lowry.

Scites for Country Seats.

I cannot understand why it is, that while city lots command a higher price here than at Pittsburgh, that scites for country seats are much more expensive in that neighborhood than at an equal distance from Cincinnati. I have under my notice several desirable spots for the purpose around our city, of which I shall refer to one merely, and to that, principally, because it is in the market. Six miles west upon the Cheviot road, a macadamised public road, and within a short distance of that place, is a ten acre lot. It lies beautifully. faces the South and is susceptible of being made a country seat, such as can hardly be seen outside of the valley of the Miami. Such a spot at an equal distance from Pittsburgh, and possessing equal natural advantages, could hardly be bought there for less than 300 dollars per acre, and this whole tract is offered for 1200 dollars.

The solution of the difficulty I refered to is probably that much of the immediate adjacency of Pittsburgh is composed of hills, too high for pleasant or convenient residences, and that the business parts of the city are too restricted in space, to allow of residences there, to the extent they exist here.

Our City Solons.

At the adjourned meeting of the city council on Friday evening, a debate sprung up on a proposition that B. F. Greenough, who is supplying a portion of the city with light by camphine, or chemical oil, be allowed to take back his lamps, in other words, that the existing arrangement with him should terminate.

Great complaints were made by members on the subject of the lamps. One member alleged that he could not walk the streets in peace on account of the various objections made by his constituents. Mr. Decamp said that Greenough appeared disposed to do as he pleased with the lights, lighting and putting out as he pleased.— Some of them burned by night, and some by day, and some were not lighted at all, the light going out as soon as the lamp-lighter left them.

The whole secret of the business seemed to be, that Mr. Greenough furnished lamps which were not adapted to the burning any other kind of oil, and thus compelled the use of the camphine. Finally Mr. Greenough was directed to take back his lamps by a vote of 13 to 7.

Some interesting facts were developed in the discussion of a motion made by Mr. Meader, to equalise the compensation of the wood measurer at the Fifth street market, and those at the river. It seems conceded that 46 feet wood at the river measure 53 feet at Fifth street market, and that what was a cord of wood at the landings becomes a cord and a quarter after being drawn up hill. This is equal to the ancient process in Cincinnati of killing cattle *for the fifth quarter i. e. the hide and tallow;* or the coinage here in 1806 of quarter dollars by dividing a spanish dollar into five equal parts, *the fifth paying the expense of the Mint.*

S. B. Star Spangled Banner.

The building of the Steamboat Yorktown, a few months since, has formed an era in steam boat architecture, and nearly all the vessels since built are indebted to that splendid boat, more or less, as a model, in which they have gained nothing by departing from its proportions or arrangements, so far as it has been done. In the opinion I thus express, my judgment and taste are amply sustained by professional men fitter qualified to decide on such subjects than I pretend to be.

Our latest specimen of modern boat-building the STAR SPANGLED BANNER, left our city the beginning of the week. I subjoin her measurements and specifications.

Hull built by *Litherbury & Lockwood.* Joiner work, *Robert Caufield.* Engine builder; *James Goodloe.* Length, 183 feet. Breadth of beam, 31 feet. Water wheels, 27 feet in diameter; length of buckets, 10 feet, and 28 inches wide. Hold 7 feet 9 inches. She has four boilers 28 feet in length, 42 inches diameter, double engines, and two 24 inch cylinders, with 9 feet stroke. She draws 4 feet water light, and hard ly more than 8 feet with 500 tons, her full cargo. She has 36 state rooms, and of course 72 berths, all appropriated to cabin passengers, the boat officers being provided with state rooms in the pilot house. This arrangement affords the officers an opportunity to attend to their appropriate duties without the annoyance and interferance of others, and dispensing with the *nuis-ance* of a SOCIAL HALL, protects the gentlemen, and especially the ladies on board, from the effluvia of cigars, which ordinarily taints the whole range of the cabins. As respects the berths, I notice as an improvement, that the lower berth projects over the line of the upper one, in this respect affording facilities for reaching the higher range without the usual incon-venience. The cabin seats are armed chairs, two feet in breadth, which supply a degree of comfort and protection to the aged or the invalid in assigning them space at the dinner table, which cannot be encroached on, and enabling them to take their meals as pleasantly as at home.

The *Star spangled Banner,* is in short built for convenience, comfort and speed, and I doubt not will prove a popular boat in the New Orleans trade for which she is designed. A speedy return with full freight and passengers to our public landing will I trust, justify all *I* expect, from the business capacities of the boat.

Her engines built by *J. Goodloe,* judging by her trial trip on last Thursday, work with unsurpassed ease and efficiency, and are highly creditable to the shop where made.

The Star spangled Banner is owned by *Richard Phillips* & *Elmore Bateman,* who are also Captain and clerk to the boat.

Tricks of the Trade.

Great Bargains! Immense Sacrifices! Selling out at cost! Selling out at 25 per cent. below cost! These are notices to be found occasionally placarded over the windows and adjoining the doors of certain dry goods houses in Cincinnati, as profusely as space permits, to catch the eye and clean the pockets of a class of customers who are not up to the tricks of trade.

In all this, however, if we examine the subject, there is no deception on the part of the sellers. "Selling off at cost", and at 25 per cent below cost are modifications of the same thing, the article being sold at the *purchaser's* cost or expense, varying never less than 25 per cent advance from what it can be bought at regular houses. This also explains the "immense sacrifice" which is what the *buyer,* not the *seller* loses.—As to the "bargains," if we look to the derivation of the word—*bar-gains,*—there is no deception also, the word itself expressing the idea of barring or excluding profits or advantages.

Occasionally, however, the seller finds in the purchaser a nut too hard for his jaws to crack. Not long since a couple of hoosiers stopped into a store on Fifth street, which held out the usual bàit, "Goods for sale, 25 per cent below cost." One of these supplied himself with a coat pat-tern, a piece domestic sheeting, calicoes, &c. taking care to inquire, "what does this cost?" article by article as he bought. His bill being made out amounted to 20 dollars. He made up a bundle of the goods, by tying them in a large handkerchief, and opening a leather pouch, counted out and handed over fifteen dollars in payment. "Five dollars more if you please," said the storekeeper, as he found no more shelling out, and bowing politely. "Five dollars more," said the hoosier. 1 guess you have got your full pay, when you take the 25 per cent off." The storekeeper tried to explain, but to no purpose. "Did you not tell me what these things cost?" "Yes." "Well, where is the 25 per cent less, or discount? The dry goods man with his clerks blustered and threatened very hard, but it was no go. The hoosiers were prepared for action, either at a magistrate's office or on *the spot,* and marched off finally, carrying their point.

City building operations.

Our city building operations for the last week or two have been partially checked by excessively hot weather, and are delayed now by the diminishing supply of materials. Shingles have advanced fifty per cent, and in the article bricks the demand and consumption has taken up the whole supply. At this time last year there were ten millions of bricks on hand. Now there are none in market, the current manufacture being required to fill existing engagements. A much larger quantity of bricks has been laid, up to the 15th July last, than for the corresponding period of the past year, so that there can be no doubt our erections of 1845 will equal those of 1844.

Portrait Painting.

A portrait painter in large practice might write a pretty book on the vanity and singularity of his sitters. A certain man came to Copley, and had himself, his wife, and seven children, all included in a family piece. 'It wants but one thing,' said, 'and that is the portrait of my first wife, for this one is my second.'

'But,' said the artist, 'she is dead, you know sir; what can I do? She must come in as a woman; no angels for me.'

The portrait was added, but some time elapsed before the person came back; when he returned, he had a stranger lady on his arm.

'I must have another cast of your hand, Copley,' he said, 'an accident befell my second wife, this lady is my third, and she is come to have her likeness included in the family picture.'

The painter complied—the likeness was introduced—and the husband looked with a glance of satisfaction on his three spouses. Not so the lady; she remonstrated, never was such a thing heard of—out her predecessors must go.

The artist painted them out accordingly, and had to bring an action at law to obtain payment for the portraits which he had obliterated.

A Legend of North Bend.

In the month of August, 1791, a man named Fuller, with his son William, a lad of 16 years of age, or thereabouts, was in the employ of John Matson Sen, and in that capacity, the Fullers accompanied Matson, a brother of his, and a neighbor, George Cullum to the Big Miami, to build a fish dam in its waters, at a place about two miles from North Bend. Old Fuller sent his son towards night to take the cows home, but the boy did not reach home, and for several days, the neighborhood turned out to hunt him up, suspecting that he had been taken by Indians. No trace of him was however obtained, nor any thing heard of him for nearly four years, when Wayne's treaty afforded an opportunity for those who had relatives captured by the Indians to ascertain their fate. Old Fuller, under the hope of learning something respecting his son, accompanied a party to Fort Greenville, and spent a week making inquiry among the Indians present, but to no purpose. One day being in conversation with *Christopher Miller*, one of Wayne's spies, and who had been taken captive himself in early years, and brought up among the Indians, he was describing his son's personal appearance, as being heavy built, cross eyed, and a little lame, when Miller exclaimed, "I can tell you where he is." He then went on to say, that he had himself made him a prisoner, that he knew where he was, and if he would come back in three weeks, he would produce him there. Fuller returned accordingly, and obtained his son, who accompanied him home. The statement of Miller was, that he was out on a scout on the Miami with two Indians, and the youth being intent on hunting the cows, had got quite near before he observed Miller. When he saw him, he attempted to run, fearing that Miller might be an Indian. Miller called out "don't run." The boy spoke up and said, "who are you?" "My name is Miller." Young Fuller supposed it to be a Thomas Miller at North Bend, and stood still waiting the other's approach. As it was now dusk, it was not until Miller had got nearly up to him, that the boy perceived his mistake, and endeavored to make his escape. Being somewhat lame, he was however soon overtaken and captured.— Miller then gave a whistle on his powder charger, when two Indians appeared. They hurried the boy across the Miami, the waters of which were quite low at the time. After traveling some distance, they encamped for the rest of the night. In the morning, the Indians discovering that Fuller was lame, and defective in his eyes, were for tomahawking him, alleging they could never make a good Indian of him, but Miller objected, saying he was his captive. He was taken to one of the Indian towns, where he remained until the treaty of 1795. He had been a bad boy hitherto, and his residence among the savages, made no improvement in him. He did no good after getting home, and associating with a gang of horse thieves, lost his life not long after in a marauding expedition, made by the party into Kentucky.

Progress of Cincinnati.

In speaking of the growth of Cincinnati, present and probable, I take care so to present the subject as to invite a scrutiny into my statements. I do not wish to sustain these merely by what reputation for judgment or veracity I may possess.

When persons abroad allege that Cincinnati claims to have built 12,000 houses within the last twelve years, as a correspondent of the Louisville Courier asserts, I deny their right to hold the city or any respectable part of it, responsible for guesses, or for any thing but statements of alleged fact, vouched by men of fair standing. I do not assume to know more of Cincinnati, than any one may, who will make it a business to watch and record its progress.

I have registered the actual increase of buildings during the last twelve years, by which I refer to dwelling houses, business offices, and store houses and work shops alone, as follows:

1833	321	1839	394
1834	300	1840	406
1835	340	1841	806
1836	365	1842	852
1837	305	1843	1003
1838	334	1844	1228

In 1840, 35 millions brick were made, as per the census returns of that year. In 1845 this quantity was increased to 80 millions. The manufacture of 1845, will shew no decrease. If this seem incredible to any of my readers, let me call their attention to the following list of public buildings now in course of erection or finishing off, which have all been commenced since January 1st, 1845, with the quantity of bricks they will consume.

Cincinnati College,		1,000,000
Masonic Hall,		660,000
Roman Catholic Church,		600,000
Odd Fellows' Hall,		400,000
Central Presbyterian Church,		395,000
Third do do		395,000
Seventh St. do do		400,000
Tabernacle do		400,000
Seven smaller Churches,		1,750,000
		6,000,000

Of private buildings, Niles' Foundry alone,

will require 500,000, the block of stores at Loring's corner, not short of 1,000,000, & the block at the corner of Fourth and Walnut, at least 500,000 more. The great aggregate of brick used is made up of 1500 buildings, which will complete the erection of 1845, and are not herein refered to.

First Church in Cincinnati--No. 2.

The first religious Society formed in Cincinnati, I have said, was of the Presbyterian order. This was organized into a congregation by Rev. David Rice, of Kentucky, who visited the place for that purpose in 1790. The inlots constituting the south half of the block bounded by Fourth, Fifth, Main and Walnut streets had been dedicated to the use of this society, which being at that day too feeble, even with such aid as they could obtain in the town to build a church edifice, the only use made of the premises was as a grave yard, where repose to this period some of our oldest citizens. Meetings for worship were held at a *Horse Mill* on Vine street, below where Third street, has since been opened, being then the foot of the hill, and also, occasionally, at private houses. *John Smith* of Columbia, then a Baptist preacher, better known since as one of the early Senators from Ohio in the U. S. Senate, and implicated in Aaron Burr's memorable project, occasionally preached to this society.

In 1791, Rev. Peter Kemper, who deceased but a few years since, was invited to take charge of this church, and was escorted from Kentucky where he resided by a number of the citizens to Cincinnati. In 1792, as already stated, the first church edifice was built. This was a plain frame about 30 by 40, roofed and weather boarded with clapboards, but neither lathed, plastered, nor ceiled. The floor was of boat plank laid loosely upon sleepers. The seats were formed by rolling in the necessary number of logs which were placed at suitable distances, and covered with boards, whipsawed for the purpose, at proper spaces for seats. There was a breast work of unplaned cherry boards which served for a pulpit, behind which the clergyman stood on a plank supported by blocks.

The congregation were required to attend with rifles, under penalty of a fine of 75 cts., which was actually inflicted upon *John S. Wallace*, formerly auditor of this county, who had left his rifle at home through forgetfulness.— Others also, doubtless, incurred fines on this account.

As a specimen of the manner in which the clergymen of that day were sustained, I annex an original receipt which I have before me.

"Received February the 14th, 1794, of Mc-Millen, Esq., the sum of three dollars, it being for Mr. Kemper's Salary for the year, 94 as an unsubscriber.

Received By me

CORNELIUS VAN NUYS."

The building referred to to above was finished in the year 1799, so as to be rendered comfortable, and stood till about 1814, when being found too small for the congregation worshiping there, it was sold, and now occupies a part of Judge Burke's lot on Vine street, being the oldest edifice, public or private, a part of Mr. D. E. Wade's house, on Congress street excepted remaining at this time.

In 1797 Rev. Peter Wilson, also from Kentucky, succeeded Mr. Kemper as pastor to the congregation, and occupied that relation until July 30th, 1799, when he deceased. He preached dressed in Kentucky jeans, and a much coarser article than bore that name at a later date. Elijah Davis was the first appointed Sexton or "Saxon," as he is called in the church minutes, to be paid at the rate of fifteen dollars per year, the salary to be raised by contributions of the Congregation. At a later date Rev. M. G. Wallace, now of Terre Haute, Indiana, was Pastor of the church, and Rev's. J. P. Campbell and John Davies were stated supplies. This state of things lasted until May 27th, 1808, when Rev. Joshua L. Wilson having accepted the charge of that church, entered on his pastoral duties.

Columbus.

There seems to be an unaccountable degree of ignorance in the American public, as to the birth place as well as the final burial place of Christopher Columbus. It is well known he was born in the State of Genoa, and has usually been considered a native of the City itself. A dispute on this point has however long existed. All debate on the subject has been lately put to rest. M. Isuardi, a Piedmontese archæologist, has discovered among the archives of Genoa, authentic proof that the illustrious navigator was born at Colognetto, a village in the republic of Genoa. It consists in a letter written by the government, dated 5th November, 1585, to their ambassador Doria, at Madrid, in which the following passage occurs: "Christopher Columbus of Colognetto, an illustrious man, as you ought to know, being in Spain, has ordered by his will, that a house shall be built at Genoa, which shall bear his name, and has instituted a fund for the preservation of this building etc. etc." A party of South Americans, on a tour upon the Continent, happening to be in Genoa when this fact was ascertained, made a pilgrimage to the palace, entered the house in which he was born, with their heads uncovered, regarding the birth place of the grand discoverer of the new world as one of the most interesting scites on their route.

Columbus died at Valladolid, in Spain, in 15-06, aged 70 years. In 1513 his remains were transported to Seville, whence they were removed in 1536 to the city of St. Domingo, and in January 1776, two hundred and sixty years after, were taken with great pomp by a Spanish squadron to Havana and placed in the wall of the Cathedral there, on the west side of the great altar. A white marble tablet has since been set in the wall to designate the spot which contains these relics. On the tablet is a medallion likeness of Columbus in profile, and beneath, the following inscription.

O! restos e ymagen del grande Colon!
Mil siglos durad guardados en la Orna,
Y en la remembranza de nuestra Nacion.
Fecit Habana, 1832.

Which may be translated thus:

O rest the image of the great Columbus!
May it endure a thousand ages, guarded in this Urn,
And in the remembrance of our nation.

I have always wondered why Columbus should have been so extensively called in Spain and Italy, Colon, his name being in Italian Columba, as in Latin, Columbus, or in English Dove.— Nor is Colon the equivalent name in the Spanish language. This discovery serves to explain the difficulty, Colon being doubtless a name which he derived from the city of his nativity. Every one familiar with the literature of the 15th and 16th centuries is aware that it was a common appellative for a distinguished man to bear a name which he derived from the place of his birth or long residence. Colon would be the di. minutive of Colognetto; the g in Italian and Spanish being thrown on to the third syllable.

A Chapter on Dunning.

In this bank note world of ours, where selling on credit, and collecting debts form so large a share of the active business of life, a good salesman, and a good collector, are two of the most valuable qualifications for employment.

Indeed, excellence in dunning, is a sure passport in the mercantile world, to patronage. I have not the design, however of lecturing on the subject, although it is worthy of a lecture, and content myself with a few anecdotes, which may interest some of my readers. They will furnish hints by which ingenious men may profit in studying the science.

Mr. G. of our city sold a pair of horses for 150 dollars to Col. ———, and after applying again and again for the money to little purpose, sent his black fellow, Jim, with positive instructions not to let him see his face again till he had got the money out of the Colonel. "Wait at his house till you get it, no odds how long he keeps you." Jim accordingly went on his mission, met the Colonel at the door, just about to leave home, applied for the money, and was put off as usual, the debtor walking away as he made his excuse. After being absent two or three hours, the Colonel returned and found Jim sitting at the door, took dinner and supper, and kept all that day ensconced in the house to escape dunning as he should come out. Jim slept at the door, and was the first object the Colonel glanced at, as he threw open his casement in the morning. "What do you want?" he abruptly inquired. "Dat money, massa,—Massa G. say mussent come home to I get it." The Colonel paused a moment; there was no dodging such pertinacity, and no telling how long Jim's visit or rather *visitation* might last. So putting the best face on the matter, "Come in Jim," said he "and get something to eat in the kitchen, and by that time I shall be ready for you." As soon as Jim had dispatched his meal, he received the money and departed with rejoicing, still further heightened when Mr. G. gave him a five dollar bill for his collecting commissions.

Mr. C———, of our city was in the dry goods business in 1836-7, and with many a worthy man went to the wall during that period. Having no means to get again into business, his financial affairs went from bad to worse, and finding it hard to scratch up as much out of his old city debts as would pay his boarding bills, he borrowed a horse, and taking along his outstanding *hoosier* accounts, set out on a collecting tour. At *Connersville* he found one of his old debtors, almost as hard up as himself. "He had nothing, was sorry to say so, would do any thing in his power to assist his friend C———. If he had had notice in time or if Mr. C——— could have called in the course of a week or two, he might have done something, he believed."— "Well," said C———, "I have never been in your place before, it seems a pleasant like neighborhood, suppose I board with you a week or two, and we will look round and see what can be done." No objection of course could be made to this under the circumstances of the case. C———, who, as a son of the emerald isle, was fond of the ladies, *had licked the blarney stone* besides, fastened on the girls, the daughters of the host, and became as constant as their shadow, palavering them to death. In short, by the time the first week was through, the young ladies were thoroughly tired of their company, whose engrossing character kept every body else at a distance, and they signified to the father that Mr. C—— must either leave the house or they should. Finally, the hoosier had to turn out, and between borrowing and collecting, he made up the bill, C—— generously forgiving the interest. C——, in telling his own story, added, "If he had not paid me, I should have boarded it out, for it was no use for me to come back without the money. I don't know who would have boarded me here."

I heard *Jonathan Young* once complain to *Esqr. Mahard*, of a person who had been employed to collect subscriptions to some benevolent object to which Young had subscribed ten dollars. "Would you believe it Squire, he called on me every day last week, and some days twice or three times. Such dunning is outrageous, don't you think so?" "Yes" said the Squire drily—"he must have had a particular spite at you, he only called once upon me."

During one period of my employment with *Macalester & Co.*, the collecting fell into my hands. P——, a debtor, who kept a drug store on Main Street, was one of our dilatory customers. It was a constant trial of skill between us, he in getting into our debt, and I in getting him out of it. On one occasion I had made out and presented his bill. He glanced it over and said he would call and settle it. After the lapse of a week I presented it again. He then set the next Monday to pay it. On Monday he had not the money; call on Thursday. On Thursday again delinquent, and so forth from the beginning of the week to the middle of it, and from that middle to the beginning of the next, and so on for six weeks. I grew very tired, but as I was determined neither to lose my temper, nor fail of my purpose, I changed my battery.— If, when I passed by his store I found him alone, or occupied behind the counter, I kept on, but if, as was often the case, he was engaged talking with his neighbors, I made it my practice to stand within sight, my file of bills displayed in my hands, and as if waiting upon others for my turn to be attended to. After tantalizing him thus for a few minutes, I would say, "Ah, I see you are busy, Mr. P——, I will call again," After doing this four or five times P—— called on my employers, and complained to Mr. Buchanan that he could not stand such dunning as his man Cist's." "Ah!" said Mr. B. in his quiet way, "I hope he is not rude to you. "No," said P——, "but he haunts me to death; he is there from Monday morning till Saturday night." "Well," said Mr. Buchanan, in a tone which mingled seriousness with pleasantry. "I would not be plagued that way by any body. I think you ought to pay him off, and send him about his business."

Another hard case I had in L——. His avowed principle, was to owe his creditor as long as he could, and as we were personal friends, acknowledged to me, that he considered the four thousand dollars, he kept open on his neighbor's books, just so much capital in his business.— At one time he had owed a balance on our books for nearly a year, six to nine months of which, I had been dunning him for the amount, and finally got him to set a day for payment. "Call," said he "next Monday, and I will pay up." As this was Tuesday, a week more was staved off. On Monday morning the first thing I did in the way of business was to call according to appointment. "You are very punctual," said he, "I generally am in business matters," I replied. "In this case however, I had another reason for being so." "Ah" said he, "what was that."— "Why," said I "if a person were to set a day to pay me money, and I did not call; it would look as though I doubted whether he meant to give it me, which," added I, "on the footing of friendship, you and I are, would be absolutely an insult; don't you think so!" He opened his eyes and stared at me, to ascertain if I was quizzing him. But I was perfectly serious and doubtless looked so. He paid the debt, and I have not a shadow of doubt, I should have had to call twenty times more for it, if I had not hit him so close.

Vine Street Hill.

As our building operations in Cincinnati, and its northern liberties have enlarged last year and the present to an extent of 1500 houses, it may be of some interest to examine their features. I take building materials for my present subject. Eighty millions of bricks were laid within those bounds in 1844. An equal if not larger quantity will be laid the current year.— Within a trifle these are all made in Cincinnati, principally within the 8th Ward. As our cellars are walled with stone, a vast amount of that article, is of course requisite for foundations of various sorts. There is no accurate means of reaching the quantity annually hauled into our city for that purpose, but it may be estimated as correctly as suffices for all practical purposes, at 150,000 perches. The number of perches hauled per day for the season compared with the actual cellar measurements establish this conclusion. As to lime, it requires 120,000 bushels for laying the brick alone, referred to above.— Probably an equal quantity of stone is required for paving and macadamizing the streets in the same bounds.

A visit I made a few days since to the hill at the head of Vine street, has enabled me to witness the operations by which our city is built up and beautified.. Through Mulberry street which connects Main street with Vine, along the edge of our northern hills, part of it having been cut *down seventy feet* for the purpose of obtaining a proper bed for it, stone has been, and still is quarried extensively, and the surplus earth cut down and carted across towards Vine street, so as to fill up the chasm between that street as it ascends the hill, and the heights to the east.— Grading and paving to the value of sixteen thousand dollars have been made in this region already, a large proportion of which has been expended upon Mulberry street. On the scite of these improvements an extensive lime kiln has been erected, which holds *fifteen hundred bushels*, and is capable of supplying three hundred bushels lime every twenty four hours. The kiln is filling and emptying all the time, cooling neither by day nor night. Th's is but one among the many kilns outside of the city which furnish us with building lime. The building stone furnished us is all taken from the hills to our north, from quarries belonging to Messrs. Torrence, Graham, Reeder, Slack and Price.

The effect of the cutting down and filling up to which I have referred, is to prepare for the connection of Cincinnati with the hill region to the north, which at no distant day must take place. Twenty years hence, additions for miles to the north will be made to Cincinnati, as a means of providing for the enlargement of the city, in the only direction in which there is room for it to extend. Spacious streets and rows of dwellings will then occupy hills and hollows, which as they now stand, seem to bid defiance to the ingenuity and resources of man in providing the means, of bringing them to a suitable level and practical grade for ascent.

Documents of last War.
HEADQUARTERS, O. M.
Lower Sandusky, Nov. 6th, 1813.
SIR:

I received yours of the 4th inst.; the information given as to the want of forage at this place is correct; my horses and those of my staff, and horse teams here, have had no forage for a long time, and in consequence have had to discharge or send back teams much wanted at portage, as I am erecting a fort there, and store and block house on the other river. Capt. Reed promised sending some grain on here but could not procure the transportation until I sent three boats round to Huron river, and I expect one will be here in five or six days. My horses have failed much, and *I* fear will die. Flour will soon be very scarce here, and beef also—a boat load is now preparing for Bass Island, and

they only have it as they can catch it, at portage. Troops passing and re-passing so frequently makes the issues very uncertain.

I have ordered a small guard to Fort Ball, and the property must and shall be protected. I shall have the balance of the British prisoners sent on from Seneca to-morrow, 76 men, women and children, under a militia escort. I am pleased with your regular exertions in your department as far as came within my notice. I thank you for the information as to the men and officers at McArthur, and will certainly call them to account for their conduct. I am glad you are sending on some artificers, provided they have tools. I wish you to inform Capt. Catterlin, as I have not time to write him, that he must be ready to send on a detachment of a subaltern and about twenty men &c., as he will receive orders to receive the detachment from here with the prisoners to go to Franklinton, and mention this to you that they may be ready and not detain the prisoners at Sandusky, as it is an object to take them to provision, instead of transporting it to them.

I am sir, yours with esteem,
JOHN S. GANO.
B. HUGHES, A. D. Q. M. G.

HEADQUARTERS, O. M.
L. Sandusky, Nov. 18th, 1813.
CAPT. B. HUGHES, *Upper Sandusky:*

Capt. Carlinton has in charge three British officers, prisoners of war, and who are on their parole. You will afford them all the accommodation in your power, and facilitate their march to Chillicothe as much as possible.

By command of Maj. Gen. Gano.
JOSEPH VANCE,
Aid-de camp.

HEADQUARTERS, O. M.
L. Sandusky, Nov. 27th, 1813.
DEAR GENERAL:

I received your letter from Buffalo on the 20th inst. Crandall that you ordered released, I am informed was released shortly after you left this place. The three Delaware Indians, and one Potawotomee, I have sent to Upper Sandusky, with directions to Mr. Stickney to deliver them as you directed. They appeared much pleased, and made very fair promises. I have been much engaged in forwarding provisions and cloathing to Detroit, sending escorts with prisoners to Chillicothe, giving orders to the different posts, and erecting a small fort at Portage, and a store and block house at the landing at the crossing place of the peninsula from this river. The weather has been so very bad I am afraid they will not be completed until spring. *I* will use every exertion to accomplish it. There have been several droves of cattle sent on to Detroit, and I presume they are well supplied as to beef. The militia have been sickly at every post, and as must be expected, some have died. I shall get the men into quarters this day, and will soon have them comfortable—they have had much fatigue and exposure, but I presume not to be compared to that of your immediate command.

My militia have been near three months in service, and have not received a cent of pay.— An idea has occured, which I think proper to communicate for your consideration, that is, as soon as a company, or a subaltern command is recruited of regulars, that they should be sent out to some of those posts under proper officers, relieve the militia and do garrison duty. It would bring them into a state of subordination and discipline by the time the spring campaign opens, it would in some measure inure them to a soldier's life, and prepare them much better than raw troops for the field, and be a saving to the United States. These observations have not arisen from sinister motives, therefore you will excuse the liberty I have taken. I have made this place my headquarters, in consequence of the large quantity of public property that was at this post, but it is now principally sent off, and as soon as the works at portage that I have laid off are in a state of forwardness that I can leave this, I wish to visit the posts, and spend some time at Urbana, where I can communicate to the left and centre line with more facility, and if permitted would make a short visit to my troops at Detroit, though I will at all times strictly conform to your orders, and do my duty, and have, and will exact it from those under my command, which has convinced them I am not seeking popularity. I have appointed as I before informed you, Major J. Lawrence Lewis my brigade Major and Inspector, from whom I have received essential service in the discipline and arrangement of my troops, and as I find Judge Huntington alias pay master and Hunt very scrupulous in their duty. I wish him or some regular officer appointed by you to muster and inspect the troops at the different posts under my command, and if it is necessary, to forward to your adjutant general my monthly reports.

I am extremely anxious to hear from you, and the lower army.

Accept Sir, the assurance of my esteem, and respect and sincere wishes for your success and happiness.

JOHN S. GANO.
Maj. Gen. Wm. H. Harrison.

Chillicothe, Jan. 29th, 1814.

Dear General:

I received yours of the 16th. Gen. Harrison has authority to arm, supply and employ all the Indians against the enemy. He is at Cincinnati. Gen. Howard goes to Detroit. Col. Campbell will in a few days send on to L. Sandusky about two companies of recruits. By direction of war department, I have ordered a detail of 1450, to be organized and held in readiness to march at a moments warning. All this will be too late to aid if the British attempt Detroit or Put in Bay. If you have no name for the new fort, and have no objections, as it was erected by you and Ohioans, and laid out by you, you may by my order call it "Fort Gano."

I shall return to Marietta on my way to Hull's trial, having been summoned; unless the Court Marshall will admit of my deposition as I have proposed. I much wish I could see you, and hope to, in the spring.

I am with much esteem,
your ob't servant,
R. J. MEIGS,
Major Gen. Gano.

Headquarters, *Cincinnati*, Jan. 16th 1814.
Dear Sir:

I have directed Major Todd Ass't. Inspector General, to proceed immediately to you to muster your whole command. Give him such directions as you may deem proper, and send in your paymasters immediately with their estimates, to receive money for their pay which shall be ready for them.

It is possible that the enemy may make an attempt to recover Detroit. We must be in readiness to fly to its relief. You will therefore be pleased to concentrate your whole force at Lower Sandusky and Fort Meigs excepting an officer and 12 or 15 men in each of the other forts, and have every thing in readiness for a forward move. Gov. Meigs will hold in readiness an additional number of militia.

If Capt. Oliver as Deputy Quarter Master General is near you, give him the necessary orders for any provision you may want. Ascertain what supplies of ammunition you have, and direct any deficiency of cartridges to be supplied. I believe there are materials some where near you.

Let me hear from you as soon as possible upon every subject connected with your command. Conciliate the Indians as much as possible. The government have determined to employ them extensively against the enemy.

Yours with great respect,
WM. HENRY HARRISON.
Major Gen. Gano,
Com'g. the O. Militia in service.

Perseverance.

"The most extraordinary and the best attested instance of enthusiasm existing in conjunction with perseverance, is related of the *founder* of the Foley family. This man, who was a fiddler, living near Stourbridge, was often witness of the immense labor and loss of time caused by dividing the rods of iron necessary in the process of making nails. The discovery of the process called splitting, in works called splitting mills, was first made in Sweden, and the consequences of this advance in art were most disastrous to the manufactures of iron about Stourbridge. Foley the fiddler was often missed from his accustomed rounds, and was not again seen for many years. He had mentally resolved to ascertain by what means the process of splitting of bars of iron was accomplished; and, without communicating his intention to a single human being, he proceeded to Hull, and thence, without funds, worked his passage to the Swedish iron-port. Arrived in Sweden, he begged and fiddled his way to the iron-foundries, where, after a time he became a universal favorite with the workmen; and, from the apparent entire absence of intelligence or any thing like ultimate object, he was received into the works, to every part of which he had access. He took the advantage thus offered, and having stored his memory with observations and all the combinations, he disappeared from among his kind friends, as he had appeared, no one knew whence or whither.

"On his return to England he communicated his voyage and its results to Mr. Knight and another person in the neighborhood, with whom he was associated, and by whom the necessary buildings were erected and machinery provided. When at length every thing was prepared, it was found that the machinery would not act,—at all events, it did not answer the sole end of its erection—it would not split the bar of iron.

"Foley disappeared again, and it was concluded that shame and mortification at his failure had driven him away forever. Not so: again, though somewhat more speedily, he found his way to the Swedish iron-works, where he was received most joyfully, and, to make sure of their fiddler, he was lodged in the splitting mill itself. Here was the very aim and end of his life attained beyond his utmost hope. He examined the works, and very soon discovered the cause of his failure. He now made drawings or rude tracings and, having abided an ample time to verify his observations, and to impress them clearly and vividly on his mind, he made his way to the port, and once more returned to England. This time he was completely successful, and by the results of his experience enriched himself and benefited the country. I hold this to be the most extraordinary instance of full and resolute purpose on record."

Raising the Wind.

Wind is an element necessary to vitality.— While it is thus an indispensible agent of nature, art and the progressive intelligence of the times have adapted it to innumerable valuable purposes. The difficulty, in many cases, is to "raise the wind," which, in a great measure, and in many instances, depends on the operator.— The last means resorted to for this purpose of which we have heard, is the following:

A fellow disguised as a gentleman, so far as good dress and address favored the personation, rode up a few days since on a high-blooded and well conditioned charger, to the door of one of those accommodating gentlemen who are always willing to lend money on deposit, and who look on laws against usury as being first among the superfluities of legislation. The equestrian alighted and addressed the comparatively obscure Rothschild in the most familiar terms, calling him by name, and briefly and frankly telling him he came to borrow money from him —a small sum—just fifty dollars, which he wanted for immediate use, and which he could not otherwise procure, the bank in which he deposited not being yet opened. He would pay it in the course of the day, and give ten dollars as a bonus, and five dollars a day so long as it might remain unpaid.

"All very fair," said Discount, "but what security!"

"My watch," said the man in search of money.

"It won't do," said Discount.

"Well, then, take my riding mare for the time being," said the individual who was hard up—"I suppose that will satisfy you?"

"I can accommodate you," said Discount; "but mind you, I shall put the mare to livery till you settle up, and you will be in for the expenses."

"Very well," said the other—"it can't be much even if they charge by the hour; because, as I have said already, I'll be in funds when the bank opens."

The terms of the transaction were drawn up and mutually signed, the fifty dollars were paid over to this modern Jeremy Diddler, and Discount took his pledge to the livery stable.

"Hallo, there," said he on reaching the stable door.

"Hallo," said the master of the horse.

"Have you got room in your stable for this mare?" said Discount.

"We'll endeavor to accommodate her, said the other coolly."

"Well, give her the very best in your stable," said Discount, "and charge your price, I like to pay well and be paid well: "live and let live is my motto."

"You are extremely liberal and disinterested." was the remark in reply; "but, pray, give yourself no uneasiness about the mare. She is mine; and I trust I shall never treat her in a manner that will draw on me the displeasure of the Society for the Prevention of Cruelty to Animals."

"Yours!" said Discount, his lip quivering with surprise and astonishment.

"Mine—yes, *mine!*" said the dealer in horse flesh. "I gave her to a gentleman to ride not more than half an hour ago, and like a good customer, he paid me five dollars in advance."

"I have got an idea," said Discount.

"So have I," said the other—"I have got an idea that some person has been fooling you."

"Fooling me, sir," said Discount—"I should'nt care about being fooled; but to be diddled—done clean out of $50—d—— me, sir, it's too bad; but I'll offer a reward of $50 more to find the fellow, and if I catch him he goes to Baton Rouge, where the State will furnish him board and lodging 'free gratis' for seven years. But never mind: when I take a deposite in live

stock again, I'll be shed for usury, that's all."
Our readers by this time will see that the sharper
hired the mare to make the raise, and that Discount, who had been himself for years shaving,
was, for the first time in his life, shaved.
N. O. Picayune.

Rise of Eminent Men.

The following extracts are taken from an in-
teresting article, to be found in the *Edinburgh
Review* for January land, upon Twiss's Life of
Lord Eldon.

Influence of Accident on Great Men.—"It
is a curious coincidence that the two greatest
Chancery Lawyers of their day should both have
been forced into the profession by incidental
circumstances. Romilly says that what principally influenced his decision was, the being
thus enabled to leave his small fortune in his father's hands, instead of buying a sworn clerk's
seat with it. At a later period of my life, after
a success at the bar which my wildest and most
sanguine dreams had never painted to me—
when I was gaining an income of $8,000 or $9,-
000 a year—I have often reflected how all that
prosperity had arisen out of the pecuniary difficulties and confined circumstances of my father.'
"Wedderburn (Lord Loughborough) began
as an advocate of the Scotch bar. In the course
of an altercation with the Lord President, he
was provoked to tell his lordship that he had
said as a judge what he could not justify as a
gentleman. Being ordered to make an apology,
he refused, and left the Scotch for the English
bar. What every one thought his ruin, turned
out the best thing that could happen to him:
"'There's a divinity that shapes our ends,
Rough hew them how we may."
"Lord Tenterden's early destination was
changed by a disappointment. When he and
Mr. Justice Richards were going the Home Circuit, they visited the cathedral at Canterbury
together. Richards commended the voice of a
singing man in the choir. 'Ah,' said Lord Tenterden, 'that is the only man I ever envied!—
When at school in this town we were candidates for a chorister's place, and he obtained it.'
"It is now well known that the Duke of Wellington, when a subaltern, was anxious to retire from the army, and actually applied to Lord
Camden (then Lord Lieutenant of Ireland) for
a commissionership of customs! It is not always true, then, that men destined to play conspicuous parts in the world have a consciousness of their coming greatness, or patience to
bide their time. Their hopes grow as their capacity expands with circumstances; honors on
honors arise, like Alps on Alps; in ascending
one they catch a glimpse of another, till the last
and highest, which was veiled in mist when
they started, stands out in bold relief against the
sky."

Human Nature.

One of these weaknesses of humanity which
seems almost universally prevalent, is a dread
of acknowledging ones age. It is not confined
to the female sex or the single life, although
most abundant in these relations of society.

Mr. Alexander, our worthy city collector,
called the other day on Mr. ———, a merchant on Pearl street, for his capitation tax.—
The merchant was busy in the warehouse cellar, and being called up, presented a head nearly bald, and a remnant of hair white as snow.
with other personal appearances which satisfied
the collector that the subject was over sixty
years years of age, and of course exempt from
further taxes. He therefore apologised for disturbing him, alleging that he had obtained his
address from his lady, and had inferred him
from the age of the wife to be a younger person.
"Who says I am sixty?" exclaimed the merchant
with great vehemence, "*I calculate to pay that
tax for fifteen years to come!*"
Another of his domiciliary visits was paid to
Mr. Jacob W———, one of our old and respectable citizens. "What do you want with
me?" said Jacob to the collector, "I am beyond
your limits: I am over sixty!" "There!" said
his wife, to whom he had been married only a
few weeks. "Mr. W———, what did you
mean by telling me not two months ago, that
you were not fifty?
I remember, in taking the census of 1840, I
obtained the necessary statistics of one family
of high respectability, from the lady. She gave
me the column, "between 20 and 30" for her
husband, and the same on the female side for
herself. She leaned over my shoulder while I
put the figures down, and not understanding my
method of entry, observed, "you are not putting me down older than my husband." "No
madam, I put you down both simply between
20 and 30." "But I want you to put him down
older than me." I took some pains to explain
that this was out of my power, every column
giving its range of ten years. I left her less than
half satisfied, and on asking a mutual acquaintance for the explanation, was told "*She is oldr
than her husband, and was afraid you would put
her down so.*"

DEATHS.

DIED—On the 22nd inst., after a protracted and painful illness, Mary Ann, infant daughter of Rev. Samuel
and Frances W. Lynn, of Boone County, Ky. aged
one year, five months, and fifteen days.

Thou hast fled, dear Spirit—to the world of repose—
Thy crown to inherit, where the Tree of Life grows;
Where the weary find rest—where the captives go free;
Where the Martyrs are blest, and thou, Jesus shalt see.
Fare thee well, dear Spirit! we remain here with those
Who, no crown inherit, where no Tree of Life grows—
Where the weary rest not, nor the captives go free—
Till with Mary Ann, blest—their Redeemer they'll see.
L.

On Thursday, the 24th inst., Rufus C. son of Robert C.
and Emeline Florer, aged 3 years and 5 months.

On Sunday the 20th inst., George M. Bryarly.

CINCINNATI MISCELLANY

CINCINNATI, AUGUST, 1845.

The Changes of human life.

Not long since I made a visit to an old friend who resides about three miles out of town, on one of those beautiful farms of high rich lands, which in almost every direction surround the city. The road for some distance lies along the line of the Whitewater canal, immediately upon the banks of the Ohio river, and from the number of steamboats, canal boats, carriages, &c. constantly passing and repassing, a person might almost fancy himself in the vicinity of London or Dublin, or some of the oldest cities of Europe.

On passing out of the city I observed an old man whom I recognized as a soldier of the revolution. I had met with him several years ago in the " far West." He returned to Cincinnati about four years since, and has resided with his son. He is eighty-four years of age, enjoys good health, and seems very happy.— These men of the revolution, whether poor or rich, always appear cheerful and happy—neither unduly elated nor depressed by circumstances, they seem to enjoy that independent, peaceful state of mind, which the world can neither give nor take away.

My friend in the country, though not a soldier of the revolution, was one of the early pioneers of the West—a race of men who suffered great privations and hardships, in the first settlement of Kentucky and Ohio. Mr. T. removed with his father and the family, from Virginia to Kentucky in 1779. He was then very young, but remembers how greatly the first settlers were harassed and perplexed, and many of them butchered by the Indians. He has seen as many as three hundred of these savages make an unsuccessful attack upon a station defended by only six men. He was in Gen. St. Clair's defeat, where nine hundred of his fellow soldiers were left dead upon the ground. He is now upwards of three score years and ten, has resided in this county for more than half a century, and witnessed the growth of Cincinnati from its very infancy. He owns a large and valuable tract of land, which twelve years ago was supposed to be worth about fifty dollars an acre: now it is worth two hundred, and some portions of it, desirable building scites, would command from three hundred to five hundred dollars per acre. I spent the summer of 1832 with my family, at this delightful place. Every thing was changed since then. Oh what changes time and death can make! Only a few

years have passed away, and where are all the members of that large and interesting household, and those who sojourned with them?— Only two remain. Six have descended to the narrow house. Some have removed from the United States, and all are scattered like the leaves in autumn.

It is a singular coincidence, that another numerous and interesting family, with whom a few years previously, I and my family had spent a very pleasant summer in the city—have all passed away but two. The father and the sons are all numbered with the dead. Mr. B— was my early and constant friend, and one of the best of men—benevolent, kind and hospitable—a worthy, good citizen, and a man of excellent taste and judgment. His old family residence, with its recent improvements by the present worthy proprietor, is one of the most splendid and beautiful mansions in this or any other city. But the men of that day will soon all have passed away, and with them much that is intimately connected with the early prosperity and history of Cincinnati. The friends who loved them, will soon follow them. It is of very little consequence where men pass their days—whether in town or country—in log-cabins or in splendid palaces. This world is not our rest. Our days are as a shadow that passeth away. Without the hope of the gospel, this would be a dark world indeed. But this blessed hope we have; it shines upon the tomb of our friends, and casts a heavenly light over the darkness of the grave.

" Hope springs exulting on triumphant wing,
    That we shall meet again in future days:
There ever bask in uncreated rays,
    No more to sigh or shed the bitter tear.
Together hymning our *Redeemer's* praise,
    In such society, yet still more dear;
While circling time moves round in an eternal
    sphere."

Our North-West Territory.

There is nothing in Cincinnati exhibits a growth as vigorous as the north-western part of our city, popularly called Texas.—What constituted originally the Seventh Ward was, only seven years ago, interspersed here and there with dwellings, but consisted principally of brick yards, cattle pastures and vegetable gardens, for the supply of our markets. Such was the unimproved condition of this region, that nearly two hundred and fifty acres occupied as pasturage, were owned by four or five individuals alone. Two hun-

11,

dred and fifty acres of pasturage in a city, and that city as thriving as Cincinnati! The whole number of dwellings, at that period, within the bounds of that Ward, were short of three hundred and fifty, and its whole population could not have reached to twenty-five hundred souls, and these the buildings and inhabitants of a section of Cincinnati more than a mile square! Now, what a change! Eleven hundred new buildings, most of them of a character for beauty, permanence, and value equal to the average of the main body of our city improvements.— The streets graded and paved to a great extent, churches and public school houses going up in its midst, and well paved sidewalks, adding to the general finish and convenience. With all these improvements, too, space has been left at the sides and in the fronts of the buildings, for that free introduction of shrubbery and flowers, which render our city so attractive to strangers, and so airy and pleasant to ourselves. It is, in short, completely *rus in urbe*, abounding in spots which combine the comfort of a country villa, with the convenience and advantages of a city residence.

It may serve to give a striking view of the magnitude and extent of the improvements in this region, to state that London street has been graded from Fulton or Mound st. west, which extent, some 1,200 feet in length, is now dug down from five to ten feet, to fill up 1,000 feet farther west and the entire width—sixty feet— of the street. The stupendous character of the work may be inferred from the volume of earth filled in, which, at the intersection of Baymiller street, measures sixteen feet in depth. The greater part of this is also paved, and progressing as fast in paving as is prudent, the graded ground being covered with stone as fast as it settles to its permanent bed. This must become one of the finest entrances to our city.— The population of this section of Cincinnati is now, doubtless, eleven thousand, the inhabitants having quintupled since 1838.

A new and important avenue to trade and marketing has been opened through this part of the city, by extending Freeman street to the Hamilton road. The effect of this will be to direct a large share of the travelling to the city, to the intersection of Fifth and Front streets, and to bring the pork wagons into direct communication with the pork-houses which must be put up on the line of the Whitewater Canal.

This avenue will also become a formidable rival to Western Row, as a connection between the adjacent parts of Indiana and Cincinnati, owing to the scandalous condition into which the upper part of that street has been suffered to dilapidate, which renders it impassable in winter, and unpleasant at all times.

What good one man may do.

The following remarkable statement forms the basis of a petition to the Massachusetts Legislature. Why may not good in this department be as extensively done here.

In the summer of 1841, John Augustus, a man in humble life, now well known to the friends of temperance in Boston, and who deserves to be through the State, visited the Police Court in Boston, and, being very much interested in the case of a poor man, who, for the vice of drunkenness, had been sentenced to the House of Correction, stepped forward and offered to become bail for him. His proposal was accepted. He paid out of his own pocket, the fees of court, amounting to a few dollars, and took the condemned man with him out of the court room. He persuaded him to sign the pledge, furnished him with food and lodgings, and at last secured employment for him, and from henceforth the rescued drunkard became an industrious and sober citizen.

Mr. Augustus, inspired by the success of his first attempt, and impelled by the yearnings of his noble heart, continued his visits to the Police Court, and from August, in the year 1841, to February of the present year, has rescued from the jaws of the House of Correction, and from the fellowship of convicted felons, one hundred and seventy-six men and fifty-six women—in all, *two hundred and thirty-two human beings*—a large portion of whom, but for the vice of intemperance, would have enjoyed an unquestionable right to the general regard of society. Fortunately for his benevolent attempt to stand between the drunkard and the customary course of law, Mr. Augustus has preserved a careful record of every case in which he has interested himself, and he is thus enabled to furnish an intelligent account of a large portion of the persons, who by his means, have been saved from confinement in South Boston. Full three-fourths of the number, or about one hundred and seventy-five, are now temperate and orderly citizens, and are gaining a livelihood. About one half of the whole number were residents of Boston, and the other half were temporary visitors to the city from the country and from neighboring States. The proportion of foreigners was much larger of the men than of the women.— The amount of costs paid by Mr. Augustus, for the release of the persons, is $976,61. This amount has nearly all been paid back to him by the persons thus rescued. Of course, this amount of costs has been saved to the towns liable for it. It will be readily seen, however; that a much larger sum has been saved, by so many intemperate persons having become useful citizens; instead of being shut up in prison at the public charge. To those towns in the country which occasionally receive large bills for the support of drunkards in the House of Correction in South Boston, this point is not unworthy of notice. These considerations are glanced at, because, indeed, they should not be overlooked; but they are of little moment in comparison with the tears which have been dried up, the hearts which have been healed, and the families which have been made happy by the restoration of so large a number of the human brotherhood, to temperance, usefulness and respectability. By the minute and unquestionable records kept by Mr. Augustus, rising eight-tenths of all the persons sent to the House of Correction are sent there for drunkenness.— Through his Samaritan efforts, the number of commitments for this dreadful vice has been largely reduced—and besides the diminished expense, consequent upon reduction, the community has been incalculably blessed by the change.

The following statement will show the actual reduction in the commitments to the House of Correction, for drunkenness, since the Washingtoninan reform commenced in Boston, but, especially, as resulting from the efforts of Mr. Augustus, In 1841, they were 605; in 1842, they were 551; in 1843, 459; in 1844, 407, On the first of January, of the present year, the number of persons remaining in the House of Correction, committed by the Police Court, was only 123; of which number 110 were committed for drunkenness, viz: 47 males and 63 females, other offences being but 13. During the first year, Mr. Augustus has saved 120 persons from the House of Correction: 20 of whom have since been sentenced to the House of Correction, the remaining 100 are doing well. It would be easy to show the actual amount, in dollars and cents, saved to the State, by a result like this, but not so easy to exhibit the blessings resulting to the rescued men, or to their families, many of the members of which would, doubtless, otherwise have become outcasts, or have found their way to our almshouses.

It is impossible to enter, in detail, into the formidable difficulties which a humble mechanic, like Mr. Augustus, has had to encounter, in order to proceed in his beneficent work. To say nothing of the formalities and liabilities which belong, alike, to all courts of law, he has, in most cases, provided a temporary home for his fallen brother, and allowed no rest to his head, until he has done his utmost to procure for him employment. It should be added, that, within a few months, a number of the 'merchant princes,' and other eminent philanthropists, of Boston, have given Mr. Augustus a substantial testimonial of their respect for his unwearied and invaluable services. Previous to this liberal act; Mr. A. had relied upon his own scanty resources, and had found it exceedingly difficult to carry into effect his praiseworthy labors.

Hints.

There is a mode of conveying ideas, of admirable efficiency, which for want of a more appropriate name, may be called *hinting*. Its brevity, which is sure to arrest attention, its obscurity, which unites it with the sublime, its irresistible energy, all render it a powerful and efficient weapon for its appropriate employment. A few examples will illustrate.

"If your honor should lose your purse before you get home," said a bar-keeper to a magistrate attending a county Court, who was leaving the house, without settling off a score which he had run up during the past week or two, "I hope you will recollect *you did not pull it out here.*"

"Have you found your watchdog which was stolen?" was a question asked a gentleman on the door step of a certain provision store. "No, not exactly, but I know where they sold the sausages" was the reply.

A miller, meeting of one of those boys (of which most villages have one) called an "idiot," asked him a question, which Jock was unable to answer. "Jock," said the miller, "you are a fool." "Yes, sir," said Jock, 'every body says so; but,' continued he, 'here are somethings I know, and some things I don't know." "Well, what do you know, then?" "I know millers always have fat pigs." "Well, and what don't you know?" again asked the miller. "Why," replied Jock, "I don't know whose meal they eat."

The best instance of the kind perhaps is the following:

"During the discussion of a ministerial measure in the House of Commons lately, Sir Robert Peel made some pungent allusion to those who, without having the power actually to defeat his policy, were yet very successful in causing *delay*. Referring to the leaders in this sort of work, he reminded the House that "when travellers in the East *do not want to go too fast* they put a *jackass* in front!"

Former Prices of Cotton.

In 1828, ten bags of Sea Island Cotton, produced 90c. a lb. The same planter, for his two succeeding crops received $1 aud $1,50 a pound. For two bags of extra kind in 1798 $2 a pound was received, the highest price ever paid for cotton. The Sea Island Cotton is superior to the best cotton produced in any part of the world. While a pound of the best produced elsewhere can be spun into a thread of only 115 miles, making 350 hanks to the pound, a pound of Sea Island from South Carolina has been spun at Manchester, in England, into a thread of over 238 miles.

An Indian Adventure in Maine.

Among the early settlers of what was then the province of Maine, a man named Smith was for many years the object of dread as well as hatred to the Indians who occupied portions of that region. He had lost several relations by their hands, and had vowed eternal enmity to the whole race. He had been twice taken by the savage tribes, but had contrived to escape from them, and had killed several of their number. He sought every opportunity to do them mischief in any way. By this course he had become so exceedingly obnoxious to the red men, that they would not even kill him directly if they could, but were constantly on the watch to take him alive for the purpose of satisfying their vengeance by the infliction of the utmost torture that barbarity could invent. Smith being aware of this disposition of theirs, was the least afraid of their bullets, and being at one period engaged splitting fence rails, in the ardor of his employment, had neglected his usual lookout, and not once thought of his antagonists, the savages, until he found himself suddenly seized at the arm by an Indian named Wahsoos, and looking around found himself surrounded by five others. Now Smit! now Smit! we got you, exclaimed the leader of the party. Smith saw it would be vain to resist, and assuming an air of composure, thus addressed his captor: "Now, Wahsoos; I will tell you what I'll do; if you will now help me to split open this log, I will then go with you without any resistance, otherwise I will not walk a step, and you will have to carry or kill me." The Indians now having him safe in their possession, and willing to save themselves trouble, agreed to split the log, if he would tell them how. Smith had already opened the end of the log with a large wooden wedge, and renewing his blows on the wedge with a beetle, he directed them to take hold of the separated parts of the log, three on each side, and pull with all their might, while he should drive in the wedge. The red men were not without their suspicions, but kept their eyes on Smith's motions, while they pulled at the sundered parts of the log. Every blow of Smith opened the crevice wider, which enabled the Indians to renew their hold by inserting their fingers deeper into the crevice, when Smith, slightly changing the direction of the beetle, struck on the side of the wedge, knocking it out of the log, which closing with great force, caught every foe by the hands, save one, who seeing the predicament of his companions, took to his heels; but was soon brought down by Smith's long barrelled gun, which he had kept near him. The other five expected no mercy, and were not disappointed. Five blows from Smith's axe, silenced their death-song.

A year or more after this affair, Smith was returning from an excursion, and passed near a bend of the Androscoggin river, about a mile above the falls on which the Lewiston Mills are now located. It was nearly dark, and he discovered an Indian making a fire on a rock by the river bank. Smith saw through the business at once: the fire was for a beacon, to guide the landing of a strong party. With unerring aim, he shot the lone savage, who pitched into the water, and Smith quickly threw the fire and fire-brands after him; and then proceeded down to the falls, and there he soon kindled another fire on a projecting rock; and then retiring up the river bank a short distance, awaited the result. He soon heard the songs of a company of warriors, who had discovered the fire, and

were steadily paddling towards it in high glee. Smith could hardly refrain from laughing aloud, as they neared the fatal beacon. Their songs were suspended by surprise, as the rapid motion of their canoes, and the hoarse roar of the falls revealed too late the dreadful truth. A brief death song uttered in savage yells, and the cries of several squaws and papooses, were all that preceded their last and dreadful plunge over the perpendicular falls.

To the Point.

We find the following in an obscure exchange. We do not remember of ever before seeing it in print, and it is too good to be lost. All the German logic or profound metaphysical research ever displayed, cannot so satisfactorily demonstrate the existence of the soul.

The Rev. James Armstrong preached at Harmony, near the Wabash, when a doctor at that place, a professed deist or infidel, called on his associates to accompany him, while he attacked the methodist, as he said. At first he asked Mr. Armstrong, "if he following preaching to save souls?" who answered in the affirmative. He then asked Mr. Armstrong "if he ever saw a soul?" "No." "If he ever heard a soul?" "No." "If he ever smelt a soul?" "No." "If he ever tasted a soul?" "No." "If he ever felt a soul?" "Yes, thank God," said Mr. Armstrong. "Well," said the doctor, "there are four of the five senses against one to evidence there is no soul!" Mr. Armstrong then asked the gentleman "if he was a doctor of medicine?" and he was also answered in the affirmative.— He then asked the doctor, "if he ever saw a pain?" "No." "If he ever heard a pain?"— "No." "If he ever tasted a pain?" "No."— "If he ever smelt a pain?" "No." "If he ever felt a pain?" "Yes." Mr. Armstrong then said, "There are also four senses against one to evidence that there is no pain; and yet, sir, you know there is pain, and I know there is a soul." The doctor appeared confounded and walked off.

Woman's Earnings.

The inadequate prices at which female labor is compensated, is a prolific source of evil in our cities. There are in Cincinnati, alone, five thousand women who sew for a living, most of them for the extensive clothing shops on Main and Front streets. Besides this, there are numbers more who reside in Fulton, Newport, Covington, and in our northern suburbs, who depend upon similar employment for a livelihood. I am not aware how low competition for employment, has reduced this description of it, but shirts have have been made heretofore as low as ten to twelve and a half cts. each. What a scandal to a christian community are such wages!

A project has been started in a New York print, by a Mr. Goin of that city, which would at once relieve the distresses of these unfortunate women, without prejudice to the interests of any class of people. It is this: To have a piece of land set apart, of government property, a good and convenient building erected thereon, and there to have all the clothing, even down to the knitting of suspenders, required for the supply of the army and navy of the United States, made by females, under female arrangement.— The government would pay to such an institution no more than it now pays to capitalists who monopolize the business of furnishing clothing for the War and Navy Departments. Large fortunes are annually made by these contractors; the articles in which they speculate are the produce of these women who are now destitute.— Why not let them retain, not only their wages, but the profit of the third person. Mr. Goin does not enter into the details of this plan; these he leaves to the Secretaries of the army and navy department.

I *goin* for this plan, and do hope that it may engage the attention of some public spirited member of Congress—Mr. Pratt of New York, for example—to press the measure into existence.

Covington and Newport.

Let those who are in doubt what is the cause why Lexington does not improve like Dayton, Cleveland, or Columbus; and Louisville, progress in the same degree with Cincinnati. Observe the progress of Newport and Covington during the last five years, and the relative decrease of the slave population in those places.

In 1840, the population of Covington was 2026
" 1845, do do 4388
Colored population in 1840, 111
do do 1845, 203
In 1840, the population of Newport was 1016
" 1845, do do 1710
Colored population in 1840,
do do 1845, 76
In 1840 the blacks of these places were as 1 to 20.

In 1845, as to the whites 1 in 22. This last is the present proportion of blacks to whites in Cincinnati. In Lexington and Louisville I presume the blacks form more than one third of the community.

I have little doubt Covington will have a population against the next census of nine thousand individuals; and Newport three thousand. They are as much one as Pittsburgh and Allegheny City, divided merely by a water course, and are both mainly built up out of Cincinnati's business and improvement. They will be in five years as populous as Lexington, probably the wealthiest city in the State; and by 1875, will surpass Louisville in population, unless the intervening period of time shall witness the extinction of slahere within the very limits of Kentucky.

Cemeteries.

Before the establishment of Rural Cemeteries near the Eastern cities, the custom prevailed of burying the dead under the churches. They were crowded in so revolting a manner, as to render the air in the churches unwholesome, considerable discussion ensued, and finally the custom was prohibited, and Cemeteries established a few miles out, in all the atlantic cities.— While the matter was in agitation, Mr PIERPONT published in the Boston papers, the following translation of an

EPITAPH,

On a celebrated French Physician.

Here lies,
Under the pure and breezy skies,
The dust
Of SIMON PETER, the devout and just,
Doctor of Medicine,
At his request.
He sleeps in Earth's sweet, wholesome breast,
Rather than in a noisy *cemetery*
Under a church, where all the great they bury,
It were, he said, a sin
Past all enduring.
A sin, which to commit, he was unwilling;
Should he, who, while alive, got fame and bread,
The sick by curing,
Entirely change his hand and go, when dead,
The well to killing.

Fort Washington Reserve.

The following proclamation is an interesting and valuable document. as it gives the history of the reservation along side of Fort Washington. I had supposed heretofore that Congress had exempted this spot at the period of granting *Symmes* his million of acres, but it seems to have been a movement of St. Clair himself. It may be worthy of notice, that the seal of the "Territory north west of the river Ohio" presents the Territorial coat of arms, the device being a *Buckeye* tree with timber in the foreground cut up into logs. The motto *"meliorem lapsa locavet."* This is doubtless the origin of our state appellative *"Buckeye."*

Proclamation.

By his excellency, Arthur St. Clair, Major General in the Service of the U. States, and Governor and Commander in Chief of their Territory north-west of the river Ohio.

THE SEAL OF THE TERRITORY OF THE U. S. N. W. OF THE RIVER OHIO.

WHEREAS, it has been represented to me, that certain persons generally known by the name of the proprietors of the Miami Purchase, have taken it upon themselves to sell and dispose of divers tracts and parcels of land, the property of the United States, lying and being to the eastward of a line to be drawn from a place upon the bank of the Ohio river, exactly twenty miles, following the several courses of the same, above the great Miami river, parallel to the general course of that river; whereby many unwary persons have been induced to make settlements upon the same, contrary to the authority of the United States, and in defiance of their proclamation, against the making settlements on any of the public lands without due authority for so doing. It is hereby made known that the lands contracted for by the honorable John Cleves Symmes and his associates, or their agents, is bounded in the manner following, viz: All that tract or parcel of land, situate, lying, and being in the Western country adjoining to the Ohio river, beginning on the bank of the same river, at a spot exactly twenty miles distant along the several courses of the same, from the place where the great Miami river empties itself into the great river Ohio, from thence extending down the said river Ohio along the several courses thereof, thence up the said Miami river along the several courses thereof, to a place from whence a line drawn due east will intersect a line drawn from the place of beginning aforesaid, parallel with the general course of the great Miami river, so as to included one million of acres within those lines and the said river, and from that place upon the great river Miami, extending along such lines to the place of beginning, containing as aforesaid, one million of acres- That the land lying to the eastward of the said parallel line, from the Ohio to where it may intersect the little Miami river, and from thence down the line to the Ohio river, and along the Ohio river to the place before mentioned, where the parallel line begins, is as yet, the property of the United States, and has not been aliened or sold to any person whosoever. That the settlements which have been made upon the same, are entirely unauthorized, and the persons who now occupy them are liable to be dispossessed as intruders,and to have their habitations destroyed; and that they are not treated in that manner immediately, is owing only to the circumstance, that they were made to believe the said proprietors of the Miami purchase had a right to the land, and to give them an opportunity to represent their case to Congress: And I do hereby strictly prohibit all persons to extend the settlements they have already made, or to form new settlements to the eastward of the aforesaid parallel line, and with that line the little Miami and the Ohio river, until the pleasure of Congress in the premises shall be made known —as they shall answer the contrary at their peril.

And Whereas, It is necessary, that a certain tract of land adjacent to and lying round Fort Washington, should be set apart and reserved for public use. I have ordered the same to be done, and it is bounded in the manner following, viz: Beginning on the Banks of the Ohio river at the middle of the street,* which passes to the westward of the house where Bartle and Strong now live, and running from thence with the said river to the east side of Deer Creek, from thence running north fifteen degrees, thirty minutes west and hundred and twenty perches, and from thence by and with a strait line to be drawn at right angles from the same until it reaches the middle of the street aforesaid, thence down the middle of the said street to the place of beginning, and all the land lying and being within these boundaries, is hereby set apart and reserved for public use until Congress shall determine otherwise—and all persons are hereby strictly forbidden to cut down, carry away or otherways destroy any timber, trees or wood that may be growing, standing or lying upon or within the same.

And Whereas, There are houses and lots at present occupied by certain persons which are included within the boundaries of this reserved tract: It is hereby made known to them, that they will be allowed to possess the same until the present crop is taken off, and no longer, unless they shall obtain permission for the same under the hand and seal of the officer commanding the Garrison or General commanding the troops upon the Ohio, and shall voluntarily submit themselves to the military laws as followers of the army.

In Testimony, whereof I have hereunto set my hand and caused the seal of the territory to be affixed this 19th day of July, one thousand seven hundred and ninety-one, and in the year of the Independence of the United States the sixteenth.

By his excellency's command,
WINTHROP SARGENT, Secretary.
ARTHUR St. CLAIR.

*Broadway.

The Herring Pie.

A STORY FOR MARRIED FOLKS.

It was a cold winter's evening; the rich banker Brounker had drawn his easy chair close into the corner of the stove, and sat smoking his long clay pipe with great complacency, while his intimate friend Van Grote, employed in exactly the same manner, occupied the other corner. All was quiet in the house, for Brounker's wife and children were gone to a masked ball, and, secure from fear of interruption, the two friends indulged in a confidential conversation.

"I cannot think," said Van Grote, "why you should refuse your consent to the marriage.—

Berkenrode can give his daughter a good fortune, and you say your son is desperately in love with her."

"I don't object to it," said Brounker. "It is my wife who will not hear to it."

"And what reason has she for refusing?"

"One which I cannot tell you," said his friend, sinking his voice.

"Oh! a mystery—come, out with it. You know I have always been frank and open with you, even to giving you my opinion of your absurd jealousy of your wife."

"Jealous of my wife? nonsense! Have I not just sent her to a masked ball?"

"I don't wonder you boast of it. I should like to have seen you do as much when you were first married. To be sure, you had reason to look sharply after her, for she was the prettiest woman in Amsterdam. Unfortunately she has taken such advantage of your love, that the gray mare has become the better horse, and you refuse an advantageous match for your son, to gratify her caprice."

"You are quite wrong, my good friend. I never allow any one to be master here but myself; and in the present instance I cannot blame Clotilda. The secret of her refusal lies in a herring pie."

"A herring pie!" exclaimed Van Grote.

"Yes, a herring pie. You may remember it was a favorite dainty of mine, and that my wife could not endure even the smell of it. Well, during the first years of my marriage, I must confess that I was a little—a very little—jealous of Clotilda. My situation obliged me to keep open house, and among the young sparks who visited us, none gave me more uneasiness than the handsome Colonel Berkenrode.— The reputation that he had already acquired for gallantry was enough to create alarm, and the marked attention he paid my wife convinced me it was well founded. What could I do? It was impossible to forbid him the house, for he had it in his power to deprive me of the government contracts; in other words, to ruin me. After pondering deeply on the subject, I decided on doing nothing until the danger should become imminent; all that was necessary was to know how things really stood; having just purchased this house, I caused a secret closet to be made behind the stove here. It communicates with my private room, and from it I could overhear every thing that passed in this apartment without risk of being discovered.— Thank God I have had no use for it for the last twenty years, and, indeed, I do not know what has become of the key. Satisfied with this precaution, I did not hesitate to leave Clotilda, when any of her admirers paid her a visit, though I promise you that some of the Colonel's gallant speeches made me wince."

"Upon my word," interrupted his friend, "you showed a most commendable patience. In your place I should have contented myself with forbidding my wife to receive his visits."

"There spoke the old bachelor. But as I did not want to drive her headlong into his arms, I went a different way to work. Day after day I was forced to listen to the insidious arguments of the seducer. My wife—I must own made a stout defence—at one time tried ridicule, at another entreaty, to deter him from his pursuit of her. He began to lose hope in proportion as I gained it, till one day he bethought himself of

threatening to blow out his brains if she would not show compassion. Moved at this proof of the strength of his passion, she burst into tears, and pleaded that she was not free—in short, she gave him to understand that I was the obstacle to his happiness. Berkenrode was too well skilled in the art of seduction not to see that he had gained a point. He raved, cursed me as the cause of his misery, and tried to obtain a promise from her, in case she should become a widow. She stopped him peremptorily; but I never closed an eye that night, and Clotilda, though she did not know that I watched her, was as uneasy as myself. On the following day a circumstance occurred that increased her agitation. While at breakfast, a message came from the cook asking to see me alone. I desired him to come in 'as I was not in the habit of interfering in domestic affairs' and communicate his business in my wife's presence.— When the man entered he was pale as a ghost, and scarcely seemed to know what he was about. At last he told me that he had received a packet containing a small bottle, three hundred guldens, and a note, in which he was requested to put the contents of the former into the first herring pie he should prepare for me. He was assured that he might do it without fear as the contents of the bottle were quite harmless, and would give a delicious flavor to the pie. An additional reward was promised if he complied with the request and kept his own counsel. The honest fellow, who was much attached to me, said he was convinced there must be something wrong in the affair, and should not be happy till bottle and money were out of his hands. I poured a few drops of the liquid on a lump of sugar, and gave it to my wife's lap dog. It fell into convulsions, and died in a few minutes. The case was now plain; there had been an attempt to poison me. Never shall I forget Clotilda's pale face as she threw herself weeping into my arms—"Poison! A murderer!" she exclaimed, clasping me as if to shield me from danger: "Merciful Heaven, protect us both!" I consoled her with the assurance that I was thankful to my unknown enemy, who was the means of showing me how much she loved me. That day Berkenrode came at the usual hour; but in vain did I take my seat in the hiding place; he was not admitted. I afterward found that she had sent him a letter, threatening that if ever he came again that her husband should be informed of all that had passed. He made many attempts to soften her resolution, but to no purpose, and in a year after he married. No acquaintance has ever existed between the families; and now you know why my wife refuses her consent to our son's marriage with Berkenrode's daughter."

"I cannot blame her," said Van Grote. "Who would have thought that Berkenrode, a soldier, and man of honor, could have been capable of such a rascally deed?"

"Ha! ha! ha!" laughed Brounker; "and do you really think it was the general who sent the poison?"

"Why, who else?"

"Myself to be sure! The whole was my own contrivance, and it cost me three hundred guldens in a present to my cook; but was money well laid out, for it saved my wife, and got rid of her troublesome lap dog at the same time."

"Do you know, Brounker, I think it was

rather a shabby trick to leave Berkenrode under such an imputation; and now that your son's happiness depends on your wife's being undeceived——"

"I am aware of all that, but to undeceive her now is not so easy as you think. How can I expect her to disbelieve a circumstance in which for the last twenty years she has put implicit faith."

He was interrupted by the entrance of Vrow Brounker. Her cheeks were flushed, and she saluted Van Grote rather stiffly.

"What! not at the ball, Clotilda?" asked her husband.

"No! I had a bad headache," she replied and Maurice has promised to take charge of his sister. But I have come to tell you that I have been thinking over his marriage with Mina Berkenrode, and have altered my mind on that subject. In short, I shall withdraw my opposition to the match."

The friends looked at each other in astonishment.

"By the by," she continued, "here is a key I found some time ago; I think it must belong to you."

"Well, Clotilda," said her husband, striving to hide his confusion as he took the key, "this is good news about the marriage——"

"Suppose you and your friend celebrate it by a supper. There is a herring pie in the house, and you need not fear that it is poisoned."

She left the room. Brounker looked foolish, and Van Grote rubbed his hands as he exclaimed, "Caught in your own trap! He who digs a pit for his enemy shall fall into it himself."

"Nevertheless," replied Brounker, "I think I have got well out of mine."

Thomas Hood.

Hood whose death may be noticed in our late papers, was one of the wittiest writers of the age. His candle burned bright to the last. The following is one of his latest.

"Mrs. Gardiner is a widow, devoted to the cultivation of flowers in her door yard garden, who has the peculiarity of identifying *herself* with each variety. Hood, standing at the little gate, compliments her on the appearance of her carnations; to which she replies,

'Yes, I've a stronger blow than any one in the place, and as to sweetness, no body can come nigh me. Would you like to walk in, sir, and smell me?'

Accepting the polite invitation, I stepped in through the little wicket, and in another moment was rapturously sniffing at her stocks, and the flower with the sanguinary name. From the walls I turned to a rose-bush, remarking that there was a very fine show of buds.

'Yes, but I want sun to make me bust. You should have seen me last June, sir, when I was in my full bloom. None of your wishy-washy pale sorts—[this was a fling at the white roses at the next door]—none of your provincials or pale pinks. There's no maiden blushes about me. I'm the regular old red cabbage!"

And she was right; for, after all, that hearty, glowing, fragrant rose is the best of the species —the queen of flowers, with a ruddy *enbonpoint*, remaining one of Rubens' beauties.

'And there's my American creeper. Miss Sharp pretends to creep, but Lord bless ye! be-

fore ever she gets up to her first floor window, I shall be running all over the roof of the villa.— You see I'm over the portico already."

Dueling.

I am glad to perceive that this senseless as well as wicked practice is falling silently into contempt. A man who in Ohio were to challenge another to a combat of this nature would expose himself to general ridicule.

The duel still lingers in some parts of the country, and certain neighborhoods, which afford facilities to evade the laws on fashionable murder, are much annoyed with the evil. The neighborhood in Delaware which adjoins Philadelphia, or rather Pennsylvania, is a retreat of this species. A late meeting of the young bloods from Philadelphia at this spot has furnished the Governor of Delaware with a plea, and a motive to demand the offender from the Governor of Pennsylvania for the purpose of being tried for the violation of the laws of the State.

They have a punishment in Delaware that is just the thing for duelists. They mount the offender on a platform 20 feet high, with his wrists and neck fastened in holes in a board. After remaining in this position an hour for the amusement of the bystanders, he is fastened to a post and receives thirty-nine lashes, well laid on.

One or two administrations of this discipline would probably guard against a repetition of the offence. It would lower a peg or two the dignity of broadcloth offenders against the laws to receive "forty stripes save one," at the hands of the public hangman.

They manage this subject admirably in Mexico. There, the man who kills his antagonist in a duel *is bound for his debts*. Hence it is a valid reason, as well as a cogent one, to refuse a meeting, where the challenger cannot show that he is clear of pecuniary obligations. It would soon put down dueling in the United States, if no one was privileged to fight a duel unless he was out of debt.

MARRIED,

On Tuesday the 29th ult., by the Rev MR. GURLEY, Mr. THOMAS FARIS to Miss RACHAEL DOERRER.

DEATHS.

At Wooster, Ohio, July 10th ult., Rev. THOMAS G. JONES, aged 67 years. Mr. Jones was a Pioneer in Ohio and formerly took an active part in the public business of the State.

In this city on Monday August 4th, MARGARET, consort of Peter Bell, Esq.. in the 79th year of her age.

On Sunday 3d EUNICE wife of Jas. Myrack, aged 65 years.

At Cummingsville July 30th, of Congestive Fever, MISS RACHAEL RUHAMAH CLOPPER youngest daughter of Nicholas Clopper, deceased.

The Buckeye.

Mr. Cist.—The remarks made in your paper of 6th August, on the Seal of the Territory of the United States, northwest of the Ohio River, suggests an origin much too respectable for the offensive nickname of Buckeye, now fastened on our State.

You say that "the seal presents the Territorial coat of arms,—the device being a *buckeye* tree, with timber cut up into logs. The motto, *Meliorem lapsa locavis*," which you consider as doubtless the origin of our state appellative of Buckeye.

My copies of the seal are less perfect than yours, being impressions after ten years longer use, and I have never been able to decipher the motto. The device is distinct, but I find no buckeye tree. In the foreground is a forest tree felledby the axe, the trunk yet resting on its stump, and the branches all cut off. In the rear and close by is a fruit tree, which, from its shape and the large round fruit, is doubtless the apple tree, and to this the motto alludes: "A better than the fallen takes its place;" or, more literally, "He (the pioneer) has set a better than the fallen." The motto is without meaning if the tree be considered a buckeye, as it certainly would be without truth, for it is the most worthless of all trees.

The buckeye served to indicate the existence of good soil, but to the early settlers it was a most useless tree: it could not be used in building, nor for fences, nor even for fuel. As a tree it consequently stood very low in the estimation of early settlers, and by a figure of speech very forcible to them, it was applied to lawyers and doctors whose capacity and attainment were of a low grade. If some of the juveniles of your bar had laboured in their profession only thirty years ago, they would have been little apt to covet the name of Buckeye, as some of them have done in later time, and had it been conferred on them by others they would have repelled the name.

The first I ever met with the name in any other than an opprobrious sense was in 1823, when reading Long's Expedition to the Yellowstone. In speaking of Cincinnati, he says (as I remember now, for I have not seen the book since) that the natives were called Buckeyes, in contradistinction to emigrants, who were generally called Yankees. This was laughed at then as a piece of amusing information, entirely new to the inhabitants. But, *tempora mutantur*, the mistake spread, and in a few years more the art and talent of your city were combined to assume the name of Buckeyes or Leatherheads, and to elevate the opprobrious epithet into dignity. In the fostering of the name they have been sufficiently successful, and if they will persist in being Buckeyes it is to be hoped that they will cause the

name to be duly honoured, meantime their elder denizens will concede the name to the native born.   J. H. J.
August 14, 1845.

My correspondent who furnishes the proof of his being a professional gentleman, in the ability with which he presents one side of a subject, seems not to have read, or if he has, appears unconvinced by, the able and witty argument of Dr. Drake, presented at our Pioneer Celebration of 1833, in favour of the Buckeye. In order that both sides may be heard, I present that article. It is of some length, but none the less valuable on that account, and deserves a more general perusal than its original publication allowed.

Mr. President and Young Gentlemen:

Being born in the East, I am not *quite* a native of the valley of the Ohio, and, therefore, am not a Buckeye by birth. Still I might claim to be a greater Buckeye than most of you who were borne in the city, for my Buckeyeism belongs to the *country*, a better soil for rearing Buckeyes than the town.

My first remembrances are of a Buckeye cabin, in the depths of a cane brake, on one of the tributary brooks of Licking River; for whose waters, as they flow into the Ohio, opposite our city, I feel some degree of affection. At the date of these recollections, the spot where we are now assembled was a Beech and Buckeye grove; no doubt altogether unconscious of its approaching fate. Thus, I am a Buckeye by engrafting, or rather by inoculation, being only in the bud, when I began to draw my nourishment from the depths of a Buckeye bowl.

The tree which you have toasted, Mr. President, has the distinction of being one of a family of plants, but a few species of which exist on the earth. They constitute the genus *Æsculus* of the botanists, which belongs to the class *Heptandria*. Now the latter, a Greek phrase, signifies *seven men;* and there happens to be exactly seven species of the genus—thus they constitute the seven wise men of the woods; in proof of which, I may mention that there is not another family of plants on the whole earth, that possess these talismanic attributes of wisdom. But this is not all. Of the seven species, our emblem-tree was discovered *last*—it is the youngest of the family—*the seventh son !* and who does not know the manifold virtues of a seventh son!

Neither Europe nor Africa has a single *native* species of *Æsculus*, and Asia but one. This is the *Æsculus Hippocastanum*, or Horsechestnut. Nearly three hundred years since, a minister from one of the courts of Western Europe to that of Russia, found this tree growing in Moscow, whither it had been brought from Siberia. He was struck with its beauty, and naturalized it in his own country. It spread with astonishing rapidity over that part of the continent, and crossing the channel, became one of the favourite shade trees of our English ancestors. But the oppressions and persecutions recounted in the address of your young orator, compelled them to cross the ocean and become exiled from the tree whose beautiful branches overhung their cottage doors.

When they reached this continent did they find their favourite shade tree, or any other species of the family, to supply its place in their affections? They did not—they *could* not—as from Jamestown to Plymouth the soil is too barren to nourish this epicurean plant. Doubtless, their first impulse was to seek it in the interior; but there the Indian still had his home, and they were compelled to languish on the sands of the sea board. The Revolution came and passed away: it was a political event, and men still hovered on the coast ; but the revolving year at length unfolded the map of the mighty West, and our fathers began to direct their footsteps thitherward. They took breath on the eastern base of the Allegheny Mountain, without having found the object of their pursuits; then scaled its lofty summits—threaded its deep and craggy defiles—descended its western slopes—but still sought in vain. The hand of destiny, however, seemed to be upon them; and boldly penetrating the unbroken forests of the Ohio, amidst savages and beasts of prey, they finally built their "half-faced camps" beneath the Buckeye tree. All their hereditary and traditional feelings were now gratified. They had not, to be sure, found the Horsechestnut, which embellished the paths of their forefathers; but a tree of the same family, of greater size and equal beauty, and, like themselves, a native of the New World. Who, of this young assembly has a heart so cold, as not to sympathise in the joyous emotions which this discovery must have raised? It acted on them like a charm,—their flagging pulses were quickened, and their imaginations warmed. They thought not of returning, but sent back pleasant messages, and invited their friends to follow. Crowds from every state in the Union soon pressed forward, and, in a single age, the native land of the Buckeye became the home of millions. Enterprise was animated; new ideas came into men's minds ; bold schemes were planned and executed; new communities organized; political states established; and the wilderness transformed, as if by enchantment.

Such was the power of the Buckeye wand; and its influence has not been limited to the west. We may fearlessly assert, that it has been felt over the whole of our common country. Till the time when the Buckeye tree was discovered, slow indeed had been the progress of society in the New World. With the exception of the Revolution, but little had been achieved, and but little was in prospect. Since that era, society has been progressive, higher destinies have been unfolded, and a reactive *Buckeye* influence, perceptible to all acute observers, must continue to assist in elevating our beloved country among the nations of the earth.

Every native of the valley of the Ohio, should feel proud of the appellation, which from the infancy of our settlements, has been conferred upon him; for the Buckeye has many qualities which may be regarded as typical of a noble character. It is not merely a native of the West, but peculiar to it; has received from the botanists the specific name of *Ohioensis*, and is the only tree of our whole forest, that does not grow elsewhere. What other tree could be so fit an emblem of our native population?

From the very beginning of emigration, it has been a friend to the " new comers." Delighting in the richest soils, they soon learned to take counsel from it, in the selection of their lands, and it never yet proved faithless to any one who confided in it.

When the first log cabin was to be hastily put up, the softness and lightness of its wood made it precious; for in those times labourers were few, and axes once broken in harder timber, could not be repaired.

When the infant Buckeyes came forth to render the solitary cabins vocal and make them instinct with life, cradles were necessary, and they could not be so easily dug out of any other tree. Thousands of men and women, who are now active and respectable performers on the great theatre of western society, were once rocked in Buckeye troughs.

In those early days, when a boundless and lofty wilderness overshadowed every habitation, to destroy the trees and make way for the growth of corn, was the great object—*hic labor, hoc opus erat*. Now, the lands where the Buckeye abounded, were from the special softness of its wood, the easiest to clear, and in this way it afforded valuable though negative assistance to the first settlers.

Foreign sugar was then unknown in these regions, and our reliance for this article as for many others, was on the abounding woods. In reference to this sweet and indispensable acquisition the Buckeye lent us positive aid ; for it was not only the best wood for troughs, but every where grew side by side with the graceful and delicious sugar maple.

We are now assembled on a spot, which is surrounded by vast warehouses, filled to overflowing, with the earthen and iron domestic utensils of China, Birmingham, Sheffield, and I should add the great western manufacturing town at the head of our noble river. The poorest and obscurest family in the land, may be, and are, in fact, adequately supplied. How different was the condition of the early emigrants! A journey of a thousand miles, over wild and rugged mountains, permitted the adventurous pioneer to bring with him little more than the Indian or the Arab carries from place to place—*his wife and children*. Elegances were unknown, even articles of pressing necessity were few in number, and when lost or broken could not be replaced. In that period of trying deprivation, to what quarter did the first settlers turn their inquiring and anxious eyes? To the Buckeye—yes, gentlemen, to the Buckeye tree; and it proved a friend indeed, because, in the simple and expressive language of those early times it was "a friend in need." Hats were manufactured of its fibres—the tray for the delicious *pone* and *johnny-cake*—the venison trencher—the noggin—the spoon—and the huge white family bowl for mush and milk, were carved from its willing trunk; and the finest "boughten" vessels could not have imparted a more delicious flavour, or left an impression so enduring. He who has ever been concerned in the petty brawls, the frolic and the fun of a family of young Buckeyes around the great wooden bowl overflowing with the "milk of human kindness," will carry the sweet remembrance to his grave.

Thus beyond all the trees of the land, the Buckeye was associated with the family circle—penetrating its privacy, facilitating its operations, and augmenting its enjoyments. Unlike many of its loftier associates, it did not bow its head and wave its arms at a haughty distance; but might be said to have held out the right hand of fellowship; for, of all the trees of our forest, it is the only one with *five* leaflets arranged on one stem—an expressive symbol of the human hand.

Mr. President and Gentlemen: I beg you to pardon the enthusiasm which betrays me into continued tresspasses on your patience. As an old friend of the Buckeye tree, I feel, that to be faithful I must dwell still longer on its virtues.

In all our woods, there is no tree so hard to kill as the Buckeye. The deepest girding will not deaden it, and even after it is cut down and worked up into the side of a cabin, it will send out young branches—denoting to all the world, that Buckeyes are not easily conquered, and could with difficulty be destroyed.

The Buckeye has generally been condemned as unfit for fuel, but its very incombustibility has been found an advantage; for no tree of the forest is equally valuable for backlogs, which are the *sine qua non* of every good cabin fire. Thus treated, it may be finally, though slowly, burned; when another of its virtues appears, as no other tree of our woods affords so great a quantity of alkali; thus there is piquancy in its very ashes!

The bark of our emblem-plant has some striking properties. Under a proper method of preparation and use, it is said to be efficacious in the cure of ague and fever, but unskilfully employed, it proves a violent emetic; which may indicate that he who tampers with a Buckeye, will not do it with impunity.

The fruit of the Buckeye offers much to interest us. The capsule or covering of the nut, is beset with sharp prickles, which, incautiously grasped, will soon compel the aggressor to let go his hold. The nut is undeniably the most beautiful of all which our teeming woods bring forth; and in many parts of the country is made subservient to the military education of our sons: who, assembling in the muster field (where their fathers and elder brothers are learning to be militia-men), divide themselves into armies, and pelt each other with Buckeye balls; a military exercise at least as instructive as that which their seniors perform with Buckeye sticks. The inner covering of the nut is highly astringent. Its substance, when grated down, is soapy, and has been used to clean fine fabrics in the absence of good soap. When the powder is washed, a large quantity of starch is obtained, which might, if times of scarcity *could* arise in a land so fertile as the native soil of this tree, be used for food. The water employed for this purpose holds in solution an active medicinal agent, which unwarily swallowed, proves a poison; thus again admonishing those who would attempt to *use up* a Buckeye, that they may repent of their rashness.

Who has not looked with admiration on the fine foliage of the Buckeye in early spring, while the more sluggish tenants of the forest, remain torpid in their winter quarters; and what tree in all our wild woods bears a flower which can be compared with that of our favourite? We may fearlessly challenge for it the closest comparison. Its early putting forth, and the beauty of its leaves and blossoms, are appropriate types of our native population, whose rapid and beautiful developement, will not be denied by those whom I now address, nor disproved by reference to their character.

Finally, the Buckeye derives its name from the resemblance of its nut to the eye of the buck, the finest organ of our noblest wild animal; while the name itself, is compounded of a Welsh and a Saxon word, belonging, therefore, to the oldest portions of our vernacular tongue, and connecting us with the primitive stocks, of which our fathers were but scions planted in the New World.

But, Mr. President and Gentlemen, I must dismiss this fascinating topic. My object has been to show the peculiar fitness of the Buckeye to be made the symbol-tree of our native population. This arises from its ·many excellent qualities. Other trees have greater magnitude, and stronger trunks. They are the Hercules of the forest; and like him of old, who was distinguished only for physical power, they are remarkable chiefly for mechanical strength. Far different is it with the Buckeye, which does not depend on brute force to effect its objects ; but exercises, as it were, a moral power and admonishes all who adopt its name, to rely upon intellectual cultivation, instead of bodily prowess.

Pittsburgh and Cincinnati.

In the "Advertiser" of the 23d ultimo, after quoting a statement in the Pittsburgh "Spirit of the Age," that as many as twelve sugar mills and engines had been manufactured in that city this season, I remarked that we had made of those articles in Cincinnati, this year already, forty-eight, and that twelve more would be completed during the current season, making sixty in all; and that, in comparing these widely different results, full justice would not be done to our business operations without adverting to the fact, that the Pittsburgh made mills and engines were of a smaller description, which at $3,500 each, were worth $42,000; while those of Cincinnati manufacture averaged $5,000 each, and made an aggregate of $240,000. My comparative statement was made for the purpose of disabusing our citizens of the impression which prevails to some extent here, that the manufacturing interest of Cincinnati is inferior in magnitude to that of Pittsburgh. I added, "abstract the rolling mills, glass and cotton yarn factories of Pittsburgh from the comparison, and in every other description of mechanical industry and products, Cincinnati is far in advance of that place."

The editor of the *Spirit of the Age* makes this statement the subject of a long article, which, as I have not room to give the whole, and dislike, on a subject of this sort, to make extracts, lest I invite suspicion of garbling the article, I shall merely say that he does both the subject and myself injustice—unintentionally, as I believe. For instance, although he quotes my closing remark correctly—the same that I have placed in this article in quotations—yet he slides, in less than six lines, from "rolling mills" to manufactures of iron, and appears throughout the article to suppose that I was desirous to exclude the entire iron manufacture of Pittsburgh from the comparisons I made. I am well aware of the magnitude of the rolling mill operations there, and

freely acknowledge that in bar iron as well as in cotton yarns our Cincinnati manufacturers are left in the background. As to glass, we do not manufacture it. And in saying that if these articles were excluded from the comparison, we were *far in advance* of Pittsburgh, I did not mean to concede that our general mechanical and manufacturing operations did not surpass those of Pittsburgh. The statistics of the census of 1840, I thought, had settled that question; for, if our manufacturing and mechanical products exceeded those of Pittsburgh in 1840, the disparity must be heightened by the lapse of later years.

After all, the true way in debates of this sort, is to furnish the statistics. If Mr. Riddle, of the Spirit of the Age, will make out a statement of the manufactures of iron and other metals, wood, leather, cotton, wool and linen, drugs, paints, chemicals, paper, food, &c., classifying it under different heads, giving the details which make up the aggregate, in short, affording the means of furnishing a corresponding statement for Cincinnati, I will pledge myself to furnish a statement in similar form of our operations, and let the figures determine the dispute. Each party holding himself liable to prove any part of the statement which may be required.

By Pittsburgh, I include all the adjacent parts, across both rivers, within one mile, and the like distance in other directions. By Cincinnati, I include the like circular distance.

The Beaten Path.

BY L. J. CIST.

" We are born—we live—we die—we are buried !"

I.

THAT BEATEN PATH! THAT BEATEN PATH!
　It goeth by the door;
And many a tale to tell it hath
　Of the days that are no more!
For o'er that path, in weal and wo,
　Earth's weary ones have trod;
And many a hurried step, or slow,
　Hath press'd its time-worn sod;
Here Childhood's mirth and Youth's glad shout
Have each its merry peal rung out;
Oft, gentle Woman's graceful tread,
In fairy motion o'er it sped;
And Manhood's care surcharged breast
A weightier step upon it press'd;
While Age's palsied footsteps, slow,
　Here last, perchance, abroad
Have feebly tottered forth, to show
Three-score-and-ten prepared to go,—
Life's journey trodden now below—
　To stay its steps with God!

II.

See'st thou yonder smiling boy,
Just escaped his mother's arms?
With what eager, gushing joy—
Heedless of her fond alarms—
Out upon THAT PATH he springs,
Light as bird with feathered wings;
Running now a frolic race,
Walking then with sober pace,
And, anon, with childish grace,
Casting down his wearied form,
With unused exertion warm,
On the grassy margin, green,
Of the pathway he is in;—
Of that path which thus, a child
Treads he first, with spirits wild;—
Of that path which he *shall* tread,
Oft in manhood's darker day,
When his weary, aching head
Gladly would he seek to lay
With the care-forgetting dead,
'Neath its grassy turf for aye!

III.

Ring out! Ring out! A joyous shout
For the fair and gentle Bride!
Make room! make room! for the gallant Groom,
In his dashing and manly pride!
For his Bridal's done!—he hath woo'd and won
The flower of the country rare;
And worthy he of his Ladye—she,
The fairest of England's fair!
Ring out! Ring out! A pealing shout!
Let Vassal to Vassal call,
Each servant gay, in his best array,
Attend in the ancient Hall:
For the Bridal train rideth on amain,
And the Lord of that Hall doth come;
By THAT PATH where, a boy, first he wandered in joy,
He bringeth his fair Bride home!

IV.

A toll!—A sad and a muffled toll
Of the deep Church-bell, for a parted soul!
The Child that in glee o'er that pathway sped—
The Youth that in beauty and manhood wed—
The Aged Lord of the Castle is dead!
Hath rested his body in solemn state,
And now 'tis borne from the Castle gate;
Sad its retainers, as mournfully slow,
Over THAT BEATEN PATH they go—
That path through which, when a child, he sped,
That path by which his fair Bride he led,
That path o'er which they now bear him—dead!
Pause they now at yon Churchyard's door,
And now—'tis entered—the pathway o'er;
THAT BEATEN PATH HE WILL PASS NO MORE!

One Day and a Half in the Life of a Tobacco Chewer.

[BY A SUFFERER.]

Saturday, July 22, 1843.—Took my hat for a walk; wife—as wives are apt to—began to load me with messages, upon seeing me ready to go out. Asked me to call at Cousin M's, and borrow for her the "Sorrows of Werter." Hate to have a wife read such namby-pamby stuff, but must humor her whims, and concluded that I had rather she would take pleasure over Werter's Sorrows, than employ her tongue in making 'sorrow' for your humble servant.

Got to Cousin M's door. Now, Cousin is an old maid, and a dreadful tidy woman. Like tidy women well enough, but can't bear your dreadful tidy ones, because I am always in dread while on their premises, lest I should offend their super-superlative neatness by a bit of gravel on the sole of my boot or such matter.

Walked in, delivered my message, and seated myself in one of her cane bottom chairs, while she rummaged the bookcase. Forgot to take out my cavendish before I entered, and while she hunted, felt the tide rising. No spitbox in the room, windows closed, floor carpeted, stove varnished. Looked to the fireplace—full of flowers, and hearth newly daubed with Spanish brown: here was a fix. Felt the flood of essence of cavendish accumulating. Began to reason with myself whether, as a last alternative, it were better to drown the flowers, redaub the hearth, or flood the carpet. Mouth in the mean time pretty well filled. To add to my misery she began to ask questions. "Did you ever read this book, ———?" "Yes, ma'm" said I, in a voice like a frog from the bottom of a well, when I wished book, aunt, and all, were with Pharaoh's host, in the Red Sea. "How do you like it?" continued the indefatigable querist. I threw my head on the back of the chair, and my mouth upward to prevent an overflow. "Pretty well," said I. She at last found the Sorrows of Werter, and came toward me. "O! dear, Cousin Oliver, don't put your head on the back of the chair, now don't—you'll grease it, and take off the gilding." I could not answer her, having now lost the power of speech entirely, and my cheeks were distended like those of a toad under a mushroom. "Why, Oliver," said my persevering tormentor, unconscious of the reason of my appearance, "you are sick; I know you are; your face is dreadfully swelled;" and before I could prevent her, her hartshorn was clapped to my distended nostrils. As my mouth was closed imperturbably, the orifices in my nasal organ were at that time my only breathing place. Judge, then, what a commotion a full snuff of hartshorn created among my olfactories.

I bolted for the door, and a hearty acheehee! relieved my proboscis, and tobacco, chyle, &c., "all at once disgorged" from my mouth, restored me the faculty of speech. Her eyes followed me in astonishment, and I returned and relieved my embarrassment by putting a load on my conscience. I told her I had been trying to relieve the toothache by the temporary use of tobacco, while, truth to tell, I never had an aching fang in my head. I went home mortified.

Sunday Forenoon.—Friend A. invited myself and wife to take a seat with him to hear the celebrated Mr. ——— preach. Conducted by neighbor A. to his pew. Mouth as usual, full of tobacco, and, horror of horrors! found the pew elegantly carpeted with white and green, two or three mahogany crickets, and a hat stand, but no spitbox. The services commenced; every peal on the organ was answered by an internal appeal from my mouth for a liberation from its contents, but the thing was impossible. I thought of using my hat for a spitbox, then of turning one of the crickets over, but I could do nothing unperceived. I took out my handkerchief, but found, in the plenitude of her officiousness, that my wife had placed one of her white cambrics in my pocket instead of my bandanna. Here was a dilemma. By the time the preacher had named his text, my cheeks had reached their utmost tension, and I must spit or die.

I arose, seized my hat, and made for the door. My wife—confound these women how they dog one about! imagining me unwell, she might have known better—got up and followed me out. "Are you unwell, Oliver?" said she, as the door closed after us. I answered her by putting out the eyes of an unlucky dog with a flood of expressed essence of cavendish. "I wish," said she, "Mr. A. had a spit-box in his pew." "So do I." We footed it home in moody silence. I was sorry my wife had lost the sermon, but how could I help it? These women are so affectionate, confound them; no, I don't mean so. But she might have known what ailed me, and kept her seat.

Tobacco! O tobacco! But the deeds of that day are not told yet. After the conclusion of the services along came farmer Ploughshare. He had seen me go out of church and stopped at the open window where I sat. "Sick to-day Mr. ——!" "Rather unwell," answered I, and there was another lie to place to the account of tobacco. "We had powerful preaching, Mr. ——; sorry you had to go out." My wife asked him in, and in he came; she might know eh would, but women must be polite. But she was the sufferer by it. Compliments over, I gave him my chair at the open window. Down he sat, and fumbling in his pockets, he drew forth a formidable plug of tobacco, and commenced untwisting it. "Then you use tobacco," said I. "A leetle occasionally," said he, as he deposited from three to four inches in his cheek. I mentally pity those using more. "A neat fence that of yourn," as flood after flood bespattered a newly painted white fence near the window. "Yes," said I, "but I like a darker color." "So do I," answered Ploughshare, "and yaller suits my notion. It don't show dirt." And he moistened my carpet with his favorite color. Good, thought I, my wife will ask him in again I guess. We were now summoned to dinner. Farmer Ploughshare seated himself. I saw his long fingers in that particular position in which a tobacco chewer knows how to put his digits when about to unlade. He drew them across his mouth; I trembled for the consequences, should he throw such a load upon the hearth or the floor. But he had no intention thus to waste his quid, and, shocking to relate, deposited it beside his plate on my wife's damask cloth.

This was too much. I plead sickness and rose. There was no lie in the assertion now, I was sick. I retired from the table, but my departure did not discompose farmer Ploughshare, who was unconscious of having done wrong. I returned in season to see him re-place his quid in his mouth to undergo a second mastication, and the church bell opportunely ringing, called him away before he could use his plate for a spit-box, for such, I am persuaded would have been his next motion. I went up stairs, and throwing myself on the bed, fell asleep. Dreams of inundation, floods and fire harassed me. I thought I was burning and smoking like a segar. I then thought the Merrimack had burst its banks and was about to overflow me with its waters. I could not escape, the water had reached my chin—I tasted it, it was like tobacco juice. I coughed and screamed, and awakening, found I had been to sleep with a quid in my mouth. My wife entered at the moment I threw away the filthy weed—"Huz, if I were you I would not use that stuff any more."

"I won't," said I. Neither fig nor twist, pigtail or cavendish has passed my lips since, nor ever shall they again.

Culture of the Grape.

ROBINSON & JONES, of our city, have lately put to press a brief practical treatise on the culture of the grape, worth fifty times the price to the purchaser, which it costs him, in the profitable hints it suggests. The author is one of a number of individuals who cultivates the grape in Hamilton county. My perusal of this manual, which gives the proper statistics on this subject, has afforded me the following conclusions:

1. Individuals in Hamilton county who have one-twentieth of their farm in grapes, make more of that portion than the entire residue.

2. The produce on an average exceeds a yield of 400 gallons to the acre, as high in some instances as 700 gallons being made from a small vineyard of eighteen hundred vines, embracing not quite an acre. At the current rate for the article---$1.50 per gallon---this would be $600 per acre as the crop value, and worth under any possible depreciation 400 dollars per acre, which would be a net profit of 250 dollars to each acre, a revenue no other crop affords.

3. The Catawba grape, which is now generally cultivated in this region, affords a wine that stands without a competitor in the world, and no degree of extension in its culture could ever reduce the price to fifty cents per gallon. At that rate, raising grapes would be more profitable than any existing crop in the West. But it is in reference to raising grapes for the table that I feel much interest on this subject. At fifty cents per bushel, Catawba grapes will furnish a very profitable crop, although the price they are now worth for making wine forbids their sale at that price; but they will be furnished at that price here in less than five years. At that price they will be as cheap as any other wholesome fruit, and ought to furnish food at the breakfast table, to the banishment of the beef-steaks and other animal food, which they would supercede. All fruit ought to be eaten, as is my practice,

early in the day, and I judge that the robust health my family enjoys should recommend the practice.

I can freely recommend this little treatise. The author insists on it, that the culture of the grape is not severe work, but rather an amusement. "You are living in the country, the newspapers contain nothing of importance [N.B. He does not take the ADVERTISER], the Oregon territory is not yet ours, and it will be a hard matter to get it, the rumor of broken banks and Swartwouters will not give you much trouble." By way of conclusion, therefore, *cultivate the grape.*

The Pardoning Power.

I observe, in a late city paper, notice, that an application will be made to obtain the pardon and release of a certain individual convicted of having counterfeit money in his possession, and sentenced for five years to the penitentiary. The alleged ground for the application is the *innocence* of the *convict.* *I* know enough of the case to be *satisfied* of his *guilt.* But without refering to what I know personally in this case, look at the absurdity of suffering the signatures to a petition to outweigh the verdict of a jury upon the subject. In such cases, men sign, frequently without looking at the petition, on simply a representation of its contents, a statement of acquittal, in an instance where twelve men on their oaths, and after proof and investigation of the circumstances, decide that he is guilty. I do not undertake to judge for others, but I would not suffer my columns thus to aid in getting a convict loose on the community for any sum offered to procure the insertion of such notices. And I lift up my voice, feeble and alone though it may be, pleading with the community to pause before they sign such applications. They are an insult to those of our fellow citizens who made the verdict; they are injurious to the community who have just got rid of disturbers of their peace or safety. I warn every man who signs such applications that he is doing all in his power to nullify all law with its safeguards and restraints, and to restore the community to its original element of society, where the weak and peaceable are made the prey of the turbulent and strong, and where every man assumes the right to judge and decide his own cause. In one word, to proclaim the supremacy of mobs and Lynch law.

Rail-Road to Xenia.

On Monday, the 17th, by invitation of the Directors of the Little Miami Rail-Road Company, the editor of the Advertiser made one of a promiscuous assemblage of travelers to Xenia, on the occasion of the Rail-Road being opened for the first time to that flourishing and beautiful village, sixty-eight miles out. The road winds through a delightful country, and follows with slight variations, the course of the Little Miami, through one of the most fertile vallies in the wide world. It may indeed be doubted whether there be a margin of bottom land of equal breadth and richness on earth, taking into view the size of the stream. Breadths of a mile in extent filled with Indian corn, in its growth the most graceful of the cereal grains, and forming a most picturesque landscape, are of repeated occurrence. Nor are the bottoms of the Little Miami, perceptibly of less magnitude, fifty or sixty miles up the stream. The road appears well finished and must create, as well as provide for, an immense travel and transportation northward, and eventually to the Lake and the Atlantic Cities. Everywhere along the road I found abundant testimony that the most ample harvest has been or is about to be gathered in, that has been known for six years, and the quality is as remarkable as the quantity. The next link in the chain will take us to Springfield, which will then enable the traveling community to connect with the line of the National Road both east and west.

The Little Miami and Sandusky Rail-Road, of which this route is the commencement, will form when completed, a most important avenue for the transportation of western produce east, and of the Atlantic Cities' merchandize west. Of what magnitude its business is destined to become, may be inferred from the amount of merchandize which is now sent to and received from Toledo, 1143 packages for the west and southwest being received in one day by one of our forwarding houses. The Canal transportation is preparing the Rail-Road transportation business, so that by the time the Rail-Road is completed, the entire Canal business will thus be turned over to the cars.

College of Dental Surgery.

Among this years' city improvements may be numbered an unassuming building of no particular order of architecture, which occupies the well known scite of Talbott's school room, on College street, and nearly covering the lot on which it is built; the edifice being 60 feet by 27, and three stories in height. This is the new College of Dental Surgery of Dr. Cook and his associates. The building is expected to be finished by the 1st of next month, and to be fitted up for theoretical and demonstrative teaching on Dental Science, by the first Monday of November, when the public lectures commence. The main hall of the college is the lecture room, capable of holding 250 persons. Other rooms will be appropriated to the library and anatomical museum and laboratory, and mechanical operations of the college.

In the testimonials which will be afforded to the public by competent and skilful professors to those who shall graduate there, must result protection from the impositions and in many cases irreparable injuries which have been inflicted on the community by mere pretenders to dental knowledge.

As a subject of city pride, it may be stated that Baltimore and Cincinnati are the only cities *in the world*, in which colleges of dental surgery exist.

Bustles.

" A Yankee" finds employment in the northwest region of our city in carding cotton for bustles. I hope the extensive scale on which he carries on his operations will reduce the price of bran, and thereby restore that article to its legitimate use. The following is his advertisement, which I insert without charge:

BUSTLES! BUSTLES!!—The undersigned having recently put in operation some cards in the building on the southwest corner of Smith and Seventh streets, would respectfully inform the fashionable part of the community that he is prepared to make any quantity of Bustles of the latest and most approved patterns, containing from four to sixteen pounds of superior carded cotton, at short notice. Bustles warranted to fit or no sale.

N. B. When not supplied with orders for the above article the machinery will be employed in manufacturing a very superior article of Batting from clean cotton, which article can be had at all times in quantities to suit, and at the right price, of   A YANKEE.

Commission.

THE SEAL OF THE TERRITORY OF THE U.S. N. W. OF THE RIVER OHIO.

By His Excellency, Arthur St. Clair, Esq., Governor and Commander in Chief of the Territory of the United States, North-West of the River Ohio, to Benjamin Perle, Greeting.

You being appointed an Ensign in the First Regiment of Hamilton County Militia, by virtue of the Power vested in me, I do by *these presents* (reposing special trust and confidence in your Loyalty, Courage and good. Conduct) commission you accordingly.—*You* are therefore carefully and diligently to discharge the duty of an Ensign in leading, ordering and exercising said Regiment in Arms, both inferior Officers and Soldiers; and to keep them in good Order and Discipline: And they are hereby commanded to

obey you as their Ensign, and *you* are yourself to observe and follow such Orders and Instructions as you shall from Time to Time receive from *me* or your superior Officers.

Given under my hand, and the Seal of the said Territory of the United States, the 21st day of August, in the Year of our Lord 1798, and of the Independence of the United States of America, the twenty-third.

By His Excellency's Command,
          WM. HENRY HARRISON,
                    Secretary.

Statistics.

It is remarkable how much worthless information goes the rounds of the press, when the exercise of a moment's reflection would detect its character. This is the business of the editor,--- if he be too lazy or too incompetent to do so, his readers will hardly take the pains.

Our fellow citizen, Nicholas Longworth, is stated in several of our city papers to have made 500 bbls. native wine this season. If these editors had known or knowing the fact had remembered it, that the season of pressing grapes had not yet arrived, this statement would hardly have been made. Mr. Longworth's wine, be the quantity what it may, will not be barreled for weeks to come.

CORRESPONDENCE.

The Calla Ethiopica.

Mr. Cist.—In your paper of last week there appeared some remarks on the Calla Ethiopica, wherein Mr. Pancoast remarked it was a native of Pennsylvania, or to that effect. If the plant alluded to be the Calla, Mr. Pancoast is much mistaken; and I presume Mr. Schnetz is a man not likely to palm on the public a native plant for that of foreign origin. The Calla Ethiopica is a native of the Cape of Good Hope, throwing up a stem two to three feet high, depending on the age of the plant. The flower is singularly formed of one whorl or vase-like calyx of pure white, in the spring. The leaf is arrow-shaped; the root, perennial and tender, will not bear the least frost, consequently cannot be a native of hist country. This plant may stand out all the winter in the south, if planted in the mud two or three feet below the surface of the water: as the root would then be sufficiently protected from frost. This plant is too generally cultivated with the lover of flowers in this part to know that it requires the warmth of a room to protect it through the winter, and may be considered a green-house plant.   T. WINTER.

August 16, 1845.

CORRESPONDENCE.

Recollections of Harmar's Campaign.

MR. C. CIST:

Dear Sir.—I forward you, as I promised, my recollections of the incidents connected with Harmar's Campaign, which fell under my observation, or in which I bore a part.

General Harmar marched his army from Fort Washington, if I recollect right, the last week of September, 1790. His expedition was designed against the Indian towns on the St. Joseph, or Maumee, near where Fort Wayne was afterwards built. The army followed the trace made by Gen. Geo. R. Clarke with the Kentucky troops, in October, 1782, as far as the Piqua towns, on both sides of the Great Miami, which were destroyed by him on that visit. Thence we had a tolerable Indian trace to where there had been a large trading establishment, *St. Mary's,* from which we had a good Indian trace to our final object, which was sixty-four miles from there into the wilderness.

There were, perhaps, one hundred and thirty of the Kentucky militia mounted and armed: one third of that force with swords and pistols, the balance with rifles. They were remarkably useful in that campaign, being found active and efficient in hunting up pack-horses or beef cattle, which were apt to stray off after night, scouring the woods for the purpose, and sometimes rousing from their concealment Indians who were watching our movements. On account of these services they were exempt from camp duty at night.

When the army got within thirty or forty miles of the Indian towns for which we were marching, there were ten or twelve of these mounted men sent out in search of some pack-horses that had been lost over night. They started a smart young Indian, took him prisoner, brought him into camp, where he was examined by two of the Kentuckians, who understood the Indian language. He spoke freely, and told all he knew respecting the movements of his people, saying that they had at first intended to make a stand and defend their towns; but after holding a council, gave up the idea, and had moved their families and property down the river, intending to burn their wigwams. When the army arrived they found all his statements true.

Two days after the army reached the Indian towns, orders were given to draft four hundred men from the different companies, with a view to send them out and see what discoveries they could make respecting the enemy. They were to draw two days provisions, and to be out over night.

About twenty of the mounted men, and, perhaps, half a dozen footmen volunteered to go along. I was one of these last. The detachment

crossed the St. Joseph where the centre of the town stood ; struck a trace on the west bank that led a west course, and followed it within one mile of the river. On the route the mounted men started two Indians and shot them both; lost one man ourselves. Pursued the trace till sunset, and found evident signs, though much scattered, of Indians. None of them appeared fresh. About sunset the six pounder in camp was fired. Col. Trotter, of Lexington, Ky., who had the command of the detachment, concluded this was a signal for our recall, and countermarching we got into camp a little after dark. The next day's tour we were placed under the command of Col. Hardin, we crossed the river where we did the day before, and struck a good Indian trace a short distance from the river, directly north; after following it four or five miles, we found considerable of fresh signs of savages. Two or three Indian dogs got in among the troops, which disappeared again shortly, discovering that they were not among their masters.

The Colonel ordered a halt, directing the different companies to station themselves on the right and left of the trace, and keep a sharp lookout. Our company went round the point of a brushy grove, which threw us out of sight of the trace, though not far from it. The Colonel sent Maj. Fountain, with eight or ten mounted men, to reconnoitre. After travelling a short distance on that trace, they came to where it crossed a small stream of water, which, being muddy on each side, pointed out plainly the fresh tracks of Indians who had been making a hasty retreat, with a view of drawing the detachment into an ambuscade. The Major returned, and reported accordingly. Colonel Hardin was so keen for pursuit, that he started off with the principal part of the troops in such a hurry, that he forgot to give us any orders. After waiting awhile we became impatient, struck the trace, and finding they were gone, followed on. We had not gone far, however, until we met Major Fountain, and Captain Faulkner, having explained that we had been directed to halt until we should get orders to march, we pressed forward to overtake the main body of our comrades.

In a short time we met two of the mounted men at full speed, each having a wounded man behind him. "Retreat," said they, "for God's sake! There are Indians enough to eat us all up." We proceeded on, however, till we had gained a high swell of ground, when we saw our troops putting back upon the trace—the Indians in pursuit, yelling and shooting. We halted, formed a line across the trace, and treed, with a view to give them a shot. They came within seventy or eighty yards of us, when they halted instantly. I expect the reason was Col. Hardin,

14

Hall, Fountain, and four or five others were on horseback close by where we were. We remained there until the retreating troops had all passed by, none of whom halted with us except the men on horseback. We covered their retreat, and marched into camp a short time after dark, under the direction of Cols. Hardin and Hall. The six pounder was discharged every hour till daylight, as a signal for the benefit of the stragglers, of which several came in that night.

Having been acquainted with Col. Hall in Bourbon County, Kentucky, and knowing he was near the front, I went to his tent next morning, to learn what had been the movements in front on the day before. He stated that the trace passed through a narrow prairie with a heavy growth of timber and underbrush on each side. At the far end it entered into a thick growth of timber. At this spot within a few feet of the trace, the enemy had kindled up a fire. Here the advance halted as soon as they came up, and just at this moment the Indians rose from their coverts on the prairie sides, and poured in a deadly fire so sudden and unexpected that it threw our troops into a confusion, from which they could not be rallied, and it was on their retreat, we being within a short distance of that prairie path, that we protected their right about movement, as I have already stated.

The army lay some days encamped, after Hardin's detachment had been thus defeated, when preparations were made for our return to Fort Washington, after destroying all the property of the enemy within reach. The first day the army marched about five miles, leaving a party of three or four mounted men with an officer on a commanding piece of ground to observe if the Indians should make their appearance and offer signs of pursuit. About two hours after the army had disappeared, the Indians began to come in by droves, hunting for hid provisions, as they had large quantities put up in that way. On learning this late in the evening, from the party left behind to watch their movements, Col. Hardin was keen to have another brush with the savages. A draft of four hundred men was accordingly made and placed under his command, in the calculation to surprise them before daylight. The detachment marched back to the post where this officer with his party had been stationed, when, taking to the left hand, Col. Hardin crossed the St. Mary's near its junction with the St. Joseph's, and pushed forward up the west bank of that river towards the Indian town built there. He was followed by Majors Fountain, M'Millan, and Wyllys. Harmar's trace crossed the Maumee River at Harmar's ford. As soon as the river was passed the town was in sight. The day was just dawning as the troops moved on, Major

Fountain, with a few mounted men in front. As they turned the point of a hazel thicket, and at a few rods distance, fifteen or twenty Indians were discovered around a fire. The Major charged right in among them, fired both his pistols, and then drew his sword; but, ten or twelve of the savages, at the time not more than as many feet off, discharged their rifles at him. One of the soldiers, George Adams by name, being close by fired on them and received four or five flesh wounds by a volley in return. Wyllys and M'Millan, with a small party of regulars, finally succeeded in drawing them into the river. Fountain although wounded in several places, and surviving but a few minutes, yet hung to his saddle. Our men took him off, and buried him under the side of a log, or under a bank, and Adams rode the horse in. When Wyllys, with the regulars, was driving the savages into the river, Hardin met them on the other side, but was compelled by inferiority of force to retire. There were many Indians killed in the skirmish of the second day; and if we had had a few more troops detached from Harmar's command, of those who were not wanted in camp, the enemy would have received the worst drubbing they ever got from the whites; as it was, they lost more men than they ever lost before in any one of our western battles. Majors Fountain and Wyllys were both killed, with other officers of inferior rank. Major M'Millan collected the scattering troops and remained on the ground until all the Indians had disappeared, and then marched into camp, which he reached before sunset.

Next morning General Harmar sent Captains Wells and Gaines, both of the Kentucky troops, as an express to Fort Washington. When they reached the bottoms of the Big Miami, at a short turn of the trace they were following, they met five Indians very unexpectedly. On the instant, Gaines wheeled to the left and Wells to the right and by the promptness of the movement saved their lives. They both made a wide circuit;— Wells got to the mouth of the Miami, and Gaines struck the river where Ripley now stands. The army, however, reached Fort Washington before either Gaines or Wells.

I knew Jacob Fowler and Ellison Williams. They were both good woodsmen and hunters. Fowler was in St. Clair's campaign, in the commissary or quarter-master's department. He had a friend, a Captain Piatt, who was killed at St. Clair's defeat. He had also a brother killed by the Indians, within a mile or two of Hamilton, while we were out on St. Clair's expedition. Williams, I believe, was in neither Harmar's nor St. Clair's campaigns.

I would be glad to have a chat with your friend John Bush. There is no doubt we could recollect many other incidents that took place in Harmar's campaign, if we had a chance of comparing notes.

The Indian prisoner, to whom I referred in the early part of this letter, was taken to Fort Washington, although afterwards sent home.

Yours,

THOMAS IRWIN.

Blue Bell, Butler County, Ohio,
August 23, 1845.

Wholesomeness of Fruit.

Such is the cheapness of meat in the United States, as compared with European countries, that the emigrants to America have acquired a taste for the indulgence, which they have transmitted to their descendants, until we have become the most *carniverous* nation on the globe. Perhaps I ought to except the *Feejee* islanders, whose principal food is the bodies of their enemies, captured or slain in battle.

I entertain great doubts of the wholesomeness of any diet, in which meat forms the largest share; and as I have all my life enjoyed an uncommon degree of good health, I must impute it to the great extent to which vegetable food enters into my entire sustenance. Lest I be misunderstood on this point, let me state briefly and explicitly, that I refer to bread and fruits.

My family of eleven persons consumes a barrel of flour every twenty days. One half my marketing is fruit, which I buy of the best quality and fully ripe.

There is no finer climate in the world for fruit than our own country, and the west surpasses the east in quality and productiveness, as far as our Atlantic region transcends Europe. France, Spain, Italy, and the Levant, furnish figs and grapes of a finer quality than ours; but our peaches, pears, and plums, taking quality and quantity together, surpass those of any other section of the world. As to apples, our middle states, from western Pennsylvania and Virginia to Indiana inclusive, raise finer and more abundantly than any where on the face of the globe. Of this region Ohio takes the lead, and in a few years will be obliged to export her surplus of the article.

I am not opposed to the moderate use of meat, but recommend by my own experience, as a preservative of health, a free use of fruit, always to be procured ripe. When grapes shall have become more abundant in our markets, as they soon must under their general culture, they ought to form a regular dish on the breakfast table.

Modern Poetry.

"The world is full of Poetry. The air
Is living with its spirit; and the waves
Dance to the music of its melodies
And sparkle in its brightness. Earth is veiled
And mantled in its beauty."

I remember when a man could read poetry, without danger of being decoyed into reading mere advertisements. But having grown wiser, I read nothing now-a-days, as the city council, ordinances, by the title. The pith or point of an article must be discovered these times, as the epigram once was, by the closing line. The subjoined article was my latest take in.

Rescued Treasure.

The spirits of the storm were out,
  Red lightnings rent the murky air,
And the tornado's battle shout
  Had roused old Ocean from his lair.
High on a ridge of serried rocks
  A gallant frigate lay impaled,
Reeling before the wild waves shocks,
  While Death the trembling seamen hailed,
He hailed them in the breaker's roar,
  He hailed them in the shrieking blast,
He hailed them when the tempest tore
  From the bruised hulk the broken mast.
And one by one they leaped and sank
  Into old Ocean's boiling breast,
Till all save one the cup had drank,
  That lulled them to eternal rest.
Boldly the last survivor springs,
  Strongly he struggles toward the land,
Till a gigantic billow flings
  Your frigate's Captain on the strand.
One treasure still his hand retains,
  That wind nor wave could make him drop;
And tightly every finger strains
  On *Chapman's Magic Razor Strop!*

Numismatology.

MONOGRAPH OF THE DOLLAR: By J. L. RIDDELL, M. D., of the New Orleans Mint. 8vo. pp. 504. Stereotyped and printed by E. Shepard, 1845.

This is a remarkable work, in which the curious and rare are blended in due proportion with the practical and every day business of life. We have all heard of the *almighty dollar*. Here is the whole history of its whole family over the globe. The author is melter and refiner in the Branch Mint, New Orleans, and Professor of Chemistry in the Medical College of Louisiana. It may readily be imagined that he is therefore thoroughly qualified for treating properly, the subjects on which he writes.

This book presents impressions of every emission of dollars which have been coined in the various mints of the world, duly classified, with a corresponding arrangement of their counterfeits, embracing specimens of all the various imitations which are spread over the United States and perhaps other countries. The variations of the genuine are 147, of the counterfeits 277. Of these 62 of the genuine, and 242 of the counterfeits, are of Mexican dollars alone. What a satire on human nature! 242 counterfeiting establishments in the United States!!

The book is replete with a great variety of knowledge, at once full and exact in its details, affording every variety of information to the banker, the coin collector, and to the general reader, much of it being rare and curious, and all of it of great practical importance. Such is the exactness of the impression that a counterfeit may be detected by it at a glance.

It is almost inconceivable that any individual, however qualified for the peculiar studies the writing of this treatise demands, could be found disposed to engage in the immense amount of labor it involves, or that a person willing to devote years of patient toil to such an enterprise should possess the necessary scientific knowledge for the purpose.

The work is admirably classified as well as arranged for reference, and for comparison of those genuine and counterfeit pieces, which correspond to each other, and in short is a book which no business man should be without.

I observe from a notice in the work that this valuable publication will probably be the precursor of a treatise on coins, foreign and domestic, perhaps more extensive and general in its nature.

I cannot close this article without referring to the typography and binding of this book, which are both creditable in a high degree to its Cincinnati getting up. The binding is by C. F. Wilstach, corner Main and Fourth streets, and will compare to advantage with any specimens of the kind from the Atlantic binderies.

City Dignitaries.

Every city has its own great men in the person of its public functionaries. We have all heard of the Lord Mayor of London, with his magnificent coach and out riders. And a London Alderman—what associations cluster round the very name! I must repeat an anecdote or two.

At a late public dinner in London, one of the company was speaking of the blessings of Providence.

"Ay!" said Alderman W., who was present, smacking his lips, "it is indeed a blessed place. We get all our turtle soup from it."

A beggar solicited food from another of these dignitaries, who directed his servant to give the applicant a crust of bread. The half famished wretch devoured it on the spot. Emboldened by the favour, he asked for other assistance.

"Pity a poor man your worship."

"Poor," exclaimed his worship, "I would give five guineas for your appetite."

Our great men are the City Council. The Mayor, it is true, is the terror of all evil doers, and discharges his functions with great zeal as well as ability. But though he has power to commit, he has none to discharge, The sublime attribute of mercy is in the hands of the Jail Committee of Council.

In 1838, Jonah Martin and myself were together members of the City Council. We were personal friends, and held the same general political principles. Beyond this we had none of the sympathies which usually hold public men in the same traces. We divided on the coffeehouse question—on the huckster licenses—on public improvements—on every thing almost. We were placed together on the Jail committee. Here we were again at issue. I had censured the Mayor for not enforcing the laws, and could not with any degree of consistency concur with my colleague in turning out culprits almost as soon as the Mayor sent them to jail. Jonah, on the contrary had an unbounded antipathy to crowding the cells and to putting in criminals for the first offence, however flagrant.

A prime minister of Spain, on a visit to Corunna, the Duke of Ossuna, liberated a galley slave that acknowledged he had been a very great rascal and deserved his punishment, while he paid no attention to the pleas which others made who alleged their innocence of the crimes laid to their charge. "Go," said he "it is not fit such a fellow as you should be here to corrupt the morals of so many honest and respectable people." Martin reversed the practise and was for turning all new offenders adrift for fear the more hardened cases would make them worse. So between us I had as much trouble to keep them in, as he to get them out.

As we approached the cells, the poor desponding wretches would creep out of the lairs in which they were disposed like so many brutes. Every step in the jail yard gave way in one progress—the eye was kindled in hope, the head bowed in reverence, and unless a flagrant case, the heart of the bondman was rejoicing in deliverance. Ours was the power to bind or to loose.

Our great men, then, are the City Council. They are the Lords President of the community. Sovereigns, three hundred and sixty-four days in the year, and servants on only one, the first Monday in April. Some of them feel accordingly like a street commissioner of that day with whom an individual was remonstrating for undue exercise of authority. " I don't know," said officer, " how long I shall continue in office, and while I *do reign*, *I mean to reign*." I propose to furnifh a gallery of portraits of these great men, the *conscripti patres of Cincinnati*, of which next week will present the first of the series.

Dayton Limestone.

The general use which is now making of this building material may give interest to the following statements.

This beautiful limestone, in its rough state, has been used for years in Dayton, but it is only of late years that its fitness for ornamental purposes by dressing its face, was rendered apparent. Messrs. Dickey, Shaeffer & Co. of that city own the most extensive quarry in its vicinity. This is three miles out of it, and its elevation is 180 feet above Dayton, which enables the proprietors to provide just such a descending grade for the cars that take it on railways into market, as to carry enormous loads.

There are four courses or strata in the quarry. One 20 inches thick, one 13 inches, one varying from 5 to 12 inches, and one uniformly 4 inches thick. It is the first description which has been so extensively used in the Miami canal locks. The four inch stone is generally used in flagging pavements, and the intermediate thickness for ordinary building purposes.

A walk through the streets will suffice to impress on the public the importance, for building purposes, of this limestone. Our public buildings are all greatly indebted for their appearance to this article, which in some instances, as the Cathedral on Plum street, and the new Cincinnati College, forms the entire front.

There is a pleasant story on the subject, which I am assured is not less true than amusing. *H. G. Phillips*, Esq. of Dayton, and one of its influential citizens, a few years since being about to build a fine dwelling for himself, visited Cincinnati to procure the cut free stone, at that time exclusively used here. Having made his purchase at one of the yards here, he called on one of his neighbours who ran a canal boat from Dayton to Cincinnati. "I have a lot of cut free stone at *Humble's* yard, I want you to bring out on your next trip. You can find the place I suppose.' 'Very easily,' replied the Captain dryly, ' I took in last week a load of our limestone and shall take another to-morrow for *Humble* to dress. He tells me they are preparing to use Dayton marble in all the best houses they are now building in Cincinnati. But it's all right, I get loading both ways by this means.'

Mary.

Inscribed in the Album of a young friend.

BY LEWIS J. CIST.

Mary!—it is a gentle name,
And they alone should bear it
Whose gentle thoughts and kindly deeds
Proclaim them meet to wear it.
Mary!—the first of whom we read
Is in the Sacred Word:
The blessed Virgin, undefiled,
The Mother of our Lord!

'Twas Mary to the Saviour knelt
And washed his feet with tears,
Sincere repentance then she felt,
For sins of other years.
With pity touched the Saviour said,
" Thy sins be all forgiven!"
And she who knelt a sinner, rose—
Mary—a child of Heaven!

Martha, we learn, remained at home,
" Troubled with many things,"
While Mary ran in haste to meet
Her Lord, the King of kings!
And He, who truly reads each heart,
Jesus, of her did say:
" Mary hath chosen that good part
Which shall not pass away!"

And when the Lord of Heaven became
The lowly, crucified,
Three Marys stood around the cross,
And wept when Jesus died.
'Twas Mary sought at early dawn
The tomb from whence he brake,
And her's the first recorded name
The risen Saviour spake.

Then, Mary, let it be your aim
To keep these still in view;
And as you bear the gentle name,
Possess their graces too!
Be meek and lowly—pure in heart—
Be every sin abhorred;
Like Mary, " Choose the better part,"
And early seek the Lord!

Printing Ink Factories.

There are three manufactories of printing ink here, which of course not only supply the home market but provide for the wants of the " Art Typographic " throughout the west, as far as the article has yet been introduced. These are the establishments of Messrs. *Henry & Co.*, *J. A. James*, and *Stearns & Co.* My further remarks apply to the last, which is the only one I have had the opportunity to examine.

Printing ink, as is generally known, is made of lampblack, or the soot which falls in the process of burning rosin or other bituminous substances. This is done by condensing the smoke in buildings suitable to the purpose. The *black* is ground in oil by means of a steam engine.

With their present fixtures Stearns & Co. can manufacture 2000 lbs. per week, and have in fact made five hundred lbs. per day for weeks. The ink is excellent and can be sold as low as any article of equal quality. This firm supplies the principal share consumed in the city offices, and sells also to the cities and towns in the interior of the State, and generally to the west and southwest, in which directions the market is constantly enlarging as the article gets into use.

Ink of every grade is made in this establishment from common news, up to the finest card ink, and at prices from 25 cts. to 100 per lb:

Sales are made nearly as fast as the article is prepared for the market, and the eastern ink, so long the sole dependence and supply in Cincinnati, is to a great extent driven from this market.

The sales of Cincinnati made ink must reach an annual value of twenty thonsand dollars.

Messrs. Stearns & Co. deserve especial credit for their success in manufacturing an article which compares to advantage with any made in our Atlantic cities, after the successive failures here of twelve or fifteen individuals in the same attempt, and in the face of the prejudice created by such failures, for its introduction into general use. The *velocity card presses of L'Hommedieu & Co. and E. Shepard*, which require for their work the finest in the market, use Stearns & Co.'s exclusively.

A Fact and a Moral.

A Pennsylvania farmer, a dutchman, was overtaken in the neighborhood of Stoystown, by a traveller, who was directing his journey to the great west on horse. The farmer was on horse also, seated on a bag of grain, about half filled with wheat, which he was taking to mill. To balance this part of the load, a large stone occupied the opposite half of the bag. The following dialogue ensued:

Traveler.—I see you have got a big stone in your bag. What is that for?

Farmer.—By shure do make de pag schteady.

T.—That stone dont steady the load. Throw it away and put half your grain on each side. Besides the sharp corners of the stone will wear your bag into holes.

Accordingly the farmer exclaims, "Py ching I neffer dought apout dat," dismounted, arranged his load as advised, the traveller assisting him for the purpose. The parties rode on a mile or two, when the traveler, tired of his slow progress, bid his neighbor good bye, and trotted forwards. After he had got out of sight, sudden misgivings seized the Pennsylvanian. "By ching it is all a tam Yenky drick. Effery potty in de Klades garries dere krice so, ant dat feller hash some getch in it." Thus soliloquising, he put back, restored the stone to its time honored place, and then pursued his journey to mill, exulting that no Yankee should get any advantage of him, no how he could fix it.

This narrative, which is an absolute fact, is in full keeping with the ideas and characters of persons in other regions, who are ready enough to suspect sinister motives where unsolicited kindness is bestowed.

Growth of New York.

We in the West who have seen villages of a few houses become large and flourishing cities in the lapse of forty years, and especially Cincinnati springing in fifty-five years from a settlement in which at that time a small garrison outweighed, in numbers, the residue of the population residing in the place, are apt to suppose that there is no parallel to these things in the Atlantic section of the republic. Such cases are doubtless rarer there, but they exist where it is hardly to be suspected, in New York for example. Sam'l Breck, an old inhabitant of Philadelphia, gives his recollections of New York in 1787, in the following language (I copy from the "National Magazine," of July last):

"In the month of June, 1787, on my return from a residence of a few years in France, I arrived in New York, and found it a neglected place, built chiefly of wood, and in a state of prostration and decay. A dozen vessels in port. Broadway from Trinity church, inclusive, down to the Battery, in ruins, owing to a fire that had occurred when the city was occupied by the enemy during the latter end of the war. The ruined walls of the burned houses standing on both sides of the way, testifying to the poverty of the place, five years after the conflagration; for although the war had ceased during that period, and the enemy had departed, no attempt had been made to rebuild them. In short, there was silence and inactivity everywhere; and the population *was very little over twenty thousand.*"

The proportional increase of New York in 58 years is fully as remarkable as that of ours, if we cofine our compa rison to population merely. It is true we have an increase of three years--- to 1848—to go upon, in order to render the comparison equal in point of age.

Street Lighting.

One of our recent city improvements is the introduction of gas pipes along the line of Fourth street, west, and the putting up lamp posts to afford light to the streets. It is greatly to be regretted, however, that the mass of foliage which the lower limbs of the shade trees presents by way of interference with the rays of light, being considerably below the range of the lamps, must diminish to a great extent the benefit of gas light to passengers on this street, and the same state of the case may be true of other streets. It will be well, therefore, for those who reside on Fourth street to give those shade trees a thorough trimming in the lower limbs, and let them not hesitate to do so under the general impression, that the spring is the proper or only season for that purpose. On the contrary, I have the authority of orchardists and others that the summer is the appropriate season for trimming, all wounds of the kind healing over more readily and perfectly now than in the spring. The late General Harrison had his whole orchard trimmed over on one occasion, in the month of August, and to better advantage, as he expressly stated, than he ever had it done in spring.

Hobson's Choice.

This is a phrase derived from the practice of John Hobson, who kept a livery stable at Oxford, England, and whose invariable rule was to let out his horses to the students in their regular routine as they occupied the stalls. This gave rise to the proverb, "Hobson's choice—that one or none."

General Wayne named his camp at Cincinnati "Hobson's Choice," why, it is not easy to conjecture. It was on the scite of the present Gas Works, reaching both above and below that spot.

I do not know a more appropriate use of the phrase, than in Beau Nash introducing Mrs. Hobson, a beautiful woman, into the Bath ballrooms, as master of the ceremonies, in these terms: "I have often heard of 'Hobson's choice,' but never had the pleasure to view it before, and you will coincide with me it reflects credit on his taste."

A Dispute.

We were comfortably situated in the stage. The horses were under way, when a young man continued a conversation which it appeared that he had broken off at the last stopping place.

"At any rate," said he, "I do not believe the story about Jonah swallowing the whale."

"And what is there so strange in that, young man," said an elderly deacon on the opposite seat.

"Strange," said the youth, "it is absurd, astonishing, impossible."

"You speak very confidently, sir, wiser men than you have believed it, continued the deacon, "and indeed why should not that be true as well as any other part of the good book?"

"I never saw it in the good book!" exclaimed the other.

"Then I am sorry to say that you are very ignorant of your Bible, young man, and it seems to me that a person who shows such a lack of religious knowledge ought not to be so confident on such a subject," and the old deacon looked at another very sober gentleman who sat opposite to him, as if for his approval.

The other gentleman opened his mouth for the first time and said—

"I perfectly agree with the young man. I do not believe in that story either."

The deacon looked thunderstruck and he stammered out—"But, sir, I thought that you told me you were a member of a church."

"Yes, sir, I am, and I believe every thing that is contained in the Bible."

"I beg your pardon, sir, but—"

"And I beg your's sir, but the young man said he did not believe that Jonah swallowed the whale."

"Jonah swallowed—whale swallowed," said the deacon, bewildered. "Did you not say, young man, that you did not believe the whale swallowed Jonah?"

"Not at all, sir—I said I did not believe that Jonah swallowed the whale."

"Well, well," said the deacon, "that alters the case, and I'm sure that I did not know what you were talking about."

Here the old gentleman opposite took a pinch of snuff, and leisurely observed that such was generally the case with religious controversy: *that one party was talking about one thing, and the other party of another.* "Therefore," said he in conclusion, "I very seldom engage in religious discussions, and more especially do I avoid them when travelling in a stage coach."

The deacon looked at the gentleman, as if he intended to know him when he saw him again, and the young man went to sleep.

A Scene at Washington.

When Mr. McLane was Secretary of State, a new minister arrived from Lisbon, and a day was appointed for him to be presented to President Jackson. The hour was set, and the Secretary expected the minister to call at the State Department for him; but McLane's French is like that of the present translator to the Department, rather difficult of comprehension, and the Portuguese misunderstood him, and proceeded to the White House alone. He rang the bell, and Jemmy O'Neal, Martin's predecessor, came to the door.

"Je suis venu voir Monsieur le President," said the minister.

"What the divil does that mane?" muttered Jemmy—"he says President though, and I s'pose he wants to see the gineral."

"Oui, oui," said the Portuguese, bowing.

So Jemmy ushered him into the green room, where the General was smoking his corncob pipe with great composure. The minister made his bow to the President, and addressed him in

French, of which the general did not understand one word.

"What does the fellow say, Jemmy?"

"Divil a know I knows—1 reckon he's a furriner."

"Try him in Irish, Jemmy," said Old Hickory.

Jemmy gave him a touch of the genuine Milesian, but the minister only shrugged his shoulders with the usual " plait-il."

" Och!" said Jemmy, " he can't go the Irish, sir—he's French, by the hill o' Howth!"

" Then send for the French cook, and let him try if he can find out what the gentleman wants."

The cook was hurried from the kitchen, sleeves rolled up, apron on, and carving-knife in hand. The minister, seeing this formidable apparition, and doubting that he was in the presence of the head of the nation, feared some treachery, and made for the door, before which Jemmy planted himself to keep him in. When the cook, by the General's order, asked him who he was and what he wanted, he gave a very subdued answer, to the astonishment of the cook, the President, and Jemmy, who now discovered for the first time the character of the stranger.

In this stage of the business McLane came in, and the minister was presented in form—but the matter could never be alluded to in Old Hickory's presence without throwing him into a passion.

Picture of Detroit.

A correspondent of the *Cleveland Herald* writes as follows:

Detroit of to day is a much greater city than the Detroit of my last visit, many years age.— And the Detroit of 1832, how different from the old French post of Fort Pontchartrain, sixty years before the peace of 1763, when the Governor and Commandant made grants of land on condition that the holder should assist in raising a May Pole every year in front of the officers' quarters! But the Detroit of to-day has remnants of the French dominion. Respectable families trace their titles and their ancestors to the days of the May Pole, and either proud of their ancient custom, or contemning of the modern, still ride through the streets in a horse cart without tires, sitting in the bottom upon a buffalo robe.

From the erection of Fort Pontchartrain to this hour, this place has had its garrison. Three companies are now here belonging to the Fifth Regiment, quartered in barracks behind the town. It is the head quarters of Brevet Major-General Brooks, who is the Colonel of the Regiment, a daring officer of the last war, who resembles Lannes, one of Napoleon's heroes, in his form, character and countenance. About three miles below town, a permanent fortification is being built, at an expense of about $200,000.

When the British frightened General Hull to surrender the place on the 16th of August, 1812, one of his excuses was that the town lay between the fort and the British, and he could not fire upon them. A brave and true man would have burned the town and then drove the British into the river.

From my window I see the ground where Pontiac lay with his Indian forces in 1764, when he was in the execution of his favourite design of driving the English from the West. You recollect the romantic circumstance of that stratagem.

On the same day Fort Mackinaw, Detroit, Fort St. Joseph's on Lake Michigan, Fort Niagara and Fort Pitt, then occupied by the English, were to be captured under the guise of friendship. The Ottowa king conducted the attack on Detroit in person, and fixed upon the day appointed for the general massacre as a council for peace within the garrison. In the evening previous, a squaw came to the Commandant with a pair of moccasins she had made for him, received her pay, and began to shed tears. After much importunity, it appeared that this officer having been kind to her and given her many moccasins to make, she wept to think that he and his family and people would be so soon among the dead. At the risk of her life she disclosed the plot. She said the Indians would appear in council, with their guns cut short and concealed beneath their blankets. When Pontiac should unwrap himself and drop his blanket on the floor, every one was to take his man, and in the struggle little doubt remained that the white man would fall. Colonel Campbell assured the squaw of safety, and proceeded to hold the talk as though nothing was known. But while Pontiac was speaking, the troops were under arms and concealed about the council room, which he did not fail to discover, and omitted to give the signal. The old Chief persisted in his assertion of friendship to the last; the warriors, although frustrated in a great enterprise at the moment of expected success, retained their composure, and many began to doubt the truth of the report of the Indian girl. But the Commandant stripped off the blanket from some of the Indians, showing their short guns, upbraided them with treachery, and, what is most singular, suffered every one to depart without harm.

"Touch Not, Handle Not."

One of those meddling gentlemen, who, like Thomas of old, are never satisfied until they have put their finger on every thing they see, was not long since observed by a friend with his hand *done up*, to use an every day phrase, in some half a dozen handkerchiefs. He accosted him with the usual question—

"What ails your hand?"

"Why," said he, " t'other day I went into the mill to see 'em saw clapboards, and I saw a thing whirling around so swift, and it looked so smooth and slick, that I thought I'd *just touch* my finger to it and see how it felt, and don't you think it took the *eend* of it right off, and then they hollered out, ' You musn't touch that—it's the *carcilar* saw that saws all the clapboards.' But they spoke half a second too late—the *eend* of my finger was gone, and I never seed it since."

Latin-English.

Coleridge gives the following artful combination of Latin so as to produce sensible English sounds, as one of the most witty productions of Dean Swift. It must be confessed that it is exquisite.

A LOVE SONG.

Mollis abuti,	Moll is a beauty,
Has ana cuti,	Has an acute eye,
No lasso finis,	No lass so fine is,
Molli divinis,	Molly divine is,
O mi de armis tres,	Oh, my dear mistress,
I mi na dis tres,	I'm in a distress,
Cantu disco ver	Can't you discover
Mias alo ver?	Me as a lover?

CINCINNATI MISCELLANY.

Cultivation of the Grape.

An article on this subject, for which many interesting facts were supplied by Mr. Schumann's valuable manual on raising grapes, just published by Robinson & Jones, was inserted in the "Advertiser" of the 20th ultimo. I have since been made acquainted with some facts on the productivenes and value of the grape as a crop, worthy of general notice.

The last years growth of Catawba was bought up for the wine manufacture, at three dollars per bushel; the wine being worth from $1 25 to $1 50 per gallon, and the prospect is that the crop will fetch this year at least as much.

As a bushel of Catawbas will make four gallons of wine, besides affording a residuum, from which vinegar can be made to profit, the permanent value of the grape as an article of purchase and sale, must be determined by the value of the wine. It is evident, plainly, that we are not cultivating sufficient now, and in the present gradual progress of the culture will, probably for years, not raise enough of the article to surpass the demand for wine, and settle to such prices as to render grapes accessible for table uses at a reasonable price. I desire, therefore, to show that the cultivation of grapes is an object worthy of being embarked in on a large scale.

There is hardly any land in Hamilton County which will not produce more bushels of grapes than of Indian corn to the acre, while on favourable scites they will produce three bushels of grapes to one of corn. I say nothing of the difference between raising a crop of which the principal labour is through with the first year, and increases in value every succeeding one, and a crop which requires the ground to be ploughed again and again every season, and every year in attending it as much toil as during the previous one. Nor shall I contrast the labour necessary to take the corn from the stalk as a crop into market, with that of gathering the grape. Nor, if the proprietor manufactures it himself into wine, can it be necessary to refer to the great profit the process affords.

In any view of the subject that can be taken, no man who feels any interest in it can fail to be strongly impressed, by Mr. Schumann's treatise, with a conviction that our Ohio hill sides will be eventually as extensively cultivated with the grape as the wine producing districts of France and Germany.

Pearces' Factory.

This is an establishment which has been gradually growing into importance for years, whose operations have been the less noticed here, that most of its manufacturing products go to the South.

J. & H. Pearce occupy the principal part of the building. One department of their business is the manufacture of cotton yarn, carpet chain, batting, &c. Of these they manufacture, with the labour of twenty-two hands, an annual value of $20,000. Another branch carried on here is the making of cotton gins, spinning machines, corn mills and shellers, &c. They employ for this purpose eighteen hands, and turn out a product of $45,000 annually.

I was shown here what may be termed, a Plantation Cotton-Spinning Machine, one of a large number finishing for the South, and designed to furnish cotton-yarn, at a single operation, from the raw material in the pod. This machine encloses in a frame less in size than a common breakfast-table, folded down, a Cotton Gin, Carding Roller, and Spinning shafts, running six parallel threads, which may be worked with such ease that one ordinary hand, in an day, performs the usual labour of ten, on the old fashioned system. These machines are distributed over the south and southwest, the proprietors keeping four members of their establishment at various points throughout the lower Mississippi valley, to see them started, and instruct the working part of that community in their use. They have already supplied that country, during the last fifteen years, with twenty-five hundred of these machines, at $130 each, their value, when set up at their place of destination. The great peculiarity of this invention is, that, as it takes the cotton from the seed and puts it into yarn, without going through the usual detached processes, which always impair the beauty and strength of the cotton fibre, it furnishes the planter with an article altogether different from, and superior to, the cotton ginned and pressed into bales. I saw specimens of yarn made by this machine, and cloth woven from the same kind of yarn. The yarn was of uncommon strength, and appeared, at a distance, rather to resemble woolen than cotton, in its filature; and the cloth, which was not fine, being designed merely for plantation wear, was remarkable for its evenness and firmness, being of durability which no factory could impart to his goods. It will readily be perceived of what consequence such a labour-saving implement must be to the lower Mississippi valley, supplying them with yarn, at their own doors, of a quality better, and at an expense less than any they can get from a distance. This machine, I was pleased to learn, in its present character, is a Cincinnati invention, and the use of it rapidly spreading throughout the south and southwest. Nothing can surpass it in beauty of fabric and exactness of performance.

Besides these operations *Henry Pearce* occupies a part of the building in executing machinery for bagging and cotton factories. Much of the machinery in use in Kentucky has been made here. He employs eighteen hands, and produces, say $40,000 value annually in his fabrics.

Pearces' factory is on the Miami Canal, not far from its mouth, and operates, of course, by water power. Its figure and elevation on an approach from the lower end of Fifth street, renders it a striking and picturesque object.

Mesmerism.---No. 1.

Nearly a year since, I presented in the "Advertiser" of that period my views on Mesmerism, or Animal Magnetism, which, it was supposed by myself and others, had to a great extent the effect of setting this agitating question at rest. But there seems to be no limits to the reign of scepticism in this age of infidelity, and the evil spirit which was supposed to be laid to "Vex the earth no more," is as rampant as ever; indeed bolder if possible.

It was formerly confined to private circles. It now speaks out in the press and the pulpit. *Dr. Cogley* has denounced Mesmerism as a phantasy and a chimera at the brimstone temple, and *Brothers Blanchard and Dyer Burgess* do not conceal their judgment, that it is the divination and sorcery that existed among the Jews in former ages. I must, therefore, buckle on my armour, and come to the rescue once more. What Professors Bronson and Stewart illustrate in public lectures, let me establish by the press.

Every intelligent and attentive observer has noticed repeatedly the power of sympathy, although unable to determine its cause or the extent of its operations; and all the well attested mesmeric phenomena are so many truths, confirmatory of the principle. My design is then to collect some facts, well known and authentic, of the existence of which others are probably as familiar as myself; and I shall argue the reality of Animal Magnetism from the evidence they afford.

In the state of Pennsylvania, and to the extent in which her emigrants may be found in the West, there exists a great variety of ascertained fact and practice, founded on the great principle of sympathy, correspondence, or magnetism, which runs through all nature. Some of these are remarkable enough, when we compare them with the kindred subjects of neurology and animal magnetism.

If a farmer there has the misfortune to cut his leg, foot, &c., in chopping wood, the axe is brought home, and hung up in the chimney corner. Twice a day it is dressed with hog's fat, and after a suitable time, of which the neighbours judge by the appearance of the axe, the man is discharged *cured*, and fit to go to work again. So in the case of treading on a nail. The nail is carefully drawn, greased, and hung up the chimney, examined from day to day, and after certain changes have taken place in the surface the cure is perfected, and the man goes to work as usual. What does this establish, if it does not prove the power of sympathy between the axe or nail, as the case may be, and the wound? They suffer together, and heal at the same time.

If a person burns or scalds himself, the usual recipe is, to breathe forcibly and repeatedly upon the injured part. The heat is withdrawn by the operator, to be breathed into the open air. This process of cure has been witnessed by hundreds living in this city, to say nothing of the vast numbers in Pennsylvania, who are constantly familiar with it.

Sometimes blood flows inordinately from the nose, by cutting an artery, bursting blood vessels, or any other cause which defies the skill of the regular physicians. In all such cases, a messenger is despatched to some individual in the neighbourhood, who has the gift of stopping blood. No odds if the operator has never seen or heard of the sufferer, all he needs is his name and place of residence, and the discharge is instantaneously arrested in a manner as striking and certain as it is mysterious.

It is useless to dispute the fact. It is as well attested as any result in laboratories of science or courts of justice. You need go no farther than Carthage, Hamilton county, to test its efficacy. I have a friend in that neighbourhood, Mr. John Hogendœblor, who in this manner can stop any discharge of blood, however violent.

I shall say nothing of the power of the divining rod, in hunting for water, minerals, &c.—How does it happen that, by its agency, not merely can water be found—for water may be found without it—but of a quality superior to any around it, nay, dug within five feet of it, and at a definite depth, frequently fifty feet nearer the surface of the earth than where the wells are dug under a different process.

Then there is the cure of the swinney in horses. I defy the ordinary farrier to reach this disease. In Pennsylvania, they take a smooth stone, and rub the horse on the part affected, then lay the stone on the grass, with the rubbed side down. Repeat this three times, and it is certain to work a cure.

There is the laying a charm or spell upon rifles, and bewitching people and cows, which prevails so extensively in the same state. I know there are multitudes with whom a sneer will weigh as much as an argument, who won't listen to a word on this subject. But every hunter knows to his sorrow, that when his rifle is in this predicament, he cannot kill game, and it is no joke to the poor sufferer to be ridden all night by witches, or his cows drained by *that accursed race* of their last drop of milk.

What shall I say of the countless operations of the moon observed in that state—perhaps elsewhere. I need only specify a few. The lower rail of a fence laid in the dark of the moon, is sure to become soon imbedded in the ground, while another, laid on the opposite side, shall remain years out of ground, if laid in the light of it. Rails split more easily in the light of the moon than in the dark. Radishes planted in one period of the moon, run all up to seed, in others, run to fibrous roots. Meat boiled at the waning, shrinks, but swells at the increase. When the circle of the moon is to the earth and she appears lying on her back, it never rains, for in that position she holds all the water. But let the position be reversed, and the horns down, the rain is pouring out all the time. Mrs. M——, of Butler county, Pennsylvania, assured me, from her own experience, that if babies diapers were rinsed in cold water, it would infallibly give the child the bellyache.

As to the mesmeric passes, I see nothing extraordinary in their effects. I can find individuals enough among the auditory of a church, put to sleep as successfully and profoundly by the right and left hand passes,—yes, and in some instances without any gesture at all—of our pulpit lecturers. I had supposed this fact sufficiently known to have rendered the kindred magnetic movement perfectly intelligible.

With one singular and curious fact, and in which we can more distinctly see the working of the magnetic or sympathetic power of nature, I shall close the article.

In Pennsylvania, the inner bark of a white walnut, or butternut, is boiled down and used for medical purposes. It is as remarkable as it is indisputable, that if the bark be scraped downwards, the application purges, if upwards it vomits. If scraped each way, it both vomits and purges. This fact is so well known, that the scraping is never confided to any persons, but those who can be depended on to scrape it the right way.

The same is equally true of the slippery elm, or of the elder bush. And I am assured by an intelligent sailor of my acquaintance, that salt water drawn from the ocean while the tide is rising, will vomit if drank, just as surely as it will purge if taken at ebb tide.

I look upon these facts, for which I can find fifty witnesses here, and thousands in Pennsylvania, equally wonderful with any thing in animal magnetism.

The City Council---No 1.

In arranging for exhibition a picture gallery of the conscript fathers of Cincinnati, a distingaished place must be allotted the presiding officer of that body.

The qualifications for a suitable president to the Council are quickness in apprehending points of order, and a degree of firmness in enforcing them, that is not incompatible with the suavity of manner which will enable him to execute his duty with the necessary promptitude, without giving personal offence.

Mr. President Strong is a Buckeye, I believe, in whose family history it is a singular circumstance, considering that Cincinnati is hardly more than fifty years of age, that both his father and grandfather are indentified with our City history and settlement, they having held honourable rank in the military service under Harmar, St. Clair and Wayne. It is a marked evidence of our advance in age here when we can furnish incumbents to this office, as we have twice done in rival candidates for the Mayoralty of Cincinnati, of individuals born here.

Mr. S. presides with great dignity of manner, and with the patience necessary to listen to the long winded harangues which members, who are thus qualifying themselves as in a debating school for more dignified offices, occasionally inflict on the president, as well as other listeners, and frequently called to decide a knotty point of order, manifests considerable skill in unraveling its intricacies, and is very prompt as well as impartial in enforcing the rules of the board. What I particularly like Mr. Strong for, is his obstinacy, or what he would call firmness, I am an obstinate man myself, and can therefore appreciate the quality in others. I asked Jonah Martin once, who he considered the two most obstinate, bigoted and prejudiced men in Cincinnati: "I don't know," replied Jonah, "unless it is you and C." "The very two persons I had in view," remarked I, "and it is the highest compliment you could pay us, for what you term obstinacy I call firmness, what you consider bigotry is simply adherence to principle, as what passes with you for prejudice, is our readiness to do our duty and take the consequences.

To return to Mr. D. E. A. Strong. He is an

eminently practical man, having been a merchant in active business; and with his understanding of the city wants, and the city interests, it is matter of regret, that he is not placed upon some of the business committees, where he could be filling a larger measure of usefulness than in presiding over the deliberations of the board.

I dislike drawing a picture, and specifying whose portrait it is, but am compelled to do it in this case. When I get among the members the likeness itself must designate the individual.

Fire Wardens.

I observe complaints made in the daily prints of the inactivity of these officers. What can persons expect from such men as Judge Torrence, or councilman Stephenson, two of the best among them? Do they imagine they can neglect their own business and spend six days of the week examining whether the houses of a large city, such as ours, are exposed to taking fire from the carelessness of neighbours? The whole system is deficient and defective. There are thirty-two fire wardens, about three to a ward, having general jurisdiction wherever they please to exercise it— which, of course, is nowhere.

If we desire to have any good result from the appointment of such officers, let the institution be remodeled. Let each block in the city have its own fire warden, who will then be interested in taking care of the block; and fine him five dollars for every fire which results from his neglect to remove all undue exposedness to it.

Nomenclature.

By accident or design, names are sometimes placed in singular collocation, and furnish new ideas to old and familiar names. Thus, we have had for years as newspaper periodicals, the *Toledo Blade*, the *Kent Bugle*, and the *Roman Citizen*, These all derive their adjectives from the town or county in which they are established. The latest thing of the kind outstrips all of them. It is the *Piketonian*, printed at Piketon, Pike county and edited by *Samuel Pike*. If Mr. P. has not yet adopted a motto, I suggest the Irish insurrectionary device of 1798: "The *Pike* shall win our way to freedom."

Free Translations.

A schoolboy, reading Cæsar's Commentaries, came to the words, "*Cæsar transit Alpes, summa diligentia;*" which, to the astonishment of his master, he translated—"Cæsar crossed the Alps on the top of a diligence!" Another in the same class translated the well-known proverb, "*Nemo omnibus horis sapit,*" as follows: "No man knows at what hour the omnibus starts."

These are admirable specimens, but not equal,

I think, to the Cincinnati law student, who, being asked to give a free translation of "*Nemo repente fuit turpissimus,*" paraphrased it: "It takes five years to make a lawyer."

New Churches.

Amidst the general advance of Cincinnati in its buildings, an uncommon share of those erected or in progress this year are of a public nature. The Cincinnati College, the Masonic and Odd Fellows Halls, the College of Dental Surgery, all bear date 1845. Then there are two Roman Catholic chapels; two Presbyterian houses of worship; one for the Welsh Church on College Street; two for the *Christian Disciples;* and four for the *Methodist Episcopal Church,* constituting an aggregate of fourteen houses of public worship, most of them handsome and spacious, for one year. I doubt if this has its equal in the United States.

Price of an Opinion.

In a cold night in November, in the year 1835, a man enveloped in a large cloak rapped at the door of one of the most distinguished advocates of Paris. He was quickly shown to the chamber of the learned lawyer.

"Sir," he said, placing upon the table a large parcel of papers. "I am rich, but the suit that has been instituted against me this day will entirely ruin me. At my age a fortune is not to be rebuilt; so that the loss of my suit will condemn me forever to the most frightful misery. I come to ask the aid of your talents. Here are the papers; as to facts, I will, if you please, expose them clearly to you."

The advocate listened attentively to the stranger, then opened the parcel, examined all the papers it contained, and said: "Sir, the action laid against you is founded in justice and morality; unfortunately, in the admirable perfection of our codes, law does not always accord with justice, and here the law is for you. If, therefore, you rest strictly upon the law, and avail yourself, without exception, of all the means in your favour—if, above all, these means are exposed with clearness and force, you will infallibly gain your suit, and nobody will afterwards dispute that fortune which you fear to lose."

"Nobody in the world," replied the client, "is so competent to do this as yourself, an opinion drawn up in the sense, and signed by you, would render one invulnerable. I am bold enough to hope that you will not refuse me."

The skilful advocate reflected some moments, taking up again the papers that he had pushed away with an abruptness peculiar to him, said that he would draw up the opinion, and that it would be finished the following day at the same hour.

The client was punctual to his appointment. The advocate presented him with the opinion, and without taking the trouble to reply to the thanks with which the other overwhelmed him, said to him rudely:

"Here is the opinion; there is no judge who after having seen that, will condemn you. Give me three thousand francs."

The client was struck dumb and motionless with surprise.

"You are free to keep your money," said the advocate, "as I am to throw the opinion into the fire."

So speaking, he advanced towards the chimney, but the other stopped him, and declared that he would pay the sum demanded; but he had only half of it with him.

He drew in fact, from his pocket-book fifteen hundred francs in bank notes. The advocate with one hand took the notes, and with the other threw the opinion into the drawer.

"But," said the client, "I am going, if you please, to give you my note for the remainder."

"I want money, bring me fifteen hundred francs, or you shall not have one line."

There was no remedy; the three thousand francs were paid. But the client to avenge himself for being thus pillaged, hastened to circulate this anecdote. It got into the papers and for a fortnight there was a deluge of witticisms of all kinds upon the disinterestedness of the great advocate. Those who did not laugh at it, said it was deplorable that a man of such merit should be tainted with a vice so degrading as avarice. Even his friends were moved by it, and some of them went so far as to remonstrate with him publicly; but the only reply he made was by shrugging his shoulders, and then, as every thing is quickly forgot in Paris, people soon ceased to talk of this.

Ten years had passed. One day the court of cassation, in its red robes, was descending the steps of the palace of justice to be present at a public ceremony. All at once a woman darts from the crowd, throws herself at the feet of the procureur general, seizes the end of his robe, and presses it to her lips. The woman was looked upon as deranged, and they tried to drag her away.

"Oh, leave me alone, leave me alone!" she cried; "I recognise him—it is he—my preserver! Thanks to him, my old age is happy. Oh, you do not know, you—one day—I was very unhappy then—I was advised to bring an action against a distant relation of my husband, who it was said, had possessed himself of a rich heritage that ought to have come to my children. Already I had sold half of my property to commence the action, when, one evening, I saw enter my house a gentleman, who said to me: 'Do not go to law, reason and morality are for you, but the law is against you. Keep the little you have, and add to it these three thousand francs, which are truly yours.' I remained speechless with surprise; when I would have spoken and thanked him he had disappeared, but the bag of money was there upon my table, and the countenance of that generous man was engraven upon my heart, never to be erased. This man; this preserver of my family is here! Let me thank him before God and before man."

The court had stopped. The procureur general appeared moved, but conquering his emotions, he said:

"Take away this good woman, and take care that no harm comes to her; I don't think she is quite right in her mind."

He was mistaken; the poor woman was not mad; only she remembered, and Monsieur Dupin had had chosen to forget.

The First Locomotive.

It is now very generally conceded, that of all the inventions of man, none holds any comparison with the steamboat. The mind can scarcely combine a calculation which may measure its importance. Some vague estimate may indeed be formed of it, by imagining what would be the state and condition of the world, at the present day, were there no steamboats; were we still to find ourselves on board sloops, making an average passage of a week to Albany, exposed to all the disasters of flaws from the "downscomer," and discomfiture of close cabins; or ascending the Mississippi in a keel-boat, pushed every inch of the way against its mighty current, by long poles, at the rate of fourteen miles in sixteen hours.

It is now almost forty years since the first steamboat ascended the Hudson, being the first practical application of a steam-engine to water conveyance. Then, no other river had seen a steamboat; and now, what river, capable of any kind of navigation, has not been bepaddled with them? It is not my purpose to enter the list of disputants, since sprung up, striving to prove that the immortal Fulton was not the first successful projector of a steamboat. In common with the world, I can but mourn over the poverty of history, that tells not of any previous successful effort of the kind. Steam, no doubt, was known before. The first tea-kettle that was hung over a fire, furnished a clear developement of that important agent. But all I can say now, is, that I never heard of a steamboat, before the "North River" moved her paddles on the Hudson; and very soon after that period, when it was contemplated to send a steamboat to southern Russia, a distinguished orator of that day, in an address before the Historical Society of this city, eloquently said, in direct allusion to the steamboat: "The hoary genius of Asia, high throned on the peaks of Caucasus, his moist eye glistening as he glances over the destruction of Palmyra and Persepolis, of Jerusalem and of Babylon, will bend with respectful deference to the inventive spirit of this western world;" thus proving conclusively, that the invention was not only of this country, but that no other country yet knew of it. In fact, the invention had not yet even reached the Mississippi; for it was not until a year after, that a long-armed, high-shouldered keel-boat man, who had just succeeded in doubling a bend in the river, by dint of hard pushing, and run his boat in a quiet eddy, for a resting spell, saw a steamboat gallantly paddling up against the centre current of that "Father of Rivers," and gazing at the scene with mingled surprise and triumph, he threw down his pole, and slapping his hands together in ecstacy, exclaimed: "Well done, old Mississippi! May I be eternally smashed, if you han't got your match at last!"

But, as before hinted, it is not my design to furnish a conclusive history of the origin of steamboats. My text stands at the head of this article; and I purpose here to record, for the information of all future time, a faithful history of "The first Locomotive." I am determined, at least that that branch of the great steam family shall know its true origin.

In the year 1808, I enjoyed the never-to-be-forgotten gratification of a *paddle* up the Hudson, on board the aforesaid first steamboat that ever moved on the waters of any river, with passengers. Among the voyagers, was a man I had known for some years previous, by the name of Jabez Doolittle. He was an industrious and ingenious worker in sheet iron, tin, and wire; but his greatest success lay in wire-work, especially in making "rat traps;" and for his last and best invention in that line, he had just secured a patent; and with a specimen of his work, he was then on a journey through the state of New York for the purpose of disposing of what he called "county rights;" or, in other words, to sell the privilege of catching rats according to his patent trap. It was a very curious trap, as simple as it was ingenious; as most ingenious things are, *after* they are invented. It was an oblong wire box, divided into two compartments; a rat entered one, where the bait was hung, which he no sooner touched, than the door which he entered fell. His only apparent escape was by a funnel-shaped hole into the other apartment, in passing which, he moved another wire, which instantly *reset* the trap; and thus rat after rat was furnished the means of "following in the footsteps of his illustrious predecessor," until the trap was full. Thus it was not simply a trap to catch a rat, but a trap by which rats trapped rats, *ad infinitum*. And now that the recollection of that wonderful trap is recalled to my memory, I would respectfully recommend it to the attention of the Treasury Department, as an appendage to the sub-Treasury system. The "specification" may be found on file in the patent office, number eleven thousand seven hundred and forty-six.

This trap, at the time to which I allude, absolutely divided the attention of the passengers; and for my part, it interested me quite as much as did the steam-engine; because, perhaps, I could more easily comprehend its mystery. To me, the steam-engine was Greek; the trap was plain English. Not so, however, to Jabez Doolittle. I found him studying the engine with great avidity and perseverance, insomuch that the engineer evidently became alarmed, and declined answering any more questions.

"Why, you needn't snap off so tarnal short," said Jabez; "a body would think you hadn't got a patent for your machine. If I can't meddle with you on the water, as nigh as I can calculate, I'll be up to you on land, one of these days."

These ominous words fell on my ear, as I saw Jabez issue from the engine room, followed by the engineer, who seemed evidently to have got his steam up.

"Well," said I, "Jabez, what do you think of this mighty machine?" "Why," he replied, "if that critter had'nt riled up so soon, a body could tell more about it; but I reckon I've got a little notion on't;" and then taking me aside, and looking carefully around, lest some one should overhear him, he "then and there" assured me in confidence, in profound secresy, that if he didn't make a *wagon* go by steam; before he was two years older, then he'd give up invention. I at first ridiculed the idea; but when I thought of that rat trap, and saw before me a man with sharp twinkling gray eyes, a pointed nose, and every line of his visage a channel of investigation and invention, I could not resist the conclusion, that if he really ever did attempt to meddle with hot water, we should hear more of it.

Time went on. Steamboats multiplied; but none dreamed, or if they did, they never told their dreams, of a steam wagon; for even the name of "locomotive" was then as unknown as "locofoco." When, about a year after the declaration of the last war with England, (*and may it be the last*,) I got a letter from Jabez, marked "private" telling me that he wanted to see me "most desperately;" and that I must make him a visit at his place, "nigh Wallingford." The din of arms, and the destruction of insurance companies, the smashing of banks, and suspension of specie payments, and various other inseparable attendants on the show and "pomp and circumstance of glorious war," had in the mean time entirely wiped from memory my friend Jabez, and his wonderful rat trap. But I obeyed his summons, not knowing but that something of importance to the army or navy might come of it. On reaching his residence, imagine my surprise, when he told me he believed he "had got the notion."

"Notion—what notion?" I inquired.

"Why," says he, "that *steam wagon* I tell'd you about a spell ago; but," added he, "it has pretty nigh starved me out;" and sure enough, he did look as if he had been on "the anxious seat," as he used to say, when things puzzled him.

"I have used up," said he, "plaguey nigh all the sheet iron, and old stove pipes, and mill-wheels, and trunnel-heads, in these parts; but I've succeeded; and for fear that some of these cute folks about here may have got a peep through the key-hole, and will trouble me when I come to get a patent, I've sent for you to be a witness; for you was the first and only man I ever hinted the notion to; in fact," continued he, "I think the most curious part of this invention is, that as yet I don't know any one about here who has been able to guess what I'm about. They all know it is an invention, of some kind, for that's my business you know; but some say it is a threshing machine, some a distillery; and of late they begin to think it is a shingle-splitter; but they'll sing another tune, when they see it spinning along past the stage coaches," added he, with a knowing chuckle, "won't they?"

This brought us to the door of an old clapboarded, dingy, long, one-story building, with a window or two in the roof, the knot-holes and cracks all carefully stuffed with old rags, and over the door he was unlocking, was written, in bold letters, "*No Admittance.*" This was his "sanctum sanctorum." I could occupy pages in description of it, for every part exhibited evidences of its uses. The patent office at Washington, like modern magazines, may exhibit finished productions of inventive genius; but if we could look into the port-folios of their contributors, in every quarter of the Union, and see there the sketches of half-finished essays, still-born poems, links and fragments of ideas and conceptions, which "but breathed and died," we might form some notion of the accumulation of "notions" that were presented to me, on entering the work-shop of Jabez Doolittle. But to my text again. "The First Locomotive." There it stood, occupying the centre of all previous conceptions, rat-traps, churns, apple-parers, pill-rollers, cooking stoves, and shingle-splitters, which hung or stood around it; or as my Lord Byron says, with reference to a more ancient but not more important invention:

"Where each conception was a heavenly guest,
   A ray of immortality, and stood
Star-like around, until they gathered to a God."

And there it stood. "the concentrated focus"

of all previous rays of inventive genius, "*The First Locomotive.*" An unpainted, unpolished, unadorned, oven-shaped mass, of double-riveted sheet-iron, with cranks, and pipes, and trunnel-heads, and screws, and valves, all firmly braced on four strongly-made travelling wheels.

"It's a curious critter to look at," says Jabez, "but you'll like it better when you see it in motion."

He was by this time igniting a quantity of charcoal, which he had stuffed under the boiler. "I filled the biler," says he, "arter I stopped working her yesterday, and it han't leaked a drop since, It will soon bile up; the coal's first rate."

Sure enough, the boiler soon gave evidence of "troubled waters," when, by pushing one slide, and pulling another, the whole machine, cranks and piston was in motion.

"It works slick, don't it?" said Jabez.

"But," I replied, "it don't move."

"You mean," said he, "the travelling-wheels don't move; well, I don't mean they shall, till I get my patent. You see," he added, crouching down, "that trunnel-head, there—that small cog wheel? Well, that's out of gear just yet; when I turn that into gear by this crank, it fits, you see, on the main travelling-wheel, and then the hull scrape will move, as nigh as I can calculate, a leetle slower than chain lightnin', and a darned leetle too! But it won't do to give it a try, before I get the patent. There is only one thing yet," he continued, "that I han't contrived—but that is a simple matter—and that is, the shortest mode of stoppin' on her. My first notion is to see how fast I can make her work, without smashing all to bits, and that's done by screwing down this upper valve; and I'll show you."

And with that he clambered up on the top, with a turning screw in one hand, and a can of soap-fat in the other, and commenced screwing down the valves, and oiling the piston-rod and crank-joints; and the motion of the mysterious mass increased, until all seemed *a buz.*

"It's nigh about perfection, ain't it?" says he.

I stood amazed in contemplating the object before me, which I confess I could not fully understand; and hence, with the greater readiness, permitted my mind to bear off to other matters more comprehensible; to the future, which is always more clear than the present, under similar circumstances. I heeded not, for the very best reason in the world, because I understood not, the complicated description that Jabez was giving of his still more complicated invention. All I knew was, that here was a machine on four good sturdy well-braced wheels, and it only required a recorded patent, to authorise that small connecting cog-wheel or trunnel-head to be thrown into gear, when it would move off, without oats, hay, or horse-shoes, and distance the mail-coaches. As I was surrounded with notions, it was not extraordinary that one should take possession of me. It dawned upon me when I saw the machine first put into motion, and was now fully orbed above the horizon of my desire; it was to see the first locomotive move off. The temptation was irresistible. "And who knows," thought I, "but some prying scamp may have been peeping through the key-hole while Jabez was at work; and, catching the idea, may be now at work on some clumsy imitation?—and if he does not succeed in turning the first trick, may divide the honours with my friend!"

"Jabez," said I, elevating my voice above the buzzing noise of the machine, "there is only one thing wanting."

"What is that?" says he, eagerly.

"Immortality," said I; "and you shall have it, patent or no patent!"

And with that, I pulled the crank that twisted the connecting trunnel-head into the travelling-wheels, and in an instant away went the machine, with Jabez on top of it, with the whiz and rapidity of a flushed partridge. The side of the old building presented the resistance of wet paper. One crash, and the "first locomotive" was ushered into this breathing world. I hurried to the opening, and had just time to clamber to the top of a fence, to catch the last glimpse of my fast departing friend. True to his purpose, I saw him alternately screwing down the valves, and oiling the piston-rod and crank-joints; evidently determined that, although he had started off a little unexpectedly, he would redeem the pledge he had given, which was that when it *did* go, it "would go a leetle slower than a streak of chain-lightnin', and a darned leetle too!"

"Like a cloud in the dim distance fleeting, Like an arrow" he flew away!

But a moment and he was *here;* in a moment he was *there;* and now *where* is he?—or rather, where is he not? But that, for the present, is neither here nor there.

The vile Moslem ridiculed the belief, so religiously cherished by the Christian Don, that in all the bloody contests that laid the cresecnt low in the dust, Saint Iago, on a white horse led on to battle and secured the triumph of the cross; but as this has now become matter of history, confirmed by the fact that on numerous occasions this identical warrior saint was distinctly seen "pounding the Moors," successfully and simultaneously in battle scenes remote from each other, thus proving his identity by saintly ubiquity; so we may safely indulge the belief that the spirit, if not the actual body and bones of Jabez Doolittle, stands perched on every locomotive that may now be seen threading its way at the rate of thirty miles an hour, to the total annihilation of space and time. The incredulous like the Moors of old, may indulge their unbelief; but for myself, I never see a locomotive in full action, that I do not also see Jabez there, directing its course, as plainly as I see the immortal *Clinton* in every canal-boat, or the equally immortal *Fulton* in every steamboat.

Unfortunately, however, these, like Jabez Doolittle, started in their career of glory without a patent, trusting too far to an ungrateful world; and now the descendants of either may (if they pay their passage) indulge the luxury that the inventive spirit of their ancestors has secured to the age.

But my task is done. All I now ask, is that although some doubt and mystery hang over the first invention of a steamboat—in which doubt, however, I for one do not participate—none whatever may exist in regard to the origin of the locomotive branch of the great steam family; and that, in all future time, this fragment of authentic history may enable the latest posterity to retrace, by "back track" and "turn out," through a long railroad line of illustrious ancestors, the first projector and contriver of "The First Locomotive," their immortal progenitor, "*Jabez Doolittle, Esq.*, nigh Wallingford, Connecticut."

Disinterested Legatees.

About forty years ago, an old man of Scottish birth, who had realised a large fortune in England, and from time to time made purchases of landed property in his native country, died after a protracted life of miserable penury, leaving only collateral relations. These persons had fully expected to be benefited by their kinsman, so that their surprise was necessarily very great when they learned that he had executed a conveyance of his whole property to a legal practitioner of Aberdeen, who had been accustomed to manage it. It appeared that the old man, under the influence of mere crotchet, or some temporary irritation, had resolved to disappoint them, at the same time that he enriched a man who had no natural claim upon his regard.

The relations had hardly recovered from the first sense of discomfiture, and the friends of Mr. C—— had scarcely begun to congratulate him upon his good fortune, when he announced to the heirs that he had destroyed the deed, and that the property would consequently pass to him as if the deceased had been intestate. He had with reluctance, he said, consented to allow of the deed being drawn up, and only for the purpose of securing the property for the rightful heirs. These individuals consequently entered upon full possession of the old man's estates and effects. They pressed upon the agent's acceptance a gift of about six thousand pounds, in gratitude for his honourable conduct. It is pleasant to record that he is still living, and a considerable land proprietor in the district where he originally practised as a solicitor or agent.

More recently, a circumstance somewhat similar took place. Two aged sisters were joint-proprietors of an estate in Perthshire. The elder was married and had a son; the other was unmarried. The elder dying first, her share of the property was inherited by her son, then an officer in the Guards. The second lady having some groundless dislike to this gentleman, bequeathed her share to a favourite nephew, far down in the family tree, and who had no expectation of such an inheritance. Finding, after the death of the old lady, how the property was destined, this gentleman lost no time in writing to his cousin—a person, we may mention, with whom he was but slightly acquainted, for they had been living at a distance from each other, and were in totally different walks in life—informing him that he could not for a moment think of taking advantage of such a will, but begged to surrender his right, without any reserve, into the hands of the heir-at-law. What added to the merit of this action, the legatee considered the whole matter as a private family affair, and said not a word about it to any beside the party principally concerned. It only became known in consequence of legal proceedings for the transference of the property to the heir-at-law, an opinion from counsel having decided that it was best to proceed upon the will, instead of holding it as null, which was the wish of the legatee.

These examples of high conscientiousness will be admired by all. They are felt to be the nobler, that public opinion would not have greatly resented a more selfish procedure in either instance. The agent might have appropriated the estate of his client, to the preclusion of all natural heirs, and still more might the junior cousin have sat quietly down in possession of his aunt's property, without forfeiting the esteem of society, seeing that they only did what the law allowed, and what hundreds would have done in their case. We therefore unavoidably accord high praise to their conduct, which we see to have sprung entirely from a genuine integrity and unselfishness of nature. But, it may be asked, is this approbation of such conduct a good sign of the public morality? We fear not; for absolutely the course taken by these two men was precisely what ought to have been taken, and no more. Their conduct only shines by reason of our believing that most men would have acted differently. Let us fully admit, then, the relative merit, seeing that most men feel as if they were well enough if they only act as their neighbours generally do, and any exception from common selfishness argues a superior nature. But still, also, let us understand that such actions ought not to be rare, nor their merit felt as calling for unusual notice or commendation.

Eclectic Medical Institute.

We have had for some time the rival Colleges, the Ohio Medical and the Botanico-Medical, and now it seems there is a third intended to combine the excellencies of both. Is there no end to human calamity, that we should have a third set of doctors let loose on the community. We shall see here calomel and lobelia, blood letting and steam, harmoniously working side by side.

This seems to be got up to introduce a set of *novi homines* into practice. The Professors in the different departments are little known in the community at any rate.

Cassius M. Clay.

The public is familiar with the fact that Mr. Clay's press has been received in this city, whither it was sent off by direction of the meeting which assembled at Lexington, for the purpose of getting rid of threatened difficulties. It was supposed that Mr. Clay, who was very ill at the time, could not survive. I learn, however, that he is on the recovery; and for myself I entertain no doubt that his first business act after arriving here, will be to set up the press in Covington, our neighbour city.

A Temperance Story.

Two young men, "with a humming in their heads," retired late at night to their room in a crowded inn; in which, as they enter, are revealed two beds ; but the wind extinguishing the light, they both, instead of taking as they supposed, a bed a piece, got back to back into one, which begins to sink under them, and come around at intervals in a manner very circumambient, but quite impossible of explanation. Presently one observes to the other:

" I say, Tom, somebody's in my bed."

" Is there," says the other ; " so there is in mine, d—n him! Let's kick 'em out!"

The next remark was:

" Tom, I've kicked my man overboard."

" Good!" says his fellow toper, " better luck than I; my man has kicked me out—right on the floor!"

The Pioneer Mothers.

It must not be infered from the narratives of Indian adventure usually published, that our Pioneer Mothers were not exposed to equal dangers with their husbands. Many of them evinced a degree of active courage which would have done honour to the sterner sex. Some of these cases occured in our own neighbourhood.

A family, consisting of the husband, the wife, and two children, one two years old, the other at the breast, occupied a solitary cabin in the neighbourhood of a block-house, where several other families resided, in the year 1789, near the Little Miami river in this state. Not long after the cabin was built the husband unfortunately died; and such was the grief and gloom of his widow, that she preferred to live alone, rather than mingle with the inhabitants of the crowded block-house, where the noise and bustle would be abhorrent to her feelings. In this solitary situation she passed several months. At night it was a common thing to see and hear the Indians around her habitation; and to secure her babes from the tomahawk, she resorted to the following precaution. Raising a puncheon of the floor, she dug a hole in the ground and prepared a bed, in which, after they had gone to sleep, she placed them side by side, and then restored the puncheon. When they awoke and required nourishment she raised it, and hushing them to sleep, returned them to their hiding place. In this way, to use her own words, she passed night after night, and week after week, with the Indians and her babes, as the sole objects of her thoughts and vigils.

The following incident displays the female character under an aspect a little different, and shows that in emergencies it may sometimes rise above that of the other sex.

About the year 1790, several families, emigrating together into the interior of Kentucky, encamped at the distance of a mile from a new settlement of five cabins. Before they had laid down, and were still sitting round the blazing brush, a party of Indians approached behind the trees and fired upon them. One man was killed on the spot, and another fled to the village, leaving *behind* him a young wife and infant child! As no danger had been apprehended, the men had not their ammunition at hand, and were so confused by the fire of the savages, that it was left for one of the mothers of the party to ascend into the wagon where it was deposited, break open the box with an axe, hand it out, and direct the men to return the fire of the enemy. This was done, and they dispersed.

The following narrative was communicated by *John Rowan* of Kentucky to Dr. Drake of our city, and is referred to by the doctor in an address which he delivered at Oxford, Ohio, in 1836.

"In the latter part of April, 1784, my father with his family, and five other families, set out from Louisville, in two flat-bottomed boats, for the Long Falls of Green river. The intention was to descend the Ohio river to the mouth of Green river, and ascend that river to the place of destination. At that time there were no settlements in Kentucky, within one hundred miles of the Long Falls of Green river (afterwards called Vienna.) The families were in one boat and their cattle in the other. When we had descended the river Ohio about one hundred miles, and were near the middle of it, gliding along very securely, as we thought, about ten o'clock of the night, we heard a prodigious yelling, by Indians, some two or three miles below us, on the northern shore. We had floated but a little distance farther down the river, when we saw a number of fires on that shore. The yelling still continued, and we concluded they had captured a boat which had passed us about midday, and were massacreing their captives. Our two boats were lashed together, and the best practicable arrangements made for defending them. The men were distributed by my father to the best advantage in case of an attack; they were seven in number including himself. The boats were neared to the Kentucky shore, with as little noise from the oars as possible. We were afraid to approach too near the Kentucky shore, lest there might be Indians on that shore also. We had not yet reached their uppermost fire (their fires were extended along the bank at intervals for half a mile or more), and we entertained a faint hope that we might slip by unperceived. But they discovered us when we had got about midway of their fires, and commanded us to come to. We were silent, for my father had given strict orders that no one should utter any sound but that of his rifle; and not that until the Indians should come within powder burning distance. They united in a most terrific yell, and rushed to their canoes, and pursued us. We floated on in silence—not an oar was pulled. They approached us within less than a hundred yards, with a seeming determination to board us. Just at this moment my mother rose from her seat, collected the axes, and placed one by the side of each man, where he stood with his gun, touching him on the knee with the handle of the axe, as she leaned it up by him against the side of the boat, to let him know it was there, and retired to her seat, retaining a hatchet for herself. The Indians continued hovering on our rear, and yelling for near three miles, when, awed by the inferences which they drew from our silence, they relinquished farther pursuit. None but those who have had a practical acquaintance with Indian warfare, can form a just idea of the terror which this hideous yelling is calculated to inspire. I was then about ten years old, and shall never forget the sensations of that night; nor can I ever cease to admire the fortitude and composure displayed by my mother on that trying occasion. We were saved, I have no doubt, by the judicious system of conduct and defence, which my father had prescribed to our little band. We were seven men and three boys—but nine guns in all. They were more than a hundred. My mother, in speaking of it afterwards, in her calm way said we had made a *providential escape*, for which we ought to feel grateful."

Nearly two years afterwards another incident occurred at a fort on Green river, which displays the dangers which beset the emigrants of that period, and illustrates the magnanimity of the female character.

About twenty young persons, male and female, of the fort, had united in a flax pulling, in one of the most distant fields. In the course of the forenoon two of their mothers made them a visit, and the younger took along her child, about eighteen months old. When the whole party were near the woods, one of the young women, who had climbed over the fence, was fired upon by several Indians concealed in the bushes, who at the same time raised the usual war-whoop. She was wounded, but retreated, as did the whole party; some running with her down the lane, which happened to open near that point, and others across the field. They were hotly pursued by the enemy, who continued to yell and fire upon them. The older of the two mothers who had gone out, recollecting in her flight, that the younger, a small and feeble woman, was burthened with her child, turned back in the face of the enemy, they firing and yelling hideously, took the child from its almost exhausted mother, and ran with it to the fort, a distance of three hundred yards. During the chase she was twice shot at with rifles, when the enemy were so near that the powder burned her, and one arrow passed through her sleeve, but she escaped uninjured. The young woman who was wounded, almost reached the place of safety when she sunk, and her pursuer, who had the hardihood to attempt to scalp her, was killed by a bullet from the fort.

Our City Watch.

It is a common subject of newspaper notice, that in connection with a stabbing affray, a riot, or a fire, that there were none of the watch to be found. But persons forget the Irishman's excuse: "Plaze your honour, could I be like a bird in two places at wunst?" It is easy finding out where the watchmen are not; the following incident will serve to show where they sometimes are.

Our well known and long respected fellow citizen, *Robert Rands*, alike for size and activity a terror to rogues, was formerly, perhaps is still a member of the night watch. Rands is or was a shoe-maker—a very appropriate occupation for the name—and had lately invented a coating of India rubber for boots and shoes, calculated to render them impervious to the slush of winter, and rain of all weathers. As this was a desideratum to the watchmen, whose duty kept them out in the most inclement seasons, the article was introduced and patronised among Rands' associates on duty; but the great difficulty was that the coating would not dry, and continually caught up in walking, various undesirable substances.

On one occasion one of the watch, Mr. B——, came off duty, and as carpenter's shavings were adhering to his boots, Butterfield, the captain of the watch, between jest and earnest, accused him of sleeping on a *shaving pile*, to the annoyance of B——, and the amusement of the rest. B—— called his attention to the India rubber: "You know," said he, "that this stuff takes hold of every thing it touches, and there were shavings swept out upon —— street, in my beat." "That may be," said Butterfield drily, "but you seem to have India rubber on your cap too," taking a shaving off it; "do you let your head stand where your feet should be?"

Colour Factories.

The wand of the enchanter which changes one substance to another in his slight of hand, or the touch of Midas, transmuting every thing to gold, are not more surprising than some of the operations of modern chemistry, which are calculated to make men that are ignorant of its powers, distrust almost the evidence of their senses. Who that beholds prussiate of potash for the first time, would suppose it any thing else than rock candy, and does not feel tempted to take the poison to his lips, and when told that this is the product of hoofs and horns, scraps of leather, hogs bristles, and stale cracklings—the most revolting of substances to sight and smell—but would smile incredulously at the statement.

Mr. Charles Dummig is engaged largely in the manufacture, having two establishments north of the corporation line, and on nearly opposite spots, upon the Miami canal. He has hardly been a year in operation, and cannot be said to be fully so yet. In a few weeks, two additional furnaces will be added to the concern, when he will be enabled to enlarge his manufacture to three thousand pounds per week. He sends almost all he makes by the Miami canal via Toledo to New York, where it commands the highest price in market.

Mr. Dummig is prepared to make Chrome yellow and green, Paris, Antwerp and mineral blue, but devotes his whole energies to the prussiate of potash, which is required in large quantities for the woolen factories and calico print works in New England. It is also purchased for rendering iron as hard as steel. The other articles named are used by painters, paper stainers, and oil cloth manufacturers, for whom they furnish blue and yellow of the deepest and most brilliant tints with all the intermediate shades.

It is inconceivable what mighty masses of offal such an establishment consumes. Four thousand pounds of animal substances, and two thousand pounds of potash, are used in Mr. D.'s factories daily. Twelve hands are constantly employed here, and the manufacturing process going on without intermission day or night.

One of these factories is forty-five by sixty-five feet; the other forty by eighty, and two stories in height. Mr. Dummig's operations will enable him to put into the market during the current year, not less than five hundred casks of this extremely valuable article, worth, at its present value at the East, $120,000.

There is an establishment on Deer creek of the same nature, belonging to *Wayne & Pleis*, of which I can give no account at present. It may serve to give a realising sense of the vast quantities of raw material consumed in them to be told, as I have been, that the supply except in the slaughtering season, falls far short of the demand, and on an average of the year barely meets it.

How much more do such businesses, in which skill and labour constitute the principal share, and raw materials an insignificant part, commend themselves to the political economist as well as philanthropist, than those heavy enterprises which exist among us, which after paying out probably eighty-five per cent. of the product for the raw material, leave a net profit, perhaps, of from five to ten per cent. to the community at large.

Ignorant Voters.

In Horace Mann's oration, delivered before the city officers of Boston, July 4, 1842, are the following remarks:

"For in the name of the living God, it must be proclaimed that licentiousness shall be liberty, and violence and chicanery the law; and superstition and craft shall be the religion, and the self-destructive influence of all sensual and unhallowed passions shall be the only happiness of that people who shall neglect the education of their children. By the census of 1840 there are in the United States 175,000 legal voters unable to read or write, who can determine the election of a President, Congress, or the Governor of a

State. The custom so prevalent at the West and South, of stump-speaking, as it is significantly, but uncouthly called, had its origin in the voter's incapacity to read. How otherwise can candidates for office communicate with ignorant voters?"

I am no apologist for ignorance; but I can tell Mr. Horace Mann, and his coadjutors, who talk so flippantly of ignorant voters, that he knows little of what he talks so fluently about. Such writers presume that school education and book knowledge are the grand panaceas to make a community intellectual and moral. Now I hold; and will furnish the examples if necessary, that an ordinary degree of education, on which knowledge of the world is engrafted, is likelier to qualify a man for becoming intelligent, than a school education which takes up a large share of the most valuable portion of human life.

Almost all the eminent names in science, literature and the arts, have been self-educated men; Franklin, Arkwright, Stephenson, Hiram Powers and Robert Burns are familiar examples, among thousands, of the fact.

I can tell Mr. M., moreover, that the voters of the West and South, who are addressed at political meetings, are as intelligent a body of men as any equal number who reside in any other section of the country; and that a man who prefers any other mode of appealing to the mass of mankind than oral addresses, whatever he may have learned at college, has yet to learn the first principles of human nature. The press is a legitimate and important engine to influence the community, but the speaker who, in the pulpit or in mass meetings, addresses a crowd, enjoys means of influence attainable in no other mode.

The ignorance of *lecturers* is, in certain instances, as remarkable as the ignorance of *voters*.

Street Loungers.

An amusing dialogue between two street loungers is published in the Knickerbocker.

"When a feller's any sort of a feller," said Nicholas, "to be ketched at home is like bein' a mouse in a wire trap. They poke sticks in your eyes, squirt cold water on your nose, and show you to the cat. Common people, Billy—low, ornery, common people, can't make it out when natur's raised a gentleman in the family—a gentleman all complete, only the money's been forgot. If a man won't work all the time, day in and day out; if he smokes by the fire, or whistles out of the winder, the very gals bump agin him, and say, get out of the way, loaf! Now what I say is this; if people hasn't had genteel fotchin' up, you can no more expect 'em to behave as if they had been fotched up genteel, than you kin make good segars out of a broom handle."

"That are a fact," ejaculated Billy Bunkers, with emphasis, for Billy had experienced, in his time, treatment at home somewhat similar to that complained of by Nicholas Nollikins.

"But, Billy, my son, never mind, and keep not a lettin' on," continued Nollikins, and a beam of hope irradiated his otherwise saturine countenance—'The world's a railroad, and the cars is comin'; all we'll have to do is to jump in, chalk free. There will be a time, something must happen. Rich widders are about yet, though they are snapped up so fast; rich widders, Billy, are special providences, as my old boss used to say, when he broke his nose in the entry, sent here like rafts, to pick up deservin' chaps when they can't swim no longer. When you've bin down twyst, Billy, and are just off agin, then comes the widder a floatin' along. Why spatterdocks is nothing to it, and a widder is the best of life-preservers when a man is most a case, like you and me."

"Well, I'm not perticklar, not I, nor never was. I'll take a widder, for my part, if she's got the mint drops and never asks no questions. I'm not proud; never was harristocratic; I drinks with any body, and smokes all the segars they give me. What's the use of bein' stuck up, stiffly? It's my principle that other folks are nearly as good as me, if they're not constables or aldermen. I can't stand them sort."

"No, Billy," said Nollikins, with an encouraging smile, "no Billy, such indiwidooals as them don't know human natur'; but, as I was goin' to say, if there happens to be a short crop of widders, why can't somebody leave us a fortin? That will be as well, if not better. Now look here; what's easier than this? I'm standin' on the wharf; the rich man tries to get aboard of the steamboat, the niggers push him off the plank; in I goes; ca-plash. The old gentleman isn't drowned, but he might have been drownded but for me, and if he had a bin, where's the use of his money then? So he gives me as much as I want now, and a great deal more when he defuncts riggler, accordin' to law and the practice of civilized nations. I'm at the wharf every day; can't afford to lose the chance, and I begin to wish the old chap would hurra about comin' along. What can keep him?"

"If it'ud come to the same thing in the end," remarked Billy Bunkers, "I'd rather the niggers would push the old man's little boy in the water, if it's all the same to him. Them fat old fellers are so heavy when they're skeered they hang on so, why I might drownded before I had time to go to bank with the check! But what's the use of waitin'? Could'nt we shove 'em in some warm afternoon ourselves? Who'd know in a crowd?"

Early Records of Cincinnati.

I copy the following memoranda from a book of field notes kept by John Dunlop, who appears to have been engaged in the surveys of Symme's purchase, as early as January 8, 1789.

"Memorandums of sundry circumstances in the Miami purchase, from the 1st day of May, 1789.

"May 21st.—*Ensign Luse*, with eight soldiers, and some citizens, going up from North Bend to a place called South Bend, was fired on by a party of Indians, the tribe they belonged to we never could learn. There were six soldiers killed and wounded, of which one died on the spot; another died of his wounds, after going to the falls of the Ohio for the doctor. There was a young man named *John R. Mills* in the boat, who was shot through the shoulder; but by management and care of some squaws he recovered and got perfectly well.

"September 20th.—The Indians visiting Columbia, at the confluence of the Little Miami, they tomahawked one boy and took another prisoner. They were sons of a *Mr. Seward*, lately from New Jersey. On the 30th same month they took another prisoner from same place.

"On the 12th December following a young man, son of *John Hilliers* of North Bend, going out in the morning to bring home the cows, about half a mile from the garrison, the Indians came upon him. They tomahawked and scalped him in a most surprising manner, took away his gun and hat, and left him lying on his back.

"On the 17th inst. following, two young men, one named *Andrew Vanemon*, the other *James Lafferty*, went on a hunting excursion across the river. When they encamped at night, and had made a fire, they were surprised by Indians, and fell a sacrifice into the hands of the savages, being killed by their first fire. They were both shot through the back, between their shoulders, the bullet coming out under their right arms. The Indians tomahawked and scalped them in a most barbarous manner, stripped them of their clothes, and left them lying on their backs quite naked, without as much as one thread on them. Next day myself and six others went over and buried them together in one grave.

"December 29th General Harmar arrived at Cincinnati, and was received with joy. They fired fourteen cannon at the garrison on his landing.

"January 1, 1790.—Governor St. Clair arrived. On his arrival they fired fourteen guns, and while he was marching to the garrison, they fired fourteen guns more. As soon as he landed they sent express for Judge Symmes, who went the next day to see him, and appoint civil and military officers for the service and protection of the settlement."

The Eclectic Series.

Besides the various mechanical fabrics which render the business relations of this city so intimate and extensive with the west and southwest, there are some heavy publishing operations which, having been carried on for some years past, have grown with our growth, and besides their regular business character, exercise a moral influence highly creditable to the reputation of Cincinnati.

I refer, particularly, in this respect to the educational publications of W. B. Smith & Co., the proprietors of what is now universally known through the Mississippi valley, by the name of the Eclectic Series of School Books, written and compiled by Professors M'Guffey and Ray. The publication of the series was, in

1842 . . . . . 75,000 volumes,
1843 . . . . . 171,500 do.
1844 . . . . . 334,000 do.

During the first six months of 1845, the issues have been 199,000, and the residue of the year will more than equal that amount, making the issue for 1845 at least 400,000 volumes, of which the value is not less than $60,000. The establishment consumes four thousand reams extra sized double medium paper annually, keeps three power printing presses constantly in motion, and gives current employment to eighty hands.

Besides supplying a large portion of the west and southwest with the series, which are in general use throughout that region, large quantities are sold to the Atlantic cities, with which country merchants supply themselves while making their general book and stationary purchases.

No series of school books eastward are put up in a neater or more durable style, as has been repeatedly acknowledged by the booksellers in our Atlantic cities. It is hardly necessary to do more than allude to the names of Professors M'Guffey and Ray as a guarantee for the scientific accuracy, pure taste, and elevated morality of the series. In this aspect of the subject, the authors, as well as publishers, have laid the great west under obligations which cannot be measured by pecuniary values.

I learn that the Eclectic Series have displaced in the schools throughout the west, the elementary books which preceded them in use.

Ball Exercises.

Every one who knows any thing of Indian sports and customs, is aware that they are among other exercises, passionately fond of ball playing. With some of the tribes, their ball plays resemble those of the whites. But some are peculiar to themselves, and have never been introduced among their civilized neighbours. A late letter from a Methodist missionary at the south west, dated Fort Coffee, Choctaw Nation, says:—

" The leading and favourite sport of the Choctaws is their ball-play. Having never witnessed one, I extract the following from the description given by the late Captain Stuart, commandant of the United States' forces, formerly stationed at this place. He says, ' It is rough and wild. The combatants engage in the contest entirely naked, except the flap. The interest and zeal which the natives of the forest take in this play, frequently attract ladies as spectators; sometimes, however, those of extreme delicacy may have occasion to blush. It is considered something of a national feast, and is often conducted by some of the leading captains with great regularity and order. Preparatory to commencing operations an extensive plain is selected, on one side of which two poles are erected about twenty feet high and placed about six inches apart at the ground, and diverging in such a manner as to be about two feet apart at the top. On the opposite side of the plain, or about two hundred yards distant two other poles are placed in the same manner. The parties to the contest, varying in number as may have been previously agreed upon, meet in the centre, when a ball is thrown up from two sticks about two feet long, with a small netting or basket-work at the end, and the strife commences. This consists in each party keeping the ball on their own side of the centre, and passing it the greatest number of times between the poles of the side to which they belong. The excitement and strife become very great; men are often hurt and sometimes killed. It sometimes requires more than a day to determine the contest. Bets usually run very high.'—This ballplay seems not unknown to the surrounding nations. The same writer says, ' It was formerly resorted to by the Indians to settle contested points of difference. A very serious difficulty which arose between the Cherokees and Creeks, about thirty years ago, was settled in that manner, and the horrors of war prevented.' "

One of the most singular results of my explorations in Indian records and narratives, has been my ascertaining that the game of *Shinny*, highly popular in my boyish days, and still in use in some parts of the United States, is of Indian parentage. Col. *James Smith*, the great uncle of the respectable family of the *Irwins* of our city, who was made prisoner by the savages and resided among them many years, describes it in such terms as serves both to identify it, and to show that the whites derived it from their Indian neighbours. It is a deeply interesting and exciting game, as all ball exercises, indeed are.

I observe that the English game of cricket, another ball exercise, is becoming introduced into Cincinnati. As an out-door game, it must be a more manly as well as moral exercise than billiards or ninepins, which in the attendant circumstances, at any rate, always deteriorate the public morals.

The Philosophy of Spitting.

Foreigners complain of our natural want of refinement and good breeding, and cite our universal practice of spitting on floors as evidence that we are barbarians. When the Irish chieftainess who had long resisted the arm of that virago Queen Elizabeth of England, was brought subdued into her presence, the Queen presented her with a handkerchief. The heroine inquired its use. To spit in, was the gracious reply. "In Ireland we spit upon the earth," rejoined the undaunted woman; "we leave it to Saxon kernes to put the spittle in their pockets."

But has it never occurred to those people that there are hidden virtues and meanings in spitting which may be said to invest the practice with a certain species of dignity. In Africa it forms an oath, or at least an attestation to treaties. The last Liberia Herald states as follows:—"The Colonies are generally prosperous. Governor Russwurm has visited an interior tribe of natives at Dena, about thirty or forty miles due east from Cape Palmas. He made a treaty of peace with them, which was duly ratified by the ceremony of "spewing water," which is the form of an oath observed by the Dena people. The covenant is performed by the chiefs of the contending tribes, after the palaver is talked, which is a kind of court held by all the head men, kings, chiefs, and all who have any influence. There is a bowl of water prepared; the king who appears to be the most willing to make peace, first dips his hands into the water, and, after slightly washing his hands, he fills his mouth, and *spits* it out on the ground a few times, and *spits*, the last time he fills his mouth, the whole mouthful into the hands of the other king, who sits before him while he performs the act. This being done, the other king gets up and goes through the same process. This being done by the kings, peace is made throughout the tribe or nation. The Governor succeeded in getting a peace of this sort made between the Dena and the Cape Palmas people, there being one of the very influential men from Cape Palmas in the company."

Nor is the practice confined to barbarous nations and modern times. Spitting, according to Pliny, was superstitiously observed to avert the effects of witchcraft and in giving a more vigorous blow to an enemy. Hence the English derive their custom in boxing, previously to a *set-to*, of spitting on their hands. Boys are accustomed to spit as a testimony or asseveration in matters of importance. In combinations of the colliers in the north of England for the purpose of raising their wages, they spit together on a stone, by way of cementing their confederacy. The English are therefore the last people who should complain of a practice they have done so much to introduce.

Coolidge's Steam Furniture Factory.

When I published lately a statement of the operations in WALTER's Steam Furniture Factory, I was under the impression that it was the only factory in Cincinnati in which furniture was made by machinery and under steam pressure. In this I made a mistake. J. K. COOLIDGE, at the corner of Smith and Front streets, has just put into operation machinery also driven by steam power, for the manufacture of the principal articles of cabinet ware, such as bedsteads; side, breakfast, and dining tables and stands, cribs, bureaus, &c.

His machinery consists of Daniel's planing machine, made by *Stewart & Kimball*, on Columbia street, two circular saws, mortice and tenon machine, boring and turning apparatus, all driven by a steam engine.

The building is forty-five feet by twenty and four stories in height.

Mr. Coolidge has placed this establishment under the charge of Mr. William Turner, an experienced cabinet maker, employs sixteen hands, and is prepared to turn out $25,000 worth of furniture during the current year. His markets are in the west, south, and southwest, a region from which our Cincinnati mechanics are rapidly driving the catchpenny and low priced eastern articles made for sale alone.

It must be apparent that fabrics cut and fitted by machinery will possess an exactness, not usually attainable by hand, which must secure and maintain a degree of strength which will enable furniture made in this mode to out last all other descriptions.

The whole district in the sixth ward, adjacent to the White Water Canal, must become filled before long with manufacturing establishments of various characters.

Artesian Wells.

In our cities an abundant supply of pure wholesome water is a blessing beyond price. It is indispensable to the luxury of the rich, the comfort of the poor, and the health of all classes. And there is hardly a city in the United States, where the supply is so inadequate to the want of the article, as in Cincinnati. I take, therefore, a deep interest in a project now agitating at Louisville, and brought forward lately before its city council to supply that city with water by *Artesian Wells*. If Louisville or Cincinnati can obtain ample supplies of wholesome water springing below the limestone formation, it is hardly possible to overrate the importance of the measure. That such wells may be obtained in certain locations, in what geologists call the secondary formation, has been successfully demonstrated both in England and France. There is one at the Episcopal palace in Fulham, one at Turnham Green, nine more in the parish of Hammersmith in Great Britain ; and besides others in France, one or more extensive wells at Paris. So that the practicability of the project is no longer a matter of doubt.

The great well of Paris is eighteen hundred

feet deep, and the expense of digging it, as may be conjectured, has been enormous. But in rocks of more recent formation, water has been obtained to flow on the level of the earth, at a depth of three hundred feet. In one case of this kind, the water ran fourteen feet above the tops of the pipes at the rate of ninety gallons per minute. I am now speaking of wells for the supply of cold, wholesome water for drinking and culinary purposes, If we go deep enough we can doubtless get it such as that supplied to Paris, which is hot enough to scald our hogs.

Nor are the benefits of such wells confined to our cities. I have no doubt that they will be found in the United States the most efficient, as well as economical agents in draining marshy lands. It is in this way the water of the Artesian well at Paris, which is used only for *jets d'eaux*, is returned into a depth where it loses itself in a permeable bed of sand, sufficing to absorb the whole. There is little doubt that any of our morasses may be drained by digging holes from twenty to fifty feet in depth.

If these views can be demonstrated as founded in fact, there is another application of the *well* principle of great importance to Cincinnati. This is the getting rid of the surplus water which, owing to the system, or to speak more correctly, want of system, in the early grading of our city, has created difficulties which must go on to increase, with the increasing discharge of water through our streets, which the improvement of Cincinnati creates. For this evil a drainage well is a cheap and efficient remedy. The expense which the wretched grades in the neighbourhood of Sycamore and Abigail streets have entailed, and are yet entailing on the city, in the shape of damages from overflow of water, would have built a dozen such wells. The culverts, which freely discharge water in ordinary rains, cannot relieve the overflow of water during storms such as we have lately had; whereas wells of this kind will let off any amount of water.

[Communication.]
Daguerreotyping.

An artist of great celebrity, just from Paris and London, says the Daguerreotypes on this side of the Anlantic are so far superior to the best of those produced on the other, that the fact could not escape the notice of an artist. This cannot be because we have made greater progress in chemistry, optics, electrics, and metrical science generally. Then why? Are we more practical and experimental, and less theoretical than our transatlantic friends? The writer imagines not —but facts are stubborn things, though we may not be able to account for them. In this country there are a great many persons practising this art, but very few who unite practical knowledge in chemics, optics, and electrics with the skill of an artist. It is this rare merit, with great experience and patience, that has given to Anthony and Edwards, of New York, and Hawkins, of this city, their deserved preeminence over all other operators in the world. We have seen pictures by the best operators from Vienna, Paris, Dresden, London, and all parts of our country—have watched the progress of this truly delightful art from its origin till the present moment, and feel proud to agree, from impartial conviction, rather than patriotism, with Mr. Healy, that our countrymen, and one of them our townsman, have no rivals—not even in Paris, where the art originated. A friend now in London, and a very competent judge, writes us lately that he compared a picture by Hawkins with those taken by Bain, (by far the best operator in London,) and that he decidedly prefers those of our fellow-citizen. Yet Bain is a clever Daguerreotypist, having taken those of Her Majesty the Queen, Prince Albert, Louis Philippe, the Duke of Wellington, &c., besides a host of minor nobles and great men of Great Britain and France. The fact is, Hawkins' Gallery of the Pioneers of this City, is the most interesting tableau vivant imaginable, and will compare advantageously with Anthony & Edwards' very interesting collection of the Heads of the American People, which no other collection we have before seen, will. One reason is, Mr. H. is at once an artist and a daguerreotypist—the father of the art in the West, an operator from predilection and not for petty lucres sake alone; but, from a passionate preference and devotion to the art—hence his success. We have no disposition to extol Mr. H. beyond his merit—to over praise or puff any one or lessen others—for good artists in this way abound in our city; but we wish our citizens to be aware that they need not cross the Atlantic for the finest daguerreotypes. It would be well for those of our merchants, importers, tourists, &c., who go abroad annually, and that have any doubts on this head, to take with them one of Mr. H.'s latest pictures. We know it would not be the first time such men as Messrs. Daguerre, Arago, Vanheim, Plaudet, Voightlander, &c., have been surprised. The continual exhibition of works of art for every department, annually displayed at Dresden and Munich, should have some specimens of our progress in Daguerreotyping; and we cannot forbear hinting to our friend H. that this would be both practical and desirable.   **Z.**

Cincinnati Churches.

In my list last week of new houses of worship, going up in our city for 1845, *two* Presbyterian are reckoned in place of *four*. This was a typographical error. There are Dr. Beecher's, a stone edifice, on Seventh street, below Western Row; the Tabernacle, brick, at the corner of Clark and John streets; the Third Presbyterian, brick, corner of Fourth and John, and the Central Presbyterian, brick, on Fifth, between Plum and Western Row. They will be ready for occupation in the inverse order in which they are named.

Fable.

" Father of men and beasts," said the Horse, approaching the throne of Jupiter, " it is said of me, that I am one of the most beautiful animals with which thou hast adorned the world ; and self love incites me to believe the character just; yet in some particulars, my appearance might admit of improvement."

" Of what kind? Inform me. I am willing to receive instruction," said the father of all, and smiled.

" I would probably run better," replied the steed, " if my legs were longer and more slender; a neck like a swan would be more becoming ; a wider chest would improve my strength ; and, since thou hast ordained me to carry thy darling, man, might I not have a natural saddle growing upon my back, instead of that with which the well meaning rider confines me?"

" Have patience," resumed the God; and with an awful voice pronounced his creative word. Life started into the dust, inert matter became alive; organised members were formed; they were joined in one consistent body ; and before the throne, arose—the hideous Camel. The horse shuddered, and shook with horror.

" See," said Jupiter, " longer and more slender legs; a neck like that of a swan; and a large chest, and a natural saddle. Would you choose to have such a shape?" The horse quaked with extreme aversion.

" Go," continued the God, " take counsel from this event; be henceforth satisfied with your condition; and, in order to remind you of the warning you have now received,"—so saying he cast on the Camel a preserving look,—" Live," said he, " new inhabitant of the world! and may the horse never see thee but with trembling aversion!"

Married by Chance.

The Count de M. lived in a state of single and independent blessedness. He was yet young, very rich, and was surrounded by every thing that could give enjoyment to life, except a wife. He had frequently thought of being a husband, but had always declared off before the knot was tied. Once, however, he found himself very nearly committing the folly of matrimony. A young person, the daughter of one of his friends, pleased him—her fortune pleased him, not less perhaps, than her person and accomplishments, and then, there were other reasons of convenience, &c., to justify the union.

The Count, who had so frequently made the first step towards matrimony, but as frequently drawn back, had not yet decided upon the course he should adopt in this case—he had promised the friends of the lady repeatedly, but had made no outward sign of performance. His future mother, however, knowing his weakness in this respect, resolved to bring matters to a termination, and therefore demanded of the Count whether he would or would not marry her daughter, and requested an immediate reply. The Count found himself in great embarrassment. At this moment his fears and hesitation returned with more force than ever, and he trembled at the consequence. To give up his cherished habits of bachelorhood, he found, was hard—it was almost impossible to abandon them. In this emergency, he resolved to appeal to chance. He wrote two letters—in the one he accepted the hand of the lady, in the other he refused it. He then put them into a hat, and called his servant.

" Take one of these letters," said he, " and carry it to the Chateau de———."

" Which, sir ?"

" Which you please."

The servant chose a letter. The Count burnt the other without opening it.

A distance of ten leagues separated the two chateaux. The domestic must be absent twenty-four hours ; twenty-four hours must elapse before the Count can know his fate. His situation is any thing but agreeable—he knows not during twenty-four hours whether he is a married man or a single one—whether he has still the power to dispose of himself, or whether he is not already disposed of. The domestic returned—he had carried the letter of acceptance, and M. de M——— is, even at this time, the happiest husband in that part of the country.

A Law Abiding Citizen.

In a county not a hundred miles off, a small-sized man went to the plantation of a certain gentleman, who was light in wit, but rather heavy in flesh, with a paper in his hand, folded in a legal form, and known by the abreviation of *'ca' 'sa.'* Having found the owner of the mansion in the field, he explained his business, drew he was required to read the *capias*, which commenced as usual, " You are hereby commanded, without delay, to take the body of," &c.

" Humph!" said the prisoner, stretching himself upon his back, " I am ready."

" Oh, but you don't expect me to carry you in my arms."

" Certainly you must *take my body*, you know. I do not resist the process of the law, understand, but submit with much cheerfulness."

" Will you wait here till I bring a cart?"

" Can't promise; I may recover my fatigue in the meanwhile."

" Well, what must I do?"

" You must do your duty."

And there he lay immoveable until the sheriff left.

MARRIED.

On the 30th August, by the Rev. Dr. Latta, Mr. Joseph James to Miss Sarah Jane Picket, all of Cincinnati.

By the Rev. Mr. J. H. Perkins, on Thursday, the 4th inst., Mr. John R. Childs, Jr., to Miss Frances P., daughter of George Wood, all of this city.

In Belpre, Ohio, on the 28th ult., by the Rev. L. C. Ford, Dr. Isaac Knapp, of Dummerston, Vermont, to Miss Abigail Baowning, of the former place.

She who hath well performed, till now,
Her duties all, in life—
As Daughter, Friend, and Sister true;
Right fittingly will, 'tis, we know,
" Her Woman's Sphere," as Wife!   C.

The Bubble of 1837, 1838.

The present generation will long remember the hot-bed speculations of 1837 and '38. A spirit adverse to making money in the usual modes was rife throughout the land. In Cincinnati we escaped the bubble and its explosion in a great measure. *Milwaukie* and *Jeffersonville* may be said to have been safety valves to us in this respect.

It was a common occurrence of that period for a man, who had made fortunate investments, though owning but a few hundreds the day before, to be considered worth as many hundreds of thousands the day after. Like all mania of the sort the decline of these brilliant prospects was generally as rapid as their rise. One or two individuals who understood the subject better, and did not suffer their judgments to be carried away into the impracticable or uncertain future, managed, however, to make hay while the sun shone, and to make it to some purpose. Let me narrate a case of the kind.

Isaac C. Elston, of Crawfordsville, Indiana, entered the section of land on which Michigan City has since been laid off and built. The land fo course cost a trifle, comparatively. He then went on to New York, where he laid it off as a town plat; had it lithographed, and advertised for sale. There was no deception in the case. This was the only port on the Lake which Indiana could ever have; and of course all the power and patronage the State could direct to that quarter, it was sure to acquire. The residue of the narrative I will give in Mr. E.'s own words, premising that having understood he had laid out a town there, which he yet had on hands, I was advising him to sell while he had a chance left, for I could assure him, I saw that building Tadmors in the wilderness had had their day, and now or never was his time. He listened very patiently, but with the air of a man that does not need advice, and then told me as follows.

" I went on to New York, as you know, and had hardly got quarters in the City Hotel there, till the speculators were all around me. They had seen the lithographs and were keen to buy, but most of them wanted to buy on credit, or at best, pay a fifth down. I told them this did not suit me; for if there was money to be made by waiting for it, I could afford to wait as well as any others. Finally, two or three Bank Directors proposed to me to give four hundred thousand dollars for my city, one half down, the residue in one and two years. I replied that I was determined not to sell unless I sold for cash, for if I had to wait, I knew that I could make more money out of it before my payments came due, than any amount I could get in the way of purchase. We talked a good while, and at last I

offered to sell them the undivided half for two hundred and fifty thousand dollars, and the company, finding me resolute, and fancying they could make more out of it by keeping me still interested in the project, accepted the last proposal, and gave me a check for that amount. I drew it out of bank in rouleaus of American gold, packed it up securely, and took it out with me to Crawfordsville, where I have since built as fine a house as any in the State. The great body of the money is still as safe as the day I got it. My wife has a roll of one thousand eagles, which she claims as hers, in her own custody; and now, my dear fellow, if I never get a cent for my share of Michigan City, it will never break me. But the truth is, this is none of your humbugs, and the place must become of vast importance; and if I have no other use for the money when the company get tired of their purchase, if they ever do, I shall be ready to buy back from them, at a fair discount. If I had not been a hard money man, I should have sold principally on credit, pocketed perhaps $20,000, and taken notes for nearly $500,000 more, of which I should never have received one cent. But my specie currency notions brought me out."

Remarkable Escape.

There never was a drama off the stage, so full of scenic effect as the French Revolution. The narrative of that event has been incorporated by Walter Scott into his life of Napoleon, with all the interest of the most *romantic spectacle.*

It was Paine, I think, who being a victim to the reign of terror, and waiting his turn for decollation, escaped with his life from the singular circumstance that the door of his cell had been left open on the morning that the attendant went his rounds to mark the victims for the day. Being intoxicated, he did not notice that the door was against the wall, and not closing on it. He chalked it accordingly, and when the myrmidon of the law went round to take away the prisoners, of course no mark appeared outside, the door being shut.

The following escape is not less remarkable:

Graf Von Schlaberndorf, was a singular person, a sort of strange German Coleridge, more however of a philosopher and a politician than a poet, living like a hermit in the bustling history of Revolutionary Paris: miserly in small things, the lord of a garret, slovenly in his attire, and cherishing a beard; but generous, even magnificent on a large scale, and actuated in all things by motives of the purest patriotism and the most disinterested benevolence, a character ready made for Sir Walter Scott. This man, as a foreigner and a German aristocrat, and also as the esteemed friend of Condorcet, Mercier, Brissot, and the unfortunate Girondist party, naturally enough during the reign of terror, fell under "suspicion of being suspected," and lay for many days, first in the Conciergerie, and then in the Luxembourg, in constant expectation of the guillotine. He escaped, however, after all; strangely enough, *saving his life by losing his boots!* Varnhagen von Ense relates the circumstance as follows:—

" One morning the death cart came for its usual number of daily victims; and Schlaberndorf's name was called out. He immediately, with the greatest coolness and good humour, prepared for departure; presence of mind in some shape, a grand stoicism or mere indifference, being common in these terrible times. And Schlaberndorf was not the man to make an ungraceful departure, when the unavoidable *must* of fate stood sternly before him. He was soon dressed, only his boots were missing; he sought, and sought, and sought, and the gaoler sought with him, in this corner and that; but they were not to be found. 'Well,' said Schlaberndorf sharply, 'to be guillotined without my boots will never do. Hark ye, my good friend,' continued he, with simple good humour to the gaoler, ' take me to-morrow; one day makes no difference; it is the man they want, not Tuesday or Wednesday.' The gaoler agreed. The wagon, full enough without that one head, went on to its destination; Schlaberndorf remained in the prison. Next morning, at the usual hour, the vehicle returned; and the victim who had so strangely escaped on the previous day, was ready, boots and all, waiting the word of command. But behold! his name was not heard that day; nor the third day, nor the fourth; and not at all. There was no mystery in the matter. It was naturally supposed he had fallen with the other victims named for the original day; in the multitude of sufferers no one could curiously inquire for an individual; for the days that followed there were enough of victims without him; and so he remained in prison till the fall of Robespierre, when with so many others he recovered his liberty. He owed his miraculous escape, not the least strange in the strange history of the Revolution, partly to the kindness of the gaoler, partly to his good temper, and above all to the circumstance that his boots were out of the way at the nick of time."

Bicknell's Conical Planing Machine.

Mr. *B.* Bicknell, a resident of our city, having some time since patented and put into operation this extremely valuable and ingenious labour-saving invention, has been harrassed with law-suits in the U. S. Courts, by the assignee for Hamilton county, of Woodworth's patent planing machine, and by others holding under the same right in Kentucky. The Kentucky case came off in May last in the U. S. District Court for that State; Judge Monroe holding that *Bicknell's* was no infringement of *Woodworth's*, even if *Woodworth's* could be sustained, either for a combination or improvement; that it did not use the carriage claimed by *Woodworth*; that it did not use his planing wheel, either horizontal or vertical; and that *Bicknell's* planing wheel is differently applied to the boards, which gave it a greater capacity to plane the surface; and that the cutter-wheels used for tonguing and grooving were not the same described by *Woodworth; Bicknell's* having cutters to give a smooth edge to the plank, which *Woodworth's* had not.

The case in Ohio came up for trial at the late July term, before Justice McLean of the U. S. Circuit Court, for that district. This trial lasted ten days. The defence consisted of five points of which it is necessary to notice the last merely, being that upon which the jury based their verdict, namely—that the machine of the defendant was so substantially different, that there was no infringement. The case was argued by some of our ablest Cincinnati lawyers, and the subject I imagine is now set to rest. The fact that we have in Cincinnati alone, fourteen planing machines in operation, turning out five millions feet of flooring boards annually; that each machine is capable of doing the work of one hundred men; and that the annual saving to the community in the United States, under this operation is $3,000,000, it may easily be imagined what a deep interest the public possesses in the result; for these decisions are not merely authority to use another machine, but they establish the fact I have known for years, that there is no point of comparison between the two, except their absolute difference, as well as the great superiority of *Bicknell's*; which not only has cut twenty-five per cent. per day and week more, but supplied a joint more perfect, and a smoother face, than any other in use.

Plato said a just man doing his duty in resistance to power and oppression, was a spectacle the Gods delighted to contemplate. Not less worthy of admiration is the conduct of *Henry M. Shreve*, in contending against the steamboat monopoly on the Ohio and Mississippi; and that of *Bicknell* against claims, which, obtained from the United States under *extraordinary and suspicious circumstances*, have aimed to close the shops of half the planing machine operators in the land. If these men had faltered or accepted shares in the monopoly, by way of compromise; in the *steamboat* case, the prosperity of the west might have been rolled back half a century; as in the *planing machine* suit, a check might have been given to our building operations in the whole west, that would have been felt for years.

This important *Cincinnati* invention will soon become, I doubt not, a source of fortune, as it already has of fame, to its inventor, as applications for rights are now pouring in, I am told, from all quarters.

The Pioneer Mothers.--No. 2.

There is an incident in the early settlement of Kentucky which has not been heretofore noticed. In the fall of the year 1779, Samuel Daviess, who resided in Bedford county, Virginia, moved with his family to Kentucky, and lived for a time, at Whitley's station in Lincoln. After residing for some time in the station, he removed with his family to a place called Gilmer's Lick, some six or seven miles distant from said station, where he built a cabin, cleared some land, which he put in corn next season, not apprehending any danger from the Indians, although he was considered a frontier settler. But this imaginary state of security did not last long; for on a morning in the month of August, in the year 1782, having stepped a few paces from his door, he was suddenly surprised by an Indian's appearing between him and the door, with tomahawk uplifted, almost within striking distance. In this unexpected condition, and being entirely unarmed, his first thought was, that by running around the house, he could enter the door in safety, but to his surprise, in attempting to effect this object, as he approached the door he found the house full of Indians. Being closely pursued by the Indian first mentioned, he made his way into the corn field, where he concealed himself, with much difficulty, until the pursuing Indian had returned to the house.

Unable as he was to render any relief to his family (there being five Indians,) he ran with the utmost speed to the station of his brother James Daviess—a distance of five miles. As he approached the station—his undressed condition told the tale of his distresses, before he was able to tell it himself. Almost breathless, and with a faltering voice, he could only say, his wife and children were in the hands of the Indians. Scarcely was the communication made when he obtained a spare gun, and the five men in the station, well armed, followed him to his residence. When they arrived at the house, the Indians, as well as the family, were found to be gone, and no evidence appeared that any of the family had been killed. A search was made to find the direction the Indians had taken; but owing to the dryness of the ground, and the adroit manner in which they had departed, no discovery could be made! In this state of perplexity, the party being all good woodsmen, took that direction in pursuit of the Indians, which they thought it most probable, they would take. After going a few miles, their attention was arrested by the howling of a dog, which afterwards turned out to be a house-dog that had followed the family, and which the Indians had undertaken to kill, so as to avoid detection, which might happen from his occasionally barking. In attempting to kill the dog, he was only wounded, which produced the howling that was heard. The noise thus heard, satisfied them that they were near the Indians, and enabled them to rush forward with the utmost impetuosity. Two of the Indians being in the rear as spies, discovering the approach of the party, ran forward to where the Indians were with the family—one of them knocked down the oldest boy, about eleven years old, and while in

the act of scalping him, was fired at, but without effect. Mrs. Daviess, seeing the agitation and alarm of the Indians, saved herself and sucking child, by jumping into a sink hole. The Indians did not stand to make fight, but fled in the most precipitate manner. In that way the family was rescued by nine o'clock in the morning, without the loss of a single life, and without any injury but that above mentioned. So soon as the boy had risen on his feet, the first word he spoke was, "*Curse that Indian, he has got my scalp.*" After the family had been rescued, Mrs. Daviess gave the following account of the manner in which the Indians had acted. A few minutes after her husband had opened the door and stepped out of the house, four Indians rushed in, whilst the fifth, as she afterwards found out, was in pursuit of her husband. Herself and children were in bed when the Indians entered the house. One of the Indians immediately made signs, by which she understood him to inquire how far it was to the next house. With an unusual presence of mind, knowing how important it would be to make the distance as far as possible, she raised both her hands, first counting the fingers of one hand, then of the other—making a distance of eight miles. The Indian then signed to her that she must rise: she immediately got up, and as soon as she could dress herself, commenced showing the Indians one article of clothing after another, which pleased them very much; and in that way, delayed them at the house nearly two hours. In the mean time, the Indian who had been in pursuit of her husband, returned with his hands stained with poke berries, which he held up, and with some violent gestures, and waving of his tomahawk, attempted to induce the belief, that the stain on his hands was the blood of her husband, and that he had killed him. She was enabled at once to discover the deception, and instead of producing any alarm on her part, she was satisfied that her husband had escaped uninjured.

After the savages had plundered the house of every thing that they could conveniently carry off with them, they started, taking Mrs. Daviess and her children—seven in number, as prisoners along with them. Some of the children were too young to travel as fast as the Indians wished, and discovering, as she believed, their intention to kill such of them as could not conveniently travel, she made the two oldest boys carry them on their backs. The Indians, in starting from the house, were very careful to leave no signs of the direction which they had taken, not even permitting the children to break a twig or weed, as they passed along. They had not gone far, before an Indian drew a knife and cut off a few inches of Mrs. Daviess' dress, so that she would not be interrupted in travelling.

Mrs. Daviess was a woman of cool deliberate courage, and accustomed to handle the gun so that she could shoot well, as many of the women were in the habit of doing in those days. She had contemplated, as a last resort, that if not rescued in the course of the day, when night came and the Indians had fallen asleep, she would rescue herself and children by killing as many of the Indians as she could—thinking that in a night attack as many of them as remained, would most probably run off. Such an attempt would now seem a species of madness; but to those who were acquainted with Mrs. Daviess, little doubt was entertained, that if the attempt had been made, it would have proved successful.

The boy who had been scalped, was greatly disfigured, as the hair never after grew upon that part of his head. He often wished for an opportunity to avenge himself upon the Indians for the injury he had received. Unfortunately for himself, ten years afterwards, the Indians came to the neighbourhood of his father and stole a number of horses. Himself and a party of men went in pursuit of them, and after following them for some days, the Indians finding that they were likely to be overtaken, placed themselves in ambush, and when their pursuers came up, killed young Daviess and one other man; so that he ultimately fell into their hands when about twenty-one years old.

The next year after the father died; his death being caused, as it was supposed, by the extraordinary efforts he made to release his family from the Indians.

I cannot close this account, without noticing an act of courage displayed by Mrs. Daviess, calculated to exhibit her character in its true point of view.

Kentucky, in its early days, like most new countries, was occasionally troubled with men of abandoned character, who lived by stealing the property of others, and after committing their depredations, retired to their hiding places, thereby eluding the operation of the law. One of these marauders, a man of desperate character, who had committed extensive thefts from Mr. Daviess, as well as from his neighbours, was pursued by Daviess and a party whose property he had taken, in order to bring him to justice. While the party were in pursuit, the suspected individual, not knowing any one was pursuing him, came to the house of Daviess, armed with his gun and tomahawk—no person being at home but Mrs. Daviess and her children. After he had stepped in the house, Mrs. Daviess asked him if he would drink something—and having set a bottle of whiskey upon the table, requested him to help himself. The fellow not suspecting any danger, set his gun up by the door, and while drinking, Mrs. Daviess picked up his gun, and placing herself in the door, had the gun cocked and levelled upon him by the time he turned around, and, in a peremptory manner, ordered him to take a seat, or she would shoot him. Struck with terror and alarm, he asked what he had done. She told him, he had stolen her husband's property, and that she intended to take care of him herself. In that condition, she held him a prisoner, until the party of men returned and took him into their possession.

Early Records of Cincinnati.--No. 2.

I continue my extracts from memoranda kept by J. Dunlop, who made the first surveys in the Miami purchase.

"April 25, 1792.—As Martin Burkhardt, Michael Hahn and Michael Lutz, were viewing some lots at the blue bank, they were fired on by Indians. Lutz was killed and scalped on the spot, besides being afterwards stabbed in different parts of the body. They shot Hahn through the body, and followed him in sight of the garrison, but finding they could not get his scalp, they fired at him a second time and killed him. Burkhardt was shot through the right shoulder, and in an effort to clear himself, took to the river to swim, but drowned, and was found at North Bend six weeks afterwards.

"Aug. 14th, 1792.—John Macnamara, Isaac Gibson, Jr., Samuel Carswell, and James Barrett, were bringing up a hand-mill stone in a canoe, and at the riffle below the station, they were fired at by the Indians. Macnamara was killed, Gibson wounded in the knee, and Carswell in the shoulder; Barrett being the only one escaping without injury.

"A copy of the speech brought in by Isaac Freeman, from the Chiefs and Warriors of the Mawme towns, to Judge Symmes.

"'Mawme, July 7, 1789.

"'Brothers! Americans!—At the Miami Warriors!—listen to us warriors, what we have to say.

"'Now Americans! Brothers,—We have heard from you, and are glad to hear the good speech you sent us. You have got our flesh and blood among you, and we have got yours among us, and we are glad to hear that you wish to exchange; we really think you want to exchange, and that is the reason we listen to you.

"''As the Great Spirit has put your flesh and blood into our hands, we now deliver them up.

"'We Warriors, if we can, wish to make peace, and then our chiefs and yours will then listen to one another. As we warriors speak from our hearts, we hope you do so too, and wish you may be of one mind as we are.

"'Brothers, Warriors,—When we heard from you that you wished to exchange prisoners, we listened attentively, and now we send some, as all are not here, nor can be procured at present, and, therefore, we hope you will send all ours home, and when we see them, it will make us strong to send all yours which cannot now all be got together.

"'Brothers, Warriors,—When we say this, it is from our hearts, and we hope you do the same; but if our young men should do any thing wrong before we all meet together, we beg you will overlook it; this is the mind of us warriors, and our chiefs are glad there is hopes of peace. We hope, therefore, that you are of the same mind.

"'Brothers, Warriors,—It is the warriors who have shut the path which your chiefs and ours formerly laid open, but there is hopes that the path will soon be cleared; that our women and children may go where they wish in peace, and that yours may do the same.

"'Now Brothers, Warriors,—You have heard from us; we hope you will be strong like us, and we hope there will be nothing but peace and friendship between you and us.'

"The following prisoners came in with Isaac Freeman, viz:

"*John White*, taken from Nelson county, Kentucky; *Elizabeth Bryant* and her child, and a child named *Ashby*, who were taken from a boat at the mouth of the Kentucky River—all its friends said to have been killed at the time. Two others who were intended to be sent in, ran off the night before Freeman left their towns, to avoid returning to the whites.

"Of those who would be sent in hereafter, was a *Mrs. Bilderback*, whose husband was killed at Mingo Bottom, at the time she was made prisoner: also, a soldier in Capt. McCurdy's company, named *Brady*. He was with a party guarding a surveyor, when made captive. Seven soldiers and several of the inhabitants were killed in the attack."

I find in reference to my notes on Symmes' settlement at North Bend, that he had ten Indian women and children, who having been made prisoners in an expedition from Kentucky to the Indian towns, had been placed in his hands by Col. Robert Patterson, for the purpose of exchanging them for white prisoners among the savages as soon as opportunity would admit. Symmes, who had always maintained towards the Indians a pacific policy, sent Freeman with a friendly Indian, then on business to North Bend, and one of the prisoners, a boy of fifteen, who speaking English, could enable Freeman and the Indian to communicate with each other; and Freeman with the Shawnese to whom he was sent.

Freeman lost his life on a later mission to the Indians, being fired on while bearing a flag of truce.

General Jackson.

The following incident occurred on a visit of mine to Washington city in 1834. Its truth may be relied on.

A widow lady in rather straitened circumstances had been keeping a boarding house for some years in that city, and during the general prostration of active business, growing out of the currency derangements of that date, had got in arrears, and to pay some of her most urgent debts, sent such of her furniture as she could possibly spare, to auction. The purchaser was a clerk in one of the Government offices; one of those public loafers of which there has always been too many at Washington and elsewhere, who run in debt as far as they can obtain credit, and without ever intending to pay. The lady called on the auctioneer, a respectable man named, *Mauro*, I believe. He called on the official who promised to pay as soon as his month's salary was due. The month rolled round, and June succeeded March, and September June, without payment being made, to the great distress of the wid-

ow and uneasiness of the auctioneer. And after further application, the office holder refused absolutely to od any thing, alleging it out of his power to pay. The sum was too large for the auctioneer to spare out of his own pocket or he would have paid it himself, so deeply did he feel for the poor creditor. In this perplexity, he concluded to call upon the President, and state the case, hoping he would suggest some relief. He waited therefore, on General Jackson with his narrative. The old man's eye flashed fire. "Have you Mr. P——'s note?" he inquired. "No," was the reply. "Call on him then, and without speaking of the purpose for which you want it, get his negotiable note and bring it here."

The auctioneer accordingly asked P—— for his note. "What do you want with the note; I don't know any body would take it," remarked the debtor, adding, however, as he sat down to write, "there it is." *Mauro* promptly returned to the President, handing him the note, who without saying a word sat down and wrote on the back of the paper "Andrew Jackson." "Now, sir," said the General, "show Mr. P—— the endorsement, and if he don't pay you, let me know it." The first man *Mauro* met as he entered Gadsby's Hotel was P——, "Ah !" said he "have you passed the note." "Not yet," said the other, "but I expect to, for I have got a first rate endorsor to it." "Nonsense," said P——, "who is it." The endorsement was shown him. He turned pale, begged the auctioneer to wait a few minutes, went out, and in a short space of time returned with the money, which was paid over to the widow that day, to the gratification of all parties. P—— kept quiet on the subject for years, but finally on a remark being made in his presence, that General Jackson did not endorse for any body whatever, remarked he knew better, for the General had endorsed once for him, and produced as evidence the note, to the surprise of all who knew not the circumstances of the case

Daniel Boone.

I left Cincinnati on Friday last, to attend the funeral pageant which took place at Frankfort, Ky., in the deposit at their final resting place, on the bank of the Kentucky, of the remains of Daniel Boone and his wife, the first man as well as the first woman in order of time, as well as in grade of character as settlers of Kentucky. Those who know nothing more of Boone than is recorded in the catch-penny biographies published of the great PIONEER, know almost nothing of that remarkable man; the rallying point alike in council or in battle among his cotemporaries, themselves men of high order of character and enterprise.

The pageant was a splendid and deeply interesting spectacle. A few survivors of his cotemporaries, gathered from all parts of the State, and a numerous train of his descendants, direct and collateral, led the van of the procession escorting the hearse, which was decorated with forest evergreens and white lilies, an appropriate tribute to the simple, as well as glorious character of Boone, and a suitable emblem of his enduring fame.

The pall-bearers bore the most respectable and distinguished names among the early settlers of the West. Generals *Taylor* and *Mc-Afee*, Col. *John Johnston*, of Ohio; Cols. *Ward* and *Boone, Richard M. Johnson*, besides other venerable looking men who were unknown to me. *Ellison E. Williams*, who accompanied him from North Carolina, had been his friend and often his associate to the day of his death, and fought under his eye, was among the most interesting objects on the ground.

The Kentucky Methodist Conference, which was in session at Frankfort, almost two hundred in force, made a part of the procession; as did in nearly equal numbers a fine looking body of officers and soldiers of the war of 1813. I judge there were not less than five thousand persons present,—and I have seen gatherings at political meetings no larger than this, which were estimated at ten to twelve thousand. The military, with the masons and odd fellows, as usual, made a part in the procession. The opening prayer was made by Bishop Soule of the Methodist Episcopal Church, and the oration or address commemorative of *Boone*, was delivered by John J. Crittenden, one of the U. S. Senators from Kentucky.

The day was propitious until one o'clock, when rain began to fall and rendered the remainder of the day unfavourable to the object for which the multitude had met. The Frankfort cemetery is a beautiful and appropriate place, still finer in its scite than ours; and the particular spot allotted to the old pioneer, whose name will never be forgotten while the west retains its existence, has been selected with singularly good taste, being on the very edge of the hill which crowns the bank of the Kentucky. Governors Owsley, Letcher, Genls. Desha, Combs, and various other distinguished public men of Kentucky, besides those named in the beginning of this article, were there.

Of the oration, I am sorry to add, that there was but one opinion expressed, and indeed felt, that it was a perfect failure; the more mortifying as Kentucky is one great school of orators, and might have furnished an hundred individuals of less established reputation than J. J. Crittenden, who would have done honor to the State in their performance.

City Solons.

A President Judge of the Butler and Allegheny District, Penn., who prided himself on his thorough scholarship, on one occasion corrected a lawyer who had asserted that in the present case an action would not lay. "*Lie*, sir, you should say; *actions lie—hens lay.*" The lawyer swallowed the dose as he best might, but soon had his revenge, the judge observing to the court, as he directed the crier to notify its adjournment, that the next day being the Fourth of July, the court would not set. "With submission to the court," observed the subject of the former rebuke, "it should be sit. *Courts sit*, and *hens set.*"

I find by the Atlas of Tuesday, that the Councilmen of the first ward, announce "they will *set* as a board," on that day. If any thing is *hatched* on the occasion worthy of notice, my readers shall be apprised in my next.

Frontier Figures of Speech.

Those who have attended musters and elections in the early days of Ohio and Kentucky, will hardly deem the following picture, taken from a Florida paper, of the "half horse half alligator" *nuisance* of that day, too highly coloured. These have been driven off in the progress of civilization, successively to Arkansas, Texas and Florida. I saw and heard a chap of this description in 1825, tell a judge in a county court in the southern section of Illinois, who had charged the jury in a case in which he was interested, as he thought very unfairly, "Wait till I catch you off that bench, and I'll make a checquer board of your face."

As we were yesterday passing by the courthouse, where an election was going on, a real "screamer from the Nob," about six feet four in height, sprang out of the crowd, and, rolling up his shirt-sleeves, commenced the following tirade: "This is *me*, and no mistake! Billy Earthquake, Esquire, commonly called Little Billy, all the way from Noth Fork of Muddy Run! I'm a small specimen, as you see,—a ramote circumstance, a mere yearling; but cuss me, if I ain't of the true 'imported breed,' and can whip any man in this section of country! Whoop! Won't *nobody* come out and fight me? Come out some of you and die decently, for I am *spileing* for a fight! I han't had one for more than a week, and if you don't come out, I'm fly blowed before sun-down, to a *certingty!* so come up to taw!

"May be you don't know who Little Billy is? I'll tell you: I'm a poor man—its a fact—and smell like a wet dog; but I can't be run over! I'm the identical individual that grinned a whole menagerie out of countenance, and made the ribbed nose baboon hang down his head and blush! W-h-o-o-p! I'm the chap too, that towed the 'Broadhorn' up Salt River, where the snags were so thick that a fish could'nt swim without rubbing his scales off!—fact, and if any body denies it, just let 'em make their will! Cock-a-doodle-doo! Maybe you never heard of the time the horse kicked me and put both his hips out of jint—if it ain't true, cut me up for cat fish bait!

W-h-o-o-p! I'm the very infant that refused its milk before its eyes were open, and called out for a bottle of old Rye! W-h-o-o-p! I'm that little Cupid! Talk to me about grinning the bark off a tree!—'taint nothing; one squint of mine at a Bull's heel would blister it! Cock-a-doodle de-doo! O I'm one of your toughest sort—live for ever, and then turn to a whiteoak post. Look at me, [said he, slapping his hands on his thighs with the report of a pocket pistol,] I'm the *ginewine* article—a *real double acting engine*, and I can out-run, out-jump, out-swim, chaw more tobacco and spit less, and drink more whiskey and keep soberer than any other man in these localities! Cock-a-doodle-doo! Darn it, [said Bill, walking off in disgust,] if that don't make 'em fight, nothing will. I wish I may be kiln-dried, and spilt up into wo͝oden shoe pegs, if I believe there is a chap among 'em that's got courage enough to collar a hen. Well! I'll go home and have another *settlement* with Jo Sykes. He's a bad chance for a fight, it's true, seeing as how he's but one eye left to gouge at, and an 'under bit' out of both ears; but poor fellow, he's *willing to do his best,* and will stay a body's appetite till the next shooting match."—Exit Little Billy, grumbling.

A Bit of Real Irish.

A jaunting car driver named Paddy Geraghty, not long since was brought before the Magistrate of the Head Police Office, Dublin, for having used threatening language to a Mr. Ellis, Hammond Lane.

The Magistrate, on hearing the statement of the complainant, directed Geraghty to give security, himself in £20, and two other persons in £10 each, that he would keep the peace.

Paddy and his friends having been ushered by the bailiff into the office of the bond-signer, or person who is to see that the bail-bond is executed, the following dialogue took place, when the bond was prepared—

Clerk.—The condition of this bond, Geraghty, is, that you will keep the peace for seven years.

Geraghty,—(scratching his head.) For seven years!

Clerk.—Yes, for seven years; and to all her Majesty's subjects.

Geraghty.—To all her Majesty's subjects! Good God! What is that for?

Clerk.—Why, it seems to be a great hardship on you to keep the peace.

Geraghty.—Is it to every one in Dublin?

Clerk.—Ay, and to every one in Ireland, too.

Geraghty.—In all Ireland?

Clerk.—Yes; in England and Scotland, also.

Geraghty.—In England and Scotland! Oh! that is on account of the union, I suppose; bad luck to it!

Clerk.—And, likewise, in all her Majesty's dominions.

Geraghty.—Is it at home and abroad?

Clerk.—Yes, certainly.

Geraghty.—Thin, certainly, by St. Patrick, I'll never sign it.

Pat was here reminded that if he did not conform to the order of the Magistrates, he would be committed, on which he reluctantly took up his pen to make the mark to the bond, exclaiming at the same time, " Oh! boys, isn't this dreadful for nothing at all?"

When the bond was signed, Geraghty shrugged up his shoulders, saying to the Clerk, with an air of sarcastic triumph, " Well, sir, you have done yer best. Thank God, you can do no more."

Clerk.—Oh! we don't want to do any more. You are now bound to keep the peace to all her Majesty's subjects.

Geraghty.—Looking at the clerk, while at the same time he was untying the whip across his shoulders,—" To keep the pace to all her Majesty's subjects! Och! then by the powers the first fellow I meet *that is not her Majesty's subject*, I'll make his head smoke."

Laving a Culprit.

The following *jeu des mot* is too good to be lost. The simplicity of the corporal appears to be *bona fide,* and there is an air of *vraisemblance* and fact about the affair which make it like enough:

" Colonel Wemyss, of the fortieth regiment, was remarkable for the studied pomposity of his diction. One day, observing that a careless man in the ranks had a particularly dirty face, which appeared not to have been washed for a twelve-month, he was exceedingly indignant at so gross a violation of military propriety. ' Take him,' said he, to the corporal, who was an Irishman, ' take the man, and lave him in the waters of the Guadiana.' After some time the corporal returned. ' What have you done with the man I sent with you?' inquired the colonel. Up flew the corporal's right hand across the peak of his cap: ' Sure and plase y'r honur, and didn't y'r honur tell me to *lave* him in the river, and sure enough I left him in the river, and there he is now, according to y'r honnur's orders.' The by-standers, and even the colonel himself, could hardly repress a smile at the mistake of the corporal, who looked like innocence itself, and wondered what there could be to laugh at."

Narrow Escape.

It is impossible to read the incident narrated below, and believe in the doctrine of chance. It occurred in reference to the late Samuel Williams, once a distinguished broker in London, and who died not long since in Boston:

One dark, stormy night, while at sea, Mr. Williams left his berth below with an intention of repairing to the deck of the vessel. He ascended the companion way, (place of entrance to, and egress from, the ship's cabin,) feeling his way along in utter darkness. The storm was howling, and every rope above him seemed strung to some strange melody, while the spray was dashing wildly over the bows of the ship. Just as Mr. W. reached the deck, the darkness on one side seemed to thicken, and the noise of the water to come in more irregularly; suddenly ropes passed over the head and along the breast of the astonished man. He seized them almost involuntarily, and held them with a convulsive grasp. An awful crash followed, and he was borne onward by the rigging on which he had siezed, while the deck which had sustained his feet had sunk beneath him.

A larger vessel had run down his own, and he and perhaps another were saved as by a miracle to tell the story of destruction, for the larger ship went booming onward in her course, and not a cry was heard from the perishing men, nor was a remnant found of the shattered bark. All were

"In the deep bosom of the ocean buried."

Steamboat Isaac Shelby.

This is a beautiful and fast running boat in the Cincinnati and Frankfort trade, on which I made a trip last Friday to witness the *Boone* pageant of Saturday last. She is comparatively a new craft, with fine accommodations and gentlemanly captain and clerk, Messrs. *Clay* and *Harlan*. As may be conjectured by the names of the officers as well as the boat, it is an entire *whole souled* Kentucky concern. A pleasanter trip can hardly be made any where from Cincinnati than to Lexington or Harrodsburg via Frankfort, to which city this boat takes passengers. I know no finer scenery than the Kentucky affords in its bold and ever changing borders, following and corresponding with the graceful sweeping of its various bends. No man accustomed to forest scenery, but must be struck with the fact that in this respect, it has not had its equal on the globe as a range for the chase. Nor is there any spot to which I would direct a foreigner, in desiring to impress him with a due sense of the fertility and beauty of the west, than to that superb country of which Lexington is the great centre.

Posers.

There is an old proverb, "Take care what you say before children and fools," which if attended to would save many a parent from getting into scrapes.

A little child, sidling up to a visiter and taking a sharp look at her eyes, was asked by the stranger what she meant by it. I wanted to see whether you had a drop in your eye. I heard mother say you had, frequently.

A boy asked one of his father's guests who his next door neighbour was, and when he heard his name, asked him if the gentleman was not a fool. "No my little friend," said the guest, "he is no fool, but a very sensible man; but why did you ask the question!" "Why," said the little boy, "my mother said the other day that you were next door to a fool, and I wanted to know who lived next door to you."

I knew an instance where a child in a religious family, after the clergyman, who was on a visit there had held family worship, ask her mother innocently, "What is the reason, ma, we never have worship only when Mr. R——— is here?"

A Careful Spouse.

At a polytechnic exhibition in Liverpool, got up by the Mechanics' Institute, a newly married man expressed a determination to "go down in the diving bell."

"Oh don't my dear," exclaimed the bride, "it must be dangerous."

The bridegroom was obstinate; and at length, finding her entreaties unavailing, his lovely Beattrice sank her demand into a compromise.

"If you will go down my dear," said she, "and peril your wife's happiness, let me beg of you to go down in *your old coat!*"

A Valuable Recipe.

The following morsel of information has been going the rounds of the papers for the last three or four weeks:

To DRIVE FLIES FROM A ROOM.—Take half a teaspoonful of well pulverized black pepper, one teaspoonful of brown sugar, and one tablespoonful of cream, mix them well together, and place them in a room on a plate, where the flies are troublesome, and, they will soon disappear.

Our friend of the United States Gazette bears testimony to the excellence of the prescription, after this fashion:

We can vouch for the correctness of the above recipe. We tried the experiment with the cream, pepper, and sugar, and in a very short time two-thirds disappeared, viz: the cream and sugar. The flies would not eat the pepper.

MARRIED.

In Dayton, O., on the 31st August, by the Rev. D. Winters, Mr. HENRY J. Ross of Cincinnati, to Miss MARGRET TRUBY, of the former place.

In Danville, Ky., on the 4th inst., by the Rev. N. L. Rice, Mr. WILLIAM W. RICE, of Louisiana, to Miss MARIA L. RICE, daughter of Mr. G. P. Rice, of Danville, Ky.

On Wednesday, the 10th instant, by the Rev. E. W. Sehon, Capt. REES PRITCHARD, Jr., to Miss MARGARET HAMILTON, daughter of Mr. Isaac Hamilton.

On the same evening by the same, Mr. JOHN Q. A. CHAPMAN to Miss ELIZABETH COFFLIN.

On Thursday, the 11th inst., by the Rev. William P. Strickland, Mr. JAMES F. DOGGETT, Esq., of Hillsborough, to Miss LAURA, daughter of the Rev. J. Cathell, of this city.

On Thursday, the 11th inst., by the Rev. George W. Maley, ENOS B. CLARK to MARY DICKSON, all of this city.

On Saturday, 13th inst., by the Rt. Rev. Bp. Purcell, EDWARD J. HUGHES of St. Louis, late of Paris, France, to Miss ELIZABETH LEWIS, daughter of Mr. John Lewis of this city.

DIED.

On Saturday morning, the 13th instant, Mrs. ANNA O. LAWRENCE, wife of Lorenzo Lawrence, deceased, aged 58 years.

On the same day, EDWIN M. son of Samuel G. and Frances D. Frazer, aged 1 year and 4 months.

Early Settlement and Settlers of Kentucky.

As a valuable and authentic contribution to the early history of the west, I have copied from the Kentucky Yeoman the following interesting synopsis from the pen of *Gen. Robert B. McAfee*, a pioneer himself, and son of one among the first who settled the State. More copious and accurate information within the same compass does not exist:

The interment of the remains of Col. Daniel Boone, and his wife at Frankfort, will of course call public attention to the early history of Kentucky; and it may not be amiss to review and notice some incidents never yet published, as I deem it a matter of some importance that our history shall contain the truth as near as we can ascertain it, especially as to the dates of important events.

It is believed that a man by the name of Finley first visited the interior of Kentucky from North Carolina, between the years 1763 and 1767. In one of his hunting trips, he was accompanied by Daniel Boone, who, in 1769, in company with Finley, John Stuart, Michael Stoner, and one or two others, came to Kentucky, and explored the country from Red River down the Kentucky. In one of their excursions Boone and Stuart were taken prisoners, and after some seven or eight days of captivity, made their escape. This was about the last of December, 1769. When they returned to their camp, they found it broken up, and their company gone. They then moved their quarters, and, it is believed, took up their residence in a *cave*, now in Meraer county, on a tract of land now owned by A. G. Talbot, Esq., (formerly Col. John Thompson's) on the waters of Shawnee run. The cave is, at its entrance, about twenty feet wide, and eight or nine high. Over the mouth of this cave, on a high bank, a tree is marked with the initials of Boone: D. B. 1770. This cave is a good deal filled up, but on digging a few feet under the ground, coals and burnt chunks were found. This point gives locality to some of Boone's wanderings; and it is believed that here, or in its vicinity, his brother, Squire Boone, found him in the spring of the year 1770, and furnished them with amunition. Stuart was killed by the Indians about this time, and Squire Boone returned to North Carolina for more amunition, and after he came back, remained in Kentucky until the spring, 1771, when they both came back home, where they remained until August, 1773, when they raised a company of about forty men, and then started to move with their families to make a permanent settlement in the country, but were attacked by the Indians, and Boone's eldest son was killed, which frustrated their whole arrangements, and he returned to Clinch river, in Virginia. And in the meantime Capt. Bullitt, with Hancock Taylor and Douglass, as surveyors, with the McAfee company, came to Kentucky in June, 1773, to mark out and survey land. Bullitt went on to the falls of Ohio with Douglass, and the McAfee company, with Hancock Taylor, came up the Kentucky river, and Robert McAfee had a survey of six hundred acres made on the 16th July, including the now town of Frankfort. They then crossed the country above Lawrenceburgh, and struck Salt river (which they called "Crooked creek") at the mouth of Hammond's creek, and surveyed nearly all the

land up to a point two miles above Harrodsburgh, and on the 31st of July started home and went up the Kentucky river, crossing the Cumberland moutain into Powell's valley, where they met Boone and his company a few days before he was attacked by the Indians. In May, 1774, Col. (then Captain) James Harrod, with thirty-one men, started from the Monongahela for Kentucky, and was soon after joined by ten others, making forty-one in all. They came down the Ohio to the mouth of Kentucky, and then up that river to the mouth of a branch now east of Salvisa, called Landing run, (now Oregon,) and thence to Harrodsburgh, where in June, 1774, they laid off a town and built five or six cabins or more, allowing each man an in and out lot, where they remained until about the 20th July, when James Cowan was killed by the Indians at "Fountainbleau," a large spring two or three miles below, when they broke up and returned home, and on their way joined Gen. Lewis and fought the Indians at the battle of the Point, October 10th, 1774.

In the meantime, Boone, having retired with his family on Clinch river, in Virginia, was commissioned as a Captain; and about the first of June, 1774, he was sent by Governor Dunmore to the falls of Ohio, to warn some companies of surveyors of the hostility of the Indians; and Boone in his route came upon Harrod and his company at Harrodsburgh, and aided in laying out the town; and, in company with a man by the name of Hinton, built a double cabin, which went by their name until burnt by the Indians. Thus Boone had the honor of laying the foundation of Harrodsburgh, nearly a year before he moved his family to Kentucky.

On the 11th day of March, 1775, the McAfee company, by the way of Cumberland gap, arrived at McAfee's station, on Salt river, seven miles below Harrodsburgh; and on the 15th day of March Capt. Harrod and the greater part of his company passed them, having came down the Ohio and up the Kentucky, and re-occupied Harrodsburgh, (then called Harrodstown,) which was never afterwards abandoned. The McAfee company, after clearing several acres of ground and planting corn, and apple and peach seeds, started home about the 10th or 11th April, leaving John Higgins and Swein Poulson to attend to the land and crops. They met Henderson and his company at Scagg's creek, on the 21st April, about ten or twelve days behind Boone, who, I believe, reached Boonesborough on the 11th of April.

In July, the Harrodsburgh and Boonesborough men who had wives returned for their families, and both parties got back in September following. Mrs. Boone and her daughters, and Mrs. McGary, Hogan, and Denton came in company; and each party arriving about the same time at Boonesborough and Harrodsburgh. Soon after, Col. (then Capt.) McGary commenced a fort about two hundred yards below their cabins, on a bluff bank of the creek, where the public square of the town was afterwards laid off. The various events which afterwards took place in the country, it is unnecessary to notice in this communication, except to say, that this fall Col. Ben. Logan came to Harrodsburgh with many others, while Simon Kenton, John Haggin, Michael Stoner, Robert Patterson, John and Levi Todd, and many others, took possession on the north side of the Kentucky, of various points, including Lexington. The year 1776 found hundreds

18

more adventurers who were searching for homes in Kentucky, which was represented as a terrestrial paradise In 1777, the Indians, aided by the Canadian British, made a simultaneous attack upon all the settlements in Kentucky, particularly on Harrodsburgh, St. Asaph's (Logan's fort,) Boonesborough, Lexington and Bryant's station. At Harrodsburgh, the attacks commenced early in March; and I cannot give a more graphic sketch of the trials and dangers of the early settlers, than is to be found in the journal of Captain John Cowan, who was then in Harrodsburgh, which will give date to many events of some importance. His journal commences March 6th, 1777, as follows, *verbatim*:

"The Indians killed Billy Ray and Thomas Shore at the Shawnee Springs. A party went out to the place in the evening. They buried Ray and Shore, and found another man alive and unhurt under a log in the cane. James Ray,—afterwards Gen. Ray, then fifteen years old—made his escape and alarmed the town, (Harrodsburgh,) and the people worked all night repairing the fort.

"March 7th.—The Indians attempted to cut off from the fort a small party of our men—a few shot exchanged. The loss on our side, some cattle killed and horses taken, and four men wounded. Their loss one killed and scalped and several supposed wounded." This attack was a little after sunrise, and a few minutes after a Mr. Thomas Wilson and his family had escaped into the fort from one of the cabins built in 1774. The Indians burnt the cabins.

"March 9th.—Ebenezer Corn arrived from the Ozark.

"March 13th.—Ebenezer Corn set off for the settlement (Virginia.)

"March 18th.—Butler and Myers arrived from Boonesborough, with accounts of one man killed and another wounded. On the 7th inst., a small party of Indians killed and scalped Hugh Wilson near the fort, and escaped.

"March 28th.—The Indians made an attack—the stragglers about the fort to the amount of thirty or forty—in which they killed and scalped Garrett Pendergrass, and took prisoner and killed Peter Flinn.

"April 3d.—Alarm about daylight.

"April 8th.—News of Jacob Huffman killed by Cherokees at Rye Cove, (place not now known.)

"April 9th, Wednesday.—Indians about.

"April 10th.—Todd and Calloway elected Burgesses. These were the two first representatives to the Virginia Legislature from the then county of Kentucky, which was made during the session of 1776.

"April 25th—Linn and Moore set out for the Mississippi. Fresh signs of Indians seen at two o'clock. They were heard imitating owls, turkeys, &c. At four o'clock sentry spied one, and shot at three soon after.

"April 28th.—Indians seen within two hundred yards of the fort. A party went out, but nothing done.

"April 29th.—The Indians attacked the fort and killed Mr. McConnell.

"April 30th.—Butler arrived from Boonesborough, and informed us that on last Thursday a body of Indians, in number forty or fifty, attacked that place, and killed and scalped Daniel Goodman, wounded Daniel Boone, Isaac Hite, John Todd and Michael Stoner.

"May 1st.—Scattered parties of Indians seen at a distance. A return was made of the people in the fort, as follows:

CENSUS OF HARRODSBURGH, MAY 7, 1777.

Men in service	81
Do not in service	4
Women	24
Children above ten years old	12
Children under ten years	58
Slaves over ten years old	12
Negro children under ten years	7
Total	**198**

"May 4th and 6th.—Indians seen several times these two days, and fired at the distance of two hundred yards.

"May 12th.—Messrs. Squire Bond and Jared Cowan arrived from the settlement.

"May 16th and 18th.—Indians seen and heard.

"May 23d.—Captain Todd, Calloway and company, set off for the settlement, (Virginia.)

"May 25th.—Indian snapped his gun at a man within forty yards of the fort, at dusk.

"May 27th.—An alarm this morning. An express arrived from Logan's and informed us that Boone's fort, (Boonesborough) was attacked on Friday morning last and a brisk firing kept up until Sunday morning, when they left the place.

"June 2d.—Indians seen round the fort. An express arrived from Logan's, and says that the Indians attacked that place last Friday, and killed William Hudson and wounded John Kennedy and Burr Harrison; and that—during the heavy firing at Boonesborough, 23d and 24th May, there were but three men wounded, and hoped not mortal; that the Indians tried hard to burn the fort, but were prevented with considerable loss.

"June 5th.—Express returned from Boonesborough, and says that Tuesday last they went within one and a half miles of the fort, and found a large body of Indians there and did not venture in.

"Capt. Harrod and Elliott set off to meet Bowman and company, (Col. Bowman was on his way with a regiment of men to protect the country.)

"Glenn and Laird arrived from Cumberland and saw Linn and Moore were safe embarked in that river on their way to Ozark.

"June 20th.—Coburn arrived from Logan's, and says Burr Harrison, who was wounded the 30th of May, died of his wound on the 13th inst. Daniel Lyon, who parted with Glenn and Lard on Green river to go to Logan's fort, had not come in yet. A part of a leather hunting-shirt was found, which was thought to be his. Indians seen to-day, and much sign.

"June 22.—Linn and Moore arrived from Kaskaskia with accounts favourable as could be expected. [As to what was their business it is not stated, except that they were sent as spies.] This evening, the Indians killed and cut off the head of Barney Stagner, above the big spring. [Stagner had taken his horse out to graze, and had been often warned not to venture so far from the fort.]

"June 25th.—Expresses arrived from Logan's and Boonesborough, and say that the Indians did not do much damage at Boonesborough, except killing cattle, and that Logan, who set out for the settlement on the 6th inst., has returned; and it is expected that Colonel Bowman is on his march out. A party of Indians (thirty) crossed Cumberland last Saturday, going towards the settlement; and Todd and Calloway and Harrod and campany had got in safe.

"July 6th.—Killed a buffalo bull at the fort. (He had come up with the cattle.)

"July 11th.—Capt. Harrod returned; says Col. Bowman is on his march here.

"July 14th and 15th.—Reaped wheat. (The first ever sown at Harrodsburgh. It was raised in a field west of the fort of not more than four acres.)

"July 16th.—Captain Harrod with a company set off to meet Bowman and inform him of the state of the fort.

"July 26th.—McGary arrived from Fort Pitt (Pittsburgh.) No prospect of peace or recovery of horses taken by the Indians.

"Harrod and his company returned, and say Colonel Bowman parted with them at the forks of the road, and is gone to Boonesborough.

"August 5th.—Ten or twelve Indians near the fort. Killed and scalped two of them, and wounded several others.

"July 28th.—Express arrived from Logan's, and says six young men, part of Col. Bowman's company who had left him, were attacked on Monday, going into Logan's, and that Ambrose Gressom was killed and scalped, and Jones Mannifee and Samuel Ingram wounded, but not mortally.

"Sept. 2d, 1777.—Court held at Harrodsburgh, and officers sworn into commission. (This was the first Court ever held in Kentucky, which shows the care of the Virginia Legislature, in the darkest days of the Revolution.)

"Sept. 7th and 9th.—The Indians seen and at—no harm done.

"Sept. 11th.—Thirty-seven men went to Captain Bowman for corn; while shelling they were fired on by the Indians; a skirmish ensued, and our men kept the ground until reinforced from town. We found two Indians dead and much blood. Eli Jared was killed, and six others wounded, one of whom died that night. The others, I hope, will survive.

"Sept. 17th.—An express sent to Williamsburgh," (Virginia.)

So far Captain Cowan's journal, which proves that Harrodsburgh was at that period the centre of business; a regular census was taken, and the first court held in the State was in the fort at this place. I do not know the names of the court; but I believe that John Cowan, Hugh M'-Gary and Ben. Logan were justices of the peace. I have seen a warrant in the hand-writing of M'-Gary, and his judgment on the back of it, which was no doubt a just decision, although not strictly legal. The warrant was for slander—one woman charged another with stealing her child's bib or cape. M'Gary decides that it is all a mistake; that, although appearances were somewhat against the woman, yet he acquitted her, and ordered the parties to say no more about it. I believe I have given the substance of the case.

In January, 1778, Col. Boone was taken prisoner by the Shawanees and taken to Detroit, where he was treated with great kindness by Governor Hamilton, who offered a hundred pounds for him, which was refused. It is said that in this extremity Boone very adroitly made use of his captain's commission from Governor Dunmore of Virginia, which was his protection from the Indians as well as the British. He however made his escape from the Indians sometime in June of this year, and got safe back to Boonesborough in time to make preparation for

the memorable siege in that year, after which he returned to his former residence in North Carolina, as his wife and father-in-law had left the country. Believing him to be dead, she did not expect to see him again. His worldly affairs being at a low ebb, he was not able to return to Kentucky until the summer, 1781, although some writers say he returned in 1780. But as we hear but little more of him until the battle of the Blue Licks, I am inclined to think it was not until the year I have stated before he got back, and this accounts for his loss of nearly all his land claims, which he entrusted to others.

As I do not intend to prolong this communication, I will only add one more statement, in relation to another matter. About a month since, a youth by the name of Stopher found a very fine tomahawk, leather shot-pouch, the remains of a powder horn, and an Indian pipe, sticking under a rocky bank of Salt river, at the mouth of a small drain on the west side, about two or three hundred yards below the mouth of the Harrodsburgh branch. On the side of the tomahawk is the name of "Thomas Walker," in fine plain letters. This ancient relict has been there some sixty or seventy years, and is yet sound and good, as it was sheltered by the rocks from the rain. I do not recollect at present the first name of Mr. Walker who ran the line between Virginia and North Carolina, or what become of him. The discovery of the tomahawk may throw some light upon the fate of the owner. It was very probably hid there by the Indians, when hovering around Harrodsburgh. I have this article in my museum; and if Thomas Walker was ever taken or killed by the Indians, his relatiods will know.

City Market Statistics.

It is impossible by a glance at figures to realise the numbers, bulk, weight and value of the immense aggregate of animal food consumed in our City Markets; nor would an European who had not visited the United States and observed the extent to which meat is used here among even the poorest families, comprehend or believe such statements.

The number of Beef Cattle sold in *Boston* last year, was 43,530; Sheep, 98,820; Hogs, 43,060. Total estimated value, $2,126,644.

The *New York* Cattle Market gives for the same period—Beef Cattle, 49,002; Cows and Calves, 2,946, and Sheep and Lambs, 75,713. Total value, $1,552,540.

In *Philadelphia*, during the same period, the sales were 37,420 Beeves; 15,121 Cows and Calves; 22,480 Hogs, and 91,480 Sheep and Lambs. Value, $1,831,620.

The number of cattle in *Baltimore*, for the same year, was 33,500 Beeves; 16,000 Cows and Calves; 24,000 Hogs, and 90,450 Sheep and Lambs, of the value of $1,755,000.

In Cincinnati the consumption of Beef Cattle, for the last twelve months, was 31,200; Cows and Calves, 15,310; Sheep and Lambs, 93,650; Hogs, 234,400. Of these, four-fifths of the Hogs, and one third of the Beef Cattle are packed up and sent to foreign markets. The value of the consumption here, $1,344,400.

RECAPITULATION.

Markets.	No. Cattle.	Value.
Boston,	185,400	$2,126,644
New York,	141,139	1,552,540
Philadelphia,	166,550	1,831,620
Baltimore,	166,950	1,755,000
Cincinnati, market,	183,416	1,344,400
Export,	194,570	3,033,520

Our finest Beef comes from the region around Bourbon county, Ky., for which not much less than one million dollars is paid annually. The Beef kept regularly at the stalls of the Berresfords, Vanaken Wunder, and John' Butcher, cannot be excelled in any market on the continent. Other butchers here, occasionally kill fine beef also.

I counted during the past year, for one week, the wagons loaded with marketing on the Market Spaces, embracing the twice-a-week markets on Fifth, Sixth, and Lower Market streets, and the daily Canal, and made out an aggregate of three thousand four hundred and sixty-three. Of these one thousand one hundred and forty-eight were at the Fifth Street Market alone.

MARKET-HOUSES.

LOWER MARKET.

There are in Lower Market street,

60 butchers stalls, which rent yearly for $50 each, - - - - -	$3,000
60 side benches, for the sale of vegetables, and rent for $12 each, - -	720
4 stalls or stands, at the end of the Market House, under the shed roof, and rent for $140, - - - - -	140

FIFTH STREET MARKET.

56 butcher's stalls, and rent for $50 each,	2,800
56 side benches, and rent for $12 each,	672
4 stalls or stands, at the end of the Market House, under the shed roof, and rent for $282, - - - - -	282

SIXTH STREET MARKET.

48 butcher's stalls, and rent for $30 each,	1,440
48 side benches, and rent for $5 each, -	240
4 stalls or stands, at the end of the Market House, under the shed roof, and rent for $15 - - - - -	15

CANAL MARKET.

38 butcher's stalls, and rent for $30 each,	1,140
38 side benches, $5 each, - - -	190

The whole amount, - - - $10,639

MARKET SPACES.

There are the following number of regularly licensed retail dealers in the markets, who deal in the following articles, and pay to the city the following prices, yearly, to wit:—

24 who sell butter and eggs, and pay $25 each, - - - - - -	$600
3 who sell butter, $20, - - - -	60
1 " sells butter, eggs, and cheese, -	35
1 " " " " " poultry, -	30
1 " " " cheese, " " -	25
4 " sell " and cheese, $25, - -	100
2 " " " " dried fruit, $30, -	60
1 " sells " bacon, and salt meat, -	40
13 bacon cutters, $25, - - - -	325
4 cheese " $20, - - - -	80
1 fish dealer, $20, - - - - - -	20
6 who sell flour, $25, - - - -	150
14 " " fruit, dried or green, $25, -	350

Whole amount, - - - - $1,875

A Chapter in Human Life.

The old proverb in regard to certain individuals is, that they are born with silver spoons in their mouths. Without any apparent effort, every thing appears to succeed in their hands. Life is to them, from beginning to end, a succession of Olympic games of feasting and enjoyment. I suppose there are commensurate drawbacks on this state of things; but they are out of sight.

Far different is the lot of another class in society, who, to preserve the figure of the proverb, enter life with wooden ladles instead of silver spoons in their mouths. Of this class was the unlucky individual with whom nothing succeeded, and who was finally led to the conclusion, that if he had been born a hatter, the Creator of all things would have constructed men without heads. Of this class was my friend Bergudd.

Charles F. Bergudd was a native of Poland—a country whose people are dissatisfied at home, and more unhappy still abroad. He was born too early and too late—too early for the last revolution—too late for the first. But he was born for revolutionary times. Of his history he never spoke, further than to say, that he could not breathe, for a single day, in any other atmosphere than that of a republic, and that "where liberty dwelt, there was his country." So he came to America; and, it was in a country town in the West, not far from Pittsburgh, that I made his acquaintance. He then spoke French indifferently, German worse, and English execrably. Of all nations on earth, the Poles appear the least fitted to acquire foreign languages; English at any rate.

He had been endeavouring to get into business, first in Pittsburgh, and afterwards in the country; but all in vain. He had no genius for labour of any description; indeed, he had all our aboriginal indian contempt for it. He felt himself fit for what he called *better things.* Perhaps, the poor progress he made when he assayed to learn some of the every-day employments, in which he found himself thrown into the shade by others, who were, intellectually, his inferiors, contributed to nourish this feeling. So, after months of well meant exertions of his friends, to tame him into civil life, he was given up as a hopeless case, and suffered to hunt, fish, and fill up his time as he saw fit. His manly feeling and good humour made him a general favourite.

After some time, as was natural, he got tired of these profitless pursuits. "I must get at something," he remarked to me one day; "this kind of life will never do. I have written to Miranda, who is now in New York, and I understand intends to make a dash at the Spanish Main, and offered myself to fill up his noble band of volunteers." In due course of time, an answer came, which sufficed to decide Bergudd to set off. A few days devoted to leave-taking for his journey, found him ready; and, followed by the best wishes of his neighbours, his old associates, he departed.

I heard nothing of Bergudd, who had promised to write as soon as he had any thing to tell, for some weeks; and the first notice conveyed of his whereabouts, was a brief letter written soon after landing—of which I shall take the liberty to furnish an abstract.

The letter was dated at some obscure town on the Spanish Main, in the rear of Cumana.

After expressing his gratification at being on Terra Firma, he proceeded to draw a vivid picture of the enthusiasm with which all classes— the priests excepted—received their advancing detachment. *Coro*, an important town in the interior, was in an insurrectionary state. *Varines* and *Angostura* were ripe to follow its example. Indeed, the whole country was receiving its liberators with open arms. Every thing he saw and heard was portrayed, as the French say, *couleur de rose*. A mighty Republic would be erected in Venezuela above all Greek, above all Roman fame; and the gallant spirits who were to carry the great enterprise into effect, would obtain a distinguished niche in the temple of history; their memories consecrated by the gratitude and happiness of the future millions of this magnificent empire. The letter wound up as it had been commenced, in the most exulting spirit; and, the writer only regreted that I could not witness and participate in his triumphs.

Well knowing the sanguine spirit of my friend, and still looking on the adventure as a wild chimera, I was folding the letter to put it in my pocket-book, when I observed a line or two which was written across on the margin, with paler ink, and doubtless of a later date. I glanced them over and deciphered. "To-mor-

row, at 10 o'clock, I shall be hung, it's a hell of a business."

Poor Bergudd! I read with melancholy interest the narrative of the final scene, which made its appearance in due time, in one of our Atlantic cities. He died as he had lived, firm and fearless, and living in the future. "Miranda will soon be here, and settle all accounts with these scoundrels. O, Liberty! dear as the breath of life to me, I die thy willing martyr!" He then submitted to his sentence.

I never saw a man who filled up in the living individual, so completely my idea of a hero. He should have died by the side of Kosciusko, when dragged to his dungeon, or Skrzynecki in the last hour of Poland's death struggle for liberty,

While mute they watched till morning's beam,
Should rise and give them light to die.

Daniel Boone.

The late funeral ceremony at Frankfort, Ky., of the 13th inst., was the occasion of bringing to light many circumstances connected with the history of this distinguished man, which otherwise would probably have been forever lost.

A chart of the family records from the days of Oliver Cromwell to the birth of *Daniel Boone*, made out in beautiful chirography by his uncle James, a schoolmaster, was produced at Frankfort, and I can truly say, I never examined a more remarkable manuscript document. A copy of it will probably appear in some future number of the "Advertiser."

It appears that the family of the Boones were Friends, or as they are more popularly named, Quakers. The immediate ancestors and their next relatives, resided at Bradninch, England, and emigrated to Pennsylvania, and settled in Exeter township, Berks county, not far from Reading, in which town Daniel Boone was born, July 14, 1732. Many of his maternal ancestors were from Wales. His father and mother, both died before he was thirteen years of age, and the children, eleven in number, under charge of James, the oldest brother, moved to the neighborhood of Winchester, Va. After residing here two years, Daniel removed to Rowan county, N. C. and was followed by two of his brothers, James and Squire, who settled on the Yadkin river. Here Boone married Rebecca Bryant, the daughter of Joseph Bryant, and remained in N. Carolina until he settled in Kentucky in 1760.

In 1773, when he attempted to remove his family to Kentucky, he started from North Carolina ; and when the Indians attacked his company, he fell back and settled on Clinch river, where he remained until the spring of 1775, when he removed to Kentucky. In the fall, 1799, he removed with his family to Missouri, and lived near the Missouri river, some 150 miles above St. Louis, where he died on the 17th day of October, 1820, at the age of 88 years. His wife died a few years before him. Daniel Boone was one of seven sons and four daughters, whose names were as follows :

Sons.—James, Samuel, Jonathan, Daniel, George, Squire, Edward.

Daughters.—Sarah, Elizabeth, Mary, Hannah.

Col. Daniel Boone had nine children, as follows :

Sons.—James, Israel, Daniel, Jesse, Nathan.

Daughters.—Susan, Jemima, Lavinia, Rebecca.

The eldest, James, was killed, 1773, by the Indians ; and his son Israel was killed at the battle of the Blue Licks, August 19th, 1782.

His son Nathan, a captain in the United States service, with his descendants, are I believe, his only posterity, bearing his name ; but an extensive and honorable collection of Kentuckians of the last and present generation, are related to the *old pioneer* by consanguinity or affinity.

The Pioneer Mothers.--No. 3.

The following incidents are taken from a letter addressed by Capt. Nathaniel Hart, of Woodford county, Ky., to Governor Morehead:

Dear Sir.—Connected with your address delivered at the celebration of the first settlement of Kentucky, at Boonesborough, the circumstances attending the escape and defence of Mrs. Woods about the year 1784 or '5, near the Crab Orchard, in Lincoln county, may not be without interest. I have a distinct recollection of them. Mr. Woods, her husband, was absent from home, and early in the morning, being a short distance from her cabin, she discovered several Indians advancing towards it. She reached it before all but one, who was so far ahead of the others, that before she could close and fasten the door, he entered. Instantly he was seized by a lame negro man of the family, and after a short scuffle, they both fell—the negro underneath. But he held the Indian so fast, that he was unable to use either his scalping knife or tomahawk, when he called upon his young mistress to take the axe from under the bed, and dispatch him by a blow upon the head. She immediately attempted it: but the first attempt was a failure. She repeated the blow and killed him. The other Indians were at the door endeavouring to force it open with their tomahawks. The negro rose, and proposed to Mrs. Woods to let in another, and they would soon dispose of the whole of them in the same way. The cabin was but a short distance from a station, the occupants of which, having discovered the perilous situation of the family, fired on the Indians, and killed another, when the remainder made their escape.

This incident is not more extraordinary than one that happened, in the fall or winter of 1781–'2, to some families belonging to our own fort at the White Oak Spring. My father settled this fort in 1779. It was situated about a mile above Boonesborough and in the same bottom of the river. It was composed principally of families from York county, Pennsylvania—orderly, respectable people, and the men good soldiers. But they were unaccustomed to Indian warfare, and the consequence was, that of some ten or twelve men, all were killed but two or three. During this period, Peter Duree, the elder, the principal man of the connexion, determined to settle a new fort between Estill's station and the mouth of Muddy Creek, directly on the trace between the Cherokee and Shawanese towns. Having erected a cabin, his son-in-law John Bullock and his family, and his son Peter Duree, his wife and two children, removed to it, taking a pair of hand mill stones with them. They remained for two or three days shut up in their cabin, but their corn meal being exhausted, they were compelled to venture out to cut a hollow tree in order to adjust their hand mill. They were attacked by Indians—Bullock, after running a short distance, fell. Duree reached the cabin, and threw himself upon the bed. Mrs. Bullock ran to the door to ascertain the fate of her husband—received a shot in the breast, and fell across the door sill. Mrs. Duree, not knowing whether her husband had been shot or had fainted, caught her by the feet, pulled her into the house and barred the door. She grasped a rifle and told her husband, she would help him to fight. He replied that he had been wounded and was dying. She then presented the gun through several port holes in quick succession—then calmly sat by her husband and closed his eyes in death. You would conclude that the scene ought to end here—but after waiting several hours, and seeing nothing more of the Indians, she sallied out in desperation to make her way to the White Oak Spring, with her infant in her arms, and a son, three or four years of age, following her. Afraid to pursue the trace, she entered the woods, and after running till she was nearly exhausted, she came at length to the trace. She determined to follow it at all hazards, and having advanced a few miles further, she met the elder Mr. Duree, with his wife, and youngest son, with their baggage, on their way to the new station. The melancholy tidings induced them, of course, to return. They led their horses into an adjoining canebrake, unloaded them, and regained the White Oak Spring fort before daylight.

It is impossible at this day to make a just impression of the sufferings of the pioneers about the period spoken of. The White Oak Spring fort in 1782, with perhaps one hundred souls in it, was reduced in August to three fighting white men —and I can say with truth, that for two or three weeks, my mother's family never unclothed themselves to sleep, nor were all of them, within the time, at their meals together, nor was any household business attempted. Food was prepared, and placed where those who chose could eat. It was the period when Bryaut's station was besieged, and for many days before and after that gloomy event, we were in constant expectation of being made prisoners. We made application to Col. Logan for a guard, and obtained one, but not until the danger was measureably over. It then consisted of two men only. Col. Logan did every thing in his power, as county lieutenant, to sustain the different forts—but it was not a very easy matter to order a married man from a fort where his family was, to defend some other—when his own was in imminent danger.

I went with my mother in January, 1783, to Logan's station to prove my father's will. He had fallen in the preceding July. Twenty armed men were of the party. Twenty-three widows were in attendance upon the court, to obtain letters of administration on the estates of their husbands who had been killed during the past year. My mother went to Col. Logan's, who received and treated her like a sister.

Diamond Cut Diamond.

When there is a scarcity of natural pigeons, sporting men by way of keeping their hands in, occasionally pluck one another. A rich case of this kind in which two of the fraternity, one a Southerner and the other a New Yorker, figured pretty conspicuously, occurred in this city last week. We give the facts as related to us; indeed they want no amplification. The whole sporting world of Gotham has had a pain in the side for several days past, in consequence of the paroxysms of laughter in which it was thrown by the denouement. We omit the names of the parties, but in other respects the statement may be relied on as full and faithful.

It appears that in the early part of last week Mr. ——, of South Carolina, an "upper crust" gambler, arrived in town, with plenty of the fluid, for the purpose of betting on the approaching race between Peytona and Fashion, and of picking up any thing verdant that might come in his way. Soon after landing from the Philadelphia boat he wended his way to a well known restaurat in Park Row, where blacklegs most do congregate, for the purpose of meeting some of his old acquaintances and making professional inquiries. He had just lighted his segar and was in the act of raising a glass of brandy and water to his lips, when the flash of a large jewel on the finger of one of the craft who was performing the same operation, arrested his attention.

"That's a fine diamond," exclaimed the Southerner, setting down his tumbler, and stooping forward to obtain a closer view of the jewel.

"Yes," remarked the other, carelessly—"it ought to be; I gave five hundred dollars for it, and got it cheap at that. I wish I had the value of it now though, for I got regularly cleaned out at ——'s, Barclay street, yesterday.

"What'll you take for it cash down," said the Southerner, who, like most of his tribe, was fond of showing bijouterie, and having a pocket full of rocks, felt remarkably self-complacent.

"Well," said the New York land shark, speaking slowly, and taking a puff at his segar, at every second word, "as I want money, and you are a pretty clever fellow, I don't care if I let you have it at four hundred and fifty dollars."

"Say four hundred, and it's a bargain."

"Well, as it's you, the half hundred dollars shant spoil a trade. You shall have it."

The ring was transferred and the money paid. By this time the parties had become the centre of a little knot of knowing ones, upon whose faces sat a sneering expression, which the Southerner, who like all gamblers, was a good physiognomist, perceived and did not relish. When the transaction was completed, his keen ear caught the sound of a sniggering whisper which ran round the little circle, and he at once concluded he was done. He showed no symptoms of suspicion, however, but called for champaigne, treated the company, declared himself delighted with the purchase, and bidding his friends good evening, left the place. Proceeding to the store of an eminent jeweller in Broadway, he placed the ring on the counter, and asked the value of "that brilliant." The jeweller looked at him and smiled. "It is paste," said he, "and worth about fifty cents."

"Have you a real stone about the same size and shape?" said the Southerner.

"I have," was the reply; and a beautiful table diamond, of which the mock stone seemed a *fac simile*, was produced.

The price was four hundred dollars. The Southerner then exclaimed that he wished to borrow it for a few days, and would leave the value in the jeweller's hands until it was returned, and pay twenty-five dollars for the use of it. The proposition was agreed to, the real diamond substituted for the counterfeit, and the Southerner left the store.

On the next evening he paid another visit to the restaurat, and found the old party assembled. They all began to quiz him; declaring that he had been regularly "sucked in;" that his ring was not worth a dollar, &c., the former owner of the trinket appearing to enjoy the joke more than the rest.

"Well, gentlemen," said the supposed dupe, with a self-sufficient air, "you may think what you please; I know it's a diamond. I've travelled some, and I'm not to be taken in so easy as you think for. I'll bet a hundred dollars this is a real brilliant."

The bet was taken up in an instant, and others offered to the amount of five or six hundred dollars more, all of which were promptly met by the Southerner. The stakes being put up, out sallied the sportsmen to find a jeweller. The first they questioned pronounced it a fine diamond, and worth from four to five hundred dollars; so said the next, and the next. The betters stood aghast!—it *was* a real diamond, and no mistake; and as the Southerner pocketed the "tin," he coolly observed: "*I told you, gentlemen, I had travelled some!*"

The following day he took the stone back to the jeweller of whom he had borrowed it, and had the composition counterfeit replaced in the ring, and in the evening he sought the restaurat for the third time. The same set were there, but looked crest-fallen. After joking with them for some time, our hero gravely addressed the cute gentleman from whom he had purchased the ring, after this fashion:

"Well, my dear fellow, I have had my laugh out of you; I don't want to rob you, and I don't want the ring. Marquand has offered me three hundred and fifty dollars for it; you shall have it for two hundred and fifty dollars, and you can go to him to-morrow if you like, and make a cool hundred out of it.

The offer was too tempting to be refused. The shark bit, and the Southerner received two hundred and fifty dollars worth of gold, and the sharper fifty cents worth of paste. The next morning the Carolinian was *non est inventus*; and the overreached sharper found lying on his table a beautiful note sealed with perfumed wax, and stamped with a figure of Mercury, the god of thieves. On removing the envelope, the note was found to contain only three words, viz: "Diamond cut Diamond."

This was a puzzle: but the first jeweller to whom our "sporting friend" showed the ring explained the mystery. The victim, unable to bear up against the ridicule brought down upon him by this *denouement*, has left town for a few weeks on urgent business.

College of Dental Surgery.

On the first Monday of November, the lectures of this Institution will commence. The professors are men of competent judgment, acquirements and experience, and I doubt not that they will acquit themselves creditably in their new relation to the science.

I have adverted two or three times to this subject, and regret that there appears so little interest manifested in it by my brother editors in Cincinnati. I suppose this results from their considering it simply a professional matter, in which the public at large have no direct interest. If so, it is a great mistake.

There are quacks in all professions, but in none are they so abundant as in dental operations, and the reason is obvious. There is no test apparent to the patient, which enables him to judge between a mere pretender and a man who understands his business. Hence, all around us we find men, who, having failed at making a subsistence in the practice of law or in retailing goods, or who have perhaps not been brought up regularly to any business, assume the practice of dentistry, to the irreparable injury of their patients. For all this there is no remedy except a regular education for this department of medical and surgical science, such as this College affords, and the evidence of it to the community in the diploma or certificate it issues.

The newly established *College of Dental Surgery* is actually a coadjutor to its neighbour, the *Ohio Medical College*, in which respect it deserves an equal share of patronage and support. It will, in the course of a few years, doubtless be felt equally influential and important, while the sphere of its operations must necessarily occupy a wider space.

Force of Habit.

In the days of my apprenticeship to the hardware business in Philadelphia, although quite young, I was salesman to our establishment. In that capacity I put up bills for the various western merchants of 1806, and of even later dates. But the lapse of forty years has made many changes in this mutable world of ours, and with the exception of *H. G. Phillips*, of Dayton; *Samuel Perry*, of our own city; *Jephthah Dudley*, of Frankfort, and *J. W. Tilford*, of Lexington, Ky., who are now all out of active business, the merchants of that day have passed off the scene of life.

Tilford and Dudley I have not seen for almost forty years, until Saturday, the 13th inst., when I made myself known to Col. Dudley, on my late visit to Frankfort. I found him at his door cutting a piece of pine shingle, the *very employment he was at forty years before, when I last saw him*

and bid him good bye, on his departure from Philadelphia. The Colonel assured me, however, that it was neither the *same knife nor the same shingle.*

The English Language.

Various have been the attempts to reduce to system, the orthography, and prosody of our language—all to little purpose.

Many and weighty are the embarrassments which the anomalies of pronunciation disfiguring the English language, inflict upon the luckless foreigner, in his attempts to master its rules.

I will give a specimen of analogies of this sort. Take and follow it out in its various pronunciations.

Bough	ow	as	cow.
Cough	off	as	doff.
Dough	ow	as	flow.
Hough	ock	as	lock.
Lough Youghiogany	} och	as	cochran.
Tough	uff	as	luff.
Fought	aw	as	law.
Through	oo	as	loo.
Thorough	u	as	hunt.
Hiccough	up	as	cup.

Here are eleven different sounds given to the same monosyllable. Is not this example at once, a comment and a satire on the labour of grammarians and lexicographers.

Koenke and his Organs.

My friend Koenke is, I find, still busy making Organs for the West. His last, is a splendid instrument of six stops, made for a Church at Lancaster, Ohio, which I would recommend all who delight in musical sounds, to examine at his shop on Williams street, north of the corporation line.

Koenke's only fault as an organ builder, is, that every instrument he turns out, excels its predecessor. This renders it difficult to determine when he will reach the *ne plus ultra* of excellence.

MARRIED.

On Sunday, the 21st., by the Rev. W. P. Strickland, Mr. ISRAEL WEAVER to Miss PHEBE JANE SMITH.

DIED.

On Tuesday, the 10th inst., Mr. JOHN R. CLINKINBEARD, in the 39th year of his age.

On Wednesday, the 17th inst., at the residence of her son, John Richards, Mrs. JANE DEE, aged 75 years.

On Thursday, the 18th inst., SAMUEL REAM, of Indianapolis, Ia.

On Friday, the 19th inst., at his residence in Storrs township, Mr. WILLIAM BICKHAM, merchant of this city, in the 46th year of his age.

CINCINNATI MISCELLANY.

CINCINNATI, OCTOBER, 1845.

Nuisances.

It has long been a settled fact, that Corporations are bodies without souls. Hence, we see individuals every day countenancing practices as a corporate body, which they personally disclaim and despise. If the members of our City Council could follow out the consequences of their legislation in their final results, it would materially affect their votes on many questions, and cover their faces with shame, if shame be left in their veins.

A few days since the City Council gave a circus company license to exhibit at the corner of Broadway and Fifth, for a series of nights. This is a region of family residences simply, and there re some ten or twelve houses of worship within gunshot of the spot. It might have been supposed that a neighbourhood in which the individuals resided patronsing such *moral and intellectual exercises*, would have been more appropriately selected for the convenience of all parties. No! Our Councilmen are friends to equal rights, and an establishment which up to eleven o'clock, and even beyond twelve o'clock, is making " night hideous " with yells and other noises, which might more appropriately come up from the bottomless pit, is placed where none of its atrons reside. What the effects of all this on ne health and comfort of the unhappy neighbours is, may be readily imagined. It is a simle fact, neither heightened by fancy " nor susceptible of being so," that there is an amiable lady dying of consumption, and whose dissolution may be momently expected, whose death ill have been hastened by these brutal orgies *censed* by the City Council.

Did I say licensed;—I retract the statement. The case is worse. The license has expired, and he circus is permitted to torment the living and he dying, without even the consolation to our ast and equitable City Solons that they have the money obtained at such a price, in the City treasury!!

All this is done in the name of *equal rights!*

The State Bank of Ohio.

It may be matter of interest to the business ublic to learn the names of the Branches of this nstitution and its officers, as the notes will soon rm the great body of our circulating medium. Ten Branches are at present organized. The otes of like denominations in all the Branches

are from the same plate, engraved by TOPPAN, CARPENTER & Co., of Cincinnati. Their general phraseology thus: " THE STATE BANK OF OHIO *will pay to bearer Five Dollars on demand at the* ————— *Branch in* —————
————— *Cashier.* ————— *President.*

The name of the Branch and its location are inserted with the pen All are signed by *G. Swan*, President of the Board of Control, and countersigned by the Cashiers of the respective Branches: as follows:

Franklin Branch in Cincinnati—T. M. Jackson, Cashier.

Mechanics' and Traders' Branch in Cincinnati —S. S. Rowe, Cashier.

Exchange Branch in Columbus—H. M. Hubbard, Cashier.

Franklin Branch in Columbus—James Espy, Cashier.

Merchants' Branch in Cleveland—Prentiss Dow, Cashier.

Chillicothe Branch in Chillicothe—J. S. Atwood, Cashier.

Xenia Branch in Xenia—F. F. Drake, Cashier.

Dayton Branch in Dayton—David Z. Pierce, Cashier.

Delaware Branch in Delaware—B. Powers, Cashier.

Jefferson Branch in Steubenville—D. Moodey, Cashier.

Miami University.

A pamphlet comprising the addresses delivered at the late inauguration of Professor M'Master, as President of the Miami University, at Oxford, Ohio, has been left on my table, by the publisher, I suppose. Cincinnati contributed no less than three addresses to the days service, one of which only appears in print—that of *Edward Woodruff*, Esq., one of its trustees, and if I mistake not, a graduate of that institution. *Rev. N. L. Rice*, and *J. W. Taylor* of the Cincinnati bar, delivered the others.

Mr. Woodruff's address evidences the good sense and sound judgment which characterises the writer. It abounds in valuable suggestions, of which a few follow:—

" My object is not to discourage the study of the ancient languages or lessen their value as a branch of classic learning; but rather to elevate the modern sciences and languages to their true importance. Any one who will examine the course of studies prescribed in most of the colleges and universities of the United States, will readily perceive that the study of the ancient classics receives much the greater share of attention, while the modern sciences and living languages, are matters of secondary consideration. If the one or the other must be neglected, either from the want of time or any other cause, let the ancients give way to the moderns."

"Another important advantage to be derived from a more general introduction of the modern sciences into the regular course of instruction, is, that they furnish new fields for the exercise of the powers of the mind, which exist in so many diversified forms, in different individuals. By elevating the sciences of agriculture, civil engineering, geology, political science, modern languages, and others of practical application, to their proper standard, so as to render them independent objects of honourable pursuit, it would greatly tend to equalize the genius and talent of the country, and prevent that unnatural and unprofitable rush which is constantly made into the ranks of law, medicine, and divinity. This immense mis-application of talent calls loudly for reform. Many who would within their appropriate spheres become highly useful members of society, often become mere *fungi* upon the body politic, wasting the best portion of their lives in slothful inactivity."

" The genius of the present age, differs essentially from that of classic antiquity. It is emphatically the age of money getting, or in one sense, the *golden age.* Almost every public and private action has for its end, pecuniary considerations, in some shape; and yet it is difficult to separate this feeling from those beneficial results which its influence exerts over the inventive faculties of man. It is said that knowledge is power, and yet we not unfrequently see that the power of money controls that of knowledge. It realizes, in no small degree, the idea of the archimedean lever. If indeed it were more liberally applied to useful purposes; if it were more frequently used in the endowment of colleges, and seminaries, and in furnishing them with libraries, philosophical apparatus, and the other appliances; if it were made subservient to the universal spread of knowledge and religion, it might indeed be considered a most substantial blessing. " The evils, however, consequent upon so inordinate a thirst for wealth, are its tendency to contract the expansive qualities of the heart and its abridgment of all the moral and social virtues. Yet with these acknowledged and obvious consequences before them, men still press on, even at the age of threescore years and ten, to the accumulation of still greater wealth; and, doubtless, it will always be more fashionable to censure the evil, than to take the lead in reforming it. To counteract so morbid an appetite, there is no better expedient than the cultivation of a literary taste; it expands and liberalizes all the better qualities of the head and heart; it is an accomplishment in society, a companion in solitude, a friend in adversity, and an ornament in old age."

I learn incidentally by this address three facts. That the *alumni* of the Miami University in the twentieth year of its existence, amount to three hundred and sixty-two, and that there are twenty-one chartered institutions of learning, nine of which are in successful operation, with an aggregate endowment of $1,500,000 yearly. The

whole annual attendance of students in all these does not exceed one thousand individuals.

The inaugural address of President M'Master, I shall not undertake to review. His Latin and Greek, are here paraded with a frequency which leads me to doubt his English scholarship, having made it a rule through life to distrust the pretensions of an author who shelters himself continually from the scrutiny of English readers, behind the thick shades of learned languages.

Seriously, if the Professor's intellect is not clearer in his Latin and Greek, than in his English, there is nothing lost to the popular reader, for his pedantry is insufferable, even in a preceptor by trade. I fear that Dr. M'Master is not the man to preside over this University, which the character of the west and of the age in which we live demands; that he wants the grand preeminent qualification, *good* sense, without which all other qualifications are of little value, and which, in the language of the poet, is

"Although no science, fairly worth the seven."

The Mother and her Family.

Philosophy is rarely found. The most perfect sample I ever met, was an old woman, who was apparently the poorest and most forlorn of the human species; so true is the maxim which all profess to believe, and none act upon invariably, viz., that all happiness does not depend on outward circumstances. The wise woman to whom I have alluded, walks to Boston, a distance of twenty or thirty miles, to sell a bag of brown thread and stockings, and then patiently walks back again with her little gains. Her dress, though tidy, is a grotesque collection of " shreds and patches," coarse in the extreme.

" Why don't you come down in a wagon?" said I, when I observed she was wearied with her long journey.

" We han't got any horse," she replied; " the neighbours are very kind to me, but they can't spare their'n, and it would cost as much to hire one as all my thread would come to."

" You have a husband—don't he do any thing for you?"

" He is a good man—he does all he can, but he's a cripple and an invalid. He reels my yarn and mends the children's shoes. He's as kind a husband as a woman need have."

" But his being a cripple is a heavy misfortune to you," said I.

" Why, ma'am, I don't look upon it in that light," replied the thread woman. " I consider that I have great reason to be thankful that he never took to any bad habits."

" How many children have you?"

" Six sons and five daughters, ma'am."

" Six sons and five daughters! What a family for a poor woman to support!"

" It's a family, surely, ma'am; but there ain't one of 'em that I'd be willing to lose. They are all as healthy children as need to be—all willing to work and all clever to me. Even the littlest boy when he gets a cent now and then for doing an errand is sure to bring it to me."

" Do your daughters spin your thread?"

" No, ma'am; as soon as they are big enough they go out to service, as I don't want to keep them always delving for me; they are always willing to give me what they can; but it's right and fair that they should do a little for themselves. I do all my spinning after the folks are a-bed."

"Don't you think you should be better off, if you had no one but yourself to provide for?"

"Why no, ma'am, I don't. If I had'nt been married I should always had to work as I could, and now I can't do more than that. My children are a great comfort to me, and I look forward to the time when they'll do as much for me as I have done for them."

Here was true philosophy! I learned a lesson from that poor woman which I shall not soon forget.

The Miami Valley Settlements.

It is hardly possible for those who are now living in Cincinnati, in the enjoyment of every comfort and luxury which money can procure, to form any notion of the privations which were suffered by the hardy settlers of the west, the pioneers of the Miami Valleys among others. Fifty-five years ago the condition of the great thoroughfares to the west—of the route across the Allegheny Mountains especially—was such as to forbid taking by the emigrants any articles but those of indispensible necessity, for a six horse road wagon, at a slow gait, could not take more than what would now be considered, over a McAdamized road, a load for two horses. When the pioneer westward had reached Redstone or Wheeling, the difficulties of transportation were not much lessened. There were no wagon roads through the intermediate country, if the hostility of the implacable savage had permitted traversing the route by land in safety; and the family boats which carried the settlers down were so encumbered with wagons, horses, cows, pigs, &c., as to have little room for any thing else but a few articles of family housekeeping of the first necessity. On reaching their destination, cabins had to be erected, the land cleared and cultivated, and the crop gathered in, in the presence, as it were, of the relentless savage, who watched every opportunity of destroying the lives of the settlers, and breaking up the lodgments as fast as made. In the meantime, supplies of food not yet raised on the improvement, had to be obtained in the woods from hunting, which in most cases was a constant exposure of life to their Indian enemies. Under these circumstances some general idea may be conceived of the sufferings and privations which those endured, who formed the van guard of civilization, and prepared the way for the present generation to enjoy the fruit of past labours and sufferings. But it is not so easy, without some specifications such as I shall furnish here, to realise the nature and extent of the privations of individuals who, in many cases, abandoned comfortable homes and the enjoyment of civilized life, at the call of duty. Especially was this the case in respect to several of the pioneer mothers.

A few notes from the recollections of one of the survivors, probably the only one of the party who landed with Major Stites at Columbia, a venerable lady of seventy-five, whose family have borne a conspicuous part in the civil, political, military, and religious history of the Miami Valley, will possess my readers of a more distinct idea of these sacrifices and privations, than they could otherwise acquire.

My informant was born and brought up in New York, her parents being in prosperous circumstances. Her husband, who was a surveyor, had been for some time in delicate health, and concluded to accompany Major Stites to his settlement at the mouth of the Little Miami. At this place, where they landed on the 18th Nov., 1788, and to which the settlers gave the name of Columbia, two or three block houses were first erected for the protection of the women and children, and log cabins were built without delay for occupation by the several families. The boats in which they came down from Limestone being broken up, served for floors, doors, &c., to these rude buildings. Stites and his party had riven out clapboards while they were detained at Maysville, which being taken down to Columbia, enabled the settlers to cover their houses without delay. The fact that the Indians were generally gathered to Fort Harmar, at the mouth of Muskingum, for the purpose of making a treaty with the whites, contributed also to the temporary security of the new settlement. Little, however, could be done beyond supplying present sustenance for the party from the woods. Wild game was abundant, but the bread stuffs they took with them soon gave out; and supplies of corn and salt were only to be obtained at a distance, and in deficient quantities, and various roots taken from the indigenous plants, the bear grass especially, had frequently to be resorted to as articles of food. When the spring of 1789 opened, their situation promised gradually to improve. The fine bottoms on the Little Miami had been long cultivated by the savages, and were found mellow as ashheaps. The men worked in divisions, one half keeping guard with their rifles while the others worked, changing their employments morning and afternoon. My informant had brought out a looking glass boxed up, from the east, and the case being mounted on a home made pair of rockers, served for the first cradle in the settlement. It had previously been set across a barrel to do duty as a table. Individuals now living in Cincinnati were actually rocked during their infancy in sugar troughs.

It was with difficulty horses could be preserved from being stolen, by all the means of protection to which the settlers could resort. In the family to which this lady belonged, the halter chains of the horses were passed through between the logs and fastened to stout hooks on the inside. But neither this precaution nor securing them with hobbles would always serve to protect horses from the savages. On one occasion a fine mare with her colt had been left in the rear of the house in a small enclosure. The mare was taken off by Indians, they having secured her by a stout buffalo tug. It appears they had not noticed the colt in the darkness of the night. As they rode her off, the colt sprang the fence after the mare, and made such a noise galloping after, that supposing themselves pursued, they let the mare go lest she should impede their escape, and the family inside of the house knew nothing of the danger to which they had been exposed until the buffalo tug told the night's adventure. On another occasion, several families who had settled on the face of the hill near where Col. Spencer afterwards resided, at a spot called Morristown, from one Morris, the principal individual in the settlement, had hung out clothes to dry. Early in the evening a party of Indians prowling around made a descent and carried off every piece of clothing left out, nor was the loss discovered until the families were about to retire for the night. Pursuit was made and the trail followed for several miles, when arriving at the place where the savages had encamped, it was found deserted, the enemy being panic struck, and having abandoned all to effect their escape. The plunder was recovered, but not until the Indians had raveled out the coverlets to make belts for themselves. But many of the settlers encountered more serious calamities than loss of property. James Seward had two boys massacred by the savages, and James Newell, one of the most valuable of the settlers at Columbia, shared a similar fate. Hinkle and Covalt, two of the settlers on Round Bottom, a few miles up the Miami, were shot dead in front of their own cabins, while engaged hewing logs.

In November, 1789, a flood on the Ohio occurred of such magnitude as to overflow the lower part of Columbia to such a height as first to drive the soldiers at one of the block houses up into the loft and then out by the gable to their boat, by which they crossed the Ohio to the hills on the opposite side. One house, only, in Columbia, remained out of water. The loss of property, valuable in proportion to its scarcity and the difficulty of replacing it, may be readily conjectured. Honour to the memories of those who at such cost, won as an inheritance for their successors the garden spot of the whole world.

Stove and Grate Manufacture.

A visit to W. & R. P. Resor's Foundry, on Plum street, has put me in possession of various interesting statistics, on a very important and extensive branch of Iron Castings—the manufacture of Stoves, which forms an indispensible class of foundry operations, as well as a distinct department of business in the sale of the article.

There are some thirty iron foundries in Cincinnati o various grades of importance, being nearly three times the number in existence at the census of 1840. And I shall confine my remarks at present to the operations of those engaged in the stove and grate manufacture, leaving the general casting business for a future article.

There are twelve foundries engaged in the manufacture exclusively, principally, or partially of these articles, two of which make grates entirely, and two others make stoves to a more or less extent, while their usual and more important business is general casting. These establishments are W. & R. P. Resor, Wolff & Brothers, Goodhue & Co., French & Winslow, Ball & Davis, Andrews, Haven & Co., Miles Greenwood, David Root, Horton & Baker, Bevan & Co., O. G. De Groff and Thomas S. Orr.

Having been familiar for years with the business of Messrs. Resor, which is probably the heaviest one of the number, I shall reserve what details I have to make on the subject as applying more especially to their operations, and close these statistics with a general view of the stove casting business at large.

Resors' establishment, including tenements for fifteen families, occupies a space of ground two hundred feet square. They have additional ground for depositing coke across Plum street. The blowing apparatus, with chimney and facing mills, are driven by a steam engine of eight horse power. The blowing apparatus was put up by Messrs. Holabird & Burns, and consists of a cylinder thirty inches in diameter and thirty-two inch stroke, and is capable of melting with ease three tons per hour with two cupolas, which are used, taking the melted iron from each alternately. The finishing shops and storing rooms are in 3 three story brick buildings of fifty-four feet front by seventy feet in depth. There are now, and have been during the year past, employed seventy-three hands, who make on the average one hundred and eighty stoves and three tons hollow ware weekly, or an annual aggregate of one thousand tons or two million pounds castings. Six to seven tons pig metal are melted daily in the establishment, and its consumption of coal exceeds eighteen thousand bushels. Eleven additional hands are employed over the sale rooms in trimming, blacking, packing, &c., the stoves for maket.

The whole of this prodigious amount of melting is through daily in three hours. No castings are made here but for the proprietors' own use or sales. The firm pays out about $500 in wages per week, and since the first of last January, the hands are paid off every Monday, to the mutual advantage of employed and employers. No running accounts are kept in the establishment. One statistic, not exactly in the casting line, I will add by stating that there is a child born on the premises every month in the year, for several years past.

Messrs. Resor were the first to introduce the neat and light patterns of stoves and hollow ware now so universally prevalent, and to demonstrate to others that stoves could be made in Cincinnati for the west, cheaper as well as of better materials—the pig iron of the Scioto region under the hot blast process—than at any other point on the Ohio.

Two thirds of the stoves made at these foundries are what are termed cooking stoves. For these there is an increasing demand, which will not slacken until every farmer in the land is supplied, economy in labour as respects providing wood, being as important to the husbandman as economy in the purchase of that article is to the city resident. There are not less than forty-five thousand stoves manufactured yearly in Cincinnati, thirty thousand of which are regular cooking stoves of various patterns and construction. The value of these articles, including the grate operations is five hundred and twelve thousand dollars annually, a business and product heavier than any city in the United States can exhibit, unless it be Albany and perhaps Troy, the great fountains of supply in this line for New York and the New England States. There are four hundred and thirty-five hands employed in these twelve establishments, on stoves, grates and hollow ware.

CORRESPONDENCE.

The Jews in America.

Mr. C. Cist:

In a former number I promised, if it should be considered interesting to your readers, to continue an article respecting the statistics, locations, and reminiscences of "God's ancient people the Israelites,"—extending the view to the whole nation dispersed throughout the world. It is well ascertained that previous to 1816, the Jewish people were not known to have located in the Mississippi Valley; and for several years subsequent, they were considered as a strange sight; —but it was necessary to the 'fulfilment of Prophecy, that the "dispersed of Israel" should inhabit every clime. There are supposed at this time to be in the city and its environs, about two thousand five hundred Israelites; and it is a matter of notoriety, that where the Jewish people are well received, that nation or city becomes happy and prosperous, and vice versa, that country or people who persecute and plunder them, are punished in an exemplary manner. What has been the end of the enemies of Israel? "That they perish for ever!" I need not quote historical reminiscences! There are some singular and remarkable facts appertaining to this people in all their locations; in being good and peaceable citizens, seeking the welfare and prosperity of the country in which they reside; not anxious to spread the tenets of their religion among the nations; but looking forward to the time when "all shall know the truth." According to their numbers, less crime is committed among them than any other class of people. *Drunkards* and *paupers* are seldom known among them: they are cleanly and abstemious in their habits and diet. In one of the congregations of this city, composed of more than eight hundred persons of all ages, there has not been a death during the past year! Very few of the towns in the west but what have more or less of them located at this period, and increased numbers are constantly emigrating from Europe. Celebrated writers in making up statistics, have been constantly underrating the numbers of this people; and it has been generally supposed there were not more than four millions in the world; at the same time rating their numbers in the United States at only five thousand. As I proceed I shall prove to the satisfaction of your readers, that they are more numerous than in the most prosperous period of their history. In this number I shall merely allude to their settlement in America. The first settlement of Jews in the Western Hemisphere, was at the Island of Cayenne, under the protection of the Dutch, in 1559. The French captured it in 1664. The Dutch inhabitants and Jews were obliged to quit. The latter went to Surinam, where they became a thriving settlement, having the full enjoyment and free exercise of their religion, rites and customs, guarantied to them by the British Government. In 1667, Surinam was taken by the Dutch, the privileges of the Jews confined to them, with all the rights of Dutch born subjects. They are now a considerable and highly respectable portion of the inhabitants of Surinam. In 1670, Jamaica and other West India Islands were visited, and considerable settlements of Jews formed, where they are now residing, being numerous, wealthy and respectable; enjoying all the privileges of citizens under the British Government, whose Colonies consequently have flourished. In 1683 the Jews were ordered to quit the French Colonies; and in 1685, all Jews found in the French Colonies were seized and their properties confiscated. What has been the result? Who has got the Canadas? And what has become of San Domingo? In 1641, a considerable number of Jews who were banished from Spain and Portugal, settled in the Brazils, formed plantations, and built towns and villages; and were protected from the Spaniards by the Dutch. In 1654, on the Portuguese obtaining possession of the Brazils, the Jews were ordered to quit, their plantations and houses confiscated; but they very *indulgently* granted them the privilege to carry away their personal property, providing a fleet of ships to carry them wherever they chose.

It is supposed that a small portion of them landed about that time at Newport, Rhode Island, and at New Amsterdam, (now New York.) Soon after that period they erected a Synagogue in Newport, the first in the thirteen Colonies. The congregation throve for about seventy or eighty years, when New York having overcome its rival in commercial pursuits, Newport declined, and the Israelites gradually withdrew to the rising city of New York, and not one family remained to protect its lonely Synagogue and burial ground. A sufficient sum was left by a legacy of the late Mr. Touro, to keep and constantly repair them, until at some future period Israelites might congregate there. This is faithfully performed by the corporation of the city. The Israelites in New York have flourished exceedingly. They have become numerous, wealthy, and respectable; nearly numbering at this time, fifteen thousand, having eight Synagogues. In 1733, forty Jews arrived in Savannah, Georgia, from London, where they and other emigrants have congregated to this day. They are highly respectable. In 1750, a congregation was founded in Charleston, which has gradually increased and become very numerous. They are many of them wealthy and respectable, having filled some of the first offices in the City and State of South Carolina. It is well known that during the War of Independence, the Jews were very active and patriotic in their exertions for their adopted country. We may also state that the late Col. David Franks, confidential aid to General Washington, was a member of the Jewish nation and religion. Since the Revolutionary War, Jewish Congregations have been established at various places in the United States and British possessions, viz: New Orleans, Mobile, Louisville, St. Louis, Little Rock, Cincinnati, Cleveland, Xenia, Albany, Troy, Buffalo, New Haven, Baltimore, Philadelphia, Richmond and Norfolk, Va.; also at Quebec and Montreal, Canada, and St. Johns, New Brunswick. There are several other locations in the U. S. not recollected. There is one important fact respecting the Jewish nation, more especially amongst those who reside in America. I have conversed and been in contact with many thousands of my brother Israelites, and have yet to meet the first *one* ignorant of reading and writing! I shall conclude this part of my subject with a general statement of the number of their Synagogues and population in America, as far as can be ascertained.

	Syn.	Pop.
New England States, - -	2	1,500
States of N. York and N. Jersey,	12	18,000
" " Pennsylvania and Delaware,	5	4,000
" " Maryland and D. Columbia,	2	2,500
" " Virginia and Kentucky,	3	3,500
" " North and South Carolina,	4	5,000
" " Georgia and Alabama,	2	2,000
" " Louisiana and Florida,	2	3,000
" " Missouri and Mississippi,	1	1,500
" " Arkansas and Texas, -	1	1,000
" " Illinois and Indiana, -	0	1,500
" " Ohio and Michigan, -	6	4,000
British Possessions, - - -	4	2,500
West India Islands, - - -	12	14,000
State of Mexico, - - -	0	1,000
States of Columbia and Central America, - - - -	0	1,000
State of South America, - -	2	8,000
	58	74,000

Cincinnati, Sept. 22, 1845.   J.

Excuses.

"Who broke this pitcher?" asked the master of the house of his lady. "It is not *broke*, my dear, it is only *cracked*." Some months afterwards he found it in the closet in fragments. "Who broke this pitcher?" he again asked. "Why that pitcher was *broke* long ago; it has been cracked more than four months."

This was a Cincinnati excuse, but, as the almanack makers say, will answer for any other meridian in our country, and in some beyond its limits. It is accordingly published for the benefit of those who have not ingenuity enough to invent excuses of their own.

Cultivation of the Grape.

The following communication addressed by the writer to the Cincinnati Horticultural Society, will be found one of the most valuable articles on the subject to which it relates, that has ever appeared in print.

CINCINNATI, Sept. 26, 1845.

Mr. President:

Upon referring to some memorandums of my father, I find amongst others, the following account kept of the produce of the vineyard since 1837. As a number of our members are cultivating the vine, I thought it would be interesting, as it is difficult to obtain a statement of the kind, kept minutely for a series of years.

It shows the actual produce, and the certainty of the crop before any other fruit in this latitude, and the difference between the Catawba and Isabella, as to the yield and certainty. The Isabella having borne a first rate crop for nine successive years, the Catawba failing occasionally from rot and the attack of insects.

The vineyard has a southern exposure, fronting on the Ohio River, was planted with rooted plants in 1834, and contained at that time seventeen hundred and seventy-five vines, placed in rows four feet apart and three feet distance in the row—the ground being previously trenched, and the stones taken out to the depth of two feet.

In the fall of 1837 the first crop was picked as follows:—164 bushels of Grapes, from which was made 667 gallons of Wine. At this time there was 1125 Isabella and Cape vines yielding 113 bushels, making 469 gallons, and 650 Catawba yielding 51 bushels, making 198 gallons.
1838—Vintage, Sept. 10th, produce 327 gallons.
1839   "   "   5th   "   440   "
1840   "   "   20, Isabella 260
                        Catawba 45—305 galls.
This year (1840) most of the Catawba rotted on the vines. From this time there were twenty-three hundred vines, about one half of each kind.
1841—Vintage, Sept. 15, Catawba 237
                        Isabella 275—512 galls.
1842   "   "   12, Catawba 166
                        Isabella 319—485 "
1843   "   "   15, Catawba 250
                        Isabella 288—538 "
1844   "   "   12, Catawba 108
                        Isabella 306—414 "
1845   "   "   9, Catawba 349
                        Isabella 283—632 "
About one-eighth of the Catawba Grapes were destroyed by bees and other insects after ripening. The quantity eaten by three families is not taken into the account.

The ground has always been thoroughly hoed in the spring and kept free from weeds; never manured until last winter, when the ground was covered and dug in, in the spring; and from the result this season it would pay well, as the vines are in better condition than they ever were, after yielding a heavy crop.

The vines have been trained to stakes, and the bearing wood cut out, after having borne one season, leaving two shoots, trained the same season, one to form the bearing hoop or bow, and the other cut to two eyes, to propagate wood for the next year, the vine never having but the hoop and the two eyes left for fruit, each year's growing at the same time.

This year the ends of the vines have been nipped and the suckers taken out four different times. The following estimate I have made from what it has cost this year, and is not far from the actual expense, although the labour has been done by the hands doing the other work on the farm, and in making wine extra hands were always employed. By planting cuttings, and preparing the ground by subsoil ploughing when it can be done, would lessen the expense. The price is what the wine was sold at from the press this season, and is a low estimate:

ESTIMATE.

2300 Vines, at 6c.,	$138.00
2300 Poles, at 2c.,	46.00
1000 do. replaced,	20.00
Trenching ground and planting,	80.00
Manuring last fall,	30.00
Two months work each year nine years,	225.00
Extra work in making wine,	150.00
Interest on investment before crop,	15.00
Cr.,	$704.00
By 4306 gallons Wine, at 75c.,	$3229.50
	$2525.50

The expense of cultivation previous to the first crop is not accounted for, nor is the press, casks, &c.; but the actual expense of cultivating an acre of grapes, when persons are hired to attend to other work, would not amount to but very little, as but a short time is required to attend to clearing the vines during the season.

Yours respectfully,
WM. RESOR.

From the Cincinnati Herald.
Medical.

There is for sale at Robinson & Jones', 109 Main street, Cincinnati, a mailable publication of some hundred pages, on the subject of Consumption of the Lungs, by W. Hall, A. M. M. D., of New Orleans, who has an office in this city during the summer. As tubercular disease is estimated to destroy one in six in civilized society, a book on this subject is more or less interesting to all. The Preface is short, and explains the design of the publication.

" The design of the following pages is to encourage such as have Consumption, or are threatened with it, to use in time those means which have saved others, and may save them.

" The Author, both before and since visiting Europe, for professional purposes, has met with the most gratifying success, and hopes to place within the reach of many whom he may never see, the means of cure.

" Difficult terms are avoided, that the most common reader may easily comprehend all that is important to be understood."

The main points stated are that—Consumption of the Lungs is a disease which admits of a perfect and permanent cure.

That it is curable in its last and worst stages

That these opinions are, and have been advocated by the most distinguished physicians of the last half century.

That it is as susceptible of cure as Bilious Fever.

That like Cholera, when taken during the premonitory symptoms, it is manageable; and less so, as the symptoms progress.

That it is not only curable, but that it can be cured in different ways; the principles of cure, however, remaining the same.

That sea voyages more frequently kill than cure.

That going to the South for lung diseases, or to a warmer climate, is a useless, injurious and fatal practice.

That, under named conditions, a cold climate is preferable to a warm one.

The nature, causes and symptoms of the disease are stated in familiar language. All the remarks are founded on one hundred and fifty consecutive cases, treated by Doctor Hall with singular success. It is not pretended to offer a specific for the disease, or to cure every case. The great point seems to be, to make the reader understand what are the premonitory symptoms of the disease, and to induce him to make a prompt effort for their removal; and encouragement is given to make an effort in the very last stage. It may with great truth be said, that every class in society is interested in the topics presented, for who has not lost a friend by this ruthless disease? Who is exempt from it?

Obituary.

The death of John H. Jones, a young and promising member of the Cincinnati Bar, on Thursday last, in the 22d year of his age, seems to call for something more than a passing notice.

Mr. J. was a young man of fine mind and bid fair for usefulness and distinction in society. "None knew him but to love him, nor named him but to praise." That such individuals should be taken away in the bud of their usefulness, while hundreds of no imaginable use to society survive, is one of those inscrutable dispensations of Providence, which are sore trials to near and dear friends.

Heaven takes the good, too good on earth to stay,
And leaves the bad, too bad to take away.

As regards the deceased, his friends have the best evidences of his preparation for future existence, in his possession of the Christian's hope, and his exemplification of the Christian's life.

To Readers.

The article on the Jews in America, is worthy of all confidence, the writer having ample opportunities of being conversant with the whole subject. I might assign another reason, however, for that community leaving Newport, R. I., than my correspondent gives. There is an old proverb "That a Jew can make a living in any part of Europe but Scotland, or America, but among the Yankees." Hence there are Jews neither among the Scotch nor New Englanders,

either class being the closest dealing people in the world, the other excepted.

Independently of the statistics, which are of deep interest, there are many singular details in "J.'s" statement, which should commend it to the reader's notice.

Early Jails.

In the last volume of the Advertiser, I spoke of the character of our early jails. *McClean*, one of the first turnkeys, was in the habit of getting drunk, and when he got into a spree, turned in and gave the whole batch of prisoners, whether such for debt or crime, a flogging all round, by way I suppose, of asserting his authority. The following document of those days speaks of other abuses:

OCTOBER 10th, 1807.

Sir,—We take this opportunity to inform you that Mr. Wheeler does not attend to his business here, as I expect, for I do not know the rules of keeping the jail; but Mr. Wheeler is absent from morning till night, and locks the keys in the cupboard, and takes the cupboard key with him, and we cant have nothing regular. When we speak to him about it he answers very abruptly and pays no attention. And in case of fire we cannot think ourselves safe or done justice by no means: And we hope you will not let these lines be known to the jailor, for it might cause disturbance between us and him, but that you will take these premises to your serious consideration, and have affairs better conducted, &c.

EVI MARTIN,
THOMAS COULTER,
JAMES HADLOCK,
JAMES NICHOLS.

To the Rev. Mr. Aaron Goforth, Sheriff, Cincinnati.

I suppose it would be difficult for a prisoner, under any circumstances, to consider his jailor an angel of light, unless he came to announce to him his deliverance; but irresponsible authority is subject to abuse, and I have seen enough of jails and penitentiaries as a grand juror and a visiter, to satisfy me that they are worthy of having been invented by the Great Spirit of Evil, whose malignity against the human race might well find gratification in the miseries they inflict and the corruption they generate. And I should devote my energies to the abolition of the whole system, and the adoption of colonising for crime by the State of Ohio, if unhappily and unwisely our State Constitution did not prohibit the measure.

MARRIED.

At St. Paul's Church, on the 30th inst., by the Rev. George D. Gillespie, Mr. John M. Huntington, of the City of New York, to Miss Jenette H., daughter of Horace Canfield, Esq., of this city.

DIED.

On Monday, the 29th inst., Ellen Amanda, only daughter of Willard and Rebecca S. Nichols, aged 22 months.

On same day, Mrs. Eliza Ann Chase, wife of Salmon P. Chase, aged 23 years and 10 months.

Conveniences of Side-Walks.

There is an article going the rounds of the press on the conveniences of a dish kettle, as follows:

"You want nothing but a dish kettle," said an an old housewife in the back woods, to her daughter who had just got married. "Why, when your father and I commenced, I had nothing but a dish kettle. I used to boil my coffee in it, and pour it into a pitcher, then boiled my potatoes in it, and set them on a warm plate, while I stewed up the meat in it, and always after a meal I fed the pigs out of the dish kettle. You can do a great deal with a dish kettle, Sally, if you are only a mind to."

It might be thought that this is carrying to its full extent the principle of putting one article to as many uses as possible, and that nothing can therefore surpass the convenience of this remarkable kitchen appendage. But we can put other things to equally accommodating purposes in Cincinnati. I refer now to our city side-walks, in its business regions.

What the original design of side-walks was, on Main street, for example, can only be matter of conjecture. They might have been, as they probably were, designed as a substitute and improvement to the boat gunnels which once formed the path-ways from the mouth of Main street to the hill at Third street. But whatever was the original purpose, they are now made to serve as many uses as the remarkable *dish kettle*, if not more.

In a walk from the river up Main street, the other day, I noticed the following "conveniences" of side-walks:

1st. Retail stores for jewelry, &c. This is a great saving to all hands, as it enables the purchaser to see what he wants at a glance; and the seller to get clear of store rent. One such, for example, is nearly in front of Mr. Joseph Alexander.

2d. Warerooms to open goods. Such as *Trevor, Woodruff & Reeves'* auction establishment. Here boxes may be opened without being in the way—of the proprietors. If a coat has an incision by an awkward blow from a hatchet, or a lady's dress torn by a straggling nail; or the passer by has his boots ruined by the operations of a saw, the victim may console himself with the reflection that it is all for the benefit of trade, and that some one of the many customers who buy at that store stand ready to make good his or her loss at fair prices.

3d. Another purpose of side-walks is to display the amount of a merchant's sales, and thus form a species of permanent and costless advertisements of his goods. Such a display I found at the door of Messrs. D. Root & Co., in stoves, grates, &c.

4th. Our Hebrew brethren, on Main street, who sell ready made clothing, find a different use—namely, to make a parlor or a drawing room of the side-walks. Here chairs are in rows for themselves and friends, and the whole air is redolent with the fumes of the cigar, and musical with the pressing invitation of "step in and see what you want," as the *subject* passes by. D. Spatz & Co. are an example of this nature.

5th. They form a counting room or store, where the merchant has no other, spacious enough. Here goods are marked, or invoiced, or packed, as the case may be. *Boylan & Co.*, for example.

6th. Lastly, where awnings are kept they form admirable shelters to the public in time of rain, and shady places in the heat of summer,—where Mrs. Smith rests with a basket or two at her feet, while she holds a deeply interesting colloquy with Mrs. Brown, who has probably a basket on each arm, to ascertain for mutual benefit the state of health of the "*old man*," or the "*darters*," or the "*byes*" of either party, which blocks up the passage long enough to give respite and rest to the weary footsteps of the business man on his way home fsom the bank or the post office.

The awning posts answer another valuable purpose, namely—to fasten horses to; and the side-walk affords at the same time a convenient stall where they may stand without being in the way of drays or wagons on the streets.

Out of the centres of business the side-walks serve other purposes also. Those sufficiently level for use, are chalked into various occult mathematical figures and horoscopes, such as Euclid never saw, or wizard never cast, with the design of playing *marbles* or *hopscot*. On ground sloping sufficiently for the purpose, the side-walks also are improved during the season of snow and ice, with hand sleds by the boys of Cincinnati. I say improved, for the foot-way is made so smooth as sometimes to enable a passenger to take but one step from the head to the foot of the hill, and get forward at the rate of a mile in two minutes, on his way into the business part of the city.

As the old lady *might have said*, "You can make a great many uses of a side walk as well as of a dish kettle."

Riches.

Almost all men desire to be rich. The exceptions are so few that they incur the imputation of affecting to undervalue what they cannot obtain, as the fox contemptuously spoke of the grapes as sour which were beyond his reach.

Yet there is no plainer proposition than that happiness is independent of wealth; and in the case of extreme wealth incompatible with it. John Jacob Astor's millions afford him his living, and do no more towards it, than the mere hundreds or thousands they possess, do to less wealthy individuals. He has innumerable cares and anxieties about his estate from which the men of the world are exempt. How would you like to take care of his large estate for your victuals and clothes? Yet this is all *he* gets. But you have nothing laid up for old age, and your children may be beggars. Not half as likely as his sons, let me tell you. Here is a decrepid old man, nearly bent double with age, and so feeble that it requires two servants to support his feeble steps as he takes his walk, or rather hobble, from the door of his dwelling to the next corner. He is nearly blind, and absolutely deaf, I understand, and his senses of taste and smell are nearly gone. What enjoyment are his millions to him? Would you barter health, youth, strength, and activity of mind and body with his infirmities, and take his wealth into the exchange? What do you envy in his possessions that the man poorer than yourself does not in yours? The rich man would give money for your appetite, as you would for that which hard labour earns.

I know a man in Cincinnati whose daily bread is supplied by his daily labour; and yet, in my standard of wealth and enjoyment, is one of the happiest and richest men in the place. If he wishes to relax from toil, he lounges in his friend Longworth's garden, eyes the beautiful shrubbery, or scents its perfumes with a sensation of exquisite enjoyment which its owner has long since lost. He contemplates the statuary or the paintings of the hospitable proprietor, with all the interest and delight which novelty imparts, and secretly feels that while the trouble and expense of keeping up such an establishment devolves on the owner, it is done all for his sake and that of hundreds in his circumstances. If he walks the streets a friend in more opulent circumstances than himself passes by in his barouche: he jumps in if he feels disposed to enjoy a ride. The gratification the owner knows, and remembers only among the things that were. The pleasurable excitement of the drive is his, the trouble and cost of maintaining the equipage another's. What wealth or luxury are to every man after the first relish is gone, may be summed up briefly as a possession, which, while it does not confer happiness in its enjoyment, distresses you in its loss.

City Solons.--Gallery of Portraits.--No. 2.

My present subject is a clear headed and sensible man, who understands his own interests well, and, of course, ought to understand those of the public,—as he does in a great measure.

He is excellent on a committee, but having been looked up to by his acquaintances in private colloquy, has acquired quite a taste for making speeches at the board. I do not accuse him of doing so for display, but place him in the same category with *Edmund Burke*, who did not desire a man's vote even when ready to give it, without first making himself sensible it ought to follow his; and as Goldsmith characterised him—

"Who still went on refining,
And thought of convincing while they thought of dining."

No. 2 is an old member, and if report has not done him injustice, has had as much influence with his successors as with his original and present colleagues, I suppose from the fact that he has been for years a lobby member of the board.

Councilman Griffin once characterized himself as the lock chain of the Council, to check a too rapid progress when they were going hill, as he thought. Number 2 is his successor in this respect in the present board.

The subject of this portrait is a pleasant, good humoured and intelligent citizen. Having a keen perception of the ludicrous, as well as a cute knowledge of human nature, he delights in *boring* appropriate cases; but as is common in such individuals, cannot himself bear to be *bored*. A diverting circumstance occurred in respect to him, a few days since, which I must relate.

The SONS OF LIGHT, who are just finishing their fine Hall at the northeast corner of Third and Walnut streets, while projecting that edifice, felt themselves short of means. As one resource, they obtained subscriptions in work to the building, a liberal one from our friend among the rest. Still they were likely to fall short; and a suggestion being made in the building committee, to call upon members of the Order among our Hebrew citizens, for money on loan subscriptions, as their Christian brethren had already been, one of the board expressed his doubts whether they would realise anything from the Jews. This led *Elam P. Langdon* to remark, that he thought differently, for there was Brother ———, (Number 2,) who had already subscribed several hundred dollars. Mr. L. thus expressed himself, being under an impression that our friend was of that nation, having probably been led into the error from his being a particular friend of *Rabbi Jonas*. The mistake was of course matter of great merriment with the party; but it was a sore joke to our friend, who could not be induced to believe it a mistake, and for weeks was not able to bear the least hint on the subject.

First Ward--Cincinnati.

I have commenced my annual enumeration of the buildings of Cincinnati. That of the First Ward follows.

There are 17 public buildings, and 828 dwellings, shops, store houses, mills and offices—Total 845. Of these 3 are stone, 530 bricks, and 312 frames.

The public buildings are two fire engine houses, an observatory, two banks, theatre, the seminary *soeurs de notre dame*, a district school house, and the post office, with nine churches, to wit—Christ Church, on Fourth street; the Wesley Chapel, on Fifth st.; Welsh Churches, on Harrison and Lawrence sts.; Disciples Church, on Sycamore; Jews Synagogue, on Broadway; Pilgrim's Church, on Lock street, and Bethel and True Wesleyan Churches—coloured. Of these the church at the corner of Lock and Fifth streets, and an engine house at the corner of Ludlow and Symmes, have been put up the current year.

Of the whole number of dwellings there were at the close of 1842—

	Stone.	Brick.	Frame.	Total.
	1	403	223	627
Built in 1843,	0	22	4	26
" " 1844,	1	71	10	82
" " 1845,	1	34	75	110
Total,	3	530	312	845

This ward, with the exception of its eastern part, has been long built on, and the great increase consequently has been in a great measure across the Miami Canal. The First Ward was originally constructed of the whole city territory north of Third and Symmes, and east of Main street.

As a general rule each year's buildings are improvements on its predecessors in value, beauty, and convenience; but this will not hold good this year, as respects the First Ward. A large share of the buildings of 1845 here, is east of the canal and on the southern brow of Deer Creek, which are to a great extent frames. The bricks of this year's erection, although not as numerous as those of 1844, are equally valuable to their number.

CORRESPONDENCE.

Pioneer Preachers.

MR. CIST:

Dear Sir,—As I have been giving you in former communications, some incidents of the early settlement of the Miami country, I will now give you some account of the pioneer preachers, for at that time we were not entirely without preaching in the stations. The first preacher I heard at North Bend was the Rev'd. John Tanner, whom I mentioned in a former communication. He then lived at Tanner's station, where Petersburgh now is, in Boone county, Kentucky. The next was the Rev'd. Lewis Dewees, who came to the same station in 1792, and after Wayne's treaty settled near North Bend, in what is now Boone county, Ky., and continued to preach for us till about the year 1804, when he settled in Indiana in the neighbourhood of Brookville, where he died about ten years ago.

They were both ministers of the Baptist Church. Next the Rev'd. James Kemper of Cincinnati, frequently visited us, and preached in the station. The Rev'd. John Smith of Columbia, a member of the United States Senate, and of Burr notoriety, preached for us occasionally.

The Methodists did not preach in the country at so early a day as some other denominations. The first Methodist I heard at North Bend, was Rev'd. Mr. Oglesby, about the year 1804 or 5. The Rev'd. John Langdon, who was well known in this country, preached in this country about the same time.

Men subject to military duty, if they went in those days to Church, were obliged to go armed and equiped, as if going to battle.

Yours respectfully,
JOHN MATSON.

North Bend, Oct. 6th, 1845.

Friends' Testimony.

At a late trial in one of our courts, a member of the Society of Friends was called on to give testimony in a case of assault, &c.

Counsel.—You were present during the affray, and have heard the preceding witnesses' statements.

Yea.

You perceive the contradictory statement of the affair as testified by those who are already examined, both as regards the manner of the assault and the way in which the plaintiff's coat was torn. One says it was torn perpendicularly; another horizontally; others again transversely and diagonally; and some give it incisions and contusions. You will, therefore, have the goodness to represent to the court and jury the precise manner in which the assault was made, and the coat torn. My client relies mainly on your testimony for redress.

"Step this way," said the witness, "and I will be brief and explicit. (Placing his hand on the lawyer's collar.) The manner was thus: friend Patrick seized the coat of friend Andrew in this way, and according to my apprehension being in a mind not savouring of peace. After various words of vanity, spoken by Patrick, which it would be unseemly to repeat, he *shook* him after this manner! As to the coat, (suiting the action to the word,) *he rent it grievously.*"

M'Colloch's Leap.

The ground where Maj. Samuel M'Colloch took the great leap to avoid being made prisoner by the Indians, is but a few rods from Wheeling, and yet such is the negligence of those who inhabit the scenes of great exploits, that we venture the remark that not one dozen men have thought of Major M'Colloch, or been upon the table land from which that leap was taken, during the last year.

We have not been to the point for five years, until last evening. We then mounted a very pleasant racker for a short ride, just as the sun was sinking behind the western hills. We cared but little where we rode, if we but found relief from suffering and the usual concomitants of that much lamented and ridiculed disease called Dyspepsia; but we had ridden but a short distance, before we felt like seeing and enjoying. We therefore turned our horse's head toward the top of the hill. In a few minutes we were at the top, and what a gorgeous scene presented itself. It was rich, magnificent, sublime. We have indeed, no language for a scene like that.

The western sun was just then sinking behind the tops of the trees on the western hills:

"With disk like target, red,
Was rushing to his gory bed,"

and great and glorious—the god of day, indeed he looked; and the western sky, like the timid maiden, blushed brighter rose, as she bade her lord goodnight. The green trees on the hill top were tipped with a golden crown, as they gracefully waved adieu; and the houses on the far off hills shone in the setting sun, as it were the light from the diamond mine, wherein the fairy queens hold revel, and their crowns and thrones, and wands of office are mingled in a brilliant mass. In the broad western valley far below you for miles you see the brown stubble, the green grass, and the waving corn chequering the earth o'er which night is already drawing her sombre veil, and which is creeping slowly up the hill sides. Westward, is the island calmly slumbering, presenting on every rod of it evidences of usefulness to the sustenance of man, yet not the less beautiful and romantic in its location, or its appearance! By it meanders our honoured river, now narrowed almost to a creek in size, and showing along each margin a broad, white gravelly beach. On its bank, and almost beneath your feet, rests Wheeling. The hum of the city is still heard, the thousand children, the still clinking hammer, the puff of the engine, and all those sounds that are made by men in masses, rise to your ears.

But no such sounds or sights as these we have imperfectly described, were seen when M'Colloch took his leap. The hill sides were then covered with trees, and the island and the eastern valley was nearly all a dense forest. Fort Henry and two or three log houses, situated near where the old court house was, could then be seen from the hill, and the little corn growing in a field north of it. These were the only evidences of civilized life to be seen: but savage life was plenty enough.

It was on the 27th of September, 1777, that Fort Henry was attacked by the Indians, led on by the notorious Simon Girty. The Indians were estimated at about five hundred warriors. The fort contained at first but forty-two fighting men; of these twenty-three were killed in the cornfield below the hill, before the attack on the fort. The siege of the fort was sustained by these nineteen men, until the next morning about daylight, when Major M'Colloch brought forty mounted men from Short Creek to their relief.

The gate of the fort was thrown open, and M'-Colloch's men, though closely beset by the Indians, entered the fort in safety. M'Colloch, like a brave officer, was the last man, and he was cut off from his men, and nearly surrounded by the Indians. He wheeled and galloped towards the hill, beset the whole way by the Indians, who might have killed him; but who wished to take him alive, that they might revenge more satisfactorily upon one of the bravest and most successful Indian fighters upon the frontier. He presumed he could ride along the ridge, and thus make his way again to Short Creek; but on arriving at the top, he was headed by a hundred savages. On the west they were gathering thick and fast up the hill, among the trees and bushes, while the main body were following in his path.

He was hemmed in on all sides but the east, where the precipice was almost perpendicular, and the bed of the creek lay like a gulf, near two hundred feet beneath him. This too, would have been protected by the cautious savage, but the jutting crags of limestone and slate, forbade his climbing or descending it even on foot, and they did not suppose that the fearless horseman or high mettled steed could survive the leap if made. But with the Major it was but a chance of deaths, and a narrow chance of life. He chose like a brave man. Setting himself back in his saddle, and his feet firmly in the stirrups, with his rifle in his left hand, and his reins adjusted in the right, he cast a look of defiance at the approaching savages, and pressing his spurs into his horse's flank, urged him over the cliff. In an instant of time the Indians saw their mortal foe, whose daring act they had looked on with horror and astonishment, merging from the valley of the creek below, still safely seated on his noble steed and shouting defiance to his pursuers.

There never was, we venture to say, in civilized or savage warfare, a more desperate or daring act, than this leap of M'Colloch. We have looked at Gen. Putnam's celebrated race ground, and we very much prefer his taste in the selection of a route for a morning ride; at least consulting our ease and convenience.—*Wheeling Times.*

The Nautilus.

The latest novelty in Cincinnati is an article designed to protect the wearer from drowning, being an ingenious substitute for the awkward "*life preserver*" heretofore relied on for that purpose. It bears an appropriate name, "The Nautilus," and may be described as follows:

Its principle is that of the distension of an air bag, so constructed as to inflate itself in being stretched to its length. No time is therefore lost in the instant of need or in the confusion of the moment for filling it, as in the old mode, and the inside springs which press and support each other upon the outer coat of the article render it impossible that the air can escape, after the *Nautilus* is once tied under the owner's arms.

Now that travelling across the Lake via Toledo, is our usual course east, no person on that journey should be without one, to guard against the dangers of fire and shipwreck, which have destroyed so many vessels on Lake Erie. The Nautilus being sufficiently portable to be carried when empty in the pocket of an overcoat, and capable of being made ready in a second of time, for the use of any person falling overboard.

Wm. Dodd, Main, below Fourth street, is the agent in Cincinnati for this article, which is as worth seeing as many an object which will attract visitors the whole length of the city.

Market Statistics.--No. 2.

In my *Advertiser* of the 24th ult., I gave the market statistics of Cincinnati, so far as beef, pork, veal, and mutton were concerned, and showed by the conclusive evidence of figures, that while our population is but one half that of Philadelphia, and one fourth that of New York, our consumption of meat fell little short of either. Two or three reasons will explain this.

The consumption of food in a given place, depends on its money, value, and the facility of earning that price. Meat is always eaten more freely and wasted, also, where it is abundant. The finest beef, pork, and lamb here, average to the consumer perhaps five cents per pound. In the Atlantic Cities it is one hundred to one hundred and fifty per cent. higher; and the comparison is wider apart with fruit and other luxuries. But this is not all; nor the most important part of the subject. The means of earning and saving are greater here, wages being higher and more steady, and other expenses lighter. Not fifteen years ago, spare ribs, such as no resident of New York or Philadelphia can purchase in the market houses of those cities, were emptied by cart loads into the river Ohio, as I have repeatedly seen, and with deep regret, knowing what a luxury they would have been alike to rich and poor elsewhere. We can now consume our spare ribs upon our tables, it is true, but even yet, a dime will get a half bushel basket filled at any of our pork houses with what is not barreled for sale.

There is another reason for the difference. There is a much more abundant supply of fresh fish as well as of better quality, there than here, and of course salt fish, also, is more extensively consumed. But the main difference is caused by the higher price of meat, compelling the mass to resort more freely to vegetable diet.

It would be curious and instructive to institute the comparative consumption of Cincinnati with some of the cities of Europe, but the materials are wanting which would do the subject justice. I observe, however, that the consumption of Paris for the half year of 1845, expiring the 30th June last, is—Beeves 40,531, Cows 9,049, Calves 40,763, and Sheep 226,476. As every live animal driven into Paris for market pays the *Octroi*, these statistics must be accurate. In Cincinnati, during the same period, the consumption was— Beef Cattle 19,450, Cows and Calves 10,245, Sheep and Lambs 50,472, Hogs 226,750. This to be sure comprehends pork put up for exporta-

tion, but after making every allowance, our consumption in a city of one fifteenth the size of Paris, must be one third of theirs. It is true there are 966 Bulls, 32 Goats and 53 Kids, and 760 Horses, to put into the Paris catalogue during the same dates; but this would not vary the proportion greatly.

It seems then that the average consumption of animal food to an individual in Cincinnati, is five times that which his fellow being in Paris uses. The difference in France is made up in soups, vegetables, and bread, of which last enormous quantities are consumed in that country. Fruit, especially grapes, constitute a share even of breakfast, there, also.

CORRESPONDENCE.

Cincinnati in 1794.

Mr. C. Cist:

Sir,—In reply to your enquiry what kind of timber first covered the scite of Cincinnati, I can state my recollections, which are very distinct on the subject.

The bank of the river had a heavy growth of beech trees, many of them very large. At *Hobson's Choice*, on the river, west of Western Row, the encampment of Gen. Wayne, they were cut down and the stumps dug out, over so much of the bank as to make a parade ground; some of the largest being left standing adjacent, for purposes of shade. Where the swamp came in between the river bank and foot of the hill, was a growth of white walnut, soft maple, white elm, shellbark hickory and white ash. On the second table of Cincinnati was spread a variety of timber, such as beech, ash, black walnut, hickory, black and red oak, generally of vigorous growth. Here and there white oak and poplar interspersed the rest. A space of perhaps one hundred and fifty acres north and west of Barr's dwelling, down to Stonemetz's ford, on Mill Creek, was filled with poplar and beech. Of the latter there is, as you know, a small grove still standing, and called Loring's woods. This is the only relic of the original growth of Cincinnati, except scattered trees. An abundant growth of spice wood was the undergrowth. They grew so thick that out at North Bend after cutting off the bush, and digging the roots loose, I have not been able, unassisted, to lift the clump out of the ground. For three or four years prior to the year 1794, there had been a large scope of *out lots*, as they were called, in a worm-fence enclosure extending from about Sixth street north to Court street, and from Main street west to the section line, which nearly follows the line of what is now John street. There was hardly a building on that space. I recollect but one—a small frame building on Main st. on the St. Clair square, between Seventh and Eighth. This had been put up by Thomas Gowdy, a lawyer of that period, as an office, but was not occupied as such, being found too much out of town for business purposes. In May of that year one of the occupants of the enclosure, being engaged in burning brush at the west end of it, the fire accidentally spread over the whole clearing, fastening on the deadened timber which had been girdled and was by this time as dry as timber could become. The wind was from the west, and was very high, which was what first caused the conflagration, and the sap wood as it burned pealed off in very large flakes, spreading the fire farther and farther east until it reached to the Main street front. It may easily be imagined what a magnificent sight was presented by more than one hundred acres of dry timber in flames. The whole population was engaged as far as practicable, in saving the rails, of which in fact, but few escaped. On Gowdy's office three or four men were stationed, while buckets of water were handed up to them from time to time. As this was the first fire in Cincinnati, so it was the most extensive as respects the space it covered. It compelled the settlers to clear the out lots much sooner than they would have done to get rid of the partially burnt timber left standing unsafely, or lying on the ground in the way of putting in the corn crop, for which they were preparing at the time.

Yours,   JOHN MATSON.
North Bend, Oct. 4th, 1845.

Population of Indiana.

New York and Indiana have been making an enumeration of their population, or rather of their white male inhabitants, over twenty-one years of age. The final return has not yet been made, I believe, in New York; but that of Indiana, as officially reported by the Auditor of State, is 154,169;—in 1840, by the United States cencus, 142,128—an increase in five years of only 12,041.

This would indicate an aggregate population in Indiana of 743,972. As the census of 1840 gave a result of 685,866 for the population of that State, this would be an increase of not quite nine per cent., or less than twenty per cent. for the decade ending in 1850. This is manifestly incorrect and falling far short of the truth, the ratio of increase from 1830 to 1840 being one hundred and one per cent., and the sources of increase nearly as copious in the present decade as the last. I cannot account for the causes, of what I have no doubt is a gross error somewhere. No intelligent man can believe that the male inhabitants of Indiana have increased within five years only 12,041, when the increase of population for the previous ten years was 354,284, a ratio which

should exhibit an increase of white male inhabitants six times as great as reported.

Taxation in Cincinnati.

As there is no feeling so deep and general as that which lies in the pocket, the following exhibit of the increase of our city taxes will interest, and may well startle our tax payers.

In another aspect of the subject, it furnishes evidence of the rapid growth of Cincinnati.

1826—Corporation and Township,	$3,157 39	
School,	1,578 69	$4,735 08
1827—Corporation and Township,	3,692 30	
School,	1,846 15	5,538 45
1828—Corporation and Township,	3,738 84	
School,	1,869 35	5,607 19
1829—Corporation,		
School,		22,257 46
Township,		
1830—Corporation,	8,191 35	
School,	11,263 11	
Township,	3,071 75	22,526 31
1831—Corporation,	9,199 50	
School,	12,661 29	
Township,	3,473 27	25,334 26
1832—Corporation,	16,127 36	
School,	16,127 46	
Township,	5,375 78	37,630 50
1833—Corporation,	16,466 93	
School,	16,466 93	
Township,	8,233 46	41,167 42
1834—Corporation,	21,724 95	
School,	16,401 80	
Township,	13,527 63	51,654 39
1835—Corporation,	31,718 42	
School,	19,166 38	
Township,	18,856 40	69,721 20
1836—Corporation,	32,969 18	
School,	21,137 73	
Township,	15,592 61	69,599 52
1837—Corporation,	32,969 18	
School,	21,137 73	
Township,	15,922 25	70,056 90
1838—Corporation,	37,011 28	
School,	26,917 29	
Township,	16,823 31	80,771 88
1839—Corporation,	50,590 38	
School,	19,686 77	
Township,	19,686 46	98,963 61
1840—Corporation,	49,325 87	
School,	18,497 20	
Township,	18,497 20	86,320 37
1841—Corporation,	63,785 85	
School,	15,107 13	
Township,	19,459 07	98,352 05
1842—Corporation,	94,343 18	
School,	20,965 15	
Township,	27,953 53	
City Road,	5,191 28	148,453 04
1843—Corporation,	94,106 74	
School,	20,965 15	
Township,	29,165 73	
City Road,	5,041 43	146,201 50
1844—Corporation,	97,233 94	
School,	20,835 84	
Township,	27,781 12	
City Road,	3,472 64	149,323 54
1845—Corporation,	102,171 50	
School,	28,602 02	
Township,	24,521 16	155,300 68

New York Two Hundred Years Ago.

New York—then New Amsterdam—had its first town watch appointed in 1653. It consisted of *six* persons. In 1658, a permanent system of watch police of eight men was established. These were divided into two reliefs, of four at a time for duty, and relieving each other from sun rise to sunset.

The first fire police was established in 1648. Fire wardens were appointed in 1650, and ordinances regulating buildings were passed between 1650 and 1656.

In 1659, it was resolved to send to Holland for two hundred and fifty leather fire buckets; but on account of the length of time which must elapse till they could be made and sent out, an effort was made by the authorities to have the buckets manufactured in New York. Proposals were issued, and the whole shoemaking craft—four in number—of the town were required to hand in offers for the contract.

After the delay of some months, answers were given as follows:—Coenrad Ten Eyck "was not minded to undertake the work." Peter Van Haalen had no materials. Finally, Remoute Remoutgen, the principal shoemaker of that day, agreed to make one hundred of the buckets at six guilders and two stuyvers. Andreas Van Laer agreed for fifty more at the same price. For one hundred and fifty years after this date, every housekeeper was compelled to have buckets in his house, which were given out to the citizens or carried to the spot in case of fire, on the ringing of the bells; and on the morning after the fire, were regularly collected at the old City Hall, and redelivered to the housekeepers.

Post Office Balances.

Every body recollects Rev. Obadiah B. Brown, who was once the "*Nick Biddle*" of the Post Office. Brown's *accounts*, of which he could give no *account* intelligible, and his *balances*, which could never be made to *balance*, are facts in American History, which, with Governor Marcy's breeches, have passed into proverbs and are enshrined in immortal remembrance. Brown was once at Saratoga Springs, N. Y., in the fashionable season when this place was crowded, and on the lookout, as the Athenians of old, for the latest novelty. A slight of hand man arrived at this juncture, and attracted immense houses. Among other exploits he balanced several dishes and plates edgewise, in so remarkable a manner as to excite general astonishment. Brown, who had taken a dislike to the performer, addressing him, observed that he had seen a man once balance three sticks, one over the other, which was still more extraordinary than the present performance. "Well," said the slight of hand man,

piqued by Brown's remarks, "You have not yet seen what I can do: I will balance anything on the spot any gentleman present will show me, except the post office accounts; and I'll balance them too, *if Mr. Brown will produce what will make the balance.*"

Post office balances now-a-days are different things from what they once were, being at the present time scales for weighing letters under the new laws of postage.

W. B. Smith & Co., have received and are selling a remarkably convenient and portable article, which, *unlike* O. B. Brown's balances, or *like* Nick Biddle's, may be kept in the pocket, either of the breeches or the vest.

John Randolph of Roanoke.

In the midst of one of his finest tirades on the extravagance of the existing administration, and while the eyes and ears of his audience in and outside the Hall of Representatives were riveted on him with breathless attention, he suddenly paused a few seconds, and as abruptly began,—" Mr. Speaker, I have found the *philosopher's stone!*"—again he paused,—no man better understood stage effect—" it is composed of four words, PAY AS YOU GO."

He had been speaking for four hours ostensibly on the Panama mission, I think it was, but actually travelled over every thing by and large, in the world, illuminating and ornamenting all that he touched, and giving way for a motion to adjourn, resumed his speech on the next day. It was in the same vein, a tissue of sarcasm and invective against the President and his Cabinet, being the string on which he fastened his pearls and diamonds of every shape and colour, but all variegated, angular and brilliant. He took occasion to refer to the Revolutionary pensioners' law, spoke of their number at the close of the revolution, the large proportion left who were found to claim the benefit of the act, and the increasing number of pensioners from year to year· under its operations. " Yesterday, Mr. Speaker, I told you I had found the *philosopher's stone.* I now tell you, sir, I have discovered the *elixir of life.* Give a man a pension and you make him immortal. Nay more, you raise him from the dead."

His sarcastic force was usually felt in some sting, brief, pointed, and generally envenomed. After some allusions to Burr; he once observed, " Wilkinson, I forbear to touch, let alone, handle. He is in the last stage of putrefaction—touch him and he falls to pieces."

The Missing Wig.

While Lord Coalstoun lived in a house in the Advocates' Close, Edinburg, a strange accident one morning befell him. It was at that time the custom for advocates and judges to dress themselves in gowns, and wig, and cravats, at their houses, and walk to the Parliament House. They usually breakfasted early, and, when dressed, were in the habit of leaning over their parlor windqws for a few minutes, before St. Gile's bell started the sounding peal of a quarter to nine, enjoying the agreeable morning air, and perhaps discussing the news of the day. It so happened, one morning, while Lord Coalstoun was prepa● ring to enjoying his mutual treat, two girls, who lived in the second flat above, were amusing themselves with a kitten, which in thoughtless sport, they had swung over the window, by a cord tied round its middle, and hoisted for some time up and down, till the creature was getting rather desperate with its exertions. His lordship had just popped his head out of the window, directly below that from which the kitten swung, little suspecting, good easy man, what a danger impended, like the sword of Damocles, over his head; when down came the exasperated animal at full career, directly upon his senatorial wig. No sooner had the girls perceived what sort of a landing place their kitten had found, than in terror and surprise they began to draw it up; but this measure was now too late, for along with the animal, up also came the judge's wig fixed full in its determined talons. His lordship's surprise on finding his wig lifted off his head was ten thousand times redoubled, when, on looking up, he perceived it dangling in its way upwards, without any means visible to him by which its motion might be accounted for. The astonishment, the dread, the awe almost of the senator below—the half mirth, half terror of the girls above—together with the fierce and retentive energy of puss between, altogether formed a scene to which language cannot do justice, but which George Cruikshank might perhaps embody with considerable effect. It was a joke, soon explained and pardoned; but assuredly the perpetrators of it did afterwards get many a lengthened injunction from their parents never again to fish over the window with such a bait for honest men's wigs.

Books of Fiction and the Bible.

The Bible contains the literature of Heaven—of eternity. It is destined to survive in human hearts every other book, and command the ultimate veneration and obdience of the world.

When Sir Walter Scott returned a trembling invalid from Italy, to die in his native land, the sight of his "sweet home" so invigorated his spirits that some hope was cherished that he might recover. But he soon relapsed. He found that he must die. Addressing his son-in-law, he said, "bring me a book." "What book?" replied Lockhart. "Can you ask," said the expiring genius, whose fascinating novels have charmed the world, but have no balm for death— "can you ask what book?—there is but one."

A Kiss for a Blow.

A visitor once went into a school at Boston, where he saw a boy and a girl on one seat, who were brother and sister. In a moment of thoughtless passion, the little boy struck his sister. The little girl was provoked, and raised her hand to return the blow. Her face showed that rage was

working within, and her clenched fist was aimed at her brother, when her teacher caught her eye. "Stop, my dear," said she, " you had better kiss your brother than strike him."

The look and the word reached her heart. Her hand dropped. She threw her arms round his neck and kissed him. The boy was moved. He could have stood against the blow, but he could not withstand a sister's kiss. He compared the provocation he had given her with the return she had made, and the tears rolled down his checks. This affected the sister, and with her little handkerchief, she wiped away his tears. But the sight of her kindness only made him cry the faster; he was completely subdued.

Her teacher then told the children always to return a kiss for a blow, and they would never get any more blows. If men and women, families and communities and nations would act on this principle, this world would almost cease to be a vale of tears. " Nation would not lift up the sword against nation, neither would they learn war any more."

Trickery in Trade.

A late number ot Hunt's Merchants' Magazine, contains an interesting memoir of Gideon Lee, from which we derive the following anecdote, illustrative of his own fair dealings, and of the usual effect of trickery in trade. No man more thoroughly despised dishonesty than Gideon Lee; and he used to remark, no trade can be sound, that is not benficial to both parties, to the buyer as well as to the seller. A man may obtain a temporary advantage by selling an article for more than it is worth; but the very effect of such operations must recoil on himself, in the shape of bad debts and increased risks. A person with whom he had some transactions, once boasted to him, that he had on one occasion obtained an advantage over such a neighbour; and " To-day," said he, " I have obtained one over you." " Well," said Gideon Lee, " that may be; and if you will promise never to enter my house again, I will give you that bundle of goat skins." The man made the promise, and took them. Fifteen years afterwards, he walked into Gideon Lee's office. At the instant of seeing him he exclaimed, " You have violated your word; pay me for my goat skins." " Oh," said the man, " I am quite poor, and have been very unfortunate since I saw you." " Yes," said Gideon, " and you always will be poor; that miserable desire for over-reaching others must ever keep you so."

Epitaph.

In a work entitled Church-yard Poetry, we find the following epitaph, copied from the marble sarcophagus of " Ladye Eudora Vennome," in one of the church-yards of Yorkshire, England:

" This shelle of stone within it keepeth,
One who dyeth not but sleepeth;
And in her quiet slumber seemeth
As if of Heaven alone she dreameth.
Her form yt was so fayre in seeminge,
Her eyne so holy in their heaminge,
So pure her heartte in everie feeling,
So high her mind in each revealing,
A band of angelles thought that she
Was one of their bright companie;
And on some homeward errand driven,
Hurried her too away to Heaven."

Cuvier and his Protegee.

Heaven be praised, the *coucous** have almost entirely disappeared from the neighbourhood of Paris! In a few years, not a trace will be left of these detestable vehicles. Under pretence of conveying travellers, these horrible machines subject unhappy mortals to the most dreadful joltings; keep them, besides, in a constant cloud of dust, and exposed to the hottest rays of the sun, as well as to every passing shower; and again, do not furnish the least protection against the winter's cold. Strange solution of that problem, how one can continue to move without advancing, it takes them two hours to travel a single league! And then, too, the surly driver, the broken winded and sorry horses, the seats, mere planks, only planed down, the stocks in which one was compelled to keep his feet. With only a few alterations, the *coucous* would have served an executioner in the middle age, as a fearful instrument of torture.

It was in one of these contrivances of affliction, on one rainy morning, that an individual was obliged to take a seat, in consequence of an accident that had happened to his own carriage. He submitted to the misfortune with a joyous, and almost child-like resignation, and seemed very much amused at the idea of terminating his journey in a *coucou*. Whilst the domestics were actively employed in raising the fallen carriage, and taking the axletree to the village blacksmith, the traveller climbed up the dangerous steps that led to the interior of the *coucou*, and took his seat; not, however, without a smile, at the grotesque appearance of the driver, whose projecting chin, flat nose, and low forehead, seemed to belong to an ourang outang, rather than to a human being. The Automedon did not appear to be in a great hurry to start, and his only unlooked for passenger did not seem to mind this delay, for he wished for some companions on his route, that he might lose none of the amusing incidents of his situation. After about twenty minutes delay, which the traveller passed in turning over the leaves of a book, and the coachman in looking around him, from his seat, but without seeing anything, like sister Anna, in the tale of Blue Beard, except the grass of the fields and the dusty road, it was at length necessary to start. The horse groaned under the lash, the wheels cracked, and the traveller hastily changed his seat from the back to the front; for such was the pitching of the *coucou*, that no one could stand the first shock it gave him. From the first seat he returned to the second, but he could not find any that were comfortable. The unfortunate sufferer began to regret that he had not remained at the village to await his own carriage, when all at once the vehicle stopped. A young girl, hardly giving the driver time to open the heavy door, sprung upon the heavy steps and seated herself on the lower seat, by the side of its occupant. He scrutinized the companion, whom chance had thus thrown into his way. A smile lightened his whole face, which, until then, had retained a serious, but l e nevolent expression. He had never seen a n or lovely maiden. Of a fair complexion, ros_y cheeks, small in size, her large blue eyes indicated at once vivacity and innocent frankness. Although the heavens were darkened by thick clouds, her golden locks seemed almost irradiated by the rays of a sun. She put a basket of flowers at her feet, adjusted the ribbons of her pretty little lace bonnet, looked by turns upon the coach-

man and her unknown companion: " Thank Heaven," said she, joyfully, " That I have arrived in time."

Without minding the rough jolts of the carriage, and as much at her ease apparently, as if she were seated in the softest arm chair, she began to look out through the glass at the trees, the country, the road, and the little birds, which were covering themselves with the moistened dust in the ruts of the road. Soon, however, the rain beat so violently against the glass that it was no longer possible for her to look out. Without showing an uneasiness at this, she took her basket upon her knees, took out the flowers it contained, and essayed to arrange them in bouqets. She did this, however, so unskillfully that the bouquet was not at all in good taste, and her travelling companion could not repress a half smile. She raised her head as gracefully as a bird, and blushing slightly, but without any show of displeasure, said:

" I do this but poorly; do I not, sir?"

He gave a friendly smile, in assent. She endeavored, but in vain, to do better. Two or three times the flowers were arranged in different ways, but neither time were they fixed tastefully. At length she gave up in despair.

The traveller had carefully watched her efforts. " You ought, indeed, sir," said she, this time, with a slight vexation, and that air of authority which youth and beauty always give, " you ought, sir, to show me how to arrange them better."

He smiled at her proposal, which seemed to amuse him mightily, and replied:

" With the greatest of pleasure, Miss."

She put all her flowers in his lap, and watched him while he arranged them. As soon as she saw the manner in which he proceeded, the young girl imitated him so well that when the *coucou* had reached the barrier, two pretty bouquets were completely finished. But it must be acknowledged the pupil had surpassed her teacher; the latter candidly confessed it.

The girl took her two bouquets, placed them in the basket, and a profound silence succeeded the intimacy which the lessons in bouquet-making had brought about between them.

The *coucou* approached the end of its route. The young girl appeared very much occupied by thoughts to which she hesitated to give utterance, and her cheeks were suffused with a beautiful blush, and she said:

" If the gentleman will accept one of these nosegays it will give me great pleasure."

" Thank you, my pretty child; your flowers are very beautiful, but I ought not to deprive those of them for whom you destined them."

This argument seemed irresistible to the young girl, for she did not insist upon it, but took from the bouquet the most beautiful pink she could find, and presented it to her neighbour.

This time he took the flower, and placed it in the red riband tied to his button hole. The young girl appeared delighted with the value which he seemed to attach to her gift. At this moment the carriage had reached the end of its journey.

The girl put her head out of the door, but soon drew it back. " It rains hard," cried she, and she gave an anxious look at her neat coloured linen dress, her black silk apron and her new buskins, which well set off her pretty foot.

" Mademoiselle," said the stranger to her, in a friendly manner, " you have shared your bouquet

* A kind of stage coach.

with me, permit me to offer you a seat in the carriage which I am going to order." As he spoke, he bestowed so liberal a sum upon their sturdy driver as almost to restore him to good nature. He ran as quickly as possible, procured a carriage, opened the door, held the large flap of his great coat over the head of the young girl, instead of an umbrella.

"Whither am I to take you?" said her companion, much amused at the confiding artlessness with which the grisette had accepted his protection.

"Rue du Pas de la Mule, No. 3."

It was some moments before the carriage reached the designated place. The unknown imitated the contrivance of the driver, to protect the dress of the young girl. When he had conducted her in safety to her door, he received the thanks of his fellow-traveller, who invited him to walk in and rest himself.

This proposal appeared to amuse him much, and he accepted it with an eagerness almost child-like.

"Since I have taught the child how to make nosegays," said he to himself, "I might as well make her a visit." Preceded by the grisette, he gaily climbed four pair of stairs. She knocked at the door: it was opened—and an old woman, followed by two girls, came out.

"Maria! dear Maria!" cried they, throwing themselves into her arms. "Good day, little mother."

She embraced and caressed them, and extended her cheek to the old woman; and, for the first time, thought of her companion.

"Pardon me," said she, naively; "I had quite forgotten you."

"I do not complain, Miss; your pretty little sisters, and your mother, are ample excuse."

"These are not my sisters; they are my children!"

"Your children!"

"Her adopted children," interrupted the old woman. "My daughter, sir—a poor woman, left in poverty by the death of her husband, an honest and industrious labourer—died of grief, in the garret above this little apartment, and left me alone, and without resources, with these two orphans. It was then necessary for us to have recourse to the hospital; for, old and infirm as I am, I could do nothing, either for myself, or for these poor creatures. My despair was noticed by those in the house; and, the same evening, I heard some one knock at the door. It was Maria, sir." "Mother Marguerite," said she to me, "I lost my mother, about three months since. I am alone in the world, without any relatives. You and these two children shall, henceforth, be mine." And since that time, sir, we have dwelt with her. To my great distress, the generous girl has to work, night and day, to meet the expenses which she has thus imposed upon herself, and which she is not fully able to do; for, every month, she is obliged to expend a small portion of her little capital of fifteen thousand francs, left her by her mother. If I was alone in the world, I would, long since, have left her, that I might not ruin my benefactress; but these two children prevent me—I have not the courage to do so. Must I take them to the hospital, sir?—my daughter's children to the hospital!"

Whilst Marguerite was speaking, Maria stood with her eyes upon the ground, confused and ashamed, as if what she was telling had not been to her credit.

"I was an orphan: I could not live alone, and without some one to love," interrupted she, as if to excuse herself. "Marguerite watches over me—her children love me—ought I not to feel under obligations to them, sir?"

"You are a good girl, Maria," replied he, much moved. "You deserve that others should take an interest in you; and I will now prove how much I take in you, by giving you a little scolding. Yes, by scolding you. Listen to me, my little friend; you should not thus travel alone in public carriages."

"Sir," interrupted Marguerite. "she has been for the last eight days to work, as a seamstress, at the house of the Marchioness de St. Vincent, who employs her."

"That is all very well, but recollect, Maria, that you ought not to converse with fellow travellers, whom you do not know, and still less make nosegays with them; and moreover, a young girl ought not to permit a person, whom she does not know, to conduct her in a carriage. God has this time thrown into your way a man in whom your beauty and your innocence have only inspired such respect and admiration as we feel for angels. But there are many others who would have made an unworthy return for your confiding frankness. Be then, for the future, more prudent and silent, when you ride in a coucou, and even suffer your pretty bonnet to be spoiled, rather than invite a stranger to your house. Now as a reward for my lesson, let me kiss this fair brow, and the fat cheeks of these charming little girls, who call you mother." He pressed his lips upon the forehead of Maria, slipped two pieces of gold into the hands of the two children, and departed without leaving his name.

"That is a very kind man," said Maria.

"Let us pray for him to-night," added Marguerite, "for he has given you good advice, my child."

Maria expected to see again the unknown, who had been so kind to her. But eight months passed without his coming again, and they were very painful ones for the poor girl! During their long and trying duration, she shed nearly as many tears as in those days of distress, when she saw her mother slowly dying before her. Old Marguerite fell sick first, after her the two young girls, Lydia and Zenais, took their turns. Maria was obliged to take care of all three, and was unable to leave their bed side either by night or by day. When at length it pleased God to put an end to these painful trials, and the old woman and the two children were at length restored to health, there no longer remained upon the cheeks of Maria, any of their late peculiar freshness. Pale, worn out by her long watches, her fatigue and anxiety, she seemed at least five or six years older. From the dreaming illusion of youth, she had passed at once into the stern realities of life. She had now seen life as it really was, and with all the cares of a mother before she had ceased to be a young maiden, she had tasted all its bitterness. Before, a smile of happiness was ever playing upon her lips; now all felt moved by a mysterious anxiety when they beheld her sad resignation and sweet contentment.

As soon as the sickness and its attendant anxieties were once fairly out of the house, it was necessary she should once more restore order and attention to her work. The cost of the physician, and the medicines, had made a sad breach in the little fund left to Maria, by her mother.

She set herself courageously to work, that she might not have to resort to it any more .

One morning, surrounded by her two children, whom she was teaching to sew, having been sewing herself since sunrise, she heard old Marguerite, all at once, utter a cry of surprise and joy, exclaimed:

"Is it indeed you, sir?" You have not, then, entirely forgotten us."

The door of her chamber opened, and the mysterious friend of this industrious little family entered. He wore a uniform that Maria did not recognize—several decorations shone upon his breast.

"I thought, sir, you had forgotten your pupil," said the maiden, smiling.

"My child, I have never once ceased to interest myself in you, and I hope soon to prove this to you. I wish to take you with me. Will you get ready and accompany me?"

"Whither are you going to take me, sir?"

"That is a secret. Be speedy; I will give you ten minutes to prepare your bewitching toilet. Your little lace bonnet, your rose-coloured robe, your black apron, and those little buskins—have you them still?"

"Alas! sir, I have not worn them once since the day on which I met you. They have not even been taken out of this wardrobe."

"So much the better; that is the dress in which I desire to see you. To your task, then, my child! Ten minutes, my dear; you hear, not one moment more."

He took out from his pocket a paper of good things, which he divided between the two little girls, and inquired, with much interest, what progress they were making in the difficult science of reading. At first somewhat afraid of him, these little rogues ended by getting on such a familiar footing with the gentleman that they played with his hat, and had climbed upon his knees, when Maria returned from her dressing room, very neatly and tastefully attired.

"You are dressed just as I wish to have you," said her unknown friend. "Embrace your children and dame Marguerite, for I do not expect to bring you back before the evening."

He offered his arm, which Maria took with some timidity. When they had descended the stairs, the young girl saw a carriage awaiting them at the door. This time it was no hack, but an elegant and convenient landau.

The coachman whipped up his horses, traversed a part of the Boulevards, crossed the Seine, entered into the court yard of the Institute, and stopped before one of the flights of steps. Maria's guide took her by the hand and led her in by a private stair-way. A small door was hastily opened, and the young girl found herself all at once in the midst of a brilliant and crowded assemblage. All eyes were directed towards him, as well as upon herself. Maria was moved, even to tears.

"My child!" whispered her protector to her, "there is a lady in this assembly, who wishes very much to make your acquaintance. She is my wife; I am going to take you to her side."

He conducted the maiden to the side of a lady of distinguished appearance and benevolent countenance. She took her hand in both of hers, just as a voice was heard to say,

"The session has now commenced."

Several gentlemen, dressed in the same uniform which the friend of Maria wore, took their seats around a large table, and one of them arose to deliver a discourse. His subject was noble and generous deeds.

"We have reserved," said the speaker, towards the close of his address, "to conclude our long series of charitable and virtuous deeds, the generous and unsolicited devotedness of a young girl, who has nobly taken upon herself the burthen of two little girls and an old grandmother of seventy years. To be able to assist them without being separated from them, she has not only passed nights of hard labour, but she has not even hesitated to sacrifice a portion of her little inheritance from her mother. For the last six months it has pleased God to subject the courage and devotion of this young maiden to a new trial; disease has prostrated her three beneficiaries. This orphan girl has exhausted her own strength, health, and her little wealth in devotion to them, and has not once given way to any discouragement, not even during the time that all three were dangerously ill. Therefore, gentlemen, let us not hesitate to adopt the suggestion of our distinguished colleague, M. George Cuvier, to decree the prize of the Institute to the Maria"

A loud burst of applause came from every part of the hall. Every one rose to look at the young girl, while the ladies showered down upon her wreaths of flowers. While her eyes were filled with tears, and she hardly realized that it was not all a dream, the illustrious naturalist came and took her by the hand, and conducted her to the president, who bestowed upon her the prize she had so worthily gained.

"Oh, sir," said she, "how happy you have made me."

"My child," said the illustrious naturalist, "this day is the most interesting one of my whole life."

This ceremony over, Cuvier took home with him, to his house, in the Garden of Plants, his lovely protegee; the young maiden dined with the family of the member of the Academy, and that evening, just as she was about to leave, she received from his hands a small portion of green morocco.

"You have expended five thousand francs of the fifteen which you inherited from your mother; the Dauphiness has directed me to present you with this sum; you have there, also, the papers of a pension of twelve hundred francs, which the King has presented to you. Thus you see, Maria, industry, virtue, and charity, are rewarded with happiness. Adieu; you will come every fortnight, on Sunday, to dine with my daughter, my wife, and myself."

We leave our readers to imagine the joy and happiness which Maria took home that evening to her little household; what blessings came from the aged lips of Marguerite, and with what fervor the whole happy family addressed that evening their prayers to God.

The day succeeding this eventful one, which had seemed to her like a dream, Maria was employed with her work near the window; in spite of herself, the recollection of all that had occurred to her the last evening caused her to let her sewing fall from her hands, while she fell into a long and sweet reverie; all at once her eyes, which were wandering vaguely around, chanced to rest upon the opposite house. Some priests were coming out with a coffin. Before them came a young man weeping bitterly. He was following the cofin of his mother. Maria could not restrain her own tears, for she felt moved with compassion, and shared the grief of the young man, recalling the day on which she had seen them carry out the coffin of her own mother.

Whether it was by chance, or whether Heaven willed that it should be so, the young man looked up and beheld the tears of the maiden, and understood that they were shed for him. Her compassion made him feel less cast down and forsaken in his grief. He no longer felt deserted by all on the earth.

That evening, when he returned to his devoted chamber, where he found no more his mother to welcome him home, he opened the window, and sat down to watch, through the panes of glass, lighted by her lamp, Maria, who was still at work, with Marguerite and the two children about her.

A month passed away. One morning, Cuvier came to make his protegee a visit. As he came out, a young man, of good personal appearance, dressed in deep mourning, was standing by his carriage.

"Excuse me, sir, for the liberty I take; but may I crave the honour of conversing with you? It is something that concerns Miss Maria."

Cuvier desired him to come into the carriage and take a seat by his side. The young man informed him that his name was Philip T——; that he was a journeyman printer, and that he loved Maria, and desired to marry her.

"I am not without means," said he, "I have a small income, amounting to a thousand francs; —besides which I earn seven francs a day, by working for my employer. Besides, sir, I lead a very correct life, and have been well educated. I would make Miss Maria happy; at least I would do my best."

Cuvier left him, and re-ascended the stairs of Maria.

"A young man, your opposite neighbour, desires to speak with you."

A blush of scarlet covered the cheeks of the young girl.

"Come, this is at least a good sign for him," added the naturalist; "I need not tell you, I see, that he loves you, and asks your hand in marriage."

"My kind protector," replied Maria, recovering from her first emotion, after a few minutes silence, "such a proposal from a worthy man, who wishes to make me his wife, and who makes that proposal through you, can only be regarded as an honour. But before I give my answer, let me tell you a few circumstances—or rather, when you have heard them, you will be so kind as to decide for me!"

"My father was a merchant; he dealt in fancy goods; he married my mother, who was well connected; the marriage met with much opposition from the families of both. This led to much sorrow, and to many dreadful scenes. Both sunk under them, and left me an orphan and alone in the world. Although thus deserted by my kindred, and although poor, sir, I hesitate to marry one who is only a journeyman. If it is wrong, sir, to feel so, I will overcome this feeling. I look to you, sir, for advice."

"I will report our conversation to Philip, and leave it to his decision.

He returned to the young man, and related to him the whole: he heard it with downcast head.

"Sir," said he at length, "entreat Maria to wait for me two years, before she thinks of marrying another. I beg of her that favour, in the name of her mother and mine, who are watching their children from above. By that time I shall have won, I hope, a name and condition in life worthy of her."

Cuvier once more ascended the four pair of stairs to Maria, to report the answer of Philip.

"This, time, Monsieur Cuvier," said she, after a few moments reflection, "I will myself deliver my answer to Philip. Do you not advise me— do you not think I would do well to place myself under the protection of one who has so noble a heart?"

Marguerite went to invite Philip to come in. "Sir," said Cuvier to him, "let me present to you your future bride."

Tears started to the eyes of the young man, and, for a moment, he was overcome with emotion.

It was not three months after this that the wedding supper took place, at the house of their benefactor, in the Garden of Plants.

At the present moment, Philip T—— is one of the most celebrated, as well as one of the most wealthy, of the printers of Paris. Maria has furnished him with efficient aid, in praiseworthy endeavours to acquire an independence.

In the parlour of the young wife stands a marble statue of Cuvier, and a bunch of dried flowers. Need we add, that it is ever with feelings of deep emotion that she contemplates either the bust or the BOUQUET OF FLOWERS.

Fair of the Mechanics' Institute.

The Eighth Annual Fair of this institution is just now in progress, and appears to have lost none of the variety, excellence and attractiveness of its predecessors.

The place of exhibition is at the corner of Pearl and Walnut streets, in what is usually known as the Assembly Rooms.

Here are displayed specimens of the useful, the ingenious and the ornamental to supply every want and please all tastes—almost. The limits of the *Advertiser* permit only a brief notice of some of the articles which grace or give value to the present Fair.

Glenn & McGregor, with locks of all descriptions; Miles Greenwood & Co., with butt hinges and malleable iron fabrics in every variety; and Teasdale with his dyeing hues of every shade and tint, and others, are back again paying their respects to visitors. Their specimens cannot be beat. Lard oil from six or seven establishments, fancy boots from two or three, and ploughs from a dozen shops, are here competing for superiority in the judgment of the spectator as well as in that of the respective committees.

A variety of fine painting, daguerreotype and statuary, generally by Cincinnati artists, decorate the walls and the tables of the exhibition. The usual display of articles of fancy work gives variety to the scene.

Of curiosities there is an ample store. Among them, an enormous Morocco skin, large enough to form a carpet for some rooms; the mastodon relics lately dug up on Main street, near the court house; a set of open work iron steps, which must be of great value where light is wanted to the basement; a type casting machine, which is at work every evening; and a printing press which daily throws off "The Artist and Artisan," the periodical of the Institute, are novelties as well as curiosities to the mass of visitors.

Let me say to my readers of every description, pay a visit to the Institute; you can hardly pass an hour more profitably. The mechanic and manufacturing interest is the right arm of Cincinnati, which is building us into population, wealth, physical and moral importance; and if you would cherish the industrious and enterprising artisan of our city, manifest the interest you take in their prosperity and *your own*, by an early visit to the Fair of the Institute.

Next week I shall go into details on the subject of articles exhibited at this time.

Steamboat Andrew Jackson.

I notice from time to time steamboats built here, merely for the purpose of marking the progress our unrivaled mechanics are making in the beautiful art of building naval craft. The ANDREW JACKSON the last trophy of Cincinnati skill, left our landing on Saturday last for New Orleans. As she has been built for a packet to ply between that port and ours, a description of her distinctive features may interest my readers.

The hull of the Andrew Jackson was built by Burton Hazen; joiners, Swain & Green; engine builder, David Griffey. Bell weighing five hundred pounds, from Coffin's Buckeye bell and brass foundry. Her measurements and equipments as follows:—length one hundred and seventy-six feet, breadth of beam thirty-one feet, water wheels twenty-five feet diameter, length of buckets ten feet and twenty-four inches wide. Her hold is but seven feet, as she has been built with as light draft as possible. She has three boilers twenty-six feet long and forty-two inches diameter. Her engine has a twenty-six inch cylinder and eight feet stroke. The boat draws three feet four inches light, and seven feet six inches with her freight on board. There are forty-eight state rooms and consequently ninety-six berths, all for passengers, the boat officers being supplied with state rooms in the pilot house. The mattrasses in the ladies' cabin are hair, and bed posts are supplied to all the berths for the purpose of hanging curtains to exclude flies, musquitoes and gnats. To the ladies' cabin there are permanent sky lights, by which the supply of warm or cold air is regulated at pleasure. Every thing is of the best quality and highest finish, convenience, strength, and ele-

gance being every where apparent. The floors are covered with the finest carpets, and the chairs of a novel pattern, equally remarkable for ease and neatness.

Ample provision is made for the security of the boat in the employment of safety guards, wire tiller and bell rope, sheet iron roof, a store of water casks on the upper decks, and one hundred and sixty feet hose, which is sufficient in case of necessity, to carry water the whole length of the boat. Nearly five hundred doors and shutters which lift from the hinges will supply floats for as many persons in any emergency that may occur.

The whole building, finishing, and furnishing interest at Pittsburgh, Wheeling, Louisville, or St. Louis, may be safely challenged to exhibit a boat of finer model or equipment. She is indeed worthy of her great name.

I close this statement in which I have briefly seized on the more important statistics, by adding that a beautiful stand of colours, and a splendid portrait of the OLD CHIEF, a copy by a Cincinnati artist of Healy's picture painted expressly for *Louis Philippe*, has been presented by the citizens of Cincinnati to the boat in honour of her name.

Thomas F. Eckert is captain, and G. R. Dudley clerk of the Andrew Jackson. Capt. Eckert I believe is the oldest Cincinnati steamboat captain in the service, having made one hundred and sixty-two entire trips on the Ohio and Mississippi.

Second Ward--Cincinnati.

The second ward is one of the oldest and most compactly built wards in the city; and late improvements have generally been made, as they must hereafter also be effected, by the removal of existing buildings. Its enumeration of dwellings, &c., follows:

Public buildings 29; store houses, workshops, offices—brick 931—frames 212. Total, 1143.

Of the public buildings there are four banks—Lafayette, Franklin, City, and Citizens'; Classical Academy, on Longworth st.; Peter's Orphan Asylum, Cincinnati and Medical Colleges, Engine Houses, on Fourth, between Walnut and Vine, and corner of Race and Centre streets; Masonic and Odd Fellows' Halls, District School House, and Mechanics' Institute. Fifteen church edifices as follows:—the First, Second, Sixth and Central Presbyterian Churches—brick—at the corner of Plum and Fourth streets; the Unitarian, Universalist, and Restorationalist Churches; St. Paul's, Episcopal, Methodist Protestant, Associate Reformed and Burke's Churches; New Jerusalem Temple, African Churches, on Baker and Third streets. All these are of brick except that last refered to, and Burke's Church, which is not only the oldest edifice of the kind in Cincinnati, but probably older than any other building here, Mr. Wade's house excepted.

Of these buildings there were at the close of the year 1842—

	Brick.	Frame.	Total.
	721	200	921
Built in 1843,	27	6	33
" " 1844,	97	5	102
" " 1845,	86	1	87
	931	212	1143

No ward in the city has received such an accession of fine buildings, especially of a public character, during the current year, as the second ward. Among the public buildings may be noticed in the order of magnitude and beauty, the Cincinnati College, Masonic Hall, Odd Fellows' Hall, and Central Presbyterian Church, the first and last being ornaments to their respective neighbourhoods. The two Engine Houses are also erections of 1845. A block of nine stores, corner of Walnut and Fourth; two store houses at the corner diagonally opposite; a spacious hotel at the corner of Walnut and Sixth, and two or three blocks of private residences are among the more important improvements of the second ward, among store houses and private dwellings.

Stultz the Tailor.

Every body has heard of Stultz who is among tailors as Rothschild among bankers—preeminent. The following from a German *Zeitung*, gives a graphic narrative of his progress to fame and fortune. It is so true to nature that it vouches its own authenticity.

In this region and throughout Germany there is now a passion for rebuilding old castles. This aristocratic fever has been raging ever since the King of Prussia removed the castle of Stolzenfels, where he is, at this moment, receiving the Queen of England. With the ruins disappear the old chivalric legends, which are replaced by very prosaic modern chronicles, like that which I gleaned on the railroad, passing by the lately re-built castle of Ortenberg.

About forty years ago, a young workman, named Stultz, born in the village of Lahr, near Ortenberg, left his country to seek his fortune in England. Stultz was a youth of good gifts; he joined to German patience and sagacity a finesse and ingenuity very rare in the land of his birth. The wily German is like a cold Southron; he has a great chance in succeeding in what he undertakes. Fortunes ought thus to smile on the young Stultz, who chose a profession of which his compatriots are fond—that of a tailor; he learnt of the best masters, then took for himself a little establishment, in which he succeeded well. He was soon in good circumstances, as to money, but this did not suffice his ambitious mind; he dreamed of wealth and glory, and wanted to be the first tailor in London. His employers were citizens, merchants and attorneys' clerks; while

doing justice to these good people, who paid him well, he felt himself worthy to clothe those of another quality. His shears trembled in his fingers as he thought of the brilliant gentlemen who set the fashions in Hyde Park and Regent street. "That," thought he, "is the custom to make a tailor illustrious and rich. But how can I ever obtain it."

At this time the famous Brummel was the king of fashion, master and model of the gilded south of London. His tailor was the only one employed by men who had pretensions to elegance. Stultz turned the whole force of his mind to the work of supplanting this unfortunate tailor, who was named, I believe, Thos. Gibson. To dispossess Gibson and assume the same position, was the aim to which he directed all his patience, sagacity and finesse.

Brummel was his hero; his object of attentive and laborious idolatry. Stultz followed him n the streets, went to all public places to watch. His justness of eye and memory served him well in his study. If he had been a painter or sculptor he would have made f om memory a portrait of this great man, being a tailor, he made exactly to his measure a delightful coat, on which he exhausted all the resources of his talent and the graces of his imagination.

When this master-piece was finished, Stultz waited one morning on Brummel, and after waiting three hours in the ante-chamber obtained the honour of an audience, on which he entered, coat in hand.

"Ah! ah!" said Brummel, "a new coat which appears charming. You are, then, one of the men of that rascal, Gibson."

"No, my lord," replied Stultz, who thought this title would propitiate the dandy.

"You are his partner, then."

"Not so, my lord, I am a tailor, little known, as yet, who expects from you his reputation and offers you this sample of his talent."

"I am in despair, my good fellow, that I can do nothing for you. If I were to wear a coat of which Gibson is not the author, it would cause a rupture between us."

"But observe, my lord, what a perfect fit it is."

"It is so, and I am astonished at it, as you have never taken my measure."

"I took it on the statue of Antonius."

"Oh! oh! flattery! that suits me very well. I receive a well deserved compliment and am willing to repay it. The coat is delightful; it has originality in its cut; grace in its details. But I cannot wear it on account of Gibson."

"Gibson would not do the same. He is growing old, falling into routine, but, my lord, I am young; I have the sacred fire, and, with a hero like you, could go far on the path of innovations."

"I believe it, but honour forbids my breaking with Gibson. Think that he has dressed me gratis for ten years."

"It was for his own advantage; the merit is not great."

"He does not, however, fail to give himself airs upon it when I receive him into audience."

"What impertinence! it is in fact he who is in your debt. I should act more conscientiously. Please, my lord, to keep my coat and examine it with care. I will return to-morrow for your definite answer."

It is well known that the delicacy of Brummel was not excessive. Wholly without fortune he lived on his position. All kinds of trades, people furnished whatever he wanted for the honour of his patronage. Stultz, knowing this, had ventured a step further and left in one of the pockets of the coat a hundred pound bank note.

Next day he returned boldly. Brummel received him graciously, observing with a perfect *a'plomb,*

" I have examined the coat, and it cannot be excelled; especially the trimming pleases me."

" I am enchanted to meet your approbation, my lord."

" Decidedly as you said yesterday, Gibson grows old; he has no new ideas now; he never would have thought of that trimming. But, tell me, Mr. Stultz, do you intend to make the same additions to all your coats?"

"Only to those I have the honour to make for you."

" Truly; but do you know that I may require many suits?"

" I will furnish you every month a coat like this in every respect. As to other clothes, you will order them at your pleasure on the same terms as with my predecessor."

"Very well; I accept your offer. From this moment you are my tailor, and I promise you the custom of all my subjects."

In fine, Gibson was dethroned. Stultz set up a splendid establishment at the West End; lords and gentlemen rushed to his shop; his fortune grew with the greatest rapidity; and he never failed to send Brummel every month a coat with the promised bank note, thus paying him in money thirty thousand francs a year, besides his clothes, which came to at least as much.

This was not the only ingenious *trait* that signalized the career of Stultz. The monarchy of fashion is no less than others, subject to revolutions. Brummel, ruined by his excesses, was obliged to leave England. Stultz, with the tact of a statesman, knew how to bend to circumstances so as to conciliate the dynasty. The monarch who succeeded Brummel was a young lord of one of the first families of England. He would not have endured having bank notes put into the pockets of his dresses; nothing in the world would have induced him to make with his tailor an arrangement not to pay his bills. He merely omitted to pay them, which as far as his convenience was concerned, amounted to the same thing.

Unluckily his disciples imitated him in this also, and Stultz found himself creditor to the young aristocracy for large sums, whose recovery seemed lost in the shades of a doubtful future. This difficulty became alarming; it was necessary to put an end to it. Stultz found in his fertile imagination an expedient.

One morning the reader found in one of the most respectable newspapers of London, this notice.

" At the moment for setting out for Bath, Lord C. (the name of the reigning king of fashion was here printed in full,) has ordered coats of the newest taste, and paid the tailor's bill. It is the fashion now among our most elegant men to settle their accounts before setting out for the watering places."

This notice excited to the highest degree the surprise of Lord C. He sent for Stultz.

" What does this notice mean?" said he, showing it to the tailor.

" It means that I am paid," replied Stultz, with his admirable German *sang-froid!*

" Paid! Has my steward taken upon nimself to pay without consulting?"

" No, my lord, your steward is incapable of betraying to such a degree the confidence which you design to bestow upon him."

" Explain to me, then, this riddle."

" I know not how to reply, my lord, unless that, as the authority of such a journal cannot be disputed, the notice is the same as a receipt in full to you."

" How do you mean, sir? I will, if I choose, remain in your debt all my life, but to take a receipt without having paid—! Do you take me for a Brummel?"

" Heaven forbid, my lord. I had not thought of wounding your delicacy; it is simply an innocent *ruse* which will do you no harm and me great good. People will believe you have paid me; what harm can that do you? This piece of originality will, without injuring you, lead all the men of fashion to do the same, and I shall be paid. Thus I have used your magic name to call in my friends, and I hope you will excuse it."

The successor to Brummel was a good Prince; he pardoned. The stratagem succeeded admirably. It was, afterwards, the fashion to pay Stultz's bill on setting off for Bath

After having realized a fortune of twelve milions, Stultz withdrew from commerce and gave up his establishment to one of his nephews who bears his name. He wished to see once more his birth place, and returned seven or oight years ago to the village of Lahr. The Grand Duke of Baden, who wished to keep this great fortune in his dominions, proposed to Stultz to buy the estate of Ortenberg, rebuild the Castle, and assume its lordship, with the title of Baron.

The tailor would thus have found himself in the first rank of the nobility of Baden. His vanity urged him to accept, his wisdom said no, and while he hesitated, Ortenberg was bought by a Russian, M. de Berkholz, who has restored it to its magnificence of the times of the Crusades, when it belonged to the sovereigns of the country. Stultz, more modest, built a hospital, he died shortly after its completion, and his countrymen have raised a monument to his memory. His nephew continuing his work, has already made a fortune equal to that of his uncle; he, too, has founded, they say, a hospital for the old and poor tailors of London. The people of Lahr hope he, too, will finish his days among them; there are many old castles in the neighbourhood to rebuild, and the Grand Duke keeps the title of Baron in abeyance for him.

Life on a Steamboat.

One of the lower country papers narrates two or three amusing incidents of steamboat life. One was the case of a steamboat ploughing along at the rate of twelve miles an hour, and hailed by a man on shore, which on rounding to, ascertained it was merely to learn whether they could take his hemp to New Orleans *next trip.* The other refered to a boat which observed a man on shore, steadily looking at the vessel and making signals with one hand and then with the other. The yawl was put off accordingly, to receive a passenger, as supposed, but on getting ashore, the fellow explained that he had only been brushing the musquitoes right and left to enable him to *read the steamboat's name.*

The following colloquy actually occurred some few trips back, between Capt. Brickell and a *customer* on the banks of the Mississippi, who was sitting on a pile of cord wood, as the boat passed by.

Captain B. hailed him—"What wood is that." "It's *cord wood,*" replied the chopper, with great unconcern.

"How long has it been cut," enquired the captain.

"*Four feet,*" said the wood merchant.

"Give her a lick ahead," said the captain, to cut short the sparring. "Tell your friends if ever you get drowned to look for you at the Falls of St. Anthony.

Corded Skirts.

In the Atlas of the 26th ult., there is a statement, partly original and partly copied from the New York Evening Post, that the ladies are in progress of exhausting the supply of coffee bags, by their consumption of the article in corded skirts. On reading that article I was led to suppose it emanated from one of those ill-natured bachelors who are continually throwing out insinuations respecting the ladies. But the advertisement of Mr. C. A. Schumann, No. 37 Main street, for two hundred coffee bags, an article never made matter of commerce heretofore, appears to give some colour to the charge that they are consumed by the milliners. Perhaps Mr. S will say what they are wanted for, and tranquilise a community which is in anxious doubt on this subject

---

The Jews.

The Englishman's fireside is proverbial for domestic happiness, "the only bliss of Paridise that has survived the fall," but of all firesides, the Jew's fireside, as far as relates to their affections, is the most abundant in good feeling. I have observed this in all families, from the most opulent to the most indigent. Let Christians, instead of yielding to the spirit of intolerance, seek the fireside of a Jewish family. They will find in many houses two or three generations—the young dutifully waiting upon the old and infirm, with a love and respect never to be excelled, and seldom to be equalled, by the members of any religion. Parent and child, husband and wife, united together in one sweet bond of union. That love which made victory bitter to David while he mourned Absalom, and which smote Jephthah to the dust while he wept for his daughter—that love still warms the heart of his descendants; and the Jew, who is not allowed to have power, or place, or country, has a home which his oppressors may

envy, where the Almighty is with him, and his children are about him. Such is the nature of their affection; it is the fruit of their religion, which abounds with love of kindred. * * * It is not, however, only in domestic life that their kind natures appear, they are distinguished for their public and private charities, for their readiness to relieve misery wherever it exists. "The Christians talk much of charity and kindness," said a bankrupt "the Jews practice it. I have experienced more kindness from the few Jews with whom I have dealt than from all my Christian customers." A friend of mine had the misfortune to lose a beloved wife in a childbirth; opposite to him lived an opulent Jew. His lady had just recovered from her confinement; she heard of my friend's loss; she immediately sent and requested that she might nurse the baby; she reared it. It is not, however, to private life that their kindness is limited; it extends to every form of benevolence.

Side-Walks.

In my last appeared an article on the conveniences of side-walks. In reply to inquiries made of me since, it may be stated that the city ordinances provide for keeping our side-walks clear of obstructions. Why standing impediments are permitted to block up the passengers' path must be therefore left to inference. The following may shed light on the subject.

In conversation a day or two since, with the officer whose business it once was to enforce the ordinances, he stated that he was offered at different times and by different persons, hats, coats, and other articles, by way of *douceur,* to wink at infractions by certain individuals, of the laws on this subject. It is but justice to Mr. Hulse, our present superintendent, that I acquit him expressly of the imputation of connivance in this case.

Gluttony.

The capacity for eating with some men is as remarkable as the intellectual capacity of others. At Mauch Chunk, Penna., lately, Thomas Farran, of Summit Hill, agreed to pay ten cents for as many raw eggs as he could eat at one time. He ate forty one and would have eaten more, but for the apprehension of the party who bore the expense, who fearing that there was no bottom to his stomach, interfered with the further betting.

In Philadelphia, during the year 1810, *John Moss,* a broker and merchant of that city, on a wager, after finishing his ordinary supper, swallowed three dozen *hard boiled* eggs. I understand Moss is still living and one of the wealthiest men in Philadelphia.

First Presbyterian Church Edifice.

Most things are great and important, or small and insignificant, by comparison, merely. To those who had been destitute of schools, as the first settlers here, the original log acadmey which occupied the scite of the present Council Chamber, nearly, was an imposing structure, although thrown into shade by its successor, which from 1816 to 1843 was known as the "Cincinnati College." This was deemed a magnificent structure when put up, as the new college is now. What this last will be considered five and twenty years hence, I must leave to the year 1870 to settle.

In like manner, tnose who had no regular place or permanent building as a house for worship, might feel proud when they got into what is now Burke's Church; and when the progress of Cincinnati justified a larger and more permanent erection, supposed they had reached the Ultima Thule of elegance and improvement, in putting up the First Presbyterian Church, on Main street, which, uncouth as ite exterior now appears, and defective as its plan and inside arrangement undoubtedly were, is a building of uncommon solidity, and well adapted in most respects to its appropriate use.

The following is the subscription list towards defraying the expense of building that edifice. It will forever form a record of the liberality of Cincinnati in its infancy; better understood and appreciated when it is recollected that four-fifths of the present wealth of Cincinnati has been created since the period when that enterprise commenced.

We, the subscribers, bind ourselves, our heirs, &c., to pay to the Treasurer of the First Presbyterian Congregation, in Cincinnati, Ohio, the sums annexed to our names, on the condition and in the manner following, viz:

1. The sums subscribed are to be appropriated for the purpose ol erecting a house of public worship in Cincinnati.

2. Each subscriber shall have an opportunity by himself or proxy, of purchasing a pew in said house at public auction, in the price of which he shall have a credit to the full amount of his subscription; and an additional credit of twenty per cent. on all that part of his subscription which he may have paid in cash: Provided, that if his pew shall have cost less than the amount of his subscription, none of the money shall be refunded.

3. The pews shall be subject to an annual tax for the support of a minister in the congregation.

4. The payment of our subscriptions shall be in cash, or such materials, produce, manufactures, merchandize or labour, as may be accepted by the Treasurer under the direction of the Trustees or their committee for the purpose of erecting the edifice; one-fourth in sixty days after public notice given in the Cincinnati papers; one-fourth in six, one-fourth in twelve, and one-fourth in eighteen months afterwards, completing the payments of the whole amount subscribed in one year and eight months after the first public notice.

In testimony whereof we have set our names, and anexed the sums to them, in the year of our Lord, 1812.

Names.	Sums.	Names.	Sums.
Jac. Burnet	$500 00	Martin Baum	$500 00
Wm. Lytle	1000 00	Danl. Symmes	400 00
David E. Wade	400 00	Jesse Hunt	400 00
Jacob Wheeler	400 00	D. Zeigler	400 00
Jas. Ferguson	400 00	Joel Williams	400 00
N. Longworth	250 00	Samuel Stitt	300 00
Francis Carr	250 00	Casper Hopple	200 00
G. Yeatman	200 00	Saml. Lowry	200 00
W. Barr	200 00	John Kidd	200 00
David Kilgour	200 00	Wm. Irwin	200 00
Jacob Williams	200. 00	W. Woodward	300 00
N. Reeder	200 00	Jesse Reeder	200 00
Wm. Betts	200 00	J. Crammer	50 00
Z. Biggs	100 00	Robt. Caldwell	150 00
J. Jenkinson	100 00	G. P. Torrence	100 00
O. M. Spencer	100 00	S. Ramsay	100 00
John Riddle	200 00	Isaac Bates	100 00
Clark Bates	100 00	E. Hutchinson	100 00
Wm. Stanley	300 00	J. B. Enness	50 00
James Riddle	250 00	Dan. Drake	75 00
Robert Allison	75 00	John H. Piatt	400 00
Isaac Anderson	100 00	Th. Ashburn	100 00
John Jones	50 00	H. Bechcle	100 00
J. Baymiller	200 00	T. Graham	300 00
Solomon Sisco	25 00	A. St Clair,Jr.	125 00
W. Noble	150 00	S. W. Davies	50 00
A. Johnston	30 00	W. C. Anderson	50 00
W. H. Hopkins	25 00	J. B. Robinson	100 00
Jeremiah Hunt	100 00	O. Ormsby	100 00
Samuel Kidd	50 00	John Brown	25 00
E. Williams	300 00	J. S. Wallace	200 00
P. Dickey	200 00	Saml. Perry	100 00
A. Dunseth	200 00	J. McIntire	100 00
Saml. Newell	100 00	E. J. Dayton	100 00
Wm. Ramsey	100 00	Joseph Prince	150 00
John S. Gano	100 00	Wm. Ruffin	100 00
J. Carpenter	100 00	C. Park	200 00
Joseph Ruffner	300 00	H. Flint	100 00
James Conn	100 00	Jos. Warner	75 00
L. Sayre	75 00	J. P. Spinning	75 00
Robert Meraie	75 00	Peter M'Nicoll	75 00
J. Reeder	75 00	A. Moore	100 00
John Mahard	50 00	Davis Embree	75 00
Geo. St. Clair	75 00	J. Gibson, Jr.	50 00
Daniel Mayo	50 00	J. Andrews	50 00
I. Spinning	100 00	A. Hamilton	50 00
Wm. Corry	100 00	C. L'Homedieu	100 00

22

John Watson	50 00	Thos. Beal	100 00
Jos. McMurray	100 00	James Dover	30 00
Andrew Hopple	50 00	Saml. Garart	100 00
Wm. Carey	50 00	Chas. Marsh	25 00
Jabez C. Tunis	50 00	J. Armstrong	200 00
Henry Hafer	50 00	Stephen Butler	25 00
J. Heighway	25 00	R. Archibald	75 00
Thos. Sloo, Jr.	50 00	Francis West	50 00
J. N. Gluer	25 00	Jonah Martin	50 00
A. Ferguson	30 00	Nath. Edson	50 00
Josiah Halley	50 00	David Wade	50 00
Andrew Mack	50 00	Benj. Cross	30 00

Emigration.

So large a city as Cincinnati not only receives continued accessions by emigration from Europe and the Atlantic regions; but furnishes a fair share of emigrants to various points west. Of the hundreds upon hundreds of individuals who have thus left Cincinnati during the last five and twenty years—settling themselves in the far west and south, I suppose the proportion that has since returned must be nine out of every ten. As far as my acquaintance extends, it is nineteen out of twenty. Indeed I cannot recollect half a dozen of these who are still residing abroad. The general testimony of those, who, in the pressures of 1834 and 1841, had returned to Cincinnati, after trying their fortune elsewhere, being that hard as the times were, they were better here than where they had been; and that if a man could not make a living here, he could not make it any where.

While engaged taking the census of 1840, I obtained the facts embodied in the following narrative from a citizen of ours, conversant thoroughly with the family refered to.

Among the emigrants from Europe in the earlier days of Cincinnati, was a Mr. L——, who after struggling long for a living in England, in his business as a coppersmith, concluded to settle in the United States. Accordingly he visited Cincinnati, where he decided on establishing himself, rightly judging it a good location for one in his business. His family consisted of the wife, two or three boys, and as many girls, all small. Mr. L—— soon got in a good business; and his boys becoming able to help him in it after the lapse of three or four years, he was fast getting into good circumstances. Unfortunately for his comfort, Mrs. L—— having few acquaintances as well as little leisure to make more, and living under a different state of manners, customs, pursuits and recreations from those existing in that part of Europe from which the family came, had never been reconciled to Cincinnati. In the enjoyment of many comforts and privileges which she did not possess at home, her thoughts dwelt with regret on those only which she had left behind, and as a consequence, by every means in her power, endeavored to induce her husband to return. His remonstrances were to no purpose, and for the sake of peace he consented, and they resumed a residence whence they originally came. A few months, however, sufficed to teach Mrs. L—— the folly of the step thus taken. Absence and time had severed old links of acquaintance and friendship; her own tastes had insensibly changed, by conforming to the state of things in a new country, and now, when too late, she perceived the various advantages and enjoyments she had abandoned in leaving the United States. The change rapidly going on in her feelings, of course, soon became apparent to her husband, but desirous that a thorough cure should take place, he forbore saying a word on the subject, well aware that it would come to a bearing in the natural course of things. One day she came home from market with a leg of veal in her basket, "There," says she, "is all I got for a guinea, I wish I was back again in Cincinnati," and setting down on her chair, fairly burst into tears. "Do you say so, my dear," said L., "we will set off then, if you please, next Monday." And on Monday they started accordingly, and were soon again in the old dwelling and shop, on Main street, where the old man spent the remainder of his days, and the boys, now among our most intelligent and wealthy citizens, are doing an active and extensive business.

There is an undoubted tendency in the West, however it may be accounted for, to dissatisfy those who have once resided in it, with a new residence in the Atlantic cities, and still more with European society and modes of life.

Ante Revolutionary Relic.

Every student of American history will remember the name of Sir William Pepperrell, the commander of the Colonial Expedition, in 1746, to Louisburg, Cape Breton. The following is an original letter of his, which has been handed me by Hon. Bellamy Storer, great grand son of the officer whose address it bears. It is publishhd—verbatim et literatim—as a feature of the times:

"KITTERY, April 18th, 1759.

"COL. JOHN STORER:

"Sir,—It fills me with great concern to hear the men returned impressed for the Canada Expedition have not attended their duty as directed.

"I expect if they don't immediately go to Castle Williams as directed, they will some of them be hanged without benefit of clergy, and it will be a scandal in this country. Here is at my wharf a schooner that designs to sail next Monday morning for Boston : if they come by that time they may go in her and all will be well; but if they don't, every officer, civil and military, and all His Majesty's subjects, should assist in apprehending them. You ought to bestir yourself in this affair; my health will not permit me.

" I am your friend and humble servant,

WM. PEPPERRELL."

Extraordinary Facts in Natural History.

The mesmeric discoveries made within the last five years, have kindled a spirit of experimenting on divers subjects, which promise remarkable results. A striking instance of the kind is recorded below.

If we go on at this rate, Natural History will soon require to be rewritten, to keep up with the progress of modern science. There are those, no doubt, who will ridicule statements [of fact as well established as those attested by Major Pillers; but with the endorsement of so respectable a print as the Charleston Courier, and the many kindred facts in mesmerism equally incredible, yet familiar to hundreds in Cincinnati and elsewhere, I do not see why the Major's testimony should be disputed.

From the Charleston Courier.

Maj. John Pillers, a farmer of great respectability in this county, informed us that while he lived at his father's in Missouri, some twenty years ago, a buzzard (is not this bird the real vulture?) was taken alive, having gorged itself over a carcase to such a degree as to prevent its flying —its weight being too heavy for its wings, when he, together with his father, brother, and a neighbour, with a small shoemakers' awl, *ripped open its eyes so that no part of the ball of either remained.* The head of the bird was then put under one of its wings, in which position it remained a few minutes, when to the surprise of all, it gradually relieved its head from its wing, shook itself as if to arrange its disordered feathers, and reappeared with two good sound eyes, free from blemish, pessessing in every degree the power of vision. This seemingly cruel experiment was repeated with the same bird on different occasions, ih the presence of different persons, fifty times, and always with the same result, and not the least injury appeared to have been occasioned by it. After the lapse of a few months the bird flew away to its accustomed haunts. I have mentioned this fact to several persons, who, though they had never "seen the like," expressed no surprise or doubt of its truth, but replied that they had always heard that the down from the inside of a buzzard's wing was a cure for blindness in horses, and one man remarked that he cured a most inveterate case of approaching blindness in himself by it. He procured the down, spread it on a bandage, applied it to his eyes, and recovered.

In corroboration of Major Pillers' statement, whose deposition is hereunto subjoined, I can state my own experience on the subject. Travelling, some three years since, on the American bottom, I staid part of a day with a friend of mine, whose step son had the day before taken a half grown buzzard—as soon as I saw the bird, the statement of Major Pillers came fresh upon my recollection; and as I had always been incredulous, I was determined to put it to the test of experiment, and accordingly mentioned the fact to the young gentleman who had the bird, and desired him to operate upon it. Having no sharp pointed instrument at hand, other than a pin, with that he punctuaed one of the eyes, and all its lustre instantly disappeared. The head was then placed under the wing of the bird, where it remained a few minutes only, and when taken out, the eye had assumed its usual brilliancy, appearing as sound as the other, with not a speck upon it. In this experiment, it is true, the eye ball was not ripped open—the operation seeming too cruel to have my participation; but, as far as it goes, it serves to inspire belief in the statement of Maj. Pillers. And why should there not be a healing virtue in the down of a buzzard's wing? No man can say why not. Do we know whence those animals and mineral sdbstances, resorted to for the cure of all maladies, derive their healing powers. The fact that certain substances possess such qualities has been ascertained by experiment, and until that infallable test has disproved the efficacy of the down, no one can say it will not cure blindness? And why should not the buzzard have the power to reproduce its eyes? There are many mysteries in nature that we shall never be able to fathom. It is a mystery that an acorn can develope itself and become an oak; that an unsightly worm can, in a short time, become a most beautiful fly; in short, the whole world is but an open volume of mysteries, which all wonder at, but few can unravel. It is true, that—

" There are more things in Heaven and earth
Than are dreamt of in our philosophy."

We know that many insects and reptiles have the power of casting their old skins every year, and appearing in an entirely new one; that the common house spider gets a new skin and a new set of legs every year; and that if you pluck off one of its legs, it will, in two or three days, have a new one in its place. The shedding the teeth and reproduction of the nails in the human species are certainly remarkable, and would be so considered, were thoy not of daily occurrence. Upon sober consideration, it cannot be regarded more wonderful that a buzzard should have the power to reproduce its eyes, tnan a spider its skin and legs, a horse his teeth and hoofs—our species their teeth and nails, or a deer his antlers. They are all remarkable phenomena of animal philosophy, and cannot be accounted for on any known principles.

The fact stated in the conclusion of the deposition, relative to the bald eagle, has not, I venture to say, arrested the attention of any one. Who would believe that the feathers of that bird cannot be plucked out? The idea of feathers and plucking are ever associated, yet you cannot get those of the bald eagle without taking the skin with them—unless, perhaps, through the agency of some chemical application, of which we " far west in the backwoods" know nothing.

SIGMA.

DEPOSITION.

I, John Pillers, a citizen of Randolph county, Illinois, do degose and say, that I am the individual alluded to in the above communication, and that the facts stated therein, so far as I am concerned, are true in every particular. The experiment of ripping open the buzzard's eyes, during the time we kept it, from February to

May, was repeated, I dare say, fifty times; and once at a log rolling, ten times in one day. An old African negro, belonging to Mr. F. Valli, Jr., of St. Genevieve, named Joseph, (though supposed to be upwards of one hundred years old,) first told me of it, and I have tried it frequently since, on different buzzards with the same result. This same negro totd me that the feathers could not be plucked out of a bald eagle. This is true. You may try it any way, and scald it, and you cannot pull out a feather.

Signed,   JOHN PILLERS.
Deposition taken before me,
Signed,   JAMES HUGHES, J. P.

Third Ward--Cincinnati.

In the enumeration of buildings to this ward, I find twelve hundred and twenty-five dwelling houses, workshops, public stables, store houses, mills, factories ond offices. Of these, seven hundred and eighty are bricks, two are of stone, and four hundred and gve are frames. Besides these there are of public buildings,—the Botanico-Medical College, and Bethel Chapel; City Water Works, an Engine House, two Public School Houses, and the new and extensive Little Miami Rail-Road Depot.

Of these buildings there were at the close of the year 1842—

	Stone.	Brick.	Frame.	Total.
	2	535	325	860
Built in 1843,	0	69	44	113
" 1844,	0	71	46	117
" 1845,	0	50	65	115
	2	725	480	1206

This ward embraces most of the original improvements of Cincinnati, in its western section; and the whole ward having bcen built on for years, there is less room for new buildings than in suburb wards. But many of the edifices put up this year and the last are of very imposing extent and character, such as the foundries of Niles & Co., on Deer Creek; Griffey, Harkness, &c., which not only cover a great space of ground; but are many stories in height. Four-fifths, at least, of this ward is built to its utmost capacity.

The Third Ward is the great beehive of Cincinnati. Planing machines; iron, bell, and brass founderies; breweries, saw, oil and rolling mills; boiler yards, boat and machine shops, &c., contribute an extensive share of its business.

Early Business Dealings here.

In the early ages of a community, and before banks and the mint afford a currency for the people, not only is one description of goods bartered for another, but debts are contracted, payable in trade. Many amusing specimens of due bills and other contracts have fallen under my notice, which illustrate this state of things in the early days of Cincinnati, and some of them have gone to press in my columns.

I have before me a due bill of a farmer of Hamilton county, dated 1793, for professional services to one of our first lawyers, *first* in every sense of the term, "for a cow and calf—payable next spring." Another due bill of the same period is for thirty dollars, the debt having been incurred on the same score, payable in pork. It seems pork has always been a staple here; but the present dwellers in Cincinnati probably do not suppose it ever formed the currency. Flour was exchanged in early days here extensively with the bakers, pound for pound, the baker making quite a iair profit under the operation. In store dealings, change was made by giving a row or two of pins or a few needles.

Such is society, always, in its first stages.

Fair of the Mechanics' Institute.

The 8th anniversary exhibition of this institution closed on Saturday last. It fell short in the number and variety of articles displayed, as compared with some of its predecessors, and the place of exhibition, the only one, on the whole, suited to its purposes, was not well adapted either for display or access. The Fair, making these allowances, however, was creditable to those concerned in getting it up. There were many splendid trophies of the ingenuity, taste, and excellence of our Cincinnati artizans, and various interestinu coutributions in the fine arts, and of curiosities both of nature and art.

I have not space in the restricted limits of my columns to notice more than a few articles, whose number corresponds with the catalogue.

No. 2. An extremely ingenious, efficient and cheap apparatus for roasting coffee thoroughly and equally, and at the same time to preserve the aroma from escaping, as it always does when burnt in an open vessel.

7 and 26. A variety of locks from Glenn & McGregor, of unrivalled excellence in structure, accuracy and finish.

13 and 25. Bank note and fancy engravings, from Rawdon, Wright & Hatch, and Tappan, Carpenter & Co., rival establishments here, equal to any thing in the United States.

14. Cards of Hinges, and a great variety of building Hardware of malleable iron from Miles Greenwood. There is nothing in the city of greater importance, in the various aspects of the subject, than Greenwood's manufacturing operations, and a minute examination there of these various articles can alone do justice to their merit and value.

30. Various specimens of book binding, by Jacob Ernst, all of the best quality, and some of them truly magnificent, especially a Doway

bible, ordered for the new Cathedral, and Mc-Kenney's Indian Biography and Portraits, intended to be sent by Bishop Purcell to Rome, as a present to the Pope.

5, 38, and 119. Daguerreotypes, from E. C. Hawkins, Abel Shawk, Faris & Plumbe, all of great excellence. A very interesting case affording the portraits of the early pioneers of Cincinnati, attracted general notice.

44. Specimens of Parlor Grates and Fire Stands, from Horton & Baker, a variety of elegant patterns, beautifully executed.

46. Various specimens of dyeing by William Teasdale, who has this year not only maintained his usual excellence, but appears to have driven his competitors from the field.

49, 13. Specimens of Umbrellas and Parasols, from I. Sleeper. The travelling umbrellas are a great convenience, and of equal excellence; all well worthy of a fuller examination than this exhibition afforded time to make.

50. Printing Ink, from Stearns & Co., of various qualities, all equal to the corresponding articles from the East.

57. An improved Hose Reel, from I. & B. Bruce, a model of taste and beauty. The lamps, brass and plating work cannot be surpassed any where.

68. A large balance of 1500 lb. capacity, by P. Medearis, of such exquisite accuracy, that, notwithstanding its great size and weight, and its resting on a solid wall, the mere passing of the visiters over the floor kept it in constant vibration.

94. A lithograph of the steamboat Yorktown, by J. B. Rowse, an admirable engraving, by a young Cincinnati artist, of one of our most splendid boats. This piece of work needs no eulogium of mine.

79, 102. Valise, Carpet-bag, and Ladies'-bag, saddle and harness. Of these it suffices to say that they are from the establishment of Isaac Young.

104. Fire Engine and Garden Hose, from Paddock & Campbell; abundant proof that these articles can be made as good and as cheap here as elsewhere.

There are a number of other articles to which I have not time to refer, particularly, as specimens of Hair Mattrass work, Marble Mantles, Lard Oil of Emery, Cheever, and others; Whips and Canes from C. Penrose; Baskets sent by Ballauf, Fancy Chairs from W. H. Ross, Hats from C. R. Camp; Japaned ware of Greenfield & Winchell; Paddle Wheel for steamboats, by Chase & Cole; Flutes by J. D. Douglass; Glass paper from J. Van Amringe; Cotton Batting of J. A. Richardson, and a Patent Detector Bank Door Lock, by Glenn and McGregor, many of which are remarkable for their ingenuity and taste, and others for their excellence in materials and workmanship.

Robert Elliott.

One of the few marble monuments in the Presbyterian burying ground, on Twelfth street, has been erected to the memory of one of the early business men of this region, and in some sense, one of the pioneers of the west. I refer to Col. Robert Elliott, who, in connection with Col. Eli Williams, of Hagarstown, Md., was one of the several contractors of supplies for Wayne's Army, on his march to the Indian country. Various incorrect accounts having been published of the circumstances attending his death, I put upon record the following from an authentic source, and which I believe is the truth in the premises.

Col. Elliott was a native of Pennsylvania; had settled in Hagarstown, and at the period to which I am to refer, 1794, was out west superintending the deliveries of his contracts. He left Fort Hamilton, accompanied by a waiter, taking what is now called the Winton road, to Cincinnati. On reaching about four miles of his journey, he was fired on by the savages in ambush and killed. He fell from his horse, which made his way back to Hamilton, followed by the servant upon the other horse. Elliott was an uncommonly large man, being both tall and heavy, and weighed nearly three hundred pounds. He wore a wig, which of course came off under the application of the scalping knife, without exhibiting marks of blood, to the great surprise of the Indians, who viewed it as a great imposition, and spoke of it afterwards as "a d——— lie." The horse was a remarkable one—worth one hundred and twenty dollars in those days, when it required a good horse to bring seventy-five dollars. He was a dark brown, but just where a pillion would have been fastened to the saddle, and exactly corresponding with it in size and shape, was a space entirely white. Elliott's body was boxed up and put into his own wagon, and sent the next day to Cincinnati for burial, the waiter accompanying it, and riding the Col's. horse. Nearly, if not exactly where Elliott had been killed the day before, a ball from Indians in ambush killed the servant also, the horse escaping as before to Hamilton, and the wagoner flying for his life. The box was broken open by the savages in expectation of it containing something of value. It was left, on discovering the contents, only the wagon horses being carried off. A party was then detached from the fort, which delivered the body at Fort Washington, and it was buried in the usual burying ground, at the corner of Main and Fourth streets. Many years after, his son, Commodore Jesse D. Elliott, then on a visit to this city, having ascertained the place of his interment, removed the body to the present burial ground of the First Presbyterian Society, erecting, as the table itself states, the monument to the memory of his father, Col. Elliott.

Steam Sash Factory.

There seems to exist a general conspiracy in Cincinnati, to put down the sales of eastern articles to the south and west of the whole United States, and a systematic effort to introduce article by article into our manufacture here by machinery of what has heretofore been fabricated merely by hand, so as to command the supply of those markets at rates which defy competition in the Atlantic cities.

I have already referred to the bedsteads, bureaus, tables, &c., made by steam propelled machinery. My present notice relates to the supply of window sash, which is now turned out under the same process.

Mr. S. *Vanemmon*, occupying the upper story of Bicknell & Jenkins' new planing machine, on Canal, between Race and Elm streets, has just put into operation an ingenious series of machinery, which takes the raw material of lumber in its roughest state, and, as its finishing touch, presents window sash of every desired size, ready fitted for use, at a saving of labour, time and expense of nearly fifty per cent. on the old system of manufacture.

The boards in their rough state are first cross cut to the necessary length by a circular saw; taken to the facing machine, where they are planed by the action of a wheel of great power and steadiness, having bitts which act successively on the surface of the boards to reduce it to an uniform evenness and smoothness. The boards are then taken to a slitting machine, where they acquire the necessary breadth for their various purposes; and thence to an instrument which adds a delicate and perfect moulding to the various parts of the sash. Lastly, the sash rails are taken to a machine which forms the mortices and tenons with great exactness, as well as rapidity, the whole operation of turning out the sash being by machinery, except the pinning together the entire frame. Some idea of the celerity of these operations may be formed by observing the movement of the slitting wheel, which performs twenty-five hundred revolutions in a minute, a degree of speed which mocks the power of the eye, to discern form or colour to the saw.

Most of the machinery is the invention of Mr. Vanemmon, and all of it is highly ingenious and efficient.

It must be obvious from this statement that sash can thus be furnished for home, and especially distant points in the west and south,

cheaper and of better quality than have heretofore been supplied to those markets.

Human Life.

It is melancholy to reflect how large a portion of life is lost or wasted before we learn its value. I do not know how it is with others; as to myself, I rarely close a day without regretting that it is not three or four hours longer. Of course I have little sympathy with those who kill time purposely and avowedly.

But take the case of a professedly industrious individual, and deduct lost and wasted time, and see even in a long life how little is left. Suppose our subject has reached his three score years and ten, a hale, vigorous old man. Deduct eight hours for sleep, and, on an average for each day, two hours for meals, between eating and waiting for them; and for dressing and undressing, washing, shaving, and other kindred employments, two hours more. Here is half the life time, or thirty-five years spent to no result.

The ordinary maladies of childhood, the diseases and accidents of maturer years, will deduct at least one day to the week, or one-seventh of the residue, say five years. This brings the period down to thirty years.

Deduct from this, time idly wasted, especially in youth in unprofitable reading, and still more unprofitable company, and it will probably reduce the residue to fifteen years, actively and profitably spent.

This calculation refers to, perhaps, the most favourable view that can be taken of the subject. What period of life can those be said to live who have left the world no better, richer, wiser or happier for their existence!

When a poor man gives, he begs.

There is a Spanish proverb, "*A poor man who gives, begs*," of which I have been forcibly reminded by the contemptible practice which many Americans, unworthy of the name, indulge in forwarding presents to crowned heads, and men of authority and wealth, in various parts of the world. The latest case is that of Mr. Day, a two penny gumeleastic manufacturer in New York City, who lately exchanged with the Bey of Tunis a pair of Indian rubber boots and breeches, accompanied with an Indian rubber boat, for a gold snuff box set with diamonds, valued at $2,500. *Allah Bismillah!* no doubt exclaimed the barbarian, when he examined his costly elastic treasure.

I well remember many years ago, a series of plough inventors or improvers sent their plough patterns to the Emperor Alexander, the mighty Czar of Muscovy, as presents. They were all graciously received and paid for like Mr. Day's presens, in rings, snuff boxes, &c. The ship-ment of ploughs increased to such an extent as to point his majesty out as the great patron of agriculture for the wide world. At last the em-peror's patience, or his rings, &c., began to give out. Accordingly, the receipt of the next plough that came was acknowledged by the present of its predecessor of the same kind, which effectu-ally stopped this species of speculation in the Russian market. I fear his Tunisian highness must send back his India rubbers in exchange for his next present, unless he is prepared to empty his treasury.

From the Wheeling Times.

History and Tradition.

We have heard some persons remark, on the strength of traditions, that our account of M'Col-loch's leap, given some days since, was not strict-ly correct as relates to the circumstances attend-ing it. The facts we related are such as they appear in the most authentic records to which we have access. There are always variations in the traditions by which all incidents are handed down; but so long as they do not change the *facts* of the case, they are of but little import-ance. History will be made up of the earliest printed accounts of transactions, and thus, wheth-er they are literally correct or not, they become established as facts.

In this sense we refer to incidents most inter-esting in the history of our town and surround-ing country. We do not profess any great knowledge of our early history; but we have of-ten referred to the productions of our former fel-low-townsman, Geo. S. M'Kiernan, who devoted much time to the examination of all the papers connected with the early history of this city and the surrounding country. We have not many of his pages at hand; but we have often perused them and others, and often reflected with regret that so few of us had taken the pains to make ourselves familiar with the history of the fron-tiersmen who settled on the ground we inhabit, when almost every leaf covered an arrow, and every tree shaded an Indian and a foe. We do not know what may be the feelings of others; but we never pass a plain grave stone standing between Wheeling and Grave Creek, without a feeling of awe, and suffering our mind to wander back to the days of Indian warfare, of blood and carnage, of war whoops, of Indians, scalping knifes, and tomahawks. That stone bears this inscription, "This humble stone is erected to the memory of Captain Foreman and twenty-one of his men, who were slain by a band of ruthless savages—the allies of a civilized na-tion of Europe—on the 25th of September, 1777.

So sleep the brave who sink to rest
By all their country's wishes blest."

This stone stands in a retired spot about seven miles from Wheeling, and just where the hill ap-proaches the river to commence what is called the Grave Creek "narrows." So fine a place for ambush could scarcely be found elsewhere, and it is by no means surprising that the Indians suc-ceeded in cutting off nearly the whole force.— Grave Creek had then a fort, having been settled by Mr. Joseph Tomlinson, only one year after the settlement of Wheeling by the Zanes, in 1770.

On the 25th of September, 1777, a smoke was seen from the Wheeling fort in the direction of Grave Creek. Apprehensions were entertained that the smoke was caused by the Indians burn-ing the fort at Grave Creek. Foreman, with forty-five men, marched down to Grave Creek, and finding all safe there, started home. When they had reached the foot of the narrows, Mr. Lynn, an old Indian fighter, advised Capt. Fore-man to return by the ridge route and thus secure themselves against any attack by the Indians, whom he presumed saw them go down from the opposite side of the river, and intended attacking them on their return.

The captain did not rely sufficiently on the opinion of Lynn, and continued up the valley, while Lynn and some of the soldiers went over the ridge. The last were safe; but when Fore-man with his men had nearly reached the place where the stone now stands, they found some trifling Indian trinket in the road before them. Their attention was attracted by it, and at the instant, half a dozen Indians stepped into the path before them, and as many in the rear, and then, as they attempted to meet their assailants, on every side, and from every bush, an Indian rose up. They were butchered without the re-motest hope of escape or successful defence. A few reached the hill; some succeeded in climbing it; but the majority were shot as they went up, and either killed or lamed. Capt. Fore-man fought well, but was among the first who fell. The number killed was twenty-two, and it is supposed that the Indian force was not less than three or four hundred. This was among the most bloody of the frontier skirmishes, and de-serves to be placed on record, not on account of any particular courage or skill, but as it shows the determined boldness of the savage foe with which our frontiersmen had to contend.

The Fuschia.

Mr. Shepherd, the accomplished conservator of the Botanical Gardens at Liverpool, is the au-thority for the following anecdote respecting the introduction of that elegant flower shrub, the Fuschia, into the green houses of Europe. Old Mr. Lee, a well known nursery-man and florist, at Greenwich, near London, about fifty years ago, was one day showing his variegated treasures to a person who suddenly turned and said, "well, you have not in your whole collection so pretty a flower as one I saw to-day in a window at Wapping!" "Indeed, and what was this Phœnix like?" "Why, the plant was beautiful, and the flowers hung down like tassels from the drooping branches, their colour was the deepest crimson, and in the centre a fold of rich purple."

Particular inquiries were made as to the exact whereabouts, and Mr. Lee posted off to the place, where he discovered the object of his pursuit, and immediately pronounced it a *new plant*. He saw and admired.

Entering the humble dwelling, he said, "my good woman, this is a nice plant of yours; I should like to buy it."

"Ah, sir! I could'nt sell it for no money, it was brought me from foreign parts by my hus-band, who has gone again, and I must keep it for his sake."

"But I must have it."

"No, sir, I can't spare it."

"Here," emptying his pockets, "here is gold,

silver and copper," (his stock amounting to more than eight guineas.)

"Well a day, sure this is a power of money."

"'Tis yours, and the plant is mine, my good woman. I'll give you one of the first young ones I rear, to keep for your husband's sake. I will, indeed."

The bargain was struck, a coach called, in which old Mr. Lee and his apparently dearly purchased flower was deposited. On returning home, his first work was to strip off and destroy every blossom and bud; the plant was divided into small cuttings which were forced into bark beds and hot beds, and again subdivided. Every effort was employed to multiply the plant. Mr. Lee became the delighted possessor of three hundred fuschias, all giving promise of fine blossom. The two which first expanded were placed in his window. A lady came in, "why, Mr. Lee, my dear Mr. Lee, where did you get this charming flower?"

"'Tis a new thing, my lady, pretty, is it not?"

"Pretty! 'tis lovely! its price?"

"A guinea, your ladyship," and one of the two plants that evening stood in beauty on her ladyship's table in her boudoir.

"My dear Charlotte! where did you get that elegant flower?"

"Oh, 'tis a new thing, I saw it at old Mr. Lee's; pretty, is it not?"

"Pretty! 'tis beautiful! what did it cost?"

"Only a guinea, and there was another left."

The visiter's horse trotted off to the suburb, and a third beauteous plant graced the spot from whence the first had been taken. The second guinea was paid, and the fuschia adorned another drawing-room of fashion. This scene was repeated as new calls were made by persons attracted by the beauty of the plant. Two plants, graceful and bursting into flower, were constantly seen on the same spot. He gladdened the faithful sailor's wife with the promised flower, and before the season closed, nearly three hundred guineas jingled in his purse, the produce of the single shrub from the window at Wapping, as a reward for old Mr. Lee's taste, skill and decision.

Benefit of Advertising.

Our fellow citizen Isaac Young, whose taste in such matters is well known, got up, some time since, a neat lithograph business card, decorated with fancy trunks and other professional devices.

A friend of his on Lower Market, being about to visit England, Mr. Y. gave him some of the lithographs to be left at Birmingham, Manchester, Sheffield, &c., which was accordingly done.

On Saturday evening, a genteel stranger, evidently an Englishman, accosted Mr. Young at his saddler shop, "Mr. Young, I presume."— Young bowed assent. "I saw your card at Ibbotson & Sons, Sheffield,"—a heavy cutlery establishment there—"and I made up my mind if I visited America to buy a trunk of you, and really, sir," added he, "I saw nothing in New York or Philadelphia in this line, like these Cincinnati articles." "They tell me," added the stranger, "that this place was a forest fifty years ago; can it be possible."

Mr. Young sold the Englishman several other articles besides the trunk, feeling as much gratification in finding Cincinnati and *himself* so well appreciated abroad, as in the profit he might have made by the sale.

Irish Ingenuity.

An intelligent traveller in Ireland recently remarked one peculiarity of the people. He says "every peasant I met asked me the same question, namely—*what time of day it was!*" An Irish gentleman bet a dozen of claret with an English officer, that he would ride from Cork to Mallow on a market day without being once asked this question—and won, too—simply by putting the question *himself* before any other person could do so.

Anecdote.

Judge Dooly, of Georgia, was remarkable for his wit, as well as other talents. At one place where he attended Court, he was not pleased with his entertainment at the tavern. On the first day of the Court, a hog, under the name of a pig, had been cooked whole and laid on the table. No person attacked it. It was brought next day, and the next, and treated with the same respect; and it was on the table on the day on which the Court adjourned. As the party finished their dinner, Judge Dooly rose from the table, and in a solemn manner addressed the Clerk, "Mr. Clerk," said he, "dismiss that hog upon his recognizance until the first day of the next Court. He has attended so faithfully during the present term, that I don't think it will be necessary to take any security."

In a Predicament.

"Hallo, Jim, how are you," inquired a young man of a friend whom he had called upon, and found *confined* to his chamber.

"I'm not well!"

"Not well! what's the matter with you?"

"I'm in a predicament."

"In a predicament! How do you make that out?"

"I have not paid my board these six weeks."

"Is that all? why my dear fellow you don't pretend to say that is the cause of your illness!"

"Yes, but I do! They won't allow me to go away till I pay my board, and they won't allow me to eat till I settle up."

His friend picked up his hat and remarked he must begone.

St. Peter's Cathedral.

The new Roman Catholic Cathedral, on Plum street, after progressing nearly five years in its erection, has become so far advanced to its completion as to admit of its consecration; and the religious rites and ceremonies peculiar to that faith will therefore be celebrated for that purpose on Sabbath, the 2d November next, which is the day following that of All Saints Day in the calendar of that church.

As much interest is felt on this subject by a share of my readers, I have prepared some interesting statistics in reference to this edifice, which, when completed, will be the finest building in the west, and the most imposing in appearance of any of the Cathedrals in the United States belonging to the Roman Catholic Church, the metropolitan edifice in Baltimore not excepted.

St. Peter's Cathedral is a parallelogram of two hundred feet in length, by eighty in breadth. It is fifty-five feet from floor to ceiling. The roof is partly supported by the side walls, which as well as the front, average four feet in thickness, but principally upon eighteen free-stone pillars, nine on each side, which are of three and a half feet diameter and thirty-three feet in height. The ceiling is of stucco work of a rich and expensive character, which renders it equal in beauty to any cathedral in the world, as I am authorized to say by competent judges, although executed in this instance by Mr. Taylor, a Cincinnati artist, for a price less than one half of what it would have cost in Europe. The main walls are built of Dayton limestone, of which this building furnished the first example in Cincinnati. The basement is of the blue limestone of the Ohio river, and forms an appropriate contrast with the superstructure. The tower and steeple are not yet finished. It is contemplated to put up a chime of the usual number and range of bells. The cathedral will be finished with a centre aisle of six feet, and two aisles for processional purposes, eleven feet each, adjoining the side-walks. The residue of the space will form one hundred and forty pews ten feet in length. The roof is composed of iron plates whose seams are coated with a composition of coal tar and sand, which renders it impervious to water. The edifice was put up under the superintendence of Mr. Henry Walter, and has cost short of $90,000, with the addition of $24,000 for the half square which it occupies in part. Not a drop of ardent spirits was consumed in its erection, and notwithstanding the unmanageable shape and size of the materials, not an accident occurred in the whole progress of the work. Every man employed about it was paid off every Saturday night; and as the principal part of the labour was performed at a season of the year when working hands are not usually employed to their advantage, the heavy disbursements have proved a seasonable and sensible benefit to the labouring class. The payments were made in cash, also, the principle of giving orders for work not being resorted to here.

Let me now advert to its interior condition, as it will exhibit itself when ready for the services of the 2d proximo. An altar of the purest Carrara marble, made by *Chiappri* of Genoa, occupies the west end of the Cathedral. This is embellished with a centre piece, being a circle with rays, around which wreaths and flowers are beautifully chiseled. It is represented to me by those who possess more knowledge and taste on such subjects than I pretend to, as a piece of exquisite design and workmanship. At the opposite end is put up an immense organ of forty-four stops and twenty-seven hundred pipes, lately finished by *Schwab*, of our city, which cost $5,400. One of these pipes alone is thirty-three feet long, and weighs four hundred pounds. There is no doubt that this is an instrument superior in size, tone and power to any on the continent, that in the German Roman Catholic Church at Baltimore, by Schwab, perhaps, excepted. The following paintings will occupy the various compartments in the Cathedral:

St. Peter liberated by the Angel.
Descent from the Cross.
Annunciation of the Blessed Virgin.
St. Jerome in the attitude of listening to the trumpet announcing the final judgment.
Christ in the Garden.
Flight into Egypt.

The *St. Peter* is by *Murillo*, well known as the head of the Spanish school; and was a present to Bishop Fenwick by Cardinal Fesch, uncle to Napoleon. The others are by some of the first artists in Europe.

The two windows next the altar are of stained glass, and serve to give us of the west an idea of that style of diffusing light to edifices devoted to religious purposes in the old world.

There will be the largest assemblage of prelates and subordinate clergy of the church on the occasion of consecrating St. Peter's, which has ever been gathered in Cincinnati. Archbishop *Eccleston*, of Baltimore; the Bishops, *Flaget*, of Louisville; *Miles*, of Nashville; *Henni*, of Milwaukie; *Kenrick*, of St. Louis; *Chanche*, of Natchez; *De la Hilandiere*, of Vincennes; *Purcell*, of Cincinnati, and the Coadjutor Bishop of N. York, *McCloskey*, attended by the usual retinue of vicars general, pastors of congregations, acolytes, &c., will perform the consecration services.

There will no doubt be an immense attendance upon that day from all parts of the west, as well as spectators from our own city.

I learn upon inquiry, that the ceremonies of

the day commence at six o'clock, A. M., and that to a great extent they will take place outside of the Cathedral and within the Cathedral grounds. Some of the rites require the floor of the building to be kept free for the passage and repassage of those engaged in the consecration services. In the afternoon the Cathedral will be thrown open for public worship.

Rev'd. J. F. Wood, a native as it were of our city, will deliver an address on that occasion to the audience assembled outside, explanatory of the exercises, &c., of the day.

I have devoted a larger share to-day to this than is usually alloted in the Advertiser to such subjects; but much inquiry has been directed to this matter, and I have collected or ascertained these facts to gratify the curious on such topics.

Journal of John G. Jungmann.

Who has not heard of the Moravians? A band of Christian brethren who were the first since the days of the Apostles to embark in the missionary enterprise; and in the lapse of an hundred years after, having wakened up in some sense to their duty various powerful and extensive denominations of Christians, are still as they always have been in proportion to their numbers at home, the largest body of missionaries in the world.

More than one hundred years since a colony of the *Unitas fratrum*, or Moravians, emigrated to Pennsylvania, and made settlements in Bethlehem and Nazareth, in Northampton, and Litiz, in Lancaster counties, in that state. Having succeeded in placing the Indians to the north and west under the influences of civilization and christianity to a great extent, they formed missionary establishments in what were then the forests of Ohio, their principal settlements being on the waters of the Muskingum. Here they succeeded also in gathering churches among the Indians of the west; and up to 1782, the period of the memorable massacre, by a horde of white savages from Western Pennsylvania and Virginia, which has rendered their memory for ever infamous, the labours of these brethren were abundantly successful in causing the desolate and solitary places to be glad, and the wilderness to blossom as the rose.

What dangers had to be met and privations endured by these missionaries, may be judged by the history of early pioneers of Keutucky and Ohio. The narrative which follows gives a graphic picture, by one of that band who laboured with Spangenberg, Zeisberger, Senseman and Heckewelder, for a long series of years in the cause. I give it from the journal—hitherto unpublished—in his own words.

"My father, J. *Jungmann*, was a Huguenot, driven from France in 1720, by the persecutions of that date. He fled to Hockenheim, Germany, where he found employment as a teacher of mathematics and music. After remaining there eleven years, he emigrated to America in 1731, landing in Rhode Island, after enduring, with others, almost unheard of sufferings on board the vessel in which he embarked from Germany. I was born in Hockenheim, shortly after his arrival there, April 19, 1720, and with the rest of the family accompanied him on the voyage.

"There had been a great emigration from Germany to America, which had been encouraged by letters received from the emigrants. My parents concluded to visit that country also, and came by water from Neckenhausen to Rotterdam, whence they sailed on a vessel bound to America, having one hundred and fifty-six passengers, besides the ship's crew, expecting to reach that country in six weeks, although provisioned for twelve. We put into Falmouth, England, where we remained three weeks, taking on more passengers. We again sailed, and twelve days afterwards the captain observed that we were now one half our journey, which filled our hearts with thankfulness and rejoicing. But we were becalmed—visited soon after with a dreadful storm—and after being eight weeks out from England, were put on short allowance of bread and water, the last four weeks having no bread at all, and but one pint of water per day to supply father, sister, and myself—my younger sister, step-mother, and her two children having died under their sufferings. We were obliged to purchase cats at one shilling and six pence, and rats and mice at six pence each, and buy what water we needed for subsistence. We found out that the villanous purpose of the captain was to starve us all to death, that he might obtain our effects, in which he succeeded to a great extent, only forty-eight of the passengers surviving to reach the land, and those only escaped by revolting on the captain, and compelling him to make the American shore, where we landed, after being twenty-five weeks on our passage from Rotterdam. Judge the state of suffering in which we all were, and our indignation on finding out that the captain and crew had secret supplies hidden in the long boat. On landing, four Indians stepped on board the vessel, of whom one of the passengers who could speak a little English, falling on his knees, supplicated a little bread and water, and assistance to take us on shore. Our ghastly looks told our sufferings, and the Indians returning for their friends, came down in a body and compelled the captain to release us all. They took us to their cabins where we were fed like little children, and by the mercy of God were restored finally to health and strength, after a long confinement. Such benevolence in savages appeared amazing to us. After being thus recruited, which took five months, my father concluded to remove to Philadelphia, and bought one hundred acres of land in the neighbourhood for fifteen pounds ten shillings."

Here the family settled down in peace and comfort, and soon prospered in their worldly circumstances. The father married again, built a distillery and brew house, and carried on a cooper shop. The son cut himself severely with an axe, and no one knowing what to prescribe, he mixed white and yolk of eggs in some fresh butter of which he made a poultice, applying it as hot as could be borne, taking *gunpowder* inwardly, and effected a cure. He now gets acquainted with the Moravians at Bethlehem, under whose preaching he becomes under religious exercise, and joins the society. I shall resume his journal in my next.

Steamer Great Britain.

It is a curious circumstance that the progress of steamboat building for ocean navigation has just brought us, as the point of perfection, to the model and proportions of the first vessel of which we have any record. I allude to the ark built by Noah. The dimensions of the Great Britain are—length three hundred and twenty-two feet, breadth of beam fifty feet, depth thirty-one and a half feet. The dimensions of the ark were—length three hundred cubits, breadth fifty cubits, depth thirty cubits. It will be seen, therefore, that the ark was nearly twice the size in depth, breadth and length of the steamboat, the cubit being twenty-two inches. Both had upper, lower, and middle stories.

If, after the experience and accumulated knowledge of forty centuries, we have not improved on the proportions of the first sea vessel, after resorting to every shape and species of water craft, have we not here an additional argument to the truth of divine revelation, that a vessel so completely adapted to its purpose, must have been planned by the Great Architect of the Universe. " As for God, his work is *perfect.*"

Irish Wit and Humour.

I was much struck with the peculiarities of the Dublin audience. The national anthem, followed by " St. Patrick's day," was invariably played in the course of every evening's performance at the Crow Street Theatre. These two airs constituted the barometer of public opinion. When pleased, Pat applauded both. But if things did'nt go to his liking, he vented his spleen on the first, and applauded his own national air in proportion. At all times, the gallery *stamped* an accompaniment to this latter, as well as to all other popular airs, besides joining in chorus. But when a new Lord and Lady Lieutenant visited the theatre for the first time, Pat's peculiarities became most diverting.

" Pat Mooney!" shouts a voice in the gallery. " Halloo!" answers Pat, from the opposite sdie. *Voice.*—Can you see 'em, Pat? (Meaning the Lord and Lady Lieutenant.)

Pat Mooney.—I can.

Voice.—Well, what's *he* like?

Pat Mooney.—Oh, mighty like a grazier, or a middle-man. Any way, he has a good long nose of his own. (Loud laughter, in which his Lordship joins.)

Voice.—Is he clever, think you?

Pat Mooney.—I'd be sorry to make him sinsekeeper. (Laughter again.)

Voice.—Does he look good-natured?

Pat Mooney.—Well he does, and enjoys a joke, too—Heaven bless him!—like a gentleman as he is.

Voice.—Then we'll not have to send him back?

Pat Mooney.—No, I don't think we shall. We may get a worse. (Roars of laughter.) They say he's mighty generous, and means to spend his money amongst us like a prince.

Gallery.—We'll keep him, then—we'll keep him. Three cheers, lads—three cheers for the Lord Lieutenant! (Cheers and laughter.)

Voice.—Well, and what's *she* like, Pat?

Pat Mooney.—Oh, nothing particular. She'd not frighten a horse. (Roars, her ladyship joining.)

Voice.—Is she tall?

Pat Mooney.—Wait till she stands up.

Voice.—May be she's stout, Pat?

Pat Mooney.—Faix! you may say that. It is'nt the likes of her lives on buttermilk. (Roars.)

Voice.—Do you think she's good-natured?

Pat Mooney.—Oh, I'll engage she is. She has the raal blood in her, and there's plenty of it. (Roars and " Bravo!" from the gallery.)

Many voices.—She'll do then, Pat?

Pat Mooney.—Och! she will—she will. I'll engage for her Ladyship.

Voices.—We may keep her then, may we?

Pat Mooney.—Och! the longer the betther—the longer the betther. (Roars.) It's her Ladyship that'll speak the good word for the man that's in thrubble, and never let the dacent woman want that's in the straw—God bless her!

Gallery.—Bravo! bravo! Three cheers for her Ladyship! Three cheers for the Lady Lieutenant! (Cheers and Laughter.)

Pat Mooney, (seeing the Lord Mayor)—My sowl to ye! Dan Finnigan, is that you?

Gallery.—Ah! ah! Is that you, Dan Finnigan!—is that you? (Hisses and laughter.)

Pat Mooney.—Faix! it's good for the likes of us to see you down among the gintry there, Dan Finnigan. (A loud laugh, at which his Lordship does not seem particularly pleased.) Och! you need'nt look up so sour at us! Many's the good time you've sat up here yourself; you know it is, you ould vinegar bottle! (Roars.)

Voice.—Sure the world's gone well with *you* any way, Dan Finnigan. Ye had'nt them white kid gloves—

Pat Mooney.—No, nor that grand cocked hat there—

Voice.—No, nor that white wand, ye cormorant! When you kept the chandler shop, and cheated Mike Kelly out of a farden's worth of pipes, and—

Gallery.—Ah! ah! Who cheated Mike Kelly?

—who cheated Mike Kelly? (Great confusion, during which the orchestra strikes up.)

But these gallery blackguards did not always let their rulers off so easily. When the Duke of Rutland, whose family name was *Manners*, with the Duchess, first visited the theatre, Mooney and his echo were in the house also. In the interval between the play and afterpiece, a *voice* was heard from one side of the gallery, " Who slept with Pig Plunket last night?" which was instantly answered on the opposite side by the reproof, " *Manners! Manners!* you blackguard." The Duke, himself not remarkable for bashfulness, could not stand this rasping down, and with his Dutchess precipitately quitted the theatre.

St, Clair,

The reverse of fortune which Belisarius is said to have experienced, when poor, old and blind, he was reduced to ask alms, *Date obolum Belisarius* is usually considered the most striking in history, and so extraordinary as to raise doubts of its truth. But the downfall of the Roman soldier was hardly more abject, than we have an authenticated case of, in the instance of St. Clair.

Arthur St. Clair was a patriot and soldier of the Revolution, high in the confidence of Gen'l. Washington, a good judge of men and their merits, and received at his hands the command of the troops raised in 1791 to chastise the aggressions of the hostile Indians of the Northwest, as well as the commission of Governor of the territory of that name.

The unfortunate issue of that expedition is well known; but it is not so well known at the present day, that St. Clair was little more successful in carrying on the government of the Territory committed to his charge, he being involved in continual difficulties with his associates in the legislative council, as well as the judicial authorities. These grew out of mistaken views of the nature and extent of his authority, and had the effect of rendering him as odious in his civil capacity as he had previously become as a soldier. Yet St. Clair, although unsuited by temper and disposition, and still more by the gout, to which he was a martyr, for the active and arduous labours devolving on him in the west, was a good man, a gallant soldier, and an accomplished scholar. But the campaigns of the west, with the exception of that of Wayne's, have never been successfully waged by other than western men. St. Clair was an European, had hardly become Americanized thoroughly, when he came to the frontiers, and never was a western man in habit or in feelings. This was in fact an unfortunate appointment, a rare exception in the exercise of a judgment of men and merits, for which Washington was remarkable.

When the territory became a state, and the people of Ohio sovereigns, St. Clair, like Othello, found his occupation gone. He had nothing to expect at their hands, and returned to Pennsylvania, where he had formerly resided. His resources limited at best, were soon exhausted by journeys to Washington to obtain the allowance of unsettled claims against the government. His pecuniary circumstances became worse and worse, and he was finally compelled as a means of support to sell *whisky by the gill and chestnuts by the quart*, to travelers crossing the Allegheny ridge.

After dragging out a miserable existence for several years in this mode, Congress granted him a small pension, which, however, he lived but a short period to enjoy, sinking to a melancholy grave under privations, which former habits ill fitted him to endure. Such was the close of a life, the prime of which was spent among the great fathers of the Revolution in council and in camp, as their leader or their equal. He had succeeded Hancock as President of the Continental Congress, and bore arms amidst the severest scenes of the Revolution, and through its whole course.

As usual, what was denied to the living was freely accorded to the dead. His countryman, Burns, was nearly starved to death. A tithe of the expense lavished on monuments to his memory, recording a nation's shame rather than the poet's glory, for it needs no such record, would have made his life comfortable. So with St. Clair. He too asked for bread and they gave him a stone. After the lapse of years, his resting place was traced out with some difficulty, his remains removed to Greensburg, Pa., where an obelisk twenty feet in height, erected by his Masonic brethren, emblazons the bitter lie that republics are not ungrateful.

Rats.

A correspondent who is greatly annoyed by rats, and finds no remedy in the various traps, dogs and cats, rat butter, &c., to which he has resorted, asks if I cannot point out some method of getting rid of these vermins. He could hardly have applied to a better source of information, and as others doubtless labour under the same difficulty, I shall communicate my reply through my own columns, for general benefit.

In Pennsylvania, as an older settlement and an extensive grain growing district, these vermins of course are abundant. There, as here, traps have been resorted to with little effect, barely serving to act upon the young and inexperienced rats. The Pennsylvania Germans, finding they cannot extirpate the race, make it a rule, when these pests become too troublesome, to get the neighbouring schoolmaster to write a notice to these rats to quit the premises, just as they would to any other tenant. The document is left in one of the rat holes and immediately gnawed to pieces, which is the usual acknowledgment of service. The rats, without delay, then take up their march, and may be seen traveling of a moonshiny night, along the public road, in battalions, to the dwelling or barn of the individual to whose premises they are directed to remove.

I annex a copy of one of these notices, issued by a farmer in Lower Saucon township, Northampton county, which may serve as a form in like cases. Perhaps if used here it had better be translated into English, as our Cincinnati rats may not understand *dutch*.

Nehmt Obacht.

Mit dem seyd ihr benachrichtet daß ihr bey Empfang dies, die von euch bisher bewohnte gebäud verlaff.n müßi, im fall ihr dies nit thut, werd ihr die j.raf empfangen von die vorgeschrieben Gesetz.

Nieder Saucon taunschip märz 10 1820.

Conrad Armig.

Ich wünsch daß ihr zum Hans Holzsperger gehn selt.

I well recollect the trial of a case before a magistrate in a German settlement in one of the western counties of Pennsylvania. *John Eisennagle* brought suit against *Jacob Breyfuss*, for damage incurred by the said John in the said Jacob sending his rats to the premises of Eisennagle. The magistrate, Esq. M——, was a man of good sense and some humour, and concluded the best way of settling such a difficulty was to let it take its course, alleging, however, that as the parties were both neighbours and on good terms with him, he proposed for the sake of saving costs, that the witnesses should be examined without being sworn, which was assented to. The parties made their statements, and the witnesses were heard. It was clearly proved that the rats had been, up to a certain period, abundant at Breyfuss' house, and scarce at Eisennagle's, and scarce at Breyfuss' and plenty at Eisennagle's at a later date. One of the witnesses proved the fact of a notice being given the rats by Breyfuss; but did not know to whom they were sent. There was much irrelevant matter, owing to the nature of the suit. After hearing the case fully, the Squire remarked that it appeared very probable that the rats at Eisennagle's were the same lot which had infested Breyfuss; but gravely remarked, that he sat there not to judge of probabilities, but by proofs, and therefore, as there was no evidence to the identity of the rats, or any one of them, he was con-

strained to give judgment against Breyfuss for costs of suit.

I have known much ill-will on this score between farmers in that neighbourhood, who were supposed thus to have exchanged rats; but this was the only instance within my knowledge in which things proceeded to extremities.

Charlemagne.

On the occasion of the late continental visit of Queen Victoria of England, at Aix-la-Chapelle, the great Cathedral was lighted up at night from roof to floor, with a brilliant display of wax tapers, which rendered the spectacle as light as day. And this at the tomb of Charlemagne, whose ashes repose in this great temple—himself its highest trophy—one of the greatest men of any age or country! Napoleon, a being better qualified to appreciate the character of Charlemagne, behaved with more dignity and in better taste on his visit to the scene. In 1804, just when Bonaparte had progressed into Napoleon, he visited Aix-la-Chapelle. Josephine, who accompanied him, indulged in the caprice of sitting upon the marble throne. But the -Emperor, though he did not control this indecorous whim of his Creole wife, attired himself for the occasion, from a deep sense of deference to that mighty name, in full regimentals, and stood, silent, motionless, and bareheaded, before the chair of Charlemagne. Charlemagne died in 814. In 1814, one thousand years afterwards, almost to an hour, occurred the fall or moral death of Napoleon. In the course of the same fatal year, the allied sovereigns visited the grave of Charles the Great, when Alexander of Russia mounted his gala uniform, in imitation of Napoleon, while Frederick William of Prussia appeared in an undress, and the Emperor of Austria in a great coat and round hat. The King of Prussia entered into all the details of the coronations of the German Emperors, with the Provost of the Chapter; but the two Emperors observed a profound silence. All these are now as silent as Charlemagne! Napoleon, Josephine, Alexander, Frederick William, and Francis II., are cold in their graves.

I say nothing of the military exploits of Charlemagne, for he has been equaled if not surpassed in this line. But the man, who in 793, conceived and commenced the plan of connecting the Rhine and the Danube, by a canal, an undertaking which he was compelled by circumstances to suspend, and which he never had an opportunity to resume, must have had a mind one thousand years in advance of his cotemporaries, and well deserved the honors, which Napoleon, in the plenitude of his glory, felt due to the illustrious dead.

The canal connecting those two great rivers of Europe, was nearly completed at the last accounts. It was to have been opened for navigation in a few days, between Nuremburg, and shortly after, through its whole extent, from the Danube to the Mayn.

Though the completion of this great work has been reserved for modern time, its conception and commencement belong to an age and generation ten centuries distant. In 793 the Emperor Charlemagne formed the purpose of establishing a water communication from one extremity of Europe to another, by means of a canal which should unite the waters of the Rhine with those of the Danube. With this object an army of workmen was assembled, the Emperor himself superintending and directing their labors, and for several months the undertaking was most industriously prosecuted. But sickness breaking out among the laborers, and distant wars demanding Charlemagne's attention, the enterprise was abandoned, only to be resumed after the lapse of more than a thousand years.

A Chapter on Business Signs.

If I had space, a volume would hardly do justice to this subject. Half a column must suffice at this time.

Some partnership firms are oddly put together. In Philadelphia a dry goods firm on Second street, bore the euphonious title of *Sheepshanks & Shufflebottom.* On Front street, the firm of *Schott & Fell* carried on business. As each side of the door bore a partner's name, it became a regular amusement of the boys to read and call out as they passed by, James *Schott*—and Jonathan *Fell.*

A sign which gave the schoolboys another reading exercise was *Speakman & Say,* apothecaries, at the corner of Market and Second streets. To this they gave, as commentators with a favourite author—a new reading, Speak, Man, and Say.

At Fairchild's corner, some years ago, Dr. D., one of our most respectable physicians, had on the Main street face, "Dr. D———, around the corner." On the Front street side was another sign, "Dr. D———, up stairs." It was no fault of the boys who passed the corner, if the whole community did not know the contents of these signs.

A German by the name of Brandt, a turner by trade, who lived back of one of our streets, put up his shingle to read thus—"Turning ☞ around the corner. Half the passers by, seem going to his shop!

We had a barber on Front street, years ago, as black as the ace of clubs, named *London Porter,* whose sign was placed conspicuously over the door. There were no coffee houses, hardly, in those days, and it was a constant jest among steamboat characters to send thirsty souls off the boats to London's to wet their whistle. Porter usually told them he could shave them; but if they wished to be half shaved they must go up on the hill.

There is a firm in Hudson, New York, of Ketchum & Cheatham, which the boys read off, Catchem & Cheatem. The friends of the firm, that it might have its true reading, proposed that the Christian name of the parties, Isaac and Uriah, should be added, which was assented to. But the artist, not being able to crowd the whole upon the board, abbreviated the names to their initials, and the sign reads—not in bad keeping for business men—" *I. Ketchum & U. Cheatham!*"

A man, still a resident in this state, named Death, kept a store on Main street, nearly opposite our old friend Jonathan Pancoast. Over the door was the sign, "Rectified Whisky," and directly underneath, the name *Absalom Death.* An old lady from the country, had been in to market with her son, who drove the wagon, and was going up Main street on her way home, when the sign caught her eye—"Stop! Rectified Whisky—Absolute Death. That's a fact, Johnny. Let me get out, there is *one honest man in Cincinnati.* I want to see what he looks like."

Fourth Ward--Cincinnati.

The public buildings of this ward are six in number. The Ohio Life Insurance and Trust Company, an Engine House, one of the Public School Houses, Disciples' Church, on Third st., and the German Reformed Church, on Second, late the Third Presbyterian Church edifice, and Cincinnati Museum. Dwelling houses, offices, workshops and store houses 1081. Of these four are of stone, of brick 589, and 488 are frames.

Of these buildings there were at the close of the year 1842—

	Stone.	Brick.	Frame.	Total.
	4	413	395	812
Built in 1843,	0	45	14	59
" " 1844,	0	75	44	119
" " 1845,	0	56	35	91
	4	589	488	1081

A very valuable description of buildings have been put up both this year and the last. Blocks of permanent store houses, spacious and convenient, adorn the intersections of Walnut and Front, and Walnut and Second streets. Resor & Co. have put up two fine warerooms at the lower end of Pearl street. Three or four fine new ware rooms and factory buildings have put up on Columbia or Second street; besides various other scattered improvements in different sections of the ward. This ward is one of the oldest improved parts of Cincinnati, and is now built up to three-fourths of its capacity. It must eventually become the seat of trade and manufactures to a much larger extent than it even now is.

Massy Herbeson's Escape from Indians.

With the heroine of the following narrative I was well acquainted in 1815. She then resided in Butler county, Pennsylvania, was a woman of great energy of character, nicknamed Bonaparte by the neighbourhood, and able to fight her way through any crowd, male or female. The child with whom she was encumbered at the time, grew to be a man in years; and at the period to which I refer above, sued his mother for a piece of land in the Butler County Court. This created great indignation among the people, and if Judge Lynch had only been present to give impulse to popular feeling the young man would probably have been tarred and feathered. He lost his case, probably as much through popular prejudice as any thing else.

An account of the sufferings of Massy Herbeson and her family, who were taken prisoners by a party of Indians.—Given on oath, before John Wilkins, Esq., one of the Justices of the Peace for the Commonwealth of Pennsylvania.

Massy Herbeson, on her oath, according to law, being taken before John Wilkins, Esq., one of the commonwealth's justices of the peace in and for the county of Allegheny, deposeth and saith, that on the 22d day of this instant, she was taken from her own house, within two hundred yards of Reed's block-house, which is called twenty-five miles from Pittsburgh; her husband, being one of the spies, was from home; two of the scouts had lodged with her that night, but had left her house about sunrise, in order to go to the block-house. and had left the door standing wide open. Shortly after the two scouts went away, a number of Indians came into the house, and drew her out of bed by the feet; the two eldest children, who also lay in another bed were drawn out in the same manner; a younger child, about one year old, slept with the deponent. The Indians then scrambled about the articles in the house; whilst they were at this work, the deponent went out of the house and hallooed to the people in the block-house; one of the Indians ran up and stopped her mouth, another ran up with his tomahawk drawn, and a third ran and seized the tomahawk and called her his squaw; the last Indian claimed her as his, and continued by her; about fifteen of the Indians then ran down toward the block-house and fired their guns at the block and store-house, in consequence of which one soldier was killed and another wounded, one having been at the spring, and the other in coming or looking out of the store-house. This deponent telling the Indians there were about forty men in the block-house, and each man had two guns, the Indians went to them that were firing at the block-house, and brought them back. They then began to drive the deponent and her children away; but a boy, about three years old, being unwilling to leave the house, they took it by the heels, and dashed it against the house, then stabbed and scalped it. They then took

the deponent and the two other children to the top of the hill, where they stopped until they tied up the plunder they had got. While they were busy about this, the deponent counted them, and the number amounted to thirty-two, including two white men that were with them, painted like the Indians.

That several of the Indians could speak English, and that she knew three or four of them very well, having often seen them go up and down the Allegheny river; two of them she knew to be Senecas, and two Muncies, who had got their guns mended by her husband about two years ago. That they sent two Indians with her, and the others took their course towards Puckety. That she, the children, and two Indians had not gone above two hundred yards, when the Indians caught two of her uncle's horses, put her and the younger child on one, and one of the Indians and the other child on the other. That the two Indians then took her and the children to the Allegheny river, and took them over in bark canoes, as they could not get the horses to swim the river. After they had crossed the river, the oldest child, a boy of about five years of age, began to mourn for his brother, when one of the Indians tomahawked and scalped him. That they traveled all day very hard, and that night arrived at a large camp covered with bark, which, by appearance, might hold fifty men; that night they took her about three hundred yards from the camp, into a large dark bottom, bound her arms, gave her some bed clothes, and lay down, one on each side of her. That the next morning they took her into a thicket on the hill side, and one remained with her till the middle of the day, while the other went to watch the path, lest some white people should follow them. They then exchanged places during the remainder of the day; she got a piece of dry venison, about the bulk of an egg, that day, and a piece about the same size the day they were marching; that evening, (Wednesday, the 23d) they moved her to a new place, and secured her as the night before: during the day of the 23d, she made several attempts to get the Indian's gun or tomahawk, that was guarding her, and, had she succeeded, she would have put him to death. She was nearly detected in trying to get the tomahawk from his belt.

The next morning (Thursday) one of the Indians went out, as on the day before, to watch the path. The other lay down and fell asleep. When she found he was sleeping, she stole her short gown, handkerchief, a child's frock, and then made her escape;—the sun was then about half an hour high—that she took her course from the Allegheny, in order to deceive the Indians, as they would naturally pursue her that way; that day she travelled along Conoquenessing creek. The next day she altered her course, and, as she believes, fell upon the waters of Pine Creek, which empties into the waters of Allegheny. Thinking this not her best course, she took over some dividing ridges,—lay on a dividing ridge on Friday night, and on Saturday came to Squaw run—continued down the run until an Indian, or some other person, shot a deer; she saw the person about one hundred and fifty yards from her —the deer running and the dog pursuing it, which from the appearance, she supposed to be an Indian dog.

She then altered her course, but again came to the same run, and continued down it until she got so tired that she was obliged to lie down, it having rained on her all that day and the night before; she lay there that night; it rained constantly; on Sunday morning she proceeded down the run until she came to the Allegheny river, and continued down the river till she came opposite to Carter's house, on the inhabited side, where she made a noise, and James Closier brought her over the river to Carter's house.

Sworn before me, at Pittsburgh, this 28th day of May, 1792. JOHN WILKINS.

Dr. Bailey.

A letter from Dayton was shown me on Saturday, in which I observe the following flattering notice:

"*Abby Kelley* is here on her way down to your city, with her friend *Foster*. Abby says that Dr. Bailey is an arrant hypocrite, and she means to prove him so. He need not think to soap her down with his deprecatory remarks."

Those who like to see their fellow-beings *rasped down*,—and there is this feature of human nature in most of us—will have rare sport when this lady, who holding to the largest liberty of tongue, gives herself great liberty of speech, makes her curtsey to Cincinnati. I anticipate a crowded house at the Tabernacle.

Progress of Cincinnati.

As late as 1809, Cincinnati was not able to sustain more than one newspaper, and at a period ten years later—1819—there were but three in existence. As late as 1832, we had only fifteen periodicals; three daily, two semi-weekly, seven weekly, one monthly and one quarterly publication. There are now published here twelve daily, fourteen weekly, and fourteen monthly periodicals; besides directories and almanacs of various descriptions. Ten of these dailies issue weeklies, and three of them tri-weeklies also.

Our progress in moral influence otherwise, is equally remarkable. As late as 1811, I believe there was but one house of worship in Cincinnati. As late as 1827, there were but twelve; in 1832, twenty-five. There are now sixty-nine.

This synopsis affords an evidence of rapid and extensive growth, which it may be safely asserted, finds no parallel in any other part of the United States, not to say in the world. It is an epitome of the progress of the great west.

Mind your Business.

Grant Thorburn, in one of his rambling reminiscences, gives the following illustration of a principle which is the foundation of success in business:

"Never leave your shop except on business. Horse, foot, or hurdle races, fishing, fowling and sailing parties will never pay your rent. When you are out on business, hurry back to your shop as soon as possible. Don't stand in the streets, talking politics, news or anything, except may be something wherein your interest is concerned. Forty years ago, when I first commenced tra-

ding, my wife was my storekeeper, my book, my housekeeper, my cook, my everything. One morning returning from the old Fly Market, foot of Maiden Lane, I met at the corner of William and Liberty streets, with a friend. At that time Bonaparte was in the full tide of manslaughter, killing at the rate of half a million per annum; that morning an arrival had brought news of his progress. We stopped probably ten minutes rehearsing the matter. When I got to my store, I inquired of my wife if any one had asked for me. 'Yes,' she replied, 'Mr. C——n called to pay his bill, but wished to see yourself.' That night he cleared for Texas. Thus I lost thirty dollars by standing in the streets, when I might have been in my store. Ever after when a friend wished me to stop in the street, 'Not here,' says I, 'but go to my store, and you may there talk all day if you please.'"

Adopting a White Man.

The chiefs of the Seneca Indians, at a late council, adopted Philip E. Thomas, of Baltimore, a benevolent Friend, a member of the Seneca tribe. After raising to his feet the Quaker gentleman, who was sitting by a table in the council, and laying his hand three times on his shoulder, the chief addressed him as follows in the Indian language:

"By this ceremony we do at this time adopt into the Seneca nation this our friend, Philip E. Thomas, by which he becomes a member of the tribe and a brother of the Swan family, and is entitled to the name of a Seneca Indian, and to all the rights and immunities of the nation. We now give him the name of Sagouan, (Benevolent Giver, or Bountiful,) by which we express our sense of his character, and under which he will hereafter be recognized among us, and we have appointed George Deer to be his cousin."

This must have been an interesting ceremony. I wonder what *Friend Thomas* thought, felt, or said, when he was painted over, the calumet put in his mouth, rings in his nose and ears, and the war club, tomahawk and scalping knife placed in his hands.

Corrections.

It seems almost impossible to correct popular errors, after they have once taken root, and mistaken efforts to do so render the matter worse.

There is a variety of apples well known in our market, which is generally called the *Peenick*, and which others, who desire to give it the correct name, term the *Phœnix*, from which appilation they suppose the other corrupted. The apple is an eastern variety like many others, and is named after the *Pennock* family of Chester county, Pa., who first raised it.

Another vulgarism which I frequently find, even in city advertisements, is *Meshannick* potatoes. This should be *Neshanock*, the name of a creek in Mercer county, Pennsylvania, on whose banks this excellent variety originated.

CINCINNATI MISCELLANY.

CINCINNATI, NOVEMBER, 1845.

Journal of John G. Jungmann.—No. 2.

" I removed to Bethlehem in 1742, and incorporated myself fully into the church; and having in 1745, married the widowed sister *Bittner*, we were sent to the missionary station at *Faulkner's Swamp*, and took charge of the nursery of Indian children there; were, however, soon recalled to Bethlehem, whence I was sent with *Spangenberg* to *Gnadenhutten* in 1746. Here I was employed building a grist and saw mill, which together with the tavern were placed under my superintendence. In 1751 we opened a school for religious instruction among the Indians, which was productive by the blessing of God of the best effects in bring the savages to a knowledge and reception of the truth. We cleared a sufficiency of land to keep the Indians employed farming; and taught them various mechanical employments. After labouring among these dear people seven years, we were recalled in 1753 to Bethlehem, whence we were sent in 1755 to *Bachgotgock*, one of our Indian stations in New England."

I must condense his narrative at this point, so as to get more rapidly forward. He works with the same spirit and energy, both in his secular and religious employments among the Indians, until the French war in 1757, suspended missionary operations there by carrying off the natives into the army: he returns to Bethlehem, whence the same year he visits *Bachgotgock*. Here he remains a year, when he is relieved and returns to Bethlehem,—is sent to *Christiansbrunn*, Pa., and subsequently made superintendent of the mission at *Wyalusing*, in the same State. I regret that the space, as well as the character of the Advertiser, forbids my copying the whole narrative, which, for its incidents, as well as the ardent and active piety of the writer, which without the least display, runs like a thread through the journal, reminds me continually of the record of Paul's labours in the Acts of the Apostles. In journeyings, fastings, sufferings, and persecutions most abundant, and continually rejoicing in every opportunity of labouring in his master's cause.

After a variety of adventures, in 1770, he is sent out to the Mission among the Indians in Ohio to a station called *Langundodaning*, probably just over the Pennsylvania line. Here the Moravian brethren, *David* and *Senseman*, had been already labouring. Jungmann set out with his wife, who accompanied him in all his journeys; and after traveling twenty days, reached his destination Oct. 28th, 1770. He was now more than four hundred miles from home, a howling wilderness occupying the whole intervening space. The missionary labours here appear to have been eminently successful. "The Indians sang and prayed, day and night without ceasing," he observes in his journal. In 1772, he removes to *Schoenbrunn*, one hundred miles further into the wilderness, where a missionary station had been maintained for several years in great prosperity. "Here," says he, " we were received with much affection."

" We saw with great gratification, our Indian brethren and sisters, industriously raising their huts for winter, and fell to work to rear our own. Schoenbrunn was a pretty, prosperous little village, having been founded only four years—having forty houses, besides the huts—three hundred Indian residents, who were all true Martyrs and Disciples of Jesus Christ and his cause;—two hundred acres of land cleared, producing excellent fruits, grains, &c. In the fifth year the unfortunate Indian war broke out—the place given up. After a happy residence of four and a half years, in April, 1776, with heavy hearts, we were compelled to start for *Lichtenau*. A council of consultation determined to give up the Moravian stations, until peace should be restored. We glorified God—sang praises for his manifold blessings and protection. We started for Bethlehem, August 6th, arriving safely on the 19th August. We remained three years with our son John at the Lehigh ferry. July, 1780, we were appointed, with our brothers *Reichel* and *Zeisberger*, to remove back to our dear Indian brethren and sisters in the Ohio stations, which we safely accomplished, July 28, 1781, having no idea of being compelled to leave so shortly again. September 2d, we were visited by a Captain of the Hurons, with six warriors, friendly shaking hands. I was making a *red cedar milk bucket*, which, fancying, they were determined to have; but I refused on account of *its* immediate wants. They then examined all my implements, and I explained their use; at which they were very much surprised. They left me in my workshop, and walked into my house—my wife absent—examining every thing there; at last left us in a friendly manner, and went their way on to *Gnadenhutten*. Next morning I received a very gloomy letter from brother

Zeisberger—September 3, 1781—stating that he could not see how matters and things relative to the welfare of our *Missionary* stations would turn out; it appears as if the very air were filled with every evil spirit; our only hope is in our Dear Saviour, and await the upshot. September 3, 1781, in the evening, brother *Ignatius* came running, out of breath, to inform us that our brethren at Gnadenhutten were taken prisoners, and that a similar fate might befall *us*; of which three runners came to inform us of its contemplation. I repaired at once to the brethren and sisters, to communicate to them, and while there, three riders came by, stopping at *my house*, and entered it. I started to meet them; found one of them to be the captain who had visited me the day previous, with his sister and a runner. The captain took me by the hand in a friendly manner, seating me beside him. The runner drew a pistol and held it to my breast, at the same time holding a rifle in his left hand. The captain told me he had come to take us, and all we had, under his protection: if we would not resist, he would keep all harmless; but if we resisted him, he would send for his warriors to cut us to pieces, and destroy our effects, to which I replied—"Use your pleasure." In this instance, our Blessed Saviour Jesus was nigh unto us; and instead of fear and dismay, courage and consolation came to our heart's fill, that *not a hair of our heads should perish.* Our interpreter was the captain's sister, who spoke good English. They took our effects, cut open our beds, scattering the feathers to the winds; the rest, they carried to the *canoes*. After clearing the house, they broke open our chests, emptying them. They went to brother *Zeisberger's;* conducted themselves in the same way. We were taken in the *canoes*, with the privilege of several of our brethren to go with us. The night was dreadfully cold—with but little clothing—nearly frozen to death. After coming half way, we were permitted to stop, make a fire, and warm ourselves; then proceeding, in sight of *Gnadenhutten*, next morning, they examined all our things, searching for silver ware, &c.—found none; detaining us in the cold; and then proceeded into town, marching and singing the war song. We were kept eight days in a small house, where they divided our effects among themselves. They permitted us to visit brother *Schebosh;* after which we were taken to *Salem.* We now began to feel the calamity which had befallen our three unfortunate missionary stations, which we were compelled to abandon. We reflected, and deeply meditated, whether, perhaps, we had not caused God's just anger to come down upon us. In deep humility we supplicated God's aid, and with compunction acknowledged our manifold sins and transgres-

sions; fell at the feet of our dear Jesus. Here now before separating, we partook of the Holy Sacrament, and leave to each a rejoicing heart. From here we were taken down the *Muskingum;* up the *Walhunding*, partly by land, partly by water; and joined by brother *Joshua* and his comrades in Christ, from *Gogoschin*—passing on to *Walhunding*, carrying the "Minister's Manuscripts;" but they were taken from us, and destroyed. In a few days we removed further; the runners gave me a very wild colt to ride, expecting it to run off and dash out my brains; but their plans failed: It moved off with me as quiet as a lamb. We arrived at Upper Sandusky, one hundred miles from our locations, in an entire dense forest—ten miles from the nearest Indian village; and told, here make your homes, and get along the best way you can. Our consolation was, *Jesus* will not suffer a sparrow to fall to the ground, and *here too*, our God will not desert us. Almost immediately, an Indian trader, hearing of us, came to our succour: he sent us corn, which we parched; and we brought—*first*, a thanks offering to Almighty God, to evince our gratitude, for his great mercy, and the fulfillment of his promises to his followers, showing that —"When need is greatest, God is nearest;" and "*Where* have ye been in want?" We could truly answer—"*Nowhere* hast thou withheld thy blessing, dear Saviour." As winter approached, we built huts. Brother David and I built one twelve feet square, with a kitchen and chimney; where we dwelt happy in the Lord.

A Legend of the War of 1812.

The Kentucky troops who bore their share, and more than their share, in the invasion of Canada during our last war with England, had among their numbers, a band of volunteers who rendesvoused at Harrodsburg, Mercer county, and formed the nucleus of the whole corps which gathered from every side, and at every day's march, in their progress towards the river Ohio, fresh accessions of forces. On leaving Harrodsburg, a mile or two out, they passed two pigs fighting, and delayed their march long enough to witness the result. After marching forward, it was observed that the victor pig was following in the route, and at night when they encamped, the animal hunted itself also a shelter and lay by too, for the night. In the morning when they put forward they were accompanied by the pig as on the day before, and thus night and morning in their progress to the river, the animal halted where they rested, and started onwards when they resumed their journey. When they came opposite Cincinnati, to which place they crossed in a ferry boat, the pig, on getting to the water's edge, promptly plunged in, waiting on the other side until the whole *cortege* crossed over, and resumed its post as customary in the flank of the moving column. In this way the animal kept on with the troops until they got to the Lake. It was finally left at Bass Island, near where Perry achieved his great naval victory, for safe keeping until the return of the troops, which were crossing near Malden for the invasion of Canada.

On the whole journey, as the men grew more familiar with their comrade, it became a pet, receiving a full share of the rations issued to the soldiers, and destitute as the troops found themselves at times, of sustenance, no one thought of putting the knife to the throat of their fellow-traveller. What they had was still shared, and if the pig fared at times, as scantily as the rest, it grunted on, and manifested as much patriotism in its own line as the bipeds it accompanied, in theirs.

After the campaign had closed, the troops recrossed the Lake, having left their horses on the American side. As soon as the line was formed, to the great surprise of many, and inspiring a deep interest in all, there was the pig at the right of the line, ready to resume his march with the rest. By this time the winter frosts had set in and the animal suffered greatly on its homeward journey. It made out, however, to reach Maysville, at which point the troops recrosed the Ohio river. There it gave out, and was placed in trusty hands by Governor Shelby; and finally taken to the Gov.'s home, where the animal passed the residue of its days in ease and indolence.

These facts I have from a gentleman who was on the compaign, who says there are more than one hundred persons living who can attest the statement.

The German Vote.

A paragraph in one of our city papers, gives a voting population of Germans in Cincinnati, at between four and five thousand. From different, and indeed, opposite motives, there seems to exist a disposition in the party political and religious presses, to overrate the numbers of both the German population and voters. A single reflection will dissipate hopes on the one and fears on the other side.

The census of 1840, as regards Cincinnati, shews that less than one-third of the population of this city were Germans and their children, three-fourths of the last having been born in the United States. In fact the exact number of Germans by birth, over twenty years, was 3,440. A very large share of these were but a short time, comparatively, in the country; and if they had all become naturalized since, the vote cannot equal that amount. Deduct the odd hundreds for those under twenty-one; and at least an equal number for those who have resided so long here as to have become one in sympathy with the native born population; and then deduct those who have earned and saved enough here to buy farms for themselves, the great object of their lives with a large number; and add the few who have arrived since, who have been naturalized elsewhere, and the aggregate can hardly exceed two thousand five hundred voters.

Pork Packing.

I learn on undoubted authority, that contracts in the aggregate for between ninety and one hundred thousand hogs, embracing the great mass of that article to arrive here from the Kentucky market, have been already made at four dollars per hundred pounds. Such a state of things *before* pork cutting up and packing has commenced, is unprecedented, and conflicts with the supposed laws of trade, in the well known disposition of buyer and seller to bargain to the best advantage. The hogs from Kentucky are always in before those of Ohio or Indiana, the córn crop ripening earlier on the side of Ohio south, than on the northern. I judge the packers, finding pork higher than they like to pay, and the farmers holding off, have concluded to take what will first arrive, in order to make themselves more independent, when those from Ohio and Indiana are brought in. I infer this the more readily as I have not heard of any *contracts* being made for any but Kentucky hogs.

"Who is Judge Story?"

This distinguished jurist, whose recent death produces a deep sensation throughout the country, was, as is generally known, a professor of law in Harvard University. It was his custom to amuse his class by relating interesting anecdotes, in illustration of principles of law, and few men have ever been more skilful and adroit in the management of this kind of instruction. The writer of this had the pleasure of hearing one of his lectures on a casual visit to Cambridge, in which he stated that the courts of England had awarded a hundred pound note to the person from whom it had been stolen, because the banker who purchased it of the thief, ought to have known from his personal appearance, that he would not be likely to own a note of such value. This rule of law, he thought, would not always operate justly in this country; and in illustration he related, in his inimitable manner, the following anecdote.

"When I came here, to Cambridge," said he, "to occupy the station which I now hold, my friends thought it proper to greet me by a public dinner, which was served up with a good deal of parade in a large room adjoining the post-office; where there was. as is not uncommon on such occasions, a good deal of noise, and a great while continued. I supposed it probable, that there was not a man, woman, or child. in this small village who did not know of this merry-making, and the occasion of it, particularly as I had occupied a seat upon the Bench in Boston for sixteen years previously, and passed sentences of death and imprisonment on numerous convicts. The bustle and noise of the dinner being over, and having for about two months pursued my avocation as lecturer on law in this place, I had occasion one day to call at the post-office and inquire for letters for *Judge Story.* '*Judge who?*' inquired the post-master. *Judge Story*, I repeated with some emphasis: ' *Judge Story, Judge Story!*' reiterated the post-master, '*who is Judge Story. I never heard of him before!*' "

"Not long afterwards," he continued, "it happened, that, on my way to Boston one day on foot, I had occasion to use the sum of fifty dollars, at the intervening village of Cambridgeport, and stepping into the Bank there, I inquired of the Cashier, whether he would pay my check for that amount on a Bank in Boston. He looked somewhat surprised, hesitated, surveyed my person, and stretching himself forward over the counter, looked particularly sharp at my feet. Finding that he did not know me, I gave him my name, when, after a few minutes conversation, as if to assure himself of my identity, he agreed to pay me the money. After he had done so, I asked him why he had hesitated, and particularly why he thought it necessary to take such a searching look at my feet. He said he did not know me, and his object was to satisfy himself whether it was probable, from my personal appearance, that I was good for fifty dollars; and he thought the best evidence would be afforded by the kind of boots I wore, which, unfortunately, on that occasion, were not such as to recommend me to his confidence."

Pioneer History.

The following interesting letter was addressed by Dr. Wm. Goforth, one of the earliest and most able physicians of Cincinnati, to one of his friends at the east.

The *South Bend* settlement or station refered to in the letter, is in the neighbourhood in which Mr. *C. A. Schumann* has been engaged cultivating the grape. The scite of Fort Miami has been washed away by the encroachments of the Ohio river, a few stones belonging to its chimney alone, being left on the bank. Fort Washington, as is well known, was on that space upon Third street, now occupied by the *Botanico Medical College*, formerly the *Bazaar* of Madame Trollope.

FORT WASHINGTON, N. W. TER.,}
Sept. 3d, 1791. }

One of the Indian captives lately died at this place,—His Excellency Gov. St. Clair gave liberty to the rest to bury the corpse according to the custom of their nation: the mode is that the body be wrapped in a shroud, over which they put a blanket, a pair of moccasons on the feet, a seven days rations by the side of the head, with other necessaries. The march from Fort Washington was very solemn; on their arrival at the grave, the corpse was let down, and the relatives immediately retired; an aged matron then descended into the grave, and placed the blanket according

to rule, and fixed the provisions in such manner as she thought would be handy and convenient to her departed friend; casting her eyes about to see if all was right, she found that the deceased was barefoot, and inquired why they had omitted the moccasons? The white person who superintended the whole business informed her that there were no good moccasons in the store, but that by way of amends they had put a sufficiency of leather into the knapsack to make two pairs, at the same time showing her the leather. With this she appeared satisfied, saying that her friend was well acquainted with making them.

The county of Hamilton lies between the two Miami rivers. Just below the mouth of the Little Miami, is a garrison called Fort Miami; at a small distance below this garrison is the town of Columbia. About six miles from Columbia is the town of Cincinnati, which is the county seat of Hamilton, and here is erected *Fort Washington*, the head-quarters of the Federal army. This Fort is pleasantly situated on the banks of the Ohio river; seven miles below this, is a settlement of eighteen or twenty families called South Bend; about seven miles from this also, on the Ohio river is the City of Miami, founded by the Hon. John Cleves Symmes. Twelve miles up the Great Miami is the settlement called Dunlap's Station; and twelve miles up the Little Miami is a settlement called Covault's Station. The number of militia in these places, according to the best accounts I have received, are, at Columbia, two hundred; Cincinnati, one hundred and fifty; South Bend, twenty; City of Miami, eighty; Dunlap's, fifteen, and at Covault's, twenty.

Old Newspapers.

The oldest living newspaper in England is the Lincoln Mercury, first published in 1695. The oldest in London is the St. James Chronicle, of 1761. The oldest paper in Scotland is the Edinburgh Evening, of 1700. The oldest in Ireland, the Belfast News Letter, of 1737.

The oldest living paper in America is the New Hampshire Gazette. It was established by Daniel Fowle, at Portsmouth, in August, 1757. It was originally printed on half a sheet of foolscap, quarto, as were all the papers of that day; but was soon enlarged to half a sheet of crown folio; and sometimes appeared on a whole sheet of crown. It is now in its 89th year, and is a well conducted paper of good dimensions.

The New Lisbon Palladium, after acknowledging the Pittsburgh Gazette as the oldest paper in existence, west of the mountains, gives the Scioto Gazette as the first paper ever published in Ohio; and the Ohio Patriot, established in New Lisbon, in 1808. These, as well as the Pittsburgh Gazette, are still in successful operation.

Newspapers were, however, published in Cincinnati before they existed in either Chillicothe or New Lisbon.

The first printing office in Ohio, was in Cincinnati; and established by *Wm. Maxwell*, who issued, on the 9th November, 1793, *The Centinel of the North Western Territory*, being the first paper published in that territory, or west of Pittsburgh, the *Lexington Gazette* excepted. It bore as a motto, " Open to all parties, but influenced by none." In 1797, *Edmund Freeman* bought out the office, and issued a paper under the title of the *"Freeman's Journal."* He continued it until 1800, when he removed to Chillicothe. On the 28th May, 1799, *Joseph Carpenter* issued the first number of the *Western Spy and Hamilton Gazette*. This was continued under various proprietors, until 1809, when it ceased to exist. There were thus three papers published here in succession, during the last century, all of which were established prior to any others in the State of Ohio.

The Last Supper, &c.

There are two interesting figure groups now exhibiting at *Fourth Street Hall*; one representing the Last Supper, the other the Trial of the Saviour. In these two pieces there are nearly forty figures—the size of life. They are modeled in good taste, and with great discrimination of character. In the *" Last Supper,"* we have the kind and affectionate *John*, the bold and forward *Peter*, and the covetous and faithless *Judas*, all clearly distinguished and represented. Above all we have the *Great Teacher*, admirably pourtrayed, the great focus to every observer's eye.

In the *" Trial of the Saviour,"* the predominant features of the piece are the human passions in action, as they are in the other, in repose. Besides the Saviour, the prominent figures are *Pontius Pilate*, the Roman governor, and *Caiaphas*, the Jewish high priest, both arrayed in their official robes. The other persons are scribes, soldiers, pages, chief priests, &c. They are in their appropriate costumes, attitudes, and employments, which enable the figures to contrast with each other to advantage, as well as to 'harmonize the general effect of the entire·groupe. The whole is a deeply interesting picture, especially to a scripture student.

Indian Mounds.

It is probably not generally known, that a systematic investigation of these mounds has been going on for some months past, in the Scioto Valley, particularly in the neighbourhood of Chillicothe, under the public spirited explorations of two individuals there.

A variety of interesting remains are reward-

ing their labours; and I observe by the last Scioto Gazette, that much light will be shed on the past by what has been already found, although the explorations have as yet reached but a very small portion of these *tumuli*. Abundant evidence has been already furnished, as more doubtless will yet be, that these mounds were erected by a race different from and superior in civilization to, those expelled from the country by the whites. They were doubtless an agicultuaalr people, and of a denser population than even now fills the Scioto country.

I have seen some of the specimens which have been found in these depositories, and can bear testimony to the skill and ingenuity of the modeling and carving they present. They would do credit to people who work with tools better adapted to their purpose than doubtless were within the reach of the aborigines.

Fifth Ward--Cincinnati.

There are in this ward, public buildings 10; pork and ware houses, dwellings, offices, workshops, mills, &c., 784; of which there are—bricks 590, frames 194.

Of these different buildings there were at the close of the year 1842—

	Brick.	Frame.	Total.
	649	663	1312
Built in 1843,	85	35	120
" " 1844,	125	57	176

I cannot compare the improvements in this ward during the past year, until I reach the seventh and tenth wards, the last having been erected during the past year, out of the 5th and 7th. These three must be compared together with the original two.

In the fifth ward, as reduced to its present size, there are 784 public and private buildings, 590 of which are of brick, and 194 are frames. The buildings of 1845, are 45 bricks, and 10 frames—Total 55. The public buildings are—a District School House, on Ninth street; the Methodist Female Seminary; the Ninth Street Baptist, St. John and Northern Lutheran Church, and the English Lutheran Church, on Ninth; the Methodist Book Room, and an Engine House. The Welsh Church, and College of Dental Surgery, and Academy of Natural Science, all on College street, are erections of 1845.

Four-fifths of this ward is built to its utmost capacity.

Growth of the West.

An ear of Indian corn was handed me last Saturday, as a specimen of the crop raised by *Major Wm. Irwin*, on his farm three miles out on the Lebanon road. He assures me that hundreds of ears as large, or nearly so, may be found in what have been gathered from the same field. It is of the large yellow grained sort, is thirteen inches long and has fourteen rows; and has eight hundred and ninety-six grains on the ear. I should like to send it to one of our Atlantic cities, that our friends at the east may have ocular evidence of the growth of the great west. If any gentleman on his way to the east, will be the bearer of it, he may be able to gratify the curiosity this statement is calculated to excite there. It is due to the Buckeye State to let our eastern brethren see some of our products. A sight of this ear of corn will illustrate and explain the *rapid growth of Ohio.*

Important Improvement.

The application of science to the business pursuits of life has hardly ever been of more signal benefit, than the following statement promises and exhibits. Such men as *Amelung & Tunis,* well known here as fully competent to judge the practical value of this important improvement in putting up beef and pork, can hardly be mistaken on this subject. There is, therefore, no doubt that its operation will effect an entire revolution in the beef and pork packing business. I give the whole article for the the benefit of my Cincinnati readers.

DR. DION. LARDNER and Mr. J. DAVIDSON, of this city, have lately perfected an apparatus for the curing of provisions, and the preservation of woods and other substances, which promises to be of vast importance.

The apparatus is very simple and compact. A cistern to hold the brine or other antiseptic fluid communicating with an air-tight cylinder, into which the meat or other substance is placed, and a common lifting or exhausting pump, which withdraws the brine from the cylinder and returns it to the cistern. This is the whole apparatus—so simple as to never get out of order, and yet astonishing in its operations. It can be made of any size, large enough to carry on the largest operations of our largest provision packers, and small enough for the use of the smallest families, and to occupy little more space than a barrel. To prove the importance of this invention, we will state a few of its actual results.

1st. Meat warm and just killed was put into the cylinder, in the hottest of summer. The animal heat was at once extracted, and the meat cured in a few hours. This was done in the presence of Mr. Amelung, the great packer and curer of St. Louis, who carried the meat so cured to St. Louis in the hottest weather of summer, and it kept as well as meat ordinarily cured in winter.

2d. It is found that the blood is completely drained out of the meat, so that the steeping in hogsheads, as in the ordinary process, is not required. By this process the cured provisions acquire very superior qualities, the juices being retained, which, in the ordinary method, are expelled. The weight is increased in proportion to the quantity of fluid infused into the meat.

3. In the presence of Mr. Tunis of Cincinnati, a practical man, pork and hams were placed in the cylinder. In six hours the former was cured. The hams were left in six hours longer—taken out, tried to the bone, found perfectly cured, and transferred to the smoke house. Mr. Tunis, of the house of James C. Hall & Co., of that place, is now in the city, and can be refered to.

4th. Meat in which were skippers (an insect very difficult to get rid of,) when placed in the cylinder, was freed at once,—as the air was gradually exhausted, the skippers made their way to the surface in search of air, where in a few minutes they perished—remaining fast on the surface of the meat, and not mingling with the meat.

5th. Old hams, black, and spoiled in appearance and taste, were well washed, scraped, and dried, and then subjected to the operation of the apparatus, with sweetened pickle; in a few hours they were taken out and smoked, and in looks and taste it was almost impossible to tell them from new hams.

6th. Some hams that were very far gone after being prepared as in the last case, were placed in the apparatus and impregnated with a weak solution of lime, afterwards taken out and thoroughly washed and dried. They were then placed in the cylinder again, and impregnated with the proper ham pickle, taken out and smoked with the same result as in the last case. They were nearly equal to sound hams.

7th. Western hams, trimmed and cleaned, and subjected to this process, could be distinguished from city cured hams only by the best judges. Lastly, besides a great many other advantages, we may say that with this apparatus, time, weather, and climate, are of no consequence. Any sort of pickle may be used,—spiced, sweetened, weak or strong brine. Meats, fish, fowl, fruit, vegetables, wood, in fact any thing which can be preserved by being impregnated with any fluid, may be effected with this apparatus. The same gentlemen have invented a machine for cutting up carcases for curing, which is only inferior in importance to the first named. This machine, almost with the speed of thought, will cut an entire carcase into pieces of the proper size and shape for curing, and this without any waste or haggling, and the pieces fall from the cutter down an inclined plane into the cylinder of the curing apparatus. With these two machines it seems to us that the ultimate of economy in time and labour is attained.

The advantages which we have particularized are developed in the application of the invention to pickling and curing. But the application of this apparatus to the curing of wood, especially for ship building and rail-road purposes, is immense. The wood is placed in the cylinder, or tank, and impregnated with a solution of salt, which for all practical purposes, (wear and use excepted,) will render it indestructible.

The proof of this, No one, we believe, has ever seen the stave of an old provision cask, which has been well saturated with brine, decomposed, even when dug out of a manure heap—nor the posts stuck in the ground in salt works where the ground is impregnated with salt. Ships are salted between the planking and lining, but the salt itself does not enter the wood—it is only the moisture or brine from it, and this only partially, while this apparatus will do it effectually. Chemical substances can even be mixed with the brine, which will colour the wood for cabinet makers,—others to render it, in a great measure, incombustible,—others to give it a greater tenacity for hoops, &c.—others to give it odour, and, in fine, there is no end to the changes which can thus be produced. Chemistry is rich enough in creations of this kind, to satisfy the most fastidious caprice. If it is desirous to *metalize*, or rather *fossilize* wood, for railways, the process is simply this: The pieces, after having been fitted by the joiner or carpenter for their places, are first cured as before mentioned; the salt fluid withdrawn, and a solution of sulphate of iron is let in from another cistern, which has a separate pipe to the cylinder—it is treated with this fluid as with the former. The wood is again withdrawn, dried, and returned to the cylinder, when a solution of muriate of lime is let in from another vessel, which coming in contact with the sulphate of iron within the wood, decomposes it and forms an insoluble of sulphate of lime or gypsum, within the wood, and the muriate of iron, the other new compound goes about its business. So the wood becomes thoroughly impregnated with stone as hard as a rock, and it is yet as tough as before. The expense of preparing two thousand sleepers, enough for a mile of railway, would not exceed $500. Some of the first engineers have expressed their confidence in the invention. What an application of it for our Mississippi valley would effect—railways built of light porous wood—the more porous the better—probably may for less than $1000 per mile, be converted into roads nearly, if not quite as durable as iron—and this cost the patentees calculated upon reducing greatly by an invention of Mr. Davidson, for supporting or sustaining the road upon an entirely new and simple principle, and for which they have applied for a patent.

It is impossible to imagine all that may be accomplished by such an invention. Meat which has to be thrown away in the summer can be saved. In the hottest region of the earth it can be cured, for once in the cylinder it is safe.—Throughout South America and the Southwest, where the skin is stripped from the carcase, and the meat thrown by, as valueless, meat will become an article of export: and in our own "far West," where we can raise enough provisions to supply the world, this invention, with its great saving of time and labour will enable us to fill every market. A gentleman of Cincinnati has, we are informed, secured a license to work under this patent in that city; St. Louis, Missouri; Lafayette, on the Wabash, and Tennessee. And we have no doubt that it will soon be in operation throughout the west. In ship-building, wood preserved in this way will take the precedence of iron, as it will in railroads, from the superior facility of its use, its cheapness and durability. We have not been able to mention half the wonders of this machine; but if any of our readers are curious on the subject, and will call at the store of Messrs. Perry, Mathews & Co., 36 Water street, in this city, they will there see pork which was brought under price in the late warm weather, when the thermometer stood from seventy to seventy-two, and cured on the same day and evening by this apparatus. The pork is there for sale and inspection, and the public can judge for themselves.

We hear the patentees intend to put up a large apparatus for the Kyanizing of wood. No other plan has ever been found effectual: various plans have been proposed and all of them were fully tested, but found too expensive for practical purposes.

The before mentioned machines have been patented by Dr. Lardner and Mr. J. Davidson, of this city, and can be seen in practical operation at the packing yard of the latter, No. 78 Sullivan street, where also licenses to work under the patent are granted.

If a one or a two horse power engine were erected, a great saving of labour would be effected in pumping the brine from the cylinders, turning the cutting machine, and chopping the lard; the steam from the boiler of which would also try up (render) the lard and tallow, and extract the grease from the bones, trimmings and coarse pieces, which cannot be sold. The bones, also, can be disposed of, and thus nothing would be lost. A still greater advantage would result from the slaughter house being attached to the curing and packing establishment, as much of the offal could be turned to account, and the blood, the most valuable of all manures, which here is thrown away, instead of being prepared, as in Paris for the West Indies—as no other manure known will produce the same quantity of sugar canes to an acre—could also be turned to account, and thus make these combined operations very profitable.

The patentees will engage to pay for the meat if it taints or spoils in the curing, provided their directions are followed in the working of the apparatus.—*N. Y. Tribune.*

Perry's Victory.

Mackenzie, in his life of Commodore Perry, while describing the battle of Lake Erie, and the horrible carnage on board the Lawrence, relates the following incident. In the hottest of the fight, Yarnall, the first Lieutenant, came to Perry, and told him that the officers in the 1st division, under his command, were all killed or disabled. Yarnall had received a wound in the forehead, and another in the neck, from which the blood flowed profusely over his face and person, while his nose, which had been struck by a splinter, was swollen to a most portentous size. Perry, after expressing some good humoured astonishment at his tragical appearance, sent him the required aid; but soon after he returned with the same complaint of a destruction of his officers, to which he replied—"You must endeavour to make out by yourself: I have no more to furnish you." In addition to other oddities of Yarnall's appearance, some of the hammocks were stuck in the nettings, and the contents of the mattresses, chiefly stuffed with the down of flag tops, or cat tails, were distributed in the air, having much the appearance of falling snow. This substance, lighting on Yarnall's face, and attaching itself to the blood, gave him, as Dr. Parsons described it, the appearance of a huge owl. When he went below, at the close of the action, even the wounded were moved to merriment, by his ludicrous appearance, and one of them exclaimed—"The devil is come for his own."

Inland Water Communication.

A keel boat with emigrants to the lower Ohio, passed our city two or three days since, which left Rochester, N. Y., last month. She came down to Lake Ontario via Genessee river to Lake Erie, via Niagara river and the Welland Canal around the falls; entered the Erie Extension, at Erie, Pa.; thence to Meadville, and down French

Creek and the Allegheny river to Pittsburgh; and thence down the Ohio nearly one thousand miles, to her final landing place. What would the East have thought thirty years ago, if it had been asserted that such a voyage would ever have become practicable?

Piling up of Jokes.

Speaking of wags, says the Picayune, what is more waggish than a dog's tail when he is pleased? Speaking of tails, we always like those that end well—Hogg's, for instance. Speaking of hogs—we saw one of these animals the other day lying in the gutter, and in the opposite one a well dressed man, the first had a ring in his nose, and the latter had a ring on his finger. The man was drunk, the hog was sober. "A hog is known by the company he keeps," thought we; so thought Mr. Parker, and off he went. Speaking of going off, puts us in mind of a gun we once owned; it went off one night, and we havn't seen it since. Speaking of guns reminds us of the "obsolete idea." We had one—a gun, not an obsolete idea—and it burst.

Poetry.

In the crowd of miscellaneous subjects which occupy the "Advertiser," the muses are elbowed out. I have been tempted to cut the following from an exchange. It bears for authorship the impress, as well as the name of our sweetest poet. I judge it to be Mrs. *Welby's* latest.

To Harriet.

FROM HER FRIEND, AMELIA.

Accept my flowers: I culled them fresh and fair
    This morning, while their leaves with dew were wet,
To deck the braids of thy rich auburn hair,
    Fair Harriet!

Thou shouldst not pine for jewels rich and rare,
    The sweet and simple flowers become thee best,
Amid thy locks their pure pale blossom wear,
    And on thy breast!

The snowy robes of sweet simplicity,
    Light floating as the zephyr's breath, were lent
For woman's lovely form, and flowers should be
    Her ornament.

Let others deck their brows with diadems.
    And glistening pearls, and corals from the sea,
But buds and flowers should be the fragrant gems,
    The gems for thee!

A Choice of Evils.

In accordance with the prejudices of past ages, rather than the more liberal spirit of modern times, the laws of Mexico deny burial to heretics. The subject came incidentally up in the last Congress, on the question of providing sepulture for those who should be killed in the service of the Republic of this class, when Senor Oliveda, one of the deputies, remarked in debate, "There is one of four things we must allow to these heretics, who die in our cause. We must either eat them; or pickle them and send them out of the country; or throw them into the field; or bury them under the ground. The former is of course impossible; to send them out of the country would be too expensive; throwing them into field would cause a pestilence; I therefore move, as the easiest and cheapest mode of disposing of them, to allow them a burial place."

Agricultural Prejudices.

At the annual meeting of the Liverpool Agricultural Society, last month, Lord Stanley, who presided on the occasion, in advocating the introduction of *iron ploughs* to supersede the lumbering wood ploughs in common use, illustrated the prejudices cherished by some farmers by an anecdote. He said a gentleman in the midland counties, who presented one of his farmers with a couple of iron ploughs, and having left the country for two years, returned and was surprised to find not only that the number of iron ploughs was not increased; but that no use was made of those he had given to the tenant. The answer he received on inquiring the cause of this, was, "Why, you—you see we have a notion in this country, that *iron ploughs breeds weeds.*"

In this country, the objection would most likely have been that "iron ploughs" turn wheat into chess.

Pioneer Church at Columbia.

Some of the first settlers of Ohio were Baptists; accordingly the *Duck Creek* Church at Columbia, was the first constituted religious society in the Miami region. Columbia was settled in 1788, and a portion of the colonists, *Stites Bailey, &c.*, formed this society. In 1789, Elder *Stephen Gano* visited this settlement; baptised three persons, of which, with those already refered to, a church was formed. After the lapse of a few years, as the settlement of Columbia decayed, the house of worship was established at Duck Creek, where it still exists, the oldest society of that faith and order in Ohio. The graveyard, a natural mound of exquisite beauty, records the former locality of the church edifice, long since perished from the earth. In the cemetery, the *Stites* and *Goforth* families of the original settlers, sleep their calm and dreamless sleep.

I understand an effort is making to resuscitate the original establishment at Columbia, and to erect a new and appropriate house of worship on the scite of the pioneer edifice.

Shoal Water.

The following curious story is related by the Concordia Intelligencer, to illustrate the accuracy of the river pilots, and the hard work by which they acquire their knowledge of depths and distances:

"An old pilot on the Arkansas once attracted our attention by pointing out a bed of rock where we could see nothing. We asked how he had studied the river—'*Why, sir, I waded from the Post to Fort Gibson, three summers, and I guess I took pains to touch bottom*'—the distance is near six hundred miles—think of that reader!

"His soundings were as follows:—*ankle!—half calf!—whole calf!—half knee!—knee!—half thigh!—thigh!—deep thigh* was as deep as he ever wished water for the Trident; she ran from that depth *down* to a bare sprinkling on the bars; at a greater depth than '*by the deep thigh*,' the order was usually given, '*head her ashore!*'"

Trifles in Verse.

Much has been said, by our city papers, since the appearance of this work, with regard to the portrait which is the frontispiece of the volume, on which subject we take occasion to say a few words.

No such embellishment was at first designed, nor was it promised in the announcement first made of the proposed work; but while in the course of publication, the artist—a friend of the author—very kindly offered to illustrate the volume with a portrait, which offer was thankfully accepted, and the drawing upon stone prepared from a Daguerreotype by Hawkins. As a *likeness* its fidelity cannot be questioned, while as a work of art the impressions first taken, were, and are still regarded, as highly creditable specimens of Lithography, when is taken into consideration the facts that the art is still in its infancy in the west, and the artist in all respects self-taught. Unfortunately, however, in the anxiety felt that the book should make its appearance duly when promised, the printing was hurried, and many indistinct and imperfect impressions were permitted to go into the binder's hands without examination, of which were most of the copies first published, including the impressions so generally animadverted upon by the editorial fraternity. Thus much of explanation, by way of the *amende honourable*, due to the artist, a modest and deserving young man, whose design upon the stone was pronounced, by judges of Lithographic drawing, as a likeness most striking, and as a work of art in a high degree meritorious and praiseworthy.

Inasmuch, however, as thus far our editors have, as it respects this volume—a Cincinnati production throughout—brought the force of their critical acumen to bear solely upon the frontispiece, it would seem to be a moot-point whether the picture does not in a great measure constitute the book. At least we think the author should feel, as he doubtless does, under much obligations to the artist for having furnished a picture which has, thus far, acted as a scape-pipe or safety-valve to all the critical steam and hot water that had otherwise no doubt alighted upon the *contents* of the volume itself.

Journal of John G. Jungmann.--No. 3.

In a short time a letter was received from *Detroit*, requesting us to remove hither; but the roads and weather rendering this impossible, we consulted the brethren and resolved, that brethren David, Heckewelder, Senseman and Edwards, with four Indians should go there: Brother *Jung* and I were to remain. We heard nothing for four weeks from our brethren, except false reports from wicked men. During this time, two of our number, God thought proper to take

home to himself: One a boy twelve years old, who had a great desire to dwell with his *Dear Saviour*, and died confidently in an acceptance with him; the other a *babe*, a grand-child of *Chief Nettuwathwehs*, both of which *I* baptised in the interest and covenant of our blessed Saviour. Brother *Micht, Jung* and *I* preached alternately under the open Heavens; and at night made fire for light and warmth, not having a house large enough. After our *departed brethren* returned from *Detroit*—expecting to remain here—we made arrangements to build a church, boil maple sugar, &c., and formed a station. But again a letter was received from the *Chief Officer* at Detroit, who commanded that all the *white* brethren and sisters "must come there forthwith." This was like a clap of thunder to our poor souls. That *we* should be separated from our dear brown brethren of the flock, we could not realize but with heartfelt *misery*. There was no alternative, but to leave them in the hands and blessings of our dear Saviour Jesus Christ.

March, 1782. we entered upon our journey, with our conductor (an officer named *Leslie*,) who, having a *noble heart*, strove to alleviate our sufferings, and smooth our rugged path. At our first night's (twenty miles) encampment, we heard news of the murder of our dear brethren at *Gnadenhutten* and *Salem*,—our feelings could not be described; but exclaimed—"Thy ways, O God, are not our ways—*but just, as thou disposeth*." We know not our own future destiny, being surrounded by murderers, and with astonishment wondered at our *thus far* preservation, by God's special interposition, in sending those runners to come and force us away, as most assuredly the same fate would have befallen us. On our journey, our sisters suffered extremely from cold; and some of us were occasionally permitted to go ahead—build up a fire to enable them to warm themselves. After we advanced, fifty miles from Lower Sandusky, a deep snow fell. At night, (making arrangements to retire under the open Heavens,) the Almighty, in mercy, sent us an Indian trader named *Rabens,* a very charitable man, who invited us to his house, (half a mile off,) which we thankfully accepted. He nourished us with *Chocolate, &c., &c.,* of which we had not partaken for a long time. Another person, one mile further on (an Indian trader,) took us to his house, and treated us with uncommon hospitality, and kept us until we could possibly pursue our journey. Here the Lord extended his special power towards me again. An Indian woman having had some misunderstanding with one of the whites, mistaking *me* for the offender—watching my entrance to the *Conductor's Lodge*, raised a tremendous billet of wood to kill me. The conductor catching the blow, and tearing it from her, saved my life. She proved to be the interpretress, who was present when we were first taken, April 14th, 1782. After three weeks detention, we started again under two new conductors, (sent by the Chief Officer at Detroit,) and arrived in sight of Detroit on my 62d anniversary, at the mouth of a river, which, connecting Lakes Erie, Huron and St. Clair, passes Detroit. This aroused heartfelt joy and great gratitude towards our Almighty God for his parental care, and more especially in reaching Detroit on the 20th April, after a very stormy voyage across the waters, coming very near foundering. We were very kindly received by the commanding officer, who furnished us with shelter, and with his wife visited us twice every day, furnishing us provision. After tarrying three months, a number of our Indian brethren followed us, which caused us to look for a location, which we found (July 29,) thirty miles from Detroit, on Huron river. We commenced building huts, cultivating land, and strove to collect our scattered flock of brethren—expecting here to remain in peace and quiet, being twenty miles from any neighbour. Our Indian brethren came in, and so fast—putting up huts and houses, that in two years time, we had a beautiful location and every convenience. A remarkable circumstance befel me, on a very rainy day. Being very thirsty, I took a bucket to a spring under the hill, on the left of which was a two foot thick Aspentree and two and a half foot Black Oak; on the right, a deep miry bog. As I was about to return to the house a terrible whirlwind arose, tearing one of the trees into fragments, and casting them all around me; the other tree torn up by the roots, and thrown down aside of me. Stunned with the terrible noise and fright, I fell to the ground; but with wonder rose, and found myself unhurt. Every one who saw and could conjecture my predicament, exclaimed, how wonderfully God protected you. To him be the praise, honour, and glory. In this our beautiful location, skirted on both sides of the Huron river, with fine fields and every thing in a very flattering and prosperous condition of 2½ years labour, we were again disturbed by the Chippeways, who sought to drive us away from it. We held consultation for removal back to our dear old location, Muskingum or Walhunding. A respite of an additional year being granted, we, during the winter, fell to work in building a Canoe, thirty-six feet long and three feet wide, with other arrangements for departing. However, it was determined that, there being few Indian brethren and enough missionaries, some should return to Bethlehem. This fell to my, and brother Senseman's lot, we being the oldest. In May, 1785, left our dear brethren at New Gnadenhutten, arrived at

Detroit, passed on Lake Erie to Fort Erie; thence to Fort Schlosser; then eight miles by land and eight miles by water to Niagara—stopped there sixteen days, (awaiting a boat from Sohinachedi, Lake Ontario;) passed to Oswego, and then on Onieda Lake and Woodcreek, to Fort Stanwix: from thence, one mile by land to Mohawk river, to Schenectady and Albany. From thence, by vessel to Newbury, and by land to Sussex, Hope, Easton; and through God's protection and blessing, safely arrived, and were friendly received by Brother Etwein, son-in-law Ebert, and Christian Heckenwelder, (whose brother's daughter we brought along with us.) We arrived safe at Bethlehem, July 8th, 1785—absent from home four and a half years (last visit.) We were now released from Missionary duties, and appointed to parish superintendence, as stewart, and as member of the "School and Missionary Directory." My dear partner through life (after forty-eight years marriage,) the Almighty thought proper to take home to Heaven, aged seventy-two years, November 22d, 1793, (Ann Margaret Jungmann.) We had eight children, (four sons and four daughters)—John, Jacob, Gottlob and Peter;—Anna Maria Brooker, (who died on Missionary Station at the Island of St. Thomas,) Mrs. Ebert, Elizabeth Gerhardt, Susan Schultz.

[J. G. Jungmann died at Bethlehem, July 17, 1808, aged eighty-eight years two months twenty-eight days. He died as he lived, solely devoted to the cause of Christ; and his whole soul absorbed in the Missionary cause and the salvation of souls.]

Original Letter of Gen'l. Wayne.

Head Quarters,
Greenville, 24th May, 1794.

Sir,—You are to march to-morrow morning at revellie with the detachment assigned you, taking under your charge and escort all the horses belonging to the Q. M. General's and Contractors's departments, for Fort Hamilton. Upon your arrival at that Fort, you are to call on the Q. M. Generals or their agents, and demand an immediate load of flour for all the horses belonging to each department, except those that may be necessary for the transport of forage for the support of those transporting the flour;—of this number Capt. Benham and Mr. Wilson will be the most competent judges.

You will take every possible precaution to guard against surprise; and if attacked, the sword, bayonet and espontoon must be your principal dependence.

You will so regulate your movements as to reach Fort St. Clair to-morrow evening, and Fort Hamilton early the next day: and in order to facilitate your early arrival at Hamilton, you will take up your line of march from St. Clair as early as you can possibly see your way in the morning; because it will be of very great advantage both to the troops and horses, to be at the end of their march before the intense heat of the day: add to this that it will give you time to have all the loading prepared and sent up the river, so as to be in perfect readiness to advance from your encampment on this side of the Miami at a very early hour on the morning of the 28th inst., and in time to reach Fort St. Clair the same evening, and this place, or Fort Jefferson, the evening following.

Your detachment will be held responsible for any depredation or plunder of the stores, until the culprit or culprits are discovered.

You will draw one gill of whisky per man for your command, from the acting Qr. Master at this place; but it will be best to reserve it until some time to-morrow,—say 12 o'clock.

Wishing you a safe tour and speedy return,
I remain with respect and esteem,
Your most humble servant,
ANTHONY WAYNE.
Capt. JACOB SLOUGH.

N. B.—Should the contractors refuse to furnish flour, load with corn, or such other articles as may be furnished by the Q M. G.

Things in Louisville.

Louisville I find in a condition much more thriving than I anticipated,—and I have only had time to visit the oldest sections of it. The more prosperous parts I understand are yet for me to see. The stores are built of greater width than ours, and the three principal business streets, which are of great length are run parallel with the river Ohio, being between the curb as wide as our widest business streets between the line of the houses; thus is a massive character given to the business of the place. There is a manifest improvement to my eyes in the appearance of the city from what it presented a year or two since. Still there is not that air of freshness and activity which is to me a great charm in the business of Cincinnati. Louisville was a place of heavy commercial operations, when Cincinnati was emerging from its village and town position. In 1826, when I first visited the former place, the greater part of the present business buildings were already in existence. Indeed, if I could trust my recollection, there was as much business done then as since. I recollect at any rate, the impression of astonishment which was fastened on me in contemplating the masses of sugar, coffee, tea, &c., with which the stores appeared filled; and this was at a period when wholesale grocery stores in Cincinnati sold one hundred and fifty to two hundred bags coffee per annum,

and other groceries in a corresponding measure.

There are a great number—too many—coffee houses here. But we of Cincinnati may well be silent on that score. There is a feature in the business of the place, however, from which we are exempt. I allude to lottery offices, of which I have seen several signs. The court house, will be, when finished, a noble building, with the exception of that at Pittsburgh, the best adapted to its purpose of any in the west. The Pittsburgh court house is, in some of its inside arrangements, inferior, however, even to this.

The *Bear grass* creek empties into the Ohio at the steamboat landing, and as it runs the course of, and for several miles back nearly parallel with the river, forms an admirable safe-harbor for coal and flat boats which require to remain any length of time in port, or are exposed to injury during winter, from ice. It must become the same thing at some future day for steamboats, as the commercial wants of the place on the one hand and its increasing capital on the other, will justify the enterprise, which although involving heavy expense, will fully justify and reimburse it.

Louisville commands the Kentucky business of the interior, until we approach the Lexington and Frankfort regions, of which it divides the trade with Cincinnati. Upper Kentucky deals entirely with our own city.

These hasty notices are all my hurried stay permit me to make. I propose to examine the city fully on my return from Memphis. A delegation of thirty have been appointed from this place, whither the proportion which attends the convention of the 12th will exceed that of ours, which is as one to four of the *appointees*.

"The Jews in America," and Things in 1808.
MR. CIST:

In your paper of October 1, 1845, I see it stated by your correspondent "J.," that " previous to 1816, the Jewish people were not known to have settled in the Mississippi Valley; and for several years subsequent they were considered as a strange sight." I think this statement is inaccurate. When I came to Ohio, about thirty-eight years ago, I had a stage companion from Philadelphia to Pittsburgh, a Mr. M., who informed me he was a " Dutch Jew." His home was Cincinnati. He was allied by marriage to an extensive connection there by the name of P——, all Israelites, and, as I understood, largely concerned in trade. Mr. M. stated that he was employed for the concern in a far ranging circuit—from Cincinnati to St. Louis and the lead regions, thence to New Orleans, Philadelphia, Pittsburgh, and home.

Mr. M. was a singular genius. He was rather

ill on the passage—more inclined to sleep than talk; but would rouse occasionally, and converse intelligently on matters within the range of his observations, which, of course, was not very limited. Our passage through Pennsylvania commenced about November 1st, 1808, and we made it in that very pleasant sort of traveling season called *Indian Summer.* We had a stage full of passengers, constituting a *well assorted* company of nine—one third of whom were ladies. There was enough of variety, of tact, of intelligence, and of *companionableness,* to cause the time to pass quite agreeably during our six day's trip; for just then they had attained such boasted speed of travelling, that, by leaving Philadelphia very early on Monday morning, driving well into each night, and rousing us for onward movement at 2 o'clock, A. M., they brought us into Old Pitt in ample time to view its then somewhat scanty improvements on the succeeding Saturday. Our mountain passages were abundantly rough, and perilous at times; especially on the night we reached Bedford. Our progress that day had been unusally dilatory. We had a shower or two, and were roused occasionally by the intonations of mountain thunder. Before reaching Bedford, we were benighted and beset with thick darkness, in descending a steep, narrow, and dangerous track—so 'twas said—and what seemed worst, the driver manifested alarm, and even fright. Most of our males took to their feet—the Jew and myself remained in the stage with the ladies—and he talked about "Bloody Ruin." It was said that a small deviation would have tumbled us headlong down some hundred feet; but, thanks to our good horses, we came down perfectly safe.

Such a company, so united for successive days, will commonly seek amusements to "while away time." With us the chief appliance was to mutual satiring Sometimes it might have seemed rather severe; but never ill-humoured. There was a merchant on board, evidently a great braggart, and from a region reputed to contain not a few of the generation of Bobadillians. He was so completely taken down that I pitied and sought to console him, though in conscience I could not much blame his assailants. There was a strapping son of Erin, of Kittaning —rather boisterous in his mirth; but entirely good humoured, in our community. Many sly satirical arrows were shot *towards* him; but they always glanced off—or if they seemed to stick, *he* never seemed to know it. He would carol away, " And a hunting we will go, go, go, and a drinking we will go!"—so merrily and heartily that the quiet mirth of the satirizers would instantly be overborne, and their arrows broken or scattered like straws. There was an Irish lady of Pittsburgh, of speech sufficiently English to pass without cavil, with tones half kindly, half quizzical, and with readiness of wit and tact, which other wits might delight to call into exercise; but none, in his right wits would choose (*hostilely*) to provoke. I was the sole representative of a certain universal nation. My turn of being attacked was to be expected—and it came. " Is it true that from among your people there came forth a great many notable sharpers?" True—perfectly true—the greatest probably on the face of the whole earth. "Indeed sir, say you so." How comes it that your people, who claim to be especially intelligent and even moral, should be marked and distinguished by the sending forth of such characters? No difficulty in explaining the matter. "Say you so, sir?—we should like to hear!" Perhaps I had better decline. "But indeed we should like to hear." And no offence? "Not the least, sir; we urge you to speak freely." Well, then, my friend, if you will urge the explanation, you shall have it in few words. Our people are intelligent and enterprising; consequently we have not only rascals as well as you; but finished, intelligent and enterprising rascals, who find abundant sphere of action and dupes to plunder among your *un*-intelligent population. Whether this reply was satisfactory I never heard; but was "put" no more to the "question." But the Jew. Was the Jew overlooked or forgotten? By no means. But it proved a bootless game. When he was wake enough to know that a shot was aimed at him, he would move—strain his eyes open—smile or rather grin—and—go to sleep again, or seem to. The "archer that shot at a frog" never engaged in more bootless archery than our fun-seekers in their attacks on the Israelite.

But we arrived at Pitt on the afternoon of Saturday, and our little community was dissolved for all time;—yet we did not all separate. The Jew, as one accustomed to the west, took in charge the unpractised Yankee; and he did it in kindness too, I have not the least hesitance in asseverating. Nevertheless, he led me into some troubles. He took me from the stage inn; that was too dear;—so a wheelbarrow man was soon engaged to transport our trunks, and away we trudged in search of cheaper lodgings. Whither away we went I can hardly now divine, for some thirty-four years elapsed before I again saw Old Pitt. But one thing I well remember—it was unconsionably muddy. We found our intended entertainer; but he had been turned out, and was in rather close quarters. We were ushered into a grog-room—rather small—full of customers, —the mud on the floor perhaps not much more than two inches thick—the grog briskly circulating, and the sights, scents, and sounds perhaps not very much inferior to the most finished exhibition of the sort in those diggins, pending the whisky rebellion. We passed on into a small room adjoining, where we were entertained with a view of culinary operations, preparatory for our supper; but these were unfortunate—all being done over a common coal grate, without any crane, was overset, and a child was badly scalded. Our repast was indifferent at best; and was rendered decidedly no better by the screams of the poor child, and multitudinous and the multifarious music in the adjoining apartment. Mr. M. declared this would never do, and we soon adjourned to a private boarding room, where we abode, pleasantly enough till Monday, when we embarked on a keel boat, Capt. M., commander, bound "low down" the Ohio. We left Pittsburgh, November 7, the water excessively low; and it took some thirty-six hours to reach Beaver—about thirty miles. Mr. M. was out of patience. We bought a skiff; he engaged four young emigrants who were working their passage in the keel (with leave of its owner) to row the skiff to Cincinnati: so away we went, merrily, merrily—but not *overly* rapid. We agreed, for the sake of dispatch, to *float at night*, an undertaking not exactly of the most comfortable kind, in such a craft and in frosty November. I essayed to *rest* in the bow—the rest where they could. M. had a buffalo rug for his comfort; but one of the rowers, a brisk, funny Irishman, seized and encircled himself with it and laid himself down to rest, with great calmness. It was rather amusing to hear the moanings of friend M., exclaiming you *stole me bool's rogue!* Finally, an amicable compromise took place. They shared the "rogue," and soon seemed lost in sound repose—of which thing I had but a very small share; the noise of the ripples and the chills in the air conspiring to invade my incipient slumbers, or prevent their occurrence. I think we floated ashore once. Myself and one of the hands took to rowing; we spied a floating light, and rowed *after* it; 'twas a family boat. They hailed—"which way are you bound?" Down river. "No! you're rowing *up*." Oh no! "Try." 'Twas so. But we went aboard, where they had a good comfortable fire; and there we gladly remained and floated till day—when we took to our skiff again. We progressed tolerably—stopped a little to look at Steubenville, then young; at Charleston (now Wellsburg,) more in years, yet a smaller place—with a wonderful row of taverns. We staid one night at Wheeling; M. seemed rather melancholy, exclaiming often, "Oh, I wish I was at *Pisburg*—wish I was at *Pisburg*." Finally he sold us his

interest in our *vessel;* and asked of me a loan of money, which he would pay at M.-when he should come down. I handed him what he desired in half eagles. I heard no more of my Jewish friend till the next spring, when, returning to M., from the country, I found he had, in an up river trip, enquired till he met a friend of mine, and left with him the lent money. He called some time after, employed me professionally, and paid handsomely.

I feel great interest in the prosperity of Jacob, and have full faith in their restoration. I know not else how the Scriptures can be fulfilled. Have you read the late discourse of M. M. Noah? He is an Israelite; would to Heaven we could add—"In whom there is no guile." But this discourse from an Israelite is well worth attention. The restoration, we suppose, will be Jewish, not Christian. What will occur after is entirely another question. Is not the way preparing? The Jews, it is fully understood, *expect* to be restored. They are waiting. The Russian Autocrat is said to be expelling them. Palestine, to a great extent, remains vacant. Egypt *may* become a dependency of Britain. A friendly power in Palestine might then be vastly important to her. Turkey is imbecile. France is swallowing the Mahommedan realms of Northern Africa. Turkey, in Europe, may soon become the prey of Austria and Russia. To sustain the balance of power, England (possibly) may seek to hand over Hanover to Prussia, and indemnify herself by serving Egypt, and replanting Palestine. But I pretend to no gift of prophecy; yet the signs of the times are surely of great and singular significance.   K.

The Assistant Editor.

With a slight variation of phraseology, the following will apply just now, as well as if it had been "expressly calculated for this meridian."

It chanced during the late summer, that a country editor fell ill of a fever. The fact was announced to his readers, along with a notice to the effect, that during his indisposition the editorial management would be confided to an assistant. Well, it turned out that the assistant contrived to please the readers of the journal better than the chief himself, and they demanded his name. The convalescent editor informed them that it would be impossible for him to divulge the name of his aid-de-camp, but that he would, in the next number of the "Squatter's Thunderbolt and Settler's Family Guide," present his patrons with a correct portrait of the assistant. Expectation balanced itself on tiptoe for a week, and when the anxiously-looked for "Guide" appeared at last, lo! and behold! at the head of the editorial column appeared a full length engraving of a portly pair of *Scissors!* Underneath were printed, in staring capitals—*Korrckt Portrait ov the 'Sisstant Editur—frum reel Life.*

Answering Letters.

The following little paragraph deserves to be written in letters of gold. It should be cut out, framed and hung up in the counting house of the merchant, as well as the office of the mechanic and professional man; or pasted upon the writing desk of every man in the habit of receiving letters, as a silent monitor of one of those minor morals of society which no true gentleman will, thus reminded, ever permit himself to offend against. Viewed in this light, no insult can be greater than that silent neglect, which says that a letter you have written is unworthy the common courtesy of an answer of some description:

Letters.—The Book of Etiquitte says "*every letter requires an answer of some kind or other*," and Madame Celwart, who is the oracle of politeness at Paris, says, "It is as proper to reply to a letter which is written to you, as to answer a question that is addressed to you."

Remarkable Incident.

A ROMANCE OF REAL LIFE.

The following singular story, which was current among the English residents in St. Petersburg at the coronation of the present Emperor of Russia, has been narrated to us by a person newly arrived from that part of the continent.

In the early part of the year 1826, an English gentleman, from Akmetch in the Crimea, having occasion to travel to France on business of importance, directed his course by way of Warsaw and Poland. About an hour after his arrival in that city, he quitted the tavern in which he had been taking a refreshment, to take a walk through the streets. While sauntering in front of one of the public buildings, he met an elderly gentleman of grave aspect, and courteous demeanor. After mutual exchange of civilities they got into conversation, during which, with the characteristic frankness of an Englishman, he told the stranger who he was, where from, and whither he was going. The other, in a most friendly manner, invited him to share the hospitalities of his house, till such time as he found it convenient to resume his journey—adding, with a smile, that it was not improbable that he might visit the Crimea himself in the course of that year, when, perhaps, he might require a similar return; the invitation was accepted, and he was conducted to a splendid mansion, elegant without and commodious within.

Unbounded liberality on the part of the Pole, produced unbounded confidence on the part of the Englishman. The latter had a small box of jewels of great value, which he had carried about his person from the time of leaving home—finding that mode of conveyance both hazardous and inconvenient in a town, he requested his munificent host to deposit it in a place of security, till he should be ready to go away. At the expiration of three days he prepared for his departure, and in asking for his box, how was he amazed when the old gentleman, with a countenance exhibiting the utmost surprise replied:

"What box?"

"Why, the small box of jewels which I gave you to keep for me."

"My dear sir, you must surely be mistaken; I never, really, saw or heard of such a box."

The Englishman was petrified. After recovering himself a little, he requested he would call his wife, she having been present when he received it. She came, and being questioned, answered in exact unison with her husband—expressed the same surprise—and benevolently endeavoured to persuade her distracted guest that it was a mere hallucination. With mingled feelings of horror, astonishment and despair, he walked out of the house and went to the tavern which he put up at, on his arrival at Warsaw. There he related his mysterious story, and learned that his iniquitous host was the richest Jew in Poland.

He was advised, without delay, to state the case to the Grand Duke, who fortunately happened at that time to be in Warsaw.

He accordingly waited on him, and with little ceremony was admitted to the audience.

He briefly stated down his case, and Constantine, "with a greedy ear devoured up his discourse." Constantine expressed his astonishment—told him he knew the Jew, having had extensive money transactions with him—that he had always been respectable, and of an unblemished character, "However," he added, "I will use every legitimate means to unveil the mystery." So saying he called on some gentlemen who were to dine with him that day, and despatched a messenger with a note to the Jew, requesting his presence.

Aaron obeyed the summons.

"Have you no recollection of having received a box of jewels from the hand of this gentleman?" said the Duke.

"Never, my lord," was the reply.

"Strange, indeed. Are you perfectly conscious," turning to the Englishman, "that you gave the box as stated?"

"Quite certain, my lord."

Then addressing himself to the Jew—"This is a very singular case, and I feel it my duty to use singular means to ascertain the truth; is your wife at home?"

"Yes, my lord."

"Then," continued Constantine, "there is a sheet of paper and here is a pen; proceed to write a note to your wife in such terms as I shall dictate."

Aaron lifted the pen.

"Now," said this second Solomon, "commence by saying—All is discovered!—There is no resource left but to deliver up the box. I have owned in the presence ᴏ the Grand Duke."

A tremor shook the frame of the Israelite, and the pen dropped from his fingers. But instantly recovering himself exclaimed—

"That is impossible, my lord. That would be directly implicating myself."

"I give my word and honour," said Constantine, "in presence of every one in the room, that what you write shall never be used as an instrument against you, farther than the effect it produces on your wife. If you are innocent you have nothing to fear,—but if you persist in not writing it, I will hold it as a proof of your guilt."

With a trembling hand the terrified Jew wrote out the note, folded it up, and as he was desired, sealed it with his own signet.

Two officers were despatched with it to his house, and when Sarah glanced over its contents, she swooned and sank to the ground. The box was delivered up, and restored to its owner—and the Jew suffered the punishment his villany deserved. He was sent to Siberia.

Button Holes on Both Sides.

A gentleman in Charleston, who entertained a good deal of company at dinner, had a black as an attendant, who was a native of Africa, and never could be taught to hand things invariably to the *left* hand of the guests at table. At length, his master thought of an infallible expedient to direct him, and as the coats were then worn in Charleston single-breasted, in the present Quaker fashion, he told him always to hand the plate, &c., to the button-hole side. Unfortunately, however, for the poor fellow, on the day after he had received this ingenious lesson, there was amongst the guests at dinner, a foreign gentleman with a double-breasted coat, and he was for awhile completely at a stand. He looked first at one side of the gentleman's coat, then at the other, and finally quite confounded at the outlandish make of the stranger's garment, he cast a despairing look at his master, and exclaiming in a loud voice, " Botton holes at both sides, massa," handed the plate right over the gentleman's head.

Managing a Husband.

This is a branch of female education too much neglected; it ought to be taught with " French Italian, and the use of the globes." To be sure, as Mrs. Glass most sensibly observes, "first catch your hare," and you must also first catch your husband. But we will suppose him caught —and therefore to be roasted, boiled, stewed, or jugged. All these methods of cooking have their matrimonial prototypes. The roasted husband is done to death by the fiery temper, the boiled husband dissolves in the warm water of conjugal tears, the stewed husband becomes ductile by the application of worry, and the jugged husband is fairly subdued by sauce and spice. Women have all a natural genius for having their own way, still the finest talents, like " the finest pisantry in the world," require cultivation. We recommend beginning soon.

When Sir William L—— was setting off on his wedding excursion, while the bride was subsiding from the pellucid lightness of white satin and bonde, into the delicate darkness of the lilac silk travelling dress, the lady's maid rushed into his presence with a torrent, not of tears, but of words. His favourite French valet had put out all the bandboxes that had been previously stored with all feminine ingenuity in the carriage. Of course, on the happiest day of his life, Sir William could not " hint a fault or hesitate dislike," and he therefore ordered the interesting exiles to be replaced. " Very vell, Sare William," said the prophetic gentleman's gentleman, " you let yourself be bandboxed now, you'll be bandboxed all your life."

The prediction of this masculine Cassandra of the curling-irons was amply fulfilled. Poor Sir William! One of his guests a gentleman whose wits might have belonged to a Leeds clothier, for, they were always wool-gathering, confounded the bridal with one of those annual festivals when people cruelly give you joy of having made one step more to your grave—this said guest, at his wedding, literally wished him many happy returns of the day! The polite admirer of the bandboxes found, however, one anniversary quite sufficient, without any returns.

The lines which follow are copied from " Trifles in Verse," a collection of Fugitive Poems, by *L. J. Cist;* just published by Robinson & Jones, of this city. The piece here given has never been in print, prior to the appearance of the volume in question:

The Blind Girl to her Sister:

ABSENT FROM HOME.

Come Home! Dear Sister!—Sad and lonely-hearted,
As o'er another ray of light withdrawn—
As for the sunshine of her home departed—
The blind girl sits and weeps, to mourn thee gone!
Gone!—The companion of her mirth and sadness,
The friend and playmate of her childish years;
Life, in thine absence, loseth half its gladness,
And this deep darkness doubly dark appears:
The long, long day is more than night without thee—
Thrice welcome night! for all sweet dreams about thee!

Come Home! Sweet Sister!—Ah! how much I miss thee—
All thy kind shielding from life's rude alarms—
From day's first dawn, when erst I sprang to kiss thee,
Till night still found me nestling in thine arms—
My lips may speak not!—but the heart's deep feeling,—
The spirit's sadness, and the low-voiced tone,—
The round full drops, that will not brook concealing,
These tell of one deep grief—I am alone!
Alone!—Without thee, dearest, what to me
Were even life's best gift—the power to see?

Come Home! Dear Sister!—Can the far-off stranger,
How kind soever, yield thee love like mine?
Can fairest scenes, through which thou rov'st, a ranger,
Give to thee joys like those which Home enshrine?
Think how for thee my lonely spirit pineth,
Through the long weary hours, as day by day
Slowly the sun down yonder west declineth,
Whilst thou, my sun of life, art far away!
Thou canst not dream how this full heart is yearning
For that bless'd day which sees thee home returning!

Come Home! Sweet Sister!—Like a dove, all lonely,
My heart sits brooding in its silent nest,
O'er joys departed!—Come! thy presence only
Can make our home with cloudless sunshine bless'd!
E'en as the bird, whose gentle mate has perished,
Droopeth, no more to notes of rapture stirred—
So pine I now, amid the scenes we've cherished;
I cannot sing, where, ever once were heard
Our strains commingled, ere thy steps did roam,—
My song is hushed:—Sister, sweet mate, Come Home!

Punning.

As a general thing, there is nothing we more abominate than puns and punsters. It is true that from among the infinity of efforts made by the latter, a good specimen of the former is occasionally produced; as by continued efforts sparks may be sometimes *forced* to scintillate from a worn-out flint; but these happy hits, coming when they do, amid the dark brood of painful abortions, of which the regular punster is usually delivered, are truly "like angel's visits, few and far between." The best puns, like the happiest similes, are always those which are suggested— not sought for; and such, we think, are the following:

"Why do you use tobacco?" said one gentleman to another. "Because I *chews*," was the prompt and witty reply.

There is no truth in men," said a lady in company. "They are like musical instruments, which sound a variety of tones."—"In other words, madam," said a wit who chanced to be present, "you believe that all men are *lyres*."

Caleb Whiteford, of punning memory, once observing a young lady very earnestly engaged at work, knotting fringe, asked her what she was doing. "Knotting, sir," replied she. "Pray, Mr. Whiteford, can you knot. "I *can not*" answered he.

Sang Froid.

The army of Mayence was attacked at Tofrou, in 1793, by Charett and Bonchamp, and, unable to resist the superior forces of the Vendeans, retreated and lost its artillery. The Republicans were on the point of being destroyed, as their retreat was about to be cut off. Kleber called the Leiut. Col. Schoudardis; "Take (said he) a company of Grenadiers; stop the enemy at that ravin; you will be killed, but your comrades will be saved." "*Oui, mon general*," replied Schouardis calmly. He marched; held the Vendeans a long time in check; and after prodigies of valour, died with his men on the spot. This "*Oui, mon general*," equals the finest specimens of antiquity.

Squeezing the Hand.

We endorse the following—every word of it. An exchange says:

"It is but lately that we understood the strange constructions that are sometimes put upon a squeeze of the hand. With some it is entirely equivalent to a declaration of love; this is very surprising indeed. We must take hold of a lady's hand like hot potatoes; afraid of giving it a squeeze lest we should burn her fingers. Very fine, truly!—Now it was our ancient custom to squeeze every hand that we got in our clutches, especially a fair one. Is it not a wonder that we have never been sued for a breach of promise? We would not give a rusty nail for one of your cold formal shakes of the hand. Every person who extends one or two fingers for your touch, (as if he were afraid of catching some cutaneous distemper,) should go to school a while to John Quincy Adams. He shakes you with a vengeance, and shakes your body too, unless you

should happen to be as thick as himself. Well, there is nothing like it; it shows a good heart at any rate, and we would rather a man would crush the very bones of our fingers, and shake our shoulder out of joint, than that he should poke our paw, as if he were about to come in contact with a bear or hyæna. The ladies may rest assured of this, that a man who will not squeeze their hand when he gets hold of it, does not deserve to have a hand in his possession; and that he has a heart seven hundred and forty-nine times smaller than a grain of mustard seed."

A Brother's Love.

There is something transcendantly virtuous in the affections of a true-hearted brother towards his gentle and amiable sister. He can feel unbounded admiration for her beauty—he can appreciate and applaud the kindness which she bestows upon himself. He can press her bright lips and fair forehead, and still she is unpolluted —he can watch the blush steal over her features when he tells her of her innocent follies, and he can clasp her to his bosom in consolation when the tears gush from her overloaded heart. With woman there is a feeling of pride mingled with the regard which she has for her brother. She looks upon him as one fitted to brave the tempest of the world; as one to whose arm of protection she can fly for shelter when she is stricken by sorrow, wronged or oppressed; as one whose honour is connected with her own: and who durst not see her insulted with impunity. He is to her as the oak is to the vine—and though she may fear all others of mankind, she is secure and confident in the love and protection of her brother. Nothing affords man such satisfaction, and nothing entwines a sister so affectionately among his sympathies and interests, as profound reliance on her virtue, and strong convictions of her diffidence and delicacy. As these two latter are far the most delightful qualities of a beautiful female, so are they the strongest spells for enticing away the affections of the other sex. A female without delicacy is a woman without principle: and, as innate and shrinking perception of virtue is a true characteristic of a pure hearted creature, so it is the most infallible union between hearts that truly beat in response to each other. There is more tenderness in the disposition of woman than of man; but the affection of a brother is full of the purest and most generous impulses; it cannot be quenched by aught on earth, and will outlive all selfish and sordid attachments. A deep rooted regard for a gentle creature born of the same parents with ourselves, is certainly one of the noblest feelings of our nature, and were every other feeling of human nature dead, save this, there would still a bright hope remain that the fountain of virtue and principle was not yet sealed.

A Guarded Answer.

In the Registration Court, Cupar Fife was called on to appear as a witness, but could not be found. On the sheriff, asking where he was, a grave elderly gentleman rose up, and with much emphasis said:

"My lord, he's gone."

"Gone! gone!" said the sheriff, "where is he gone?"

"That I cannot inform you," replied the communicative gentleman, "but he's dead."

Appleby's the Man.

By the author of the "Little Pedlington Papers."

In Drury Lane Theatre there was, during many years, a man, a character, whose name was Appleby. He was messenger to the establishment, and, besides, did a variety of little odd jobs for the performers. To describe his person would be to do an unkindness to his memory:— "*De mortuis—;*" and little Appleby has long been sleeping in his little grave. Yet let us endeavour, in a delicate way, to convey to you some notion of what manner of man he was, and this may be done least offensively by negatives. He was not qualified, then, for the adequate representation of Coriolanus—his stature and deportment were against it; nor for that of Lothario —his face was not in its favour; nor for Romeo —his voice did not sound "silver sweet by night" --nor, indeed, by day either; nor could he have succeeded as Harlequin, for (not his eyebrows, but) his shins being finely arched, they would have endangered his personal comfort as often as he had to risk them in a leap through a brick wall or a dripping pan. But his voice having been, what a late noble orator might have called, his most remarkable "feature," it is necessary to say farther of it, that it possessed considerable charms for those who delight in a compound of a snuffle and a lisp.

At the time when Appleby flourished, there flourished also in the same theatre with him, many persons of high distinction; amongst those were Sheridan, the finest comic dramatist that has ever existed since Congreve and Farquhar; John Kemble, a tragedian as yet unapproached, if not unapproachable; and two others to whom the same remarks will apply—Mrs. Siddons and Mrs. Jordan. Now, as Appleby frankly and honestly admitted the importance of those persons to the establishment to which they and he were attached, so was he unscrupulous in asserting his own: and for so long a period had he filled his situation, that, at last, he considered himself an integral part of the theatre, which could no more exist, and he not in it, than a watch perform its functions if one of its wheels were removed. Having said thus much, it will at once be perceived, that of Appleby's mind, the grand characteristic was vanity—not a small, sneaking, timid vanity, which is contemptible, but a vanity bold, boundless, and indomitable, compelling admiration. It was not of his person he was vain, his great soul was above such weakness—but of his abilities. He fancied not only that he could do every thing, but also that he could do every thing better than any body else. This he always thought, and never hesitated to say. Now, as occasions for the declaration of this opinion of himself were constantly occurring, a long phrase for the purpose would have been inconvenient: it would have caused a ruinous waste of time: he compressed his sentiment, therefore, into one short, compact, and most expressive sentence, consisting of only three words:—"Appleby's the Man!"

But in addition to his settled notion that whatever he did was right and best, he would have it believed also that he could do no wrong. He never would admit that he had made a mistake, or had lapsed into negligence. To err might be human, but error was a frailty from which little Appleby always contended that little Appleby was exempt.

But mere description is insufficient to do justice! we must exhibit him in action, and make him speak for himself.

One day, just at the termination of a rehearsal, Wroughton, the stage manager, received a message from Mrs. Siddons. She informed him that she was suddenly taken ill, and that unless she should recover within a few hours, it would be impossible for her to act that evening. She requested, therefore, that, in case of the worst, he would be prepared for some change in the performances; but assured him that she would exert herself to the utmost to render any such change unnecessary.

What was to be done? It was too late to change the play (which was Macbeth) altogether! the manager's only resource, therefore, was to be prepared with a substitute for Mrs. Siddons. He wrote a note to Mrs. Powell, acquainting her with the circumstance, and requesting her attendance at the theatre that evening, in case her services should be required.

Appleby, the messenger, was sent for; and, in order to guard against any mistake, the manager was precise in his directions to him.

"Appleby," said Mr. Wroughton, "here is a note to Mrs. Powell; it is of great importance; you must not lose a moment in the delivery of it. And now, observe, if you do not find her at home, you must follow her to wherever she may be, and put the note into her own hands."

"That'll do, sir—note of importance—enough said, sir—Appleby's the man." Appleby's compound of snuffle and lisp, which defies the printer, the reader must supply—if he can.

"Then go; and lose no time."

"Lose time, sir? Beggin' your pardon, sir, Appleby never loses time, sir. I tell you what, Mr. Wroughton, there are some people in this theatre—and some of what I call the big wheels in the machine, too,—who do lose time; but beggin' your pardon, sir, for never losing time, Appleby's the man."

"Now, sir," said the manager sharply, "unless you go instantly with that note, I shall send somebody else with it."

"Beggin', your pardon, sir, there is nobody in this theatre can take this note but little Appleby. 'Tisn't a common note, sir—any body can take a common note, sir—but you told me very distinctly that—now beggin' your pardon sir, for not allowing myself to be interrupted, you did tell me very distinctly that this is a note of great importance; and for delivering a note of great importance, Appleby's the man."

"Then go at once, and make no mistake."

"Now beggin' your pardon, sir, I never made a mistake in my life; and I tell you what, Mr. Wroughton, I'm the only man in the world that can say as much—at least in Drury Lane Theatre, and this theatre is what I call the world in mini'tur', so that it's the same thing. Could make a mistake as well as any body else, if I tried, I dare say; but beggin' your pardon, sir, for never making a mistake, Appleby's the man."

Appleby quitted the presence; and Mr. Wroughton drew up, and despatched to the printer, a notice, which, in case of need, was to be posted at the doors of the theatre, prior to their opening. In the days of Kembles, and Siddonses, and Jordans, ladies and gentlemen, did not presume to "condescend" to do that which it was their duty to their employers and the public to do, even though that duty might in-

26

volve the performance of a second rate part of Shakespeare's;* so the notice ran simply thus:

"Owing to the sudden indisposition of Mrs. Siddons, the indulgence of the public is entreated for Mrs. Powell, who has undertaken the part of Lady Macbeth, at a very short notice."

At the period in question, the entertainments commenced at half-past six, and the doors were opened at half-past five. Long, long before that time, however, the various entrances were besieged by crowds who were anxiously waiting to witness the sublime performance of Kemble and his sister. Mr. Wroughton had taken a hasty dinner, and at five o'clock was again at the theatre. His first question to the stage door keeper was, "Is Mrs. Siddons here?" To this the reply was in the negative.

"Then is Mrs. Powell come, or has she sent any messenger?" inquired the manager.

To this double shotted question, the reply was as before.

"Then send Appleby to me instantly," said he; and he proceeded to his room.

But Appleby was no where to be found. It was ascertained that he had left the theatre, when ordered, with the letter to Mrs. Powell, but had not since been seen. Now Appleby was the Magnus Apollo of a small circle who frequented a public house near the stage door (which was then in Drury Lane;) he was the dictator, the unquestioned and unquestionable authority in all matters theatrical. The most profound secrets of the manager's room, stories of the most private doings of the principal performers, the last night's receipts to a fraction, the plot of the forthcoming, or even of the yet unfinished play, would all be communicated by Appleiy to his auditors; and as he enjoyed their implicit reliance upon the correctness of any thing he told them, however improbable or absurd it might be, so did they, when disseminating the information they had received from him, command the belief of their hearers by the unanswerable—"I had it from Appleby!" In that scene of his glory was Appleby sought for, but in vain: wonderful to tell he had not been there that day! The time for the opening was drawing near: it was necessary that something should instantly be determined upon. Mr. Wroughton himself went to Mrs. Powell's house, which was in the immediate neighbourhood of the theatre. He was informed by one of her servants that she believed her mistress had not received any note from him, for that only half an hour ago she had set off to visit a sick friend at Hampstead. All hope of her assistance, therefore, was at an end, so that he could not issue the notice he had prepared. What should he do? He was mightily perplexed; so he did what many people, who are quite as wise as he was, do when they find themselves in a scrape—he resolved to trust to the chapter of accidents for getting out of it. Nevertheless, that nothing might be wanting on his part, he went to Mrs. Siddons; he made her acquainted with the difficult position in which the theatre was placed; and that lady though scarcely capable of the exertion of acting, yet undertook to play that night. The evening's performances consisted of nothing more than the tragedy of Macbeth, with Kemble and Siddons in its lead-

ing parts, and the farce of "High Life below Stairs;" yet was the house as crowded as if the classic stage of Drury had presented a cage of wild beasts for the play, and Jim Crow, the elegant and the edifying, for the afterpiece.

Before the conclusion of the play, Mrs. Powell came into the green-room, she confirmed the statement made by her servant, that she had not received Mr. Wroughton's note, and added that Appleby had not been at her house at all on that day. Shortly afterwards it was announced that Appleby had at length made his appearance. The culprit, who exhibited symptoms of having been indulging in potations of a stronger kind than water, was forthwith summoned into the manager's room.

The manager, assuming his severest look and sternest tone, thus began:—"Now, sir, what is the reason that——"

"Now, beggin' your pardon, sir, that isn't the point: ther's four hundred and eighty-six pounds in the house, at first account, this blessed night, and who have you to thank for it? I tell you, sir, Appleby's the man."

"None of your foolery, sirrah, but tell me why——"

"Beggin' your pardon, sir; I don't mean to say that Mrs. Siddons is to go for nothing—in all machines there are wheels—big wheels and little wheels—wheels within wheels, as I say. Sometimes the big wheel does the work, sometimes the little wheel. Mrs. Siddons is a wheel, a big wheel—Mr. Kemble is a big wheel—but Appleby also is a wheel, and—now, please, beggin' your pardon, sir, don't interrupt me—I say Appleby's a wheel, though he is but a little wheel. Now, to-night the little wheel has done it. Four hundred and eighty-six pound, first account—Appleby's the man." And Appleby, with an air of importance, drew himself up to his utmost height.

Wroughton, angry as he really was, could scarcely suppress a laugh; and aware of the man's weakness, and perhaps amused by his exhibition of it, he allowed him to make out his case in his own way.

"Appleby, I gave you a note for Mrs. Powell; the fact is you lost it."

"Oh!—now I understand you, sir. You accuse me of losing the note. Beggin' your pardon, sir, I never lost a note in all my life." Here, with an air of triumph, he drew the note from his pocket, and threw it down upon the table. "Now, Mr. Wroughton. I hope you'll confess your *un*-justice. You accuse me of losing the note, and there it is. No, no, sir; you may think what you please, but beggin' your pardon, rely upon what I tell you—little Appleby's the man."

"Why, this is making the matter worse and worse. Instead of obeying my orders, you have been passing the whole of the afternoon in some public house."

"*In* course I have, sir," replied Appleby, in a manner the most unconcerned. "*In* course; and where's the harm of it, when I had nothing else to do?"

"What! when I positively ordered you to deliver that note into Mrs. Powell's own hands!"

"*In* course you did: you're a perfect gentleman, Mr. Wroughton, and I don't mean to contradict you: but, beggin' your pardon, sir, there was no need to employ an *Appleby* for such a thing as *that*."

"What do you mean, sirrah?"

---

* In the bills of the Theatre Royal ——— (the play being Hamlet,) it positively stands recorded of a second rate actor of the present day, that —"upon which occasion, and for that night only. Mr. ——, will kindly condescend to perform the part of the Ghost.'

SEGMENT

"I'll tell you what I mean, sir. Any man in this theatre can deliver a note when he is ordered to do so: any *common* messenger can do that; but for knowing when to *deliver* a note, and when *not* to deliver a note, beggin' your pardon, sir, Appleby's the man. Now—now—please, sir, don't interrupt me. Setting the case I had done as you ordered me, what would have been the consequence? First place, Mrs. Powell would have got the note; second place she'd have come to the theatre; third place, you would have put up at all the doors, a notice of change; fourth place, more than eight-eighths of the people would have gone away—taken their money to the Garden, perhaps;* fifth place, you'd have had seventy pound in the house. Now, sir, owing to my not delivering that note, there's four-eighty-six, first account, and who have you to thank for it? Beggin' your pardon, sir, Appleby's the man."

And having satisfied himself, not only that he had done no wrong; but, that on the contrary, he had rendered a considerable service to the theatre, he without waiting for another word from the manager, strutted out of the room.

There was in the theatre a bricklayer, who was constantly retained for the purpose of giving his professional assistance upon any sudden emergency; but as those occasions were not of daily occurrence, he did duty also as a relief to the stage door keeper. This man was a tall, athletic Irishman, named Billy Brown. It had happened that Brown being employed upon some necessary repairs, Appleby had (to use Brown's words,) "dropt an insult upon him which he would never forgive." What was the nature of that insult we have never been able to learn: it seems to have been entirely between the parties, for it never was brought to light. The offence, however, must have been heavy; for, the first time after its perpetration that the parties met, (which was in the hall of the theatre,) Brown caught Appleby up in his arms and *actually threw him behind the fire.* From this perilous situation he was instantly released by persons who were present, and all he suffered was some damage to his clothes. But Brown never forgave the insult, nor Appleby the injury; and when they met, as sometimes they could not avoid doing, they always passed each other in silence and with a sullen scowl.

On the morning after Appleby's interview with the manager, Brown was in attendance at the stage door. Appleby came as usual. Greatly to his astonishment, he was saluted with, "Good morning to you, Misthur Appleby." But the value of the salute was considerably diminished in Appleby's estimation, by the sneering tone in which it was uttered. Appleby made no reply, but was passing on, when his progress was prevented by Brown's placing his huge arm across the doorway.

"None of your nonsense, beggin' your pardon, Mr. Brown: I'm Appleby!"

"Then you'll walk out of this, Misthur Appleby: you are discharged."

* Meaning thereby Convent Garden Theatre. "You have had a bad house to-night," said some one to"S——, who was for many years the box book keeper at Drury Lane Theatre. "Sorry to say, sir, very bad, sir," was that most civil functionary's reply. And with upturned eyes, a pious look, and a hand upon his heart, he added: "But Providence is very kind to us, sir, notwithstanding, sir; thank God it is a great deal worse at the Garden, sir."

"Discharge Appleby! pooh! Let me know who'll discharge Appleby, and I'll soon let them know that Appleby's the man?"

"Then you'll let Misthur Wroughton know it, Misthur Appleby, for it's by his orders; so walk out of this, I tell you."

"I'll see Mr. Wroughton himself," said Appleby, attempting to force a passage under Brown's guard.

"Then you'll see him in the sthrate, for out of this you must go—and quietly, if you plase." Brown uttered these words with a malignant grin, at the same time pointing significantly at the fire. The hint was sufficient, the burnt child made no reply, but hastily shuffled out into the street.

Discharged! *Appleby* discharged! The doom of Drury was pronounced. The thing could not be; it was an invention of his old enemy, Brown, for the purpose of annoying him. Such were the thoughts of Appleby as he paced up and down, outside the stage door, in expectation of the arrival of Mr. Wroughton. At length that gentleman made his appearance.

"Beggin' your pardon, sir," said Appleby, taking off his hat, but standing erect and looking the manager full in the face—" beggin your pardon, sir, I have news that will astonish you: Appleby's discharged."

"Well, and what then?" said Mr. Wroughton, in a tone of indifference.

"Beggin' your pardon, sir, I'm afraid you don't understand me: I say Appleby's discharged, and you say, 'what then?' *Appleby's* discharged: Appleby! that's all."

"I have discharged you in consequence of your negligence yesterday. You will be paid the full week's wages, but you will not be wanted here again. You are discharged." Saying this, Mr. Wroughton entered the theatre, leaving Appleby utterly bewildered by this confirmation of his disgrace.

He staggered over to the other side of the way, and looked up at the building from which he was so unnaturally dissevered, as if he expected nothing less than that its fall must ensue.

"Can't go on," at length he muttered; "can't go on, that's *very* certain; a wheel out of the machine. Poor Drury! I'm sorry for poor old Drury. Appleby *out?* Can't be! Mr. Wroughton's a wheel—a big wheel, I don't deny it; but Mr. Sheridan's a bigger wheel. Now we'll see what Mr. Sheridan will say to this."

Appleby proceeded directly to the house of the "bigger wheel." Here he was informed that Sheridan was gone down to the House of Commons. Thither he followed him. He found him in one of the committee rooms. He scribbled something upon a piece of paper, which was handed up to Sheridan, who, with evident alarm read the words,—*Don't be frightened, sir, but I have bad news for you.*

Sheridan hurriedly led the way out of the room. "What in the name of Heaven is the matter," inquired he, "is the theatre on fire, or what?"

"Not exactly that, sir, only beggin' your pardon, the concern can't go on."

"Oh, the old story, I suppose; the performers have struck for arrears of salary."

"No, sir; but the thing will never enter your head, so I'll tell you: Appleby's discharged."

"Well, and is that all? is that why you have dared to disturb me?"

"All!!" exclaimed Appleby. Beggin' your pardon, sir, allow me to ask you a question. Suppose I took a wheel out of your watch—a little wheel, we'll say—what would happen?"

"Why, booby the watch would stop."

"That'll do, sir; that's all I want; for getting at once to the rights of things Appleby's the man. Now, Mr. Sheridan, this is why the concern can' go on; a little wheel is taken out of the machine: Appleby's discharged. *That's all.*"

Sheridan, who knew and enjoyed the humour of the man, burst out laughing in spite of his vexation at the interruption. "Who has discharged you?" said he, "and why? I suppose you have done something to deserve it."

"I am discharged out of gratitude, sir. Four hundred and eighty-six pound in the house last night, at first account, letting alone the half-price, and who is to be thanked for it? *You* know me of old, Mr. Sheridan; so I needn't tell *you*—Appleby's the man."

Sheridan, having patiently listened to Appleby's story (which he told after his own fashion,) desired him to meet him at the theatre in an hour, promising to intercede in his behalf with Mr. Wroughton.

Appleby, who now considered his reinstatement in office as a settled thing, loitered about the neighbourhood of the House of Commons till Mr. Sheridan came out, and unperceived by him he followed him to the theatre. He entered at the same moment with Sheridan.

"Oh, here you are, Appleby," said Sheridan, who had not till then observed him, "come along with me."

"Good morning to you this time, Mr. Brown," said Appleby, as he strutted past his redoubtable foe.

The result of Sheridan's intercession was, as might have been expected, Appleby's restoration to his place:—a severe rebuke, and a fine of ten shillings, for example's sake, being his only punishment. Appleby did not venture down to the hall until he had satisfied himself that all persons who might be there, but chiefly Brown, were informed of his being again in power. He then made his appearance with a handful of letters for delivery. Of the fine and rebuke he said nothing; but, placing himself in the very centre of the hall, he folded his arms across his breast, and looking Brown steadily in the face, cried, "Discharge Appleby!" Then, striking his hat firmly down upon his head, he added, "Appleby's the man!"

But poor Appleby did not long live to enjoy his triumph. In his last moments, a friend was with him, who vainly entreated him to send for a clergyman.

"My good fellow," said the friend, "you wish to enter heaven?"

"In course," replied Appleby, faintly: "wheels—beggin' your par——big wheels—little—"

"Then if that be your wish," resumed the friend—"if you wish to enter heaven, how can you expect it, unless—"

"Leave that to me," said Appleby—"Appleby's the man." And having uttered these, his last words, he turned his head upon his pillow, and expired.

Appleby is no more; but the race of those *qui ne pensent pas petite bierre d'eux memes* is not extinct.

Journal of Rev. David Jones, in 1773.

Communicated by H. G. Jones, Jr., of Leverington, Pa.

Genius.—The Shawanese naturally, are an active, sensible people; in common not so large and well made as the Delawares. They are the most cheerful and merry people I ever saw; all their study seems to be some kind of drollery, consequently both men and women are the greatest laughers I ever met in any nation. At the same time they are the most deceitful that perhaps exist in human shape. They are also very suspicious that white people have some design to enslave them. This made me fare the worse, for they surmised that the white people had sent me as a spy. What the Cretian sage remarked concerning that nation, is true when applied to the Shawanese, viz: "They are always liars, evil beasts," &c. This I found to be a craft among them; if they imagined any thing in their own heart about you, and they could not find out whether it was true or not, they would come and tell you that some one told them such things, and all this cunning is to find out your thoughts about them.

Government.—This people are unacquainted with civil power or authority. Every town has some head men, some of whom are called kings by us; but by what I can learn, this appellation is given to none by the Indians only as they have learned it from us. These head men have no power; nor do they pretend to have any, only to give their advice in councils, especially in war affairs. These are also made use of in conversing with us on any occasion. They have no laws among them to redress the oppressed. They are much given to stealing, both from white people and each other. When any one among them steals, the sufferer steals as much from that person, as he judges satisfactory; and I am persuaded that the second thief has the best bargain, for he is not easily satisfied. In case any person kills another, there is nothing said or done; but if the murdered person has a friend, he often kills the murderer in some drunken fit, and 'tis likely intoxicates himself for this purpose, for an Indian has not much resolution without a dram. Mrs. Henry told me that it was not uncommon for women to hang their children, or drown them, and never regard them so much as to bury them afterwards; nor are they guilty of this inhumanity secretly, nor is any thing said on the occasion any more than if a puppy had been drowned. This gentlewoman told me that during her captivity, she has known this to be done, with many other acts of barbarity that could scarcely be imagined. When white captives were brought in, they would run a knife through between the wrist bones, and passing deer sinews through would tie them up naked in their long house and make all the diversion possible of them; sometimes coming up and taking hold of the captives nose, and to divert themselves and make sport, would cut off the nose. After all diversion was past, they would lead them out and kill them.

Customs.—This nation make considerable lamentation for their dead, if the person is of note. It is common for the survivor to dress good victuals and lay it at the head of the grave for several nights after the person is buried, supposing that the deceased eats it; but in truth if they were to dress a buffalo every night, their hungry dogs could dispose of it, without one morsel for the dead. They have no form of marriage, only the man and woman agree, and make a bargain for so many bucks, that she shall live with him. I think from information, and what I saw, that it may be said they have no more natural affection than the beasts of the field, for no woman marries out of any love she has for the person, the only motive being the reward which he gives her; and if his features are not so agreeable, she regards it not, if he has only enough to give her. There may be some of a different turn; but what I have said will be found true among the general part of them. 'Tis said by those who have been best acquainted with them, that women are purchased by the night, week, month or winter, so that the chief way that women support themselves is by fornication, which is esteemed no crime or shame. Polygamy is not considered a crime, and it is common to have several wives at the same time, and as common to part on the least dislike. It often proves offence enough if a woman prove with child; but this does not often happen, for their women seldom have many children, nor can they, while whoredom is so common. It is probable if they do as they have done only for one century, that there will be few of them on the earth. The whole nation of the Shawanese, according to Mr. Henry's calculation, does not exceed six hundred, including men, women, and children, and I am persuaded from what I saw and heard, that this account is full large enough.

Diversions.—In the winter season they spend a great part of their time in playing cards, and a game something like dice, called *Mamundis.* They have a kind of game, which consists in pulling a greasy thong, by which they gain prizes. They are most indefatigable dancers, i the winter nights: their musical instruments are a keg with a skin stretched over it, and a gourd which has a parcel of grains of corn in it. But all sing as they dance, so that the echo of their united voices may be heard for near a mile. Fishing and hunting employ the men in summer, and raising corn is the occupation of the women: indeed they are the only drudges; but they have all the profits and riches of the nation, for what the men make in the summer, they give to the women for their winter's lodging. Among the diversions of this people may be reckoned their Mock Devils, three of which I saw myself, and if I had not heard that Mr. Brainerd described such, I should have been more surprised. These they call manitous. Not long before my departure, a young Indian came into the house where I lodged, and told me that the manitous were coming, and if we did not give them something they would bedaub us with all nastiness. Upon which I looked out and saw them near one hundred yards off. All the Indians knew me, and therefore the manitous seeing me, I apprehend intended to scare me. Each had a stick in his hand, and one stooped down by a tree as if he was going to shoot at me; but I could see that he had no gun. Afterwards he came towards me, with all the pranks imaginable, making as hideous noises as he could possibly invent: each made the same noise. Each had false faces of light wood, and all were dressed in bear skins, with the black hair on, so that they had no appearance of any thing human. The foremost one had a great red face, with a huge, long nose, and prodigious large lips, his head above being covered with bear skin. As he came near me, he made a wonderful rattling, with a great dry tortoise shell, having an artificial neck and head, and being filled with grains of corn, and other trinkets. The other two had black faces, resembling the countenance of a bear, with very long chins. They came around me with an abundance of pranks, making a noise nothing like the voice of a man. After some time, I asked them what they wanted; but manitous cannot speak. They continued their racket, and at last showed me a pipe, by which I understood they wanted tobacco. Upon the reception of any gift, they make some kind of obeisance and depart, dancing the strangest capers that are possible. In short, their looks, voice and actions, are such that I thought if they had got their samples from beneath, the scene could not be much exceeded. This apparel is used also by their powwowers in their attempts at conjuvation.

Religion.—The Shawanese, as well as all other Indians, that I either saw or heard of, say they believe there is a good manitou and a bad manitou; but they neither worship one nor the other. It is wrong to say they worship the devil, for they give themselves no concern about God or the devil: they have not one thought worthy of

206

a God. They never in any way acknowledge any mercy or judgment as from God. They look on it that he made the world at first, but have no conception that he has any concern with it as a governor. They never, in any distress, call upon any higher power to help them, neither do they apprehend that he is displeased with any of their actions, for they have no thought that any thing is a sin. It was never known that they have any reproof of conscience for any crime committed; so that it may well be said they are without any kind of religion, good or bad. There is a great deal of noise in the world about natural religion, but I am now fully convinced that there is no such thing existing; for if men had neither tradition nor revelation, they would concern themselves about God, no more than the brutes that perish.

I know some will say that there have been heathen who wrote well concerning God. I know what they have said, and also know that whoever reads Grotius on Revelation, will see how they came by their knowledge; but this will prove nothing, till it is first proved that these persons had no tradition to begin on, and whoever considers that the world was then comparatively young, will see that tradition was not extinct. I could wish that these vain talkers (who call the improvements which men make on revelation, natural religion,) would only go and see the Indians who are least acquainted with us, and I am persuaded they would be convinced of the falsity of their principles, and readily give up the point and acknowledge that if God had not revealed himself to us, we would never have made it our study to concern ourselves about him. Notwithstanding that this is the deplorable case, I am of the opinion that is peopleth might be brought into a civilized state in a short time, if the matter became one of public concern, and authority would interpose.

Literary Notices.

The Artist, Merchant, and Statesman, by C. E. Lester, late U. S. Consul at Genoa, is the title of a new work, the first part of which has just reached here, and which we have looked over with considerable interest. The volume before us is principally devoted to a subject interesting to every American, and especially to Cincinnatians, viz: the early history and later efforts of the first Sculptor of the age, Hiram Powers, written by Mr. Lester, from conversations held in his Studio with the Sculptor himself. The following passage we extract, as well on account of its intrinsic interest—being the artist's own narration of his first attempt in modelling a bust from life—as from its deserved mention of one of our most worthy fellow-citizens, whose well known taste and discrimination in the fine arts, were never more strikingly shown, than in his early discernment and encouragement of the genius of the now world-renowned Sculptor.

After mentioning his introduction to a gentleman engaged in modelling a bust of Gen'l. Jackson, which operation he closely watched, the artist says:

"I determined to make a trial myself, and anticipating that on my first work, occupied as I was in other matters, I should consume much time, I concluded to work in wax instead of clay; and accordingly I procured several pounds of beeswax, and in melting it, stirred in a quantity of colouring matter to render it sufficiently opaque. When it was all prepared, I began a reduced copy of a head of the Venus de' Medici which some Italian plaster-worker had brought to Cincinnati. I had a little apartment in the garret of the clock-factory which I used for a *studio*. A gentleman to whom I showed this work was so well pleased he desired me to make a bust of his daughter only four years old. This gentleman was Mr. John P. Foote. This head, too, I did in wax, and finished it as I had the other, in the garret of the clock-factory; and I can say, with all honesty, that when I compare it with other busts I have made, that so far as the likeness and finish of it are concerned, I have never surpassed it, nor could I improve it now, if I except some portions of the hair. This was my *first order*, and I received for it all I asked, which was deemed a very reasonable sum by the child's father, who assured me it would give him pleasure to pay me more if I would consent to receive it. The work was finished in plaster, and my price for it was twenty-four dollars."

The cast thus referred to is still in existence, and should long be preserved—a memento no less of the early talent of the artist, than of the infantile grace and beauty of the fair subject.

Bating a good deal of needless glorification of Mr. C. Edwards Lester, himself, in the dedication, prefatory letter, and other *fillings up* of the book, we commend this little volume to the public, as one with which we have been much pleased, and one which cannot but be interesting to the friends of the great Sculptor, in this city.

The Groves of Blarney, by Mrs. S. C. Hall: —An Irish novel! and by Mrs. Hall, and it, too, all about—

"The Groves of Blarney, so charming!"

Who would not wish to read it? We have done so, and can honestly advise all the admirers of one of the most graceful and pleasing lady writers of the age to do the same. The characters, without being strikingly new, are natural and well drawn; the plot is simple, and the incidents are of sufficient interest to fix the attention, while *Mrs. Hall's* charming descriptive powers, and graceful flow of sprightly dialogue, are always such as to please the most determinately not-to-be-pleased reader.

Novelists do not generally make good tale writers, and *vice versa*. JAMES' stories, and those of other novelists, whose efforts that way we have read, were always "lame and impotent conclusions;" and we would not give the poorest of SIMMS' novels for all the tales with which he has bored the public through the Annuals and Magazines of the day. Hence we think that novel writing is not Mrs. Hall's *forte*—her short simple tales, each story a picture, finished and perfect, no matter how short, far excel her more laboured efforts. While we cannot rank the "Groves of Blarney," with "The Old French Drawing Master," "It's only a drop," and fifty others that we could name of her smaller tales, yet we believe the candid reader will agree after its perusal with all we have said of its merits.

THE MERCHANT'S DAUGHTER, by Miss PICKER-ING, though not equal in point of merit, we think, to "Nan Darrell," or "The Grumbler," or (our especial favourite of Miss P.'s delightful novels,) "The Grandfather," is yet a story of much interest, and will well repay its readers for the time spent in its perusal. No imaginative writings of the day are more worthy of commendation than the novels of Ellen Pickering.

LECTURES ON THE ENGLISH COMIC WRITERS, by HAZLITT; THE TWINS AND HEART, by M. F. TUP-PER, author of the Crock of Gold; and LAMB'S SPECIMENS OF THE ENGLISH DRAMATIC POETS, form No. 27 to 30, inclusive, of Wiley & Putnam's excellent "Library of Choice Reading." We have not yet had time to give them a reading, and can only therefore take them upon trust, from the reputation of their respective authors.

Critical Consolation.

Authors, no less than artists, whose works are frequently found fault with by those whom they regard as not peculiarly qualified to play a critical part, are apt to find a fund of consolation in the philosophy of the following:

The celebrated painter, Jarvis, was keenly sensitive to criticism, especially coming from those whom he knew to be unskilled in the rules of his favourite art. Being once told that Judge ———, had expressed himself in terms of decided disapprobation of one of his late productions, Jarvis testily exclaimed—"What of that—he's not a judge of painting, he's only Judge of Probate!"

Errors of the Press.

Some little experience in the amusement of proof-reading, both prose and verse, enables us to vouch for the following, as being drawn to the life. There is quite as much of truth as poetry in it. We could parallel Miss Biddy Fudge's

vexations by others, almost as ludicrous, and not less provoking, in our own experience:

AN ERRATUM.—Miss Biddy Fudge, in the History of the Fudges in England, recounting the miseries of authors, says, that—

"Though an angel should write, 'tis devils must print;" and gives the following instance of the havoc made by the printers in one of her effusions:

But a week or two since, in my Ode upon Spring,
Which I meant to have made a most beautiful thing,
Where I talked of the "dew drops from freshly blown roses,"
The nasty things made it "from freshly blown noses."

Here is a soap story, in the manufacture of which, we should say, no small quantity of *lie* was found necessary:

Jim Black, of Beargrass.

Jim Black was one of those persons usually designated "hard customers," and in his case the term applied. A careless fellow that could whip his weight in wild cats, and care no more for a tustle with a bear than a fisticuff with one of his neighbours, for Jim was "cock of the walk" on the head waters of Beargrass. Although he had the good will of most of his neighbours, yet none of the folks in "them diggins" felt inclined to a nearer relationship with him. Of this fact he seemed pretty well satisfied, for he never attempted any flirtation with any of the fair ones of Beargrass. It happened that when Jim had reached twenty-eight years, a new family arrived, in which were "two of the tallest gals you ever did see," as Jim described them. One of them, Nancy, took his eye "tarnation strong," and he concluded to "sit right up to her." Jim had heard that it always took two to make a bargain, but the possibility of a third person coming into a contract never for a moment entered his mind. Things progressed smoothly, and we may say rapidly, for a short time; when Nancy's father took it into his head he ought to have something to say in the matter. This bothered Jim amazingly, and came near a broken bone or two for the old gentleman; but, finally Jim was ordered from the premises, with the request that he would forever keep as far as possible from that plantation. This was a sad go for Jim; but, having a stout heart, he determined to never give it up so, and he set his wits to work to out general the old man. The gal was on his side, and why shouldn't he?—"The track of real genuine love was always crooked," as the poet didn't express it, but as Jim did. Jim laid his plans and waited for an opportunity to carry them into effect. It was not long before he obtained a sight of the fair one, who readily entered into his plot, and as the family were to vacate the cabin on the following Sunday, and be gone the whole day, it was proposed that Jim should spend the day with Nancy, that they might mature their plan for putting the blind upon the old folks.

Sunday came, and according to agreement the family left home to visit a neighbour, and Jim left home to visit Nancy. The day passed off as days will under like circumstances, until near sundown. It occurred to Nancy that there could be no impropriety in just stepping to the door to see if the old folks were coming. "Oh, crackee, Jim, here they come home; hide yourself or the old man will *hide* me. Here, jump into this barrel, quick." "Tarnation?" said Jim, as he soused himself into the barrel. "By golly, Nancy, there's soap in this ere barrel, and it smarts like creation." "Well it does hoss, but you must do it, they are right here, so keep still."

Nancy had hardly time to cover over the barrel before the old folks entered the door. All were soon seated about the room, and commenced talking about the way they had passed the day, and when it came Nancy's turn to speak she said, "Well I'd a done very well, I s'pose if it hadn't been for that ugly bear that was trying to take the pigs off."

"What pigs?" asked the old gentleman.

"Why the pigs out on the other side of the cornfield."

No sooner were the words out of her mouth than the old folks and young ones too, except Nancy and Jim, were off to see after the pigs. "I say, Nance, it's a mighty hot place here," said Jim; "can't a feller come out now?" he asked.

"Well I guess he can Jim; but you must clear out quick, for they will be back right away."

Jim cleared the barrel at one bound.

"If that ain't the hottest place about this house then I give in," said Jim. "But I say Nance, that yarn of yourn about the pigs is full out as slick as that soft soap, and it don't hurt so bad. So good bye; I'm for the Beargrass—gracious how the stuff burns! Good bye, Nance, I'm off—gosh I'm raw all over."

His doings at the creek we must give in his own words:

"Well, in I went—for may be I warn't mad. The water felt mighty cool and comfortable, I tell you. I scrubbed and washed until I got the truck off me, when I began to feel a little better. But if Beargrass didn't run soap suds for a week after that, then I wouln't tell you so."

Choice Recipes.

IMPROVED COOKERY.—*To Make a Match.*—Catch a young gentleman and lady, the best you can; let the young gentleman be raw, and the young lady quite tender. Set the gentleman at dinner table; put in a good quantity of wine, and whilst he is soaking, stick in a word or two every now and then about Miss: this will help to make him boil. When getting red in the gills take him out into the drawing room, set him by the lady, and sop them both with green tea; then set them at the piano and blow the flame till the lady sighs: when you hear the gentleman sigh it is time to take them off, as they are warm enough. Put them by themselves in a corner of the room or on a sofa, and there let them simper together the rest of the evening. Repeat this three or four times, taking care to place them side by side at dinner, and they will be ready for marriage whenever you want them. After marriage great care should be taken, as they are apt to turn sour.

To COMMIT MURDER.—Take a pretty young lady—tell her she has a pretty foot—she will wear a small shoe—go out in wet spring weather —catch a cold—then a fever—and die in a month. This remedy never fails.

ANOTHER.—Take a pretty young lady—tell

her she has a small waist—she will lace tighter than ever—her lungs will be compressed—a cough will ensue—neglect follows—consumption *attends*—and death does not *wait* long.

He is a rich man, who lives within his income, be it ever so small; he is a poor man, who exceeds it, be it ever so large.

If the best man's faults were written on his forehead, he would pull his hat over his eyes.

As the gem cannot be polished without friction, so neither can man be perfected without adversity.

Mother, Home, and Heaven, are the three most beautiful words in the English language.

Never marry a woman who keeps a lap dog—for she who can bring her mind down to love so contemptible a thing, can never elevate it to that dignity which man requires.

Some writer very justly compares a coquette to those light wines which every body *tastes*, and nobody *buys*; and another no less strikingly says, "A coquette is a rose from which every lover plucks a leaf, while the thorns are left for her future husband."

There is more truth than poetry in the following definition of "independence," taken from an exchange:

"INDEPENDENCE.—Speaking your mind freely where it cannot possibly hurt your interests."

An old maid eyes a single gentleman with the same feelings that we look at a street dog in dog-days, viz: wondering whether he intends to *bite*.

To Young Men.

There is no object so beautiful to me as a conscientious young man. I watch him as I do a star in the heavens; clouds may be before him, but we know his light is behind them, and will beam again; the blaze of others' popularity may outshine him, but we know that though unknown he illuminates his own true sphere. He resists temptation, not without a struggle, for that is not virtue; but he does resist and conquer; he hears the sarcasms of the profligate, and it stings him, for that is the trial of virtue, but he heals the wound with his own pure touch. He heeds not the watchword of fashion, if it leads to sin; the atheist who says, not only in his own heart, but with his lips, "there is no God," controls him not; he sees the hand of a creating God and rejoices in it.

Woman is sheltered by fond arms and loving council; old age is protected by its experience, and manhood by its strength, but the young man stands amid the temptations of the world, like a self-balanced tower; happy he who seeks and gains the prop of morality.

Onward, then, conscientious youth!—raise thy standard and nerve thyself for goodness. If God has given thee intellectual power, awaken in that cause; never let it be said of thee he helped swell the tide of sin, by pouring his influence into its channels. If thou art feeble in mental strength, throw not that drop into a polluted current. Awake, arise, young man! assume the beautiful garb of virtue!—It is fearfully easy to sin; it is difficult to be pure and holy. Put on thy strength then! let thy chivalry be roused against error! let the truth be the lady of thy love—defend her.—*Southern Rose*

Western Poetry.

Among the many beautiful books which are expected to see the light about the time of the Holidays, is one which will be welcomed by all admirers of flowers and poetry. We allude to "The Floral Year," by Mrs. Anna P. Dinnies, of St. Louis, published by Coleman, New York. As "*Moina*," Mrs. Dinnies, when only fifteen, acquired by her "Wedded Love," and "The Wife's Appeal," an enviable reputation, which the later efforts of her muse have served to confirm. "The Floral Year," is designed to illustrate, by the flowers of poesy, the natural flowers of the various seasons of the year. It will be an acceptable token to every fair lover of flowers—as what fair lady is not?

The Broadway Journal announces as in press, a volume of poems by William Wallace, formerly of Louisville, Ky., who, although for some years past a resident of the Eastern Cities, we still claim as a *Western* Poet, and therefore announce his work as another volume of Western Poetry. Mr. Wallace is a poet of true genius—possessed of a brilliant imagination, combined with great vigor of thought, and power of expression. We are much pleased to see the announcement of a volume from his pen.

Literary Chit-Chat.

The "*Excelsior*," is announced as the title of a new Literary Journal which is about to be established in the City of New York, to be edited by Charles Fenno Hoffman, the poet and author of "A Winter in the West," and which, as its name indicates, is expected to take high ground in American periodical literature.

It is stated also that Park Benjamin, having removed to Baltimore, is about to take the editorial charge of a new literary paper in that city. Mr. Benjamin is one of the first American poets and critics, and no better guaranty than his sound discrimination and correct taste, as formerly displayed in his management of the "New World," can be desired, as assurance that a paper established under his editorial conduct, must become highly popular and successful.

In the west we have also two or three similar undertakings talked of; all of which are, however, as yet, in a state of *embryo*, with a single exception. Mr. L. A. Hine, one of the editors of the late "Western Literary Journal," proposes to publish a "*Quarterly Journal and Review*," at the extremely low price of one dollar per annum. If published, we wish Mr. H. better luck than fell to his share in his connection with the Western Literary Journal.

The "*Southern Literary Messenger*," published at Richmond, Va., and one of the most substantial of the monthlies, has published the bans of matrimonial alliance, with W. Gilmore Simms' "Monthly Magazine and Review," a work commenced about a year since at Charleston, S. C. —the union to be consummated at the commencement of the new year. This will give additional force to the "Messenger," already and for some time past, in our opinion, one of the best literary periodicals in the country.

A Nuisance.

Traversing, a few days since, the length of Fourth street, about the middle of the afternoon, we encountered opposite the Second Presbyterian Church, a gang of boys, some ten or a dozen in number, engaged in kicking a foot ball, now in the middle of the street, and now upon the sidewalks, as chance directed the course of the ball, not a little to the annoyance of ladies, and other passers by. The indulgence of the boys of our city in this sport, in the public streets (seldom we believe in so thronged a thoroughfare as is that of Fourth street,) is a *nuisance* which should not for a moment be tolerated. There are plenty of commons and open lots in which our city juveniles may play, without turning the streets into "camping grounds," to the risk of the shins of either themselves or others, not desirous of partaking in the sport.

Another, and a yet greater nuisance—because of the actual danger to passers by, with which it is attended—is the practice of our boys playing at *Shinny* or *Shindy*, (as it is not in our copy of Webster, we will not stake our reputation upon the orthography of the word,) along the sidewalks. The clubs with which they play it, are generally of stout hickory, and of weight sufficient to knock over a small man, coming in contact with one of them unawares; and the way the young shavers usually swing them around when preparing to strike the ball a blow, with a total recklessness of the possible consequences to those who may be near, is a truly edifying specimen of Republican Independence! Add to this, that the ball used is generally a *stone* of sufficient size and weight to inflict a pretty serious indentation upon the shins of the luckless passenger who is not quick-sighted and nimble-footed enough to dodge it, in its rapid advance along the pavement to meet him, and we think our objections to this, the present *fashionable* amusement of our young hopefuls, will be deemed valid and sufficient. We are always pleased at the sight of boys engaged in any proper and harmless play, but really this practice of *Shinnying* stones and brickbats along the crowded side-walks, which we have been accustomed to regard as devoted to other and very different uses, has become a nuisance which we must protest against, as indeed "most tolerable and not to be endured." We have frequently heard ladies say lately, that they are afraid to walk the streets on this account; and our wonder is, that the practice is not oftener attended with results of a more serious and fatal character.

A Hint to Mothers.

There are many things which are better left to chance; precaution is sometimes more mischievous than negligence. The late Sir W—— C—— was one day expected at a large dinner party, at Mr. M—d—y's, in Russel square. The worthy baronet's nose, it will be remembered, was, to say the least of it, remarkable. Before the company assembled, Mr. M—— suggested to his lady, that upon this particular occasion, it would be *safer* that little Alfred should *not* (as at other times) be introduced along with the dessert after dinner; for that, the said Alfred, a fine child of seven years old, having a propensity to make observations upon all personal defects or deformities, from a pimple to a bump, from a crooked finger to a cork leg, might possibly say something not altogether agreeable to Sir W. "Leave that to me," said the lady; "I'll contrive it nicely." Accordingly she proceeded to the nursery, and thus addressed the little gentleman,— "Alfred, my dear, we have a gentleman coming to dinner to-day who has a monstrous ugly nose. Now, if you will promise to be a good boy, and *not make any observations on it*, you may come down after dinner, and you shall have an orange. But remember the nose!" Master Alfred acceded to the terms of the treaty, and, in due time, was ushered into the dining room. After the lapse of a quarter of an hour, the young gentleman, finding the reward of his forbearance still in arrear, took advantage of a dead pause in the conversation, and cried out from the further end of the table, "Mamma, it is time *now* for me to have the orange you promised me, if I didn't say anything about that gentleman's monstrous ugly nose."

The Trysting Tree.
From "Real Life, or the Portfolio of a Chronicler."

Journeying one day along a muirland road not far from Stirling, we passed a very fine old tree in a field at a short distance. I remarked its beauty, to which Simon assented, but seemed for a while absorbed in recalling recollections associated with it. At last, he said, pausing and looking back on the tree; 'That sturdy old plant of other years, reminds me of an incident which displayed a striking trait of character of the true old Scottish breed. That is, or was, called the Trysting Tree, and there a country lass had consented to meet her sweetheart one winter night, to arrange matters for the wedding. The night came, cold and foggy, and the girl, true to her appointment, set off silently in the hopes of being back again before she was missed. It soon came on a heavy snow, and snowed all night. The girl was not to be found; and all the roads round being not only impassible but invisible, from the depth of the drift, a whole week passed before any communication was possible with the neighbouring farms, all which time nothing could be heard of her. At length the news reached her lover, who was lost and bewildered in contending feelings of wonder, fear, and jealousy. On inquiry as to the time when his bride had been last seen, he found it was the night of their assignation and the first of the snow. The Trysting Tree flashed upon his mind, and thither with a sturdy band of volunteer pioneers he bent his course. On reaching the tree they commenced digging all round it, and soon came to a solid hammock. Their spades and shovels were then exchanged for the simple labour of their hands, with which they gathered up and flung out the snow by gowpens, and ere this had been long continued, they succeeded in extricating the very girl, exactly eight days from the time she had been buried. You may guess it was a moment of agonizing perturbation which succeeded the discovery that she was alive!

On coming to the tree and not finding her lover there, she drew her plaid tight round her, and sat down to wait. She conjectured that the cold had made her drowsy, and the snow falling thick upon her, when she awoke she was unable to move, and felt herself as if alive in her grave, and cut off from the living world. Her lover was full of sorrow and of explanations. 'If he had but thought she could have ventured out on such a night, he never would have failed to keep his word,' &c., &c., &c. Every young man's mind will suggest the proper thing to be said on the occasion; but Lizzy, who could scarcely be suspected of bestowing any but *cold* looks at such a time, took no notice of him whatever. The country people who had accompanied him had a supply of cordials, and he was loud and earnest in enjoining them to 'give her something warm instantly;' and a glass of spirits was offered, which she gravely pushed aside. 'Give me a glass of water,' said she; '*it's a cauld heart that canna warm a drink to itsel'.*'

Her Joe was ardent in his adresses, but she repulsed him with endless scorn. Whether she ever took a husband or not, I have forgotten, but it is certain she never married him.

Food for Digestion.

In the following, taken from a Scotch paper, we hardly know which is tougher—the story, or the tripe. If, however, the "sonsie lassie" managed to bolt *the one*, as narrated, our readers, we think, should make no difficulty of swallowing *the other*.

TOUGH TRIPE.—A sort of original character of a servant girl belonging to this neighbourhood, engaged as dairy maid at Craignish, in Argyllshire, last summer, and the first night after going home, as the family had supped on tripe before she could get her work in the byre brought to a close, Kate was told by her mistress that she would find her share in a pot on the fire. Impelled by a pretty sharp appetite, which the fresh air of the Highlands had imparted, Kate approached one of the two pots on the fire, carrying it off into the corner, and then and there commenced an attack on what she conceived to be about a square yard of tripe. She found it darkish in the colour, and about the toughest fabric of human provender which had ever encountered her ivory; but as she was young and blate, and, moreover, had never before tasted tripe, she felt ashamed to reject that of which she had been told all the family had partaken, and, therefore, tore away at it, now using her teeth, now her hands, and at times, breaking it over her knees, till she managed to bolt the whole of it; inwardly ejaculating, "it was mair like the hide, than the inside of ony beast ever she saw."

All night her horrid night-mare moans so loudly indicated that Kate's digestive powers were being severely tested, that the guid wife cannily administered a bead of the small-still aqua, to master the tripe. It was found next morning, when the household assembled at breakfast, that Kate had taken the wrong pot from the fire, and had swallowed the *dish clout*, which had been left in the water to wash the dishes! Kate thinking it was a trick, her blood got up, and she seized an old claut, with which she unceremoniously dislocated the shoulder blade of the farmer's eldest son, and shouting as a sort of war-cry, that "naebody suld make a ropewalk o' her stamach," let skelp at all and sundry, and charged them from one room to another, till she fairly put the whole establishment to rout. A reconciliation was ultimately effected, but till the day she left the house, the "brawniest chiel" among them dared not mention the word "tripe" in Kate's presence.

A Rising Genius.

Timothy Sly's own Epistle, (not the Master's.)—Dear Dick: I copied my school letter to father and mother ten times before one was good enough, and while the teacher is putting the capitals and flourishes in I shall slip this off on the sly. Our examination was yesterday and the table was covered with books and things bound in gilt and silk for prizes, but were all put away again and none of us got none, only they awarded Master Key a new fourpenny bit for his essay on Locke, because his friends live next door; and little Coombe got the toothache, so they would not let him try his experiments on vital air, which was very scurvy. It didn't come to my turn, so I did not get a prize; but as the company was to stop to tea I put the cat in the water butt which they clean out in the hollidays, and they will be sure to find her: and we were all re-ted with tea, and I did not like to refuse as they might have suspext something. Last night we had a stocking and bolster fight after we went to bed, and I fought a little lad with a big bolster; his name is Bill Barnacle, and I knocked his eye out with a stone in my stocking; but as nobody knows who did it, because we were all in the dark, so I could see no harm in it. Dear Dick, send me directly your Wattses Hymns to show, for I burnt mine and a lump of cobblers wax for the master's chair on breaking up day; and some small shot to pepper the people with my quill gun and eighteen pence in copper to shy at windows as we ride through the village and make it one and ninepence, for there's a good many as Ive a spite against and if father wont give it you ask mother and say its for yourself and meet me at the Elephant and Castle and if there's room on the coach you can get up for I want to give you some crackers to let off as soon as we get home while they are all kissing of me your affectionate brother Timothy Sly.

A Strong Verdict.

About the commencement of the present century, a black man, who had lived at the north end of Boston, suddenly disappeared, and it was thought that he had drowned himself. Accordingly diligent serach was made, and at the end of two days his body was found in a dock in Charlestown. As is usual in such cases, a jury was called together; and as the story goes, (which is true for all we know,) they were all men of "colour." After some deliberation, they brought in a verdict as follows: "Dat, going home one berry dark night, he fell from the wharf and was *killed;* and the tide coming in strong, it floated him over to Charlestown, and he was *drowned; dat de wedder being berry cold, he froze to death!*" The coroner who was a bit of a wag, notwithstanding the solemnity of the occasion, said "you might as well add, *died in the wool!*"

A Poser.

"An' Cuff, will ye be afther tipping us a little bit of a song this cold mornin'?" exclaimed a son of the Emerald Isle to a brother of the sable race, a co-labourer in the division and sub-division of wood.

"Golly, massa, I can't sing!"

"Can't sing! An' what's your leg stuck in the middle of yer fut for, like a bird's, if ye can't sing?"

The follov i g was probably written by some old bachelor, who was paying the penalty of his neglect, in early life, to perform "the whole duty of man" to the gentler sex. We have reason to think there is a good deal of truth in his observations on the subject.

Benefits of Matrimony.

I went to one neighbour and solicited a donation for public objects: he replied, "I approve of your object, and would assist you—but you know I have a family, and 'Charity begins at home.'"

I called upon a second: he replied that such as were able ought to be liberal, and that he had every disposition to aid me;—"but," he added, "there are stronger claims than yours, which I am bound to regard—those of my children."

A public charity demanded that a messenger should be sent from the city to a remote country. A person was selected whose talents were well adapted to the mission. He replied that nothing would give him more pleasure, but it was absolutely impossible on account of his family. He was excused.

Two merchants, partners in business failed. At a meeting of the creditors, it was resolved that one should be forthwith released; but the other, because he was a bachelor, might yet, as was his duty, go to work and pay a small dividend.

A public office was about to appoint a secretary. There were, as usual, twenty applicants. In the discussion of the board of directors, the talents of many were set forth; when a member rose, and said that the candidate whom he should propose was a man of moderate capacity, but he was a poor man with a family. He succeeded, and holds the office still.

A mercantile friend wished me to procure a person to fill a responsible station. A gentleman came who seemed well fitted for the office. I asked him how much salary he expected. He replied, smilingly, "I am a married man"—which I understood to be $1,500 per annum. He has the place. No bachelor would have had over a thousand.

Two criminals were tried for forgery at the Old Bailey, and condemned to death. The King pardoned the one who was married, on account of his wife and children. The other paid the forfeit of his life, because he was a bachelor.

In short would you avoid trouble of many kinds, excite sympathy, procure office, or escape punishment, you have only to get married.

The following admirable *Jeu d'esprit* was written many years since, and published in a London Magazine, during the lifetime of the "Prince of modern Punsters." Alas! for the lovers of genuine humour, that which was then but a jest, (albeit on a *grave* subject,) has since become a sad reality. This epitaph is so much in Hood's own vein, that, but for its subject, we should be tempted to attribute it to his pen.

AN EPITAPH
PROPOSED FOR THOMAS HOOD,
Author of "Whims and Oddities."

—

Reader, whoe'er you are—
Perchance a youth
That loves the truth—
Drop now a natural tear;
For one who loved it too, is lying here,
He and his lyre are both laid down in sooth;
And oh, ye Artists—ye who draw afar,
Draw near!
Ye bards who merely blow a reed,
Now read a blow
Which funless fate has just decreed:
Hood is below!
Not Admiral, but admirable Hood,
Who wore no sword, but gave us cuts—in wood
As well as verse,
In lines all quaint and terse;
Who made us laugh, and very often cry
" That's good!"
And without trouble
Contrived to make us see each sentence double,
Who turned our ill-used language inside out,
And round about,
And searched it low and high;
Who voyaged on with all his wits unfurled,
And every day discovered a new world,
An island pun far off and dim,
If out of sight, 'twas all the same to him;
And when no new joke met his eye
He turned the old,
Melted them down, or made another mould;
And when at last you thought, " well now he's done,"
He'd find another pun
Hid in the small and secret cells
Of most impracticable syllables;
Just like a nun!
And when he wished to give us raps,
He'd put his puns, like children, in SMALL CAPS!
To him no dactyll ever came amiss,
And spondees were his bliss.
For every joke a plot was made
That of itself, appeared the work of ages;
And for each pun a plot was laid
That, like a king's, employed a dozen pages.
Thus he pursued his trade:
Yet, ah! with all this weight or worth,
His witty things he very seldom spoke,
And ne'er in private gave away a joke;
But like Mount Ætna, frequently sent forth
Volumes of smoke.

Reverence for the Sex.

The subjoined, written by Addison, more than a century ago, is as true as if it had been penned but yesterday. Our own sentiments precisely, and our own case exactly!

" I have found that men who are really most fond of the society of ladies, who cherish for them a high respect, nay reverence, are seldom the most popular with the sex. Men of more assurance, whose tongues are lightly hung, who make words supply the place of ideas, and place compliment in the room of sentiment are the favourites. A true respect for women leads to respectful actions towards them, and respect is usually distant action, and this great distance is mistaken by them for neglect and want of interest."

Journal of Rev. David Jones in 1773.—No. 2
Communicated by H. G. Jones, Jr., of Leverington, Pa.

At present there is one difficulty that I never thought of till I got there, viz: this people live a vagrant life, remaining for the most part but a short time, in any one place. If they were persuaded and assisted to farm, and learned to read, they would soon be civilized. 'Tis strange to me that nothing has been done by the Provinces bordering on these Indians: but under all these disadvantages, if there was no rum bought among them, I am apprehensive I could have done something. Some have been of the opinion, that the traders prejudiced the Indians against me; but though some of them have not that fear of God which I could wish they had, in their hearts, yet I solemnly think there was not one trader in the nation but assisted me what he could; at least they did me no harm. I have reason to acknowledge both their civility and generosity, when I remember that I was well entertained by Mr. Henry and Mr. Irwine, and when I came away neither would take one farthing for their kindness. At present it is not safe for any person to venture himself among such a lawless company of people as these savages are, that really have no conscience about shedding innocent blood. Some of the traders have said that the Indians only designed to scare me, but I am persuaded this is not the opinion of Mr. Henry or Mr. Irwine, who were the best judges in the case, being present when the Indians sought after me. I would now dismiss the subject of these Indians, only I remember I have said nothing of their apparel. In this respect they are like other Indians, the men wearing shirts, match coats, breech clouts, leggins and moccasons: their ornaments are silver plates on their arms above and below the elbows—rose jewels are also common. They paint their faces and cut the rim of their ears so as to stretch them very large; and their head is dressed in the best mode, with a black silk handkerchief about it. The women wear short shifts, sometimes a calico bed-gown, over their shoulders, which is in place of a petticoat. Their hair is parted and tied behind; they paint none except in spots: their ears are never cut, but have about ten silver rings in them. One squaw will have five hundred broaches stuck in her shift and leggins. Both men and women are very proud, but of the two the men are the more haughty. 'Tis said that neither men nor women suffer any hair to grow on any part of their body only their head. Some pull out not only their beard but also their eyebrows.

But to return to my travels. Having got a horse, which cost me twenty-five dollars, through the kindness of Mr. Irwine, and being somewhat furnished with provisions for my journey, on Monday, the 8th of February, I parted with my friends, and left Chillicothe about ten o'clock, alone, and passing Pickaweeke I came to Kicka-pookee, which is situated on a creek that soon empties into the Scioto, the town being about one mile from the river: it is more than twenty miles from Chillicothe, about N. E. and N. For the first eight miles I was not without some appre-hensions of being persued; but afterwards I was very little disturbed in mind. At this town I lodged with Mr. Richard Butler, brother to Mr. William Butler, before mentioned: he used me very kindly and prepared some wheat cakes for my journey; and as I had no goods he gave me two pairs of leggins to barter for provisions by the way, for these Indians, as yet, have not the use of money. In the morning my horse could not be found till near twelve o'clock, and by those means I missed some company. Howev-er, about one o'clock I passed over the river Scioto in a canoe in company with Mr. Butler, for I could not speak their language, and I did not know what to say to the Indian who kept the ferry. The boy who brought me over was a white captive, and could not speak any English, which made my heart sorry to hear him answer me, motta keeno toleeh, that is, I do not under-stand you. There remains a considerable num-ber of captives in this nation, all of whom were to be delivered up at the conclusion of the last peace: without a doubt, the agent has not done his duty in this point. This day I travelled alone through an excellent land, only there were so many bogs, or as they may be called fresh marshes, that it does not promise equal health to some other parts; but I am persuaded it will be an unparalleled land for stock: this day's journey was twenty-two miles in a northeast course. As I passed the Great Lick I saw the last flock of parrots, for these birds are not fond of extreme cold. I had only a small path, and night came on in this wide wilderness, which was more dis-agreeable than I can express. However, I arri-ved safe before nine o'clock at Mr. McCormick's at the Standing Stone, on a creek called Hock-hocking. Here is a town of Delaware Indians,

but as I had no interpreter, I could say nothing to them. The land about this creek is indeed as rich as heart could wish for; but the water is al-ways muddy, occasioned by the intermixture of the soil. Though this creek is narrow and very crooked, yet it soon grows deep enough to carry large canoes, and by these they transmit their peltry to Fort Pitt. Here I overtook Mr. David Duncan, a trader of Shippy's town, who was go-ing to Fort Pitt. Wednesday 10, set out early, for we expected to travel about forty miles before night: our course was more north than northeast. The land was for the most part low and level; consequently when the horses broke through it was very bad road, but the soil was good. Be-fore night we came to a small town known by the name of Dan. Ellet's wife's: here were some Shawanese and some Delawares. We lodged in a negro house, which was vacated for our use this night. This Shawanese is very rich in cat-tle, horses, and captive negroes. We got plenty of milk, and corn for our horses at a very expen-sive rate; but Mr. Duncan paid for me here, as well as in the remaining part of my journey while we traveled together. About a mile before we came to this town we crossed a large creek, called Salt Lick creek, which empties into the * Mooskingung, on which the chief town of the Delawares is situated. Thursday 11th, set out for a place known by the name of Conner's: we traveled near a northeast course. The land ap-peared very good, and the distance was not so great as the journey of the preceding day, so that we came to this small town some time before night: it is not situated near any stream as I saw. The land is level and the timber chiefly black oak, so that good wheat might be propuced if the trial were made. Mr. Conner, who is a white man and a native of Maryland, told me he in-tended to sow wheat this year, and was resolved to proceed to farming at all events. 'Tis proba-ble that he will be as good as his word, for he is a man who seems not to fear God, and it is likely that he does not much fear man. There are some circumstances favourable to him in such attempts, for he and the chief man of this town are in their way married to two sisters. These women were captives among the Indians, and it is likely from their childhood, for they have the actions of Indians; and I cannot tell whether the Indian's wife can speak but very little English. Notwithstanding Mr. Conner is one of the worst swearers that I have met with, yet he was kind and respectful to me. This town is a mixture of Shawanese and Delawares, and dwell in tolera-ble log houses. Friday 12th, set out for New Comer's town in company with Mr. Duncan: in

_____
* The present Muskingum.

a few miles we came to a town called the Little Shawanese Woman's Town. This woman is very rich, and as she is the chief person, the town is named after her. It is situated on the west side of the Mooskingung, and consists chiefly of Shawanese. Here we tarried only to warm ourselves and crossed the river in a canoe, our horses swiming by its side. The country now began to be hilly and broken, interrpersed with barren plains. We passed Capt. White Eye's Town, but this noted Indian was with my interpreter down the river Ohio, so that I had not the satisfaction of seeing him this visit, though I saw him several times during my first journey. He was the only Indian that I saw in all my travels who had any design of accomplishing any thing future. He told me he intended to be religious and have his children educated. He saw their way of living would not answer much longer—game grew scarce—they could not pretend to live much longer by hunting, but must farm, &c.: but he could not attend to matters of religion just now, for he intended to make a great hunt down the Ohio, and take his skins to Philadelphia himself. This he accomplished, going down the Mississippi and round by the Gulf of Florida. On this occasion I thought of that text of Scripture which says, " One went to his farm, and another to his merchandise," and it may be said the Indian went to his hunting. This was the case last year, and it may be something as important may employ the time this year. Some miles north of White Eye's Town, there is another small town of Delawares: at this we drove our horses into the river and obliged them to swim over, following them in a canoe belonging to the Indians. Thence we traveled over very hilly land, till we came within three miles of New Comer's Town; and from thence to the town is fine level land, covered with black oak and hickory, for the most part. We arrived at the town before night, and found it was a great triennial feast; consequently little could be done, till that expired. From the great town, Chillicothe, to this great metropolis of the Delawares, is about one hundred and thirty miles: the course may be estimated as northeast, though it varies in many places as the path goes.

" Pickled Cockles."

A parrot, the property of a lady, was one day detected by the enraged cook, for the fiftieth time, in the act of lar e y, in stealing pickle l cockles. The matter was upon him, and she inflicted a summary punishment on the green-headed delinquent. " What! you've been at the pickled cockles again, have you?" said she, hurling a ladle of hot soup at him. The feathers of his head were scalded off, and from being excessively talkative, he became mute, bald and solemn for nearly a year.

At last, the stubs began to peep out on his pate; and the mistress' father came from the country to see her;—the old man was bald. The bird had never seen him before, and was doubt ess struck with the coincidence of naked heads; for the moment the old gentleman entered the room, the parrot broke his long silence by vociferating with immense emphasis and glee,— " What, you've been at the pickled cockles again, have you?"

A Negative Compliment.

One of those individuals, who seem to be peculiar to every house, store, and office, familiarly known as "idlers," "loungers," &c., but more appropriately as "loafers," stepped into a store on Market street the other day, and proceeding to a clerk very busily engaged at the desk, assailed him with a string of interrogatories, something after the following style:
" Young man, is Mr. Readymoney within?"
" No."
" Do you know how long it will be before he returns?"
" No."
" Do you know where he has gone?"
" No."
" You know where he lives at, I suppose, don't you?"
" No."
For the information of the reader, be it observed, that each negative had, in due proportion, been delivered with an increased elevation of tone, and the effect of the finisher will be " better imagined than described," as the intruder demanded with some indignation:—
" Is that the way you answer a gentleman?"
" No!"
A clap of thunder was a fool to it, and the loafer was extinguished.

Changes of Fortune.

A Boston paper, published in 1787, illustrates by the following examples in the lives of distinguished Englishmen, the extraordinary changes which a few short years often produce in the condition of individuals:

In 1777, Mr. Hastings received an humble petition from Shaw-Allum, the Great Mogul, for relief against his enemies. In 1787, Mr. Hastings is on his knees before the House of Lords, taken into custody by a servant of the House of Commons, and obliged to give bail to insure his not flying from his country.

In 1777, Mr. Burke was reckoned the best speaker in the House of Commons, and the first formidable opponent of the Ministers. In 1787, Mr. Burke is either coughed down or not attended to, and is formidable only to the opposition that he acts with.

In 1777, Lord North managed the helm of state, and directed all the public affairs of the kingdom. In 1787, we read in a newspaper, that poor Lord North was led out of Westminster Abbey by one of his daughters.

In 1777, Sir —— was a very smart and active waiter at a public tavern. In 1787, Sir —— is a nabob, a baronet, and a knight of the shire.

In 1777, one Arnold headed the American troops that retired from Canada at Saratoga. In 1787, this same Arnold is closeted at St. James', where he and his Majesty are one.

In 1777, Col. Conway, Sir Henry Clinton's

aid-de-camp, offered to fight a duel for the sake of a woman. In 1787, this same gentleman preached a sermon on the following text:—" *If any one strike thee on the left cheek, offer him the other.*"

In 1775, Dr. Prettyman went to the gallery of the House of Commons to hear Mr. Pitt's speech, and was turned out. In 1787, Dr. Prettyman rose in his seat in the House of Lords, in defence of a drayman, while Mr. Pitt stood below the bar to hear him.

Such are the changes that may happen in ten years!

To those who only know the lamented Laman Blanchard, as the wit and humourist—one of the ablest, as he was one of the earliest, contributors to the Punch newspaper—the following verses, which breathe of the purest spirit of poetry, will be at once new and acceptable.

Saturday Night.

BY LAMAN BLANCHARD.

The water! the water, who brings?
Run, Lucy, the water, while yet there is light
    You can go to the first of the springs;
To-morrow, remember, the Sabbath bell rings,
And this (how the weeks fly!) is Saturday night.

Where's the pitcher? there's water within it—
Not half enough;—here, skim away down the path,
    The rogue will be stript in a minute,
His little heart, feel, how it pants to be in it,
And longs, like a frolicksome bird, for the bath.

Now, then, all is ready, and here,
Ah! here is the water, a feast for the sight,
    Pour it in till its sparkles appear—
Why the child's very forehead is scarcely more clear,
And his eye, though it glistens, is only as bright.

There's a bath for young beauty! so in,
In, sweet little bather, one splash and its o'er;
    We'll sprinkle you just to begin—
There, there. now it's over, he's up to his chin,
And the silver drops down from his gold ringlets pour.

With his wet hand he rubs his wet nose,
And he shuts up his eyelids and lips like a book;
    And as down each drop trickling goes,
His flushed cheek resembles a dew-dripping rose,
And his brow seems a lily just snatched from a brook.

Now his other hand dashes away
The drops that are trickling his forehead and chin;
    And he opens his eyes in his play,
Like some quaint little water-sprite peering for day,
With glances that seemed to ask how he got in.

But anon comes his time of delight:
The bather begins to breathe after the dip;
    Much more is he now like a spirite,
And now will he celebrate Saturday night
With the play of his limbs and the power of his lip.

Just hear how his small voice can shout.
While he sparkles and splashes there, much like a fish;
    How he scatters the bright drops about—
How he laughs, and leaps up, and look prankish! no doubt
He would turn o'er the bath, if he had but his wish!

At last the ablution is done;
The wild little innocent's gambols are o'er—
    The dripping limbs dried one by one;
And the mother breathes kisses all over her son,
And thinks he was never so lovely before.

Her arms round her darling she twines,
And his flower-like senses in sleep are up-curled;
    So he lies—till the Sabbath sun shines,
When, waking, his Saturday dress he resigns,
And puts on the prettiest frock in the world.

May he, when his childhood's resigned,
With its dress, and the rough paths of life are in sight,
    As immediately wash from his mind
The dust and the stains of the world—may he find
Before him, a Sabbath of love and delight!

Passing Strange.

"Where will you pass the winter Tom?"
"Upon my soul I do not know;
    The times to such a pitch have come,
That nothing *passes* nowhere now."

Philosophy.

A story is told of a love smitten professor in some College, who after conversing awhile with his Dulcinea on the interesting topic of matrimony, concluded at last with a declaration, and put the emphatic question of—

" Will you have me?"

" I am sorry to disappoint you," replied the lady, " and hope my refusal will not give you pain; but I must answer no."

" Well, well, that will do, madam," said her philosophical lover, " and now *suppose we change the subject!*"

A Valuable Index.

A gentleman was wading through the index of some law reports the other day, and under the " G.'s" he found " Great mind—Mr. Laing," and knowing that his worship was not possessed of a very large body, he was naturally curious to learn something of the dimensions of his mind, and turning to the page refered to, he found the following, " Mr. Laing said he had a great mind to commit John Thomas for the misdemeanor.

Definitions.

RING.—A circular link put through the snouts of swine, and on the fingers of women, to hold them both under subjection.

TINDER.—A thin rag, such as modern female dresses, intended to catch sparks, raise a flame and light a match.

GUARDIAN ANGELS.—Cautious mamas, with a dozen frolicksome daughters.

An old maid eyes a single gentleman with the same feelings that we look at a street dog in dog-days, viz: wondering whether he intends to *bite.*

"Variety's the Spice of Life."

Reader whoever you may be, whether a traveled agent, or an exclusive book-worm—whether you have inspected high and low life in London, or seen the cat jump nine ways for Sunday in these diggins, it matters not—you have not seen a rarer curiosity we venture, than the bill which follows, which we copy verbatim, and which was actually paid. Pope, we guess, it was, who said—

"Various the mind of desultory man."

But we poets and philosophers of Florida, are constrained to cry out,

Various the *professions*—of some folks.

Major ———,
1840.   To ———,   Dr.
Oct. 10—To 2,000 *Shingles*, at $6 25 $12 50
  "   One pair of *Shoes*   -   -   2 50
      By Cash   -   -   -   8 50
  "   Repairing *Coat*   -   -   -   1 50
      By Cash   -   -   -   12 00
  "   Playing the *Fiddle* one night   10 00
  "   Jacket and pair Pants for Negro   9 00
  "   Mending *Boots*   -   -   -   2 00
  "   Playing the *Fiddle* another night   10 00
  "   Setting four panes *Glass*   ;   1 00
  "   *Sawing* a load of wood   -   1 00
  "   *Scouring* Coat   -   -   -   1 75
  "   Making a thousand *Brick*   -   4 50
  "   *Painting* Dog House   -   -   2 50
  "   *Butchering* a Beef   -   -   4 00
  "   *Pulling six teeth* for Negro boy *Ike*   75
  "   Curing your gray Horse of colic   5 00
                                    ————
                                    $88 50

And then the way the fellow added debts and credits all together, must have been somewhat distressing to the gentleman whose imperative duty it became to "I am up" the gross amount.—*Florida Journal.*

Manners.

It is bad manners for a gentleman to run against a lady in the street, and when he does so, he should gracefully fall back a step or two, take off his hat, make a low bow, and humbly beg her pardon.
It is decidedly bad manners to stare a pretty girl out of countenance. She don't like it. A pretty girl likes to be noticed, feels proud of admiration; but a stupid, vulgar, impudent stare, disgusts her. It is better to look at her when she don't notice you, and to let your eye fall when it meets her's.
It is not considered correct for a lady and gentleman to walk in a fashionable prominade, arm in arm, in the day time, unless they are engaged or married, or one is a stranger in the city, or it is a public day, and the crowded streets require it. It is proper in unfashionable streets, or when you get into the country. At the East, walking arm in arm, in the day time, unless with the exceptions we have made, is considered equal to a publishment in the parish church.
It is shocking bad manners not to give a lady the wall when walking with her. When you meet, in general, it is best to turn to the right, as that prevents any confusion, and when the walks are crowded, it is absolutely necessary.
We have decided that it is most distinctly bad manners for a gentleman to offer to shake hands with a lady, with whom he is on terms of but common acquaintance, but that should the lady offer her hand, she has a right to do so according to the laws of gallantry and chivalry, and in such a case, it is optional with the gentleman to shake, squeeze or kiss it. The prettiest and best behaved girl we ever saw, always sprang forward, and gave us both hands, when we had not seen her for a day or two. She was a bit of a romp, to be sure, but we like such romps.

Juvenile Balls.

The early developement of the passions which the present system of education calls forth, cannot be elucidated by any thing so forcible as the following anecdotes:—A Lilliputian in long clothes, throwing herself languishingly upon a sofa, on her return from church, cried lately to her mother, "I really must decline going to church in future, at least we must have our places changed." "Why so, my dear?" asked her astonished parent. "Because there is a person in an adjoining pew who stares at me like a pest, and I do assure you, mamma, I never gave him the slightest encouragement." This incipient coquette had attained the respectable age of seven years. The eldest daughter of a gentleman in Russel square, aged six, received a card which ran thus: "Miss B——— at home at seven, punch at eight, quadarilles." It was for the same evening—rather short notice, to be sure, for a fashionable assemblage. It elicited the following reply, the father being somewhat of our way of thinking in these matters:—"Miss R——— presents her compliments to Miss B———, and regrets to say that she is to be well whipped at seven, and in bed by eight."—*Monthly Magazine.*

New Music.

We have received from Messrs. Peters & Co., the following pieces of new Music, which have just been published by them in a neat and elegant style.
"*We'll go to Sea no More*," a popular Scotch Ballad, written by J. Haskin: Music arranged by Wm. C. Peters. This little Song, as we have heard it sung, we can commend as a sweet and beautiful Ballad.
"*Thou Sweet gliding Kedron*," is a Sacred Song and Chorus, the music of which, by John Candy of Louisville, should be (if there be any virtue in a name,) a *sweet* thing.
"*Vespers for the Assumption and other Festivals*," and "*Alma Redemptoris*," an Anthem for Advent," from Pleyel, are sacred pieces, adapted more especially for the worship of the Catholic Church, to the members of which they will no doubt be highly acceptable.
"*The Departed*, written by Park Benjamin, Esq.; composed and arranged as a Duett, and dedicated to Mrs. R. S. Nichols, of this city, by Lewis J. Cist," is the title of a new piece, also published and for sale by Messrs. Peters & Co., East Fourth street. Price 25 cents, nett.

CINCINNATI MISCELLANY.

CINCINNATI, DECEMBER, 1845.

John S. Wallace.

An incident or two in the pioneer history of John S. Wallace, one of the earliest settlers of Cincinnati, and a resident here until his death, which occured but a few years since, are worthy of being recorded from the oblivion to which the greater share of the narratives of those days is rapidly hastening.

Mr. *Wallace* was, with most of the first settlers of Cincinnati, a native of Pennsylvania, and had been engaged in trading voyages on the Ohio, at a date even prior to the first settlement of our city.

On his second visit to Cincinnati, in 1789, he was informed that Capt. *Strong's* company of regulars, who had been stationed at Fort Washington to protect the infant settlements in Judge Symmes' purchase, were about to abandon the post for want of provisions, supplies from stations higher up the Ohio having given out. Wallace called on the Captain, and suggested to him, that he could probably buy as much corn at Columbia as would furnish bread-stuffs for some time, while he—Wallace—would take the woods with a hunter or two in company and supply the meat rations. The suggestion was well timed as well as judicious, and readily adopted. Strong, accompanied by Capt. Kearsey, rode up to Columbia, applied to Capt. *James Flinn,* for his corn, which he refused, alleging that when the government paid him for corn which he had supplied at *Belleville* to the garrison at *Fort Harmar,* he would furnish more. While they were thus engaged, *Luke Foster,* still living and now residing in Springfield township, interposed and asked what was the difficulty. The Captain remarked, " Difficulty enough, we are out of provisions below, and will have to retreat on starvation, for we have nothing left for the garrison to eat." Foster thereupon offered to lend them one hundred bushels corn, which he did, getting it back in small parcels the next season. How opportune this offer was may be judged by the fact that the corn in the hands of Flinn and Foster constituted two-thirds of the whole supply of Columbia and Cincinnati.

In the meantime Wallace started to the woods, accompanied by two of the early settlers, *Drennan* and *Dement.* Drennan did not understand much of hunting, and Dement had never attempted it, but they were both serviceable in the only department in which they were needed by Wallace, that is in packing the meat—Indian fashion—on their backs—Dement, especially. They went down the river in a canoe, some ten miles below Cincinnati, on the Kentucky side, where they secreted their craft in the mouth of a small branch, fearing the Indians might be induced to lie in ambush for their return, if it fell under their notice. Here they struck into the woods and secured an abundant supply of buffalo, deer and bear meat, to last the troops, about seventy in number, for six weeks—until provisions should arrive from Pittsburgh.

This supply was of great importance. Without provisions the military station here must have been relinquished, to the prejudice of its speedy re-occupation, and to the necessary discouragement of persons settling at the place, as well as tempting the abandonment of the existing settlements of Cincinnati and Columbia.

Early in January, 1791, Wallace, accompanied *Abner Hunt,* who was a surveyor, with two other persons, *Sloan* and *Cunningham,* on surveys on the west bank of the Great Miami. On the night of the 7th, they encamped there. Next morning after they had been roasting venison, on which they breakfasted, they set out to explore the Miami bottoms above, where the Colerain settlement or station, was located. They had hardly left their camp seventy yards behind, when they were beset by the savages on their rear, who fired a volley of eight or ten guns. Cunningham was killed on the spot. Hunt, having been thrown from his horse, was made a prisoner before he could recover, and Sloan, although shot through his body, kept his seat and made his escape, accompanied by Hunt's loose horse. Two of the Indians pursued Wallace more than a mile and a half, but owing to his uncommon activity he made out to overtake Sloan with the spare horse, which he mounted and succeeded in crossing the Miami in Sloan's company. In his flight on foot, he was twice shot at, but without effect. His leggings had been getting loose, and at the moment of the first shot, he tripped and fell. Supposing him struck by the bullet, the Indians raised a shout, *Wah! hoo!* calculating to a certainty on his scalp; but hastily tying his leggings, he resumed his flight and effected his escape. After crossing the Miami Sloan complained of faintness from his wound, when Wallace advised him to thrust part of his shirt into the bullet hole to stop the flow of blood. Leaving the river they directed their course to Cincinnati. On traveling six miles or more, they fell into the trace from Dunlap's station, since called Colrain, to Cincinnati. Here they held a consultation, the result of which was, to visit the post, and put the settlers there on their guard. That night it rained, froze and finally snowed six or seven inches in depth. On the 9th they buried the slain man, and returned to the station, which the Indians invested the next day at sunrise—just as the women were milking the cows. Hunt was compelled to ask and urge its surrender, which in the hope of saving his life he did in the most pressing terms, promising that life and property should both be held sacred. Lieutenant *Kingsbury*, who was stationed there with a mere handful of soldiers, promptly rejected all such propositions, telling the Indians that the garrison had despatched a man to Judge *Symmes'*, who would soon be up to their help, with the whole settlement at the river. He failed in imposing this upon them, they replying that it was a lie, as they knew that Symmes was in New Jersey. The invaders were nearly three hundred in force, and commanded by the infamous *Simon Girty*, as was subsequently ascertained through a man who had been taken prisoner a few days before the attack, at a short distance from the fort; after his return from a seven year's captivity.

Finding their party unsuccessful, the Indians commenced a fire on the fort, which they kept up all that day and part of the night. At ten o'clock that night Wallace made an effort to escape for the purpose of obtaining a reinforcement from Gen'l. *Harmar* at Fort Washington, but was obliged to return, the Indians encompassing him on every side. At three o'clock in the morning, however, he left the station, accompanied by a man named *Wiseman*, crossed the river in a canoe, took the bushes, descended the river bottoms a mile or so, attempted to cross the river through the running ice, but the water proving too deep, returned, ran a mile further down, crossed the river and took the woods to Cincinnati. Six miles out from that place he met Capt. John S. Gano, at the head of a company of Columbia militia, and returned with him to the station. On their arrival, they found that the Indians, despairing of success and apprehensive of reinforcements arriving, had abandoned the siege. Hunt was found dead, his brains beaten out, a brand applied to his bowels, and two *war clubs* laid across his breast. He had been also stripped of his scalp, as well as of his clothes. In their retreat, as the tracks shewed, the savages had filed off, right and left, from the fort. On the first fire the Indians shot into the

building where the hand-mill was kept, through the logs which had not been chunked, by which they wounded one man and killed another. Of the assailants a number were killed and two scalps taken, one of which Wallace dressed and presented to General Harmar, on his return to Fort Washington. The station was particularly exposed to assault, as the houses, contrary to the usual and proper plan, presented their lower edges outside, some of them being so low that my informant stated to me he saw a dog which had been shut out of the station, leap from a stump outside on to the roof of one of the cabins. In the progress of the seige, the most active efforts of the assailants were directed to setting the roofs of the houses on a blaze, both by fire arrows, and by carrying brands of fire. One Indian ran with a burning brand to a building, which he had just reached as a volley stretched him lifeless. The party from Columbia was under the command of Lieutenant *Foster*, as that from Cincinnati was in charge of Lieutenant *Scott Traverse*, the whole being a detachment of sixty men. After remaining long enough to assist Col. *Shaumburg* in strengthening the fortifications, they returned home.

In the month of June, 1791, Wallace, with his father and a lad, were hoeing corn in a lot immediately north of where the Cincinnati Hospital now stands; and at the same time two men named *Scott* and *Shepherd* were engaged near what is now the corner of Western Row and Clinton streets, ploughing corn. They had drawn a few furrows across the lot, when five or six Indians jumped the fence, raised the yell, and gave chase to the ploughman, but to no effect. On hearing the yell, Wallace snatched up his rifle which lay in the row before him, directing those with him to make their escape to town, as fast as possible. On stepping cautiously into the adjacent lot, he discovered an Indian about eighty yards from him about to enter the bushes. He shot at him, probably without effect, as he left the ground in haste; at the same instant he saw two Indians riding the plough horses away at full speed. The party of savages left eight blankets and blanket capots behind, together with a leg of bear meat, a horn full of powder and some trifling trinkets. The alarm was given and eleven of the best woodsmen and hunters were started on foot in pursuit, followed by eleven others on horse, having all the horses in the place, each man supplied with some pone and venison wrapped in his blanket for both horsemen and footmen. About sunset they encountered a severe thunder storm, accompanied with heavy rain. By the time it became dark the rear party overtook the advance on foot, and making their horses fast to the trees, encamped for the night. In the morning they took the trail, and found that the Indians had lain all night in a prickly ash thicket a short distance in advance where they had eaten a part of a fawn raw, and left the rest. The enemy was pursued to the river at a point where the Indians had crossed, just above where the town of Hamilton now stands. Owing to the tremendous rains which had fallen, the river was bank full, and the pursuing party were obliged to return home. During the same year *Van Cleve* was killed near where the Hospital stands, and *Cutter* was made prisoner in the same vicinity.

These were the last instances in which a savage rifle was fired within the present limits of Cincinnati, later 'depredations being connected with the bow and arrow, which enabled them to destroy cattle while prowling through our streets by night without creating an alarm. On one of these visits they shot an arrow with a stone head into an ox with such force that it went entirely through the carcase. Stealing horses from this time until Wayne arrived in 1793, constituted the principal injury inflicted by our red brethren upon their white neighbours in Cincinnati.

The Memphis Convention.

MEMPHIS, November 15th 1845.

Owing to an uncommon scarcity of water, boats of a large class, the Diomed, Duke of Orleans, and Andrew Jackson, all stuck fast at various points on the Lower Ohio or immediately below the mouth of that river. We lost every night but Tuesday, on the Jackson from this cause, having out traveled the rise which preceded us, and being constrained to lay by at night at shoal places to allow it to overtake us. We passed the Steamboat Henry Bry at *Randolph*, snagged the night before. We reached here on Wednesday evening, and found Memphis overflowing with population, the number of delegates alone being almost six hundred, a very large share of whom were from various points at a distance. The convention organized temporarily on Wednesday and adjourned to this morning, when John C. Calhoun was appointed President, with the usual allowance of Vice-Presidents and Secretaries; J. S. Hawkins in the former capacity, and T. B. Drinker in the latter, representing Ohio. There are some of the most distinguished men in Congress and the State Legislatures in attendance as members. Gen. Gaines, in part, represents Louisiana, and was received on entering, by a general rising of the convention in acknowlment of his gray hairs, as well as his patriotic services. Mr. Calhoun on taking the chair made admirable address, characterized by the most enlarged, patriotic, and statesman-like views, and widely different in its features with one or two exceptions from what had been my expectation on that score. He spoke for forty-five minutes with the entire sympathy of the assembly.

I have been thus far highly gratified in this visit. The Andrew Jackson runs fast and smoothly; has a captain who makes every thing move in its proper orbit, being himself always at his post. The table was excellent, and what is not usually enjoyed by men in this kind of traveling, the sleeping accommodations were all I could desire. I fear I shall be detained by the important and various business which will occupy the convention, longer than I had contemplated at my departure, but feel it my duty to see its necessary business transacted before I leave Memphis.

What pork is in Cincinnati, and more, is cotton in Memphis, because while pork is but one of our important exports, cotton is the great staple here, as high as nine hundred bales having been received here this week, from the interior, in one day. What the quantity of groceries and other goods furnished to the wealthy region which supplies this cotton crop, may be infered accordingly. Memphis is in fact a place of great commercial activity for its size, and the extent of its improvements bears testimony to that fact. The population—nine thousand inhabitants—indicates its position as the most important town in Tennessee, Nashville excepted.

November 15th, evening.—The convention has just adjourned. Our Cincinnati dailies have recorded its doings as far as the journals point them out. It may be of interest to notice some things which lie out of sight.

The south and southwest came to the convention to carry a rail-road to Memphis under the patronage of the general government, or at any rate to unite the interests of the several states through which it should pass, so as to secure the necessary state patronage to the measure. Mr. Calhoun's address compeled them to the latter course. He said distinctly at the outset, that the United States could do nothing on its behalf.

The jealousy of states right men who were members of that convention, constituting as they did a majority there, choked off every thing in the way of public improvements, except where the improvement lay within their own territory. It was in vain that we furnished evidence that the Ohio and its tributaries turned out more manufactured and agricultural products than any other river in the United States. All that the Ohio delegation could obtain was a general recommendation to the improvement of the Ohio, along with that of the Mississippi. The Louisville delegation in the committee, wily, persevering, and adroit, staved off any direct recommendation of a new canal or widening the old one, or making either free, by embarrassing our action with the wild and absurd proposition of making a slackwater navigation of the Ohio river from Pittsburgh to its mouth.

What the west needs to have done for itself this session of Congress, must be done by public meetings, held in every Congressional district affected by the great interest in which the whole west has a common stake. In this way the mails, the navigation of the Ohio, national depots, armories &c., will all be settled as the west requires them lo be disposed of.

There were many distinguished public men from all quarters, present at Memphis, the most fluent speakers generally being from the south and southwest. In this respect, however, Mr. Briggs of Cleveland, and Mr. Elwood Fisher of our own city amply sustained the honour of Ohio. Fisher's readiness at repartee rendered him very troublesome to some of the St. Louis delegation, who were thereby made by him sufficiently rediculous. Dr. Evans of *Evansville*, Indiana, and Mr. Russell of Wheeling, made brief but very effective speeches, also. J. B. Butler of Pittsburgh, sustained a marked influence in the various committees of which he made part, as might be expected from his experience in public business.

Rail-Road to the Pacific.

The projected enterprise by Mr. *A. Whitney*, of constructing a railroad from the western borders of Lake Michigan to the shores of the Pacific, which has been for several months before the public, and will be brought before the Congress of the United States at its present session, demands such vast means for its accomplishment, and comprehends such important consequences in its results, alike in its moral, political and pecuniary bearings, as to justify and require a thorough analysis. Much of what has appeared in the periodical press is deficient in the statistics of the subject, and vague notions of its character, have prevailed to such an extent that the only individual—Judge Douglass, of Illinois—who has yet thought proper to oppose the measure imputes as objections to it, three important features, which do not belong to the project. If a writer, usually intelligent, has committed such gross errors on a subject to which he addresses himself, what must be the general ignorance of those who have merely glanced at the sketchy and indefinite statements on this subject, which have been presented by the press. Discussing the project for the last three weeks, I have found no individual, myself included, who had any distinct or accurate notion of the enter-

prise until he had thoroughly examined the whole subject.

What then is the project?

Mr. Whitney has memorialized the Congress of the United States for a grant of the public lands, sixty miles wide, from the western shores of Lake Michigan to the Pacific ocean. The sales of this belt of land are to build the road. He proposes that commissioners on behalf of the United States shall be appointed by the President, who in conjunction with himself shall make the titles. He to effect the sales and they to receive the money, which they will disburse as fast and as far as the road progresses. The sales of one mile on the road, extending the breadth of the grant—sixty miles—will furnish means to build two miles of the road. In this way the road sells the land, and the land makes the road, and the final result is the settlement of the country and *with it* the OREGON QUESTION.

As regards the route, with its points of commencement and termination, there is nothing in the nature of the enterprise which determines the precise location except that the rail-road *must* traverse the south pass of the Rocky Mountains in latitude forty-two degrees thirty minutes. It cannot commence as low as *Milwaukie*, because the lands on that parallel are so extensively taken up as to forbid a location much below *Greenbay*, and it may terminate at the mouth of the Columbia river, or what is infinitely preferable, at or near *San Francisco* in California, should that country fall within our limits in the course of ten or fifteen years. It is not necessary for nearly that space of time to determine the point at which the road shall strike the Pacific.

Mr. Whitney proposes not only to make the road, but to keep it in repair for the fifteen years which may elapse before its completion.

This rail-road is designed to be free except for such an amount as may be necessary to keep up repairs. The ownership of the road is in the people of the United States, and such residue of the lands as may not be requisite for its construction becomes finally the property of Mr. Whitney.

If the project fails in any stage of its progress, the lands become as they always have been, the property of the people.

It will be seen then, and should be distinctly understood and recollected by my readers in the farther prosecution of this topic,

That, this is no joint stock company.

That it is no land company speculation, and,

That it is in no shape an irresponsible corporation.

If there be any danger of failure in accomplishing the enterprise, it is at the risk of the projector, the government or rather the people of the United States hazard nothing, and in the event of success, contribute nothing but wild lands, three-fourths of which will be of no value otherwise for a century to come, and could doubtness now be bought of Congress for five cents per acre.

Journal of Rev. David Jones in 1773.--No. 3. *Communicated by H. G. Jones, Jr., of Leverington, Pa.*

Saturday, 13th February, 1773, I was so happy as to learn that Joseph Peappi, a Moravian Indian, who is a good interpreter, was in town. I made application to him for his assistance in speaking to the king. He engaged, and spoke very kindly on the occasion, and consequently the king was informed that I was in town and would wait on him presently. Joseph carried the message and was to remain until I came: on this occasion the king's brother and some of his friends were gathered in the king's house. When I thought it suitable I went in, desiring Joseph to let him know I was the man he expected, upon which he gave me the right hand of friendship and appeared to receive me in a kind manner, inviting me to sit down. I told him I was the man who wrote two letters to him last year, one from Monongahela and the other from Fort Pitt, asking if he had received them with a belt of wampum. He said he had received all, and I might see them if I pleased. I replied that it was not necessary to be at that trouble; if he had received them that was enough. I proceeded to let him know that my design in coming was the same that was specified in the letters; that I was a minister who was desirous to instruct them in the knowledge of that God who had made us all; that now I was ready to speak to him and his people, if he was pleased to grant me liberty. He replied that in these matters he could do nothing without the advice of his council, but he would inform them of it, and I should have an answer as soon as the great feast was over. This was not only what they call a feast, but also a time of great dancing and gaming, and nothing else could be attended to 'till these were finished; therefore I concluded to visit the Moravian Indian towns to employ the time till they consulted about the matter. Sabbath 14th, Mr. Duncan and I set out for the Moravian town which is situated on the same river, about ten miles up the stream: the road was very icy, so that we were obliged to go into the woods, which made it late before we came to the town: when I arrived worship was not finished. I went in and found the minister instructing them in the English tongue by an interpreter; but after a few sentences he stopped. This town stands on high-level ground, east of the Mooskingung, and is laid out in regular form, the buildings being on each side of the street. These Indians came here in August, 1772, and so industrious have they been, that they have built neat log houses for themselves, and a good house for worship about twenty-two feet by eighteen; well seated, with a good floor and chimney. They are a mixture of Stockbridge Indians, Mingos and Delawares. Since the last war they have lived about Wyoming, until their removal. Their conduct in time of worship is praiseworthy—their grave and solemn countenances exceeding what is common among us at such times. Their minister, the Rev. David Zeisberger, a native of Moravia, seems to be an honest man: he has been quite successful among these poor heathen. They used no kind of prayer—their worship beginning and ending with singing a hymn in the Indian language. In the evening they met again for worship; but their minister, either inconsiderately or by design, spoke in the German language, so that I knew not what he said. Mr. Zeisberger told me that between the two towns there were near eighty families, and two ministers besides himself; and I was informed that one of them whose name is Youngman, is a person of good abilities. From what I saw I must say that the conduct of the Moravian Society toward the heathen is commendable; they have behaved like Christians indeed, while others have in the most shameful manner, neglected these poor fellow creatures, or else made only faint attempts by persons not suitably qualified. Indeed from all that I have heard of Mr. David Brainerd, he was sincerely engaged, and well qualified, but his time was short. In the evening I told Mr. Zeisberger that I had a desire to speak to the Indians; he replied with some coldness that I might have an opportunity in the morning. I am apprehensive he was afraid to countenance me much, lest I might be of some disadvantage by drawing away disciples, but perhaps his reservedness was from his natural disposition. Monday, 15th, early in the morning I parted with my kind fellow traveler, Mr. Duncan, who went on his way towards Fort Pitt. The Indians convened —Joseph Peappi was interpreter. I told them when I came from home I had no design to speak for them, for I did not know of their removal; but seeing Providence gave me an opportunity I had a desire to speak to them. I proceeded to observe that all the disciples of our Saviour Jesus Christ separated themselves from the course of this world, no longer to live as the world lived; as other people were bad, they might expect difficulties and persecutions, but to be strong in heart, as God would give them rest—that they should be watchful and beware of falling back to living as other Indians, but as God had opened their eyes, to keep on their way until they came to eternal rest with Christ. I suppose my discourse continued about half an hour. I felt much of the assistance of God, and by the great solemnity, it might be judged that the word was felt with power. I could not go to the other town, by reason of the ice. These Indians understand carpenter work and farming, and intend to live as we do, and I am certain that in a few years they will be rich and live well, for the land is exceedingly good for wheat. While I was here one of the Indians asked the minister when Easter Sunday was. Mr. Zeisberger seemed to evade any discourse about it and merely told him that it was not for some time, and that he should have notice when it arrived. Perhaps I should have thought nothing of it, if I had heard such a question among white people; but the case was quite different here, for I ruminated on it with anxiety to think that any man would presume to teach a heathen to observe that which God Almighty never taught him, for since the heathen were made, God never taught any one to observe Easter Sunday. My thoughts rested not here, but I began to think what superstitious relics of the Romish Church were kept alive among us, and among others, I fixed on Christmas as an abomination which God never commanded to be observed.

I returned to Newcomers' Town in the afternoon, and went to see Capt. Killbuck, who is a sensible Indian, speaks good English, and treats a white with some of the complaisance of a gentleman. He received me very kindly and conversed freely on the subject of preaching, and was to meet next morning to converse farther: he invited me to make free in coming to see him. I soon perceived that he was the person who bore all the sway in their affairs, and could do more than the king himself. Tuesday 16th, met Capt. Killbuck, and talked on many subjects. In our discourse he told me that some years ago two Presbyterian ministers visited them—that though they did not incline to let them stay, yet they had been thinking of the matter ever since, and intended to have a minister and a schoolmaster, but would not have Presbyterians, because their ministers went to war against them, and therefore they did not like to be taught now by those who formerly were for killing them. I found Indian prejudice very great and unreasonable, and therefore observed that they might receive the Moravians, for they never fought against them. He replied that the Moravians did not belong to our kingdom, but were of Germany, and could not save their people alive in time of war. Upon this he related very exactly all the distresses and dangers of the Moravian Indians last war, and how they were preserved in the Barracks in Philadelphia; adding that for all the assistance the Moravians could give their Indians would have been killed, consequently it did not signify to be of that religion which would not protect them in war time. He said they intended to go home to the king and tell him that they would be of the same religion that he was, and desired a minister and schoolmaster of his choosing. I told him I approved of his speech, but was apprehensive that they were too poor to go, and thought they would not get much help. He informed me that they had nearly forty pounds now in money, and intended to make an early hunt, and go in the fall. I encouraged the attempt, willing to resign the civilising of them to the king and council; but I am persuaded that the service of the Church of England, as it now stands, will never be prescribed to the Indians, for they would not like a religion which takes a person a great part of his lifetime to learn its ceremonies.

Steamboat Traveling.

For the benefit of those readers of the Advertiser who are not regular steamboat travelers, I submit a few hints which they may improve to their advantage. The moral I desire to inculcate is, be careful always on what steamboat you travel. Those who infer that one steamboat is about as good as another for a man on a journey, will probably become undeceived, if they take western steamboats repeatedly. Let me supply a contrast for public benefit.

I started to Memphis with my fellow members, to attend the Convention there, on board the Steamboat *Andrew Jackson*, Capt. *Eckert*, commander. Every comfort and enjoyment within reach of an individual at his own home, was at our hands. The river was lower than usual, and after leaving Louisville, we grounded every night waiting for a slight rise, which we had outtraveled. Whatever difficulty had been, from time to time created by low water, was overcome by the ingenuity, perseverance and energy of the captain, who was always found by me at his post day and night, watching over our safety, deducting occasionally an hour or two through the day, in which he slept, and depending on getting into port for an opportunity of posting up his sleeping account. Every thing moved like clock work about the boat, a look or a word from the captain sufficing for his subordinates. In this way we got down to Memphis, regreting that we should not have the opportunity of returning by the same conveyance, and arriving twenty-four hours in advance of all the other delegates from Cincinnati, Pittsburg and Louisville.

Now for the contrast—I left Memphis, accompanied by others of our city delegation, on the

Brownsville, a new boat which started from Memphis on Tuesday, 18th ult. The boat, although small, had a double engine, and bore a fair reputation for speed. She was new, and kept remarkably neat and in good order. Every thing in short as to her appearance, was perfectly a decoy. Her captain was a gentlemanly man, but, as well as his officers, destitute of experience, and indeed fitness for his business. On onr way up, and below *Mills' point*, he halted to take a lot of boilers and heavy machinery, which had been left during high water on a bluff bank, and which any man of sense or judgment, could have discovered at a glance, could not be got aboard without endangering the safety alike of boat and passengers, and for one half of which there was not stowage room, at any rate. After spending three hours in an undecided state, swung to and fro alternately, by the advice of their owner and the passengers, he concluded at last to leave them. At *Cairo* he left half a dozen passengers for *St. Louis*. This took him *three hours* more. At *Golconda* the boat stopped to take in 67 tons pigmetal for *Louisville*. Here an hour was spent adjusting the price of freight, and nine hours more in getting the iron on board —an operation that might have been done in two, had the necessary preparation been made. We never rounded to for passengers or freight, at a less delay than an hour, even when ten minutes would have sufficed Capt. Eckert for the purpose. All these stoppages were noted by the watch. As may be infered from all this, we were nearly six days on our way from Memphis to Louisville, although we had two feet more water, in the Ohio than when we went down on the *Andrew Jackson*.

I make this statement, not to gratify the griefs of myself and associates, or to injure the Brownsville, which is owned as I understand, by her captain, clerk, pilot and engineers, but simply, to point out to those who are inexperienced in such matters, the importance of finding out the character and competency, not only of a boat, but of her officers.

John C. Calhoun.

I think it likely, by what I saw and learned at the Memphis Convention, that this distinguished statesman's opinion on various public questions have been undergoing of late a considerable change, which if of no other effect, will render him less an abstractionist than heretofore. In this he is but reflecting the popular sentiment of his own state, which is fast assuming a practical cast, *and for his sake.*

In saying that Mr. Calhoun, at Memphis, was the rallying point of notice, justice is hardly done that individual. The truth is that he towered immeasurably higher than whoever there might have been considered next to himself. The exemplary candor and frankness which characterized every thing he said and did; the marked ability and dignity with which he presided over its deliberations, and above all the winning, yes, seductive charm of his address, won their way to the hearts of all the members. I cannot conceive how any one can resist the influence of that address.

I ascertained from Mr. Calhoun that urgent business compelled his return via New Orleans, but that he would pay us a visit to Cincinnati in the course of next summer. He is not unaware of the character of the Valley of the Miamis, and Lexington, Ky., region for beauty and exuberant fertility, and anticipates great pleasure from the visit.

Mr. Calhoun returns to the Senate of the United States. I say this *on the highest authority* short of his own. He is, in my opinion, one of the greatest as well as the most interesting men of the age, and in saying this, it is but fairness to add, that I have come to that conclusion since I went to Memphis, and in the face of prepossessions against him of various kinds, long and ardently indulged. At Memphis, as at New Orleans, he was received with honour and respect by every body without distinction of party.

Domestic Markets.

One of my exchanges, a country paper, hits off with great success, the miserable apings by some of our western towns and cities of the "State of the market" articles in the New York and Philadelphia prints.

"Hay was so abundant last Saturday as to furnish the town cows with a belly full apiece free of expense. A small quantity of homony was brought in by a shivering boy in a linen apron, which went off rapidly at a bit a gallon, and a couple of opossums, that delicious epicurean rarity, were sold in less than no time at fifteen cents each."

Washington Correspondents.

If ever there was a class of men making any pretensions to character, more corrupt and unprincipled than the professional Washington correspondents to the press in various parts of the country, I cannot point out its existence. There business being to gratify public curiosity, or to create a sensation, they are constantly tempted to falsify, to invent, and to exaggerate. It is common to talk of the corrupting influence of the party press, but this is undoubtedly its worst feature. Every intelligent man at our seat of government, State or National, knows, that as a general rule, there is not an assertion or statement in letters of this description, to be relied on. The "Spy in Washington," and Bennett's various correspondents at the sessions of Congress, have done more to corrupt the morals of this class of writers, than any conservative or restorative influence of later date and purer minds can do to purify and correct.

It is time that the independent and moral part of the press should speak out on this subject.

Pioneer Recollections.

MR. CIST:

Sir,—It may serve to fill up the picture of the past, which you are sketching in the "Advertiser," to say something of the journeys which our early settlers were sometimes compelled to take through the wilderness, when business or necessity called us to our former homes and neighbours.

The savages were so hostile, that such journeys were not often undertaken. When they were the traveler would start to Limestone by river, in a canoe or periogue, from Fort Washington or Fort Miami, as the case might be. Flatboats were always used to descend the Ohio, but were of course not adapted to ascend it. The traveler always took provision with him, and kept on what was termed the Virginia side, so called from the Virginia land claims. From Limeston his route lay to Lexington sixty-four miles, a wilderness except a station at the Blue Licks, erected by a gentleman named Lyons, who carried on making salt. He had a family of coloured people and entertained travelers. As this was the only supply of salt to the emigrants at that period, and Mr. L. dealt with great fairness with the settlers, he was very popular, and had a great run of custom for that day. From Lexington the traveler proceeded to the Crab Orchard, leaving written notices at Lexington that a party would leave the Crab Orchard at such a date. These notices or advertisements were posted at stations or on trees. This was the means of making a party from the various stations, or settlements of such as were desirous also to journey east. At the appointed time the party would assemble to proceed on horseback with their rifles to the old settlements from which they came. But though traveling in this mode in numbers and with their arms in their hands, they were often attacked by Indians, and several at different times lost their lives.

Every thing brought by the emigrants to the west, was taken out on pack horses, but as the children, both white and black, had to be taken this way also, only a few articles of the first necessity could be added. It is easy to judge the privations and sufferings of the early settlers, by this circumstance.

The first printing press in Kentucky, was set up in Lexington, by Mr. John Bradford, and the first one in Ohio, by William Maxwell, whose office was on Sycamore street, on the left hand side as you go to the river. Maxwell was son-in-law to Judge McMillan.

I traveled once in the way of which I speak in 1789 from Columbia, designing to accompany my husband on his way east as far as Lexington, where his father and mother resided, with whom I intended to stay until his return. He was on a journey to New York and Philadelphia. We left Maysville—then Limeston—with the agree-

ment not to speak a word to each other after leaving Washington, until we should reach the Blue Licks, twenty-two miles. At Washington, four miles on our journey, we learned that the Indians had attacked a party the day before of movers to Lexington. This we considered good encouragement to proceed, as the Indians would be off as rapidly as possible through fear of pursuit. They are a very cautious people, and will not attack except at an advantage. We remained at Lyons, all night, and after reaching Lexington next day, my husband set out for the Crab Orchard on his way over the mountains. In due time I received a letter from him which was taken through the wilderness by a party of settlers coming out on their way to the west. The party was attacked by Indians, and the man who had the letter killed, and the letter which had been on his person was very much stained with his blood. Others of the same party were killed at the same time. Occasionally, travelers would go up the Ohio to Wheeling, by periogue or canoe poling or paddling all the way, but most persons went the route which I have described. In ascending the river, they always kept the Virginia side, as the safest.

When the courts were first established in Cincinnati, the officers who lived in Columbia, went down in canoes, or walked the distance, but always on the Virginia side, for fear of Indians. They were obliged to take their provisions with them, as there were very few inhabitants in Cincinnati, and no boarding houses there at that period.

Navigation of the West.

It is necessary only to visit the lower Ohio and the adjacent parts of the Mississippi, to be rendered sensible of the gross neglect which the Ohio and upper Mississippi interests are sustaining at the hands of the General Government. Since I left home, were to be found the Steamboat Reindeer snagged just below Memphis, the Henry Bry sunk near Randolph, the Manhattan snagged just above Cairo, all in the Mississippi; and the Richmond broke on a rock at the Grand Chain, and the Swiftsure snagged near Golconda, both on the Ohio. All this occurred within a space of three hundred miles in distance, and seven days in time. Here then are five boats destroyed in so short a space of time, and all by sunken rocks and trees, which would not be permitted to lie unremoved a single day, if they lay in the bed of one of our eastern rivers.

My visit to Memphis, has satisfied me that the West has as little to expect from the south and south west, as she has heretofore received from the north and the east, and must concentrate her strength within her own bounds, and let Congress know that if justice be refused her now, she will be apt, under the representation of 1850, in that body, not only to claim her rights for the future, but settle up the arrearages of the past.

Rail-Road to the Pacific.---No. 2.

ITS OBJECTS AND RESULTS.

In my last, my readers were presented with a brief statement of the actual character of this project of Mr. *Whitney*. I shall now advance by sketching the physical, moral and pecuniary results, which, when accomplished, it must effect.

By the time this great road shall have been completed to its *terminus* at the Pacific, connecting lines of rail-road will have been laid from the great centres of commerce and manufactures over our whole country. The rail-road communications from *Boston, New York*, and *Philadelphia*, in less than two years will be made at least as far west in the Lake regions as *Sandusky*. That from *Cincinnati* to the same point, will be effected at a still earlier date. From *Sandusky*, these routes must continue by following the north lines of Ohio and Indiana, and striking the great Pacific road, either by turning round *Lake Michigan* to the point where the road commences, on the western shore of that Lake, or take such direct line from the south end of Lake Michigan as shall enable the two roads to connect at some suitable point east of the Mississippi river, where the great rail-road crosses that stream—probably about *Prairie de Chien*. The various routes from *New Orleans, St. Louis, Natchez, &c.*, would connect these last with the various business centres of the Atlantic, south and southeast. Or if Virginia and South Carolina should strike at and cross the Ohio river, they would connect with the routes which Kentucky, Ohio, Illinois and Indiana, would make from their southern lines. Maryland, and perhaps Pennsylvania, would connect with the same route, which would extend from Cincinnati to *Lake Erie*. When this road shall have been built, the great general result will be accomplished of bringing the most distant parts of the earth, which have heretofore required a voyage of six months, to receive or return cargoes in their intercourse with each other, into a thirty days access, by land and water. From the Mississippi, which will then become the great business centre of this Republic, if not of the whole world, we can communicate in four days with our *Atlantic* or *Pacific* shores, or with the *Gulf of Mexico*. By steam vessels we can reach *Amoy*, in China, the port nearest the silk and tea provinces, from the Pacific coast in fifteen days, the distance not much greater than from *New York* to *Liverpool*. The superior facilities of rail-road travel, in saving time and expense of transportation, will, to a great extent, supercede the existing river navigation of the United States. The entire traveling of two-thirds of the world, will be across our continent, and the valley of the Mississippi must become the garden and granary of the world.

In my next, I propose to examine and render apparent the great changes, pecuniary, moral and physical, which this vast project must operate on the fabric of society throughout our country, to say nothing of the world.

Buildings in St. Louis.

The buildings put up in 1844, in St. Louis have been *estimated* by some of the newspapers there at twelve hundred, and the erections this year variously *supposed* by contractors to reach from twelve hundred to two thousand. Why cannot the actual number be ascertained by enumeration as easily in St. Louis as in Cincinnati? There can be no doubt that St. Louis is in a very thriving condition, but one statistic furnished by the editor who states these particulars convinces me that the buildings are overrated either in number or importance. He gives from what he asserts to be reliable authority, the quantity of bricks thus consumed this season at forty two millions. Our consumption of bricks for fifteen hundred houses built last year, was eighty millions, and though I have not thus far ascertained the quantity made in 1845, yet from the facts that our buildings of this year will equal those put up during the last, while they will far surpass them in magnitude, it may be safely stated at one hundred millions. If then forty-two million of bricks sufficed to do the building of twelve hundred houses, after deducting the requirement of bricks for other purposes, they must have been of only half the size of ours. This is incredible. On the other hand, if fifty millions of bricks were used in the building of such ware and dwelling houses as we put up they could not have built more than five hundred houses.

This will be better understood when I state what is susceptible of easy proof, that thirty-one buildings alone of the fifteen hundred erections of this year in Cincinnati and its adjacency, have consumed more than eight millions of bricks.

To those like myself, who are unwilling to take guesses in these matters, and who know nothing of St. Louis but by information, a regular ascertainment in actual count by some individual in that city of the houses there, would be interesting and satisfactory.

Landscape and Map Engraving.

This is a line of business in Cincinnati entirely distinct from bank note engraving, and has been carried on extensively and successfully by Messrs. Doolittle & Munson, here, for the last fifteen years. They are in fact the oldest engravers in the west. The engraving and printing of maps is their principal business, and their maps of the United States, Ohio, Illinois and Indiana, are extensively distributed throughout the whole country, and especially the west. Their standard maps are as follows:—

1. The United States, 54 by 42 inches.
2. Ohio, 54 by 60 inches.
3. Map of Illinois and Indiana, in townships.
4. Map of Iowa and Wisconsin.
5. Same, sectional.
6. Same, in townships.

They have also executed a fine map of the Mississippi river, exhibiting its various bends, reaches, cut offs and bars, with the respective plantations on its margin, which is the fullest and and most accurate steamboat guide extant.

Of the Ohio map, which has been for several years before the public, they have sold to the value of twelve thousand dollars. Of the United States map, which has only been a year before the public, they have disposed of four thousand copies. This is the only map yet published of the United States, which includes Texas, and that Republic is here represented in its various counties and other geographical divisions. In the preparation of these maps there are twelve thousand yards of bleached muslin six quarters wide, annually consumed, with map paper of a quality equal to seventeen dollars per ream. One ream of this size makes one hundred maps. This firm maintains agencies at New York, Providence, R. I.; Richmond, Va., and Baltimore, and sells its publications extensively at Philadelphia itself, along side of the great map producing establishments of that city. Our Cincinnati maps will compare in accuracy and beauty with those made in any part of the United States.

Twenty-four persons are kept in employment in the various departments of the establishment.

Our Red Brethren.

It is probably known to most of my readers that the Cherokees settled beyond the Mississippi are enjoying most of the blessings of civilization, a newspaper and national legislature among the rest. This periodical, which is called "The Cherokee Advocate," is an excellent publication, and might shame many of its competitors for dispensing knowledge among the whites; but the *National Committee*, as they call their legislature, is indeed *sui generis* in character, business, and nomenclature.

On the 22d Oct., the petition of *Messenger Tiger* for a divorce was rejected, not coming, as they correctly judged, within the purview of their appropriate business. I commend their example to the Legislature of Ohio.

October 23d, a bill regulating payment of sub-

scriptions to the Cherokee Advocate was passed. Happy printer, whose collections are attended to by the public authorities! Same day two *public cooks* were appointed by the legislature. It seems thus in legislating for the public the Committee does not neglect its own welfare.

On the 28th, Mr. *Six Killer* proposed the passage of "a bill for the more effectual suppression of the introduction and vending of intoxicating spirits in the country:"—refered to a committee of which Six Killer was chairman.

Nov. 1st, *Bark Flute* offered an amendment to the act creating solicitors and defining their duties. Read and laid on the table.

The Staff of Life.

Flour has risen, owing to the prospect of famine in the British Islands. In the same measure the baker's loaf has diminished here in size and increased in value. This must set numbers to baking their own bread.

To make good bread two or three things are requisite. First, good flour; secondly, an oven of bricks, or a good cooking stove; and, thirdly, skill in mixing and baking.

But I do not design to inflict an essay on this subject, important though it be. I hold to the philosophy which teaches by example, and invite my acquaintances, saying nothing of friends, to call at my office and partake of a baking, which will illustrate what good bread is, and what every body ought to have within reach; in good flour, first rate cooking stoves, and proper baking. Let them come if they do not mean to live and die in ignorance. They will then find out who sells the best flour in the city.

A lunch, not *a la fourchette*, but *au doigt*, may be found accordingly at my office, this day at two o'clock. Those who are afraid to spoil their appetites by partaking it at that hour, may confine themselves to a *taste*, or even to a *glance*.

I hold that not one man in ten in Cincinnati buys flour such as he ought to; that not one in twenty has the kind of cooking apparatus he should possess, and that not one in fifty knows the luxury of a fine home made loaf, such as is within the reach of most, and of which I propose to furnish a sample.

Destroying the Romance.

A capital story is told of a young fellow, who one Sunday strolled into a village church, and, during the service, was electrified and gratified by the sparkle of a pair of brilliant black eyes, which were riveted upon his face. After the service, he saw the possessor of the bewitching orbs leave the church alone, and emboldened by her glances, he ventured to follow her, his heart aching with rapture. He saw her look behind, and fancied she evinced some emotion at recognising him. He then quickened his pace, and

she actually slacked hers, as if to let him come up with her—but we will permit the young gentleman to tell the rest in his own way:—
"Noble young creature!" thought I—"her artless and warm heart is superior to the bonds of custom."

I reached within a stone's throw of her. She suddenly halted and turned her face towards me. My heart swelled to bursting. I reached the spot where she stood. She began to speak, and I took off my hat, as if doing reverence to an angel.

"Are you a pedlar?"

"No, my dear girl, that is not my occupation."

"Well, I don't know," continued she, not very bashfully, and eyeing me very sternly—"I thought when I saw you in the meeting house, that you looked like the pedlar who passed off a pewter half dollar on me about three weeks ago, and so I determined to keep an eye on you. Brother John has got home now, and he says if he catches the feller, he'll wring his neck for him; and I ain't sure but you are the good-for-nothing rascal after all."

Ohio against the World.

The fine steer Distribution, seven years old, raised by one of the Renicks, the great cattle feeders of the Scioto Valley, has been lately purchased by Messrs. Vanaken Wunder and John Butcher, two of our long established victualers, for the approaching holydays. He is estimated to weigh almost four thousand pounds, and will furnish doubtless an article of splendid beef, such as has not lately been seen in our markets, fine as they usually are in this line. The animal may be seen in the wagon yard of Mr. Marchant, corner of Ninth and Sycamore streets, and is worth a visit. I have not seen so fine a brute since Col. Chapin of New York, exhibited in 1808, his superb stall fed oxen *Maximus* and *Magnus*.

The Moustache.

Fashions and customs, apparently absurd, are generally founded on reason, although the reason may sometimes be difficult to trace. We all know that many fashions have been introduced in the courts of Europe to conceal the personal blemishes or defects of kings or other potentates, such as the wearing of the hair long, &c., and the introduction of cravats for the concealment of wens and scars. • But I was not aware until a day or two since that the *Moustache*, or beard on the upper lip, was suffered to grow for a special and deliberate purpose. The custom originated with the diplomacy of France. A well trained diplomatist, however excited, internally keeps his eye and cheek under such discipline as to betray nothing of his sentiments or intentions. But it is found impracticable by the mere exercise of will to arrest the play of the muscles of the upper lip, and to hide the least vestige of motion there, the moustache is permitted to grow.

I know not what apology can be made for the tuft on the chin or under the lip, which assimilate man, or rather the *mannee* to the goat.

The Bridegroom to his Bride.

Four years ago dear love!
And we were strangers; in a distant land
Long had it been my lonely lot to rove;
And I had never touched that gentle hand,
Or looked into the lustre of those eyes,
Or heard that voice of lovely melodies,
Winning its way unto the listener's heart,
And gladdening it, as a fresh stream doth part
The grass and flowers, and beautifies its road
With fresher hues, by its sweet tide bestowed.
Then I had never heard that name of thine,
Which on this blessed day hath merged in mine!

Three years ago, mine own,
And we had met—'twas but acquaintanceship;
There was no tremor in the courteous tone
Which, greeting thee, flowed freely to my lip
At every interview. Thy beauty seemed
Indeed the very vision I had dreamed
Of woma 's loveliest form; but that it shrined
So bright a gem, so true and pure a mind,
I did not early learn: for thou art one
Whose gentle, kindly actions ever shun
The glare of day. I knew not *then* the power
That seems thy richest gift at this blest hour.

Another year went by,
And we were *friends!*—"dear friends" we called
each other—
We said our bosoms throbbed in sympathy,
That we were like a sister and a brother.
Ah! but do brothers' hearts thrill through each
chord,
At a dear sister's smile or gracious word!
Do sisters blush, and strive the blush to hide,
When a fond brother lingers at her side?
Do friends, and nothing more, shrink from sur-
mise,
And dread to meet the keen world's scrutinies,
And tremble with a vague and groundless shame,
And start when each doth hear the other's name?

One little year ago,
And we were lovers—lovers pledged and vowed—
The unsealed fountains of our hearts might
flow;
Our summer happiness had scarce a cloud.
We smiled to think upon the dubious past,
How *could* so long our self-delusions last?
We laughed at our own fears, whose dim array
One spoken word of love had put away.
In love's full blessed confidence we talked,
We heeded not who watched us as we walked;
And day by day hath that affection grown,
Until this happy morn that makes us one.

Beloved! 'tis the day,
The summer day, to which our hearts have
turned,
As to a haven that before them lay,
A haven dim and distantly discerned.
Now have we reached it, and our onward gaze
Must henceforth be beyond earth's fleeting days,
Unto a better home, when having loved
ONE more than e'er each other—having proved
Faithful to HIM, and faithful to the vow
That in our hearts is echoing even now
We two shall dwell His glorious throne before,
With souls, not *bound*, but blended evermore.

Maria Edgeworth.

In my late visit to Memphis, I met with an intelligent young Irishman, who having resided here some years, has lately revisited his native country. I gathered at his hands several interesting notices of *Maria Edgeworth*, who resides in the town where my new acquaintance was brought up. I shall state but one or two at present.

Miss Edgeworth, as is well known, after the publication, more than thirty years since, of *"Patronage,"* had given nothing to the press. But the Edinburg reviewers having taken occasion to insinuate that the works of fiction bearing her name, had been written by her father, *Richard Lovel Edgeworth*, as had been rendered apparent by their cessation, after his death; Miss Edgeworth was piqued into a reappearance on the literary arena with *"Helen."* The copy right of this she sold at twenty-five hundred pounds sterling, more than twelve thousand dollars. On Sir Walter Scott's visit to her, he made her sensible that she had disposed of the book at a sacrifice, and as a consequence, she has refused various offers for a work on which she has been since employed, intending to be her own publisher *henceforth.* Miss E. is over eighty years of age, but with unfaltering health and spirits. The title of the new volume is, *"As you like it."*

My Memphis acquaintance was employed by Maria Edgeworth in transcribing "Helen" for the press. Of course he is thoroughly acquainted with her and her writings. While he does full justice to her talents, he represents her as destitute of patriotic feeling, and so thoroughly English in her tastes, partialities, and prejudices, as to be rendered incapable of doing justice to Irish character and feeling.

My own estimate of Miss Edgeworth, if I may state it without presumption, is entirely different. She never wrote but for the direct purpose of inculcating some great moral principle, and has done more for the world in this respect than all the novel writers of the last fifty years, Walter Scott inclusive. She wrote for the London market and English readers.

Shut the Door.

A hint in time is like a stitch in time, and not only saves additional hinting, but much ill-humour in the breast of suffering humanity. Of all nations under the sun, there are none which may compare with Americans in trespassing on the the score of leaving doors open, and this when the thermometer is probably down to zero.

I remember traveling a few years since with an observing and intelligent Englishman. "Every nation," he remarked to me, "has its dis-

tinctive peculiarities, and if I were to point out the characteristic feature of your countrymen, it would be that they never shut doors after them. In the course of nearly two years traveling through the United States you are the first individual I have noticed shutting a door after him." I laughed, and expressed an opinion that the case could not be so general as he thought. "If you find any man between here and Columbus shut a door after him, I will pay your bill when we leave that city." We were then at Sharon, and I suppose that on our journey we stopped at thirty different places to take our meals or water the horses. It was as inclement a spell of weather as ever I traveled in. At every public house there were blazing fires in the bar-rooms, and yet the very individuals whose first movement after they got in was to punch the fire afresh, invariably left the doors wide open, even in cases where they led direct to the road or the street. "Landlord," said I, in one case, where a carpenter was employed repairing the door, what do you keep doors to your room for?" He stared as if to enquire what I meant. "Why," said I, "there is no earthly use for a door in a country where nobody shuts it. There have been twenty persons out and in through the opposite door since we came, and I have not seen the first man shut it." Turning to my English acquaintance, I then said, "I give up the debate."

Citizens and Strangers.

The inhabitants of a city acquire from coming into daily contact with numbers in the various relations and occupations of life, a character and appearance, which enables them to detect a stranger from our interior towns at a glance. He may get his clothes or his hat or boots, or any thing else, from our most fashionable establishments. Still there is something in his gait or want of easy self-possession, or a difference in shuffling over city side-walks, which points him out as at once the stranger. In this manner our dry goods clerks know a young lady from the interior of Ohio or from Kentucky on her very entrance, and act the salesman accordingly. There are other marks still more palpable which expose persons visiting a large city to imposition and even robbery, from which the citizen is exempt. If a stranger walks our street, as he may occasionally be seen, eating an apple in the streets, perhaps with a knife open in his hand, such an individual is sure to be followed, and in all probability victimized, by some of the loafing gentry which infest every large city. Stopping on the side-walks to converse, or at a picture or fancy shop to look at fineries, also marks out a subject to depredators. Opening a pocket book in the streets to examine if its contents are safe, exposes the individual doing it to dangers of the same sort. Hence we find that most cases of picking pockets or street robbery, are perpetrated on strangers, while citizens are visited and plundered by breaking into their houses.

Reminiscences of the War of 1812.

The Hon. Lemuel Sawyer, who was a member of Congress in 1812, furnishes the following interesting reminiscences in a letter to the editor of the New York Courier and Enquirer:

I well remember the occasion of the presentation by Mid. Hamilton, of the flag of the Macedonian. I was present, though unintentionally, at the grand naval ball, given about the 14th of December, 1812, by the citizens of Washington, to Capt. Stewart, in return for one he had given them a little previous, on board his ship.

The ball was held at Tomlinson's Hotel, on Capitol Hill, where I boarded; and being somewhat indisposed, I had retired to bed just as the ball opened. The music, and the regular vibration of the floor to the motion of the dance, kept me awake. I considered as I was thus condemned to suffer the evil of the ball, I might as well compensate myself by its gratification. I found it well filled with the beauty and fashion of the place, and honoured with the presence of Mr. and Mrs. Madison, and the Heads of the Departments, among whom was Paul Hamilton, the Secretary of the Navy, his lady and two handsome daughters.

In the midst of our enjoyment, at about eleven o'clock, a messenger came to the door and communicated some news secretly to the manager. They were then observed to whisper something to Mr. Hamilton, who had a private conversation with the President. Immediately it was buzzed about that a messenger had come and was waiting below, with the glad tidings of a signal victory of one of our ships over one of the British, with equal force.

In a moment, and without the least noise or confusion, an arrangement was made by the managers, to give full effect to the fortunate co-incident. The Secretary's impatience to run down stairs and meet his son, was restaained, and a delegation of three gentlemen were appointed to wait on Mid. Hamilton and invite him up, with the trophy of victory of which he was the bearer, the flag of the Macedonian.

An opening was left through the crowd of spectators, from the door to the part of the room. Secretary Hamilton and his family were placed at the bottom of the passage, and in front of the door, while the President and his lady, with the members of the cabinet, were placed on each side. A breathless silence prevailed. The ladies stood up on the back seats, between the columns that supported the ceiling, the whole length of the room, gazing with intense interest at the door.

It may be mentioned that Mid. Hamilton had been absent two years, and that he had escaped, by a miracle, from the conflagration of the Richmond theatre, the winter before, by breaking through the sash of one of the upper windows, and leaping to the ground, a distance of thirty feet. At length the head of the procession entered the room, consisting of Mid. Hamilton, supported on each side by a member of the committee, followed by a train of gentlemen, having the captured flag.

Young Hamilton, seeing his parents waiting his approach with outstretched arms, with modest demeanor and accelerated steps threw himself into the arms of his mother, who hid her face in his bosom, overcome by her feelings of silent joy; from thence he tore himself to grasp his father's hand in a long and cordial shake, and ended by returning the enraptured embrace of his sisters.

As soon as this highly dramatic scene was over, one sudden burst of huzzas resounded through the room, The flag was paraded, and marched through the room to the tune of Hail Columbia —after which it was brought before Mrs. Madison, and laid at her feet, but she did not tread on it, as some of the opposition papers alleged. You may well expect that this new and unexpected feature in the ceremony, gave an increased zest to the entertainment, and that it went off with charming and enhanced gusto.

Young Hamilton was a very handsome officer, and invested as he was, with the virgin honours of this great naval victory which dissolved the charm of British invincibility on the ocean, was the cynosure of all the fair eyes present; but he bore his triumph meekly. He was promoted to a lieutenancy, and in that capacity was cut in two by a chain shot, in the action of the President with the Endymion, or rather a British squadron off the coast of Rhode Island, a few months after, while he was bravely discharging his duty under the gallant Decatur.

A Western Simile.

At Memphis, I met with a very intelligent coloured Baptist clergyman, from Jackson, Tennessee. Finding out I was from Cincinnati, among other questions he asked me, "Do you know a preacher there, Dr. S.?" "Perfectly," I replied. "Well sir," said he, "he lived five or six years in our town, and I heard he had gone to your place. He is a most wonderful man, don't you think so?" "I don't know," I replied, "we have abler preachers than the Doctor in Cincinnati, I think." "That's what I think too," replied my acquaintance—He scatters like a shot gun. Those who know how a shot gun stands in the estimation of a western man, as compared with the rifle, will understand, and relish accordingly the simile. It was so apposite that I gave way to a hearty burst of merriment. And I shall never hear a preacher of that description, without thinking of the shot gun.

Anecdote of Gen. Jackson.

A distinguished politician of Cincinnati, on a visit to Washington in 1835, was accounting to, Gen. Jackson for the defeat at a recent election, of the party to which he belonged, by alleging that "they had not used proper policy, and that a little management in the disposal of a certain question, would have doubtless rendered their party successful," with other remarks of similar tenor. The general heard him through without making the slightest comment, after which, walking up to the fire place, he knocked the ashes out of the pipe he had been smoking, which he deposited on the mantel, then turning to his visitor, he observed : " Mr. ——, you are a young, as I am an old man—suffer me to give you a word of advice: never use that abominable word *policy*, again, in that sense, nor practice the principle. Rely on it sir, honesty is as much the best policy in politics as it is in any thing else.

Journal of Rev. David Jones in 1773.--No. 4.
Communicated by H. G. Jones, Jr., of Leverington, Pa.

Wednesday 17th, Killbuck's son was kicked badly by a horse, therefore no business could be done, for he could not leave him. Thursday 18th, in the afternoon, Killbuck told me that the young men were very desirous to hear me preach; consequently I concluded to preach next day. In the evening conversed with Joseph Peappi, who was willing to interpret for me, but when I told him my Society allowed me only to pay five pound a month, he said he would have seven pounds. I find the Indians from the greatest to the least, are mercenary and excessively greedy of gains; indeed they are so lazy, that they are always needy, and must be so, if they do not apply themselves to cultivating their land, for deer are scarce, so that the great part of the year, they rather starve than live. Mr. Evans, who is a trader in this town, told me that last summer they supported themseves by sucking the juice of green cornstalks. Friday 19th, I expected to preach, but Killbuck told me that they were not yet fully united on the point. I found the king was not much for it, though he said little; neither have I any reason to believe that Joseph was desirous of it, for I was often told by the traders that the Moravians taught their Indians to disregard others, and by Joseph's talk I believe there is too much reason for the report. I asked Killbuck why they were not agreed about my preaching; he said if I had come last fall while they were in the notion of it, it would have been otherwise. But I found by conversing with him, that they were jealous, lest the white people had some design of enslaving them, or something of that nature. He said that a Highland officer took one of their Indian women as his wife and went to Maryland near Joppa, and he had heard—from a gentleman of Philadelphia—that there he sold her as a slave: as they never could see the squaw, they were ready to conclude the case was so. I told him I never heard of it, and was certain that it could not be true that she remained in slavery; for if the officer was so bad as to be guilty of such a crime, the law of our land allowed no Indian to be a slave, and the magistrates would surely set her free. He said their people did not know our law, and therefore such reports as this made

them afraid of us, and said he, what has become of the woman, for she has never come back to us again? I replied that I could not tell—perhaps she was dead, or if alive, did not choose to come.

By this time I was almost starved, for what they call a feast, with us would be considered a fast; no meal was to be had for love or money. I bought milk for nine pence a quart, and butter for two shillings a pound, but could not be half supplied. From the king I bought the rump of a deer, dried after their fashion in the smoke to preserve it, which made it very disagreeable. I had coffee, chocolate and tea, but sugar was very scarce, so that I could not often use it. Therefore, on Saturday 20th, I made enquiry for a guide to go with me towards the Ohio. The season was as cold as severely cold weather at Philadelphia, so that the king and Capt. Killbuck would not suffer me to go, for they said the cold was so great that it would kill an Indian, and therefore would surely kill me. The weather continued so intensely cold that I was convinced that travelling was impracticable—though my continuance was very disagreeable, for notwithstanding the traders of this town were very civil, yet they had no taste for religion, so that I was alone and had no suitable sustenance, waiting the permission of Providence to depart homewards. Sabbath 21st.—This was a remarkable cold day. I spent part of it conversing with Capt. Killbuck on several subjects, in which I enquired into the belief of the Delaware Indians; —in particular I asked him if they believed there was a God who created all things. He said they all believed in this. Then I asked if they believed that when a person died, his soul went either to a happy place or a bad one;—he said this was their belief. Then I enquired whether they knew that God would by his great power raise all the dead to life again—to which he replied that this they knew nothing of, until lately they had heard it among the Moravian Indians. But these Indians have been so long acquainted with us, that it is not easy to determine what they have learned of us. To-day Killbuck told me, that as they had concluded their feast, if I had an interpreter, I might preach as much as I pleased; but he would not accept of Joseph, for he said I might as well not speak as to have Joseph, for instead of delivering what I said he would say what his own heart thought. I soon perceived that Killbuck had such an aversion to Joseph, that nothing could be done if he was made use of: therefore all I spoke in the way of preaching was in the council, using Capt. Killbuck as my interpreter. He is a sensible man in common affairs, but knows not half as much as Joseph in matters of religion. I saw now, that through the want of Mr. Owens, my old interpreter, I was altogether frustrated in this visit and could do nothing. To-day the king and council concluded that no more rum should be drank in this town, and that there should be no dancing except at their Triennial Feast. This made me think of the laws of New Jersey about horseracing, in which there were such reserves as evidently demonstrated that some of the assembly loved the sport. Monday 22d, Captain Killbuck told me they were making up a speech to Governor Penn, who had written to them last fall, and that I must wait and carry it—telling me at the same time not to concern myself about a guide, as they would provide one. Tuesday 22d, the same message was sent, informing me that for six dollars I should have a guide to see me to the Ohio. This news was not the most agreeable, as the wages of the guide were unreasonable, and my daily expenses were similar. It was impossible to get a piece of bear's flesh or venison ham. This people live very poorly—their land, however, is good, but the price is in fool's hands. In the afternoon a messenger came for me to wait on the king and council. I attended, and found about twenty persons convened in their council house, which was sixty feet by twenty-eight. It had one post in the middle,— there were two fires around which the Indians sat on skins, nearly all having long pipes which they kept in constant use. They prepared a stool for me, and presented me with a bowl of homony, of which they were eating, but they had a great advantage over me by reason of their very wide mouths which suited the broad ladle, used by them instead of a spoon—one ladle serving for four or five Indians. After our repast a sheet of paper was brought, and Killbuck being interpreter informed me that it was their desire that I should write to Governor Penn from them, desiring him to let his people know, that, if they or any white man or Indian brought rum to their side of the Allegheny or Ohio, they had appointed six men on penalty of death, to stave every keg; and that he would let Gov. Franklin know that they desired all the Jersey Indians to move to them, as their country was large enough. According to request I drew up a letter and had every word of it interpreted by Capt. Killbuck and an assistant. This I delivered to his honour Richard Penn. Wednesday 24th, I was called to the council, and was desired to deliver a speech to the Quakers of Philadelphia; but there was nothing in the message worthy of writing, and hence I delivered it verbally to Mr. Thomas Wharton of Philadelphia. As I was to start on my journey the next day, I took leave of them at this meeting—giving them all the advice I thought proper, which they seemed to receive in a friendly manner—so that we parted in love and peace.

These Indians are not defective in capacity, and their long acquaintance with us has given some of them better notions than many other savages hold. They are as void of government as the Shawanese—their virtues are few—their vices nearly the same as those of other Indians. Their apparel and customs are similar to those of the Shawanese; but they do not paint as much, and they have a great feast once in three years. I asked Killbuck the reason of this, to which he replied that it might have had some meaning at first, but it was only observed as an old custom. These Indians have no kind of worship but incline to have learning among them, and are beginning to farm. Indeed it appears to me that a schoolmaster and minister may go with safety and success among them, if they keep their conclusion to suffer no rum to be used in their country. On this subject I spoke much, and they answered with loud voices, *Kehellah*, which is the strongest affirmation. They were very civil to me, and honour a minister. Their number, including men, women and children, is about six hundred: they increase much more than the Shawanese, licentiousness and polygamy not being so common. This town is in no regular form. Neither these nor the Shawanese claim any distinct property in land, nor do they know where their boundaries are. *Nectotwhealemon* is among them styled a king, and is considerably honoured—his house has a good stone chimney—a good loft and stairs. Providence seems to point out the civilizing of these Indians, for a farming life will lead to law, learning, and government to secure property. Capt. Killbuck told me he saw there was a need of a magistrate to recover debts and expected by and by they would have one; but their people did not yet understand matters. This I can say; though the want of an interpreter and provisions, rendered my continuance impracticable, yet I left them with a heart full of pity, considering them my fellow creatnres.

Thursday 25th, having got a guide ready, who cost six dollars, I set out about eleven o'clock for the river Ohio. My guide was a Jersey Indian named Pontius Newtimus, who spoke good English, but was almost as great a stranger to the woods as myself, and we had no road only a small part of the way. The spot on the Ohio at which I aimed lay a little south of east from Newcomer's Town—traveled fifteen miles and encamped by a brook, where we were surrounded by an abundance of howling wolves: we made a large fire and slept well. Friday 26th, we set out about eight o'clock, and traveled over exceedingly fine land for wheat—covered with excellent timber and gooseberry bushes. Crossing a number of brooks running southwardly, we came at last to a creek about fifteen feet wide running southeast, where we encamped. We could not tell whether this run into the Ohio or Mooskingung; however we slept safe on its bank in the midst of the wilderness, having traveled at least thirty miles.

Saturday 27th, we soon left this creek and went through the woods an east course, until at length we came to a creek which we followed, and a little before sunset came to the river Ohio, opposite Wheeling. This creek comes into the Ohio against an island and was not mentioned in Hutchins' map; therefore, as I gave information of it, in the map it will bear my name. Sabbath 28th, I parted with my guide in great love and friendship, having traveled at least seventy-five miles together in the solitary wilderness; and though he behaved very well, yet I must say that I was not without some fear lest he might have done me an injury. I went about four miles down the river and came to a place opposite Mr. Wm. McMeeken's, from whence I took the water for the Shawanese. The river had much driving ice in it, yet when I called Mr. McM. came over in a small canoe and took me over safely, having left my horse behind on account of the ice, but in a few days I obliged him to swim over. When I set my feet on shore on that side of the Ohio, I felt as if I was at home and hope rose high in expectation of seeing New Jersey once more. Here I tarried some weeks, waiting for my brother and Mr. Clark to return with corn from the Monongahela, for I could not set out however until I saw them, because I had left part of my clothes with them. As I am now about to depart from this famous country, I think it proper to say something on a subject which I forgot when speaking of it before. The land itself I have justly described—but this is not all the excellency of this new world, for its waters abound with the greatest abundance of famous fish that are any where to be met with. There is a kind called white perch, which is much larger than a shad and is very agreeable food; the yellow perch, called sun fish, are here as large as shad. There is another fish called Buffalo fish which is much larger than our sheep's head. Catfish of an extraordinary size are taken—some weighing one hundred pounds, and we took one from which fourteen persons ate and then part was given to the Indians. Large salmon are also to be found—some sturgeon—prodigious large pike, with herrings, chubs, mullets, and various kinds of small fish, and what is remarkable, they are found not only in the Ohio, but in the creeks. There is also a soft shell turtle, which is good food. This country abounds with an abundance of turkeys, some of which are very large—wild geese, ducks; and some swans are also seen—

and after you go near the Great Kanawha, large flocks of small green parrots are to be seen—not many pigeons—some few quails—considerable numbers of pheasants—abundance of eagles and and ravens, but very few crows and black birds. The wild animals are bears, panthers, wolves, wild cats, foxes, very few rabbits, deer, buffalo, moose deer, which are commonly called elks,—but in the Delaware language moose—some few squirrels, and plenty of raccoons, beavers and otters. Thus I have described this country and that of the Indians, together with some remarkable occurrences, and would now leave the reader; but as God was pleased to bring me through some very trying scenes, I have thought proper to communicate the same. Before doing so I wish to remark that I made many inquiries for the Welsh Indians—all accounts pointed out their residence beyond the Mississippi in the latitude of forty degrees, or thereabouts. But the accounts are so various that it is a doubt with me whether there is any such people on the continent; but if there is, a few years will discover them, for we gain knowledge fast of this western world. Friday, March 19th, I left the Ohio, and slept alone in the solitary, wild wilderness, among wild beasts, but God kept me safe and undisturbed.

On the 25th of March, I was crossing the Allegheny mountains and the snow was nine inches deep. Came to Old Town the 28th, and preached in the evening at Col. Cresap's. On my way in the following week, was taken with the pleurisy, and lay at David Bowen's, west side of the Connicocheague. On Saturday, 30th of April, had blood let and gained so much relief that in the afternoon I fell into a pleasant sleep, and had such a representation of the state of my family at home, that when I awoke I told the people that I believed my son was dead, and I found when I came home that he had died about that very time. From that time my spirit sank in me with unaccountable sadness. I would infer from this circumstance that God may reveal some things in the sleep, but in common no regard ought to be placed in slumbering imaginations. After recruiting I started home—passing through New Castle county, Delaware, having some business that way. On Thursday 22d, at a town called Chester, about sixteen miles from Philadelphia, I was informed that my favourite son was dead. Though I much expected it, the tidings struck me through the very heart with such sorrow that my soul was ready to expire. Sorrowfully I rode to Philadelphia, where I was prevailed on to stay over Sabbath. I had buried two children before, but as Jacob's heart and life were bound up in Benjamin, so were mine in this son.

Recollections of the Last Sixty Years.

BY J. JOHNSTON, Esq., *of Piqua.*

UPPER PIQUA, Nov. 26th, 1845.

MR. C. CIST, *Sir*—

In conformity to a promise made you in Cincinnati, last summer, that I would write you some account of my rambles over the mountains and throughout the west, more than a half century ago, having some weeks of leisure, during a sojourn at the Harrodsburg Springs, in August and September last, I employed the time in putting on paper what had then occurred to my mind. In the hurry of packing up my baggage, or in the confusion at Frankfort on the occasion of the funeral of the remains of Boone and his wife, I lost my manuscript, and since my return to Piqua, I have been so much occupied with the affairs of the farm, together with occasional bad health, that I could not until the present redeem my promise.

I was at Carlisle, in Pennsylvania, at sixteen years old, behind the counter in the store of a good honest Presbyterian Elder, Judge John Creigh, when it first entered my head to become an adventurer in the far west. Many of the troops who perished in the defeat of St. Clair, in 1791, rendesvoused at Carlisle, were there disciplined, prepared for the field, and marched westward. The United States owned extensive grounds and barracks there, erected during the Revolutionary War, and used at the present day as a military depot. Here some of the officers returned after the carnage at which is now called Recovery. Among these was Major Thomas Butler, who was shot in the leg, and who commanded all the troops collected at Carlisle, for the army under Gen'l. Wayne. I thus early became familiar with persons who had been in the west, heard the beauty and extent of the country described; its large lakes and rivers, boundless forests, extensive prairies; and I was determined to behold with my eyes what had been so often described in my hearing. Accordingly, the son of my patron, Judge Creigh, and myself, set out about January 7, 1793, for the Ohio, with a mercantile establishment. I crossed the mountains on foot, with the waggons, for the protection of the property, young Creigh, having preceded me on horseback to make arrangements for transporting the goods down the river. After a tedious and harassing journey in the midst of winter, through frost and snow, averaging twelve to fourteen miles a day, for there were no turnpike roads then in Pennsylvania, I reached Pittsburgh in safety with my goods, and descended the Ohio to Fort Washington, now Cincinnati, without encountering the the smallest accident. We took in for a passen-

ger at Pittsburgh, a French lady from Paris, in pursuit of her husband, an emigrant some time settled at the French grant—Gallipolis. The meeting of the parties in that wild country was interesting and affecting in the extreme. Previous to the finding of her husband, the lady's caresses were all bestowed upon a favourite dog, which had accompanied her from her own fair France. He eat with her and slept with her; but on meeting with her long lost husband, the poor dog, as was to be expected, was no longer noticed. He evidently felt the neglect, and by his looks and manner sensibly rebuked his mistress. We were detained a day and night at the station, to share in the joy of our passenger, for we had treated her kindly, and she was very grateful. In 1793, the French inhabitants at Gallipolis had a fort built, and a regular military organization for their safety from the Indians. The officers wore blue as uniform, with white facings, after the fashion of their own country. In the fall of 1794, in ascending the river to Pittsburgh, I called at Gallipolis to see our former friend madame; found her in good health, much altered in dress and appearance, alarmed about the Indians, tired of the country, and urgent upon her husband to abandon it and return to France. All kinds of merchandise were high in price, and in demand at Fort Washington. The army was cantoned at Hobson's Choice, just below where is now the city of Cincinnati. Money plenty:—the currency, with the exception of some specie, was all of the paper of the old Bank of the United States. A great proportion of the circulation was in bills of three dollars, three dollars being then the monthly pay of a private soldier. It was a common expression with the troops to call the bank bills *oblongs*. This was more especially the case at the gambling tables. Gambling was much practised among the officers and retainers of the army. The principal merchants and traders with the army at Cincinnati, in 1793 and 4, were Abijah Hunt and brothers, Smith and Findlay, the late Gen. James Findlay, O. Ormsby, Tate, afterwards Bullock, Ferguson, Wilson, Creigh, and others not remembered. Traders with the produce of the upper country were constantly coming and going. The pack horses, for transporting supplies to Forts Hamilton, St. Clair, Jefferson and Greenville, were all procured in Kentucky. Captain Benham had the command of the pack-horse department, and was called pack-horse master general. He was assisted by John Sutherland, Wallen, and others, as subordinate captains, each having the care and management of 40 horses with the requisite number of divisions. This branch of the service was very laborious and dangerous, the drivers being

30

often killed by the Indians. Ox teams were also employed in transporting supplies to the out posts above named. Several generally went together and were protected by escorts of troopers or dragoons. Pack-horse companies often went unprotected, because they went quicker and were not so liable to be attacked by the Indians.

A certain Scott Traverse owned an ox team, with wagon, frequently passing alone as far as Greenville, unharmed. He never would wait for an escort. Go always when he was ready, he prided himself on his good fortune. At last, on one of his trips, near Fort Hamilton, he was overtaken by the Indians and himself and his oxen killed, his wagon burnt, and the loading carried off and destroyed. He was often cautioned against his fool hardiness.

Elliott, the partner of Elliott and Williams, the army contractors, was killed in the summer of 1794, between Cincinnati and Fort Hamilton. He was on his way coming in from the head quarters of the army, at Greenville, having, as was reported, settled up all his business previous to the commencement of the campaign, and was not to revisit the army any more. The body when recovered was abused and mutilated by the Indians. It was brought into Cincinnati and intered. I think it was in June, 1794, I went to Greenville in an escort commanded by Major Winston of the dragoons. There were several ox teams, with pack horses, quarter masters' men, and others along; some on foot and some mounted. The late Daniel Conner of Cincinnati, and myself, were together on foot. The escort was large, extending on the road a considerable distance. A few miles in advance of Griffin's station the front of the line was fired on by the Indians, and several men killed and scalped by them, before the dragoons came up. They had detained at the station, and not a man of them came up until the mischief was all over. The officer in command was blamed, but not brought to court martial. Had his force been properly distributed in front and rear no attack would have been made. No doubt at all the Indians, as was their constant practice, had their scouts watching our progress, and finding the dragoons remiss in their duty they availed themselves accordingly. They got little or no booty I often learned from the Indians in after times, that no detachment of troops ever left the Ohio without their progress being daily watched by the Indian spies.

Kentucky against the World.

When I refered, last week, to the fine steer DISTRIBUTION, raised in Ohio, and recently bought by Messrs. *Wunder & Butcher*, for the approach-

ing holydays, as having no rival of his kind in the United States, I was not aware that an equally remarkable animal from Kentucky would be here to divide public attention and admiration in this line.

It is worth a walk the whole length of the city, to see a remarkable heifer raised by Mr. *Roberts*, of Kentucky, for which two hundred dollars has been paid by the same persons, *Vanaken Wunder* and *John Butcher*, for the purpose of gracing their stalls during the Christmas and New Years festivals. She weighs sixteen hundred pounds, and has been pronounced both the *fattest and largest heifer in the world*, by those who are familiar with the subject. They may both be seen at the stables of Mr. Isaac Marchant, corner of Ninth and Sycamore streets.

I learn that the BERRESFORDS, a family of our oldest established victualars, will have an ample supply of splendid beef and other meats during the festive season which closes the year, which I propose to notice more particularly next week.

Sleepy Worshipers.

Mr. ——, a mason by trade, having worked hard all the week, was disposed while at church on Sunday, to take a snooze. He had kept awake until the preacher had progressed some way in his sermon, when he fell into a sound sleep, and dreaming in his soporific obliviousness that he was about his work, cried out in a stentorian voice—"*Mort! more Mort!!*" The effect upon the congregation, says the Portland Argus, may be imagined.

I recollect a worthy member of the Society of Friends in Philadelphia, named *Hunson Waters*, who kept a dry goods store on Third, between Market and Arch streets. He was a man of lethargic habit, and, of course, easily overcome by sleep while attending the silent meeting of his sect. One hot summer day, while at his post at meeting, he had been full of some business reverie, and fancying himself at his own store, taking his yearly inventory, he bawled out to the scandal of his brethren and his own deep mortification—"Three thousand pieces short yellow nankins; five shillings per piece; *set that down John.*"

Ancient Bills of Lading.

The following curious document is worthy of special notice, on various accounts. It serves, in the first place, to shew that in 1729, while the House of Burgesses, in Virginia, was remonstrating against the introduction of slaves into Virginia, that New England shipping was carrying on a traffic in negroes. The continued reference to the *grace of God*, and the blending piety with commerce in this bill of lading, was perfectly characteristic of the region and the date to which it refers, although similar language in such documents would now pass for arrant hypocrisy.

The document is perfectly authentic and *verbatim*, as respects the language:

Shipped by the Grace of GOD, in good Order and well conditioned, by William Pepperell on his account and risque, in and upon the good Briga, called, the Culner,—whereof is Master under GOD for this present Voyage, Walter Osborne, and now riding at Anchor in the harbor of Piscataqua,—and by GOD'S Grace bound for Martinique, To say, ONE NEGRO MAN, call'd James, Being Marked and Numbered as in the Margent, and there to be delivered in like Order and well Conditioned, at the aforesaid Port of Martinique (the Danger of the Seas only excepted) unto Capt. Benj'a. Clark, or to his Assigns, he or they paying Freight for said Goods Nothing, with Primage and Average accustomed. In witness whereof the Master or Purser of the said Briga hath affirmed to two Bills of Lading, all of this Tenor and Date, one of which two Bills being Accomplished, the other to stand void. And so GOD send the good Briga to her desired Port in safety, AMEN.

Dated in Piscataqua, the 9th day of Feb'ua., 1729. WALTER OSBORN.

I have seen bills of lading from Liverpool, England, dated as late as 1807, very much in the same strain; and a remarkable one of the sort may be seen preserved in a frame, at the office of the Firemens' Insurance Company, corner of Main and Front streets.

A Story of Pocket Picking.

The adroitness of the nimble fingered gentry who make pocket picking their *profession* is often a matter of astonishment to the unpractised. We have heard of a case which illustrates the *legerdemain* of this wide spread and dangerous species of villany, more thoroughly than any other we have heard of. It may be relied upon as authentic.

A few weeks since, a gentleman at the Astor House, in New York, suddenly missed a gold watch, which was worth more to him than it could be to any one else. He marvelled much at its absence, for he knew he had only been in and out of the office and reading room of that hotel since he noted the hour by it. In the hope of recovering it, he advertised his loss and offered a reward of fifty dollars. The same day he received a note, informing him that he could have his watch by calling at a certain house in an obscure part of the city. After some little hesitation he resolved to go. The watch was too valuable to him to be given up without at least this attempt to recover it. So he went. His call at the door was promptly answered by a very gentlemanly looking person, who in reply to his inquiries, replied that he had in his possession the advertised watch, and that on payment of the offered reward he would deliver it up. The loser promised to pay the fifty dollars provided he was convinced the watch was his. It was exhibited, and the gentleman recognised it at once, paid the reward, and gladly placed the recovered treasure in its place in his vest pocket. As he was turning to go away he remarked,

"I am glad, as you may suppose, to get my watch back again, but I should really be pleased to know how you took it from me."

"That I will inform you," readily replied the pick pocket. "Do you remember holding an animated conversation with two other gentlemen in the reading room of the Astor on the morning you lost your watch."

"I do," replied the loser.

"Well, do you not also remember that a gentleman who stood close by, left his newspaper, drew near, and finally joined in the discussion."

"Very distinctly," replied the other, "and also that he engaged in it with much warmth."

"Precisely," continued the narrator, "and do you not remember that he at one time, in his earnestness, tapped you two or three times on the left breast, *thus?*" (suiting the action to the word.)

"Yes," replied the gentleman.

"*Then* I took your watch," said the other, and turning, shut the door and disappeared.

The gentleman returned to the Astor, musing on this strange occurrence, and while relating it to some of his wondering friends, was astonished to find that his watch was again missing. When the adroit knight of the nimble fingers described to him how he *once* filched from him his watch, he took it again! So the gentleman finally lost his watch, after having paid to the thief the reward for its recovery!

Responsibilities.

When a Brazilian introduces you to an acquaintance, he says, "This is my friend Mr. so and so. *I will be responsible for any thing he steals.*" Such a responsibility would be dangerous in some places.

I should have thought this a caricature, but for a circumstance of a kindred nature, which it recalls to my remembrance.

Many years ago I was a clerk to an individual, whose great infirmity was a suspicious nature. He appeared to have no confidence at all in mankind. On one occasion a gentleman from the south, a wealthy planter, who had bought a large bill of goods at the store, after taking supper with my employer, was spending the evening in the counting room. After sitting to a late hour, the gentleman rose to depart. The counting room communicated with the store, through a long and dark passage, and his path to the street was through the store. Handing me a candle my employer addressed me—"Mr. Cist will you be good enough to light Mr. —— to the door:" then sinking his voice to a whisper, audible but to me—"*and see that he steals nothing by the way.*"

A Recollection of the Stage.

William B. Wood, Esq., formerly manager of the Philadelphia Theatre, took a benefit at the Baltimore Theatre, after having been forty-seven years on the stage, and always sustaining the character of a gentleman. His father taught school in the large building in the rear of Trinity Church, and young Wood was usher. He was afterwards a clerk in the auction store of Hoffman

& Gloss. He is about seventy-four years of age. Forty years ago I saw *William B. Wood* and *Syencer H. Cone* performing in the same piece on the boards of the Philadelphia stage. Until I saw this paragraph I was not aware that Mr. W. was still living. Cone soon after left the stage, united with the Baptist Church under the care of Dr. *Staughton,* an eminent divine of that denomination, prepared for the ministry, and has been ever since a successful and venerated minister of the gospel in the City of New York. How widely different has been the course of these men, once rival candidates for public favour. I cannot but believe Mr. Cone made the wiser choice. Mr. Wood's private character was always considered irreproachable; but at the close of a long life, can he look back to the influence he has exerted on society with the same consciousness that his cotemporary must feel, that the community has been the wiser and better for his existence?

A Fairy Story.

It may be considered impertinent, were I to explain what is meant by a changeling; both Shakspeare and Spenser have already done so, and who is there unacquainted with the Midsummer Night's Dream, and the Fairy Queen?

Now Mrs. Sullivan fancied that her youngest child had been changed by "faries' theft," to use Spenser's words, and certainly appearances warranted such a conclusion; for in one night her healthy blue eyed boy had become shrivelled up into almost nothing, and never ceased squalling and crying. This naturally made poor Mrs. Sullivan very unhappy; and all the neighbours, by way of comforting her, said, that her own child was beyond any kind of a doubt, with the good people, and that one of themselves had been put in its place.

Mrs. Sullivan, of course, could not disbelieve what every one told her, but she did not wish to hurt the thing; for although its face was so withered, and its body wasted away to a mere skeleton, it had still a strong resemblance to her own boy: she, therefore, could not find it in her heart to roast it alive on the griddle, or to burn its nose off with the red hot tongs, or to throw it out in the snow on the road-side, notwithstanning these and several like proceedings were strongly recommended to her for the recovery of her child.

One day who should Mrs. Sullivan meet but a cunning woman, well known about the country by the name of Ellen Leah (or Ellen Gray.) She had the gift, however she got it, of telling where the dead were, and what was good for the rest of their souls; and could charm away warts and wens, and do a great many wonderful things of the same nature.

"You're in grief this morning, Mrs. Sullivan," were the first words of Ellen Leah to her.

"You may say that Ellen," said Mrs. Sullivan, "and good cause I have to be in grief, for there was my own fine child whipped off from me out of his cradle, without as much as by your leave, or ask your pardon, and an ugly dony bit of shrivelled up fairy put in its place: no wonder then that you see me in grief, Ellen."

"Small blame to you, Mrs. Sullivan," said Ellen Leah; "but are you sure 'tis a fairy?"

"Sure!" echoed Mrs. Sullivan, "sure enough am I to my sorrow, and can I doubt my own two eyes? Every mother's soul must feel for me?"

"Will you take an old woman's advice?" said Ellen Leah, fixing her wild and mysterious gaze upon the unhappy mother; and after a pause, she added, "but you'll call it foolish?"

"Can you get me back my child—my own child, Ellen?" said Mrs. Sullivan, with great energy.

"If you do as I bid you," returned Ellen Leah, "you'll know." Mrs. Sullivan was silent in expectation, and Ellen continued. "Put down the big pot, full of water, on the fire; and make it boil like mad; then get a dozen new laid eggs, break them, and keep the shells, but throw away the rest; when that is done, put the shells in the pot of boiling water, and you will soon know whether its your own boy or a fairy. If you find that it is a fairy in the cradle, take the red hot poker and cram it down his ugly throat, and you will not have much trouble with him after that, I promise you."

Home went Mrs. Sullivan, and did as Ellen Leah desired. She put the pot on the fire, and plenty of turf under it, and set the water to boiling at such a rate that if ever water was red hot —it surely was.

The child was lying, for a wonder, quite easy and quiet in the cradle, every now and then cocking his eye, that would twinkle as keen as a star in a frosty night, over at the great fire, and the big pot upon it; and he looked on with great attention at Mrs. Sullivan breaking the eggs, and putting down the egg-shells to boil. At last he asked with the voice of a very old man, "What are you adoing mammy?"

Mrs. Sullivan's heart, as she said herself, was up in her mouth ready to choke her, at hearing the child speak. But she contrived to put the poker in the fire, and to answer, without making any wonder at the words, "I'm brewing, a vick" (my son.)

"And what are you brewing, mammy?" said the little imp, whose supernatural gift of speech now proved beyond question that he was a fairy substitute.

"I wish the poker was red hot," thought Mrs. Sullivan; but it was a large one, and took a long time heating; so she determined to keep him in talk until the poker was in a proper state to thrust down his throat, and therefore repeated the question.

"Is it what I'm brewing, a vick," said she, "you want to know?"

"Yes, mammy; what are you brewing?" returned the fairy.

"Egg-shells, a vick," said Mrs. Sullivan.

"Oh!" shrieked the imp, starting up in the cradle, and clapping his hands together, "I'm fifteen hundred years in the world; I never was at a brewery of egg-shells before!"

The poker was by this time quite red, and Mrs. Sullivan seizing it, ran furiously towards the cradle; somehow or other her foot slipped, and she fell flat on the floor, and the poker flew out of her hand to the other end of the house. However, she got up without much loss of time, and went to the cradle intending to pitch the wicked thing that was in it into the pot of boiling water, when there she saw her own child in a sweet sleep, one of his soft round arms resting upon the pillow—his features were as placid as if his repose had never been disturbed, save the rosy mouth which moved with a gentle and regular breathing.

Who can tell the feelings of a mother when she looks upon her sleeping child? Why should I, therefore, endeavour to describe those of Mrs. Sullivan at again beholding her long lost boy? The fountain of her heart overflowed with the excess of joy—and she wept! tears trickled silently down her cheeks, nor did she strive to check them—they were tears not of sorrow, but of happiness.

Rail-Road to the Pacific.--No. 3.

Pecuniary Results.—The whole commerce of Europe, with the unnumbered millions of China and India, and the islands of those seas must pass entirely by this route, rendering us the carriers of the largest and most lucrative commerce on the globe. In the next place, it would enable the vast and productive valley of the Mississippi to reach, with its bulkiest articles, our whole country at profitable rates, and to dispose of an export of Indian corn to Hindustan and China, greater than the whole present crop of that article, immense as it now is, and at a price which would forever secure forty cents per bushel as a minimum rate throughout the whole valley of the Mississippi. Let me illustrate this for a moment. Rice, the great staple of those countries, usually sells there at $1 25 the *picul*—one hundred thirty-three pounds—which is of course about one cent per pound. This equalizes Indian corn to sixty cents per bushel. Corn will be taken on this rail-road to the shores of the Pacific for fifteen cents per bushel—thence to China and India for five cents more, netting forty cents per bushel to the owner.

The last year's crop of Indian corn in the United States, was nearly four hundred million bushels. This would not be a bushel to each inhabitant of those countries, and at twenty-five cents per bushel, which is the lowest average value over the whole west, must produce one hundred million dollars, almost twice the value of the cotton crop of the United States; now and for some years past, its most valuable article of export.

There is no deficiency of wealth in China to purchase our produce, for she lays the whole world under contribution by the sale of her silks, teas, &c.; and until the United States exported to that country lead and domestic cottons, which even yet form but a small part of the means to pay for our imports thence, we paid for her teas, silks, porcelain, &c., in Spanish dollars. China is in fact, so far as the accumulation of money makes a nation rich, the richest nation on the globe. And when the means of transportation, at a cheap rate, of the necessaries and luxuries which America produces for the food of mankind are thus afforded, a market will be opened there for American produce, of which we have now not the faintest idea.

Border Incident.

During the continuance of the Indian war, from 1790 to 1795, it was customary for the inmates of all the garrisons to cultivate considerable fields of Indian corn and other vegetables near the walls of their defences. Although hazardous in the extreme, it was preferable to starvation. For a part of that time no provisions could be obtained from the older settlements above, on the Monongahela and Ohio; sometimes from a scarcity amongst themselves, and always at great hazard from Indians, who watched the river for the capture of boats. Another reason was the want of money; many of the settlers having expended a large share of their funds in the journey on, and for the purchase of lands, while others had not a single dollar; so that necessity compelled them to plant their fields. The war having commenced so soon after their arrival, and at a time when not expected, as a formal treaty was made with them at Marietta, in January, 1789, which by the way was only a piece of Indian diplomacy, they never intending to abide by it any longer than suited their convenience, and no stores being laid up for a siege, they were taken entirely unprepared. So desperate were their circumstances at one period, that serious thoughts of abandoning the country were entertained by many of the leading men. Under these circumstances R. J. Meigs, then a young lawyer, was forced to lay aside the gown, and assume the use of both the sword and the plow. It is true that but little ploughing was done, as much of the corn was then raised by planting the virgin soil with a hoe, amongst the stumps and logs of the clearing, after burning off the brush and light stuff. In this way large crops were invariably produced; so that nearly all the implements needed were the axe and the hoe. It so happened that Mr. Meigs, whose residence was in Campus Martius, the garrison on the east side of the Muskingum river, had planted a field of corn on the west side of that stream in the vicinity of Fort Harmar. To reach this field the river was to be crossed near his residence in a canoe, and the space between the landing and his crop, a distance of about half a mile, to be passed by an obscure path through a thick wood.

Early in June, 1792, Mr. Meigs, having completed the labour of the day a little before night, set out on his return home in company with Joseph Symonds and a coloured boy, which he had brought with him as a servant from Connecticut. Immediately on leaving the field they entered the forest through which they had to pass before reaching the canoe. Symonds and the boy were unarmed; Mr. Meigs carried a small shot-gun, which he had taken with him for the purpose of shooting a turkey, which at that day abounded to an extent that would hardly be credited at this time. Flocks of several hundred were not uncommon, and of a size and fatness that would excite the admiration of an epicure of any period of the world, even of Apicius himself. Meeting, however, with no turkies, he had discharged his gun at a large snake which crossed his path. They had now arrived within a few rods of the landing, when two Indians, who had been for some time watching their movements and heard the discharge of the gun, sprang into the path behind them, fired and shot Symonds through the shoulder. He, being an excellent swimmer, rushed down the bank and into the Muskingum river; where, turning on his back, he was enabled to support himself on the surface until he floated down near to Fort Harmar, where he was taken up by a canoe. His wound, although a dangerous one, was healed, and I knew him twenty years afterwards. The black boy followed Symonds into the river as far as he could wade, but being no swimmer, was unable to get out of reach of the Indian who pursued them, and was seized and dragged on shore. The Indian who had captured him was desirous of making him a prisoner, which he so obstinately refused, and made so much resistance that he finally tomahawked and scalped him near the edge of the water. To this alternative he was in a manner compelled, rather than lose both prisoner and scalp; as the rangers and men at Campus Martius had commenced firing at him from the opposite shore. The first shot was fired by a spirited black man in the service of Commodore Abraham Whipple, who was employed near the river at the time.

From some accident, it seems that only one of the Indians was armed with a rifle, while the other had a tomahawk and knife. After Symonds was shot, Mr. Meigs immediately faced about in order to retreat to Fort Harmar. The savage armed with the rifle, had placed himself in the path, intending to cut off his escape, but had no time to reload it before his intended victim clubbed his gun and rushed upon his antagonist. As he passed, Mr. Meigs aimed a blow at his head, which the Indian returned with his rifle. From the rapidity of the movement, neither of them were seriously injured, although it staggered each considerably, yet neither fell to the ground. Instantly recovering from the shock, he pursued his course to the fort with the Indian close at his heels. Mr. Meigs was in the vigour of early manhood, and had, by frequent practice in the race, become a very swift runner. His foeman was also very fleet, and amongst the most active of their warriors, as none but such were sent into the settlements on marauding excursions. The race continued for sixty or eighty rods with little advantage on either side, when Mr. Meigs gradually increased his distance a-head, and leaping across a deep run that traversed the path, the Indian stopped on the brink, threw his tomahawk, and gave up the pursuit with one of those fierce yells which rage and disappointment both served to sharpen. It was distinctly heard at both the forts. About eight years since, an Indian tomahawk was plowed up near this very spot, and was most probably the one thrown at Mr. Meigs; as the rescue and pursuit from Fort Harmar was so immediate upon hearing the alarm, that he had no time to recover it. With the scalp of the poor black boy, the Indians ascended the abrupt side of the hill which overlooked the garrison, and, shouting defiance to their foes, escaped in the forest.

The excitement was very great at the garrison, and taught the inmates an useful lesson; that of being better armed and more on their guard when they went out on their agricultural pursuits. Had Mr. Meigs tried any other expedient than that of facing his enemy and rushing instantly upon him, he must inevitably have lost his life,

as the Indian was well aware of his gun being unloaded. On his right was the river, on his left a very steep and high hill; beyond him the pathless forest, and between him and the fort his Indian foe. To his sudden and unexpected attack, to his dauntless and intrepid manner, and to his activity, he undoubtedly owed his life.

The Wheat Crop of 1845.

It is now rendered certain that there is a serious deficiency in the English, and a partial failure in the European crops. The price of bread stuffs have, in consequence considerably advanced in our markets. Under these circumstances it is fortunate that our harvests have proved so abundant. The wheat and corn crops of this country are far heavier, this year, than ever before—notwithstanding their unpromising aspect early in the season. The wheat crop of this year is moderately estimated at 125,000,000 of bushels, which is an excess of 22,000,000 over the crop of 1842, (viz. 103,000,000) the largest ever before raised in the United States. We shall thus be able to feed our brethren across the Atlantic, and still have an abundance left for ourselves. The Albany Argus has the following paragraphs, which will not be uninteresting in this connection:—

The wheat crop of Michigan is comparatively larger than that of any other State in the Union. With a population of not over 400,000, she raises this year at least 7,000,000 bushels of wheat. The quality is also of the very best. The Wolverines are glorying in their abundance, and they say they can furnish Europe with all the bread she may need. The central rail-road now brings down to Detroit 10,000 bushels of wheat daily, but the supply is so very heavy at Marshall and the other depots at this busy season, that the motive power cannot take it off as fast as the forwarders require. This will give some idea of the production of Michigan. The recent advance in prices will most fortunately afford a fair profit to the producer, and thus with an immense crop he reaps a high price—which fortunate combination is all that is wanted to ensure a sound and enviable prosperity.

This fall the western States are not only peculiarly fortunate in their large crops, but also in acquiring intelligence of the late rise before the whole crop was in second hands.

The following table, which we find in the N. Y. Herald, affords material for reflection, as exhibiting the variations in our crops arising from the caracter of the season.

The production of grain in the United States for four years, according to the returns issued from the office of the Commissioner of Patents, has been as annexed:

QUANTITY OF GRAIN GROWN IN THE U. STATES.

	1840.	1842.	1843.	1844.
	Bushels.	Bushels.	Bushels.	Bushels.
Wheat,	84,822,272	102,317,34?	100,310,856	95,6?7,000
Barley,	4,161,504	2,871,622	3,230,721	3,627,000
Oats,	123,071,341	150,883,?17	145,929,666	172,247,009
Rye,	18.645,567	22,772,952	24,289,281	26,450,000
Buckwheat,	7,291,743	9,483,480	7,959,410	9,071,000
Ind. Corn,	377,531,875	441,829,246	494,618,3?6	424,953,000

Yet from the diversity of our soil, extent of country, and variety of climate, the word ABUNDANCE better exprsses the garnerings in, of every harvest.

The amount of Indian corn raised, seems a matter of wonderment. The half starved operatives of Europe may well look at those returns with glistening eyes, for it affords twenty-two bushels of corn alone for every man, woman and child in this country. Indian corn will rarely bear exportation, and therefore but little is carried abroad. It is nearly all consumed at home. Our cattle enjoy an abundance of that food which would be deemed a luxury in Europe. Such is the prolific fertility of our soil and and the extent of production under the competition of freeman.

Egypt was once called the granary of the world, but America, in the extent of its wheat production as well as the production of its quality, will throw into the shade even the fables of Herodotus.

To Readers.

No 1 of an interesting series of "Recollections of the last sixty years," being a narrative referring principally to the actual condition of things, and progress of events, in the west during that period, is this day published in the Advertiser, and will be followed by other numbers from the same pen. The writer is *John Johnston*, Esq., of *Piqua*, well known and highly appreciated in the community as a man of integrity and capacity, and who in the character of Indian agent, which he sustained for many years to the United States, has had means of becoming conversant with many interesting facts in the history and condition of those tribes who formerly inhabited the great State of Ohio, the Delawares, Shawanese and Wyandots.

I anticipate valuable materials for the future historian in the correspondence of Mr. J.

Anecdote of Napoleon.

Bonaparte, having made a visit to an aqueduct, prepared for his return to Suez: it was a dark night when he reached the coast. The flow of the tide had begun, and it was proposed to encamp and spend the night on the shore, but Bonaparte refused; he called the guide, and commanded him to lead the way. The guide, confounded by an order from a person whom the Arabs regarded as a prophet, mistook the ford, and the passage was lengthened by about half an hour. They were scarcely half way, when the waves of the flowing tide began to rise round the legs of the horses—the rapidity of the swell on the coast was great—the darkness hindered them from seeing the distance they had yet to go. General Caffarelli, whose wooden leg prevented him from holding firm in the saddle, cried out for assistance. The cry was deemed a signal of distress; the little caravan was instantly thrown into disorder; everybody fled his own way. Bonaparte alone continued tranquilly to follow his guide. Still the water rose, his horse became frightened, and refused to advance—the position

was terrible; the least delay was death. One of the guides, remarkable for his great height and Hurculean strength, leaped into the sea, took the General on his shoulders, and, holding fast by the horse's tail, carried Bonaparte like a child. In a few minutes the water rose to his arm-pits, and he began to lose his footing; the sea rose with frightful rapidity; five minutes more, and the fortunes of the world would have been changed by the death of a single man. Suddenly the Arab shouted, he felt he touched the shore; the guide, quite exhausted, fell upon his knees—the General was saved at the moment his strength was gone.

On how little more than a thread the destinies of Europe for thirty years, depended at that moment.

Powers' Greek Slave.

A foreign correspondent of the N. Y. Mirror, who has seen the work of Powers, thus eloquently writes:—

I have seen it—and I want words to express my admiration. It is so beautiful, so true, so chaste. The *treatment* of the subject, too, is admirable in detail. The figure, you are aware, is that of a young female; her manacled hands reveal her enthraled condition. She is a slave! while the classic lineaments of her calmly beautiful face, and the adjuncts of her Greek cap and drapery—arranged to form the support of the figure—delicately but intelligently announced that she is the daughter of

The clime of the unfortunate brave
Whose land, from plain to mountain cave,
Was freedom's home or glory's grave!

The figure itself is unencumbered with drapery, the position is easy, natural, unrestrained; the face thoughtful, unimpassioned, (perhaps *too calm* —that is, one might say so, if determined to find some exception,) the limbs exquisitely moulded, perfectly proportioned, displaying the perfection of female beauty in its greatest delicacy, without the slightest *nuance* of grossness. The disposal of the slight chain is most happily conceived and executed, and materially assists the sentiment of *pudeur* that pervades the composition. Indeed, the figure seems to breathe an atmosphere of purity, and to be surrounded by a halo of virgin innocence; and you gaze on the charms that the artist's hand has revealed with feelings of reverence and admiration, unmixed with a thought of earthly passion. All the world acknowledges the sculptor's triumph.

Beauty of Cincinnati.

Cincinnati is proverbially clean in its streets and avenues; a thing greatly helped by the fact that it is seated upon hilly ground, which give the streets a rapid descent for water. In its general aspect it so strikingly resembles Philadelphia that in some parts of the city I could almost believe myself there. Some Quaker angels seem to have clubbed together, and by their united strength, taken up the old city of Brotherly Love, and, bearing it over the tops of the Alleghanies, to have deposited it, joyfully, on the banks of the Ohio, in the very midst of the rich soil of "Symmes' Purchase." *There she sits*, in new-born majesty, "apparent queen." To a staid and moderate European politician the thing would seem a miracle. Here is a beautiful city, of nearly a hundred thousand inhabitants, where but fifty years ago nothing was to be seen but boon Nature's wild luxuriance of wood and soil and stream. It is such a transmutation as can be witnessed nowhere but in our beloved land; and the more one contemplates it the more will a sanguine spirit be inclined to cry—

"Visions of glory! spare my aching sight;
Ye unborn ages, crowd not on my soul!"

New Map and Gazetteer of the United States.

Messrs. SHERMAN & SMITH of New York, have recently published one of the best maps of the United States, as well as the largest, in use, being seventy-two by eighty-four inches. The agent, Mr. Moulton, is offering it to our citizens, and I can recommend it accordingly.

This Map is accompanied by a new and valuable Gazetteer of the United States. If the ably condensed article refering to Cincinnati be a fair specimen of the book at large, as I presume it to be, this volume will prove a valuable topographical dictionary for general use.

Getting to the Fire.

Every one has heard the anecdote of Dr. Franklin, who when traveling upon a raw and gusty day, stopped at a tavern, and found the bar-room fire entirely pre-occupied by a set of village loafers, who could not budge an inch, in the way of civility to a stranger. He called for a peck of oysters for his horse, and when the unmannerly cubs all went to the stable to witness the novel spectacle of a horse eating oysters, the doctor selected a comfortable place at the fire " to roast his oysters and warm himself." Of course the *horse didn't* eat the oysters, but the *doctor did.* About as good a story is told in the Spirit of the Times, of a captain in the recruiting service at the west, where were a lot of loungers, and no one offered him a seat. Knowing every thing about the grocery he went behind the counter, and seizing a keg marked " powder," threw it upon the fire exclaiming, " Gentlemen, it's my opinion that we've lived long enough." The way they evacuated the premises wasn't slow. Of course the keg was empty.

Tea and Toast.

One day last week the London Dock Company, at the opening of their new range of tea-ware-houses, gave a party to the tea division of the mercantile interest of London. The " usual

toasts" were given on the occasion; and though, no doubt, these toasts were, so to speak, buttered, we believe that they were not exactly that description of toast which is " usually given" at tea. On the health of Souchong being proposed,

Souchong (through his representative) declared that he had never risen—in the market or anywhere else—under circumstances so flattering as the present. He had been often drunk; though he was never either tipsy himself, nor the cause of intoxication in others; for his was the draught that cheered but not inebriated. Around him were the merchant princes of London; though he must regret the absence of one who was at once a merchant prince and a merchant tailor. He felt that he had now been on his legs long enough, and could only return his best thanks for the honour that had been done him.

Gunpowder felt himself ready to explode with gratitude for the distinction which had just been conferred upon him. He hoped to continue to give satisfaction—in a friendly way: he was not that gunpowder that feared to be superceded by steam: he respected steam for its connection with boiling water—which was his element. It was his boast to load the caddies, and not the cannons, of his country. Allied as he trusted ever to be, with the milk of human kindness and the sugar of free labour, it should ever be his aim to promote universal peace.

Green Hyson, in acknowledging the compliment that he had just received, would notice with pride an epithet which had been applied to him. He had been called evergreen: he felt thus associated with the laurel; and if the laurel bound the poet's temples, he had often to boast of stimulating the poet's brain: he was aware that it had been insinuated that he was hostile to the nervous system; this was a calumny and he took that public opportunity of making the assertion.

Young Hyson, after the eloquent speech just made by his brother, would merely express his thanks. He was unaccustomed to public speaking; his experience being limited to the silent spouting of the kettle.

" The Genuine Leaf " having been proposed—

A stranger rose to respond. He claimed the appellation which had just been mentioned: he was the British Leaf. (*Indignant cries of "Turn him out!"*)

A scene of indescribable confusion here ensued, amid which the pretender was expelled from the room. Order having at length been restored, harmony resumed her sway, and several sentimental and comic songs having been sung, the company separated at an advanced hour.—*Punch.*

New Zealand Melody.

Wallaloo! Wallaloo!
Love white man and eat him too!
Stranger white, but that no matter!
Brown man fat, but white man fatter!
Put him on hot stone and bake him!
Crisp and crackling soon we'll make **him!**
Round and round the dainty goes;—
Eat his fingers! eat his toes!
His body shall our palates tickle!
Then we'll put his head in pickle.

CHORUS.

On the white man dine and sup,
Whet our teeth and eat him up.

Recollections of the Last Sixty Years.--No. 2.

BY J. JOHNSTON, ESQ., *of Piqua.*

After the peace with the Indians, and after I became agent for many of the tribes, my acquaintance with their distinguished men was of long continuance, and in many cases highly instructing and interesting. The following are the names of some, which after a lapse of more than forty years now occur to my mind:—of the Delawares, Kithtuleland or Anderson, the principal chief, a half-breed, the son of Mr. Anderson by a Delaware woman, who resided prior to the Revolutionary War, below Harrisburg, on the Susquehanna, and who gave name to the ferry, long within my remembrance, called "Anderson's ferry." This chief was a very dignified man in character and appearance, upwards of six feet high, well proportioned; a man of great benevolence and goodness; of excellent understanding, but not a public speaker; was greatly beloved by his people. In 1823, he must have been about sixty years old. In pursuance of treaty stipulations with the United States, I removed the whole Delaware tribe, consisting of twenty-four hundred souls, to their new home southwest of Missouri river, near the mouth of the Kansas, in the years 1822 and 23. Such is the fate of this once war-like and powerful tribe, that there were many persons among them in the years mentioned who were born and raised within thirty miles of Philadelphia, and who have gone at our bidding into the far west. There no doubt they will communicate to the wild tribes of that country the overreaching craft, cunning, and deceit of the white man. I will give an instance to shew that the Indians are capable of performing some of the highest acts of humanity and magnanimity. During the last war, the Delawares claimed and received the protection of the United States. The tribe were committed to my keeping during the war of 1813. C. M., a plain country farmer, came to my house at Upper Piqua to see his benefactor, the chief Anderson. This man then resided two hundred miles below Cincinnati, near the Ohio river, and his only errand was to return his acknowledgments to the aged and humane chief who had once spared the lives and property of himself and family. It appeared that he was emigrating to the west, in 1792, on the Ohio river, in a Kentucky boat; that near the mouth of the Scioto, a number of Indians, who afterwards proved to be Delawares, pursued him in canoes and finally got before him, so that escape was impossible. He did not at all fire on the Indians, and this doubtless contributed to his ultimate escape; but making a virtue of necessity, turned his boat to the shore and landed among the Indians. Himself and all

his people were immediately taken out and conducted prisoners over some hills to the camp where was Anderson and other head men. The prisoners being seated and C. M. interrogated through an interpreter, after a warm discussion among the Indians, the chief, Anderson, informed the white people they were at liberty to depart with their boat and all it contained; and cautioned them to be on their watch further down, as there were other Indians waylaying the river, who would certainly murder and rob them if they fell into their hands. They found every thing in the boat as they had left it, and after dividing liberally their stock of provisions with the Indians, they put off with light hearts and many thanks to their uncouth benefactors, and reached their place of destination in safety. The head of this family hearing that Anderson and his people were stationed at Piqua, in the war of 1812, came a long journey of over two hundred miles to see and thank his benefactor. The interview took place in my then "Log Cabin," and in my presence. At our treaty with the Delawares, in 1817-18, at my instance a pension of one dollar a day was settled upon Anderson, which he continued to receive during his life. The second chief of the Delawares was Lapauchlie, a full blooded Indian, also a very large, fine looking man. At the treaty above mentioned, a pension of fifty cents a day was settled on him, during his life. These two chiefs died since their removal westward,—both beloved and popular men of the Shawanese. There was Kituwekasa or Blackhoof, the principal chief, a great orator, small of stature—died at Wapaghkonetta, Allen county, Ohio, at the age of more than one hundred years, some time before the tribe emigrated westward. He was probably in more battles than any living man in his day. His first great affair was at the defeat of Braddock. He was born in Florida, and his nation being the most restless and warlike, was a continual thorn in the side of the Southern English Colonies, warring against them continually. They hovered along the frontiers of the Carolinas and Virginia, until they entered Pennsylvania, giving names to several of the rivers and places within that province and Maryland. The other chiefs of this tribe, we the Shemenetoo or the Snake, Biaseka or the Wolf, Lolaway or Perry. Tecumtha was of this tribe, but not a chief, until he threw off the authority of his nation and became the chief of a banditti, for his followers at Tippecanoe were composed chiefly, if not altogether, of outlaws from all the surrounding tribes. His father was a renowned chief, and killed in a fort at the mouth of Kanawha, before the Revolutionary War, under the following circumstances:—the

Indian chiefs were invited to a truce by the commanding officer, when a soldier crossing the Kanawha river to shoot tnrkies, was waylaid by some Indians, killed and scalped. His comrades going over and finding the body, returned enraged, rushed into the fort, and despite of the entreaties and authority of their officers, fell on and murdered the ambassadors of peace, leaving not one of them alive. This, with other cases of atrocity, which has been related to me by the Indians, was assigned as a cause for the deep rooted hatred which Tecumtha always manifested towards our race. His feelings were so intense on this head that he often said he never looked upon the face of a white man without being horror struck or feeling his flesh creep. Although he was unquestionably a true patriot and brave man, it is nevertheless a fact that in the first fight he was engaged in with the Kentuckians, on Mad river, he ran away, leaving his brother, wounded, to take care of himself; but was never known to flinch afterwards. He was undoubtedly among the great men of his race, and aimed at the independence of his people by a union of all the Indians north and south, against the encroachments of the whites. Had he appeared fifty years sooner he might have set bounds to the Anglo-Saxon race in the west: but he came upon the stage of action too late—when the power and resources of the Indians were so much impaired and weakened as to render them unable to effect any thing against their powerful neighbours. This celebrated man was about five feet ten inches in height, square, well built form for strength and agility; about forty eight or fifty years old when he fell at the battle of the Thames, during the last war. Tecumtha signifies in English, a wild cat or panther crouching ready to spring upon its prey. The Shawanese successively inhabited in Ohio, the country on the Scioto at Chillicothe, and Old Town, the Mad river country at Zanesfield, Bellefontaine, Urbana and Springfield, the Great Miami at Staunton, Lower and Upper Piqua. From the latter place they were routed by the Kentuckians, when they took refuge on the Auglaize and Hog Creek, extending their settlements down as low as Defiance. Latterly they had chiefly congregated at and near Wapaghkonetta, twenty-nine miles north of Piqua, from whence they finally emigrated southwest of Missouri in 1826 and 1833. The Shawanese were divided into four tribes, viz. the Chillicothe, Mequochake, Piqua and Kiscopokee. Tecumtha was of the last named tribe, and on account of their restless, warring propensities, this tribe numbered very few fighting men when they left Ohio. The prophet, Elsquatawa, was a twin brother of

Tecumtha, a man void of talent or merit, a brawling, mischievous Indian demagogue.

Ladies' Fair.

This is the season of fairs: And I am desired to say to my readers that the ladies belonging to the Central Presbyterian Church, will continue for a night or two more in the basement of the church edifice, on Fifth street, between Plum and Western Row, the Fair for the sale of useful and fancy articles, which was opened last evening, the 23d inst. They rely on the liberality of their neighbours and friends in purchasing the avails of their industry, to furnish means for the payment of sundry debts, contracted in their department of the church enterprise. I trust to behold there the usual complement of bright eyes and happy faces appropriate to the season and the scene. " The Christmas Guest," I suppose will make its reappearance and two or three curiosities exhibited of great local interest. One of these is the original list of subscriptions to the erection of the oldest permanent house of worship here—the First Presbyterian Church, on Main street. Here may be seen the autographs of the early settlers whose liberality put up that building contributions, in which shame the public spirit of the present age. Some of them yet survive in the midst of the community which they have aided to build up, and it is right that the inhabitants of Cincinnati should know who those are to whom they are thus indebted.

Lastly, I take occasion to say that some specimens of that fine bread which attracted so much admiration last week at my office, will be offered for exhibition and taste, to those who have not yet enjoyed that luxury. I am determined that the citizens of this place shall learn what flour ought to be and can be made to be.

A Relic of Revolutionary Days.

The following letter, published now for the first time, was written by Gen. M'Dougal to Judge Goforth of New York, afterwards one of the first settlers of Columbia:

FISH KILL, February 7th, 1780.

My Dear Sir:—This will inform you that I have been at quarters here, since the 6th of December last, in order to get rid of an old complaint of the stone. The symptoms have so far yielded to medicine, as to render them more tolerable than they were.

I have seen the report of the committee of the convention of Massachusetts Bay of a constitution to be offered the people for their approbation. From some sentences in it, I think they have not wholly lost sight of an establishment. I am inclined to believe this was occasioned by their dread of the clergy; for if the convention declared against such a measure, they would exert themselves to get a negative put on it. when it should be proposed to the people. But independent of this subject, I think the people will not approve of it, or any other form, which gives energy to the government or social security to the people. To give security to a people in the frame of a government, they must resign a portion of their natural liberty for the security of the rest. There is a large county in that state that will not suffer a court of justice to sit to do any business. These very people have become so licentious that they have taken flour by force of arms from a magistrate in this state, who was retaining it here according to law to supply the army, which has been frequently distressed for the want of that article. From this specimen you may form a judgment what kind of constitution will suit that people. There is a great deal of good sense among them; but I have my doubts of its having effect in the frame of government.

I want some small articles from your town. I shall be much obliged to you to inform me how much higher dry goods are than they were before the war *for hard money?* What can the best leather breeches be bought for in like specie?

Your old subaltern is well.

I wish to hear from you by post on the subject of my request as soon as possible.

I am, dear sir, your humble ser't,

ALEX. M'DOUGAL.

Judge W. GOFORTH, New York.

Ice.

It is some alleviation of the hardship to which we are exposed for a few weeks of paying double price for fuel, that the same cause, the intense freezing during the last fifteen days, has furnished our ice houses with abundant supplies of ice, some of it twelve inches thick. The article will be plenty and cheap next season without doubt. bringing a wholesome article of the comforts, if not luxuries of life, within the reach of all classes.

Our Ancestors.

Statistics are considered by many persons as dry subjects. But they serve to shed light and elicit truth on many topics, which they illustrate distinctly by means of facts and figures.

It is a common prejudice to suppose that extravagance and luxury are of modern date. Hence our grandfathers and grandmothers are usually contrasted with their descendants as paragons of economy and thrift. I propose to set this matter on a different basis, by showing thet fashion and luxury are the same in all ages, when the means of expenditure are alike.

An account of disbursements more than one hundred years ago, on behalf of a lady residing in New England, niece of Sir John Sherburne, formerly Governor of Nova Scotia, has been handed to me in the original manuscript. It is a great curiosity throughout, although my extracts must be brief. For convenience sake, I have thrown the amounts into dollars and cents, although kept in pounds, shillings and pence.

One satin dress, *nineteen* yards, with four yards flounce, - - - -	$533 00
One piece fine lawn, - - -	113 50
One silk petticoat, - - - -	150 00
One fan—mounted, - - -	26 00
Bill of lace per particulars, - -	484 33
One pair silk shoes, - - -	35 67
One *full suit* rich brocade, *eighteen yards,*	666 67
Two very rich brocaded night gowns,	600 00
One long cloth riding hood, - -	166 67
One sett yellow moreen bed curtains,	443 50
One sett crimson do complete,	250 00
One pair sconces, - - - -	312 67
Two sconce glasses, - - -	186 67
One pair stays, - - - -	60 00
Three yards fine crimson, $12 50, -	37 50
	$4066 18

It will hardly surprise my readers after perusing this specimen, to learn that the bill or running account, of which the above is part, was £9023, 17s. and 10d., which at $3 33—the New England six shillings to the dollar—is more than *thirty thousand dollars!*

The account to be sure, ran for several years —like all such bills—without settlement, or indeed payment in whole, or in part. Such a woman is indeed of more value than *pearls* or *rubies.*

I have growled at having to buy ten yards for a dress; but " eighteen" or " nineteen" yards leads all things. I suppose this was the era of hoops.

I trust when my New York exchanges copy this precious document, that the ladies there who have been teasing their husbands for " *those fifteen hundred dollar shawls,*" will send me a vote of thanks to encourage my further explorations into the past.

Powers, the Sculptor.

A literary friend handed us yesterday the following extract of a letter he has just received from Powers, the American Sculptor, now at Florence. We gladly give it to our readers as a matter of interest:

" The death of Mr. Carey grieves me more than I can tell, or you would perhaps believe, and what adds to my grief and makes the circumstances still more sad to me, is, that the bust of " Proserpine," upon which I had spent so much pains and time, arrived *too late to be seen by him.* I did my best to have it done sooner, but the difficulty of procuring workmen to execute to a *certain extent,* my works, has all along perplexed me. There are plenty of them, but I find but few of them capable of performing precisely what I wish them to do. Besides I had previously commenced another for Mr. Carey which I had laid aside, mainly because it had no basket attached to it.

"My Slave has proved more successful in England than I had ever hoped for. I have already orders for three copies of it—and lately have received an order for an original work—*a female statue*—the subject left entirely to my own choice. One of these orders is from America, the others from England. I am now engaged on a bust of Princess Demidoff, a daughter of Jerome Bonaparte. She has a very handsome face, and I am taking much pains with it. Her husband desires me to make his bust also. I have quite as much work therefore as I can do.

The daguerreotypes all failed, although I made many trials. The marble is too white for the process, it burns up the surface before the shadows have time to take effect. I gave two or three of them to Mr. Lester, but the impressions were so false that they would not admit of being engraved. I intend soon to have a careful drawing made, both of that and my second Eve, and if I succeed better, I shall send copies to you. At all events I shall not forget you. I hope soon to have it in my *power* to make a suitable return for kindness received.

"With the best wishes for your welfare and happiness, I am sincerely and truly your friend,

HIRAM POWERS.

Manufacture of Boots and Shoes.

Every day is adding to the variety, as well as extent, of our manufacturing operations. When I took the statistics in this line, for the census of 1840, for Cincinnati, although the value of the leather annually manufactured in the place, was $335,000, yet at that period the entire consumption of leather here was for customers by the boot and shoemakers, and the amount of raw material beyond that demand was exported east, whence it came back to a great extent worked up into the cheaper qualities of ready made boots and shoes.

Within the last three years a beginning and successful progress has been made in changing this course of things. L. CHAPIN & Co., who are now in active operation as wholesale boot and shoe manufacturers, at the corner of Elm and Second streets, made a commencement in this line in 1842, and there is no doubt, that in the course of ten years or less, not a pair of boots or shoes will be brought here of New England manufacture; and a high probability exists, that within a few years more we shall be supplying the very markets in which we now purchase.

A brief statement of some of the operations of this firm will illustrate the subject. Their manufactory is twenty-five feet on Elm, by one hundred feet on Second street, and is four stories high, with convenient cellars and attics besides. Their operations are in fine and coarse shoes and boots, principally the last. The leather, with the exception of a small portion of hemlock tanned soal, is all made in this city. They work up calf skins and upper leather yearly, to the value of $15,000, and require an annual supply of thirty-five thousand pounds of soal leather, and twelve hundred dozen sheep skins for their operations. They use up, during the same period, three thousand pounds boot nails, three hundred bushels shoe pegs, and three hundred dollars worth of lasts. As their materials are all manufactured here, these facts exhibit the manner and extent to which this, as every other new branch of business embarked in here, aids existing manufacturing operations, or contributes to the establishment of new ones.

Every description of boots and shoes, as has been ascertained at this factory, can be made as cheap here as at the Eastward, and the finer kinds much cheaper; and the country merchant can buy always to better advantage in the west, not merely in the saving of traveling expenses and freight or carriage, but in the certainty of getting his goods almost at his door at a day's notice, and of individuals within reach of responsibility for the wares they manufacture.

Messrs. Chapin & Co. employ one hundred and seventy-five hands in the various branches of their business, principally journeymen; although a large share of the rough work is done by boys, and the stitching and binding by women. It was pleasant to me to learn that one beneficial result of this enterprise has been to find employment for the poor and the destitute. I was refered to a case where a woman with three boys earned in this business three dollars a week, and each of the boys three more; and of another in which an elderly man, who was out of employment when he came to Cincinnati, was now earning, with three or four children, twenty dollars per week. These are samples that employment for our poor, is of more efficiency as well as less burthensome to the community than the periodical efforts made to relieve distress in the community, after it is rendered apparent.

The firm is doing a business of $100,000 for the year. There is little doubt that its operations for 1846 will enlarge fifty per cent. They now supply probably not more than one twentieth of the boots and shoes sold in stores of that description in Cincinnati, their customers being dispersed over every part of the west.

Fuel.

The people of Cincinnati have been lately taught, at some expense in acquiring the lesson, too, the importance of protecting themselves from imposition and extortion in the supply of wood and coal for winter use. The scarcity of coal, when winter bursts upon us so unexpectedly, because so early, as the beginning of December, has led to much suffering and privation, which it will be our own fault if we again endure. To crown our misfortune in this line, of five coal boats which were on their way from the Meigs county mines to this place, four were sunk on the way, and the fifth, after landing here, has since sunk, having been cut to pieces by ice. We are now consequently at the mercy of the weather until a favourable change sends us further supplies.

S. W. Pomeroy, agent for the Meigs county mines, has made the public a liberal proposition for furnishing the coal wanted here by families, which I judge is for the interest of all to accept. He offers to supply coal on subscriptions at ten cents per bushel, one half the price payable at the time of subscribing, and the residue on the delivery of the coal during the spring and summer months ensuing.

This is obviously so advantageous a bargain to coal purchasers, as to invite general acceptance, and I learn that subscriptions have already been made for the article, not only for family and office uses, but from the smaller manufacturers also, who are persuaded that this is the cheapest mode of supplying themselves.

One of the most favourable aspects of this arrangements to me is, that it will create a supply in due season, for those will attend to getting their coal in time, when they have half paid for it, that could not be depended on thus to provide for their families, if that motive did not secure their punctuality. And whatever amount of coal is thus disposed of withdraws just so many buyers from the regular coal market, and to that extent protects the rest of the community.

Christmas Beef.

The splendid beef offered for sale in our market is continually stimulating fresh efforts from those engaged in the business to rival and surpass previous efforts in this line, and no expence seems spared to secure the finest beef in the world for our citizens. I refered last week to the fine bullock and heifer exhibited by Messrs. *Wunder & Butcher*, which have been since sold at their stalls in Fifth Street Market, objects of admiration to the spectators, many whom were strangers to the city, aud have never seen such beef at home.

On Monday last, Mr. Samuel Berresford brought over from Bourbon county, Kentucky, eighteen head of beef cattle of a quality unsurpassed to the number, in supplies of Christmas beef, heretofore. A remarkably fat *Buffalo heifer* also contributed a part of the procession through our streets, and one hundred and eight extra fat sheep of the Bakewell breed, brought up the rear.

Four of the finest and heaviest of the cattle, with the buffalo and a dozen of the mutton, will be disposed of at Messrs. Berresford's long established stalls in Lower Market st., at to-day's market there. Finer or fatter meat has never graced our stalls. One of our city epicures was noticed contemplating the display on Tuesday, who after gazing at it awhile, turned away from the spectacle, feeling the water springing to his mouth and eyes.

Mr. Berresford has bought a lot of twenty-three head of cattle from Gen. James Shelby, Fayette county, Ky., for $100 each, which he challenges to the world to surpass or even to equal.

Fire Engine.

I noticed by calling at Messrs. Paddock & Campbell's a few days since, an elegant new six and a half inch chamber suction fire engine, and inquiring its destination, learned that it had been built for the City of Frankfort, Kentucky; but left on their hands, the citizens having had a larger one built in lieu of it at their establishment. It struck me that it might suit for a place of two or three thousand inhabitants who might be tempted to protect themselves in this way from the ravages of fire, to which this season of the year exposes the community, if they knew that an engine could be procured without delay. With this view I state that it can be got at a fair price, under guarantee of its power and efficiency. Such of my exchanges as reside in towns needing an engine of such dimensions as may be readily worked by twenty or twenty-five hands will do well to notice this for the benefit of their neighbours.

Sugar Crop of Louisiana.

It must always be a matter of deep interest to our community to know the state of supply of this article, which habit has rendered a necessary of life. I have made the following synopsis of the subject from late and authentic communications to the press and to the Treasury Department, from responsible sources.

In 1828, there were three hundred and eight sugar plantations in Louisiana, valued at thirty-four millions of dollars. In 1830, the estates had increased to six hundred and ninety-four, and the capital employed was estimated at fifty millions of dollars. The plantations are now—1845 —twelve hundred and nine.

The last year's crop, was, as may be infered from this synopsis, a very heavy one, and it is supposed the coming one will not fall short of it.

Seventy-two sugar mills and engines were put up the current year in Louisiana, from N. York, Philadelphia, Pittsburgh, Louisville, and Cincinnati, principally from the last, the number manufactured here for that market being precisely forty-eight—two-thirds of the whole.

There will be one hundred and thirty-two put up the ensuing season; supplied as follows:— New York 10, Louisville 10, New Orleans 15, Pittsburgh 25, Cincinnati 72; more than one half being from our own establishments.

Importance of Right Emphasis.

A stranger from the country, observing one of *Carpenter's Roller Counting-House Rules*, lifted it, and enquiring the object, was answered—" It is a rule for *counting* houses." Too well bred, as he construed politeness, to ask unnecessary questions, he turned it over and over, and up and down repeatedly, and at last, in a paroxysm of baffled curiosity, enquired—" How in the name of nature, do you *count houses with this?*"

There is another good story on the subject of emphasis. " Boy," said a visitor at the house of a friend to his little son, " step over the way and see how *old Mrs. Brown is?*" The boy did the errand, and on his return reported that Mrs. Brown did not know how *old* she was, and that she said he might find out by his own learning.

Cotton and Wool Cards Machines.

There are few inventions more remarkable than AMOS WHITTEMORE's machine for making cotton and wool cards.

A correspondent of the Concordia Intelligencer, who lately visited the great factory at West Cambridge, built by this inventor and still in operation, writes as follows:—" Whittemore's machine for making cotton and wool cards has saved to the world an amount of manual labour, which places him among the greatest benefactors of his race. When the circumstances of the inventor are considered, the machine appears a most remarkable creation of native genius, and is an extraordinary instance of a mind undrilled by education, unaided by science, and unpracticed even in mechanical labour, eliminating a series of the most complicated and beautiful combinations known to us in mechanics. On beholding its rapid, delicate, and almost incredible operations, one can scarce avoid the impression that the inventor has created something more than a machine;—that he has given it volition and intelligence. There being a factory in the village, built by the inventor still in operation,

we did not fail to pay it a visit. On entering the factory we beheld some twenty of these machines, each occupying a space of about four feet by twelve, at work in most industrious activity, making a noise like the combined ticking of a thousand clocks, and moving by some invisible power, and acting apparently without any superintendence; for, at the moment of our entrance there was no one in the apartment. One boy, we were told, could attend ten or twelve machines; for there was little to be done, but to change the leather as the cards are completed. To describe the machine, is to me impossible;—I can only tell you some of the results of its operations. A piece of leather, of the size of the card to be made, is inserted in two long clamps, that stretch it and hold it firm in the machine;—the wire is put on a reel, like a skein of yarn, and the end of it given to the machine, which is set in motion by a small band, revolving over a drum moved by a small steam engine, in an apartment below, and in a few minutes the active little automaton completes, without any human agency, one of the finest cards used at Lowell, perfect and ready to be placed on the carder. The beauty and delicacy of its movements excel those of any machine I ever saw before. After the leather is placed in the machine and the wire given to it, the first motion brings up to the leather a curved head of a small iron snake, with a forked tongue, fine as the most delicate cambrick needle, with which it darts at the leather and perforates it;—in a wink, a pair of small fingers rise with a tooth in their hold and insert it in the scarce perceptible punctures made by the snake's sting, and then disappear, and out darts again the reptile's head;—when the wire is inserted in the leather by the little digital nippers. The two prongs of the card tooth are straight, but the instant it is driven through the leather, a small hammer, on the opposite side, gives it a slight blow, by which it is bent into its hook shape. The rapidity of these movements is so great when the machine is running at its usual speed as to render it difficult to follow them with the eye. I scarcely dare trust my memory to state the number of teeth it forms and inserts in a minute;—I am confident that it is as large as five hundred, and I believe it is almost as high as nine hundred. To have any just conception of this extraordinary achievement of human ingenuity, consider what wonderful precision, exactness and delicacy is required in a machine, first to form the fine tooth of the exact shape and size; then to perforate the leather and insert the pronged wire into the almost invisible holes. Each part, remember, is performed by successive motions of independent parts of the machine, moving with a rapidity that inserts, say five hundred in a minute;—counting the motions of the hammer, the bending of the wire, the perforations and insertion of the teeth, there are not less than two thousand independent, successive acts of the machine every instant of time that it is running.

" Incredible as it may appear, this machine of such beautiful combinations of varied, yet simple movements, came forth at once perfect and complete from the brain and hand of the inventor. The first machine cast and built from his original model in wood, I saw in operation and was told that it was as perfect as any one in the factory;—after near forty years use of it, no improvement has been suggested to the original conception of the author of this ingenious and wonderful piece of mechanism.

This fact will appear still more surprising when the history of the inventor is known, and the adverse circumstances, which attended his labours, are related. In early life he was extremely poor. Amos Whittemore, the inventor, was at first a day labourer;—having an aptness for mechanical labour, he took up the humble employment of an itinerant tinker; and for many years supported a wife and increasing family by repairing "pans, cans, and the whole kitchen trade" of the farmers in the regions about Boston. As he advanced in mechanical dexterity and knowledge, he added a higher branch of the arts to his profession, and became a cleaner and repairer of old clocks. He at last resigned the itinerant wagon, and took a shop in his native town of Cambridge, and put forth a shingle on which it was announced, "*Watches and Clocks repaired here.*" It was while engaged in this respectable mechanical trade, that he formed the first conception of his card machine. He was too poor to undertake the construction of it without aid, and no one could be found who had faith enough in his talents to risk an hundred dollars on the success of the invention. After many discouraging efforts to obtain assistance, he entered into an agreement with a younger brother, who was labouring at "*the awl and last;*" and it was stipulated that the latter should divide the amount of his weekly earnings, between his own and brother's family, while Amos was employed in constructing his machine and putting it in operation; and if the invention proved valuable, the two brothers were to share equally the advantages of the patent. It was difficult by the labour of one man, to preserve two large families from suffering through a New England winter; but the machine slowly advanced, and hope sustained them in the struggle with want and poverty;—spring came and saw it almost completed;—summer arrived, and the lone labourer who had been hidden from the world for six months in an old obscure building, *giving form and shape to the conceptions of his own brain, came forth with one of the most remarkable inventions of his age, complete in all its parts, and so perfect in its operations,* that a child could perform the labour of fifty adults. When success had been made sure, aid was no longer reluctantly withheld. Patents were secured in this country, England, and France; and the rights to the use of the machine in Europe, was sold for a sum sufficient to commence the business here, on a large scale. The demand in this country at that time, principally for hand cards, was immense, and the projector of the machine for setting the teeth, immediately commenced a machinery for the boards and handles for the ordinary domestic card; this he soon completed; and the whole process of constructing a card from the wire in the skein, and the unpunctured leather in the hide, and the board and handle from the rude block of wood, was done by machinery, with the exception of nailing the leather on the board.

"The Whittemores, instead of selling the right to the machine, retained a monopoly of the business in their own hands. The embargo having occurred soon after the establishment of their factory, and the war of 1812 succeeding the former event, people were forced into the use of homespun and domestic manufactures, which greatly enhanced the demand for cards;—and

the families of the two brothers, who had often in former days looked forward with solicitude for means to procure an humble meal, began to roll in wealth, and adopt a style of magnificent and luxurious living. Before the expiration of their first patent, as a tribute of national gratitude, and a reward of the extraordinary mechanical ingenuity displayed by the invention, Congress passed a special act for renewing the patent for double the time for which they were then granted. Soon after procuring this grant from the country, the original patentees sold out their right to a stock company for a large sum and retired from all active pursuits, with an ample fortune, and with the intention of passing the remainder of their lives in "otium cum dignitate."

"But how often are the apparently surest prospects of life delusive; how dangerous is it for a man "to say unto his soul, take thine ease;"—a mind that had displayed the most extraordinary powers of combination, and which, without claiming any new discovery in science, or the application of new powers, had excelled in mechanical ingenuity, all the great inventors of the age, sunk into a lethargy, after it had lost its accustomed stimulus to action, and its powers declined, till in a few years, the great inventor became a confirmed hypocondriac. The strangest idea he imbibed, and which became inveterately fixed in his mind, was that his legs had became vitrified, and that these useful members of his person, had turned to *glass*. With this notion irradically fixed in his head, he had two long narrow canes made and lined with downy cushions in which he placed his legs, to secure them from injury; and it was his employment all day, seated in a recumbent position, and his leg in a horizontal position, with a long wand in his hand, to keep people at a respectable distance, and to warn them not to approach incautiously his fragile limbs. Various expedients were adopted to remove the strange hallucination; but although his mind on all subjects not relating to his own physical condition, was rational, yet on this point the dictates of reason, and the evidence of his senses were impotent to remove the false impression. Fear, nor joy, nor the most violent passions could for a moment break the delusion;—he could by no means be forced to use his limbs;—placed within the reach of the approaching tide, or surrounded by a conflagration, he would drown or suffer the tortures of the stake, rather than risk the integrity of his fragile limbs, in an attempt to escape. Although the functions of the bodily organs were regular, his strength declined with the powers of his mind;—and with growing weakness, and aberrations of his intellect, his fortune wasted away; and he died at last, within eight years after he relinquished business, in a premature dotage, and with little more money than he had at the commencement of his fortunate career;—and to the last breath of his life insisted that his legs were glass.

"His brother and partner after having well filled his purse, became afflicted with violent political aspirations to the gratification of which his lack of education was an insurmountable barrier in New England. Failing in the object of his ambition at the East, in 1818 he went to Kentucky where, in that early period, he thought his wealth would give him more consideration.—Among the first acquaintances he made, was that of Prentice the celebrated speculator in lands and produce, and who at one time controlled the whole financial and commercial operations of the community along the Ohio. Drawn into the fascinating toils of that arch intriguer, he entrusted the management of his funds to his new friend, who in one day stript him of every dollar he possessed, and within one year from the period of his departure, he returned to Boston, with less worldly means than he had when he gained his daily bread by his awl and lapstone.

"Some may censure the publication of these details of private life;—but as they relate principally to a man whose character and fame has become a subject of history, and as they contain a moral for the government of our desires of wealth, and one for the employment of our physical and mental powers, teaching us that idleness in age as well as youth destroys the strength and health of the strongest and noblest faculties. I trust you will be excused for giving them to the world."

The Weather.

We have had to Tuesday last, twenty-eight successive days which as an average of cold have had no parallel for the past in the Miami Valley. The thermometer has ranged during three of those mornings from two to six degrees below zero, and the average of cold during the whole period, must have been twelve to fifteen degrees below the freezing point. I place this on record for future comparisons.

Popping the Question.

We forgot where we met the following laconic example of "popping the question:" "Pray, madam, do you like buttered toast?" "Yes, sir." "Will you marry me?" The mode adopted by an eccentric physician is almost as condensed. A lady came to consult him. He prescribed and took his guinea. "Madam," said he, "I wish to see you to-morrow. In the interval, take the medicine here prescribed, and ere we meet again, made up your mind to give me a plain YES or NO to the question I now put to you. I am inclined to wed, not to woo. Will you allow me to lay out my fee in the purchase of your wedding ring?"

Tricking a Landlord.

I find the following in one of my exchanges:— "A man lived in a house between two blacksmiths, and was disturbed by the noise they made. At last they promised to remove, on condition that he should give them an excellent dinner, which he readily agreed to do. When the promised feast was ended, he asked them whither they intended to transfer their domicils. "Why," answered one of them, "my neighbour will remove to my shop and I to his."

I can parallel this without going out of Cincinnati.

A heavy property holder here had a tenant named Jones, who had been delinquent so long for rent, that the landlord in despair offered to forgive his arrears if he would remove. In reply, the tenant observed that he would like to accommodate his creditor, and that he had a house in view, but the owner required payment of the rent in advance. Rather than retain a tenant rent free, the landlord agreed to advance Mr. Jones the price of a month's rent, giving him an uncurrent note at ten per cent. discount. In the evening when the landlord's agent came to report the day's business and pay over his receipts, there was the identical note of ten dollars. The landlord it seems had paid him a premium to remove from one of his houses to another one.

Poetry.

The question is sometimes asked, what is the use of poetry? The noble sentiments so loftily and beautifully expressed in the following verses makes the blood course livelier through the veins, and animate the desponding and the weary in the good fight of faith. These stanzas are worthy the lyre of Robert Burns, whose spirit they breathe. They are from a late number of the Dublin Nation.

Our Faith.

The slave may sicken of his toil,
    And at his task repine—
The manly arm will dig the soil
    Until it reach the mine;
No toil will make the brave man quail,
    No time his patience try,
And if he use the word "to fail,"
    He only means—"to die."

What is a year in work like ours?
    The proudest ever planned—
To stay Oppression's withering powers,
    And free our native land!
Oh! many a year were bravely past,
    And many a life well lost,
If blessings such as these, at last,
    Were purchased at their cost!

The seed that yields our daily bread
    Not for a year we reap,
But when the goodly grain we spread,
    We hold the labour cheap—
Yet ere the winter's snow appears,
    Must other seeds be sown,
For man consumes the golden ears
    As quickly as they're grown.

Not so the harvest Freedom yields,
    'Twill last for ages long,
If those who till her glorious fields,
    Be steadfast, brave and strong;
Shall we, then, hopelessly complain,
    Because its growth is slow,
When thousands die before the grain
    Is ripened, which they sow?

MARRIED.

At North Bend, on Tuesday, the 16th of December, by the Rev. Geo. W. Walker, Mr. JOHN B. ROWSE to Miss MARGARET M. SILVER, of that place.

Recollections of the Last Sixty Years.--No. 3.

BY J. JOHNSTON, Esq., *of Piqua.*

The Wyandotts were a part of my agency also. They occupied the Sandusky country, the country of the river Huron, in Michigan, and a tract of land near Malden, in Upper Canada. Their principal chief was Tarhee or the Crane, who resided at Upper Sandusky, where he died twenty-five years ago; and from the treaty of Greenville with Gen. Wayne, in 1795, was a steadfast friend of the government and people of the United States. About forty years ago this tribe contained twenty-two hundred souls, and in March, 1842, when as commissioner of the United States, I concluded with them a treaty of cession and emigration, they had become reduced to eight hundred of all ages and both sexes. Before the [Revolutionary War, a large portion of the Wyandotts had embraced christianity in the communion of the Roman Catholic Church. In the early part of my agency the Presbyterians had a mission among them at Lower Sandusky, under the care of Rev. Joseph Badger. The war of 1812 broke up this benevolent enterprise. When peace was restored the Methodists became the spiritual instructors of these Indians, and continued in charge of them until their final removal westward of Missouri river, two years ago. The mission had once been in a very prosperous state, but of late years had greatly declined, many of the Indians having gone back to habits of intemperance and heathenism: a few continued steadfast to their christian profession. Of this number was "Grey Eyes," a regularly ordained minister, of pure Wyandott blood, a holy, devoted and exemplary christian. This man was resolutely opposed to the emigration of his people, and was against me at every step of a long and protracted negotiation of twelve months continuance. I finally overcome all objections; on the last vote, more than two-thirds of the whole male population were found in favour of removal. The preacher had always asserted that, under no circumstances would he ever go westward. His age was about forty-eight years; his character forbade any approaches to tampering with him; and although I felt very sensibly his influence, yet I never addressed myself to him personally on the subject of the treaty: but as soon as the whole nation in open council, had voted to leave their country and seek a new home far in the west, I sent an invitation to the preacher to come and dine with me and spend the evening in conversation; he came accordingly. I told him that in consequence of his sacred character, I had abstained from using any means to influence his course in

relation to the pending negotiation; that my business with him had no concealment; it was open, and communicated to all men, women and children; and as many of their white friends as desired to hear me in open council; that I came to them with the words of their great father, Harrison; and although the lips that first uttered these words were cold in death, still they were the words of truth—which all must acknowledge were for their present and future good; that in the treaty I was about to sign in a few more days with their chiefs, ample justice was done their whole nation, and this too as well on account of my own character as the character of him who had sent me to treat with them; that if he—the preacher "Grey Eyes"—was called to preach the gospel to his nation and race, it was his duty to go with them westward and do them all the good in his power; that in a few more years the Indians would be all gone from Ohio and Michigan, and he well knew he could not, by reason of his ignorance of our language, minister to the whites, and that it must therefore be evident to all that the Providence of God called loudly upon him to go westward with his people; and there administer as he had done to their spiritual and temporal wants. He replied that during the progress of the treaty, he had opposed me to the utmost extent of his power; that now the nation having decided by a large majority on selling their lands and removing to the west, he had determined on uniting his fate with it, and would prepare to go along and do all the good he could for his people. From this time forward the preacher and myself were very good friends. He frequently called and ate with me, on all which occasions I called on him for a blessing, which he pronounced in his own language, in a very devout and becoming manner. When I had brought my business with the Wyandotts to a close, and was on the point of leaving there, I sent for my good friend the preacher and gave him all my remaining provisions and stores, not of large amount, remarking to the Indians present, to prevent their being jealous, that their minister being the servant of Jesus Christ, devoting his time to the care of their souls and bodies, to the neglect of himself and family, it was proper therefore that I should provide for him as far as lay in my power: to which they very readily assented. The Wyandotts were always a leading tribe among the Indians of the Northwest: with them was the sacred fire deposited at Brownstown, Michigan; and here was the great council of the confederacy held and peace and war decided upon in the war of 1812. The place was polluted with the spilling of blood in battle, and no council could ever after be held there.

There is nothing in the history of the settlement and extension of the English and their descendants upon this continent so melancholy to the mind of the christian and philanthropist as the case of the Indians, the primitive inhabitants and lords of the country. Since the first landing of the Europeans to the present day, hundreds of tribes of the natives have been swept away by the avarice, cupidity and vices of the white man, leaving not a single individual to testify that they ever had an existence; and what is most disreputable in this matter to our race up to the present moment, not a single effectual attempt has been made by the English government during our Colonial vassalage, nor since the American revolution by the Congress and President of the United States, to lay the foundation of a system to preserve the unhappy race of the red man from final extinction. All our plans have been directed to shifts and expedients to acquire their lands and push them further back, without in the least altering the tenure of their possession. The last story on our part was, go southwest of Missouri and we will never call upon you for the cession of another acre. In reference to this very matter, in my farewell speech to the Wyandotts, they were told that the white people loved land; it was their food; that they in the course of time might be called on in the west to sell the lands which I had assigned them by the treaty; but no matter who invited them to council for such a purpose, if it was the President himself in person, to shut their ears and obey no such call; never for a moment entertain a proposition of the kind. If you do this you will be safe: if you once listen you are undone, for the white man will overcome you with money and goods. What do we see already? While I am writing this sheet we read that a deputation of the Potawatomies is on a visit to the President at Washington imploring him to put a stop to the demands made upon them to abandon their present homes; and yet it is but a few years, certainly not more than twenty, since those same Indians left Indiana, the country near Chicago, and Michigan at our bidding, and to make room for our population. Is it any wonder that the Indians cannot be civilized; and that all confidence on their part in our race is at an end? Seeing that our avarice, overreaching and encroachments upon their homes has no limits, nothing can save them but a total change in our policy towards them. I had been officially connected with the Indian service upwards of thirty years and had reflected much upon their deplorable condition. The result was communicated many years ago to the men in power at Washington, through Gen. Joseph Vance, our then as at present representative in Congress. My plan

was predicated upon the basis that without a local government, adapted to the condition and wants of the Indians, and for their exclusive use and benefit, their race must perish. Nething has since occurred to change that opinion, but much to confirm and strengthen it.

A territorial government, under the authority of Congress, should be established over the Indians to be composed of a Governor, Council and House of Representatives: the Governor to be appointed in the usual way by the President and Senate, the Council to be composed of the Indian agents for the time being, and the House of Representatives to be composed exclusively of persons elected by the various tribes, and in all cases to be Indians by blood, each member so elected and admitted to a seat to receive from the United States Treasury $2 or $3 per day for his attendance, and $2 or $3 per day for each thirty miles travel going to and returning from the seat of the Indian government, a delegate in Congress as a matter of course. A plan of the kind here proposed, would gradually introduce among the Indians a knowledge of civil government and its blessings, and pave the way for their civilization: without something of the kind their race msut perish. That it is a sacred debt due to the primitive inhabitants of the land, from the representatives of the American people in Congress assembled, no man acquainted with the wrongs of the red man will attempt to deny. Connected with the providing a government for them must be a solemn covenant on the part of Congress that no attempt shall ever be made to purchase or alienate any part of the Indian territory, and the total abandonment of the practice of removing competent and faithful agents for political cause. The longer an honest and competent agent is in office, the better for both the government and the Indians. So mischievous in its effects has been this practice of removing men in the Indian service, that I have known persons under Gen. Jackson's administration to receive the appointment of Indian interpreter, who knew not a single word of Indian; and another who received the appointment of blacksmith and held the place for several years, and never performed a day's work at the anvil and bellows. Notorious, wicked, and incompetent men have in many instances been appointed agents and commissioners for managing their affairs; and a course of measures pursued towards them for the last sixteen years, in violation of treaties, law and right that has banished from the minds of the Indians every vestige of confidence they ever had in us. Wholesale frauds have been practised upon them by men in office, to the disgrace of the government and people of the United States.

Our Observatory.

Cincinnati is advantageously known abroad by her artists and men of science. *Powers* has made the name of the Queen City a familiar lesson in geography to civilized Europe; and *Locke* and *Mitchell* are as well known in the academies and halls of science east as at home. Indeed *John Locke* of America is as distinguished a man in Europe as *John Locke* of England, although in different departments of science.

Our Observatory has directed the attention of the *savans* of Europe to our youthful city, and we have already received unequivocal testimony of the interest it inspires abroad, in the transmission of the following documents from various places:

1. The twenty-first volume of the *Annals of the Astronomical Observatory at Vienna:* Forwarded by its director, by order of the Emperor of Austria.

2. Six volumes folio of *Meteorological and Magnetical Observatories.* This was transmitted by the Minister of France in Russia, Baron Cancrini.

3. A volume of *Observations* made at the Imperial Observatory, *Dorpat,* Russia. From the director of that institution.

4. A volume describing the *North Equatorial,* in London. Forwarded by the Duke of Northumberland.

5. A sett of *Magnetical Observations,* made in Canada by Col. Sabine.

These have all been received lately, within a short space of time, many of them from distant places, which but for the erection of our Observatory, would never have heard of Cincinnati, and which now know it as other scientific establishments in Europe will shortly, as a seat of science and the arts.

Who is there here, with the least degree of self-respect, that does not, in the knowledge of such facts, feel himself repaid for the contribution he has made to establish our Observatory.

Western Mails.

The Committee of the Memphis Convention on the subject of Western Waters, have just published their report.

They point out the injustice done the west in the neglect to establish the same continuity of line along the great business points west and southwest of Louisville, while the lines of mail communication at the east are by rail-roads and mail steamers along the coast. They suggest the reorganization of the western mails as follows:

1st. A main daily steamboat river line should be established to run from Pittsburgh or Wheeling to New Orleans, (or at least from Cincinnati to New Orleans,) which should connect at the mouth of the Ohio with a branch from the Mississippi and Missouri rivers.

2d. This line should be divided into different sections so that boats might be constructed to suit each section of the river.

3d. During the fall months, if necessary, the sections above Cincinnati might be discontinued, and the mails upon that portion of the river line

4th. The main river line should be intersected at the chief towns on the river, by a daily stage or rail-road line, leading from thence to the capitol of each of the Valley States.

5th. A daily line of post coaches should connect the Charleston and Georgia railroads with the Decatur and Tuscumbia rail-road, and thence with the main river line at Memphis or some other central point.

Human Life.

A letter from New York gives the following picture of business in the fancy line:

" You may judge of the business and prospects of the city in the last few years, dating, perhaps, by some *accidental coincidence,* from the passage of the tariff law, when I tell you, that being last night in a magnificent French store in Broadway, I asked him the rent. Three years ago, he answered, I took it for seven years, at $1500, but now I could get $2500 a year for the remainder of my lease. The magnificence of some of those stores, and the costliness of their wares, are almost incredible. Sets of China, $300, and single chairs, belonging to sets, $100 a piece, and yet *they find purchasers!* In plate glass, the French beat the world, until now, it is said the English equal them, after having expended immense sums in the race of competition. In *gilding* furniture, great perfection has been attained. The Romans could only make seven hundred and fifty leaves of gilding, four inches square, out of one ounce of gold—while now, a single grain of gold may be stretched out to *cover a house.*"

It is just such gilding which sets of thousands of the human race, as well as furniture at New York and elsewhere, and the gold leaf is beat out just as thin for this purpose as to cover the house.

The Temperance Mess.

Soon after our declaration of war against Great Britain, in 1812, had taken place, a call was made on Gov. SNYDER, of Pennsylvania, for a detachment of the militia of that State to serve a six months tour of duty on the shores of the Delaware. The enemy was just commencing that course of laying waste the accessible parts of our coasts, which afterwards inflicted so much distress upon the inhabitants of the lower parts of Maryland and Virginia.

Snyder, in place of drafting the necessary number, out of the militia, issued a proclamation calling for volunteers, which was promptly responded to, by an offer of service from three of the volunteer corps of Philadelphia, two of which were old established companies that had filled up their ranks under the existing patriotic impulse, while the third was a new company, formed within three days of their tender of service. One of the first alluded to was commanded by Captain *Samuel Borden*, for many years prior to his death, a resident of Cincinnati. *Condy Raguet*, a lawyer of Philadelphia, distinguished afterwards as an able writer on the currency and free trade questions, was captain of the last named corps. I belonged to this last. With the exception of our commander, there was not a man in it older than twenty-one; a large proportion being, in fact, eighteen and nineteen years of age. A majority of the corps were the sons of respectable and influential persons of that city.

Our services were accepted, and the detachment, numbering three hundred and forty-eight men, placed under the command of Col. *Lewis Rush*, mustered, inspected, and ordered by the commanding officer of that military district, to an encampment some thirty miles south of Philadelphia, which bore the name of *Shellpot Hill*. It appeared that an attack was apprehended on *Dupont's* powder mills, in that neighbourhood, a very important object of defence, in the existing general want of preparation for war, extending over the whole country.

As soon as we reached our encampment ground, and the tents had been pitched, kitchens *dug*, wood cut for cooking, and other arrangements made, we were formed into messes of *seven* each. This was more to a mess than desirable, during the warm season of August, which was the second month of our engagement; but the scarcity of tents did not permit us to reduce the size of our messes. Each one of these messes had a non-commissioned officer in command of it. Ours was Sergeant *Thomas I. Wharton*, a member of a highly respectable family in Philadelphia, and now distinguished as an able counsellor at law in in that city.

In due season rations were issued out to each mess, comprehending meat, bread, salt, vinegar, soap, and *whiskey*. The uses of all these were well understood by our whole mess, except the last article. Of the one hundred and twenty men composing the company, I judge not half a dozen had ever either tasted or smelt whisky at home; those who drank used beer or wine, and a few, brandy; the great mass, however, were too young to have acquired any taste or relish for drinking at all. Judge the horror with which the taste and smell of whisky, inspired most of us. Our men, after a brief consultation, which showed we were all of one opinion, authorized me, in the re-

ceipt of the rations which fell to our share, to commute the whiskey ration into bread or beef, at my choice. I did so; and not one gill of whiskey was consumed by our mess, during our whole absence from Philadelphia. What the other messes did, I do not recollect distinctly; but believe that they generally received it, and that the whiskey was drank, by parts only of each mess; but its presence, and the convivial spirit of those days, doubtless led too many to contract a relish for ardent spirits, which brought individuals in after periods of their lives to a premature grave.

After our tour of duty was performed, the company to which I allude, returned, and on the recurrence of peace, the members gradually scattered, some changing the place of their residence south, west and north; some left for distant parts of the world; some silently disappeared from the scene of human life, and the regular operations of time and disease, carried a portion more to their graves; and after a lapse of nineteen years, when an invitation for the survivors to meet in Philadelphia, brought together the persons or names of those who were yet alive, it was ascertained that only thirty-three of the original one hundred and twenty survived. Not a mess, as originally constituted, numbered more than two among the living, except the mess to which I belonged, who were *all either present or accounted for by letters*. Thirteen years more, or thirty-two years, have passed since the service alluded to was performed, yet the *whole seven survive to this date*, as far as I know or believe. I am not aware that a single one of the seven I have thus refered to, was a temperance man, in the modern use of the phrase; but the circumstances in this case explain and illustrate the philosophy of the modern movement. They were placed in circumstances, which for half a year removed them out of the influences to which they were exposed at home; and for the same period they put aside the temptation to contract habits of drink, by which their comrades were assailed. The effect to me and I believe to the rest, was to imbibe a dislike to the taste and smell of most descriptions of ardent spirits.

Honoured forever be the memory and example of that good and great MAN, who, as President of the United States in 1832, set the example of offering pure water as refreshment at his levee, and directed the spirit ration to be abolished in the supplies of the army and navy of the United States. Thousands of lives and reputations would have been saved, and an incalculable amount of misery spared to our country, had that reform been made by his illustrious predecessor who first occupied the chair of state.

Public Halls in Cincinnati.

For many years there has been a great deficiency of Public Halls of a suitable extent and arrangement to suit the various wants of our growing city. This was in part remedied by the construction of Concert and Washington Halls, but it is only since the new College and the Masonic and Odd Fellows Halls, and the spacious saloon which constitutes an important feature in Mr. Williams' new erection at the corner of 4th and Walnut streets, that provision has been made for our wants. The public hall of the Odd Fellows is forty-nine by sixty-two and eighteen feet high; that of Mr. Williams is sixty by ninety, and twenty-four feet high; of the Masonic building is fifty-one by one hundred and twelve, and twenty-three feet high; and of the College edifice, sixty-five by one hundred and thirty-two, and twenty-two feet high. These are of sufficient capacity for any public assemblage except mass meetings; and almost any of the larger of these will hold a public meeting of three thousand citizens, as many as can brought together except on extraordinary occasions.

History of Newspapers.

Newspapers are of Italian origin, whence the term Gazette from *Gaceta*, is derived. This is a small coin, which was the price of one paper, and became the badge of the periodical as the Picayune—six cents—is that of a well known New Orleans print. The first issue was at Venice, in 1536, ninety years after the discovery of printing; so it seems books in the modern form, first printed in 1479, are older than newspapers. This was a private enterprise, and was soon suppressed by the public authorities there—at all times one of the worst tyrannies the world ever knew. I re-established in 1558, under censorship and by authority, *" con licenzia."*

The oldest newspaper in Paris was the Mercure de France, which appeared as early as 1605. There was in that city twenty-seven papers, in 1779, thirty-five.

A newspaper was established in Scotland by Cromwell, in 1652. One was permanently established at Glasgow in 1715 during the era of the first Pretender. The oldest paper still in existence is the Edinburg Evening, of which the first number was issued in 1700.

In 1696, there were but nine newspapers in London—all weekly. The first daily was issued in 1709, at which date there were eighteen published of all descriptions. In 1724, the number was twenty, to wit—3 daily, 6 weekly, 7 tri-weekly, 3 penny post, and a semi-weekly London Gazette.

In 1792, there were thirteen daily and twenty semi-weekly papers. The oldest existing papers are the Whitehall Evening Post, commenced in 1794; the St. James Chronicle, 1793; and the Morning Chronicle, 1769.

The number of dailies in London since 1792, has decreased to nine; and these are all the dailies in England. The aggregate of their issues has however increased prodigiously. The London annual issues of all descriptions exceed sixty millions.

The oldest newspaper in Ireland is the Belfast Newsletter. It is still in existence.

I have too few data to give any statement of the newspapers in America, except to say that in 1743, there was no newspaper in New York; and at the date 1792, when there were thirty-three periodicals in London we had none in Cincinnati. Now there are sixty-nine of various descriptions in New York, and forty-eight in Cincinnati.

The issues of the American press are greater than those of England, being nearly double. The history of American newspapers is yet to be compiled.

Firemen's Fair at the Masonic Hall.

A Fair for the benefit of Relief Fire Company No. 2, on George street, opened at the public hall in the new Masonic Buildings, corner of Walnut and Third streets, on Christmas Eve, and will continue until the ensuing 8th of January.

The usual amount of useful and fancy articles, with the *refreshing* influences of ice cream, soda and cake, bright eyes and rosy cheeks, welcomed the thronging guests of that evening, opening their hearts and their purses. Besides a very great number of season ticket admissions, three thousand seven hundred and thirty persons must have been present in the course of that evening, as testified by the receipts at the door, so that their visitors on that occasion could not have fallen short of four thousand persons: indeed hundreds were shut out who came to witness the scene. And well do these, a division of our gallant firemen, deserve all the pecuniary support they receive.

In a room one hundred and twelve feet by fifty-one, filled around with novelties and curiosities upon the tables which line the sides, there was of course such a variety and extent of objects worthy of notice, as the limits of my columns would not afford space to describe. I shall therefore refer to but an article or two as a sample of the attractions of the evening.

A rich pagoda or pavilion occupies nearly the centre of the hall, constructed for the occasion, fitted up in the room by the skill and ingenuity of some of the mechanics of the company, and furnished by the exquisite taste of the ladies of their acquaintance. It is an octagon with fluted columns and pannel work at the sides, festooned with pink curtains and canopied in gorgeous style. In the centre a temporary building was erected to serve as a post office. The pavilion will no doubt be purchased at the conclusion of the fair for a summer house, by some our citizens. It is admirably adapted to that purpose. Opposite, and occupying a position corresponding with this, is a new hose reel made by *I. & B. Bruce*, for the company, which surpasses for excellence of work, exactness of proportion and fit, taste in design, and elegance in finish, anything brought from the east. The wood work is hickory, oak and ash of the best qualities, as the samples of the original woods there, clearly indicate. The iron work is as light as the necessary strength of the article would permit, and is coated entirely with plated brass. On the main pannel on one side is the frigate Constitution ploughing a rough sea; on the other, Gen. Wayne taking leave of the officers at Fort Washington in 1793. Both views are tastefully surrounded with groups of the national flag. The corner pannels are decorated with figures of firemen in their appropriate costume, with hose pipe in hand and trumpet to the mouth. The carved work, painted or gilt, the arch of the reel with its braces, the pillars and scroll work, and the lamps, are all specimens of beauty and taste which I cannot stop minutely to describe. But I must say one word respecting the bells. These are in number five, of clear, delightful tone, and hung and balanced with such accuracy that the most mechanical eye cannot detect a hair's breadth in the range of the springs or yokes which support them. The reel itself, on the whole, must be seen to be properly appreciated. It is a splendid trophy of the skill and ingenuity of Cincinnati mechanics and artists.

For the design, and the execution in part, of this reel, the company is indebted to Mr. *M. Ruffner,* and his associates of the building committee.

Two charming wreaths of white roses, contributed for the purpose by the Misses *Baker*, on Fourth street, decorate the apparatus in appropriate style.

The Lost Child.

A correspondent of the St. Louis Weekly Gazette gives the following account of a hunt for a lost child, in one of the thinly peopled neighbourhoods of the west:

About ten o'clock in the morning, was heard loud shout at the gate—"Ho! Mr. W., ho!"

"What's wanting!"

"O'Leary's boy is lost—little Johnny!"

This was enough to secure a father's aid, and on the road to shout the same at every door he passed. Little Johnny! said I, and my heart burst forth at the very sound. He was a fair and lovely child, little Johnny, and had a gentle and affectionate mother, with an ardent and sacrificing love which few mothers feel. His father was a bold hunter—his horses and hounds and rifle, had more of his heart than all the world besides; but little Johnny nestled there; indeed he was a great pet with the neighbours, and won more caresses and more sympathies than all the rest of the children together. Such appeals are always sovereign; but few perhaps, have ever met with a more quick or general response than his—every body turned out—the news flew like lightning; and men and boys for ten miles around came in to assist in the search, while women and children were running to and fro, and hailing every passer by, to learn the progress of the work. Never before I may dare to say, was there such a neighbourly union as now pervaded this motley mass—the same gush of sympathy, the same fearful apprehension, and the same images of death and wo, pervaded every home and heart. It seemed as if one vast cloud of gloom enwrapped the region around, from which shone out in lurid glare, and to which every eye was turned, and every pulse beat true—*the lost child!*

Little Johnny was about four years old; he had been out in the field, with his father and the black man, who were harvesting corn—and started for home about 2 o'clock, P M. On returning at night, they ascertained that the child had never been seen. It was nearly dark, but the alarm was given, and some fifteen or twenty neighbours commenced the search. The corn, where he was last seen, was the first object of course; here they took single rows and scoured the field in vain. They then scattered through the adjoining wood; the father frantic, often calling out in a voice of thunder—"Ho! John—ho!—ho John!" Then fearing the boy might be alarmed and afraid to answer, he would soften down into the gentle winning tone of the fireside—"Johnny, Johnny my dear, father's come." It was a cloudy evening; and though, perhaps, he had never bowed the knee "before Jehovah's awful throne," he prayed—O how earnestly he prayed the Lord it might not rain that night. The air was damp and chilly, so that if the child were alive with his bare feet and light jacket, he must be suffering cruelly from cold. But the wolves!—ah this was the fear, this the terror, which all felt, but none dared to breathe. A wolf had been seen prowling around the premises—indeed they had a common path across the prairie—and the point where several beside myself, had heard the cries of distress, was a famous haunt for them. Even in the midst of the anxious search, a distant growl would now and then burst on the ear, picturing forth the den, the cubs, the————————. The dogs were very eager in the field, especially wolf dogs. Winder, one of the best, would run no other trail. O'Leary knew this, and watched with most intense anxiety his every move. He scents—he scents—he runs—"Oh my God, he's got my boy!" He leaps from his horse, he sees the foot print of his own dear Johnny in the gopher hill by the side—he tracks him to the wood, and off from Winder's trail: ah! now he breathes again.

The search was continued until midnight, when a part thought it best to relieve their horses, and wait for daylight to begin afresh. But the father, with three of his hunting friends, who had re-solved not to eat or sleep till they had found the boy, still kept on—sometimes riding, sometimes walking—calling and shouting, if for no other purpose than to keep the wolves at bay. At length they stationed themselves within hearing distance of each other, and sat down to protect the child, to rush to his rescue, in case they should hear him attacked, to watch until the morning.

At early dawn, about fifty new horsemen arrived, and the search commenced anew. The field was again examined for the track, which was pursued with some doubt, as he had been there three successive days. On tracing the path which led towards the wolf woods, the imprints of Johnny's little feet were again discovered, as he appeared to be running, and the mark of his bag dragging along by his side. Here the father's anguish gushed anew, as the fears of the preceding night were justified and corroborated. They now agreed to take a station of about fifteen rods abreast, go up one side of the branch and down the other, till the whole surface of an extensive area, (farther than he could possibly have traveled,) had been explored. They had completed one side, and were returning, when the signal was given—Johnny was found! The noisy shouting and repeated peals of the hunters' winding horns, soon grouped [the excited cavalcade. But O'Leary, though foremost in the hunt, fell back at the first note of the summoning horn, nor did he speak a word, or scarcely breathed, till he snatched his own dear Johnny from the arms of his delighted bearer, and pressed him with a frantic fondness to his now bursting heart. The dear boy was found about two miles from home, in a thicket of hazel, picking filberts, with his bag of corn still on his arm. He looked bright and happy; and when asked where he was going, said he was going home, but it was *so far*. He said he hadn't seen anybody, but he heard some one call him, and that he was afraid, that he run away till he was tired, and then he laid his little head down on his bag, and cried—that while he was crying, he saw a big carriage go by him with candles in it, (the thunder and lightning,) and then it grew very dark, and he asked God to take care of little Johnny, and went to sleep.

Putting Resolutions into Practice.

At a missionary meeting held amongst the negroes at Jamaica, these three resolutions were agreed upon:

1. We will all give something.
2. We will all give as God has enabled us.
3. We will all give willingly.

So soon as the meeting was over, a leading negro took his seat at the table, with pen and ink, to put down what each came to give. Many came forward and gave, some more and some less. Amongst those that came was a rich old negro, almost as rich as all the others put together, and threw down upon the table a small silver coin. " Take dat back again," said the negro that received the money, " Dat may be according to de first resolution, but its not according to de second." The rich old man accordingly took it up, and hobbled back again to his seat in a rage. One after another came forward, and as almost all gave more than himself, he was fairly ashamed of himself, and again threw down a piece of money on the table, saying, " Dare, take dat!"

It was a valuable piece of gold, but it was given so ill-temperedly, that the negro answered again, " No! dat won't do yet. It may be according to de first and second resolutions, but not according de last," and he was obliged to take up his coin again. Still angry at himself and all the rest, he sat a long time, till nearly all had gone, and then came up to the table, with a smile on his face, and very willingly gave a large sum to the treasury. " Very well," said the negro, " Dat will do. Dat according to all de resolutions."

Royalty.

A leaf from the account book of the Lord Steward or head cook of Queen Victoria's royal household, for the last year, gives the following items. The amounts are thrown into American currency, that they may be understood at a glance.

Butcher's meat	$17,000
Bread	10
Milk and cream . . .	7,000
Poultry	18,000
Fish	10,000
Bacon, cheese and eggs, . .	25,000
Groceries	23,000
Oil	8,600
Fruit and confectionary . .	8,250
Vegetables, . . .	2,000
Wine, ale and beer—liquors, &c. .	47,050
Wax and tallow candles .	11,000
Lamps, ...	23,000
Fuel, ...	24,000
Stationery	1,000
Turnery	1,700
Braziery, ...	4,400
China, glass, &c. . . .	6,550
Linen	4,420
Washing table linen . .	15,500
Plate	1,740
	$316,000

Such are the blessings of royalty. The relative disbursements for bread and wine, beer and ale have had no parallel since the days of Sir John Falstaff. "Oh monstrous!—four penceworth of bread to all this sack," and is another striking illustration how true to nature Shakspeare wrote.

A Lawyer's Portrait.

A painter, the other day, in a country town, made a great mistake in a characteristic, and it was discovered by a country farmer. It was the portrait of a lawyer—an attorney who from humble pretensions had made a good deal of money, and established thereby his pretensions, but somehow or other not very much enlarged his respectability. To his pretensions was added that of having his portrait put up in the parlour as large as life. There it is, very flashy, and true; one hand in his breast and the other in his small clothes pocket. It is market day; the country clients are called in—opinions are passed (the family present,) and all complimentary,—

such as, "Never saw such a likeness in the course of my born days: as like un as he can stare." "Well, sure enough, there he is." But at last there was one dissentient! "'Taint like —not very—no, 'taint," said a heavy, middle-aged farmer, with a rather dry look, too, about the corners of his mouth. All eyes were upon him. "Not like! How not like?" exclaimed one of the company, and who knew the attorney —"say where it is not like?" "Why, don't you see," said the man, "he has got his hand in his breeches pocket. It would be as like again if he had it in some other body's pocket!" The family portrait was removed, especially, as after this, many came on purpose to see it; the attorney was lowered a peg or two, and the farmer obtained the reputation of a connoisseur as well as a wit.

Scripture Quotations.

A late city paper quotes as a scripture text, "that he that runs may read," "and that the wayfaring man, though a fool, need not err therein." The second member of the quotation is undoubtedly taken from the Bible, although not literally correct in the quotation, but the first part, although cited as above in many periodicals, is neither a scripture phrase nor a scripture idea, and cannot be found from Genesis to Revelations. It would be an employment conducive to the accuracy of certain editors if they would brush up their acquaintance with the Bible, as a means of enabling them to quote it correctly. They might probably derive other benefits in the perusal. There are various other *texts*, such as—" God tempers the wind to the shorn lamb,"—"In the midst of life we are in death,"—What shadows we are, and what shadows we pursue," supposed even by persons otherwise intelligent to be derived from the scriptures, which originated from far different sources. The first is in Tristam Shandy, by Sterne; the last was written by Edmund Burke. I cannot trace the origin of the second, but believe it to be an aphorism of one of the puritan writers of England.

Diplomacy.

The following incident occurred lately at Washington. Straws shew which way the wind blows:—

At a dinner at M. Bodisco's, Mr. Buchanan, Mr. Ritchie, and the British Minister were among the guests. After dinner, Mr. Ritchie, filling his glass, proposed to Mr. Bodisco, as a toast: "The immediate affinity of the Russian and United States Territory on the Northwest coast." Mr. Bodisco, turning to Mr. Packenham, said—" Will you drink that?" "I am not thirsty," said Mr. Packenham, filling his glass with water. Some time afterwards, Mr. Buchanan accosted Mr. Ritchie, "Come, I will drink your toast again!" There was diplomacy for you, in the quiet reply of the British Minister!

From the Snow-Flake Annual for 1846.

The Memory of the Past.

BY GEORGE P. MORRIS.

One balmy summer night, Mary,
    Just as the risen moon
Had cast aside her fleecy veil,
    We left the gay saloon.
And, in a green sequestered spot,
    Beneath a drooping tree,
Fond words were breathed, by you forgot,
    That still are dear to me, Mary,
    That still are dear to me.

Oh we were happy then, Mary—
    Time linger'd on his way,
To crowd a life-time in a night,
    Whole ages in a day!
If star and sun would set and rise
    Thus in our after years,
This world would be a Paradise,
    And not a vale of tears, Mary,
    And not a vale of tears.

I live but in the past, Mary—
    The glorious days of old!
When love was hoarded in the heart,
    As misers hoard their gold;
And, often like a bridal train,
    To music soft and low,
The by-gone moments cross my brain,
    In all their summer glow, Mary,
    In all their summer glow.

These visions form and fade, Mary,
    As age comes stealing on
To bring the light and leave the shade
    Of days forever gone!
The poet's brow may wear at last
    The bays that round it fall;
But love has rose-buds of the past
    Far dearer than them all, Mary,
    Far dearer than them all.

A Professional Hit.

Dr. Elliott, as is well known, was a merry, eccentric little being, who talked pretty much at random, and oftentimes with no great reverence for the subjects which he talked upon.

On one occasion he called upon a patient, Henderson, the celebrated actor, to inquire how his medicine had succeeded, and in his northern accent demanded of the patient,

"Had he taken the *palls* that he sent him?"

"He had."

"Well, and how did they agree? what had they done?"

"Wonders," replied Henderson; "I survived them."

"To be sure you did," said the doctor, "and you must take more of them, and live for ever. I make my patients immortal.

"That is exactly what I am afraid of," doctor, rejoined the patient.

CINCINNATI MISCELLANY.

CINCINNATI, JANUARY, 1846.

Coal.

I refered a short time since to a proposal made by Mr. S. W. Pomeroy, of our city, to supply coal on contract for the ensuing season, at ten cents per bushel, one half payable at the time of subscribing, and the residue on delivery. I find great misapprehension exists as to the character of this project and its advantages to the public, which in both its pecuniary and moral aspects, I propose to remove.

It has been objected to me, that this is too high a price. "We have bought coal," say individuals, "when plenty, at nine cents per bushel, and even less. Mr. Pomeroy himself sells coal at six and seven cents by the boat load, and why should he charge such a difference to families?" In fact I have been told that I have been doing the community an injury by advocating the project, and an insinuation was made more than once that it was done by me for interested purposes.

As to the unworthy motives imputed to me, as there never was a public servant who did his duty, that escaped such treatment, I shall endure it, satisfied if a great public good shall have been accomplished by this project. As to the character of the proposal, a word or two.

When coal first became an article of fuel here for family purposes, it was sold at twelve and a half to fifteen cents, by *Ephraim Jones*, who introduced it here into general use. As others got into the business it became an article for speculation, commanding in time of scarcity as high as thirty, and even forty cents per bushel. To remedy this, the Fuel Company was established, and stock to the value of $30,000 taken. The larger share of this has been absorbed in improvements, stock and fixtures, some thirteen thousand dollars being applied annually to the purchase of coal, hardly enough to supply four hundred of the eight thousand families here, who consume the article, and in fact not a sufficiency for the supply of two hundred, if we deduct what is needed for the use of manufacturers who are stockholders. Well, the Fuel Company sold upper country coal at twelve and a half to fifteen cents, and in a great measure checked the spirit of monopoly and extortion that was at work. A permanent market being thus opened, coal was landed here in large quantities, and for one sea-son the Fuel Company was undersold, and its operations temporarily checked, by the public affording no further patronage, being led to suppose that the desired effect on the coal market had now been accomplished in a permanent reduction of its price.

What next? Here we have had a long period of low water, succeeded by a month of suspension of river navigation by ice, while our consumption of coal has increased more than double the amount of 1840, and the result has been that from thirty to eighty cents per bushel has been exacted for coal. Truly is it recorded that the love of money is the *Root* of all evil. Alas! that men, for the sake of making a few dollars, should be guilty of extorting from the pockets of the destitute the last dime of their wretched pittance. We have all now learnt a lesson. Let it be considered how to profit by it. And now for Mr. Pomeroy's proposition.

In the first place, coal delivered at the doors of private houses is as cheap as it can be permanently done. Ask any manufacturer who buys by measurement and pays his hawling himself, how much cheaper he gets it than the man who buys it by the cart load. One cent per bushel, probably. Is this too great a difference? But it has been bought at nine or even eight cents, when the market was glutted. But did not this glut put the next season's consumption to you at sixteen cents, and was not the average thus made, higher than the price now proposed?

But if there are those who believe they can buy to better advantage without making such engagement as I recommend, is not this very arrangement the means of enabling them to do so. By withdrawing a large portion of purchasers out of the private yards, will it not lessen the usual demand there, which has served to keep up or advance the price; and did not the Fuel Company operate as far as they went, to this very effect?

As to the Fuel Company, it must enlarge its sphere before it can protect the community. Men have not only had to pay extra price elsewhere for what they have needed, but the benevolent have been disabled from assisting with this article as many of the destitute as they would otherwise have done.

I will make a fair proposition to any one who does not agree in these views, to test their value. I shall buy three hundred bushels of Mr. Pomeroy, under this arrangement, for my own use. Let any person who thinks he can economise by purchasing the same quantity in any other mode, invest thirty dollars in the article. At the close of the winter, let it be ascertained who has most on hands. Let the value of what is left be paid to the Orphan Asylum, by whoever shall have the least quantity unburnt, or the value of a load by him who shall first run out.

The importance of the subject must excuse the length of this article.

Cincinnati Steamboats of 1845.

I have procured for publication a list of steamboats enroled as belonging to this district, together with the names of two others which were built here, but finished, the Belle Creole of 448 tons, at Louisville, and the Bulletin of 499 tons, at New Albany.

Magnolia -	-	-	596	50,000
Bulletin -	-	-	499	37,000
Belle Creole	-	-	449	33,000
Hercules -	-	-	371	20,000
Jamestown	-	-	338	27,000
Cincinnati	-	-	326	22,000
Sea -	-	-	310	21,000
George Washington -	-	303	24,000
Metamora	-	-	297	25,000
Hard Times	-	-	291	20,000
Alhambra	-	-	290	24,000
Star Spangled Banner	-	275	25,000
Pike No. 8	-	-	247	20,000
Andrew Jackson	-	229	22,000
Selma	-	-	227	18,000
Undine -	-	-	193	15,000
Wm. R. McKee	-	165	13,000
Mary Pell	-	-	159	11,000
Reliance -	-	-	156	9,000
War Eagle	-	-	156	14,000
Sultan	-	-	125	6,000
Clermont -	-	-	121	6,000
Rob Roy -	-	-	111	8,000
Eureka -	-	-	110	7,000
Mentoria -	-	-	108	6,500
Matilda Jane -	-	87	8,000
Henri	-	-	56	3,500

27 boats. Total, 6609 505,500

The building here in 1840, was thirty-three boats of 5361 tons, at a cost of $592,500; of 1844, thirty-two boats of 7838 tons, and a value of $542,500. The gradual diminution in value of of aggregates, results from the reduction in the price of materials of late years, and the disproportion of price of cost, compared with tonnage, and in the War Eagle and Reliance of the same tonnage, costing, one nine and the other fourteen thousand dollars, in the absolute difference of finish and equipment.

The steamboats and barges built last year, as far as I can make up a list, were at

	Number.	Tonnage.	Cost.
New Albany,	11	1,959	$118,500
Louisville,	16	4,152	270,000
Cincinnati,	27	6,609	505,500

As soon as I get the Pittsburgh and St. Louis lists I shall add them to this.

Several boats are on the way here—two of them nearly finished, which are not included in my list.

CORRESPONDENCE.

Mr. C. Cist,—Sir:

I am not much given to speculation, nor can I be charged with favouring any of those extensive projects by which our citizens have been plundered or the city involved in debt. Yet when an enterprise perfectly practicable, and of immense importance to the public, has been proposed, although it may involve an outlay of money, I have not withheld my assent.

A few years only can elapse—not exceeding ten—before we shall have a railway connecting the Capitol of the State of Indiana with Cincinnati. The distance is about one hundred and ten miles, and the route must be through the Whitewater Valley to Hamilton, thence to the city on the line of the canal.

Our citizens and the city corporation have a grade for twenty-five miles of the road already, in the bed of the Whitewater Canal. Upon this bed, timbers and rails can be laid down for about $4,000 per mile, making the cost of our portion of the work when completed, $100,000. The east end of the Whitewater Canal, terminating at Cincinnati, it is the general impression, will never yield anything, as revenue, to the owners, while used as a canal; but when abandoned for the grade of a rail-road, the stockholders will receive at least six per cent. upon the whole cost of grade and rails. Such will be the impetus given to trade and travel in the direction of Indianapolis, by the extension of this work even to the Indiana line, that the people of that state will soon make provision for its completion to their capitol.

The controversy now waging between the owners of property on the line of the contemplated street and Market Space, between Walnut street and Western Row, and the city, must end in embarrassment to both parties, if not soon terminated. By the abandonment of the Market Space, between Elm street and Western Row, and only taking ground for a fifty-three feet street, room can be had for the passage of the railway from

Western Row to Walnut street, and the difficulty may be settled. This track may be made so as to touch the south end of Green street, and afford space for warehouses, and a depot on the whole line from Western Row, without encroaching upon Pearl street. The rails may be laid upon a level with the bottom of the canal at the east end, and allow the cars to pass under the cross streets to the terminus, without obstruction or damage to the thoroughfares of the city, and without any opposition on the part of the citizens; and *this is the only way and the only route by which a railway will ever be permitted to enter the city.* The importance of a depot from Indiana and Hamilton, in the centre of the city, must be seen at a glance; and on looking over our city plat, covered with expensive and permanent improvements, it must be admitted that I am right in my conclusion that this is the only route left.

In view then of securing the money already invested in the Whitewater Canal, of terminating a costly and vexatious litigation, and of affording to our merchants the only opportunity of a railway termination in the centre of the city, I hope our City Council and others interested, may take up this project and give it a full and candid examination.   C.

January 1, 1836.

Fire Engines.

A new engine called "Relief No. 2," built by Paddack & Campbell for the Fire Company on George street bearing that name, and intended to match the superb hose reel now exhibiting at their Fair at the Masonic Hall, was brought out on trial a few days since.

In the construction of this engine Messrs. Paddack & Campbell have not only surpassed everything heretofore brought from the east—the Fame for example—but also all their own previous efforts in this line. This can readily be made apparent.

The Fame throws the farthest of any of our Eastern engines, as the Cincinnati does of those made here. The Fame has thrown water after repeated trials two hundred and four feet, and the best performace of the Cincinnati was two hundred and ten; both from the gallery. These are respectively of $7\frac{1}{2}$ and $7\frac{1}{4}$ chambers, and of corresponding power in other respects, and constitute a class of engines which usually throw thirty to forty feet farther than the smaller class of six inch chambers, which is the size of the *Relief.* Yet the last engine, in an unfinished state, on her first and only trial, has thrown water by measurement, two hundred feet, level distance, through a nosel, also, one sixteenth of an inch larger than that of the Fame.

The Relief is now in the hands of her painters,

I. & B. Bruce, and will doubtless settle on her next trial the question, what we shall gain by sending to our Atlantic Cities for fire apparatus.

The Relief costs less than the Fame, and besides being of greater power, as a double suction engine, is not as heavy by from twelve to fourteen hundred pounds in weight.

It gratifies me to find our Cincinnati mechanics justifying my guarantee that they will make as good if not better work, at as cheap if not cheaper rates, than the same description of articles cost in Boston or Philadelphia.

Adventure with a Bull.
(From Scenes and Adventures in Spain.)

It was a fine afternoon in August. On the old *plaza* the rays of a canicular sun were shed with scorching intensity, and a strong stream of light gilded the pavement under the arch, and for a short distance beyond it.

As I emerged from the heated region into the cool, solitary street, but adorned and irradiated with bright eyes and gracious smiles from the ranges of balconies above, the effect was singular. Advancing towards my quarters, intending merely to take leave of my *patron* and his family, I saw my servant with the horses waiting for me at the door according to my directions. In the balconies were the young ladies and some Senoritas, their friends. A good distance beyond, and where the street was somewhat broader, there was a mass of people looking down another street which branched off, occasionally peering round the corner, and starting back as though dreading some encounter.

In a few minutes a *Novillo,* or rather a young bull, rushed, prancing and butting, into the street, maddened and urged on by hundreds of vociferations, from the crowd by whom he was pursued. My servant dragged his horses through the gateway, doubtless expecting me to follow, but I did not choose to do so. How could I, when so many bright eyes were bent down upon me? So I bade him shut the gate.

" 'Tis only a *Novillo,*" said I to myself.

And here let me explain that, in the northern provinces of Spain, and, I believe, in many others, it is the custom, on festive days, to enjoy a sport called *Novillo,* that is a yearling bull is secured by the horns with rope several fathoms in length, and then he is cast free, as it were, and excited by hootings, shrieks, and an infinity of discordant sounds, until he runs the whole length of his tether, when he is brought up with a jerk. All get out of his way as well as they can. Some, however, tantalize him by shaking their cloaks, jackets, or handkerchiefs before his eyes, and imitating the tricks and manœuvres of professed bull-fighters.

Well, I was alone, in the narrow part of the street, quite despising the *Novillo.* All at once he came full tear down the street, the whole *posse* of tormentors howling after him. I stood resting on my cane, which was a stout one, with a long gilt ferrule at the end; but the *Novillo* was butting right at me, and, to my dismay, I perceived that he had very sharp, and, by no means, short horns.

There was no possibility of a retreat. The case was a desperate one. I was between the infuriated animal's pointed horns and the wall, against which he seemed fully bent on pinning me.

How it came into my head I know not, but instantaneously I wedged the thick end of the cane between the upper part of my arm and my chest, as I had seen the *picadores* do with their spears, at the bull-fights, and firmly grasping the projecting portion in the hand, presented the ferruled point to the animal, who came on most furiously, head down, horns just at the proper tossing angle, and tail lashing his flank. I kept my eye upon him, and just as he made at me, I thrust my cane with all my might and main. I meant to do so into his shoulder in *picador* style, but luckily for me, I think, it buried itself in his flank, and threw him down with great force, turning him on his back, his feet trembling in the air, and his tongue lolling out of his foaming mouth.

I slipped aside, and was greeted with *rivas* from all the balconies, the ladies waving their handkerchiefs to me, my own fair *patrones* being among the most energetic. I coolly took off my cap, bowed right and left, and passed along amidst enthusiastic cheers, until I again passed the archway into the *plaza*.

When I arrived there, I stood still, marveling at my escape, and at the manner which I had hit upon to effect it. The whole scene did not occupy a twentieth part of the time it has taken me to describe it. I returned presently to my street, in which there were several groups in animated conversation. I was soon recognised, and again cheered as *El torero Yngles*. Nothing could have happened more calculated to make an individual popular than an event of this kind, any feat of agility or *sang froid* in encounters of this kind, being quite to the taste of the people all over Spain, though there was no merit on my part, no prowess; it was a case of self-preservation; and, not only did my poke in the *Novillo's* short ribs force the breath out of his body, but the pavement of Vitoria is proverbially slippery; so that when he once lost his legs, there was no recovering them. I had only time to say adieu to my friends, to receive their warm congratulations, to enjoy a hearty laugh with them at my curious adventure; and to depart, as I had a long ride before me, and was anxious, lest any sudden march at head-quarters should occur during my absence.

Recollections of the Last Sixty Years.--No. 4.

BY J. JOHNSTON, ESQ., *of Piqua.*

During my agency at Fort Wayne, the Miamis were a part of my charge. They formerly inhabited this river, the Miami of Ohio, and here where I live was their principal towns—extending from the mouth of Loramie's creek, including the ground occupied by my farm down to, and including lower Piqua, the present town of Piqua. The Miamis, in the old French war, which terminated with the peace of 1763, took part with the French, and were obliged to abandon their towns here; and sought a refuge on the upper waters of the Wabash and the Miami of the Lake, near the mouth of the Saint Joseph and Saint Mary's rivers, where Fort Wayne stood. The Shawanese and Delawares adhered to the

British interests, and were the occasion of the expulsion of the Miamis from this point. The Miamis were anciently called the Tewightewees; and after them the Shawanese took their places here, and gave it the name of Piqua, from one of their tribes. Of this tribe, the Miami was Meshekenoghqua or Little Turtle, a celebrated orator and chief who sig ed the treaty of Greenville with Gen. Wayne; a man of great wit, humour, and vivacity, fond of the company of gentlemen, and delighted in good eating. When I knew him he had two wives living with him under the same roof in the greatest harmony; one an old woman about his own age—fifty—the choice of his youth, who performed the drudgery of the house; the other a young and beautiful creature of eighteen, who was his favourite, yet it never was discovered by any one that the least unkind feeling existed between them. This distinguished chief died at Fort Wayne about twenty-five years ago, of a confirmed case of the gout, brought on by high living, and was buried with military honours by the troops of the United States. The Little Turtle used to entertain us with many of his war adventures, and would laugh immoderately at the recital of the following:—A white man, a prisoner of many years in the tribe, had often solicited permission to go on a war party to Kentucky, and had been refused. It never was the practise with the Indians to ask or encourage white prisoners among them to go to war against their countrymen. This man however had so far acquired the confidence of the Indians, and being very importunate to go to war, the Turtle at length consented, and took him on an expedition into Kentucky. As was their practise, they had reconnoitred during the day, and had fixed on a house recently built and occupied, as the object to be attacked, next morning a little before the dawn of day. The house was surrounded by a clearing, there being much brush and fallen timber on the ground. At the appointed time the Indians, with the white man, began to move to the attack. At all such times no talking or noise is to be made. They crawl along the ground on hands and feet; all is done by signs from the leader. The white man all the time was striving to be foremost, the Indians beckoning him to keep back. In spite of all their efforts he would keep foremost, and having at length got within running distance of the house, he jumped to his feet and went with all his speed, shouting at the top of his voice, Indians! Indians! The Turtle and his party had to make a precipitate retreat, losing for ever their white companion; and disappointed in their fancied conquest of the unsuspecting victims of the log cabin. From that day forth this chief would never trust a white man to accompany him again to war.

During the Presidency of Washington, the Little Turtle visited that great and just man at Philadelphia, and during his whole life after, often spoke of the pleasures which that visit afforded him. Kosciusko, the Polish chief, was at the time in Philadelphia, confined by sickness to his lodgings, and hearing of the Indians being in the city, he sent for them, and after an interview of some length, he had his favourite brace of pistols brought forth, and addressing the chief, Turtle said—I have carried and used these in many a hard fought battle in defence of the oppressed, the weak, and the wronged of my own race, and I now present them to you with this injunction, that with them you shoot dead the first man that ever comes to subjugate you or despoil you of your country. The pistols were of the best quality and finest manufacture, silver mounted, with gold touch-holes.

The white people, by their knowledge of letters, are enabled always to exhibit a long catalogue of grievances against the Indians, whilst they not possessing the same advantages, their wrongs are in a great measure unrecorded and unknown. I will cite two instances of many that occured during my long intercourse with the Indians, which for cold blooded, unprovoked, and premeditated cruelty, has never been exceeded and seldom equaled, among savage or civilized people.

In the time of sugar making, 1824, one of the subordinate chiefs of the Seneca Indians, with eight of his people, were hunting within the limits of Madison county, Indiana, a new county then, and thinly populated. Having spent the previous fall and winter there, they were distinguished for their inoffensive, orderly and peaceable conduct. In March of that year, Bridge, Sawyer, Hudson, and a youth under age, the son of Bridge, with another person whose name I have forgot, and who made his escape to Texas, the common refuge of all bad men, matured and perpetrated a plan for murdering the unoffending Indians. Those five white persons repaired early on a certain day to the hunting cabin of the Indians under a pretence that they had lost their horses, and asked the two Indian men to go with them in the woods in different directions to search for them, each party taking an Indian. When they got them out a sufficient distance they basely murdered them; and after covering up the bodies, returned towards the Indian camp. The poor women seeing the white men return without their husbands, came out to meet them. One of them in front, who was a Delaware, half white, and spoke English, asked, much agitated, for her husband. They told her that he would come by and by, and to turn and go into the house. It appeared by the confession of these monsters in human shape, that they had not the heart to shoot her down facing them, but as soon as she turned away from them, they shot her, though not mortally. She fell on her knees, imploring mercy for the sake of the Lord Jesus Christ, telling them she was of their own flesh—alluding to her colour—and in that condition they knocked out her brains with a homony pounder, and with knives, tomahawks, and the same instrument, they murdered the remaining women and children; whole number murdered nine. To cap the climax of this tragedy. and to shew what a degree of callous, hard-hearted depravity, men calling themselves christians may arrive at, the whole of these murderers were next day found in attendance on their knees at a religious meeting in the neighbourhood. As soon as the murder was known among the Indians, many of whom were in the neighbourhood hunting, having met, the declared if the murderers were not secured and punished, satisfaction would fall upon innocent persons, as they could not restrain their young men. The frontier became alarmed; the murderers apprehended with the exception of the one who fled to Texas. An express was sent to myself with the news; I repaired to the spot, took immediate measures for the security of the prisoners, reported the case, first to the Governor of Indiana, who declined acting, and second to the Secretary of War, Mr. Calhoun, who promptly acted, giving me ample powers to prosecute to conviction and execution, and to spare no expense. The conduct of this upright and able secretary in this and many other cases which fell under my notice, placed him above all praise. He filled that department, in my estimation, better than any other man since the days of Washington. At the time of Gen. Jackson's coming into power, I was at the seat of government settling my accounts. A friend of holding office, called on him to solicit his influence with the President in favour of his being continued. Mr. Calhoun appeared to be surprised that any fears should exist on the part of any faithful, competent man, and expressed his utter abhorrence at having anything to do, pro or con, with such dirty work.

Foreign Correspondence.

I am in receipt of a letter from *Buenos Ayres,* from our late fellow-citizen, *T. B. Coffin,* under date of October 22d, being the latest advices from the Argentine Republic. At that date the port of Buenos Ayres had been thirty days under blockade by the English and French squadrons on that coast, and all business in the city was in an absolute paralysis.

The Buenos Ayreans were in an exasperated state of feeling, the British having not long before taken possession of their national fleet at *Montevideo*, and the Argentine Legislature was at that date deliberating on a declaration of war against those powers. The allied invaders had made a descent on *Gualaguchu*, in the province of *Entre Rios* and on the river *Uruguay*, and after being guilty of the most atrocious violence, had carried off a booty of $150,000 in value. The writer adds, that there is no doubt that Great Britain is about to take the same steps to force a commerce up the *La Plata*, *Parana*, and *Uruguay*, as she has done with *China* and would up the *Mississippi* and *Ohio*, if she had to do with same kind of people.

Going the whole Figure.

At the late meeting in New York of Robert Owen's Convention for National Reform, the principle was laid down that no one should be permitted to hold more land than would constitute a suitable farm. This was going a step farther than that body laid down " the principle" in 1844, when they resolved that the General Government had no right to dispose of the public lands, which they alleged belonged to the whole country, and should first be allotted to the settlers free of cost—to the extent they would be needed for that purpose. But revolutions neither go backward nor stand still, as the following colloquy which appeared in a late New York paper, serves to prove:

" Bill," said one fellow to another, " I'se a National Reformer, I is."

" Vy, is that our party?"

" Vy, yes, hossy, it *is* that. If you puts in a vote for that ere party, you votes yourself a farm."

" Vell, I don't go that onless they'll go a little further. I vants a farm, and *somebody to work it besides.*"

This is carrying out " the principle," and reminds me of the views expressed by a sailor, during a nautical *row* in New York in the time of the " long embargo."

" What do you want, my good fellow?" asked the Mayor of the city, in a deprecating tone.

" Want?" exclaimed the spokesman, an old weather-beaten tar, about " three sheets in the wind"—" we want our *rights*. No land-lubber should be allowed to live on fried halibut, sea-pie and soft tommy, while poor Jack is starving on mouldy biscuit and salt junk. We want an equal division of property and provisions!"

" My good friend," exclaimed a sedate and portly-looking alderman, if we should comply with your demands, and make an equal division of all property, in less than a month you would be as destitute as ever."

" Perhaps so," replied the old tar, with a sly wink and a significant grin, " and *then we will divide again!*"

Transcendentalism.

The Chinese and Hindoos occasionally furnish us specimens of " orphic sayings," which throw into the shade their brother savans of Germany and Boston City. The following letter was written during our last war with Great Britain, by a merchant in extensive business at Calcutta. It is a curious document, and in no respect more remarkable than in the writer's ability to express himself in good English when he comes to treat of money matters.

CALCUTTA, 10th December, 1831.

Sir:—Having favoured with your kind Epistle of the 16th December, 1812, and received it with the best promulgation of Joy, with a view of renewing our reciprocal friendship again to its former state, but it solely partitioned by the present serious warlike intercourse existed between you and the British Government, which commonly occasioned an obscurity amongst the inclination of the Mankind, who originally entered to improve their Commodities in Traffics. However we confide these serious resistances will not remain for a longer, and will accordingly orifice an way on a reasonable time to enable us to promote our Mercantile purposes, as it was before.— We had once learned that an amicable arrangement on the subject have had taken place, and which caused to demonstrate our Joy, and accordingly we had the honour to sent the intelligence in circulation under cover of the Envelopes, but it instantly regreted us by perusing the advertisement, announcing the refreshment of the American War over again; however we hope that the Providence may determine the present hostility, and exist a tranquility between your territories and the Great Britain.

In regard the remittance of the Proceeds of Peace Goods, I beg leave to request you that if you think the present war to be immediately concluded and your coming out to Bengal will be taken place, I hope you will bring the amount with you, otherwise you will please to remit the same to Messrs. Farlie, Bonham & Co. of London, directing them to send the amount by a bill of Exchange to Ramdullol Day.

I hope this will meet you and family in a perfect health and happiness.

And remain with due respect, Sir,
Your most Obedient and Humble Servant,
RAMNARAIN GHOSS.
To G. W. J., Philadelphia.

The Dutch of Pennsylvania.

A traveler through York county, Pennsylvania, having lost his way, hailed a man he saw in a garden hoeing cabbages. " Hallo! I say, can you tell me the way to Daudel's mill." The man thus accosted, and who was, to use a Pennsylvania simile, as dutch as Hiester's horse, turned round and replied—" Py sure; I gin dell you so pesser als any potty. You see dat pridge; yoost make dat pridge ofer, den durn the riffer up schtream, biss you gum to a finker bose py a gross rote; dake down dirty oder forty bannels of fence on dat rote and you will gum on a gavern house mit a pick jerry dree at the toor, durn de gavern round und yoost pefere you is my prudder Hans' parn schinkled mit schtraw. When you kit upon his house you ax him, und he gin dell you so pesser als me."

"Let me see," said the traveler, reflecting— "make a bridge over, turn the river up stream, turn a house around and take forty pannels of fence down; my gracious what a day's work I have before me! Good bye."

Chronological Table.

Jan 1st—New Year's Day. Anthony Wayne, born, 1745.

2d.—Edmund Burke, born, 1730. Lavater, died, 1801.

3d.—Battle of Trenton, N. J., 1777. General Monk, died, 1670.

4th.—C. C. Pinckney, died, 1812; Roger Ascham, 1568; Sir Isaac Newton, 1642.

5th.—Duke of York, died, 1827.

6th.—The Epiphany, an *Appearance* or apparition is kept in commemoration of the manifestation of our Saviour to the Gentiles, and first observed A. D., 813—Old Christmas Day.

7th.—Fenelon, died, 1715.

8th—Battle of New Orleans, 1815. Galileo, died, 1742.

9th.—Archbishop Laud, beheaded, 1645.

10th.—Stamp Act passed, 1765. James Watt, born, 1736. Linnaeus, died, 1778.

Review.

A Sermon on Witchcraft. By J. L. WILSON, D. D.: preached at the First Presbyterian Church, November 9, 1845. pp. 23. Published by request.

This is a remarkable production, which exhibits all the learning, fidelity to duty, deference to the word of God, and boldness in avowing most unpopular opinions, which have characterised the whole course of the writer's life. The author holds that witchcraft has existed for ages, as he proves by the word of God; that it still exists, in the Papacy, in the New Jerusalem Church, the Shakers, the Mormons, and among the practitioners of the Mesmeric art. He adjudges the miracles wrought by Prince Hohenlohe and the Holy Coat of Treves, effected by the power o witchcraft; Emanuel Swedenborg to be no impostor, but deceived by lying spirits, and as such became the "prince of modern necromancers;" and mesmerism he considers founded on the same principle. He insists that the vain pretences to witchcraft which have been made in all ages, are just as full evidences of the existence of that art as the presence of a counterfeit note is of the fact that there are genuine ones, since without an original, there could be neither imitation nor copy.

I cannot concur with Dr. Wilson in all his views; and regard Mormonism as simply an unprincipled movement of artful deceivers, whose dupes are sufficiently ready to be deceived. What is new of Shakerism and Mesmerism is not true, and what is true is not new. A considerable share of the phenomena in both these, is referable to the nervous system; the residue a sheer imposture of men who begin dupes and end deceivers. In this category I place the whole horde of neurologists, mesmerists, clairvoyants, &c.; such as Professor *Brownson*, Drs. *Buchanan*, *Parnell* and *June.* Nor can I perceive in what respect these men are working miracles, any more than Signor Blitz or the Fakir of Ava.

Dr. Wilson's pamphlet is, however, worthy of a careful perusal by all who take an interest in the subject on which he treats.

The Sermon is from Donogh's press, and is a beautiful specimen of Cincinnati typography.

Address at the Fair of the Hamilton County Agricultural Society, at Carthage, Sept. 18, 1845. By JOHN W. CALDWELL, President. pp. 12.

I should not have felt called to review this production, but for the vigour and originality of the author's views and illustrations.

He commences by elevating to a proud eminence the agricultural employment. "What would our cities be without the farmer?" he asks. True, if we had not known it before, we should have found it out since we have had to pay five dollars per cord for wood. But it is not merely in provisioning us, we are under obligations to the sons of the soil, in the author's judgment.

"The very population itself of your crowded cities, is gathered from, and replenished by, the bands of healthful yeomanry, who till the soil. No city could long exist in prosperity, were it not for the commingling of its blood with that of the robust sons and daughters of the field."

This is hardly stating the case fairly and fully, for we are getting an admixture also of Saxon blood from German emigrants to renew the Heptarchy element in our ancestors, now nearly run out.

Mr. *Caldwell* contrasts agriculture as a profession, with that of the pulpit, the bench, the bar, the faculty, the political press, and the ranks of commerce and of the mechanic arts, of all which, as a class, he speaks with sufficient irreverence, although making the necessary exceptions.

I must turn him over to brothers Drinker or

Taylor, for his attacks on the political press. As to the bar, of which Mr. C. is a member, wait till the lawyers catch him in court, for him to get jesse.

He is in his element, as I have intimated, when he eulogises the farmers. Even Dr. *Overton* at Memphis, did not lay it on with a trowel, heavier, when he pronounced that convention the most able, enlightened, intelligent and influential body of men that ever had assembled or ever would assemble in the vast succession of ages to come, on the face of the wide earth. Still Mr. C. has a few things against his friends, the farmers. He thinks log cabins should be entirely obsolete—that the farmers ought to read more, and mind what they read. Above all they should pay the printer. I like the last suggestion—as such; but not the insinuation it conceals. My farmer subscribers do not want dunning, and are the best pay in the world.

Besides these things he hints to them that they are raising but thirty bushels corn, and a large share even less than that, where one hundred have heretofore been raised, unstinted both in grain and ear. And he tells them boldly if they don't spur up and remedy this state of things, the Dutch—who can produce on two acres as much as our farmers do upon ten, will get possession of their land and take the country. Hear this ye Native Americans and blow the trumpet in time!

The author closes his address in these words, every one of which is as true as it is important, and all said in the right spirit and taste.

" Indulge me, fellow-citizens, in the expression of a hope that the day is not far distant when the effort will be as well to improve the mind, as the crops of the tiller of the soil; when no farmer will consider his whole duty accomplished, whilst his children have not the facilities and opportunities of a good education; and when farmers will be men of literature and science, capable of analyzing their own soils, of applying science to their art, and of gracing the journals of the day with interesting reports of their operations. Then, and not till then, will you know and feel the full strength of your order; then, and not till then, will you obtain your true position, that which a high grade of intelligence, united to your permanent wealth and overwhelming numbers, will entitle you.

The *Debate on Slavery*, held at the Second Advent Tabernacle, in Cincinnati, by Rev. Jona Blanchard and N. L. Rice, D. D. pp. 482. Published by W. H. Moore & Co., Cincinnati.

This " Debate," long looked for by the thousands who were present at it, and the tens of thousands who have heard of it and take a deep interest in the subject, is at length before the public. As an individual, I have my own opinion which side has a right to claim the victory in argument, but it is not necessary, and would be in-

vidious in me to use these columns for that purpose. I can, however, freely and truly say, so far as I am competent to judge, that the debatants are men of signal ability, who have left little to be said on the subject beyond what is presented in this volume. My business with the book rather refers to its character for paper, printing, binding, &c., than to its subject.

The volume then is beautifully got up, the paper clear and white, the typographical arrangement neat and perspicuous, and the binding and general outside appearance surpassing that of any volume of the Cincinnati book issues heretofore. In this respect it is a perfect contrast to its predecessor, the " *Debate on Universalism*," which was on inferior paper and in an inferior style of cover and binding, and disfigured with such a profusion of italics and small capitals as to mar the general effect of its being read to advantage.

I can freely, therefore, recommend the volume to thousands who need light on the interesting subject to which it relates.

Clerical Eccentricity.

Rev. Mr. S. was a man of many eccentricities; and not a very animated or interesting preacher. As he advanced in years he became even less engaging, and his people—although they respected their good old pastor, and were disposed to keep the right side of him in expectation of a legacy —felt it quite a relief if they could find a plausible excuse for absenting themselves from his meetings. When any family was absent two or three Sabbaths in succession, Mr. S. would publicly state to the congregation that as Mr. ——'s family had been for some time absent from public worship, he presumed there was sickness or trouble in their household, and would appoint a prayer meeting at their house on the next Tuesday afternoon. For a while this answered the purpose, and it was found that the people preferred even to hear Mr. S. preach in the great congregation, than to have the almost exclusive benefit of his prayer meetings. He was, however, at times, obliged to adopt other measures to fill his house; for although the families took care to be represented on the Sabbath, they took special care not to come out *en masse*, so that the hearers of the parson, in his spacious temple, were generally few and far between. On one Sabbath afternoon, he told his people that he should take a journey the next day and be absent for a short time; but he would take care that some person should come from Boston on the next Saturday and supply his desk the next Sabbath. On the next Sabbath morning, the meeting house was filled. The whole town turned out to hear the Boston minister. They waited awhile in eager expectation of his entrance, when in marched the Rev. Mr. S., and walked up the broad aisle as he had been accustomed to do for many years gone by. On ascending his pulpit he smiled graciously upon his large audience and said, " I am glad, my dear hearers, that I have got you out—you're all here as you ought to be —and I hope your minds are prepared to receive instruction—I came from Boston yesterday myself!"

Flour Mills in St. Louis and Cincinnati.

I propose to institute a comparison between the flour milling operations in St. Louis and Cincinnati. It will be recollected that it is only within a few years we have manufactured any considerable quantity of flour in the city, while it has been an established business for many years in St. Louis. Under these circumstances the comparison is quite favourable for Cincinnati.

The number of mills here is fifteen, all but one of which are steam mills. The water mill belongs to Mr. Chouteau, and is propelled by water from the pond bearing his name.

Page's Mill,	. .	8 run of 4½ feet stones.
Union,	. . .	3 do of 5 feet do.
Star,	. . .	3 do of 4½ feet do.
Eagle,	. . .	2 do of 4½ feet do.
Washington,	. .	2 do of 4½ feet do.
Missouri, .	. .	2 do of 4½ feet do.
Phœnix,	. . .	2 do of 4½ feet do.
City,	. . .	2 do of 4½ feet do.
McKee's, .	. .	2 do of 4½ feet do.
Franklin,	. .	2 do of 4½ feet do.
Tucker, .	. .	3 do of 3 feet do.
Mound,	. . .	2 do of 3 feet do.
Park,	. . .	2 do of 3 feet do.
Pearle,	. . .	1 do of 3 feet do.
Chouteau,	. .	3 do of 4½ feet do.

Making,   40 run of stones.

In the above there are *three* run of stones of five feet diameter, *twenty-four* of four and a half feet, and *fifteen* run of three feet diameter—being equivalent to *upwards* of twenty-eight run of four and a half feet diameter.

I copy the above from the St. Louis New Era of the 20th ult. Our city mills are—

C. S. Bradbury, .	. . .	5 runs.
West & Co.,	. . . .	4 do.
Atkins & Blair, .	. . .	3 do.
John Elstner, .	. . .	3 do.
C. C. Febiger, .	. . .	3 do.
Atkins & Co., .	. . .	3 do.
Franklin Mills, .	. . .	3 do.
Fagin's, .	. . . .	3 do.

Twenty-seven, all of four and half feet stones. Hardly more than one run of stones as a difference.

I was surprised to find so little disparity in the two products, under the circumstances of the case. I do not know the amount of flour actually manufactured in St. Louis. This is both there and here, far short of the actual capacity of the mills. We make in Cincinnati more than one hundred and twenty thousand barrels annually, all beyond our home consumption, until this year, for shipment to New Orleans and the Atlantic Cities. Owing to the late flour operations, we have sent this year largely to the Lake Erie ports. At Union mills, St. Louis, on two run of stones —five feet—they make one hundred barrels flour per day. At Bradbury's, here, on four run four and a half feet, one hundred and thirty to one hundred and fifty barrels daily. This is

about equal. West & Co., on three pair of four and a half feet, have made in three consecutive weeks three thousand and thirty-three barrels, which is an extraordinary performance. Our city mills usually command a small advance on other brands, even of first rate quality.

Our capacity being within a fraction equal to that of St. Louis, I presume the actual manufacture is in about the same proportion, probably greater, as besides our supply of grain from the interior of Ohio, we get ample consignments of wheat from the St. Louis region itself.

Unaccountable.

A remarkable fact, and one which all my previous experience in statistics affords me no means to account for, may be found in the following circumstance.

The pews of the newly erected Central Presbyterian Church afford a remarkable contrast in the appearance of the backs. The ends next their doors are all distinctly marked at their upper edges with dark shade, as of coal dust pressed out against the paint by the men who occupy that part. The inside ends on the contrary, have the same impression made from the ladies' dresses, some twelve inches above the seat.

I hope the announcement of this remarkable contrast will not produce a *bustle* to ascertain the cause of the difference refered to.

Dr. Buchanan.

The following letter explains itself. I am perfectly willing that the Dr. should be heard through these columns, so far as his letter goes. The extracts accompanying that document, although termed "short" by the Dr., would take up more room than I can spare in my columns. They are the testimony of a writer in the Democratic Review, to the originality as well as the value of Dr. Buchanan's neurological discoveries. As to the "best minds" refered to in the letter, what determines their right to that attribute? Who shall indorse the indorsers? *Quis custodiet ipsos custodes?*

CINCINNATI, July 8, 1846.

Mr. C. CIST,—*Sir:*

Having been accustomed to very courteous relations with the gentlemen of the press, I regret to observe in your paper of yesterday a paragraph equally uncourteous and unjust, in which my name is associated with others in a sneering allusion.

Whatever you can justly say of myself, you are welcome to say; but as men are judged by their associates, I beg that my name shall not on any occasion be connected with those of men with whom I have as little sympathy, affinity, or connection as yourself and Dr. Wilson.

Whether my investigations of the brain receive public honour or censure, troubles me very little; but I am not willing that my friends should be annoyed and my position mystified with the public, by using my name in the company in which you have placed it.

Although editors are not bound to be omniscient, they are at least bound to be just in what they do say; and as your columns have a tone of independence and conscientiousness, I would request you to rectify this matter by a short extract which I herewith send you, which will serve *in some degree* to define my position for your readers.

Legitimate, and even insolent and unfair opposition I expect as a matter of course, but I am not prepared to submit to any *personal degradation* as a proper reward for investigations which some of the best minds of our country already regard as the commencement of a new era in the science of mind.

Very respectfully yours,

JOS. R. BUCHANAN.

The Way Americans go Down Hill.

But who has not been both wearied and amused with the slow caution of the German drivers? At every little descent on the road that it would almost require a spirit level to discern that it was a descent, he dismounts and puts on his drag. On a road of the gentlest undulations, where a heavy English coach would go at the rate of ten English miles an hour, without drag or pause, up and down, he is continually alighting and patting on one or both drags, alighting and ascending with a patience that amazes you. Nay, in many states, this caution is evinced also by the government, and is enforced by a' post on the side, standing on the top of every slope on the road, having painted on a board a black and conspicuous drag, and announcing a fine, of commonly six florins (ten shillings) on any loaded carriage which shall descend without the drag on. In everything they are continually guarded against those accidents which result from hurry, or slightness of construction.—*Howitt's Moral and Domestic Life in Germany.*

The stage in which we traveled across "tht Alleghenies," was one of the then called "Transi Line." It was, as the driver termed it, a "rushing affair," and managed by a refined cruelty to the dumb beasts, to keep a little ahead of the "Opposition," that seemed to come clattering in our rear like some ill-timed spirit, never destined exactly to reach us. The drivers of our different "changes" all seemed to be made upon the go-ahead principle, looking upon nothing as really disgraceful but being behind the stage that so perseveringly pursued us. Unfortunately, too, for our safety, we went in an "extra," and managed, by a freak of fortune, to arrive at the different stations, when drivers and horses were changed, just as the former had got comfortably to bed, and it was not the least interesting portion of my thoughts, that every one of those Jehus made the most solemn protestations that they would "upset us over some precipice, not less than three hundred and sixty-five feet high, and knock us into such a perfect nonentity, that it

would save the coroner the trouble of calling a jury to sit upon our remains."

It is nine years since, and if the winter of that year is not "remarkably cold" in the almanacs, it shows a want of care in those useful annuals. We say it was nine years since we crossed the Alleghenies. At the particular time we allude to, the "oldest inhabitant" of the country, and we met him on the road side, informed us that he had no recollection of such a severe season. How we lived through it has puzzled us quite as much as it did Capt. Ross, after he returned to England, from his trip to the north pole. The fire in every house we passed smoked like a Pittsburgh furnace, and around its genial warmth were crowded groups of men, women and children, that looked as if they had been born in the workshop of Vulcan. The road over which we traveled was McAdamized, and then frozen; it was as hard as nature will permit and the trampling of the horses' feet upon it sounded in the frosty air as if they were rushing across a continuous bridge.

The inside of the stage coach is a wonder; it is a perfect denial of Newton's theory, that two things or twenty cannot occupy the same place at the same time. The one we traveled in was perfectly full of seats, and their backs straw, buffalo robes, hat-boxes, rifles, flute cases, small parcels, and yet nine men, the very nine muses at times, (all the cider along the road was frozen and we drank the heart of it.) stowed themselves away within its bowels, but how, we leave to the invention of exhausted air-pumps and hydraulic presses. We all of course froze more or less, but it was in streaks; the curtains of the stage were fastened down and made tight, and then like pigs we quarreled ourselves into the snuggest possible position and place, it being considered fortunate to be most *in the middle*, as we then parted with the least heat, to satisfy the craving appetite of Jack Frost, who penetrated every little hole and nook, and delighted himself in painting fantastic figures upon the different objects exposed to his influence, out of our misery and death.

By one of these extraordinary phenomena, exhibited in the light of our favoured country, we unexpectedly found ourselves traveling over a road that was covered with frozen sleet; cold as was the season, there was no snow, the horses' shoes had no corks on them worth noticing, and the iron bound wheels on this change in the surface of the earth, seemed to have so little hold upon the road, that we almost expected they would make an effort to leave it, and break our necks as a reward for their aspirations. On we went, however, and as night came on, the darkness enveloped us in a kind of cloud, the ice-glazed surface of the ground reflecting a dull mysterious light upwards. Our whereabout never troubled us, all places between the one we were anxious to reach and where we were, made no impression upon us, and perhaps we would never have known a single particular place but for the incident we are about to detail.

I think that all my companions as well as myself were asleep, when I was awakened by that peculiar sawing motion a stage-body makes upon its springs when suddenly stopped. "What's the matter now?" was the general exclamation of the "insides" to the driver, who was discovered through the glass windows on the ground, beating his arms around his body with a vehemence that almost raised him into the air.

"Matter!" he exclaimed, sticking his nose above a woolen blanket that was tied around his face, which from the cold and his breath, wss frosted like a wedding cake, "Matter, matter enough—here we are on the top of 'Ball Mountain,' the drag chain broken, and I am so infarnal cold, I couldn't tie a knot in a rope if I had eighteen thousand hands!"

It was a rueful situation, truly. I jumped out of the stage, and contemplated the prospect near and at a distance with mixed feelings. So absorbed did I soon become, that I lost sight of the unpleasant situation in which we were placed, and regarded only the appearance of things about me disconnected with my personal happiness. There stood the stage upon the very apex of the mountain, the hot steaming breath of my half smothered fellow travelers pouring out of its open door in puffs, like the respiration of a mammoth. The driver, poor fellow, was limping about, more than half frozen, growling, swearing and threatening. The poor horses looked about twenty years older than when they started, their heads being whitened with the frost. They stamped with impatience on the 'hard ribbed ice;" the polished iron of their shoes looked as if it would penetrate their flesh with blighting cold. But such a landscape of beauty, all shrouded in death, we never saw or conceived, and one like it is seldom presented to the eye. Down the mountains could be traced the broad road in serpentine windings, lessening in the distance until it appeared no wider than a foot-path, obscured by the ravines and forest trees through which it ran. On either side were deep yawning chasms, at the bottom of which the hardy pines sprung upward a hundred and fifty feet, and yet they looked from where I stood like creeping plants. The very mountain tops spread out before me like pyramids. The moon shone upon this vast prospect, coming up from behind the distant horizon, bathing one eleventh in light, and another in darkness, or reflecting her silvery rays across the frozen ground, in sparkling gems, as if some eastern prince scattered diamonds upon a marble floor, then starting in bold relief the shaggy rock-born hemlock and poison laurel, penetrating the deep solitudes, and making "darkness visible" where all before had been deep obscurity. There, too, might be seen the heat driven from the earth in light fogs by the intense cold, floating upwards in fantastic forms, and spreading in thin ether as they sought more elevated regions. As far in the distance, in every direction, as the eye could reach, were the valleys of Penn, all silent in the embrace of winter and night, calling up most vividly the emotions of the beautiful and sublime.

"How are we to go down this outrageous hill, driver?" bawled out a speculator in western lands, who had amused us through the day past with nice calculations of how much he could have saved the government and himself, had he had the contract of making the "National road" over which we were traveling. The reply of the driver was exceedingly apt and characteristic.

"There is no difficulty in getting *down the hill*, but you well know there are a variety of ways in doing the same thing; the drag-chain would be of little use, as the wheel tire would make a runner of it. I think you had all better take your places inside, say your prayers, and let me put off, and if yonder grinning moon has a wish to see a race between a stage-coach and four horses down

'Ball mountain,' she'll be gratified, and see sights that would make a locomotive blush."

The prospect was rather a doleful one; we had about ninety chances in a hundred that we would make a "smash of it," and we had the same number of chances of being frozen to death if we did not take the risk of being smashed, for the first tavern we could get to was at the foot of the mountain. The driver was a smart fellow, and had some hostage in the world worth living for, because he was but three days married—had he been six months we would not have trusted him. The vote was taken, and it was decided to "go ahead."

If I were to describe an unpleasant situation, I should say that it was to be in a stage, the door closed upon you, with the probabilities that it will be opened by your head thrusting itself through its oak pannels, with the axle of the wheel at the same time falling across your breast. It seemed to me that it would be, with my companions, if I entered that stage, to be buried alive; so I mounted the driver's seat with a degree of resolution that would have enabled me to walk under a falling house without winking.

At the crack of the whip, the horses, impatient at delay, started with a bound, and ran a short distance, the boot of the stage pointing to the earth: a sudden reverse of this position, and an inclination of our bodies forward, told too plainly that we were on the descent. Now commenced a race between the gravitation and horse-flesh, and odds would have been safely bet on the former. One time we swayed to and fro as if in a hammock; then we would travel a hundred yards side ways, the wheels on the ice sparkling with fire and electricity, and making a grating sound, as terrible to my nerves as the extracting of a tooth. The horses frightened at the terrible state of things in the rear, and the lashing of the whip, would pull us around for a moment, and away we would go again, sideways, bouncing; crashing about like mad. A quarter way down the mountain, and still perfectly sound: but by this time the momentum of our descending body was terrible, and the horses, with reeking hot sides and distended nostrils, lay themselves down to their work, while the lashing whip cracked and goaded in their rear to hasten their speed. The driver, with a coolness that never forsook him, guided his vehicle, as much as possible, in zig zag lines across the road. Obstacles no larger than pebbles would project us into the air as if we had been an India rubber ball, and once, as we fell into a rut, we escaped upsetting by a gentle tap from the stump of a cedar tree, upon the hub of the wheel, that righted us with the swiftness of lightning. On we went, the blood starting in my chilled frame, diffusing over me a glowing heat, until I wiped huge drops of perspiration from my brow, and breathed in the cold air as if I were smothering. The dull, stunning sound that now marked our progress was scarcely relieved by the clattering hoofs of the horses, and the motion became perfectly steady, except when a piece of ice would explode from under the wheel, as if burst with powder. Almost with the speed of thought we rushed on, and the critical moment of our safety came. The slightest obstacle, the stumbling of a horse, the breaking of a strap, a too strongly drawn breath almost, would have, with the speed we were making, projected us over the mountain side, as if shot from a cannon, and buried us beneath the frozen ground and hard rock below. The driver, with distended eyes, and an expression of intellectual excitement, played his part well, and fortune favoured us. As we made the last turn in the road, the stage for a moment vibrated between safety and destruction—running for several yards upon one side, it exposed two wheels in the air, whirling with a swiftness that rendered them almost invisible. With a severe contusion it righted, the driver shouted, and we were rushing *up an ascent.* For a moment the stage and horses went on, and it was but for a moment; for the heavy body, lately so full of life, settled back upon the traces a dead weight, dragging the poor animals in one confused heap downwards, and shaking violently upon its springs, it stood still.

" A pretty severe tug," said one of the insides, to the driver, as he stretched himself with a yawn.

"Well, I rather think it was," said Jehu, with a smile of disdain.

" I've driv on this road fifteen years, but I never was so near——as to-night. If I was on t'other side of ' Ball mountain,' and my wife on this (only three days married, recollect,) I would not drive that stage down ' Ball mountain' as I have to-night to keep her from running away with another."

"Why, you don't think there was any great danger, do you?" inquired another "inside," thrusting his head into the cold air.

" I calculate I do; if that off leader, when I reached the ' devil's rut,' had fallen, as he intended, your body would now be as flat as either of the back seat cushions in that stage."

" Lord bless us, is it possible," sighed another "inside;" but it is all very well, we have escaped, and one must run a *little risk*, rather than to be delayed in a journey.

Appreciating the terrible ordeal through which I had passed better than my fellow-travellers, I have often in my dreams, fancied myself on a stage coach, just tumbling down the ravines that yawn on the sides of " Ball mountain;" and when I have started into wakefulness, I have speculated on that principle of the American character, that is ever impelling it forward; but it never so forcibly struck me as a national peculiarity, until I read Howitt's journey down hill, among the sturdy Germans of the Old World.

The latest from Ireland.

NEWTON LIMAVADY, Dec. 15, 1845.
Dear James:—

I received your dutiful letter from Cincinnati a week or so since, and sends my best love and my blessing in return to ye. By what you say of America it must be a wonderful country. I don't wonder that the Yankees are so yellow complected as you say they are, seeing they haven't the potatoe to live on. I suppose if an Irishman was born in America it would be all the same.

But there's one thing weighs heavy on my mind. I am afraid that the people in America streetch the blanket, as we say here, and that my own James is learning to do the likes. Mr. Mulhollan was reading to me in an " Old Countryman," which was sent over to him, that " Money in New York was plenty in the streets," on the

14th, which was the day before the packet sailed. I am doubting that same story; for why would not the poor people pick it up if it lay in the streets? But what is this to what you tell me about the hogs near Cincinnati—that you give them corn *in the ear* to save trouble. Oh James! James! would you make your old mother believe that the pigs there swallow through the ear any more than in Ireland. Don't deceive your own mother so.

My blessing on ye! all the boys and *one of the girls* sends love to ye.

Recollections of the Last Sixty Years.—No. 5.
BY J. JOHNSTON, Esq., *of Piqua.*

After a year's delay the prisoners were tried, convicted and ordered for execution. His Honour Judge Wick, presided. My chief counsel was the late General James Noble, one of the Senators in Congress from Indiana, assisted by three others. Bridge, Sawyer and Hudson suffered; young Bridge, being a minor, was pardoned at the place of execution by the consent of the Indians. Three of them witnessed the awful scene, the Governor attending a mile off to act as circumstances might require. This affair cost the United States from first to last, seven thousand dollars. The justice of the country was vindicated in the eyes of the Indians, and they were satisfied. Thanks be to the distinguished man then at the head of the war department, who disdaining the popularity of the mob, chose to obey the dictates of duty and honour.

The other case happened with the Wyandotts of Sandusky, about seven years ago, in Hancock county, Ohio. One of their beloved chiefs and counsellors of the Christian party, took a hunting excursion with his family: his camp was visited in the evening by three white men with axes, who proposed to the Indian to lodge all night at his camp. This being readily agreed to, the women gave them their suppers, after which the Indian, agreeable to his uniform custom, kneeled down and prayed in his own language, and then lay down with his wife to sleep, little suspecting that these fiends in human shape, who had been so hospitably and kindly entertained by himself and his wife, were at that moment plotting their destruction. As soon as the man and his wife were sound asleep, the white men rose on them with the axes they brought and killed them in the most brutal manner, and then robbed the camp, taking off the horses. The murderers living not many miles off, were soon discovered and apprehended, committed to prison, and afterwards permitted to break jail and escape. I was not in the service at the time of this murder, or a very different fate would have awaited these villains. In 1841 and 2, when as

United States Commissioner I was treating with the Wyandotts, one of these murderers was reported to me as being in the jail of Wood county, Ohio, under a charge of passing counterfeit money, and of course within our reach. I immediately reported the fact to the Commissioner for Indian affairs at Washington, asking for authority and funds to proceed against the offender. No money would be furnished to sustain a prosecution against the offender, although there was no lack of proof, and the murderer escaped. This time I had not John C. Calhoun to sustain me and see justice done to the Indians.*

Cases innumerable, and nearly as bad as the foregoing, have occurred during my long acquaintance with the Indians. In a period of fifty three years since I first came to the west, an instance of white men being tried, convicted, and executed under our laws for the murder of Indians has not come to my knowledge, other than the one given in this narrative. I had very great difficulty in persuading the Indians to witness the execution in Indiana. They said they would take my word that the murderers had been hung. I told them no—they must witness the fact with their eyes, being well aware that bad white men would tell them we had deceived them, and permitted the murderers to escape. When the culprits were cast off and the death struggle ensued, the Indians could not restrain their tears. They had witnessed death in every shape, but never before by hanging.

During my negotiations with the Wyandotts, in 1841 and 42, I ascertained a fact which had previously escaped my notice—that they had no horses previous to 1755. The year of Braddock's defeat, the first owned by the Wyandotts were captured in that disastrous campaign.

My agency embraced all the Indians in Ohio, as well as the Delawares of Indiana, who would not consent to be separated from me. In addition to these enumerated, were the remains of the Munseys, Mohegans, Nanticokes, a part of the Mohawks, Senecas, and Ottawas. The two last

* My partiality for Mr. Calhoun has reference to his former position as an executive officer; for I should be loth to endorse his waywardness in politics, especially his doctrine of State Rights and Nullification. His late speech as President of the Memphis Convention has gone far, however, to redeem his former errors. The broad and liberal ground taken there in regard to the duties of the General Government in assuming the care of the navigation of the Mississippi and all its tributaries accessible to steam power, considering his high standing in the South, and the almost certainty of his again coming to the Senate, is a great point gained to us of the west. It will be remembered that Gen. Jackson refused his assent to an appropriation for improving the Wabash river, and yet that stream is included in Mr. Calhoun's tributaries of the Mississippi, for it is navigated by steamboats.

had rights in the soil of Ohio, which they ceded to the United States by joint treaty with the Shawanese and Wyandotts. There is not now an acre of land owned or occupied by an Indian in Ohio. Fifty-one years ago they owned the whole territory. Does not the voice of humanity cry aloud to the Congress of the United States to give them a country and a home in perpetuity, and a government adapted to their condition? Will impartial history excuse this people and their government if they permit the destruction of the primitive race to happen without one adequate effort being put forth to save them? I shall, during the long nights of the winter, prepare you some further notice of the natives and the first settlement of Ohio by the whites.

Your friend and obd. servt,
JOHN JOHNSTON.
Charles Cist, Esq., Cincinnati.

Pioneer Adventure.

I have taken down the following from the lips of an old citizen here, as a specimen of the every day dangers which the early pioneers encountered in the settlement of the west. There is a great deal of the fire of the flint in these old fellows yet. At the last Presidential election, being on board a steamboat, an upstart, dandy lawyer, with whom he differed in politics, forgot himself so far as to call our veteran an old tory. The words were hardly out of the young fellow's mouth when he found himself in tight grips carried to the edge of the boat, and would have been dropped overboard like any other puppy, but for the intercession of some of the passengers. But to the story.

" In 1795, soon after the defeat of the Indians by Gen. Wayne, I started for Detroit, where my brother William had been working for some time. My main business was to sell a stud horse there. I succeeded in obtaining five hundred dollars in cash and trade for the beast. A part of the trade was a first rate gelding, the finest brute I ever owned, and for which I got at Dayton afterwards, one hundred and twenty-five dollars, although half the money would buy a pretty good horse in those days. My brother accompanied me on my way home to Cincinnati. At Fort Defiance we fell in with an old man, a cripple, who also kept company with us. When we got within ten or twelve miles of Dayton, which had been just laid out and a few houses built there, we encamped, turned our horses loose to graze, and prepared to cook a meal's victuals and rest ourselves. While I was kindling a fire for this purpose, I heard the old man, who had occasion to turn aside into the brush, call out that the Indians were catching our horse. The horses were in the high weeds and brush; the weeds being as high as themselves we could not see them at a short distance. As I ran up I saw an Indian who had caught my gelding, trying to mount him, but to no purpose. I stepped forward, laid my hands on the back of his shoulders, and jerked him heels over head. The villain struck me twice with his butcher knife and cut me through the arm with great violence. I knocked him down with my fist and stamped on him, and but for the persuasions of my party, would have killed him. My brother was about to interpose in an early period of the scuffle, when the other Indian leveled his rifle at him, exclaiming in very good English, " *Let them fight it out.*" Our whole party were unarmed, not apprehending any trouble; and it was almost a miracle that we all got off alive and safe from two Indians, who both had rifles."

Chronological Table.

Jan. 11th.—Dr. Dwight, died, 1817.
" 13th.—C. J. Fox, born, 1749.
" 14th.—Halley, died, 1742.
" 15th.—Queen Elizabeth crowned at Westminster, 1559. Charleston burnt, 1778. Dr. Aikin, died, 1747.
" 16th.—Gibbon, died, 1794. Battle of Corunna, 1809.
" 17th.—Dr. B. Franklin, born, 1706.
" 18th.—Battle of Cowpens, 1781.
" 19th.—Copernicus, born, 1473.
" 20th.—American Independence acknowledged by Great Britain, 1783.

State Census of 1845.

Most of the States take a census midway between those of the General Government. During the late year I have compiled such as have been published in their respective states. These are—

	1840.	1845.
New York,	2,428,921	2,601,374
Ohio,	1,519,467	1,732,832
Indiana,	685,866	854,321
Georgia,	691,392	774,325
Alabama,	590,756	624,827
Illinois,	476,183	705,011
Michigan,	212,367	304,285
	6,604,952	7,596,925
		6,604,952

Increase in five years, ... 992,023

It will be perceived that the per cent. ratio of increase during the last five years in these States is—New York 7, Ohio 14, Indiana 24, Georgia 22, Alabama 6, Illinois 48, Michigan 43.

There must be some inaccuracy in the statement of population in Alabama, the increase there being unquestionably larger than in Georgia.

Judging by the returns thus far, the entire population of the United States must be very nearly 19,500,000. This will agree with the calculation already made of 22,500,000 for 1850, which corresponds with the uniform ratio of increase at every census for fifty years past, which is so regular that the national progress can be as well determined by calculation as by enumeration. The largest share of increase at the next census will be in Michigan, Illinois, Missouri, Iowa, Wisconsin, Indiana, Ohio and Texas.

The Memphis Reunion.

Between forty and fifty editors and ex-editors, after the adjournment of the Convention there, sat down to an *apician* entertainment, given by the corps editorial of that city to the craft. Most of these editors have been giving their recollections of the scene, and I shall follow their example.

Of the whole corps, but three abstained from wine. Two of them—both from Ohio—sat together, to sustain each other, I suppose. One of these editors, who sat opposite, having been honoured with a toast, was called upon for a speech, which he made in these terms:—We have ascertained, Mr. President, this day, through Dr. Overton, that the Memphis Convention was the most dignified, intellectual, and influential body of men that ever had assembled or ever would assemble in all ages; and, Mr. President, we all know that the Mississippi is *the* deepest and *the* broadest, *the* longest and *the* fastest stream in the universe. Still her waters need improvement, and this, I suppose, was one great object for which our convention assembled. My brethren from Ohio opposite, however, are strict constructionists—They have *constitutional* scruples on this subject; they are for leaving these waters as they are, and sir—added the speaker—I am on the *opposite side*, as you see, and while I fill this tumbler—almost—with water—it is that of the Mississippi I believe:—I feel it my duty to go for *the improvement of our western waters*, and mingle the pure cogniac with its contents.

So said, so done; and the annexation of France and the United States being happily cemented, the speaker drank the contents, and sat down amidst a shout of applause.

Scripture Quotations.

A late city paper quotes as a scripture text, "that he that runs may read," "and that the wayfaring man, though a fool, need not err therein." The second member of the quotation is undoubtedly taken from the Bible, although not literally correct in the quotation, but the first part, although cited as above in many periodicals, is neither a scripture phrase nor a scripture idea, and cannot be found from Genesis to Revelations. It would be an employment conducive to the accuracy of certain editors if they would brush up their acquaintance with the Bible, as a means of enabling them to quote it correctly. They might probably derive other benefits in the perusal.

There are various other *texts*, such as—" God tempers the wind to the shorn lamb,"—" In the midst of life we are in death,"—What shadows we are, and what shadows we pursue," supposed even by persons otherwise intelligent to be derived from the scriptures, which originate from far different sources. The first is in Tristram Shandy, by Sterne; the last was written by Edmund Burke. I cannot trace the origin of the second, but believe it to be an aphorism of one of the puritan writers of England.

Safety of New York.

The New York Plebeian scouts the idea of that city being exposed to hazard in case of war with Great Britain and a consequent landing of her troops on our shores. He holds this language:—

" We chance to know that any fears as to the city being bombarded are absurd, *because* there are regulations of law that *prevent it*. By the provisions of the statute in such case made and provided, in section seventeen of article third, of title second, of chapter XIV of volume first, of the Revised Statute, page 422, it is made the bounden duty of the health officer, Dr. Van Hovenburgh, to enter on board of ' *every vessel* immediately on her arrival, and to make strict search and inquiry into the *state* and *condition* of the vessel;' and in case he finds it would be *dangerous* to permit such vessel to visit the city, he is to subject her to quarantine nine miles below New York. * * The Legislature also, with an eye to the public safety, in its far-seeing wisdom, has provided, lest the health officer might not be able to detect every vessel desirous to approach the city, that they shall not move from quarantine towards the city, without first having the permission of the health officer."

Circuitous Preaching.

Dr. Elliott, of the Western Christian Advocate, having lately a congregation of but two persons in Indianapolis to address, relates the following singular occurrence:

" Our mind was involuntarily led back to 1822, to an occasion on which we preached a sermon to one poor Mohawk woman, aided by two interpreters. The woman had traveled fourteen miles on foot, and carried her child on Sunday morning, to hear me preach. Between-the-logs knew Wyandott and Mohawk, but no English! My interpreter knew only Wyandott and English. But by my preaching in English, and Jonathan, my interpreter, converting into Wyandott, and then Between-the-logs giving this in Mohawk, we all three made out to preach to the poor Indian woman, as she sat at the root of of a large oak. with her child fastened on a board in her arms."

To my Wife.

Pillow thy head upon this breast,
　My own, my cherished wife;
And let us for one hour forget
　Our dreary path of life,
And let me kiss thy tears away,
　And bid remembrance flee
Back to the halcyon days of youth,
　When all was hope and glee.

Fair was the early promise, love,
　Of our joy-freighted barque;
Sun-lit and lustrous, too, the skies
　Now all so dim and dark;
Over a stormy sea, dear wife,
　We drive with shattered sail,
But love sits smiling at the helm,
　And mocks the threat'ning gale.

Come, let me part those clustering curls,
　And gaze upon thy brow—
How many, many memories
　Sweep o'er my spirits now!
How much of happiness and grief—
　How much of hope and fear—
Breathe from such dear loved lineaments,
　Most eloquently here!

Though, gentle one, few joys remain
　To cheer our lonely lot;
And storms have left our paradise
　With but one sunny spot,
Hallow'd forever be that place
　To hearts like thine and mine—
'Tis where our youthful hands upreared
　Affection's earliest shrine.

Then nestle closer to this breast,
　My fond and faithful dove!
Where, if not here, should be the ark
　Of refuge for thy love?
The poor man's blessing and his curse,
　Alike belong to me:
For, shorn of worldly wealth, dear wife,
　Am I not rich in thee?

Cooking Stoves.

These were an unknown article thirty years ago, and cooking was performed in the chimney, which served to boil, roast, and bake our wives, daughters and mothers as well if not as thoroughly as their various objects of cooking. Thanks to the ingenuity of the inventers of the cooking stove, all this is now dispensed with. The stove is brought out into the kitchen and serves, besides its principal function of cooking, to warm the room so effectually as to make a given quantity of wood afford twice as much warmth as when burnt in the chimney.

But the first cooking stove was like the first steamboat, the application of a principle merely, leaving to later projectors the honour as well as benefit of bringing out of the invention by further improvements, the perfection in economy and comfort of which it might be found susceptible. The latest improvement, perhaps the greatest ever made in these stoves, is STRAUB's *Flame encircled oven Cooking Apparatus.*

This is a stove that claims to combine all that is valuable in the existing cooking stoves, with certain improvements peculiar to itself, which unite in a remarkable degree the equalization of heat throughout the whole baking department, with an economy of fuel which I have noticed in no other article of the kind.

The stove is constructed so as to pass a flue entirely round the oven; the heat being thus used twice, once under, and once over the oven, with an enlarged air chamber through which all the heat must pass. Consequently, every part of the oven must be heated alike. It is this mode of applying the flame and heat which produces the saving of fuel also.

I regard Mr. Straub as having solved a difficult and long sought problem—the passing the heat twice round without impairing the necessary draught of the stove. This is effected in the enlargement of the air chamber, which affords increased space for the rarefaction of air, and compensates for the usual disadvantage of a circular draught.

The plates of this stove are thicker than most others, which enables them to retain heat a longer period, and to cool more gradually.

The thickness also renders the plates less liable to warp. I deem this a valuable improvement.

Indian Portraits.

I would call attention to the advertisement of Messrs. Stanley & Dickerman, in this day's Advertiser. I have seen the Gallery of Portraits while in their progress on the canvass, know they have been taken from the living subject, and consider them of inconceivable value as a commentary on the past and present condition and character of that interesting race, the Indians of the west. The day will come when this collection will command an extravagant price, for a national or great public museum.

Cincinnati Directory for 1846.

The new City Directory of *Robinson & Jones*, long wanted and expected, is now out. I shall take the liberty of commenting upon this publication *ex cathedra;* claiming as I do to know something from experience, what a Directory should be.

The names appear to be alphabeted carefully, and care to have been taken in getting the German names correctly spelt, and the given names of all persons, as far as possible supplied: all this goes to contribute much of the value of a Directory.

An admirable map forms a frontispiece to the volume, embracing not only the city itself, but a circuit of two and a half miles adjacent to it in all directions, in which are designated the subdi-

visions, canal, turnpikes, hills, and every other natural or artificial object of any importance, and serves to direct the stranger to the various points of this vicinity, as fully and distinctly as a guide book.

This Directory is the first of a series which Robinson & Jones propose to issue annually. They design in each successive volume to add such improvements as the progress of the enterprise may suggest. I have no doubt myself, that the experience of a year or two will supply any deficiency that may be found in this issue, and render its successors equal for comprehensiveness and accuracy to similar publications of long standing in our Atlantic cities.

Errors of the Press.

A capital story is told of a "mistake of the printer" in the Baltimore Argus. A merchant employed an engraver to cut a plate for a business card; the plate was sent to the printer, who worked off five hundred cards and it was then returned to the engraver, who, at a glance, discovered two C's where there should have been but one. Without delay, he altered the plate, taking out the extra C. This was just accomplished when the clerk of the merchant called with one of the cards, and pointed out the error to the engraver, who appeared much surprised, and at once produced the plate on which the cards had been printed. This not having on it the extra C, it was at once decided that it must be a mistake of the printer. The story is not without a moral.

Our Great Staple.

As a heavy pork market, Cincinnati is in the receipt of hogs, which, for size and fatness, would appear incredible to those who know nothing of the west but by description. I am not aware, however, whether the following statement has been paralleled in the Miami Valley. It is taken from the last "Chillicothe Advertiser."

"On Thursday last, the finest lot of hogs that we have ever seen, was killed at the slaughter house of John Marfield, in this city. They were owned by John H. Maxwell, of Green township, in this county. There were fifty-four hogs in the lot, and their average weight was 360 pounds. Fifty of these averaged *three hundred and seventy* pounds each!! We give herewith the weight of nine, *all of one litter.* We doubt whether this has ever been beaten in the Union:—386, 454, 456, 452, 456, 526, 534, 516, 444.

"These nine averaged a fraction less than *four hundred and seventy* pounds each."

Mr. Maxwell's lot of hogs for 1843, were eighty in number, and an average of 335 pounds in weight.

Pioneer Adventure of two Scouts.

What is preserved of the Pioneer history of the west, serves to shew the value of that which has perished. Bold enterprise and hair breadth escapes are constant features in the settlement of the west.

As early as the year 1790, the block-house and stockade, above the mouth of the Hockhocking river, was a frontier post for the hardy pioneers of that portion of our State from the Hockhocking to the Scioto, and from the Ohio river to our northern Lakes. Then nature wore her undisturbed livery of dark and thick forests, interspersed with green and flowery prairies. Then the axe of the woodman had not been heard in the wilderness, nor the plough of the husbandman marred the business of the green prairies. Among the many rich and luxuriant valleys that of the Hockhocking was pre-eminent for nature's richest gifts—and the portion of it whereon Lancaster now stands, was marked as the most luxuriant and picturesque, and became the seat of an Indian village, at a period so early, that the "memory of man runneth not parallel thereto." On the green sward of the prairie was held many a rude gambol of the Indians; and here too, was many an assemblage of the warriors of one of the most powerful tribes, taking counsel for a "war path" upon some weak or defenceless frontier post. Upon one of these war-stirring occasions, intelligence reached the little garrison above the mouth of the Hockhocking, that the Indians were gathering in force somewhere up the valley, for the purpose of striking a terrible and fatal blow on one of the few and scattered defences of the whites. A council was held by the garrison, and scouts were sent up the Hockhocking, in order to ascertain the strength of the foe, and the probable point of attack. In the month of October, and on one of the balmiest days of our Indian summer, two men could have been seen emerging out of the thick plumb and hazel bushes skirting the prairie, and stealthily climbing the eastern declivity of that most remarkable promontory, now known as Mount Pleasant, whose western summit gives a commanding view to the eye of what is doing on the prairie. This eminence was gained by our two adventurers and hardy scouts, and from this point they carefully observed the movements taking place on the prairie. Every day brought an accession of warriors to those already assembled, and every day the scouts witnessed from their eyrie, the horse-racing, leaping, running and throwing the deadly tomahawk by the warriors. The old sachems looking on with indifference—the squaws, for the most part, engaged in their usual drudgeries, and the papooses manifesting all the noisy and wayward joy of childhood. The arrival of any new party of warriors was hailed by the terrible war whoop, which striking the mural face of Mount Pleasant, was driven back into the various indentations of the surrounding hills, producing reverberation on reverberation, and echo on echo, till it seemed as if ten thousand fiends were gathered in their orgies. Such yells might well strike terror into the bosoms of those unaccustomed to them. To our scouts these were but martial music strains which waked their watchfulness, and strung their iron frames. From their early youth had they been always on the frontier, and therefore well practised in all the subtlety, craft and cun-

ning, as well as knowing the ferocity and blood-thirsty perseverance of the savage. They were therefore not likely to be circumvented by the cunning of their foes; and without a desperate struggle, would not fall victims to the scalping knife. On several occasions, small parties of warriors left the prairie and ascended the Mount; at which times our scouts would hide in the fissures of the rocks, or lying by the side of some long prostrate tree, cover themselves with the sear and yellow leaf, and again leave their hiding places when their uninvited visiters had disappeared. For food they depended on jerked venison, and cold corn bread, with which their knapsacks had been well stored. Fire they dared not kindle, and the report of one of their rifles would bring upon them the entire force of the Indians. For drink they depended on some rain water, which still stood in excavations of the rocks, but in a few days this store was exhausted, and M'Clelland and White must abandon their enterprise or find a new supply. To accomplish this most hazardous affair, M'Clelland being the elder, resolved to make the attempt—with his trusty rifle in his grasp, and two canteens strung across his shoulders, he cautiously descended to the prairie, and skirting the hills on the north as much as possible within the hazle thickets, he struck a course for the Hockhocking river. He reached its margin, and turning an abrupt point of a hill, he found a beautiful fountain of limpid water now known as the Cold Spring, within a few feet of the river. He filled his canteens and returned in safety to his watchful companion. It was now determined to have a fresh supply of water every day, and this duty was to be performed alternately. On one of these occasions, after White had filled his canteens, he sat a few moments, watching the limpid element, as it came gurgling out of the bosom of the earth—the light sound of footsteps caught his practiced ear, and upon turning round, he saw two squaws within a few feet of him; these upon turning the jet of the hill had thus suddenly come upon him. The elder squaw gave one of those far-reaching whoops peculiar to the Indians. White at once comprehended his perilous situation,—for if the alarm should reach the camp, he and his companion must inevitably perish. Self-preservation impelled him to inflict a noiseless death upon the squaws, and in such a manner as to leave no trace behind. Ever rapid in thought, and prompt in action, he sprang upon his victims with the rapidity and power of a panther, and grasping the throat of each, with one bound he sprang into the Hockhocking, and rapidly thrust the head of the elder woman under the water, and making strong efforts to submerge the younger, who, however, powerfully resisted. During the short struggle, the younger female addressed him in his own language, though almost in inarticulate sounds. Releasing his hold, she informed him, that, ten years before, she had been made a prisoner, on Grave Creek flats, and that the Indians, in her presence, butchered her mother and two sisters; and that an only remaining brother had been captured with her, who succeeded on the second night in making his escape; but what had become of him she knew not. During the narrative, White, unobserved by the girl, had let go his grasp on the elder squaw, whose body soon floated where it would not, probably, soon be found. He now directed the girl hastily to follow him, and with his usual energy and speed, pushed for the Mount. They had scarcely gone two hundred yards from the spring, before the alarm cry was heard some quarter of a mile down the stream. It was supposed that some warriors returning from a hunt, struck the Hockhocking just as the body of the drowned squaw floated past. White and the girl succeeded in reaching the Mount, where M'Clelland had been no indifferent spectator to the sudden commotion among the Indians, as the prairie parties of warriors were seen to strike off in every direction, and before White and the girl had arrived, a party of some twenty warriors had already gained the eastern acclivity of the Mount, and were cautiously ascending, carefully keeping under cover. Soon the two scouts saw the swarthy faces of the foe, as they glided from tree to tree, and rock to rock, until the whole base of the Mount was surrounded, and all hopes of escape cut off.

In this peril nothing was left, other than to sell their lives as dearly as they could; this they resolved to do, and advised the girl to escape to the Indians, and tell them she had been a captive to the scouts. She said no! death, and that in presence of my people, is to me a thousand times sweeter than captivity—furnish me with a rifle, and I will show you that I can fight as well as die. This spot I leave not! here my bones shall lie bleaching with yours! and should either of you escape, you will carry the tidings of my death to my remaining relatives. Remonstrance proved fruitless; the two scouts matured their plans for a vigorous defence—opposing craft to craft, expedient to expedient, and an unerring fire of the deadly rifle. The attack commenced in front where, from the narrow backbone of the Mount, the savages had to advance in single file, but where they could avail themselves of the rocks and trees. In advancing the warrior must be momentarily exposed, and two bare inches of his swarthy form was target enough for the unerring rifle of the scouts. After bravely maintaining the fight in front, and keeping the enemy in check, they discovered a new danger threatening them. The wary foe now made every preparation to attack them in flank, which could be most successfully and fatally done by reaching an insulated rock lying in one of the ravines on the southern hill side. This rock once gained by the Indians, they could bring the scouts under point blank shot of the rifle; and without the possibility of escape,

Our brave scouts saw the hopelessness of their situation, which nothing could avert but brave companions and an unerring shot—them they had not. But the brave never despair. With this certain fate resting upon them, they had continued as calm, and as calculating, and as unwearied as the strongest desire of vengeance on a treacherous foe could produce. Soon M'Clelland saw a tall and swarthy figure preparing to spring from a cover so near the fatal rock, that a single bound must reach it, and all hope be destroyed. He felt that all depended on one advantageous shot, although but one inch of the warrior's body was exposed, and that a distance of one hundred yards—he resolved to risk all—coolly he raised his rifle to his eyes, carefully shading the sight with his hand, he drew a bead so sure, that he felt conscious it would do—he touched the hair trigger with his finger—the hammer came down, but in place of striking fire, it crushed his flint into a hundred fragments! Although he felt that the savage must reach the

fatal rock before he could adjust another flint, he proceeded to the task with the utmost composure, casting many a furtive glance towards the fearful point. Suddenly he saw the warrior stretching every muscle for the leap—and with the agility of a deer he made the spring—instead of reaching the rock he sprung ten feet in the air, and giving one terrific yell he fell upon the earth, and his dark corpse rolled fifty feet down the hill. He had evidently received a death shot from some unknown hand. A hundred voices from below re-echoed the terrible shout, and it was evident that they had lost a favourite warrior, as well as been foiled for a time in their most important movement. A very few moments proved that the advantage so mysteriously gained would be of short duration; for already the scouts caught a momentary glimpse of a swarthy warrior, cautiously advancing towards the cover so recently occupied by a fellow companion. Now, too, the attack in front was resumed with increased fury, so as to require the incessant fire of both scouts, to prevent the Indians from gaining the eminence—and in a short time M'Clelland saw the wary warrior behind the cover, preparing for a leap to gain the fearful rock—the leap was made, and the warrior turning a somerset, his corpse rolled down towards his companion: again a mysterious agent had interposed in their behalf. This second sacrifice cast dismay into the ranks of the assailants; and just as the sun was disappearing behind the western hills, the foe withdrew a short distance, for the purpose of devising new modes of attack. The respite came most seasonably to the scouts, who had bravely kept their position, and boldly maintained the unequal fight from the middle of the day.

Now, for the first time was the girl missing, and the scouts supposed that through terror she had escaped to her former captors, or that she had been killed during the fight. They were not long left to doubt, for in a few moments the girl was seen emerging from behind a rock and coming to them with a rifle in her hand. During the heat of the fight she saw a warrior fall, who had advanced some fifty yards before the main body in front. She at once resolved to possess herself of his rifle, and crouching in undergrowth she crept to the spot, and succeeded in her enterprise, being all the time exposed to the cross fire of the defenders and assailants—her practised eye had early noticed the *fatal rock*, and hers was the *mysterious hand* by which the two warriors had fallen—the last being the most wary, untiring and blood thirsty *brave* of the Shawanese tribe. He it was, who ten years previous had scalped the family of the girl, and been her captor. In the west, dark clouds were now gathering, and in an hour the whole heavens were shrouded in them; this darkness greatly embarrassed the scouts in their contemplated night retreat, for they might readily lose their way, or accidentally fall on the enemy—this being highly probable, if not inevitable. An hour's consultation decided their plans, and it was agreed that the girl, from her intimate knowledge of their localities, should lead the advance a few steps. Another advantage might be gained by this arrangement, for in case they should fall in with some out-post, the girl's knowledge of the Indian tongue, would perhaps enable her to deceive the sentinel: and so the sequel proved, for scarcely had they descended one hundred feet, when a low "whist" from the girl, warned them of present danger. The scouts sunk silently to the earth, where by previous agree-ment, they were to remain till another signal was given them by the girl,—whose absence for more than a quarter of an hour now began to excite the most serious apprehensions. At length she again appeared, and told them that she had suc-ceeded in removing two sentinels who were di-rectly in their route to a point some hundred feet distant. The descent was noiselessly resumed— the level gained, and the scouts followed their in-trepid pioneer for half a mile in the most pro-found silence, when the barking of a small dog, within a few feet, apprized them of a new dan-ger. The almost simultaneous click of the scouts' rifles was heard by the girl, who rapidly ap-proached them, and stated that they were now in the midst of the Indian wigwams, and their lives depended on the most profound silence, and im-plicitly following her footsteps. A moment af-terwards, the girl was accosted by a squaw from an opening in a wigwam. She replied in the In-dian language, and without stopping pressed for-ward. In a short time she stopped and assured the scouts that the village was cleared, and that they were now in safety. She knew that every pass leading out of the prairie was safely guarded by Indians, and at once resolved to adopt the bold adventure of passing through the very cen-tre of their village as the least hazardous. The result proved the correctness of her judgment. They now kept a course for the Ohio, being gui-ded by the Hockhocking river—and after three days march and suffering, the party arrived at the Block-House in safety. Their escape from the Indians, prevented the contemplated attack: and the rescued girl proved to be the sister of the intrepid Neil Washburn, celebrated in Indian history as the renowned Scout to Capt. Kenton's bloody Kentuckians.

The Eclectics.

"We have had for some time the rival Colle-ges, the Ohio Medical and the Botanico-Medical, and now it seems there is a third intended to combine the excellencies of both. Is there no end to human calamity, that we should have a third set of doctors let loose on the community. We shall see here calomel and lobelia, blood-let-ting and steam, harmoniously working side by side.

"This seems to be got up to introduce a set of novi homines into practice. The Professors in the different departments are little known in the community at any rate."—Western General Ad-vertiser.

The above complimental notice did not until recently present itself to our observation—neither are we aware that any such sheet as the Western General Advertiser is at present issued from the Cincinnati press. Of one thing we are very cer-tain, however: if the above scrap is to be taken as a specimen of the taste and intelligence of its editor, we pity the deplorable and despicable state of moral and intellectual degradation of that brainless functionary, who, it seems, has un-dertaken to instruct his readers (if he has any) on a subject of which he is wholly and totally ig-norant, not only in reference to the principles and practice of the Eclectic School of Physicians and Surgeons, but also the general reputation and standing of the members of the Faculty of said Institute. For example, in the closing cogi-tations of this senseless wiseacre, it is asserted that the members of the Faculty "are little

known in the community"—so far from this be-ing the case it may be safely asserted that as many as two or three of the members of the Faculty are not only as favourably, but as extensively known as any in this or any other country, not only as practitioners, but as teachers of Medical science. This is especially true of one, who enjoys at this moment a more extensive reputation as a Medi-cal man than the most distinguished authors, teachers or practitioners of the Healing Art, either in Europe or America.

We neither know nor care who the editor of the "Advertiser" is, but we hope if he has any self-respect he will endeavour to furnish himself with something like definite information on this as well as other subjects before he commits his thoughts to paper hereafter.—Western Medical Reformer, Dec., 1845.

Wonders will never cease.

I supposed if there was any thing certain in this city of ours, the fact that I was by trade a collector of statistics, was a fixed fact of ab-solute notoriety. Even the existence of the Fakir of Ava, or of Rees E. Price might be as reasona-bly a disputed fact. But the "Eclectics" have dis-covered that "on that subject"—themselves—"as on all others," the editor of the General Western Advertiser has no "definite information."

As to "that subject," I confess my ignorance. I have been for years discovering that what I know, compared with that I am ignorant of, is as a drop to the bucket, every additional step in the acquisition of light I make, serving to reveal to me the existence of darkness around me. On this principle I imagine I am beginning to pene-trate the mysteries of the Eclectic practise, for familiar as my pursuits render me with the citi-zens of Cincinnati, such men as Doctors Cox, Hill, Morrow, Jones, et genus id omre, never fell under my notice. I neither met with them in the halls of science, nor in the respectable walks of private life. I have, it is true, the names of some of them in my directories, but they were taken from their signs. But it seems that un-known as they are to me, they are well known to fame. "Two or three are as favourably and "as extensively known as any in this or any other "country, not only as practitioners, but as teach-"ers of medical science! This is especially true "of one, who enjoys at this moment a more ex-"tensive reputation as a medical man than the "most distinguished authors, teachers or practi-"tioners of the Healing Art, either in Europe or "America!!"

Old as I am, I trust I am not too old to learn, and ignorant as I may be, not unwilling to be enlightened. I suppose those who know me will admit that there is nobody has a higher opinion of Cincinnati talent, energy, learning, ingenuity and enterprise than myself; and now, I want to know who those two or three, and especially this one, are, whose fame as authors, teachers and practitioners transcends that of Velpeau, Roux, and Andral, of the Paris, and Liston, Stokes, Graves, Cusack and Lawrence, of the London and Dublin Schools of Medicine and Surgery; or that of M'Clellan, Mott, Warren, Gibson and Jackson, who belong to America, but whose fame is not limited to this side of the Atlantic. I feel it a disgrace to remain longer in ignorance. Let him be produced, and we will have him exhibited at the hall of the Eclectic Institute as a greater curiosity than the skeleton giant of Tennessee, or the mastodon of Dr. Koch. Let him be produced, that the TEACHER, *Author* and *Practitioner* may receive the notice he deserves at home, as well as enjoys throughout Europe and America!

An Impregnable Safe.

It would be a pleasant thing to possess money to the utmost extent of our wants and desires, if it were not for the difficulty and anxiety of keeping it safe. If it is to be kept ready for use at a moment's notice, it is usually deposited in an iron safe or a bank, both which sometimes betray their trust; and if the money is invested in property, it cannot be realised and withdraw nat a moment's warning. The proprietor of a gold mine, Senor *Yriarte*, living at Cossalo, Mexico, has overcome this difficulty in a manner equally ingenious and simple. Although he owns the richest mine in the universe, he works it only to the extent of his current expenses—some one million five hundred thousand dollars per annum —alleging as a reason to those who asked why he did not mine it more extensively—" *My gold is safer in the mine than anywhere else.*"

The Little Miami Rail-Road.

The third annual report of the *Little Miami Rail-Road Company*, of which I lately published a synopsis, ought to be in the hands of every public man in the west. It serves to give some idea of what the products from the great west are rapidly becoming. This is, however, not so easily realised by figures as in other respects.

The Company erected, last fall, an immense depot, as was supposed of sufficient capacity to provide for the reception of the various freight received at this point, and accumulating for two or three days at a time. The building was brick, three hundred feet long and fifty feet wide. The rail-way enters it at the west, running within fifty feet of its entire length. A floor of thirteen thousand five hundred square feet, graded to the level of the cars, enables them to discharge their burthens on a level, whence they are taken to the Front street face of the building and loaded in wagons and drays.

Large, however, as is this building, it has been found inadequate to the heavy and increasing demands of the business done on the line. When the road shall have been completed, by next October, to Sandusky City, the great staples of flour, whiskey, pork, bacon, lard, &c., of great magnitude in bulk and value, as they are, will afford a splendid prize for the competition of our Atlantic Cities, in their respective routes. When the Buffalo and Sandusky rail-road shall have been completed, we shall have a continuous rail-road to New York and Boston. Philadelphia is preparing to complete a rail-road to Cleveland by filling up the intervening links between the two points.

Thanksgiving Goose.

Turkies are the general market standard for thanksgiving day, but sometimes a goose is prefered. In a neighbouring city, a gentleman in market was attracted by the sight of a plump, extra sized, well cleaned goose. " Is it a young one?" said he to a bonny rosy cheeked country lass. " Yes sir, indeed it is," was the ready reply. " And how much do you want for it?" " A dollar, sir." " That is too much, I think; say eighty-seven and a half cents, and here's your money." " Well, sir, as I would like to get you for a steady customer, take it away." The goose was taken home and roasted; but it was found difficult to carve, and when cut up, so tough as to be uneatable. The gentleman went to market again, on the following day, as usual, and there met with his fair poulterer. " Did you not tell me that goose was young, which I bought of you?" " Yes sir, I did, and so it was. Don't you call me a young woman? I am only nineteen." " Yes I do." " Well, I have heard mother say, many a time, that it was nearly six weeks younger than me."

Mesmerism, Neurology, &c.

It was to be hoped, after the remarkable and authenticated cases I have published of things " most surely believed," in Pennsylvania and elsewhere, analogous to the phenomena exhibited here by various lecturers on these subjects, that the lips of incredulity would have been put to silence. But infidels still exist and perhaps will, always.

A friend of mine lately received a letter from a distinguished physician of Kentucky, in which he says: " You need not laugh at Mr. Cist's testimonials on the subject of extract of white walnut or butter nut. It may all be depended on. They will vomit if the bark be scraped *up*, and purge if scraped *down*, as he says. They still do more than this, for they will vomit and purge at the same time, if scraped both up and down, and they will neither vomit nor purge if scraped crosswise from the tree. All this I know from my own experience."

For facts corroborative of certain other points of Pennsylvania faith and practise, I refer to the communication which follows. It is from as intelligent an individual as resides in the county or state, who having devoted much time during a long life, to storing his mind with useful knowledge, the fruit of both reading and observation, is now well qualified to employ, with profit to my readers, his leisure hours in the communications for my columns, which he has given me reason to expect from time to time.

Mr. C. CIST,—*Sir:*

I know not how you will class what follows; you may call it what you please. You have published things much like it, and may do so with this.

It is rather more than fifty years since I began housekeeping in Philadelphia. A good supply of hickory was laid up for the winter; but as it generally happens, towards the spring there remained a pretty considerable assortment of the largest logs left,—knotty, knurly affairs,—the rejected of the pile, while better could be got at; still they must be burnt, and a sort of industrious fit having come on me, I determined to split them up into sizeable wood myself. Axe, maul and wedges, were had, and things went on pretty well for a time, but one morning—a cold morning—as I was entering a wedge with the poll of the axe, the wedge slipped from my fingers, and the axe came on my thumb. I don't believe it made me faint, as I never did see, nor ever did hear of, any well-certified faint in man or woman, unless there was some other person near to take care of the sufferer. You may have seen, as I have, how utterly helpless a young woman becomes—as limber as a wet rag—on such occasions, when a young man has to lift her up, to lay her on the sofa—and how prettily and nicely she will revive after her hands have been duly chafed—what pretty little sighs —and how the eyelids gently unclose, &c. I imagine that about nine and a half times in ten cases, the proper orthography of the word is *feint.* Your lady readers must not suppose that I am a horrid, hard-hearted unbeliever, for I do think that it may be possible for a lady to come to an actual faint, even when alone. I know that I, even I myself, felt a mighty queer sort of a dizziness as I sat on the cellar steps, and did not remember how I got there; and it may be, had any one been present, a real, downright faint might have been perpetrated. When I went up stairs one of my family—it then was composed of the smallest possible number to constitute a family—doctored the unfortunate thumb with a poultice of salt and vinegar, but without much, if any, good effect. The next day I was in the book store of the late worthy Thomas Dobson: he noticed my little doll-baby of a thumb, and having informed him what was the matter, he told me he could remove the pain. I said he

could not, for I had no faith. He did not care whether I had or not, and bid me to lay my hand on the counter, which was done. He moved his hands over mine, but I heard him say nothing. In about, perhaps, a minute, he asked if the pain was gone—*it had gone*—but I told him it was worse than ever. He continued his operations for a short time, and then told me he knew it was gone; and I had to laugh and own it was so.

Nearly opposite the "stone house" of Mr. Dobson, lived Robert Haydock, plumber, one of whose men got burnt from shoulder to wrist by melted lead. The pain could not be allayed by the physician, or the care and attention of Robert and his kind, good lady. They were Friends, "after the most strictest sect." "Robert," said this good lady, "I am much troubled in mind about John; I have done all I can, and the doctor has nothing further to advise but patience. Did thee never hear that neighbour Dobson hath the gift, as it is called, of extracting pain, when all remedies have failed? "Tut, tut, wife, I wonder thee can believe in such nonsense; it is only the effect of imagination. "Nay, but Robert, if it is only the effect of imagination, if John imagines the pain is gone, he will get a good night's rest; and at all events, I do not see that any evil can arise." After a little more opposition the wife had her way—a thing of course,—John went to neighbour Dobson, and in about ten minutes came back—*as he imagined*—free from pain. This was told me by a "Friend" in high standing in the Society, to whom I had related my thumb business. I asked him what he thought of such things? Well, he didn't know—he had heard of many wonders of the power of imagination, and yet he knew of a strange cure of a horse, which he could not ascribe to that. He then related that a few years previous he had some meeting-business to attend to in Chester county, and on his way home, three or four miles beyond Darby—you know the little town well,—his horse was suddenly struck lame; after riding a few rods the creature seemed to suffer so much that he got off and led him to the tavern in Darby, which was kept by a friend.—I believe in those days all the inhabitants were of that sect.— The ostler—all ostlers are *ex officio* horse doctors —was called to see what was the matter, but could discover no cause of lameness, and proposed taking him to a "straw doctor" a short distance from the place. My friend, an unbeliever in such things, objected, but as the tavern keeper allowed that the "doctor" had made some surprising cures, and as it could do no harm any how, the ostler was sent with the horse, and in about half an hour returned riding him back. The ostler stated that the "doctor" examined the horse whether he was corked, which he was not, and then cut a square sod, with which he rubbed the horse, and then replaced it in the ground. His charge for "medicine and attendance," was a quarter dollar. My friend rode the horse home, and never observed any ill consequences from the witchcraft cure. Others may think as they please; I firmly believe all I have stated; yet I am not so easy of belief as Sancho, who told his master, the Don, that the story was so very true, that any one who only *heard* it might safely and conscientiously make oath that he *saw* it; nor does my unbelief equal that of the old Dutch tory, on Long Island, who when told that Cornwallis was taken, said "it was a tam'd lie just as dat dat was told dree or four years ago dat Sheneral Burgoyne was daken.

All this may be too long for your columns, but if any part will do, you may cut and slash to suit yourself.   H.

January 19th, 1846.

Diplomacy of the United States.

For centuries the diplomatic intercourse of the civilized world had been carried on, upon the principle of deceit and lying, bribery and espionage. During that period all was considered fair in diplomacy, as it is now by some in politics. And the only disgrace felt or experienced, was in detection or failure. Almost the first public act of America, after we became a nation, was to teach the world that in *all things* honesty is the best of policy. Franklin set this example in France. It has been followed by our various Ambassadors abroad, from John Adams down, and by our department of state under every incumbent. And the result is, that our national character for fair and direct dealing stands higher than that of most other nations in the world.

Many interesting incidents have been recorded on this subject. I propose to furnish one which rests on undoubted authority, which has, however, as far as my knowledge goes, never yet appeared in print.

During the administration of Mr. Van Buren, *George M. Dallas*, our present Vice-President, was sent as Minister Plenipotentiary to Russia, to negociate a commercial treaty with that Empire. As soon after presenting his credentials and being accredited in that capacity at the Court of St. Petersburg as afforded him, in his judgment, a proper opportunity, he addressed a letter to Count *Nesselrode*, the Russian Minister of State, in which he made known the object for which he was sent, and politely inquired of his Excellency when it would suit his convenience to attend to the business. The receipt of the letter was duly acknowledged, and the assurance given of his Excellency's high consideration of the writer, nothing being, however, said on the

main subject of the epistle. Mr. Dallas, unwilling as the representative of the youngest nation on earth, to transgress the laws of etiquette, waited a while and finally wrote a second and a third note, to which he received answers pretty much to the same purpose as had been made to the first. Finding himself unable to progress in this way, he determined to come to the point at once, and despatched a letter stating to the Minister, that finding himself unable to accomplish the object of his mission, and unwilling to remain for any other purpose, he would ask of his Excellency that his imperial majesty might furnish him with the necessary passports for his departure. This brought things at once to a crisis. The Emperor—Nicholas—a man of great energy and directness of purpose,—probably thought the better of the young republican for his frankness, and told his minister, "Ask him what he wants." Dallas, who was prepared for any issue, replied by handing in a draft of the treaty, which being read to the Autocrat of the Russians, he promptly said, "I agree to it—ask him if he wants anything more." Dallas, emboldened by this gracious treatment, then added, "I should like to receive the treaty on His Majesty's birth-day." The birth-day, or rather the Saint's Day, after whom the reigning monarch was named, was but a few days off, being St. Nicholas Day, the 6th December, O. S., by which the Greek Church yet reckons. Accordingly, on that day the usual levee was held, at which all the foreign Ambassadors attended—all but Mr. Dallas in stars, ribbons and embroidery—he in a plain black suit of citizen's dress. They were introduced in the court order of precedence, the Envoy from Austria taking the post of honour, and the British Ambassador next, &c., Mr. Dallas so far in the rear as to be out of sight, when the Austrian Minister stepped forward to make his compliments. As he advanced, the Emperor called out in a tone which rang through the hall of audience, "Is the American Minister here?" "Yes sire." "Ask Mr. Dallas to step forward." Mr. Dallas made his bow and offered the usual congratulations. The Emperor, in the kindest manner, expressed his thanks, handing Mr. D. the treaty at the same time. The rest of the corps diplomatique stared, and well they might, for the document, with its seals and ribbons, proclaimed its character, and the whole deportment of the Emperor taught them a lesson, that in diplomacy and politics, honesty and directness of conduct is, as in all things else, the best policy.

Tossing in a Blanket.

Nearly all my readers have perused the admirable work of *Cervantes—Don Quixote*—and most of them will distinctly recollect the blanketing of Sancho Panza, his esquire. I venture to say, however, that not more than one reader in ten thousand—that being probably the proportion who have ever witnessed the tossing in a blanket of some luckless wight—has any accurate idea of the exercise.

My attention has been frequently called to the subject by engravings and paintings refering to the scene in Don Quixote, in every one of which there was the same want of truth to nature, which satisfied me the artist had never witnessed a performance of the kind. The universal notion entertained on the subject, being that the victim is lifted from the ground on a blanket and thrown or tossed up by the flinging up of the arms of those who hold the blanket. The smallest amount of reflection, however, would teach that a man in this mode could not be raised more than a foot or two from the level of the breasts of those who conduct the exercise.

A few words will explain the operation. As large and stout a blanket as possible being obtained, and the victim laid on it and surrounded by as many as can possibly get hold of the edges of the blanket, thereby preventing his escape, the whole body holding on, make a quick and vigorous *pull* from the common centre. It is this tightening process simply, which springs the culprit into the air, and the height to which he may in this mode be projected, is hardly conceivable to those who have not witnessed the exercise. The subject instinctively grasps the slack of the blanket, by way of resisting the impulse; an useless and absurd effort. Useless because it serves not his purpose; and absurd because it is this very holding on, *and nothing else*, which produces the punishment. By this grasp, his head and shoulders are the last part going up, and in the process of elevation, as he turns over and over, he is sure to fall in some constrained and unnatural posture, which makes him feel, after a night's rest, as if every bone in his body was bruised: so much so that I have known individuals who have been kept too long under the discipline, groan under their pain, upon turning in their beds, during their night's rest after it.

I have known this exercise, during the war of 1812, resorted to by way of punishment to troublesome fellows in camp for getting drunk, or other minor offences. One of the culprits, who was undergoing it for the second time, had the sagacity as soon as the blanket began to tighten, to bring himself to his feet. In this position he shot perpendicularly up, and enjoyed what he afterwards spoke of as the pleasantest exercise in his life, making finally a hole through the blanket, and thereby a close to the punishment, both for himself and others.

Etymologies.

It would be interesting, as well as instructive, to trace the sources whence our western towns derive their names. I shall take up the subject and apply it to Ohio, next week. At present I shall barely glance at Kentucky.

Lexington, in Massachusetts, gave name to its beautiful namesake in Kentucky, news of the first battle in the war of Independence, reaching the spot at the moment the settlers were deliberating on its proposed name. Cynthiana was given its name by the individual who laid it out, by compounding the names of his two daughters, *Cynthia* and *Anna*.

Frankfort owes its title to the following incident, which I have from Ellison E. Williams, who bore a part in it, and who still survives, residing in Covington, Kentucky.

In the year 1780, Wm. Bryant, who was one of the founders of Bryant's Station, Nicholas Tomlin, Ellison E. Williams, Stephen Franks, and others, were on their way from Bryant's Station and the fort of Lexington, to Mann's Salt Licks for the purpose of procuring salt, and while encamping on the bank of the Kentucky river, where the town of Frankfort now stands, were attacked by a company of Indians. Franks was instantly killed, and Tomlin and Bryant were both wounded. The rest of the company escaped unhurt. From this circumstance—the killing of Franks—the place was called *Frankfort*.

Unpublished Historical Fact.

Publicity has just been given to an interesting fact connected with the repulse and defeat of the British at New Orleans, in 1814.

Those who are old enough to remember the war of 1812, may recollect a remarkable instance of bravery in the defence of the American privateer, *General Armstrong*, Capt. *Samuel C. Reed*, which was attacked while lying in the harbour of *Fayal*, in the Western Islands, by the boats of three of the enemy's ships of war, consisting of the *Rota* frigate, the *Plantagenet* 74, and the *Carnation* brig, on the 26th September, 1814—in which engagement, out of the attacking force, nearly four hundred strong, the British lost between two and three hundred, killed and wounded, while on the part of the Americans, only two were killed and seven wounded. I remember the sensation which this news produced on its arrival in our seaport cities, as one of the most brilliant exploits in naval warfare.

It now seems, and the fact is abundantly sustained by documentary evidence, that this engagement, with its results, delayed Admiral Lloyd, who had charge of the squadron above alluded to, ten days at Fayal, whence he sent the severely wounded home to England on the Thais and Calypso sloops of war. He then proceeded to Jamaica, where Admiral Cochrane and General Packenham had been waiting for him several days, who were highly indignant at both the loss and the delay, and loaded him with bitter reproaches. Well might they have done so, if they could have foreseen the fruits of that ten days' delay! Cochrane's fleet of eighty-six sail of vessels arrived at the mouth of the Mississippi on the 6th December, 1814. Gen. Jackson had reached New Orleans on the 2d, only four days before. The Kentucky and Tennessee troops did not arrive until the 16th; nor were they fully supplied with arms, and especially gun-flints, until a later date. If, therefore, the invading fleet and army had arrived ten or twelve days sooner, say on the 25th November, what was there to interpose the slightest impediment to their conquest and sack of the beautiful city of New Orleans, destitute of military forces or defences, and a population hardly long enough a part of the American community, to possess the requisite spirit and patriotism for resistance?

If my limits permitted, I should like to have copied the evidence of these facts. The whole subject clearly points out an overruling Providence watching over our national existence.

Church Livings at Auction.

Going down one day to the Auction Mart, Bartholomew Lane, I found George Robbins—the celebrated London auctioneer—in the act of commencing the sale of several church livings. "Now, gentlemen," said he, addressing the crowd of clergymen, "I have some prime things for you to-day. The church, let me remind you, gentlemen, is now become the only good speculation. It is the only line in which you can establish your sons like gentlemen, and with a chance of success. The church, my friends, that's the only genteel, gentlemanly, and 'certain' profession. And why certain? Because you can certainly 'buy' the best livings, you that have the money, and here's, in the first place, a specimen of what's to be had. Let me see—the income of this living is altogether £1,000; now the tithes are commuted, which are themselves, £1,000 and no bother about collecting. It's a rent, now, gentlemen, it's a rent and comes in cheerfully, easily, graciously—almost of itself. It's within thirty miles of London, in a fine sporting neighbourhood and——"

"How old's the incumbent?" shouted a short, thick man, in rusty black, with a great bundle of papers in his hand.

"Old? why, my friend, you could not well wish him older. He is turned eighty."

"And means to live a hundred," cried another voice.

"Is he ill?" bawls another.

"Is he ill?" says Robbins. "That's a delicate point gentlemen. I do not like to enter into delicate matters; but my learned friend here," turning to a pale young man sitting under the desk, the legal broker of church livings—" my learned friend has seen him lately; I dare say he can tell you."

"Is he ill, old——?"

"Why, no, not *ill* exactly. I should not say *ill*; but he's not strong.

"My friend is cautious, gentlemen. The worthy old man, he says, is not *ill*, but he's not *strong*; and when a man is turned *eighty*, and is not *strong*, why I leave you to judge for yourselves. Depend upon it he's soon for *kingdom come*."

The next presentation was knocked down for £1,000.—*Howitt.*

Little Willie.

The nursery shows thy pictured wall,
 Thy bat, thy bow,
Thy hat and horse, thy club and ball,
 But where art *thou?*
A corner holds thy empty chair—
Thy playthings idly scattered there
But speak to us of our despair.

Even to the last thy every word,
 Too glad, to grieve,
Was sweet as sweetest song of bird
 On summer's eve;
In outward beauty undecayed,
Death o'er thy beauty cast no shade,
And like a rainbow thou didst fade.

We mourn for thee; when blind blank night
 The chamber fills,
We pine for thee, when morn's first light
 Reddens the hills!
The sun, the moon, the stars, the sea,
All, to the wall flower and wild pea,
Are changed—we see the world throngh thee.

And though, perchance, a smile may gleam
 Of casual mirth,
It doth not own, what'er may seem,
 An inward birth;
We miss thy small step on the stair;
We miss thee at our evening prayer;
All day we miss thee, *every where.*

Farewell, then—for a while, farewell—
 Pride of my heart;
It cannot be that long we dwell,
 Thus torn apart;
Time's shadows like the shuttles flee;
And, dark howe'er night's life may be,
Beyond the grave, I'll meet with thee!

Chronological Table.

Jan. 21st.—Louis XVI. guillotined, 1793.
" 22d.—Massacre on the River Raisin, 1813.
   Lord Byron, born, 1788.
" 23d.—Wm. Pitt, died, 1806.
" 24th.—Frederick the Great, born, 1712.
" 25th.—Robert Burns, born, 1759.
" 26th.—Brazil discovered, 1496. Jenner, died, 1823.
" 27th.—Mozart, born, 1755.

Narrative of John Hudson,

A Revolutionary Soldier, and now resident in Cincinnati.

I have been induced, from my long acquaintance with Mr. *Hudson*, as well as the high opinion of his uncommon mental and bodily energies, with which that knowledge has inspired me, to take ample notes from his own lips, of one of the most important events in our revolutionary struggle—the entire movement of the French and American forces, which led to the investment of Lord Cornwallis at Yorktown, Virginia, and his surrender there, which virtually put an end to the War of Independence. Mr. Hudson's reputation for intelligence and veracity is such that implicit confidence may be placed in his narrative, and a degree of interest is confered upon his statements by the uncommon circumstance, that he is amply qualified to make that statement, by the fact that he was actor in his own sphere throughout the principal part of the scene, and eye witness to all in which he did not participate. Most military narratives are taken from the lips of general officers, the mere soldier being rarely competent to give an intelligent history of passing events, of which, however, his personal knowledge is greater than that of his officers.

I deem this narrative of the more importance as there is no circumstance in the revolutionary struggle so little understood as the whole history of the events connected with the surrender of Cornwallis. I give the narrative in Mr. Hudson's own words.

" I was born in *Westchester*, New York, on the 12th June, 1768, and am now, of course, nearly seventy-eight years of age. In April, 1781, there was a levy raised for the defence of the state from domestic enemies, to enable the regular troops of the New York line to march to such points as might be required. In this levy I enlisted, in what was then called *King's district*, Albany county, and is now *Canaan*, in Columbia county, marched to *Saratoga*, where having been drilled one week as a soldier, I enlisted in the Continental service, in which I remained to the end of the War of Independence, mounting guard repeatedly over the very graves of those who fell in our battles with Burgoyne. I remained at Saratoga until the middle of July, 1781, when *Col. Van Schoyck's* regiment, to which I belonged, was directed to join the combined armies at Dobbs' ferry, on the Hudson river, under the command of Gen. *Washington* and Count *Rochambeau*. On the march I carried a British grenadier's musket, as much longer and heavier than the old-fashioned Continentals, as these would outweigh and outreach with their bayonets, the modern article made at Springfield or Harper's ferry. On this musket I carried a bayonet, which never left it only when it was taken off to be cleaned and polished, for it had no scabbard. Besides this weight I bore a cartouch box, with forty rounds ball cartridge, and knapsack with twenty rounds more, and my clothes, blanket and four days provisions. After reaching the grand army, we started up the east side of the *Hudson river* to *Verplank's Point*, and crossed over to *Stony Point*, memorable as the spot where *Gen. Wayne* retaliated on the British troops—the surprize and massacre of *Paoli*. I helped to draw cannon up into that very fort, which it became necessary to fortify when we were about to leave for Virginia. We carried on our march boats so large that it took a wagon and eight horses to draw them, and two inch plank in quantities, by the same conveyance. These were to enable us to form flotillas to cross our troops upon the water courses which lay on our route. In this way, after passing the Hudson, we crossed the *Delaware*, at *Trenton*, N. J., and marched by the way of *Brandywine* creek to the head of *Elk* river, now *Elkton*, but then nothing but an old frame warehouse there. Here we lay three days, and during this period I received the only pay I ever drew for my services during the war, being six French crowns, which were a part of what *Robert Morris* borrowed on his own credit from the French commander, to supply the most urgent necessities of the soldiers. My comrades received the same amount. Those three days were spent in getting our heavy munitions from the Delaware across the Elk river. Here the cannon, &c., were sent by water to *Baltimore*, and thence by the *Chesapeake Bay* into Virginia. The army marched—crossing the Susquehanna at *Havre de Grace*, on their way—to Baltimore, where they encamped at *Howard's hill*, where six hundred head of cattle were slaughtered and salted for our use. Thence we sailed to the mouth of *James river*, encountering an equinoctial storm of remarkable fury, which lasted eight days, checking our progress that entire period, sweeping our decks fore and aft, and drenching us all to the skin. To crown our troubles we had nothing to eat but coarse barley bread, baked for the horses, which had become mouldy and wormy, but we were fain to use it, as an alternative to starvation. On the 25th Sept. we reached our place of debarkation, 40 miles up the James river, six miles from *Williamsburg*, the then seat of government of Virginia. The object of our expedition was to capture the English army under Lord *Cornwallis*, which lay entrenched at *Yorktown* on the York river, southeast of the point we had struck, which enabled us to gain the rear of his position. The *Marquis de la Fayette* we found stationed at *Williamsburg*, expecting our arrival and support."

Gallery of Indian Portraits.

So many catchpenny exhibitions have been paraded before our citizens, and so freely have our city editors puffed every thing which was advertised in their columns, that it seems difficult to press the claims of modest merit to an audience or a visit.

Mr. Stanley, the painter of this fine collection of pictures, has employed the last three years of his life in the praiseworthy effort to collect and perpetuate the likenesses of distinguished chiefs, orators and warriors of our aborigines. He proposes in April next to resume his interesting employment in other and yet unexplored fields of labour, and now opens the exhibition for the purpose of testing the interest the American people are disposed to take in the enterprise.

For my own share I can say with truth, that while these paintings as works of art, in my judgment, will sustain the criticism of connoiseurs, they especially commend themselves to the simple taste of the mass, who in the language of *Sterne*, " are pleased they know not why, and care not wherefore," in my opinion always the true test of excellence.

This is not only a collection of portraits, but of far west scenery, and of incidents in Indian life. It is an exhibition of costume and character, and a museum of specimens of art and fancy work of the most interesting nature, and well calculated to illustrate the pioneer history of Kentucky and Ohio.

No man who feels any interest in such subjects should neglect to visit this Gallery of Portraits.

Derivations.

Besides those names of things which have undergone so little change as to furnish palpable evidence of their origin, there are a few which have been traced out of less obvious character, which are very curious. Thus curmudgeon—a miserly fellow—is from the French *Coeur Mechant*—bad heart. John Dory—a fish of this name—from *il janetore*, the door keeper—this fish being called in Italy, also, *San Pietro*, after the Apostle of that name, popularly supposed there the door keeper of Heaven. Jerusalem Artichoke derives its adjectival name from a corruption of *Girasole*, Italian—turning to the sun, it being the sun-flower variety of that plant. Currant is a corruption of *Corinth*, or grape of Corinth, as damsons, properly Damascene, of the plum of *Damascus*.

The Geneting apple is derived from *Jeanneton*, or Jane of Navarre, in France, who gave it her name. The Mayduke cherry is a corruption of *Medoc*, in Burgundy. Asparagus is termed by

many persons Sparrowgrass. Tuberose, which is neither " tubes" nor " roses," is derived from the adjective botanical title *Tuberosa*, that is tuberous. In the same manner gilliflower takes its name from the season of its flowering in England —July.

I will add andiron to this list, the name changed from *end* iron—an iron to receive the ends of logs. The term bankrupt is from the Italian phrase *bancorotto*, broken bench, which refers to the state of things during early ages, in the banking or money changing community there. In the *bourse* or exchange halls in Lombardy, the money changers had stalls or benches, whence the title bank or banco, at which they transacted their business. When any one of these gentry failed to meet his engagements or became insolvent, his bench was broken and thrown into the street, and the name *bancorotto* or bankrupt given him. Our old English dramatists use the orthography *bankerout*, from the same source. It is both purer English and of clearer significance.

I was forcibly reminded of this term as well as its derivation, during the mob riot which resulted in the destruction of the Exchange Bank, at the corner of Third and Main streets, some three years since. After the rioters had destroyed or mutilated everything else within their reach, they seized the counter, which they carried into the street and broke into pieces there.

Equivoques.

I gave an instance or two in a late paper on the subject of proper emphasis. and now add one or two more. Appropriate gesture is equally important.

An anecdote is related of an English clergyman who was tormented by a termagant wife. By and by, she paid " the debt of nature." Her husband personally officiated at the funeral. His speech was devoted in part to the " thousand ills which flesh is heir to," and was concluded by a scripture quotation. Extending his right hand toward the grave, he said, " There the wicked cease from troubling"—and then placing the same hand on his heart, he added, " and the weary are at rest."

But there are equivocal expressions, which it is out of the power of either emphasis or gesture to illustrate; as a late advertisement in a New York paper, for two girls to *feed* on a double Adams power press. Or the case of the individual in Pennsylvania, in a neighbourhood where each farmer, in harvest, killed in turn for the common benefit, who observed that he did not know whether he should *kill* himself or *eat* a piece of his father.

The latest notice in this line is an advertise-ent of two sisters who *want washing*, and another of a maiden lady, particularly fond of children, that *wishes for two or three, or other employ*ent.

More about Sausages.

When I was in Brussels, Mrs. Stratton, the other of the General, tasted some sausages, hich she declared the best things she had eaten France or Belgium; in fact, she "had found it little that was fit to eat in this country, for very thing was so Frenchified and covered in avy, she dare not eat it; but there was some thing that tasted *natural* about these sausages; e had never eaten any as good, even in Ameri,," and she sent to the landlady to inquire the ame of them, for she meant to buy some to take ong with her. The answer came that they were lled "Saucisses de Lyons," (Lyons Sausages,) d straightway Mrs. Stratton went out and pur ased half a dozen pounds. Professor H. G. erman, (the antiquarian,) soon came in, and a learning what she had in her package, he re arked—

"Mrs. Stratton, do you know what Lyons usages are made of?"

"No," she replied; "but I know that they are st rate!"

"Well," replied Sherman, "they may be good, t they are made from donkeys!"—which really the fact.

Mrs. Stratton said she was not to be fooled so sily—that she knew better, and that she should ck to the sausages.

Presently Mr. Pinte, our French interpreter, tered the room.

"Mr. Pinte," said Sherman, "you are a enchman, and know everything about edibles; ay tell me what Lyons sausages are made of."

"Of asses," replied the inoffensive professor, r. Pinte.

Mrs. Stratton seized the package; the street ndow was open, and in less than a minute, a 'ge brindle dog was bearing the "Lyons sau zes" triumphantly away! Mrs. Stratton was ken violently sick at the stomach, and kept her d when I left Brussels, two days afterwards!—rnum's Letters.

Apologies and Excuses.

Some of these are remarkable enough. I an x a specimen of each kind:

1. The *reasonable.*—"Mrs. Grimes, lend me ur tub!" "Can't do it! all the hoops are off! s full of suds; besides I never had one, because vash in a barrel.

2. The *conclusive.*—A distinguished clergyman the Universalist denomination—now resident New York—was accused, while in Lowell, of violently dragging his wife from a revival meet g, and *compelling* her to go home with him." replied as follows:

1. I have never attempted to influence my fe in her views, nor her choice of meetings.

2. My wife has not attended any of the revival etings in Lowell.

3. I have not attended even one of these meet s, for any purpose whatever.

4. Neither my wife, nor myself, has any inclination to attend these meetings.

5. *I never had a wife!*

3. The *comprehensive.*—A postmaster, acting as agent to an Eastern print, writes his employer as follows:—It would doubtless be well to erase the name of J. S. from your books, and give up as gone that $7.60. He says, in the first place, he never ordered the paper, and if he did he never got it, and if he did get it, it was as an agent; and besides he thinks he paid for it long ago, and if he didn't, he's got nothing to pay, and if he had, he could plead the statute of limitation, for the debt has stood nine years.

New Orleans Picayune.

They tell a good story at Northampton, Mass., about the editor of the New Orleans Picayune. He stopped at the stage house, with the intention of spending some days in that beautiful town. After a reasonable time he became dry, and called for a glass of brandy. "No," says the landlord, "we have no license to sell spirits—we don't keep the article." The editor visited the other public houses,—looked into the groceries and cellars, made close inquiries, but found them tetotallers. He returned to the stage house with a long face—"Landlord," says he, "tell me the nearest place where I can get a glass of brandy, for I'm too dry to stay here any longer."—"I guess you can get it at Greenfield, for they grant licenses there, and it is said they sell spirits." "How far is it?" "Twenty miles." "What time does the stage start?" "Twelve o'clock at night." "Well, landlord, book me for Greenfield."

So it has grown into a proverb in that part of Massachusetts, that when one calls for liquor, he says, "Book me for Greenfield," and when he is corned he is said to be "Booked for Greenfield."

Chronological Table.

Jan. 28th.—Peter the Great, born, 1725. Admiral Byug, shot by sentence of Court Martial, 1757.

Jan. 29th.—Swedenburg, born, 1689. Constantinople, burnt, 1730.

Jan 30th.—Charles I., beheaded, Whitehall, 1648.

Jan. 31st.—Guy Fawkes, executed, 1606.

Feb. 1st.—Battle of Brienne, 1814.

" 2d.—B. Trumbull, died, 1820.

Flattery in Rags.

There is an excellent anecdote, which furnishes a fine lesson in the study of human nature. A miserable looking beggar, in piteous accent implored the charity of a well dressed lady who was passing by, but he was not graciously received. "I have no small change," said she, with a repulsive look. "Then, most charming madam," said the philosopher in rags, "allow me the privilege of kissing your beautiful, lily-white hand?" "No, my friend," replied the fair one with a smile, "I cannot do that, but there's half a crown."

Thoughts of Heaven.

No sickness there,—
No weary wasting of the frame away;
No fearful shrinking from the midnight air,
No dread of summer's bright and fervid ray!

No hidden grief,
No wild and cheerless vision of despair,
No vain petition for a swift relief;
No tearful eyes, no broken hearts are there.

Care has no home
In all the realms of ceaseless prayer and song!
Its billows melt away and break in foam
Far from the mansions of the spirit throng.

The storm's black wing
Is never spread athwart celestial skies!
Its wailings blend not with the voice of Spring,
As some too tender flower fades and dies!

No night distils
Its chilling dews upon the tender frame;
No moon is needed there: The light which fills
That land of glory from its Maker came!

No parted friends
O'er mournful recollections have to weep!
No bed of death enduring love attends
To watch the coming of a pulseless sleep.

No blasted flower
Or withered bud celestial gardens know!
No scorching blast or fierce descending shower
Scatters destruction like a ruthless foe!

No battle word
Startles the sacred host with fear and dread!
The song of peace Creation's morning heard
Is sung wherever angel minstrels tread!

Let us depart
If Home like this await the weary soul!
Look up thou stricken one! Thy wounded heart
Shall bleed no more at sorrow's stern control.

With faith our guide
White-robed and innocent to lead the way,
Why fear to plunge in Jordan's rolling tide.
And find the ocean of eternal day!

Early Steamboat Statistics.

It is remarkable how little is known, or at least recollected, of the character of the first steamboat performances.

The first steamboat in operation in America, or indeed any where else, was in 1787, when *James Rumsey* made a short voyage on the Potomac, with a boat about fifty feet long, propeled by the reaction of a stream of water drawn in at the bow and forced out at the stern, by means of a pump worked by a steam engine. The boat moved at the rate of three or four miles an hour when loaded with three tons burthen. The weight of the engine was one-third of a ton. The boiler held five gallons, and the entire machinery occupied but the space required for four barrels of flour, and she consumed from four to six bushels of coal per day.

In 1787, *John Fitch* put a boat in motion on the Delaware, which performed at the rate of three miles per hour. His next effort was to construct a passenger boat without decks, the *Perseverance*, in which he went, October 12th, 1788, from Philadelphia to Burlington, on the Delaware river, twenty miles, in three hours. This, it may be remarked, was a better performance than any of *Fulton's* early efforts.

The earliest steamboat trip in the world for practical purposes, was by Fulton, in the *Clermont*, of eighteen horse power, which made its passage from New York to Albany in the Hudson river in thirty-five hours, or at the rate of five miles per hour. Such is the difference between progress at the east and in the west, that as late as August, 1816, the Albany Argus, in speaking of the cheapness and expedition of traveling, remarked " That steamboats leave Albany for New York every Monday, Wednesday, Friday and Saturday, at 9 A. M., and New York the same day at 5 P. M. The fare is only *seven dollars*, and the trip is made in twenty-four hours!"

The trip has been made of late years in *ten hours*, and at but one dollar passage money expense; and there is hardly an hour in the day a which a boat may not be taken from New York to Albany.

The first steamboat on the western waters— the Orleans, of 300 tons—was built at Pittsburgh in 1812, and the Vesuvius, 390 tons, in 1813. The first steamboat arrival at New Orleans from Louisville, was on the 30th of May, 1815, of the Enterprise. A steamboat constructed by Fulton commenced running to Providence from the city of New York, in 1815.

The following notice appeared in Niles' Weekly Register, of the 30th September, 1813:—" A project is on foot at New York, to build a steamer of 350 tons, to serve as a packet between New York and Charleston, South Carolina, in which it is estimated the passage will be made in four days. Those whose opinions are entitled to the fullest confidence, decidedly believe that the voyage may be made with at least as much safety as in other vessels."

The steamboat Enterprise arrived at Charleston, 23d July, 1816, from Savannah, and excited a great deal of curiosity—it being the first steamboat ever seen in Charleston. Great as was the surprise, the editors of the newspapers then prophesied that " ten years hence such a boat would be no novelty anywhere in the United States, where there was water enough to float one."

In 1817, the persons engaged in fishing on the Potomac, petitioned the Virginia Legislature, that steamboats might be prevented from running during the month of April—as the noise could be heard several miles, and the agitation of the a and water, frightened all the fish from the river.

The steamship Savannah sailed from Savannah, in 1819, for Liverpool, where she arrived after a passage of twenty-six days, being the first steamer that ever crossed the Atlantic.

Belmont County, Ohio.

The original counties of this State were Washington and Hamilton, the river Muskingum marking between them a division line of the State into east and west. In 1797, Jefferson and Adams were taken off the upper end of Washington and Hamilton counties. In 1798, Ross was formed in the interior of the State. To these were added, in 1800, Fairfield, Clermont, and Trumbull, the latter then comprehending the entire Western Reserve. In 1801, Belmont was taken from Jefferson, the document below being the first move in the matter. It was designed to build up a county seat of Pultney, a settlement on the Ohio, some seven miles below Wheeling, but the public buildings were located at St. Clairsville, and Pultney is now, like some other *Tadmors* in the wilderness, among the things that *once* were.

To his Excellency Arthur St. Clair, Esquire, Governor of the North Western Territory of the United States, and northwest of the river Ohio.

The Petition of sundry subscribers, inhabitants of Jefferson county, in the said Territory, respectfully sheweth—

That, whereas, a division of the said county of Jefferson is contemplated.—Your memorialists are of opinion, that when a division is made that the line between Jefferson county and the said county, which is to be formed from part of Jefferson county, ought to be run thus, viz:—

Commence on the bank of the river Ohio, and at the middle of the fourth township and second range; or in other words, to commence on the bank of the river Ohio, three miles from the northeast corner of said fourth township and second range, which will be two miles and about one quarter from the mouth of Short Creek—and from the bank of the river Ohio, as aforesaid, to run a due west, until the same shall intersect, or in other words, touch the range line between the sixth and seventh range of the seven ranges of townships, and from thenceforth along said range line until the same shall touch the northwest corner of the sixth township and sixth range; and from thence a due east until the same shall touch the river Ohio, or as far to the southern extremity, for the forming of the new county, as may be considered advisable; and from thence north along said river Ohio until the place of beginning—which boundary your memorialists are individually and collectively of opinion ought to form the new county.

And your memorialists are of opinion that the most eligible and proper situation for the seat of justice would be at the town of Pultney, formerly known by the name of the Wetzel Bottom, which being upon the bank of the river Ohio, and laid off in a large bottom, which contains nearly one thousand acres, and is about eight miles south of Wheeling, and about thirty-one miles south of Steubenville, the present seat of justice of Jefferson county; and being a thriving settlement, rapidly increasing in population and improvements. From these circumstances, as well as the central position, it must certainly have a decided preference over any other town that may be put in competition with it: And we are decidedly of opinion that the town of Pultney ought to made the seat of justice for the said new county. And your memorialists shall ever pray, &c.

James Archibald,	John M'Cune,
Samuel Stewart,	John M'Clure,
James Alexander,	Isaac M'Alister,
Peter Mander,	John Mitchel,
Wm. Pickary,	Patrick M'Elheny,
Robert M'Millan,	Stephen Workman,
Charles Irwin,	John Graham,
Henry Hardesty,	

Churches in the East and West--1846.

Denominations.	N. Y.	Phila.	Cinc.
Baptist, - - -	29	17	3
Roman Catholics, - -	20	11	5
Christian, - - -	0	1	1
Do. Disciples, -	0	1	4
Dutch Reformed, - -	18	2	0
Episcopal, - - -	38	20	4
Friends, - - -	4	7	2
German Reformed, -	0	3	2
Jews' Synagogues, -	9	2	2
Lutheran, - - -	5	5	5
Mariners, - - -	0	2	1
Methodist Episcopal, -	40	26	12
Moravian, - - -	1	1	0
New Jerusalem, - -	2	2	1
Presbyterian, - -	40	32	12
Unitarian, - - -	2	1	1
Universalist, - - -	4	4	1
Congregationalist, -	5	1	0
Coloured Churches, -	0	12	6
Millerite, - - -	0	0	1
	172	151	63

This is, for

Cincinnati one Church to 1,300 persons.
Philadelphia one "   to 2,000   "
New York one "   to 2,500   "

In other words, New York has but one half the Churches, in comparison to her population, that are in Cincinnati; and applying the same rule to Philadelphia, she has but two thirds as many as we have.

Another feature of comparison is the different proportions in these different cities. The Baptists, Episcopalians, and Dutch Reformed, constitute nearly one half the religious societies in New York, while they form not one eighth of the whole number here. On the other hand, there are more of the Disciples' Churches (Campbellite) here, than in both the other cities, and as many German Lutheran as in Philadelphia, where there were three Churches of that denomination before there was a Church of any description in Cincinnati. There are, at this moment, in Cincinnati, more houses of worship in which the services are conducted in the German language than in Philadelphia, although a much larger emigration of that people has lodged there than here. The difference is ascribable to the circumstance that our Germans require preaching in that language, only a small portion being familiar with the English, whereas in Philadelphia they and their descendants have lost their native tongue, to a very great extent, by long residence in this country.

In fifty years there will hardly be a house of worship in Cincinnati in which the services will be conducted in the German language, such having been the overpowering influence of the English in our own country everywhere that that it has come in contact with foreign languages for the every day business of life.

Etymologies of County Towns in Ohio.

There are eighty counties in the State of Ohio, and consequently as many county towns, or seats of justice. Of these seventeen—West Union, Georgetown, Springfield, Wilmington, Lancaster, Cambridge, Hillsborough, Norwalk, Troy, Mount Vernon, Burlington, Newark, Chester, Somerset, Portsmouth, New Philadelphia, and Lebanon—derive their names from older settlements in the Atlantic States, and received them from the settlers—as a general rule—in compliment to the neighbourhoods from whence they came. Another class of names are taken from towns and cities of antiquity, or of eminence in foreign countries, as Lima, Athens, New Lisbon, Cadiz, London, Toledo, Medina, Ravenna and Canton. Four bear the names of their respective founders—as Cleveland, Millersburg, M'Connellsville and Zanesville. The heroes and sages of the revolution have given names to eleven—to wit: Jefferson, Hamilton, Van Wert, Marion, Paulding, Warren, Carrollton, Greenville, Washington, Wooster, and Steubenville. Three owe their names to Americans of later date, as Piketon, Jackson, Perrysburg. But two only are named after Governors of the State—St. Clairs-

ville and Tiffin. Four bear the name of early pioneers to the State—Kenton, Findlay, Eaton, and Dayton.

The Indian aboriginals are few—Coshocton, Bucyrus? Delaware, and Chillicothe are all, I believe. Logan is named after the celebrated Indian Chief, whose memory will endure as long as the letters exist which compose his memorable speech. Gallipolis signifies the city of Frenchmen. Three owe their name to local features—as Bellefontaine, from a fine spring in the town; Circleviile, from the ancient circular fortifications found there, and corresponding to which the centre of the town was laid out; Defiance, from the old Fort of that name, erected by Gen. Wayne. Marietta was named after Marie Antoinetta, Queen of France, by compounding the first and last four letters of her name. Kalida is a formation from a Greek word, signifying beautiful. Sandusky, properly *Sodowsky*, from a trader of Polish descent, who lived many years in that region of country. Xenia, Sidney, Chardon and Elyria, were merely fancy names, in all probability. St. Mary's from the river of that name, so called by Jesuit missionaries. The origin of Woodsfield, Marysville, Mansfield and Akron, I cannot state, or even conjecture. Columbus, the capitol of the State, as well as of Franklin county, bears the proud name of the discoverer of America; and the modern scourge of nations, Napoleon, has given his name to the seat of justice for Henry county.

If any of my readers or correspondents can correct errors or supply deficencies in this article, their communications for that purpose will be very acceptable. The utmost industry would not suffiice to make a first effort of the kind perfect.

What's in a Name?

I observe that there is a bill before the Legislature of Ohio, to change the name of *Montague L. Moses* to *Moses L. Montague.* This name reminds me of a pleasant little incident in English parliamentary history, which runs as follows:

There were two members of Parliament—*Montagu Matthew* and *Matthew Montagu*, Esqs. They formed the contrast in size there, which Messrs. *Wentworth* and *Douglass* do in the present Congress of the United States, who being two feet difference in height are said to be nicknamed in Washington, "The long and short of the matter." Montagu Matthew was almost a giant in height, and Matthew Montagu, on the contrary, was considerable under the usual size. Their names being so much alike, they were sometimes mistaken for each other in debate, greatly to the annoyance of the former, who affected great contempt, personal and political, for his namesake. On one occasion where this mistake had occurred under some especially provoking circumstances, he rose and remarked that, certain honourable gentleman, by the manner they confounded names, did not appear aware that there was any difference between Montagu Matthew and Matthew Montague. If they were, however, to take a look at us both, they would see there is as much resemblance between us as between *a chestnut horse and a horse chestnut.*

Original Letter of Th. Jefferson.

WASHINGTON, Dec. 21, 1802.

Sir:—I informed General Kosciuszko of your kind attention to the location of his lands, and of your refusal to accept of anything for it, expressing pleasure at an opportunity of rendering him a service; and he in answer desires you to be assured how sensible he is of this mark of recollection and friendship, and the pleasure he has received from this testimony of regard from an old brother soldier. Having sold the lands to Madame Louisa Frances Felix, who is now come over to settle on them with her family, and leaves this place in a few days for that purpose, I have, in pursuance of a power of attorney from the General, given her a written power to enter into possession of the lands and to hold them according to the contract of conveyance from the General. Should there be any difficulty in finding the lands, I trust that your good disposition towards the General will lead you to render her any information necessary for that purpose.

Accept my respects and good wishes.

TH. JEFFERSON.

Col. JOHN ARMSTRONG, Cincinnati.

Novel Mode of Leeching.

During the mania for leeches, which prevailed some years ago in France, a country doctor in Bretagne had ordered some to be applied to a patient suffering with the sore throat. On calling to see the effect of his remedy, the first person he met, on entering the house, was the peasant's wife.

" Well, my good woman," said the doctor, ' how is your husband to-day? better no doubt?"

" Oh, yes, surely!" answered the woman, "he is as well as ever and gone to the field."

" I thought so," continued Monsieur le Docteur, " the leeches have cured him! Wonderful effect they have! you have got the leeches of course?"

" Oh yes, Monsieur le Docteur, they did him a great deal of good, though he could not take them all."

" Take them all!" cried our friend, " why how did you apply them?"

" Oh, I managed it nicely," said the wife, looking quite contented with herself; " for variety's sake I boiled one half and make a fry of the other. The first he got down very well, but they made him sick. But what he took was quite enough," continued she, seeing some horror in the doctor's countenance, " for he was better the next morning, and to-day he is quite well."

" Umph!" said the doctor, with a sapient shake of the head, " if they have cured him it is sufficient; but they would have been better applied externally."

Cincinnati Literature.

A distant correspondent says,—" Cincinnati boasts of her common schools, and the consequent diffusion of knowledge in your community. Pity that they had not been established so many years earlier as to benefit your editors in the orthography of the language in which they write or publish. I observe in the first line of an advertisement, which appears in most of your papers, the vulgarism,

' I dreampt that I dwelt in marble halls.'

" Errors may occur at times without impeaching the knowledge of an editor, but an error of this description, common to your whole press, and which a school boy or girl of seven years of age would promptly detect, I consider disgraceful to the literature of the editorial fraternity of your city."

How *Dr. Bailey* and *Professor Mansfield*, literary men of no mean pretensions, should have committed such blunders, is to me inscrutable.

Titles.

My correspondents will do me a favour by dispensing with the title Esq. after my name.

For this I have several reasons—

1st. It is indistinct, being applied to all manner of persons, honourable and dishonourable, in public and in private life.

2d. It is inapplicable to me. Esquire is derived from the French *Ecuyer,* a stable boy or ostler. I have not cleaned out a stable for *forty years.*

3d. It is anti-republican. A good democrat desires no better name than to combine the appellative given him in baptism with that which he inherits by descent. He wants as a handle neither *Mr.* at one end nor *Esq.* at the other of his legitimate appellation.

In this respect, as in many others, the Society of Friends set a first rate example, neither giving nor taking titles.

The Iron Manufacture of the United States.

How deeply the United States is interested in the Tariff question, may be judged by the following statistics, which have been gathered by a Convention of iron masters and coal mine proprietors, lately assembled in Philadelphia.

The product of the whole United States is over 500,000 tons of pig iron, and 300,000 tons of bar, hoops, &c. The following estimate, in detail, of the Iron business in the United States, for 1845, will give our readers an idea of the value and extent of this branch of business.

24) blast furnaces, yielding 486,000 tons pig iron—average of 900 tons to the furnace per annum,   486,000 tons.
950 bloomeries, forges, rolling and slitting mills, and yielding—291,600 tons of bar, hoops, &c.

Blooms,	30,000 tons.
Castings, machinery, stove plates, &c.,	121,500 tons.

which, at their present market value, would stand thus:

291,600 tons of wrought iron, at $80 per ton,	$23,328,000
121,500 tons of castings, at $75 per ton,	9,112,500
30,000 tons of bloomery iron, at $50 per ton,	1,500,000
	$33,949,500

To which must be added to the quantity imported for the last year:

46,000 tons bar iron, rolled, at $60 per ton,	$2,760,000
17,500 tons hammered, at $80 per ton,	1,500,000
16,050 tons, pig iron, converted into castings, at $75 per ton,	1,950,750
5,750 tons scrap iron, at $35 per ton,	201,950
4,157 tons sheet, hoops, &c., at $130 per ton,	540,410
2,800 tons steel, at $335 per ton,	938,000
	$41,744,640

Pennsylvania, it is estimated, has a population of 400,000 persons, in various relations to the Iron business.

To Readers.

Since the establishment of the Advertiser I have been in the receipt of various friendly and approbatory notices of my little sheet from the corps editorial at home and in other places, which I felt unwilling to publish, deeming them personal matters merely. But I am not sure whether there has not been false delicacy in this. The Advertiser embodies a great amount of statistical and other subjects, for a large share of which I am indebted to correspondents—most of which is of great value now, and will be of inappreciable interest in future years for comparison and reference. And it is probable that there is no one who takes it at present and files it away, but at a future period could obtain a greatly enhanced price on what it cost, in years to come, if disposed to part with it.

My paper enjoys a fair support at home, considering how many publications exist to drain the pockets and consume the reading leisure of the community here. But it might, and perhaps ought to have, five hundred additional subscribers in this neighbourhood, devoted as it is to the collection and preservation of every thing connected with the West, that can shed light on the past or afford it to the future.

With these views I republish a friendly notice from the *Dayton Journal & Advertiser*, of the 02th inst.:

"One of the best papers we receive is Cist's Advertiser, published at Cincinnati, and we find its contents sufficiently readable to induce us to lay it by for a leisure hour, so that we may read it through without interruption. In the last number of that paper we find the following *spirited* sketch of a scene at the Memphis Convention.

"We give it, not for the purpose of sanctioning the peculiar mode of improving the Western waters which is set forth, but as a lively and amusing sketch which may bring a smile from a Washingtonian without any discredit to his pledge or profession.

"We may as well add in this place, that the Advertiser contains much useful statistical information, and many interesting facts and narratives connected with the early settlement of the West. It is a paper unlike any other that we know of, and we cannot but believe that if its merits were more generally known, it would have a large circulation, in the West especially. It is published weekly at $2 per annum."

Coal Mines of Pennsylvania.

The coal of Pennsylvania is of more value to her morally, physical and pecuniary, than the gold mines of Mexico and Peru to those empires.

The value of the coal refered to in the table below must be of more than twelve millions of dollars.

The Miner's Journal, at Pottsville Pennsylvania, contains some valuable statistics on the Schuylkill coal region. The following is the official statement of the quantity of coal sent to market from the different regions in 1845, compared with 1844:—

		1845.	1844.	*Increase.*
Schuylkill	R. R.,	829,237	441,491	378,845
	Canal,	263,550	308,443	134,884
				[*decrease.*
		1,083,796	839,934	243,862
Lehigh,		432,080	377,821	54,259
Lackawanna,		269,469	251,005	18,464
Wilkesbarre,		178,401	114,906	63,495
Pinegrove,		47,928	34,976	13,012
Shamokin,		10,000	13,087	
		2,051,674	1,631,669	*tons.*
		1,631,669		
Increase in 1845,		390,005		

American Artists Abroad.

We are gratified to learn of the constant marks of respect and esteem received by our young countrymen, POWERS, the Sculptor, and his friend and associate, KELLOGG, the Painter—both gentlemen of fine genius and destined to shed lustre on American arts. We learn that Mr. Kellogg, returning recently to Italy from a tour of some extent in the East, was presented, while in Constantinople, by a high functionary of the Turkish empire, with a magnificent cup, studded with upwards of a hundred diamonds, as a testimony of friendship and respect.

Sixth Ward,--Cincinnati.

This is the southwest section of the city, and a region which our increasing demands for room will soon bring into dense occupation, fronting as it does, a mile and a half on the Ohio river.

The number of its public buildings are 12—St. Aloysius' Orphan Asylum, Gas Works, a Public School House, two Friends' meeting houses, Morris Chapel, Trinity Church, on Fifth street, Third Presbyterian Church, *Christ*ian Church, on Fourth, near Stone street, Baptist Church, on Pearson street, and an Engine House on Fifth st.

The entire number of buildings in the ward is 1183, of which 593 are of brick, and 590 are frames.

Of these there were, at the close of 1842,

	Bricks.	Frames.	Total.
	229	501	730
Built in 1843,	157	39	196
" " 1844,	89	28	117
" " 1845,	118	22	140
	593	590	1183

Several important manufacturing establishments were put up in 1844, and a few of the same character have been added in 1845. All these are of brick.

More than one half of this ward is built upon. There are probably more persons in it owning the houses which they occupy, in proportion to the number, than can be found in any other section of the city.

John Randolph.

I am old enough to have witnessed the whole progress of this remarkable man, from the commencement of his Congressional career to the close of his natural life. He has left very imperfect traces behind him on the course over which the chariot wheels of his genius were driven, and posterity finding but little preserved that gives any idea of the prodigious effect of his political speeches, or rather *diatribes*, will doubtless attribute it to his own peculiar manner of saying things.

This undoubtedly had its share of influence, but any one who has read the cotemporary reports of his speeches in Congress, negligently and inadequately as they were reported—for there were no reporters deserving of the name at that date —must have been sensible that there was as much at least in the matter, as in their mode of delivery. His wonderful command of language, in which he delighted to illustrate the energy and eloquence of the Saxon English stile, his unrivalled power of sarcasm and ridicule, his remarkable perspicuity of thought as well as of expression, furnishing ideas to the intellectual, and comprehension to the mass—imparted greater influence to his ges-

ture and management of voice, remarkable as these were than they derived from such characteristics.

Randolph aspired to become a political leader, a position for which he had neither the necessary temper or tact; and when his failure as such became manifest, even to himself, he gradually assumed his natural place, not merely in opposition, but in that Ishmaelite warfare which he was willing should lift every man's hand against him, so long as he felt free to lift his hand against every man.

But it is not my object to write his history, or even fully pourtray his character. For these employments I have neither the talent nor the limits—so far as these columns are refered to. I have heard him often on the floor of Congress, and always, if not with pleasure, with deep interest. But I cannot trust myself to recollect the brilliant passages which have since faded on my memory, one excepted. He was speaking on the Yazoo land claims, a subject that always stirred up his bile, and took occasion to glance at other objects, with the ferocity that tinctured too many of his speeches—" As to Wilkinson, he is in the last stage of putrefaction—*touch him and he falls to pieces.*"

One or two characteristic anecdotes of Randolph, hitherto unpublished, as I believe, will close this article. They are perfectly authentic.

During one of the suspensions of specie payments, in his day, Mr. R. was on a visit to New York, on business. He had occasion to present a check to a large amount for payment at the Merchants' Bank of that city, for which he refused to accept any thing but specie, which the tellers of the bank as obstinately refused to give. Randolph disdained to bandy words, with either clerks or principals on their conduct, which in his own way of thinking, amounted to swindling, but withdrew and had a handbill issued at the next printing office, which in two hours was posted up over the whole city, stating that—

" John Randolph, of Roanoke, being on a visit to New York, will address his fellow-citizens on the banking and currency questions, from the *steps* of the Merchants' Bank, at six o'clock this evening."

A crowd began to gather more than an hour before the appointed time, enlarging so rapidly and amply that before the hour assigned to address it had arrived, the officers of the bank took the alarm, and finding out his lodging place, sent one of the clerks with the amount of the check in gold, which Randolph received with a sardonic smile and the apt quotation—*Chartaciam invenit, auream reliquit.* He left New York in one of the stages which at that period anticipated day light, and as he was hardly known in that city, 'the notice passed off for a more hoax on the public.

After leaving the Merchants' Bank, he called at the Mechanics' Bank to transact some money business there, involving a discount of a few dollars. Randolph, with his peculiar notions on such subjects, felt as though these had been stolen out of his pocket. He said nothing, however, until getting to the door of entrance, where the effigy of a huge arm swung as huge a hammer, he asked what that meant. "The badge of our institution, sir, you know this is the Mechanics' Bank," was the explanation of the teller. "You had better take it down and substitute a currier's knife," was Randolph's brief and bitter reply.

JOE LOGSTON.

The elder Logston, whose name was Joseph, and his wife, whose name was Mary, with an only son bearing his name, lived, when I first knew them, in Virginia, near the source of the north branch of the Potomac, in one of the most inhospitable regions of the Allegheny mountains, some twenty or thirty miles from any settlement. There never was, perhaps, a family better calculated to live in such a place. Old Joe (for they were soon known as Old Joe and Young Joe Logston,) was a very athletic man, with uncommon muscular strength. The old lady was not so much above the ordinary height of women, but like the Dutchman's horse, was built up from the ground; and it would have taken the strength of two or three common women to equal hers. The son was no discredit to either in the way of strength, size, or activity. In fact he soon outstripped his father. What little he lost in height was more than compensated in the thickness and muscle of the mother, so that when he came to his full size and strength, he went by the name of Big Joe Logston. I would not venture to say his physical powers were equal to those of the strong man of old, but such they were as to become proverbial. It was often said to stout looking, growing young men, "You will soon be as big as Big Joe Logston."

Joe sometimes descended from the mountain heights into the valleys, in order to exchange his skins for powder, lead, and other articles for the use of the family. While in society he entered, with great alacrity, into all the various athletic sports of the day. No Kentuckian could ever, with greater propriety than he, have said, "I can out-run, out-hop, out-jump, throw down, drag out, and whip, any man in the country." And as to the use of the rifle, he was said to be one of the quickest and surest centre shots to be found. With all this, as is usual with men of real grit, Joe was good natured, and never sought a quarrel. No doubt many a bullying, braging fellow would have been proud of the name of having whipped Big Joe Logston, but that, on taking a close survey of him, he thought "prudence the better part of valour," and let him return to his mountain without raising his dander.

About the time Joe arrived at manhood, his father, and perhaps his mother, were called hence, leaving him single handed to contend, not only with the Spitzbergen winters of the mountains, but with the bears, panthers, wolves, rattlesnakes, and all the numerous tribes of dangerous animals,

reptiles and insects, with which the mountain regions abound. Joe, however, maintained his ground for several years, until the settlements had begun to encroach on what he had been accustomed to consider his own premises. One man sat down six miles east of him, another about the same distance in another direction, and finally one, with a numerous family, had the temerity to come and pitch his cabin within two miles of him. This Joe could not stand, and he pulled up stakes and decamped to seek a neighbourhood where he could hear the crack of no man's rifle but his own.

Of all the men I ever knew he was the best qualified to live on a frontier where there were savages, either animal or human to contend with. His uncommon size and strength, and inclination to be entirely free from restraint, made him choose his residence a little outside of the bounds of law and civil liberty. I do not know the precise time he left the Alleghenies, but believe it was between the years 1787 and '91. The next that we heard of Joe was, that he had settled in Kentucky, south of Green river, I think on Little Barren river, and of course, a little in advance of the settlements. The frontiers were frequently compelled to contend with the southern Indians. There was not a particle of fear in Joe's composition; that ingredient was left out of his mixture. I never knew such a man in my life. There he would be. He soon had an introduction to a new acquaintance. So far he had been acquainted only with savage beasts, but now savage man came in his way, and as it "stirs the blood more to rouse the lion than to start a hare," Joe was in his delight. The Indians made a sudden attack, and all that escaped were driven into a rude fort for preservation, and, though reluctantly, Joe was one. This was a new life to him, and did not at all suit his taste. He soon became very restless, and every day insisted on going out with others to hunt up the cattle. Knowing the danger better, or fearing it more, all persisted in their refusals to go with him.

To indulge his taste for the woodman's life, he turned out alone, and rode till the after part of the day without finding any cattle. What the Indians had not killed were scared off. He concluded to return to the fort. Riding along a path which led in, he came to a fine vine of grapes. He laid his gun across the pommel of his saddle, set his hat on it, and filled it with grapes. He turned into the path and rode carelessly along, eating his grapes, and the first intimation he had of danger, was the crack of two rifles, one from each side of the road. One of the balls passed through the paps of his breast, which, for a male, were remarkably prominent, almost as much so as those of many nurses. The ball just grazed the skin between the paps, but did not injure the breast bone. The other ball struck the horse behind the saddle, and he sunk in his tracks. Thus was Joe eased off his horse in a manner more rare than welcome. Still he was on his feet in an instant, with his rifle in his hands, and might have taken to his heels; and I will venture the opinion, that no Indian could have caught him. That, he said, was not his sort. He had never left a battle ground without leaving his mark, and he was resolved that that should not be the first. The moment the guns fired, one very athletic Indian sprang towards him with tomahawk in hand. His eye was on him, and his gun to his eye, ready, as soon as he approached near enough to make a sure shot, to let him have it. As soon as the Indian discovered this, he jumped behind two pretty large saplings, some small distance apart, neither of which were large enough to cover his body, and to save himself as well as he could, he kept springing from one to the other.

Joe, knowing he had two enemies on the ground, kept a lookout for the other by a quick glance of the eye. He presently discovered him behind a tree, loading his gun. The tree was not quite large enough to hide him. When in the act of pushing down his bullet, he exposed pretty fairly his hips. Joe, in the twinkling of an eye, wheeled and let him have his load in the part exposed. The big Indian then, with a mighty "Ugh!" rushed towards him with his raised tomahawk. Here were two warriors met, each determined to conquer or die,—each the Goliah of his nation. The Indian had rather the advantage in size of frame, but Joe in weight and muscular strength. The Indian made a halt at the distance of fifteen or twenty feet, and threw his tomahawk with all his force, but Joe had his eye on him and dodged it. It flew quite out of the reach of either of them. Joe then clubbed his gun and made at the Indian, thinking to knock him down. The Indian sprang into some brush, or saplings, to avoid his blows. The Indian depended entirely on dodging, with the help of the saplings. At length Joe, thinking he had a pretty fair chance, made a side blow with such force, that missing the dodging Indian, the gun, now reduced to the naked barrel, was drawn quite out of his hands, and flew entirely out of reach. The Indian now gave another exulting "Ugh!" and sprang at him with all the savage fury he was master of. Neither of them had a weapon in his hands, and the Indian, seeing Logston bleeding freely, thought he could throw him down and dispatch him. In this he was mistaken. They seized each other and a desperate scuffle ensued. Joe could throw him down, but could not hold him there. The Indian being naked, with his hide oiled, had greatly the advantage in a ground scuffle, and would still slip out of Joe's grasp and rise. After throwing him five or six times, Joe found, that between loss of blood and violent exertions, his wind was leaving him, and that he must change the mode of warfare or lose his scalp, which he was not yet willing to spare. He threw the Indian again, and without attempting to hold him, jumped from him, and as he rose, aimed a fist blow at his head, which caused him to fall back, and as he would rise, Joe gave him several blows in succession, the Indian rising slower each time. He at last succeeded in giving him a pretty fair blow in the burr of the ear, with all his force, and he fell, as Joe thought, pretty near dead. Joe jumped on him, and thinking he could dispatch him by choaking, grasped his neck with his left hand, keeping his right one free for contingencies. Joe soon found the Indian was not so dead as he thought, and that he was making some use of his right arm which lay across his body, and on casting his eye down discovered the Indian was making an effort to unsheath a knife that was hanging at his belt. The knife was so short and so sunk in the sheath that it was necessary to force it up by pressing against the point. This the Indian was trying to effect, and with good success. Joe kept his eye on it, and let the Indian work the handle out, when he suddenly grabbed it, jerked it out of the sheath, and sunk it up to the handle in the Indian's breast, who gave a death groan and expired.

Joe now thought of the other Indian, and not knowing how far he had succeeded in killing or crippling him, sprang to his feet. He found the crippled Indian had crawled some distance towards them, and had propped his broken back against a log and was trying to raise his gun to shoot him, but in attempting to do which he would fall forward. and had to push against his gun to raise himself again. Joe seeing that he was safe, concluded he had fought long enough for healthy exercise that day, and not liking to be killed by a crippled Indian, he made for the fort. He got in about nightfall, and a hard looking case he was—blood and dirt from the crown of his head to the sole of his foot, no horse, no hat, no gun—with an account of the battle that some of his comrades could scarce believe to be much else than one of his big stories in which he would sometimes indulge. He told them they must go and judge for themselves.

Next morning a company was made up to go to Joe's battle ground. When they approached it Joe's accusers became more confirmed, as there was no appearance of dead Indians, and nothing Joe had talked of but the dead horse. They, however, found a trail as if something had been dragged away. On pursuing it they found the big Indian, at a little distance, beside a log, covered up with leaves. Still pursuing the trail, though not so plain, some hundred yards farther, they found the broken backed Indian, lying on his back with his own knife sticking up to the hilt in his body, just below the breast bone, evidently to show that he had killed himself and that he had not come to his end by the hand of an enemy. They had a long search before they found the knife with which Joe killed the big Indian. They at last found it forced down into the ground below the surface, apparently with the weight of a person's heel. This had been done by the crippled Indian. The great efforts he must have made, alone, in that condition, show, among thousands of other instances, what Indians are capable of under the greatest extremities.

Some years after the above took place, peace with the Indians was restored. That frontier, like many others, became infested with a gang of outlaws, who commenced stealing horses and committing various depredations. To counteract which a company of regulators, as they were called, was raised. In a contest between these and the depredators, Big Joe Logston lost his life, which would not be highly esteemed in civil society. But in frontier settlements, which he always occupied, where savages and beasts were to be contested with for the right of soil, the use of such a man is very conspicuous. Without such, the country could never have been cleared of its natural rudeness so as to admit of the more brilliant and ornamental exercises of arts, sciences and civilization.

Professional Etiquette.

The following amusing incident of professional etiquette, I had from Dr. Joel Lewis, of Pittsburgh, an eminent physician, who flourished there twenty-five or thirty years since.

The Dr. had a valuable cow, which became sick and seemed likely to die. He asked an Irish servant who lived with him, if he knew any body who followed cow doctoring. "It's meself dis that same," said the man, "there's Jemmy

Lafferty can cure any cow in the world, barring she's at the lift." "Well, then," replied the Dr., " go for Lafferty." The cow doctor accordingly came, drenched and physiced the brute for four or five days, in the lapse of which time he waited on Dr. Lewis and pronounced her cured. The Dr., greatly delighted, put his hand to his pocket-book, "Well, Lafferty, what do I owe you?" "Owe me," replied Jemmy, drawing himself up with great dignity, "sorra the haporth! *We doctors niver take money of one another.*"

" My first impulse," said the Dr., while telling the story, which he gave me directly after the incident happened, " was to kick the fellow out of the house, and throw his fee after him, but on second thought, the whole affair seemed so ridiculous that I bowed him my acknowledgments with as much gravity as I could assume, and as soon as he left the house lay down on the carpet, rolling over and over to indulge the fit of laughter which I must give way to, or burst."

Narrative of John Hudson,
A Revolutionary Soldier, and now resident in Cincinnati.—No. 2.

I neglected to state, in its proper place, a remarkable circumstance which occurred while I was at Saratoga, which may as well be brought in here as at a later stage of this narrative.

When I reached *Saratoga,* the levy of which I formed a part, was stationed in a hovel made of slabs, which was opposite *Schuyler's* saw-mill. Here we lay on the bare ground, having not even a bundle of straw to put under us. Some few nights after we took possession of these lodgings, and in the course of a pitch dark night, our acting adjutant roused us up, and demanded of the officer in command, a detachment of a sergeant, corporal, and twelve privates for immediate service. Of these twelve I was made one, and in the course of a few minutes we were all ready, and followed the adjutant to Gen. Schuyler's residence. We were there taken into a bed room where there were two men prisoners, who were pinioned by the arms. The adjutant, giving them in charge to the sergeant in command with strict exhortations to watch them carefully, departed with the guard whose place we were about to take. The next morning about nine o'clock, *Capt. Austin,* in whose company I afterwards enlisted, came marching down with his command and five drums and fifes, a black silk handkerchief on each drum, and all the drums snared. A negro accompanied the party as hangman, who on entering the room fastened ropes around the men's necks, who were then taken out and marched off. I was at this time a boy of thirteen years of age, fresh from the peaceable employments of a country life, and the awe and

horror with which these preparations inspired me may be readily conjectured. Our own party remained behind in the bed room, waiting further orders. Gen. Schuyler was at this period commander-in-chief of the northern frontier, and absent at the time from home, and I was informed that Mrs. Schuyler, with some feeling of jealousy that her husband's authority should be infringed, sent a note to the commander of the garrison, inquiring of him how he expected to account to the General, his superior officer, for the lives of men about to be executed without a trial, or even an examination. I understood that this had the effect of taking the prisoners down from the tree to which they were already fastened. They were then brought back to the bed room with the same solemnity as they had been taken away, and a boat being prepared at the Hudson river, not more than a quarter of a mile distance, they were put in charge of a guard of regulars and sent down to Albany. One of these men was *Solomon Meeker,* a private in Capt. Austin's company, and the other was a British deserter named *John Higginbottom,* who it was judged was in reality a spy, and had been tampering with Meeker to lead him to desert, if not for worse purposes. Meeker, I believe, never was put to trial, for we took him out of Albany jail on our march to the Chesapeake. As to Higginbottom, many years after the period of which I am now speaking, and long after the war was at a close, I became acquainted with him, recognising him as soon as I saw him, and reminding him of these things. He acknowledged himself to be the man, and stated that he had got clear at Albany by representing himself as a deserter, which led them at last to let him off. He confessed to me that he had been, however, a spy, and as such had come to Saratoga, and that he had entered that fort at daylight, and in a few hours would have been off and discovered enough to the British forces to bring on a body of Indians and tories from Canada sufficient to have destroyed every human being about the place. We see by this, on how narrow a pivot very important events turn, and the necessity of prompt and vigorous action in time of danger. Let me now resume the narrative of our Virginia campaign, and first let me state the cause of my enlistment in the regular service.

The levies mounted guard with the regular troops, and one morning just after being relieved at the usual hour, I had gone into our quarters and was sitting on the ground with my gun between my knees, when it went off accidentally and apparently without cause, the ball passing out of the hovel, but injuring no one. However, it was an offence punishable with one hundred lashes, and the corporal of the quarter guard immediately came in with a file of men and took me to the guard house. Here a conversation took place between the sergeant major and quartermaster sergeant, and one of them remarked with an oath, that it was a shame to give a boy like this an hundred lashes for what was notoriously an accident. This was said, purposely loud enough for me to hear. Then turning to me he added—"Come my lad, the best way for you to get out of this, will be to enlist—come along with us." I jumped up immediately, and had my name entered on the muster roll of the company, which was that of Captain Austin, and now I was fairly entered for the campaign.

We landed, as I have already stated, on the 25th September, 1781, and here we drew provisions, and made the first meal for eight days in any degree of comfort. As evening approached, we took up our line of march for Williamsburg, which we reached some time that night, and a very dark one it was. As soon as we arrived I was put in the commissary's guard. Williamsburg was six miles from our landing place and twelve from Yorktown, our destined theatre of employment. Every six men, on their march had a tent and tent poles, and camp kettle, and in addition to the heavy load I have already stated I was carrying, that tent was thrown over my shoulders in my regular turn of carrying it. At that time I was advanced in my fourteenth year, only from the 12th of June to the 25th of September. We found *Lafayette*, with the American troops under his command, at Williamsburg, it being his head quarters, and a body of French troops, landed by Admiral *De Barras*, a few days before, to reinforce his detachment. As I was up all night in the service assigned me, I had ample opportunity of noticing the bustle of marching and preparing to march, which kept others as well as myself awake the whole night. As the morning dawned I saw nothing but small parties which were following the army; probably piquet guards, whose duty not being over till daylight, had delayed them, and who were now pushing on to overtake the main body of the army. The exposure of that night made me very unwell and I rode part of the day on the commissary's wagon. In the course of that afternoon we caught up with the army, when I was relieved from this post and rejoined my own company.

That Iron Safe.

It is an old saying, "If you want news of home, always look for it abroad." A Philadelphia paper states the following:—

"There is being constructed at Cincinnati, a large iron safe intended for an appendage to a jail in the interior of Louisiana. It is eleven feet wide, twelve feet long, and eight in height."

We all recollect this safe and know its appear-ance, although hundreds doubtless saw it who could not conjecture its design. Let me briefly explain it.

The lower Mississippi country does not produce stone for building purposes. The walls of the jails and penitentiaries there are built of bricks accordingly, which of course are an inadquate security against violence. To form an inner lining to a room about to be built in one of the jails south, this *Safe*, as it is not inaptly called, was designed and made. It is formed of iron bars 2½ inches broad by ¾ inches thick, which are riveted together where they cross each other, and form a cube of the size stated above, and an enclosure which will defy the efforts alike of cunning and force.

I make this correction to a paragraph, which as it goes the rounds will lead its readers to suppose that the safe is to secure money rather than robbers or murderers.

Derivations.

Mr. CIST:—

You invite corrections and explanations to the list of Ohio county towns published in your last. Accordingly I suggest that Elyria, from Mr. Ely, proprietor of the place, and Woodsfield, laid off by Mr. Woods, of Wheeling, are names of places commemorating their respective founders. Mansfield is in honour of the great English jurist of that name, as Sidney is of his conntryman Sir Philip Sidney, the great light of chivalry. Akron is Greek, for an elevation or higher place, as Acropolis, a high city. Xenia, in the same language, signifies hospitality. I have never yet experienced much of this cardinal virtue there but what I paid for; what I might have received had I been in necessitous circumstances, I cannot say. Marysville was named in honour of the daughter of its original proprietor.

You speak of Bucyrus, doubtfully, as an aboriginal name. I judge it is a corruption by some half taught schoolmaster, of Busiris who conformed the termination to the name of the celebrated King of Persia, and first tetotaller of antiquity. D.

Cincinnati, January 31, 1846.

The Railway Speculation.

Punch "has found the diary and pocket-book of a railway speculator, who from being a footman, rose into a millionaire. An inventory of the pocket-book shows the following contents. Three tavern bills, paid; a tailor's ditto, unsettled; forty-nine allotments in different companies, twenty-six thousand seven hundred shares in all, of which the market value we take, on an average, to be ¼ discount; and in an old bit of paper; tied with pink ribbon, a lock of chesnut hair, with the initials M. A. H.

" In the diary of the pocket book was a journal, jotted down by the proprietor from time to time. At first the entries are insignificant; as

for instance:—' January 3d—Our beer in the Su-
vats' Hall so *precious* small at this time that I
reely *muss* give warning, & wood, but for my
dear Mary Hann.' 'February 7—That broot,
Screw, the butler, wanted to kiss her, but my dear
Mary Hann boxt his hold hears, & served him
right. I *datest* Screw,'—and so forth. Then
the diary relates to Stock Exchange operations
until we come to the time when, having achieved
his success, Mr. Jeames quitted Berkley Square
and his livery, and began his life as a speculator
and a gentleman upon town. It is from the latter part of his diary that we make the following
"EXTRAX.

" When I announced in the Servants' All my
axeshn of forting, and that by the exasize of my
own talince and ingiannity I had reerlized a
summ of £200,000—(it was only 5, but what's
the use of a man depreshiating the quality of his
own muckyrel?)—wen I enounced my abrupt intention to cut—you should have seen the sensation among hall the people. Cook wanted to
know whether I wouldn like a sweatbread or the
slise of a brest of a Cold Turky. Screw, the butler,) womb I always detested as a hinsolent ho-
verbearing beest,) begged me to walk into the
Hupper Servants' All, and try a glass of Shupe-
rior Shatto Margo. Heven Visk, the coachman,
eld out his and, & said:—' Jeames, I hopes there's
no quarralling betwigst you & me, & I'll stand
a pot of beer with pleasure.'

" The sickofnts!—that very Cook had spilt on
me to the Housekeeper ony last week (catchin
me priggin some cold turtle soop, of which I'm
remarkable fond.) Has for the butler, I always
ebomminated him for his precious sneers and im-
perence to all us Gents who woar livery, (he
never would sit in our parlor, fasooth; nor drink
out of our mugs;) and in regard to Visp—why, it
was ony the day before the vulgar beest hoffered
to fite me, and threatened to give me a good iding
if I refused. ' Gentlemen and ladies,' says I, as
haughty as may be, ' there's nothink that I want
for that I can't go for to buy with my hown
money, and take at my lodgings in Halbany, letter Hex; if I'm ungry I've no need to refresh myself in the *kitching*.' And, so saying, I took a
dignafied ajew of these minial domestics; and as-
ending to my epartment in the 4 pair back,
brushed the powder out of my air, and, taking
hoff those hojous livries for hever, put on a new
soot, made for me by Cullin, of St. Jeames street,
and which fitted my manly figger as tight as
whacks.

" There was *one* pusson in the ouse with womb
I was rayther anxious to avoid a personal leave-
taking—Mary Hann Oggins, I mean—for my art
is natural tender, and I can't abide seeing a pore
gal in pane. I'd given her previous the infoma-
tion of my departure—doing the ansom thing by
her at the same time—paying her back £20,
which she'd lent me six months before; and paying her back not only the interest, but I gave her
an andsome pair of scissors and a silver thimbil,
by way boanus. ' Mary Hann,' says I, ' suckm-
stances as altered our rellatif positions in life. I
quit the Servants' Hall for hever, (for has for your
marrying a person in my rank, that my dear is
hall gammon,) and so I wish you a good by my
good gal, and if you want to better yourself halways refer to me.'

" Mary Hann didn't hanser my speech, (which
I think was remarkable kind,) but looked at me
in the face quite wild like, and burst into something betwigst a laugh & cry, and fell down with

her ed on the kitchen dresser, where she lay until her young misses rang the dressing-room bell.
Would you believe it? she left the thimbil &
things, & my check for £20 10s. on the tabil,
when she went to hanser the bell. And now I
heard her sobbing and vimpering in her own room
nex but one to mine, with the dore open, perhaps
expecting that I should come in and say good by.
But, as soon as I was dressed I cut down stairs,
hony desiring Frederick, my fellow servant, to
fetch me a cab, and requesting permission to
take leave of my lady & the family before my
departure."

* * * * * *

" How Miss Hemly did hogle me to be sure!
Her ladyship told me what a sweet gal she was
—hamiable, fond of poetry, plays the gitter.
Then she hasked me if I liked blond bewties and
haubin air. Haubin, indeed! I don't like car-
rits! as it must be confest Miss Hemley's his—and
has for *blood buty* she as pink I's like a Albine,
and her face looks as if it were dipt in a brann
mash. How she squeezed my and as she went
away!

" Mary Hann now *has* haubin air, and a complexion like roses and hivory, and I's as blew as
Evin.

" I gev Frederick two and six for fetchin the
cabb, as been resolved to hact the gentleman in
hall things. How he stared!"

" 25th.—I am now director of forty-seven had-
vantageous lines, and have passed hall day in the
Citty. Although I've hate or nine new soots of
close, and Mr. Cullin fits me heligant, yet I fancy
they hall reckonise me. Conshns whispers to me
—'Jeames, you'r hony a footman in disguise after
all.' "

" 28th.—Been to the Hopra. Music tol lol.
That Lablash is a wopper at singing. I couldn
make out why some people called out ' Bravo,'
some ' Bravar,' and some ' Bravee.' ' Bravee,
Lablash,' says I, at which heavery body laft.
" I'm in my new stall. I've add new cushins
put in, and my harms in goold on the back. I'm
dressed hall in black, excep a goold waiscoat and
dimid studds in the embridered busum of my sha-
meese. I wear a Camallia Jiponiky in my button ole, and have a double-barrel opera-glass, so
big, that I make Timmins, my second man, bring
it in the other cab.
" What an igstronry exhabishn that Pawdy
Carter is! If those four galls are fairies, Tellioni
is sutnly the fairy Queend. She can do all that
they can do, and something they can't. There's
an indiscrible grace about her, and Carlotty,
my sweet Carlotty, she sets my art in flams.
" Ow that Miss Hemly was noddin and winkin
at me out of their box on the fourth tear?
" What linx i's she must av. As if I could
mount up there!
" P. S. Talking of *mounting hup*, the St. Helena's walked up 4 per cent. this very day."

" *2nd July.*—Rode my bay oss Desperation in
the park. There was me, Lord George Ring-
wood (Lord Cinqbar's son,) Lord Ballybunnion,
Honourable Capting Trap, and several young
swells. Sir John's carridge there in coarse. Miss
Hemly lets fall her book as I pass, and I'm oble-
ged to get hoff and pick it hup, and get splashed
up to the hies. The gettin on hoss back again is
halways the juice and hall. Just as I was hon,
Desperation begins a poring the hair with his 4

feet, and sinks down so on his anches, that I'm blest if I didn't slip hoff agin over his tail; at which Ballybunnion and the other chaps rord with lafter."

Going West.

Mr. Wentworth, of Illinois, in his late speech at Washington—observed that, he knew a man who had lived in Ohio when it was a frontier State. But this man had been moving and moving away from the inroads of society, until he had reached the banks of the Mississippi, and was about to move again. Wentworth asked him his reason. He said it was the dying advice of his father, " to keep twenty miles beyond *law* and *calomel*, and a doctor and lawyer were within fifteen miles, and he thought it time to go."

Correction.

I acknowledge obligations for the following, which is from a man of intelligence, as may be judged by its tenor. The subject is not of sufficient consequence to justify controversy on the derivative refered to, but I would remind my correspondent that the French *ecuyer*, as well as the English *equerry*, have a common root in *Equus*, and however dignified now by subsequent application of the title, had their origin in the home of the horse—the stable. The esquire who attended the knight to the lists, after all, as far as the horse was concerned, was a mere groom.

My correspondent's interesting illustrations only serve to shew that the title Esquire, like various others, has changed its original meaning, by a gradual perversion of its application. In the same manner *clericus*, or clerk, was a writer and a clergyman, because originally, writing was confined to that profession. Hence, the benefit of clergy, I suppose was not so directly intended to protect the lives of monks but of men who could write, and were therefore not so easily to be spared by the community as others. A clerk now-a-days is a title applied to any penman, and is even extending itself to mere salesmen in business establishments.

I should be glad to make the acquaintance of my correspondent, for more reasons than one.

To the Editor of the " Advertiser."

Sir:—Will you allow me to differ with you as to the derivation of the word *Esquire*, which in your last paper you request your correspondents to omit when addressing you. The first reason you give for wishing to dispense with the title, is certainly a sufficient one, however. The word Esquire was first introduced into England by the Normans, and is derived, as you say, from the French *Ecuyer*, which word bears, however, no reference to a stable. The *Ecuyer* was anciently the person that attended a Knight in time of war, and carried his lance, and often

thus serving a noviciate to the " noble science of arms." A lady's gentleman usher was also signified by this term; and the addition of a final *e*, by which French words are generally made to change their genders, makes it *ecuyere*, a female equestrian. The French derived the word from the Latin *armiger*, from *arma*, arms for the body, and *gero*, to bear or carry; and thus in classical history we meet with the term *armigera Dianae*, applied to the nymph who bore the goddess' bow and quiver. The French ecurie is a stable, and ecureur may with propriety be translated a " stable boy or ostler," but in my opinion the words *ccuyer* and *ecurie* bear very little if any, analogy to each other. PHIL.

Western Poetry.

The following delightful morceau, is worth a dozen of the fugitive pieces of English origin which go the rounds of our periodicals. It is from the last *Rock Island Advertiser*, published amidst scenery which is well fitted to inspire the poet's muse to such spirited flights as this:

A Beau Ideal.

A hazel eye with jetty fringe,
A dewy lip of ruby tinge,
The features Grecian, soft and fair,
The contour classic, rich and rare,
Long raven tresses wild that play,
And in most wanton frolic stray
Aronnd a neck of swan-like gace,
And o'er a Parian shoulder trace
Their curls, that well might put to flight
The " saintship of an anchorite."
So purely beautiful and fair,
You fondly dream an angel there,
Until her smile dispels the fear,
And bids your swelling heart draw near:
So heavenly, yet so earthly too,
You really know not which to do,
Creation's lord, to bow thy knee,
Or clasp that heaving breast to thee;
Her heart as orient pearl is pure,
Her voice Ulysses might allure,
Although he braved the syren's wiles,
And steered his bark through Grecian isles.
Her boundless love for me alone—
The spell has broke, my vision gone,
And though this phantom is not real,
What think you of my Beau Ideal?
GLAUCUS.

Davenport, I. T.

After explaining the difference between double and triple time, a musical teacher, pointing to the figures on the staff, said—" Can any one tell me what time it is?" " Five minutes to nine!" was the prompt and innocent reply.

" They *cure* excellent hams at Davis'," said Dan to his friend John. " Do they cure shoulders, too?" asked the latter. " Certainly." " Well, then, I'll just step in and get the rheumatism *cured* in mine."

It is rare that we meet with anything more true to nature than the following little gem, descriptive of frontier life, which is taken from the Cleveland Herald:

The Backwoodsman.

In the deep wild-wood is a lonely man,
And he swings his broad-axe like a slight ratan—
His garb is uncouth, but his step is proud,
And his voice when he speaketh, is firm and loud;
The forest recedes, as his strong arm swings,
And light out of darkness around he brings.

His hut is of logs, and his infant brood
Tumble forth to rejoice in that solitude.
They chase the honey bee home to its store,
And the old tree gives up what it never bore.
They hide in the brake, they rush thro' the stream,
And flit to and fro like the things of a dream,

The mother is pale like the sweet moonlight,
But they say, in her youth no rose was so bright,
She moves in the cabin with gentle grace,
And the homeliest things have their regular place:
She sings as she works with a placid smile,
And her far off home is in vision the while.

The Beadle and the Countryman.

A short time since, one of the beadles of N—— took a quantity of butter from a countryman because it was deficient in weight; and meeting him a few days after, in a public house, said to him—

"You are the man I took the twenty pounds of butter from the other day."

"No, I ben't," replied Hodge.

"I am sure you are," replied the beadle.

"I tell you I ben't," replied the countryman, "and if thou likest, I'll lay thee a guinea on't."

"Done," replied the beadle, and the money was quickly posted.

"Now," said the countryman, "thee did take lumps of butter from me, but if they had been twenty pounds, you'd have no right to take 'em, and this," continued he, very coolly pocketing the money," "will just pay me for the loss of the butter."

The Corrector Corrected.

My respected exchange, the Richmond Watchman & Observer, in undertaking to correct my article on Scripture Quotations, has placed himself by an oversight, in the very position he seeks to place me. It was not through ignorance of the passage he quotes, but because of my knowl-

edge of it, that I made the broad declaration, that neither the expression nor the idea "so plain that he that runs may read," was not to be found from Genesis to Revelations. The passage he offers as one he supposes me to have overlooked, inculcates a different, if not opposite charge. Obviously "so plain that he that runs may read," is a very different precept from "so plain, that he may run that readeth. The reader is to run, rather than the runner to read. The editor of the Watchman & Observer, however, is in good company in his mistake, as he may find by examining Matthew Henry's notes on the passage refered to.

Retort Courteous.

A heavy produce dealer in the lower part of Cincinnati, who has been operating largely in flour, during the late excitement, and of course lost money instead of making it, was accosted near the post office, by an acquaintance, a dealer in whisky, with a knowing look, and asked what was the state of the flour market. The whisky dealer not only sold spirits wholesale, but patronised the *ardent* by retail, and when he asked the question, was *full of the subject.* "Flour," replied his friend, "is giving way—I need not ask you what whisky is doing, *for I see it holds its own.*"

Chronological Table.

Feb. 5th.—Sir Robert Peel, born, 1788. Cato stabbed himself at Utica, in Africa, 45, B. C.

6th.—Dr. Priestly, died, 1804.

7th.—Mary Queen of Scots, beheaded at Fotheringay Castle, 1587. George Crabbe, died, 1833.

8th.—Earthquake in London, 1760.

9th.—Georgia settled by Gen. Oglethorp. Savannah laid out, 1733. Gen. W. H. Harrison, born, 1773.

10th.—Cincinnati inundated, the Ohio river having risen sixty-three feet above low water mark, 1832. Queen Victoria, married, 1840.

An exchange paper, in an article on the state of the market, has the following:—" Pigs' tails. These were rather *drooping*—but we observe that they have *taken a turn!*"

CINCINNATI MISCELLANY.

CINCINNATI, FEBRUARY, 1846.

Recollections of the Last Sixty Years.--No. 6.
BY J. JOHNSTON, ESQ., *of Piqua.*

In the present degenerate state of the country, divided as it is into factions, the frequent abandonment of principles by public men in the pursuit of popularity and office; the extension and perpetuation of slavery by the authority of the general government, and that at a period too, when a large portion of the christian world were uniting to put the evil down; that the free states of this Union should be found aiding and assisting in such a policy, and for the purpose of giving it the largest possible scope, despoiling a friendly neighbouring power of one of its most valuable provinces, will be recorded among the blackest pages of the history of the nineteenth century. Amidst all these appaling and national grievances, it is some consolation to recur to the character of a patriot, soldier, and statesman, who lived for his country, and who for purity of design, honesty and fidelity in the discharge of public duty, would advantageously compare with the purest men of Greece, Athens, or Rome. I shall therefore devote a part of this communication to some of the incidents which came under my notice in the life and services of the late President Harrison. Every thing connected with his name forms part and parcel of the history of the west. I first saw Lieut. W. H. Harrison at Hobson's Choice, in 1793, where Gen. Wayne's army was then cantoned. He was one of the aid-de-camps; a young man of popular manners and very prepossessing appearance, a great favourite with the soldiers and the whole army; had the character of a peace maker, and from the relation in which he stood to the commander-in-chief, exercised much influence. I had no personal acquaintance with him at the time, nor after until he became Governor of Indiana, where as an officer in the Indian department, I became subject to his control and government: but I often heard him spoken of by the soldiers and others, as a kind hearted, humane and generous man, dividing his stores with the sick and the needy. He entered the army at Philadelphia, during the first Presidency of Washington. I heard him relate the circumstances. He went to that city for the purpose of finishing his medical education; troops were at the time raising for the protection of the western frontier, laid open and exposed to the in-

cursions of the Indians, by the entire defeat of St. Clair's army, in November, 1791. To use his own language, he fell in love with the drum and fife, applied to Gen. Washington for a commission, who appointed him an ensign. In 1792, and immediately—as well as I can recollect—without going home to his family, he repaired to the Ohio and joined the army. Duels were frequent in the army, and from the warm temperament of Gen. Wayne, it was said that he rather encouraged than forbade them. Not so with Harrison: I often heard that he was a successful pacificator in many quarrels between the officers. Some fatal duels took place after the army reached Greenville: one resulted in the death of both the principals, Lieutenants Bradshaw and Huston; both Irishmen, and both fell mortally wounded. The cause of the quarrel was a very trivial matter—a mere point of etiquette. Bradshaw was what was called a gentleman in his own country; bred a physician. Huston was by profession a weaver. The former shewed some slight towards the latter, probably over their cups. A challenge ensued, and they were buried within three hours of each other. Writing occasionally for the quarter-master, I had access to all Bradshaw's papers. He had kept a regular journal of all his travels, which shewed him to be a scholar and a person of accurate observation. Among his papers were several letters from a beloved sister in Ireland, urging his return. It was evident they were people of rank and distinction. Alas! she was never more to behold that beloved brother, so much longed after. He had a duelist's grave; not a stone or stick to mark where he lay. Capt. Tom Lewis, one of the aids, and Major Thomas H. Cushing also had a duel. The watch of the latter saved his life. Lewis' pistol bullet having lodged directly in the centre of Cushing's gold watch, the watch was destroyed, but it saved his life. Another duel, threatening at first the death of both parties, took place under the following circumstances at Wilkinsonville, on the Ohio:—The officers having dined together in mess—as was too often the case in those days—got drunk before quitting the table. Capt. Frank Johnston, a near relative of my own, and Mr. Dinsmore, quarreled and agreed to fight with pistols, across the table. The weapons were got and loaded: the other officers seeing such a scene of murder about to be acted, became sobered, ran out of the hut and kept peeping through the cracks to see how the affair would terminate. It seems Johnston fired first and struck the pistol arm of his adversary at the wrist, and shattered it above the elbow, and thus ended the affair. My friend Johnston closed his life not long after by hard drinking.

At the second Treaty of Greenville, in 1814, I was on the ground two weeks before the arrival of Gen. Harrison, the principal commissioner on the part of the United States. I had pitched my markee on an elevated spot near the creek, for the convenience of water, and a flag staff erected with my flag flying. On his arrival the General sent for me, and said he wanted as a favour, that I would permit the location of the flag to be changed, and the staff to be erected on the spot where Gen. Wayne's quarters were in 1795, at the date of his celebrated treaty with the Indians. He said the ground was consecrated to him by many endearing recollections, which could never be effaced from his memory, and that he wanted all the details of the great treaty about to be held, to conform as near as could be to the one which had preceded it nineteen years before. I, of course, assented, and our flag waved over the spot on which General Wayne's quarters stood It was at this first treaty of Greenville, 1814, that the Indians were first formally invited by the United States to take up the hatchet and make common cause with us against the English. Fortunately the treaty of peace which was soon afterwards signed at Ghent, rendered the services of our new allies unnecessary. I happened to be at Washington, in 1812, at the time Congress was deliberating on a declaration of war. Governor Hull was there also. The Secretary of War, Dr. Eustis, sent for me to call at his house in the six buildings, early on a morning. His wife, the daughter of John Langdon, of New Hampshire, was up and in readiness to receive me, and said they expected me for breakfast. They married late in life and had no children. The Secretary soon came down stairs, and at once told me he wanted to consult me about Indian affairs; that Congress would, in a few days, declare war against Great Britain; that he wanted me to return to my station in Ohio as soon as possible; (I had at this time been transfered from the agency at Fort Wayne to a new agency at Piqua, having in charge all the Indians of Ohio, with the Delawares of Indiana,) and to go direct to Pittsburgh to conduct a detachment of troops through by land, the safest and best route to Detroit. I replied that I could not do this, being at the time engaged in the transportation of a large amount of public property from Philadelphia, Baltimore and Georgetown, which must go by

Cumberland, Brownsville, Pittsburgh, Cincinnati, and Piqua, as it could not go by the Lakes from the danger of capture by the enemy, and that I must attend to this duty in person. He then interrogated me about the Indians—how will they conduct in the war between us and the English; can they be kept quiet? I answered promptly and decidedly, that the Indians would be for or against us in the war; that we must immediately engage their services or they would go over to the enemy; that they were altogether mercenary in their feelings, and governed by a thirst for blood and plunder, and did not much care on which side they fought; but that they would be on one side or the other was most certain—and I urged him to take the most prompt and decisive measures in time to engage them. I offered to raise a thousand Indians within my agency, provided their families were fed and supported by the United States, and such a force would be fit to beat any two thousand of the same kind which the enemy could raise. The Delawares, Shawanese, Wyandotts, and Senecas of my charge, constituted the veterans of the Indian army in all former wars, and they were anxious to take part with us. The Secretary replied that the President—Mr. Madison—on this point was immovable; that no entreaty could induce him to consent to the employment of such a force; and further, he remarked that Governor Hull, who was there, assured him that he could keep the Indians neutral; that (using a figure) he had only to beckon with his finger and they would obey. The counsels of Governor Hull prevailed; the consequences was most disastrous; the loss of some of the best blood of the country; the temporary disgrace and loss of Michigan, and the loss of forty millions of the treasury of the United States, all of which I fearlessly assert might have been prevented by the employment of the Indians named in the beginning of the war; and furthermore, the Upper Province of Canada taken from the enemy the first campaign. Whilst at Washington, I learned that Hull was an applicant for the command of the North Western Army. Gov. Worthington was then in the Senate. I took the liberty of warning him against the appointment. The people of the country where he was to operate had no confidence in him: the Indians despised him;—he was too old, broken down in body and mind to conduct the multifarious operations of such a command. The nomination was made, objected to, refered to a committee, reported on favourably, and confirmed. On the very same day he passed the Senate, the poor, vain, weak old man was seen in full dress uniform, parading the streets of Washington, making calls. When the army rendevoused at Dayton, Hull requested me to send him twelve or fifteen trusty Indians to accompany the army into Canada, as spies and guides. The requisite number went. On parting with them, they were requested, as soon as discharged, to return, find me out and make report. They did so. They left the army at the river Canard, between Sandwich and Malden. The Chief Butler, son by a Shawanese woman, of Gen. Richard Butler, who fell at St. Clair's defeat, an intelligent and observant man, was the speaker. He said they left the army doing no good; would he thought do no good, and at last be defeated; that the Indians from the north were coming down like a swarm of bees, and by and by would eat them all up. This Butler was at the defeat of St. Clair, and it has been often reported, put an end to the life of his own father. The story runs thus: General Butler, being mortally wounded early in the battle, was, by his own request, set up leaning against a tree with his pistols loaded and cocked; that an Indian rushing towards him, was fired at and missed, when the savage dispatched him with his tomahawk. I never asked the Indian, Butler, to give me any information on the subject, knowing the repugnance they always feel to speak about such matters. I never saw General Butler, the reputed father of the Shawanese chief, but the Indian was a marked half breed, and very closely resembled both in person, features, and character, all the members of the family I ever did see. He had one sister who bore the same striking resemblance to the parent stock. The General was a trader among the Shawanese before the revolutionary war. His last wife was a Semple from near Carlisle, Pennsylvania, lived at Pittsburgh in my time, and enjoyed a pension from the United States.

The following is on a street in which lawyers abounded, and at the bottom of which many boats were found:—

" At the top of the street the attorneys abound,
And down at the bottom the barges are found;
Fly, honesty, fly, to some safer retreat,
For there's craft in the river and craft in the street."

Shakspeare makes one of his characters say—

"How sweet the moonshine sleeps upon this bank."

The modern reading about banks and moonshine is this—

"How sweet these banks do sleep upon this moonshine!"

Not Bad.

A friend of ours. says a New York paper, who had recently made a trip up the Hudson, was asked what he thought of St. Anthony's Nose. " Why it was once a great curiosity," he replied, " but now they are blowing it all to pieces!"

Bell and Brass Foundry.

This is an important item of manufacturing industry in Cincinnati, and of increasing value. Its importance consists not more in the amount of industry which it stimulates, than in the incidental aid it supplies to other business, by concentrating to this point, the entire demand for bells north, south, and west of us. In 1840 there were eight of these establishments, with sixty-two hands, which have been increased at this date to twelve foundries, with one hundred and six hands, all engaged in the various operations of casting and finishing of articles in brass, of which the article of bells is of the greatest magnitude, affording an aggregate value of $135,000 for the past year. As an example of its character and operations, I select the business for the last three years, of G. W. Coffin, at the *Buckeye Foundry*, on Columbia street, whose bell business is of greater magnitude than all the other establishments combined, but whose brass business, generally, would not constitute more than an average of the general aggregate. In 1843, Mr. Coffin made, all to order,

36 steamboat bells, from	150 to 706 lbs.	each.
8 plantation do	50 to 360	do.
2 foundry do	150 to 350	do.
11 college, academy, and		
school house bells,	50 to 350	do.
1 court house,	350	do.
1 engine house,	326	do.
38 church do	80 to 3,363	do

Besides 206 of lighter sizes of which no register has been kept. The whole weighing 40647 pounds, including the iron works connected therewith—worth more than twenty thousand dollars. The entire operations in brass, in this foundry reached the value of $31,000.

During the year 1844, there were made in this establishment:

39 steamboat bells, weighing	11,660 lbs
31 plantation farm bells	3,406
6 foundry, factory, and engine bells	376
9 school house and college bells	1,000
8 court house and fire engine bells	3.630
57 church bells	19,758
21 hotel do	694
	40,525

Exclusive of the iron work connected with the bells.

The value of bells made in the *Buckeye Brass and Bell Foundry* for 1844 was 31,000 dollars; of all manufactured articles of brass and bell metal, 39,000 dollars, being an increase of 25 per cent on the business of 1843. I presume there is a proportionate increase in the other establishments, Mr. Coffin being in bells, and theirs in brass foundry, generally. He has lately put up a new Foundry, where bells only will be made.

During the past year, bells have been made at this foundry for the following boats:

Blue Ridge	200	Doctor Watson	326
J. E. Roberts	82	Mary Pell	200
Daniel Boone	50	Clermont	150
Felix Grundy	500	Isaac Shelby	326
War Eagle	200	Belle Creole	500
Daniel Boone	200	Princess	500
Isaac Shelby	220	Cadmus	100
Daniel Boone	100	Bulletin	720
Lancet	226	James Dick	500
Confidence	225	Andrew Jackson	500
Richmond	500	Geo. Washington	500
Dove	150	Reindeer	500
Pike No. 8	350	Eureka	100
Convoy	500	Hercules	500
Queen City	500	Huntsville	500
Windsor	350	Pride of the west	700
Magic	170	Edward Shippen	350
C. Connor	350	Belle Air	300
Jim Gilmer	224	Albatross	500
Magnolia	625	Old Hickory	500
Belle of the West	300	American Eagle	500
Sea	500	W. R. M'Kee	200
		Mentoria	200

45 steam boat bells, 15,492

28 plantation and farm bells,

262	262	262	80	35	40	262
500	31	150	80	35	40	260
100	35	100	80	35	224	350
100	80	100	80	50	80	226
262						——3,977

5 foundry, factory and furnace,

82	50	326	100	84	——642

20 school house and college,

50	120	50	100	50	100	50
100	100	30	60	50	158	60
100	100	50	120	100	100	
						——1,648

3 fire engine house bells,

774	700	700
		——2,174

61 churches,

383	120	326	110	720	120	500	500
279	120	700	110	326	224	275	275
326	150	326	116	720	100	332	275
326	120	326	220	1300	170	700	350
700	200	326	100	500	125	400	300
450	120	326	170	326	400	300	362
400	100	350	262	362	200	326	100
200							——19,596

20 hotels,

51	25	31	25	35	22	30	35	25	40	25
35	35	35	25	25	35	40	50	25	——649	

The value of the bells and brass castings made here, during the past year, is about equal to that of the year 1844, and would have been much greater, had not has spacious building improve-ments during the heaviest period of the business season, disabled Mr. Coffin from pushing his foundry operations to the extent he is now prepared to do.

I speak advisedly when I say that the *Buckeye Bell and Brass foundry* is the most extensive establishment in the manufacture of bells, of any in the United States.

Narrative of John Hudson,

A Revolutionary Soldier, and now resident in Cincinnati.—**No. 3.**

On reaching my company I heard discharges of cannon fired in quick succession, and the sound of their balls striking some object. Inquiring what was doing, of my associates, I was told, that they had raised a redoubt the morning of their arrival and that the balls were from the enemy, who were striking a large oak tree in front of the redoubt. On that very day, as I afterwards learnt, *Col. A. Scammel*, who was out with a reconnoitering party was taken prisoner by Tarleton's light horse and inhumanly murdered after his capture. I was told also, that the night before, the Marquis de la Fayette, with a party of Frenchmen who had been landed from the fleet, had stormed two batteries of two twelve pounders to each battery, putting every man to the sword—literally—as the very privates among the French wore that weapon. These events all took place on the 26th September, 1781, and I refer particularly to this date to remove an impression erroneously but extensively prevalent, that the important events of this siege were crowded all into one night at a later date.

Our army was composed of three divisions, and throughout the siege of Yorktown, which had now commenced, each division was twenty-four hours in the works and forty-eight in the camp. One of these divisions was under command of *Brig. Gen. James Clinton*, and to this was attached the New York line. I belonged to the oldest company of the oldest regiment of these troops, which of course was the head of the column. We left the camp a short time before sundown, and marching along a road, came to a high mound of earth, and wheeling short round to the right, we reached within a few feet of the end of a cause way, made of pitch-pine logs recently put down, perhaps fifteen or twenty rods long. This crossed a marsh, otherwise impassable. Yorktown was virtually an island, the river passing at an elbow, two sides of it—and an extensive deep marsh faced the other side.

We marched over the causeway to the batteries which I have already stated were stormed by Lafayette. I saw two embrasures to each battery, which proved that there had been the same number of cannon. These, with the dead, had been all removed, and the batteries being thirty feet apart, we marched between the two. Every thing that I could see there was covered with blood.

We passed these batteries a short distance, the night approaching, when we were halted, every man directed to sit down, and neither to talk nor leave his place. As I had been sick through that day, and had, like the rest, my knapsack on my back, I laid my cartouch box under my head, and with my musket in my arms, soon fell asleep. During my repose a sudden and violent rain came on, falling in torrents, which failed, however, to wake me, such had been my fatigue. In the course of the night—I cannot tell at what time—the non-commissioned officers came along the ranks, and without saying a word, woke us all and got us to our feet. I rose up with the rain dripping from my clothes. We were directed to shift our arms to the right shoulder, and each man to put his right hand on the shoulder of his file leader, marching in two ranks, the right in front. The road being clear of all obstructions, our progress was uninterrupted, although nothing was visible—no man being able even to see his comrade. We finally halted, and every man had a spade put into his hands. Shortly afterwards—the rain still pouring down—a party of men, with gabions, came along. I will describe them, for the better comprehension of my narrative. Sticks are cut about five feet in length, of the thickness of a man's wrist; one end is sharpened and set in the ground, in a circle of perhaps three feet diamater. Flexible brush, about the size of a hoop-pole, with such branches as adhere to them, are interlaced as in making a basket, working upwards from the bottom. The gabion thus made is thrown on its side, a long pole run through it, and passed on the shoulders of as many men as can get beneath it. These were placed, when brought to the ground for use, in such position as the engineer judged proper, the stakes being, as before, pressed into the earth. We were then directed, and as at first, merely by signs, to commence three feet inside of where they had been placed, and shovel up earth sufficient to fill the gabions. The ground was of sand, which being thoroughly wet by the rain, was very easy digging. We shoveled until we filled these gabions, and finished by throwing up a bank in front, when the work was completed. The gabions being side and side the earth formed a solid line of breast works, through which a cannon ball could not pass. From what I afterwards saw of the efficacy of this description of defence in repeling cannon balls, there is no doubt that it is a better protection than a stone wall six feet thick, and has this advantage, that it can be made in a few hours. Not a single cannon ball penetrated this defence during the whole siege.

It ceased raining just as the day was about to dawn, when we observed that our artillery had thrown up a battery a few rods from our right, and on the bank of the river; and had raised a lofty flag staff with the star spangled banner streaming to the wind upon it. This was called *Matchem's bettery*, being erected under the direction of a captain of that name, who retained it as his command during the siege. I wish it distinctly understood, that we were so near the British lines with these defences that there never were any other works erected in our front, in the whole progress of the campaign. After it was fully daylight, the British had the hardihood to come out with a six pounder, immediately in front of the battery I had assisted to construct, and so near to us that a horseman could have shot any one of these artillerists with his pistol. There they stood firing their piece rapidly for half an hour, battering at the fortification without any apparent effect. After they found that we treated them with silent contempt, for we took no notice of them, they desisted and returned to their own lines. Our allies, the French, who occupied our left, were doubtless busy, but in what way I had no means of knowing.

I am very confident that there was no firing on our part upon the enemy for eight days; while they were keeping up a constant cannonade, night and day, during that period. *General Washington* and *Count Rochambeau* used to ride to the rear of the works, side by side, each equipped with a spy glass, of which they made frequent use. This was repeated every day while we were raising other works, assisting the French, and strengthening batteries. On the ninth day—the 4th or 5th of October—the generals, as usual, came down, attended with their retinue, and General Washington, not seeing Captain Matchem, inquired where he was. He was shewn where the Captain lay asleep upon a plank, in the open air. The General chid him gently for thus exposing himself, asking him why he did not go into his marquee. He answered spiritedly, that he would never enter his marquee till he had stopped that bull dog from barking—alluding to a twelve pounder in the wall of the town, which had been playing night and day on his battery, annoying him greatly. Washington then directed him to open his battery immediately, the Generals riding back as customary. There was now a general shout among the soldiers, that we should now see some fun. In my simplicity, I asked "what fun?" Up to this time I had never seen a cannon fired. "Don't you see those matchets burning," they replied. I looked and saw them on staffs, four or five feet long, at the side of the guns.

Review.

REPORT OF THE COMMITTEE—Appointed at the Meet'ng of the Citizens of Cincinnati, held at the Council Chamber, January 22d, 1846: on the subject of improving the navigation around the Falls of the Ohio river.

This is a document of great ability, comprehensive as well as minute in its researches, and cogent in its conclusions. It covers the whole canal question, in its difficulties and the remedies; and manifests the impolicy and injustice of the present facilities, or rather want of them, as a means of conveying the vast freights of the west to and from their appropriate markets. The remedy proposed in this report for the vexatious and oppressive burthens imposed by the existing state of things, is the construction of a new canal on the Indiana side, of dimensions greatly larger than that on the Kentucky side, which the present commerce of the upper Ohio has years since outgrown. The objections for relying on any alteration or enlargement of the canal on the Kentucky side, as a remedy or relief to present and future difficulties, are stated thus:—

"We are opposed to the alteration of the present canal, because we think the increasing commerce of the river will require two canals, before the desired alterations could be completed. To verify the truth of this assertion, it is only necessary to examine the extent of territory embraced in the Valley of the Mississippi. By reference to a map of the United States, it will be perceived, that the territory of the Union is divided into three distinct Geographical Sections. The first being the Atlantic slope, extending from the Atlantic ocean to the Allegheny mountains; the second, from the Alleghenies to the Rocky mountains, and the third from the Rocky mountains to the Pacific ocean;—the first division, presenting an area of about 400,000 square miles; the second, or Valley of the Mississippi, including some southern rivers, which empty into the Gulf stream, about 1,200,000 square miles; and the third, or Pacific slope, about 425,000 miles. Thus you will perceive that the Ohio and Mississippi rivers are the main avenues, on which the commerce of this middle section is to be conducted—which nearly doubles in extent of territory the two other divisions of the Union.

"In this vast region nature has been most bountiful in scattering over the whole land all the valuable minerals, including the most extensive coal formations known to the world. Every portion of the country is interspersed with streams, affording water power, and every elementary principle furnished, which could be desirable for manufacturing industry.

"Our climate is admirably adapted to all kind of agricultural productions; and even our most extensive mineral regions, may be explored under ground by the miner, whilst the agriculturalist is raising abundant crops on the surface of the same soil.

"A large portion of this valley is yet a wilderness, or uninhabited prairies; but we already number a population equal to nearly half the Union. The value of property annually floating upon onr western rivers is still more astonishing. If we can depend upon statements furnished through committees at different points, and Custom House registers, we may estimate the annual value of property, transported on our great rivers, at a sum over two hundred millions of dollars, which is a much lager amount than the exports and imports of the United States from foreign nations.

"In our agricultural productions we far exceed any people in the world, compared with the number of our population.

"From Mr. Peyton's report made to Congress, in 1844, we find that the surplus of grain raised in the Mississippi Valley in 1843, was one hundred and fifty-nine millions of bushels, whilst the surplus of the Atlantic States, for the same year, was two millions. Scarcely thirty years have passed, since steamboats were fairly introduced upon our western whters, and we may now estimate the number at six hundred, exceeding, by forty thousand tons, the entire steamboat commercial tonnage of the British Empire.

"The introduction of steam upon these great rivers gave the first impulse to the rapid growth of the west, and the life and energy of western commerce depends mainly upon the engine of the steamboat. It is therefore important to protect and foster all the connexions with this element of our prosperity. If it were possible to estimate the future growth of our country, and our commerce by what has taken place, we might take our city as an evidence of increase. Within half a century we have acquired a population of eighty thousand inhabitants, who build yearly from thirty to fifty steamboats, and export from ten to twelve millions of dollars worth of their own manufactures.

"A very important portion of the Mississippi Valley, which produces two of the great agricultural staples of the country, cotton and sugar, has but one natural outlet to the Atlantic ocean. This being the mouth of the Mississippi river, in time of war, it might be easily blockaded by a superior naval force. Under such circumstances these products would have to find a market in the Atlantic States by ascending the Mississppi and Ohio rivers, necessarily passing through the canal around the Falls, unless the Ohio was at more than ordinary height.

"To give an idea of the facilities necessary at that point for this change of commerce, we will take the export of cotton from New Orleans for the last year, as given in the Commercial Review; and the sugar crop of Louisiana for the last year, as reported by the New Orleans Chamber of Commerce.

"The export of cotton is stated at 984,616 bales of four hundred pounds each, which reduced to tons, would amount to 196,923.

"The sugar crop is stated at 204,913 hogsheads of 1000 pounds each, which would give, in tons, 102,456, making in cotton and sugar, 299,379 tons, which would require for transportation nineteen hundred ninety-five steamboats carrying one hundred and fifty tons each. Allowing these boats two hours each, the usual time for passing the present canal, and you will find that it would require one hundred and sixty days, or a period of more than five months to accommodate the ascending navigation through the canal, of these two items of trade. If we add to this, the molasses connected with the sugar trade, and the enormous exports of lead, hemp, and tobacco from St. Louis, which would have to be diverted from its natural channel up the Ohio river, it would be clearly demonstrated, that to pass all the commerce, which now passes through the mouth of the Mississippi from these two States, the present canal would be occupied all the time by their export trade."

" If it be asked upon what principles we call upon the National Government to furnish another canal? we answer, that these great rivers are under the control of the nation, and, as national highways, beyond the influence of States bordering on them, they are properly speaking " inland seas," entitled to the same protection of the General Government, as all other harbours and defences of the country, which have received the fostering care of the nation, since the establishment of our government.

" We ask it, because we have contributed our blood in defence of the country during war, and our treasure annually to support its expenditures; and here we may state, that the nation is largely our debtor for nearly one hundred millions of dollars, received for sales of the public lands, whilst all the appropriations in return for internal improvements is not one tithe of that sum. Let us, for a moment, look at the expenditures of the government since our independence, which, according to the annual register, for fifty-six years, amounts to nearly one thousand millions of dollars. Of this sum the Valley of the Mississippi has received but a small proportion of the disbursements for Public Works.

" We ask the government to furnish another canal, because the nation is greatly interested in the public domain yet unsold, which must be benefitted in proportion to the advantages derived from national improvement.

" We would also urge the necessity of this work as an important improvement connected with the military defences of the nation. It is probable that the most effective naval force of the country must, in future, consist of steam vessels; and the cheapnesss, convenience, and abundance, of iron, coal, lead, hemp. and provisions, on the Ohio river, render this valley the most eligible source of supply for the material and construction of war vessels. Therefore, to bring such vessels into service, and to give efficiency to our military resources, the enlarged canal around the Falls is indispensably necessary."

I make no apology for the length of these extracts. The subject is of vast importance, addressing itself to the interests of two thirds of the people of the United States, and of direct pecuniary relation to the whole west.

The committee close their report with five resolutions, in which they assert the necessity for a new canal; the injustice done for the past fourteen years to the West by the general government, as principal stockholder in the Louisville and Portland Canal Company, imposing a ruinous tax on the Ohio river commerce; the national obligation to remove the existing obstructions, and, finally, protest against any alteration of the Louisville and Portland Canal as an interruption to the whole business of the country and productive of incalculable loss and expense.

This report is understood to have been prepared by George Graham, the chairman of that committee, and is highly creditable to his judgment and statistical researches.

THE QUARTERLY JOURNAL AND REVIEW. Vol. 1., No. 1. Cincinnati. L. A. Hine, Editor and Proprietor.

The tendency and tone of this work are good, and it evinces an ability in the editor for strong and useful disquisition, quite beyond the ordinary editorial standard. He certainly deserves the credit of having risen above his pretensions. So far I am quoting the language of Dr. Bailey of the Herald, for the purpose of adopting the judgment, and establishing it by the testimony of more than one witness. There is a vigour and freshness in the style, as well as independence in thought which I like; at the same time a squinting to the mysticism of the German school of philosophy which I disapprove. Mr. H. would have made an admirable pupil of Fourier and the transcendentalists if they had laid hold of him in his earlier life.

No man who takes this periodical will, I think, doubt his obtaining the equivalent and more, of its remarkable low price—one dollar per annum. For sale at Robinson & Jones', 109 Main street.

Chronological Table.

Feb. 11.—De Witt Clinton, died, 1828. Shenstone, died, 1763.

12th.—Lady Jane Grey and her hussband beheaded in the Tower, 1554.

13th.—Massacre of Glencoe, 1691. Sir William Blackstone, died, 1780. Schwarz, died, 1798. Duc de Berri, assasinated, 1821.

14th.—VALENTINE'S DAY.—Captain Cook, killed at Owyhee, 1779.

17th.—Battle of St. Albans, 1461. Michael Angelo, died at Rome, 1564.

18th.—Martin Luther, died, 1564.

Seventh Ward,--Cincinnati.

This ward lies between Race and John streets, and includes all between Sixth street and the Corporation Line. The upper half has been devoted to building purposes only for the last three years, and is occupied by our German population, who have been, during that period, making extensive and permanent improvements.

The public buildings in this ward are 12,—the Commercial Hospital, Cincinnati Orphan Asylum, Engine House, on George st.; Churches —Methodist Protestant, on Elm; Fifth Presbyterian, corner of Elm and Seventh; Elm Street Baptist; German Reformed, on Elm street; Second Advent Tabernacle, corner John and Seventh; Reformed Presbyterian, on George; Grace Church—Episcopal—on Seventh; Ninth Street Methodist Chapel, and the Roman Catholic Cathedral, nearly finished and occupied since November last.

The entire number of buildings in the Seventh Ward is 1531—of which 756 are bricks, and 775 are frames.

Of these there were, at the close of 1842,

	Bricks.	Frames.	Total.
	352	588	940
Built in 1843,	112	40	152
" " 1844,	146	73	219
" " 1845,	146	74	210
	756	775	1531

There have been put up a considerable number of neat and even substantial buildings during the past year in this ward—especially on Court street. The largest share of its improvements, however, are beyond the canal. Fine improvements are also going on in the northwestern section of this ward, in the neighbourhood of Betts, Hopkins and Clark streets. Three-fifths of this ward, as accurately as I can judge, is built to its full capacity.

The two Baskets.

I was perambulating the streets of Darmstadt with my German friend Von Holst, when a gentleman passed, whom he recognised; and they bowed to each other.

"You saw that gentlemanly person pass," said he. "It is the handsome and wealthy Baron de B."

"I observed him," said I.

"Would you believe it possible," continued my friend, "that he has had a basket sent to him?"

"Has he?" said I, somewhat mystified—for I did not perceive any reason why he should not have a basket of game or choice fruit sent to him, as well as any body else.

"Yes," said my friend, "and you will be the more surprised, when I tell you that the Baron's mind, disposition, and fortune, are as unexceptionable as his person."

"Extraordinary," said I, for want of something else to say, for I did not see anything extraordinary in the matter.

As we sauntered on, I began considering and guessing what could be the contents of the basket, the reception of which by the Baron seemed to strike my friend as so extraordinary, and as the cause of this remark. At last it struck me that I had hit upon an explanation of the mystery; some little contretems in connection with the tender passions, and the intimation conveyed to him in this very unequivocal fashion—or it might be some low cabal, got up to work upon the Baron's generosity or his fears, to compromise the feelings of his noble family.

My friend Von Holst, observing that I appeared to be ruminating on what he had told me, presently added, in a still more impressive tone than before—"I see that you are much interested for the poor Baron. What then will you say when I tell you that he had received TWO baskets sent to him—actually TWO baskets.

I was now more puzzled than ever, and all I could do was to shrug up my shoulders with a sort of despairing no meaning; look foolish, and utter an ejaculatory, "Oh!"

Meantime my friend continued, "Yes, actually two!" Now the first did not so much surprise me, coming as it did from the daughter of the Counsellor of State, Count P——. But the second, I own, astonished me, as Mdlle. S——, is only the daughter of the Banker S——, who is not reputed rich, and has, moreover, a very large family.

I grew puzzled and mystified more and more every moment. It was clear that my solution of the difficulty was very far from the right one, yet I had gained no clue to any other.

My face, I supposed, expressed my surprise, and my friend again remarked—

"Only think! that so excellent a fellow as the Baron to receive two baskets both one after the other."

"I could hold out no longer. But what the deuce did the baskets contain?"

"Contain?" said Von Holst; "why, what should they contain? Of course, nothing but the refusal."

"The refusal," I exclaimed; "the refusal of what?"

"Don't you know?" exclaimed my friend—now puzzled in his turn. "The refusal of an offer of marriage, to be sure!"

The mystery was solved at last.

In point of fact the belles of Darmstadt when they object to the addresses of a lover, and will not take any milder course, fairly basket him.

Steamboat Building of the West, in 1845.

	Boats.	Tonnage.	Cost.
New Albany,	11	1959	118,500
Louisville,	16	4152	270,000
St. Louis,	10	2912	180,500
Cincinnati,	27	6609	505,500

This does not include for Cincinnati, several boats under way—two of them nearly finished. The whole number of steamboats built in 1845, on the waters of the Ohio and Mississippi, will not fall short of one hundred, an aggregate of twenty-two thousand tons, and a value of sixteen hundred thousand dollars.

The above tonnage is custom house measurement—the actual capacity in freight being more than thirty thousand tons.

George the Third's Mother.

The Princess of Wales had always loved the Duke of Gloucester the least, although the most meritorious of her children. She thought him insuperably dull; nor was he bright. One day in his childhood she ridiculed him before his brothers and sisters, and bade them laugh at the fool. He sat silent and thoughtful.

"What! now, are you sullen?"

He replied, "No, he was thinking."

"Thinking!" replied the mother, with scorn, "and pray what were you thinking of?"

"I was thinking what I should feel if I had a son as unhappy as you make me."

Recollections of the last Sixty Years.—No. 7.

By Col. J. JOHNSTON, *of Piqua.*

In the year 1803, the French government ceded the whole of Louisiana to the United States, and in 1804, Governor Harrison was appointed by President Jefferson to receive possession of the Upper Province, and to organize its government. He repaired to St. Louis for the porpose. Many of the Indians came in from a distance to meet their new father, as was the invariable custom. The Governor ordered provisions to be issued to them. To his utter astonishment, they refused to receive any. At this he and all present were greatly surprised, for it was known they had come far, and must be hungry. They were urged for their reasons for conduct so unusual. They were for some time silent. The Indians are exceedingly averse to saying any thing calculated to hurt the feelings of those whom they meet in council. The speaker, seeing that a reply was expected, at length addressed the Governor:—Father we have traveled far to see you and are both weary and hungry; but father we are afraid to take your bread and meat, for we hear you Americans are very greedy for land that you love, and eat it; and therefore we think if we take your provisions you will want some of our land in return. The Governor having assured them he had no such intention, the Indians took the provisions daily while their visit continued. Gen. John Gibson was Gov. Harrison's Secretary for the Indiana Territory; the same person who accompanied Lord Dunmore, the royal governor of Virginia, in 1774, in his expedition against the Indians on the Scioto; and was the interpreter of the celebrated speech delivered by Logan, the Mingo Chief, and recorded in Jefferson's Notes on Virginia, about the year 1797. The genuineness of this speech, which Jefferson pronounces to be equal in eloquence to any thing ever produced in the old world, was questioned in many of the newspapers and periodicals of the day. I think the ample testimony accompanying the notes has settled the question. But I had it from Gen. Gibson's lips, that every word of that admirable production, as published in the notes, was communicated from Logan through him to Governor Dunmore. Gibson was many years an Indian trader, and spoke the Delaware tongue fluently; was an officer in the Virginia line on Continental establishment in the Revolutionary War; a very old man when I knew him, nearly blind; and could render very little assistance to Gov. Harrison in the business of the Territory. He was poor, and the emoluments of the office necessary to his comfortable support. In those days the old servants of the the country, if honest and capable, were not

turned out of office upon the cold charities of the world.

Twenty-eight years ago, on the death of the great chief of the Wyandotts, I was invited to attend a general council of all the tribes of Ohio, the Delawares of Indiana, and the Senecas of New York, at Upper Sandusky. I found on arriving at the place, a very large attendance. Among the chiefs was the noted leader and orator, Red Jacket, from Buffalo. The first business done, was the speaker of the nation delivering an oration on the character of the deceased chief. Then followed what might be called a monody, or ceremony, of mourning and lamentation. Thus seats were arranged from end to end of a large council house, about six feet apart. The head men and the aged, took their seats facing each other, stooping down their heads almost touching. In that position they remained for several hours. Deep, heavy, and long continued groans would commence at one end of the row of mourners, and so pass round until all had responded; and these repeated at intervals of a few minutes. The Indians were all washed, and had no paint or decorations of any kind upon their persons, their countenances and general deportment denoting the deepest mourning. I had never witnessed any thing of the kind before, and was told this ceremony was not performed but on the decease of some great man. After the period of mourning and lamentation was over, the Indians proceeded to business. There was present the Wyandotts, Shawanese, Delawares, Senecas, Ottewas and Mohawks. The business was entirely confined to their own affairs, and the main topic related to their lands, and the claims of the respective tribes. It was evident, in the course of the discussion, that the presence of myself and people, (there were some white men with me) was not acceptable to some of the parties, and allusions were made so direct to myself, that I was constrained to notice them, by saying that I came there as the guest of the Wyandotts, by their special invitation; that as the agent of the United States, I had a right to be there, or any where else in the Indian country; and that if any insult was offered to myself or my people it would be resented and punished. Red Jacket was the principal speaker, and was intemperate and personal in his remarks. Accusations, pro and con, were made by the different parties, accusing each other of being foremost in selling lands to the United States. The Shawanese were particularly marked out as more guilty than any other; that they were the last coming into the Ohio country, and although they had no right but by permission of the other tribes, they were always the foremost in selling lands. This brought the Shawanese out, who retorted through their head chief, the Black Hoof, on the Senecas and Wyandotts with pointed severity. The discussion was long continued, calling out some of the ablest speakers, and was distinguished for ability, cutting sarcasm, and research; going far back into the history of the natives, their wars, alliances, negotiations, migrations, &c. I had attended many councils, treaties, and gatherings of the Indians, but never in my life did I witness such an outpouring of native oratory and eloquence, of severe rebuke, taunting, national and personal reproaches. The council broke up late, in great confusion, and in the worst possible feeling. A circumstance occurred towards the close, which more than any thing else exhibited the bad feeling prevailing. In handing round the wampum belt, the emblem of amity, peace, and good will, when presented to one of the chiefs, he would not touch it with his fingers, but passed it on a stick to the person next him. A greater indignity, agreeable to Indian etiquette, could not be offered. The next day appeared to be one of unusual anxiety and despondency among the Indians. They could be seen in groups everywhere near the council house in deep consultation. They had acted foolishly, were sorry, but the difficulty was, who would first present the olive branch. The council convened late, and was very full; silence prevailed for a long time; at last the aged chief of the Shawanese, the Black Hoof, rose—a man of great influence, and a celebrated orator. He told the assembly they had acted like children and not men, on yesterday; that him and his people were sorry for the words that had been spoken, and which had done so much harm; that he came into the council by the unanimous desire of his people present, to recall those foolish words, and did there take them back—handing strings of wampum, which passed round and was received by all with the greatest satisfaction. Several of the principal chiefs delivered speeches to the same effect, handing round wampum in turn, and in this manner the whole difficulty of the preceding day was settled, and to all appearance forgotten. The Indians are very courteous and civil to each other, and it is a rare thing to see their assemblies disturbed by unwise or ill-timed remarks. I never witnessed it except on the occasion here alluded to, and it is more than probable that the presence of myself and other white men contributed towards the unpleasant occurrence. I could not help but admire the genuine philosophy and good sense displayed by men whom we call savages, in the transaction of their public business; and how much we might profit in the halls of our legislatures by occasionally taking for our example the proceedings of the great Indian council at Sandusky.

The Indians have a great and abiding reverence for the places of their dead. I have known the Munceys and Nanticokes to raise the remains of their friends many years after interment, and carry them to their new homes and reinter them. The virtuous dead and those who have been useful and beloved in life, are long remembered and mourned after. I have seen the head chief of the Putawatimies, Onoxa, burst into tears in speaking of the Sun, a man who was distinguished as a preacher of peace among the tribes; who went about settling difficulties, healing the sick, and to use the language of the chief when he told me of the death of his friend and benefactor, "he was constantly traveling about among us doing good, and died on his road."

In 1820, the Wyandott chief, "The Cherokee Boy," came to me in great distress, stating that his dead was buried on land now owned by a white man in the Sandusky country, and that the man was clearing and preparing to plow up the graves, and wanted my assistance to prevent the apprehended desecration. I told him I had no authority over the case; that the man had purchased the ground from the government, and could do as he pleased with it: and the only relief to his feelings which I could think of, was for him to raise the dead and remove them to his own land. It was then summer, and if he would do this, I would write a letter to the man, asking him to suffer the place of his dead to be undisturbed until the winter, at which time they should be removed. The old chief readily assented. I wrote the letter, and accordingly he removed the dead to his own land.

I have known Indians, not under the teachings of Missionaries of the Gospel, at the approach of death, have very clear hopes and expectations of going to Heaven. I have never known any that did not believe in the immortality of the sou and a future existence.

Eighth Ward,--Cincinnati.

This is greatly the largest ward in the city, and exceeds a mile square in extent. In conjunction with the Sixth Ward it forms the entire western front of Cincinnati, and is the only ward in the city which is not more than half built up. Seven years ago, with trifling exceptions, it was a region of extensive pasture fields, brick yards, and vegetable gardens. Now it has 1250 dwellings and business houses, many of them of a spacious and elegant character, and the ward comprehending more neat and comfortable dwellings of the modern style of buildings, than any other in the city.

The public buildings are in number 11. These

are—one Engine and two School Houses; the Disciples', New Wesleyan, and United Brethern Churches; the Tabernacle, at the corner of Clark and John streets; a new Episcopal Church, at the corner of Clinton and Laurel; the Pest House; the old Tabernacle, on Betts street.

The entire number of buildings in this ward are 1252—bricks 491, frames 761.

Of these there were, at the close of 1842,

	Bricks.	Frames.	Total.
	145	504	649
Built in 1843,	138	51	189
" " 1844,	126	106	226
" " 1845,	88	100	188
	491	761	1252

Sixth and Eighth streets have been rendered, during the past year, beautiful and important avenues to the city, by reason of the extent to which they have been graded and paved. More work has been done for Cincinnati in this respect, in 1845, than in any equal period of the past.

An Adventure.

A late American traveler in Germany, complains in his narrative of the use and abuse of feather beds in that country, every where prevalent. He says,—" You are smothered with feathers, as you are invariably packed down between a feather bed beneath and another above."

This reminds me of an adventure of mine, many years since, in the village of *Harmonie,* Pennsylvania, a place originally built and occupied by *Rapp* and his followers. These people, holding no intercourse with their American neighbours, were as German in their language, customs, and habits, at the time I refer to, as the the day they settled in that part of Pennsylvania.

I had been one of a party of pleasure who rode out from Pittsburgh to Harmonie, and as we had to lodge for the night in this village, I was shewn into a large room in which were six or eight beds, apparently all alike.

The landlord lighted me to the room, and leaving the candle, withdrew, wishing me a good night's rest.

I observed, without being much struck with their appearance, that the under beds were very round, resembling bags of cotton rather than any thing else, and supposed the manner in which they were filled, resulted from a disposition to spare no expense to provide the best of every article—as was their reputation, and judged therefore they had put as many feathers in the ticks as they would hold. So in I sprang, blew out the light, and composing myself to slumber, being very tired, I fell asleep in a few minutes.

I was awakened to consciousness in a very few minutes more, by a loud noise and the sudden and peculiar sensation produced by my rolling out from the bed to the floor. I gathered myself up in considerable ill-humour, and as well as I could in the dark, regained my place in the bed, which was as round as ever—I was not as heavy then as now, by some sixty pounds—and in a brief space of time Somnus once more shed his poppies over my eyelids. Again, alas! I pitched to the floor with the same violence as at first. What to do now I did not know,—the building was nearly as extensive as a barrack, and I was in the third story, and had not noticed the way by which I came, and was apprehensive I might break my neck by falling through some place or other in the dark, if I were to attempt a return down stairs. The night, too, was excessively cold.

Well, I climbed up a third time, making a virtue of necessity, and getting asleep, found myself on the floor, suddenly—with a sensation in my arm as if I had broken it. All sleep and desire for it was gone by this time. And merely hoping to be able to get and keep warm until daylight, I pulled one of the upper beds to the floor, and taking another for a covering, again composed myself to rest. By this time I had become thoroughly chilled through, and after vainly lying still for some minutes to get warm, I rose, dressed myself, and, *neck or nothing,* groped my way out, feeling for the stairs, by which at last I made my way down to the ground floor. The bar-room was locked;—so was the kitchen. At last I made my way to an out-building, used as a wash-house, through a window of which I saw the welcome light of a waning fire, and getting hold of a chair, I brought myself within the influence of the chimney embers about to expire. I fell asleep directly, dreaming sweetly and pleasantly—how long I know not—but was again wakened by finding I had fallen head foremost into the hot ashes. I had been, through up-stairs annoyances, in a sufficiently bad humour, but this last misadventure made me swear out right at the landlord, and the whole race of Dutch, their beds particularly, and every thing about them generally. Brushing the ashes as well as I could from my clothes, I walked out and patroled the village until daylight, singing and whooping at the top of my voice to rouse somebody to my relief, —all to no purpose. So I was kept on the patrole till daylight.

As soon as the house was opened I made my way to the bar-room, in a delightful humour to knock the landlord down if he gave me the slightest chance for a quarrel. I found him at the bar, and asked what he meant by putting a guest on such sacks as he kept, and then went on detailing what I had gone through. He expressed much regret, and explained that the bed should have been pressed and beaten down with my hands before I had got in. "But did you not hear me in the streets." "Yes," replied he, "and would have got up if I had known it was you, but I thought it was some one of our Irish neighbours who had got drunk and lost his way into our village, as they sometimes do, when in that plight."

So all the sympathy and consolation for my night's troubles I had met at last, was to be taken for a drunken, brawling rowdy by these quiet, sober Germans.

To Readers.

My correspondent "H." in his article, "Yankee Tricks," gives the history of a pork operation, the point of which may be no more obvious, at first sight, to my readers than it was to me. But if we make out the bill, we can as readily discover the *shave*, as doubtless did the clerk at the sale.

Had the purchasers selected the hogs as the seller expected—the man taking the best who paid the highest, and the poorest hogs going with the lowest price, the bill would have been—

First choice,	7 hogs,	200—1400	at 3 cents	$42.00
Second "	7 hogs,	100—700	at 1 "	7.00
Third "	7 hogs,	50—350	at ½ "	1.75
				$50.75

But as the choice was made—

7 hogs, 50—350 at 3 cents,	$10.50
7 " 100—700 at 1 cent,	7.00
7 " 200—1400 at ½ cent,	7.00
	$24.50

This was a *neat* thing, and according to the laws of trade, fairly and lawfully done.

Life in Florida.

A public meeting of the citizens of Jacksonville, Florida, appointed a committee to memorialize the Legislature of that State, to supply the Supreme Court Rooms of a newly erected Court House with the necessary furniture. I quote the suggestions of the committee in their own language.

"The committee recommend the immediate purchase of the following articles of furniture, and that as the expense attendant will be too enormous to borne by the public, they sincerely trust that the Governor will be patriotic enough to "run his face" for them.

"One pine table, for the lawyers to sit upon; four rush bottomed chairs, for the lawyers to put their feet upon; one pine bench, large enough for the witnesses and lawyers, that have nothing to do, to go to sleep upon; and one yellow pine spittoon, six feet by six.

"Your committee, in suggesting the purchase of this article, would respectfully represent, that the old one, which was only three feet by three, was broken over the head of an eminent leading counsel, during a little difficulty, and that it is advisabte to have one in future, that cannot be lifted, and that can afford ample accommodations for the whole bench and bar, and assembled witnesses."

We may smile at Floridian notions of convenience, but there are accommodations alluded to—the sleeping bench particularly—if made suficiently large, which would be very desirable elsewhere as a place of repose during the long winded harangues of some of the lawyers.

"Yankee Tricks."

This is a common term for anything very smart, done in the way of trade, no matter in which of the States the doer was born. I approve of the old saying—"Let every tub stand on its own bottom." I am no Yankee, but have been well acquainted with many of them in the way of business and friendly intercourse. They are generally pretty cute, cautious, and saving men, though liberal promoters of charitable and public institutions, to which objects a single Yankee State, (the Old Bay,) or perhaps the town of Boston only, has, within the last thirty years, given more than the whole of the States south of Mason & Dixon's line have done since their first settlement; and of what these have given, it is probable more than half was from Baltimore alone. Let any Yankee take a journey south on a real good horse, and when he returns see if the beast he rides does not shew he has been out yankeed. He is some how or other induced to trade or swap till it ends in a bit of carrion, unless indeed his good horse is stolen, for horse fanciers (thieves) are as plenty as he goes along south as they are scarce in the New England States. Jockeys are no doubt to be found in all the States. We have them in Ohio, but all that I have known came here from south of the line. If such folks are otherwise respectable, the only way is to *put them upon their man*—describe the horse you want and about the price you would be willing to give, and you will seldom be disappointed in price or quality. I remember reading in a southern paper of a Yankee trick. It stated that some bales of *cotton* were returned from Glasgow, that were made up of cotton seeds and trash—the sweepings of the warehouse, with a nice plating of excellent Sea-Island. I heard the late Col. Humphreys, Sen., of Philadelphia, tell of a parcel of pitch—of which he used a large quantity in his business of ship building—which on melting proved to be about seven-eighths stones. I was told in a southern city, a story about half a large grindstone, which was returned as not being tobacco:—with it came the warehouse marks, by which the honest planter was easily discovered. The merchant who was the original shipper of the tobacco, *kept shady*, but afterwards sold the planter a barrel of sugar in which was the said grindstone; and, wonderful to relate, it was never discovered—at least it may be so surmised—as the buyer never mentioned it. Another " Yankee trick" I can vouch for:—A hogshead of tobacco came from the same southern city, to New York; it was there sold and paid for—but before delivery, a letter came from the shipper, directing that it should be particularly examined, as another hogshead of the same crop had been sold to a manufacturer, which, on breaking up, was found to be a cheat. It was accordingly examined, particularly; and in the centre was a very large oval pebble stone, which weighed, I think, three hundred and twenty pounds. To fix it in its place, long, slender oak pins were driven at short distances all round it, and very neatly done. Above and below, and all round it, the tobacco was excellent, and the whole appearance of the hogshead was such as would warrant an inspector to pass it, or a purchaser to buy it on sight; particularly if the tobacco was undergoing its sweat, as at such time opening it, by letting in the air is injurious and causes mouldiness. I was once riding with an esteemed friend, and we met with a man who had grossly cheated him. Said my friend to his brother Yankee, "it is such rascals as you who when driven from home, settle where you are not known, but are soon found out in your old dirty tricks, that forty or fifty miles round give a bad name to all New England." As to the dealers in horn gun flints and wooden nutmegs, I give them up to be buffeted. though the nutmeg business was not so very bad after all. A country store-keeper, who had dealt in the article, on being asked about it, said they were very pretty looking nutmegs—made he believed of saw-dust; that those made of sassafras were reasonably good, but those of elm or beech, wasn't worth a curse.

I once saw a very neat specimen of Yankee cuteness when traveling south. Some where below Baltimore the stage was delayed crossing a stream, by being behind several wagons which would have to cross over before it. It was a cold morning, and the stage passengers got out and crossed over in the first boat, to a country store near the ferry, so as to warm themselves before the stage got over. One of the passengers was a quiet-looking, youngish man, evidently one of the " Universal Yankee Nation." He had little or nothing to say while in the stage, except when answering a question, which he did modestly and understandingly. In the store were

several tall, lathy-looking men, who had probably came there to take their morning bitters. One of them addressed our passenger with—" I say, stranger, a'n't you a Yankee?" " Yes I be one of the people so called." " Well, you Yankees are said to be good at guessing, now I'll bet you a pint of rum I'll guess *nearer* the weight of that roll of tobacco than you can." " I don't drink rum, but will take my share in gingerbread." The man then took up the roll of pigtail, and after a short handling, said—" The weight is four pounds, ten ounces and a half; now what do you say?" His opponent handled the roll for some time;—" Well, what do you say?" asked the other. " Why I say four pounds, ten ounces and a half." This raised a general laugh at the proposer, who said it was not fair, and it was left to the company to decide; but, honour bright, his own companions, wild-looking creatures though they were, gave it against their friend.

Some years since, a sloop was drifting with the tide up a river in Old Virginia; a boat was ahead, as if towing her, but the men only occasionally gave a pull or two, merely to keep the sloop in the channel. She had a cargo of notions, consisting of Boston china, (Hingham wooden ware) onions, apples, coffins in nests, cheese, potatoes, and many other articles, " too tedious to mention." At a house near the river, a large number of people were gathered, and the captain, thinking some trade could be made, came to anchor and went on shore, with his mate and one of his seamen. He found there was to be a sale of the personal property of a deceased planter or farmer. Before the sale began he made a pretty considerable trade for his notions. The sale commenced with the live stock, part of which consisted of hogs, which were put in three lots of seven each; terms, cash down, for live weight, sinking the offal. Part of the drove were very fine and fat, but they decreased in quality and weight down to lean shoats and small pigs, most of them so feeble as to be hardly able to raise a squeal or grunt, without laying down or leaning against the wall. The first choice of seven would average, say, two hundred pounds net weight; the next best one hundred pounds, and the last about fifty. Well, the captain purchased the first lot at $7 per hundred; the mate the next at $1; and the sailor the last at 50 cents. When the delivery was made, the captain, to the astonishment of Old Virginia, chose the seven lightest. An honest buckskin said—" Why, captain, what a d——d fool you are; don't you know you have the choice?" " Yes I do, and I choose these nice little roasters." The mate made choice of the next in size, so that the *leavings* fell to the poor sailor. The grunters were all put on board and the sloop went her way up the river with a new article of trade. H.

CORRESPONDENCE.

Mr. C. Cist: *Dear Sir*,—

I do not pen this communication for the purpose of publication; neither do I write in a spirit of controversy, the subject being of too trifling a nature: but I wished to submit to your excellent judgment another derivation of the word *Ecuyer*, instead of the word *equus*, which, with great plausibility of correctness, you gave in your last. You very properly correct my derivation of the term; but in my first communication, I merely wished to say, the *corresponding* word, answering to the English *esquire* and French *ecuyer* in its *application*, was the Latin *armiger*. Our *equerry*, I agree with you, has its root in *equus*; but will you allow me to suggest another, and in my opinion, more probable derivation of the word, viz: the Latin *scutum*, a shield, from whence the French *ecu*, also a shield or buckler. The transition from ecu to ecuyer, would be easy enough. If the word in dispute is derived from *equus*, we must suppose that esquire and equerry denote the same thing—a groom of the horse: But the term has had a too widely known meaning, as signifying an honourable title, amongst the Romans as *armigeri*, the French as ecuyer, and English esquire, to allow us to suppose it derived from such a menial source.

February 9th, 1846. PHIL.

Covington.

Cincinnati has progressed in her improvements to a point, which in the advanced value of ground, brings into competition as advantageous scites to dwellings and factories, our neighbours of Covington, Newport, and the adjacent parts of Delhi, Fulton, and Millcreek townships.

A recent visit to Covington has impressed me strongly with the conviction that a large portion of our citizens must find homes across the river, as a necessary consequence of our rapidly increasing density of buildings. Streets are being laid out in the new parts of Covington, in which lots have been extensively sold at prices advancing, from time to time, in nearly the same ratio as in our suburbs, to the north and west. These have principally been taken by individuals who continue to carry on business on this side of the Ohio.

I shall take an early opportunity of pointing out some of the features which especially mark the progress of our sister city, refering at present merely to the fact that a new and extensive rolling mill and steam grist mill, are about being erected by *A. L. Greer & Co.*, of Covington, immediately west of the bagging factory of *M. J.*

Blair & Co., nearly opposite the Franklin Cotton Factory of our own city. This new establishment will make the *sixth* for the supply of iron to the Cincinnati market. Ten years will not elapse before our city will lead Pittsburgh as far in the market for this article as we now do in all other manufactures—glass and cotton yarn excepted.

Covington is already, I suppose, the fourth city in Kentucky for magnitude and population. By the census of 1850 it will probably be the second; and if it shall maintain for forty years its present ratio of improvement, must eventually become the great city of that state.

Building for 1846.

Although the weather is still of chequered and unsettled character, yet spring is evidently advancing, and with its approaching revival of buds and of flowers, is a revival of building operations. All over the city there are extensive preparations for putting up dwellings and stores to supply the increasing wants of the city. The unprecedentedly low water of last year shut out the regular supply of lumber to this market and checked various building operations here, which would otherwise have been made, and which will therefore add to the regular annual improvements of Cincinnati.

The buildings of the year past I judge will reach in the computation now in progress 1250; nearly the same as for 1845. It must be recollected, that independently of the reason just given why part of the improvements of 1845 will be thrown into 1846, that the buildings—brick especially—of last year, are of a character greatly superior to those of its predecessors in magnitude and importance, and consuming at least twenty millions more bricks in their construction. The public edifices alone of 1845, are of greater extent, value and consequence, than almost all other public buildings in existence heretofore. In this estimate it must be understood is included the great *Cathedral*, which, although in progress of erection for four years, has not been rendered ready for service until 1845, and is even yet not entirely finished.

Notwithstanding the number of dwellings putting up in Newport and Covington, and Storrs, Delhi, Fulton, and Millcreek townships, whose owners or occupants are doing business in Cincinnati, a greater number of buildings will be put up in Cincinnati for 1846, than has ever yet been known.

One at a Time.

In a western city, which shall be nameless, a sheriff's deputy in attendance on the courts of justice, was ordered by the judge to call John Bell and Elizabeth Bell. He immediately began, at the top of his lungs—

"John Bell and Elizabeth Bell!"

"One at a time," said the judge.

"One at a time—*one at a time*—ONE AT A TIME!" shouted the crier.

"Now you've done it," exclaimed the judge, out of patience.

"Now you've done it—*now you've done it*—NOW YOU'VE DONE IT!" yelled the deputy.

There was no standing this; the court, bar and bystanders broke into a hearty laugh, to the perfect surprise and dismay of the astonished crier.

Legislative Wit.

During a late debate in the Ohio Legislature, on what are called the Black Laws, one of the representatives from the Western Reserve—*Cheesedom*, as it is nicknamed at Columbus—in advocating their repeal, disclaimed any local interest on the subject, there being few negroes in that part of the State. This brought out a Mr. Stanley, who remarked in reference to the disclaimer—"I believe it. Yankees and negroes cannot well live together. Negroes generally follow shaving for a livelihood, and *we* Yankees are in the habit of shaving ourselves." "Yes," added Mr. Gallagher, our city representative, "and every body else." (Great merriment.)

Notice.

The "Young People's Magazine," as well as the Literary Emporium, two of the New York monthlies for January and February, have been laid on my editorial table. I take pleasure in recommending them to readers who are cloyed with the preserved citron of sentimental narrative which pervades generally the periodical literature of the East.

Derivations.

In my article on derivations, I omitted to notice two or three.

The origin of the name *Doomsday book*, was for a long time hidden in obscurity. At last a persevering explorer ferreted out, by ascertaining its original title in a black letter manuscript —that the term doomsday was merely a corruption of *Domus Dei*—the house of God, i. e. the religious house in which it had been kept for safety.

A more amusing instance of corrupting a word, or phrase, is the expression, *Tit for tat*, evidently a childish pronunciation of "this for that," being probably a slap or punch retaliatory.

Chronological Table.

Feb. 19th.—Galileo, born, 1564.
20th.—Voltaire, born, 1694.
21st.—Archbishop Cranmer, burnt, 1556.
22d.—GEORGE WASHINGTON, born, 1732.
Sir Joshua Reynolds, died, 1792.
23d.—The Peacock taken, 1813.

Errors of the Press.

Typographical blunders are sometimes so detrimentally and strangely wrong, that it would seem as if they were not always accidental. In a publisher's announcement, instead of "Cricket on the Hearth, a Fairy Tale of Home—for sale at the bookstores," the following travestie appears: "The Critic on the Heat, a Fiery Tale of Rome, for sale at the bootstores."

Iron Steamboat Hunter.

This boat, which is propeled by the submerged horizontal propelers, invented by the officer whose name she bears, left Cincinnati on Friday, the 8th inst., for Louisville. She made her run to the mouth of the Great Miami—twenty-two miles —in one hour and twenty minutes—nearly sixteen miles an hour. This is a rate of speed unprecedented for any boat like the Hunter—but one hundred feet in length—and seems to indicate that the propelers have not had fair play at the East, where they have been considered a failure.

Shakspeare and the Bible.

An obscure Scotch peasant, calling on business at a gentleman's house, in Edinburg, saw a bust of Shakspeare, and these lines from the Tempest, inscribed beneath it:—

"The cloud capt towers, the gorgeous palaces
The solemn temples, the great globe itself
Yea, all which it inherit, shall dissolve
And like the baseless fabric of a vision,
Leave not a wreck behind."

The gentleman seeing the peasant's eyes attracted by these lines, asked him if he had ever seen anything equal to them in sublimity. His reply was just and striking. "Yes I have. The following passage from the Book of Revelation is much more striking:—

"'*And I saw a great white throne and Him that sat upon it, from whose face the earth and the heaven fled away, and there was no place for them.*'"

Journal of Memphis Convention.

I observe this journal is published at last. Will my brethren of the Enquirer or Eagle have the kindness to see that the copies due to the Ohio delegation, for which they paid in advance, will be forwarded by the individual whose business it may be to do so?

Law Literature.

The last number of Hunt's Merchants' Magazine has an article humorously illustrative of the necessity for members of the bar, especially in the United States, to make themselves better acquainted with mercantile subjects and terms than is generally the case:—

"Many ludicrous mistakes," says the writer, "have occurred by reason of the ignorance of judges and lawyers upon general and commercial subjects. It is related of an English barrister, that in examining a witness he asked, "where a ship (in question) was at a particular time?" "Oh," replied the witness, "the ship was then in quarantine." "In Quarantine was she? and pray sir, *where* is Quarantine?"

Mr. Chitty, whose writings are well known to the bar, mentions the case of a judge, who after being engaged six hours in the trial of an insurance case, on a insurance policy upon Russia duck, on his charge to the jury complained that no evidence had been given to show how the Russia duck, (mistaking the cloth of that name for the bird,) could be damaged by sea water and to what extent

Turkish Punishment.

The celebrated French author, Dumas, in his pleasing account of "A Fortnight at Sinai," narrates the following characteristic anecdote of punishment on the person of a baker at Cairo, who had been convicted of fraud. He was nailed to his own doorway by one ear, and at such a distance from the ground that the whole weight of the body rested on the great toes, and no relief could be procured without tearing the ear, to which no Mussulman of honour can submit. M. Dumas was at first inclined to intercede for him, but, on seeing his ears bored, with holes like a seive, he thought him too old an offender to be worthy of his efforts; and placing himself opposite, made a sketch of him instead. While so occupied, he overheard the following curious dialogue between the culprit and the guard placed over him, to see the chastisement fulfilled. "Brother," said the baker, "there is a law of our Holy Prophet, which says, 'that we ought to aid each other.'" The guard continued to smoke without making any reply. "Brother," again said the baker, "hast thou heard me?" The guard gave no other sign of attention than puffing out a large mouthful of smoke. "Brother," resumed the offender, "one of us two might help the other, and be agreeable to the Prophet!" The puffs of smoke continued to follow each other with provoking regularity. "Brother," persevered the sufferer, in a melancholy tone, "put a stone under my feet, and I will give you a piaster"—worth about three pence English—absolute silence. "Two piasters"—a pause—"three piasters"—smoke—"four piasters." "Ten," said the guard. The ear and the purse of the baker had a long struggle; at last pain gained the ascendency, and the ten piasters rolled at the feet of the guard, who picked them up, counted and pocketed them, placed his chibook against the wall, rose, procured a small pebble, placed it under the feet of the baker, and resumed his smoking. "Brother," said the delinquent, "I do not feel any thing under my feet." "Nevertheless," answered the guard, "there is a stone. I have chosen one proportioned to the sum; give me a talari. (four shillings English,) and I will put a stone under thy feet so beautiful, and so adapted to thy situation, that when thou art in paradise thou shalt regret the place thou didst occupy at the door of thy shop." Again did pain get the better of the baker, who had the stone, and the guard his talari.

Small Pox.

The inhabitants of the good city of Boston were thrown into a great excitement last week, by the startling announcement that a crier had been heard ringing his bell, and proclaiming, "*lots of small pox in Nashua street.*" On examination, however, it was discovered that a slight error had been committed, the crier having said—"Lost, a small box, in Nashua street." This altered the complexion of things materially.

What is Luxury?

A candle would have been a luxury to Alfred; a half-crown cotton gown to his Queen. Carpets in lieu of rushes, would have been luxuries to Henry VII. Glass windows in lieu of horn to his nobles. A lettuce to Henry VIII's Queen; silk gloves and stockings to Queen Elizabeth; and so on, *ad infinitum.* Mr. Charles Waterton, the author of some works on natural history, in his account of his family, tells us that one of his ancestors, in the time of Henry IV, "was sent into France by the King, with orders to contract a royal marriage, and was allowed 13s. a day for his trouble and traveling expenses."

Recollections of the last Sixty Years.—No. 8.

By Col. J. Johnston, *of Piqua.*

In the year 1801, the Society of Friends belonging to the yearly meeting of Baltimore commenced their labours of love among the Miamis of the Wabash, thirty-five miles southwest of Fort Wayne. William and Mahlon Kirk, with other assistants, were sent out from Maryland to conduct the agricultural operations, and introduce among the Indians such of the mechanic arts as were suited to their condition. The Friends were gaining fast upon the confidence of the Miamis, until the traders, whiskey, and rum sellers, with other bad men in the Indian country, began to poison the minds of the Indians against their best friends, for such were the Quakers; and the benevolent enterprise was finally, after some years given up, and the mission transfered to the Shawanese of Ohio, and continued until their final removal southwest of Missouri. The society, at a very considerable expense, introduced farming among the Shawanese; built them a grist and saw mill, at Wapaghkonetta; and the writer of these sheets was made the almoner of a female friend in Ireland—whose name he was not permitted to know—to the amount of one hundred pounds sterling, to be expended in stock and implements of agriculture among the Indians of his agency, which trust he faithfully executed, sending an account of the expenditure, with a suitable address from the chiefs, through the hands of the committee of Friends for Indian concerns at Baltimore. Acts such as the preceding, with the accounts transmitted through the Delawares of the just and humane government of the Quakers in Pennsylvania towards the primitive Indians, has made them all repose great confidence in persons of their society; and if I were young, in the prime of my years, and once more placed in the management of the Indians, I would take for my assistants in the service none but Quakers, and with such, and just men in the administration of the government, I would want no soldiers to keep the Indians in subjection. See how the Cherokees are distracted with interminable and bloody feuds, by reason of Schermerhorn's treaty, made with about one tenth of the nation; and with the knowledge of this fact, ratified by the Senate and President of the United States. Already some of the best men in the nation have been assassinated in consequence; and at this moment the United S. dragoons are in the Cherokee country—Lieutenant Johnston, my own son among them—hunting up the murderers and trying to restore peace. The latter is impracticable: the cause lies too deep—too much blood already shed;—and all this by the unjust acts of the general government, in wresting their country from them under the solemn mockery of a treaty made

with a handful of irresponsible persons. And now, amidst all the contentions for the acquisition of territory to the Union, already too large for its good, no voice is raised in Congress to secure to the natives a perpetual inheritance in the soil. They are still to be creatures of a temporising policy, to be pushed back out of the way as our race approaches them, until, as the Black Hoof once remarked to myself in reference to this matter,—"We will go any where you please, if you will afterwards let us alone, but we know from past experience, you will keep driving us back until we reach the sea on the other side of the Rocky Mountains, and then we must jump off,"—meaning there would be no country or home left for the Indians at last: and does not our past and present policy towards this unhappy race but too clearly tend to confirm these apprehensions.

In 1817, I was charged by Governor Cass with the management of the Ohio and Indiana Indians, in bringing them to the treaty of Miami rapids. I collected seven thousand, with which we moved to the treaty ground. Much rain had fallen on the way, and we were long on the journey. Provisions became scarce; the hunters were seldom successful in procuring game. Such of the Indians as were not encumbered with women and children, with myself and some of the interpretors, left the main body, stating that we would proceed on to a noted camping ground in the prairie called the Big Hill and there await the coming up of the main body; that when we got all together we could consult and determine upon our future course of operations. In a few days the whole were assembled at our encampment: a grand council held. The result was that they did not intend leaving that place until they made a sacrifice to the Great Spirit. I urged in the council to omit this on the present occasion; that we were then behind our time several days; that we were suffering for want of provisions; that the commissioners of the United States were anxiously waiting for us, as no business could be done before our arrival; that plenty awaited us the moment we reached the treaty ground. The council decided that the Indians could not leave the spot until they sacrificed; and requested me to write to the Gov'r. their determination, and to ask for some things which they needed to complete their arrangements for the sacrifice: namely, tobacco, and some white muslin to dress the priests. We wanted flour, meat, and salt for provisioning our party, all of which I wrote for;—distance to the treaty ground twenty miles;—sent down runners, with horses sufficient to bring back what was wanted. The commissioners, on the receipt of my communication, were indignant at the delay; would send us nothing but the provisions—writing me positive orders to bring the Indians on immediately; that they could not wait the delay of their sacrifice. The chiefs were called together, the commissioners' letter read and explained, to which they instantly replied, that they could not and would not go to the treaty ground until after they sacrificed; that the Great Spirit would not aid them; and that if they were not indulged in doing what they had always been accustomed to do, on entering on any important business, they would forthwith return home. The result was communicated to the commissioners, with an earnest request, that the Indians should be indulged in what they believed to be a conscientious duty; that the articles wanted might be sent up; that I would hurry the arrangement. The commissioners finally assented to my request, and forwarded the articles ordered. The Indians held their sacrifice, after which we proceeded in a body to the treaty; remained on the ground six weeks; procured a large cession of country, and all of us white men connected with the service, elated with our success. All Northwestern Ohio was at this time ceded to the United States. The greatest opposition was experienced from the Wyandotts, who by the cession were cut off from the lake shore, and placed sixty miles interior. They reserved a spot of one hundred and sixty acres on Sandusky Bay, for a camping place in their occasional journyes to visit their friends in Canada. The attachment of the Wyandotts was ardent for their native country. The night they agreed to give it up many of the chiefs shed tears.

During the war of 1812, Gen. Harrison had his head quarters part of the time at Piqua, and occasionally sojourned with his staff at my log cabin. There was but one fire place in the house, chimney of *cat and clay*—a phrase well known to backwoodsmen,—and in the cold weather the family and guests made quite a circle. The women, in cooking the supper, were often compelled to step over the feet of the General and his aids; and then at bed time such a backwoods scene! The floor would be covered with blankets, cloaks, buffalo robes, and such articles as travelers usually carry with them for the purpose of camping out. No one ever looked for a bed in those times. It was not unusual for twenty and thirty persons to lodge with us for a night. The Indians frequently were of the number. Missionaries of all denominations, Catholics and Protestants, were alike welcomed. We lived on the extreme verge of the frontier, where travelers could no where else find accommodations. We obeyed to the letter the injunction of the Apostle—given to hospitality I was some times censured by my protestant friends for entertaining catholic priests. This proceeded from an un-

happy spirit, and chiefly the result of ignorance, and produced no difference with myself or that excellent woman who shared so largely in all my labours growing out of those troublesome times. The Ministers of Jesus Christ of whatever name, always found the latch string of our cabin door —as the lamented Harrison said to the old soldier —"hanging out." My aged mother lived with me at the time. On the General taking leave of us, setting out for the north, he asked for garden seeds. The old woman immediately took him up by saying—what do you want with a garden; are you not going right on to retake Detroit, and drive the British out of Canada. The General knew full well he could do nothing effectual towards the reconquest of Michigan without the co-operation of Commodore Perry, and his fleet was not yet ready to go on the lake.

On several occasions during the war I was requested by the General to copy his confidential communications to the war department. I am not at liberty, even at this late day, to disclose any part of that correspondence; but I may nevertheless be permitted to say, in justice to my old and valued friend, that in the prosecution of the war, he was often thwarted in his designs by the secretary of the department; and that this was especially the case while Gen. Armstrong presided over it—a functionary who did the greatest injustice to Gen. Harrison, and in the end was the occasion of his retiring from the command of the army. He could not serve in justice to his own honour under such a man. His slanderous history, put forth pending the contest for the Presidency in 1839, and for the purpose of effecting the prospects of Gen. Harrison, failed of its object, and only proved the malice and premeditated baseness and hatred of the author. And Mr. C. J. Ingersoll has lately thought it his duty to put forth another history of the war to traduce and vilify the illustrious dead. He has, however, received so many severe rebukes from distinguished living witnesses, as to render the work totally harmless as a chronicler of the truth. It is not very extraordinary that a man who boasted that if he had lived in the days of the revolution he would have been a tory, should delight in slandering him in whose veins flowed some of the best blood of the patriots and sages of that memorable struggle.

Duelling.

The absurdity of duelling has been pointed out in a thousand ways. There is one feature of it, however, which is supremely ridiculous—the trivial and even ludicrous provocations which in many cases have instigated such meetings.

Col. *Montgomery* was shot in a duel which was owing to a dispute between the merits of two dogs. Capt. *Ramsay* lost his life because he would not relinquish his servant to brother officer. Lieut. *Featherstone* last his on a recruit. The father of *Lawrence Stone* was shot owing to a difficulty respecting a goose.

Col. D——, who was an Irishman, challenged a brother officer because he smiled incredulously, when D—— told him he had seen an acre of anchovies in a field near Smyrna. They met, twice exchanged shots without injury, and were about to fire a third time, when the Colonel, suddenly recollecting himself, exclaimed, was it anchovies I said? by —— it was capers I meant. This, of course, settled the difficulty, which might have cost one or more lives.

Captain *Smith* was challenged for merely asking his opponent to partake of a second goblet. General *Barry*, for declining to take a pinch of snuff; and Major *McDermot* for doing the same with a glass of wine, although he pleaded on the spot that it always made his head ache: and Lieutenant *Crowther* lost his life in a duel because he had been refused admittance into a club of pigeon shooters.

I do not recollect, however, anything which places the ridicule of its practice in a stronger light, than an incident which took place some years since in Cincinnati. I was acquainted with the parties and can vouch for the facts. The circumstance occurred at a period when duelling, although rare, occasionally took place here.

Mr. L——, a young man of the *finest honourable feelings*, was told that a certain young gentleman on Main street, was the author of a communication in a newspaper of that day, which Mr. L. considered an aspersion on his character. Fired with indignation, he repaired to the residence of the reputed author, and finding him at the door, in spite of all explanation, remonstrance, and resistance of his victim, inflicted on him an unmerciful cowhiding.

A few days after, the real offender came to light, and L——, feeling it his duty to make an apology for his *mistake*, called upon the young man he had chastised, and acknowledged his error, said he was sorry for what had passed, that he bore no malice in the case; and if that explanation was not perfectly satisfactory, he should hold himself ready and willing to afford the *usual and proper satisfaction* on the Kentucky shore, if a call for that purpose was made.

I forget how the matter terminated. It was certainly not by the meeting in Kentucky, L.'s antagonist probably thinking a cowhiding past was less unpleasant than a bullet lodging in his carcase might prove. One thing I do remember, that I censured L. very freely for his conduct, and was surprised to find most persons disposed to justify it. "What more could he do than offer satisfaction?" said they. "It was but a mistake on his part at first."

The Masonic Hall.

This fine edifice stands at the northeast corner of Walnut and Third streets, occupying a front of one hundred and fifteen feet on its southern, and sixty-six feet on its western exposure, and is eighty feet high from the pavement to the top of the angle buttress. It was erected at an expense of thirty thousand dollars, and its appropriate furniture and decorations will cost, when completed, five thousand more. It is in the castellated style of the Gothic architecture of the Elizabethan era. The lower story is partitioned into eight store rooms, three of which adjacent to Walnut street, will be occupied by the Cincinnati post office.

The front is divided by buttresses two feet face, and eight inches projection. These buttresses run above the battlements, the tops of which are finished with openings in the ancient castle style. The windows to the principal hall are sixteen feet high, and are divided by a heavy centre mullion and cross rail, making four parts in each. Each window is surmounted by a hood of fine cut stone. The windows of the third story are nearly of the same size, order, and finish. At each end of the building on the south front, two of the buttresses are elevated a few feet above the centre, and returned on the west front the same distance. Each angle of the west front, is made to correspond with each angle of the south front. The centre of the west front is gabled; in the centre of which is a shield, with an inscription bearing the name of the building and date of its erection, together with the era of masonry. An iron balcony surrounds the building, on a level with the floor of the main hall in the second story. This is designed for public assemblies, and is one of the most spacious in Cincinnati, being fifty-one by one hundred and twelve feet fronting west, and twenty-three feet high, with an orchestra on the east end. The ceiling and cornice of this hall are finished in the richest style.

The third story is designed as a hall, for the use of the several lodges of the city, together with the chapter, council, and encampment, and will be eighty by fifty-one feet on the floor, and twenty feet in height. There are various passages, antechambers, and committee rooms, which fill up the residue of this story. The chapter room proper, is fifty-one by twenty-eight feet. The finish of these rooms, especially the ceilings and cornices, are truly elaborate. The exterior of the edifice is to be rough cast, and the roof will be slate.

The furniture of the chapter room is of mahogany, with Gothic open panel work, on a rich crimson satin ground. That of the Masonic Hall is of bronzed work of the same character, excepting that the satin is of mazarine blue. The carpets are of ingrain, of the best quality of Mosaic work pattern, with tessellated borders. Seven splendid Gothic chandeliers ornament the various halls—these will be lighted with gas.

The entrance to the public hall is from Third street—that to the Masonic Hall, on Walnut street.

There are various rooms for dressing, and refreshment purposes, which communicate with the public hall, and render it the most convenient place in the city for holding public dinners, &c.

Narrative of John Hudson,

A Revolutionary Soldier, and now resident in Cincinnati.—No. 4.

Captain *Matchem* accordingly fired his field piece, which was a twelve pounder. The ball, however, had been directed too low, and struck the bottom of the embrasure. He then corrected his aim and threw the second shot, which struck the mouth of his enemy's cannon, in rather an oblique direction, commencing a breach about eighteen inches from the muzzle of the piece, and tore off its side for that distance. This I had the curiosity and opportunity to ascertain exactly, after the surrender of the place. The fire thus opened from the battery, served as a signal to the French on the left, who commenced firing from their whole train of artillery. I was informed by competent persons at the time, that the combined forces were prepared to fire as much as sixty shot, or shells, at a volley, in less time than once every minute, and frequently did so. Inside the walls of Yorktown, and visible above those walls, were several frame buildings, which soon were battered to pieces under the allied fire, the shattered fragments flying in all directions, and killing and wounding by their fall, without doubt, numbers of the British troops.

South of the town, and at the left wing of the French forces, the ground rose up into land of considerable height, where the enemy had several out posts, one of which, and the largest, annoyed the French excessively, destroying the lives of numbers in their lines. In consequence of this the commanders-in-chief decided to carry them at the point of the bayonet, which was accomplished by the French grenadiers, who bore in this service the hand grenades, from which that species of troops derive their title, and which they only employ when about to storm an entrenchment. These grenades are bombs in miniature They are about the size of a mock orange, and being carried to the ground in the haversacks of the grenadiers are hurled in showers into the works, as their assailants advance. On the same

night the *Marquis de la Fayette*, with the American troops, stormed the walls of the town in front of Matchem's battery. The Marquis and his party obtained possession of the British guns, which were immediately turned upon their own defences, and kept in the hands of the storming force until daylight enabled the enemy to concentre their troops and drive the assailants off. The ordinary narrative of the siege of Yorktown condenses the whole history of it into this bloody and eventful night, as though that period embraced every event of importance in that campaign; but this is not the fact, for from the opening of our works by the first fire from the battery of Capt. Matchem, on the 4th or 5th October, there was an incessant cannonading kept up on both sides, which lasted until the evening of the 19th October, when the surrender took place.

Such was the vivacity of both attack and defence of Yorktown, that between the flashes from the guns and from the fuses of the shells, it was rendered light enough for us to attend to all necessary work during any portion of night, through the whole period of fifteen days which I have alluded to.

One night during the siege a major of the 43d regiment, sallied out on the besiegers with his command of several hundreds, and actually captured one of the French batteries, spiking their guns. By this time the whole line had taken the alarm, and he met with so warm a reception, tha he was glad to regain the town, with such of his troops as he was not obliged to leave behind in dead and wounded upon the field.

After this, and as a consequence of this incident, we had a piquet guard placed in advance of our batteries, and just under the muzzle of the enemy's guns. I was myself one of that guard one night. We had double centinels placed all along under the line of the British works, who were stationed each with one knee to the ground and the gun cocked lying on the other, our hail being to give three smart taps on our cartouch boxes. Our instructions were to fire instantly when the same signal was not repeated. Those taps resembled greatly the flapping of the wings of the turkey buzzard, which abounded from the number of the unburied dead lying in the neighbourhood, and would have been ascribed by the enemy to these birds, if the din of the cannon had permitted the signal, during any interval of their discharges, to be heard and noticed.

During the siege there had been remarked conspicuously a large house, built of white marble, which Capt. Matchem had spared, knowing it to be the property of Gen. *Hugh Nelson*, whose estate lay in the neighbourhood. The General, on his arrival, which took place a few days after, inquired why he did not fire on that building.

Matchem accordingly gave the reason. Never mind my property, replied the Gen.; rap away at it. Matchem then fired one ball, which made its way through the house. Where the ball entered, it made a small breach, but where it came out it forced a very large opening. After the surrender, I learned that there were a number of the British officers had made it their quarters, but they abandoned it as soon as this shot was fired, fearing more would follow. But this was the first and the last, as I distinctly recollect.

Lord *Cornwallis,* finding that he had no prospect of obtaining relief from *Sir Henry Clinton,* determined finally to surrender, which he did on the evening of the 19th October. On the 20th, we marched into Yorktown, and relieved the British guard there. On the 21st, the enemy's troops marched out and laid down their arms. On the 22d, they were marched off with a heavy escort, for Lancaster, Pennsylvania. On the 23d, as I was informed, the Marquis de la Fayette embarked for France, to carry tidings of the welcome event which was then generally supposed the close of the revolutionary struggle.

Our army staid at Yorktown until cold weather set in, for the purpose of leveling the works. We found hundreds of shells which had not exploded, from the circumstance of the fuse falling undermost, in which case they do not go off. These we gathered up in wagons, and put them on board vessels to take to Gen. *Greene,* who was still carrying on the war in South Carolina. There was a party of French prisoners who had gathered up a four horse wagon load of these shells. By some mismangement, not easily explained, an explosion took place, which tore the wagon to fragments; killed the horses, and twelve of the Frenchmen employed in the service. I saw these twelve men neatly laid out in a marquee all in a row with white linen burial clothes. This would not have been done for them, or any one else, during the progress of the sige.

The Cincinnati College.

This is a modern edifice of the Grecian Doric order, with pilaster fronts, and facade of Dayton marble. It occupies the scite of the former college, which building was destroyed some time since by fire; being on the east side of Walnut, between Fourth and Fifth streets. It is of three stories, exclusive of an attic, the whole front being one hundred and forty feet front by one hundred in depth, and sixty in height. The edifice was commenced in April last, and will be finished in the course of April next; at a cost of $35,000.

The ground story in front is divided into eight spacious rooms for stores. In the rear of these are three spacious halls, originally intended for the Temperance Societies, being respectively 40 by 19, 40 by 35, and 40 by 60. The front range on the second floor is designed for the accommodation of the *Young Mens' Library Association* and *Merchants' Exchange and Reading Rooms.* The exchange will be 45 by 59; the reading and library rooms each 45 by 29. There is also a room 14 by 16 for the use of the directors. In the rear of these will be the great hall of the building for public meetings of the citizens, which will be one of the finest rooms in the city, being 136 long by 50 feet broad and 31 feet high.

The various study and recitation rooms appropriate to the college itself are in the third story, and occupy a space of 45 by 136 feet, being the whole length of the building.

The attic is subdivided into a gallery for the academy of fine arts, 59 by 25, a room for chemical and philosophical apparatus, and the lecture room of the law school connected with the college. Fourteen spacious offices occupy the entire range in the rear.

The whole will be thoroughly lighted by gas, and is properly ventilated with suitable passages and openings, and an ample amount of daylight secured in the rear for the benefit of the rooms and offices which face in that direction.

The entire building is roofed in the most substantial manner; is finished with projecting stone cornice, and will be surmounted with a cupola modeled on a design taken from the tower of the winds at Athens.

One million of bricks, besides a large quantity of building and ornamental stone, has been employed in the construction of this edifice.

The Covington Bridge.

A bridge over the Ohio, to connect Covington with our city, is exciting great interest, and at the same time no little controversy and prejudice. For myself I have no hesitation in expressing a favourable opinion of the project, if it shall prove that a suspension bridge *without piers* can be constructed for the general convenience. But I should deem it unwise to risk the safety of our landings, and freedom from obstruction to the Ohio channel by the erection of piers in the river.

The following, which is copied from the "Union," of the 10th, is more to the point than any thing I can write. I must, however, correct Mr. *Roebling* on the width of the Ohio, which has been ascertained to be over eight hundred yards—double the breadth he assigns it.

We have been shown a letter addressed to a highly respectable citizen here—from John A. Roebling, Esq.—the architect of the new Monongahela suspension bridge—from which we make an extract, below. In the opinion of Mr. Roebling, the project of a bridge across the Ohio, at the point proposed, seems clearly feasible—and we give place to such portions of the letter, as will be interesting to our citizens—and those who feel an interest in the success of the undertaking. The letter dates at—

PITTSBURGH, Jan. 31, 1845.

A Wire Suspension Bridge can be constructed at Cincinnati, which would span the Ohio, in *one single arch*, leave the river entirely unobstructed, form a perfectly safe communication with the Kentucky side at all seasons of the year, prove the best paying stock, and the same time, a great ornament to the city, and one of the most remarkable works of modern engineering. A span of 1200 feet, (which I believe is the width of the river at the contemplated site,) is perfectly practicable, and *far* within safe limits of the capacity of well constructed Wire Cables. The size of the cables, and other means applied, must of course be in proportion. The distance from the ends of the approaches to the centre of the river would be sufficient to admit of a general ascent of, say forty feet. Add to this the height of the abutments of, say from fifty to sixty feet, and you have a height of ninety to one hundred feet above the river, sufficient to clear steamboats at a high stage of water.

If economy were a great object, two piers might be resorted, for the support of a centre span, of six to seven hundred feet, and two end spans of lesser dimensions. But I for one, would say, do not obstruct " La belle riviere"—there is but one in the world.

The Monongahela Suspension Bridge was opened to-day for wagons, and was literally covered with teams from one end to the other, without showing any signs of the *fever and ague;* it proves *more* steady and firm than a wooden bridge;—it will present a very pretty appearance when entirely finished. I am yours,

Very respectfully,
JOHN A. ROEBLING.

Legal Ingenuity.

A farmer attending a fair with a hundred pounds in his pocket, took the precaution of depositing it in the hands of the landlord of the public house at which he stopped. Having occasion for it shortly afterwards, he resorted to mine host for the bailment, but the landlord, too deep for the countryman, wondered what hundred he meant, and was quite sure that no such sum had been left in his hands by the astonished rustic, After ineffectual appeals to the recollection, and finally to the honour of mine host, the farmer applied to Curran for advice.

" Have patience, my friend," said the counsellor—" speak to the landlord civilly, and tell him you might have left your money with some other person. Take a friend with you, and leave with him another hundred in the presence of your friend, and come to me."

He did so, and returned to his legal friend.

" And now, sir, I don't see how I am to be better off for this, if I get my second hundred again; but how is that to be done?"

" Go and ask him for it when he is alone," asid the counsellor.

" Ay, sir, but asking won't do, I'm afraid, without my witness at any rate."

" Never mind, take my advice," said the counsellor, " do as I bid you and return to me."

The farmer returned with his hundred, glad to find them safe in his possession.

" Now, sir, I must be content, but I don't see I'm much better off."

" Well then," said the counsellor, " now take your friend with you and ask the landlord for the hundred pounds your friend saw you leave with him."

We need not add that the wily landlord found that he had been taken of his guard, while our honest farmer returned to thank his counsel, exultingly, with both hundreds in his pocket.

Pork Packing.

The putting up of Pork has been so important a branch of business in our city, for five and twenty years, as to have constituted its largest item of manufacture, and acquired for it the *soubriquet* of Porkopolis. Requiring as it does, in the various processes, from the killing of the hogs, to their being finally made ready for shipment, a great extent of room in the Pork houses, there are few things which make a more vivid impression on the visitor, who sees Cincinnati for the first time, than the magnitude and extent of the various buildings connected with this business; many of them with four stories, extensive fronts, and reaching in depth from street to street. If he should be here during the packing, and especially the forwarding season of the article, he becomes bewildered in the attempt to follow, with the eye and the memory, the various and successive processes he has witnessed, in the putting up; and the apparently interminable rows of drays, which in great numbers, and from early dawn to dark, are filling the streets leading to the river, and the immense surface of ground on the side walks, on lower floors of stores, and on the public landing, occupied with pork barrels, bacon hogsheads, and lard kegs.

Our pork business is the largest in the world, not even excepting Cork, or Belfast, in Ireland, which puts up and exports immense amounts in that line; and the stranger who visits Cincinnati during the season of cutting and packing hogs, should, on no account, neglect making a visit to one or more slaughter houses, and pork packing establishments in the city.

It may appear remarkable in considering the facility for putting up pork which many other points in Illinois, Indiana, Ohio and Kentucky possess, in their greater contiguity to the neighbourhoods which produce the hogs, and other advantages which are palpable, that so large an amount of this business is engrossed at Cincinnati. It must be observed, however, that the raw material in this business—the hog—constitutes 80 per cent. of the value when ready for sale, and being always paid for in cash, such heavy disbursements are required in large sums, and at a day's notice, that the necessary capital is not readily obtainable elsewhere in the west, than here. Nor in an article, which in the process of curing, runs great risks from sudden changes of weather, can the packer protect himself, except where there are ample means in extensive supplies of salt, and any necessary force of coopers, or labourers, to put on in case of emergency, or disappointment in previous arrangements. More than all, the facilities of turning to account in various manufactures, or as articles of food in a dense community, what cannot be disposed of to profit elsewhere, renders hogs, to the Cincinnati packer, worth ten per cent. more than they will command at any other point in the Mississippi valley.

The following table serves to show the progress of this business since it first became of sufficient importance to preserve its statistics:

1832	. . . . .	85,000
1833	. . . . .	123,000
1834	. . . . .	162,000
1835	. . . . .	123,000
1836	. . . . .	103,000
1837	. . . . .	182,000
1838	. . . . .	190,000
1839	. . . . .	95,000
1840	. . . . .	160,000
1841	. . . . .	220,000
1842	. . . . .	250,000
1843	. . . . .	240,000
1844	. . . . .	173,000
1845	. . . . .	275,000

The value of the pork put up in 1840, was $3,208,790. It will exceed $5,000,000 the present year.

As a specimen of the amazing activity which characterizes all the details of packing, cutting, &c., here, it may be stated that two hands, in one of our pork houses, in less than thirteen hours, cut up eight hundred and fifty hogs, averaging over three hundred pounds each, two others placing them on the block for the purpose. All these hogs were weighed singly on scales, in the course of eleven hours. Another had trimmed the hams—seventeen hundred pieces, in Cincinnati style, as fast as they were separated from the carcases. The hogs were thus cut up and disposed of at the rate of more than one to the minute. It may be added that this is very little better than the ordinary day's work at the pork houses.

A Paris Joke.

A rich and very avaricious capitalist of Paris, returned home one evening after having spent the afternoon as usual at his club. To his astonishment he saw the staircase decorated with splendid exotics; the upholsterers had taken possession of his apartments and had arranged throughout the most tasteful decorations.— "What does this mean?" cried the rentier in surprise. "These are preparations for a ball which Monsieur gives this evening." "I a ball!" The upholsterer exhibited th written

order, which was in an unknown hand; it was a complete mystification. While the rentier was yet beside himself, came the confectioner, with a train of tarts and ices; champaign bottles were already standing in close batteries before the sideboard; cold edibles stood ready in great baskets, and to complete his embarrassment, Musard, the son, appeared at the head of a powerful orchestra. The guests were not long in coming, and the rentier was compelled to put a good face upon the joke. The supper was delicious; the poor man received a thousand flatteries about his good taste; and the next day paid the bills to avoid a suit, which would have made him the talk of Paris.

Life in Mississippi.

The hotels at Jackson are celebrated for sumptuous entertainments, but instead of printed bills of fare, they call out every dish with a loud voice, frequently giving the price and history of their dishes. For instance, at the Mansion House, a negro boy takes a prominent position in the hall, and after the guests are all seated he begins:—Fresh butter, costs thirty cents per pound; eggs, fried, boiled, and scrambled; biscuit made from the best St. Louis flour and costs eight dollars per barrel; spare ribs, genuine Berkshire spare ribs, south-down mutton chops, we use no other kind at the Mansion House; if any gentleman at breakfast wishes to buy some, let him write to Col. C., of Adams county, who furnishes these. Venison from the free state of Rankin, &c. &c.

At McMakin's, the polite General discharges this duty himself, and when seated for dinner he begins:—Roast beef, roast mutton, roast turkey, boiled ham, boiled mutton, McMakin's ducks, Philip's potatoes, Scott county peas; after which comes old fashioned peach pies, buttermilk, sweet milk, cheese, crackers and molasses. Gentlemen don't neglect my liquors. *Gentlemen we are a great people.*

CORRESPONDENCE.

Cincinnati, Feb. 23, 1846.

Mr. Chas. Cist:—

I was greatly interested, as doubtless others were, in your article, published a few weeks since, on the important bearing which the gallant defence, in 1814, of the privateer, Gen. Armstrong, in the harbour of Fayal, had upon the issue of the battle of New Orleans, and the safety of that city which was its result. But the narrative had an additional interest from the circumstances connected with the subject of that vessel, which I shall proceed to narrate.

So brave and spirited an action, in which a force so superior was defeated, with the loss of nearly three hundred, killed and wounded, on the the part of the assailants, while our gallant countrymen lost only seven, killed and wounded, made an extraordinary impression among the Portuguese residing at that port, and filled the Americans there with patriotic pride. When the termination of the war soon after, rendered privateering obsolete, our Consul at Fayal, Mr. Dabney, obtained the privateer's figure head, an effigy of General Armstrong in uniform and installed it in his garden, where it crowned an arch in the centre, every successive 4th of July. As a part of the paraphernalia of the day, it was decked with flowers and evergreens. There, encompassed by our national flag in festoons around it, the head made a conspicuous figure in the eyes of the Portuguese, who regarded it that of the American patron saint, and the 4th of July as the saint's day, Americans and natives drinking the General's health with great gusto. The natives considering this as the only saint we have in the calendar. **P.**

Ambiguous Compliment.

The following appeared in the Nashville *Orthopolitan:*—

"We, the undersigned, passengers on board the steamer *Felix Grundy,* subscribe our names to this certificate, of the good behaviour of the chambermaid Jane. We found her kind and attentive to the wishes of the passengers, and *prompt on all occasions to gratify their wants.*"

Thirteen names were signed to the bottom of the card.

A Valuable Slave.

A bill passed the Legislature emancipating, by desire of his master, a servant named Horace King, belonging to Mr. John Goodwin, of Russell county.

The servant, says the Montgomery *Journal,* is well known for his intelligence and skill as a mechanic, which is displayed in many of the important bridges in this section. He has been very valuable and faithful to his master; and it was stated in the Legislature, he had earned for him some *seventy-five or eighty thousand dollars.* His master has refused *fifteen thousand dollars for him.* —*Mobile Herald.*

Chronological Table.

Feb. 25th.—Sir Christopher Wren, died, 1723.
　26th.—Napoleon escaped from Elba, 1815.
　27th.—Dr. Arbuthnot, died, 1735.
　28th.—Montaigne, born, 1533.
March 1st—St. David's Day.
　2d.—John Wesley, died, 1791. De Witt Clinton, born, 1769.
　3d.—Boileau, died, 1711. Otway, born, 1631.

The West.

A few weeks ago a well known master mechanic of Louisville, Ky., who was sojourning at the Tremont House, in Boston, walked into the dining room at the summons of the bell, and seeing in the long row of chairs one that was turned up against the table, to indicate that it was appropriated to some particular individual, he deliberately took it and commenced his dinner. In about five minutes, a young dandy, in whiskers and moustache, walked up behind him, and remarked in a supercilious tone—' Sir, you have got my plate." "Have I?" said Jim, carelessly,

"well, you are perfectly welcome to it," handing his empty soup-plate over his shoulder. A loud laugh ensued, and the man in the moustache beat a very precipitate retreat.

The Farmer's Progress.
1776.
Man to the plough,
Wife to the cow,
Girl to the yarn,
Boy to the barn,
And all dues were netted.
1837.
Man a mere show,
Girl piano,
Wife, silk, satin,
Boy, Greek, Latin,
And all hands Gazetted.
1845.
Man all in debt,
Wifes in a pet,
Boys mere muscles,
Girls snuff and bustles,
And every one cheated.

Almanac and Picture of Cincinnati,—1846.

A neat and portable volume bearing this title, has just made its appearance at the publishing establishment of Robinson & Jones, having recently issued from the press.

It embraces a description of the city, comprehending its public institutions and edifices, business operations, city government, courts of justice, business directory, periodicals, and a great variety of useful and interesting matter not easily reducible to heads, furnishing a great amount of useful intelligence to our own citizens and a guide book to strangers, which exists in no other shape.

I extract, as specimens of the publication, two or three articles from that department of the work which is made up of my contributions. They will be found under the heads, "The Masonic Hall," "The Cincinnati College," and "Pork Packing."

An Almanac for reference and one for memoranda, form a valuable department of the "Picture of Cincinnati," which is also illustrated by a new and accurate map of the city.

"You told me, neighbour Twist, when I paid Tim Doolittle in advance, on his promising to work for me in haying time, that I should find him *as good as his word.*" "To be sure I did, for I always knew his *word was good for nothing!*"

A New Church in Texas.

Our pork and flour dealers whose business carries them up Sycamore street to the Canal, have doubtless noticed the handsome improvement which has transformed the well known *Black Bear* Tavern, kept for many years by our respected fellow citizen, *Isaac Marchent*, from an old fashioned frame, into a spacious and extensive brick hotel, hardly surpassed any where for beauty and convenience. Our friend Marchent still commands the post, and the time honored Black Bear yet occupies his station as guardian to the establishment. Being well aware that the frame tenements of Cincinnati, as fast as they give way to brick buildings, generally *emigrate to Texas*, I kept a bright look out for *Fort Marchent* during my late explorations of the Eighth Ward, and had nearly completed it, without recognizing the emigrant. Finally, however, it made its appearance at the corner of *Clinton* and *Laurel* streets, but in so changed an exterior that nothing but my long acquaintanceship enabled me to recognize it. The whole establishment had been remodeled and repainted in and outside, a neat cupola now crowned its gable front, and rendered it obvious that it was being converted to some public purposes. The Clinton street front I found fitted up for a *Temperance* hall; the rear and out building constituting a family dwelling, and the upper part of the building had undergone the necessary change to fit it for a Church, by taking out all above the second story and putting up a suitable dome. All this was so neatly and appropriately done as to take me by surprise. The building is amply lighted and ventilated, and is of dimensions sufficiently lofty and spacious for religious services. The whole expense of the enterprize is nine hundred dollars, and as the ground rent is but twenty dollars per annum, the congregation is at a rent,—calculating interest on their disbursement—of but seventy-five dollars per annum. To meet this and afford a revenue to defray other expenses, they rent the dwelling and Temperance hall for one hundred and eighty-five dollars yearly.

I have read of Theatres being converted into Churches, and Distilleries into Temperance halls. Here is a tavern transformed into a temple for the promotion both of morality and piety. The bar where ardent spirits were sold and drank, becomes the stand for the lecturer on total abstinence; and the second story, as in apostolic days, is made an *"upper room"* for devotional purposes, capable of holding as many as in that period constituted the whole church of Christ.

Here is an example of the extensive good which may be accomplished at comparatively trifling expense by a few energetic public spirited men.

I should add that this is denominationally an *Episcopalian* enterprize. I wish them all success, and that they may stimulate other religious persuasions to "go and do likewise."

As an out post of civilization and christianity on the extreme borders of our city, I take the deeper interest in this movement. This church must be nearly two miles from our first house of worship, then the centre of Cincinnati.

Thrilling Adventure.

I had just turned over in my berth, in hopes to resume a very pleasant dream, the thread of which had been broken by some noise on deck, and was about closing my senses to external delight, when a cry of "Sail ho!" caused me to jump up, and make haste on deck. I met Mr. Tompkins in the gangway, coming down to call me. "Where is she sir?"

"On the lee beam."

"A ship?"

"No sir, I believe a schooner, but I can't make her out."

"Steward, hand up my glass."

The day had scarcely dawned, and by the grave and uncertain light, unassisted by the glass, I could only make out an object, but the moment I put my telescope to her, I saw she was a schooner with raking masts, standing to the westward, with a square sail set. We were heading south, close hauled, with a light air from the eastward, momentarily expecting the Trade Winds. As the day dawned more perfectly, and we were perceived by the stranger, his square sail came in and he hauled his wind with such celerity, that I did not hesitate to pronounce him a slaver or a pirate, which indeed, are synonymous terms in blue waters.

"Call all hands, Mr. Tompkins; hoist our colours."

"Ay, ay, sir."

The stranger showed Portuguese colours in reply to ours. This did not relieve the anxiety which had seized on me the moment I had a fair view of the schooner, for that nation was still actively engaged in the slave trade, and we were just in the track of outward bound vessels to the coast of Africa and the Cape de Verd Islands, also where they often stop to refresh and refit. Our crew consisting of only two men, besides officers, cook and steward, were soon mustered aft.

"I have called you, my boys," said I, "to state my intentions in regard to that vessel to leeward, which I suspect to be a rogue. We will prepare for as stout a resistance as possible. If he is honest, I can see by your actions which of you I can really depend upon, and there will be nothing lost; and if a rogue, we must take it for granted that, if we give up like cowards, we shall have our throats cut; and as this is to be our fate whether we resist or not if he boards us, let us make up our minds to sell our lives as dearly as possible; and remember men, one man devoted to a good cause is able to beat off a dozen engaged in robbery and murder." They gave a simultaneous shout of approbation in good spirits.

It was now broad daylight, and we could plainly perceive that the stranger gained to windward, though he dropped astern a little, rendering it somewhat doubtful whether he was superior to us in sailing. Our good bark was reputed a first-rate sailor on the wind in her best trim; but she was pretty deeply laden with a full cargo of cotton bale goods, and about one hundred thousand dollars in specie, and it could not be supposed that we could sail with a clipper schooner on the wind or in any other way. Our ship's armament consisted of two six pounders, twelve muskets, and the same number of boarding pikes, and a brace or two of pistols; my private armament consisted of a good rifle, a large ducking-gun, a double barrelled Joe Manton, a pair of duelling pistols capable of discharging six balls in as many seconds; and I accounted myself a good shot with all of them.

At eight o'clock it was nearly calm, the chase about two miles on the lee quarter, and heading directly for us.

Mr. Tompkins was a six footer, a real down east Yankee, who had been mate of the Ark, for all I knew, and was equal to any man in that capacity, although he might be taken for twenty years of age, if seen going aloft; there were people who had known him at least that time as chief mate. He had always obeyed orders promptly, never failed to have an answer ready, and exacted from all under him the same prompt and strict obedience that he paid to his superior officer.— My crew were all active young men, and the cook (or Doctor, as he was called,) was a real specimen of a first-rate runaway Virginia slave; he could cook as well as he could fiddle, and on Saturday night he would amuse all hands by a tale of a 'possum hunt or a deer drive. Having now described our crew, our vessel, and all we knew of the stranger, I will hasten to put the patient reader in possession of the facts for which he is anxiously looking. My orders were as follows, and they were obeyed in as short a time as I shall take to write them:

"Mr. Tompkins, load the small arms, one ball and four buckshot in each; look to the flints; also load the great guns with round and canister."

"Ay, ay, sir."

"Doctor, put two iron bolts in the fire, and keep them red hot, and fill your coppers with boiling water."

"Mr. Turner, muster all the hats and peajackets, and stick one on each handspike near about the ports; it will make him think that we are well manned; and trice up all the ports, sir, and put a log of wood out of each, and give them a dab of black paint."

"Mr. Tompkins, send old Brown to the helm, and tell him to steer small."

These arrangements being completed, I went down below and loaded my arms, and on examining the Doctor, I found that he was quite familiar with the instrument of death, the rifle; I accordingly gave him my flask and bag of balls and other materials, telling him I should call upon him to load for me when the time came.

"Oh, neber fear, Massa—gib us breeze and him no catch us so easy," said he, grinning from ear to ear, and whetting his long knife on a stone.

I put a ball and four slugs into my double barrel, and a handful of buckshot into my "ducker," and a quantum sufficit of balls into the pistols. I had scarcely made these arrangements when Tompkins called—

"He's sweeping his bow off, sir, and I reckon he's going to slap 'long Tom' into us."

I jumped on deck, and, as it was now dead calm, it was too evident this was his intention.

"Down flat upon deck, every soul of you," shouted I. All obeyed except Tompkins, who coolly looked through the glass.

"There she flashes, sir," and in another instant a heavy shot whistled through our main-top-galiant-sail.

"He shoots well, that's a fact," said Tompkins.

I looked as the smoke lazily curled away, and saw that he had not the same flag flying. "Tompkins, what is that at the peak?"

"It looks, sir, like a red shirt with the Doctor's head in it, and a couple of bones rigged across his chin."

Sure enough, it was a red flag, with a black death's head, and marrow-bones painted on it. I cannot say that I felt relieved at these symptoms; yet my mind was made up that we were lost, and it remained only for us to die game. There seemed nothing short of Providence to save us; if it remained calm, he would bore us through with his long gun; if it breezed up, he could outsail us.

"Mr. Tompkins, keep an eye to him, and let me know of any movement. Mr. Turner, bend on the weather studding sails, all ready to run out; perhaps we can out sail him off the wind when the breeze comes."

This order was scarcely obeyed, when Tompkins reported—"They are getting a tackriggin', sir, to hoist out their launch and board us, by Heavens!"

"I like that, Mr. Tompkins, for the rascally captain and half his crew will come in her, certain of an easy prey; but if my aim don't fail me, few of that boat's crew will return, be they more or less. Mr. Turner, hoist those two guns up on the poop at once, for if we want them at all, it will be over the stern. Are you a good shot, Mr. Tompkins?"

"When I was young, sir, I was called a leetle the best shot in Kennebunk, and I guess I could fetch a turkey at a hundred yards now with a straight rifle."

"Then, sir, do you take charge of the twelve muskets, and let Jim load for us as fast as you fire, while the Doctor and I will keep my own tools busy?"

The pirate's launch was now manned and pulling ten oars at us lustily, while a group of men were collected forward and in the stern sheets of her, perhaps twenty or twenty-five altogether scarcely a mile astern, and as we were almost entirely becalmed, gained rapidly on us. There was no occasion to call the people aft to give my orders, for they were collected round the capstan with anxious faces and blanched cheeks.

"If they succeed in getting alongside, boys," said I, "we will retreat with our arms to the cabin, and let them board us, and through the windows and cabin door we may clear the decks; if not, I shall reserve my last pistol for the powder magazine, which is at hand, and we will all go together, and disappoint the rascals."

"But I trust it will not be necessary to come to that. Nail down the forecastle, Mr. Turner. If they get alongside, mind every one retreat to the cabin, or die like a dog on deck, if he pleases."

"There they shoot, sir, and pull ahead as if after a whale," said the mate; "and here comes a little breeze too—perhaps it will strike us before the villains get near enough."

"They are in the range of the rifle, sir."

"No, sir, wait until they get near enough to be sure of the leader—within a hundred yards.

There she breezes, thank God! 'Good full,' Brown, and nothing off. We have the breeze before the schooner, but it is very light yet, and the launch gains fast. Now, Doctor, stand by, mind you, ram the balls home, be cool, never mind the patches. Stand by, Tompkins, aim at the group in the bow, while I take the stern; are you ready?"

" Yes sir!"

" Fire!" and down went the rascal at the tiller, and one also at the bow.

" Load her quick, Doctor, and let me give them Joe Manton; in the mean time fire away Tompkins, as fast as you please, only take good aim—be cool."

" Cool as a cucumber, sir."

My double-barrelled gun dropped one oar in the water, and caused some confusion in the after part of the boat.

" Put it into them, sir—we have not lost a ball yet. Give me the rifle, Doctor."

" Yes, sir, she is ready. I spit on the bait for luck."

This discharge caused them, with the increased breeze, to lay on their oars an instant, and then pull round for the schooner; they had only six oars out.

" Three cheers my lads, and fire as long as you can reach them. There, the schooner begins to feel the breeze. Mr. Turner, run up the weather studding sails—keep her off two points, for he must pick up his boat. There, she breezes, thank Heaven! steady, Mr. Brown, steady."

" Steady, sir."

" Keep her straight, for your life. Steward, give the lads a glass of grog at once."

By the time the schooner had picked up her boat and hoisted her on board, we had gained a mile or two, and we were now going eight or nine knots with a free wind.

" Watch her close, Tompkins; let me know if she gains on us."

" Ay, ay, sir."

" Mr. Turner, we are a little by the stern; carry every thing portable chock forward—carpenter's chest, harness; roll those two after casks forward—be lively, sir. Swab those guns out, Doctor, we'll have another dab at them yet, I fear, for he sails like a witch."

" Yes, sir, him going to Africa, ivory and gold dust—dat's what they call nigger trading."

" She gains, sir, but slowly; he hasn't got the bsst of the breeze yet, perhaps."

" So, that will do, Mr. Turner, now get a small pull of your weather top-sail and top-gallant braces. Well, sir—well all!"

" They are hoisting that great square sail, sir, and she springs to it like a tiger."

" Mr. Turner, slack a little of your top-mast, and top-gallant backstays to the windward—carefully, sir, not much—and then send all chock forward—every pound will help."

" Four bells, sir; hold the reel."

" No, never mind the bells, nor the reel, Tompkins; what use is it to us now? Keep your eye on the schooner, and let me know when the six pounders will tell on him; and we may shoot away his top-mast by good luck."

" Ay, ay, sir."

Tompkins was so mechanically correct in every thing that he would, no doubt, have brought his quadrant on deck and observed for the sun, if it had been noon, and I had not interfered. He was as cool as possible, and his conduct seemed to put nerve into the men.

" He gains fast, sir; I can see the red cap on the rascal at the helm—let me give him a shot, sir."

" Well, sir, fire away if you think you can reach him. Doctor, bring your loggerhead, and when I give the word, touch her quick! So, lift her breech a little Tom, so, so, stand by—give it to her!" and away went our little shot and struck the water about two-thirds of the way to the schooner.

" Load up again, Tompkins, and leave out the canister, and the shot will go straighter; aim higher than before, say the royal—now give it to him!"

" Plump into her square sail, sir; but forty thousand such would'nt hit him hard. Oh, if we only could borrow his Long Tom for an hour or two. The Sarpint is sure of us or he would fire it himself."

At this crisis the chase was only a mile or a mile and a half astern, and could easily have bored us through; but I presume he was afraid to yaw his vessel round to bring the gun to bear, and it would no doubt kill his wind in a considerable degree, and, as he was gaining preceptibly, he calculated to be alongside of us long before night.

" Load up again, sir, and I will try my luck for it must be a mere chance shot that does him any harm."

" All ready, sir."

" Stand by, Doctor, and when I give the word touch her quick—fire."

The shot struck the water just under the bow. " Now for the other gun; I shall do better—ready—fire! His top-mast totters! it falls, by heavens!"

A spontaneous cheer from our crew seemed to assure us of safety. " Give me the glass boy. They are cutting the wreck away as fast as possible, still determined to overhaul us. Keep off two points, round in the weather braces a full, run out that lower studding-sail—be handy, lads. Watch the rascals, Mr. Tompkins, and let us know if we gain on him."

" Ay, ay, sir."

The breeze was now fresh, well on the quarter, and we were sure to gain on him until his top-mast can be replaced, which, with a large and active crew, bent on revenge, would cost him but an hour's work.

" She drops, sir, she drops! I can but just see that nigger's head on the flag; half an hour ago I could see the marrow bones."

" Very well, sir, let the people get a bite of dinner, for we shall have more work to do yet to get clear of him, if we do at all."

" I don't know what more we can do sir, unless we grease the bottom," said Tompkins, with a smile.

" We have yet one principal resort, my dear sir, and we will do it the moment we get something to work upon, if he gains upon us."

Tompkins cut a new quid of tobacco, of which he had made uncommonly free use that morning, and by that only did he show any sign of anxiety.

" Get your dinners, Mr. Tompkins and Mr. Turner; I can't go down to eat while that fellow is dogging us. Send me a bite of biscuit, and a glass of wine,"

" Ay, ay, sir."

It was now about one o'clock, and the schooner dropping slowly, while the preparation to fit a new top mast were accordingly progressing.—

In ten minutes all hands were again on deck, anxiously watching. As Tompkins came on deck, I heard him say to Turner—

"Consarn me, if I know what the old man is going at; we've done all human nature can do, and he's not given to praying."

"How long, Tompkins, will it take him to catch us, when he makes all sail again, at the rate he gained before?"

"Three or four hours, sir. He will be alongside before sunset, I reckon."

By two o'clock, his top-sail and tog-gallant were again set; and twenty minutes more, in his studding sails, royal and ringtail, and it was evident that he began to gain apace, though now more than four miles astern.

"Mr. Tompkins, we will now try our last resort."

"Ay, ay, sir."

"Break open the hatches, saw the rail and bulwarks off abreast them, and tumble up those bales as fast as possible."

This idea had evidently never entered into the heads of any of the crew or officers; and the long faces with which they had seen the pirate gaining on us, were instantly changed to faces of hope. In ten minutes the cook and the second mate had sawed off the rail and bulwarks, the hatches were off, and the bales coming up faster than any ever before came out of her, and overboard.

"Look to your trim, Mr. Tompkins, do not take too many from one side. Send boy Jim on the poop to keep an account of the number as they pass by. Over with them, boys, you are now working for your lives." But no encouragement was necessary, for the men, striped to their trousers only, worked like tigers.

"Mr. Tompkins, cut away the stern boat; every little helps—let her go, sir, at once—that's it. These large bales will oblige him to steer wild or to run against them."

We continued this work for nearly an hour, before we began perceptibly to gain on the schooner. But by four o'clock he had dropped more than a mile; yet to make sure, we did not abate our exertions until five o'clock, when four hundred out of a thousand bales had been thrown over. During the operation I could hardly refrain from laughing at the remarks which escaped from the men after we began to gain.

"Huzza, boys!" said one, "over with them, the under-writers are rich."

"Watch there—watch!" cried another, as he rolled a bale over; "them will do for him to buy niggers with."

"I wish my old woman had a bale of that," said the Doctor.

As soon as the pirate discovered that we were gaining, he gave us several shots from his Long Tom, but the distance was too great, and by sunset he was hull down from the poop; a few minutes after he hauled in his square-sail and studding-sails, and rounded too; and when last seen, was very busy in picking up the bale goods, which would no doubt come in play, though not quite so acceptable to him as the dollars would have been, sweetened with blood. At dusk, we could but just discern the villain, lying to.

"See all secure in hold, Mr. Tompkins, and put on the hatches; and as we have a steady trade-wind, let her go till midnight South South-West; and let all hands get some rest. I must do the same, for I am nearly done up."

The excitement being over, I was nearly pros-

trate, and after thanking God with more fervor and sincerity than I prayed before, I threw myself into my berth, but had a feverish and dreamy sleep till twelve o'clock, when my trusty mate called me according to orders.

"Twelve o'clock, sir."

"How is the wind and weather?"

"Fresh trade, sir—clear and pleasant—moon just rising—going nine, large."

"Take in the lower studding-sail, Tompkins, and haul up South and East, if she'll go it good full."

"Ay, ay, sir."

It is sufficient to inform the patient reader that we saw no more of the pirate, and made much better progress now that our bonny barque was in ballast trim only. We finished our passage without further trouble. Many were the jokes cracked by all hands, as they talked over the events of that day's excitement. The underwriters not only paid for the cargo thrown overboard at once, on receiving the news, but, on learning the particulars, voted a piece of plate for me, and a gratuity in cash for the mates and men in equal value.

In conclusion, I have merely to remark, that the above tale is founded on facts, and is not expected to interest any, except nautical men, being too full of technicalities to amuse the general reader, and too imperfect to claim the notice of the literati.

Recollections of the last Sixty Years.--No. 9.

By Col. J. Johnston, of Piqua.

I spent some of my early years in the ancient town of Carlisle, Pennsylvania, in the family of an aged, respectable citizen—the late Judge John Creigh. Gen. Armstrong was born in that town—the son of Gen. John Armstrong of the revolution—who was from the same parish in the county of Fermanagh, Ireland, from which my honoured father and mother emigrated to the United States, sixty years ago, and where I was born, in the year 1775. In passing home from Washington to the west, I think in 1809, I took the town of Carlisle in my route; and called to see my old and venerable preceptor, Judge Creigh. The conversation turned upon Gen. Armstrong, then the Minister of the United States in France. The old Judge remarked—he was born here; I have known him from infancy; was a bad boy, is a bad man; and although possessed of talents, he never had any good principles—and added, that the President could not have sent a more suitable tool to the Court of St. Cloud—alluding to the total disregard of the just rights of nations and individuals which dictated the policy of Bonaparte. This was the opinion of one who knew the author of the Newburg letters, and corresponded exactly with that which I afterwards formed of the man, on reading some of his orders to Gen. Harrison—orders which if carried out, would have disgraced any civilized nation in the world.

Governor Harrison was superintendent of Indian affairs within Indiana, Ohio, Illinois, and Michigan. His power and patronage were very extensive; in a great measure unlimited. Mr. Jefferson had the most unbounded confidence in his patriotism, wisdom, and integrity. I have no recollection of the Executive ever having negatived any of his recommendations. His numerous treaties with the Indians of the Northwest were conceived and executed in the spirit of paternal kindness and benevolence: his government over them was distinguished for mercy and liberality, wisdom and justice. In 1840 I received a message from Caldwell, the Putawatimie chief, as follows:—My old friend and father Johnston, I still hold you fast by the hand, even up to the shoulder, (meaning that nothing could break his friendship for me.) I have been for three years past invited by my father, (meaning the representative of Mr. Van Buren) to come and make a treaty with him. I have shut my ears against him, for he is a liar and speaks with two tongues. But I hear my old friend and father, Harrison, is soon to become President, and when he becomes my father again, I will go and settle the business of my nation with him. And although I fought hard against him last war I know him to be honest, and will not cheat or tell me lies. About the same time I received many messages of gratulation from other Indian chiefs. They were all delighted at the prospect of Harrison becoming their great father. Poor fellows, his death blasted all their hopes. More than once the President declared in my hearing his firm purpose of having a total change made in the government of the Indians. They and the old soldiers of the campaigns of Harmar, St. Clair, and Wayne, were looking up to him for justice long delayed. Had Providence spared him they would not have been disappointed. Years before his election he told me he was so annoyed by the applications of old soldiers that he thought he should be compelled to spend a winter at Washington, in order to make known their claims to Congress; but he said his finances would illy justify the expense.

Pending the presidential election in 1840, Gen. Harrison was occasionally an inmate at Upper Piqua. He was there a few months previous to the death of my beloved wife, she had enjoyed his acquaintance for almost forty years, and took a deep interest in all that concerned his happiness and fame. She was an humble, pious and devoted christian, and cherished a sincere desire to see all others in possession of those hopes which sustained her through a life spent in the wilds of the west under circumstances of more than ordinary trial and difficulty. She sought an opportunity of conversing with the General on the subject of religion, urging upon him that as he was getting old it was time he should turn his attention to the close of his earthly career, and seek his peace with God in the gospel of his Son. He replied that he was long convinced it was his duty to make a public profession of christianity, that the people of the United States had made him a candidate for the Presidency, that if he was then to unite with the church it would be ascribed to a desire for popularity, and would do the cause of religion a serious injury and make himself the subject of uncharitable remarks in the political journals, but, said he, as soon as this contest for the Presidency is over, let it be adverse or prosperous to myself, it is my purpose if my life is spared, to make a public profession of religion after the inauguration. It is well known that the President had the proper understanding with the Rev. Doctor Hawley of St. John's Church in Washington, to become a member of that church on Easter Sunday, April, 1841. The Dr. stated this fact over his remains. Late in March, 1841, I went to the President's house on a Sunday evening, the whole house was filled with visitors of all sorts, I was pained to see this, on account of the character of its incumbent; at last an opportunity occured of my speaking to the President, I told him I was sorry to see the house the resort of such a multitude of idle persons on the Sabbath day, that I feared those matters would get into the newspapers and injure his character. He said he regreted much himself that persons would visit him on that day, that the city was full of people and all wanted to see him, but as soon as the crowd dispersed and went home, that house in future would be closed against all visits on the Sabbath day. He remarked further, to shew you how much I have been engaged since coming into this house, I do not know a servant in it but the porter at the door, I do not know the man that cooks my dinner. Both before and after the inauguration, the President had seen fit to notice myself on several occasions, and made me the medium of confidential communication between himself and others; this gave me out of doors, with many persons, the character of a favourite. I was therefore frequently called upon to present persons to the President elect and the President defacto. I evaded this as much as possible, because the calls were so frequent as to give the General the most serious annoyance. At times I had so many individuals to present that it became necessary to have a written list of the names and read them off at the presentation. At length I concluded to decline all further service in that way, out of regard to the value of the President's time, his comfort and peace. A few days before I left the city, a member of Congress called on me to present a friend of his to the President, remarking that he had not time to go himself. I said I had declined taking any one there for some days, but to oblige him would take his friend, and named the hour at which I would be ready. The gentleman came, and we repaired to the White House; I introduced my friend, the Rev. Mr. Hand, of the Methodist church, from the lower counties of Pennsylvania. The President replied, I am under obligations to the Methodists, for they all voted for me. Yes, said I, General, and all the praying people of the U. States voted for you. I believe it was so, was his reply. I spoke to him twice in favour of some democratic gentlemen in office who were apprehensive of being displaced. I knew them to be good officers, and as far as I could ascertain had not interfered with the elections of the people. He said he did not wish to turn any deserving man out of office, but the office holders had so generally perverted their official influence and power to control the elections every where, that he believed if he did justice to the country very few of them could be retained; if his life was spared he would see that in future they would let the people do their own voting. An old resident in Washington remarked to myself, your President will be the most popular man in Washington of any that has ever occupied the White House. Although he has been here but a month, he is so much out among the people that more persons know him already than knew Mr. Van Buren in all his four years.

A Glossary.

The modern peripatetics who go about picking pockets by law, take as many liberties with the English language as they do with the public at large. They not only call themselves by new names, as other depredators on society are known by *aliases*, but they assume time honored titles which have been borne by some of the most distinguished names in Science and the Arts. As a landmark for future reference, I propose to record what these titles once meant, lest that meaning should be lost sight of, as is threatened by their innovations and assumptions.

A *professor* once signified a man who having devoted almost a lifetime to the study of some particular Science, became so eminent for his knowledge as to be called to teach it within the walls of an University. *Porson* on Philology, *Davy* and *Faraday* on Chemistry, *Lardner* on Astronomy, were known as *Professors* world wide. *McClellan* and *Mott, Silliman, Hare* and *Locke* have sustained the same title in our own country, in various departments of Science with honor to themselves and the community of which they make a part. *Now* we have for Professors such men as *Gouraud, Smith, Bronson,* &c., mere vagabond empirics in mnemotechny, mesmerism, neurology, &c.

Originally the title Doctor signified learned and wise, and it has accordingly been confered in past ages upon men distinguished above their fellows in theology, law, medicine, &c. Now, every man, however illiterate, who practices medicine is a Doctor, equally with the most renowned physician. Every apothecary's boy also is dubbed Doctor now-a-days.

Once the performer on the fiddle was a fiddler, on the harp, a harper, on the fife, a fifer, on the drum, a drummer. These are now new named by themselves. The fiddler is a *violinist*, or *violincellist*, the harper, a *harpist*, the piano and flute players are *pianists* and *flutists*. I believe we have not got so far yet as to honor the drummer and fifer by the title drummist or fifist—this, if they exhibited themselves in public halls, would doubtless have been long since the case.

What was once a milliner is now a *modist*. Do not mistake the word for *modest*. The two terms have nothing in common. The writing master is metamorphosed into a *calligraphist*, as the editor will doubtless soon be into a *paragraphist*. The old fashioned pastry cook is now an *artiste*. What was a public singer in former days is in modern times a vocalist, if a squaller in petticoats, a *cantatrice*. Cockatrice I should think a more expressive and appropriate term. An impudent hussy, whose exposure of her nakedness would once have brought blushes on the cheeks of the spectators, is a *danseuse*—Fanny Elsler for example. Let me not forget in this list of these distinguished characters the corn curer. He is in modern days a *chiropedist*.

The Ne Plus Ultra of Rivalry.

At New York and Philadelphia, as well as at Cincinnati and New Orleans, the security of Iron Fire Safes forms a subject of lively interest. But I have never seen the professional spirit, as well as local characteristics, more fully developed than in a late *New Orleans* print, in which one safe dealer proposes to his competitor to submit their respective Safes to the usual ordeal of fire, *each party to be locked up in his own safe!* as test of the sincerity of his confidence in its incombustibility. His antagonist declines it, *only*, as he says, because it would bring the parties under the stringent provisions respecting duelling incorporated into the new constitution of Louisiana!!

The Masonic Hall.

Only two years since and Cincinnati was more deficient in halls for concerts or lectures, than any city of equal size and importance in our republic. We have now reversed this order of things in the erection of *Concert* Hall, *Washington* Hall, *Masonic* and *Odd Fellows* Halls, the hall in Mr. *Williams'* buildings, corner Fourth and Walnut, and the great hall in the new *College* edifice. The last three are not finished, of course their, acoustic character and capacity for public use cannot be accurately known. But the hall of the Masonic building has now been fully tested, and the result is truly gratifyi: g to our city pride. It has been pronounced by those who have given concerts within its walls to be unique in its adaptation to such purposes. Those who have exhibited in the *Musical Fund* Hall, Philadelphia, the *Apollo* Hall, Louisville, and the *Armory* Hall, New Orleans, which bear a high reputation in this line, give the MASONIC Hall the preference, and indeed assert that if this last were furnished in the style of the Armory Hall, it would be unrivaled for concert exhibitions by any saloon they have seen in *London* itself.

I can furnish responsible names for this testimonial, and of persons who have traveled professionally through all the prixcipal places in the United States.

The Masonic Hall room it will be recollected, is 51 by 112 feet on the floor, and 23 feet in height.

Small Pox and Vaccination.

Rules and hints to the Physicians and the People.

1st. Vaccine matter should always be selected, and none taken except from perfectly healthy subjects.

2d. The longer the pustule continues after vaccination the more perfect the protection will be, and the better will be the matter to vaccinate others with.

3d. As a general rule, I would take no matter from any subject, to vaccinate others with, that had not passed at least fifteen days from the time of vaccination; I should never take matter from any patient that had broken the pustule, by scratching or any other means; nor if local inflammation had been caused by taking cold, or otherwise.

4th. The patient should be examined on the fourth day after vaccination. If there be any doubt as to its having taken effect, he should be vaccinated in the other arm. The patient should be examined also on the eighth or ninth day. If there be no fever, or other constitutional symptoms, such as soreness of the axiliary glands, &c. he should be vaccinated in the other arm. He should be seen again on the sixteenth day. If the pustule shall have become dry, and crust perfect, it should then be taken off, if it can be, if not, another examination on the 17th or 18th day will be necessary.

5th. If the pustule dries up, forming a scab, before the 15th day, I should consider it imperfect, and vaccinate the patient again. Because in many cases the vaccine disease is a mere local affection—and when it is so it can of course afford no protection against Small Pox. This local character is readily seen in the absence of fever on the eighth or ninth day, absence of soreness in the axillary glands, and in the short duration of the pustule.

6th. I recommend re-vaccination in all cases in which there is any doubt of its previous efficiency.

In such cases I never depend upon the appearance of the scab, nor the memory of the patient as to the soreness of the arm, &c., nor upon any other testimony than that of the Physician who vaccinated the patient the first time. If this be not satisfactory, according to the above rules, I re-vaccinate.

I have never seen a person that I *knew* had been perfectly vaccinated, take either vaccination a second time, or varioloid, or small pox.

The scar is not to be depended upon. It can only inform us that vaccination has been *attempted*—the pustule may have been scratched, or opened in some other way; a common sore may have left the scar. Non-medical people are not good judges as to the perfection of vaccination. I have in numerous instances produced the perfect vaccine disease in persons that showed good scars, and who said they had been well vaccinated, that their arms were "*very sore,*" &c. &c.

I was vaccinated in the fall of 1818. I have repeatedly, even an hundred times, vaccinated myself since—last fall, (1845) particularly, I vaccinated myself ten times—but it did not, in any one instance, take effect. When the Small Pox was so prevalent, in the years 1822, 1823, and 1824, I was constantly amongst it, often having an hundred or more patients at a time among the poor. I never had the slightest symptom of the disease.

I believe the present prevalence of Small Pox to be owing to inattention to patients after the insertion of the virus. The common price for vaccination ($1) is a mere nominal affair—it does not pay a physician for even three, to say nothing of *four* visits. Hence it is often the case that the Physician inserts the matter in the arm, and never sees the patient afterwards. The mere fact of the operation satisfies the patient and his friends. It may not have taken effect at all; it may have taken, but some accident destroyed its effect upon the constitution. And hence this great preventive of one of the most terrible scourges of the world is brought into disrepute. I do not believe that the preventive effects of *perfect* vaccination ever "wear out." My own experience is upwards of 27 years. From 1819 to 1822, inclusive, I vaccinated upwards of 33,000 persons. I have seen great numbers of them since, time and again, but have never found one that had taken Varioloid or Small Pox. But I have always been particular in the selection of matter to vaccinate with. I prefer that which has been on the arm full fifteen, and from that up to 17, 18, or even 20 days; and that from *full grown persons, when possible;* robust and healthy patients always; rejecting that from all others. I never take matter from doubtful sources.

I feel very certain, that, if these hints could be taken and acted upon by all our physicians and the people, the Small Pox would be completely extirpated in a month. I offer them with much diffidence, and certainly with due deference to the faculty.

GIDEON B. SMITH, M. D

An Indian Name.

One of the most beautiful and picturesque villages on Long-Island, has for many years been doomed to the infliction of the name of Oyster, or Clam Bay. The inhabitants have recently restored its ancient and euphonic Indian name of Syosset, and the Postmaster General has consented to the change.

Ninth Ward,--Cincinnati.

This is the region of Cincinnati which lies north of Sixth and east of Main streets; and as it embraces, north of the Miami Canal, the original German settlement in our city, it is pretty compactly built up—at least in its western sections. The public buildings of this ward are 14—in number as follows: the Woodward and St. Xavier Colleges; Court House and Public Offices adjacent; Jail; Engine Houses, on Sycamore and Webster streets; School House, on Franklin st.; German Reformed Church, on Webster street; Episcopal, on Pendleton; Methodist, on Webster; Roman Catholic, on Sycamore strees, and the Coloured Methodist, on New street.

The aggregate of buildings in the Ninth Ward is 1299; bricks 564, frames 733, stone 2.

Of these there were, at the close of 1842,

	Bricks.	Frames.	Total.
	352	633	985
Built in 1843,	81	34	115
" " 1844,	45	35	80
" " 1845,	86	31	117
	564	733	1297

The only part of the ward which admits of much future occupation with buildings, is the northeast corner, being the territory lying north of the Lebanon road and east of Broadway.

Chronological Table.

March 4th.—First meeting of Congress at New York City; Washington chosen President, 1789. Saladin, died, 1193.

5th.—Battle of Barossa, 1811. Dr. Parr, died, 1825.

6th.—Battle of Alamo, in which Col. Crocket was killed, 1836. Michael Angelo, born, 1475.

8th.—Raphael, born, 1483. William III, died, 1702.

9th.—David Rizzio, assassinated, 1566.

10th.—Death of Benjamin West, in London, 1820.

Irish Advantages.

"Recollect, Mr. Falcon, I positively wont go to Ireland unless the situation is permanent, and the country quiet." "Dublin is as safe as London, my dear," said Falcon; "indeed safer, if possible, for I am told it has lately been fortified. I know something about fortifications. When I was Deputy store-keeper at the Tower"—— "I don't like the idea of living in fortified places," replied the mother Falcon, not waiting for the close of this interesting chapter in her husband's life. "It's not pleasant to think of being besieged, sacked, and ransacked. I have heard of women being sacked; they do it in Turkey constantly, and throw them into the Phosphorous. I'm not a coward, I flatter myself I'm as stout as any woman, and I was never ashamed to own it; but I do not like to be *horse de combat*."—

"Indeed, mamma," said Emily, "Ireland is quite as safe a country to live in as England. Nobody is ever shot but a tyrannical landlord occasionally."—*The Falcon Family; or Young Ireland.*

To Readers.

The great extent to which emigration to Cincinnati prevails, serves to keep up scattering cases of small pox here. On this account, and for the benefit alike of medical men and their patients, I publish an article on vaccination, from the pen of Dr. Smith, an eminent physician of Baltimore, which embodies valuable testimony as well as advice on this important subject.

I consider it the most explicit and intelligent, as well as conclusive evidence in favour of the absolute security afforded by vaccination which has ever fallen under my notice.

Smart Boy.

A wealthy squire had a little son whose name was Tommy, and Tommy had a little drum. He one day lost his drumstick in a draw well, much to his mortification; but great as was his loss, he too well knew that no one would go to the bottom to recover his toy. So Tommy dropped a silver punch ladle into the well. The ladle was missed, and a hue and cry was raised. "I think," said Tommy, "I saw something shining down the well." The groom was ordered into a bucket to make a voyage of discovery, and was lowered to the bottom, where sure enough, he found the ladle. The handle was put in motion to raise him from the well, when Tommy, squeezing his head between the servants who clustered round the mouth, squeaked down to the groom, "Perhaps, while you are there, you'll get me my drum-stick!"

Period of Lives.

A boar rarely exceeds twenty years, yet we have known bores much older; lions are long lived—except the lion of the day; a squirrel or hare, seven or eight years—but gray hairs are often much older; rabbits seven.

Epicures live broad but not very long. Mules seldom die. The life of the sea-serpent is thought to be circular. The moon gets old every lunar month, and young as often. Methusaleh's gander is thought to be yet living. A boat at sea lives till it gets swamped. Clover, on prairie lands, generally dies out the second year. The horse radish, like the red horse, lives till it is killed. Human life is said to be but a *span*—which we presume means single and not married life. Men and things generally die when they can't live any longer.

A Pertinent Reply.

It is said a subject of the King of Prussia, a talented mechanic, being about to emigrate to America, was arrested and brought before his majesty.

"Well, my good friend," said the king, "how can we persuade you to remain in Prussia."

"Most gracious sire, only by making Prussia what America is."

He was allowed to emigrate.

CINCINNATI MISCELLANY.

CINCINNATI, MARCH, 1846.

Recollections of the last Sixty Years.—No. 10.

By Col. J. Johnston, *of Piqua.*

I was a member of the Harrisburg Convention, and in order to perform all the service I could to my old and honoured chief, and with a view of mixing with the middling and lower classes of the people as much as possible, I performed the whole journey, going and returning, on horseback, always stopping at the taverns frequented by wagoners, farmers, mechanics and working men. I thus had unrestrained access to the rank and file of the political army. I could tell them more about Old Tip, as they called him, than ever they had heard before. I had large audiences;—some times the bar-room could not contain the people; dozens would be pressing me to drink with them because I could tell them so many good things about Old Tip;—his popularity was unbounded: payment of my tavern bills were often refused because I was his friend and of the convention that was going to make him President, for from the day I set out for Harrisburg until the election was over, I never once doubted of his success: the evidence met me at every step of my journey. The last time that Gen. Harrison slept under my roof, was in the summer of 1840. He was expected in the town of Piqua in the evening. I went down to meet him, and for the purpose of bringing him home, that he might be quiet and refreshed with comfortable quarters, a good bed and sleep, all of which he greatly needed. He had reached the town, and was surrounded at Tuttle's hotel, with an immense crowd, so that it was some time before I could get near to him. The people were already making a platform of boxes in the street, to get him out to speak. He had rode near fifty miles the same day, and delivered three speeches. I asked if he had any refreshment since his arrival? None whatever. I ordered some tea, ham, and bread and butter, and after partaking, he was on the stand and spoke an hour. Col. Chambers took his place, and I slipped the General through the crowd to my house, three miles off. After supper we sat up late, talking about old times. He asked me how I got along since being turned out of the service by Gen. Jackson. I replied, as well as I could; that I had not wealth, but a competency; kept out of debt, and made the two

ends of the year meet. He said he could not do so well; and asked me, why did you not speculate and make a fortune, as other men did in the service? I told him he had always enjoined upon his subordinates, that we should never apply the money of the public to private purposes, and that he had always enforced this rule, both by precept and example; and in a pleasant mood observed—if there is any one to blame why I have not made a fortune, it is yourself. He laughed at my rejoinder. I must have handled from first to last, a million and a half of the public money, and I am very confident that I never applied one hundred dollars of that sum to private purposes, over and above my stated compensation. The practise of doing so was unknown to the service in those times. Governor Harrison would never touch the public money, but would always give drafts on the proper department, accompanying the bills and accounts rendered. If Providence had spared him he would have proved a blessing to the whole nation. Honest and without guile himself, he would, as far as lay in his power, make the public servants honest also.

Among the numerous persons who visited Gen. Harrison at my house, was the venerable Boyer, at that time eighty-seven years of age; beyond all dispute the last survivor of Washington's guard, for the original discharge I have seen and copied and could verify the same, as being in the proper hand writing of Col. Cobb, the aid-de-camp, and bearing the genuine signature of the commander-in-chief. The following notice of the death of this aged patriot soldier, was published at the time:—

From the Ohio State Journal.

Mr. Scott:—I will thank you to republish from the last Piqua Register, the obituary notice of the venerable Boyer, who died in my county (Miami,) on Saturday, the 23d ultimo. Many of your readers in this city will doubtless remember the iron frame and commanding person of the patriot whig soldier, who rode the white horse, with the war saddle equipments of Washington, in the great Whig Convention of 1840, carrying the banner inscribed—"the last of Washington's life guards."

He was my neighbour for more than thirty years past; an ardent, unwavering whig; and it was my purpose to have made the effort of taking him to Baltimore, as my colleague to the Whig National Convention, in May next. Death, which destroys all the hopes of man, has in this case, alas! disappointed me. My old friend—the friend, follower, and protector of Washington in many a well fought field, has gone to the grave full of years and full of honours. It will be seen by the date of his discharge, that he served to the latest period, the revolutionary army having been disbanded many months before.

JOHN JOHNSTON,
Of Piqua, Ohio.

Columbus, October 2, 1843.

From the Piqua Register, September 30.

DEATH OF A SOLDIER.

DIED—At his residence in this vicinity, on Saturday evening last, Lewis Boyer, a patriot of the revolution, aged eighty-seven years. As the highest testimony that could be offered of the fidelity with which he served his country in the dark hour of her severest trials, we publish the copy of his discharge from the American army at the close of the revolution. The original, to which is attached the name of the commander-in-chief, in his own hand-writing, was carefully preserved by the deceased until the day of his death; and has been kindly furnished by one of the family for the purpose of copying.

By His Excellency George Washington, Esq.,
General and Commander-in-Chief of the forces
of the United States of America:

The bearer, Lewis Boyer, private dragoon in the independent troop of horse, commanded by Major Van Herr, being enlisted for the war, and having served the term of his engagement, consented to continue in the service until the 31st day of December inst., from which date he is hereby discharged from the American army; and in consequence of his attention and fidelity, the commander-in-chief, being authorized by a resolution of Congress, presents him with the horse, arms and accoutrements now in his possession, as a gratuity.

Given at Philadelphia, this 10th day of December, 1783.

(Signed) GEORGE WASHINGTON.
By His Excellency's command,
(Signed) DAVID COBB, Aid-de-Camp.

The deceased had enjoyed remarkable health throughout his whole life. When taken ill he refused all medical aid; and stated that he had never at any time during his long life, " taken medicine," but nature, which had always been his physician, could no longer act efficiently. His time had come; the last enemy was before him; the courage of his youth sustained him;—

he died as he had lived, a true soldier. At his own request, made some time ago, he received a military burial. The Piqua Light Infantry, commanded by Col. Adams, and the Cavalry, under Capt. Barney, performed the solemn duty. The funeral was attended by two thousand persons.

A few more years and those brave hearts,
Once so faithful and so true,
Will all be cold in death. Those
Who linger yet a while,
As the last bough upon a tree,
Are sear and shrivelled as the autumn leaf. Their season has been a long and honourable one;—they, too, have one more battle to fight, after which may they have—
" Rest, eternal rest."

In this, my second communication for your paper, I have written more than intended in the beginning. The character and services of Gen. Harrison, is a theme which requires an abler pen than mine. It is delightful to hold up such a man to the example of his country. The paltry sum of $24,000 was grudged to his widow and children by the demagogues and mock patriots of the day; yet four times that sum, nor any sum of money, would be but a poor price for the legacy left to his country by a long life of high and holy patriotism; of unsullied integrity and honour in the discharge of the innumerable important public trusts committed to him in a period of forty years service.

By the conflagration of the establishments of the Indian department at Fort Wayne, by the Indians, last war, I lost nearly all my books and papers, and have to write altogether from memory. If spared life and health, you may expect further communications.

Your friend and ob't serv't,
JOHN JOHNSTON.
CHARLES CIST, ESQ.

Cotton Cloth.

It has always been matter of surprise to me that the Yankees, with their characteristic ingenuity, should not have contrived to manufacture, out of our great national staple, *Cotton*, an article superior to the woollen cloths which now constitute the winter's wear of the United States. There can be no question that cotton, woven thick and properly napped, is a warmer dress than can be made of wool, the thickness of the two being alike. This is both the philosophy and the fact in the case. Cotton is a better non conductor of heat than wool, as the *Canton flannel* of the stores serves to prove. It will doubtless be objected that cotton cloth cannot be made to receive as handsome a finish, or dye as perfect as the rival fabric; that it must always be exposed to stains and splashes, which will not brush out as in woolen cloth. Some of these difficulties have never been fairly tested and might be overcome. At any rate there can be little doubt that a thick, well napt, and warm cloth, might be made for those who desire an article to work in, which would not cost one fourth the price of woolen cloth, and be equally comfortable. The very fact of the sale and use of such an article would lower the price of woolen cloths in proportion to the extent to which the cotton cloths would be supplied for use.

The great amount of cassinets, Kentucky jeans and other mixtures of wool and cotton have superceded cloth of wool alone, is an encouragement to the experiment of what may be made of cotton entire.

Eastern Periodicals.

Few people are aware of the extent to which the cheap publications and periodical literature of the East, are supported in the great West. Some interesting details on the subject in the late "*Picture of Cincinnati*," shew the magnitude of contributions here on that score, so far as the books of the principal book and periodical depot in Cincinnati—that of Robinson & Jones—exhibit it.

Statement of the number of Foreign Periodicals disposed of by Robinson & Jones, during the year ending December 31st, 1845.

MAGAZINES AND PERIODICALS.

	Number.
Graham's Magazine, Philadelphia,	7,785
Godey's Lady's Book do,	4,828
Columbian Magazine, New York,	2,312
National do, Philadelpha,	4,425
Arthur's do, do,	1,250
Blackwood's Edinburgh Magazine,	665
London, Westminster, Foreign and Edinburgh Quarterly Reviews,	208
Democratic Review, New York,	180
American and Whig Review, New York,	208
Eclectic Magazine, Brownson's Reviews, &c.,	336
Littell's Living Age—weekly—Boston,	2,120
Medical Publications,	985
Ferrett's Musical Publications,	1,526
Total,	26,828

NEWSPAPERS.

	No. of copies.
Saturday Evening Post, Philadelphia,	2,600
Saturday Courier do,	3,900
Neal's Saturday Gazette, do,	3,000
Dollar Newspaper, do,	2,600
Bennett's Weekly Herald, New York,	4,500
New World, six months, do,	250
Broadway Journal, New Music, &c., do,	1,040
Old Countryman, do,	1,500
Miscellaneous,	800
Foreign Newspapers, including the Pictorial Times and News, Punch, Dublin Nation, Bell's Life in London, &c.,	5,200
Total,	25,390

Besides the depot of Robinson & Jones, there are several other agencies for periodicals; and a great many papers are received directly by subscribers through the mail.

Is it any wonder that we have been heretofore unable to maintain and extend the influence of western literature? And yet we have periodicals —*Mrs. Nichols' "Guest,"* published here—for instance—with which in moral elevation, poetical beauty, and strength of sound teaching, there is nothing at the East to compare.

The Hog Season of 1846.

The Pork Packing season being at an end, the returns of the putting up throughout the west are generally in. The following table furnishes a synopsis of these operations·

	1844.	1845.	1846.
Cincinnati,	240,000	173,000	287,000
Ohio at large,	214,200	149,900	225,600
Ohio,	454,200	322,900	512,600
Indiana,	183,200	119,300	162,600
Illinois and Missouri,	84,000	39,000	59,500
Kentucky and Tennessee,	102,000	75,000	140,500
Totals,	823,400	556,200	875,200

It will be seen that the general aggregate of 1846 does not much surpass that of 1844, the difference being but six per cent. An equal difference at least exists, however, in the quality and weight, the hogs of the present year being, as a body, the finest ever brought into market. This is owing to the vast increase of the corn production of the west, and the probability, since realised, that pork would bring good prices, inducing farmers to feed hogs, rather than supply distilleries. It must be recollected that the increase of this year has been effected to some extent, by the scarcity of corn in North Carolina and Virginia, which has prompted the drovers from Tennessee and southern Kentucky, to take their hogs to Louisville and Cincinnati. To this extent there was no actual increase of the pork market in the whole country, nor taking into view the late commercial changes in England, is there any probability that the price of pork can fall. On the contrary, it must undoubtedly rise.

Tenth Ward,--Cincinnati.

This ward comprehends that part of the city which lies between Main street and the line of the Miami Canal on Plum street, and between the same canal on the south and the northern Corporation Line. By the formation of this ward, which was taken, nearly a year since, from the Fifth and Seventh Wards, the Fifth has ceased to be what it has always heretofore been —an outside ward.

The public buildings of the Tenth Ward are 9—Cincinnati Orphan Asylum; the Methodist Protestant and German Reformed Churches, on Elm street, St. Mary's Catholic, German Methodist and German Reformed on Walnut and Thirteenth streets, German Lutheran, on Bremen st., School House, on Thirteenth street, and an Engine House.

The buildings of this ward are—bricks 485, frames 740. Total, 1225.

Of these there were, at the close of the year 1846—

	Bricks.	Frames.	Total.
	363	700	1063
Built in 1845,	122	40	162
	485	740	1225

This ward is hardly more than one half occupied with buildings, the residue serving as board-yards and burial grounds, and receptacles of temporary sheds, shops and stables.

Virginia; Its History and Antiquities.

This is a work of great interest and value. It is at once a *History* and a *Gazetteer*, the narrative being embellished and popularised, and the Gazetteer enlivened with a great variety of interesting revolutionary and pioneer adventures, as well as local facts, not usual in such books. This volume is one of a series of which "New York and New Jersey" and "Pennsylvania," have preceded it, and "Ohio" is proposed as the next. Mr. Howe, the indefatigable and accomplished author, has just left Cincinnati to explore the State for that purpose. I hazard nothing in asserting that the most interesting History of Ohio which has yet appeared will be the fruit of his labours, if individuals in each county who are qualified for the employment, will contribute the necessary local information to the great aggregate.

The plan of these series seems to be—a general outline history of the State from its first settlement, forms the first department; a miscellany, statistical and descriptive, makes up the second division: the last and most extensive section of the book is a delineation of the State by counties, illustrated by various narrative and pictorial sketches. This department is alphabeted. This volume is a rich treat to the antiquirian, for whom it has extracted much valuable fact and incident, a large share of which is to be found no where else; and the residue deriving additional value for being now arranged in the proper place for preservation and reference.

No expense seems to have been spared in getting up this publication, paper, typography and

binding, all being of the best description. Besides innumerable wood cuts of rare excellence, there are various steel engravings of equal merit, including a new map of Virginia.

Among these is a very fine whole length engraving of Washington, in his prime, in full regimentals, standing at his horse's head, from the original painting of Col. Trumbull, pronounced by the Marquis de la Fayette the only likeness competent to do justice to the personal appearance of that great man.

I shall make extracts from time to time for the Advertiser, which shall serve to give some idea of the design and character of this publication.

The Flatboatman of the West.

BY T. B. THORPE.

Occasionally may be seen on the Ohio and Mississippi rivers singularly hearty-looking men, that puzzle a stranger as to their history and age. Their forms always exhibit a powerful development of muscle and bone; their cheeks are prominent, and you would pronounce them men enjoying perfect health in middle life, were it not for their heads, which, if not bald, will be sparsely covered with steel-gray hair. Another peculiarity about this people is, that they have a singular knowledge of all the places on the river; every bar and bend is spoken of with precision and familiarity; every town is recollected before it was half as large as the present, or no town at all. Innumerable places are marked out where once was an Indian fight, or a rendesvous of robbers. The manner, the language, and the dress of these individuals are all characteristic of sterling common sense—the manner modest, yet full of self-reliance; the language strong and forcible, from superiority of mind rather than education; the dress studied for comfort, rather than fashion —on the whole, you become attached to them and court their society. The good humour, the frankness, the practical sense, the reminiscences, the powerful frame—all indicate a character, at the present day anomalous; and such indeed is the case, for your acquaintance will be one of the few remaining people now spoken of as the "last of the flatboat men."

Thirty years ago the navigation of the western waters was confined to this class of men; the obstacles presented to the pursuit in those swift-running and wayward waters had to be overcome by physical force alone; the navigator's arm grew strong as he guided his rude craft past the "snag" and "sawyer," or kept off the no less dreaded "bar." Besides all this, the deep forests that covered the river banks concealed the wily Indian, who gloated over the shedding of blood. The qualities of the frontier warrior associated themselves with the boatmen, while he would, when at home, drop both these characters in the cultivator of the soil. It is no wonder, then, that they were brave, hardy, and open-handed men: their whole lives were a round of manly excitement; they were hyperbolical in thought and in deed, when most natural, compared with any other class of men. Their bravery and chivalrous deeds were performed without a herald to proclaim them to the world—they were the mere incident of a border life, considered too common to outlive the time of a passing wonder. Obscurity has nearly obliterated the men, and their actions. A few of the former still exist, as if to justify their wonderful exploits, which now live almost exclusively as traditions.

Among the flatboatmen there were none that gained more notoriety than *Mike Fink*. His name is still remembered along the whole of the Ohio as a man who excelled his fellows in every thing,—particularly in his rifle-shot, which was acknowledged to be unsurpassed. Probably no man ever lived who could compete with Mike Fink in the latter accomplishment. Strong as Hercules, free from all nervous excitement, possessed of perfect health, and familiar with his weapon from childhood, he raised the rifle to his eye, and, having once taken sight, it was as firmly fixed as if buried in a rock. It was Mike's pride, and he rejoiced on all occasions where he could bring it into use, whether it was turned against the beast of prey or the more savage Indian; and in his day these last named were the common foe with whom Mike and his associates had to contend. On the occasion that we would particularly introduce Mike to the reader, he had bound himself for a while to the pursuits of trade, until a voyage from the head-waters of the Ohio, and down the Mississippi could be completed. Heretofore he had kept himself exclusively to the Ohio, but a liberal reward, and some curiosity, prompted him to extend his business character beyond his ordinary habits and inclinations. In accomplishment of this object, he was lolling carelessly over the big " sweep" that guided the " flat" on which he officiated; the current of the river bore the boat swiftly along, and made his labour light; his eye glanced around him, and he broke forth in ecstasies at what he saw and felt. If there is a river in the world that merits the name of beautiful, it is the Ohio, when its channel is

" Without o'erflowing, full."

The scenery is everywhere soft; there are no jutting rocks, no steep banks, no high hills; but the clear and swift current laves beautiful and unadulterated shores, that descend gradually to the water's edge. The foliage is rich and luxuriant, and its outlines in the water are no less distinct than when it is relieved against the sky. Interspersed along its route are islands, as beautiful as ever figured in poetry as the land of the fairies; enchanted spots indeed, that seem to sit so lightly on the water that you almost expect them, as you approach, to vanish into dreams. So late as when Mike Fink disturbed the solitudes of the Ohio with his rifle, the canoe of the Indian was hidden in the little recesses along the shore; they moved about in their frail barks like spirits; and clung, in spite of the constant encroachments of civilization, to the places which tradition had designated as the happy places of a favoured people.

Wild and uncultivated as Mike appeared, he loved nature, and had a soul that sometimes felt, while admiring it, an exalted enthusiasm. The Ohio was his favourite stream. From where it runs no stronger than a gentle rivulet, to where it mixes with the muddy Mississippi, Mike was as familiar with its meanderings as a child could be with those of a flower-garden. He could not help noticing with sorrow the desecrating hand of improvement as he passed along, and half soliloquizing, and half addressing his companions, he broke forth:—" I knew these parts afore a

squatter's axe had blazed a tree; 'twasn't them pulling a —— sweep to get a living; but pulling the trigger business. Those were times to see; a man might call himself lucky. What's the use of improvements? When did cutting down trees make deer more plenty? Who ever found wild buffalo or a brave Indian in a city? Where's the fun, the frolicking, the fighting? Gone! Gone! . The rifle wont make a man a living now—he must turn nigger and work. If forests continue to be used up, I may yet be smothered in the settlement. Boys, this 'ere life won't do. I'll stick to the broadhorn 'cordin' to contract; but once done with it, I'm off for a frolic. If the Choctaws or Cherokees on the Massassip don't give us a brush as we pass along, I shall grow as poor as a starved wolf in a pitfall. I must, to live peaceably, point my rifle at something more dangerous than varmint. Six months and no fight would spile me worse than a dead horse on a pararee."

Mike ceased speaking. The then beautiful village of Louisville appeared in sight; the labour of landing the boat occupied his attention—the bustle and confusion that followed such an incident ensued, and Mike was his own master by law until his employers ceased trafficking, and again required his services.

At the time we write of, there were a great many renegade Indians who lived about the settlements, and which is still the case in the extreme southwest. These Indians generally are the most degraded of their tribes—outcasts, who, for crime or dissipation, are no longer allowed to associate with their people; they live by hunting or stealing, and spend their precarious gains in intoxication. Among the throng that crowded on the flatboat on his arrival, were a number of these unfortunate beings; they were influenced by no other motives than that of loitering round in idle speculation at what was going on. Mike was attracted towards them at sight; and as he too was in the situation that is deemed most favourable to mischief, it struck him that it was a good opportunity to have a little sport at the Indians, expense. Without ceremony, he gave a terrific war whoop; and then mixing the language of the aborigines and his own together, he went on in savage fashion and bragged of his triumphs and victories on the war-path, with all the seeming earnestness of a real " brave." Nor were taunting words spared to exasperate the poor creatures, who, perfectly helpless, listened to the tales of their own greatness, and their own shame, until wound up to the highest pitch of impotent exasperation. Mike's companions joined in; thoughtless boys caught the spirit of the affair; and the Indians were goaded until they in turn made battle with their tongues. Then commenced a system of running against them, pulling off their blankets, together with a thousand other indignities; finally they made a precipitate retreat ashore, amid the hooting and jeering of an unfeeling crowd, who considered them poor devils destitute of feeling and humanity. Among this crowd of outcasts was a Cherokee, who bore the name of Proud Joe; what his real cognomen was, no one knew, for he was taciturn, haughty—and, in spite of his poverty and his manner of life won the name we have mentioned. His face was expressive of talent, but it was furrowed by the most terrible habits of drunkenness. That he was a superior Indian was admitted; and it was also understood that he was banished from his mountain home, his tribe being then numerous and powerful, for some great crime. He was always looked up to by his companions, and managed, however intoxicated he might be, to sustain a singularly proud bearing, which did not even depart from him while prostrated on the ground. Joe was filthy in his person and habits—in this respect he was behind his fellows; but one ornament of his person was attended to with a care which would have done honour to him if surrounded by his people, and in his native woods. Joe still wore with Indian dignity his scalp-lock; he ornamented it with taste, and cherished it, as report said, that some Indian messenger of vengeance might tear it from his head, as expiatory of his numerous crimes. Mike noticed this peculiarity, and reaching out his hand, plucked from it a hawk's feather, which was attached to the scalp-lock. The Indian glared horribly on Mike as he consummated the insult, snatched the feather from his hand, then shaking his clenched fist in the air, as if calling on Heaven for revenge, retreated with his friends. Mike saw that he had roused the savage's soul, and he marvelled wonderfully that so much resentment should be exhibited; and as an earnest to Proud Joe that the wrong he had done him should not rest unrevenged, he swore he would cut the scalp-lock off close to his head the first convenient opportunity he got, and then he thought no more about it.

The morning following the arrival of the boat at Louisville was occupied in making preparations to pursue the voyage down the river. Nearly every thing was completed, and Mike had taken his favourite place at the sweep, when looking up the river bank he beheld at some distance Joe and his companions, and perceived from their gesticulations that they were making him the subject of conversation.

Mike thought instantly of several ways in which he could show them altogether a fair fight, and then whip them with ease: he also reflected with what extreme satisfaction he would enter into the spirit of the arrangement, and other matters to him equally pleasing, when all the Indians disappeared, save Joe himself, who stood at times reviewing him in moody silence, and then staring round at passing objects. From the peculiarity of Joe's position to Mike, who was below him, his head and upper part of his body relieved boldly against the sky, and in one of his movements he brought his profile face to view. The prominent scalp-lock and its adornments seemed to be more striking than ever, and it again roused the pugnacity of Mike Fink: in an instant he raised his rifle, always loaded at his command, brought it to his eye, and, before he could be prevented, drew sight upon Proud Joe and fired. The ball whistled loud and shrill, and Joe, springing his whole length into the air, fell upon the ground. The cold-blooded murder was noticed by fifty persons at least, and there arose from the crowd an universal cry of horror and indignation at the bloody deed. Mike himself seemed to be much astonished, and in an instant reloaded his rifle, and as a number of white persons rushed towards the boat, Mike threw aside his coat, and, taking his powder horn between his teeth, leaped, rifle in hand, into the Ohio, and commenced swimming for the opposite shore. Some bold spirits determined Mike should not so easily escape, and jumping into the only skiff at command, pulled swiftly after him. Mike watched their movements until they came within a hundred yards of him, then turning in the water, he supported himself by his feet alone, and raised

his deadly rifle to his eye. Its muzzle, if it spoke hostilely, was as certain to send a messenger of death through one or more of his pursuers, as if it were lightning, and they knew it; dropping their oars and turning pale, they bid Mike not to fire. Mike waved his hand towards the little village of Louisville, and again pursued his way to the opposite shore.

The time consumed by the firing of Mike's rifle, the pursuit, and the abandonment of it, required less time than we have taken to give the details; and in that time, to the astonishment of the gaping crowd around Joe, they saw him rising with a bewildered air; a moment more and he recovered his senses and stood up—at his feet lay his scalp-lock! The ball had cut it clear from his head: the cord around the root of it, in which were placed feathers and other ornaments, held it together; the concussion had merely stunned its owner; farther, he had escaped all bodily harm! A cry of exultation rose at the last evidence of the skill of Mike Fink—the exhibition of a shot that established his claim, indisputable, to the eminence he ever afterwards held—the unrivaled marksman of all the flatboatmen of the western waters. Proud Joe had received many insults. He looked upon himself as a degraded, worthless being; and the ignominy heaped upon him he never, except by reply, resented: but this last insult was like seizing the lion by the mane, or a Roman senator by the beard—it roused the slumbering demon within, and made him again thirst to resent his wrongs with an intensity of emotion that can only be felt by an Indian. His eye glared upon the jeering crowd around like a fiend; his chest swelled and heaved until it seemed that he must suffocate. No one noticed this emotion. All were intent upon the exploit that had so singularly deprived Joe of his war-lock: and, smothering his wrath, he retreated to his associates with a consuming fire at his vitals. He was a different man from an hour before; and with that desperate resolution on which a man stakes his all, he swore by the Great Spirit of his forefathers that he would be revenged.

An hour after the disappearance of Joe, both he and Mike Fink were forgotten. The flatboat, which the latter had deserted, was got under way, and dashing through the rapids in the river opposite Louisville, wended on its course. As is customary when nights set in, the boat was securely fastened in some little bend or bay in the shore, where it remained until early morn.

Long before the sun had fairly risen, the boat was again pushed into the stream, and it passed through a valley presenting the greatest possible beauty and freshness of landscape the mind can conceive.

Mexican Ladies.

Management of their Dresses, &c.—The following clever sketch is from one of the letters of the correspondent of the London Times in the city of Mexico. The same thing which strikes this writer—the way the Mexican ladies manage their dresses in threading a cord—has often surprised us, and the manner which the women of the middle and lower classes of Mexico can dispose of themselves upon the floor at a fandango, or other merry-makings, is even more singular. We have seen a dozen of them seat themselves upon a space on the floor that would hardly afford standing-room for that number of females of any other land, and how they did it was a mystery. But this has nothing to do with the extract from the London Times, which is as follows.—*N. O. Pic.*

I have never gone to the theatre without being surprised at the talent with which a Mexican belle pilots her way through the avenues of chairs in her box to that particular seat which is reserved for her nightly use. Fashion having ordained that every body shall not wear less than from seven to eleven petticoats, all starched to the highest degree, and rendered more balloon-like by mainstays of canvass equally stiffened, it is impossible for her safely to pass through any space less than five yards wide. But as young ladies must slide between half a dozen chairs, not two feet apart, each is compelled to reduce that quart bottle of her dress to a pint decanter, and that without deranging the general symmetry or disturbing the flowing outline. She, therefore, leaving the upper part of her dress to swell to its greatest extent, attaches firmly both hands to that part below the knee, and thus clasping it fore and aft, she glides through the projecting rocks of the chairs in question like a cutter working its way through the narrow passage of a reef; with canvass ten times its bulk swelling in the breeze, with the graceful craft itself is scarcely seen until it reaches the desired point in safety. When the Mexican belle has secured her place, the volume of dress rises at each side to an immense extent. She sits in the midst of fleecy hosiery, covered with gauze, in clouds of vapory muslin, or many-coloured silks, like Mr. Green's Vauxhall balloon. We see only a face, shoulders and waist.

Bartlett's Commercial College.

Newspaper recommendations are fast becoming mere inscriptions on tomb-stones, so indiscriminate and so flattering are their notices. It is therefore probable that their testimony will soon be regarded of as little value. The subject and the writer of this notice will, however, I hope, be alike exempt from that system of puffing which recommends with equal energy every thing, from the shooting star of the theatre to the last patent itch ointment.

R. M. BARTLETT, who has not only reduced book-keeping to a scientific study, but has varied and adapted its details to every practical purpose in life, has been engaged in this pursuit for the last thirteen years, during which period he has qualified as many hundred individuals, by the rigid and efficient discipline of his college, not only to open and keep a set of books for the most extensive mercantile houses in our country, but to take charge, without embarrassment, of any set of books already in existence, and carry them out upon whatever principles they may be kept. All business men will understand the value and rarity of the last qualification. So general is the complaint that book-keeping, as taught in schools, does not fit the pupil for applying his knowledge to the set of books placed in his hands, and the business which he is called to register on their pages, that I must confess my own convictions as an accountant have hitherto been,

that such preparation is of little value in qualifying an individual for a counting-room in our business regions. I have been induced to change my views on this subject, however, not more from a rigid examination of the system and practice in his college rooms, than by the uniform and explicit testimony of a large share of the book-keepers in our principal houses, who have been trained to their business by Mr. Bartlett himself, and who, of course, are conclusive witnesses on the subject. The testimony of such persons is explicit to the value for practical purposes of Mr. Bartlett's system of instruction.

The system of Mr. B. is both analytical and synthetical. It is the taking to pieces, as a study, a complicated but exact machine, to contemplate and learn the relation of the several parts to each other and to the machine, and the putting it together to make it operate accurately, and without embarrassment. With this view the student is required to give a reason for every thing he does, to take up an every day transaction and put it through the books to its final close, to shew why one given entry is accurate or any other one incorrect, in short under the severest drilling to render it apparent that he has mastered the theory of book-keeping, as well as reduced it to practice.

The *Diploma* which Mr. Bartlett furnishes his pupils, who have finished a regular course, is one of the finest specimens of design and engraving that has ever fallen under my notice. It was executed at the establishment of *Rawdon, Wright & Hatch*, in our city, and is a credit to Cincinnati.

I regard this establishment, which numbers in its pupils young men from every district of country in the west, and which has supplied book-keepers not only to this region, as well as the south and southwest, but even prepared them for Boston, New York, and Philadelphia counting-rooms, as one of a number of public institutions, giving a high reputation abroad to Cincinnati.

Yankee Financiering.--A True Story.

A farmer "Down East," (a possessor of a voracious appetite) took with him to a neighbouring town, to market, a fine fat *turkey*. A tavern-keeper espying it, inquired of him *his price.*

"Wall," said the Yankee farmer, "if you would like *to buy*, I will let you have it for one dollar *in cash*,—with the understanding that I am to have a dinner from the turkey besides."

The tavern-keeper, unconscious of the farmer's *devouring abilities*, finally accepted the proposition.

When the dinner-hour arrived, in walked the farmer, and seated himself at the table, upon which was *steaming* the turkey, cooked in fine style, and all the *et ceteras.*

All preliminaries having been *dispensed with,* the Yankee immediately commenced operations. Down went one leg of the turkey, succeeded by a wing, another leg and wing, and so on, until all (*minus bones*) followed in their course. The company present looked first at the farmer and turkey, and then at each other, wondering *where* would be the limits of his appetite,—when up jumped the Yankee, having finished his dinner *and the turkey*, leaving his astonished companions to reconcile themselves as they best could to their deprivation.

Off went the Yankee farmer with his *one dollar in cash, turkey, dressing, and all*, doubtless feeling assured that he had *satisfactorily disposed of* a portion of his marketing.

Rail-Road Anecdote.

One day last week while a train of cars on the Little Miami Rail-Road, stopped at the depot at Waynesville, a fellow, who had never seen the like before, stepped on the locomotive, which for the time being had been dislocated from the cars, and being curious to know and see every thing about it, happened to place his hands on a screw, which he turned, and in an instant the locomotive started off in full speed, with the fellow upon it, hallooing and bellowing at the pitch of his voice to stop the *tarnation thing*, while at the same time he would pray to God to have mercy upon him. The locomotive ran about seven miles, when, by accident, it left the track and stopped, without any material injury, either to the unfortunate passenger or locomotive.—*Germantown Gazette.*

Chronological Table.

March 11th.—Birth of Tasso, 1544. Emperor Napoleon married the Archduchess of Austria, 1810.

12th.—British garrison, at Mobile, surrendered to the Spaniards, 1780.

13th.—Sir John Herschel discovered a new planet, which he named Georgium Sidus, 1781. Dr. Priestly, born, 1738.

14th.—Klopstock, died, 1803.

15th.—Andrew Jackson, born, 1767.

16th.—Gustavus III., King of Sweden, assassinated, 1792. Battle of Culloden, 1746.

17th.—St. Patrick, Tutelary Saint of Ireland, died at Ulster, 493. Gen. Washington marched into Boston after it had been evacuated by the British, 1776.

The Cantatrice and the Empress.

The arrival of the, for a time, " great attraction," Gabrielli the *cantatrice*, at the Russian capital, made a sensation of course, at the Court of Catharine.

" What are we to do for this young beauty?" said the Empress, who comes from Naples expressly for us; or rather my child, speak—what terms do you expect for your engagement at our court?

" Madame," Gabrielli replied, " I perceive that I shall be at a considerable expense for furs this winter, and I am poor. Shall I ask too much if I ask of your majesty 20,000 rubles?"

At this demand the brow of the Empress lowered, a slight flash was visible on her cheek, and her eyes glittered—but it was only for a moment. Nevertheless, (continues Gabrielli,) I was afraid,

and I regretted my words; but, woman like, I would not for the world have withdrawn them in the presence of the young officer, who was then gazing on me with such interest.

" Twenty thousand rubles!" exclaimed Catherine. " Do you know what you ask, child? For twenty thousand rubles I can have two field-marshals!"

" In that case, perhaps, your majesty will engage two field-marshals that can sing," I replied, in the most deliberate manner imaginable. I do not know what possessed me—it must have been some evil spirit, for as I uttered the words I saw my fate balancing between Siberia and the Hermitage. But my good fortune saved me.

" You are bold, young woman," said the Empress; and then quickly resuming the pleasant smile with which she first greeted me; " but go," she said, " go, and consider yourself as *two field-marshals*.

Married Life.

Most young men associate the idea of great expense and the necessary income to meet it, with married life. But it might easily be shewn, that a young man, a clerk on a salary, for example, could support a wife on what it cost him to live. I know of cases where men recently married have actually paid out less than while they were single. As a family enlarges, other expenses doubtless increase, but the industry and economy which a judicious, prudent wife would stimulate will always provide on that score.

The March of Science.

What next?—The Miners' Journal, printed at Pottsville, Pa., says—" We have written on paper manufactured from iron, and seen a book whose leaves and binding are both of the same material."

Truly the mechanical and chemical transformations of the present age throw into the shade all the magic of the east—ancient and modern.

Thunder and Lightning.

A fellow was lately swigging at the bung-hole of a gallon jug, with all the ardour of one who really loved its contents. The jug, in reply to his drafts, went *clug, clug, clug*,—on which an anxious expectant, standing by, remarked:— " Jim, you'd better stop; don't you hear the thunder?" " No," replied Jim, " but I perceive the jug begins to *lighten.*"

Good Credit.

The members of a certain society having become somewhat remiss in their attendance, it was proposed to pay their debts, and dissolve the concern. " Pay our debts, indeed!" said a wag, " let us adjourn now, while we can do so with *credit.*"

Buildings for 1845---Cincinnati.

I have now completed the enumeration of the buildings in this city—by wards, during 1845, as follows:—

	Bricks.	Frames.	Total.
First,	35	75	110
Second,	86	11	97
Third,	50	65	115
Fourth,	56	35	91
Fifth,	45	10	55
Sixth,	118	22	140
Seventh,	101	76	177
Eighth,	88	100	188
Ninth,	86	31	117
Tenth,	122	40	162
	789	463	1252

The buildings for 1844, were 1225. Those for 1843, were 1003. The advance of 1845 over 1844 in the number of buildings has not progressed at the same rate as that of the previous year; but is much greater, if we refer to the character of the buildings. I have no doubt that 10,000,000 more bricks have been used in this year's erections. The public buildings alone, put up this year, have consumed as many bricks as would have sufficed to put up one hundred and fifty private dwellings of the usual size.

The total number of buildings in this city, exclusive of frame stables and out-buildings of every description, is 11,560.

I propose to furnish a comparative table of buildings of such of the various cities as have put their improvements on record—and commence with—

	Population	Buildings in 1845	Improvement—per ct.
Cincinnati,	85,000	1252	15
Washington, D. C.,	33,000	336	10
Columbus (Ohio),	10,016	202	20

Capture of John Andre.

One of them ost remarkable episodes of the American revolution, and threatening if successful, most disastrous consequences to the issue of that great event, was the treasonable plot of *Benedict Arnold* to deliver West Point, together with the person of the commander-in-chief, if possible, into the hands of the British forces. That incident teaches a valuable lesson in morals and politics, and has consigned the name of the great traitor to a signal and unenviable pinnacle of infamy.

Connected with the treason and defection to the enemy, of Gen. Arnold, is recorded the romantic history of the brave and unfortunate *Andre*, whose life paid the penalty of the enterprise, on its failure.

It is not with the view of furnishing a general history of what is already on record as facts, that the following narrative is prepared for the press, but for the correction of various important errors in the statement of Andre's apprehension, by the three militiamen, *Paulding, Williams* and *Van Wert.* I derive the information from Mr. John Hudson, whose narrative of the capture of Cornwallis, has lately appeared in the "Advertiser." Mr. H. was for many years of his life a resident in the immediate neighbourhood where the events occurred, and was personally acquainted with all three of the captors, from whose lips he had the statements he makes. I shall give the narrative in his own language.

"I have conversed with these men, being a resident of the neighbourhood where they dwelt, and was well acquainted with Paulding and Van Wert. Williams was a small man, in middle life, and I did not know so much of him as of the rest. Van Wert was a shoemaker by trade, and a large athletic man. Paulding was tall, well built, of a commanding figure; and at the period of these events, in the twenty-second year of his age. He had been left an orphan, and was brought up by his grandfather, an independent farmer, who resided within four miles of Tarrytown.

"*Col. Delancey,* at the head of the refugees and tories, had been engaged scouring that part of the State, seizing the persons of those who were considered well affected to the cause of liberty, and taking them on to New York City, where they were consigned to the custody of the provost marshal, Cunningham—an absolute antechamber to the grave. Hundreds fell victims to the barbarities of the enemy, and numbers, to escape that treatment, enlisted in their service; generally with the design of deserting at the first favourable opportunity. Paulding fell into these men's hands, and like others, enlisted, as the only means offering an escape with life. He soon afterwards, in the dress, and with the arms and accoutrements of a British soldier, deserted accordingly and returned home, where he was appointed a corporal of militia; and having Van Wert and Williams assigned him as a patrol, was occupied scouting over the neutral ground—so called because between the lines of both armies, although occupied by neither. Within this territory, parties of militia on the one side, and tories on the other, were constantly on the alert and look-out for the benefit of their respective sides. The neutral ground comprehended the country between Spikenduyvel creek and Croton river.

"On the hill just above Tarrytown, is level, table land, to a considerable extent. The post-road from New York to Albany, crossed the elevation, and the *White Plains* road entered it here, nearly at right angles; a few rods south stood a poplar or tulip tree, the most remarkable one I have ever seen, although I have since seen thousands in the west, and many of great magnitude. The trunk was smooth and round, as generally is the case with that description of tree. It was at least six feet through, and extended forty to fifty feet without a limb; and what is unusual with the poplar, the branches spread out to a great length, forming the greatest extent of shade which I have ever seen to any tree. This I suppose was owing to its standing alone; no other tree being within a considerable distance of it.

" Under the shade of this tree, these three men —Paulding, Williams and Van Wert—were playing cards, their guns resting against its trunk. Andre, as soon as his return by water by the Vulture had been cut off, it seems had been directed by Arnold, a circuitous route which took him into the White Plains road, and thence into the post-road to N. York, as I have already stated, a few rods north of this tree. As he approached the party, observing Paulding in the dress and with the accoutrements of a British soldier,he very naturally concluded he belonged to his own side. He rode up accordingly and accosted the party— ' My lads, am I past all the rebel guards.' From the fact of his being Adjutant General to the troops, the person of Andre was perfectly known to every soldier in the British lines, and Paulding, of course, recognised him at once. He rose up therefore, approached Andre as if to address him, and seizing the horse by the bridle, ordered the rider to dismount. Andre promptly produced his pass signed by General Arnold, as bearer of a flag of truce. Paulding's judgment led him to think it highly improbable that a man of Andre's rank would be employed in that capacity, and appearing to hesitate as to what he ought to do, Major Andre proposed to him that he should dispatch one of his men with a letter to Arnold, which being assented to, he sat down and wrote, sending it off by Williams, on Andre's own horse. As soon as he was gone, Andre began to tamper with the others, offering his watch and purse of gold, and rising in his offers to them as they refused them; and finally making such promises if they would escort him into the British lines as convinced Paulding that there was something wrong in the case, and probably of great importance to the American interests to detect. He accordingly proceeded to search his prisoner, and drawing off his boots, found a variety of papers, which disclosed the whole transaction, as well as Arnold's connection with it. Among these were a plan of West Point, minute returns of the forces, ordnance and defences of that post, with critical remarks on the works. His captors then took him to *Sing Sing*, where there was a ferry kept by one *Jerry Stuyvers.* There they crossed to the west side of the Hudson and proceeded down to *Tappan*, where the main body of the American troops were encamped. *Gen. Washington* was absent at the time, but arrived in a few minutes. The rest is on the page of history.

" So near had Andre effected his return to the British lines, that the Vulture sloop of war, was in sight of Paulding's party at the time of Andre's capture, waiting only the proper signal to send off a boat to the shore. He suffered as a spy on the 2d October, 1780.

" The poplar tree I have alluded to was in the centre of the road, and from these circumstances became an object of such notoriety that stage passengers made it a constant practice to chip or cut off pieces of it as mementos. Many years afterwards it was struck by lightning so severely as not only to split it open, but to tear it absolutely out of root."

It will be readily comprehended by the foregoing narrative, that it was the British uniform of Paulding which led Andre into the mistake which cost him his life; and a reason is now furnished for his conduct on that occasion, which serves to explain what was heretofore unaccounted for— his neglect to produce his pass from Arnold, at once.

The main Chance.

The Pennsylvania Germans are a people, who by keeping their eye on the main chance, between earning and saving, have generally become rich, because always independent of pressure for money. It is curious to observe the operation of the money saving principle in these people.

A wealthy German from Eastern Pennsylvania, named Z——, purchased the village of Harmonie, on the road from Pittsburgh to Erie, after Rapp and his associates who had built it, left for the Wabash. Although a keen, sagacious business man, he could hardly read, and his writing extended no farther than to sign his name; but having had one of his sons qualified in these accomplishments so far as to keep his accounts by single entry, he devolved that business on him.

One day the old man being absent from home, a man named *Musselman* in his employ and family, while engaged in raising a barn, fell with a heavy piece of timber across him, which broke his leg, as well as inflicted other injuries. As soon as the poor fellow was brought home on a litter it was suggested to Mrs. Z., that a physician should be sent for. "Dat's drue," remarked the provident lady—"Ape"—her son Abraham—"you look off the pook unt see if dere's any ting gumin to *Musselman.*" *Ape* accordingly examined the account and found it unposted, and after hunting up all the charges and credits for six months, out of a day-book which contained the original entries of accounts with three hundred persons, at least, it was ascertained finally, that there were some three dollars due the sufferer, who was lying unattended to all this time. "Well," exclaimed Mrs. Z, addressing a younger son, "Sam, you run for the toctor unt dell him to gum to Musselman, unt tont forket to dell him we wont bay more dan is on de pooks."

I have been reminded of the above incident by the article in another column—"The Lost Boy" —taken from a correspondent to the *Morning Herald* of our city.

Patrick Henry.

Many years ago, I was at the trial, in one of our district courts, of a man charged with murder. The case was briefly this:—the prisoner had gone, in execution of his office as a constable, to arrest a slave who had been guilty of some misconduct and bring him to justice. Expecting opposition in the business, the constable took several men with him; some of them armed. They found the slave on the plantation of his master, within view of the house, and proceeded to seize and bind him. His mistress seeing his arrest, came down and remonstrated vehemently against it. Finding her efforts unavailing, she went off to a barn where her husband was, who was presently perceived running briskly to the house. It was known he had always kept a loaded rifle over his door. The constable now desired his company to remain where they were, taking care to keep the slave in custody, while he himself would go to the house to prevent mischief. He accordingly ran toward the house. When he arrived within a short distance of it, the master appeared coming out of his door with his rifle in his hand. Some witnesses said as he came to the door he drew the cock of the piece, and was seen in the act of raising it in the position of firing. But upon these points there was not an entire agreement of evidence. The constable, standing near a small building in the yard at this instant, fired, and the fire had a fatal effect. No previous malice was proved against him, and his plea upon trial was that he had taken the life of his assailant in necessary self-defence.

A great mass of testimony was delivered. This was commented upon with considerable ability by the lawyer for the commonwealth, and by another lawyer engaged by the friends of the deceased for the prosecution. The prisoner was also defended in elaborate speeches by two re spectable advocates. These proceedings brought the day to a close. The general whisper through a crowded house was that the man was guilty, and could not be saved.

About dark, candles were brought in, and Henry arose. His manner was exactly that which the *British* Spy described with so much felicity; plain, simple and unassuming. "Gentlemen of the jury," said he, " I dare say we have all been very much fatigued with this tedious trial. The

prisoner at the bar has been well defended already, but it is my duty to offer you some further observations in behalf of this unfortunate man. I shall aim at brevity. But should I take up more of your time than you expect, I hope you will hear me with patience, when you consider *that* BLOOD IS CONCERNED."

I cannot admit the possibility that any one who never heard Henry speak should be made fully to conceive the force of the impression which he gave these few words, " *blood is concerned.*" I had been on my feet through the day, pushed about in the crowd, and was excessively weary. I was strongly of opinion, too, notwithstanding all the previous defensive pleadings, that the prisoner was guilty of murder; and I felt anxious to know how the matter would terminate. Yet when Henry had uttered these words, my feelings underwent an instantaneous change; I found every thing within me answering at once, yes, since blood is concerned, in the name of all that is righteous, go on—we will hear you with patience till morning's sun. This bowing of the the soul must have been universal; for the profoundest silence reigned, as if every breath had been suspended. The spell of the magician was upon us, and we stood like statues around him. Under the touch of his genius every particular of the story assumed a new aspect, and his cause became continually more bright and promising. At length he arrived at the fatal act itself. " You have been told, gentlemen, that the prisoner was bound by every obligation to avoid the supposed necessity of firing by leaping behind a house, near which he stood that moment. Had he been attacked with a club, or with stones, the argument would have been unanswerable, and I should feel myself compelled to give up the defence in despair. But surely I need not tell you, gentlemen, how wide is the difference between sticks or stones, and a double triggered *loaded rifle cocked at your breast?*" The effect of this terrific image, exhibited in this great orator's peerless manner, cannot be described. I dare not attempt to delineate the paroxysm of emotion which it excited in every heart. The result was, that the prisoner was acquitted; with the perfect approbation, I believe, of the numerous assembly who attended the trial. What was it that gave such transcendent force to the eqoquence of Henry? His reasoning powers were good; but they have been equalled, more than equalled, by those of other men. His imagination was exceedingly quick, and commanded all the stores of nature as materials for illustrating his subject. His voice and delivery were inexpressibly happy. But his most irresistible charm was the vivid feeling of his cause with which he spoke. Such feeling infallibly communicates itself to the breast of the hearer.—*Howe's Virginia.*

The Lost Boy.

Mr. Editor:—Under the head of " The Lost Child," in your paper of the 28th ult., you relate a story which brought to my recollection a circumstance which occurred many years ago in Orange county, New York; and I do not think the affair was ever made a matter of newspaper notoriety. If you think it is worth its room in your paper, I will give you the story as it was related to me, more than thirty years ago, by the friends and neighbours of the parties. Philip D. in early life was poor, but robust and industrious; consequently he was thrifty. His motto was, "to make every thing count." He used to say, (by the bye he was a Dutchman,) "When I can kit a tollar a tay, I takes it, and when I can kit put a shilling a tay, I takes tat. I lose no time." After he had accumulated some property, he cast about for a help-mate. He ultimately married Elizabeth W., an Irish girl, of a very respectable family; though not rich in this world's goods—Elizabeth had, however, obtained (there was reason to believe) a " better inheritance." Through their united efforts, they became wealthy, and raised a family. The number of daughters I do not now remember, but they raised three sons, viz: Jacob, Joseph and Philip. I would here premise, that Mr. D. was rather singular in his composition—as an instance or two will go to establish. He thought his wife, whom he used to called " Lish," was one of the best women in the world—and I believe other people thought so too. Well, on a certain occasion Mrs. D. was taken violently ill. Dr. M. of M———, was sent for, and after administering to, and prescribing for Mrs. D., when he was about to leave, Mr. D. accosted him with, " Well toctor, I wants you to too the pest you can for Lish, for I would rather lose the best horse I've cot, as to lose her." On another occasion, he was taken very ill himself. Dr. M. was sent for in the evening—administered to, and prescribed for him, and left. In the morning the Dr. called again, and found Mr. D. lying on his back, with his eyes closed; and stepping up softly, and taking him by the hand, enquires—" How do you feel this morning Mr. D?" The patient was speechless. The Dr. repeats the enquiry, in an elevated tone,—" Mr. D. how do you feel this morning?" The patient felt his risibles, and in a peevish tone, cries out to his wife—" Lish, wy tont you schpeke, and tell te toctor? You know *I* can't schpeke?"

Well, in the fulness of time, when young Philip was full ten years old, he came up missing one evening. An enquiry was set on foot. No body had seen him since early in the evening. A search was made through the house, the barn, the out-houses, and even the farm—no Philip. The neighbours were alarmed, and the news spread far and wide, " Young Philip is lost." The consternation became general. He is certainly destroyed by the wolves, (for at that time, wolves often made incursions into the settlement from the "Shawangunk" mountains, and destroyed the sheep, calves, &c.) The neighbours —some fifty or sixty of them were out—and kept up the hunt with dogs and horns, until all hope was at an end, and it was given up, that Philip was lost. The neighbours, between midnight and day, sorrowingly returned to their homes, and the family sat down in the family room, to mourn over their loss; the almost broken hearted mother seated in one corner of the room, giving vent to her grief for the loss of her youngest child. Mr. D. stood petrified—he could not shed tears, nor could he bear the sight of his " Lish taking on so." He at length took his seat beside her, for the purpose of consoling her, and laying his hand on her knee, exclaimed " vell my tear Lish, ve has got one more *farm* as ve has got sons now!" That you know was consoling.

Well, at long and last, the family made preparation for bed, when, on pulling out the trundle bed from under the old family concern, lo, and behold! young Philip safe and snug, sound asleep in his usual place of repose, and totally uncon-

scious of the affliction he had brought on his family and friends.

I was acquainted with him when he was a young man, and I never met with Philip D., but I thought of the " Lost Boy."

Yours, &c., R. S.

Frankfort, Ross Co., Feb. 6th, 1846.

Anecdotes.

The following *naive* lover's promise was offered as an irresistible temptation to a filially given inamorata:—"1 like you," sighed the girl to her suitor, " but I can't leave home. I'm a widow's only darling; no husband can ever *equal* my parent in kindness." " She is kind," pleaded the wooer, " but be my wife, we will all live together, and see if I don't *beat your mother.*"

A Bristol bride, whose French was "somewhat of the oddest," after listening to her intended's various schemes for the honey moon tour, said modestly, " I don't care where we go in reason, Mr. Hadams, honly let us avoid *Hecla!*"

A Yorkshire lad, who had lately gone to service, having had salad served up for dinner every day for a week, ran away; and when asked why he had left his place, he replied:

" They made me yeat grass i'th summer, and I wur afraid they'd make me eat hay i'th winter —and I could not stand that, so I wur off."

Our Markets.

Some idea of the extent and character of the delicacies we enjoy in Cincinnati, may be inferred from the following list of marketing, brought in by one person alone, who supplies the city from the counties of Jay and Randolph, Indiana.

74 Deer—entire carcasses.

270 Deer Saddles.

172 Opossums.

4300 Rabbits.

483 Squirrels.

2290 Pheasants.

10100 Partridges, or Quails.

90 Wild Turkeys.

340 small Birds.

6 *Coons.*

These were all sold in our market within the first of December and twentieth of February last. They were brought in by *Mr. Charles Comfort,* from whose lips the statement is given.

I suggest to the Ohio Legislature, at its next session, to alter the name of *Comfort* to that of *Luxury.* He well deserves the change.

During the same period there have been sold 2500 cans Baltimore oysters—equal to 1800 bushels and 1500 bbls. oysters with the shell, brought up from New Orleans and across the mountains.

It is not only in the abundance and quality of our table enjoyments, but in their price—bringing them within the reach of all classes, that the subject may be refered to. The venison has not averaged higher per pound than four to five cts.; Rabbits, ten to twelve cents each; Squirrels, fifty to sixty cents per dozen; Wild Turkeys, seventy-five cents each; Partridges, sixty to seventy-five cents; and Pheasants one dollar fifty cents to two dollars per dozen.

Oysters are of course higher for family use than in Philadelphia or Baltimore. But they can be purchased at eating houses for refreshment, as cheaply as at those places.

Hide your diminished heads, ye New York and Philadelphia epicures!

The Faculty.

It detracts greatly from the specimens of various good things in the shape of anecdotes, that we are often led to doubt whether they are "founded on facts." For the following, which is peculiarly rich, I hold myself responsible.

Professor Miller, in his valedictory to the late medical class graduating at the Louisville Medical College, advised the newly manufactured doctors to go and settle where they were not known! Was this simplicity or archness?

Our own Artists.

One of our Cincinnati Artists, under the direction of Mr. Charles A. Jewett, has lately furnished a fine *Mezzotint* of Bishop Hamline of the Methodist Episcopal Church. This is the first mezzotint ever engraved in Cincinnati, and will compare favourably with the efforts of practised engravers at the east. Specimens may be seen at Mr. Jewett's office, on Third street, opposite the Mayor's office.

Those who want work of this kind hereafter, will find competent artists at home to execute it.

CORRESPONDENCE.

The late Gen. Harrison.

Mr. C. Cist,—*Sir:*

In the summer of 1791, William H. Harrison was in the City of Philadelphia, pursuing the study of medicine under the direction of Doctor Rush; where he formed a determination to abandon the study of his profession, and join the army. To accomplish his purpose, he made known his determination to his friends, Robert Morris and Thomas Willing, one of whom was his guardian, he being then a minor; and requested them to apply to the President for a commission. They attempted to dissuade him from his purpose; but finding that to be impossible, they waited on the President, who told them that there was no appointment at his disposal, worthy of the acceptance of Mr. Harrison—that he could not offer him any thing above an ensigncy.

They reported the result of their application, under a hope that he would decline it, and they advised him to do so. His reply was:—Gentlemen, it is all I want.

The result was made known to the President,

who immediately gave him the commission of an ensign, and he started forthwith for Cincinnati. The date of the commission is not known to me, but on the 31st of October, the President reported to the Senate, that he *had* appointed Wm. H. Harrison an ensign in the army, vice Thompson promoted. Of course his mind was decided, and he had entered the service before the unfortunate battle of General St. Clair was fought, which was on the 4th of November, after his appointment.

General Wayne was appointed to command the army in April, 1792. He spent the principal part of the next summer at Pittsburgh. The following winter—1792-3—he was at Legionville, and did not proceed to Cincinnati till late in the summer of 1793.   J. BURNET.

Cincinnati, March 13th, 1846.

Chronological Table.

March 18th.—James Madison, born, 1751. Horne Tooke, died, 1812.

19th.—The first eclipse of the moon of which we have any record was observed on this day, 720 B. C.

20th.—Sir Isaac Newton, died, 1727.

21st.—Duc D' Enghien, shot, 1804.

22d.—Goethe, died, 1832.

25th.—Queen Elizabeth, died, 1603.

A Mistake.

It was thought a few years since that Charles Carroll, of Carrollton, was the last of the signers to the Declaration of Independence. This must be a mistake. A late Vicksburgh Intelligencer, says—" The signers to the Declaration of Independence are on board a flatboat at the foot of Jackson street. Visit them—they are worth seeing."

A Hard Witness.

Ordinarily, a lawyer has the advantage of a witness in the "colloquies at court." Sometimes, as in the following case, the lawyer fares second best:

Everybody in Philadelphia and out of Philadelphia, we believe, knows or has heard of Gottlieb Scherer, a tall, robust, well-formed German, with a small twinkling eye, and a *look* that tells you quite as distinctly as language, that he "knows a thing or two." Being called upon the stand as a witness on one occasion, he was catechised rather severely by (so the story goes) Mr. Dallas, who expected to make out a strong point by eliciting something from the following questions:—

" Were you at Harrisburg, Mr. Scherer, in December?"

"At Harrisburg in December, did you say, Mr. Dallas?"

" Yes, sir, I said at Harrisburg in December."

Putting his head down thoughtfully for a moment, he replied, " No, sir, I was not."

" Were you at Harrisburg in *January*, Mr. Scherer?"

"At Harrisburg in *January*, did you say, Mr. Dallas?"

" Yes, sir, I said at Harrisburg in January.

Relapsing into a thoughtful mood for a moment—" No, sir, I was not at Harrisburg in January."

" Well, Mr. Scherer, were you at Harrisburg in *February?*"

" Did you say at Harrisburg in February, Mr. Dallas?"

" Yes, sir,—answer me if you please—I said at Harrisburg in February."

Studying for a moment or two, as before— " No, sir, I was not at Harrisburg in February."

Getting somewhat out of patience with him, Mr. D., elevating his tone, demanded—"At *what time*, then, sir, *were* you at Harrisburg?"

" At Harrisburg? at Harrisburg, Mr. Dallas? —*I never was at Harrisburg in my life, sir?*"

Of course the Court adjourned instanter.

The Flatboatman of the West.---No 2.

BY T. B. THORPE.

It was spring, and a thousand tints of green developed themselves in the half-formed foliage and bursting buds. The beautiful mallard skimmed across the water, ignorant of the danger of the white man's approach; the splendid spoon-bill decked the shallow places near the shore, while myriads of singing birds filled the air with their unwritten songs. In the far reaches down the river, there occasionally might be seen a bear stepping along the ground as if dainty of its feet, and, snuffing the intruder on his wild home, he would retreat into the woods. To enliven all this, and give the picture the look of humanity, there might also be seen, struggling with the floating mists, a column of blue smoke, that came from a fire built on a projecting point of land, around which the current swept rapidly, and carried every thing that floated on the river. The eye of the boatman saw the advantage of the situation which the place rendered to those on shore, to annoy and attack, and as wandering Indians, in those days, did not hesitate to rob, there was much speculation as to what reception the boat would receive from the builders of the fire.

The rifles were all loaded, to be prepared for the worst, and the loss of Mike Fink lamented, as a prospect of a fight presented itself, where he could use his terrible rifle. The boat in the mean time swept round the point; but instead of an enemy, there lay, in profound sleep, Mike Fink, with his feet toasting at the fire; his pillow was a huge bear, that had baen shot on the day previous, while at his sides, and scattered in profusion around him, were several deer and wild turkeys. Mike had not been idle. After picking out a place most eligible to notice the passing boat, he had spent his time in hunting, and he was surrounded by trophies of his prowess. The scene that he presented was worthy of the time and the man, and would have thrown Landseer into a delirium of joy, could he have witnessed it. The boat, owing to the swiftness of the current, passed Mike's resting place, although it was pulled strongly to the shore. As Mike's companions came opposite to him, they raised such a shout, half exultation of meeting him, and half to alarm him with the idea that Joe's friends were upon him. Mike, at the sound, sprang to his feet, rifle in hand, and as he looked around, he raised it to his eyes, and by the time he discovered the boat, he was ready to fire. " Down with

your shooting-iron, you wild critter," shouted one of the boatmen. Mike dropped the piece, and gave a loud halloo, that echoed among the solitudes like a piece of artillery. The meeting between Mike and his fellows was characteristic. They joked, and jibed him with their rough wit, and he parried it off with a most creditable ingenuity. Mike soon learned the extent of his rifleshot—he seemed perfectly indifferent to the fact that Proud Joe was not dead. The only sentiment he uttered, was regret that he did not fire at the vagabond's head, and if he hadn't hit it, why, he made the first bad shot in twenty years. The dead game was carried on board of the boat, the adventure was forgotten, and every thing resumed the monotony of floating in a flatboat down the Ohio.

A month or more elapsed, and Mike had progressed several hundred miles down the Mississippi; his journey had been remarkably free from incident; morning, noon, and night, presented the same banks, and the same muddy water, and he sighed to see some broken land, some high hills, and he railed and swore, that he should have been such a fool as to have deserted his favourite Ohio for a river that produced nothing but alligators, and was never at best half finished.

Occasionally, the plentifulness of game put him in spirits, but it did not last long; he wanted more lasting excitement, and declared himself as perfectly miserable and helpless as a wild-cat without teeth or claws.

In the vicinity of Natchez rises a few abrupt hills, which tower above the surrounding lowlands of the Mississippi like mountains; they are not high, but from their loneliness and rarity they create sensations of pleasure and awe.

Under the shadow of one of these bluffs, Mike and his associates made the customary preparations to pass the night. Mike's enthusiasm knew no bounds at the sight of land again; he said it was as pleasant as " cold water to a fresh wound;" and, as his spirits rose, he went on making the regions round about, according to his notions, an agreeable residence.

" The Choctaws live in these diggins," said Mike, " and a cursed time they must have of it. Now if I lived in these parts I'd declare war on 'em just to have something to keep me from growing dull; without some such business I'd be as musty as an old swamp moccasin. I could build a cabin on that ar hill yonder that could, from its location, with my rifle, repulse a whole tribe if they came after me. What a beautiful time I'd have of it! I never was particular about what's called a fair fight; I just ask half a chance, and the odds against me, and if I then don't keep clear of snags and sawyers, let me spring a leak and go to the bottom. Its natur that the big fish should eat the little ones. I've seen trout swallow perch, and a cat would come along and swallow the trout, and perhaps, on the Mississippi, the alligators use up the cat, and so on to the end of the row. Well, I will walk tall into varmint and Indian; it's a way I've got, and it comes as natural as grinning to a hyena. I'm a regular tornado, tough as a hickory, and long-winded as a nor'-wester. I can strike a blow like a falling tree, and every lick makes a gap in the crowd that lets in an acre of sunshine. Whew, boys!" shouted Mike, twirling his rifle like a walking-stick around his head, at the ideas suggested in his mind. " Whew, boys! if the Choctaw divils in them ar woods thare would give us a brush, just as I feel now, I'd call them gentlemen. I must fight something, or I'll catch the dry rot—burnt brandy won't save me." Such were some of the expressions which Mike gave utterance to, and in which his companions heartily joined; but they never presumed to be quite equal to Mike, for his bodily prowess, as well as his rifle, were acknowledged to be unsurpassed. These displays of animal spirits generally ended in boxing and wrestling-matches, in which falls were received, and blows were struck without being noticed, that would heve destroyed common men. Occasionally angry words and blows were exchanged, but, like the summer storm, the cloud that emitted the lightning purified the air; and when the commotion ceased, the combatants immediately made friends and became more attached to each other than before the cause that interrupted the good feelings occurred. Such were the conversation and amusements of the evening when the boat was moored under the bluffs we have alluded to. As night wore on, one by one of the hardy boatmen fell asleep, some in its confined interior, and others protected by a light covering in the open air. The moon rose in beautiful majesty; her silver light, behind the highlands, gave them a power and theatrical effect as it ascended; and as its silver rays grew perpendicular, they finally kissed gently the summit of the hills, and poured down their full light upon the boat, with almost noonday brilliancy. The silence with which the beautiful changes of darkness and light were produced made it mysterious. It seemed as if some creative power was at work, bringing form and life out of darkness. In the midst of the witchery of this quiet scene, there sounded forth the terrible rifle, and the more terrible war-whoop of the Indian. One of the flatboatmen, asleep on deck, gave a stifled groan, turned upon his face, and with a quivering motion, ceased to live. Not so with his companions—they in an instant, as men accustomed to danger and sudden attacks, sprang ready-armed to their feet; but before they could discover their foes, seven sleek and horribly painted savages leaped from the hill into the boat. The firing of the rifle was useless, and each man singled out a foe and met him with a drawn knife.

The struggle was quick and fearful; and deadly blows were given amid screams and imprecations that rent the air. Yet the voice of Mike Fink could be heard in encouraging shouts above the clamour. "Give it to them, boys!" he cried, "cut their hearts out! choke the dogs! Here's hell a-fire and the river rising!" then clenching with the most powerful of the assailants, he rolled with him upon the deck of the boat. Powerful as Mike was, the Indian seemed nearly a match for him. The two twisted and writhed like serpents,—now one seeming to have the advantage, and then the other.

In all this confusion there might occasionally be seen glancing in the moonlight the blade of a knife; but at whom the thrusts were made, or who wielded it, could not be discovered.

The general fight lasted less time than we have taken to describe it. The white men gained the advantage; two of the Indians lay dead upon the boat, and the living, escaping from their antagonists leaped ashore, and before the rifle could be brought to bear they were out of its reach. While Mike was yet struggling with his antagonist, one of his companions cut the boat loose from the shore, and, with powerful exertion, managed to get its bows so far into the current, that it swung round and floated; but before this was accomplished, and before any one interfered with Mike, he was on his feet, covered with blood, and blowing like a porpoise: by the time he could get his breath, he commenced talking. "Ain't been so busy in a long time," said he, turning over his victim with his foot; "that fellow fou't beautiful; if he's a specimen of the Choctaws that live in these parts, they are screamers; the infernal sarpents! the d——d possums!" Talking in this way, he with others, took a general survey of the killed and wounded. Mike himself was a geod deal cut up with the Indian's knife; but he called his wounds blackberry scratches. One of Mike's associates was severely hurt; the rest escaped comparatively harmless. The sacrifice was made at the first fire; for beside the dead Indians, there lay one of the boat's crew, cold and dead, his body perforated with four different balls. That he was the chief object of attack seemed evident, yet no one of his associates knew of his having a single fight with the Indians. The soul of Mike was affected, and, taking the hand of his deceased friend between his own, he raised his bloody knife towards the bright moon, and swore that he would desolate "the nation" that claimed the Indians who made war upon them that night, and turned to his stiffened victim, that, dead as it was, retained the expression of implacable hatred and defiance, he gave a smile of grim satisfaction, and then joined in the general conversation, which the occurrences of the night would naturally suggest. The master of the "broad horn" was a business man, and had often been down the Mississippi. This was the first attack he had received, or knew to have been made from the shores inhabited by the Choctaws, except by the white men, and he, among other things, suggested the keeping of the dead Indians until daylight, that they might have an opportunity to examine their dress and features, and see with certainty who were to blame for the occurrences of the night. The dead boatman was removed with care to a respectable distance; and the living, except the person at the sweep of the boat, were soon buried in profound slumber.

Not until after the rude breakfast was partaken of, and the funeral rites of the dead boatmen were solemnly performed, did Mike and his companions disturb the corses of the red men. When both these things had been leisurely and gently got through with, there was a different spirit among the men.

Mike was astir, and went about his business with alacrity. He stripped the bloody blanket from the Indian he had killed, as if it enveloped something disgusting, and required no respect. He examined carefully the moccasins on the Indian's feet, pronouncing them at one time Chickasas, at another time, the Shawanese. He stared at the livid face, but could not recognise the style of paint that covered it.

That the Indians were not strictly national in their adornments, was certain, for they were examined by practised eyes, that could have told the nation of the dead, if such had been the case, as readily as a sailor could distinguish a ship by its flag. Mike was evidently puzzled; and as he was about giving up his task as hopeless, the dead body he was examining, from some cause, turned on its side. Mike's eyes distended, as some of his companions observed, "like a choked cat," and became riveted. He drew himself up in a half serious, and half comic expression, and pointing at the back of the dead Indian's head, there was exhibited a dead warrior in his paint, destitute of his scalp-lock, the small stump which was only left, being stiffened with *red paint.* Those who could read Indian symbols learned a volume of deadly resolve in what they saw. The body of Proud Joe was stiff and cold before them. The last and best shot of Mike Fink cost a brave man his life. The corpse so lately interred, was evidently taken in the moonlight by Proud Joe and his party, as that of Mike's, and they had risked their lives, one and all, that he might with certainty be sacrificed. Nearly a thousand miles of swamp had been threaded, large and swift running rivers had been crossed, hostile tribes passed through by Joe and his friends, that they might revenge the fearful insult, of destroying *without the life,* the sacred scalp-lock.

A Good One.

We understand that a petition was presented to the House of Representatives, praying the passage of an act to legalize a lottery for the purpose of completing the Catholic Cathedral, at Natchez. Mr. McCaughan opposed the petition, saying "he had no objection to the erection of a church to worship our Saviour in, but was opposed to calling on the devil to build it."—*Vicksburg Intel.*

The Guest.

The first number of this periodical, which is a semi-monthly quarto, made its appearance last Friday. The editor, *Mrs. R. S. Nichols,* is well and favourably known to the literary world —east and west—of our country, and she seems sustained by several spirited contributors, some of them of great ability. The paper, typography, and mechanical arrangement are unexceptionable, and the *Guest,* for the extent and character of its original matter, is one of the cheapest family papers of the day.

Of a writer like Mrs. Nichols, whose fugitive pieces have been so highly appreciated by the reading public, it is hardly necessary to speak, and it may suffice to say, that if she can keep up in this new enterprize an array of correspondents and contributors equal to those who have sent in their pieces to the first number, a literary sheet will be furnished for the west, of a higher order of merit than most of the eastern periodicals, either weekly or monthly.

I recommend the " *Guest*" to all who desire a good paper for the family circle.

Pleasant Hill Academy.

The semi-annual examination of this institution commences this day and continues until this day week, the 25th inst. This establishment is the germ out of which is about to be formed " The Farmers' College," a novel enterprize, although justified, and indeed, demanded not only by our republican institutions, but by the commanding influence which the " *sons of the soil,*" as the great mass of the voters of our country, are

destined to exert in the community of which they form a part. To what extent the educational privileges of this institution will diffuse themselves through our farming community, may be judged from the fact that more than five hundred youth have already passed through a course of study at this Academy.

I recommend a general attendance of those whose avocations permit a visit on the occasion from this city.

A Curiosity.

The following is a verbatim copy of a quit claim Mormon bill of divorce, found on the bank of the river opposite Nauvoo, a few days since:

Noo no all men buy thes presence that I Margaret Wilcox have settled all my afairs and difficulties with Silas Wilcox my former husband and hold no more claim on him for any coevnant that has been made hear to fore and air williug that we both do part in friend ship hoping that the blessings of God may rest upon as and we be prospered both in time and eternity and live as brother and sister in the church of Jesus Christ of Laterday saints.

the City of Joseph Oct. 9th 1845.

or so long as we both continue in the faith or in the feloship of the church.

MARGRIT WILCOX.

J. P. Harmon, Witness.
    her
Sarah ✕ Harmon, Witness.

The party interested can have the above by " proving property and paying charges."

Does any body want Twins?

We copy the following *unique* advertisement from the Detroit Free Press:

" TWINS.—The undersigned, having recently lost his wife, and leaving a pair of daughters, which he would give to some good family that would like to adopt them as their own. The infants can be seen at the house of Mr. H. E. Perry, Woodward Avenue, Detroit.

ISAAC DIEFFENDERFER."

Religion and Oysters.

They do such strange things out west that they no longer surprise us. The St. Louis Gazette of the 5th says: "This evening, in the Tobacco warehouse, our Baptist brethren make their first call—we should rather say, *offer,* of a fine entertainment—an Oyster Supper—good cheer, musical airs, &c.—and all for one dollar. We hope, we expect, we know, there will be a rush for the Oysters."

Kindness.

" What! Mr. Brown a brute! why he writes to his wife every packet!" " Yes, he writes a parcel of flummery about the agony of absence, but he has never remitted her a shilling. Do you call that kindness?" " Decidedly, *unremitting* kindness."

Juvenile Precocity.

" Boy what is your name?" " Robert, sir." " Yes, that is your christian name, but what is your other name?" " Bob, sir."

Nomenclature.

A survey of the last British Tariff, which I have lately made, suggests some curious statistics, as respects names.

Among the articles imported into Great Britain, are,—Acorns, Aristolochia, Asses, Bastropes, Glass Bugles, Singing Birds, Clinkers, Bullrushes, Caviare, Chillias, Civet, Culm, Codilla, Coir, Coker, Cutch, Divi divi, Flocks, Granilla, Inkle, Jet, Latten, Lentiles, Medlars, Orchal, Orsidew, Safflower, Salep, Stavesacre, Talc, Tarras, Tincal, Tornsal, Truffles, Vallonia, Weld, Woad, and Zaffre. All these are subject to duty. Most of these things are as much known to the general reader as if their names were in Arabic; and it must be matter of surprise that many of those which are known should be subjects of duty, or even importation.

How far the cheap luxuries of our country are denied to the mass in Great Britain, may be infered from the duty on mead—5s. 6d. per gallon —about *one dollar and forty cents*; and cider £10 10s., or fifty-two dollars per *tun*. It may be said these duties are designed as prohibitory, but if even so, they indicate the price at home of these articles, since it is never necessary that a prohibitory duty should exceed, or even equal, the value of the domestic article.

Sugar Refinery.

Before twenty years shall have elapsed, a manufacturing interest will have sprung into existence in and around Cincinnati, of which we have no example in the U. States. In but the growth of our infancy we have already the great amount of $20,000,000 as an annual product of our mechanical and manufacturing industry. What we shall become when the manufactures of cotton, woolen, and iron, which are either not now in existence here or which have been in operation only upon a limited scale, shall have reached their utmost capacity of profitable establishment, may be infered from our progress in this line of the last twenty years, at the commencement of which period our manufacturing products reached barely three millions of dollars in value. When capital shall be directed to this point from abroad to such an extent as to enable us to manufacture the bar and sheet iron of the west, and to make cotton sheetings and printed goods for the United States and foreign markets, which will be done here within twenty years, we shall then behold a concentration of business and population at Cincinnati which will surpass the most sanguine expectations of its citizens at this time.

I am aware of the ridicule which men of petty minds and narrow views may cast upon such predictions, but I entrench myself on the fact that the most liberal estimate for the future of the progress of Cincinnati, made by myself or any other person hitherto, through the medium of the press, has always fallen far short of the reality, when the period to which it refered arrived, and the views I entertain of our ultimate destiny are now being shared by a much larger portion of our inhabitants than had sustained my former anticipations of the progress of Cincinnati.

I shall, therefore, allude now to a branch of productive industry which the lapse of a few years will establish here, and to an extent of which few persons are now aware. I refer to the refining of New Orleans sugar.

It is matter of surprise to me, that in a city now approaching a population of one hundred thousand souls, no sugar refinery exists, while in St. Louis, destitute of our advantages for their establishment, there are four or five. A mere glance at the subject must satisfy almost every one that the demand upon Cincinnati for the articles of refined sugar and molasses, must be equal to that of St. Louis, at least.

During the past year the whole region east and west of the Lakes has been added to the already extensive markets which our manufactures and the foreign goods business have supplied to Ohio, Indiana, and parts of Kentucky, Virginia, and Illinois.

The Miami Extension Canal opens at once what our Sandusky Rail-Road will more extensively effect; since by transporting produce at lower rates, a market to Western New York, Northern Ohio, Indiana, Illinois, and Southern and Eastern Michigan, for groceries, will be created which must shortly close the supplies from the Empire City, in that line.

When our rail-road shall extend to the Lake, forty thousand additional hogsheads New Orleans sugar, and molasses in proportion, will be needed for the region alluded to. The basis of this estimate is found in the fact that Louisiana sugar can be put down at the terminus of the canal and rail-road, for at least one cent per pound less than it can be supplied via New York. The figures which establish this are few and easily comprehended. The freight from plantation to Cincinnati is ¼ cent per pound; from Cincinnati to the Lake ½ cent. Contracts for any amount of freight can be made at this price now, the toll being but 12½ cents per hundred, or $1.25 per thousand. Now the average of freight from plantation to New York is all of fifty cents per hundred, or five dollars per hogshead. Freight, including tolls, from New York to Buffalo, ½ cent additional; and the insurance requisite to pass it by way of New York, equal to 3-8 cent. Here are then 1½ cent per pound charges via N. York, against ¾ cent via Cincinnati. And the market for the article is principally west of Buffalo, which will make a further difference in favour of the Ohio route of at least ¼ cent per lb. to take it as far west as the terminus of our canal or rail road. All these calculations serve to show that sugar, molasses, &c., can be sent as far as Utica, N. Y., before New York City can fairly compete with us in prices, and the consumption of sugar in the region west of Utica is known to exceed fifty thousand hogsheads annually.

In these estimates the expenses of transhipment by both routes are assumed to be equal, but it might easily be shown that the charges here are always lighter than at New York, where the expense in every shape of carrying on business is greater than in Cincinnati.

All that has been thus exhibited of superior access with crude sugar to western and northern markets, applies with still greater force to refined sugar, as an article in which less bulk and weight to higher value has an important bearing in charges of transportation.

When we recollect that every item of expense in manufacturing is less costly here than at St. Louis, it becomes evident that sugar and molasses, refined from crude sugar, with which we are now extensively supplied from that place, will be manufactured in this city in the course of a year or two.

Alligator Killing.

In the dark recesses of the loneliest swamps, in those dismal abodes where decay and production seem to run riot; where the serpent crawls from his den among the tangled ferns and luxuriant grass, and hisses forth its propensities to destroy unmolested; where the toad and lizard spend the live-long day in their melancholy chirpings; where the stagnant pool festers and ferments, and bubbles up its foul miasma; where the fungi seems to grow beneath your gaze; where the unclean birds retire after their repast, and sit and stare with dull eyes in vacancy for hours and days together; there originates the alligator; there, if happy in his history, he lives and dies. The pioneer of the forest invades his home; the axe lets in the sunshine upon his hiding places: he frequently finds himself, like the Indian, surrounded by the encroachments of civilization, a mere intruder in his original domain, and under such circumstances only does he become an object of rough sport, the incidents of which deserve a passing notice.

The extreme southern portions of the United States are exceedingly favourable to the growth of the alligator: in the swamps that stretch over a vast extent of country, inaccessible almost to man, they increase in numbers and size, live undisputed monarchs of their abodes, exhibiting but little more intelligence, or exerting but little more volition than the decayed trunk of the tree, for which they are not unfrequently taken. In these swamp regions, however, are frequently found high ridges of land, inviting cultivation. The log cabin takes the place of the rank vegetation; the evidences of thrift appear; and as the running streams display themselves, and are cleared for navigation, the old settler, the alligator, becomes

exposed, and daily falls a victim to the rapacity of man. Thus hunted, like creatures of higher organization, he grows more intelligent, from the dangers of his situation; his taste grows more delicate, and he wars in turn upon his only enemy; soon acquires a civilized taste for pork and poultry, and acquires also a very uncivilized one for dogs.

An alligator in the truly savage state is a very happy reptile: encased in an armour as impenetrable as that of Ajax, he moves about unharmed by surrounding circumstances. The fangs of the rattlesnake grate over his scales as they would over a file; the constrictor finds nothing about him to crush; the poisonous moccasin bites at him in vain; and the greatest pest of all, the musquito, that fills the air of his abode with a million stings, that burn the flesh like sparks of fire, buzz out their fury upon his carcass in vain. To say that he enjoys not these advantages, that he crawls not forth as a proud knight in his armour, that he treads not upon the land as a master, and moves in the water the same, would be doing injustice to his actions, and his habits, and the philosophical example of independence which he sets to the trembling victims that are daily sacrificed to his wants.

The character of an alligator's face is far from being a flattering letter of recommendation. It suggests a rude shovel; the mouth extends from the extreme tip of the nose backwards until it passes the ears; indeed, about one-third of the whole animal is mouth, with the exact expression of a tailor's shears; and this mouth being ornamented with a superabundance of rows of white teeth, gives the same hope of getting out of it, sound in body and mind, if once in, as does the hopper of a bark-mill. Its body is short and round not unlike that of a horse; its tail is very long and flattened at the end like an oar. It has the most dexterous use of this appendage, propelling along, swiftly, and on land it answers the purpose of a weapon of defence.

The traveler through the lonely swamp at nightfall often finds himself surrounded by these singular creatures, and if he is unaccustomed to their presence and habits, they cause great alarm. Scattered about in every direction, yet hidden by the darkness, he hears their huge jaws open and shut with a force that makes a noise, when numbers are congregated, like echoing thunder. Again, in the glare of the camp-fire, will sometimes be seen the huge alligator crawling within the lighted circle, attracted by the smell of food —perchance you have *squatted* upon a nest of eggs, encased with great judgment in the centre of some high ground you yourself have chosen to pass the night upon. Many there are, who go unconcernedly to sleep with such intruders in their immediate vicinity; but a rifle-ball, effectively fired, will most certainly leave you unmolested, and the dying alligator, no doubt comforts itself that the sun will not neglect its maternal charge, but raise up its numerous young as hideous and destructive as itself.

The alligator is a luxurious animal, fond of all the comforts of life, which are, according to its habits, plentifully scattered around it. We have watched them, enjoying their evening nap in the shades of tangled vines, and in the hollow trunk of the cypress, or floating like a log on the top of some sluggish pool. We have seen them sporting in the green slime, and catching, like a dainty gourmand, the fattest frogs and longest snakes;

but they are in the height of their glory, stretched out upon the sand-bar, in the meridian sun, when the summer heats pour down and radiate back from the parched sand, as tangibly as they would from red hot iron. In such places will they bask and blow off, with a loud noise, the inflated air and water, that would seem to expand within them as if confined in an iron pipe, occasionally rolling about their swinish eyes with a slowness of motion, that, while it expresses the most perfect satisfaction, is in no way calculated to agitate their nerves, or discompose them by too suddenly taking the impression of outward objects. While thus disposed of, and after the first nap is taken, they amuse themselves with opening their huge jaws to their widest extent, upon the inside of which, instinctively settle, thousands of musquitoes and other noxious insects that infest the abode of the alligator. When the inside of the mouth is thus covered, the reptile brings his jaws together with inconceivable velocity, gives a gulp or two, and again sets his formidable trap for this small game.

Some years since, a gentleman in the southern part of Louisiana, "opening a plantation," found, after most of the forest had been cleared off, that in the centre of his land was a boggy piece of low soil, covering nearly twenty acres. This place was singularly infested with alligators. Among the first victims that fell a prey to their rapacity, were a number of hogs and fine poultry; next followed most of a pack of fine deer hounds. It may be easily imagined that the last outrage was not passed over with indifference. The leisure time of every day was devoted to their extermination, until the cold of winter rendered them torpid, and buried them up in the mud. The following summer, as is naturally the case, the swamp, from the heat of the sun, contracted in its dimensions; a number of artificial ditches drained off the water, and left the alligators little else to live in than mud, about the consistency of good mortar: still the alligators clung, with singular tenacity, to their native homesteads as if perfectly conscious that the coming fall would bring them rain. While thus exposed, a general attack was planned, carried into execution, and nearly every alligator of any size was destroyed. It was a fearful and disgusting sight to see them rolling about in the thick mud, striking their immense jaws together in the agony of death. Dreadful to relate, the stench of these decaying bodies in the hot sun produced an unthought-of evil. Teams of oxen were used in vain to haul them away; the progress of corruption under the sun of a tropical climate made the attempt fruitless. On the very edge of the swamp, with nothing exposed but the head, lay a huge monster, evidently sixteen or eighteen feet long; he had been wounded in the melee, and made incapable of moving, and the heat had actually baked the earth around his body as firmly as if imbeded in cement. It was a cruel and singular exhibition, to see so much power for destruction so helpless. We amused ourselves in throwing things into his great cavernous mouth, which he would grind up between his teeth. Seizing a large oak rail, we attempted to run it down his throat, but it was impossible; for he held it for a moment as firmly as if it had been the bow of a ship, then with his jaws crushed and ground it to fine splinters. The odd fellow, however, had his revenge; the dead alligators were found more destructive than the living ones, and the plantation for a season had to be abandoned.

In shooting the alligator, the bullet must hit just in front of the fore legs, where the skin is most vulnerable; it seldom penetrates in other parts of the body. Certainty of aim, therefore, tells, in alligator shooting, as it does in every thing else connected with sporting. Generally, the alligator, when wounded, retreats to some obscure place; but if wounded in a *bayou*, where the banks are steep, and not affording any hiding-places, he makes considerable amusement in his convolutions in the water, and in his efforts to avoid the pain of his smarting wounds. In shooting, the instant you fire, the reptile disappears, and you are for a few moments unable to learn the extent of injury you have inflicted. An excellent shot, that sent the load with almost unerring certainty through the eye, was made at a huge alligator, and, as usual, he disappeared, but almost instantly rose again, spouting water from his nose, not unlike a whale. A second ball, shot in his tail, sent him down again, but he instantly rose and spouted: this singular conduct prompted a bit of provocation, in the way of a plentiful sprinkling of bits of wood, rattled against his hide. The alligator lashed himself into a fury; the blood started from his mouth; he beat the water with his tail until he covered himself with spray, but never sunk without instantly rising again. In the course of the day he died and floated ashore; and on examination, it was found that the little valve nature has provided the reptile with, to close over its nostrils when under water, had been cut off by the first shot, and thus compelled him to stay on the top of the water to keep from being drowned. We have heard of many since who have tried thus to wound them, and although they have been hit in the nose, yet they have been so crippled as to sink and die.

The alligator is particularly destructive on pigs and dogs, when they inhabit places near plantations; and if you wish to shoot them, you can never fail to draw them on the surface of the water, if you will make a dog yell, or pig squeal; and that too, in places where you may have been fishing all day, without suspecting their presence. Herodotus mentions the catching of crocodiles in the Nile, by baiting a hook with flesh, and then attracting the reptile towards it by making a hog squeal. The ancient Egyptian manner of killing the crocodile is different from that of the present day, as powder and ball have changed the manner of destruction; but the fondness for pigs in the crocodile and alligator, after more than two thousand years, remains the same.

Manufactures of Cincinnati.

The productive industry of Cincinnati is employed in manufacturing articles requiring manual labour, more than those made by machinery. In this respect it differs greatly from Pittsburgh. The manufactures in wood, iron and other metals, leather, cotton, wool, linen and hemp, etc., of Cincinnati, amounted in the year 1841, to nearly $17,500,000, and employed 10,640 hands. Of these manufactures there were five steamboat yards producing $592,500 per annum, and employing 306 hands; thirteen foundries and engine shops, employing 563 hands, and producing $668,657; four machinists employing 42 hands, and producing $77,000; two rolling mills employing 148 hands, and producing $394,000; five sheet iron works employing 33 hands, and producing $58,000; eight brass foundries employing 62 hands, and producing $81,000; thirty-two copper, brass, sheet iron, and tin plate shops employing 208 hands, and producing $311,300; in the manufactures of leather, making boots, shoes, saddlery, and the material itself, there were 988 hands employed, producing $1,768,000; the manufactures of cotton, wool, linen and hemp—consisting of awning and sail making, coach lace, fringe and military equipments, cotton-yarn factories, oil cloth factories, cordage and rope factories, etc.—employed 352 hands, and produced $411,190.

Besides these, there are manufactories of white lead, oil for machinery etc., paper, flour, clothing, (the clothing stores alone employ 813 hands, and produce $1,223,800 per annum,) hats, soap, candles, powder, etc., etc.

From the above statement we are struck with the great extent to which the productive industry of Cincinnati has arrived. Many other articles might have been added to it, but we have only selected those which are most required for military and naval forces.

The manufactures of Cincinnati are noted throughout the west for their superiority of workmanship, and their excellence of material; hence they command better prices than those from the east. This city is also famed for its steamboat building; some of the finest and largest boats on the western waters have been constructed there. In 1840 there were thirty-three steamboats of 5631 tons built, at a cost of $592,000.

Albert and Victoria.

The present Royal Family of England consists of six persons; Alexandria Victoria, twenty-six years of age; and Albert Francis Augustus Charles Emanuel—we delight, like the good Vicar of Wakefield, in giving the full name—her royal husband, who is three months younger than the lady; his wife and Queen. The eldest child, will be five years old in November, and rejoices in the mellifluous appellative of Victoria Adelaide Mary Louisa. The next child is a boy, and will be four years old the 9th of November. He will be the king hereafter, if he outlives his mother, and the Kingdom endures; the boy taking precedence of the sister, although younger. His name is Albert Edward, and his style the Prince of Wales. The second Princess Royal—two years old—is Alice Maud Mary. The Royal Prince born the 6th of August last, is named Alfred Ernst Albert.

Advantage of Advertising.

A lady in Providence, R. I., having ordered an advertisement of "money lost," in one of the papers, returned home and found it in the drawer of her work-table.

To Readers.

There is an admirable publication of T. B Thorpe, called "The Mysteries of the Backwoods," which affords a more accurate idea of the manners, habits and sports of the west than any thing else I recollect seeing. The chapter on Alligator killing in the southwest is a specimen of the sort, and I shall publish one or two more on other subjects. The book is for sale at Robinson & Jones', on Main street.

The March number of "The Commercial Re-

view of the South and West," published at New Orleans by J. D. B. DeBow, is to hand. The article in to-day's Advertiser—"Manufactures in Cincinnati"—is from this publication, and affords a striking picture—far short of the reality however—of our business and industry.

Chronological Table.

March 27th.—Embargo, 1794. Peace of Amiens, 1802.

28th.—Gen. Abercrombie, died, 1801. Raphael, born, 1483.

29th.—The planet Vesta, discovered by Dr. Olbers of Bremen, 1807. Swedenborg, died, 1772. Siege of Acre, 1799.

30th.—Dr. Hunter, died, 1783. The Allied Sovereigns entered Paris. 1814.

31st.—Beethoven, died, 1827.

Western Literature.

It is not often that western talent is recognised in our Atlantic Cities, and western literature finds a market there. Geo. W. Cutter, of our neighbouring city of Covington, however, has found a publisher in New York for his poems, in one of the first houses there, and the handsome compensation of one thousand dollars as the price of the copy right. The volume is in course of preparation for the press, and will make its appearance in the course of a few months.

Vicissitudes.

The following is a picture of human life. Mr. William A. Welles, a journeyman printer, at a late typographical celebration in Rochester, New York, gave a synopsis of his ups and downs through life, to this effect:

He commenced active life in the office of Alderman Seymour, of New York. His associates were Commissary Gen. Chandler, Mr. Mayor Harper, and Gen. Geo. P. Morris. Here he pulled the first sheet of the New York American; set the early numbers of Salamagundi and the Sketch Book of Washington Irving. He went thence to Boston, where he set from manuscript, Gibbs' Hebrew Lexicon, which included nineteen different languages, living and dead. Tired of such employment, and obtaining a midshipman's warrant, he then went to sea on board the Brandywine, Com. Morris, in which Gen. Lafayette returned to France, from his visit to America, in 1825. After leaving Lafayette at home, on board the Brandywine, he makes the circumnavigation of the Globe, almost.

As a printer he had worked in almost every city in the United States; besides building a saw mill, and mill dam across Bear Lake, Western Michigan. He has acted in every capacity in a printing office, from devil to editor and publisher of a city daily press.

Among other vicissitudes, he was incarcerated at *Buenos Ayres*, in the same dungeon of the *Carcal* with *Don Manuel Rosas*, now President of the Argentine Republic, although for different offences. Rosas was confined for treason—in all ages a gentlemanly crime—at least in despotic governments; Welles for slipping a dirk between the ribs of a *Gaucho*, who attempted his life.

How much of human life is made up of such vicissitudes; and what varied adventure is within the recollection of hundreds of our citizens here.

CORRESPONDENCE.

To CHARLES CIST,—*Sir:*

Your correspondent D. has corrected your error in relation to the derivation of the name of Bucyrus, which is, as he states, a corrupt orthography of the fabled Egyptian King, Busirus, who sacrificed all foreigners to Jupiter, whence it means *the tomb of Osiris*. But my object is to correct D. in relation to the village of Mansfield, which was not so named in honour of the Chief Justice of that name, at whom Junius hurled his violent attacks, but in memory of Col. J. Mansfield, a citizen of our state, then Surveyor General and a distinguished mathematician.

Whilst I have my pen in hand allow me to copy the following, which may throw some light on the subject of your controversy with *Phil.*

"Esquire (from the French *Escu*, Latin *Scutum*, in Greek *Skutos*,) signifies a hide, of which shields were anciently made, for in the times of of the Saxons, the shields were covered with leather; so that an Esquire was he who attended a knight in war, and carried his shield, whence he was called Escuier in French, and Scutifer or Armiger in Latin. Those which the French call Esquires, were a military kind of vassals, having *jus scuti*, viz: liberty to bear a shield, and in it the ensigns of their family, in token of their dignity."

In conclusion, you will not wish to make the acquaintance of   XANTIPPE.

What becomes of our Coffee Bags?

A few days since, during that delightful blending of cold air and bright sunshine which characterized the atmosphere of week before last, and which forms weather which no other country than America can boast of, in walking up Fourth street to my office, it was my fortune to overtake a couple of charming girls, whom I knew but a few years since as Sabbath scholars. In the interval they had ripened into womanhood, and are now among the most graceful of that large class of beings which toil not nor spin, and yet are not surpassed in attractiveness by the fairest and finest of the lilies and roses oi our gardens. After the usual salutations and inquiries had been exchanged, in walking a few paces, I happened to cast my eyes on one of the young ladies' skirts, and discovered what I supposed a stray dark coloured thread, and stretched out a friendly hand to remove it. Mistaking its character, as well as its degree of resistance, I failed to effect my design, and making a second effort, I discovered it to be a thread of Manilla sea grass. "What is this, my dear?" I exclaimed. The young lady blushed scarlet and made no reply; and regreting the embarrassment I had created, I turned off as soon as the next corner was near enough to furnish an excuse to leave my company.

Eureka! I exclaimed, as I extended my solitary walk; the secret is discovered—the problem what becomes of the coffee bags, is solved at length. No wonder Mr, *C. A. Schumann*—doubtless as commission merchant to the fashionable dress makers—was compelled to advertise for three hundred Havana coffee bags. What a pity that the coffee of Rio Janeiro has superceded so extensively that of Havana in the American markets.

A long Street.

Front street is not only the longest continuous street in Cincinnati, but with the exception of one or two streets in *London*, the longest in the world. It extends from the three mile post on the *Little Miami Rail-Road*, through *Fulton* and Cincinnati as far west as *Storrs* township, an extent of seven miles. In all this range there are not ten dwellings which are three feet distant from the adjacent ones, and two-thirds of the entire route is as densely built as is desirable for business purposes and dwelling house convenience.

The Battle of the 8th January.--No. 1.

BY A HUNTER OF KENTUCKY.

It is the confidence we place in a narrative in which the narrator is relating facts within his own knowledge, and the conviction of reality thus inspired, which gives autobiography—the charm it possesses over history compiled from other sources. The following, which I condense from a late *Louisville Democrat*, will commend itself to the perusal of my readers.

It was in the fall of 1814, that word came, that the British had landed in Louisiana, or were about to land; and pretty soon, there was a draft of Kentucky militia, to go down and help old Jackson dress their jackets. I drew clear, but somehow or other I wasn't much rejoiced when the blank ticket came out, for I felt a sort of hankering to go. I had a notion that Old Hickory would shew us something worth seeing, and besides, I felt as if I wanted to help our brave fellows thrash the British ragmuffins, for coming on our soil where they had no business. Well, it wasn't long, before I met one of my neighbours, who had been drafted and didn't want to go. He was a wealthy man, and had so much business at home, he said, he did not see how in the world he could get off. He offered forty dollars for a substitute, and asked me if I knew where he could get one. "Well," said I, "that's easily done. I have got all my crops well housed and the old woman and children are pretty well fixed to live through the winter, so if you'll give me the forty dollars, and let me have credit for the tour of service, I'll go myself!" He agreed to that, and we soon clinched the bargain. When I told my wife what I had done, she did look a little blank, but she was good game and didn't make any fuss. She soon rigged me out with a yellowish green hunting shirt of homemade jean, a couple of pairs of trowsers of the same, with a blanket and some other nick-nacks for camp use. Then I bought a stout wool hat with a low crown and broad brim, and shouldering my rifle I set off from Nelson county to join the army at Louisville.

We rendesvoused at Shippingsport on the 10th of November, and next day marched to Louisville and drew provisions. I belonged to Captain John Farmer's Company, 15th Regiment, Kentucky militia, commanded by Colonel Slaughter. The day after we had drawn provisions we went into an election for company officers, all except Captain and Orderly Sergeant. When we had mustered for that purpose Captain Farmer told us, that it was his right to choose our officers, but he didn't want to do so; he wanted us to choose for ourselves, so that we should be better satisfied. Every man in the company, he said, must be a candidate, and whoever had the most votes should be elected. Then we began to look round to see who should be our lieutenant, and several were spoken of, but finally we pitched upon Willoughby Ashby. He was a perfect stranger, and was neither a drafted man nor a substitute. He had joined the company at Louisville, purely of his own free will, and when we were about to choose a lieutenant he stepped out in front of the line, and spoke up in this way:—"Boys," said he, "I served in Canada, and was taken prisoner at the river Raisin, where I was a good deal mislisted by the British. Now I am going down with you to get satisfaction out of them for it, and if you choose to elect me an officer, I'll do my best to do what's right. I'm willing to go as a private or as an officer, or any how you please—so we give the British a good drubbing it's all one to me." This kind of talk took our fancy, and as he was a good looking fellow and seemed the right kind of stuff, we thought we couldn't do better—so we all stepped out to him and elected him unanimously. Then we elected John Figg, a fine young man, from Nelson county, Ensign; and after that we appointed our Sergeants and Corporals.

We remained at Shippingsport some fifteen or twenty days, while preparations were making for stores and boats to convey us down the river. About the 39th of November, the 13th and 15th regiments embarked in about twenty flatboats—each company occupying one. Our men were all dressed according to their fancy. Some had hunting shirts, some long tailed coats, and some roundabouts. The only thing that made them look like being in uniform, was the materials out of which their clothes were made, which were either homemade jeans, or tanned buckskin. The only regular uniform coat in our company, was Lieutenant Ashby's. He had one of blue cloth, turned up with red; and I am not sure but his having an officer's coat was one reason why we elected him. He had also epaulettes, but he wore a common hat, trowsers, and jacket. Our captain was dressed in common clothes like the rest of us, and, indeed, the lieutenant only appeared in his fine coat on parade days and very important occasions. If we didn't look much like regular soldiers, however, we were all full of spirits and devilment. Most of us had a tolerable good idea of the use of the rifle, and we felt a reasonable confidence that if we drew sight on a red-jacket within anything like shooting distance, we should be pretty certain to make a hole in it.

When we got down to the mouths of the Cumberland and Tennessee, we fell in with the 14th regiment, parts of which had come down both those rivers. We lay at Cumberland Island three days, collecting the different detachments, and then proceeded on down the river, the three regiments in company.

At New Orleans, as soon as we were disembarked, we were formed into a line, a little below the city. The main part of the army was then about seven miles below, at the breastworks, where the battle afterwards took place. Our line had scarcely been formed before a drum came round, beating for volunteers to go down to the lines, and assist the Tennesseeans, who had been on fatigue duty for several days. I stepped out after the drum, and in a few minutes, about four or five hundred of us were on the march. We got down to the breast works a little after dark, and there we laid under arms till morning. Some were laying or sitting on the ground, but the greater part of us stood up all night, ready for an attack. None took place, and the next morning we were marched back to join our companies. It was about one o'clock in the day when we arrived, and immediately there was another call for volunteers to go down and spend the next night. A good many of us were so wiry-edged and so keen to see and know every thing that was going on, that though we had no time to get any thing to eat, we volunteered again; and thus we had no sooner marched up to the city than we had the pleasure of marching back to the lines. This night passed as did the one before. There was no alarm and nothing took place worthy of note. Next morning we were marched up to the city as before, but when we arrived we found our regiment paraded, and that orders had been given for the whole army to proceed down to the breastworks. A third expedition, on such short notice, was one more than we had bargained for in our own minds, but there was no help for it. We had but just time to tumble into the ranks, before the word was given to march.

We got down a little before sundown on the evening of the 7th, and formed about a couple of hundred yards from the breastwork. Directly after our line had been formed, there were three rockets discharged from the British camp. The first struck the ground just behind the breastwork; the second passed high above our heads, but the third came waving over the breastwork, and passed right through our line. Our company parted to the right and left to let it pass. It went through between William Grubb and Geo. Phillips, so close that the sparks flew upon both of them. It struck the ground a few rods behind us, near a grey horse that was feeding on the commons. The horse was terribly frightened. He snorted, jumped and made off as fast as his legs could carry him.

After these rockets had been discharged we were hastily marched up to the breastwork, where we remained until after dark, but nothing farther occurring, we were marched back to our former position and dismissed; with orders for every man to keep up his arms and to be ready at a moment's notice. By this time some of us were so hungry that we felt rather savage. We had had nothing to eat since the morning we landed at New Orleans. Each time in marching from the lines up to the city, we had came back without having time to procure or cook our rations; the first time our own eagerness to be on the second volunteering party, had prevented us from getting our allowance; and the second time we had no chance, as we found the whole army paraded and ready to march. As good luck would have it, one of our mess had a little flour, which he made into dough with some water, and another having hunted up an old skillet, we baked it over a few coals. I had for my share a piece about half as big as the palm of my hand. We passed the night sitting, standing, or lying, as we could find opportunity, but with our rifles ready for use at a moment's warning. Most of the men were sulky with fatigue and hunger, and there was not much conversation. It was a very dark night, there being no moon until twelve o'clock, and a considerable fog rendered it still more gloomy.

Just at dawn of day—it was a foggy, hazy morning—we heard the firing of our picket guard. For an instant or two, there was a confused noise all along the front of our line, as if a high wind was rushing over a field of ripe corn. Then there were a few dropping shots, and directly volleys of musketry, as our guard retreated. Our troops instantly ran up to the breastwork, and we heard the British troops coming on, like a confused mass and yelling like devils.

Our regiment—the 15th—was about the centre of the line. The 14th regiment was on our left, between us and the swamp, and the regulars were on our right towards the river. The Tennesseeans were scattered about amongst us, I don't exactly know how. At any rate, a good many of them got mixed up with us before the battle was over. Our company was exactly under the leaning oak, which stood about half way between the river and the swamp. We were formed into sections five deep, with orders for the sections to advance and fire alternately. The section I was in, was composed of Henry Spillman, John Anderson, Barnet Bridwell, and I think, Matthew Kane and James Glass. The other individuals around me, as near as I can recollect, were Lieut. Ashby, Ensign Weller, Orderly Sergeant Isaac Chambers, Isaac Wilcox, Alex. Robinson, Thomas Anderson, and Abram Springston. These were my acquaintances whom I remember seeing about me at the commencement of the battle. It was so dark, however, that one could see but little.

Captain Farmer was that morning commander of the picket guard, and, of course, did not join us until after the battle had commenced. During the night, one of our regular soldiers had deserted to the enemy, and had given them the countersign and watchword. While on guard, Captain Farmer, being dressed in dark clothes, had let the guard fire, and passing through his own line of sentinels, approached so near that of the British that he could hear them talking. He heard them speak of the deserter, and the advantage they would have from knowing our passwords. It didn't turn out any advantage, though, for as soon as Capt. Farmer returned they were changed.

The Dress of Authors.

Anthony Magliabechi, who passed his time among his books, had an old cloak, which served him for a gown in the day, and for bed-clothes at night; he had one straw chair for his table, and another for his bed, on which he generally remained fixed, in the midst of a heap of volumes and papers, until he was overpowered with sleep. Emerson, the mathematician, made one hat last him the greater part of his lifetime, the rim generally lessening bit by bit, till little remained except the crown. Another "shocking bad hat," which belonged to a celebrated geologist of the present day, is honoured with a place among the curious relics of costumes in the Ashmolean Museum at Oxford, to which valuable collection it was presented by some waggish university youths. In the "History of Holy Ghost Chapel, Basingstoke" (1819), it is stated that the Rev. Samuel Loggon, a great student of antiquities, "used to wear two old shirts at once, saying that they were warmer than new ones." Dr. Paris, in his "Life of Sir Humphrey Davy," tells us that this great philosopher was, in the busiest period of his career, so sparing of time, that he would not afford a moment to divesting himself of his dirty linen, but would slip clean linen over it. This practice he would continue, until as many as even six shirts were on his back at a time. When at length he had found leisure to extricate himself from all except the one that was clean, his bulk was so visibly and suddenly reduced, that his friends, not knowing the cause, would remark that he was getting thinner with alarming rapidity. But their fears of his being in a consumption would shortly be removed, when shirt over shirt began to accumulate again. He was then like a plump caterpillar, existing under several skins. In later days, Davy became more attentive to the toilet; in fact the thinking and busy philosopher merged into a frivolous fop, cultivating curls, and wearing piebald waistcoats of patchwork pattern. Shenstone was somewhat of an exquisite. He loved showy colours in dress, delighted in trinkets and perfumes, designed patterns for snuff-boxes, played music, sung, and painted flowers. He had, however, great antipathy to card playing and dancing; yet he says that ecstatic, rough, unsophisticated dancing, is one of the most natural expressions of delight, for it coincides with jumping for joy; but when it is done according to rule, it is, in his opinion, merely *cum ratione insauire*. Benjamin Stillingfleet generally wore a full dress suit of cloth of the same uniform colour, with blue worsted stockings. In this dress he used frequently to attend Mrs. Montague's literary evening parties, and as his conversation was very interesting, the ladies used to say,—"We can do nothing without the blue stockings;" hence arose the appellation of *bas bleu*, or "blue stockings" to literary ladies. Mezerai, the French historian, was so extremely susceptible of cold, that immediately on the setting in of winter, he provided himself with twelve pairs of stockings, all of which he sometimes wore at once. In the morning he always consulted his barometer, and, according to the greater or less degree of cold put on so many more or fewer pairs of stockings. In reference to the general seediness of literary costume, a recent writer has justly remarked, that to laugh—as has been the custom since the days of Juvenal—at the loutish manners, threadbare cloak, and clouted shoe of the mere man of letters, is a stale and heartless joke, for the poorest, threadbare, ungainly scholar (if he be indeed a scholar) is a gentleman in his feelings.

Building for 1846.

Early as is the season for building operations, preparations for that purpose are to be seen on every side. Not less than one hundred and fifty cellars are in various stages of progress already, and the prospect is that the erections of 1846 will be as numerous as those of the past year, while the private buildings will doubtless exceed their predecessors in elegance, covenience, and value.

As regards public edifices, a new Disciples' Church, fifty by seventy-four feet, for the congregation lately worshiping on Sycamore street, is now building at the southwest corner of Walnut and Eighth streets, the basement of which will be laid off for business purposes. A new Jewish Synagogue—*Kal a Kodesh Beni Jeshurun*—fifty-five by seventy-five feet, will also be put up this year, under the direction of Mr. Henry Walters, Architect. The Synagogue will be erected on Lodge, between Fifth and Sixth streets.

Sound the loud timbrel o'er valley and sea,
The cord is now broken that bound thee to me:

As the Hoosier belle apostrophized her corset, on learning that the article had gone out of fashion.

Error of the Press.

An exchange mentions the appointment, by and with the consent of the Senate, of Mr. John Smith, as "Master of *Chicanery*." In the opinion of the uninitiated, the printer was not far wrong, as the difference between *chicanery* and *chancery* is not very great.

Oysters and the Mails.

In my last week's article—"Our Markets"—I adverted to the abundant supply of oysters to this market. One circumstance was, however, omitted, of some statistical importance, of not less consequence to the *gastronome* as an index to the state of supplies in this article, in respect to freshness and quality, than is the thermometer to the brewer, or any other manufacturer, as a criterion of atmospheric temperature. It is this, that in the exact degree of punctuality with which the Eastern mail arrives, the can oysters are left behind; and to the extent in which the oysters are received, the Eastern letters and papers are missing. This is a very singular and curious coincidence.

It follows, therefore, that the annunciation of mail failures, which are so frequently made by our editors, is equivalent to an advertisement by our friends, *Selves* and *Ringgold*, "*that they have this day received a fresh lot of oysters*," with which they are ready to supply customers.

The Great Lakes.

The Boston Journal observes that but few persons are really aware of the magnitude of the great Lakes of the West. They are truly inland seas, and navigation there is as dangerous, and subjected to all the vicissitudes which are connected with the navigation of the Baltic, Black Sea, or the Mediterranean. The following is an authentic tabular statement of the extent of those fresh water seas, embraced in a report of the State Geologist of Michigan:

Lakes.	Mean length.	Mean breadth.	Area sq. miles.
Superior,	400	80	32,000
Michigan,	320	70	22,000
Huron,	240	80	20,000
Green Bay,	100	20	2,000
Erie,	240	40	7,400
Ontario,	180	35	6,300
St. Clair,	20	14	360
			90,060

The same tabular statement exhibits also the depth and the elevation of each above tide-water:

Lakes.	Mean depth.	Elevation.
Superior,	900 feet.	696 feet.
Michigan,	1000	578
Huron,	1000	578
St. Clair,	20	570
Erie,	84	565
Ontario,	500	232

It is computed that the Lakes contain above fourteen thousand miles of fresh water; a quantity *more than half of all the fresh water on earth.* The extent of country drained by the lakes, from Niagara to the northwestern angle of Superior, including also that of the lakes themselves, is estimated at 335,515 square miles.

A paper in the west abuses a professional gentleman as a "*briefless lawyer.*" The Louisville Journal takes his cotemporary to task and admonishes him never to abuse a man *without a cause.*

"Out for Five Minutes."

A lawyer who was in the habit of leaving such a *mem.* as the above, on his office door, when ever business or pleasure called him out, was rebuked by an *addenda* to his card, in the following words—"for *one* minute *in.*"

He never hung out that shingle again.

Legislative Statistics.

I have compiled in tabular form the component ingredients of such of our State Legislatures as my statistical information on the subject provided me with the necessary data. These are those of Mississippi, Ohio, Kentucky, and Maryland.

Occupations.	Md.	Ky.	Ohio.	Miss.
Farmers,	50	75	62	89
Lawyers,	17	40	22	26
Physicians,	4	5	5	11
Mechanics,	5	6	11	3
Teachers,	1		2	
Merchants,	4	9	6	1
Innkeepers,	1	2	1	
Ages—Youngest,		26	29	23
Oldest,		68	76	63
Married,			101	
Single,			7	

Birthplace.	Ky.	Ohio.	Miss.
Ohio,	8	28	
Pennsylvania,	6	24	1
New York,		14	4
Virginia,	34	8	21
Kentucky,	81	5	10
Maryland,		5	5
Connecticut,	1	8	
Illinois,			1
Maine,		2	1
New Hampshire,	2	2	2
New Jersey,		2	1
Alabama,			3
District Columbia,	1	1	
North Carolina,	3		18
South Carolina,	1		30
Tennessee,	6		14
Vermont,	1		1
Georgia,			11
Mississippi,			10
Native Americans,	126	104	129
Ireland,	2		
Wales,	1		
Germany,	1		
France,			1

It were desirable that fuller statistics on this interesting topic should be furnished by the several State Legislatures. It would serve to shed light upon the formation of our national character. Imperfect as these are they supply many valuable inductions, to the cause of knowledge.

Farmers and planters constitute the largest portion in the legislatures, as they do of the people. All classes have probably a fair representation—lawyers excepted. These always exist in the legislatures, both state and national, in a proportion which forms a great and crying evil. It will be found, I apprehend, that they are the great cause why so much time is wasted in mere talking, to the great disadvantage of getting through business. I say not this out of disrespect to the profession, in whose ranks are to be found a full share of business tact and talent. But as the very nature of that profession cannot permit its members to become legislators but at the absolute sacrifice of their business, the effect of sending lawyers to the seat of government is, as a general rule, to take them from men of fourth and fifth rate calibre. It appears to me, too, that the tendency itself of the lawyer's employment, to try what can be said on both sides, begets an undue distrust of ones own judgment, and a desire to protract coming to a decision, which is the common failing in deliberative bodies.

Not the least striking feature in these statistics is, that the proportion of natives of other countries does not form much more than one out of one hundred members. I had no idea that the proportion was so small.

Value of Property.

Our public sales are the true average of the value of real estate. On Thursday last, Wright & Graff sold at auction, a lot on the southwest corner of Walnut and Third streets, and the adjacent lots on both Walnut and Third streets. The corner twenty-five feet by seventy-five feet, brought $2.200, or $328 per front foot. The adjacent one on Walnut, same front and depth, was sold for $5.150, or $23 per front foot; and the Third street front, twenty-five feet by but fifty feet deep, was disposed of at $2.250, being $90 per foot front. These prices indicate a steady advance in the value of property; and although there are brick buildings on the premises, every one knows that these lots would have brought as much if they had been destitute of improvement; in fact the business wants of Cincinnati will compel the erection of buildings adapted for stores and offices, at not only this corner, but at the opposite one.

These prices seem high, but I am warranted in pronouncing the purchase safe and prudent. I can state on the best authority, that the Masonic Lodge, in whom is vested the title to the property, extending from the opposite corner to the alley next the Lafayette Bank, have a day or two since *refused four hundred dollars* per front foot, for twenty-five feet west of Watson's barbering establishment.

What would an individual unacquainted with Cincinnati think of the progress of our city to be told the indubitable fact, that this twenty-five feet for which $10,000 have been refused form one eighth, and the least valuable eighth part of a lot, bequeathed by William McMillan, in 1804, to the Masonic fraternity, and deemed of so little value at that period that the legatees suffered it to be sold for taxes, and did not deem it worth redemption until 1810. The naked lot would now command at sheriff's sale one hundred thousand dollars.

Cincinnati Grocery Trade.

That Cincinnati is the largest interior market, not only in the West, but in the United States, is a fact no longer disputed. The extent of its operations, however, is, we believe, very inadequately appreciated. To give some idea of its business, we show below, the receipts of Coffee, Molasses, and Sugar, the three great staples in the Grocery trade, during the last two years. The aggregates are as follows:

	1845.	1844.
Coffee, sacks,	55,490	46,809
Molasses, barrels,	22,928	18,099
Sugar, hhds.,	12,287	11,404
Do. brls.,	6,832	4,118
Do. boxes,	649	1,421

I copy the above from the ATLAS. It suggests a powerful contrast to the past, while it furnishes one among many evidences of our rapid growth in every department of business. What that progress is may be infered from the following incident.

In 1816, Adam Moore and Nathaniel Reeder brought up seventy bags coffee from New Orleans, and offered it for sale to a firm, at that time one of the principal grocers in the place. Before taking the responsibility of making so heavy a purchase, one of the partners went round town, and having ascertained that the whole stock on hand in Cincinnati—their own included —did not equal that quantity, they purchased it, under considerable hesitation that the price of the article might fall before they were able to dispose of their whole supply—less than one hundred bags.

In the business season, it is no uncommon circumstance now for one of our largest houses to have two thousand bags on hand at once. And this too when the daily arrival of steamboats from New Orleans in short passages affords a constant opportunity of replenishing a lighter supply.

Steel Bells.

Much mischief is occasionally done by the press, not only in stating facts which are untrue, but in extending their circulation by copying extracts which a moment's reflection would exclude from their columns.

An article has gone the rounds, stating that " Steel Bells are now manufactured by an ingenious mechanic in Cincinnati. A bell of steel weighing fifty pounds, will cost only thirty dollars, and can be heard two miles, or more. They are so cheap and good, therefore, that every church may have a bell of a clear, brilliant, and musical tone, while the lightness of this species of bells requires no strength of belfry to support

it. It is rung with a crank which can be moved by a mere boy. For about two hundred dollars a chime of steel bells can be bought."

It is needless for me to say to residents here that this is an entire fabrication, without the least foundation in fact.

Dr. Bailey of the Herald and myself, have been put to trouble and expense by repeated applications through letter and otherwise, from this silly paragraph. Probably other publishers also. I hope this explanation will put inquiries at rest.

The manufacture of steel bells was attempted in New England some years since, and proved an absolute failure.

In 1815, after Napoleon's return from Elba, a violent royalist exclaimed to his confessor, who happened to dine with him at Ghent—" What, Henry III. and IV. were assassinated, and nobody can be found to rid us of the usurper Bonaparte!" The priest fetched a deep sigh:—" Ah, my dear sir," said he, " there is no longer any religion in the world in these days!" Napoleon is said to have been much amused with this anecdote.

The Battle of the 8th January.--No. 2.
BY A HUNTER OF KENTUCKY.

The British made their attack in three divisions. That next the river, after forcing the picket guard, followed it right into the works. I did not see this part of the attack, of course, but I heard from Capt. Farmer, Joseph Smithy (Drum Major of our regiment,) and William Reasoner, all of whom were on the guard, that the British were completely mixed up with them, when they came to the gate which led through the breastwork. A British soldier kept hunching Reasoner with his elbow, telling him to " form—form—form." Finding after a while that Reasoner was an American—in the darkness it was difficult to distinguish friend from foe—he fired his musket at him and knocked the cock off Reasoner's gun. At this the latter turned and finding the lock spoiled, he clubbed the rifle and broke it over the Englishman's head. Captain Farmer was one of the last of the picket guard that passed through the gateway, and just at that moment he noticed the matchman of the thirty-two pounder that was placed at that point, brightening his match. The Captain turned to look— the old thirty-two went off, cutting a wide lane through the dense mass of red coats, that had by this time crowded up to its very muzzle. In a minute it was loaded again with grape and canister shot, and the Captain had an opportunity to see the effect of a second fire, just as he had turned to pass up the line and join his company. It seemed to cut another lane through the British, taking down every man within several feet of its range on either side. Still they came rushing on. A British officer jumped on the works and began spiking a canon. I heard say it was Colonel Gibbs. He exclaimed to his men, " come on boys, the day's our own!" but just as he had got the words out of his mouth, Joe Smithy stepped up to him, saying, " you're not so sure of that," and fired a pistol right in his face. Down went the officer. Several shots must have been fired at him at the same time, for I was told that seven bullets had passed through him before he fell.

When we first ran up to the breastwork, at our part of the lines, some of our men began firing, and orders were passed along rapidly, " cease that firing—cease that firing." Some said the men we heard coming were the picket guards coming in. Col. Smily, from Bardstown, was the first one who gave us orders to fire from our part of the line; and then, I reckon, there was a pretty considerable noise. There were also brass pieces just on our right, the noisiest kind of varmints, that began blazing away as hard as they could, while the heavy iron cannon, towards the river, and some thousands of small arms, joined in the chorus and made the ground shake under our feet. Directly after the firing began, Capt. Patterson—I think he was from Knox county, Kentucky, but an Irishman born—came running along. He jumped up on the breastwork, and stooping a moment to look through the darkness as well as he could, he shouted with a broad North of Ireland brogue, " shoot low, boys! 'shoot low! rak them—rak them! D—— them!—they're a comin' on their all fours!"

The official report said the action lasted two hours and five minutes, but it did not seem half that length of time to me. It was so dark that little could be seen, until just about the time the battle ceased. The morning had dawned to be sure, but the smoke was so thick that every thing seemed covered up in it. Our men did not seem to apprehend any danger, but would load and fire as fast as they could, talking, swearing, and joking, all the time. All ranks and sections were soon broken up. After the first shot, every one loaded and banged away on his own hook. Henry Spillman did not load and fire quite so often as some of the rest, but every time he did fire he would go up to the breastwork, look over till he could see something to shoot at, and then take deliberate aim and crack away. Lieut. Ashby was as busy as a nailor, and it was evident that the River Raisin was uppermost in his mind all the time. He kept dashing about, and every now and then he would call out, " we'll pay you now for the River Raisin, d—— you! We'll give you something to remember the River Raisin!" When the British had come up to the opposite side of the breastwork, having no gun he picked up an empty barrel and flung it at them. Then finding an iron bar he jumped up on the works and hove that at them.

At one time I noticed, a little on our right, a curious kind of a chap named Ambrose Odd, one of Captain Higdon's company, and known among the men by the nickname of " Sukey," standing coolly on the top of the breastwork and peering into the darkness for something to shoot at. The balls were whistling around him and over our heads, as thick as hail, and Col. Slaughter coming along, ordered him to come down. The Colonel told him there was policy in war, and that he was exposing himself too much. Sukey turned round, holding up the flap of his old broad brimed hat with one hand, to see who was speaking to him, and replied: " Oh! never mind Colonel—here's Sukey—I don't want to waste my powder and I'd like to know how I can shoot till I see something?" Pretty soon after, Sukey got his eye on a red coat and no doubt made a hole through it, for he took deliberate aim, fired and then coolly came down to load again.

During the action a number of Tennessee men got mixed with ours. One of them was killed about five or six yards from where I stood. I did not know his name. A ball passed through his head and he fell against Ensign Weller. I always .thought, as did many others who were standing near, that he must have been accidentally shot by some of our own men. From the range of the British balls, they could hardly have passed over the breastwork without passing over our heads, unless we were standing very close to the works, which were a little over breast high, and five or six feet wide on the top. This man was standing a little back and rather behind Weller. After the battle, I could not see that any balls had struck the oak tree lower than ten or twelve feet from the ground. Above that height it was thickly peppered. This was the only man killed near where I was stationed. It was near the close of the firing. About the time that I observed three or four men carrying his body away, or directly after, there was a white flag raised on the opposite side of the breastwork and the firing ceased.

The white flag, before mentioned, was raised about ten or twelve feet from where I stood, close to the breastwork and a little to the right. It was a white handkerchief, or something of the kind, on a sword or stick. It was waved several times and as soon as it was perceived we ceased firing. Just then the wind got up a little and blew the smoke off, so that we could see the field. It then appeared that the flag had been raised by a British officer wearing epaulets. I was told he was a Major. He stepped over the breastwork and came into our lines. Amongst the Tennesseeans who had got mixed with us during the fight, there was a little fellow whose name I do not know; but he was a cadaverous looking chap and went by that of Paleface. As the British officer came in, Paleface demanded his sword. He hesitated about giving it to him, probably thinking it was derogatory to his dignity, to surrender to a private all over begrimed with dust and powder and that some officer should shew him the courtesy to receive it. Just at that moment, Colonel Smily came up and cried, " G—— d—— you! give it up —give it up to him in a minute!" The British officer quickly handed his weapon to Paleface, holding it in both hands and making a very polite bow.

A good many others came in just about the same time. Amongst them I noticed a very neatly dressed young man, standing on the edge of the breastwork, and offering his hand, as if for some one to assist him down. He appeared to be about nineteen or twenty years old, and, as I should judge, from his appearance, was an Irishman. He held his musket in one hand while he was offering the other. I took hold of his musket and set it down, and then giving him my hand, he jumped down quite lightly. As soon as he got down, he began trying to take off his cartouch box, and then I noticed a red spot of blood on his clean white under jacket. I asked him if he was wounded and he said that he was, and he feared pretty badly. While he was trying to disengage his accoutrements, Capt. Farmer came up, and said to him, " let me help you my man!" The Captain and myself then assisted him to take them off. He begged us not to take his canteen, which contained his water. We told him, we did not wish to take any thing but what was in his way and cumbersome to him. Just then one of the Tennesseeans, who had ran down to the river, as soon as the firing ceased, for water, came along with some in a tin coffee-pot. The wounded man observing him, asked if he would please to give him a drop. "O! yes," said the Tennesseean, "I'll treat you to any thing I've got." The young man took the coffee-pot, and swallowed two or three mouthfulls out of the spout. He then handed back the pot and in an instant we observed him sinking backwards. We eased him down against the side of a tent, when he gave two or three gasps and was dead. He had been shot through the breast.

On the opposite side of the breastwork, there was a ditch about ten feet wide, made by the excavation of the earth of which the work was formed. In it, was about a foot or eighteen inches of water, and to make it the more difficult of passage, a quantity of thornbush had been cut and thrown into it. In this ditch, a number of British soldiers were found at the close of the action; some dead, and many who had sought to get close under the breastwork, as a shelter from our fire. These, of course, came in and surrendered.

When the smoke had cleared away and we could obtain a fair view of the field, it looked, at the first glance, like a sea of blood. It was not blood itself which gave it this appearance, but the red coats in which the British soldiers were dressed. Straight out before our position, for about the width of space which we supposed had been occupied by the British column, the field was entirely covered with prostrate bodies. In some places they were laying in piles of several, one on the top of the other. On either side, there was an interval more thinly sprinkled with the slain; and then two other dense rows, one near the levee and the other towards the swamp. About two hundred yards off, directly in front of our position, lay a large dapple grey horse, which we understood to have been Packenham's. Something like half way between the body of the horse and our breastwork, there was a very large pile of dead, and at this spot, as I was afterwards told, Packenham had been killed; his horse having staggered off to a considerable distance before he fell. I have no doubt that I could have walked on the bodies, from the edge of the ditch to where the horse was lying, without touching the ground. I did not notice any other horse on the field.

When we first got a fair view of the field in our front, individuals could be seen in every possible attitude. Some laying quite dead, others, mortally wounded, pitching and tumbling about in the agonies of death. Some had their heads shot off, some their legs, some their arms. Some were laughing, some crying, some groaning and some screaming. There was every variety of sight and sound. Amongst those that were on the ground, however, there were some that were neither dead nor wounded. A great many had thrown themselves down behind piles of slain, for protection. As the firing ceased, these men were every now and then, jumping up and either running off or coming in and giving themselves up.

Amongst those that were running off we observed one stout looking fellow, in a red coat, who would every now and then stop and display some gestures towards us, that were rather the opposite of complimentary. Perhaps fifty guns were fired at him, but as he was a good way off, without effect. Just then, it was noticed, that Paleface was loading his rifle, and some one called out to him, "hurra, Paleface! load quick and give him a shot. The d—— rascal is patting his butt at us!" Sure enough, Paleface rammed home his bullet, and, taking a long sight, he let drive. The fellow, by this time, was from two to three hundred yards off, and somewhat to the left of Packenham's horse. Paleface said he drew sight on him and then run it along up his back till the sight was lost over his head, to allow for the sinking of the ball in so great a distance, and then let go. As soon as the gun cracked the fellow was seen to stagger. He ran forward a few steps, then pitched down on his head and moved no more. As soon as he fell, George Huffman, a big stout Dutchman belonging to our company, asked the Captain if he might go and see where Paleface hit him. The Captain said he didn't care, and George, jumping from the breastwork over the ditch, ran out over the dead and wounded till he came to the place where the fellow was lying. George rolled the body over till he could see the face, and then turning round to us, shouted at the top of his voice, "mine got! he ish a nager!" He was a mulatto, and he was quite dead. Paleface's ball had entered between the shoulders and passed out through his breast. George, as he came back, brought three or four muskets which he had picked up. By this time our men were running out in all directions, picking up muskets, and sometimes watches and other plunder. One man who had got a little too far out on the field was fired at from the British breastwork, and wounded in the arm. He came running back a good deal faster than he had gone out. He was not much hurt but pretty well scared.

Tales of the Hospital.

Under this title Mrs. *Nichols* of the "Guest," is publishing a series of articles of deep interest. The second number affords an example of the power of presence of mind, united to moral courage, to allay the fury of maniacal violence. The story is that of a madman who had escaped from his cell, and to the exceeding terror of the *Matron*, is found by her on lifting up her eyes from work, confronting her presence. Dreadfully alarmed, she springs off and makes her escape, although pursued by the maniac. Her husband, the *Steward* of the Hospital, having made his appearance at this juncture, arrested his movement by stepping forward and observing in a pleasant tone,— "Ah Grant, where are you going?" The madman glared at him a moment, and then replied in a similar tone—"to take a walk," "Take my arm," said the Steward, with a good natured smile, "and we will walk together." The man complied immediately, and drawing his arm within his own, the Steward conducted him very slowly back to his cell, talking pleasantly to him till they reached it, when being joined by the keeper, they refastened the chains and secured the door more firmly than before.

I too can tell a tale of the Hospital, which the narrative, of which I have extracted merely one of the incidents, brings to my recollection.

In taking the census of 1840, it became my duty to enumerate the wretched inmates of our city Hospital, and acquainting its officers with my business, William Crossman, one of the township trustees, accompanied me through its wards to afford me the information which the tenants themselves could not impart. It was my first visit to such abodes of horror and wretchedness, and it is hardly necessary to add, that the spectacle made a deep impression on me. After visiting the wards in which were lodged those whose derangement was of a mild type, I was pointed to a wretched object crawling like a brute on all fours. Having been told his history, Mr. Crossman led me to a chamber opposite, and unlocking the door, its inmate, a half naked woman, who had succeeded by some means in divesting herself of the strait jacket, sprang forward, and having a stout piece of cord wood in her hand, brandished it over his head and saluted him with,— "There, d—— you, I have got you now and will kill you." Crossman, with a degree of self-possession I thought wonderful, simply smiled and said in his blandest tones—"Why, Elizabeth, who has been ill-treating thee so?" She paused a moment, let fall the stick, and whimpering said they would not let her have her cup of tea any longer. "Well," said our friend, "I must see that thee gets it, and find out who is keeping thee out of it. But let me fix thy dress a little." So saying he adjusted and secured the strait jacket as quietly and unresistedly as though he had been fitting an apron to a child, and bidding her good bye, withdrew and relocked the door. During this scene, I trembled for a valuable life, which I could make no attempt to save, for when first accosted and threatened, the door was not more widely opened than sufficed for him to fill the space. He was left to depend upon himself, and the least faltering would no doubt have brought the blow down upon his uncovered head. I never before so fully appreciated the value of self-possession and presence of mind.

Modern Relics.

When we hear or read of "Relics," we naturally associate with the subject the church of Rome. But the protestant churches, and even the no-church—the world at large—have relics; as highly prized, if we should judge by the prices paid for them, as those held by the Papal church.

A few years since a chair which had been the property of "the Dairyman's daughter," was produced at one of the New York anniversaries. It was, as might have been expected, a rough article, which but for its associated ideas, would not have brought a dime at public sale. As it was, an individual offered one hundred dollars on the spot for it. This relic and rarity mania is, however, more prevalent in Europe than in this country. Prince Albert has presented to Greenwich Hospital the coat worn by Nelson, in which he received his death wound, at Trafalgar. The ivory chair of Gustavus Vasa was sold in 1823, for fifty-eight thousand florins—nearly $30,000. The coat worn by Charles XII. at the battle of Pultowa, brought, at Edinburg, in 1825, the enormous sum of twenty-two thousand pounds sterling—over $100,000. A tooth belonging to Sir Isaac Newton, was sold to the celebrated Shaftsbury for seven hundred and thirty pounds —$3.500. As far as we may judge by another relic of this sort, this was far below the value.

Lenoir, the founder of the French museum, while engaged transporting the remains of Abelard and Heloise to the Petits Augustins, was offered by a wealthy Englishman one hundred thousand francs—nearly $20,000—for one of the teeth of Heloise. At Stockholm, on the contrary, the whole head—teeth included—of Descartes, was sold for barely ninety francs—$18—what a sacrifice!

Voltaire's cane brought five hundred francs; Rousseau's waistcoat nine hundred and sixty-nine, and his copper watch five hundred francs. The wig of Kant, the founder of transcendentalism, brought only two hundred francs, while that of Sterne was sold in London for two hundred guineas—almost $1000. A hat wore by Napoleon, was purchased by M. Lacroix for nineteen hundred francs. To do this, he had to out bid thirty-two competitors. Sir Francis Burdett paid five hundred pounds sterling for the two pens used to the signature of the treaty of Amiens.

Our City Business.

The sales of Dry Goods, Groceries, &c., this Spring, although not fairly opened as yet, surpass all previous example, and indicate that our city will soon supply the surrounding country to the west, north and northwest, as extensively as she now does in her own manufactures. Pearl street, and the business parts of Front, Second, and Main streets, are putting up and sending off by drays and wagons, goods of every description, to an extent which blocks up the side walks, while it impedes the passage even of the streets. I know of one firm whose March sales will reach to one hundred thousand dollars, while there are others very little behind this in extent. And the prospect is, that the April sales will equal those of March. What kind of stocks we have on hand for the supply of country customers, may be inferred from a single statistic. I saw in one large dry goods house twenty-two thousand pieces spring and summer prints. Every thing else was proportionately abundant.

The western and northern merchants are now finding out that they can lay in their goods to better advantage here than at the east, by buying as low in Cincinnati, carriage added, as at New

York or Philadelphia, while they save time and expense in traveling, by the change. If they go east, it involves a loss of nearly a month, while here they can buy oftener, at a loss of a day or two, and just as much as they want from month to month. In this way they can avoid the accumulation of goods which injure by keeping or going out of fashion.

Growth of our Cities.

Population.	1840.	1846.
Cincinnati, ...	46,382	83,450
Columbus, ...	6,048	10,016
Cleveland, ...	6,071	10,135
Dayton, ...	6,067	10.192

It is remarkable what a neck and neck race the three last places have been running, both in 1840 and at present. Thirty-three hundred and fifty-four individuals—probably one half of the adult population of Cleveland—are not natives of the United States. We have obviously then less foreigners in proportion in Cincinnati, although I was not previously made aware of the fact.

Boot-Making---Quick Work.

The Dover, Mass., Gazette, says:—Mr. Chas. Mulloy, a journeyman boot and shoe-maker, in the employ of Mr. D. M. Clark, South Berwick, made throughout (after they were cut) twenty-four pair of thick boots in one week; the work being done in a substantial manner, and to the entire satisfaction of his employer. This is considered to be the work of four journeymen.

A correspondent at Clintonville, N. Y., calls our attention to the above, and says:—Mr. Martin Clark, a journeyman boot and shoe-maker, in the employ of L. W. Paige, of this place, made throughout (after they were cut) *twenty-five pair* of thick boots in one week, in a good workmanlike manner, to the entire satisfaction of his employer, and he calls upon his friend, the "Down Easter," to go it again, while he pledges to do the work of five men in one week, if twenty-four pair is the work of four men.

Confident by what I have seen in other industrial departments, that our Cincinnati workmen are *equal* to any in the world, both for skill and activity, I handed the above statement to L. Chapin of the firm of *L. Chapin & Co.*, who are largely engaged in the manufacture here of boots and shoes. He authorizes me to say, that he has a journeyman in his employ, *Mr. Thomas Starkey*, whose regular day's work, and of eight hours to the day only, is six pairs of boots of the description here alluded to—equal to thirty-six pair per week, and that he has as many as three times, made twelve pairs of these boots at sittings of fifteen hours in each instance; and what is more, he will do it again, in the presence of any individual Messrs. Clark or Paige may commission at this place to see it done.

As the eastern working hours are at least ten to the day, Mr. Starkey's work is equal to *forty-five* pairs in a week of six days of ten hours each.

A pair of these boots are left at my office for a few days to satisfy those who take an interest in this subject, of the quality of the article. They are equal to the No. 1 coarse boots, which are warranted, being stamped L. Chapin & Co.

Messrs. Chapin & Co., authorize me further to say to Messrs. Clark, Paige, or any other individual east, that if they desire to see the performance of Mr. Starkey and take a lesson in the science of boot-making, that if Mr. S. does not in their presence make a pair of boots in workmanlike style in sixty minutes, which shall be warranted to wear six months at least, that their expenses to Cincinnati and home, will be reimbursed by the proprietors of this establishment.

A new Seal Device.

I have to acknowledge the receipt of public documents from our Representative in Congress, James J. Faran. The envelope bears the impression on its seal of 54 deg. 40 sec., which is, of course, the flag under which Mr. F. ranges himself on the Oregon question.

Brick Manufacture.

The Albany papers state the manufacture of building bricks in that city for the past year, at fifteen millions. We have made at least six times that quantity, during the same period, at the brick yards in Cincinnati.

Iron Safes.

Although the public attention has been called to the Iron Safes of Mr. Charles Urban, in the columns of the Advertiser and in other quarters, there are individuals here who appear to be ignorant that as good an article as Wilder's or Rich's Salamander Safes can be bought here at a price as low as at New York—ten cents per pound—while the expense of carriage is saved and a guarantee secured on the spot, which if offered in New York is worth nothing to the purchaser when he ascertains at the distance of Cincinnati from that place, that his safe is defective in any respect.

As to the quality of the article it is not necessary to refer to the recommendations of those who have bought. For those who need a safe, by calling at the store of Messrs. Thompson & Campbell, on Second street, between Main and Sycamore, may see one of Urban's Salamander Safes, and by comparing it with other Safes of New York, Philadelphia or Pittsburgh manufacture, they can discover where the superiority of manufacture lies.

One of these Safes was submitted to the action

of a fire for twenty-four hours, during which nineteen and a half cords of hickory and sugar tree wood were burned beneath and around it.

On opening it several hundred dollars in bank notes deposited within, were found to be uninjured by this test, severe as it was.

When may a Person be called Drunk?

"Well, Doctor, pray give us a definition of what you consider being *fou*, that we may know in future, when a cannie Scot may, with propriety, be termed drunk."

"Well gentlemen," said the Doctor, "that is rather a kittle question to answer, for you must know there is a great diversity of opinion on the subject. Some say that a man is sober as long as he can stand upon his legs. An Irish friend of mine, a fire-eating, hard drinking captain of dragoons, once declared to me on his honour as a soldier and a gentleman, that he would never allow any friend of his to be called drunk, till he saw him trying to light his pipe at the pump. And others there be, men of learning and respectability too, who are of opinion that a man has a right to consider himself sober as long as he can lie flat on his back without holding on by the ground. For my own part I am a man of moderate opinions, and would allow that a man was fou without being just so far gone as any of these. But with your leave, gentlemen, I'll tell you a story about the Laird of Bonniemoon, that will be a good illustration of what I call being fou.

"The Laird of Bonniemoon was gae fond of his bottle—in short just a poor drunken body, as I said afore. On one occasion he was asked to dine with Lord B———, a neighbour of his, and his lordship being well acquainted with the Laird's dislike to small drinks, ordered a bottle of cherry brandy to be set before him after dinner, instead of port, which he always drank in preference to claret, when nothing better was to be got. The Laird thought this fine heartsome stuff, and on he went, filling his glass like the rest, and telling his cracks, and ever the more he drank, the more he praised his lordship's *port*. It was a fine, full bodied wine, and lay well on the stomach, not like that poisonous stuff, claret, that makes a body feel as if he had swallowed a nest of puddocks. Well, gentleman, the Laird had finished one bottle of cherry brandy, or as his Lordship called it, 'his particular port,' and had just tossed of a glass of the second bottle, which he declared to be even better than the first, when his old confidential servant, Watty, came stalking into the room, and making his best bow, announced that the Laird's horse was at the door. 'Get o' that, ye fause loon,' cried the Laird, pulling off his wig, and flinging it at Watty's head. 'Don't ye see, ye blethering brute, that I'm just beginning my second bottle?'

"But Maister," says Watty, scratching his head, "amaist twall o'clock." "Weel what though it be?" said the Laird, turning up his glass with drunken gravity, while the rest of the company were like to split their sides with laughing at him and Watty. "It cannot be ony later my man, so just reach me my wig and let the naig bide a wee." Well gentlemen, it was a cold frosty night, and Watty soon tired of kicking his heels at the door; so in a little while, back he comes, and says he, Maister, Maister, it's amaist ane o'clock! "Well, Watty," says the Laird,

with a hiccup—for he was far gone by this time —"it will never be ony earlier, Watty, my man, and that's a comfort, so ye may just rest yoursel' a wee while langer till I finish my bottle. A full belly makes a stiff back, you know, Watty." Watty was by this time dancing mad; so after waiting another half hour, back he comes, in an awful hurry, and says he, "Laird, Laird, as true as death the sun's rising." "Weel Watty," says the Laird, looking awful wise, and trying with both hands to fill his glass, "let him rise my man, let him rise, he has further to gang the day than aither you or me, Watty."

This answer fairly dumbfounded poor Watty, and he gave it up in despair. But at last the bottle was finished; the Laird was lifted into the saddle, and off he rode in high glee, thinking all the time the moon was the sun, and that he had fine daylight for his journey. "Hech Watty, my man," said the Laird, patting his stomach; and speaking awful thick, "we were nane the worse for that second bottle this frosty morning."— "Faith," said Watty, blowing his fingers and looking as blue as a bilberry, "your honour may be nane the worse for it, but I'm nane the better; I wish I was." Well, on they rode fou cannily, the Laird gripping hard at the horse's mane, rolling about like a sack of meal; for the cold air was beginning to make the spirits tell on him. At last they came to a bit of a brook that crossed the road; and the Laird's horse being pretty well used to have his own way, stopped short to take a drink. This had the effect to make the poor Laird lose his balance, and away he went over the horse's ears, into the very middle of the brook. The Laird, honest man, had just sense enough to hear the splash, and to know that something was wrong, but he was that drunk, that he did not the least suspect that it was himself. "Watty!" said he, sitting up in the middle of the stream, and stammering out the words with great difficulty, 'Watty, my man, Watty.' Faith you may say that, replied Watty, like to roll off his horse with laughing, for its just yourself, Laird! "Hout fie, Watty," cried the Laird, with a hiccup between every word, "it surely canna be me, Watty, for *I'm here!*"

Now gentlemen, continued the Doctor, here is the case in which I would allow a man to be drunk, although he had neither lost his speech nor the use of his limbs.

A Razor Strop Trade.

"I calculate, sir, I couldn't drive a trade with you to-day," said a true specimen of a Yankee pedlar, as he stood at the door of a merchant of St. Louis.

"I calculate you calculate about right, for you cannot," was the sneering reply.

"Well, I guess you needn't get huffy about it. Now here's a dozen genuine razor strops, worth two dollars and a half—you may have 'em for two dollars."

"I tell you I don't want any of your trash, so you had better be going."

"Wal, now, I declare! I'll bet you five dollars if you make me an offer for them ere strops we'll have a trade yet."

"Done," replied the merchant, placing the money in the hands of a bystander.

The Yankee deposited the like sum—when the merchant offered him a picayune for the strops.

"They're your'n," as he quietly fobbed the stakes. "But," he added with great apparent honesty, "I calculate a joke's a joke, and if you don't want them strops, I'll trade back!"

The merchant's countenance brightened.

"You're not so bad a chap after all; here are your strops—give me tne money.

"There it is," said the Yankee, as he received the strops and passed over the picayune. A trade's a trade—and now you're wide awake in airnest; I guess the next time you trade with that are pic, you'll do better than to buy razor strops."

And away walked the pedlar with his strops and the wager, amid the shouts of the laughing crowd.

Second Municipality.

John Archangel, charged with stealing some silver spoons from Mrs. Dewees, was sent to the Criminal Court yesterday.—*N. O. Tropic.*

This was, as Milton says, "Not less than Archangel, ruined."

A Cincinnati Convention.

Arrangements are about taking place in Kentucky, to hold a convention of delegates in Cincinnati, from every point on the Ohio interested in removing the obstructions in that river and improving its navigation. The meeting of the convention is proposed for the 11th May ensuing It will, without doubt, embody a large attendance. As respects Cincinnati, I trust that her delegation will be select and able rather than large in numbers, and that mere talkers will not form any portion of their ranks.

Chronological Table.

April 1.—Napoleon married to Maria Louisa, 1810.

2.—Florida discovered, 1512. Nelson victory at Copenhagen. 1801. Mirabeau, died, 1791.

3.—Crucifixion of Christ. Napier, died, 1617.

4.—Oliver Goldsmith, died 1774.

5.—Resurrection of Christ. Robert Raikes, the introducer of Sunday Schools, died, 1821.

6.—Richard *Cour de Lion,* died, 1199. Laura, the beloved of Petrarch, died, 1388. Lalande, the astronomer, died, 1804.

An Austrian Yankee.

Before Prince Metternich attained the exalted station he now holds, he was particularly fond of practical jokes, and equally anxious to perpetrate *outre* revenge for annoyances suffered, as he is at the present moment. A Jew banker, at Vienna, was so desirous to become possessor of an Arabian horse, a great favourite of the Prince's, that he constantly called on him to sell it—his highness was constantly refusing. At last, the Prince, being worn out with the banker's impornities, said to him, "I will not sell the horse; but I will part with it only on one condition." "Name it—name it," exclaimed the banker. "It is this," replied the Prince, "I will give you two sound whippings at times proposed by yourself, and a third on a day appointed by me: after

the last beating the horse shall be yours." The Jew asked for the first whipping then, which was administered with right good will; after which rubbing his sore shoulders, he exclaimed, "Well, Prince, give me the second," which was done, and then, scarcely able to stand, he prayed the Prince to appoint a day for the third: "Certainly, sir," said his highness, chuckling; "this day seven years, when, you know, according to our agreement, the horse becomes your property; good morning, sir," continued the Prince, and politely bowed the suffering banker out of the room.—*Morris' Nat. Press.*

Anecdote.

A worthy old sea captain of our acquaintance once took on board a large number of passengers at a port in the Emerald Isle, to bring to this country. On appoaching our coast, he as usual, sounded, but found no bottom.

"And did you strike ground, Captain," inquired one of the Irishmen.

"No," was the reply.

"And will you be so good as to tell us," rejoined Pat, "*how near ye came to it.*"

Faith, Hope and Charity.

A student at a University, being called upon for a definition of these Christian virtues, made his reply as follows:

Quid est Fides? Quod non vides.
Quid Spes? Van res.
Quid Charitas? Magna raritas.

TRANSLATION.

What is Faith? What you cannot see.
What Hope? A thing too vain to be.
What Charity? A great rarity.

Erratum.

My compositor made me say in last weeks's "Advertiser," while stating the length of Front street, that there were not ten houses in the entire length of the street which were *three feet* apart. It should have been three *hundred*, the last word escaping by oversight. An error like this is a great annoyance, for the correction in many cases never follows the error through its various travels.

"Shepherd," said a sentimental young lady (who fancied herself a heroine in the golden groves of Arcadia,) to a rustic who was tending some sheep, "why have you not got your pipe with you?" "Bekase, ma'am, I ha'nt got no '*backer.*"

"Make way, here," said a member of a political deputation, "we are the representatives of the people," "Make way yourself," shouted a sturdy fellow from the throng, "we are the people themselves."

Said an old man, "When I was young, I was poor; when old I became rich. But in each condition I found disappointment. When the faculties of enjoyment were bright, I had not the means, when the means came, the faculties were gone."

The Battle of the 8th January.--No. 3.

By a Hunter of Kentucky.

I had not much opportunity to see what passed on the field after the battle, for we had scarcely time to give a hasty glance on what I have just attempted to describe, when orders came for our company and five others, to cross the river and reinforce our troops that had been beaten on the west bank. We were hastily mustered, and leaving one man from each mess to take care of the baggage, the rest of us moved off up the river at a sharp trot. We soon got up to the city, where we were to cross, running a good part of the way. As we passed along the levee to the upper faubourg, crowds of men, women, and children ran down to see us. They were singing, dancing, shouting, and cutting all manner of antics. The whole city seemed crazy with joy. Some rolled out barrels of bread and biscuit, and there were hundreds of baskets of cakes, cold meat and nicknacks held out to us as we ran along. We had no time to stop and eat, and we were so full of excitement, that though we had been on foot and fasting nearly the whole time, for three days and nights, we got little or nothing of the abundance that was offered us. Some of us snatched a biscuit or two and thrust them into the bosoms of our hunting-shirts. Some nibbled a little as they went, but there wasn't many that felt either hungry or tired. When we came to the barge there were three marked boards prepared for us to run in on, and in a few minutes we were pushing over.

As soon as we landed on the other side, cartridges were served out to those men who had not a full supply. Some of these were worth nothing. They contained raw cotton, cotton seed, and some of them a few small shot; or a ball, with scarcely powder enough to drive it out of the gun. A good many men got supplies of these false cartridges. The cheat was not discovered until the next day, when it created considerable excitement, but I never heard who was to blame.

We took our position behind a little breastwork that had been thrown up. At dark the picket guard was detailed. When the Orderly came round, I took the place of one of our men, who was sick, though I had then half a dozen tours ahead. We were marched out about half way between our post and that of the British, who occupied a small fort from which they had driven our troops in the morning. The sentinels were placed about thirty or forty feet apart, along a small ditch that had been cut through a sugarfield to the swamp. George Phillips was on my right hand and Robert Brown on my left. Next to Brown was Wm. Grubb. We four were within speaking distance of each other. We were posted on the bank thrown up from the ditch; but thinking this was rather a conspicuous position, I placed my blanket against the side of the bank and sitting down on it, rested my feet on the opposite edge of the ditch, so that the water ran trickling under me. Two hours was our regular tour of duty, when we ought to have been relieved, but it seems that Sergeant Houston, who was but a very young man and had been, like the rest of us, on constant fatigue duty for three days and nights, fell asleep by the watch fire and did not wake until we had been nearly four hours on our posts. This was rather severe, but we stood it out. Brown, my next neighbour on the left, soon laid down on the ground and went to sleep. Phillips and Grubb were constantly trying to wake him. He was a son of one of their neighbours. They had promised his parents to take care of him, and were fearful that he would be discovered asleep on his post and punished or disgraced. I told them to let him alone—the poor fellow was perfectly worn out with fatigue, and as there could be no danger unperceived by us, there would be no harm done and we could wake him before the relief came round. In fact, just before this conversation occurred, I was satisfied that the British had abandoned the fort and gone off.

During the evening they had set fire to a sugar-house, and some other out buildings, just in the rear of the fort. By the light of this fire, from the place where I sat, I could very plainly see the fort and the British soldiers passing to and fro about it. Sometime towards eleven or twelve o'clock, I observed three men start out from the fort and come in a straight line towards the spot where I was stationed. The moon by this time had got pretty well up, and though the night was rather hazy, by the light of the moon and fire together, I could see all their motions very distinctly. They were, apparently, ignorant of our position, and seemed to be coming right on to us. For a few moments I was thinking of the chances of a rencounter. I examined my rifle to see that every thing was right, brought my tomahawk and knife round so that I could readily grasp them, and then waited to see what would come of this manœuvre. When they had advanced to within about a hundred yards, they suddenly halted. A moment after, they wheeled short round to the right and marched some three or four hundred yards towards the river; then, wheeling to the right again, they returned to the fort. Immediately after this I saw the British troops parading; and in a few minutes they disappeared in the darkness towards the river. I felt certain that they had evacuated the fort and gone down the river.

Sometime after this the relief came round. I then went to the guard fire, and sat down on a bunch of sugar cane till morning. About daylight I was on post again, and when the sun was about an hour high, old Looksharp brought me something like a pound of sugar and a loaf of bread. This was the first good meal I had had for four days, and I made a capital breakfast.

About eight o'clock, we were called off post, and the troops paraded to make an attack upon the fort. While the line was forming, I observed Major Harrison coming along the line on horseback, and not liking to address him directly, I spoke up pretty loudly to Grubb, "what the deuce are they making all this fuss for? There's no use in going to attack the British. They're all gone." "I know that," says Grubb. The Major rode along, but in a few minutes he came back and asked who it was that said the British were all gone. "It was me, sir," said I. "How do you know?" said he. "I saw them go last night when I was on guard," said I. "Very good news if it is true!" said he. We then marched up to within a short distance of the fort and formed in line. Major Harrison and several other officers rode up close to the fort and soon returned. The Major rode up near where I was standing, and said, "right, old man, the British are all gone!" It was found that the fort had been evacuated, as I had supposed, and we had nothing more to do but march back to New Orleans, which we did to the tune of Yankee Doodle, every one full of joy and gladness. We re-crossed the river and got down to our lines, near the battle ground, about two o'clock that day.

When we got back to the camp, on the battle ground, the British were lying about two miles below. By this time the field was cleared of the dead. There were, scattered about, a few caps and fragments of clothing, generally shot to pieces; and stains of blood, with many other marks of the dreadful carnage that had been there. Packenham's horse was still lying in the same place, now the only occupant of the bed where his master and so many hundreds of others laid with him the day before.

The second day after the battle, the drums beat up for volunteers to attack the British redoubt. Plenty of men turned out, all eager for the attempt. I don't know who were the projectors of this attack, but so it was, that just after the men had paraded and taken leave of their comrades, and while they were as wolfish and full of fight as it was possible for that number of animals to be, here came an order from Old Hickory for every man to face to the right-about and go to cooking and eating. This was quite a damper. The men could not exactly tell what to make of it, but they knew if Jackson said so it had to be done. They didn't fully understand the long and short of it, but so it was.

A few days after this, I was walking about the levee at New Orleans, when I saw three officers passing on horseback. As they came up I turned to give them the usual salute, when who should I see but Col. Andrew Hines, then one of Jackson's aids, and who I had been well acquainted with when he kept store at Bardstown. "Why, halloo! old man," said he, "are you here?" "Yes, Colonel," said I, "I'm knocking about with the rest." With that we shook hands and he asked me about my family. After a few words had passed, I told him I'd like to ask a question, if he didn't think it improper—that I didn't want to ask him any thing that was improper to be told; but there was one thing I had some curiosity to know. "Well, what is it;" said he, "I'll tell you any thing I can consistently." "Then," said I, "I'd just like to know what was the reason that old Jackson ordered us all out of the field the other day, when we had got ready to go and fight the British." "O!" said he, "I'll tell you with freedom. General Jackson has got more wisdom than all of us put together. He knew that we had gained one of the greatest victories that ever was heard of, and he was determined to keep it. He said, if we attacked the redoubt there would be a great many good men killed, and that it was better to drive off the enemy without the loss of our own men."

About a week or ten days after the battle—I don't recollect the exact time now—the British broke up their camp and went over to Lake Ponchartrain. The night they left, I was out on picket guard, about half way between the camps. I did not notice any thing remarkable during the night, except the old bluetailed bomb shells that were discharged at them from our lines, every half hour. They would go whizzing over our heads, leaving a long streak of bluish light with a sprinkling of sparks in their rear. We heard a great screaming at the moment one of them fell. As I afterwards heard, it smashed through the roof of a little negro house, where a lieutenant and fourteen men were sleeping, every one of whom were killed or wounded.

Just at daylight, an Irishman who had deserted came to the sentinels, with whom he remained until the relief came round. He told us the British had all gone, and said, that as they were marching off, he pretended to have left something behind, and handing his gun to a comrade to hold, he ran back as if to look for it; but instead of doing so he ran as fast as he could towards the American camp. He soon heard a party in pursuit of him, and took refuge in a little negro hut, crawling up the chimney. His pursuers entered the house, and he said his heart beat so while they were hunting him, that he was afraid they would hear it thumping. They did not think of the chimney, however, and the poor fellow escaped. As soon as they had gone he made his way to our line and came in. I heard of the execution done by the bomb shell, at the time we heard the screaming. This man afterwards came to Kentucky and is, or was a few years ago, living in Nelson county, where he became a very respectable citizen.

After the British moved down to the Lake, they remained for some time near the mouth of Villery's Canal, embarking in flats. Whilst they were there, a certain number of men were detailed from our camp, every three days, to serve as swamp guards. The Lake was skirted by a cypress swamp, which, as is the usual character of that kind of swamp, was very miry and full of water. Along the Lake edge of this swamp, the British had sentinels, posted on logs of timber cut for them to stand or lie upon; and in like manner our sentinels were stationed in the same way, along the other edge of the swamp on the land side. At some places where the swamp was narrow and the timber thin, we could see the British sentinels on their posts very plainly. Amongst the rest, there was one that attracted particular attention. He had a plank laid upon some logs along which he walked backwards and forwards. His red coat, with the steel about his accoutrements, and particularly, the plate upon his cap, glistened very conspicuously in the sun. Whether it was because the men had nothing else to do but look at him, or because he was the most conspicuous object, or for what precise reason, I do not know, but he became a sort of an eye-sore. So about ten o'clock in the morning, Col. Ben Harrison, of Bardstown, spoke up to some men, who were lounging about the guard fire. "Boys," said he, "I'll give five dollars to any one of you that will go and shoot that darned red-coat, and a suit of clothes to boot, as soon as we get home." With that, a little, slender, palefaced fellow, belonging to Higdon's company, named Dick Pratt, jumped up and declared he'd try it any how. He wiped out his rifle, and having loaded it to his mind, he put into the swamp. Dick went crawling along among the roots, wading in the water and dodging about behind the trees and brush, pretty much as if he was trying to get a shot at a scurvy duck. The Englishman kept on walking up and down his plank, probably little thinking of being game for a Kentucky hunter. He might have been thinking of a wife and children or a sweetheart at home, poor fellow! But our men who knew what was on foot, watched the result with breathless interest, though, if the truth must be told, without much thinking of pity. The general impression was, that the British had come there to kill our men, if they could, and it was only serving them as they deserved, to shoot them whenever there was an opportunity. They soon lost sight of Dick who had disappeared in the swamp, but they kept their eyes on the sentinel. It was pretty near half an hour before any thing took place. At last a little puff of smoke spouted up from behind a log in the middle of the swamp, which was quietly followed by a sharp crack of Dick's rifle. The poor Englishman instantly dropped his musket and threw his hands above his head. He then staggered backwards and forwards on his plank for a moment or two—the next, he tumbled head foremost into the water. A sharp fire of grape and canister shot was immediately opened from the British boats, which made the mud and water fly in good earnest; but Dick, the cunning varmint, as soon as he had fired ran off rapidly from his smoke to one side, instead of retreating in a direct line, and thus fooled them. He came off scot free, but the British kept up such a fire that our guards were compelled to retreat from their stations on the edge of the swamp. After this there were no more British sentinels in sight or within reach of our men. Dick got his five dollars, and after we got home, I saw him one day in a suit of clothes, which he said, was the reward of that exploit.

Next day after returning from swamp guard, I was detached to go to New Orleans, to attend some of my comrades who were sick in the hospital. Four of our company were sick, but they all got well except Barnett Bridwell. He, poor fellow! died of a complication of diseases. I saw nothing more of the army until we started home. We left New Orleans about the 20th of March, ninety of us in company, and arrived safely in Kentucky about the 1st of April.

A Grizzly Bear Hunt.

The every-day sports of the wild woods include many feats of daring that never find a pen of record. Constantly in the haunts of the savage, are enacting scenes of thrilling interest, the very details of which would make the denizen of enlightened life turn away with instinctive dread. Every Indian tribe has its heroes, celebrated respectively for their courage in different ways exhibited. Some for their acuteness in pursuing the enemy on the war-path, and others for the destruction they have accomplished among the wild beasts of the forest. A great hunter among the Indians is a marked personage. It is a title that distinguishes its possessor among his people as a prince; while the exploits in which he has been engaged hang about his person as brilliantly as the decorations of so many oders. The country in which the Osage finds a home possesses abundantly the grizzly bear, an animal formidable beyond any other inhabitant of the North American forests: an animal seemingly insensible to pain, uncertain in its habits, and by its mighty strength able to overcome any living obstacle that comes within its reach, as an enemy. The Indian warrior, of any tribe, among the haunts of the grizzly bear, finds no necklace so honourable to be worn as the claws of this gigantic animal, if he fell by his own prowess; and if he can add an eagle's plume to his scalp-lock, plucked from a bird shot while on the wing, he is honourable indeed. The Indian's "smoke," like the fire-side of the white man, is often the place where groups of people assemble to relate whatever may most pleasantly while away the hours of a long evening, or destroy the monotony of a dull and idle day. On such occasions, the old "brave" will sometimes relax from his natural gravity, and grow loquacious over his chequered life. But no recital commands such undivided attention as the adventures with the grizzly bear; and the death of an enemy on the war-path hardly vies with it in interest.

We have listened to these soul-stirring adventures over the urn, or while lounging on the sofa; and the recital of the risks run, the hardships endured, have made us think them almost impossible, when compared with the conventional self-indulgence of enlightened life. But they were the tales of a truthful man: a hunter, who had strayed away from the scenes once necessary for his life, and who loved, like the worn-out soldier, to "fight his battles over," in which he was once engaged. It may be, and is the province of the sportsman to exaggerate; but the "hunter," surrounded by the magnificence and sublimity of an American forest, earning his bread by the hardy adventures of the chase, meets with too much reality to find room for colouring—too much of the sublime and terrible in the scenes with which he is associated to be boastful of himself. Apart from the favourable effects of civilization, he is also separated from its contaminations; and boasting and exaggeration are "settlements" weaknesses, and not the products of the wild woods.

The hunter, whether Indian or white, presents one of the most extraordinary exhibitions of the singular capacity of the human senses to be improved by cultivation. The unfortunate deaf, dumb, and blind girl, in one of our public institutions,[*] selects her food, her clothing, and her friends, by the touch alone—so delicate has it become from the mind's being directed to that sense alone. The forest hunter uses the sight most extraordinarily well, and experience at last renders it so keen, that the slightest touch of a passing object on the leaves, trees, or earth, seems to leave deep and visible impressions, that to the common eye are unseen as the path of the bird through the air. This knowledge governs the chase and the war-path; this knowledge is what, when excelled in, makes the master-spirit among the rude inhabitants of the woods: and that man is the greatest chief, who follows the coldest trail, and leaves none behind by his own footsteps. The hunter in pursuit of the grizzly bear is governed by this instinct of sight. It directs him with more certainty than the hound is directed by his nose. The impressions of the bear's footsteps upon the leaves, its marks on the trees, its resting-places, are all known long before the bear is really seen; and the hunter, while thus following "the trail," calculates the very sex, weight, and age with certainty. Thus it is that he will neglect or chose a trail: one because it is poor, and another because it is small, another because it is with cubs, and another because it is fat, identifying the very trail as the bear itself; and herein, perhaps, lies the distinction between the sportsman, and the huntsman. The hunter follows his object by his own knowledge and instinct, while the sportsman employs the instinct of domesticated animals to assist his pursuits.

The different methods to destroy the grizzly bear, by those who hunt them, are as numerous as the bears that are killed. They are not animals which permit of a system in hunting them; and it is for this reason they are so dangerous and difficult to destroy. The experience of one hunt may cost a limb or a life in the next one, if used as a criterion; and fatal, indeed, is the mistake, if it comes to grappling with an animal whose gigantic strength enables him to lift a horse in his

* Hartford Asylum for the Deaf and Dumb.

is one terrible exception to this rule; one habit of huge arms, and bear it away as a prize. There the animal may be certainly calculated on, but a daring heart only can take advantage of it.

The grizzly bear, like the tiger and lion, have their caves in which they live; but they use them principally as a safe lodging-place when the cold of winter renders them torpid and disposed to sleep. To these caves they retire late in the fall, and they seldom venture out until the warmth of spring. Sometimes two occupy one cave, but this is not often the case, as the unsociability of the animal is proverbial, they prefering to be solitary and alone. A knowledge of the forests, and an occasional trailing for bear inform the hunter of these caves, and the only habit of the grizzly bear that can with certainty be taken advantage of, is that of his being in his cave alive, if at a proper season. And the hunter has the terrible liberty of entering his cave single-handed, and there destroying him. Of this only method of hunting the grizzly bear we would attempt a description.

The thought of entering a cave, inhabited by one of the most powerful beasts of prey, is calculated to try the strength of the best nerves; and when it is considered that the least trepidation, the slightest mistake, may cause, and probably will result in the instant death of the hunter, it certainly exhibits the highest demonstration of physical courage to pursue such a method of hunting. Yet there are many persons in the forests of North America who engage in such perilous adventures with no other object in view than the "sport" or hearty meal. The hunter's preparations to "beard the lion in his den," commence with examining the mouth of the cave he is about to enter. Upon the signs there exhibited he decides whether the bear is alone; for if there are two, the cave is never entered. The size of the bear is also thus known, and the time since he was last in search of food. The way this knowledge is obtained, from indications so slight, or unseen to an ordinary eye, is one of the greatest mysteries of the woods. Placing ourselves at the mouth of the cave containing a grizzly bear, to our untutored senses there would be nothing to distinguish it from one that was empty; but if some Diana of the forest would touch our eyes, and give us the instinct of sight possessed by the hunter, we would argue thus: "From all the marks about the mouth of the cave, the occupant has not been out for a great length of time, for the grass and the earth have not been lately disturbed. The bear is in the cave, for the last tracks made are with the toe marks towards the cave. There is but one bear, because the tracks are regular and of the same size. He is a large bear; the length of the step and the size of the paw indicate this; and he is a fat one, because his *hind feet do not step in the impressions made by the fore ones*, as is always the case with a lean bear." Such are the signs and arguments that present themselves to the hunter; and mysterious as they seem, when not understood, when explained they strike the imagination at once as being founded on the unerring simplicity and the certainty of nature. It may be asked, how is it that the grizzly bear is so formidable to numbers, when met in the forest, and when in a cave can be assailed successfully by a single man? In answer to this, we must recollect that the bear is only attacked in his cave when he is in total darkness, and suffering from surprise and the torpidity of the season. These three things are in this method of hunting taken advantage of; and but for these advantages, no quickness of eye, no steadiness of nerve or forest experience, would protect for an instant the intruder to the cave of the grizzly bear. The hunter, having satisfied himself about the cave, prepares a candle, which he makes out of the wax taken from the comb of wild bees, softened by the grease of the bear. This candle has a large wick, and emits a brilliant flame. Nothing else is needed but the rifle. The knife and the belt are useless; for if a struggle should ensue that would make it available, the foe is too powerful to mind its thrusts before the hand using it would be dead. Bearing the candle before him, with the rifle in a convenient position, the hunter fearlessly enters the cave. He is soon surrounded by darkness, and is totally unconscious where his enemy will reveal himself. Having fixed the candle in the ground in firm position, with an apparatus provided, he lights it, and its brilliant flame soon penetrates into the recesses of the cavern—its size of course rendering the illumination more or less complete. The hunter now places himself on his belly, having the candle between the back part of the cave where the bear is, and himself; in this position, with the muzzle of the rifle protruding out in front of him, he patiently waits for his victim. A short time only elapses before Bruin is aroused by the light. The noise made by his starting from sleep attracts the hunter, and he soon distinguishes the black mass, moving, stretching, and yawning like a person awaked from a deep sleep. The hunter moves not, but prepares his rifle; the bear, finally roused, turns his head towards the candle, and, with slow and wading steps, approaches it.

Now is the time that tries the nerves of the hunter. Too late to retreat, his life hangs upon his certain aim and the goodness of his powder. The slightest variation in the bullet, or a flashing pan, and he is a doomed man. So tenacious of life is the common black bear, that it is frequently wounded in its most vital parts, and will still escape or give terrible battle. But the grizzly bear seems to possess an infinitely greater tenacity of life. His skin, covered by matted hair, and the huge bones of his body, protect the heart, as if incased in a wall; while the brain is buried in a skull, compared to which adamant is not harder. A bullet, striking the bear's forehead, would flatten, if it struck squarely on the solid bone, as if fired against a rock; and dangerous indeed would it be to take the chance of reaching the animal's heart. With these fearful odds against the hunter, the bear approaches the candle, growing every moment more sensible of some uncommon intrusion. He reaches the blaze, and either raises his paw to strike it, or lifts his nose to scent it, either of which will extinguish it, and leave the hunter and the bear in total darkness. This dreadful moment is taken advantage of. The loud report of the rifle fills the cave with stunning noise, and as the light disappears, the ball, if successfully fired, penetrates the eye of the huge animal—the only place where it would find a passage to the brain; and this not only gives the wound, but instantly paralyzes, that no temporary resistance may be made. On such chances the American hunter perils his life, and often thoughtlessly courts the danger.

CONTENTS OF VOLUME I.

CONTENTS OF VOLUME II.

The First American Frontier

AN ARNO PRESS/NEW YORK TIMES COLLECTION

Agnew, Daniel.
A History of the Region of Pennsylvania North of the Allegheny River. 1887.

Alden, George H.
New Government West of the Alleghenies Before 1780. 1897.

Barrett, Jay Amos.
Evolution of the Ordinance of 1787. 1891.

Billon, Frederick.
Annals of St. Louis in its Early Days Under the French and Spanish Dominations. 1886.

Billon, Frederick.
Annals of St. Louis in its Territorial Days, 1804-1821. 1888.

Littel, William.
Political Transactions in and Concerning Kentucky. 1926.

Bowles, William Augustus.
Authentic Memoirs of William Augustus Bowles. 1916.

Bradley, A. G.
The Fight with France for North America. 1900.

Brannan, John, ed.
Official Letters of the Military and Naval Officers of the War, 1812-1815. 1823.

Brown, John P.
Old Frontiers. 1938.

Brown, Samuel R.
The Western Gazetteer. 1817.

Cist, Charles.
Cincinnati Miscellany of Antiquities of the West and Pioneer History. (2 volumes in one). 1845-6.

Claiborne, Nathaniel Herbert.
Notes on the War in the South with Biographical Sketches of the Lives of Montgomery, Jackson, Sevier, and Others. 1819.

Clark, Daniel.
Proofs of the Corruption of Gen. James Wilkinson. 1809.

Clark, George Rogers.
Colonel George Rogers Clark's Sketch of His Campaign in the Illinois in 1778-9. 1869.

Collins, Lewis.
Historical Sketches of Kentucky. 1847.

Cruikshank, Ernest, ed,
Documents Relating to Invasion of Canada and the Surrender of Detroit. 1912.

Cruikshank, Ernest, ed,
The Documentary History of the Campaign on the Niagara Frontier, 1812-1814. (4 volumes). 1896-1909.

Cutler, Jervis.
A Topographical Description of the State of Ohio, Indian Territory, and Louisiana. 1812.

Cutler, Julia P.
The Life and Times of Ephraim Cutler. 1890.

Darlington, Mary C.
History of Col. Henry Bouquet and the Western Frontiers of Pennsylvania. 1920.

Darlington, Mary C.
Fort Pitt and Letters From the Frontier. 1892.

De Schweinitz, Edmund.
The Life and Times of David Zeisberger. 1870.

Dillon, John B.
History of Indiana. 1859.

Eaton, John Henry.
Life of Andrew Jackson. 1824.

English, William Hayden.
Conquest of the Country Northwest of the Ohio. (2 volumes in one). 1896.

Flint, Timothy.
Indian Wars of the West. 1833.

Forbes, John.
Writings of General John Forbes Relating to His Service in North America. 1938.

Forman, Samuel S.
Narrative of a Journey Down the Ohio and Mississippi in 1789-90. 1888.

Haywood, John.
Civil and Political History of the State of Tennessee to 1796. 1823.

Heckewelder, John.
History, Manners and Customs of the Indian Nations. 1876.

Heckewelder, John.
Narrative of the Mission of the United Brethren. 1820.

Hildreth, Samuel P.
Pioneer History. 1848.

Houck, Louis.
The Boundaries of the Louisiana Purchase: A Historical Study. 1901.

Houck, Louis.
History of Missouri. (3 volumes in one). 1908.

Houck, Louis.
The Spanish Regime in Missouri. (2 volumes in one). 1909.

Jacob, John J.
A Biographical Sketch of the Life of the Late Capt. Michael Cresap. 1826.

Jones, David.
A Journal of Two Visits Made to Some Nations of Indians on the West Side of the River Ohio, in the Years 1772 and 1773. 1774.

Kenton, Edna.
Simon Kenton. 1930.

Loudon, Archibald.
Selection of Some of the Most Interesting Narratives of Outrages. (2 volumes in one). 1808-1811.

Monette, J. W.
History, Discovery and Settlement of the Mississippi Valley. (2 volumes in one). 1846.

Morse, Jedediah.
American Gazetteer. 1797.

Pickett, Albert James.
History of Alabama. (2 volumes in one). 1851.

Pope, John.
A Tour Through the Southern and Western Territories. 1792.

Putnam, Albigence Waldo.
History of Middle Tennessee. 1859.

Ramsey, James G. M.
Annals of Tennessee. 1853.

Ranck, George W.
Boonesborough. 1901.

Robertson, James Rood, ed.
Petitions of the Early Inhabitants of Kentucky to the Gen. Assembly of Virginia. 1914.

Royce, Charles.
Indian Land Cessions. 1899.

Rupp, I. Daniel.
History of Northampton, Lehigh, Monroe, Carbon and Schuykill Counties. 1845.

Safford, William H.
The Blennerhasset Papers. 1864.

St. Clair, Arthur.
A Narrative of the Manner in which the Campaign Against the Indians, in the Year 1791 was Conducted. 1812.

Sargent, Winthrop, ed.
A History of an Expedition Against Fort DuQuesne in 1755. 1855.

Severance, Frank H.
An Old Frontier of France. (2 volumes in one). 1917.

Sipe, C. Hale.
Fort Ligonier and Its Times. 1932.

Stevens, Henry N.
Lewis Evans: His Map of the Middle British Colonies in America. 1920.

Timberlake, Henry.
The Memoirs of Lieut. Henry Timberlake. 1927.

Tome, Philip.
Pioneer Life: Or Thirty Years a Hunter. 1854.

Trent, William.
Journal of Captain William Trent From Logstown to Pickawillany. 1871.

Walton, Joseph S.
Conrad Weiser and the Indian Policy of Colonial Pennsylvania. 1900.

Withers, Alexander Scott.
Chronicles of Border Warfare. 1895.